For the School of Law,

David Dorkin

1967-70

Litigation Library

THE LAW AND PRACTICE OF COMPROMISE

AUSTRALIA
Law Book Co.
Sydney

CANADA & USA
Carswell
Toronto

HONG KONG
Sweet & Maxwell Asia

NEW ZEALAND
Brookers
Wellington

SINGAPORE AND MALAYSIA
Sweet & Maxwell Asia
Singapore and Kuala Lumpur

LITIGATION LIBRARY

THE LAW AND PRACTICE OF COMPROMISE

WITH PRECEDENTS

by

David Foskett, Q.C., LL.B., F.C.I.Arb.,
of Gray's Inn, Barrister
Bencher of Gray's Inn
A Recorder

and contributors

Sixth Edition

LONDON
SWEET & MAXWELL
2005

First Edition	1980
Second Edition	1985
Third Edition	1991
Fourth Edition	1996
Fifth Edition	2002
Sixth Edition	2005

Published by
Sweet & Maxwell Limited of
100 Avenue Road, Swiss Cottage, London NW3 3PF
www.sweetandmaxwell.co.uk
Typeset by LBJ Typesetting Ltd of Kingsclere
Printed and bound in Great Britain by William Clowes Ltd, Beccles, Suffolk

No natural forests were destroyed to make this product,
only farmed timber was used and replanted

British Library Cataloguing in Publication Data

A CIP catalogue record for this book
is available from the British Library

ISBN 0–421–90300–7

All rights reserved. Crown copyright material
is reproduced with the permission of the Controller of
HMSO and the Queen's Printer for Scotland.

No part of this publication may be reproduced or transmitted, in any form
or by any means, or stored in any retrieval system of any nature without
prior written permission, except for permitted fair dealing under the
Copyright, Designs and Patents Act 1988, or in accordance with the terms
of a licence issued by the Copyright Licensing Agency in respect of
photocopying and/or reprographic reproduction. Application for permission
for other use of copyright material including permission to reproduce
extracts in other published works shall be made to the publishers. Full
acknowledgment of author, publisher and source must be given.

©
David Foskett
2005

Contributors

David Hodge Q.C., B.A. (Oxon.), B.C.L.,
of Inner Temple and Lincoln's Inn, Barrister
Bencher of Lincoln's Inn
A Recorder

Jonathan Cohen Q.C., B.A.,
of Lincoln's Inn, Barrister
A Recorder

Michael Black Q.C., LL.B., F.C.I.Arb., F.Inst.C.E.S.,
of Middle Temple, Barrister
A Recorder

Adrian Lynch Q.C., LL.B.,
of Gray's Inn, Barrister

Nigel Giffin Q.C., M.A. (Oxon.),
of Inner Temple, Barrister

William Edis, B.A. (Oxon.), Dip. Law (City University),
of Lincoln's Inn, Barrister

Michelle Stevens-Hoare, LL.B., LL.M.,
of Middle Temple, Barrister

"Discourage litigation. Persuade your neighbors to compromise whenever you can. Point out to them how the nominal winner is often a real loser—in fees, expenses, and waste of time. As a peacemaker the lawyer has a superior opportunity of being a good man. There will still be business enough."

Abraham Lincoln, 16th president of the United States of America (1809–1865), Notes for a Law Lecture 1850.

"Has anybody here seen my old friend, Abraham,
Can you tell me where he's gone?
O, he freed a lotta people, but it seems the good die young, yeah,
I just looked around and he was gone."

From "Abraham, Martin and John", composed by Richard Holler (© 1968), as recorded by Marvin Gaye (1939–1984) in 1970.

To

Lord Lane

and

Professor A.G. Guest

FOREWORD TO THE FIRST EDITION

"I'm happy to be able to tell your Lordship that you will not be troubled by this case; the parties have settled their differences." Those words, so welcome to the judicial ear mean much more, however, than an unexpected round of golf for the judge. If it were not that a high proportion of cases are compromised long before they reach court the administration of justice would soon grind to a halt; the courts would be overwhelmed by the volume of work. Moreover, the skilful practitioner, be he barrister or solicitor, who can accurately gauge the strength of his own case and that of his opponent will often be able to save his client great trouble and expense by judicious and timely compromise.

When one realises the importance of these skills, and how much of some practitioners' time is taken up in attempts to settle litigation, it is surprising that there is so little written guidance on the subject. It may look easy, but there is much to learn and many pitfalls.

Mr. Foskett has in his comprehensive and scholarly review covered every aspect of the subject, not overlooking the vital area of professional ethics. The reputation of being a straightforward honest negotiator is worth any number of dubiously achieved settlements.

This is a book which anyone handling litigation would do well to read.

The Right Hon. Lord Lane, A.F.C.,
Lord Chief Justice of England

FOREWORD TO THE FOURTH EDITION

The law loves compromise.

It has good reason to do so, since a settlement agreement freely made between both parties to a dispute ordinarily commands a degree of willing acceptance denied to an order imposed on one party by court decision. A party who settles forgoes the chance of total victory, but avoids the anxiety, risk, uncertainty and expenditure of time which is inherent in almost any contested action, and escapes the danger of total defeat.

The law reflects this philosophy, by making it hard for a party to withdraw from a settlement agreement, as from any other agreement, and by giving special standing to an agreement embodied, by consent, in an order of the court. Rules of practice are framed so as to encourage settlement, by exposing the substantial loser of an action to a heavy burden of costs and enabling the maker of a reasonable offer, even if the offer is refused, to obtain some protection against that burden.

But there is, as always, a catch. To negotiate a final and binding settlement agreement; to make sure that all necessary matters are covered; to express the terms clearly and unambiguously; to make sure that the agreement is simply and inexpensively enforceable; to advise where one party claims that he has been misled or pressured into making an agreement by the other side; all this may call for as much skill, including legal skill, as fighting the action.

In this, as in other legal fields, there is no substitute for a sound grasp of legal principle, an understanding of the special rules governing the subject matter and a knowledge of the up-to-date case law. That is what this valuable book provides, and that is why a Fourth Edition is so welcome.

If, as is greatly to be hoped, the movement towards settlement of disputes out of court, by mediation or conciliation, gathers pace, the learning which this book contains will become even more relevant and necessary. It is the right book, in the right place, at the right time.

The Right Honourable Lord Bingham of Cornhill
Lord Chief Justice of England

The Law Courts
The Strand
London

June 4, 1996

FOREWORD TO SETTLEMENT UNDER THE CIVIL PROCEDURE RULES

Under the Civil Procedure Rules offers to settle have become one of the most important elements of the civil justice system. The message of the new regime is that you should not be involved in litigation except as a last resort. Protocols will assist in bringing this about.

However, disputes cannot be avoided. What is required is to resolve the disputes when they arise expeditiously and in a sensible and reasonable way. The new rules should help to achieve this. They will enable the parties to take steps to ensure that they can obtain disclosure so as to form a realistic assessment of the merits of a case without litigation. Both sides will be in a position to make realistic offers to settle without having to commence proceedings. A well judged offer to settle should be the turning point in most disputes.

However, to make such an offer will involve a detailed knowledge and understanding of the rules. The same is true of the emphasis which is now placed on ADR. A mistake could have serious repercussions in the form of adverse orders for costs and interest. This is why I am particularly pleased that David Foskett has written this excellent commentary on making settlements under the new rules. He knows the rules as to settlement intimately. This is because he was one of their principal architects. This book provides practitioners with the information they need to make the best use of their new tools. I congratulate David Foskett on this excellent and comprehensive work which I know will be of immense value to practitioners.

The Right Honourable the Lord Woolf
Master of the Rolls

PREFACE

In the four years since the text was last updated, a number of significant developments have taken place. In the context of the general law, the House of Lords has considered the difficult legal issue of the effect that a settlement between two parties may have upon another party with direct or indirect links to the dispute (*Heaton v Axa Life, etc.*) and the important practical issue of advice given at the doors of the court on a settlement (*Moy v Pettmann Smith*). The Court of Appeal has dealt with the question of a mistake of law affording the basis for setting aside a compromise (*Brennan v Bolt Burdon*), the issue of mistake generally *"The Great Peace"*, the whole question of mediation (*Halsey v Milton Keynes General NHS Trust*) and a significant number of issues arising from Part 36, including the important question of the extent to which an offer in a money claim may be made other than by a payment into court (*Crouch v King's Healthcare NHS Trust* and *The Trustees of Stokes Pension Fund v Western Power Distribution (South West) Plc*). The role of *Calderbank* offers in the matrimonial jurisdiction has been the subject of detailed consideration by the Court of Appeal in *Norris v Norris*.

These are but a few examples of decisions that impact on the process of settlement in significant areas. The revision of the text in these and other areas has been timely.

Publication of this edition coincides with the 25th anniversary of the publication of the First edition. This affords an opportunity for me to look back briefly.

In those 25 years the book has gone from a single-author slim volume comprising 191 pages to something rather larger at 670 pages with a number of contributors in specialist areas. Quite what is to be deduced from these statistics is debatable. However, for me it is gratifying to find that the seeds of an idea sown over a quarter of a century ago has developed into what now seems to a permanent feature in the landscape of legal literature. Citation with approval in courts both at home and abroad and anecdotal evidence of the value the profession attaches to the book have made the time and effort to update it every few years worthwhile. The emergence of new and unexpected situations in which legal and practical problems can arise in the context of compromise keeps alive one's interest in whole area. The sheer volume of disputation, coupled with the high settlement rate, means that the subject will never go away.

The anniversary also affords an opportunity for a few expressions of thanks. To the publishers for having the vision to run with the idea from the beginning and to continue with their support ever since. To my distinguished team of contributors for coming on board and staying on board. To Lord Woolf for his kind words in the Foreword to "Settlement under the Civil Procedure Rules", published in 1999, the revised text of which now appears in Chapters 13–26. To Lord Bingham for his generous endorsement of the book in his Foreword to the Fourth edition. And to my wife (to whom the First edition was dedicated) for her continued support and encouragement throughout this prolonged venture—and to my two daughters for cheerfully putting up with the consequences of authorship from time to time.

My final thanks, however, on this occasion are reserved for two people to whom I have taken the liberty of dedicating this edition.

I first met Lord Lane when he was Mr Justice Geoffrey Lane. He had been invited to judge a university mooting competition in which I was participating. With that slender connection I wrote to him some years later (before, incidentally, news of his appointment as Lord Chief Justice was known) asking whether he would be prepared to write a Foreword to the First edition. He agreed immediately and I have always been very grateful for the words he used about even the then slim volume. I would like to think that the book has grown into the description he gave it.

I met Professor A.G. (Tony) Guest when I was an undergraduate at King's College London where he endeavoured to teach me the law of contract. He kindly agreed to read the manuscript of the First edition, thus ensuring that the content was at least moderately on target.

I am convinced that their combined support at that stage gave the book a kick-start but for which it may not have gathered its subsequent momentum. I remain very grateful to them both.

As for this 25th anniversary edition, I believe the text is up-to-date as at August 1, 2005.

David Foskett Q.C.
August 15, 2005

Postscript to Preface

I have learned only today, whilst on holiday abroad, that Lord Lane has died. His death occurred exactly a week after I had written the Preface and had told the publishers that he was to be one of the two dedicatees of this edition.

It is, of course, a very sad event for his family. From my point of view I am disappointed that I shall not now be able to send him a copy of this edition with his name appearing on the dedication page. I was able during his lifetime to thank him personally for his support for and endorsement of the First edition, but would have welcomed very much the opportunity to present him with a copy of the edition published 25 years later. It was not to be.

By the time the Preface and this Postscript is read there will have been many tributes and personal anecdotes about Lord Lane from distinguished sources. My far less distinguished contribution is merely this: he said something nice about my potential advocacy skills when I was an undergraduate, something very generous about the First edition some 10 years later, gave me a nod of recognition when I was called "within the Bar" in his court 11 years after that, was charming to my wife when he met her and was always very friendly when our paths crossed from time to time. His reputation for being approachable is one I can confirm. In addition I have one abiding personal recollection. As his Foreword hints, he was an enthusiastic golfer. On one occasion during his tenure as Lord Chief Justice he was playing in a Gray's Inn Golfing Society meeting at Woking Golf Club. Only he and I were in the main corridor of the clubhouse when I discovered him playing the fruit machine. I told him how much I wished that I had a camera in my hands at that moment. Those who knew him well can imagine his reply.

I am very saddened by his passing.

D.F.
August 28, 2005

CONTENTS

	page
Foreword to First Edition (Lord Lane)	ix
Foreword to Fourth Edition (Lord Bingham)	xi
Foreword to "Settlement under the Civil Procedure Rules" (Lord Woolf)	xiii
Preface	xv
Table of Cases	xxxv
Table of Statutes	xci
Table of Statutory Instruments	xcvii

PART 1: LEGAL FOUNDATION AND CONSEQUENCES OF COMPROMISE

(David Foskett Q.C.)

	para.
1. Introduction	1–01
2. Nature of a Dispute	
Must be a dispute before a compromise	2–01
Actual dispute	2–02
Potential dispute	2–08
The unarticulated dispute?	2–12
Law or fact	2–15
Must be bona fide	2–19
3. Essential Requirements of a Valid Compromise	
Introduction	3–01
Consideration	3–02
Promised or actual forbearance to sue	3–03
Compromise proper	3–07
No consideration	3–10

An identifiable agreement	3–22
General	3–22
Some examples	3–23
Presentation of cheque sent in settlement	3–30
A complete and certain agreement	3–49
General principle	3–49
Failure to agree all material terms	3–50
Terms too vague	3–51
Agreement to agree and the "future document"	3–55
Problem of the "conditional" compromise	3–58
Compromise of part of dispute	3–65
Agreement reached in "without prejudice" negotiations	3–67
Intention to create legal relations	3–68
Formalities	3–71
Land	3–72
Guarantee	3–74
Deeds	3–75

4. Impeachment of a Compromise

Incapacity	4–02
Children	4–02
Mentally disordered persons and patients	4–03
Legal advisers	4–06
Non-legal advisers and representatives	4–07
Expert witnesses	4–08
Companies	4–09
Local authorities	4–10
Partners	4–11
Representative parties	4–12
Represented parties acting personally	4–13
Mistake	4–14
General	4–14
Relief sought or given	4–15
Mistake in compromise	4–16
Misrepresentation	4–37
General	4–37
Are compromises contracts *uberrimae fidei?*	4–38
Some examples	4–42
Relief available	4–51
Duress and undue influence	4–52
General	4–52
Examples in the context of compromise	4–54
Effect	4–70
Illegality	4–71
General	4–71

Compromise of disputes involving issues of illegality	4–72
Illegal compromises	4–75

5. Terms of a Compromise

Preliminary	5–01
Construction	5–02
General problems and approach	5–02
Subjective intentions or understandings and extrinsic evidence	5–10
Post-compromise words and deeds	5–17
"Rules" of construction	5–18
Releases	5–23
The "*contra proferentem*" rule	5–34
Relevance of jurisdiction of court when construing consent order or judgment	5–36
Implied terms	5–42
General	5–42
Implications as to time	5–43
"Permission to apply" omitted	5–45
No implication of consent order or judgment	5–47
Implied term pending agreed order	5–48
Costs	5–60

6. Effects of a Compromise

Effects as between the parties	6–01
End of dispute	6–01
Identifying the disputes resolved	6–03
Matters left out	6–07
Other effects of compromise	6–18
Financial accounting involving other parties following a settlement	6–55
Preservation of rights against other parties in partial settlements of multi-party litigation—some illustrations	6–59
Effects upon and in connection with third parties	6–62
Imposition of liability	6–63
Acquisition of rights	6–64
Impeachment by or on behalf of third parties	6–74
Effects of impeachment by parties on third parties	6–82
Effects in connection with assignment	6–85

7. Satisfaction and Discharge of Obligations under a Compromise

Performance	7–02

Payment by cheque	7–03
Payment by instalments	7–04
Entire compromise	7–05
Agreement collateral to compromise	7–06
Mutually dependent obligations	7–07
Discharge other than by performance	7–08

8. Effects of a Breach of a Compromise

General	8–01
Promised or actual acts	8–03
Anticipatory breach of compromise	8–11
Renunciation	8–12
Self-created impossibility	8–13
Implied term as to co-operation	8–14
Innocent party's choice if available	8–15

PART 2: MACHINERY, PRACTICE AND ENFORCEMENT OF A COMPROMISE

(David Foskett Q.C.)

9. Means by which Compromises are Effectuated

General and preliminary	9–01
The aim	9–02
Costs	9–03
The methods of compromise	9–07
Exchange of letters	9–07
A deed or memorandum of agreement	9–08
Making an agreement an order or rule of court	9–09
Simple consent judgment for the payment of money	9–10
Consent judgment providing time for payment	9–13
Payment of money without judgment	9–16
Consent judgment or order involving terms other than mere payment of money, including Tomlin order	9–18
Other cases	9–34
Acceptance of Pt 36 payment	9–42

10. Practice of Compromise

General	10–01
Attitude of the courts to compromise	10–02
Reality of the consent	10–03
Recording of the consent	10–04
Indorsement of counsels' briefs	10–05

Jurisdiction	10–06
Practice of obtaining a consent order	10–17
Information required by court	10–20
Settlements reached just before or during trial	10–21
Settlements requiring approval of the court	10–22
Notification of settlement to court	10–25
Settlement of appeals	10–27
Confidentiality	10–28

11. Enforcement of a Compromise

General	11–01
Where there is no order or judgment	11–02
Where there is an order or judgment	11–04
Where agreement is filed and made a rule of court	11–06
Where the terms are incorporated in a Tomlin order	11–21
Where the terms are part of an order that does not reflect finality	11–28
Agreed order that recites the terms of agreement	11–29
Injunction by consent or undertaking	11–33

PART 3: PRACTICE ON IMPEACHMENT OF A COMPROMISE

(David Foskett Q.C.)

12. Practice on Setting Aside a Compromise

Compromise agreement	12–02
Compromise embodied in an order or judgment	12–03

PART 4: THE SETTLEMENT PROCESS IN CIVIL JUSTICE

(David Foskett Q.C.)

13. Present Landscape in Civil Litigation

Negotiation	13–04
Exchange of information	13–05
Pre-action costs	13–08
Indemnity costs	13–09

14. Structure of Pt 36

Introduction	14–01
Not a complete code	14–02

Freedom of contract	14–03
Privileged nature of offers within Pt 36	14–06

15. Pre-action Offers

Background	15–01
The offer itself	15–03
Further requirements—money claims	15–10
Further requirements—non-money claims	15–12
Can a pre-action offer be accepted after proceedings have started?	15–13

16. Essential General Requirements of a Pt 36 Offer and a Pt 36 Payment Notice

Introduction	16–01
Form	16–02
Matters to which either can relate	16–03
"The whole of the claim"	16–04
Interest	16–06
Parts and issues	16–07
Liability up to a specified proportion	16–10
Counterclaims	16–11
Interim payments	16–12

17. Particular Requirements of a Pt 36 Offer

Definition	17–01
Time given for acceptance	17–02
Alteration of Pt 36 offer	17–07
Court's permission to accept a Pt 36 offer	17–08

18. Particular Requirements of a Pt 36 Payment and a Pt 36 Payment Notice

Definition of a Pt 36 payment	18–01
Part 36 payment notice	18–08
Mechanics of payment	18–10
Mechanics of service of the notice	18–11
Increased payment into court	18–12
The 21-day rule	18–13
Effectiveness of a Pt 36 payment outside the 21-day rule	18–16
Withdrawal of a Pt 36 payment	18–17

19. Mixed Money and Non-money Claims

The old rules	19–01

The CPR	19–02
An offer to settle the whole of a mixed claim	19–03

20. Clarification of Pt 36 Offers and Payment Notices

Introduction	20–01
The rule	20–02
Offeree's options and their impact on costs	20–04

21. Acceptance other than with the Court's Permission

Introduction	21–01
The mechanics of acceptance	21–02
Costs consequences of acceptance of a defendant's offer	21–04
Costs consequences of acceptance of an offer or payment by one or more of several defendants	21–07
Costs consequences of acceptance of a claimant's offer	21–10
The mechanics of payment out	21–11
Interest	21–12
Consequences of acceptance for the proceedings	21–13

22. Acceptance with the Court's Permission

Introduction	22–01
Children and patients	22–02
Several defendants	22–05
Late Pt 36 offer and/or late acceptance	22–06

23. Failing to beat a Pt 36 Offer or a Pt 36 Payment

Introduction	23–01
Defendant's offer—money claim	23–02
Defendant's offer—non-money claim	23–04
Defendant's offer—mixed claim	23–06
Departure from general rule on grounds of injustice	23–08
Failing to "beat" a claimant's offer	23–09
A. The amount on which, and the period for which, increased interest is payable	23–13
B. The rate of interest	23–14
C. How are these choices made?	23–15
Unjust to make the order?	23–27
The "tactical offer"	23–30

24. Narrow Beating of, or a Failure to Beat, a Pt 36 Offer or Pt 36 Payment

	24–01

25. Miscellaneous Matters Relating to Pt 36

Introduction	25–01
Pt 20 claims	25–02
Small claims	25–05
Provisional damages	25–07
Periodical payments award in a personal injury case	25–10
Converting an ordered payment into court to a Pt 36 payment	25–11
Apportionment of money accepted in settlement of a Fatal Accidents Act claim	25–12

26. Offers outside Pt 36

A "without prejudice" offer	26–04
A *Calderbank* offer	26–05
An open offer	26–08

27. The "Without Prejudice" Rule

Introduction	27–01
When are negotiations without prejudice?	27–04
Express stipulation	27–06
Implied stipulation	27–07
"Opening shots"	27–09
"Parting shots" and responses to without prejudice letters	27–13
When will the without prejudice veil be lifted or disregarded?	27–15
A. The fact of agreement	27–20
B. Delay and adverse inferences from apparent lack of communication	27–21
C. Where a without prejudice document would prejudice the recipient	27–22
D. Matters independent of or collateral to the subject-matter of the dispute	27–25
E. "Unambiguous impropriety"	27–28
F. Estoppel	27–45
G. Waiver and mutuality	27–46
When will the disclosure of documents be protected by operation of the rule?	27–47
When can without prejudice negotiations be referred to at interim applications?	27–52
Want of prosecution	27–52
Security for costs	27–54
Interim payment applications	27–56

At what stage in proceedings may objection be
taken to a proposal to adduce evidence of the
content of without prejudice negotiations?   27–57

PART 5: ROLE OF LEGAL ADVISERS IN COMPROMISE

(David Foskett Q.C.)

28. Professional Ethics and Responsibilities

General	28–01
"Confidential" matters disclosed by client or opponent	28–03
Conflicts of interest	28–05
Unfounded claims	28–07
Informing client of offer of settlement	28–09
Overall duties to client in compromise	28–10
Keep court informed	28–12

29. Authority to Compromise and Liabilities of Legal Advisers Arising from Compromise

Authority to compromise—general	29–01
The law	29–04
Actual authority and ostensible (or apparent) authority to compromise	29–04
Ostensible (or apparent) authority	29–15
Misunderstandings between client and legal advisor	29–17
Liabilities of legal advisers arising from compromise	29–22
What constitutes negligence in this context?	29–25
Legal advisers in the investigation of negligence	29–32

PART 6: INSURANCE INTERESTS AND COMPROMISE

(David Foskett Q.C.)

30. Insurance Interests and Compromise

Introduction	30–01
Settlement with third party—the effects for the third party	30–03
General principle	30–03
Insured and uninsured losses	30–04
Settlements with third party—the effect as between insurer and insured	30–11
Settlement with third party—the effect on a co-insurer	30–14
Reinsurance and "follow the settlements" clauses	30–15
Nature of the "settlement" of an insured's claim	30–18

PART 7: CHANCERY LITIGATION

(David Hodge Q.C.)

31. The Settlement of Chancery Litigation

Insolvency	31–03
Companies	31–03
Individuals	31–06
Appeals	31–09
Liquidators and trustees in bankruptcy	31–10
Unfair prejudice	31–11
Disqualification orders	31–12
Court-appointed receivers	31–17
Trustees and personal representatives	31–18
Charities	31–23
Probate claims	31–25
Practice and procedure	31–30
Agreed orders	31–30
Appeals	31–31
Declarations	31–33
Interim applications	31–34
Masters	31–40
Release from undertaking	31–42

PART 8: MATRIMONIAL, FAMILY AND INHERITANCE DISPUTES

(Jonathan Cohen Q.C. and David Foskett Q.C.)

32. Compromise of Disputes between Husband and Wife

Agreements not necessarily involving divorce or judicial separation	32–02
Compromise of proceedings under Married Womens' Property Act 1882, s.17	32–03
Maintenance (and separation) agreements	32–08
Matrimonial Causes Act 1973, ss.34 and 35	32–10
Agreements concerning disposal of divorce or judicial separation suit itself	32–20
Agreements involving interim stages of divorce or judicial separation proceedings, including interim financial provision	32–23
Interim applications proper	32–23
Interim financial provision	32–27
Agreements relating to final disposal of financial and property applications	32–31

Preliminary	32–31
Nature and relevance of an agreement in this context	32–33
Securing an order reflecting a prior agreement	32–54
Disregarding agreements and setting aside consent orders	32–71
Agreements made "a rule of court" and variations	32–128
Agreements relating to children	32–136

33. Settlement of Inheritance Act Disputes

Preliminary	33–01
Contracting out	33–02
Effect of previous compromise or consent order	33–06
Effect and variation of previous "maintenance agreement"	33–09
Compromise proper of claims under the Act	33–10
Setting aside and enforcement	33–16
Practice	33–17

34. Offers of Settlement in Matrimonial Finance Cases

Preliminary	34–01
General approach to costs	34–04
Making an offer that may affect the costs order	34–08
The effect, if any, of the offer on costs	34–14
Children's cases	34–17

PART 9: SETTLEMENT OF SERIOUS PERSONAL INJURY CLAIMS INVOLVING CHILDREN OR PATIENTS

(William Edis)

35. Settlement of Serious Personal Injury Claims Involving Children or Patients

Introduction	35–01
Consequences of failing to obtain approval	35–10
Effect of approval and setting aside consent orders on the basis of a change of circumstances	35–14
Court of Protection	35–19
Various principles in settlement in personal injury cases	35–23
A. Provisional damages	35–24
B. Structured settlements/orders for periodical payments	35–29

C. The recoupment of benefits	35–54
D. Costs	35–56
E. Money laundering	35–64

PART 10: EMPLOYMENT CONTRACTS AND COMPROMISE

(Adrian Lynch Q.C.)

36. Employment Contracts and Compromise

Introduction	36–01
Contractual claims	36–04
General Release	36–05
Stress related personal injury	36–07
References	36–09
Statutory claims	36–14
Settlement achieved through intervention of conciliation officer	36–25
Compromise agreements	36–29
The particular complaint or proceedings	36–33
Statutory compromise agreements, ACAS conciliation and continuity of employment	36–34
Transfer of Undertakings (Protection of Employment) Regulations 1981 ("TUPE")	36–35
Mechanics of settlement in Employment Tribunals	36–39
Setting aside an agreed settlement	36–43
Setting aside a consent order	36–44
Statutory arbitration scheme	36–47
Conclusion	36–51

PART 11: LANDLORD AND TENANT AND DISPUTES OVER LAND

(Michelle Stevens-Hoare)

37. Landlord and Tenant

Business tenancies	37–04
Introduction	37–04
Contracting out	37–05
Parties agree upon the grant of a new tenancy	37–12
Parties agree that a business tenant will vacate	37–26
Residential tenancies	37–29
Introduction	37–29
No contracting out	37–31
Statutory framework and the court's jurisdiction	37–34

Obtaining an "agreed" order in practice	37–39
Residential occupants without statutory protection or with "restricted contracts"	37–43
Subsequent variation and enforcement of orders	37–45
Tenancy springing from the compromise	37–49
Forfeiture and relief from forfeiture	37–50

38. Disputes over land

General	38–01
Boundaries	38–07
During court proceedings	38–10

PART 12: CONSTRUCTION LITIGATION

(Michael Black Q.C.)

39. Construction Disputes

Introduction	39–01
Long-term issues	39–03
Certificates and retentions	39–09
Multiple issues	39–16
Multiple parties	39–27
Claims for contribution to settlements reached with other parties	39–39
The principle in *Biggin v Permanite*	39–40
Relevance and admissibility of advice received	39–51
Amendment of pleadings between date of offer and judgment or award	39–59
Value added tax	39–63
Adjudication	39–64

PART 13: ADMINISTRATIVE COURT PROCEEDINGS

(Nigel Giffin Q.C.)

40. The Resolution by Agreement of Administrative Court Proceedings

Introduction	40–01
Alternative dispute resolution	40–05
The power to compromise	40–07
Nature, enforcement and effect of compromise	40–11
Withdrawal of proceedings	40–14

Obtaining agreed order	40–16
Costs upon withdrawal or settlement of judicial review proceedings	40–20
Continuation of proceedings after fresh decision	40–24
Agreement at the permission stage	40–27

PART 14: ARBITRATIONS

(Michael Black Q.C.)

41. Settlement of Arbitrations

General	41–01
Essential principles concerning compromise	41–02
Enforcement of compromise	41–06
Who decides whether compromise concluded?	41–09
Setting aside consent award	41–14
Offers and costs	41–15

PART 15: APPEALS AND ADR

(David Foskett Q.C.)

42. Settlement of Appeals

Court of Appeal	42–02
Judge	42–09

43. Settlement through ADR

Introduction	43–01
Court's role in encouraging mediation and costs consequences to parties of failing to embrace it	43–03
Merits of the case	43–10
Other attempts at settlement	43–11
Whether mediation had reasonable prospects of success	43–12
Legal parameters of a mediation and mediated settlement	43–14

APPENDIX 1: Precedents

Section 1: Precedents for Part 36	A1–01
Section 2: Draft Consent Orders and Judgments—General	A1–12
Section 3: Chancery Precedents	A1–15
Section 4: Precedents for Serious Personal Injury Claims by Children or Patients	A1–21

Section 5: Landlord and Tenant Cases and
Boundary Disputes   A1–22
Section 6: Administrative Court Proceedings   A1–29

APPENDIX 2:

CPR Part 36 and Part 36 Practice Direction   A2–01

APPENDIX 3:

Extract from CPR Part 21 and Part 21 Practice Direction   A3–01

APPENDIX 4:

Extract from CPR Part 40 and Part 23 Practice Direction   A4–01

APPENDIX 5:

Part 36 Forms   A5–01

APPENDIX 6:

Text of Lecture entitled "The Tomlin Order:
three score years and ten"   A6–01

APPENDIX 7:

Extract from *B–T v B–T*   A7–01

TABLE OF CASES

Note: C.A.T. denotes Court of Appeal transcript.

A v A (Maintenance Pending Suit: Provision for Legal Fees); sub nom. A v A (Maintenance Pending Suit: Provision for Legal Costs) [2001] 1 W.L.R. 605; [2001] 1 F.L.R. 377; [2001] 1 F.C.R. 226; [2001] Fam. Law 96; (2000) 97(44) L.S.G. 45; (2000) 144 S.J.L.B. 273; *The Times*, November 14, 2000; *Independent*, December 11, 2000 (C.S), Fam Div. 32–27

AG Securities v Vaughan; Antoniades v Villiers [1990] 1 A.C. 417; [1988] 3 W.L.R. 1205; [1988] 3 All E.R. 1058; (1989) 21 H.L.R. 79; (1989) 57 P. & C.R. 17; [1988] 47 E.G. 193; (1989) 86(1) L.S.G. 39; (1988) 138 N.L.J. Rep. 325; (1988) 132 S.J. 1638; *The Times*, November 11, 1988, HL; reversing [1988] 2 W.L.R. 689; [1988] 2 All E.R. 173; (1988) 20 H.L.R. 212; (1988) 56 P. & C.R. 168; [1988] 06 E.G. 112; (1988) 85(7) L.S.G. 38; (1988) 138 N.L.J. Rep. 23; (1988) 132 S.J. 301, CA (Civ Div)........................... 37–31

Abada v Gray (Costs), *The Times*, July 9, 1997, CA (Civ Div)............ 23–08

Abbott (Bankrupt No.8 of 1980), Re; sub nom. Trustee of the Property of the Bankrupt v Abbott [1983] Ch. 45; [1982] 3 W.L.R. 86; [1982] 3 All E.R. 181; 126 S.J. 345, Ch D................................. 6–75

Abraham v Jutsun [1963] 1 W.L.R. 658; [1963] 2 All E.R. 402; 107 S.J. 357, CA; reversing (1962) 106 S.J. 880, DC..................... 28–07

Action for Negligence, Re, *The Times*, March 5, 1993, Ch D...... 14–08, 27–57

Adams v Adams (Separation Agreement) [1941] 1 K.B. 536, CA........... 7–11

Adamson v Adamson (1907) 23 T.L.R. 434........................... 32–12

Advanced Technology Structures Ltd v Cray Valley Products Ltd [1993] B.C.L.C. 723; *The Times*, December 29, 1992, CA (Civ Div).. 4–81, 39–34

Agromet Motoimport Ltd v Maulden Engineering Co (Beds) Ltd [1985] 1 W.L.R. 762; [1985] 2 All E.R. 436, QBD........................ 41–06

Ainsworth v Wilding (No.1) [1896] 1 Ch. 673, Ch D............... 4–32, 6–20

Alabama New Orleans Texas & Pacific Junction Railway Co, Re [1891] 1 Ch. 213, CA.. 1–01

Alcove Properties v Fraser and Fraser (1966) C.A.T. 124A............... 37–44

Alderson v Beetham Organisation Ltd [2003] EWCA Civ 408; [2003] 1 W.L.R. 1686; [2003] B.L.R. 217; [2003] H.L.R. 60; (2003) 100(23) L.S.G. 39; (2003) 147 S.J.L.B. 418; [2003] N.P.C. 47; *The Times*, April 19, 2003, CA (Civ Div).................................. 39–18

Ali Shipping Corp v Shipyard Trogir [1999] 1 W.L.R. 314; [1998] 2 All E.R. 136; [1998] 1 Lloyd's Rep. 643; [1998] C.L.C. 566; *Independent*, January 26, 1998 (C.S.), CA (Civ Div)..................... 43–16

Alizadeh v Nikbin, *The Times*, March 19, 1993, CA (Civ Div)..... 27–37, 27–41

TABLE OF CASES

Al-Kandari v JR Brown & Co [1988] Q.B. 665; [1988] 2 W.L.R. 671; [1988] 1 All E.R. 833; [1988] Fam. Law 382; (1988) 85(14) L.S.G. 50; (1988) 138 N.L.J. Rep. 62; (1988) 132 S.J. 462, CA (Civ Div); reversing [1987] Q.B. 514; [1987] 2 W.L.R. 469; [1987] 2 All E.R. 302; (1987) 84 L.S.G. 825; (1987) 137 N.L.J. 36; (1987) 131 S.J. 225, QBD. 29–31
Allcard v Walker [1896] 2 Ch. 369, Ch D. 4–16
Alliance Bank Ltd v Broom (1864) 2 Drew. & Sm. 289. 3–05
Allied Irish Bank v Hughes (1994) C.A.T. 1055; *The Times*, November 4, 1994, CA. 4–35
Allied Maples Group Ltd v Simmons & Simmons [1995] 1 W.L.R. 1602; [1995] 4 All E.R. 907; [1996] C.L.C. 153; 46 Con. L.R. 134; [1955–95] P.N.L.R. 701; (1995) 145 N.L.J. 1646; [1995] N.P.C. 83; (1995) 70 P. & C.R. D14, CA (Civ Div). 29–27
Allsop v Allsop (1980) 11 Fam. Law 18; 124 S.J. 710, CA (Civ Div). 32–72
Allsuch v Kaye (1978) C.A.T. 840. 5–38
Alonso v Alonso (1974) 4 Fam. Law 164; (1974) 118 S.J. 660, CA (Civ Div). 53–83
Amber v Stacey [2001] 1 W.L.R. 1225; [2001] 2 All E.R. 88; [2001] C.P. Rep. 26; [2001] C.P.L.R. 37; (2001) 3 T.C.L.R. 20; [2001] 2 Costs L.R. 325; (2000) 150 N.L.J. 1755; *Daily Telegraph*, November 28, 2000, CA (Civ Div). 18–02, 23–29
Amey v Amey [1992] 2 F.L.R. 89; [1992] F.C.R. 289. .... 3–61, 32–43
Amoco (UK) Exploration Co v Amerada Hess Ltd [1994] 1 Lloyd's Rep. 330, Ch D. 4–75
Anderson v Pacific Fire & Marine Insurance Co (1871–72) L.R. 7 C.P. 65, CCP. 4–42
Antaios Compania Naviera SA v Salen Rederierna AB (The Antaios) [1985] A.C. 191; [1984] 3 W.L.R. 592; [1984] 3 All E.R. 229; [1984] 2 Lloyd's Rep. 235; (1984) 81 L.S.G. 2776; (1984) 128 S.J. 564, HL; affirming [1983] 1 W.L.R. 1362; [1983] 3 All E.R. 777; [1983] 2 Lloyd's Rep. 473; [1983] Com. L.R. 262; (1983) 127 S.J. 730, CA (Civ Div). 5–08
Anufrijeva v Southwark LBC; R. (on the application of N) v Secretary of State for the Home Department; R. (on the application of M) v Secretary of State for the Home Department; sub nom. R. (on the application of Anufrijeva) v Southwark [2003] EWCA Civ 1406; [2004] Q.B. 1124; [2004] 2 W.L.R. 603; [2004] 1 All E.R. 833; [2004] 1 F.L.R. 8; [2003] 3 F.C.R. 673; [2004] H.R.L.R. 1; [2004] U.K.H.R.R. 1; 15 B.H.R.C. 526; [2004] H.L.R. 22; [2004] B.L.G.R. 184; (2003) 6 C.C.L. Rep. 415; [2004] Fam. Law 12; (2003) 100(44) L.S.G. 30; *The Times*, October 17, 2003; *Independent*, October 23, 2003, CA (Civ Div); affirming in part [2002] EWHC 3163; (2003) 6 C.C.L. Rep. 25, QBD. 40–07
Apley Estates Co Ltd v De Bernales [1947] Ch. 217; [1947] 1 All E.R. 213; 63 T.L.R. 71; [1947] L.J.R. 705; 176 L.T. 182; 91 S.J. 12, CA; affirming [1946] 2 All E.R. 338, Ch D. 6–41
Apple Computer Inc v Popiolek [1984] V.R. 156, Sup Ct (Vic). 9–37
Appleton v Aspin [1988] 1 W.L.R. 410; [1988] 1 All E.R. 904; (1988) 20 H.L.R. 182; (1988) 56 P. & C.R. 22; [1988] 04 E.G. 123; 132 S.J. 374, CA (Civ Div). 37–31
Archital Luxfer Ltd v Henry Boot Construction Ltd [1981] 1 Lloyd's Rep. 642, QBD. 41–19, 41–21, 41–22, 41–27

Ardandhu, The. *See* Owners of Cargo of the Kronprinz v Owners of the Kronprinz
Argolis Shipping Co SA v Midwest Steel and Alloy Corp (The Angeliki) [1982] 2 Lloyd's Rep. 594, QBD (Comm)....................... 41–28
Arnold v National Westminster Bank Plc (No.1) [1991] 2 A.C. 93; [1991] 2 W.L.R. 1177; [1991] 3 All E.R. 41; (1991) 62 P. & C.R. 490; [1991] 2 E.G.L.R. 109; [1991] 30 E.G. 57; [1991] E.G.C.S. 49; (1991) 135 S.J. 574; *The Times*, April 26, 1991, HL; affirming [1990] Ch. 573; [1990] 2 W.L.R. 304; [1990] 1 All E.R. 529; (1990) 59 P. & C.R. 389; [1990] 01 E.G. 58; (1990) 87(7) L.S.G. 35; (1990) 134 S.J. 1010; *The Times*, November 20, 1989; *Independent*, November 24, 1989, CA (Civ Div); affirming [1989] Ch. 63; [1988] 3 W.L.R. 1229; [1988] 3 All E.R. 977; (1989) 58 P. & C.R. 175; [1988] 45 E.G. 106; (1988) 85(46) L.S.G. 41; (1988) 138 N.L.J. Rep. 218; (1988) 132 S.J. 1639; *The Times*, July 11, 1988; *Independent*, July 7, 1988, Ch D.. 6–11
Arrale v Costain Civil Engineer [1976] 1 Lloyd's Rep. 98; (1975) 119 S.J. 527, CA (Civ Div)...... 2–08, 3–15, 4–47, 5–11, 5–17, 5–25, 5–32, 5–34
Arthur JS Hall & Co v Simons; Barratt v Woolf Seddon; Cockbone v Atkinson Dacre & Slack; Harris v Scholfield Roberts & Hill; sub nom. Harris v Scholfield Roberts & Hall; Barratt v Ansell (t/a Woolf Seddon) [2002] 1 A.C. 615; [2000] 3 W.L.R. 543; [2000] 3 All E.R. 673; [2000] B.L.R. 407; [2000] E.C.C. 487; [2000] 2 F.L.R. 545; [2000] 2 F.C.R. 673; [2001] P.N.L.R. 6; [2000] Fam. Law 806; [2000] E.G.C.S. 99; (2000) 97(32) L.S.G. 38; (2000) 150 N.L.J. 1147; (2000) 144 S.J.L.B. 238; [2000] N.P.C. 87; *The Times*, July 21, 2000; *Independent*, July 25, 2000, HL; affirming [1999] 3 W.L.R. 873; [1999] 1 F.L.R. 536; [1999] 2 F.C.R. 193; [1999] Lloyd's Rep. P.N. 47; [1999] P.N.L.R. 374; [1999] Fam. Law 215; [1998] N.P.C. 162; *The Times*, December 18, 1998; *Independent*, December 18, 1998, CA (Civ Div); affirming [1998] 2 F.L.R. 679; [1999] P.N.L.R. 208; [1998] Fam. Law 524, QBD.... 10–02, 13–05, 20–01, 29–02, 29–03, 29–17, 29–23
Ascon Contracting Ltd v Alfred McAlpine Construction Isle of Man Ltd, 66 Con. L.R. 119; (2000) 16 Const. L.J. 316; [2000] C.I.L.L. 1583, QBD (TCC)... 39–04
Aspden (Inspector of Taxes) v Hildesley [1982] 1 W.L.R. 264; [1982] 2 All E.R. 53; [1982] S.T.C. 206; 55 T.C. 609; [1981] T.R. 479; *The Times*, December 1, 1981, DC.................. 11–08, 32–129, 32–130
Assi v Leeds Metropolitan University [2001] EWCA Civ 641, CA (Civ Div) 3–53
Assicurazioni Generali SpA v CGU International Insurance Plc [2004] EWCA Civ 429; [2004] 2 All E.R. (Comm) 114; [2004] 2 C.L.C. 122; [2004] Lloyd's Rep. I.R. 457; (2004) 148 S.J.L.B. 475, CA (Civ Div); affirming [2003] EWHC 1073; [2003] 2 All E.R. (Comm) 425; [2003] 2 C.L.C. 852; [2003] Lloyd's Rep. I.R. 725, QBD (Comm).. 30–16
Associated Deliveries Ltd v Harrison (1985) 50 P. & C.R. 91; (1984) 272 E.G. 321, CA (Civ Div)... 37–51
Atkinson v Atkinson [1984] Fam. Law 305, CA (Civ Div)................ 32–62
Atkinson v Castan, *The Times*, April 17, 1991, CA (Civ Div).. 5–46, 5–57, 5–58, 9–09, 9–19, 9–30, 9–40, 11–29, 11–30
Atlee v Backhouse (1838) 3 M. & W. 633............................. 4–60

TABLE OF CASES

Attorney General v HRH Prince Ernest Augustus of Hanover; sub nom. Prince Ernest of Hanover v Attorney General [1957] A.C. 436; [1957] 2 W.L.R. 1; [1957] 1 All E.R. 49; 101 S.J. 60, HL; affirming [1956] Ch. 188; [1955] 3 W.L.R. 868; [1955] 3 All E.R. 647; 99 S.J. 871, CA; reversing [1955] Ch. 440; [1955] 2 W.L.R. 613; [1955] 1 All E.R. 746; 99 S.J. 220, Ch D. 32–16
Auriema Ltd v Haigh and Ringrose Ltd (1988) 4 Const. L.J. 200, QBD (OR). 3–30, 3–42
Awwad v Geraghty & Co; sub nom. Geraghty & Co v Awwad [2001] Q.B. 570; [2000] 3 W.L.R. 1041; [2000] 1 All E.R. 608; [2000] 1 Costs L.R. 105; [1999] N.P.C. 148; *Independent*, December 1, 1999, CA (Civ Div). 4–79
Azzarito v Pinkett & Eastern British Road Services Ltd (1979) C.A.T. 628.. 3–27

B (A Child) v Secretary of State for Social Security [2001] EWCA Civ 498; [2001] 1 W.L.R. 1404; [2001] Lloyd's Rep. Med. 297; (2001) 98(22) L.S.G. 36; (2001) 145 S.J.L.B. 120; *The Times*, May 3, 2001, CA (Civ Div). 35–34
B v B [1994] 1 F.C.R. 585. .... 32–85, 32–100, 32–108
B v B [1995] 1 F.L.R. 9; [1995] Fam. Law 70, Fam Div.... 32–49, 32–78, 32–94
B-T v B-T (Divorce: Procedure) [1990] 2 F.L.R. 1; [1990] F.C.R. 654; [1990] Fam. Law 294. .... 32–115, 32–116, 32–117, 32–122
BCT Software Solutions Ltd v C Brewer & Sons Ltd [2003] EWCA Civ 939; [2004] C.P. Rep. 2; [2004] F.S.R. 9; (2003) 26(9) I.P.D. 26057; (2003) 100(35) L.S.G. 35; (2003) 147 S.J.L.B. 874, CA (Civ Div).... 9–04, 9–05
BG Plc v Nelson Group Services (Maintenance) Ltd [2002] EWCA Civ 547, CA (Civ Div). 4–42
BNP Paribas v Mezzotero [2004] I.R.L.R. 508; (2004) 148 S.J.L.B. 666, EAT. 27–44
Babcock v Lawson (1879–80) L.R. 5 Q.B.D. 284, CA; affirming (1878–79) L.R. 4 Q.B.D. 394, QBD. 6–83
Backhouse v Backhouse; sub nom. B v B [1978] 1 W.L.R. 243; [1978] 1 All E.R. 1158; (1977) 7 Fam. Law 212; 121 S.J. 710, Fam Div... 4–53, 32–31
Baker v Baker (1886) 55 L.T. 723. 11–03
Balfour Beatty Civil Engineering Ltd v Docklands Light Railway Ltd [1996] C.L.C. 1435; 78 B.L.R. 42; 49 Con. L.R. 1; (1996) 12 Const. L.J. 259, CA (Civ Div). 39–09
Balkanbank v Taher (No.2) [1995] 1 W.L.R. 1056; [1995] 2 All E.R. 904; *The Times*, December 1, 1994, CA (Civ Div). 5–36, 5–41, 6–05
Bank of Credit and Commerce International SA (In Liquidation) v Ali (No.1) [2001] UKHL 8; [2002] 1 A.C. 251; [2001] 2 W.L.R. 735; [2001] 1 All E.R. 961; [2001] I.C.R. 337; [2001] I.R.L.R. 292; [2001] Emp. L.R. 359; (2001) 98(15) L.S.G. 32; (2001) 151 N.L.J. 351; (2001) 145 S.J.L.B. 67; (2001) 145 S.J.L.B. 70; *The Times*, March 6, 2001, HL; affirming [2000] 3 All E.R. 51; [2000] I.C.R. 1410; [2000] I.R.L.R. 398; *The Times*, May 10, 2000, CA (Civ Div); reversing [1999] 2 All E.R. 1005; [1999] I.C.R. 1068; [1999] I.R.L.R. 226; (1999) 96(7) L.S.G. 35; (1999) 149 N.L.J. 53; *The Times*, January 25, 1999, Ch D...... 2–10, 3–16, 5–05, 5–10, 5–19, 5–22, 5–23, 5–24, 5–29, 5–31, 6–30, 6–39, 36–05, 36–28, 39–22
Banque Keyser Ullmann SA v Skandia (UK) Insurance Co (No.2) [1988] 2 All E.R. 880; [1988] 1 F.T.L.R. 360; (1988) 138 N.L.J. Rep. 31, QBD (Comm). 6–55, 6–58

Banyard v Banyard [1985] Fam. Law 120, CA (Civ Div)................. 32–62

Barber v Staffordshire CC [1996] I.C.R. 379; [1996] I.R.L.R. 209; (1996) 140 S.J.L.B. 43; *The Times*, January 29, 1996; *Independent*, February 2, 1996, CA (Civ Div)... 36–40

Barclays Bank Plc v O'Brien [1994] 1 A.C. 180; [1993] 3 W.L.R. 786; [1993] 4 All E.R. 417; [1994] 1 F.L.R. 1; [1994] 1 F.C.R. 357; (1994) 26 H.L.R. 75; (1994) 13 Tr. L.R. 165; [1994] C.C.L.R. 94; [1994] Fam. Law 78; [1993] E.G.C.S. 169; (1993) 143 N.L.J. 1511; (1993) 137 S.J.L.B. 240; [1993] N.P.C. 135; *The Times*, October 22, 1993; *Independent*, October 22, 1993, HL; affirming [1993] Q.B. 109; [1992] 3 W.L.R. 593; [1992] 4 All E.R. 983; [1993] 1 F.L.R. 124; [1993] 1 F.C.R. 97; (1993) 66 P. & C.R. 135; (1992) 11 Tr. L.R. 153; [1992] C.C.L.R. 37; [1993] Fam. Law 62; (1992) 89(27) L.S.G. 34; (1992) 142 N.L.J. 1040; (1992) 136 S.J.L.B. 175; [1992] N.P.C. 74; *The Times*, June 3, 1992; *Independent*, June 17, 1992; *Financial Times*, June 10, 1992, CA (Civ Div).......... 4–66, 4–69, 6–31

Barclays Bank Plc v Willowbrook International [1987] B.C.L.C. 717; [1987] F.T.L.R. 386, CA (Civ Div); reversing; *Financial Times*, July 9, 1985, Ch D.. 6–73

Barden v Barden (1921) 21 S.R.N.S.W. 588, S.C..................... 27–27

Barder v Caluori; sub nom. Barder v Barder [1988] A.C. 20; [1987] 2 W.L.R. 1350; [1987] 2 All E.R. 440; [1987] 2 F.L.R. 480; [1988] Fam. Law 18; (1987) 84 L.S.G. 2046; (1987) 137 N.L.J. 497; (1987) 131 S.J. 776, HL; reversing [1987] Fam. 24; [1986] 3 W.L.R. 145; [1986] 2 All E.R. 918; [1987] 1 F.L.R. 18; [1986] Fam. Law 331; (1986) 83 L.S.G. 1996; (1986) 136 N.L.J. 561; (1986) 130 S.J., CA (Civ Div)... 4–19, 32–76, 32–84, 32–91, 32–97, 32–100, 32–101, 32–104, 32–107, 32–108, 32–111, 32–112, 35–16

Bargain Pages Ltd v Midland Independent Newspapers Ltd [2003] EWHC 1887; [2004] F.S.R. 6; (2003) 26(9) I.P.D. 26059, Ch D...... 9–26, 9–27

Barings Plc (In Liquidation), Re (No.2); sub nom. Barings Plc (In Liquidation) (No.7), Re [2002] 1 B.C.L.C. 401; [2002] B.P.I.R. 653, Ch D (Companies Ct)... 31–10

Barrell Enterprises, Re [1973] 1 W.L.R. 19, CA (Civ Div).............. 35–10

Bartlett v Conley, July 2, 1999, CA.................................. 3–64

Barton v Fincham [1921] 2 K.B. 291, CA...................... 37–34, 37–39

Basaran v Nevar Investments Ltd (1979) C.A.T. 181................ 4–75, 6–23

Bath's Case. *See* Norwich Provident Insurance Society (Winding Up), Re

Bayoumi v Women's Total Abstinence Educational Union Ltd; sub nom. Perkins v Women's Total Abstinence Educational Union Ltd [2003] EWCA Civ 1548; [2004] Ch. 46; [2004] 2 W.L.R. 181; [2004] 3 All E.R. 110; [2004] 2 P. & C.R. 11; [2004] W.T.L.R. 133; (2003) 100(47) L.S.G. 21; (2003) 147 S.J.L.B. 1307; [2003] N.P.C. 135; [2004] 1 P. & C.R. DG9; *The Times*, November 11, 2003, CA (Civ Div); reversing [2003] EWHC 212; [2003] Ch. 283; [2003] 2 W.L.R. 1287; [2003] 1 All E.R. 864; [2003] W.T.L.R. 317; (2003) 100(10) L.S.G. 27; [2003] N.P.C. 4; [2003] 1 P. & C.R. DG21; *The Times*, February 4, 2003; *Independent*, March 17, 2003 (C.S), Ch D....... 31–32

Beaufort Developments (NI) Ltd v Gilbert-Ash (NI) Ltd [1999] 1 A.C. 266; [1998] 2 W.L.R. 860; [1998] 2 All E.R. 778; [1998] N.I. 144; [1998] C.L.C. 830; 88 B.L.R. 1; 59 Con. L.R. 66; (1998) 14 Const. L.J. 280; [1998] E.G.C.S. 85; (1998) 95(24) L.S.G. 33; (1998) 95(31) L.S.G. 34; (1998) 148 N.L.J. 869; (1998) 142 S.J.L.B. 172; [1998] N.P.C. 91; [1998] N.P.C. 93; *The Times*, June 8, 1998, HL (NI); reversing [1997] N.I. 142; 83 B.L.R. 1; (1997) 13 Const. L.J. 321, CA (NI)... 39–09

Beesly v Hallwood Estates Ltd [1961] Ch. 105; [1961] 2 W.L.R. 36; [1961] 1 All E.R. 90; 105 S.J. 61, CA; affirming [1960] 1 W.L.R. 549; [1960] 2 All E.R. 314; 104 S.J. 407, Ch D........................ 4–45

Behar, Ellis and Parnell v Territorial Investments Ltd. (1973) C.A.T. 237.. 37–18

Beighton v Beighton (1974) 4 Fam. Law 119, CA (Civ Div)........ 3–56, 32–29

Bell v Galynski; Bell v A Kings (Loft Extensions) Ltd [1974] 2 Lloyd's Rep. 13, CA (Civ Div).. 3–36, 3–39

Bell v Lever Brothers Ltd; sub nom. Lever Bros Ltd v Bell [1932] A.C. 161, HL; reversing [1931] 1 K.B. 557, CA............................. 4–38

Bell Electric Ltd v Aweco Appliance Systems GmbH & Co KG [2002] EWHC 872; [2002] C.L.C. 1246; [2002] Eu. L.R. 443, QBD........ 8–15

Bellamy v Sheffield Teaching Hospitals NHS Trust [2003] EWCA Civ 1124, CA (Civ Div)... 16–03, 23–11

Bellcairn, The (1885) L.R. 10 P.D. 161, CA................. 4–32, 6–84, 9–40

Belt v Basildon and Thurrock NHS Trust [2004] EWHC 783, QBD....... 27–40

Bennett v Bennett [1952] 1 K.B. 249; [1952] 1 All E.R. 413; [1952] 1 T.L.R. 400, CA; affirming [1951] 2 K.B. 572; [1951] 1 All E.R. 1088; [1951] 1 T.L.R. 873; 115 J.P. 355; 95 S.J. 286, KBD........ 32–09

Benson v Benson (dec'd) [1996] 1 F.L.R. 692; [1996] 3 F.C.R. 590; [1996] Fam. Law 351, Fam Div..................... 32–112, 32–114, 32–121

Benstall v Swain (1829) Tamlyn 288 at 295........................... 3–60

Beoco Ltd v Alfa Laval Co Ltd [1995] Q.B. 137; [1994] 3 W.L.R. 1179; [1994] 4 All E.R. 464; 66 B.L.R. 1; (1994) 144 N.L.J. 233; *The Times*, January 12, 1994, CA (Civ Div)........................ 39–60

Berry Trade Ltd v Moussavi (No.3) [2003] EWCA Civ 715; (2003) 100(29) L.S.G. 36; (2003) 147 S.J.L.B. 625; *The Times*, June 3, 2003, CA (Civ Div).. 27–40

Beswick v Beswick [1968] A.C. 58; [1967] 3 W.L.R. 932; [1967] 2 All E.R. 1197; 111 S.J. 540, HL; affirming [1966] Ch. 538; [1966] 3 W.L.R. 396; [1966] 3 All E.R. 1; 110 S.J. 507, CA; reversing [1965] 3 All E.R. 858; (1965) 116 N.L.J. 245, Chancery Ct of Lancaster......... 6–64

Beta Investments SA v Transmedia Europe Inc [2003] EWHC 3066, Ch D.. 3–56

Biggin & Co Ltd v Permanite Ltd [1951] 2 K.B. 314; [1951] 2 All E.R. 191; [1951] 2 T.L.R. 159; 95 S.J. 414, CA; reversing in part [1951] 1 K.B. 422; [1950] 2 All E.R. 859; (1950) 66 T.L.R. (Pt. 2) 944, KBD.... 39–39, 39–44, 39–49, 39–54, 39–55, 39–56, 39–58

Binder v Alachouzos [1972] 2 Q.B. 151; [1972] 2 W.L.R. 947; [1972] 2 All E.R. 189; [1972] 1 Lloyd's Rep. 524; 116 S.J. 139, CA (Civ Div).... 2–17, 2–18, 2–19, 4–72, 37–31

Birse Construction Ltd v Haiste Ltd [1996] 1 W.L.R. 675; [1996] 2 All E.R. 1; [1996] C.L.C. 577; 76 B.L.R. 31; 47 Con. L.R. 162; [1996] P.N.L.R. 8; (1996) 93(2) L.S.G. 29; (1996) 140 S.J.L.B. 25; *The Times*, December 12, 1995, CA (Civ Div); reversing......... 6–52, 39–28

Bishop v Berkshire HA [1999] P.I.Q.R. P92; [1999] Lloyd's Rep. Med. 16; (1999) 46 B.M.L.R. 67; *Independent*, October 26, 1998 (C.S.), QBD 3–56

Black v Doncaster MBC [1999] 1 W.L.R. 53; [1998] 3 All E.R. 631; [1998]
P.I.Q.R. Q139; (1998) 95(29) L.S.G. 27; (1998) 142 S.J.L.B. 199;
The Times, July 14, 1998; *Independent*, June 29, 1998 (C.S.), CA
(Civ Div)... 15–14
Blackham v Entrepose UK [2004] EWCA Civ 1109; (2004) 101(35) L.S.G.
33; (2004) 148 S.J.L.B. 945; *The Times*, September 28, 2004, CA
(Civ Div)... 23–02
Blackpool BC v F Parkinson Ltd, 58 B.L.R. 85; (1993) 9 Const. L.J. 29... 39–10
Blackspur Group Plc (No.3), Re; sub nom. Secretary of State for Trade and
Industry v Davies (No.3); Secretary of State for Trade and Industry v
Eastaway (Undertakings) [2001] EWCA Civ 1595; [2004] B.C.C.
839; [2002] 2 B.C.L.C. 263, CA (Civ Div); affirming (2001) 98(26)
L.S.G. 43; (2001) 151 N.L.J. 889; (2001) 145 S.J.L.B. 155; *The
Times*, July 5, 2001, Ch D... 31–16
Blair v Assets Co Ltd [1896] A.C. 409, HL............................. 28–09
Blenkinsopp v Blenkinsopp (1852) 1 De G.M. & G. 495.................. 6–81
Blexen v G Percy Trentham Ltd, 54 B.L.R. 37; 21 Con. L.R. 61; [1990] 42
E.G. 133, CA (Civ Div).. 39–61, 39–62
Blythe Ex p. Banner, Re; sub nom. Blythe, Re v Ex p. Banner (1881) L.R.
17 Ch. D. 480, CA.. 2–19, 6–75
Boag v Standard Marine Insurance Co Ltd [1937] 2 K.B. 113; (1937) 57 Ll.
L. Rep. 83, CA; affirming [1936] 2 K.B. 121; (1936) 54 Ll. L. Rep.
320, KBD.. 30–11
Board v Hoey, 65 T.L.R. 43; [1948] W.N. 448; 92 S.J. 661............. 5–43
Bolkiah v KPMG; sub nom. HRH Prince Jefri Bolkiah v KPMG [1999] 2
A.C. 222; [1999] 2 W.L.R. 215; [1999] 1 B.C.L.C. 1; [1999]
P.N.L.R. 220; (1999) 149 N.L.J. 16; (1999) 143 S.J.L.B. 35; *The
Times*, April 20, 1999; *Independent*, January 12, 1999, HL; reversing
[1999] 1 All E.R. 517; [1999] C.L.C. 175; (1998) 95(42) L.S.G. 33;
(1998) 148 N.L.J. 1602; (1998) 142 S.J.L.B. 268; *The Times*,
October 22, 1998; *Independent*, October 22, 1998, CA (Civ Div);
reversing, *The Times*, September 25, 1998, Ch D.................. 28–05
Bolton v Mahadeva [1972] 1 W.L.R. 1009; [1972] 2 All E.R. 1322; 116
S.J. 564, CA (Civ Div)... 7–05
Boots the Chemists Ltd v Pinkland; Thorn EMI v Pinkland [1992] 28 E.G.
118... 37–18
Bothe v Amos [1976] Fam. 46; [1975] 2 W.L.R. 838; [1975] 2 All E.R.
321; (1975) 5 Fam. Law 86; 119 S.J. 150, CA (Civ Div)............. 32–04
Boustany v Piggott (1995) 69 P. & C.R. 298; [1993] E.G.C.S. 85; [1993]
N.P.C. 75, PC (Ant).. 4–67
Bovis Lend Lease Ltd (formerly Bovis Construction Ltd) v RD Fire
Protection Ltd; Huthco Ltd v Bovis Lend Lease Ltd (formerly Bovis
Construction Ltd); sub nom. Hutcho Ltd v Bovis Lend Lease Ltd
[2003] EWHC 939; 89 Con. L.R. 169, QBD (TCC).............. 39–56
Bowman v Fels [2005] EWCA Civ 226; (2005) 155 N.L.J. 413; (2005) 149
S.J.L.B. 357; *The Times*, March 14, 2005, CA (Civ Div)............ 35–64
Braben v Emap Images Ltd [1997] 1 W.L.R. 1507; [1997] 2 All E.R. 544;
(1997) 147 N.L.J. 14; *The Times*, January 3, 1997, Ch D........... 19–01
Bradstock Group Pension Scheme Trustees Ltd v Bradstock Group Plc
[2002] EWHC 651; [2002] I.C.R. 1427; [2002] O.P.L.R. 281;
[2002] Pens. L.R. 327; [2002] W.T.L.R. 1281; (2002) 99(36) L.S.G.
40; *The Times*, July 10, 2002, Ch D............................... 31–18
Brady v Curran (1868) I.R. 2 C.L. 314................................. 29–15

Bremer Oeltransport GmbH v Drewry [1933] 1 K.B. 753; (1933) 45 Ll. L. Rep. 133, CA... 41–06
Brennan v Bolt Burdon; sub nom. Brennan v Bolt Burden; Brennan v Islington LBC [2004] EWCA Civ 1017; [2005] Q.B. 303; [2004] 3 W.L.R. 1321; [2004] C.P. Rep. 43; (2004) 101(34) L.S.G. 31; (2004) 148 S.J.L.B. 972; [2004] N.P.C. 133; *The Times*, August 27, 2004, CA (Civ Div); reversing [2003] EWHC 2493; [2004] 1 W.L.R. 1240; *The Times*, November 7, 2003, QBD.............................. 4–20
Brent v Brent ((1841) 10 L.J. Ch. 84..................................... 4–56
Brill v Proud [1984] Fam. Law 59, CA (Civ Div).................... 33–08
Brister v Brister; sub nom. B (GC) v B(BA) [1970] 1 W.L.R. 664; [1970] 1 All E.R. 913, PDAD................................ 6–23, 9–12, 32–29, 32–82
Bristol Myers Squibb Co v Baker Norton Pharmaceuticals Inc (Costs) [2001] EWCA Civ 414; [2001] R.P.C. 45; (2001) 24(6) I.P.D. 24035; *The Times*, April 26, 2001, CA (Civ Div)................... 5–44
Bristow v Grout, *The Times*, November 9, 1987, CA (Civ Div); affirming, *The Times*, November 3, 1986............................. 2–11, 2–12
British Movietonews v London and District Cinemas 1952] A.C. 166; [1951] 2 All E.R. 617; [1951] 2 T.L.R. 571; 95 S.J. 499, HL; reversing [1951] 1 K.B. 190; [1950] 2 All E.R. 390; 66 T.L.R. (Pt. 2) 203; 94 S.J. 504, CA... 5–10
British Russian Gazette & Trade Outlook Ltd v Associated Newspapers Ltd; Talbot v Associated Newspapers Ltd [1933] 2 K.B. 616, CA... 3–03, 3–30, 8–03
British Steel Plc v Customs and Excise Commissioners (No.1) [1997] 2 All E.R. 366, CA (Civ Div); reversing [1996] 1 All E.R. 1002, QBD..... 1–02
Brocklesby v Armitage & Guest [2002] 1 W.L.R. 598; [2001] 1 All E.R. 172; [1999] Lloyd's Rep. P.N. 888; [2000] P.N.L.R. 33; [2001] 1 E.G.L.R. 67; [2001] 14 E.G. 150, CA (Civ Div).................... 39–20
Brockwell v Brockwell (1975) 6 Fam. Law 46, CA (Civ Div)....... 32–09, 32–49
Broderick, Re [1986] 6 N.I.J.B. 36....................................... 3–17, 3–43
Brown v Kirrage (1981) 11 Fam. Law 141, CA........................ 32–62
Brown v Raphael [1958] Ch. 636; [1958] 2 W.L.R. 647; [1958] 2 All E.R. 79; 102 S.J. 269, CA... 4–42
Brownton Ltd v Edward Moore Inbucom Ltd [1985] 3 All E.R. 499; (1985) 82 L.S.G. 1165, CA (Civ Div)....................... 4–80, 6–88, 6–91
Brunsden v Humphrey [1884] 14 Q.B.D. 141......................... 39–21
Brunsdon v Allard (1859) 2 Ell. & Ell................................... 194–13
Buckbod Investments v Nana-Otchere [1985] 1 W.L.R. 342; [1985] 1 All E.R. 283; (1985) 82 L.S.G. 929; (1985) 129 S.J. 172, Ch D........ 31–31
Buckinghamshire CC v Moran [1990] Ch. 623; [1989] 3 W.L.R. 152; [1989] 2 All E.R. 225; 88 L.G.R. 145; (1989) 58 P. & C.R. 236; (1989) 139 N.L.J. 257; (1989) 133 S.J. 849, CA (Civ Div); affirming; 86 L.G.R. 472; (1988) 56 P. & C.R. 372; *The Times*, March 2, 1988, Ch D.. 27–09, 27–12
Buckland v Palmer [1984] 1 W.L.R. 1109; [1984] 3 All E.R. 554; [1985] R.T.R. 5; (1984) 81 L.S.G. 2300; (1984) 128 S.J. 565, CA (Civ Div).. 30–08, 30–09, 30–03
Bunge SA v Kruse [1977] 1 Lloyd's Rep. 492; *The Times*, November 5, 1976, CA (Civ Div); affirming [1976] 1 Lloyd's Rep. 357; 119 S.J. 794, QBD (Comm)... 3–26, 3–34
Burke v Burke (1973) [1974] 1 W.L.R. 1063; [1974] 2 All E.R. 944; 118 S.J. 98, CA (Civ Div).. 3–23

Burns v Burns [2004] EWCA Civ 1258; [2004] 3 F.C.R. 263, CA (Civ
Div).. 35–16, 35–18
Burrell & Son v Leven (1926) 42 T.L.R. 407........................... 3–11
Burrows v Brent LBC [1996] 1 W.L.R. 1448; [1996] 4 All E.R. 577; [1997]
1 F.L.R. 178; [1997] 2 F.C.R. 43; (1997) 29 H.L.R. 167; [1997] 1
E.G.L.R. 32; [1997] 11 E.G. 150; [1997] Fam. Law 246; (1996)
93(43) L.S.G. 26; (1996) 146 N.L.J. 1616; (1996) 140 S.J.L.B. 239;
[1996] N.P.C. 149; The Times, November 4, 1996; Independent,
November 8, 1996, HL; reversing (1995) 27 H.L.R. 748; (1996) 72
P. & C.R. 261; [1995] E.G.C.S. 128; [1995] N.P.C. 124; The Times,
July 21, 1995; Independent, August 22, 1995, CA (Civ Div)........ 37–49
Bushwall Properties Ltd v Vortex Properties Ltd [1976] 1 W.L.R. 591;
[1976] 2 All E.R. 283; (1976) 32 P. & C.R. 334; 120 S.J. 183, CA
(Civ Div); reversing [1975] 1 W.L.R. 1649; [1975] 2 All E.R. 214;
(1974) 119 S.J. 846, Ch D.................................... 3–22, 3–68
Butcher v Wolfe [1999] C.P.L.R. 112; [1999] B.L.R. 61; [1999] 1 F.L.R.
334; [1999] 2 F.C.R. 165; [1999] Fam. Law 80; [1998] E.G.C.S.
153; (1998) 95(48) L.S.G. 31; (1998) 95(43) L.S.G. 33; The Times,
November 9, 1998, CA (Civ Div)..... 9–04, 15–01, 15–04, 23–04, 26–06,
26–07
Butler Machine Tool Co v Ex-cell-o Corp (England) [1979] 1 W.L.R. 401;
[1979] 1 All E.R. 965; 121 S.J. 406, CA (Civ Div)................. 3–22
Butler v Knight (1866–67) L.R. 2 Ex. 109, Ex Ct....................... 29–28
Butlin's Settlement Trusts, Re; sub nom. Butlin v Butlin (1974) 118 S.J.
757.. 31–19
Butt v Butt [1987] 1 W.L.R. 1351; [1987] 3 All E.R. 657; [1987] F.S.R.
574; (1987) 84 L.S.G. 2194; (1987) 131 S.J. 1286, CA (Civ Div)... 31–38

C, Re [1993] 2 F.L.R. 799; [1993] Fam. Law 675..... 32–116, 32–122, 32–127
C v C (Financial Provision: Non-Disclosure) [1994] 2 F.L.R. 272; [1995] 1
F.C.R. 75; [1994] Fam. Law 561, Fam Div...................... 32–113
C v C (Costs: Ancillary Relief) [2003] EWHC 2321; [2004] 1 F.L.R. 291;
[2004] Fam. Law 18, Fam Div................................ 34–06
C v FC (Children Proceedings: Costs) [2004] 1 F.L.R. 362; [2004] Fam.
Law 104, Fam Div.. 34–17
C&H Engineering v F Klucznik & Sons Ltd (No.2) [1992] F.S.R. 667; The
Times, March 26, 1992, Ch D........................... 26–07, 27–14
CIBC Mortgages Plc v Pitt [1994] 1 A.C. 200; [1993] 3 W.L.R. 802; [1993]
4 All E.R. 433; [1994] 1 F.L.R. 17; [1994] 1 F.C.R. 374; (1994) 26
H.L.R. 90; (1994) 13 Tr. L.R. 180; [1994] C.C.L.R. 68; [1993] Fam.
Law 79; [1993] E.G.C.S. 174; (1993) 143 N.L.J. 1514; (1993) 137
S.J.L.B. 240; [1993] N.P.C. 136; The Times, October 22, 1993;
Independent, October 22, 1993, HL; affirming (1993) 25 H.L.R. 439;
(1993) 66 P. & C.R. 179; [1993] E.G.C.S. 66; [1993] N.P.C. 61; The
Times, April 7, 1993, CA (Civ Div).............................. 4–66
CPL Contracting Ltd v Cadenza Residential Ltd [2005] T.C.L.R. 1, QBD
(TCC)... 39–13, 39–67
CTN Cash and Carry Ltd v Gallaher Ltd [1994] 4 All E.R. 714, CA (Civ
Div).. 4–61
Cable & Wireless Plc v IBM United Kingdom Ltd; sub nom. Cable &
Wireless Plc v IBM UK Ltd [2002] EWHC 2059; [2002] 2 All E.R.
(Comm) 1041; [2002] C.L.C. 1319; [2003] B.L.R. 89; [2002]
Masons C.L.R. 58; (2002) 152 N.L.J. 1652, QBD (Comm)......... 3–55
Cadmus Investment Ltd v Amec Building Ltd [1998] A.D.R.L.J. 72, QBD.. 39–62

Cadogan v Cadogan [1977] 1 W.L.R. 1041; [1977] 3 All E.R. 831; (1978) 35 P. & C.R. 92, CA (Civ Div); reversing [1977] 1 All E.R. 200; (1976) 32 P. & C.R. 388; 121 S.J. 443, Ch D.................... 6–81

Calderbank v Calderbank [1976] Fam. 93; [1975] 3 W.L.R. 586; [1975] 3 All E.R. 333; (1975) 5 Fam. Law 190; 119 S.J. 490, CA (Civ Div).. 14–06, 26–01, 26–02, 26–04, 26–05, 26–06, 26–07, 27–14, 34–06, 34–08, 34–09, 34–13, 34–15, 34–16, 35–60, 41–29

Callisher v Bischoffsheim (1869–70) L.R. 5 Q.B. 449, QB........... 2–19, 3–08

Camm v Camm (1983) 4 F.L.R. 577; (1983) 13 Fam. Law 112, CA (Civ Div)................ 32–09, 32–31, 32–48, 32–77, 32–78, 32–79, 32–80

Cape & Dalgleish v Fitzgerald [2002] UKHL 16; [2002] C.P. Rep. 51; [2002] C.P.L.R. 509; [2003] 1 C.L.C. 65, HL; affirming [2001] Lloyd's Rep. P.N. 110, CA (Civ Div).................. 5–09, 6–30, 6–38

Capital Bank Plc v Stickland [2004] EWCA Civ 1677, CA (Civ Div)...... 14–11, 15–14, 18–17, 22–12

Capon v Evans, unreported, April 11, 1986........... 3–24, 5–12, 6–04, 30–05

Cardshops Ltd v John Lewis Properties Ltd [1983] Q.B. 161; [1982] 3 W.L.R. 803; [1982] 3 All E.R. 746; (1983) 45 P. & C.R. 197; (1982) 263 E.G. 791; 126 S.J. 625, CA (Civ Div)........................ 37–27

Carecraft Construction Co Ltd, Re [1994] 1 W.L.R. 172; [1993] 4 All E.R. 499; [1993] B.C.C. 336; [1993] B.C.L.C. 1259, Ch D...... 31–13, 31–14, 31–15, 31–16, 33–13

Carillion Construction Ltd v Felix (UK) Ltd [2001] B.L.R. 1; 74 Con. L.R. 144, QBD (TCC)... 39–37

Carney v Herbert [1985] A.C. 301; [1984] 3 W.L.R. 1303; [1985] 1 All E.R. 438; (1984) 81 L.S.G. 3500, PC (Aus)........................ 4–71

Carrs Bury St Edmunds Ltd v Whitworth Partnership; Carrs Bury St Edmunds Ltd v Barnes Group, 84 B.L.R. 117; (1997) 13 Const. L.J. 199, QBD (OR).. 21–06, 21–09

Carson v Carson [1983] 1 W.L.R. 285; [1983] 1 All E.R. 478; (1981) 2 F.L.R. 352; 125 S.J. 513; *The Times*, July 7, 1981, CA (Civ Div).... 53–83

Carter v Carter [1980] 1 W.L.R. 390; [1980] 1 All E.R. 827; (1979) 10 Fam. Law 117; 124 S.J. 203, CA (Civ Div)....................... 32–62

Caudery v Finnerty (1892) L.J.Q.B. 496, (1892) 66 L.J. 684.............. 5–40

Cave v Robinson Jarvis & Rolf; sub nom. Robinson Jarvis & Rolf v Cave; Cave v Robinson Jarvis & Rolfe [2002] UKHL 18; [2003] 1 A.C. 384; [2002] 2 W.L.R. 1107; [2002] 2 All E.R. 641; [2003] 1 C.L.C. 101; 81 Con. L.R. 25; [2002] P.N.L.R. 25; [2002] 19 E.G.C.S. 146; (2002) 99(20) L.S.G. 32; (2002) 152 N.L.J. 671; (2002) 146 S.J.L.B. 109; *The Times*, May 7, 2002; *Independent*, April 30, 2002, HL; reversing [2001] EWCA Civ 245; [2002] 1 W.L.R. 581; [2001] C.P. Rep. 66; 78 Con. L.R. 1; [2001] Lloyd's Rep. P.N. 290; [2001] P.N.L.R. 23; (2001) 17 Const. L.J. 262; [2001] 9 E.G.C.S. 229; [2001] N.P.C. 36; *Independent*, April 9, 2001 (C.S), CA (Civ Div)... 39–20

Chainrai v Boston [2002] EWHC 1895, QBD......................... 18–11

Chandless-Chandless v Nicholson [1942] 2 K.B. 321; [1942] 2 All E.R. 315, CA................................. 6–22, 9–12, 10–04, 37–54

Chanel Ltd v FW Woolworth & Co Ltd [1981] 1 W.L.R. 485; [1981] 1 All E.R. 745; [1981] F.S.R. 196; 125 S.J. 202; *The Times*, November 14 1980, CA (Civ Div).................. 5–36, 6–22, 31–38, 32–26, 32–83

TABLE OF CASES

Channel Tunnel Group Ltd v Balfour Beatty Construction Ltd; France Manche SA v Balfour Beatty Construction Ltd [1993] A.C. 334; [1993] 2 W.L.R. 262; [1993] 1 All E.R. 664; [1993] 1 Lloyd's Rep. 291; 61 B.L.R. 1; 32 Con. L.R. 1; [1993] I.L.Pr. 607; (1993) 137 S.J.L.B. 36; [1993] N.P.C. 8; TheTimes, January 25, 1993, HL; affirming [1992] Q.B. 656; [1992] 2 W.L.R. 741; [1992] 2 All E.R. 609; [1992] 2 Lloyd's Rep. 7; 56 B.L.R. 23; (1992) 8 Const. L.J. 150; (1992) 136 S.J.L.B. 54; [1992] N.P.C. 7; *The Times*, January 23, 1992; *Financial Times*, January 29, 1992, CA (Civ Div)............. 4–75

Chapman's Settlement Trusts (No.1), Re; Downshire Settled Estates, Re; Blackwell's Settlement Trusts, Re; sub nom. Chapman v Chapman (No.1); Marquess of Downshire v Royal Bank of Scotland; Blackwell v Blackwell [1954] A.C. 429; [1954] 2 W.L.R. 723; [1954] 1 All E.R. 798; (1954) 47 R. & I.T. 310; (1954) 33 A.T.C. 84; [1954] T.R. 93; 98 S.J. 246, HL; affirming [1953] Ch. 218; [1953] 2 W.L.R. 94; [1953] 1 All E.R. 103; (1953) 46 R. & I.T. 64; 97 S.J. 29, CA...... 2–01, 31–18, 31–20

Charge Card Services Ltd, Re [1989] Ch. 497; [1988] 3 W.L.R. 764; [1988] 3 All E.R. 702; (1988) 4 B.C.C. 524; [1988] B.C.L.C. 711; [1988] P.C.C. 390; [1988] Fin. L.R. 308; (1989) 8 Tr. L.R. 86; (1988) 85(42) L.S.G. 46; (1988) 138 N.L.J. Rep. 201; (1988) 132 S.J. 1458; *The Times*, July 7, 1988; *Independent*, July 6, 1988; *Financial Times*, July 8, 1988; *Guardian*, July 7, 1988; *Daily Telegraph*, July 7, 1988, CA (Civ Div); affirming [1987] Ch. 150; [1986] 3 W.L.R. 697; [1986] 3 All E.R. 289; [1987] B.C.L.C. 17; [1987] P.C.C. 36; [1987] E.C.C. 91; [1987] Fin. L.R. 1; (1986) 83 L.S.G. 3424; (1986) 130 S.J. 801, Ch D................................. 3–30

Charles v NTL Group Ltd [2002] EWCA Civ 2004; [2003] C.P. Rep. 44; *Independent*, February 10, 2003 (C.S), CA (Civ Div)............... 18–06

Charm Marine Inc v Elborne Mitchell, CA (Civ Div)............. 23–01, 23–11

Charm Maritime Inc v Kyriakou [1987] 1 Lloyd's Rep. 433; [1987] 1 F.T.L.R. 265, CA (Civ Div)............................. 24–02, 24–03

Charman v Guardian Royal Exchange Assurance [1992] 2 Lloyd's Rep. 607, QBD (Comm)... 30–17

Chaudhuri v Chaudhuri [1992] 2 F.L.R. 73; [1992] 2 F.C.R. 426; [1992] Fam. Law 385, CA (Civ Div).................... 32–85, 32–104, 32–109

Cheddar Valley Engineering Ltd v Chaddlewood Homes Ltd [1992] 1 W.L.R. 820; [1992] 4 All E.R. 942; (1992) 89(27) L.S.G. 35; *The Times*, April 7, 1992, Ch D..................................... 27–05

Cherkas v F&P Barretta, B1/2000/0030, CA (Civ Div).................... 3–29

Chimimport Plc v G D'Alesio SAS (The Paula D'Alesio) [1994] 2 Lloyd's Rep. 366, QBD (Comm)................................. 41–05, 41–10

Chocoladefabriken Lindt & Sprungli AG v Nestle Co Ltd [1978] R.P.C. 287, Ch D... 27–08, 27–57

Chown v Parrott (1863) 14 C.B............................. 29–25

Cinderby v Cinderby; sub nom. Pekesin v Pekesin, 122 S.J. 436; *The Times*, April 27, 1978, CA (Civ Div)............................. 11–33

Clarion Ltd v National Provident Institution [2000] 1 W.L.R. 1888; [2000] 2 All E.R. 265, Ch D... 4–39

Clark v Clark (Costs) [1906] P. 331, PDAD......................... 6–90

Clark (Florence Edith) v Clark (Sidney John) [1939] P. 257, PDAD....... 32–13

Clarke, Re; sub nom. Debtor Ex p. v S Aston & Son Ltd [1967] Ch. 1121; [1966] 3 W.L.R. 1101; [1966] 3 All E.R. 622; 110 S.J. 923, DC..... 6–83

xlv

TABLE OF CASES

Clarke v Nationwide Anglia Building Society [1998] E.G.C.S. 47; (1998) 95(12) L.S.G. 29; [1998] N.P.C. 45; (1998) 76 P. & C.R. D5, CA (Civ Div)... 3–28
Claughton v Price; sub nom. Trustee in Bankruptcy of Arthur Knapton v Price (1998) 30 H.L.R. 396; [1997] E.G.C.S. 51; (1997) 74 P. & C.R. D15, CA (Civ Div).. 4–67
Clegg v Burnley, Pendle and Rossendale HA, unreported, July 17, 2001... 35–31
Cloutte v Storey [1911] 1 Ch. 18, CA....................... 2–03, 5–36, 6–05
Cocks v Thanet DC [1983] 2 A.C. 286; [1982] 3 W.L.R. 1121; [1982] 3 All E.R. 1135; 81 L.G.R. 81; [1984] R.V.R. 31; 126 S.J. 820, HL....... 1–02
Cohen v Jonesco [1926] 2 K.B. 1, CA; reversing [1926] 1 K.B. 119, KBD... 9–40
Colchester BC v Smith; Colchester BC v Tillson [1992] Ch. 421; [1992] 2 W.L.R. 728; [1992] 2 All E.R. 561, CA (Civ Div); affirming [1991] Ch. 448; [1991] 2 W.L.R. 540; [1991] 2 All E.R. 29; (1991) 62 P. & C.R. 242, Ch D.. 2–18
Collet v Bromsgrove DC; sub nom. Collett v Bromsgrove DC (1996) 160 J.P. 593; [1997] Crim. L.R. 206; (1996) 160 J.P.N. 697; *The Times*, July 15, 1996; *Independent*, July 8, 1996 (C.S.), DC............... 40–15
Combe v Combe; sub nom. Coombe v Coombe [1951] 2 K.B. 215; [1951] 1 All E.R. 767; [1951] 1 T.L.R. 811; 95 S.J. 317, CA; reversing [1950] 2 All E.R. 1115; 66 T.L.R. (Pt. 2) 983; [1950] W.N. 552; 95 S.J. 30, KBD.. 3–05, 3–06
Company (No.003324 of 1979), Re [1981] 1 W.L.R. 1059; [1981] 2 All E.R. 1007; 125 S.J. 287, Ch D........................... 31–11, 31–65
Company (No.000928 of 1991) Ex p. City Electrical Factors, Re [1991] B.C.L.C. 514... 31–65
Computer Machinery Co Ltd v Drescher [1983] 1 W.L.R. 1379; [1983] 3 All E.R. 153; (1984) 81 L.S.G. 123; (1983) 127 S.J. 823, Ch D..... 26–04
Comyn Ching & Co (London) Ltd v Oriental Tube Co Ltd [1981] Com. L.R. 67; 17 B.L.R. 47, CA (Civ Div)..................... 39–57, 39–58
Conlon v Conlons; sub nom. Conlon v Conlans [1952] 2 All E.R. 462; [1952] 2 T.L.R. 343; [1952] W.N. 403; 96 S.J. 547, CA........... 29–04
Connex South Eastern Ltd v MJ Building Services Group Plc [2005] EWCA Civ 193; (2005) 149 S.J.L.B. 296, CA (Civ Div); reversing [2004] EWHC 1518; [2004] B.L.R. 333; 95 Con. L.R. 43, QBD (TCC).... 39–35
Conolan v Leyland (1884) L.R. 27 Ch. D. 632, Ch D.................... 9–12
Conquer v Boot [1928] 2 K.B. 336, KBD............................. 39–21
Cook v Cook [1984] Fam. Law 121; *The Times*, December 13, 1983, CA (Civ Div).................. 5–58, 32–11, 32–68, 32–85, 32–104, 32–109
Cook v Lister (1863) 13 C.B. N.S. 543................................ 6–73
Cook v Wright [1967] N.Z.L.R. 1034, Sup Ct............... 2–01, 3–20, 6–02
Cooke v United Bristol Healthcare NHS Trust; Sheppard v Stibbe; Page v Lee [2003] EWCA Civ 1370; [2004] 1 W.L.R. 251; [2004] 1 All E.R. 797; [2004] P.I.Q.R. Q2; [2004] Lloyd's Rep. Med. 63; (2004) 78 B.M.L.R. 1; (2003) 100(43) L.S.G. 32; *The Times*, October 24, 2003, CA (Civ Div)... 35–43
Coop v Hastings (1993) 91 L.G.R. 608.............................. 37–08
Cooper v Cooper (Preece) (1973) C.A.T. 425......................... 4–19
Cooper v Williams [1963] 2 Q.B. 567; [1963] 2 W.L.R. 913; [1963] 2 All E.R. 282; 107 S.J. 194, CA... 9–28

Cooperative Retail Services Ltd v Taylor Young Partnership Ltd; Cooperative Retail Services Ltd v Hoare Lea & Partners; Cooperative Retail Services Ltd v Carillion Construction Ltd (formerly Tarmac Construction (Contracts) Ltd); Cooperative Retail Services Ltd v East Midlands Electricity Electrical Installations Services Ltd (t/a Hall Electrical) (In Liquidation) [2002] UKHL 17; [2002] 1 W.L.R. 1419; [2002] 1 All E.R. (Comm) 918; [2003] 1 C.L.C. 75; [2002] B.L.R. 272; [2002] T.C.L.R. 9; 82 Con. L.R. 1; [2002] Lloyd's Rep. I.R. 555, HL; affirming [2000] 2 All E.R. 865; [2000] B.L.R. 461; (2001) 3 T.C.L.R. 4; 74 Con. L.R. 12; [2001] Lloyd's Rep. I.R. 122; (2000) 16 Const. L.J. 347; *Independent*, October 2, 2000 (C.S); *Independent*, July 14, 2000, CA (Civ Div); affirming [2000] 1 All E.R. (Comm) 721; (2000) 16 Const. L.J. 204; [2000] E.G.C.S. 6, QBD (TCC)... 39–30, 39–33
Corby DC v Holst & Co [1985] 1 W.L.R. 427; [1985] 1 All E.R. 321; 28 B.L.R. 35; (1985) 82 L.S.G. 681; (1985) 135 N.L.J. 56; (1985) 129 S.J. 172, CA (Civ Div)............................... 18–07, 26–05
Cornhill Insurance Plc v Barclay (1992) C.A.T. 948..... 5–36, 5–41, 6–04, 6–05, 7–04
Cornick v Cornick (No.1) [1994] 2 F.L.R. 530; [1994] 2 F.C.R. 1189; [1994] Fam. Law 617, Fam Div................ 32–101, 32–103, 32–109
Cory v Bretton (1830) 4 C.&P. 462................................... 26–04
Cott UK Ltd v FE Barber Ltd [1997] 3 All E.R. 540, QBD................ 4–75
Cotton v Official Solicitor [1989] C.L.Y. 3045........................ 31–21
Council of Engineering Institutions v Maddison [1977] I.C.R. 30; (1976) 11 I.T.R. 272, EAT.. 36–15
Courage Take Home Trade v Keys [1986] I.C.R. 874; [1986] I.R.L.R. 427, EAT.. 36–17
Cowan v Kitson Insulations [1992] P.I.Q.R. Q19, HC.................... 35–31
Cox v Sun Alliance Life Ltd [2001] EWCA Civ 649; [2001] I.R.L.R. 448; [2001] Emp. L.R. 660, CA (Civ Div)........................... 36–11
Craddock Bros Ltd v Hunt [1923] 2 Ch. 136, CA; affirming [1922] 2 Ch. 809, Ch D... 4–31
Crane v Lewis (1887) 36 W.R. 480................................... 4–11
Crawford v Clarke (Extension of Time); sub nom. Crawford v Clark [2000] E.G.C.S. 33; (2000) 97(12) L.S.G. 45; (2000) 80 P. & C.R. D5, CA (Civ Div)... 37–54
Credit Lyonnais Bank Nederland NV v Burch [1997] 1 All E.R. 144; [1996] 5 Bank. L.R. 233; [1997] C.L.C. 95; [1997] 1 F.L.R. 11; [1997] 2 F.C.R. 1; (1997) 29 H.L.R. 513; (1997) 74 P. & C.R. 384; [1997] Fam. Law 168; (1996) 93(32) L.S.G. 33; (1996) 146 N.L.J. 1421; (1996) 140 S.J.L.B. 158; [1996] N.P.C. 99; (1996) 72 P. & C.R. D33; *The Times*, July 1, 1996; *Independent*, June 27, 1996, CA (Civ Div)... 4–67
Credit Suisse First Boston (Europe) Ltd v Lister [1999] 1 C.M.L.R. 710; [1999] I.C.R. 794; [1998] I.R.L.R. 700; (1998) 95(44) L.S.G. 35; (1998) 142 S.J.L.B. 269; *The Times*, October 22, 1998; *Independent*, November 9, 1998 (C.S.), CA (Civ Div)....................... 36–35
Cristel v Cristel [1951] 2 K.B. 725; [1951] 2 All E.R. 574; 95 S.J. 561, CA 5–45, 32–83
Croft v Croft (1922) 38 T.L.R. 648................................... 11–08

Crouch v King's Healthcare NHS Trust; Murry v Blackburn, Hyndburn and
    Ribble Valley Healthcare NHS Trust [2004] EWCA Civ 1332; [2005]
    1 W.L.R. 2015; [2005] 1 All E.R. 207; [2005] Lloyd's Rep. Med. 50;
    (2004) 101(44) L.S.G. 29; (2004) 154 N.L.J. 1616; (2004) 148
    S.J.L.B. 1245; *The Times*, November 9, 2004, CA (Civ Div)   14–03, 18–01,
                                   18–04, 18–06, 18–07, 35–61, 35–62
Crown Estate Commissioners v John Mowlem & Co Ltd, 70 B.L.R. 1; 40
    Con. L.R. 36; (1994) 10 Const. L.J. 311, CA (Civ Div)............   39–10
Crowther v Farrer(1850) 15 Q.B.677..................................   8–03
Crozier v Crozier [1994] Fam. 114; [1994] 2 W.L.R. 444; [1994] 2 All E.R.
    362; [1994] 1 F.L.R. 126; [1994] 1 F.C.R. 781; [1994] Fam. Law
    244; (1993) 143 N.L.J. 1784; *The Times*, December 9, 1993;
    Independent, December 9, 1993, Fam Div....... 32–100, 32–110, 32–121,
                                                                         32–122
Cumper v Pothecary [1941] 2 K.B. 58; [1941] 2 All E.R. 516, CA........   18–17
Cundy v Lindsay; sub nom. Lindsay v Cundy (1877–78) L.R. 3 App. Cas.
    459; [1874–80] All E.R. Rep. 1149; (1878) 42 J.P. 483; (1878) 14
    Cox C.C. 93; (1878) 26 W.R. 406; (1878) 47 L.J. Q.B. 481; (1878)
    38 L.T. 573; 15 Sask. R. 233, HL; affirming (1876–77) L.R. 2 Q.B.D.
    96, CA; reversing (1875–76) L.R. 1 Q.B.D. 348, QBD..............   6–83
Curwen v James [1963] 1 W.L.R. 748; [1963] 2 All E.R. 619; 107 S.J. 314,
    CA...   35–15
Cutts v Head [1984] Ch. 290; [1984] 2 W.L.R. 349; [1984] 1 All E.R. 597;
    (1984) 81 L.S.G. 509; (1984) 128 S.J. 117; *The Times*, December 14,
    1983, CA (Civ Div)... 14–03, 14–06, 18–04, 23–01, 26–04, 26–05, 27–01,
                                                    27–16, 27–17, 27–23

D v A & Co [1900] 1 Ch. 484, Ch D..........................   11–34, 32–24
D v D (1974) 5 Fam. Law 61; (1974) 118 S.J. 715....................   32–16
D (A Child) v Walker; sub nom. Walker v D (A Child) [2000] 1 W.L.R.
    1382; [2000] C.P.L.R. 462; [2001] H.R.L.R. 1; [2000] U.K.H.R.R.
    648; [2000] P.I.Q.R. P193; (2000) 97(22) L.S.G. 44; *The Times*, May
    17, 2000; *Independent*, June 12, 2000 (C.S), CA (Civ Div)..........   4–08
D&C Builders Ltd v Rees [1966] 2 Q.B. 617; [1966] 2 W.L.R. 288; [1965]
    3 All E.R. 837; 109 S.J. 971; *The Times*, November 13, 1965, CA...   3–13,
                                                                          4–59
DSL Group Ltd v Unisys International Services Ltd (No.1) (1994) B.L.R.
    117, 41 Con. L.R. 33, QBD (OR).........................   39–53, 39–54
DSND Subsea Ltd (formerly DSND Oceantech Ltd) v Petroleum Geo
    Services ASA [2000] B.L.R. 530, QBD (TCC).....................   39–37
Daintrey Ex p. Holt, Re [1893] 2 Q.B. 116, QBD.. 27–09, 27–19, 27–22, 27–24
Dalgety Foods Holland BV v Deb-its Ltd [1994] F.S.R. 125, Ch D.........   3–57
Darley (Trustee of Baines) v Tulley (1923) 155 L.T.Jo. 128..............   10–04
Dashwood v Dashwood, (1927) 71 S.J. 911; *The Times*, May 8, 1964....   11–13,
                                                                         11–21
Dattani v Trio Supermarkets Ltd [1998] I.C.R. 872; [1998] I.R.L.R. 240;
    (1998) 95(9) L.S.G. 29; (1998) 142 S.J.L.B. 77; *The Times*, February
    20, 1998, CA (Civ Div)............ 5–10, 5–14, 5–15, 5–18, 6–02, 6–06
Davies v Collins [1945] 1 All E.R. 247, CA............................   6–86
Davies v Davies [1986] 1 F.L.R. 497; [1986] Fam. Law 138.............   32–62
Davies v London and Provincial Marine Insurance Co (1878) L.R. 8 Ch. D.
    469; (1878) 26 W.R. 794, Ch D.................................   4–43
Davies v Sweet [1962] 2 Q.B. 300; [1962] 2 W.L.R. 525; [1962] 1 All E.R.
    92; 105 S.J. 1083, CA...   3–22

Davies v Taylor (No.1) [1974] A.C. 207; [1972] 3 W.L.R. 801; [1972] 3 All
E.R. 836; 116 S.J. 864, HL; affirming [1972] 1 Q.B. 286; [1971] 3
W.L.R. 515; 115 S.J. 774, CA (Civ Div)......................... 35–24
Davis v Hedges (1870–71) L.R. 6 Q.B. 687, QB...................... 39–22
Davy-Chiesman v Davy-Chiesman [1984] Fam. 48; [1984] 2 W.L.R. 291;
[1984] 1 All E.R. 321; (1984) 81 L.S.G. 44; (1983) 127 S.J. 805; *The
Times*, November 21, 1983, CA (Civ Div)........................ 28–08
Dawson v Great Northern & City Railway Co [1905] 1 K.B. 260, CA;
reversing [1904] 1 K.B. 277, KBD............................... 6–89
Day v McLea (1889) L.R. 22 Q.B.D. 610, CA..................... 3–34, 3–41
De Lasala v De Lasala [1980] A.C. 546; [1979] 3 W.L.R. 390; [1979] 2 All
E.R. 1146; [1980] F.S.R. 443; (1979) 123 S.J. 301, PC (HK)....... 6–20,
11–10, 32–09, 32–05, 32–06, 32–13, 32–29, 32–32, 32–33, 32–34,
32–37, 32–74, 32–82, 32–84, 32–88, 32–89, 32–91, 32–130
Dean v Dean [1978] Fam. 161; [1978] 3 W.L.R. 288; [1978] 3 All E.R.
758; (1978) 8 Fam. Law 171; 122 S.J. 211, Fam Div........ 32–09, 32–49,
32–67, 32–79
Deanplan Ltd v Mahmoud [1993] Ch. 151; [1992] 3 W.L.R. 467; [1992] 3
All E.R. 945; (1992) 64 P. & C.R. 409; [1992] 1 E.G.L.R. 79; [1992]
16 E.G. 100; [1992] E.G.C.S. 30; [1992] N.P.C. 31; *The Times*,
March 3, 1992, Ch D.. 6–46
Debtor (No.27 of 1927), Re [1929] 1 Ch. 125, Ch D.................... 6–75
Debtors (No.13–MISC-2000 and No.14–MISC-2000), Re (2000) 97(16)
L.S.G. 40; (2000) 144 S.J.L.B. 174; *The Times*, April 10, 2000;
Independent, May 15, 2000 (C.S.), Ch D........................ 29–06
Defries v Milne [1913] 1 Ch. 98, CA................................ 6–89
Denne v Denne (1977) C.A.T. 474B................................. 9–05
Dennis v McDonald [1982] Fam. 63; [1982] 2 W.L.R. 275; [1982] 1 All
E.R. 590; (1982) 12 Fam. Law 84; 126 S.J. 16, CA (Civ Div);
affirming [1981] 1 W.L.R. 810; [1981] 2 All E.R. 632; 125 S.J. 308;
The Times, February 26, 1981, Fam Div........................ 32–04
Densham (A Bankrupt), Re; sub nom. Trustee Ex p. v Densham [1975] 1
W.L.R. 1519; [1975] 3 All E.R. 726; 119 S.J. 774, Ch D........... 6–76
Derby & Co Ltd v ITC Pension Trust Ltd [1977] 2 All E.R. 890; (1977)
245 E.G. 569, Ch D... 37–17
Derrick v Williams [1939] 2 All E.R. 559; (1939) 55 T.L.R. 676, CA 9–28, 9–31
Di Placito v Slater; sub nom. Placito v Slater [2003] EWCA Civ 1863;
[2004] 1 W.L.R. 1605; [2004] C.P. Rep. 21; [2004] W.T.L.R. 407;
The Times, January 29, 2004, CA (Civ Div); affirming [2003] EWHC
1233; [2003] W.T.L.R. 805, Ch D...................... 31–29, 31–41
Dicker v Scammell [2005] EWCA Civ 405, CA (Civ Div); reversing [2003]
EWHC 1601; [2003] N.P.C. 90, QBD............................ 38–08
Dickinson v Jones Alexander & Co [1993] 2 F.L.R. 521; [1990] Fam. Law
137; (1989) 139 N.L.J. 1525; *The Times*, October 19, 1989;
Independent, October 18, 1989; *Guardian*, December 13, 1989,
QBD.. 29–30, 29–31
Dietz v Lennig Chemicals Ltd [1969] 1 A.C. 170; [1967] 3 W.L.R. 165;
[1967] 2 All E.R. 282; (1967) 111 S.J. 354, HL; affirming [1966] 1
W.L.R. 1349; [1966] 2 All E.R. 962; 110 S.J. 448, CA. 3–61, 4–43, 4–48,
6–20, 35–10, 35–12
Dimmock v Hallett (1866–67) L.R. 2 Ch. App. 21; (1866) 12 Jur. N.S.
953; (1866) 15 W.R. 93, CA in Chancery........................ 4–38

xlix

TABLE OF CASES

Dimskal Shipping Co SA v International Transport Workers Federation
(The Evia Luck) (No.1) [1986] 2 Lloyd's Rep. 165, QBD (Comm)... 4–62,
4–64
Dinch v Dinch [1987] 1 W.L.R. 252; [1987] 1 All E.R. 818; [1987] 2
F.L.R. 162; [1987] Fam. Law 267; (1987) 84 L.S.G. 1142; (1987)
131 S.J. 296, HL.................................... 32–33, 32–60, 32–61
Dipper v Dipper [1981] Fam. 31; [1980] 3 W.L.R. 626; [1980] 2 All E.R.
722; (1979) 10 Fam. Law 211; (1981) 145 J.P.N. 391; 124 S.J. 775,
CA (Civ Div)... 32–11, 32–62
Dixon v Evans; sub nom. Agriculturist Cattle Insurance Co, Re; Dixon's
Case (1871–72) L.R. 5 H.L. 606, HL; reversing (1869–70) L.R. 5 Ch.
App. 79, CA in Chancery................................. 4–09, 6–02
Dixons Stores Group Ltd v Thames Television Plc [1993] 1 All E.R. 349,
QBD... 26–11, 27–07
Dora v Simper [2000] 2 B.C.L.C. 561, CA (Civ Div); affirming [1999]
B.C.C. 836; *The Times*, May 26, 1999, Ch D.............. 27–40, 27–59
Dorimex Srl v Visage Imports Ltd, CA (Civ Div)........................ 4–64
Doyle v Wallace [1998] P.I.Q.R. Q146; (1998) 95(30) L.S.G. 25; (1998)
142 S.J.L.B. 196; *The Times*, July 22, 1998, CA (Civ Div).......... 35–24
Drinkall v Whitwood [2003] EWCA Civ 1547; [2004] 1 W.L.R. 462;
[2004] 4 All E.R. 378; (2003) 100(47) L.S.G. 21; (2003) 147 S.J.L.B.
1308; *The Times*, November 13, 2003, CA (Civ Div).............. 35–07,
35–12, 35–13
Drive Yourself Hire Co (London) Ltd v Strutt [1954] 1 Q.B. 250; [1953] 3
W.L.R. 1111; [1953] 2 All E.R. 1475; 97 S.J. 874, CA; reversing
[1953] 2 W.L.R. 593; [1953] 1 All E.R. 1036; 97 S.J. 317, QBD..... 6–64
Duck v Mayeu [1892] 2 Q.B. 511, CA................................ 6–41
Dunlop Pneumatic Tyre Co Ltd v Selfridge & Co Ltd [1915] A.C. 847, HL;
affirming [1914] W.N. 59, CA..................................... 6–64
Dunnett v Railtrack Plc [2002] EWCA Civ 303; [2002] 1 W.L.R. 2434;
[2002] 2 All E.R. 850; [2002] C.P. Rep. 35; [2002] C.P.L.R. 309;
(2002) 99(16) L.S.G. ; *The Times*, April 3, 2002, CA (Civ Div)..... 43–06
Duport Furniture Products Ltd v Moore; sub nom. Moore v Duport
Furniture Products Ltd [1982] I.C.R. 84; [1982] I.R.L.R. 31; 126 S.J.
98, HL; affirming [1980] I.C.R. 581; 124 S.J. 645, CA (Civ Div);
affirming [1979] I.C.R. 165; [1978] I.R.L.R. 544; 122 S.J. 729,
EAT.. 36–25
Durabella Ltd v J Jarvis & Sons Ltd, 83 Con. L.R. 145, QBD (TCC)...... 39–38
Dutfield v Gilbert H Stephens and Sons [1988] Fam. Law 473........... 32–77
Dyson Appliances Ltd v Hoover Ltd (Costs); sub nom. Dyson Ltd v Hoover
Ltd [2002] EWHC 2229; [2003] F.S.R. 21; (2002) 25(12) I.P.D.
25087; (2002) 99(45) L.S.G. 34; *The Times*, November 6, 2002, Ch
D (Patents Ct).. 21–04

E v E [1990] Fam. Law 297...................................... 34–02, 34–08
EF Phillips & Sons v Clarke [1970] Ch. 322; [1969] 3 W.L.R. 622; [1969]
3 All E.R. 710; 113 S.J. 837, Ch D.................. 5–46, 9–21, 11–22
Eagle v Chambers (No.2) [2004] EWCA Civ 1033; [2004] 1 W.L.R. 3081;
[2005] 1 All E.R. 136; [2005] P.I.Q.R. Q2; [2004] Lloyd's Rep. Med.
413; (2004) 154 N.L.J. 1451; (2004) 148 S.J.L.B. 972; *The Times*,
August 30, 2004, CA (Civ Div); reversing in part [2003] EWHC
3135, QBD... 35–34

l

Eagle Star Insurance Co Ltd v Cresswell; sub nom. Eagle Star Insurance Co
  Ltd v JN Cresswell [2004] EWCA Civ 602; [2004] 2 All E.R.
  (Comm) 244; [2004] 1 C.L.C. 926; [2004] Lloyd's Rep. I.R. 537;
  (2004) 148 S.J.L.B. 632, CA (Civ Div); reversing [2003] EWHC
  2224; [2004] 1 All E.R. (Comm) 508, QBD (Comm)....... 30–14, 30–16
Earl v Cantor Fitzgerald International, unreported, May 2000, QBD...... 23–16,
  23–24, 23–25, 23–26
Earl of Strafford (dec'd), Re; sub nom. Royal Bank of Scotland Ltd v Byng
  [1980] Ch. 28; [1979] 2 W.L.R. 459; [1979] 1 All E.R. 513; 123 S.J.
  50, CA (Civ Div); affirming [1978] 3 W.L.R. 223; [1978] 3 All E.R.
  18; 122 S.J. 472, Ch D.. 31–18
East West Corp v DKBS 1912 (Costs); Utaniko Ltd v P&O Nedlloyd BV
  (Costs); sub nom. East West Corp v Dampskibsselskabet AF 1912 A/S
  (Costs); Dampskibsselskabet AF 1912 A/S v East West Corp (Costs);
  P&O Nedlloyd BV v Utaniko Ltd (Costs) [2003] EWCA Civ 174;
  [2003] 1 Lloyd's Rep. 265; [2003] C.P.L.R. 319; [2003] 4 Costs L.R.
  531; (2003) 100(14) L.S.G. 27; (2003) 147 S.J.L.B. 234; The Times,
  February 21, 2003, CA (Civ Div); affirming [2002] EWHC 253;
  [2002] 2 Lloyd's Rep. 222, QBD (Comm)................. 23–11, 23–30
Eastbourne BC v Foster (No.1) [2001] EWCA Civ 1091; [2002] I.C.R. 234;
  [2001] Emp. L.R. 1079; (2001) 3 L.G.L.R. 53; [2001] B.L.G.R. 529;
  (2001) 98(33) L.S.G. 30; The Times, August 17, 2001; Independent,
  July 18, 2001, CA (Civ Div)............................... 4–10, 4–15
Easyfind (N.S.W.) Pty Ltd v Paterson (1987) 11 N.S.W.L.R. 98............ 4–27
Eden v Humphries & Glasgow [1981] I.C.R. 183, EAT.... 36–44, 36–45, 36–46
Eden v Naish (1877–78) L.R. 7 Ch. D. 781, Ch D..................... 11–03
Edgar v Edgar [1980] 1 W.L.R. 1410; [1980] 3 All E.R. 887; (1981) 2
  F.L.R. 19; (1980) 11 Fam. Law 20; 124 S.J. 809; The Times, July 24,
  1980, CA (Civ Div)... 32–09, 32–31, 32–37, 32–45, 32–48, 32–49, 32–66,
  32–72, 32–74, 32–77, 32–78, 32–88, 32–90
Edmonds v Edmonds [1990] 2 F.L.R. 202; [1990] F.C.R. 856; The Times,
  February 16, 1990, CA (Civ Div)................. 4–19, 32–102, 32–104
Electricity Supply Nominees Ltd v Farrell [1997] 1 W.L.R. 1149; [1997] 2
  All E.R. 498; [1998] 1 Costs L.R. 49; The Times, March 10, 1997;
  Independent, March 10, 1997 (C.S.), CA (Civ Div)................ 21–13
Ellis v Torrington [1920] 1 K.B. 399, CA............................. 6–89
Elstein's Affairs, Re [1945] 1 All E.R. 272............................ 6–20
Emanuel v Emanuel [1982] 1 W.L.R. 669; [1982] 2 All E.R. 342; (1982) 12
  Fam. Law 62, Fam Div....................................... 32–25
Ernst & Young v Butte Mining Plc [1996] 1 W.L.R. 1605; [1996] 2 All E.R.
  623; (1996) 146 N.L.J. 553; The Times, March 22, 1996, Ch D..... 9–36
Essexcrest Ltd v Evenlex Ltd (1988) 55 P. & C.R. 279; [1988] 01 E.G. 56,
  CA (Civ Div).. 37–06, 37–09
Esso Petroleum Co Ltd v Mardon [1976] Q.B. 801; [1976] 2 W.L.R. 583;
  [1976] 2 All E.R. 5; [1976] 2 Lloyd's Rep. 305; 2 B.L.R. 82; 120 S.J.
  131, CA (Civ Div); reversing in part [1975] Q.B. 819; [1975] 2
  W.L.R. 147; [1975] 1 All E.R. 203; (1974) 119 S.J. 81; The Times,
  August 2, 1974, QBD... 4–42
Everglade Maritime Inc v Schiffahrtsgesellschaft Detlef von Appen GmbH
  (The Maria) [1993] Q.B. 780; [1993] 3 W.L.R. 176; [1993] 3 All
  E.R. 748; [1993] 2 Lloyd's Rep. 168, CA (Civ Div); affirming [1993]
  1 W.L.R. 33; [1992] 3 All E.R. 851; [1992] 2 Lloyd's Rep. 167, QBD
  (Comm)..................................... 23–04, 41–15, 41–25

Ewart v Ewart [1959] P. 23; [1958] 3 W.L.R. 680; [1958] 3 All E.R. 561;
   123 J.P. 63; 102 S.J. 861, PDAD........................ 32–08, 32–09
Excelsior Commercial & Industrial Holdings Ltd v Salisbury Hamer Aspden
   & Johnson (Costs); sub nom. Excelsior Commercial & Industrial
   Holdings Ltd v Salisbury Hammer Aspden & Johnson [2002] EWCA
   Civ 879; [2002] C.P. Rep. 67; [2002] C.P.L.R. 693; *Independent*,
   June 18, 2002, CA (Civ Div)............................ 13–09, 13–10
Ezekiel's Settlement Trusts, Re; sub nom. National Provincial Bank Ltd v
   Hyam [1942] Ch. 230, CA..................................... 31–19

F v F (Ancillary Relief: Substantial Assets) [1995] 2 F.L.R. 45; [1996] 2
   F.C.R. 397; [1995] Fam. Law 546, Fam Div...................... 32–30
F (A Minor) (Custody: Consent Order: Procedure), Re [1992] 1 F.L.R. 561;
   [1992] Fam. Law 330; *The Times*, November 15, 1991; *Independent*,
   September 9, 1991, CA (Civ Div)............................. 32–139
Faccenda Chicken Ltd v Fowler; Fowler v Faccenda Chicken Ltd [1987]
   Ch. 117; [1986] 3 W.L.R. 288; [1986] 1 All E.R. 617; [1986] I.C.R.
   297; [1986] I.R.L.R. 69; [1986] F.S.R. 291; (1986) 83 L.S.G. 288;
   (1986) 136 N.L.J. 71; (1986) 130 S.J. 573; *The Times*, December 11,
   1985, CA (Civ Div); affirming [1985] 1 All E.R. 724; [1984] I.C.R.
   589; [1984] I.R.L.R. 61; [1985] F.S.R. 105; (1984) 134 N.L.J. 255;
   The Times, November 16, 1983, Ch D........................... 31–01
Factortame Ltd v Secretary of State for the Environment, Transport and the
   Regions (Costs) (No.1); sub nom. R. v Secretary of State for
   Transport Ex p. Factortame Ltd (Costs: Part 36 Payments) [2002]
   EWCA Civ 22; [2002] 1 W.L.R. 2438; [2002] 2 All E.R. 838; [2002]
   C.P.L.R. 385; (2002) 152 N.L.J. 171, CA (Civ Div).............. 23–29
Faircharm Investments Ltd v Citibank International Plc [1998] Lloyd's Rep.
   Bank. 127; *The Times*, February 20, 1998, CA (Civ Div)........... 30–11
Fairfield-Mabey Ltd v Shell UK Metallurgical Testing Services (Scotland)
   Ltd [1989] 1 All E.R. 576; 45 B.L.R. 113; 27 Con. L.R. 1, QBD.... 39–46
Family Housing Association (Manchester) v Michael Hyde & Partners
   [1993] 1 W.L.R. 354; [1993] 2 All E.R. 567; [1993] 2 E.G.L.R. 239;
   [1992] E.G.C.S. 150; *The Times*, December 15, 1992, CA (Civ
   Div)... 27–53
Farrage v North Wiltshire DC; sub nom. Trustees of Chippenham Golf
   Club v North Wiltshire DC (1992) 64 P. & C.R. 527; (1992) 156
   L.G. Rev. 863; [1991] E.G.C.S. 135; [1991] N.P.C. 139; *The Times*,
   December 31, 1991; *Independent*, January 13, 1992 (C.S.), CA (Civ
   Div); reversing, 89 L.G.R. 785; (1991) 62 P. & C.R. 643, Ch D..... 3–72
Farrow (dec'd), Re [1987] 1 F.L.R. 205; [1987] Fam. Law 14............ 33–05
Fearon v Earl of Aylesford (1884–85) L.R. 14 Q.B.D. 792, CA; reversing
   (1883–84) L.R. 12 Q.B.D. 539, QBD............................. 7–07
Ferguson v Davies [1997] 1 All E.R. 315; *Independent*, December 12, 1996,
   CA (Civ Div)...................... 2–07, 2–04, 3–14, 3–28, 3–30, 3–34
Field v Railways Commissioner (1957) 32 A.L.J.R. 110.................. 27–27
Finch v Wilson, unreported, May 8, 1997.................... 27–33, 27–57
Firle Investments Ltd v Datapoint International Ltd [2001] EWCA Civ
   1106; [2001] C.P. Rep. 101; [2001] N.P.C. 106, CA (Civ Div);
   reversing, HT-99–119, QBD (TCC)............................. 24–03
Fitzroy v Cave [1905] 2 K.B. 364, CA................................ 6–88

TABLE OF CASES

Fleet Mortgage & Investment Co Ltd v Lower Maisonette 46 Eaton Place Ltd; Lower Maisonette 46 Eaton Place Ltd v Crown Lodge (Belgravia) Ltd [1972] 1 W.L.R. 765; [1972] 2 All E.R. 737; 116 S.J. 434, Ch D.. 37–47
Fletcher & Stewart Ltd v Peter Jay & Partners, 17 B.L.R. 38, CA (Civ Div).. 39–44, 39–50
Flint (A Bankrupt), Re [1993] Ch. 319; [1993] 2 W.L.R. 537; [1993] 1 F.L.R. 763; (1992) 136 S.J.L.B. 221; The Times, July 16, 1992, Ch D.. 6–76
Flower v Sadler (1882–83) L.R. 10 Q.B.D. 572, CA; affirming (1881–82) L.R. 9 Q.B.D. 83, QBD.. 4–54
Flynn v Scougall [2004] EWCA Civ 873; [2004] 1 W.L.R. 3069; [2004] 3 All E.R. 609; [2004] C.P. Rep. 37; (2004) 148 S.J.L.B. 880; The Times, July 21, 2004; Independent, July 16, 2004, CA (Civ Div).... 18–17
Foakes v Beer; sub nom. Beer v Foakes (1883–84) L.R. 9 App. Cas. 605, HL; (1882–83) L.R. 11 Q.B.D. 221, CA.. 3–13, 3–18
Foley v Classique Coaches Ltd [1934] 2 K.B. 1, CA.. 3–49
Ford v GKR Construction Ltd [2000] 1 W.L.R. 1397; [2000] 1 All E.R. 802; [1999] C.P.L.R. 788; The Times, November 4, 1999, CA (Civ Div).. 23–29
Foreningen af Arbejdsledere i Danmark v Daddy's Dance Hall A/S (C324/86) [1988] E.C.R. 739; [1989] 2 C.M.L.R. 517; [1988] I.R.L.R. 315, ECJ (3rd Chamber).. 36–35
Forster v Baker [1910] 2 K.B. 636, CA.. 6–91
Forster v Friedland, C.A.T 1052, CA (Civ Div).... 27–04, 27–19, 27–23, 27–28, 27–34, 27–36, 27–41
Fraser v Elger Tavern Pty [1982] V.R. 398, Sup Ct (Vic).. 8–05
Fray v Voules (1867–68) L.R. 3 Q.B. 214, QB.. 29–27
Freedman (t/a John Freedman & Co) v Union Group Plc [1997] E.G.C.S. 28, CA (Civ Div).. 2–19
Freeman v Sovereign Chicken [1991] I.C.R. 853; [1991] I.R.L.R. 408; The Times, September 24, 1991, EAT.. 36–25
Freud Lemos Properties v Secretary of State for the Environment, CO/2839/91.. 40–22
Fritz v Hobson (1880) L.R. 14 Ch. D. 542, Ch D.. 5–45
Fryer v London Transport Executive, The Times, December 4, 1982, CA (Civ Div).. 27–56
Fullard (dec'd), Re; sub nom. Fuller (dec'd), Re [1982] Fam. 42; [1981] 3 W.L.R. 743; [1981] 2 All E.R. 796; (1981) 11 Fam. Law 116; The Times, February 3, 1981, CA (Civ Div)............. 33–05, 33–07, 33–13
Fullerton v Provincial Bank of Ireland [1903] A.C. 309, HL (UK-Irl).. 3–03, 3–05
Furneaux v Furneaux (1973) 118 S.J. 204.. 32–16

G v G (Maintenance Pending Suit: Legal Costs) [2002] EWHC 306; [2003] 2 F.L.R. 71; [2002] 3 F.C.R. 339; [2003] Fam. Law 393, Fam Div.. 32–27
Gaisberg v Storr [1950] 1 K.B. 107; [1949] 2 All E.R. 411; 65 T.L.R. 485; [1949] W.N. 337; 93 S.J. 600, CA.. 32–09
Galloway v Galloway (1914) 30 T.L.R. 531.. 4–17
Gandolfo v Gandolfo (Standard Chartered Bank, Garnishee) [1980] Q.B. 359; [1980] 2 W.L.R. 680; [1980] 1 All E.R. 833; (1979) 10 Fam. Law 152; 124 S.J. 239, CA (Civ Div).. 11–34
Gannon v Chubb Fire Ltd [1996] P.I.Q.R. P108, CA (Civ Div)....... 3–50, 5–62

liii

Gardiner v Moore (No.2) [1969] 1 Q.B. 55; [1966] 3 W.L.R. 786; [1966] 1
  All E.R. 365; (1965) 110 S.J. 34; *The Times*, December 14, 1965,
  QBD.. 6–41, 29–16, 29–32
Gardiner v South Essex HA, unreported, December 10, 1998, QBD........ 3–56
Garlick v Royal Trust Bank, CA................................ 1–02, 3–21
Garner v Cleggs [1983] 1 W.L.R. 862; [1983] 2 All E.R. 398, CA (Civ
  Div).. 15–14
Garner v Garner [1992] 1 F.L.R. 573; [1992] Fam. Law 331; (1992) 156
  J.P.N. 202, CA (Civ Div)....................................... 32–135
Garratt v Saxby [2004] EWCA Civ 341; [2004] 1 W.L.R. 2152; [2004]
  C.P. Rep. 32; (2004) 101(11) L.S.G. 35; (2004) 148 S.J.L.B. 237, CA
  (Civ Div)... 14–08
Garrett v Camden LBC [2001] EWCA Civ 395, CA (Civ Div)............ 36–08
Garthwaite v Garthwaite [1964] P. 356; [1964] 2 W.L.R. 1108; [1964] 2
  All E.R. 233; 108 S.J. 276, CA; reversing [1964] 2 W.L.R. 531; 108
  S.J. 76, PDAD... 10–09
Gaskins v British Aluminium Co Ltd [1976] Q.B. 524; [1976] 2 W.L.R. 6;
  [1976] 1 All E.R. 208; (1975) 119 S.J. 848; *The Times*, November 7,
  1975, CA (Civ Div)...................................... 14–11, 15–14
Gaynor v Blackpool FC, unreported, December 10, 2001, CC (Oldham)... 23–30
Gee v Gee (1972) 116 S.J. 219, CA (Civ Div).................. 32–05, 32–62
General Accident Fire and Life Assurance Corp, Ltd v Inland Revenue
  Commissioners; sub nom. Lacy's Settlement Trustee v Inland Rev-
  enue Commissioners [1963] 1 W.L.R. 1207; [1963] 3 All E.R. 259;
  (1963) 42 A.T.C. 313; [1963] T.R. 321; 107 S.J. 870, CA; affirming
  [1963] 1 W.L.R. 421; [1963] 1 All E.R. 618; (1963) 42 A.T.C. 3;
  [1963] T.R. 1; 107 S.J. 315, Ch D.................... 5–10, 6–04, 6–05
Gibbons v Caunt (1799) 4 Ves. 849................................. 4–38
Gibbs v Ebbetts, unreported, October 20, 1997, CA............... 5–09, 5–14
Gibson v Manchester City Council [1979] 1 W.L.R. 294; [1979] 1 All E.R.
  972; 77 L.G.R. 405; [1979] J.P.L. 532; 123 S.J. 201, HL; reversing
  [1978] 1 W.L.R. 520; [1978] 2 All E.R. 583; 76 L.G.R. 365; [1978]
  J.P.L. 246; 122 S.J. 80, CA (Civ Div)............................ 3–22
Gilbert Ash (Northern) Ltd v Modern Engineering (Bristol) Ltd; sub nom.
  Modern Engineering (Bristol) Ltd v Gilbert Ash (Northern) Ltd
  [1974] A.C. 689; [1973] 3 W.L.R. 421; [1973] 3 All E.R. 195; 1
  B.L.R. 73; 72 L.G.R. 1; 117 S.J. 745, HL; reversing, 71 L.G.R. 162,
  CA (Civ Div)... 39–09
Gilbert v Endean (1878) L.R. 9 Ch. D. 259, CA...................... 4–43
Gilbert v Kembridge Fibres [1984] I.C.R. 188; [1984] I.R.L.R. 52; (1984)
  134 N.L.J. 256, EAT... 36–25
Giles v Thompson; Devlin v Baslington; Sanders v Templar [1994] 1 A.C.
  142; [1993] 2 W.L.R. 908; [1993] 3 All E.R. 321; [1993] R.T.R.
  289; (1993) 143 N.L.J. 884; (1993) 137 S.J.L.B. 151; *The Times*,
  June 1, 1993, HL; affirming (1993) 143 N.L.J. 284; *The Times*,
  January 13, 1993, CA (Civ Div)................................ 4–79
Gissing v Gissing [1971] A.C. 886; [1970] 3 W.L.R. 255; [1970] 2 All E.R.
  780; (1970) 21 P. & C.R. 702; 114 S.J. 550, HL; reversing [1969] 2
  Ch. 85; [1969] 2 W.L.R. 525; [1969] 1 All E.R. 1043; (1969) 20 P.
  & C.R. 276; 113 S.J. 187, CA (Civ Div)........................ 32–04
Glegg v Bromley [1912] 3 K.B. 474, CA............................. 6–89
Gloystarne & Co Ltd v Martin [2001] I.R.L.R. 15, EAT.................. 36–25

Gnitrow Ltd v Cape Plc [2000] 1 W.L.R. 2327; [2000] 3 All E.R. 763; [2001] C.P. Rep. 21; (2000) 150 N.L.J. 1109; *The Times*, July 18, 2000, CA (Civ Div).. 27–50
Gojkovic v Gojkovic [1992] Fam. 40; [1991] 3 W.L.R. 621; [1992] 1 All E.R. 267; [1991] 2 F.L.R. 233; [1991] F.C.R. 913; [1991] Fam. Law 378; *The Times*, May 1, 1991, CA (Civ Div)   34–11, 34–12, 34–05, 34–09
Goldsworthy v Brickell [1987] Ch. 378; [1987] 2 W.L.R. 133; [1987] 1 All E.R. 853; (1987) 84 L.S.G. 654; (1987) 131 S.J. 102, CA (Civ Div)   22–05
Gooday v Gooday [1969] P. 1; [1968] 3 W.L.R. 750; [1968] 3 All E.R. 611; 112 S.J. 785, CA (Civ Div)....................................... 34–04
Goodinson v Goodinson [1954] 2 Q.B. 118; [1954] 2 W.L.R. 1121; [1954] 2 All E.R. 255; 98 S.J. 369, CA..................................... 32–09
Goodman v Robinson (1887) L.R. 18 Q.B.D. 332, QBD................... 6–91
Gordon v Gordon (1816–19) 3 Swans. 400............................ 4–38
Gorman v Gorman [1964] 1 W.L.R. 1440; [1964] 3 All E.R. 739; 108 S.J. 878, CA.. 32–15
Goucher v Clayton (1865) 13 W.R 336............................... 6–06
Goymour v Pigge (1844) 13 L.J. Ch.322.............................. 4–38
Grains & Fourrages SA v Huyton [1997] 1 Lloyd's Rep. 628, QBD (Comm)   4–18
Graves v Graves (1893) 69 L.T. 420...................... 5–47, 9–09, 11–15
Great Atlantic Insurance Co v Home Insurance Co; sub nom.Great Atlantic Insurance Co v American Foreign Insurance Association; Great Atlantic Insurance Co v CE Heath & Co (International); Great Atlantic Insurance Co v Frank Elger & Co [1981] 1 W.L.R. 529; [1981] 2 All E.R. 485; [1981] 2 Lloyd's Rep. 138; 125 S.J. 203, CA (Civ Div); affirming [1981] 2 Lloyd's Rep. 219,QBD (Comm)....... 27–46
Great North West Central Railway Co v Charlebois [1899] A.C. 114, PC (Can)... 4–09
Great Peace Shipping Ltd v Tsavliris Salvage (International) Ltd [2002] EWCA Civ 1407; [2003] Q.B. 679; [2002] 3 W.L.R. 1617; [2002] 4 All E.R. 689; [2002] 2 All E.R. (Comm) 999; [2002] 2 Lloyd's Rep. 653; [2003] 2 C.L.C. 16; (2002) 99(43) L.S.G. 34; (2002) 152 N.L.J. 1616; [2002] N.P.C. 127; *The Times*, October 17, 2002; *Independent*, October 22, 2002, CA (Civ Div); affirming (2001) 151 N.L.J. 1696, QBD (Comm)..................... 4–14, 4–15, 4–17, 4–22, 4–66
Greater London Council v Rush & Tomkins (1984) 81 L.S.G. 2624; (1984) 128 S.J. 722, CA (Civ Div).............................. 6–22, 27–16
Green v Briscoe, May 9, 2005, unreported............................ 31–26
Green v Collyer-Bristow [1999] Lloyd's Rep. P.N. 798; [1999] N.P.C. 56, QBD... 29–32
Green v Crockett; Crockett v Green (1865)34 L.J.Ch.606............... 29–13
Green v Duckett (1882–83) L.R. 11 Q.B.D. 275, QBD................... 4–60
Green v Rozen [1955] 1 W.L.R. 741; [1955] 2 All E.R. 797; 99 S.J. 473, QBD.. 5–47, 9–09, 9–28, 11–14
Greenhalgh v Mallard [1947] 2 All E.R. 255, CA....................... 6–11
Greenhaven Motors Ltd, Re [1999] B.C.C. 463; [1999] 1 B.C.L.C. 635, CA (Civ Div); reversing [1997] B.C.C. 547; [1997] 1 B.C.L.C. 739, Ch D... 31–10
Greenwich LBC v Regan (1996) 28 H.L.R. 469; (1996) 72 P. & C.R. 507; [1996] E.G.C.S. 15; [1996] N.P.C. 10; *The Times*, February 8, 1996, CA (Civ Div).. 37–49
Greenwood, Re (1911) 105 L.J. 509.................................. 31–19
Greenwood v Fitts (1961) 29 D.L.R. 260...................... 27–31, 27–34

TABLE OF CASES

Grenfell v Grenfell [1978] Fam. 128; [1977] 3 W.L.R. 738; [1978] 1 All E.R. 561; (1977) 7 Fam. Law 242; 121 S.J. 814, CA (Civ Div); affirming, 121 S.J. 355.................................... 32–21, 34–04
Guinle v Kirreh; Kinstreet Ltd v Balmargo Corp Ltd; Interfisa Management Inc v Hamam [2000] C.P. Rep. 62, Ch D........................ 43–04
Gurney v Grimmer (1932) 44 Ll. L. Rep. 189, CA; reversing (1932) 43 Ll. L. Rep. 481, KBD... 1–01
Guy v Walker (1892) 8 T.L.R. 314............................ 7–06, 11–03

H v H (Financial Relief: Non-disclosure: Costs) [1994] 2 F.L.R. 94; [1994] 2 F.C.R. 301; [1994] Fam. Law 497, Fam Div.............. 32–11, 32–49
HFC Bank Plc v HSBC Bank Plc (formerly Midland Bank Plc) [2000] C.P.L.R. 197; (2000) 97(19) L.S.G. 43; (2000) 144 S.J.L.B. 182; *The Times*, April 26, 2000; *Independent*, April 3, 2000 (C.S.), CA (Civ Div); affirming [2000] F.S.R. 176; (1999) 22(12) I.P.D. 22119; *The Times*, September 28, 1999, Ch D............................. 10–26
HSS Hire Services Group Plc v BMB Builders Merchants Ltd; HSS Hire Services Group Plc v Grafton Group (UK) Plc [2004] EWHC 2013, QBD... 14–09
Hadfield v Knowles (Practice Note) [1996] 1 W.L.R. 1003; [1996] P.I.Q.R. Q97; (1997) 34 B.M.L.R. 55; (1996) 93(28) L.S.G. 29; (1996) 140 S.J.L.B. 148; *The Times*, May 27, 1996, CA (Civ Div)............. 42–06
Hadley v Baxendale, 156 E.R. 145; (1854) 9 Ex. 341, Ex Ct............. 39–48
Halifax Financial Services Ltd v Intuitive Systems Ltd [1999] 1 All E.R. (Comm) 303; (2000) 2 T.C.L.R. 35; [1999] C.I.L.L. 1467, QBD..... 4–75
Hall v Hall, *The Times*, June 30, 1972................................ 32–129
Halsey v Milton Keynes General NHS Trust; Steel v Joy [2004] EWCA Civ 576; [2004] 1 W.L.R. 3002; [2004] 4 All E.R. 920; [2004] C.P. Rep. 34; [2004] 3 Costs L.R. 393; (2005) 81 B.M.L.R. 108; (2004) 101(22) L.S.G. 31; (2004) 154 N.L.J. 769; (2004) 148 S.J.L.B. 629; *The Times*, May 27, 2004; *Independent*, May 21, 2004, CA (Civ Div)............... 35–63, 40–05, 43–01, 43–04, 43–06–43–14, 43–21
Hambleton v Brown [1917] 2 K.B. 93, KBD........................ 6–91
Hamlin v Edwin Evans (A Firm), 80 B.L.R. 85; 52 Con. L.R. 106; (1997) 29 H.L.R. 414; [1996] P.N.L.R. 398; [1996] 2 E.G.L.R. 106; [1996] 47 E.G. 141; [1996] E.G.C.S. 120; (1996) 93(27) L.S.G. 29; (1996) 140 S.J.L.B. 167; [1996] N.P.C. 110; *The Times*, July 15, 1996; *Independent*, July 24, 1996, CA (Civ Div)........................ 39–23
Hammond v Schofield [1891] 1 Q.B. 453, QBD...................... 6–84
Hammond v Travers, unreported, May 7, 1999, QBD................. 11–25
Hanlon v Hanlon [1978] 1 W.L.R. 592; [1978] 2 All E.R. 889; 122 S.J. 62, CA (Civ Div)... 32–09
Harford v Birmingham City Council (1993) 66 P. & C.R. 468, Lands Tr. . 29–06
Hargrave v Hargrave (1850) 12 Beavan 408at413..................... 5–52
Hargreaves Construction (Limeside) v Williams, *The Times*, July 3, 1982, Ch D... 14–01
Harley v Samson (1914) 30 T.L.R.450............................... 6–91
Harper v Gray & Walker [1985] 1 W.L.R. 1196; [1985] 2 All E.R. 507; (1983) 1 Const. L.J. 46; [1984] C.I.L.L. 106; (1985) 82 L.S.G. 3532; (1985) 129 S.J. 776, QBD...................................... 25–04
Harris, Re (1875) 32 L.T. 417..................................... 27–07

Harris (formerly Manahan) v Manahan [1996] 4 All E.R. 454; [1997] 1 F.L.R. 205; [1997] 2 F.C.R. 607; [1997] Fam. Law 238, CA (Civ Div); affirming, Fam Div.... 32–31, 32–32, 32–93, 32–78, 32–89, 32–116, 32–118, 32–121, 32–122
Hart v O'Connor [1985] A.C. 1000; [1985] 3 W.L.R. 214; [1985] 2 All E.R. 880; [1985] 1 N.Z.L.R. 159; (1985) 82 L.S.G. 2658; (1985) 129 S.J. 484, PC (NZ)... 4–03
Hart v Hart (1881) 18 Ch.D.670.................................... 4–66
Harte v Harte (1976) C.A.T. 423A.......................... 11–03, 32–67
Hartman v South Essex Mental Health and Community Care NHS Trust [2005] EWCA Civ 6; [2005] I.C.R. 782; [2005] I.R.L.R. 293; [2005] E.L.R. 237; (2005) 149 S.J.L.B. 115; *The Times*, January 21, 2005; *Independent*, January 25, 2005, CA (Civ Div).................... 36–08
Harvey v Croydon Union Rural Sanitary Authority (1884) L.R. 26 Ch. D. 249; (1884) 53 L.J. Ch. 707, CA............................... 29–13
Hawick Jersey International Ltd v Caplan, *The Times*, March 11, 1988, QBD... 27–34, 27–41
Hawkins Ex p. Troup, Re [1895] 1 Q.B. 404, CA...................... 6–75
Hayler v Chapman [1989] 1 Lloyd's Rep. 490; *The Times*, November 11, 1988, CA (Civ Div).. 30–03, 30–10
Hazell v Hammersmith and Fulham LBC [1992] 2 A.C. 1; [1991] 2 W.L.R. 372; [1991] 1 All E.R. 545; 89 L.G.R. 271; (1991) 3 Admin. L.R. 549; [1991] R.V.R. 28; (1991) 155 J.P.N. 527; (1991) 155 L.G. Rev. 527; (1991) 88(8) L.S.G. 36; (1991) 141 N.L.J. 127; *The Times*, January 25, 1991; *Independent*, January 25, 1991; *Financial Times*, January 29, 1991; *Guardian*, January 25, 1991; *Daily Telegraph*, February 4, 1991, HL; reversing [1990] 2 W.L.R. 1038; [1990] 3 All E.R. 33; 88 L.G.R. 433; [1990] R.V.R. 140; (1990) 87(20) L.S.G. 36; (1990) 134 S.J. 637, CA (Civ Div); reversing in part [1990] 2 W.L.R. 17; [1989] R.V.R. 188; [1989] R.V.R. 188; [1990] C.O.D. 112; (1990) 87(2) L.S.G. 36; (1989) 134 S.J. 21, QBD....... 4–10, 40–07
Heard v Heard [1995] 1 F.L.R. 970; [1996] 1 F.C.R. 33; [1995] Fam. Law 477, CA (Civ Div)... 32–104
Hearn, Re, [1913] W.N. 103........................ 5–46, 9–29, 9–30, 11–30
Heaton v Axa Equity & Law Life Assurance Society Plc [2002] UKHL 15; [2002] 2 A.C. 329; [2002] 2 W.L.R. 1081; [2002] 2 All E.R. 961; [2002] C.P. Rep. 52; [2002] C.P.L.R. 475; [2003] 1 C.L.C. 37; *The Times*, May 15, 2002, HL; affirming [2001] Ch. 173; [2000] 3 W.L.R. 1341; [2000] 4 All E.R. 673; [2001] C.P. Rep. 10; [2000] C.P.L.R. 505; *The Times*, June 7, 2000; *Independent*, July 3, 2000 (C.S), CA (Civ Div); reversing; *The Times*, July 19, 1999, Ch D..... 2–10, 5–23, 6–37, 6–39, 6–40, 39–36
Henderson v Henderson [1843–60] All E.R. Rep. 378; (1843) 67 E.R. 313; (1843) 3 Hare 100, Ct of Chancery.. 6–06, 6–09, 6–12, 6–14, 6–16, 6–17, 6–29, 16–04
Henderson v Stobart (1850) 5 Ex. 99................................. 8–03
Hennessy v Craigmyle & Co [1986] I.C.R. 461; [1986] I.R.L.R. 300; (1986) 83 L.S.G. 2160; (1986) 130 S.J. 633, CA (Civ Div); affirming [1985] I.C.R. 879; [1985] I.R.L.R. 446; *The Times*, July 11, 1985, EAT.. 4–65, 36–25, 36–43
Henry Boot Building v Croydon Hotel & Leisure Co, 36 B.L.R. 41; (1986) 2 Const. L.J. 183, CA (Civ Div).............................. 39–15
Herbert v Herbert (1978) 122 S.J. 826.............. 11–12, 11–13, 11–14

lvii

Heselwood v Collett [1999] P.I.Q.R. Q136; [1999] Lloyd's Rep. Med. 42, QBD.. 3–56
Heywood v Wellers (A Firm) [1976] Q.B. 446; [1976] 2 W.L.R. 101; [1976] 1 All E.R. 300; [1976] 2 Lloyd's Rep. 88; (1975) 120 S.J. 9; *The Times*, November 15, 1975, CA (Civ Div)................... 29–31
Hickman v Berens [1895] 2 Ch. 638, CA................... 4–66, 6–20, 12–07
Hill v Mercantile & General Reinsurance Co Plc; Berry v Mercantile & General Reinsurance Co Plc [1996] 1 W.L.R. 1239; [1996] 3 All E.R. 865; [1996] L.R.L.R. 341; [1996] C.L.C. 1247; [1996] 5 Re. L.R. 461; (1996) 93(35) L.S.G. 32; (1996) 146 N.L.J. 1313; (1996) 140 S.J.L.B. 192; *The Times*, August 15, 1996, HL; reversing [1995] L.R.L.R. 160; [1995] 4 Re. L.R. 1; *The Times*, July 25, 1994, CA (Civ Div)... 30–16
Hill v William Hill (Park Lane) Ltd [1949] A.C. 530; [1949] 2 All E.R. 452; 65 T.L.R. 471; [1949] L.J.R. 1383; 93 S.J. 587, HL............... 4–74
Hinde v Hinde [1953] 1 W.L.R. 175; [1953] 1 All E.R. 171; 97 S.J. 47, CA.................. 5–36, 10–02, 10–06, 10–11, 32–04, 32–60, 33–10
Hirachand Punamchand v Temple [1911] 2 K.B. 330, CA............... 6–73
Hirschfeld v London Brighton & South Coast Railway Co (1876–77) L.R. 2 Q.B.D. 1, QBD... 4–29, 4–46
Hitachi Sales (UK) v Mitsui Osk Lines [1986] 2 Lloyd's Rep. 574, CA (Civ Div).. 5–44
Hobin v Douglas (No.2) [2000] P.I.Q.R. Q1; (1999) 96(4) L.S.G. 37; (1999) 143 S.J.L.B. 21; *The Times*, December 29, 1998; *Independent*, December 14, 1998 (C.S.), CA (Civ Div)........... 16–07, 23–04, 26–06
Hodgkinson & Corby Ltd v Wards Mobility Services Ltd (No.2) [1998] F.S.R. 530, CA (Civ Div); reversing [1997] F.S.R. 178, Ch D....... 27–45
Hodgson v Guardall Ltd [1991] 3 All E.R. 823, QBD.................. 21–06
Hoghton v Hoghton (1852) 15 Beav. 278............................ 26–04
Holland Hannen & Cubitts (Northern) Ltd v Welsh Health Technical Services Organisation, 35 B.L.R. 1; 7 Con. L.R. 1; [1985] C.I.L.L. 217, CA (Civ Div)... 39–45
Hollingsworth v Humphrey, *Independent*, December 21, 1987, CA (Civ Div)............................ 9–23, 9–26, 9–27, 9–28, 9–31, 21–16
Holsworthy Urban DC v Holsworthy Rural DC [1907] 2 Ch. 62, Ch D.... 2–16, 6–02
Holt v Jesse (1876) L.R. 3 Ch. D. 177, Ch D........................... 6–20
Homeguard Products (N.Z.) Ltd v Kiwi Packaging Ltd [1981] 2 N.Z.L.R. 322... 3–48
Hooper v Secretary of State for Work and Pensions; Withey v Secretary of State for Work and Pensions; Naylor v Secretary of State for Work and Pensions; Martin v Secretary of State for Work and Pensions; sub nom. R. (on the application of Hooper) v Secretary of State for Work and Pensions [2003] EWCA Civ 813; [2003] 1 W.L.R. 2623; [2003] 3 All E.R. 673; [2003] 2 F.C.R. 504; [2003] U.K.H.R.R. 1268; 14 B.H.R.C. 626; (2003) 100(29) L.S.G. 35; *The Times*, June 28, 2003; *Independent*, June 25, 2003, CA (Civ Div); affirming [2002] EWHC 191; [2002] U.K.H.R.R. 785, QBD (Admin)............... 40–05, 40–09
Hope, The (1883) L.R. 8 P.D. 144, CA............................. 4–13
Hope-Smith v Hope-Smith [1989] 2 F.L.R. 56; [1989] F.C.R. 785; [1989] Fam. Law 268; (1989) 153 J.P.N. 630; (1989) 139 N.L.J. 111, CA (Civ Div)........................... 32–85, 32–89, 32–104, 32–106
Hopmeyer v Silverman (1980) C.A.T. 147.......................... 8–06

Horizon Technologies International Ltd v Lucky Wealth Consultants Ltd
[1992] 1 W.L.R. 24; [1992] 1 All E.R. 469; (1992) 89(2) L.S.G. 32;
(1991) 135 S.J.L.B. 204; *The Times*, November 21, 1991, PC (HK).. 7–04,
9–12, 9–15, 10–29, 11–25, 11–26
Horry v Tate & Lyle Refineries [1982] 2 Lloyd's Rep. 416, QBD.... 4–53, 4–68
Horse, Carriage and General Insurance Co. v Petch (1916) 33 T.L.R. 131 30–11
Houghton, Re; sub nom. Hawley v. Blake [1904] 1 Ch. 622, Ch D...... 31–19
Hounslow LBC v McBride (1999) 31 H.L.R. 143, CA (Civ Div).......... 37–38
Howard & Wyndham v Healthworks UK, unreported, August 21, 1989,
CA (Civ Div)... 5–53, 5–56
Huck v Robson [2002] EWCA Civ 398; [2003] 1 W.L.R. 1340; [2002] 3
All E.R. 263; [2002] C.P. Rep. 38; [2002] C.P.L.R. 345; [2003] 1
Costs L.R. 19; [2002] P.I.Q.R. P31, CA (Civ Div)... 15–07, 23–30, 23–31
Huddersfield Banking Co Ltd v Henry Lister & Son Ltd (No.2) [1895] 2
Ch. 273, CA......................... 2–14, 2–16, 4–17, 4–51, 6–20
Hudson v Elmbridge BC [1991] 1 W.L.R. 880; [1991] 4 All E.R. 55; *The
Times*, November 29, 1990, CA (Civ Div)........................ 21–05
Hudson v Yonkers Fruit Co. (1932) 179 North Eastern Reps. 373.... 3–45, 3–47
Hughes v Singh, *The Times*, April 21, 1989; *Independent*, April 24, 1989,
CA (Civ Div)... 35–15
Hulton v Hulton [1917] 1 K.B. 813, CA; affirming [1916] 2 K.B. 642,
KBD.. 32–12
Hunt v RM Douglas (Roofing) Ltd [1990] 1 A.C. 398; [1988] 3 W.L.R.
975; [1988] 3 All E.R. 823; (1989) 86(1) L.S.G. 40; (1988) 138
N.L.J. Rep. 324; (1988) 132 S.J. 1592, HL................ 9–06, 11–20
Hurst v Leeming [2002] EWHC 1051; [2003] 1 Lloyd's Rep. 379; [2002]
C.P. Rep. 59; [2003] 2 Costs L.R. 153; [2002] Lloyd's Rep. P.N.
508, Ch D... 35–63, 43–06
Hurst Stores & Interiors Ltd v ML Europe Property Ltd [2004] EWCA Civ
490; [2004] B.L.R. 249; 94 Con. L.R. 66; (2004) 148 S.J.L.B. 421,
CA (Civ Div); affirming [2003] B.L.R. 391, QBD (TCC)............ 4–09
Hussain v Heywood [2001] 7 C.L. 73, CC (Sheffield).................... 23–16
Hussain v Hussain [1986] Fam. 134; [1986] 2 W.L.R. 801; [1986] 1 All
E.R. 961; [1986] 2 F.L.R. 271; [1986] Fam. Law 269; (1986) 83
L.S.G. 1314; (1986) 136 N.L.J. 358; (1986) 130 S.J. 341, CA (Civ
Div).. 11–34
Hussey v Horne-Payne (1878–79) L.R. 4 App. Cas. 311, HL; affirming
(1878) L.R. 8 Ch. D. 670, CA.................................. 3–22
Hutchinson v Tamosius, 1997 H 4888, QBD..................... 3–51, 4–65
Huyton SA v Peter Cremer GmbH & Co [1999] 1 Lloyd's Rep. 620; [1999]
C.L.C. 230, QBD (Comm).................................. 3–22, 4–61
Hyams v Coombes (1912) 28 T.L.R. 413............................. 3–11
Hydrocarbons Great Britain Ltd v Cammell Laird Shipbuilders and Automotive Products Ltd (t/a Ap Precision Hydraulics) and Redman
Broughton and Black Clawson International, 53 B.L.R. 84, CA (Civ
Div); reversing, 25 Con. L.R. 131, QBD (OR)..................... 6–60
Hyman v Hyman; Hughes v Hughes [1929] A.C. 601, HL; affirming [1929]
P. 1, CA.. 32–09, 32–42, 32–48
Hynes v Twinsectra Ltd (1996) 28 H.L.R. 183; (1996) 71 P. & C.R. 145;
[1995] 2 E.G.L.R. 69; [1995] 35 E.G. 136; [1995] E.G.C.S. 42; *The
Times*, March 8, 1995; *Independent*, May 22, 1995 (C.S.), CA (Civ
Div)... 37–53

Igbo v Johnson Matthey Chemicals [1986] I.C.R. 505; [1986] I.R.L.R. 215; (1986) 83 L.S.G. 2089; (1986) 130 S.J. 524, CA (Civ Div); reversing [1986] I.C.R. 82; [1985] I.R.L.R. 189; (1985) 82 L.S.G. 1011, EAT. 36–16
Imperial Loan Co Ltd v Stone [1892] 1 Q.B. 599, CA. 4–03
Independent Research Services v Catterall [1993] I.C.R. 1, EAT... 27–43, 27–44
Indian Rubber, Guttapercha, and Telegraph Works Company Ltd v Chapman (1926) 20 B.W.C.C. 184, CA. 27–07
IRC v Hoogstraten [1985] Q.B. 1077; [1984] 3 W.L.R. 933; [1984] 3 All E.R. 25; (1984) 81 L.S.G. 1368; (1984) 128 S.J. 484, CA (Civ Div).. 6–20, 10–10, 10–06
IRC v West [1991] S.T.C. 357; 64 T.C. 196; [1991] S.T.I. 527, CA (Civ Div). 4–07
Instance v Denny Bros Printing Ltd, unreported, December 21, 1999, CA.. 43–16
Insurance Co of Africa v Scor (UK) Reinsurance Co Ltd [1985] 1 Lloyd's Rep. 312, CA (Civ Div); reversing in part [1983] 1 Lloyd's Rep. 541; [1983] Com. L.R. 81, QBD (Comm). 30–15
International Military Services Ltd v Capital & Counties Plc [1982] 1 W.L.R. 575; [1982] 2 All E.R. 20; 80 L.G.R. 83; (1982) 44 P. & C.R. 83; (1982) 261 E.G. 778; 126 S.J. 293, Ch D. 37–27
Investment Corporation v Skibs A/S Avanti [1976] 1 Lloyd's Rep 293. 4–70
Investors Compensation Scheme Ltd v West Bromwich Building Society (No.1); Investors Compensation Scheme Ltd v Hopkin & Sons; Alford v West Bromwich Building Society; Armitage v West Bromwich Building Society [1998] 1 W.L.R. 896; [1998] 1 All E.R. 98; [1998] 1 B.C.L.C. 531; [1997] C.L.C. 1243; [1997] P.N.L.R. 541; (1997) 147 N.L.J. 989; *The Times*, June 24, 1997, HL; reversing [1998] 1 B.C.L.C. 521; [1997] C.L.C. 363; [1997] P.N.L.R. 166; [1997] N.P.C. 104; *The Times*, November 8, 1996, CA (Civ Div); affirming [1998] 1 B.C.L.C. 493; [1997] C.L.C. 348; *The Times*, October 10, 1996, Ch D. 5–03, 5–10, 5–17, 5–35, 6–39
Isaacs v Robertson [1985] A.C. 97; [1984] 3 W.L.R. 705; [1984] 3 All E.R. 140; (1984) 81 L.S.G. 2769; (1984) 134 N.L.J. 745, PC (StV). 10–10
Islam v Askar (1994) 138 S.J.L.B. 215, *The Times*, October 20, 1994, CA (Civ Div). 4–31, 4–32, 4–33, 9–12, 9–30, 10–31, 11–27
Ivory Gate Ltd v Spetale (1999) 77 P. & C.R. 141; [1998] L. & T.R. 58; [1998] 2 E.G.L.R. 43; [1998] 27 E.G. 139; [1998] E.G.C.S. 69; [1998] N.P.C. 72; (1998) 76 P. & C.R. D14, CA (Civ Div); reversing in part [1996] N.P.C. 186, QBD. 37–52

J Sainsbury Plc v Broadway Malyan, 61 Con. L.R. 31; [1999] P.N.L.R. 286, QBD (OR). 39–53
Jackson v Jackson [1971] 1 W.L.R. 1539; [1971] 3 All E.R. 774; 115 S.J. 723, CA (Civ Div); affirming [1971] 1 W.L.R. 59; [1970] 3 All E.R. 854, Ch D. 3–23
Jameson v Central Electricity Generating Board (No.1) [2000] 1 A.C. 455; [1999] 2 W.L.R. 141; [1999] 1 All E.R. 193; [1999] 1 Lloyd's Rep. 573; [1999] P.I.Q.R. Q81; (1999) 96(5) L.S.G. 37; (1999) 143 S.J.L.B. 29; *The Times*, December 17, 1998, HL; reversing [1998] Q.B. 323; [1997] 3 W.L.R. 151; [1997] 4 All E.R. 38; [1997] P.I.Q.R. Q89; (1997) 141 S.J.L.B. 55; *The Times*, February 25, 1997, CA (Civ Div). 6–36, 6–39, 6–40, 6–41

TABLE OF CASES

Jenkins v Livesey (formerly Jenkins) [1985] A.C. 424; [1985] 2 W.L.R. 47; [1985] 1 All E.R. 106; [1985] Fam. Law 310; (1985) 82 L.S.G. 517; (1985) 134 N.L.J. 55, HL; reversing, 1985] Fam. Law 180, CA (Civ Div)...... 4–19, 4–39, 4–44, 32–04, 32–27, 32–28, 32–29, 32–34, 32–43, 32–51, 32–53, 32–54, 32–60, 32–74, 32–76, 32–84, 32–85, 32–88, 32–91, 32–92, 32–101, 32–116, 32–129, 32–131,33–10, 33–15
Jennery, Re; sub nom. Jennery v Jennery [1967] Ch. 280; [1967] 2 W.L.R. 201; [1967] 1 All E.R. 691; 110 S.J. 910, CA.................... 33–17
Jessel v Jessel [1979] 1 W.L.R. 1148; [1979] 3 All E.R. 645; 123 S.J. 404, CA (Civ Div).. 11–10, 11–11
John Mowlem Construction Plc v Secretary of State for Defence, 82 Con. L.R. 140, QBD (TCC).. 39–26
Johnson v Davies [1999] Ch. 117; [1998] 3 W.L.R. 1299; [1998] 2 All E.R. 649; [1999] B.C.C. 275; [1998] 2 B.C.L.C. 252; [1998] B.P.I.R. 607; (2000) 79 P. & C.R. 14; [1998] L. & T.R. 69; [1998] 3 E.G.L.R. 72; [1998] 49 E.G. 153; (1998) 95(19) L.S.G. 23; (1998) 142 S.J.L.B. 141; [1998] N.P.C. 50; *The Times*, March 31, 1998, CA (Civ Div); affirming [1997] 1 W.L.R. 1511; [1997] 1 All E.R. 921; [1997] 1 B.C.L.C. 580; [1997] B.P.I.R. 221; [1997] 1 E.G.L.R. 42; [1997] 19 E.G. 157; (1996) 146 N.L.J. 1814, Ch D.................... 6–43, 6–46
Johnson v Gore Wood & Co (No.1); sub nom. Johnson v Gore Woods & Co [2002] 2 A.C. 1; [2001] 2 W.L.R. 72; [2001] 1 All E.R. 481; [2001] C.P.L.R. 49; [2001] B.C.C. 820; [2001] 1 B.C.L.C. 313; [2001] P.N.L.R. 18; (2001) 98(1) L.S.G. 24; (2001) 98(8) L.S.G. 46; (2000) 150 N.L.J. 1889; (2001) 145 S.J.L.B. 29; *The Times*, December 22, 2000; *Independent*, February 7, 2001 (C.S), HL; reversing in part [1999] C.P.L.R. 155; [1999] B.C.C. 474; [1999] Lloyd's Rep. P.N. 91; [1999] P.N.L.R. 426; [1998] N.P.C. 151, CA (Civ Div).... 6–06, 6–12, 6–14, 6–16, 6–17, 6–29
Joint Committee of the River Ribble v Croston Urban DC [1897] 1 Q.B. 251, QBD.. 6–05
Jon Beauforte (London) Ltd, Re; Grainger Smith & Co (Builders) Ltd's Application; John Wright & Son (Veneers) Ltd's Application; Lowell Baldwin Ltd's Application [1953] Ch. 131; [1953] 2 W.L.R. 465; [1953] 1 All E.R. 634; 97 S.J. 152, Ch D........................ 4–09
Jones (Joseph) v Director of British Empire Shipping Co (1860) 8 H.L. Cas. 338, HL.. 4–60
Jones v Foxall (1852) 15 Beav. 388.................................... 26–04
Jones v Merionethshire Permanent Benefit Building Society [1892] 1 Ch. 173, CA; affirming [1891] 2 Ch. 587, Ch D..................... 4–77
Jones v Price [1965] 2 Q.B. 618; [1965] 3 W.L.R. 296; [1965] 2 All E.R. 625; 109 S.J. 415, CA... 38–01
Jones v Sherwood Computer Services Plc [1992] 1 W.L.R. 277; [1992] 2 All E.R. 170; *The Times*, December 14, 1989, CA (Civ Div)......... 4–75
Joseph Finney Plc v Vickers (t/a Mill Hotel), unreported, March 7, 2001, QBD (TCC)... 39–68
Joyce v Rigolli [2004] EWCA Civ 79; (2004) 148 S.J.L.B. 234; [2004] 1 P. & C.R. DG22, CA (Civ Div)..................................... 3–73

Kavangh v Kavangh (1978) C.A.T. 571.................................. 11–33
Kearley v Thomson (1890) L.R. 24 Q.B.D. 742, CA..................... 4–78
Keary Developments Ltd v Tarmac Construction Ltd [1995] 3 All E.R. 534; [1995] 2 B.C.L.C. 395; 73 B.L.R. 115, CA (Civ Div)............. 27–55
Keir v Leemen (1846) 9 Q.B. 371...................................... 4–77

lxi

TABLE OF CASES

Kellar v Williams (2004) 148 S.J.L.B. 821, PC (TCI).................... 4–79
Kelley v Corston [1998] Q.B. 686; [1998] 3 W.L.R. 246; [1997] 4 All E.R. 466; [1998] E.C.C. 141; [1998] 1 F.L.R. 986; [1998] 1 F.C.R. 554; [1998] P.N.L.R. 37; [1998] Fam. Law 399; (1997) 94(32) L.S.G. 28; (1997) 147 N.L.J. 1276; (1997) 141 S.J.L.B. 206; [1997] N.P.C. 111; *The Times*, August 20, 1997, CA (Civ Div).................. 29–23
Kenburgh Investments (Northern) Ltd (In Liquidation) v David Yablon Minton (A Firm); sub nom. David Yablon Minton (A Firm) v Kenburgh Investments (Northern) Ltd (In Liquidation) [2000] C.P.L.R. 551; [2001] B.C.C. 648; [2001] B.P.I.R. 64; [2000] Lloyd's Rep. P.N. 736; (2000) 97(29) L.S.G. 46; *The Times*, July 11, 2000, CA (Civ Div).. 6–30
Kennedy v Claude Williams Motors Ltd (1975) C.A.T. 135.............. 6–20
Kensington Housing Trust v Oliver (1998) 30 H.L.R. 608; [1997] N.P.C. 119, CA (Civ Div)... 37–46
Keys v Harwood (1846) 2 C.B. 905..................................... 8–13
Kiam v MGN Ltd (Costs) [2002] EWCA Civ 66; [2002] 1 W.L.R. 2810; [2002] 2 All E.R. 242; [2002] C.P. Rep. 30; [2002] E.M.L.R. 26; *Independent*, March 25, 2002 (CS), CA (Civ Div)................. 13–10
Kinch v Walcott [1929] A.C. 482, PC (Bar)................. 6–02, 6–20, 9–40
Kinetics Technology International SpA v Cross Seas Shipping Corp (The Mosconici) [2001] 2 Lloyd's Rep. 313, QBD (Comm)....... 20–03, 24–03
King v Thomas McKenna Ltd [1991] 2 Q.B. 480; [1991] 2 W.L.R. 1234; [1991] 1 All E.R. 653; 54 B.L.R. 48; *The Times*, January 30, 1991, CA (Civ Div)... 41–18
King v Weston-Howell [1989] 1 W.L.R. 579; [1989] 2 All E.R. 375; (1989) 139 N.L.J. 399; (1989) 133 S.J. 750, CA (Civ Div)......... 18–15, 18–16
Kingsley (dec'd) v Secretary of State for Transport; sub nom. Estate of M Kingsley, Re [1994] C.O.D. , QBD....................... 40–14, 40–18
Kirin-Amgen Inc v Transkaryotic Therapies Inc (No.2); sub nom. Kirin-Amgen Inc's European Patent (No.148605) (No.2); Kirin-Amgen Inc v Hoechst Marion Roussel Ltd (No.2) [2004] UKHL 46; [2005] 1 All E.R. 667; [2005] R.P.C. 9; (2004) 148 S.J.L.B. 1249, HL; affirming [2002] EWCA Civ 1096; [2003] E.N.P.R. 4; [2003] R.P.C. 3; (2002) 25(11) I.P.D. 25076, CA (Civ Div); reversing in part [2002] R.P.C. 2; (2001) 24(8) I.P.D. 24051; (2001) 98(24) L.S.G. 45; *The Times*, June 1, 2001, Ch D (Patents Ct)............. 6–20
Kirk v Eustace [1937] A.C. 491, HL; reversing [1937] 1 K.B. 278, CA.... 10–11, 32–08
Kitcat v Sharp (1882) 48 L.T.64...................................... 27–29
Kitchen Design & Advice Ltd v Lea Valley Water Co [1989] 2 Lloyd's Rep. 221; *The Times*, March 14, 1989, QBD............... 2–09, 2–12, 30–03
Kleinwort Benson Ltd v Lincoln City Council; Kleinwort Benson Ltd v Birmingham City Council; Kleinwort Benson Ltd v Southwark LBC; Kleinwort Benson Ltd v Kensington and Chelsea RLBC [1999] 2 A.C. 349; [1998] 3 W.L.R. 1095; [1998] 4 All E.R. 513; [1998] Lloyd's Rep. Bank. 387; [1999] C.L.C. 332; (1999) 1 L.G.L.R. 148; (1999) 11 Admin. L.R. 130; [1998] R.V.R. 315; (1998) 148 N.L.J. 1674; (1998) 142 S.J.L.B. 279; [1998] N.P.C. 145; *The Times*, October 30, 1998; *Independent*, November 4, 1998, HL............ 3–70, 4–20, 4–45
Knowles, Re; sub nom. Knowles v Birtwell [1966] Ch. 386; [1966] 3 W.L.R. 51; [1966] 2 All E.R. 480 (Note); 110 S.J. 549, Ch D...... 33–17
Knowles v Roberts (1888) L.R. 38 Ch. D. 263, CA................. 6–01, 6–02

Korea Foreign Insurance Co v Omne Re SA, unreported, April 14, 1999,
CA.................................... 1–01, 7–04, 8–07, 8–08, 8–10
Kristjansson v R Verney & Co Ltd, unreported, June 18, 1998, CA (Civ
Div).. 27–54
Kumar (A Bankrupt), Re; sub nom. Lewis v Kumar [1993] 1 W.L.R. 224;
[1993] 2 All E.R. 700; [1993] B.C.L.C. 548; [1993] 2 F.L.R. 382;
[1993] Fam. Law 470, Ch D................................... 6–75
Kurttz and Co v Spence & Sons (1877) L.J.Ch.238................... 27–31
Kuwait Airways Corp v Iraqi Airways Co (No.8) (Petition for Variation of
Order) [2001] 1 W.L.R. 429; [2001] 1 Lloyd's Rep. 485; (2001)
98(11) L.S.G. 44; (2001) 145 S.J.L.B. 84; *The Times*, February 14,
2001; *Daily Telegraph*, February 20, 2001, HL.................... 6–20

L v L (Lump Sum Payments) (1981) 11 Fam. Law 57; 124 S.J. 828........ 4–19
L Figueiredo (L) Navegacas SA v Reederei Richard Schroeder KG (The
Erich Schroeder) [1974] 1 Lloyd's Rep. 192, QBD (Comm)......... 41–15
Lambert v Mainland Market Deliveries Ltd [1977] 1 W.L.R. 825; [1977] 2
All E.R. 826; [1978] 1 Lloyd's Rep. 245; 121 S.J. 477, CA (Civ
Div)....................................... 9–28, 9–31, 30–07, 30–10
Landall v Dennis Faulkner & Alsop [1994] 5 Med. L.R. 268, QBD....... 29–23
Langford v Hebran [2001] EWCA Civ 361; [2001] P.I.Q.R. Q13, CA (Civ
Div); affirming, QBD.. 35–25
Larkfield of Chepstow v Milne [1988] I.C.R. 1, EAT...... 36–43, 36–45, 36–46
Lathom Construction Ltd v Cross (1999) C.I.L.L. 1568.... 39–65, 39–66, 39–67
Launder, Re (1908) 98 L.T. 554............................. 11–34, 32–24
Lawlor v Gray [1984] 3 All E.R. 345, Ch D......................... 6–11
Leake (formerly Bruzzi) v Bruzzi; sub nom. Leake v Bruzzi [1974] 1 W.L.R.
1528; [1974] 2 All E.R. 1196; 118 S.J. 831, CA (Civ Div)......... 32–04
Lee v Showmen's Guild of Great Britain [1952] 2 Q.B. 329; [1952] 1 All
E.R. 1175; [1952] 1 T.L.R. 1115; 96 S.J. 296, CA................ 4–75
Legal & General Assurance Society Ltd v Drake Insurance Co (t/a Drake
Motor Policies at Lloyd's) [1992] Q.B. 887; [1992] 2 W.L.R. 157;
[1992] 1 All E.R. 283; [1991] 2 Lloyd's Rep. 36; [1992] R.T.R. 162;
(1992) 89(2) L.S.G. 30; *The Times*, January 15, 1991; *Financial
Times*, January 15, 1991, CA (Civ Div); reversing [1989] 3 All E.R.
923, QBD... 30–14
Legal Aid Board v Russell [1991] 2 A.C. 317; [1991] 2 W.L.R. 1300; *The
Times*, May 22, 1991; *Independent*, May 24, 1991, HL; affirming
[1990] 2 Q.B. 607; [1990] 3 W.L.R. 526; [1990] 3 All E.R. 18, CA
(Civ Div)... 11–20, 32–16
Lennox, Re; Ex p. Lennox (1885) 16 Q.B.D. 315..................... 6–75
Levi v Taylor (1904) 116 L.T.Jo. 64.............................. 9–12
Lewis's v Lewis (1890) L.R. 45 Ch. D. 281, Ch D.................... 6–20
Lievesley v Gilmore (1865–66) L.R. 1 C.P. 570, CCP................. 9–12
Lim Poh Choo v Camden and Islington AHA [1980] A.C. 174; [1979] 3
W.L.R. 44; [1979] 2 All E.R. 910; 123 S.J. 457, HL; affirming in part
[1979] Q.B. 196; [1978] 3 W.L.R. 895; [1979] 1 All E.R. 332; 122
S.J. 508, CA (Civ Div); affirming, 122 S.J. 82; *The Times*, December
8 1977, QBD.. 35–24

Linden Gardens Trust Ltd v Lenesta Sludge Disposals Ltd; St Martins
Property Corp Ltd v Sir Robert McAlpine & Sons [1994] 1 A.C. 85;
[1993] 3 W.L.R. 408; [1993] 3 All E.R. 417; 63 B.L.R. 1; 36 Con.
L.R. 1; [1993] E.G.C.S. 139; (1993) 143 N.L.J. 1152; (1993) 137
S.J.L.B. 183; *The Times*, July 23, 1993; *Independent*, July 30, 1993,
HL; reversing in part, 57 B.L.R. 57; 30 Con. L.R. 1; (1992) 8 Const.
L.J. 180; *The Times*, February 27, 1992; *Independent*, March 6,
1992; *Financial Times*, February 20, 1992, CA (Civ Div); reversing,
52 B.L.R. 93; 25 Con. L.R. 28; [1991] E.G.C.S. 11, QBD........... 6–64
Lindner Ceilings Floors Partitions Plc v How Engineering Services Ltd;
How Engineering Services Ltd v Lindner Ceilings Floors Partitions
Plc (Appeal Against Costs [2001] B.L.R. 90; (2001) 3 T.C.L.R. 12,
QBD (TCC)... 41–24, 41–26
Line Trust Corp Ltd v Fielding, unreported, July 26, 1999, CA........... 2–08,
5–09, 5–22, 6–07
Little v George Little Sebire & Co (Enhanced Interest), *The Times*,
November 17, 1999, QBD.............................. 23–15, 23–25
Little v Spreadbury [1910] 2 K.B. 658, KBD........................... 29–26
Liverpool City Council v Irwin [1977] A.C. 239; [1976] 2 W.L.R. 562;
[1976] 2 All E.R. 39; (1984) 13 H.L.R. 38; 74 L.G.R. 392; (1976) 32
P. & C.R. 43; (1976) 238 E.G. 879; [1976] J.P.L. 427; 120 S.J. 267,
HL; affirming in part [1976] Q.B. 319; [1975] 3 W.L.R. 663; [1975]
3 All E.R. 658; 74 L.G.R. 21; (1976) 31 P. & C.R. 34; 119 S.J. 612,
CA (Civ Div)... 5–42
Liverpool Properties v Oldbridge Investments [1985] 2 E.G.L.R. 111;
(1985) 276 E.G. 1352, CA (Civ Div).......................... 37–51
Liverpool Roman Catholic Archdiocesan Trustees Inc v Goldberg (No.1)
[2001] 1 All E.R. 182; [2000] Lloyd's Rep. P.N. 836; [2001]
P.N.L.R. 19; *The Times*, July 18, 2000, Ch D..................... 39–20
Livingstone v Hepworth Refractories Plc [1992] 3 C.M.L.R. 601; [1992]
I.C.R. 287; [1992] I.R.L.R. 63; (1992) 89(5) L.S.G. 31; *The Times*,
December 23, 1991, EAT....................................... 36–28
Lloyds Bank Ltd v Bundy [1975] Q.B. 326; [1974] 3 W.L.R. 501; [1974] 3
All E.R. 757; [1974] 2 Lloyd's Rep. 366; 118 S.J. 714, CA (Civ Div)   4–52
Lockley v National Blood Transfusion Service [1992] 1 W.L.R. 492; [1992]
2 All E.R. 589; [1992] 3 Med. L.R. 173; *The Times*, November 11,
1991; *Independent*, November 4, 1991, CA (Civ Div).............. 34–15
Lofts, Re; sub nom. Lofts v Kenwright [1968] 1 W.L.R. 1949 (Note);
[1969] 1 All E.R. 7 (Note); (1968) 112 S.J. 968, Ch D............ 33–17
Logan v Uttlesford DC (1984) 134 N.L.J. 500; *The Times*, February 21,
1984, QBD.. 6–51
London & South Western Railway Co v Blackmore (1869–70) L.R. 4 H.L.
610; (1870) 39 L.J. Ch. 713, HL............................... 5–31
Longford, The (1889) L.R. 14 P.D. 34, CA............................ 32–16
Lord Napier and Ettrick v RF Kershaw Ltd (No.1); Lord Napier and Ettrick
v Hunter [1993] A.C. 713; [1993] 2 W.L.R. 42; [1993] 1 All E.R.
385; [1993] 1 Lloyd's Rep. 197; (1993) 137 S.J.L.B. 44; *The Times*,
December 16, 1992; *Independent*, December 11, 1992, HL; reversing
[1993] 1 Lloyd's Rep. 10; *The Times*, July 17, 1992; *Financial Times*,
July 22, 1992, CA (Civ Div); reversing in part, Ch D.............. 30–13
Luke v South Kensington Hotel Co (1879) L.R. 11 Ch. D. 121, CA;
reversing (1877–78) L.R. 7 Ch. D. 789, Ch D..................... 31–19

Lumbermens Mutual Casualty Co v Bovis Lend Lease Ltd (Preliminary Issues); sub nom. Lumbermen Mutual Casualty Co v Bovis Lend Lease Ltd (Preliminary Issues) [2004] EWHC 2197; [2005] B.L.R. 47; [2005] Lloyd's Rep. I.R. 74; [2004] 42 E.G.C.S. 160, QBD (Comm)... 39–58
Lunt v Merseyside TEC Ltd [1999] I.C.R. 17; [1999] I.R.L.R. 458, EAT.. 36–33

M (dec'd), Re [1968] P. 174, PDAD.................................. 33–02
M v H (Costs: Residence Proceedings) [2000] 1 F.L.R. 394; [2000] Fam. Law 313, Fam Div... 34–17
M v M, *The Times*, January 9, 1982................................ 32–130
MH Smith (Plant Hire) v DL Mainwaring (t/a Inshore) [1986] 2 Lloyd's Rep. 244; *The Times*, June 10, 1986, CA (Civ Div)............... 30–01
Macedonia Maritime Co, Alcionis Maritime Co, Kozani Maritime Co and Vassiliki Maritime Co v Austin & Pickersgill (The Fayrouz I-IV) [1989] 2 Lloyd's Rep. 73, QBD (Comm)........................ 9–39
Maersk Co Ltd v Wilson [2004] EWCA Civ 313, CA (Civ Div)........... 23–29
Maersk Colombo. *See* Southampton Container Terminals Ltd v Hansa Schiffahrts GmbH
Magee v Pennine Insurance Co [1969] 2 Q.B. 507; [1969] 2 W.L.R. 1278; [1969] 2 All E.R. 891; [1969] 2 Lloyd's Rep. 378; 113 S.J. 303, CA (Civ Div).. 2–14, 4–17
Magnus v National Bank of Scotland (1888) 58 L.T. 617.......... 9–40, 10–04
Mahmud v Bank of Credit and Commerce International SA. *See* Malik v Bank of Credit and Commerce International SA (In Liquidation)
Malhotra v Dhawan [1997] 8 Med. L.R. 319, CA (Civ Div)............. 14–01
Malik v Bank of Credit and Commerce International SA (In Liquidation); sub nom. Mahmud v Bank of Credit and Commerce International SA (In Liquidation); BCCI SA, Re [1998] A.C. 20; [1997] 3 W.L.R. 95; [1997] 3 All E.R. 1; [1997] I.C.R. 606; [1997] I.R.L.R. 462; (1997) 94(25) L.S.G. 33; (1997) 147 N.L.J. 917; *The Times*, June 13, 1997; *Independent*, June 20, 1997, HL; reversing [1995] 3 All E.R. 545; [1996] I.C.R. 406; [1995] I.R.L.R. 375; (1995) 145 N.L.J. 593; *The Times*, April 12, 1995; *Independent*, March 17, 1995, CA (Civ Div); affirming [1994] I.R.L.R. 282; *The Times*, February 23, 1994; *Independent*, March 21, 1994 (C.S.), Ch D....................... 5–24
Manku v Seehra, 7 Con. L.R. 90...................................... 15–14
Mannai Investment Co Ltd v Eagle Star Life Assurance Co Ltd [1997] A.C. 749; [1997] 2 W.L.R. 945; [1997] 3 All E.R. 352; [1997] C.L.C. 1124; [1997] 1 E.G.L.R. 57; [1997] 25 E.G. 138; [1997] 24 E.G. 122; (1997) 16 Tr. L.R. 432; [1997] E.G.C.S. 82; (1997) 94(30) L.S.G. 30; (1997) 147 N.L.J. 846; (1997) 141 S.J.L.B. 130; [1997] N.P.C. 81; *The Times*, May 26, 1997, HL; reversing [1995] 1 W.L.R. 1508; [1996] 1 All E.R. 55; (1996) 71 P. & C.R. 129; [1996] 1 E.G.L.R. 69; [1996] 06 E.G. 140; [1995] E.G.C.S. 124; (1995) 139 S.J.L.B. 179; [1995] N.P.C. 117; *The Times*, July 19, 1995, CA (Civ Div).. 5–07
Marchant v Marchant (1967) C.A.T. 26................... 9–21, 11–13, 11–35
Margetson and Jones, Re [1897] 2 Ch. 314, Ch D...................... 4–13
Markos v Goodfellow (No.2) [2002] EWCA Civ 1542; (2002) 146 S.J.L.B. 231, CA (Civ Div)... 5–44
Marly Laboratory's Application, Re (No.2) [1952] 1 All E.R. 1057; (1952) 69 R.P.C. 156; [1952] W.N. 195; 96 S.J. 261, CA................. 6–91

Marsden v Marsden [1972] Fam. 280; [1972] 3 W.L.R. 136; [1972] 2 All
  E.R. 1162; 116 S.J. 415, Fam Div................... 6–20, 29–15, 29–20
Marshall v Marshall, unreported, October 8, 1998, CA................... 4–38
Martin v Martin [1976] Fam. 335; [1976] 3 W.L.R. 580; [1976] 3 All E.R.
  625; (1976) 6 Fam. Law 246; 120 S.J. 503, CA (Civ Div); reversing
  in part [1976] Fam. 167; [1976] 2 W.L.R. 901; 120 S.J. 233, Fam
  Div... 6–80, 34–04
Martin (BH) v Martin (D) [1978] Fam. 12; [1977] 3 W.L.R. 101; [1977] 3
  All E.R. 762; (1977) 7 Fam. Law 175; 121 S.J. 335, CA (Civ Div).. 28–10
Masefield v Alexander (Lump Sum: Extension of Time) [1995] 1 F.L.R.
  100; [1995] 2 F.C.R. 663; [1995] Fam. Law 130; *The Times*, August
  19, 1994; *Independent*, August 22, 1994 (C.S.), CA (Civ Div)....... 32–60
Masterman-Lister v Brutton & Co (Costs); Joseph v Jewell [2003] EWCA
  Civ 70, CA (Civ Div)... 35–02
Mathews, Re; sub nom. Oates v Mooney [1905] 2 Ch. 460, Ch D........ 11–03
Mattei v Vautro (1898) 78 L.t. 682...................................... 4–02
Matthew Hall Ortech Ltd v Tarmac Roadstone Ltd, 87 B.L.R. 96, QBD
  (OR)... 39–10
Matthews v Baxter (1872–73) L.R. 8 Ex. 132, Ex Ct..................... 4–03
Matthews v Munster (1888) L.R. 20 Q.B.D. 141, CA................... 29–13
Maundy Gregory Ex p. Norton, Re [1935] Ch. 65, CA.................. 6–75
May v May [1929] 2 K.B. 386, CA...................................... 7–11
Macaulay v Polley [1897] 2 Q.B. 122, CA............................. 29–13
McCallum v Country Residences; sub nom. McCallum v Country Res-
  idences [1965] 1 W.L.R. 657; [1965] 2 All E.R. 264; 109 S.J. 293,
  CA.................................... 5–47, 5–53 - 5–57, 6–18, 8–01
McCallum v Westridge Construction Co [1971] C.L.Y. 9360............. 14–03
McCann v Sheppard [1973] 1 W.L.R. 540; [1973] 2 All E.R. 881; [1973] 1
  Lloyd's Rep. 561; 117 S.J. 323, CA (Civ Div)..................... 35–15
Macdonald v MacDonald [1964] P. 1; [1963] 3 W.L.R. 350; [1963] 2 All
  E.R. 857; 107 S.J. 630, CA..................................... 32–13
McDonnell v McDonnell; sub nom. MacDonnell v McDonnell [1977] 1
  W.L.R. 34; [1977] 1 All E.R. 766; (1976) 6 Fam. Law 220; 121 S.J.
  87; 120 S.J. 250, CA (Civ Div)..................... 26–05, 34–04, 34–16
McDonnell v Woodhouse & Jones, *The Times*, May 25, 1995, QBD...... 23–11
McDowell v Hirschfield Lipson & Rumney [1992] 2 F.L.R. 126; [1992]
  Fam. Law 430; *The Times*, February 13, 1992, QBD............... 27–27
McFadden v Snow (1952) 69 W.N. N.S.W 8........................... 27–21
McIlraith v Grady [1968] 1 Q.B. 468; [1967] 3 W.L.R. 1331; [1967] 3 All
  E.R. 625; 111 S.J. 583, CA (Civ Div)............................ 11–33
McMillan Williams (A Firm) v Range [2004] EWCA Civ 294; [2004] 1
  W.L.R. 1858; [2005] E.C.C. 8; (2004) 148 S.J.L.B.; *The Times*, April
  16, 2004, CA (Civ Div)... 43–13
McNamara v Martin Mears & Co (1983) 127 S.J. 69.................... 29–29
McPhilemy v Times Newspapers Ltd (Costs) [2001] EWCA Civ 933; [2002]
  1 W.L.R. 934; [2001] 4 All E.R. 861; [2002] C.P. Rep. 9; [2001] 2
  Costs L.R. 295; [2001] E.M.L.R. 35; *The Times*, July 3, 2001, CA
  (Civ Div).. 23–22
Mellor v Mellor [1992] 1 W.L.R. 517; [1992] 4 All E.R. 10; [1992] B.C.C.
  513; [1993] B.C.L.C. 30, Ch D.................................. 31–17
Mercantile Investment & General Trust Co v International Trust Co of
  Mexico [1893] 1 Ch. 484 (Note), CA............................. 2–01
Merkuria Foreign Trade Corporation v Dateline Electric Company Ltd and
  Dateline International Ltd (1979) C.A.T. 413..................... ??–??

Merrett v Babb [2001] EWCA Civ 214; [2001] Q.B. 1174; [2001] 3 W.L.R. 1; [2001] B.L.R. 483; (2001) 3 T.C.L.R. 15; 80 Con. L.R. 43; [2001] Lloyd's Rep. P.N. 468; [2001] P.N.L.R. 29; [2001] 1 E.G.L.R. 145; [2001] 8 E.G.C.S. 167; (2001) 98(13) L.S.G. 41; (2001) 145 S.J.L.B. 75; *The Times*, March 2, 2001; *Independent*, February 23, 2001, CA (Civ Div).. 39–32
Metroinvest Ansalt v Commercial Union Assurance Co [1985] 1 W.L.R. 513; [1985] 2 All E.R. 318; 7 Con. L.R. 73; (1985) 82 L.S.G. 523; (1985) 129 S.J. 86, CA (Civ Div)... 15–14
Metrostore Ltd v British Railways Board, unreported, January 20, 1989... 11–03
Michel v Mutch (1886) 54 L.T. 45... 10–04
Middleton v Elliot Turbomachinery, *The Times*, October 29, 1990; *Independent*, November 16, 1990, CA (Civ Div)...................... 35–28
Milburn v Newton Colliery (1908) 52 S.J. 317............................ 11–34
Miles v New Zealand Alford Estate Co (1886) L.R. 32 Ch. D. 266, CA.... 3–05, 3–09, 3–20
Milestone School of English v Leakey [1981] I.R.L.R. 3, EAT............ 36–40
Millensted v Grosvenor House (Park Lane) Ltd [1937] 1 K.B. 717, CA.... 14–08
Miller v Davies, unreported, September 14, 2001, CC (Liverpool)......... 3–33
Milne v Milne [1981] 2 F.L.R. 286, CA..................................... 32–70, 32–131
Minton v Minton [1979] A.C. 593; [1979] 2 W.L.R. 31; [1979] 1 All E.R. 79; 122 S.J. 843, HL; affirming, 122 S.J. 31, CA (Civ Div).. 11–11, 32–09, 32–31
Misa v Currie; sub nom. Currie v Misa (1875–76) L.R. 1 App. Cas. 554, HL; affirming (1874–75) L.R. 10 Ex. 153, Ex Chamber............. 3–02
Mitchell v Alasia [2005] EWHC 11, QBD.................................. 35–02
Mitchell v CC Sanitation Co (1968) 430 S.W. (2d) 933................... 4–61
Mitchells (A Firm) v James (Costs); sub nom. Mitchell v James [2002] EWCA Civ 997; [2004] 1 W.L.R. 158; [2003] 2 All E.R. 1064; [2002] C.P. Rep. 72; [2002] C.P.L.R. 764; (2002) 99(36) L.S.G. 38; (2002) 146 S.J.L.B. 202; *The Times*, July 20, 2002; *Independent*, July 18, 2002, CA (Civ Div).................... 16–03, 18–06, 23–11, 41–20
Monksfield v Vehicle and General Insurance Co [1971] 1 Lloyd's Rep. 139, MCLC... 30–14
Moorcock, The (1889) L.R. 14 P.D. 64; [1886–90] All E.R. Rep. 530, CA; affirming (1888) L.R. 13 P.D. 157, PDAD........................ 5–42
Moore v Peachey [1891] 2 Q.B. 707, QBD................................. 6–20
Moorish v Moorish [1984] Fam. Law 26, CA (Civ Div)............ 34–05, 34–08
Moriarty v London Chatham & Dover Railway Co (1869–70) L.R. 5 Q.B. 314, QB.. 27–53
Morris v Baron & Co [1918] A.C. 1, HL; reversing (1856) 18 C.B. 587, CA   8–03
Morris v Wentworth-Stanley; sub nom. Morris v Molesworth [1999] Q.B. 1004; [1999] 2 W.L.R. 470; [1999] 1 F.L.R. 83; (1998) 95(39) L.S.G. 34; (1998) 148 N.L.J. 1551; (1998) 142 S.J.L.B. 258; *The Times*, October 2, 1998, CA (Civ Div)........... 5–36, 6–29, 6–30, 6–73
Morss v Morss [1972] Fam. 264; [1972] 2 W.L.R. 908; [1972] 1 All E.R. 1121; 116 S.J. 143, CA (Civ Div)...................................... 5–20
Morton v Morton (1942) 58 T.L.R. 158.................................... 3–57
Morton v Quick (1878) 26 W.R. 441....................................... 9–28
Mostcash Plc (formerly UK Paper Plc) v Fluor Ltd (No.1) [2002] EWCA Civ 975; [2002] B.L.R. 411; 83 Con. L.R. 1; (2003) 19 Const. L.J. 200, CA (Civ Div); reversing [2002] EWHC 265, QBD (TCC)...... 39–22
Mostyn v Brooke (1869–70) L.R. 4 H.L. 304, HL......................... 4–38

Mouat-Balthasar v Murphy [1967] 1 Q.B. 344; [1966] 3 W.L.R. 695; [1966] 3 All E.R. 477; 110 S.J. 603, CA. 37–46
Moy v Pettman Smith (A Firm) [2005] UKHL 7; [2005] 1 W.L.R. 581; [2005] 1 All E.R. 903; [2005] P.N.L.R. 24; (2005) 102(11) L.S.G. 31; (2005) 155 N.L.J. 218; (2005) 149 S.J.L.B. 180; [2005] N.P.C. 15; *The Times*, February 4, 2005, HL; reversing [2002] EWCA Civ 875; [2002] C.P.L.R. 619; [2002] Lloyd's Rep. P.N. 513; [2002] P.N.L.R. 44; *Independent*, June 28, 2002, CA (Civ Div); reversing, QBD. 28–09, 29–25
Mulholland v Mitchell (No.1) [1971] A.C. 666; [1971] 2 W.L.R. 93; [1971] 1 All E.R. 307; 115 S.J. 15, HL. 35–15, 35–16
Muller v Linsley & Mortimer [1996] P.N.L.R. 74; (1995) 92(3) L.S.G. 38; (1995) 139 S.J.L.B. 43; *The Times*, December 8, 1994, CA (Civ Div). 26–04, 27–01, 27–16, 27–18, 27–19, 27–49
Mullins v Howell; sub nom. Mollins v Howell (1879) L.R. 11 Ch. D. 763, Ch D. 6–23
Muman v Nagasena [2000] 1 W.L.R. 299; [1999] 4 All E.R. 178, CA (Civ Div). 43–04
Murphy v Stone-Wallwork (Charlton) Ltd; sub nom. Murphy v Stone-Wallwork (Charlton) [1969] 1 W.L.R. 1023; [1969] 2 All E.R. 949; 7 K.I.R. 203; 113 S.J. 546, HL. 35–15, 35–16
Murrell v Healy [2001] EWCA Civ 486; [2001] 4 All E.R. 345; [2002] R.T.R. 2; *The Times*, May 1, 2001, CA (Civ Div). 27–50

N v N (Consent Order: Variation) [1993] 2 F.L.R. 868; [1994] 2 F.C.R. 275; [1993] Fam. Law 676; *The Times*, July 29, 1993; *Independent*, August 23, 1993 (C.S), CA (Civ Div). 32–133
N v N (Divorce: Agreement Not to Defend) [1992] 1 F.L.R. 266; [1991] F.C.R. 690; [1992] Fam. Law 145. .... 32–21, 32–49, 32–76, 32–135
Naqvi v Stephens Jewellers Ltd [1978] I.C.R. 631, EAT. 36–15
National Bank of Sharjah v Dellborg, unreported, July 9, 1997, CA. . 5–09, 5–21
National Benzole Co Ltd v Gooch [1961] 1 W.L.R. 1489; [1961] 3 All E.R. 1097; 105 S.J. 930,CA. 42–01
National Farmers Union Development Trusts, Re; sub nom. NFU Development Trust, Re [1972] 1 W.L.R. 1548; [1973] 1 All E.R. 135; 116 S.J. 679, Ch D. 1–01
National Westminster Bank Plc v Morgan [1985] A.C. 686; [1985] 2 W.L.R. 588; [1985] 1 All E.R. 821; [1985] F.L.R. 266; (1985) 17 H.L.R. 360; (1985) 82 L.S.G. 1485; (1985) 135 N.L.J. 254; (1985) 129 S.J. 205, HL; reversing [1983] 3 All E.R. 85; (1983) 133 N.L.J. 378, CA (Civ Div). 3–15, 4–52, 4–66, 4–68
National Westminster Bank v Smillie, unreported, February 4, 1999. 10–18
Naylor v Winch (1824) 1 Sim. and St. 555. 3–10
Neale v Gordon Lennox [1902] A.C. 465, HL; reversing [1902] 1 K.B. 838, CA. 6–20, 29–18
Neath Canal Co v Ynisarwed Resolven Colliery Co (1874–75) L.R. 10 Ch. App. 450, CA in Chancery. 11–34
Neave v Neave (Costs) [2003] EWCA Civ 325; (2003) 100(14) L.S.G. 27, CA (Civ Div); reversing [2002] EWHC 966, QBD. 18–06
Neste Production v Shell UK [1994] 1 Lloyd's Rep. 447, Ch D. 4–75
Neuchatel Asphalte v Barnett [1957] 1 W.L.R. 356; [1957] 1 All E.R. 362; (1957) 101 S.J. 170, CA. 2–06, 3–25, 3–32, 3–34, 5–16

New Zealand Shipping Co Ltd v AM Satterthwaite & Co Ltd (The Eurymedon); sub nom. AM Satterthwaite & Co Ltd v New Zealand Shipping Co Ltd [1975] A.C. 154; [1974] 2 W.L.R. 865; [1974] 1 All E.R. 1015; [1974] 1 Lloyd's Rep. 534; 118 S.J. 387, PC (NZ); affirming [1972] 2 Lloyd's Rep. 544, CA (NZ); reversing [1971] 2 Lloyd's Rep. 399; [1972] N.Z.L.R. 385, Sup Ct (NZ)................ 3–22
Newen, Re; sub nom. Carruthers v Newen [1903] 1 Ch. 812, Ch D...... 29–25
Newton v Newton [1990] 1 F.L.R. 33; [1989] F.C.R. 521; [1990] Fam. Law 25; (1989) 153 J.P.N. 642, CA (Civ Div).................... 34–02
Newton Moor Construction Ltd v Charlton (1997) 13 Const. L.J. 275, CA (Civ Div)... 2–05, 3–32
Nicholls v Kinsey; sub nom. Nicholas v Kinsey [1994] Q.B. 600; [1994] 2 W.L.R. 622; (1995) 69 P. & C.R. 438; [1994] 16 E.G. 145; [1994] E.G.C.S. 9; [1994] N.P.C. 9; *The Times*, February 3, 1994; *Independent*, February 7, 1994 (C.S.), CA (Civ Div)................ 10–10, 37–08
Nicholson v Revill (1836) 4 Ad. & El. 675............................ 6–47
Nicolene Ltd v Simmonds [1953] 1 Q.B. 543; [1953] 2 W.L.R. 717; [1953] 1 All E.R. 822; [1953] 1 Lloyd's Rep. 189; 97 S.J. 247, CA; affirming [1952] 2 Lloyd's Rep. 419, QBD................................. 3–54
Niemann v Niemann (1890) L.R. 43 Ch. D. 198, CA.................... 4–11
Nikko Hotels (UK) Ltd v MEPC Plc [1991] 2 E.G.L.R. 103; [1991] 28 E.G. 86, Ch D... 4–75
Noel v Becker [1971] 1 W.L.R. 355; [1971] 2 All E.R. 1186; 115 S.J. 157, CA (Civ Div)................................... 10–02, 10–09, 32–60
Nolan Davis Ltd v Catton, unreported, March 6, 2001, QBD (TCC)....... 4–36
Norfolk Finance Ltd v Newton, CA (Civ Div)................... 2–16, 2–19
Norglen Ltd (In Liquidation) v Reeds Rains Prudential Ltd; Mayhew-Lewis v Westminster Scaffolding Group Plc; Levy v ABN AMRO Bank NV; Circuit Systems Ltd (In Liquidation) v Zuken-Redac (UK) Ltd [1999] 2 A.C. 1; [1997] 3 W.L.R. 1177; [1998] 1 All E.R. 218; [1998] B.C.C. 44; [1998] 1 B.C.L.C. 176; 87 B.L.R. 1; (1997) 94(48) L.S.G. 29; (1997) 147 N.L.J. 1773; (1998) 142 S.J.L.B. 26; (1998) 75 P. & C.R. D21; *The Times*, December 1, 1997, HL; affirming [1996] 1 W.L.R. 864; [1996] 1 All E.R. 945; [1996] B.C.C. 532; [1996] 1 B.C.L.C. 690; *The Times*, December 6, 1995; *Independent*, January 12, 1996, CA (Civ Div); reversing [1994] E.G.C.S. 21, Ch D.. 4–81, 39–34
Normid Housing Association Ltd v Ralphs & Mansell (Third Party Rights: Mareva Injunction); Normid Housing Association Ltd v Assicurazioni Generali SpA; sub nom. Normid Housing Association Ltd v R John Ralphs; Normid Housing Association Ltd v John S Mansell [1989] 1 Lloyd's Rep. 265; 21 Con. L.R. 98; *The Times*, November 15, 1988, CA (Civ Div)... 30–19
Norris v Norris; Haskins v Haskins [2003] EWCA Civ 1084; [2003] 1 W.L.R. 2960; [2003] 4 Costs L.R. 591; [2003] 2 F.L.R. 1124; [2003] 3 F.C.R. 136; [2003] Fam. Law 721; (2003) 100(36) L.S.G. 37; *The Times*, August 26, 2003, CA (Civ Div); affirming [2002] EWHC 2996; [2003] 1 F.L.R. 1142; [2003] 2 F.C.R. 245; [2003] Fam. Law 301, Fam Div.................................... 34–06, 34–08, 34–12
North Ocean Shipping Co v Hyundai Construction Co (The Atlantic Baron) [1979] Q.B. 705; [1979] 3 W.L.R. 419; [1978] 3 All E.R. 1170; [1979] 1 Lloyd's Rep. 89; 123 S.J. 352, QBD (Comm).............. 4–70
Norwich Provident Insurance Society (Winding Up), Re; sub nom. Bath's Case; Hesketh's Case, Re (1879–80) L.R. 13 Ch. D. 693, CA; reversing (1879) L.R. 11 Ch. D. 386, Ch D........................ 4–09

Norwich Union Life Insurance Society v Waller (Tony) (1984) 270 E.G. 42; (1984) 81 L.S.G. 899; (1984) 128 S.J. 300,Ch D. 27–10, 27–12
Nowmost Co Ltd, Re [1997] B.C.C. 105; [1996] 2 B.C.L.C. 492, Ch D. . . 31–03
Nweze v Nwoko [2004] EWCA Civ 379; [2004] 2 P. & C.R. 33; (2004) 101(17) L.S.G. 30; (2004) 148 S.J.L.B. 472; [2004] N.P.C. 50; [2004] 2 P. & C.R. DG1; *The Times*, May 6, 2004, CA (Civ Div). . . 3–73, 38–06

Oben v Blackman; sub nom. Debtor (No.510 of 1997), Re; Blackman (A Debtor), Re [1999] B.C.C. 446; [2000] B.P.I.R. 302; *The Times*, June 18, 1998, Ch D. 31–08
O'Boyle v Leiper; sub nom. Boyle v Leiper (1990) 87(10) L.S.G. 36; (1990) 134 S.J. 316; *The Times*, January 26, 1990, CA (Civ Div). 2–11
Occidental Worldwide Investment Corp v Skibs A/S Avanti (The Siboen and The Sibotre) [1976] 1 Lloyd's Rep. 293, QBD (Comm). 4–59, 4–70
O'Connor v Mohammend Din (1993) C.A.T. 150. 32–121
Official Receiver v Cooper [1999] B.C.C. 115, Ch D. 31–15
Ogur BC v Knight [1994] T.L.R. 22, CA. 42–04
Oliver v Davis [1949] 2 K.B. 727; [1949] 2 All E.R. 353; [1949] L.J.R. 1661; 93 S.J. 562, CA. 3–02
Olympia Sauna Shipping Co SA v Shinwa Kaiun Kaisha Ltd (The Ypatia Halloussi) [1985] 2 Lloyd's Rep. 364, QBD (Comm). 4–26
O'Reilly v Mackman; Millbanks v Secretary of State for the Home Department; Derbyshire v Mackman; Dougan v Mackman; Millbanks v Home Office [1983] 2 A.C. 237; [1982] 3 W.L.R. 1096; [1982] 3 All E.R. 1124; 126 S.J. 820, HL; affirming [1982] 3 W.L.R. 604; [1982] 3 All E.R. 680; (1982) 79 L.S.G. 1176; 126 S.J. 578, CA (Civ Div); reversing, 126 S.J. 312; *The Times*, March 16, 1982, QBD. 1–02
Orion Insurance Co Plc v Sphere Drake Insurance Plc [1992] 1 Lloyd's Rep. 239, CA (Civ Div); affirming [1990] 1 Lloyd's Rep. 465; *Independent*, February 1, 1990, QBD (Comm). 3–68
Ormes v Beadel (1860) 2 Giff. 166. 4–58
Orton v Orton (1959) 109 L.J. 50. 32–16
O'Sullivan v Williams [1992] 3 All E.R. 385; [1992] R.T.R. 402; (1992) 142 N.L.J. 717; *The Times*, March 13, 1992; *Independent*, March 20, 1992, CA (Civ Div). 6–54
OT Africa Line Ltd v Vickers Plc [1996] 1 Lloyd's Rep. 700; [1996] C.L.C. 722, QBD (Comm). 3–22, 4–27
Overton v Bannister (1844) 3 Ha. 504. 4–02
Owners of Cargo of the Kronprinz v Owners of the Kronprinz (The Kronprinz and The Ardandhu) (1887) L.R. 12 App. Cas. 256, HL; affirming (1886) L.R. 11 P.D. 40, CA. 9–36, 9–38, 9–40
Oxford University (t/a Oxford University Press) v John Stedman Design Group (1991) 7 Const. L.J. 102, QBD (OR). 39–51

P v P (Ancillary Relief: Proceeds of Crime); sub nom. P v P (Divorce: Ancillary Relief) [2003] EWHC 2260; [2004] Fam. 1; [2003] 3 W.L.R. 1350; [2003] 4 All E.R. 843; [2004] 1 F.L.R. 193; [2003] 3 F.C.R. 459; [2003] W.T.L.R. 1449; [2004] Fam. Law 9; (2003) 100(41) L.S.G. 33; (2003) 153 N.L.J. 1550; (2003) 147 S.J.L.B. 1206; *The Times*, October 14, 2003, Fam Div. 35–64

P v P (Divorce: Financial Provision: Clean Break) [2002] EWCA Civ 1886; [2003] 1 F.L.R. 942; [2003] 1 F.C.R. 97; [2003] Fam. Law 314, CA (Civ Div); reversing [2002] EWHC 887; [2002] 2 F.L.R. 1075; [2002] 3 F.C.R. 513; [2002] Fam. Law 656, Fam Div............. 34–06
P v P (Financial Relief: Illiquid Assets); sub nom. LJP v GRGP [2004] EWHC 2277; [2005] 1 F.L.R. 548, Fam Div..................... 34–03
P&O Developments Ltd v Guy's & St Thomas NHS Trust; Guy's & St Thomas NHS Trust v P&O Developments Ltd [1999] B.L.R. 3; 62 Con. L.R. 38; (1999) 15 Const. L.J. 374, QBD (TCC)...... 39–48, 39–54, 39–55, 39–58
P&O Property Holdings Ltd v Norwich Union Life Insurance Society; sub nom. Norwich Union Life Insurance Society v P&O Property Holdings Ltd (1994) 68 P. & C.R. 261, HL; affirming [1993] 1 E.G.L.R. 164; [1993] 13 E.G. 108; [1993] E.G.C.S. 69; [1993] N.P.C. 1, CA (Civ Div)... 4–75
Pace (Formerly Doe) v Doe [1977] Fam. 18; [1976] 3 W.L.R. 865; [1977] 1 All E.R. 176; 120 S.J. 818, Fam Div............................ 32–16
Pacific Associates v Baxter [1990] 1 Q.B. 993; [1989] 3 W.L.R. 1150; [1989] 2 All E.R. 159; 44 B.L.R. 33; 16 Con. L.R. 90; (1989) 139 N.L.J. 41; (1989) 133 S.J. 123; *The Times*, December 28, 1988; *Independent*, January 6, 1989, CA (Civ Div); affirming, 13 Con. L.R. 80, OR.. 39–15
Paddock v Forrester (1842) 3 Man. & G. 903.................. 26–04, 27–07
Page v Page (1972) C.A.T. 383.............................. 6–20, 32–06
Page v Plymouth Hospitals NHS Trust [2004] EWHC 1154; [2004] 3 All E.R. 367; [2004] P.I.Q.R. Q6; [2004] Lloyd's Rep. Med. 337; (2004) 101(26) L.S.G. 27; (2004) 154 N.L.J. 853, QBD................. 35–34
Pagnan SpA v Tradax Ocean Transportation SA; sub nom. Tradax Ocean Transportation SA v Pagnan [1987] 3 All E.R. 565; [1987] 2 Lloyd's Rep. 342, CA (Civ Div); affirming [1987] 1 All E.R. 81; [1986] 2 Lloyd's Rep. ; *Financial Times*, July 8, 1986, QBD (Comm)........ 32–37
Palmer v Townsend (1979) 123 S.J. 570, CA (Civ Div)................. 11–33
Panayiotou v Sony Music Entertainment (UK) Ltd (1994) [1994] E.C.C. 395; [1994] E.M.L.R. 229; (1994) 13 Tr. L.R. 532; *The Times*, June 30, 1994; *Independent*, June 24, 1994; *Guardian*, July 2, 1994, Ch D... 2–17
Pardy v Pardy [1939] P. 288, CA....................................... 32–13
Parkman Consulting Engineers v Cumbrian Industrials Ltd; sub nom. BICC Ltd v Parkman Consulting Engineers; Cumbrian Industrials Ltd v Parkman Consulting Engineers; BICC Ltd v Cumbrian Industrial Ltd [2001] EWCA Civ 1621; [2002] B.L.R. 64; [2002] T.C.L.R. 28; 79 Con. L.R. 112; [2002] Lloyd's Rep. P.N. 526, CA (Civ Div); affirming, 78 Con. L.R. 18, QBD (TCC)......................... 39–31
Parr v Wyre BC; sub nom. R. v Wyre BC Ex p. Parr (1981) 2 H.L.R. 71; *The Times*, February 4, 1982, CA (Civ Div)...................... 40–25
Patten v Burke Publishing Co Ltd [1991] 1 W.L.R. 541; [1991] 2 All E.R. 821; [1991] F.S.R. 483, Ch D..................... 10–02, 31–33, 38–03
Peacock v Harper (1877–78) L.R. 7 Ch. D. 648, Ch D.................. 27–06
Peacock v Peacock (1991) [1991] 1 F.L.R. 324; [1991] F.C.R. 121; [1991] Fam. Law 324.. 32–45, 32–48
Penrice v Williams (1883) L.R. 23 Ch. D. 353, Ch D.................... 5–45
Penrose v Penrose [1994] 2 F.L.R. 621; [1994] 2 F.C.R. 1167; [1994] Fam. Law 618, CA (Civ Div)... 32–104

TABLE OF CASES

Pereira v Inspirations East Ltd. (1992) C.A.T. 1048..... 3–34, 3–35, 3–44, 3–45, 3–47
Perkins, Re; sub nom. Poyser v Beyfus [1898] 2 Ch. 182, CA............. 5–33
Perry v Day [2004] EWHC 1398, Ch D................................ 6–17
Petrotrade Inc v Texaco Ltd [2002] 1 W.L.R. 947 (Note); [2001] 4 All E.R. 853; [2001] C.P. Rep. 29; [2000] C.L.C. 1341; [2002] 1 Costs L.R. 60; *The Times*, June 14, 2000; *Independent*, July 10, 2000 (C.S), CA (Civ Div); affirming, 1998 Folio 1348, QBD (Comm)....... 23–16, 23–11, 23–12, 23–15, 23–24, 23–25
Pettitt v Pettitt; sub nom. P v P [1970] A.C. 777; [1969] 2 W.L.R. 966; [1969] 2 All E.R. 385; (1969) 20 P. & C.R. 991; 113 S.J. 344, HL; reversing [1968] 1 W.L.R. 443; [1968] 1 All E.R. 1053; (1968) 19 P. & C.R. 245; 112 S.J. 111, CA (Civ Div)......................... 32–04
Philex Plc v Golban, *The Times*, July 9, 1993, Ch D.................... 28–08
Pick v Pick (1981) 11 Fam. Law 187.................................... 34–15
Piglowska v Piglowski [1999] 1 W.L.R. 1360; [1999] 3 All E.R. 632; [1999] 2 F.L.R. 763; [1999] 2 F.C.R. 481; [1999] Fam. Law 617; (1999) 96(27) L.S.G. 34; (1999) 143 S.J.L.B. 190; *The Times*, June 25, 1999, HL; reversing, CA (Civ Div).......................... 34–02
Pitts v Adney [1961] N.S.W.R. 535..................................... 27–21
Plaschkes v Jones and Jones (1982) C.A.T. 438.................. 37–35, 37–42
Platform Home Loans Ltd v Oyston Shipways Ltd [2000] 2 A.C. 190; [1999] 2 W.L.R. 518; [1999] 1 All E.R. 833; [1999] C.L.C. 867; (1999) 1 T.C.L.R. 18; [1999] P.N.L.R. 469; [1999] 1 E.G.L.R. 77; [1999] 13 E.G. 119; [1999] E.G.C.S. 26; (1999) 96(10) L.S.G. 31; (1999) 149 N.L.J. 283; (1999) 143 S.J.L.B. 65; [1999] N.P.C. 21; *The Times*, February 19, 1999; *Independent*, March 5, 1999, HL; reversing [1998] Ch. 466; [1998] 3 W.L.R. 94; [1998] 4 All E.R. 252; [1998] P.N.L.R. 512; [1998] 1 E.G.L.R. 108; [1998] 13 E.G. 148; [1997] E.G.C.S. 184; (1998) 95(1) L.S.G. 26; (1998) 142 S.J.L.B. 46; [1997] N.P.C. 185; *The Times*, January 15, 1998, CA (Civ Div); reversing in part [1996] 2 E.G.L.R. 110; [1996] 49 E.G. 112; [1996] E.G.C.S. 146, Ch D................................ 31–01
Plumley v Horrell (1869) 20 L.T. 473........................... 3–60, 6–01
Poteliakhoff v Teakle [1938] 2 K.B. 816, CA..................... 3–11, 4–74
Potter v Potter [1990] 2 F.L.R. 27; [1990] F.C.R. 704; [1990] Fam. Law 59, CA (Civ Div)... 32–62
Potts v Potts (1976) 6 Fam. Law 217, CA (Civ Div).............. 5–45, 32–83
Pounds v Pounds [1994] 1 W.L.R. 1535; [1994] 4 All E.R. 777; [1994] 1 F.L.R. 775; [1994] Fam. Law 436; (1994) 144 N.L.J. 459; *The Times*, March 17, 1994; *Independent*, March 3, 1994, CA (Civ Div)................................... 32–43, 32–60, 32–72, 32–78
Povey v Povey [1972] Fam. 40; [1971] 2 W.L.R. 381; [1970] 3 All E.R. 612; 115 S.J. 95, PDAD.. 34–04
Powell v Brodhurst [1901] 2 Ch. 160, Ch D.......................... 6–53
Powell v Marshall Parkes & Co [1899] 1 Q.B. 710, CA................. 8–13
Powell v Powell [1900] 1 Ch. 243, Ch D............................. 4–67
Powell v Smith (1872) L.R. 14 Eq. 85................................ 4–66
Practice Direction (Ch D: Minutes of Order) [1960] 1 W.L.R. 1168; [1960] 3 All E.R. 416; [1960] 1 Lloyd's Rep. 720; 104 S.J. 866, Ch D..... 10–02
Practice Direction (Ch D: Compromise of Probate Actions) [1972] 1 W.L.R. 1215; [1972] 3 All E.R. 319; [1972] 2 Lloyd's Rep. 90, Ch D.. 33–13

Practice Direction (Ch D: Grants of Representation: Endorsement of Orders) [1979] 1 W.L.R. 1; [1978] 3 All E.R. 1032; [1979] 1 Lloyd's Rep. 122; 122 S.J. 780, Ch D............................... 33–17
Practice Direction (Crown Office List: Uncontested Proceedings) [1982] 1 W.L.R. 979, QBD... 40–17
Practice Direction (Crown Office List: Consent Orders) [1997] 1 W.L.R. 825; [1997] 2 Cr. App. R. 338; *The Times*, May 14, 1997, QBD.... 40–17
Practice Direction (CA: Consolidation: Notice of Consolidation) [1999] 1 W.L.R. 1027; [1999] 2 All E.R. 490; *The Times*, April 26, 1999, CA (Civ Div).. 42–08
Practice Direction (Fam Div: Ancillary Relief: Costs Estimates) [1988] 1 W.L.R. 561; [1988] 2 All E.R. 63; [1988] 1 F.L.R. 452, Fam Div... 34–08
Practice Direction (Fam Div: Consent Summonses and Notices of Application) [1976] 1 W.L.R. 74; [1976] 1 All E.R. 272, Fam Div....... 32–55
Practice Direction (Fam Div: Matrimonial Causes Rules 1977: Rule 76A: Consent Orders); sub nom. Practice Direction (Fam Div: Financial Provision: Consent Order) [1986] 1 W.L.R. 381; [1986] 1 All E.R. 704; [1986] 1 F.L.R. 337, Fam Div............................ 32–55
Practice Direction (Fam Div: Financial Provisions: Agreed Terms) [1972] 1 W.L.R. 1313, Fam Div....................................... 32–129
Practice Direction (Fam Div: Financial Statement) [1984] 1 W.L.R. 674, Fam Div... 32–57
Practice Direction (Fam Div: Matrimonial Causes Rules 1977: Rule 76A: Consent Orders); sub nom. Practice Direction (Fam Div: Divorce: Consent Orders: Minute of Order) [1990] 1 W.L.R. 150; [1990] 1 All E.R. 382, Fam Div.. 32–55
Practice Direction (Fam Div: Procedure: Divorce Registry: Consent Applications: Attendance) [1974] 1 W.L.R. 937; [1974] 2 All E.R. 1120, Fam Div... 32–55
Practice Direction (QBD: Admin Ct: Establishment); sub nom. Practice Direction (QBD: Admin Ct: Review of Crown Office List) [2000] 1 W.L.R. 1654; [2000] 4 All E.R. 1071; [2000] 2 Lloyd's Rep. 445; [2000] 2 Cr. App. R. 455; [2000] C.O.D. 290; *The Times*, July 27, 2000, QBD.. 40–01
Practice Direction (QBD: Trial: Setting Down Action: London) [1981] 1 W.L.R. 1296; [1981] 3 All E.R. 61, QBD....................... 40–01
Prenn v Simmonds [1971] 1 W.L.R. 1381; [1971] 3 All E.R. 237; 115 S.J. 654, HL... 5–03, 6–04
Prestwich v Poley (1865) 18 C.B..................................... 29–25
Proetta v Times Newspapers [1991] 1 W.L.R. 337; [1991] 4 All E.R. 46, CA (Civ Div)... 15–14
Prudential Assurance Co Ltd v Fountain Page Ltd [1991] 1 W.L.R. 756; [1991] 3 All E.R. 878,QBD...................................... 27–51
Prudential Assurance Co Ltd v McBains Cooper [2000] 1 W.L.R. 2000; [2001] 3 All E.R. 1014; [2001] C.P. Rep. 19; [2000] C.P.L.R. 475; (2000) 97(24) L.S.G. 40; (2000) 150 N.L.J. 832; *The Times*, June 2, 2000, CA (Civ Div)................................ 1–03, 6–01, 10–02
Prudential Assurance Co Ltd v Prudential Insurance Co of America; sub nom. Prudential Insurance Co of America v Prudential Assurance Co Ltd [2003] EWCA Civ 1154; [2004] E.T.M.R. 29, CA (Civ Div); affirming [2002] EWHC 2809; *The Times*, January 2, 2003, Ch D.. 27–04
Pubmaster Ltd v Gibb [2002] EWHC 2236, Ch D...................... 11–21

lxxiii

TABLE OF CASES

Purcell v FC Trigell Ltd (t/a Southern Window & General Cleaning Co) [1971] 1 Q.B. 358; [1970] 3 W.L.R. 884; [1970] 3 All E.R. 671; 114 S.J. 668, CA (Civ Div).............................. 6–22, 6–23, 32–118
Pym v Campbell (1856) 6 E. & B. 370................................. 3–61

Q v Q (Costs: Summary Assessment); sub nom. Q v Q (Family Proceedings: Costs Order) [2002] 2 F.L.R. 668; [2002] Fam. Law 804; (2002) 99(32) L.S.G. 33; The Times, July 16, 2002, Fam Div............. 34–17
QBE Insurance (UK) Ltd v Mediterranean Insurance and Reinsurance Co Ltd [1992] 1 W.L.R. 573; [1992] 1 All E.R. 12; [1992] 1 Lloyd's Rep. 435, QBD (Comm)... 21–09
Quorum A/S v Schramm (Costs) [2002] 2 All E.R. (Comm) 179; [2002] 2 Lloyd's Rep. 72; [2002] C.L.C. 77; [2002] Lloyd's Rep. I.R. 315; (2003) 19 Const. L.J. 224, QBD (Comm)................. 23–10, 54–04

R, Re [1995] 1 F.L.R. 123... 32–138
R v R [1997] 2 F.L.R. 95.. 34–17
R (A Minor) (Consent Order: Appeal), Re [1995] 1 W.L.R. 184; [1995] 2 F.L.R. 123; [1994] 2 F.C.R. 1251; [1995] Fam. Law 123; The Times, July 18, 1994, CA (Civ Div)....................................... 32–138
R. (A, B, X and Y) v East Sussex CC (2005) 8 C.C.l.P. 228.............. 40–05
R. v Aylesbury Vale DC Ex p. Chaplin (1998) 76 P. & C.R. 207; [1997] 3 P.L.R. 55; [1998] J.P.L. 49; The Times, August 19, 1997; Independent, October 6, 1997 (C.S.), CA (Civ Div); affirming [1996] E.G.C.S. 126; The Times, July 23, 1996, QBD........................ 40–10
R. v Bassetlaw DC Ex p. Aldergate Estates Ltd (Costs), CO/4387/99, QBD.. 40–22
R. v Bassetlaw DC Ex p. Oxby [1998] P.L.C.R. 283; [1997] N.P.C. 178; The Times, December 18, 1997; Independent, December 16, 1997, CA (Civ Div); reversing [1997] J.P.L. 576, QBD................... 40–18
R. v Bloomsbury and Marylebone County Court Ex p. Blackburne (1985) 275 E.G. 1273, CA (Civ Div); affirming (1984) 14 H.L.R. 56; The Times, March 21, 1984, QBD...................... 10–02, 37–34, 37–44
R. v Central Criminal Court Ex p. Propend Finance Property Ltd; sub nom. R. v Secretary of State for the Home Department Ex p. Propend Finance Pty Ltd [1996] 2 Cr. App. R. 26; [1994] C.O.D. 386; The Times, April 5, 1994; Independent, March 29, 1994, QBD......... 40–22
R. v Commissioner for Local Administration Ex p. H (A Minor) [1999] E.L.R. 314, CA (Civ Div); affirming (1999) 1 L.G.L.R. 932; [1999] C.O.D. 382; (1999) 96(5) L.S.G. 37; (1999) 143 S.J.L.B. 39; The Times, January 8, 1999; Independent, January 11, 1999 (C.S.), QBD.. 40–13
R. v Entry Clearance Officer Ex p. Makkari, unreported, February 18, 1999... 40–25
R. v Hackney LBC Ex p. Rowe [1996] C.O.D. 155, DC................. 40–22
R. v Holderness BC Ex p. James Robert Developments Ltd (1993) 5 Admin. L.R. 470; (1993) 66 P. & C.R. 46; [1993] 1 P.L.R. 108; [1993] J.P.L. 659; (1993) 157 L.G. Rev. 643; [1992] N.P.C. 156; The Times, December 22, 1992; Independent, December 21, 1992 (C.S.), CA (Civ Div); affirming (1992) 64 P. & C.R. 100; [1991] E.G.C.S. 128; [1991] N.P.C. 128, QBD....................................... 40–22
R. v Immigration Appeal Tribunal Ex p. Probakaran [1996] Imm. A.R. 603, QBD.. 40–03

R. v Independent Appeals Tribunal of the Local Education Authority of Hillingdon LBC Ex p. Governors of Mellow Lane School [2001] E.L.R. 200, QBD... 40–18

R. v Independent Television Commission Ex p. Church of Scientology [1996] C.O.D. 443, QBD....................................... 40–22

R. v IRC Ex p. Opman International UK [1986] 1 W.L.R. 568; [1986] 1 All E.R. 328; [1986] S.T.C. 18; 59 T.C. 352; (1986) 130 S.J. 373, QBD... 40–21

R. v IRC Ex p. Woolwich Equitable Building Society 18572

R. v Inner London Education Authority Ex p. Ali (1990) 2 Admin. L.R. 822; [1990] C.O.D. 317; (1990) 154 L.G. Rev. 852; *The Times*, February 21, 1990; *Independent*, February 15, 1990; *Guardian*, March 6, 1990; *Daily Telegraph*, February 22, 1990, QBD......... 40–12

R. v Judge Willes Ex p. Abbey National Building Society [1954] 1 W.L.R. 136; 98 S.J. 44, QBD; reversing (1953) 103 L.J. 416.............. 10–07

R. v Kensington and Chelsea RLBC Ex p. Ghebregiogis (1995) 27 H.L.R. 602; [1994] C.O.D. 502, QBD................................. 40–22

R. v Lambeth LBC Ex p. A1 and A2(1997) 30 H.L.R. 933............... 40–25

R. v Liverpool City Council Ex p. Muldoon; R. v Liverpool City Council Ex p. Kelly; R. v Rent Officer Service Ex p. Kelly; sub nom. R. v Rent Officer Service Ex p. Muldoon [1996] 1 W.L.R. 1103; [1996] 3 All E.R. 498; (1997) 29 H.L.R. 163; (1996) 8 Admin. L.R. 552; [1996] C.O.D. 495; (1996) 160 J.P. Rep. 875; (1996) 93(33) L.S.G. 25; (1996) 146 N.L.J. 1057; (1996) 140 S.J.L.B. 184; *The Times*, July 11, 1996, HL; affirming (1996) 28 H.L.R. 208; 94 L.G.R. 1; (1995) 7 Admin. L.R. 663; [1995] C.O.D. 329; *The Times*, April 18, 1995; *Independent*, May 8, 1995 (C.S.), CA (Civ Div); affirming [1994] C.O.D. 388, QBD.. 40–18

R. v Liverpool City Council Ex p. Newman (1993) 5 Admin. L.R. 669; [1993] C.O.D. 65; *The Times*, November 3, 1992, QBD........... 40–21

R. v Newcastle under Lyme Justices Ex p. Massey; R. v Newcastle under Lyme Justices Ex p. Mudryj; R. v Newcastle under Lyme Justices Ex p. Coxon; R. v Stoke on Trent Magistrates Court Ex p. Knight; R. v Stoke on Trent Magistrates Court Ex p. Tudor [1994] 1 W.L.R. 1684; [1995] 1 All E.R. 120; (1994) 158 J.P. 1037; (1994) 158 J.P.N. 786; (1994) 144 N.L.J. 1444; *The Times*, October 13, 1994; *Independent*, October 7, 1994, DC............................. 40–23

R. v Newcastle upon Tyne CC Ex p. Thompson (1988) 20 H.L.R. 430; [1988] 26 E.G. 112; *The Times*, March 18, 1988; *Independent*, March 22, 1988, QBD........................... 37–34, 37–36, 37–41

R. v North and East Devon HA Ex p. Coughlan [2001] Q.B. 213; [2000] 2 W.L.R. 622; [2000] 3 All E.R. 850; (2000) 2 L.G.L.R. 1; [1999] B.L.G.R. 703; (1999) 2 C.C.L. Rep. 285; [1999] Lloyd's Rep. Med. 306; (2000) 51 B.M.L.R. 1; [1999] C.O.D. 340; (1999) 96(31) L.S.G. 39; (1999) 143 S.J.L.B. 213; *The Times*, July 20, 1999; *Independent*, July 20, 1999, CA (Civ Div); affirming (1999) 2 C.C.L. Rep. 27; (1999) 47 B.M.L.R. 27; [1999] C.O.D. 174; *The Times*, December 29, 1998, QBD.. 40–12

R. v Panayiotou (Andreas); R. v Antoniades (Agis) [1973] 1 W.L.R. 1032; [1973] 3 All E.R. 112; (1973) 57 Cr. App. R. 762; [1973] Crim. L.R. 445; 117 S.J. 464, CA (Crim Div)................................. 4–77

R. v Parliamentary Commissioner for Administration Ex p. Balchin (No.1) [1998] 1 P.L.R. 1; [1997] J.P.L. 917; [1997] C.O.D. 146; [1996] E.G.C.S. 166; [1996] N.P.C. 147, QBD........................... 40–10

R. v Secretary of State for the Home Department Ex p. Alabi [1997] I.N.L.R. 124; [1998] C.O.D. 103, CA (Civ Div).................. 40–25
R. v Secretary of State for the Home Department Ex p. Gashi (Shefki); R. v Secretary of State for the Home Department Ex p. Gjoka, unreported, June 15, 2000, QBD................................... 40–14
R. v Secretary of State for the Home Department Ex p. Salem [1999] 1 A.C. 450; [1999] 2 W.L.R. 483; [1999] 2 All E.R. 42; (1999) 11 Admin. L.R. 194; [1999] C.O.D. 486; (1999) 96(9) L.S.G. 32; (1999) 143 S.J.L.B. 59; *The Times*, February 12, 1999, HL; affirming [1999] Q.B. 805; [1999] 2 W.L.R. 1; [1998] C.O.D. 406; *The Times*, March 18, 1998, CA (Civ Div).. 40–26
R. v Special Adjudicator Ex p. Gnanavarathan; sub nom. Gnanavarathan v Special Adjudicator; R. v Secretary of State for the Home Department Ex p. Gnanavarathan; R. v Special Adjudicator Ex p. Norbert [1995] Imm. A.R. 64; *Independent*, October 3, 1994 (C.S.), CA (Civ Div)... 40–03
R. v Wandsworth County Court, Ex p. Wandsworth LBC [1975] 1 W.L.R. 1314; [1975] 3 All E.R. 390; 74 L.G.R. 62; 119 S.J. 529, DC....... 6–33
R. v Worthing BC Ex p. Bruce; sub nom. Bruce v Worthing BC (1994) 26 H.L.R. 223; [1994] 24 E.G. 149; [1993] E.G.C.S. 173; *Independent*, November 8, 1993 (C.S.), CA (Civ Div); affirming (1992) 24 H.L.R. 261; [1992] C.O.D. 42, QBD...................... 10–02, 37–32, 37–34
R. (on the application of Bowhay) v North and East Durham Health Authority [2001] A.C.D. 159.................................... 40–22
R. (on the application of Boxall) v Waltham Forest LBC (2001) 4 C.C.L. Rep. 258, QBD (Admin)... 40–22
R. (on the application of Cowl) v Plymouth City Council; sub nom. Cowl v Plymouth City Council; Cowl (Practice Note), Re [2001] EWCA Civ 1935; [2002] 1 W.L.R. 803; [2002] C.P. Rep. 18; (2002) 5 C.C.L. Rep. 42; [2002] A.C.D. 11; [2002] Fam. Law 265; (2002) 99(8) L.S.G. 35; (2002) 146 S.J.L.B. ; *The Times*, January 8, 2002, CA (Civ Div); affirming [2001] EWHC Admin 734; (2001) 4 C.C.L. Rep. 475, QBD (Admin)............................ 40–05, 40–06, 43–06
R. (on the application of Davies) v HM Deputy Coroner for Birmingham (Costs); sub nom. R. (on the application of Davies) v Birmingham Deputy Coroner (Costs) [2004] EWCA Civ 207; [2004] 1 W.L.R. 2739; [2004] 3 All E.R. 543; [2004] 4 Costs L.R. 545; (2004) 80 B.M.L.R. 48; (2004) 148 S.J.L.B. 297; *The Times*, March 10, 2004; *Independent*, March 18, 2004, CA (Civ Div)..................... 40–23
R. (on the application of Garland) v Secretary of State for the Environment, Transport and the Regions (2001) 3 L.G.L.R. 26, QBD (Admin).... 40–13
R. (on the application of Hopley) v Liverpool HA [2002] EWHC 1723; [2003] P.I.Q.R. P10; [2002] Lloyd's Rep. Med. 494, QBD (Admin).. 35–31
R. (on the application of L) v Barking and Dagenham LBC; sub nom. R. v L; R. v Barking and Dagenham LBC Ex p. L [2001] EWCA Civ 533; [2001] 2 F.L.R. 763; [2002] 1 F.C.R. 136; [2001] B.L.G.R. 421; (2001) 4 C.C.L. Rep. 196; [2001] Fam. Law 662; *The Times*, June 11, 2001, CA (Civ Div); affirming [2001] B.L.G.R. 86; (2001) 4 C.C.L. Rep. 5, QBD.. 40–12
R. (on the application of Meredith) v Merthyr Tydfil CBC [2002] EWHC 634, QBD (Admin).. 40–18
R. (on the application of Nurse Prescribers Ltd) v Secretary of State for Health [2004] EWHC 403, QBD (Admin)......................... 40–05

R. (on the application of Towry Law Financial Services Ltd) v Financial
 Ombudsman Services [2004] EWCA Civ 1701, CA (Civ Div). 40–10,
 40–23
R. (on the application of Tshikangu) v Newham LBC; sub nom. Tshikangu
 v Newham LBC [2001] EWHC Admin 92; [2001] N.P.C. 33; *The
 Times*, April 27, 2001, QBD (Admin). 40–26
R. (on the application of Umo) v Commissioner for Local Adminstration in
 England [2003] EWHC 3202; [2004] E.L.R. 265, QBD (Admin). . . . 40–13
R. (on the application of Veja) v Secretary of State for the Home
 Department [2004] EWHC 1188, QBD (Admin). 40–22
R. (on the application of Wirral HA) v Mental Health Review Tribunal; R.
 (on the application of Wirral HA) v Finnegan [2001] EWCA Civ
 1901; (2002) 99(2) L.S.G. 27; (2001) 145 S.J.L.B. 270; *The Times*,
 November 26, 2001, CA (Civ Div); affirming [2001] EWHC Admin
 312, QBD (Admin). 40–18
RWJ Sutherland & Co v Hannevig Bros Ltd [1921] 1 K.B. 336; (1920) 5
 Ll. L. Rep. 154, KBD. 41–05
Rabin v Mendoza & Co [1954] 1 W.L.R. 271; [1954] 1 All E.R. 247; 98
 S.J. 92, CA. 27–07, 27–51
Rajbenback v Mamon; sub nom. Rajenback v Mamon [1955] 1 Q.B. 283;
 [1955] 2 W.L.R. 21; [1955] 1 All E.R. 12; 99 S.J. 29, QBD. 37–33
Ranasingham v Cooray (1978) C.A.T. 302. 6–84
Rawlings v Coal Consumers Association (1874)30 L.T. 469. 4–77
Read v Edmed [2004] EWHC 3274; *The Times*, December 13, 2004,
 QBD. 23–11, 23–31
Reardon Smith Line Ltd v Hansen-Tangen (The Diana Prosperity);
 Hansen-Tangen v Sanko Steamship Co Ltd [1976] 1 W.L.R. 989;
 [1976] 3 All E.R. 570; [1976] 2 Lloyd's Rep. 621; 120 S.J. 719, HL;
 affirming [1976] 2 Lloyd's Rep. 60; 120 S.J. 329, CA (Civ Div). 3–25,
 5–03, 5–10, 6–04
Rediffusion Simulation Ltd v Link Miles Ltd (Admissibility) [1992] F.S.R.
 195, Ch D. 27–58
Redmond v Redmond [1986] 2 F.L.R. 173; [1986] Fam. Law 260. 32–128
Reed Executive Plc v Reed Business Information Ltd (Costs: Alternative
 Dispute Resolution) [2004] EWCA Civ 887; [2004] 1 W.L.R. 3026;
 [2004] 4 All E.R. 942; [2004] 4 Costs L.R. 662; [2005] F.S.R. 3;
 (2004) 27(7) I.P.D. 27067; (2004) 148 S.J.L.B. 881; *The Times*, July
 16, 2004, CA (Civ Div). 41–15, 43–11
Rees v Sinclair [1955–95] P.N.L.R. 56; [1974] 1 N.Z.L.R. 180, CA (NZ). . 29–22
Rees v West Glamorgan CC [1994] P.I.Q.R. P37; (1993) 143 N.L.J. 814,
 CA (Civ Div). 5–13, 35–55
Reid Minty (A Firm) v Taylor [2001] EWCA Civ 1723; [2002] 1 W.L.R.
 2800; [2002] 2 All E.R. 150; [2002] C.P. Rep. 12; [2002] C.P.L.R. 1;
 [2002] 1 Costs L.R. 180; [2002] E.M.L.R. 19, CA (Civ Div). 13–10
Richardson v Peto (1840) 1 Man. & G. 896. 29–13
Richardson v Richardson (No.1) [1994] 1 W.L.R. 186; [1994] 1 W.L.R.
 187; [1993] 4 All E.R. 673; [1994] 1 F.L.R. 286; [1994] 1 F.C.R. 53;
 [1994] Fam. Law 188, Fam Div. 32–62, 32–94

Ridehalgh v Horsefield; Allen v Unigate Dairies Ltd; Antonelli v Wade Gery Farr (A Firm); Philex Plc v Golban; Roberts v Coverite (Asphalters) Ltd; Watson v Watson (Wasted Costs Orders) [1994] Ch. 205; [1994] 3 W.L.R. 462; [1994] 3 All E.R. 848; [1994] B.C.C. 390; [1994] 2 F.L.R. 194; [1955–95] P.N.L.R. 636; [1994] Fam. Law 560; [1994] E.G.C.S. 15; (1994) 144 N.L.J. 231; [1994] N.P.C. 7; *The Times*, January 28, 1994; *Independent*, February 4, 1994, CA (Civ Div)... 28–08, 32–78

Ridsdel, Re; sub nom. Ridsdel v Rawlinson [1947] Ch. 597; [1947] 2 All E.R. 312; [1947] L.J.R. 1486; 91 S.J. 483, Ch D.................. 31–18

Riverlate Properties Ltd v Paul [1975] Ch. 133; [1974] 3 W.L.R. 564; [1974] 2 All E.R. 656; (1974) 28 P. & C.R. 220; 118 S.J. 644, CA (Civ Div); affirming (1973) 227 E.G. 333....................... 4–31

Roache v News Group Newspapers Ltd [1998] E.M.L.R. 161; *The Times*, November 23, 1992; *Independent*, December 31, 1992, CA (Civ Div)... 23–01, 23–04, 26–06

Roberts, Re; sub nom. Roberts v Roberts [1905] 1 Ch. 704, CA..... 4–15, 4–49, 12–02

Robinson v Robinson (Practice Note); sub nom. Practice Note (Fam Div: Final Orders) [1982] 1 W.L.R. 786; [1982] 2 All E.R. 699; (1983) 4 F.L.R. 102; (1982) 12 Fam. Law 175; 126 S.J. 360, CA (Civ Div).. 32–37, 32–89, 32–116, 32–122

Robson v Drummond (1831) 2 B. & Ad. 303......................... 6–86

Roche v Roche (1981) 11 Fam. Law 243, CA (Civ Div)................ 32–25

Roebuck v Mungovin [1994] 2 A.C. 224; [1994] 2 W.L.R. 290; [1994] 1 All E.R. 568; [1994] 1 Lloyd's Rep. 481; [1994] P.I.Q.R. P209; (1994) 91(13) L.S.G. 36; (1994) 144 N.L.J. 197; (1994) 138 S.J.L.B. 59; [1994] J.P.I.L. 164; *The Times*, February 4, 1994; *Independent*, February 8, 1994, HL; reversing [1993] P.I.Q.R. P444; *Independent*, April 26, 1993 (C.S.), CA (Civ Div)............................ 27–53

Rofa Sport Management AG v DHL International (UK) Ltd [1989] 1 W.L.R. 902; [1989] 2 All E.R. 743; (1989) 133 S.J. 1202, CA (Civ Div)... 9–28

Rogers and Parry (in liquidation) v Thornham Construction Co., High Court, Official Referee's Business Liverpool District Registry Case No. 91R5647, O/R No. 112/9 1, unreported, May 21, 1992........ 27–54

Rooker v Rooker [1988] 1 F.L.R. 219; [1988] Fam. Law 55, CA (Civ Div)... 32–106

Ropac Ltd v Inntrepreneur Pub Co (CPC) Ltd [2001] C.P. Rep. 31; [2001] L. & T.R. 10; (2000) 97(26) L.S.G. 36; *The Times*, June 21, 2000, Ch D... 6–24, 37–55

Rose v Rose [2002] EWCA Civ 208; [2002] 1 F.L.R. 978; [2002] 1 F.C.R. 639; [2002] Fam. Law 344; (2002) 99(11) L.S.G. 36; (2002) 146 S.J.L.B. 66; *The Times*, March 12, 2002, CA (Civ Div)............. 32–44

Rossiter v Langley [1925] 1 K.B. 741, KBD........................... 37–46

Roth, Re ((1896) 74 L.T. 50... 31–19

Rowe v Rowe [1980] Fam. 47; [1979] 3 W.L.R. 101; [1979] 2 All E.R. 1123; (1979) 10 Fam. Law 57; 123 S.J. 352, CA (Civ Div)......... 32–20

TABLE OF CASES

Roy v Kensington and Chelsea and Westminster Family Practitioner Committee [1992] 1 A.C. 624; [1992] 2 W.L.R. 239; [1992] 1 All E.R. 705; [1992] I.R.L.R. 233; (1992) 4 Admin. L.R. 649; [1992] 3 Med. L.R. 177; (1992) 142 N.L.J. 240; (1992) 136 S.J.L.B. 63; *The Times*, February 10, 1992; *Independent*, February 11, 1992, HL; affirming (1990) 2 Admin. L.R. 669; *The Times*, March 27, 1990, CA (Civ Div); reversing (1990) 2 Admin. L.R. 29; *The Times*, March 7, 1989, QBD. 1–02
Royal Bank of Scotland Plc v Etridge (No.2); Barclays Bank Plc v Coleman; Barclays Bank Plc v Harris; Midland Bank Plc v Wallace; National Westminster Bank Plc v Gill; UCB Home Loans Corp Ltd v Moore; Bank of Scotland v Bennett; Kenyon-Brown v Desmond Banks & Co (Undue Influence) (No.2) [2001] UKHL 44; [2002] 2 A.C. 773; [2001] 3 W.L.R. 1021; [2001] 4 All E.R. 449; [2001] 2 All E.R. (Comm) 1061; [2002] 1 Lloyd's Rep. 343; [2001] 2 F.L.R. 1364; [2001] 3 F.C.R. 481; [2002] H.L.R. 4; [2001] Fam. Law 880; [2001] 43 E.G.C.S. 184; (2001) 151 N.L.J. 1538; [2001] N.P.C. 147; [2002] 1 P. & C.R. DG14; *The Times*, October 17, 2001; *Daily Telegraph*, October 23, 2001, HL; affirming in part [1998] 4 All E.R. 705; [1998] 2 F.L.R. 843; [1998] 3 F.C.R. 675; (1999) 31 H.L.R. 575; [1998] Fam. Law 665; (1998) 95(32) L.S.G. 31; (2001) 151 N.L.J. 1538; (1998) 148 N.L.J. 1390; [1998] N.P.C. 130; (1998) 76 P. & C.R. D39; *The Times*, August 17, 1998, CA (Civ Div)... 4–66, 4–67, 4–69
Royal Brompton Hospital NHS Trust v Hammond (No.1) [1999] B.L.R. 162; (2000) 2 T.C.L.R. 92; 66 Con. L.R. 42; (1999) 15 Const. L.J. 395; (1999) 149 N.L.J. 89; *Independent*, January 25, 1999 (C.S.), QBD (TCC). 39–49, 39–50, 39–55
Royal Brompton Hospital NHS Trust v Hammond (No.3) [2002] UKHL 14; [2002] 1 W.L.R. 1397; [2002] 2 All E.R. 801; [2002] 1 All E.R. (Comm) 897; [2003] 1 C.L.C. 11; [2002] B.L.R. 255; [2002] T.C.L.R. 14; 81 Con. L.R. 1; [2002] P.N.L.R. 37; *The Times*, April 26, 2002, HL; affirming, 69 Con. L.R. 145; [2000] Lloyd's Rep. P.N. 643, CA (Civ Div); affirming [1999] B.L.R. 385, QBD (TCC). 6–52
Royal Brompton Hospital NHS Trust v Watkins Gray International (UK) (2001) 3 T.C.L.R. 3, CA (Civ Div). 39–31, 39–33
Royal Society of Literature v Lowenthal (1978) C.A.T. 182. .... 11–12, 11–17
Rundle v Rundle [1992] 2 F.L.R. 80; [1992] 2 F.C.R. 361; [1992] Fam. Law 388, CA (Civ Div). 32–89, 32–104
Rush & Tompkins Ltd v Greater London Council [1989] A.C. 1280; [1988] 3 W.L.R. 939; [1988] 3 All E.R. 737; 43 B.L.R. 1; 22 Con. L.R. 114; (1988) 138 N.L.J. Rep. 315; (1988) 132 S.J. 1592, HL; reversing [1988] 2 W.L.R. 533; [1988] 1 All E.R. 549; 40 B.L.R. 53; (1988) 138 N.L.J. Rep. 22; (1988) 132 S.J. 265, CA (Civ Div). 27–01, 27–04, 27–06, 27–08, 27–16, 27–19, 27–26, 27–29, 27–40, 27–47
Rushforth v Rushforth (1976) C.A.T. 91. 32–62
Rustenburg Platinum Mines Ltd v South African Airways and Pan American World Airways Inc [1979] 1 Lloyd's Rep. 19, CA (Civ Div); reversing [1977] 1 Lloyd's Rep. 564, QBD (Comm). 3–31
Ryan Developments Ltd, Re [2002] EWHC 1121; [2002] 2 B.C.L.C. 792; [2003] B.P.I.R. 482, Ch D. 31–03

S, Re; sub nom. S v S [1965] P. 165; [1965] 2 W.L.R. 986; [1965] 1 All E.R. 1018; 109 S.J. 194, PDAD. 33–02

S v B (Ancillary Relief: Costs) [2004] EWHC 2089; [2005] 1 F.L.R. 474, Fam Div.. 34–03, 34–08
S v Dudley MBC (Costs) [2000] Ed. C.R. 410; (1999) 149 N.L.J. 1904, QBD.. 40–23
S v S (Financial Provision) (Post-Divorce Cohabitation) [1994] 2 F.L.R. 228; [1994] 2 F.C.R. 1225; [1994] Fam. Law 438, Fam Div...... 32–122
S v S (Ancillary Relief: Consent Order); sub nom. S v S (Divorce: Setting Aside Consent Order) [2002] EWHC 223; [2003] Fam. 1; [2002] 3 W.L.R. 1372; [2002] 1 F.L.R. 992; [2002] Fam. Law 422; (2002) 99(15) L.S.G. 34; (2002) 152 N.L.J. 398; (2002) 146 S.J.L.B. 78, Fam Div.. 32–111
Saif Ali v Sydney Mitchell & Co [1980] A.C. 198; [1978] 3 W.L.R. 849; [1978] 3 All E.R. 1033; [1955–95] P.N.L.R. 151; 122 S.J. 761, HL; reversing [1978] Q.B. 95; [1977] 3 W.L.R. 421; [1977] 3 All E.R. 744; 121 S.J. 336, CA (Civ Div)..... 28–03, 29–22, 29–23, 29–24, 29–25
Saint Anna, The (No.2) [1983] 1 W.L.R. 895; [1983] 2 All E.R. 691; [1983] 1 Lloyd's Rep. 637, QBD (Admlty)....................... 41–06
Salomon v Akiens [1993] 1 E.G.L.R. 101.................................. 37–22
Salter v Lask (No.1) [1924] 1 K.B. 754, CA; reversing [1923] 2 K.B. 798, KBD.. 37–34
Sampson v John Boddy Timber Ltd (1995) 145 N.L.J. 851; *Independent*, May 17, 1995, CA (Civ Div).. 26–09, 26–11, 27–02, 27–04, 27–05, 27–11
Sandford v Sandford [1986] 1 F.L.R. 412; [1986] Fam. Law 104, CA (Civ Div); affirming [1985] Fam. Law 230........................... 32–62
Saunders v Ford Motor Co [1970] 1 Lloyd's Rep. 379, QBD........ 2–08, 4–47
Saunders v Saunders (1978) 8 Fam. Law 206, CA (Civ Div)............... 4–32
Savings & Investment Bank Ltd (In Liquidation) v Fincken [2003] EWCA Civ 1630; [2004] 1 W.L.R. 667; [2004] 1 All E.R. 1125; [2004] C.P. Rep. 16; (2004) 101(2) L.S.G. 30; *The Times*, November 25, 2003, CA (Civ Div); reversing [2003] EWHC 719; [2003] 3 All E.R. 1091, Ch D... 27–40
Savings & Investment Bank Ltd v Gasco Investments (Netherlands) BV (No.1) [1984] 1 W.L.R. 271; [1984] 1 All E.R. 296; (1984) 81 L.S.G. 657; (1984) 128 S.J. 115, Ch D................................. 27–57
Scammell v Dicker; sub nom. Dicker v Scammell [2001] 1 W.L.R. 631; [2001] C.P. Rep. 64; [2001] C.P.L.R. 188; (2001) 98(7) L.S.G. 41; (2001) 145 S.J.L.B. 28; [2001] N.P.C. 1; *The Times*, February 14, 2001, CA (Civ Div)..................................... 15–15, 17–04
Schebsman (dec'd) Ex p. Official Receiver, Re; sub nom. Trustee v Cargo Supertintendents (London) Ltd [1944] Ch. 83; [1943] 2 All E.R. 768, CA; affirming in part [1943] Ch. 366, Ch D....................... 6–66
Schering Corp v Cipla Ltd [2004] EWHC 2587; (2004) 101(47) L.S.G. 30; *The Times*, December 2, 2004, Ch D........................... 27–10
Scheyer v Wontner (1890) 90 L.T. Jo.116................................ 29–15
Scholefield v Templer (1859) 4 De G.J.E. 429........................... 6–83
Scott Paper Co. v Drayton Paper Works Ltd [1927] 44 R.P.C. 151...... 27–17
Scruttons Ltd v Midland Silicones Ltd; sub nom. Midland Silicones Ltd v Scruttons Ltd [1962] A.C. 446; [1962] 2 W.L.R. 186; [1962] 1 All E.R. 1; [1961] 2 Lloyd's Rep. 365; 106 S.J. 34, HL; affirming [1961] 1 Q.B. 106; [1960] 3 W.L.R. 372; [1960] 2 All E.R. 737; [1960] 1 Lloyd's Rep. 571; 104 S.J. 603, CA; affirming [1959] 2 Q.B. 171; [1959] 2 W.L.R. 761; [1959] 2 All E.R. 289; [1959] 1 Lloyd's Rep. 289; 103 S.J. 415, QBD.. 6–64

Seaton v Burnand; sub nom. Seaton v Heath [1900] A.C. 135, HL; reversing [1899] 1 Q.B. 782, CA.................................. 4–39
Secretary of State for Trade and Industry v Banarse; sub nom. PS Banarse & Co, Re [1997] B.C.C. 425; [1997] 1 B.C.L.C. 653; *The Times*, November 1, 1996, Ch D....................................... 31–15
Secretary of State for Trade and Industry v Rogers [1996] 1 W.L.R. 1569; [1996] 4 All E.R. 854; [1997] B.C.C. 155; [1996] 2 B.C.L.C. 513, CA (Civ Div)... 31–13, 31–16
Selectmove, Re [1995] 1 W.L.R. 474; [1995] 2 All E.R. 531; [1995] S.T.C. 406; [1994] B.C.C. 349; 66 T.C. 552; *The Times*, January 13, 1994; *Independent*, January 17, 1994 (C.S.), CA (Civ Div)........... 3–18, 4–07
Selig v Lion [1891] 1 Q.B. 513, QBD.................................. 9–28
Seven Seas Properties Ltd v Al-Essa (No.2) [1993] 1 W.L.R. 1083; [1993] 3 All E.R. 577, Ch D.. 39–47
Shaw, Re; sub nom. Smith v Shaw [1918] P. 47, CA....... 9–09, 11–08, 11–12, 11–13, 32–130
Shears v Shears (1973) C.A.T. 288.................. 3–22, 3–23, 5–43, 32–04
Shenton, Re [1935] Ch. 651, Ch D..................................... 31–18
Shepherd v Robinson [1919] 1 K.B. 474, CA.................... 6–20, 29–19
Shepherd Construction Ltd v Mecright Ltd [2000] B.L.R. 489, QBD (TCC).. 39–66, 39–67
Sheppard (Trustees of the Woodland Trust) v Inland Revenue Commissioners (No.1) [1992] 3 All E.R. 58; [1991] S.T.C. 460, Ch D....... 4–07
Shipman v Shipman [1991] 1 F.L.R. 250; [1991] F.C.R. 628; [1991] Fam. Law 145... 32–25
Shipping Co Ltd v Lakeview Trading Co SA (1979) C.A.T. 317........... 5–10
Shirayama Shokusan Co Ltd v Danovo Ltd [2004] EWHC 390; [2004] 1 W.L.R. 2985; (2004) 101(13) L.S.G. 34; *The Times*, March 22, 2004, Ch D... 43–04
Shusella, Re, 126 S.J. 577; *The Times*, June 23, 1982, Ch D............. 31–03
Sibtree v Tripp (1846)15 M. & W.23................................... 8–03
Siebe Gorman & Co Ltd v Pneupac Ltd [1982] 1 W.L.R. 185; [1982] 1 All E.R. 377; 125 S.J. 725, CA (Civ Div)....................... 6–22, 9–12
Sill v Thomas (1839) 8 C.& P. 762.................................... 28–09
Simaan General Contracting Co v Pilkington Glass Ltd [1988] Q.B. 758; [1988] 2 W.L.R. 761; [1988] 1 All E.R. 791; 40 B.L.R. 28; [1988] F.T.L.R. 469; (1988) 138 N.L.J. Rep. 53; (1988) 132 S.J. 463, CA (Civ Div) [1987] 1 W.L.R. 516; [1987] 1 All E.R. 345; (1987) 3 Const. L.J. 300; (1987) 84(0) L.S.G. 819; (1986) 136 N.L.J. 824; 131 S.J. 297, QBD (OR)......................... 27–53, 27–54, 27–55
Simister v Simister (No.2) [1987] 1 F.L.R. 194; [1987] Fam. Law 50...... 32–15
Simons and Simons v Winder and Winder (1982) C.A.T. 369............. 10–03
Singer (formerly Sharegin) v Sharegin; sub nom. Sharegin v Sharegin [1984] Fam. Law 58; *The Times*, June 28, 1983, CA (Civ Div)...... 34–02, 34–05
Sir Lindsay Parkinson & Co v Triplan Ltd [1973] Q.B. 609; [1973] 2 W.L.R. 632; 117 S.J. 146, CA (Civ Div); affirming [1973] 2 All E.R. 273; (1972) 117 S.J. 36, QBD.................................... 27–55
Skandia International Corporation v NRG Victory Reinsurance Ltd, unreported, March 16, 1998, CA................................... 30–15
Skinner v Thames Valley & Aldershot Co Ltd and Layson, CA............ 6–20
Slack v Greenham (Plant Hire) [1983] I.C.R. 617; [1983] I.R.L.R. 217, EAT... 36–26

Smallman v Smallman [1972] Fam. 25; [1971] 3 W.L.R. 588; [1971] 3 All
E.R. 717; 115 S.J. 527, CA (Civ Div).... 3–61, 5–52, 8–14, 32–43, 32–47,
32–80
Smith v McInerney [1994] 2 F.L.R. 1077; [1994] 2 F.C.R. 1086; [1995]
Fam. Law 10, Fam Div.................................... 32–11, 32–49
Smith v Poulter [1947] K.B. 339; [1947] 1 All E.R. 216; 62 T.L.R. 736;
[1947] L.J.R. 847; 91 S.J. 149, KBD............................ 37–34
Smith v Shirley and Baylis (1875) 32 L.T. 234......... 8–04, 8–10, 8–11, 11–28
Smith v Smith (1974) 5 Fam. Law 125, CA (Civ Div).............. 2–03, 6–05,
6–07, 32–100
Smith v Smith; sub nom. Smith (dec'd), Re [1992] Fam. 69; [1991] 3
W.L.R. 646; [1991] 2 All E.R. 306; [1991] 2 F.L.R. 432; [1991]
F.C.R. 791; [1991] Fam. Law 412; (1991) 141 N.L.J. 309; *Independent*, February 28, 1991; *Daily Telegraph*, March 18, 1991, CA (Civ
Div).. 32–107
Smythe v Smythe (1887) L.R. 18 Q.B.D. 544, QBD..................... 11–14
Sneath v Valley Gold Ltd [1893] 1 Ch. 477, CA....................... 2–01
Snelling v John G Snelling Ltd [1973] Q.B. 87; [1972] 2 W.L.R. 588;
[1972] 1 All E.R. 79; 116 S.J. 217, QBD.. 3–51, 3–68, 3–69, 6–72, 11–03
Snowden, Re; sub nom. Shackleton v Eddy Henderson; Henderson v
Attorney General; Snowden v Eddy Henderson; Shackleton v Methodist Missionary Society; Henderson, Re [1970] Ch. 700; [1969] 3
W.L.R. 273; [1969] 3 All E.R. 208; 113 S.J. 545, Ch D........... 31–24
Snuggs v Seyd and Kelly's Credit Index Co [1894] W.N. 95............. 15–01
Society of Lloyds v Kitson's Environmental Services (1994) 67 B.L.R. 102
at 116... 39–52
Solectron Scotland Ltd v Roper [2004] I.R.L.R. 4, EAT................. 36–35
Solicitors (A Firm), Re [1992] Q.B. 959; [1992] 2 W.L.R. 809; [1992] 1 All
E.R. 353; (1991) 141 N.L.J. 746; (1991) 135 S.J.L.B. 125; *The
Times*, June 20, 1991; *Independent*, June 26, 1991, CA (Civ Div)... 28–06
Somatra Ltd v Sinclair Roche & Temperley (No.1); Sinclair Roche &
Temperley v Somatra Ltd [2000] 1 W.L.R. 2453; [2000] 2 Lloyd's
Rep. 673; [2000] C.P.L.R. 601; (2000) 97(35) L.S.G. 37; *The Times*,
September 22, 2000, CA (Civ Div); reversing in part [2000] 1 Lloyd's
Rep. 311, QBD (Comm)....................................... 27–46
Somerset v Ley; sub nom. Ley's Will Trusts, Re [1964] 1 W.L.R. 640;
[1964] 2 All E.R. 326; 108 S.J. 299, Ch D........................ 5–61
South American and Mexican Co Ex p. Bank of England, Re [1895] 1 Ch.
37, CA............................... 3–63, 4–32, 6–02, 9–15, 10–02
South East Thames RHA v YJ Lovell (London) Ltd 32 B.L.R. 127; 9 Con.
L.R. 36, QBD... 4–80, 39–34
South Shropshire DC v Amos [1986] 1 W.L.R. 1271; [1987] 1 All E.R.
340; [1986] 2 E.G.L.R. 194; (1986) 280 E.G. 635; [1986] R.V.R.
235; (1986) 83 L.S.G. 3513; (1986) 136 N.L.J. 800; (1986) 130 S.J.
803, CA (Civ Div)....................................... 27–10, 27–12
Southampton Container Terminals Ltd v Hansa Schiffahrts GmbH (The
Maersk Colombo); sub nom. Southampton Container Terminals Ltd
v Schiffahrisgesellsch "Hansa Australia" MGH & Co; Southampton
Container Terminals Ltd v Hansa Schiffahrtsgesellschaft mbH [2001]
EWCA Civ 717; [2001] 2 Lloyd's Rep. 275; (2001) 98(24) L.S.G. 43;
(2001) 145 S.J.L.B. 149; *The Times*, June 13, 2001, CA (Civ Div);
affirming [1999] 2 Lloyd's Rep. 491; [1999] C.L.C. 1814, QBD
(Admlty)................................... 18–03, 18–04, 18–06

Spiro v Glencrown Properties Ltd [1991] Ch. 537; [1991] 2 W.L.R. 931; [1991] 1 All E.R. 600; (1991) 62 P. & C.R. 402; [1991] 02 E.G. 167; (1991) 141 N.L.J. 124; (1990) 134 S.J. 1479; *The Times*, December 13, 1990; *Independent*, December 5, 1990; *Financial Times*, December 14, 1990; *Daily Telegraph*, December 17, 1990, Ch D. 3–72

Spring v Guardian Assurance Plc [1995] 2 A.C. 296; [1994] 3 W.L.R. 354; [1994] 3 All E.R. 129; [1994] I.C.R. 596; [1994] I.R.L.R. 460; (1994) 91(40) L.S.G. 36; (1994) 144 N.L.J. 971; (1994) 138 S.J.L.B. 183; *The Times*, July 8, 1994; *Independent*, July 12, 1994, HL; reversing [1993] 2 All E.R. 273; [1993] I.C.R. 412; [1993] I.R.L.R. 122; (1993) 12 Tr. L.R. 33; (1993) 143 N.L.J. 365; (1993) 137 S.J.L.B. 47; *The Times*, December 22, 1992; *Independent*, January 26, 1993, CA (Civ Div); reversing [1992] I.R.L.R. 173; (1992) 11 Tr. L.R. 100; *The Times*, February 10, 1992, QBD. 36–09

Standrin v Yenton Minster Homes, *The Times*, July 22, 1991, CA (Civ Div). 27–09, 27–12

Steadman v Steadman [1976] A.C. 536; [1974] 3 W.L.R. 56; [1974] 2 All E.R. 977; (1975) 29 P. & C.R. 46; 118 S.J. 480, HL; affirming [1974] Q.B. 161; [1973] 3 W.L.R. 695; [1973] 3 All E.R. 977; (1973) 26 P. & C.R. 249; 117 S.J. 794, CA (Civ Div). 3–72, 32–05

Steamship Mutual Underwriting Association Ltd v Trollope & Colls (City) Ltd , 33 B.L.R. 77; 6 Con. L.R. 11; (1986) 2 Const. L.J. 224, CA (Civ Div); affirming, 11 Con. L.R. 91; (1986) 2 Const. L.J. 75, DC. 39–22, 39–25

Steeds v Steeds (1889) L.R. 22 Q.B.D. 537, QBD. 6–53

Stein v Blake (No.1) [1996] A.C. 243; [1995] 2 W.L.R. 710; [1995] 2 All E.R. 961; [1995] B.C.C. 543; [1995] 2 B.C.L.C. 94; (1995) 145 N.L.J. 760; *The Times*, May 19, 1995; *Independent*, May 19, 1995, HL; affirming [1994] Ch. 16; [1993] 3 W.L.R. 718; [1993] 4 All E.R. 225; [1993] B.C.C. 587; [1993] B.C.L.C. 1478; *The Times*, May 13, 1993; *Independent*, June 14, 1993 (C.S.), CA (Civ Div). 6–93

Stephens v Bateman (1778) 1 Bro.C.C. 22. 3–10

Stephenson v Stephenson (1974) 4 Fam. Law 124, CA (Civ Div). 32–29

Stewart v Engel [2000] B.C.C. 741; [2000] 2 B.C.L.C. 528; [2000] B.P.I.R. 383; [2000] Lloyd's Rep. P.N. 234; *The Times*, November 19, 1999, QBD (Merc). 6–20

Stewart v Kennedy (No.2) (1890) L.R. 15 App. Cas. 108; (1890) 17 R. (H.L.) 25, HL. 6–20

Stock v London Underground Ltd, *The Times*, August 13, 1999, CA (Civ Div). 39–25

Stokes Pension Fund Trustees v Western Power Distribution (South West) Plc [2005] EWCA Civ 854; (2005) 102(30) L.S.G. 28; *The Times*, July 28, 2005; *Independent*, July 15, 2005, CA (Civ Div)... 18–05A, 18–07

Stone v Godfrey (1854) 5 De G.M. & G. 76. .... 4–66, 6–83

Stotesbury v Turner [1943] K.B. 370, KBD. 26–04, 41–14

Stour Valley Builders v Stuart [2003] T.C.L.R. 8; *The Times*, February 22, 1993; *Independent*, February 9, 1993, CA (Civ Div).... 3–34, 3–36, 3–39, 3–45, 3–47, 3–48, 6–73

Stratton (R J) v Wallis Tomlin & Co [1986] 1 E.G.L.R. 104; (1985) 277 E.G. 409, CA (Civ Div). 37–17, 37–19, 38–10, 40–12

Strauss v Francis (1866) 4 F. & F. 939. 29–15

Sugden v Sugden [1957] P. 120; [1957] 2 W.L.R. 210; [1957] 1 All E.R. 300; 121 J.P. 121; 101 S.J. 109, CA; reversing [1956] 3 W.L.R. 1010; [1956] 3 All E.R. 874; 100 S.J. 876, PDAD.................. 10–11
Sullivan v Pearson Ex p. Morrison (1868–69) L.R. 4 Q.B. 153; (1868) 9 B. & S. 960, QB.. 4–13
Supamarl v Federated Homes, 9 Con. L.R. 25............................. 8–02
Sutcliffe v Thackrah [1974] A.C. 727; [1974] 2 W.L.R. 295; [1974] 1 All E.R. 859; [1974] 1 Lloyd's Rep. 318; 118 S.J. 148, HL; reversing [1973] 1 W.L.R. 888; [1973] 2 All E.R. 1047; [1973] 2 Lloyd's Rep. 115; 117 S.J. 509, CA (Civ Div)... 39–14
Sutherland v Network Appliance Ltd [2001] I.R.L.R. 12, EAT............. 36–13
Suttill v Graham [1977] 1 W.L.R. 819; [1977] 3 All E.R. 1117; (1977) 7 Fam. Law 211; 121 S.J. 408, CA (Civ Div)........................ 32–04
Sutton v Sutton [1984] Ch. 184; [1984] 2 W.L.R. 146; [1984] 1 All E.R. 168; [1984] Fam. Law 205; (1984) 81 L.S.G. 591; (1984) 128 S.J. 80, Ch D.. 3–42, 3–72
Syed Hussain bin Abdul Rahman bin Shaikh Alkaff v AM Abdullah Sahib & Co [1985] 1 W.L.R. 1392; (1985) 82 L.S.G. 2701; (1985) 129 S.J. 891, PC (Sing)................................... 37–31, 37–33, 37–43
Syros Shipping Co SA v Elaghill Trading Co (The Proodos C) [1981] 3 All E.R. 189; [1980] 2 Lloyd's Rep. 390; [1981] Com. L.R. 80, QBD (Comm)... 3–20

T v T (Financial Provision); sub nom. T (Divorce: Interim Maintenance: Discovery), Re [1990] 1 F.L.R. 1; [1990] F.C.R. 169; [1989] Fam. Law 438; (1990) 154 J.P.N. 153.. 34–02
T v T (Consent Order: Procedure to Set Aside) [1996] 2 F.L.R. 640; [1997] 1 F.C.R. 282; [1997] Fam. Law 15, Fam Div..................... 32–113
Tadmor v Tadmor (1976) C.A.T. 432....................................... 3–52
Talbot v Berkshire CC [1994] Q.B. 290; [1993] 3 W.L.R. 708; [1993] 4 All E.R. 9; [1993] R.T.R. 406; [1993] P.I.Q.R. P319; (1993) 157 L.G. Rev. 1004; (1993) 143 N.L.J. 402; *The Times*, March 23, 1993, CA (Civ Div)... 6–16
Tameside MBC v Barlow Securities Group Services Ltd [2001] EWCA Civ 1; [2001] B.L.R. 113; 75 Con. L.R. 112, CA (Civ Div)....... 39–14, 39–18
Tanfern Ltd v Cameron-MacDonald [2000] 1 W.L.R. 1311; [2000] 2 All E.R. 801; [2001] C.P. Rep. 8; [2000] 2 Costs L.R. 260; (2000) 97(24) L.S.G. 41; *The Times*, May 17, 2000; *Independent*, May 16, 2000, CA (Civ Div)... 6–25
Taylor v O Wray & Co [1971] 1 Lloyd's Rep. 497, CA (Civ Div)......... 30–05
Taylor v Taylor (1976) C.A.T. 228A....................................... 4–66
Technocrats International Inc v Fredic Ltd (No 2) [2004] EWHC 1206, QBD.. 3–09
Temple v Temple [1976] 1 W.L.R. 701; [1976] 3 All E.R. 12; (1976) 6 Fam. Law 107; 120 S.J. 403, CA (Civ Div)............... 32–09, 32–13
Thakrar v Ciro Citterio Menswear Plc (In Administration) [2002] EWHC 1975, Ch D... 11–26
Thoday v Thoday [1964] P. 181; [1964] 2 W.L.R. 371; [1964] 1 All E.R. 341; 108 S.J. 15, CA... 8–01
Thomas Bates & Son Ltd v Wyndham's (Lingerie) Ltd [1981] 1 W.L.R. 505; [1981] 1 All E.R. 1077; (1981) 41 P. & C.R. 345; (1980) 257 E.G. 381; 125 S.J. 32, CA (Civ Div); affirming (1980) 39 P. & C.R. 517, Ch D.. 4–31

Thompson v Elmbridge BC [1987] 1 W.L.R. 1425; (1987) 19 H.L.R. 526;
   86 L.G.R. 245; (1988) 152 L.G. Rev. 129; (1987) 84 L.S.G. 2456;
   131 S.J. 1285, CA (Civ Div)................................... 6–33
Thompson v Howley [1977] N.Z.L.R. 16............................ 29–06
Thompson v Smiths Shiprepairers (North Shields) Ltd; Mitchell v Vickers
   Armstrong Ltd; Gray v Smiths Shiprepairers (North Shields) Ltd;
   Nicholson v Smiths Shiprepairers (North Shields) Ltd; Blacklock v
   Swan Hunter Shipbuilders Ltd; Waggott v Swan Hunter Shipbuilders
   Ltd [1984] Q.B. 405; [1984] 2 W.L.R. 522; [1984] 1 All E.R. 881;
   [1984] I.C.R. 236; [1984] I.R.L.R. 93; (1984) 81 L.S.G. 741; (1984)
   128 S.J. 225, QBD... 35–24
Thompson v Thompson (Financial Provision) [1991] 2 F.L.R. 530; [1992]
   1 F.C.R. 368; [1992] Fam. Law 18; [1991] N.P.C. 95, CA (Civ
   Div)............. 32–26, 32–60, 32–83, 32–89, 32–101, 32–102, 32–104
Thompson v Thompson (Costs) [1993] 2 F.L.R. 464; [1994] 1 F.C.R. 97;
   [1993] Fam. Law 626, CA (Civ Div)............................ 34–08
Thompson v Walon Car Delivery [1997] I.R.L.R. 343, EAT............. 36–38
Thorne v Smith [1947] K.B. 307; [1947] 1 All E.R. 39; 63 T.L.R. 55;
   [1947] L.J.R. 596; 91 S.J. 54, CA............................. 37–48
Thwaite v Thwaite [1982] Fam. 1; [1981] 3 W.L.R. 96; [1981] 2 All E.R.
   789; 125 S.J. 307, CA (Civ Div).... 32– 16, 32–31, 32–34, 32–91, 32–130
Tigner-Roche & Co v Spiro, 126 S.J. 525, CA (Civ Div).................. 6–22
Tilly v Tilly 91979) Fam. Law 79...................................... 32–95
Times Newspapers v Fitt [1981] I.C.R. 637, EAT....................... 36–44
Tiney Engineering v Amods Knitting Machinery, unreported, May 15,
   1986, CA (Civ Div).. 3–14
Tinsley v Milligan [1994] 1 A.C. 340; [1993] 3 W.L.R. 126; [1993] 3 All
   E.R. 65; [1993] 2 F.L.R. 963; (1994) 68 P. & C.R. 412; [1993]
   E.G.C.S. 118; [1993] N.P.C. 97; *The Times*, June 28, 1993; *Independent*, July 6, 1993, HL; affirming [1992] Ch. 310; [1992] 2 W.L.R.
   508; [1992] 2 All E.R. 391; (1992) 63 P. & C.R. 152; (1991) 88(33)
   L.S.G. 32; (1991) 135 S.J.L.B. 108; [1991] N.P.C. 100; *The Times*,
   August 22, 1991, CA (Civ Div)................................ 4–71
Tolhurst v Associated Portland Cement Manufacturers (1900) Ltd; Associated Portland Cement Manufacturers (1900) Ltd v Tolhurst [1903]
   A.C. 414, HL; affirming [1902] 2 K.B. 660, CA; reversing [1901] 2
   K.B. 811, KBD... 6–86, 6–88
Tomlin v Standard Telephones & Cables Ltd [1969] 1 W.L.R. 1378; [1969]
   3 All E.R. 201; [1969] 1 Lloyd's Rep. 309; 113 S.J. 641, CA (Civ
   Div)................................. 3–26, 3–65, 3–67, 11–03, 27–20
Tommey v Tommey [1983] Fam. 15; [1982] 3 W.L.R. 909; [1982] 3 All
   E.R. 385; (1983) 4 F.L.R. 159; (1982) 12 Fam. Law 148; 126 S.J.
   243, Fam Div..................................... 32–34, 32–91, 32–130
Topliss Showers v Gessey & Son [1982] I.C.R. 501, QBD............... 4–82
Toprak Enerji Sanayi AS v Sale Tilney Technology Plc [1994] 1 W.L.R.
   840; [1994] 3 All E.R. 483; [1994] 1 Lloyd's Rep. 303, QBD
   (Comm)... 16–07
Tottenham Hotspur Football & Athletic Co Ltd v Princegrove Publishers
   Ltd [1974] 1 W.L.R. 113; [1974] 1 All E.R. 17; (1974) 27 P. & C.R.
   101; (1973) 118 S.J. 35, QBD......................... 37–10, 37–11
Townsend v Stone Toms & Partners (No.1) [1981] 1 W.L.R. 1153; [1981]
   2 All E.R. 690; 125 S.J. 428, CA (Civ Div)...... 6–31, 6–55, 6–56, 21–06

TABLE OF CASES

Tramountana Armadora SA v Atlantic Shipping Co SA (The Vorros) [1978] 2 All E.R. 870; [1978] 1 Lloyd's Rep. 391, QBD (Comm)... 41–16, 41–20, 41–24, 41–26

Trendtex Trading Corp v Credit Suisse [1982] A.C. 679; [1981] 3 W.L.R. 766; [1981] 3 All E.R. 520; [1981] Com. L.R. 262; 125 S.J. 761, HL; affirming [1980] Q.B. 629; [1980] 3 W.L.R. 367; [1980] 3 All E.R. 721; 124 S.J. 396, CA (Civ Div)...................... 4–79, 6–89

Trustees of the Dennis Rye Pension Fund v Sheffield City Council [1998] 1 W.L.R. 840; [1997] 4 All E.R. 747; (1998) 30 H.L.R. 645; (1998) 10 Admin. L.R. 112; (1998) 162 J.P.N. 145; *The Times*, August 20, 1997, CA (Civ Div)... 1–02

Trustees of Chippenham Golf Club v North Wiltshire District Council. *See* Farrage v North Wiltshire DC

Tucker v Woodroof, *The Times*, March 18, 1993, CA (Civ Div)........... 5–39

Tudor Grange Holdings Ltd v Citibank NA [1992] Ch. 53; [1991] 3 W.L.R. 750; [1991] 4 All E.R. 1; [1991] B.C.L.C. 1009; (1991) 135 S.J.L.B. 3; *The Times*, April 30, 1991, Ch D............................. 2–10

Turner v Green [1895] 2 Ch. 205, Ch D............................. 4–39

Turner v Turner; Hall v Turner (1880) L.R. 14 Ch. D. 829, Ch D... 5–25, 5–30

Underwood v Cox (1912) 4 D.L.R. 66, Ontario Div. Ct................. 27–30

Unilever Plc v Procter & Gamble Co [2000] 1 W.L.R. 2436; [2001] 1 All E.R. 783; [2000] F.S.R. 344; (2000) 23(1) I.P.D. 23001; (1999) 96(44) L.S.G. 40; (1999) 143 S.J.L.B. 268; *The Times*, November 4, 1999; *Independent*, November 5, 1999, CA (Civ Div); affirming [1999] 1 W.L.R. 1630; [1999] 2 All E.R. 691; [1999] F.S.R. 849; (1999) 22(5) I.P.D. 22042; (1999) 149 N.L.J. 370; *The Times*, March 18, 1999, Ch D (Patents Ct).. 27–01, 27–03, 27–24, 27–28, 27–31, 27–38, 27–39, 27–45, 43–17

United Dominions Trust (Commercial) v Eagle Aircraft Services; sub nom. United Dominions Trust (Commercial) v Eagle Aviation [1968] 1 W.L.R. 74; [1968] 1 All E.R. 104; (1967) 111 S.J. 849, CA (Civ Div); reversing (1967) 117 N.L.J. 324................................... 3–62

United Dominions Trust (Commercial) Ltd v Parkway Motors Ltd [1955] 1 W.L.R. 719; [1955] 2 All E.R. 557; 99 S.J. 436, QBD.............. 6–87

United States v Motor Trucks Ltd [1924] A.C. 196, PC (Can)............. 4–31

Universal Cargo Carriers Corp v Citati (No.1) [1957] 1 W.L.R. 979; [1957] 3 All E.R. 234; [1957] 2 Lloyd's Rep. 191; 101 S.J. 762, CA; affirming [1957] 2 Q.B. 401; [1957] 2 W.L.R. 713; [1957] 2 All E.R. 70; [1957] 1 Lloyd's Rep. 174; (1957) 101 S.J. 320, QBD........... 8–13

Upfield v Marshall (1976) C.A.T. 142................................ 3–37

VSEL Ltd v Cape Contracts Plc; sub nom. Vickers Shipbuilding & Engineering Ltd v Cape Contracts Plc [1998] P.I.Q.R. P207, QBD........... 27–50

Vandepitte v Preferred Accident Insurance Corp of New York; sub nom. Vandepitte v Preferred Accident Insurance Co of New York [1933] A.C. 70; (1932) 44 Ll. L. Rep. 41, PC (Can)...................... 6–66

Vaughan-Armatrading (Noel) v Sarsah (Alexander K) (1995) 27 H.L.R. 631, CA (Civ Div)... 37–49

Von Hatzfeldt Wildenburg v Alexander [1912] 1 Ch. 284, Ch D.......... 3–56

WEA (A Debtor), Re [1901] 2 K.B. 642, CA...................... 6–30, 6–47

WH Smith Ltd v Colman (t/a Cherished Domains) [2001] F.S.R. 9, CA (Civ
    Div)... 27–40
Wachtel v Wachtel (No.2) [1973] Fam. 72; [1973] 2 W.L.R. 366; [1973] 1
    All E.R. 829; 117 S.J. 124, CA (Civ Div); affirming in part [1973] 2
    W.L.R. 84; [1973] 1 All E.R. 113; (1972) 116 S.J. 762; *The Times*,
    October 5, 1972, Fam Div..................................... 32–79
Wade v Simeon (1846) 2 C.B. 548................................... 2–19
Wagstaff v Colls [2003] EWCA Civ 469; [2003] C.P. Rep. 50; [2003] 4
    Costs L.R. 535; [2003] P.N.L.R. 29; (2003) 147 S.J.L.B. 419; *The
    Times*, April 17, 2003; *Independent*, April 11, 2003, CA (Civ Div)... 9–23,
                                                                        9–28
Waldridge v Kennison (1794) 1 Esp. 142.................... 27–25, 27–26
Wales v Wadham [1977] 1 W.L.R. 199; [1977] 1 All E.R. 125; (1976) 7
    Fam. Law 19; 121 S.J. 154; *The Times*, June 26, 1976, Fam Div..... 4–39,
                                                                        4–44, 4–50
Walford v Miles [1992] 2 A.C. 128; [1992] 2 W.L.R. 174; [1992] 1 All
    E.R. 453; (1992) 64 P. & C.R. 166; [1992] 1 E.G.L.R. 207; [1992]
    11 E.G. 115; [1992] N.P.C. 4; *The Times*, January 27, 1992;
    Independent, January 29, 1992, HL; affirming (1991) 62 P. & C.R.
    410; [1991] 2 E.G.L.R. 185; [1991] 28 E.G. 81; [1991] 27 E.G. 114;
    [1990] E.G.C.S. 158; *Independent*, January 15, 1991, CA (Civ Div);
    reversing [1990] 1 E.G.L.R. 212; [1990] 12 E.G. 107, QBD......... 3–55
Walker v Northumberland CC [1995] 1 All E.R. 737; [1995] I.C.R. 702;
    [1995] I.R.L.R. 35; [1995] P.I.Q.R. P521; (1994) 144 N.L.J. 1659;
    The Times, November 24, 1994; *Independent*, November 18, 1994,
    QBD.. 36–08
Walker v Wilsher (1889) L.R. 23 Q.B.D. 335, CA......... 26–04, 27–06, 27–21
Wallersteiner v Moir (No.1); sub nom. Moir v Wallersteiner (No.1) [1974]
    1 W.L.R. 991; [1974] 3 All E.R. 217; 118 S.J. 464, CA (Civ Div).. 10–02,
                                                                        31–33, 38–03
Walsh v Lonsdale (1882) L.R. 21 Ch. D. 9, CA...................... 37–11
Wandsworth LBC v Fadayomi [1987] 1 W.L.R. 1473; [1987] 3 All E.R.
    474; [1988] 1 F.L.R. 381; (1987) 19 H.L.R. 512; 86 L.G.R. 176;
    [1988] Fam. Law 131; (1987) 84 L.S.G. 2535; (1987) 131 S.J. 1285,
    CA (Civ Div).. 37–34
Ward (Robert Lloyd), Re; Barry, Re (1843) 7 Scott N.R.499, QBD....... 4–54
Warden v Warden [1982] Fam. 10; [1981] 3 W.L.R. 435; [1981] 3 All E.R.
    193; 125 S.J. 530, CA (Civ Div).............................. 32–16
Warren v Warren (1983) (1983) 13 Fam. Law 49, CA (Civ Div).......... 4–19
Watkins v Watkins [1896] P. 222, CA................................ 6–90
Watters v Smith (1831) 2 B. & Ad. 889.............................. 6–47
Watts v Aldington; Tolstoy v Aldington [1999] L. & T.R. 578; *The Times*,
    December 16, 1993; *Independent*, January 25, 1994, CA (Civ Div)... 6–36,
                                                                        6–41, 6–43, 6–48
Waugh v HB Clifford & Sons Ltd [1982] Ch. 374; [1982] 2 W.L.R. 679;
    [1982] 1 All E.R. 1095, CA (Civ Div) 29–06, 29–07, 29–11, 29–04, 29–25
Weaver v Mogford [1988] 31 E.G. 49, CA (Civ Div)................... 37–53
Websdell v Jenkins (1902) 46 S.J. 484.............................. 5–45
Welfare v Welfare (1977) 8 Fam. Law 55; 121 S.J. 743............... 32–22
Wellington v Wellington, 122 S.J. 296; *The Times*, March 22, 1978, CA
    (Civ Div).. 11–33
Wells v Wells; sub nom. W v W (Financial Provision: Company Shares)
    [2002] EWCA Civ 476; [2002] 2 F.L.R. 97; [2002] Fam. Law 512,
    CA (Civ Div); reversing [2001] Fam. Law 656, Fam Div........... 34–08

Welsh v Roe (1918) 87 L.J. K.B. 520.................................. 29–15
Wentworth v Bullen (1829) 9 B. & C. 840............................ 9–12
Wessex RHA v HLM Design Ltd, 71 B.L.R. 32; (1994) 10 Const. L.J. 165,
 QBD.. 6–61
West London Commercial Bank Ltd v Kitson; West London Commercial
 Bank Ltd v Porter; West London Commercial Bank Ltd v Woodward
 (1883–84) L.R. 13 Q.B.D. 360, CA; affirming (1883–84) L.R. 12
 Q.B.D. 157, QBD... 4–46
West of England Fire Insurance Co v Isaacs [1897] 1 Q.B. 226, CA;
 affirming [1896] 2 Q.B. 377, QBD....................... 30–03, 30–11
Westbury v Sampson [2001] EWCA Civ 407; [2002] 1 F.L.R. 166; [2001]
 2 F.C.R. 210; [2002] Fam. Law 15; (2001) 98(20) L.S.G. 44, CA
 (Civ Div).. 32–95
Westminster Building Co Ltd v Beckingham [2004] EWHC 138; [2004]
 B.L.R. 163; [2004] B.L.R. 265; [2004] T.C.L.R. 8; 94 Con. L.R. 107,
 QBD (TCC)... 39–08
White (Pamela) v White (Martin) [2001] 1 A.C. 596; [2000] 3 W.L.R.
 1571; [2001] 1 All E.R. 1; [2000] 2 F.L.R. 981; [2000] 3 F.C.R. 555;
 [2001] Fam. Law 12; (2000) 97(43) L.S.G. 38; (2000) 150 N.L.J.
 1716; (2000) 144 S.J.L.B. 266; [2000] N.P.C. 111; *The Times*,
 October 31, 2000; *Independent*, November 1, 2000; *Daily Telegraph*,
 November 7, 2000, HL; affirming [1999] Fam. 304; [1999] 2 W.L.R.
 1213; [1998] 4 All E.R. 659; [1998] 2 F.L.R. 310; [1998] 3 F.C.R.
 45; [1998] Fam. Law 522; *The Times*, July 13, 1998; *Independent*,
 June 29, 1998 (C.S.), CA (Civ Div)............................. 32–111
Whiteley, Re (1910) 1 Ch. 600................................. 31–19, 31–23
Whiting v Whiting [1988] 1 W.L.R. 565; [1988] 2 All E.R. 275; [1988] 2
 F.L.R. 189; [1988] F.C.R. 569; [1988] Fam. Law 429; (1988) 152
 J.P.N. 574; (1988) 138 N.L.J. Rep. 39; (1988) 132 S.J. 658, CA (Civ
 Div)... 32–55, 33–04
Whitworth Street Estates (Manchester) Ltd v James Miller & Partners Ltd;
 sub nom. James Miller & Partners Ltd v Whitworth Street Estates
 (Manchester) Ltd [1970] A.C. 583; [1970] 2 W.L.R. 728; [1970] 1
 All E.R. 796; [1970] 1 Lloyd's Rep. 269; 114 S.J. 225, HL; reversing
 [1969] 1 W.L.R. 377; [1969] 2 All E.R. 210; 113 S.J. 126, CA (Civ
 Div).. 3–22
Wigan v English and Scottish Law Life Assurance Association [1909] 1 Ch.
 291, Ch D... 3–04, 3–05
Wilding v Sanderson [1897] 2 Ch. 534, CA...................... 4–24, 6–20
Williams v Bayley (1866) L.R. 1 H.L. 200, HL..................... 4–77
Williams v Roffey Bros & Nicholls (Contractors) Ltd [1991] 1 Q.B. 1;
 [1990] 2 W.L.R. 1153; [1990] 1 All E.R. 512; 48 B.L.R. 69; (1991)
 10 Tr. L.R. 12; (1990) 87(12) L.S.G. 36; (1989) 139 N.L.J. 1712,
 CA (Civ Div).. 3–16
Williams v Settle [1960] 1 W.L.R. 1072; [1960] 2 All E.R. 806; 104 S.J.
 847, CA.. 10–07
Willis v Willis [1928] P. 10, CA.. 7–10
Willson v Ministry of Defence; sub nom. Wilson v Ministry of Defence
 [1991] 1 All E.R. 638; [1991] I.C.R. 595, QBD............. 25–09, 35–26
Wilson & Whitworth Ltd v Express & Independent Newspapers Ltd [1969]
 1 W.L.R. 197; [1969] 1 All E.R. 294; [1969] F.S.R. 1; [1969] R.P.C.
 165; (1968) 113 S.J. 65; *The Times*, December 19, 1968, Ch D..... 3–51,
 4–34, 5–02, 9–20

Wilson Smithett & Cape (Sugar) v Bangladesh Sugar and Food Industries
 Corp [1986] 1 Lloyd's Rep. 378, QBD (Comm)..................... 3–70
Wiltshire CC v Frazer (Writ of Restitutuion) [1986] 1 W.L.R. 109; [1986]
 1 All E.R. 65; (1986) 52 P. & C.R. 46; (1985) 82 L.S.G. 3448;
 (1985) 135 N.L.J. 1080; *The Times*, September 27, 1985, QBD...... 6–33
Windhill Local Board of Health v Vint (1890) L.R. 45 Ch. D. 351, CA..... 4–77
Windle (A Bankrupt), Re; sub nom. Trustee Ex p. v Windle [1975] 1
 W.L.R. 1628; [1975] 3 All E.R. 987; 119 S.J. 808, Ch D........... 6–75
With v O'Flanagan [1936] Ch. 575, CA............................... 4–43
Wood v Wood (1979) C.A.T. 49..................................... 32–137
Woodhead v Woodhead (1978) C.A.T. 147...................... 4–05, 10–03
Woolwich Building Society (formerly Woolwich Equitable Building Society)
 v Inland Revenue Commissioners [1993] A.C. 70; [1992] 3 W.L.R.
 366; [1992] 3 All E.R. 737; [1992] S.T.C. 657; (1993) 5 Admin. L.R.
 265; 65 T.C. 265; (1992) 142 N.L.J. 1196; (1992) 136 S.J.L.B. 230;
 The Times, July 22, 1992; *Independent*, August 13, 1992; *Guardian*,
 August 19, 1992, HL; affirming [1991] 3 W.L.R. 790; [1991] 4 All
 E.R. 577; [1991] S.T.C. 364; (1991) 135 S.J.L.B. 46; *The Times*, May
 27, 1991, CA (Civ Div); reversing [1989] 1 W.L.R. 137; [1989]
 S.T.C. 111; (1989) 133 S.J. 291, QBD............................ 2–13
Worlock v Worlock [1994] 2 F.L.R. 689; [1994] 2 F.C.R. 1157; [1994]
 Fam. Law 619, CA (Civ Div)......................... 32–104, 32–122
Worman v Worman (1890) L.R. 43 Ch. D. 296, Ch D.............. 6–07, 6–16
Worthington & Co Ltd v Abbott [1910] 1 Ch. 588, Ch D................ 9–12
Wright v Wright [1970] 1 W.L.R. 1219; [1970] 3 All E.R. 209; 114 S.J.
 619, CA (Civ Div)... 32–09
Wyvern Developments, Re [1974] 1 W.L.R. 1097; [1974] 2 All E.R. 535;
 118 S.J. 531, Ch D... 3–05

Xydhias v Xydhias [1999] 2 All E.R. 386; [1999] 1 F.L.R. 683; [1999] 1
 F.C.R. 289; [1999] Fam. Law 301; (1999) 96(6) L.S.G. 34; (1999)
 149 N.L.J. 52; *The Times*, January 13, 1999; *Independent*, January
 21, 1999, CA (Civ Div)..................... 3–57, 32–36, 32–39, 32–41

Yat Tung Investment Co Ltd v Dao Heng Bank Ltd [1975] A.C. 581;
 [1975] 2 W.L.R. 690; 119 S.J. 273, PC (HK)...................... 6–11
Yorwerth v Sonnyplaster (1973) C.A.T. 255............................ 3–50
Yorweth v Sonnyplaster (1973) C.A.T. 2555–62............................
Young v Black Sluice Commissioners (1903) 73 J.P. 265................. 19–01

Zamet v Hyman [1961] 1 W.L.R. 1442; [1961] 3 All E.R. 933; 105 S.J.
 911, CA... 33–02
Zaniewski v Scales, 113 S.J. 525..................................... 5–62

TABLE OF STATUTES

1677 Statute of Frauds (29 Car.2 c.3) 3–74
1838 Judgments Act (1&2 Vict. c.110) 32–16
    s.17 5–40
    s.18 .... 5–40, 11–20
1859 Matrimonial Causes Act (22 & 23 Vict. c.61 32–14
1873 Supreme Court of Judicature Act (36 & 37 Vict. c.66)
    s.49 35–14
1882 Married Women's Property Act (45 & 46 Vict. c.75) 3–23
    s.17 .... 2–03, 6–76, 32–02–32–07, 32–16, 32–25
1883 Patents, Designs and Trade Marks Act (46 & 47 Vict. c.57)
    s.32 27–31
1908 Bills of Exchange Act (8 Edw.7)
    s.21(2)(b) 3–48
1920 Increase of Rent and Mortgage Interest (Restriction) Act (10 & 11 Geo.5 c.17) 37–29
1925 Trustee Act (15 &16 Geo.5 c.19)
    s.15 .... 31–18, 31–19, 31–20, 31–23
    (1) 33–02, 33–03, 33–06
    Law of Property Act (15 & 16 Geo.5 c.20) .. 6–87
    s.31(1)(h) 32–118
    s.40 3–72
    s.54(2) 3–73

1925 Supreme Court of Judicature (Consolidation) Act (15&16 Geo.5 c.49)
    s.190(2) 10–11
1934 Law Reform (Miscellaneous Provisions) Act (24 & 25 Geo.5 c.41) 25–12
1938 Inheritance (Family Provision) Act (1 & 2 Geo.6, c.46) 33–02
1946 Furnished Houses (Rent Control) Act 37–44
1950 Arbitration Act (14 Geo.6 c.27) 39–61
    s.36 6–94
1954 Landlord and Tenant Act (2 & 3 Eliz.2 c.56) 8–06, 37–04, 37–08, 37–09, 37–10, 37–11, 37–17
    Pt II 37–04
    ss.24–28 .... 37–10, 37–11, 37–26
    s.25 .... 37–17, 37–22
    s.28 37–17
    s.29 37–12
    s.30 37–27
    s.37 37–27
    s.38(A) 37–05, 37–08, 37–09, 37–10, 37–26
    s.38(1) 37–05, 37–26
    (4) 37–05, 37–11, 37–12
1957 Maintenance Agreements Act (5 & 6 Eliz.2 c35) 32–10, 32–14, 32–16
    s.1(1) 32–08

Year	Statute	Reference
1958	Matrimonial Causes (Property and Maintenance) Act (6 & 7 Eliz.2 c.35)	
	s.7	32–03
	(7)	32–03
	Variation of Trusts Act (6 & 7 Eliz.2 c.53)	31–18
1965	Matrimonial Causes Act (11 Eliz.2 c.72)	32–33
	s.23(2)	32–08
1967	Misrepresentation Act (11 Eliz.2 c.7)	
	s.2(2)	12–02
1968	Civil Evidence Act (11 Eliz.2 c.64)	
	s.3(1)(a)	27–42
1969	Divorce Reform Act (11 Eliz.2 c.55)	32–03
1970	Taxes Management Act (11 Eliz.2 c.9)	4–07
	Equal Pay Act (11 Eliz.2 c.41)	36–21
	Matrimonial Property and Proceedings Act (11 Eliz.2 c.45)	32–03, 32–14
1971	Guardianship of Minors Act (c.3)	32–13
	s.12A	32–13
	Town and Country Planning Act (c.78)	
	s.120	27–10
1972	Defective Premises Act (c.35)	39–18
	s.1(5)	39–18
	Local Government Act (c.70)	
	s.111	40–08
	s.222	40–08
1973	Matrimonial Causes Act (c.18)	6–78, 6–79, 28–10, 32–08, 32–29, 32–69, 33–01, 33–11, 33–15
	s.5	32–22
	(1)	32–10
	s.22	32–27
	s.23	32–16, 32–60, 32–86, 32–131, 33–01
	(2)(d)	32–27
	s.24	32–16, 32–60, 32–86, 32–131, 33–01
1973	Matrimonial Causes Act—cont.	
	s.25	4–39, 32–37, 32–52, 32–53, 32–58, 32–78, 32–79, 32–86, 32–108
	s.25A	5–58
	s.25(1)	32–86
	s.27	32–13
	(3)	32–13
	s.27(3A)	32–13
	s.28(1A)	32–135
	(1)(a)	10–11
	s.31	32–82, 32–95
	(1)(e)	32–33
	(g)	33–05
	(4)	32–33
	(7)A	32–16
	s.33A	32–32, 32–81, 32–51, 32–56, 32–57, 32–96
	ss.34–36	32–08, 32–14, 32–17
	s.34	3–11, 32–09, 32–11, 32–42
	(1)	32–11, 32–16
	(2)	32–08, 32–10, 32–42
	s.35	7–11, 32–09
	(2)	32–15
	(3)	32–16
	(4)	32–16
	s.36	10–11, 32–16
	s.37	6–76, 32–25
	(4)	6–79
	s.39	6–76
	s.42	32–137
	(1)	32–137
	s.52(1)	32–137
	s.86	32–52
	Guardianship Act (c.29)	32–13
1975	Inheritance (Provision for Family and Dependants) Act (c.63)	6–78, 6–79, 31–01, 33–01, 33–12
	s.1(1)	33–01
	(e)	33–13
	(2)(b)	33–06
	s.2	33–01, 33–02, 33–09
	(1)	33–13
	s.3	33–12
	(1)	33–14
	s.4	33–01

1975	Inheritance (Provision for Family and Dependants) Act—*cont.*		1977	Housing (Homeless Persons) Act (c.48) 37–39
	s.5	33–09	1978	Interpretation Act (c.30)
	s.10	6–76		s.12 40–10
	(2) 6–79, 6–80			Employment Protection (Consolidation) Act (c.44)
	(b)	6–79		s.74 36–17
	(6)	6–79		s.134 4–65
	s.15 .... 33–02, 33–04			s.140 36–43
	s.15A	33–02		s.140(1)(b) 36–17
	(1)	33–02		Civil Liability (Contribution) Act (c.47) 6–28, 6–38, 6–43, 6–50, 6–61, 39–28, 39–31
	s.15(1) 32–55, 33–02, 33–03, 33–06			
	s.17	33–02		
	(2)	33–09		s.1 .... 6–37, 39–29
	s.18	33–09		(1) 6–52, 39–29
	s.19(1)	33–16		(3) 6–51
	(3)	33–17		(4) 6–49
	Resevoirs Act (c.23)			s.3 6–29, 6–28, 6–30, 6–37
	s.7	39–28		s.4 6–28
	Inheritance (Provision for Family and Dependants) Act (c.63) 31–40			s.5 6–54
			1979	Sale of Goods Act (c.54)
				s.31(2) 7–04
	Sex Discrimination Act (c.65) 36–21, 36–27, 36–29, 36–30, 36–39		1980	Partnership Act (c.39)
				s.5 4–11
				Housing Act (c.51) 37–30
	s.77	36–21		Limitation Act (c.58)
	Policyholders Protection Act (c.75) 35–34			s.5 39–18
				s.8 39–18
1976	Fatal Accidents Act (c.30) 6–40, 25–12			s.14A 39–23
				s.32 39–19
	Restrictive Trade Practices Act (c.34) 4–82			(1) 39–19
				(b) 39–20
	Race Relations Act (c.74) 36–27, 36–29, 36–30, 36–39			(3) 39–19
				s.35 9–36
			1981	Supreme Court Act (c.54) 32–118
	s.72	36–21		
	Rent (Agriculture) Act (c.80) 37–30			s.9 38–10
				s.17 32–118
	s.6(1)	37–34		(2) 32–118
1977	Torts (Interference with Goods) Act (c.32) .. 6–54			s.18(1)(f) 35–15
				s.32A 35–25
	Patents Act (c.37)			s.39 11–22
	s.70	27–38		s.61(1) 31–41
	Rent Act (c.42) 37–30, 37–36, 37–49			s.64 .... 31–01, 32–126
				s.65 31–01
	s.2	37–48		Sch.1 31–41
	s.19	37–43	1982	Civil Jurisdiction and Judgments Act (c.27)
	s.98	37–41		
	(1)	37–34		
	s.100	37–46		s.25 5–41

TABLE OF STATUTES

1982	Civil Jurisdiction and Judgments Act—*cont.*
	s.34 6–94

Administration of Justice Act (c.53)
    s.6 35–25

1983 Mental Health Act (c.20) 35–01
    Pt VII 4–04
    s.1(2) 35–01
    s.94(2) 35–01

1984 County Courts Act (c.28) 10–07
    s.18 10–06
    s.23 31–01
    s.24 .... 10–06, 31–01
    s.52 35–26
    s.76 32–118

1984 Matrimonial and Family Proceedings Act (c.42)
    s.7 .... 32–32, 32–51
    s.9 33–02
    s.17 33–02
    s.25 33–02
    s.31(7) 32–29

1985 Companies Act (c.6)
    s.459 31–11

Enduring Powers of Attorney Act (c.29) 35–22

Administration of Justice Act (c.61)
    s.49 .... 31–28, 31–29
    (2) 31–27

Housing Act (c.68) 37–30, 37–32, 37–49
    s.81 37–32
    s.84 37–34
    s.85 37–46

1986 Insolvency Act (c.45) ... 31–12
    s.127 .... 31–03, 31–05
    s.129 31–03
    s.165(2)(a) 31–10
    (b) 31–10
    s.167(1)(a) 31–10
    s.283(1) 6–76
    (3) 6–76
    s.284 6–76
    s.314(1)(a) 31–10
    s.339 .... 6–76, 32–07
    ss.339–342 6–75

1986 Insolvency Act—*cont.*
    s.340 32–07
    s.375(2) 31–09
    Sch.4, para.2 31–10
    para.3 31–10
    Sch.5, para.6 31–10
    para.7 31–10

Company Directors Disqualification Act (c.46) 31–12, 31–16
    s.1A 31–16

1988 Legal Aid Act (c.34)
    s.17(1) 14–03, 34–08, 34–15
    s.18 34–16

Housing Act (c.50)
    s.7 37–34
    s.9 37–46
    s.12 37–48
    s.36 37–43

1989 Social Security Act (c.24)
    s.22 5–13

Law of Property (Miscellaneous Provisions) Act (c.34) 3–75
    s.1 3–75
    (2)(a) 3–75
    (b) 3–75
    (3) 3–75
    (11) 3–75
    s.2 .... 37–20, 38–02
    (1) 3–72, 38–07
    (2) 3–72
    (3) 3–72
    (5)(a) 3–73
    (8) 3–72

Children Act (c.41) 32–16, 32–17, 32–137
    s.1(1) 32–137
    (5) 32–137
    s.8 32–137
    s.10(1) 32–137
    s.15(1) 32–18
    Sch.1, para.3(1) 32–18
    (2) 32–18
    para.10(1) 32–17
    (2) 32–17
    (3) 32–18
    (5) 32–18

1991	Child Support Act (c.48) 32–09, 32–10, 32–17, 32–18, 32–19, 32–27, 32–100, 32–109, 32–110		1996	Employment Tribunals Act (c.17) 36–36
	s.8(7) 32–19			s.18 .... 36–18, 36–26
	(8) 32–19			(1) 36–18
	s.9 .... 32–08, 32–11			(2) 36–25
	(1) 32–10, 32–19			(3) 36–25
	(2) 32–19			Employment Rights Act (c.18) 36–19, 36–21, 36–36, 36–38
	(3) 32–19			Pt V 36–20, 36–21
	(4) 32–11			Pt VI 36–20
	s.10 32–27			Pt VII 36–20
	(2) 32–19			Pt X 36–20
1992	Trade Union and Labour Relations (Consolidation) Act (c.52) 36–22			s.8 36–20
				s.13 36–20
				s.15 36–20
				s.18 36–20
				s.21 36–20
	s.64 36–22			s.28 36–20
	s.68 36–22			s.80 36–20
	s.70(B) 36–22			s.92 36–20
	s.86 36–22			s.135 36–20
	s.137 36–22			s.203 .... 36–15, 36–21
	s.138 36–22			(1) 36–15, 36–18
	s.146 36–22			(2) 36–18
	s.164 36–22			(e) ... 36–18, 36–26
	ss.168–170 36–22			(f) 36–18
	s.188 .... 36–23, 36–37			(3) 36–29
	s.190 .... 36–23, 36–37			Arbitration Act (c.23) ... 1–01, 4–75, 41–01
	s.212A 36–47			s.5 41–07
	s.288 36–22			s.6 41–07
	(2C) 36–33			s.9 41–10
	Sch.A1, para.156 36–22			(4) 41–10
1993	Charities Act (c.10)			s.30 .... 41–05, 41–10
	s.26 31–23			s.32 41–12
	s.27 31–24			s.38(3) 41–11
	Trade Union Reform and Employment Rights Act (c.19)			s.47 41–04
				s.49(3) 41–10
				s.51 .... 41–02, 41–04
	s.39 36–26			ss.52–58 41–02
1995	Pensions Act (c.26)			ss.59–65 41–02
	s.75 31–18			s.61 41–10
	Law Reform (Succession) Act (c.41) 33–01			s.66 .... 41–06, 41–07
				(3) 41–07
	Act (c.50) 36–27, 36–30			s.67 41–10
				s.68 41–14
	s.9 36–21			(1) 41–14
1996	National Health Service (Residual Liabilities) Act (c.15) 35–33, 35–62			(2)(g) 41–14
				s.70(3) 41–14
				ss.89–91 41–01
				Family Law Act (c.27) .. 32–24
				s.66 32–51

1996	Damages Act (c.48)	
	s.1(1)	35–45
	s.2	35–37
	s.2B	35–52
	s.2(4)	35–46
	s.4	35–34
	Housing Grants Construction and Regeneration Act (c.53)	39–01, 39–66
	s.104	39–64
	s.108	39–64
	(3)	39–64
1997	Social Security (Recovery of Benefits) Act (c.270	35–54
	s.15	35–55
	(1)	35–55
1998	Employment Rights (Dispute Resolution) Act (c.8)	
	s.7	36–47
	National Minimum Wage Act (c.39)	36–01
	s.49	36–21
	Competition Act (c.41)	4–82
	Human Rights Act (c.42)	40–07
1999	Access to Justice Act (c.22)	
	s.55	31–09
	Employment Relations Act (c.26)	
	ss.10–13	36–21
1999	Contracts (Rights of Third Parties) Act (c.31)	6–39, 6–63, 6–64
	s.1	6–69
	(1)	6–67
	(a)	6–67
	(b)	6–68
	(2)	6–68
	(3)	6–67
	s.2	6–69
	s.4	6–69
	s.10(2)	6–67
2000	Local Government Act (c.22)	40–08
	s.2	40–08
	Trustee Act (c.29)	
	s.1(1)	31–18
	s.40(1)	31–18
	Sch.2, Pt II, para.20	31–18
	Insolvency Act (c.39)	
	s.5	31–12
	s.6	31–16
2002	Land Registration Act (c.9)	38–02
	Proceeds of Crime Act (c.29)	35–64
2003	Courts Act (c.39)	
	s.100	25–10, 35–37, 35–52
	s.101	25–10
2005	Mental Capacity Act	35–02

TABLE OF STATUTORY INSTRUMENTS

1965 Rules of the Supreme
 Court (SI 1965/
 1776) 6–24, 26–05
 Ord.15, r.13(4) 31–21
 Ord.16, r.10 15–01
 Ord.18 22–02
 Ord.21, r.2(4) 40–14
 Ord.22 ...... 14–01, 41–27
   r.1 19–01
   r.1(1) 15–01
   r.1(5) 6–57, 20–03
   rr.1–3 16–07
   r.3(1) 18–15
   r.3(4) 19–01
   r.4 22–05
   r.7(1) 14–08
   r.14 26–05
     (1) 15–01,
           16–07
 Ord.33, r.4A 15–01
 Ord.38, r.37 27–51
 Ord.42, r.2 5–43
   r.5A 31–30
 Ord.62, r.5(4) 21–05,
           21–09
   r.9(1) 15–01
   r.9(1)(d) 16–07

1977 Matrimonial Causes Rules
 (SI 1977/344)
 r.76A 32–28

1981 County Court Rules (SI
 1981/1687) 26–05
 Ord.5, r.6(3) 31–21
 Ord.10 22–02
 Ord.11 14–01
   r.10 26–05
 Ord.22, r.3 5–44
 Ord.37, r.1 32–121,
           32–122
   r.6 32–120
     (1) 32–124
     (5) 32–124
 Ord.38, r.9 .... 5–38, 5–39

1981 Transfer of Undertakings
 (Protection of
 Employment)
 Regulations (SI
 1981/1794) 36–01,
     36–34, 36–35, 36–36,
         36–37, 36–38
 reg.5 36–35
 regs 10–11 .. 36–36, 36–37
 reg.10 36–37
 reg.11 36–37
   (9) 36–37

1986 Insolvency Rules (SI
 1986/1925)
 r.4.15 31–03
 r.4.19 31–03
 r.6.31 31–07
 r.6.32 31–07
 r.7.47(2) 31–09
 r.7.48(2) 31–09
   Form 4.8 31–03
   Form 6.21 31–03
   Form 6.31 31–06

1991 Family Proceedings Rules
 (SI 1991/1247) .. 32–121,
           34–06
 r.2.24(3) 32–20
 r.2.36 32–20
 r.2.53(2)(b) 32–55
 r.2.61 ...... 32–28, 32–51,
     32–57, 32–58, 32–96,
           33–15
 r.2.61D 31–45
 r.2.61E 31–45
 r.2.61E(3) 34–13
 r.2.61E(5) 34–13
 r.2.61F 34–03
 r.2.61(3) 32–55, 32–59
 r.2.64 32–22
 r.2.65 32–126
 r.2.69B 34–06
 r.2.69B–D 34–14
 r.2.69D 34–06, 34–14
 r.2.69D(e) 34–06
 r.2.69(1) 34–10

TABLE OF STATUTORY INSTRUMENTS

1993	Employment Tribunals (Constitution and Rules of Procedure) Regulations (SI 1993/2687) 36–40

Employment Appeal Tribunal Rules (SI 1993/2854)
    r.33 36–45
    reg.11 36–45

1996 Employment Protection (Recoupment of Jobseekers' Allowance and Income Support) Regulations (SI 1996/2349) 36–42

Employment Protection (Continuity of Employment) Regulations (SI 1996/3147) 36–34

1997 Social Security (Recovery of Benefits) Regulations (SI 1997/2205) 35–54

1998 Working Time Regulations (SI 1998/1833) 36–01
    reg.35 36–21

Civil Procedure Rules (SI 1998/3132)   4–75, 5–44, 6–21, 6–24, 6–21, 9–04, 11–05, 23–11, 40–14, 42–05
    r.1.2 .... 22–11, 23–15
    r.1.2(b) 21–14, 25–03
    r.1.4(1) 43–03
        (2) 43–03
           (b) 16–06
           (d) 16–06
           (f) 10–02, 16–06, 20–02
    Pt 1 31–21
    r.2.3(1) 21–02
    r.2.4 10–08
    r.3.1(2)(a) 21–01
    r.3.1(3) 21–01, 25–11
    rr.3.1(3)–(7) 13–06
    r.3.1(5) 25–11
    r.3.4 32–127
    r.3.9(1)(e) 13–06
    r.3.10 4–12

1998 Civil Procedure Rules—*cont.*
    Pt 3 42–10
    r.6.2(1) 18–11
    r.6.2(1)(e) 18–11
    r.6.3(2) 18–11
    r.6.10 18–11
    Pt 7 35–12
    Pt 8 .... 35–07, 35–12, 35–27, 40–01
    r.19.3 6–53
    r.19.6 4–12
    r.19.6(1) 4–12
    r.19.6(4) 4–12
    r.19.6(4)(a) 4–12
    r.19.6(4)(b) 4–12
    r.19.7 .... 4–12, 31–21, 31–28
    r.19.7(1) 4–12, 31–21
    r.19.7(2) 31–21
    r.19.7(5) 4–12, 31–21
    r.19.7(6) 4–12, 31–21
    r.19.7(7) 4–12, 31–21
    r.19.8A 31–22, 31–28
    r.19.8A(1) 31–22
    r.19.8A(2) 31–22
    r.19.8A(8) 31–22
    r.20.2 16–11
    r.20.2(1) 25–02
    r.20.3(1) 25–02
    Pt 20 .... 25–01, 25–02, 25–03, 25–03, 25–04
    r.21.1(2) 35–04
    r.21.1(2)(a) ... 4–01, 35–01
    r.21.1(3) 35–04
    r.21.2(1) 35–04
    r.21.10 4–04
    r.21.10(1) ... 22–02, 35–05
    r.21.10(2) 22–02
    r.21.10(2)(a) 35–07
    r.21.10(2)(b) 35–07
    r.21.11 22–02
    Pt 21 35–04
    Pt 21 PD 10–22
            para.1.7 .. 35–11
            para.6.1 .. 35–07
    r.23.8 31–30
    r.23.8(a) 10–19
    Pt 23 .... 10–19, 20–02, 21–16, 31–26, 35–50
    Pt 23 PD 10–19, 10–20
            para.5 31–30
            para.10.4   31–30

1998 Civil Procedure Rules—
cont.
    Pt 24 .... 32–13, 39–65
    r.25.1(1)(k) 16–12
    r.25.7(1)(a) 27–56
    r.25.7(1)(b) 27–56
    r.25.7(1)(c) 27–56
    r.26.4 43–04
    r.27.2(1)(g) 25–05
    r.27.14(2) 25–05
    r.27.14(3) 25–05
    r.27.14(4) 25–05
    Pt 28 PD, para.4.1 .. 37–12
    r.31.11 4–12
    r.35.7 4–08
    r.35.8 4–08
    r.35.12(5) 4–08
    r.36.1(1)(b) 14–02
    r.36.1(1)(2) 41–20
    r.36.1(2) 14–02, 14–04,
        18–03, 18–05, 23–11,
        25–04, 35–61, 41–20
    r.36.2 14–02
    r.36.2(1) 18–01
    r.36.2(3) 18–01
    r.36.2(4) 18–01, 18–06
    r.36.2(4)(a) .. 17–01, 18–16
    r.36.2(5) 25–05
    r.36.2A 18–01, 25–10
    r.36.2A(2) 25–10
    r.36.2A(4) 25–10
    r.36.2A(5) ... 25–10, 35–43
    r.36.2A(7) 25–10
    r.36.3 .... 14–03, 18–01
    r.36.3(1) 16–10, 18–01,
        25–02
    r.36.4 21–15
    r.36.4(2) 19–05
    r.36.4(3) 19–05
    r.36.4(4) 19–06
    r.36.4(20) 23–07
    r.36.5(1) 14–03, 16–02
    r.36.5(2) 16–03
    r.36.5(3) 6–57
    r.36.5(3)(a) 16–03
    r.36.5(3)(b) 16–11
    r.36.5(3)(c) 16–06
    r.36.5(4) 14–09, 16–10
    r.36.5(5) 16–12
    r.36.5(6)(a) .. 17–02, 17–05
    r.36.5(6)(b) .. 17–02, 18–06
    r.36.5(6)(b)(ii) 17–04

1998 Civil Procedure Rules—
cont.
    r.36.5(7) 17–02, 17–05
    r.36.5(8) 15–15, 17–03,
        17–05
    r.36.6 .... 25–03, 25–11
    r.36.6(1) 16–03
    r.36.6(2) 6–57, 16–02,
        18–08, 18–11
    r.36.6(2)(b) 16–03
    r.36.6(2)(c) 16–11
    r.36.6(2)(d) 16–12
    r.36.6(2)(e) 16–06
    r.36.6(3) 18–11, 25–12
    r.36.6(4) 18–11
    r.36.6(5) 17–05,18–17
    r.36.7(1) 25–07
    r.36.7(2) 25–07
    r.36.7(3) 25–07
    r.36.7(4) 25–08
    r.36.7(6) 25–09
    r.36.8 14–03
    r.36.8(1) 15–04, 17–02
    r.36.8(2) 18–11
    r.36.8(3) 17–07
    r.36.8(4) 18–11
    r.36.8(5) 21–02
    r.36.9 .... 6–57, 15–04,
        16–11
    r.36.9(1) 20–02
    r.36.9(2) 20–02
    r.36.9(3) 20–02
    r.36.10 ..... 15–03, 15–07,
        18–01
    r.36.10(1) ... 15–01, 17–01
    r.36.10(2)(a) 15–03
    r.36.10(2)(b) 15–03
    r.36.10(2)(c) 15–03
    r.36.10(3) ... 14–03, 15–10
    r.36.10(4) 15–13
    r.36.10(5) 15–03
    r.36.11 15–03
    r.36.11(1) ... 18–14, 21–02
    r.36.11(2) 18–14
    r.36.11(2)(a) 14–11
    r.36.11(2)(b)(ii) 14–11
    r.36.12(1) 21–02
    r.36.12(2) 22–11
    r.36.12(3) 22–11
    r.36.13(1) 21–04
    r.36.13(2) 21–05
    r.36.13(3) 21–04
    r.36.13(4) 21–04

1998 Civil Procedure Rules—
cont.
r.36.14 21–10
r.36.15 14–10
r.36.15(1) ... 21–13, 30–06
r.36.15(2) ... 21–15, 21–16
r.36.15(3) ... 21–06, 21–14
r.36.15(4) 22–03
r.36.15(6) 21–16
r.36.16 21–11
r.36.17(2) 21–07
r.36.17(4) ... 21–08, 22–05
r.36.18(1) 22–02
r.36.18(1)(b) 22–02
r.36.18(2)(a) 22–02
r.36.18(2)(b) 22–02
r.36.19 14–09
r.36.19(1) 14–06
r.36.19(2) ... 14–07, 14–08
r.36.19(3)(a) 14–09
r.36.19(3)(b) 14–10
r.36.19(3)(c) 14–09
r.36.20 ...... 14–05, 17–01
r.36.20(1)(a) 23–02
r.36.20(1)(b) 23–02
r.36.20(2) ... 23–02, 23–03
r.36.21 ..... 13–09, 14–03,
  14–05, 15–07, 17–01,
  23–11, 23–15, 23–16,
  23–20, 23–21, 23–22,
  23–29, 23–31, 23–32
r.36.21(1) ... 23–11, 23–12,
  23–32
r.36.21(2) ... 23–22, 23–12,
  23–14, 23–31
r.36.21(3) ... 23–22, 23–12,
  23–31
r.36.21(3)(a)   23–11, 23–12
r.36.21(3)(b) 23–14
r.36.21(4) ... 23–22, 23–12
r.36.21(5) 23–21
r.36.21(5)(c) 23–29
r.36.21(6) 23–13
r.36.22 16–06
r.36.22(1) 16–06
r.36.22(2) 16–06
r.36.23(2) 18–01
r.36.23(4) 35–54
r.36.51 41–28
Pt 36 .... 9–41, 13–03,
  13–04, 14–01–14–09,
  15–04, 15–07, 15–10,

1998 Civil Procedure Rules—
cont.
Pt 36—cont.
  15–11, 16–01–16–04,
  16–06, 16–08–16–12,
  17–01–17–08,
  18–01–18–04, 18–07,
  18–08, 18–11–18–17,
  19–02, 19–04, 19–05,
  19–06, 20–01, 20–02,
  21–01–21–07, 21–10,
  21–12–21–15,
  22–01–22–06, 22–10,
  22–11, 23–01, 23–02,
  23–04–23–08, 23–10,
  23–11, 23–16, 23–19,
  23–22, 23–29, 23–31,
  24–02, 24–04, 25–03,
  25–04–25–11, 27–55,
  30–06, 35–42, 41–18,
  41–20, 41–28
Pt 36 PD ... 18–01, 18–10,
  18–15, 26–01, 26–02,
  26–03, 26–05, 35–54
Pt 36 PD,
  paras.7.2–7.3 20–02
  para.8.6 21–02
  para.8.7 21–03
  para.8.10 21–12
  paras 9.1–9.4 21–11
  para.9.4 21–07
  para.9.5 21–11
  para.12.3 21–12
  para.12.4 21–12
r.37.2(1) 25–11
r.37.2(2) 25–12
r.37.4(1) 25–12
Pt 37 PD 25–11
r.38.2(2) 40–14
Pt 38 .. 9–36, 31–25, 40–14
r.40.2 6–20
r.40.2(1)(c) 10–17
r.40.3 6–20
r.40.3(1) 6–20
r.40.3(6)(f) 14–09
r.40.6   6–20, 10–20, 10–24,
  21–15, 31–30
r.40.6(2) 6–20, 10–17,
  10–19
r.40.6(3) 10–17, 10–18,
  10–19

1998 Civil Procedure Rules—
cont.
r.40.6(3)(b)(ii) 21–15
r.40.6(5) 10–19
r.40.6(6) 10–19
r.40.7 10–19
r.40.11 .... 5–44, 9–11,
11–22
r.40.11(a) 9–15
r.40.20 31–33
Pt 40 21–15
Pt 40 PD ... 10–02, 10–03,
10–04, 35–48
para.3 31–30
para.8.1 ... 5–44
Pt 40C PD ... 35–49, 35–50
para.4 ... 35–50
para.5 ... 35–50
r.41.5 35–41
r.41.9 35–46
Pt 41 .... 25–09, 35–40
Pt 41 PD, para.4.1 .. 35–28
Pt 41B PD 35–52
r.44.3 .... 18–05, 35–61
r.44.3(2) 22–13, 23–02,
43–08
r.44.3(2)(a) .. 14–02, 34–06
r.44.3(2)(b) 24–03
r.44.3(4) 9–04, 14–02,
20–04, 24–03, 43–08
r.44.3(4)(c) .. 14–09, 15–02,
18–16, 26–03
r.44.3(5) 9–04, 13–07,
14–02, 43–08
r.44.3(5)(a) 13–06
r.44.3(5)(b) 23–10
r.44.3(6) 21–14, 24–03
r.44.3(6)(d) 13–08
r.44.3(6)(g) 13–08
r.44.4 23–17
r.44.4(2) 13–09
r.44.4(3) 13–09
r.44.5 23–17
r.44.12(1)(b) 21–04
r.44.12(1)(c) 21–10
Pt 44 PD,
para.4.4(4) 31–07,
31–09
r.48.5 35–54
Pt 51 PD 35–54
r.52.1(3)(b) 42–11
r.52.3(1) 6–25

1998 Civil Procedure Rules—
cont.
r.52.6(2) 40–27
Pt 52 .... 40–15, 42–09
Pt 52 PD 42–11
para.2.1 42–11
para.8.1 42–09
para.8.10 42–09
para.9.1 42–10
para.12 ... 31–31, 42–11
para.12.4 .. 40–19, 42–04
para.13 42–11
para.13.1 40–19
para.13.3 42–07
Pt 52 PD,
para.13.4 .. 42–06, 42–07
r.54.1(2)(e) 40–01
r.54.5(2) 40–27
r.54.7(b) 40–18
r.54.18 40–29
Pt 54 .... 40–01, 40–14
Pt 54 PD, para.17 .. 40–16,
40–18
r.56.3(2) 37–12
r.57.2(2) 31–01
r.57.5 31–28
r.57.10 31–25
r.57.11(1) 31–25
r.57.11(2) ... 31–25, 31–26
r.57.13(2) 31–01
Pt 57 31–25
Pt 57 PD 31–25, 31–27
Pt 57 PD, para.6.1 .. 31–25,
31–28
Pt 60 39–01
r.62.18(5) 41–06
Pt 62 41–14
r.64.1(3) 31–01
Pt 70 11–05
Sch.1, Ord.44, r.2 .. 31–21,
31–22
Ord.45, r.1 ... 10–10
r.5 ... 10–10
r.8 ... 11–12
1999 Family Proceedings
(Miscellaneous
Amendments) Rules
(SI 1999/1012)
r.4(1)(6) 34–06

1999 Transnational Information and Consultation of Employees Regulations (SI 1999/3323)
　　reg.41 36–21
Family Proceedings (Amendment No.2) Rules (SI 1999/3491) 34–03
2000 Part-time Workers (Prevention of Less Favourable Treatment) Regulations (SI 2000/1551)
　　reg.9 36–21
2001 Court of Protection Rules (SI 2001/824) 35–19
Court of Protection (Enduring Powers of Attorney) Rules (SI 2001/825) 35–22
ACAS Arbitration Scheme (England and Wales) Order (SI 2001/1185) 36–47, 36–49
　　Sch., paras.31–34 ... 36–49
2002 Fixed-term Employees (Prevention of Less Favourable Treatment) Regulations (SI 2002/2034) 36–21
Social Security Amendment (Personal Injury Payments) Regulations (SI 2002/2442) 35–34
National Assistance (Assessment of Resources) (Amendment) (No.2) (England) Regulations (SI 2002/2531) 35–34

2003 Merchant Shipping (Working Time: Inland Waterways) Regulations (SI 2003/0000) 36–21
Employment Equality (Religion or Belief) Regulations (SI 2003/1660) 36–21
Employment Equality (Sexual Orientation) Regulations (SI 2003/1661) 36–21
Regulatory Reform (Business Tenancies) (England and Wales) Order (SI 2003/3096) 37–04, 37–07
　　Sch.1 37–05
　　Sch.2 37–05
　　Sch.3 37–05
　　Sch.4 37–05
2004 Employment Tribunals (Constitution and Rules of Procedure) Regulations (SI 2004/1861)
　　Sch.1, regs 22–24 ... 36–28
European Public Limited-Liability Company Regulations (SI 2004/2326) 36–21
ACAS (Flexible Working) Arbitration Scheme (Great Britain) Order (SI 2004/2333) 36–47
Civil Procedure (Amendment No.3) Rules (SI 2004/3129) 18–01, 35–42
2005 Damages (Variation of Periodical Payments) Order (SI 2005/841) 35–52
　　art.5 35–52

PART 1

Legal Foundation and Consequences of Compromises

CHAPTER 1

Introduction

Compromise can be defined as the settlement of dispute by mutual concession,[1] its essential foundation being the ordinary law of contract. This combined definition and assertion of principle[2] is good for most purposes although it does not comprehend all matters discussed in this work. A more practical and, perhaps, more apt definition would be the complete or partial resolution by agreement of differences[3] before final adjudication by a court or tribunal of competent jurisdiction. However, the search for a suitable definition is, it is suggested, a somewhat barren exercise. Identifying the contexts in which "compromise" operates may be more useful.

1–01

Broadly speaking, compromise occurs most frequently in the private law context[4] where disputes arise between individuals or other legal *personae*. The law is the framework of rules by reference to which disputes are

1–02

---

[1] See *Shorter Oxford Dictionary*. In *Gurney v Grimmer* (1932) 38 Com.Cas. 12 at 18, Lawrence L.J. said that when a matter has been compromised it "assumes that a mutual concession has been made by both parties and that each party has got something less than he claimed". In *Re NFU Development Trust* [1972] 1 W.L.R. 1548 at 1555, Brightman J., as he then was, said that "the word 'compromise' implies some element of accommodation on each side". See also Re *Alabama, New Orleans, Texas and Pacific Junction Railway Co* [1891] 1 Ch.213 at 243. And see Ch.2, below.

[2] Quoted with approval in *Korea Foreign Insurance Company v Omne Re SA*, unreported, April 14, 1999, CA, *per* Evans L.J., noted at para.8–08, below.

[3] "Differences" for this purpose are taken to include differences during the interim stages of litigation. In the Arbitration Act 1996 the expression "dispute" is defined as including "any difference": see Ch.41, below. In *Garlick v Royal Trust Bank*, unreported, February 10, 1999, CA, Peter Gibson L.J. said that it had been undisputed that "a compromise is merely a contract which emerges from the course of negotiations, that there must be some underlying dispute before a true compromise could be said to have emerged [and] that a compromise is designed to bring an end to the dispute . . .".

[4] For the distinction between private and public law remedies, see *O'Reilly v Mackman* [1983] 2 A.C. 237 and *Cocks v Thanet District Council* [1983] 2 A.C. 286. See further the discussion in de Smith and others, *Principles of Judicial Review* (1999), Ch.3. *cf. Roy v Kensington and Chelsea and Westminster Family Practitioner Committee* [1992] 1 A.C. 624; *British Steel Plc v Customs and Excise Commissioners (No.1)* [1997] 2 All E.R. 366; *Trustees of the Dennis Rye Pension Fund v Sheffield City Council* [1998] 1 W.L.R. 840.

resolved. Courts and other tribunals exist for the purpose of administering the law and thereby resolving disputes. Since 1999 a case-managed system of civil justice has been in place, albeit a system based upon an adversarial process. In that adversarial system it is for the parties to bring their disputes before the appropriate forum. Procedural rules govern the form and manner in which disputes are litigated. These are designed to identify and clarify the issues between the parties, to encourage a state of readiness for the trial of those issues and to assist thereby the ultimate resolution of the particular dispute or disputes from which the litigation arose. Subject to the existence of any right of appeal and the pursuit of such an appeal to its conclusion, the decision or judgment of the appropriate tribunal represents the final word on the matter as between the parties. The matter is said to be *res judicata*.[5] It cannot be ventilated again. The only matter which might occasion further recourse to the tribunal is the enforcement of the decision or judgment or some incidental question such as costs. More or less identical consequences follow if the parties choose arbitration to resolve their dispute.[6]

1–03 At any stage of the whole process the parties may draw back from asking the court or other tribunal to adjudicate upon their dispute.[7] They may, by agreement, resolve it themselves. Indeed, they may have resolved it before embarking on any litigious process. Except in certain cases[8] they have complete freedom to do so without interference from the court. Having resolved their dispute in this way it is no less binding upon them and final than if they had asked the court to resolve it for them.[9]

1–04 Whilst in many cases the agreement represents the final resolution of the original dispute, questions can arise on issues such as whether some aspect of the prior negotiations invalidates the compromise, precisely what it means, the manner of its enforcement—and so on. In consequence a body of law, founded essentially on the ordinary law of contract, has grown up with special reference to the situation of parties engaged in, or who have engaged in, the resolution or attempted resolution of their disputes. This constitutes the subject-matter of the law of compromise. The manner in which parties conclude their agreement and the use to which they put the court process to give effect to it, or to set it aside, constitute features of the practice of compromise.

---

[5] The full Latin expression is *res judicata pro veritae accipitur*: a thing adjudicated is received as the truth. See Ch.6, below.
[6] See Ch.41, below.
[7] However, the fact that parties compromise litigation between the conclusion of the trial and before a reserved judgment is given may not necessarily result in the court not handing down the judgment: *Prudential Assurance Co Ltd v McBains Cooper* [2000] 1 W.L.R. 2000, CA.
[8] See, *e.g.* Ch.35, below.
[9] See Ch.6, below.

Compromise is not confined solely to the private law context. The growth of litigation in the public law sector has led inevitably on occasion to situations in which the parties have achieved a complete or partial resolution of the differences leading to that litigation. Whether this is compromise *stricto sensu* is debatable, but it is an area that merits attention.[10]

I–05

---

[10] See Ch.40, below.

CHAPTER 2

Nature of a Dispute

MUST BE A DISPUTE BEFORE A COMPROMISE

2–01 Bearing in mind its essential nature, a compromise in the true sense of the term does not arise until some dispute or difference of view exists between the parties which, by agreement, they resolve.[1] It is not necessary for there to be pending litigation,[2] but there must be some "actual" or "potential" dispute.[3] The meaning to be given to the word "potential" in this context has widened somewhat in recent years.[4]

ACTUAL DISPUTE

2–02 An "actual" dispute will not exist until a claim is asserted by one party which is "disputed" by the other. Where no such dispute about an issue can be discerned, no subsequent agreement between the parties will be found to have compromised that issue.[5] This can be illustrated by a number of examples:

---

[1] See para.1–01, above. There is a close relationship between this proposition and the principle that consideration is required to sustain the validity of a compromise: see, paras 3–07 *et seq.*, below.

[2] *Cook v Wright* (1861) 1 B. & S. 559; *Mercantile Investment and General Trust Co v International Company of Mexico* [1893] 1 Ch. 484 at 494, *per* Lindley L.J.

[3] In two cases concerning alleged compromises of shareholders' rights, it was emphasised by the Court of Appeal that any rearrangement of those rights could not be said to be a true compromise unless a dispute as to those rights or their enforcement existed: *Sneath v Valley Gold Ltd* [1893] 1 Ch. 477; *Mercantile Investment and General Trust Co v International Company of Mexico*, n.2, above. See also *Chapman v Chapman* [1995] A.C. 429, referred to at para.31–18, below.

[4] See paras 2–07 *et seq.*, below.

[5] This issue may also arise in connection with whether a purported "without prejudice" offer is admissible in evidence. If there is no dispute, or no extant dispute, at the time it is made it will not be subject to the "without prejudice" privilege: see paras 27–09 *et seq.*, below.

In *Smith v Smith*,[6] following a divorce, W made two applications to the court in respect of the former matrimonial home: one was under s.17 of the Married Women's Property Act 1882, by virtue of which she claimed a beneficial interest in it; the other was under the divorce jurisdiction by virtue of which she claimed a property adjustment order in relation to it. At that time she made no application for lump sum provision. When the applications came to be heard in April 1971, it transpired that because of certain charges on the house its net value at that time was nil. W abandoned the two applications and acknowledged, as part of a consent order, that she had no beneficial interest in the house. Some two years later, after the house had increased substantially in value, she applied for leave to claim a lump sum, the only source of such a lump sum being the net proceeds of sale of the house. H sought to allege that she was precluded from doing so by virtue of the consent order made in 1971 and said, in effect, that she had agreed as part of the compromise not to seek a lump sum. This argument was rejected on the basis that merely abandoning claims for specific relief in relation to the property could not be construed as agreeing not to claim a lump sum from its proceeds of sale.

2–03

In other words, at the time of the agreement in 1971, W had not asserted a claim for relief by way of lump sum provision and there was thus no "dispute" about it. It follows, therefore, that this claim could not have been compromised.[7]

In other cases a fair analysis of the discussions between the parties may reveal that, whatever other specific differences lie between them, certain matters are not in dispute and may even be admitted. These undisputed and admitted matters cannot thereafter be invested with a contentious character in order to found an argument that they have been the subject of a compromise. This situation arises not infrequently where a sum of money is in truth paid "on account" of some (yet to be determined) final figure and an attempt is then made to suggest that it was tendered or paid "in full and final settlement" of an alleged dispute.[8] The following cases illustrate the way in which the court will react to such a suggestion:

2–04

In *Newton Moor Construction v Charlton*,[9] C did building works for D and submitted a bill for £18,612 comprised of the price for the works originally ordered plus sums for extra items with deductions for items omitted. On October 25, D's solicitors wrote saying that he was prepared to pay £8,847 and set out how this sum was arrived at. The letter indicated that he took the tender amount for the original work (£11,020) and made certain deductions for items omitted. He made a further deduction for some delay which he claimed to be entitled to set off and added a series of sums for extras, two of

2–05

---

[6] (1974) 5 Fam. Law 125, CA. See also *Cloutte v Storey* [1911] 1 Ch. 18, CA.
[7] A party who should have disputed a matter at the time of a compromise reflected in a consent order or judgment may be prevented from disputing it later: see paras 6–07 *et seq.*, below.
[8] This part of this paragraph was cited with approval in *Ferguson v Davies* [1997] 1 All E.R. 315, CA, noted at para.2–07, below.
[9] (1981) C.A.T. 555. And see n.11, below. Also see paras 3–12 *et seq.*, below.

which he said were agreed figures and the remainder at figures he said were reasonable. The letter concluded as follows: "In these circumstances [D] has handed to me for despatch to you a cheque for £8,847 in full and final settlement of your account concerning the work . . . If you are not prepared to accept this payment we have instructions to accept service of any proceedings concerning same. Will you please acknowledge receipt of this letter and cheque".

The cheque was received by C, paid into C's account and met. On October 30, C's solicitors wrote acknowledging the letter and saying this: "With regard to the cheque for £8,847 our clients are accepting this cheque in part payment". In due course C sued for the balance of the bill and was met by the defence that there had been an accord and satisfaction by acceptance of the cheque sent in full and final settlement. The Court of Appeal held that there had been no accord and satisfaction. Sir David Cairns said that the letter of October 25, when properly analysed, was no more than an admission that the sum of £8,847 was due for the reasons set out in the letter. There was, therefore, no consideration "for any agreement that could be said to be implied from the letter of October 25, the cheque and the acceptance of that cheque". Eveleigh L.J. said that the cheque was not accepted on the basis upon which it was offered and the parties were not, therefore, *ad idem*. Lawton L.J. said that there was no evidence of accord and satisfaction.

2–06   In *Neuchatel Asphalte Co Ltd v Barnett*,[10] C, a company with its head office in London, contracted through its Birmingham office to do certain work for D at an agreed price of £250. The total amount charged was £259 to take account of an extra item. After the works were completed D objected to the additional £9 and had some queries in relation to the main works carried out. Initially D sent a cheque for £125 expressly "on account" pending a reply to the queries he had raised. D discussed the queries with C's representative in Birmingham, but they had not been resolved by the time a statement for the outstanding amount of £134 had been sent by the London office. D returned the statement to the London office asking it to liaise with the representative in Birmingham. About a week later, but before the Birmingham representative had dealt with the matter, D sent a letter and a cheque for £75 to C's London office. The letter was as follows: "With further reference to account, in spite of repeated requests for allowance to which I am entitled, you have failed to advise me in this matter. I am therefore enclosing my further cheque for £75 in respect of this work". On the back of the cheque D had typed the words "in full and final settlement of account" and made provision for a signature and date. Upon receipt of the cheque, a secretary indorsed it by rubber stamp over a 2d stamp and signed it. In proceedings brought by C for the balance, D sought to argue that, having presented the cheque for payment,[11] C must be taken to have settled the dispute. One of the facts found by the trial judge was that a reduction of £59 was far greater than any allowance C was likely to grant D in relation to the disputed items. The Court of Appeal held that, having regard to the terms of the letter sent by D with his cheque, it was plain that the £75 was sent on account and not by way of a settlement proposal.

2–07   In *Ferguson v Davies*,[12] C and D entered into a contract whereby C sold his stock of specialist records, tapes and discs to D in return for D's promise to provide C with similar goods up to the value of £600 by a certain date in

---

[10] [1957] 1 W.L.R. 356.
[11] For other cases concerning cheques sent "in full and final settlement", see paras 3–30 *et seq.*, below.
[12] See n.8, above.

default of which D was to pay to C the value of the goods supplied by C in cash. That value was in the region of £1,700. In fact D only delivered goods to the value of £143.50 and made a single payment of £5. C had originally limited his claim to £486.50 (possibly to keep within the small claims jurisdiction) and issued a default summons in Form N1. When Form N1 was sent to D it was accompanied by Form 9B which, *inter alia*, asked the question "How much of the claim do you dispute?". D originally ticked the box "I dispute the full amount claimed", but then crossed the tick out and intialled the erasure. He then ticked the second box opposite "I admit the amount of £ . . ." and inserted £150. D did not complete certain parts of the form that followed, but then answered a later question, "Do you dispute the claim because you have already paid it?", with the answer "Yes, I paid £450 to the plaintiff over this period", giving details of when the sums were paid. This assertion was rejected by the trial judge who found the facts as indicated above. D did send a cheque for £150 to C as he was encouraged to do by Form 9B which indicated that "If [he disputed] part only of the claim [he] must either pay the amount admitted to [C] . . . [and] send this defence to the court" or "complete the . . . admission form and send it to the court with this defence". D wrote two letters on the day he sent the cheque (February 17), one to C enclosing the cheque which he described "as a full payment on the County Court Summons" and expressing the hope that "this will now resolve the matter". The other letter was to the court in which he indicated that he did not dispute the fact that he owed C money, but that he did dispute the amount being claimed. C, who discussed the position with a member of the county court staff, took the view that he was entitled to accept the cheque in part payment of the larger sum and to pursue that larger sum. He presented the cheque and following its clearance he wrote to D informing him that he was proposing to enlarge his claim to a sum in excess of £1500. In due course he was given leave to amend his claim to increase it to £1,745.79. This claim was met by a defence of accord and satisfaction. This was not dealt with as a preliminary point. The judge found that a further £1400 was due to C from D, but held that the presentation for payment of the cheque for £150 compromised the claim and the action failed. The Court of Appeal held that this conclusion was wrong. The sending by D of the cheque for £150 was simply an unequivocal and formal admission of indebtedness and he was not giving C any additional benefit on top. Accordingly (*per* Henry L.J.), there was no consideration for the accord suggested. Evans L.J. expressed no view on the question of lack of consideration, but was unable to interpret D's letter to C as containing an unequivocal offer to pay £150 only upon the basis that, if C accepted it, he would withdraw the balance of the claim. C was entitled to understand D's offer as simply being to the effect that £150 was admittedly due, and was being paid, leaving the balance in dispute.

POTENTIAL DISPUTE

Parties frequently seek to compromise "potential" issues between them even if those issues have not yet been elevated to the status of an actual dispute. A familiar and well-established formula for settling disputes is in the following (or similar) terms: 2–08

"A agrees to accept from B the sum of [figure] in full and final settlement of all claims which he has or may have arising from [the specified incident or other state of affairs."[13]

The intention of wording of this nature is plain. It is intended that the payment should discharge finally all claims that have not merely already been advanced, but also those which might subsequently be advanced in connection with whatever incident or state of affairs had brought the parties into dispute. It follows that the intention of the agreement underlying the use of this formula is that an issue not yet identified or formulated is also to be regarded as comprehended in the settlement. The phraseology has been subjected to judicial scrutiny:

2–09   In *Kitchen Design and Advice Ltd v Lea Valley Water Co*,[14] C sustained damage to its stock, fixtures and fittings at its premises as a result of flooding caused by a burst water main owned by D. C made a claim against its own insurers initially only for the physical damage arising from the flooding and this claim was settled by the insurers for about £18,000. C's insurers, who were subrogated to C's rights against D, sought to recover that sum from D's insurers. After negotiations D's insurers paid C's insurers the sum of £15,000 and the latter signed a form of discharge which expressly stated that the sum of £15,000 was accepted "in full satisfaction, liquidation and discharge of all claims we have or may have against [D] in connection with a burst water main in [place identified] on [date recorded]". Some four months after this agreement was concluded, C advanced to its insurers for the first time a claim for loss of profit in consequence of business interruption. This was settled as between C and its insurers for about £17,000 and C's insurers then sought to claim this from D's insurers. The latter took the point that the entirety of C's claim had been settled by the payment of the sum of £15,000 having regard to the terms of the form of discharge. Phillips J., as he then was, held that D's insurers were correct in this contention. One of the arguments advanced on behalf of C's insurers was that the phrase "all claims we have or may have" meant that the settlement was restricted to claims which C's insurers "either had advanced or were in a position to advance at the time the form of discharge was signed" and that the subject-matter of the agreement "was limited to the claims that were actually discussed" between the insurers' representatives. In relation to these arguments Phillips J. said that the phrase "was clearly designed to cover, not merely claims actually advanced in relation to the burst main, but other claims not advanced which might be advanced".

---

[13] Another form sometimes seen in personal injuries cases is "in settlement [or full and final settlement or full satisfaction and discharge] of all claims, whether now or hereafter to become manifest, arising directly or indirectly from [the defined accident]": see, *e.g. Saunders v Ford Motor Co* [1970] 1 Lloyd's Rep. 379; *Arrale v Costain Civil Engineering Ltd* [1976] 1 Lloyd's Rep. 98, CA. In *Line Trust Corporation Ltd v Fielding*, unreported, July 26, 1999, CA, the provision in the Tomlin order the subject of the argument was in the following terms: "All parties . . . release all claims which they or any of them have or may have against each other in respect of the subject matter of this action or arising out of these proceedings". As Peter Gibson L.J. said, the use of the expression "may have" showed that the settlement comprehended "any future claim".
[14] [1989] 2 Lloyd's Rep. 221.

He went on to say that the fact that the insurers' representatives had only been negotiating in respect of specific items of physical damage "cannot detract from the natural meaning of the phrase . . .".

2–10 It is submitted, with respect, that this approach is clearly correct. The "buying off" of a potential claim has long been recognised as a matter of importance and the courts have never stood in the way of this being achieved in appropriate circumstances.[15]

This approach has been confirmed by the House of Lords as potentially applicable to claims of which the parties could not at the time of the compromise have been aware. It has been said that, in principle and provided the appropriate language is used, a party may be bound by a compromise agreement supported by valuable consideration in which he agrees "to release claims or rights of which he is unaware and of which he could not be aware [and] even claims which could not on the facts known to the parties have been imagined".[16] The phraseology of an agreement giving rise to such a consequence will, of course, depend upon the subject-matter of the dispute giving rise to the agreement and to the general nature of the agreement into which the parties have entered. A clause along the following lines[17] may have efficacy in this regard:

> "This agreement is in full and final settlement of all claims and potential claims of whatsoever nature and kind (including interest, costs and any claims that at the date hereof have not or may not have been foreseen or may not have been capable of being foreseen, either factually or legally, by the parties hereto) which the parties have or may have against each other under or in respect of or arising out of or in connection with, whether directly or indirectly, [*the specified and identified matters giving rise to the dispute*] and without prejudice the generality of the foregoing, the parties hereto agree not to commence or prosecute any proceedings against one another arising out of or in connection with such matters."

2–11 Indeed, the release of an unforeseen claim may be achieved even in circumstances where a formula of the kind to which reference has been made above has not been used expressly by the parties:

---

[15] *cf.* paras 5–18 *et seq.*, below. A submission that a provision such as that referred to in para.2–06, above must satisfy the "reasonableness test" within the Unfair Contract Terms Act 1977 in order to be binding was rejected in *Tudor Grange Holdings Ltd v Citibank NA* [1992] Ch. 53.
[16] *Bank of Credit and Commercial International SA v Ali* [2002] 1 A.C. 251, *per* Lord Bingham of Cornhill, with whom Lord Browne-Wilkinson agreed, at 259. See also Lord Nicholls of Birkenhead at 265 and Lord Clyde at 282. Lord Hoffmann, who dissented in the result, was also of the view that a release could operate effectively to exclude a claim which could not have been foreseen at the time of the release. For further consideration of this case, including the form of the release, see paras 5–23 *et seq.*, below.
[17] Adapted from the clause considered in *Heaton v AXA Equity and Law Life* [2002] 2 A.C. 329. See paras 6–39 *et seq.*, below.

In *Bristow v Grout*,[18] C was injured in an accident in January 1982 in respect of which there was no issue concerning D's liability. C's solicitors wrote to D's insurers indicating that C claimed "damages for the personal injury, losses, expenses and inconvenience arising from the accident". At that stage C's injuries appeared to be confined to his face. After further correspondence, C's solicitors wrote to the insurers saying that C "is prepared to accept your offer in the sum of £1,500" in relation to general damages. In that letter there was further reference to certain expenses and disbursements and also to special damages. After further correspondence C's solicitors wrote again confirming that C was prepared to accept general damages "already agreed at £1,500 together with special damages in the sum of £147 comprising examination fees £12, telephone calls £15 and the travelling expenses. The overall settlement figure is therefore £1,647 . . . subject to payment of costs. . .". The letter indicated that the costs were £565.01. The next day D's insurers sent two cheques to C's solicitors for £1,647 and £565.01 respectively, both of which were presented and met. At that time, unbeknown to C, he was beginning to suffer from a condition of the hip possibly attributable to the accident. In 1985 a consultant orthopaedic surgeon concluded that his symptoms, which by then had substantially increased, were as a result of the accident. The Court of Appeal held that C was not entitled to seek damages either for the "original" injuries or the further symptoms since it was plain that the agreement was intended to be in full and final settlement of his claim in negligence for personal injuries arising out of the accident in January 1982 which was the claim made in the letter before action. May L.J. said that it was "quite clear . . . that [C] cannot in subsequent proceedings be heard to say that, as a result of the accident and claim so compromised, he in fact sustained further damage of which he was earlier unaware".

THE UNARTICULATED DISPUTE?

2–12 It has been suggested above[19] that the absence of a dispute, actual or potential, precludes the emergence of a compromise in its true sense. An actual dispute[20] will invariably be articulated expressly by the parties. Even a potential dispute[21] will be articulated expressly in the sense that the parties will have identified the essential legal and factual matrix or substratum from which the potential dispute might arise.[22] Andrews[23] has contended for what is arguably a third situation, namely, one where parties

---

[18] (1987) C.A.T. 1134; *The Times*, November 9, 1987, CA. See also *O'Boyle v Leiper*, *The Times*, January 26, 1990, CA.
[19] See paras 2–01 *et seq.*, above.
[20] See paras 2–02—2–07, above.
[21] See paras 2–08—2–11, above.
[22] In a straightforward personal injury case, for example, the parties will identify the material accident and the overall claim for damages (as was done in *Bristow v Grout*: see para.2–11, above). By settling all claims that the claimant has or may have the parties have expressly articulated the potential existence of claims going beyond those actually formulated at the time of the settlement: *Kitchen Design and Advice Ltd v Lea Valley Water Co*: see para.2–09, above.
[23] N.H. Andrews, "Mistaken settlement of disputable claims" (1989) 4 L.M.C.L.Q. 431.

reach an agreement "without [having spelt] out a dispute, [but sensing] that an underlying problem might grow into a fully articulated disagreement".[24]

The distinction between this situation and that of a compromise of a potential dispute as previously defined[25] is, it is thought, that no "underlying problem" has been contemplated by the parties in respect of the latter: each has effectively said to the other "If there is something arising from the state of affairs that brought us into dispute which we have not yet identified, we expressly forego any further claims or counterclaims arising therefrom". In the former situation each party is effectively recognising internally that some dispute might emerge from the shadows, but neither has raised it expressly with the other or in a way that identifies the area in shadow. Andrews argues[26] that an agreement reached in such a situation should be characterised as an "implied settlement", the word "settlement" being preferred to "compromise" because of the latter's association with the need for disputation to exist before a compromise can be said to have arisen. An "implied settlement" is defined as one where an agreement is made "in circumstances of doubt", a classic example being afforded by the payment made by an insurer to an insured who has made a claim under the contract of insurance between them. The payment made by the insurer is generally to be regarded as closing the matter[27] even if possible disputes as to the liability to make payment exist, albeit in unarticulated form. 2–13

For many practical purposes the distinction between the compromise of a potential dispute and an implied settlement as defined[28] would be of no great importance: the law will strive to uphold an agreement plainly designed to bring to an end any latent disputation between the parties. The difficulty with the foregoing formulation of an implied settlement is that it does not sit happily with a number of well-established authorities.[29] It is submitted that the existence of an actual or potential dispute remains the foundation of a true compromise and that settlements of claims under insurance policies need to be seen as a category of their own,[30] whilst recognising that in many such cases a true compromise of a disputed liability will take place and in others something closely analogous thereto will result. Since it is now clear that even "unimagined" claims (which, by definition, could not have been articulated so as to give rise to a dispute at the time of the compromise[31]) can be the subject of a compromise, there 2–14

---

[24] *ibid.*, p.437.
[25] See n.22, above.
[26] Andrews, n.23, above.
[27] *cf. Woolwich Building Society v IRC* [1993] A.C. 70 at 165, *per* Lord Goff of Chieveley.
[28] See para.2–13, above.
[29] For example *Magee v Pennine Insurance Co* [1969] 2 Q.B. 507 and *Huddersfield Banking Co v Lister* [1895] 2 Ch. 273, referred to at paras 4–19 and 4–20, below. And see Andrews, n.23, above, pp.445–449.
[30] See para.30–18, below.
[31] See para.2–10, above.

can be no doubt that unarticulated disputes may be the subject of a true compromise.

Law or fact

2–15 A dispute may involve questions of law or fact or a combination of both. The disputation may be conducted orally or by written communications and within or outwith the context of litigation.

2–16 The assertions, denials and counter-assertions comprising the dispute need have no foundation in fact or in law provided they are made in good faith.[32] If a party to a compromise attempts to escape its consequences by alleging that the claim had no legal or factual foundation, the court will decline to investigate such an allegation.[33] In many cases, for example, a claimant will allege the fact of the defendant's negligence which the defendant denies. The law does not permit a defendant who has compromised a claimant's claim for damages based on the alleged negligence subsequently to pursue the suggestion that he was not in fact negligent for the purpose of avoiding the compromise. Not infrequently, in cases between landlord and tenant, the tenant will seek to claim damages for the failure of the landlord to effect certain external repairs in breach of an alleged implied covenant to that effect. In many situations no such covenant is implied by law and yet the landlord might, for example, reduce his own claim for arrears of rent against the tenant because of the tenant's claim. He would not be permitted subsequently to allege that the compromise of the rent claim should be set aside because the tenant's claim was unfounded in law.

2–17 In *Binder v Alachouzos*,[34] D borrowed a total of £65,000 from C, relatives of C and companies with which C was closely associated. D gave cheques by way of repayment of the loans and agreed interest, but the cheques were not met. The various lenders commenced actions against D on the dishonoured cheques. In his defence, D alleged that the loans were made in the course of carrying on the business of moneylending and were void and unenforceable. Shortly before the trial of those actions an agreement was reached which provided, *inter alia*, that the actions should be discontinued and that D should

---

[32] The proposition in the text should not be confused with the principle that a fundamental mistake, going to the root of the compromise itself, may vitiate the compromise: see Ch.4, below. For proviso as to good faith, see para.2–19, below.
[33] For example *Huddersfield Banking Co v Lister* [1895] 2 Ch. 273 at 278 (fact); *Holsworthy UDC v Holsworthy RDC* [1907] 2 Ch. 62 at 73 (law). See also *Norfolk Finance Ltd v Newton*, unreported, October 15, 1998, CA.
[34] [1972] 2 Q.B. 151. See also *Panyiatou v Sony Music Entertainment (UK) Ltd*, The Times, June 30, 1994.

pay C the sum of £86,565, with interest at 18 per cent, by instalments of £10,000 per month payable on a particular day each month. It was further expressly agreed by D that:

(a) none of the transactions the subject of the actions was a transaction to which the Moneylenders Acts applied; and
(b) no defence should be raised in any action on the agreement other than as to the quantum of the moneys that had been paid.

D paid two or three instalments and then defaulted. In C's action to recover the balance of the sums owing under the agreement, D sought to raise again the issue of the Moneylenders Acts and suggested that the compromise was not binding. The Court of Appeal held that he was not entitled to put forward these arguments since there had been a bona fide compromise of an issue of fact in the previous action, namely whether the original loans were unlawful moneylending transactions.

In *Colchester Borough Council v Smith*,[35] C and D had been in dispute about D's occupation of certain land. D had asserted through his solicitors that he had acquired possessory title to the land, an assertion rejected by C. In due course, after further correspondence and a threat by C to bring possession proceedings, D entered into a tenancy agreement in relation to the land and, as part of that agreement, he acknowledged that he had "not gained any right title or interest to or in it by adverse possession". That agreement was made in November 1983. In November 1984 C instituted proceedings seeking possession of the land relying upon the terms of the tenancy agreement. In those proceedings D sought to argue, *inter alia*, that he had acquired possessory title to the land. At first instance it was held on the evidence that D had, prior to the tenancy agreement, acquired possessory title to certain parts of the land, but that he was estopped by contract or convention from disputing C's title to it having regard to the agreement. The Court of Appeal held, following *Binder v Alachouzos*, that there had been a bona fide compromise of a disputed issue in the agreement of November 1983 and that D was prevented from going behind it.

2–18

Must be bona fide

A want of good faith in the assertion of a claim or the maintenance of a denial, in circumstances where there is no foundation in fact or law to support them, may operate to invalidate a compromise founded thereon.[36] It would seem that provided a claimant believes that he has a right to make the claim he asserts, even if he has little confidence in its ultimate success, a compromise of it is valid.[37] If, on the other hand, he makes a claim which

2–19

---

[35] [1992] Ch. 421.
[36] *Callisher v Bischoffsheim* (1869) L.R. 5 Q.B. 449; *Re Blythe Ex p. Banner* (1881) 17 Ch.D. 480; *Holsworthy UDC v Holsworthy RDC* [1907] 2 Ch. 62; *Binder v Alachouzos* [1972] 2 Q.B. 151.
[37] *Callisher v Bischoffsheim*, n.36, above; *Re Blyth Ex p. Banner*, n.36, above. In *Freedman v Union Group plc* [1997] E.G.C.S. 28, Peter Gibson L.J. said that it is "common for a person genuinely to believe in the rightness of a claim, but still to harbour doubts whether it would in fact succeed".

he knows to be unfounded and derives an advantage from its compromise, his conduct will be considered fraudulent and the compromise liable to be set aside.[38] In the former case the compromise will be upheld even if the party against whom the claim is made believes that it has no foundation. By compromising it, he puts an end to troublesome litigation.[39] In the latter case, however, if the lack of foundation of a claim is known by the other party, any agreement purporting to be based upon it cannot truly be said to be a compromise since no real dispute as such exists. The legal effect of such an agreement will often arise in connection with third party rights.[40] As between the parties it may be operative.[41]

---

[38] *Callisher v Bischoffsheim*, n.36, above, *per* Cockburn C.J. at 452; *Wade v Simeon* (1846) 2 C.B. 548. See Ch.4, below.
[39] See Ch.3, below.
[40] See Ch.6, below.
[41] *ibid*. On the one hand, it could be argued that, since no consideration is furnished by either party, the apparent agreement is a *nudum pactum*; on the other hand, the agreement may be seen simply as the equivalent of a release of an "unimagined" claim: *cf.* n.31, above.

CHAPTER 3

Essential Requirements of a Valid Compromise

INTRODUCTION

Since a compromise is merely a contract, the ordinary principles of contract law apply with as much force as in other contractual contexts. Under the ordinary law a contract will not be found to have arisen unless: 3–01

   (i) consideration exists[1];
   (ii) an agreement can be identified which is complete and certain;
   (iii) the parties intend to create legal relations; and
   (iv) in some cases, certain formalities have been observed.[2]

The significance of each of these requirements in the context of compromise will be examined briefly.

CONSIDERATION

The usual approach to consideration under the general law is to define it as the accrual of some benefit to one party or the suffering of some detriment by the other.[3] Consideration may consist of the exchange of mutual promises or the performance by one party of an act in return for a promise by the other to do some act.[4] In standard terminology, consideration must "move from the promisee".[5] 3–02

---

[1] Except, of course, in cases of contracts under seal.
[2] *Chitty on Contracts* (29th ed., 2004), Vol.1, Chs 2 and 4.
[3] *Currie v Misa* (1875) L.R. 10 Ex. 153 at 162, *per* Lush J.
[4] *Chitty on Contracts* (29th ed., 2004), Vol.1, para.3–008.
[5] *ibid.* paras 3–036 *et seq*. It need not, but usually does, "move to the promisor".

Promised or actual forbearance to sue

3-03 In compromise, consideration is often furnished by the promised or actual forbearance of one party to pursue a claim against another in return for some promised or actual act by the other.[6] Such act may constitute a benefit to the claimant or a detriment to the performer or indeed both. The promised or actual forbearance may be for a specified time or, where no time is specified, for a reasonable time.[7]

3-04   An example of a promised forbearance is afforded by a situation in which in return for a promise by a creditor to forbear from taking immediate proceedings on a debt, the debtor promises to create, or actually creates, a charge on his house in favour of the creditor for the amount of the debt.[8] The respective benefits and detriments are obvious.

3-05   An example of an actual forbearance arises where a creditor forbears in fact from taking immediate proceedings on a debt, though not in pursuance of an express promise to that effect, on the basis of which the debtor promises to create a charge on his house for the amount of the debt. The actual forbearance is said to constitute the consideration for the debtor's promise.[9] But it must be referable to the debtor's promise[10] and arise (probably[11]) from an express or implied request therefor by him:

3-06   In *Combe v Combe*,[12] H, following a divorce, promised W permanent alimony at the rate of £100 per annum. When he failed to keep his promise, W sought to enforce it as an agreement arguing, *inter alia*, that she had given the consideration for it by her forbearance to take proceedings for maintenance. The Court of Appeal held, on this argument, that the alleged consideration did not exist because H had not requested W, expressly or impliedly, to forbear from taking proceedings and the actual forbearance could not be said to be referable to H's promise.[13]

---

[6] Any doubt concerning the efficacy of a promise as constituting good consideration was resolved by the decision in *British Russian Gazette and Trade Outlook Ltd v Associated Newspapers Ltd* [1933] 2 K.B. 616. A promised or actual forbearance from pursuing a claim against a third party in return for a promised or actual act by another party will furnish good consideration (*cf. Oliver v Davis* [1949] 2 K.B. 727 at 743) although the doctrine of privity of contract may preclude the third party from enforcing the agreement thus reached: see Ch.6, below.
[7] *Fullerton v Provincial Bank of Ireland* [1903] A.C. 309 at 313.
[8] *cf. Wigan v England & Scottish Law Life Assurance Association* [1909] 1 Ch. 291 at 297–298.
[9] See *Alliance Bank v Broom* (1864) 2 Drew & Sm. 289; *Re Wyvern Developments* [1974] 1 W.L.R. 1097 at 1103–1104; *cf.* the majority of the Court of Appeal in *Miles v New Zealand Alford Estate Co* (1886) 32 Ch.D. 26 and the suggested distinction between it and the *Alliance Bank* case in *Chitty on Contracts* (29th ed., 2004), Vol.1, para.3–057.
[10] *Combe v Combe* [1951] 2 K.B. 215; *Wigan v English and Scottish Law Life Assurance Association* [1909] 1 Ch. 291.
[11] *Combe v Combe* n.10, above; *Fullerton v Provincial Bank of Ireland* n.7, above; *cf. Alliance Bank v Broom* n.9, above.
[12] See n.10, above.
[13] Even if W had agreed not to proceed for maintenance as a direct result of a request by H, public policy would have prevented enforcement of the agreement: see *per* Asquith L.J. at p.226 and see Ch.32, below.

Compromise proper

The emphasis of the foregoing discussion has been upon situations where the promised or actual forbearance to sue has been met by an act which was not itself a promised or actual forbearance to raise some defence to the intended claim, or to pursue some counterclaim. However, such matters manifestly represent good consideration for the original claimant's promised or actual forbearance to sue. In this situation, where consideration of this nature "moves each way", one can legitimately say that a contract of compromise has been concluded by the parties. The nature of the consideration has been described judicially thus: 3–07

> "Every day a compromise is effected on the grounds that the party making it has a chance of succeeding in it, and if he bona fide believes he has a fair chance of success, he has a reasonable ground for suing, and his forbearance to sue will constitute a good consideration. When such a person forbears to sue he gives up what he believes to be a right of action, and the other party gets an advantage, and, instead of being annoyed with an action, he escapes from the vexations incident to it . . .".[14] 3–08

> ". . . if an intending litigant bona fide forbears a right to litigate a question of law or fact which it is not vexatious or frivolous to litigate, he does give up something of value. It is a mistake to suppose it is not an advantage, which a suitor is capable of appreciating, to be able to litigate his claim, even if he turns out to be wrong. It seems to me it is equally a mistake to suppose that it is not sometimes a disadvantage to a man to have to defend an action even if in the end he succeeds in his defence; and I think therefore that the reality of the claim which is given up must be measured, not by the state of the law as it is ultimately discovered to be, but by the state of the knowledge of the person who at the time has to judge and make the concession. Otherwise you would have to try the whole cause to know if the man had a right to compromise it."[15] 3–09

No consideration

In the normal course of events the adequacy of the consideration given or received is not open to question.[16] Since, however, consideration must be real, there are circumstances in which the court will decline to uphold the existence of a consideration that apparently exists. 3–10

---

[14] *Callisher v Bischoffsheim* (1870) L.R. 5 Q.B. 449 at 452, *per* Cockburn C.J.
[15] *Miles v New Zealand Alford Estate Co* (1885) 32 Ch.D. 266 at 291, *per* Bowen L.J. See the analysis of the facts in *Technocrats International Inc v Fredic Ltd* [2004] EWHC 692 (QB) at [30]–[33].
[16] *Chitty on Contracts* (29th ed., 2004), Vol.1, paras 3–014—3–021. See also *Stephens v Bateman* (1778) 1 Bro.C.C. 22 and *Naylor v Winch* (1824) 1 Sim. and St. 555.

3-11 **Baseless, frivolous, vexatious or illegal claim.** From the authorities already referred to, it would seem that a forbearance from pursuing a claim:

(a) known by the claimant to be baseless[17]; or
(b) which is vexatious or frivolous,[18]

would constitute no consideration for a compromise based upon it. Equally, a forbearance to pursue an illegal claim, for example one made illegal by the Gaming Act 1845, would represent no consideration.[19] So too a forbearance which itself is prohibited by law or is contrary to public policy is no consideration.[20]

3-12 **Existing debts and part payment thereof.** The general law of contract provides that past consideration is no consideration unless given at the request of the promisor.[21] It has already been noted[22] that an actual forbearance to sue will constitute consideration only if afforded at the request of the debtor. Thus, an actual abstention from pursuing an existing debt will be good consideration for some promise of the debtor, for example to give security for it, only if it results from some express or implied request therefor.

3-13 It should be recalled in this context that, in general terms, an agreement to accept part payment of a debt or liquidated demand is not binding because no consideration is furnished by the debtor.[23] This would seem to be so even if, as a matter of fact, the creditor is content to avoid the process of litigation with a view to securing the money indisputably due to him.[24] If, however, the debtor gives something other than mere part payment of the debt, for example he pays at a different time or place or in a different currency, sufficient consideration is furnished.[25] There are, furthermore, a number of exceptions to the general rule expressed above and the doctrine of equitable estoppel may intervene to protect the debtor.[26] An agreement of the nature under discussion may not, perhaps, in any event be regarded as a compromise in the true sense of the term. There is no dispute settled by mutual concession.[27]

---

[17] See para.2-19, above.
[18] See n.15, above.
[19] *Hyams v Coombes* (1912) 28 T.L.R. 413; *Burrell & Son v Leven* (1926) 42 T.L.R. 407; *Poteliakhoff v Teakle* [1938] 2 K.B. 816. See *Chitty on Contracts* (29th ed., 2004), Vol.1, para.3-166; and see Ch.4, below.
[20] For example Matrimonial Causes Act 1973, s.34, discussed in Ch.32, below.
[21] *Chitty on Contracts* (29th ed., 2004), Vol.1, paras 3-029 *et seq.*
[22] See paras 3-03 *et seq.*, above.
[23] *Foakes v Beer* (1884) 9 App.Cas. 605; *D. & C. Builders Ltd v Rees* [1966] 2 Q.B. 617.
[24] *cf.* paras 3-07—3-09, above.
[25] *Chitty on Contracts* (29th ed., 2004), Vol.1, para.3-122.
[26] *ibid.*, paras 3-128—3-136.
[27] See para.1-01, above.

In *Tiney Engineering Ltd v Amods Knitting Machines Ltd*,[28] C and D engaged **3–14**
in a transaction involving the sale of a knitting machine. C's case was that it
had been agreed that upon sale of the machine a commission of 10 per cent of
the price should be paid. D's case was that 5 per cent was the agreed
percentage. The sale went through and C submitted an invoice to D on the
basis of 10 per cent. A meeting took place at which C's representative
initialled the invoice, which had been amended to 5 per cent commission,
underneath the words "accepted in full and final settlement". £3,000 was then
paid immediately, but C thereafter claimed the balance of a commission based
on 10 per cent. It was found as a fact at the trial that the original agreement
had been that a 10 per cent commission would be paid. The Court of Appeal
held that, on the facts found, a sum based upon a 10 per cent commission was
admittedly due and all that was given when the sum of £3,000 was paid was
part payment of that sum. There was, accordingly, no consideration for the
agreement to accept the lesser sum and C was entitled to the balance.

In *Arrale v Costain Civil Engineering Ltd*,[29] C was injured in an accident **3–15**
when employed by D in the building of a harbour wall at Dubai in the Persian
Gulf, as a result of which his left arm had to be amputated. According to the
Workmen's Compensation Ordnance of the Trucial States 1965, which was
operative in Dubai, C was entitled to a fixed sum of money (calculated by
reference to a schedule) by way of compensation for his injuries. A provision
of the Ordnance entitled D, if they elected to do so, to seek to prove "to the
Court that [C] deliberately contravened instructions issued to safeguard his
health and person or displayed serious negligence in executing those instructions", whereupon C would not have been entitled to compensation under the
Ordnance. As a matter of policy D had decided not to rely on this provision.
The sterling equivalent of the sum to which C thus became entitled was £490.
This sum was paid to C upon C signing a receipt acknowledging that the sum
was accepted "in full satisfaction and discharge of all claims in respect of
personal injury whether now or hereafter to become manifest arising directly
or indirectly from" the accident. C thereafter sought to pursue a claim for
compensation at common law. D argued that C could not do so having regard
to the terms of the receipt. The Court of Appeal held that C was entitled to
proceed. The majority[30] held that the receipt, on its true construction, did not
operate to exclude the common law claim.[31] All members of the court held
that if the receipt did so operate, D had given no consideration for any such
agreement. Lord Denning M.R.[32] appeared to equate the position with
accepting a lesser sum in discharge of a greater sum, drawing attention to the
fact that D had paid C the exact sum to which he was entitled under the
Ordnance. However, he did go on to suggest that this was a conclusion that
could only be reached if the two claims were "to be regarded as severed into
two or combined into one" which, he continued, "would be a poor way of
deciding whether an agreement is binding". He preferred to regard the
position as one of inequality of bargaining power, where no one had explained

---

[28] (1986) C.A.T. 440; [1987] C.L.Y. 412. In *Ferguson v Davies*, referred to in para.2–07, above, Henry L.J. (with whom Aldous L.J. agreed) based his decision upon the ground that no consideration was furnished by D.
[29] [1976] 1 Lloyd's Rep. 98, CA.
[30] Lord Denning M.R. and Stephenson L.J.
[31] This aspect of the decision is noted further in paras 5–32 and 5–34, below.
[32] [1976] Lloyd's Rep 98 at 102.

to C that he might have a claim at common law, and thus one in which there could have been no agreement to bargain away the common law claim. Geoffrey Lane L.J. (as he then was), having taken the view that C had promised not to sue at common law, said that D gave no consideration because:

> (a) by paying the sum under the Ordnance, they were doing no more than performing an obligation already cast upon them by law; and
> (b) having decided in this case never to invoke the provision referred to above, they gave nothing up in this regard in return for C's promise.[33]

On the issue of consideration Stephenson L.J. agreed with the reasons given by Lord Denning M.R. and Geoffrey Lane L.J., but was not prepared to regard it as a case of inequality of bargaining power having regard to certain findings of fact made by the trial judge.[34]

3–16 *Arrale's* case is a difficult one in some respects, particularly having regard to the differing judicial views and emphases on the various issues canvassed.[35] On the question of consideration, it is submitted, with respect, that the first reason given by Geoffrey Lane L.J. (with which Stephenson L.J. agreed) is the most persuasive and most consistent with ordinary contractual principles.[36] The second reason is also consistent with the principle that illusory consideration is no consideration,[37] but there are features of this principle that require further examination in the context of compromise.[38]

3–17 There are other examples in the reported cases of situations where this issue has arisen for consideration:

> In *Re Broderick*,[39] the Inland Revenue obtained judgment for nearly £14,000 and costs against B on the basis of an assessment to tax. Shortly after issuing enforcement proceedings, B's solicitors asked the Revenue for, and were granted, eight weeks to arrange settlement. Some two weeks later B's solicitors sent a "without prejudice" letter to the Revenue stating that B was in a position to make an offer of £7,500 in settlement of the amount due. The Revenue replied saying that the amount offered would be accepted without prejudice, but that B's proposals for clearing the balance would be expected within about two months. Shortly before the expiration of the deadline for

---

[33] *ibid.*, at 106.
[34] *ibid.*, at 104–105. Any reference in the judgments to the principle of "inequality of bargaining power" must be read in the light of *National Westminster Bank plc v Morgan* [1985] A.C. 686 at 708.
[35] It was referred to without disapproval in the narrative of relevant cases by Lord Bingham of Cornhill in *Bank of Credit and Commercial International SA v Ali* [2002] 1 A.C. 251 at [16]. See further at paras 5–23 *et seq.*, below.
[36] *Chitty on Contracts* (29th ed., 2004), Vol.1, paras 3–121 *et seq. cf. Williams v Roffey Bros and Nicholls (Contractors) Ltd* [1991] 1 Q.B. 1, CA.
[37] *Chitty on Contracts* (29th ed., 2004), Vol.1, para.3–023.
[38] See para.3–17, below.
[39] [1986] 6 N.I.J.B. 36.

these further proposals, B's solicitors sent a cheque for £7,500 "in full and final settlement of all monies due" in the enforcement proceedings. The cheque was presented and paid into an Inland Revenue account. A few days later the Revenue wrote to B's solicitors asking for proposals as to the balance. In subsequent bankruptcy proceedings B contended that there had been an accord and satisfaction. Carswell J. held that:

(i) there had been no accord and satisfaction[40]; and
(ii) if there had been an agreement to accept £7,500 in settlement, there was no consideration for that agreement.

3-18 In *Re Selectomove*[41] S Company was in debt to the Inland Revenue for unpaid PAYE and NIC. Discussions took place in about July 1991 as to how the debt might be discharged. S Company contended that it had been agreed in those discussions that the Revenue would take no action on the debt in return for a promise that payment of the debt would be made by instalments of £1,000 per month from February 1992 together with future PAYE and NIC contributions as they fell due. Payments were made pursuant to the alleged agreement, although some were late, until the Revenue demanded payment of the debt in full and presented a winding-up petition. It was contended on S Company's behalf that, since the Revenue would have received a practical benefit from receiving the instalment payments, there was good consideration for the Revenue's alleged promise not to enforce the debt. The Court of Appeal held that, although the facts did not support the existence of the alleged promise, even if they had done so this argument had to be rejected because it had been raised and rejected by the House of Lords in *Foakes v Beer*.[42]

3-19 **Intention to pursue claim?** One final matter arises in the context of the question whether consideration exists to support a compromise. Does a person who bona fide sets up a claim against another, but who does not in fact intend to pursue it to court, furnish consideration by "forbearing" from pursuing it? An example would be afforded where, say, an elderly lady is injured as the result of another person's alleged negligence and is advised by her legal advisers that she has a reasonable case for claiming damages. Although she is prepared for her solicitors to intimate a claim, and even commence proceedings on her behalf, in the hope that some offer of compromise is made, because of her age and fear of giving evidence in court she is firm in her intention of not pursuing the claim to court. Assuming such facts to be susceptible of proof, would any compromise of the apparent claim be considered a nullity on the basis that she had furnished no consideration?

---

[40] See paras 3-32 *et seq.*, below.
[41] [1995] 1 W.L.R. 474. See Peel, "Part Payment of a debt is no consideration" (1994) 110 L.Q.R. 353.
[42] See n.23, above.

3-20   There is some authority[43] to suggest that no consideration is furnished in such a situation. In *Arrale*'s case[44] one basis for the Court of Appeal's decision was that since the defendants had no intention of raising a form of defence to one part of the plaintiff's overall claim, they were not entitled to say that by not raising it they had furnished consideration for his promise not to pursue the rest of his claim.[45] It is submitted that this was a plainly correct analysis of the situation in that case and reflects the principle that illusory consideration is no consideration.[46] However, it is not thought that this establishes (any more than do the other authorities) that an intention to pursue a claim (or, of course, a defence) to court must be maintained throughout the period until a compromise is concluded. Indeed, other authority[47] suggests that the "reality of the claim made and the bona fides of the compromise" represents the real consideration.

3-21   It is submitted that the better view is that consideration is furnished in a situation such as that described. It might fairly be regarded as furnished by the giving up of the right on the part of the claimant to a change of heart about not proceeding, such right existing, of course, until the expiration of the relevant limitation period or until the claim is dismissed for want of prosecution. Needless to say, the potential defendant "buys off" the risk of such a change of heart although he will probably regard it as "buying off" an intended claim.[48] Perhaps the correct view is that a person is entitled to pursue a bona fide claim to the point of compromise and that thereafter his intention to pursue the claim to court cannot be called into question.

AN IDENTIFIABLE AGREEMENT

General

3-22   In many instances the existence of a compromise will not be in doubt. Usually it will be found in, or evidenced by, an exchange of correspondence, a written memorandum of agreement or a consent order or

---

[43] *Miles v New Zealand Alford Estate Co* (1886) L.R. 32 Ch.D. 266 at 291, *per* Bowen L.J. who refers to an "intending litigant"; in *Cook v Wright* (1861) 1 B. & S. 559 at 569 reference is made to a claim which is "bona fide intended to pursue". See also *Syros Shipping Co SA v Elaghill Trading Co; The Proodos C* [1980] 2 Lloyd's Rep. 390 at 392.
[44] See n.29, above.
[45] "It is no consideration to refrain from a course of action which it was never intended to pursue": *ibid.*, *per* Geoffrey Lane L.J. at 106.
[46] See n.37, above.
[47] *Cook v Wright* (1861) 1 B. & S. 559 at 570, *per* Blackburn J.; adopted by Fry L.J. in *Miles v New Zealand Alford Co* (1886) 32 Ch.D. 266.
[48] In *Garlick v Royal Trust Bank*, unreported, February 10, 1999, the Court of Appeal quoted the view expressed in the text without express approval, but equally without express disapproval. In the circumstances of that case it was said that there was "no evidence that [D] had decided not to proceed, or never intended to proceed" in relation to the particular matter in dispute.

judgment. However, there may be circumstances in which it is difficult to discern whether the parties have in fact concluded an agreement. The essential task is to determine whether the parties' negotiations have crystallised into a contractually binding agreement. In order to achieve this the traditional approach, applying an objective test, is to seek to identify a definite offer by one party and a definite acceptance of that offer by the other party.[49] It is not proposed to consider the refinements of this approach in this work.[50] Some examples taken from cases involving compromise will be considered below. Each involves the exercise of construing objectively the parties' negotiations.[51]

The court will look at the whole course of the negotiations to see whether agreement is reached at any point.[52] If such a point is identified, the mere fact that negotiations are continued thereafter will not of itself affect the existence of the agreement already concluded.[53] If the continued negotiations disclose an agreed rescission of that agreement then the position is different.[54]

Some examples

Binding agreements. In the following cases, the court concluded that a binding compromise had been achieved: 3–23

> In *Shears v Shears*,[55] during the pendency of proceedings brought by W under s.17 of the Married Womens' Property Act 1882, solicitors; letters to the following effect were exchanged:
>
> (a) from W indicating that she would be prepared to accept £500 as one lump sum in settlement of her claim, expressing the hope that H would do everything possible to raise the sum so that the matter could be disposed of once and for all;
>
> (b) a reply from H indicating that he would be able to raise £500 "within the next two months", but indicating that he needed time to make arrangements, and inviting W's solicitors to take instructions;

---

[49] This traditional approach may not always be that helpful: see *New Zealand Shipping Co Ltd v A.M. Satterthwaite & Co Ltd* [1975] A.C. 154 at 167, *per* Lord Wilberforce; *Butler Machine Tool v Ex-Cell-O. Corpn (England)* [1979] 1 W.L.R. 401 at 404, *per* Lord Denning M.R. But see *Gibson v Manchester City Council* [1979] 1 W.L.R. 294, HL.
[50] See *Chitty on Contracts* (29th ed., 2004), Vol.1, Ch.2.
[51] The objective nature of the exercise is exemplified in *O.T. Africa Line Ltd v Vickers Plc* [1996] 1 Lloyd's Rep. 700, where Mance J., as he then was, held that D was bound by an agreement arising from acceptance by C of a mistaken offer of £150,000 in settlement made by D's solicitor when D's intention was that $155,000 should be offered. See para.4–28, below. See also *Huyton SA v Peter Cremer GMBH & Co* [1999] 1 Lloyd's Rep. 620; referred to at para.4–61, n.45 below.
[52] *Hussey v Horne-Payne* (1879) 4 App. Cas. 311; *Shears v Shears* (1973) C.A.T. 288; *Bushwall Properties Ltd v Vortex Properties Ltd* [1976] 1 W.L.R. 591, CA.
[53] *James Miller & Partners Ltd v Whitworth Street Estates (Manchester) Ltd* [1970] A.C. 583. See also *Chitty on Contracts* (29th ed., 2004), Vol.1, para.2–026.
[54] *Davies v Sweet* [1962] 2 Q.B. 300; *Shears v Shears*, n.55, below.
[55] (1973) C.A.T. 288.

(c) from W saying that she would accept £500 cash and "appreciates it may take a few weeks to raise that amount";

(d) a number of letters from H thereafter asking if (but not insisting that) W would accept a £50 reduction on account of some liability of the parties to a third party.

The Court of Appeal held, construing the correspondence as a whole, that a concluded agreement that W would accept £500 in full settlement of her claim to be paid "within a reasonable time" of (c) could be discerned.

3–24   In *Capon v Evans*,[56] C was involved in a road traffic accident for which D was responsible. C's car was damaged and she also sustained personal injuries. The damage to her car was covered by her own insurance policy, but the claims she wished to advance for loss of use of the car and for her personal injuries represented uninsured losses. D was not covered by a policy of insurance in relation to this accident. C instructed solicitors to pursue her uninsured losses, her insurers having met the cost of repairing the damage to her car. C's insurers sought to recover their outlay (some £1,646) from D separately. D instructed solicitors to deal with the claims being made against him and correspondence ensued between those solicitors, on the one hand, and C's solicitors and C's insurers, on the other. The following material letters passed:

March 2—D's solicitors wrote to C's insurers saying that they would like to discuss "the question of your outlay and [C'S] claim for uninsured losses". They asked whether they should communicate with the insurers or C's solicitors in this regard.

March 4—C's insurers replied saying that D's solicitors should communicate with C's solicitors concerning the uninsured losses and with them (the insurers) regarding their outlay.

March 9—D's solicitors wrote:

(a) to C's solicitors expressing their understanding that they (C's solicitors) were communicating with other insurers as agents for the Motor Insurers Bureau in connection with the personal injury claims and asked for details of the other uninsured losses; and
(b) C's insurers asking for details of their outlay.

March 12—C's insurers wrote to D's solicitors giving the figure of £1,646 as their outlay.

March 31—C's solicitors replied to (a) above indicating that hiring charges for an alternative vehicle represented the only uninsured losses being pursued against D which were not covered by the Motor Insurers Bureau.

June 3—D's solicitors wrote to C's solicitors offering a sum in respect of vehicle hire. (The letter did not purport to deal with anything else.)

July 6—D's solicitors wrote to C's insurers disputing the quantum of their outlay, but indicating that D would be prepared to discharge whatever liability he may have to them by instalment payments.

---

[56] (1986) C.A.T. 413; [1987] C.L.Y. 413.

August 12—C's solicitors replied to D's solicitors' letter of June 3, saying that C would be prepared to "concede a proportion of the hire charges and would accept £100 plus VAT towards those charges". The letter concluded with these words: "If the above is acceptable to your client, we can say that there will be no other claim by our client on yours arising out of this accident".

September 17—D's solicitors wrote back to C's solicitors indicating acceptance of the proposal in the letter of August 12, "on the basis that there will be no other claim by your client on ours arising out of this accident". In this letter they sent a cheque for £115 (*i.e.* £100 plus VAT) which they asked C's solicitors to hold to their order until C had signed a form of "receipt and indemnity" which acknowledged that the sum of £115 was "in full and final settlement of all . . . claims against [D] arising from the motor accident . . .". The form of receipt was duly signed and the cheque presented and met.

In due course C's insurers sought to pursue their outlay against D and were met by the defence that there had been an accord and satisfaction in respect of all C's losses, including the insured losses. On the trial of the preliminary point, the trial judge held that there had been no compromise of the insured losses and in arriving at that conclusion he had received evidence concerning C's state of mind when effecting the settlement with D. The Court of Appeal also held that there had been no settlement of the insured losses, but said that C's "subjective understanding as to the effect of the words used [in the settlement agreement] . . . cannot have been relevant and admissible evidence, in the absence of any plea of mistake or rectification". It was further held that the agreement was not to be found solely in the receipt but it comprised of: 3–25

(a) the offer in the letter of August 12;
(b) the counter-offer in the letter of September 17; and
(c) the acceptance of that counter-offer by the signing of the receipt and the acceptance of the cheque.

The letter of August 12 dealt solely with C's uninsured losses relating to hiring charges and prior thereto D's solicitors had been "manifestly content to treat the [claim for damage to the car] as being the claim of the insurers themselves", something evidenced by the previous correspondence. It was said that "a reasonable person, standing in the shoes of the offeree, would reasonably have construed the offer in the letter of September 17 . . . in the same sense as [C'S] solicitors' letter of August 12, . . . namely that it related to the uninsured losses only".[57] It was permissible to look at the letter enclosing the receipt to determine its true effect.[58]

---

[57] Relying upon *Reardon Smith Line Ltd v Yngvar Hansen-Tangen* [1976] 1 W.L.R. 989 at 996–997.
[58] Relying on *Neuchatel Asphalte Co Ltd v Barnett* [1957] 1 W.L.R. 356, noted at para.2-06, above.

3–26   In *Tomlin v Standard Telephones and Cables Ltd*,[59] C sustained injuries on board D's ship in an accident in June 1964. Negotiations ensued between C's solicitor and D's insurers before proceedings were issued. In a letter from the insurers to C's solicitor they said that they were "only prepared to deal with the case on a 50/50 basis" and then went on to make an offer of a specific sum of money. C's solicitor replied in these terms: "Whilst, as you appreciate, I take the opposite view . . . on the question of liability, my client has instructed me to say that he will agree to settle his case on a 50/50 basis as you propose and accordingly this leaves only the question of quantum to be disposed of". There was no letter subsequent to that letter in which the proposition of liability being agreed on a 50/50 basis was accepted specifically. However, there were letters from D's insurers thereafter referring to the "50/50 agreement come to between us for settlement of this claim" and to the effect that it had been agreed that it was a "50/50 case". The suggestion that all that was left was quantum was never rejected or controverted in the subsequent correspondence. The Court of Appeal[60] held that a concluded agreement on the issue of liability had been reached, the counter-offer contained in the letter from C's solicitor having been accepted by the course of correspondence thereafter. Sir Gordon Willmer said[61] that "[O]n the whole . . . those repeated recitals of the existence of an agreement can be, and should be, construed as an acceptance of [C's] counter-offer".[62]

3–27 **No binding agreement.** In the following case no binding agreement was found:

In *Azzarito v Pinkett & Eastern British Road Services Ltd*,[63] there were written negotiations between C's solicitors and D's insurers concerning C's personal injuries claim. D's solicitors offered "£800 inclusive in full and final settlement of your client's claim", after stating that they considered special damages to be approximately £384 and general damages to be £400. C's solicitors replied saying that their client "is prepared to accept £800 plus our costs herein in settlement of this claim".

They then indicated a precise figure for costs and the constituent elements of that sum. D's solicitors replied sending a cheque for £800 "in full and final settlement of his claim" and raised a query as to one of the constituent elements of the costs figure. After further correspondence, D's solicitors said

---

[59] [1969] 1 W.L.R. 1378. This case is further referred to in para.27–20, below, concerning the circumstances in which the "without prejudice" veil can be lifted. An interesting contrast to this decision, in which part of a dispute was held to have been compromised, is afforded by *Bunge SA v Kruse* [1980] 2 Lloyd's Rep. 142, CA; affirming [1977] 1 Lloyd's Rep. 492. In that case, an issue arose as to whether the whole or merely part of a commercial dispute had been compromised. The Court of Appeal held that the commercial background to the negotiations showed that the whole dispute was intended to be compromised even though the literal interpretation of the telexes constituting the agreement did not suggest this.
[60] Danckwerts L.J. and Sir Gordon Willmer; Ormrod J. dissenting on the construction of the correspondence.
[61] [1969] 1 W.L.R. 1378 at 1387.
[62] The correspondence carried the suggestion that there had been some telephone contact between C's solicitor and the insurers although there was no evidence of this. In the absence of such evidence, the acceptance of the offer can best be seen as one manifested by conduct: see *Chitty on Contracts* (29th ed., 2004), Vol.1, para.2–028.
[63] (1979) C.A.T. 628. See also para.3–50, below.

that they would be prepared to agree a lesser sum for costs than the figure suggested by C's solicitors. By then, C had decided not to accept the sum offered, and the cheque for £800, which had not been cashed, was returned. The Court of Appeal held that the correspondence, on its true construction, did not give rise to an agreement by C to be bound by the figure of £800 for his damages. His solicitors' first letter amounted to a counter-offer to the effect that he was prepared to accept £800 plus the specified figure for costs in full and final settlement of his claim. That counter-offer was never accepted by D's insurers.

In *Ferguson v Davies*,[64] Evans L.J. held that C was entitled to treat the sending by D of the cheque for £150 as merely being in respect of an undisputed amount and not as an unequivocal offer of a sum in final settlement of the whole of C's claim. 3–28

In *Cherkas v F & P Barretta*,[65] D, floor contractors, did flooring work at C's property. C raised complaints about the work, which D disputed. Arrangements were made for D to return to the property to carry out remedial works. D alleged that they had agreed to do this in order to resolve all outstanding issues. C, however, asserted that they had agreed to D's return, but not so as to preclude them from seeking to recover from D their outlay in terms of costs arising from the investigation and pursuit of their complaints. The correspondence between the parties' solicitors that preceded D's return to the property indicated that D did not wish to contribute to C's outlay, but that whilst C were happy for D to return, they wanted reimbursement of their outlay. The Court of Appeal held that there was no binding agreement of compromise. 3–29

Presentation of cheque sent in settlement

The issue. A question that frequently arises in this context is whether the presentation of a cheque sent "in full and final settlement" of a dispute amounts to an unqualified acceptance of the offer reflected in the sending of that cheque on those terms. The question is often posed on the basis of whether the presentation of the cheque for payment constitutes an "accord and satisfaction" of the disputed claim.[66] Having regard to the classic definition of "accord and satisfaction",[67] and indeed to the ordinary contractual principles reflected in that definition, the issue is more accurately stated as being confined initially to whether an accord has been 3–30

---

[64] See para.2–07, above and nn.69 and 80, below. See also *Clarke v Nationwide Building Society* (1998) 76 P. & C.R. D5, where the sending of a cheque purportedly "in full and final settlement" was held to be merely a gesture of goodwill.
[65] Unreported, May 12, 2000 (Buxton L.J. and Hooper J.).
[66] See, *e.g. Auriema Ltd v Haigh and Ringrose Ltd* at para.3–42, below.
[67] "Accord and satisfaction is the purchase of a release from an obligation whether arising under a contract or tort or by means of any valuable consideration, not being the actual performance of the obligation itself. The accord is the agreement by which the obligation is discharged. The satisfaction is the consideration which makes the agreement operative": *British Russian Gazette and Trade Outlook Ltd v Associated Newspapers Ltd* [1933] 2 K.B. 616 at 643.

reached in the circumstances, satisfaction depending on whether acceptance of the cheque *per se* is sufficient or whether payment on presentation of the cheque is required.[68]

Whether an "accord" has been reached depends on whether, construed objectively, the actions of the recipient of the cheque constitute acceptance of the offer reflected in the sending of the cheque. Before this issue arises for determination two preliminary matters may need to be considered:[69]

3–31 *(i) Cheque must be offered in "full and final settlement".* The evidence must show that a definite offer has been made to settle on a "full and final" basis. Without this no question of an equivalent acceptance on that basis can arise.

> In *Rustenburg Platinum Mines Ltd and Johnson Matthey and Matthey Bishop Inc v South African Airways and Pan American World Airways Inc*,[70] C were the owners of two boxes of platinum which were flown into Heathrow Airport from South Africa by D1 and were due to be flown to the United States by D2. Whilst the boxes were in the effective custody of D2, one was stolen. C sought the value of the lost platinum (about £60,000) from their insurers who, in due course, made claims against D1 and D2. By a letter, D2 authorised D1 to settle the claim and advised them that they (D2) regarded their maximum liability to be about £200 having regard to the terms of the Warsaw Convention. A few weeks later D1 sent a cheque in that sum to C's insurers' agents, informing them of the terms of D2's letter. On the reverse side of the cheque was a short printed form of receipt including the words "In payment of claim TC 1546/70". The agents forwarded the cheque to C's insurers who signed the receipt and banked the cheque. In the insurers' subsequent subrogated action to recover the full amount of the claim, D2 contended, *inter alia*, that the claim had been settled by the signing of the receipt and the acceptance of the cheque. Ackner J. (as he then was) held[71] that D1's letter to C's insurers' agent did not constitute an unequivocal offer for the full and final settlement of C's claim. The Court of Appeal confirmed this view. Sir David Cairns said[72] that "[v]ery clear words would be needed to show that an offer of [£200] was to be understood as an offer to settle a claim amounting to [£60,000]. . . . The only possible offer was [D1's letter to C's insurers' agents], and this did not make it at all plain that the [£200] was offered in full and final settlement".

3–32 *(ii) Cheque offered "in full and final settlement" must seek to settle a dispute.* The need for there to have been an actual or potential dispute before a compromise can be said to have arisen has been noted pre-

---

[68] There is a presumption that a payment made by cheque is conditional on the cheque being honoured, but the presumption can be rebutted by showing an express or implied intention that the cheque is taken in total satisfaction of the relevant liability: *Re Charge Card Services Ltd* [1989] Ch. 417; *Chitty on Contracts* (29th ed., 2004), Vol.1, para.21–074. An interesting question that might arise in this context is whether an offeree of a cheque sent "in full and final settlement", and who decides to present the cheque, thereby binds himself to the amount proffered on the cheque as the settlement sum in the event of it being dishonoured. Provided there is nothing in the circumstances to displace the foregoing presumption, it is thought that he would not be so bound.
[69] These two issues may merge in some circumstances: see, *e.g. Ferguson v Davies*, *per* Evans L.J., referred to in para.2–07 and n.28, above.
[70] [1979] 1 Lloyd's Rep. 19, CA.
[71] [1977] 1 Lloyd's Rep. 564, Commercial Ct.
[72] [1979] 1 Lloyd's Rep. 19 at 25, CA.

viously.[73] If a cheque is sent purporting to be "in full and final settlement" of something, but the background shows the sending of the same merely to constitute an admission that the amount on the cheque is owing, the question of whether there has been an overall settlement will not arise. This was the situation in *Newton Moor Construction Ltd v Charlton*[74] and *Neuchatel Asphalte Co Ltd v Barnett*.[75]

How is the issue determined? On the assumption that an offer "in full and final settlement" of some real dispute is clearly made at the time the cheque is sent, will its acceptance and/or presentation amount to an acceptance of the offer? 3–33

(a) Fact or law? Despite a comment of Lord Denning M.R. in one case to the contrary,[76] the balance of authority supports the proposition that neither of these acts of itself, as a matter of law, constitutes an acceptance. Whether there has been an "accord" by virtue of the acceptance and/or presentation of the cheque is a question of fact determined on the evidence in each case where the issue arises. Many years ago the matter was put authoritatively in this way[77]:

> "If a person sends a sum of money on the terms that it is to be taken, if at all, in satisfaction of a larger claim; and if the money is kept, it is a question of fact as to the terms upon which it is so kept. Accord and satisfaction imply an agreement to take the money in satisfaction of the claim in respect of which it is sent. If accord is a question of agreement, there must be either two minds agreeing or one of the two persons acting in such a way as to induce the other to think that the money is taken in satisfaction of the claim, and to cause him to act upon that view. In either case it is a question of fact."

In *Bunge SA v Kruse*[78] Lord Denning M.R. said of the foregoing passage: 3–34

> "I do not agree [that the question of accord and satisfaction is one of fact]. At any rate, when everything is on paper, in the telexes and correspondence between the parties, it is a question of law."

This comment has been the subject of further analysis by the Court of Appeal in two subsequent cases. In *Pereira v Inspirations East Ltd*[79] Rose L.J. (with whom Glidewell and Nolan L.JJ. agreed) said this:

---

[73] See Ch.2, paras 2–01 *et seq.*, above
[74] Certainly so far as Sir David Cairns was concerned: see para.2–05, above.
[75] See para.2–06, above.
[76] See n.78, below.
[77] *Day v McLea* (1889) 22 Q.B.D. 610 as 613, *per* Bowen L.J. Lord Esher M.R. gave a judgment to the same effect (at 612–613) and Fry L.J. (at 613) agreed that the earlier unreported case of *Miller v Davies* was conclusive on the issue.
[78] [1977] 1 Lloyd's Rep. 492 at 495.
[79] (1992) C.A.T. 1048. See para.3–44, below.

"For my part, save in relation to analysis of the matter as being a question of law or fact, I do not see anything in Lord Denning's judgment which is inconsistent with the approach of Bowen L.J. in *Day v McLea*. In any event, it seems to me that although ultimately whether there is accord and satisfaction must be a matter of law, equally clearly, the resolution of that legal question must depend upon the facts of the particular case."

Further, in *Stour Valley Builders v Stuart*[80] Lloyd L.J., as he then was, having referred to the final sentence of the quotation from Lord Denning's judgment referred to above, said this:

"The qualification is important. The construction of correspondence is always a question of law. But there is nothing in *Bunge v Kruse* to support the view that accord and satisfaction is a question of law in every case . . . *Day v McLea* has not, in my opinion, been qualified by *Bunge v Kruse* except in the sense which I have already mentioned in relation to negotiations conducted in writing."[81]

3–35 *(b) The resolution of the issue of fact.* Since the issue is one of fact then, unless there is some irrebuttable presumption that the acceptance and/or presentation of such a cheque is to be taken as acceptance of the terms upon which it is offered, each case will depend upon its own facts. It is clear from the authorities already referred to and from those further cases to which reference will be made below, that no such irrebuttable presumption operates: if such a presumption were to operate it would effectively negate the rejection by the courts of the proposition that acceptance and/or presentation of the cheque itself constitutes acceptance as a matter of law.[82]

3–36 The starting point for addressing the analysis of the facts in any case where the issue falls for consideration is that an objective construction must be placed on the material events:

---

[80] (1992) C.A.T. 1281; *Independent*, February 9, 1993; noted at para.3–40, below. See also *Ferguson v Davies*, referred to in para.2–07, above, *per* Evans L.J. at 325.

[81] It is not thought that there is any significant conflict between the views of the Court of Appeal in *Pereira* and those expressed in *Stour Valley Builders*. If there is, some interesting questions of precedent would arise. The judgment in *Pereira* was given on November 9, 1992, some six weeks before the judgment in *Stour Valley Builders*. The former case was not cited in the latter, but equally the earlier Court of Appeal decision in *Neuchatel Asphalte Co Ltd v Burnett* [1957] 1 W.L.R. 356 (to which decision Denning L.J. was a party) in which *Day v McLea* was cited and relied upon by Morris L.J., was not cited in *Pereira*. The *Neuchatel Asphalte* decision was cited and relied upon in *Stour Valley Builders*.

[82] In *Pereira*, Rose L.J. said that "Any presumption that might otherwise have arisen that payment of the cheque into the Plaintiff's bank account . . . gave rise to an inference that he was accepting the Defendant's offer was plainly rebutted by him simultaneously sending his letter to the Defendants".

In *Bell v Galynski and Kings (A.) Loft Extensions*,[83] C lived in a semi-detached house. D1 either lived in or controlled the other half of the building. C became aware that damage had occurred to the party wall in his loft and that certain rubble had been deposited on the insulating material covering the floor of the loft, as a result of loft conversion works carried out in D1's part of the building by D2. C informed D1's solicitors that he held D1 responsible and said that he would forward the account for the remedial works in due course. He also notified them that he would additionally claim compensation for "any further deterioration of my property due . . . to the development work already carried out". The account for the remedial works was subsequently sent and C sought reimbursement. In his letter C expressly made his claim "without prejudice to any further claim which might result from the building work affixed to my property". D2 sent a cheque to C for the amount of the account under cover of a letter which stated that it was sent "in full and final settlement of your claim against [D1] with regard to damage caused to party wall". Some three weeks later, and before the cheque had been cleared through C's bank, D2 wrote advising C that they would not be held responsible "for any further claims for any damage allegedly arising due to construction of the loft conversion unless we are allowed to inspect such 'alleged damage' prior to repair". Thereafter the cheque was cleared. In due course C sought to claim from D1 and D2 further damages arising from the original loft conversion works and the issue arose as to whether any such claim had been compromised by the acceptance of the cheque.

The Court of Appeal held that such claim had indeed been compromised. Since the cheque was tendered "in full and final settlement" and C did not make clear his intention at that stage of claiming further compensation, his action "in clearing the cheque without any demur or further qualification must be regarded as excluding him from prosecuting a further claim for alleged additional damage caused [by D1 and D2]" (*per* Edmund Davies L.J.). Megaw L.J. emphasised that the words and actions of C must be judged objectively and without regard to what C may have intended and understood.

The approach thus adopted to this particular question would seem to be that the presentation for payment of a cheque tendered "in full and final settlement" of a dispute, without demur or qualification, will be taken as an objective manifestation of an intention to accept the offer of settlement thus made. This approach is further illustrated by the following cases: 3–37

In *Upfield v Marshall*,[84] the parties were in dispute about the balance due under an outstanding account. D wrote to C enclosing a cheque for £167 "in full and final settlement of the work done so far and the items supplied to date". C paid in the cheque and issued no response to the letter for seven weeks when solicitors he had instructed in the meantime wrote saying that the sum was not accepted "in full and final settlement".

The Court of Appeal held that the payment in of the cheque amounted to an acceptance of the offer and there was a binding agreement. (The agree-

---

[83] [1974] 2 Lloyd's Rep. 13, CA. See also *per* Lloyd L.J. in *Stour Valley Builders v Stuart*: "As with any other bilateral contract, what matters is not what the creditor himself intends but what, by his words and conduct, he has led the other party as a reasonable person . . . to believe".
[84] (1976) C.A.T. 142.

ment, of course, related only to the matters which were then in dispute, *i.e.* "the work done so far and the items supplied to date".)

3–38   In *Merkuria Foreign Trade Corporation v Dateline Electric Company Ltd and Dateline International Ltd*,[85] D1 sent to C a cheque for £6,696 under cover of a letter of July 4, 1975 expressed to be "in full and final settlement" of any claims against D2 and, in effect, said that if the cheque was presented to D2's bank in Jersey it would be cleared pursuant to the terms of the letter enclosing the cheque. That letter had been preceded by a telex making the same offer and a further letter to the same effect was sent on July 17, 1975. C did present the cheque for payment and it was cleared on July 23. Subsequently, C sought to argue that it had received the money merely as part payment of its claim. The Court of Appeal rejected this argument: *per* Stephenson L.J.: "they did not qualify or seek to qualify in any way, as they could have done, the terms under which they were accepting it. They did not say 'We are accepting it without prejudice to other claims'; they did not say 'We are accepting it on account'"; *per* Robert Goff L.J.: "by paying the cheque into their bank account without in any way objecting that they were not receiving it on those terms [*i.e.* in the letter] the plaintiffs clearly bound themselves by those terms".

3–39   In each of the foregoing cases there was a clearly definable and not insignificant delay between the receipt of and/or the payment in of the cheque and the subsequent manifestation of an intention not to accept the proceeds of the cheque other than as part payment. In *Bell v Galynski*[86] the plaintiff had retained the cheque for over three weeks and thereafter paid it into his bank. The question arises of whether there is any clear dividing line between those cases where the delay is not sufficient to give rise to the inference of acceptance, and those where it is. The answer was provided by Lloyd L.J. in *Stour Valley Builders v Stuart*[87]:

> "Cashing the cheque is always strong evidence of acceptance, especially if it is not accompanied by immediate rejection of the offer. Retention of the cheque without rejection is also strong evidence of acceptance depending on the length of the delay. But neither of these factors are conclusive; and it would . . . be artificial to draw a hard and fast line between cases where the payment is accompanied by immediate rejection of the offer and cases where objection comes within a day or a few days."

3–40   In that case, C, a small firm of builders, carried out some work for D at his home. On July 5, 1991 C sent D an itemised bill which showed an amount of £10,204 after certain payments on account had been taken into account. D queried a number of items which had been charged as extras and complained about other items for which he claimed compensation. On July 18, C sent a

---

[85] (1979) C.A.T. 413.
[86] See para.3–36, above.
[87] See n.80, above.

detailed reply in which it was accepted that there had been some very minor errors in the original account. The revised account came to £10,163. On July 23 D sent a detailed reply, the amount in dispute being about £3,000. D made an offer to settle in the sum of £8,471 in the following terms:

> "I am prepared to settle this matter now. I am enclosing a cheque in full and final settlement of all charges for £8,471. This figure includes all charges, compensation, savings and does not leave any retention outstanding."

The cheque arrived on July 25, and one of C's proprietors (C1) gave it to his secretary to pay in. He spoke to his fellow proprietor the same day and contacted his solicitor the following day, sending him the papers. On July 29, the cheque had been cleared. On July 31, the solicitor advised C1 by telephone and C1 then spoke to D on the telephone saying that the cheque could not be accepted in full and final settlement. D asked why the cheque had been paid in and C1 said he needed the money. On August 1, C wrote a letter before action claiming the difference between £8,471 and £10,163. The judge found as a fact that there had been no agreement between the parties that the cheque was to be accepted in full and final satisfaction of C's claim. The Court of Appeal held that this finding was open to the judge on the facts and would not be disturbed. It was held that the judge had asked himself the correct question, namely whether what C had done had caused D to think that the money had been taken in satisfaction of the claim and that he was entitled, on the evidence, to conclude that it did not.

The following also illustrate circumstances in which the court has held that no accord could be discerned: 3–41

> In *Day v McLea*,[88] C was claiming a considerable sum from D. Before proceedings were commenced D sent a cheque for £102 18s 6d, being less than the amount claimed, stating that it was in full satisfaction of all demands and enclosing a form of receipt to be signed by C in those terms. C replied saying that the cheque was taken "on account" and had been placed to D's credit, a receipt on account being sent together with a request for the balance of the claim. The Court of Appeal held that, the matter being one of fact, the judge had been entitled to conclude that there had been no accord and satisfaction.

> In *Auriema Ltd v Haigh and Ringrose Ltd*,[89] D contracted with T to install high-level alarms for spheres at T's oil refinery. D subcontracted the supply of the detectors to C for a total sum of just over £9,900. Following the supply and installation of the alarms a dispute arose between C and D. D alleged that they had incurred expenses of £5,205 because of defects in the detectors. C denied liability for these expenses, the basis for this denial of liability being set out in a detailed letter. This detailed letter did not come to the attention of the person within D who wrote to C in the following terms: 3–42

>> "In order that this matter may be concluded we enclose a cheque to cover the differences between [the contract sum which C claimed and the sum of

---

[88] (1889) 22 Q.B.D. 610.
[89] (1988) 4 Const. L.J. 200.

£5,205]. Your banking of the cheque will be taken as acceptance of our proposal as full and final settlement and we would waive the right to pursue further costs."

C replied in the following terms: "We have accepted this payment as part-payment towards our invoice [for the full amount of the claim] . . . and do not accept the suggestion that this was in full and final settlement of our invoice". That letter appears to have been written on the day the cheque was banked. His Honour Judge James Fox-Andrews Q.C., Official Referee, held that there was evidence, in the form of C's letter in reply, that C did not intend to accept the offer and that there had not been the necessary accord: "If the cheque had been banked without demur or qualification by [C], that would have been compelling evidence that [C] intended to accept [D'S] offer".

3–43   In *Re Broderick*,[90] the principal ground for the decision was that the essential element for an accord and satisfaction was missing as there was no agreement between the minds of the parties, and the Inland Revenue had done nothing to induce B's solicitors to think that the money was taken in satisfaction of the claim.

3–44   In *Pereira v Inspirations East Ltd*,[91] C booked a touring holiday through D, travel agents. The holiday took place in December 1989. C did not regard the holiday as successful and upon his return made various complaints to D. He asked D to refund his money "plus costs and losses". By a letter of January 6, 1990 D sent a cheque for £225 to C "in full and final settlement of this matter". On March 24, 1990, C paid the cheque into his bank account and sent a letter to D dated January 11, 1990, saying that the cheque was "accepted on account", claiming the balance of the monies he had paid to D and indicating that he was awaiting D's "revised offer in short course". The letter did not say that C was paying the cheque into his account. C's letter was received by D on March 26, 1990 and the cheque was cleared by debit of D's bank account on March 27, 1990, after 3pm. The Court of Appeal held that, assessing C's conduct objectively, the simultaneous sending of the letter with the payment of the cheque into his bank showed clearly that he was not accepting D's offer.

3–45 **The American rule.** The balance of authority in the United States is that "[as] a matter of law, the use or retention of [a cheque sent on condition that it is accepted in full and final settlement of a dispute] by the creditor, with knowledge of the condition, is regarded as an assent to it".[92] The contention that this rule applies (or should apply) in the English courts has been rejected twice by the Court of Appeal.[93] The advantage of certainty that the operation of the rule would bring has been acknowledged. Lloyd L.J. said this in *Stour Valley Builders v Stuart*[94]:

---

[90] [1986] 6 N.I.J.B. 36; [1987] C.L.Y. 2644; discussed at para.3–17, above.
[91] See n.79, above.
[92] *Williston on Contracts* (3rd ed.), para.1854; *Hudson v Yonkers Fruit Co* (1932) 179 North Eastern Reps. 373.
[93] It was rejected explicitly in *Stour Valley Builders v Stuart* and implicitly in *Pereira v Inspirations East Ltd*.
[94] (1992) C.A.T. 1281, *Independent*, February 9, 1993.

"I can see the advantages of having such a rule. But there are analytical and conceptual difficulties. Accord and satisfaction depends on the debtor establishing an agreement between the parties whereby the creditor undertakes for valuable consideration to accept a sum less than the amount of his claim . . . If the creditor at the very moment of paying in the cheque makes clear that he is not assenting to the condition imposed by the debtor, how can it be said that, objectively, he has accepted the debtor's offer?"

The debate about which approach is the better one and which is more consistent with established contractual principles[95] highlights two classic confrontations: first, that between the objective and subjective analyses of a set of facts; secondly, that between the need for certainty in the law (particularly in commercial dealings) and the desire for flexibility to meet the perceived justice of a particular situation. As things stand, the English courts have elected for the flexibility that is denied by the American rule. That flexibility enables the court in appropriate circumstances to prevent advantage being taken by a debtor of the precarious financial situation of the creditor. Cash flow is the lifeblood of many small businesses and the sending of a cheque for a lesser sum than the claim purporting to be "in full and final settlement", may, in reality, be no more than an attempt to put pressure on the creditor in need of an immediate injection of revenue.

Conversion of the cheque or its proceeds. A consequence of the American rule[96] is that the recipient of a cheque sent in full and final settlement who banks that cheque in violation of the condition imposed by the sender is guilty of converting the cheque or its proceeds.[97] That the same legal consequence may flow from the same factual situation under the English law appears to have been acknowledged by the English courts.[98] Whilst in *Pereira v Inspirations East Ltd*[99] the Court of Appeal appeared to accept that where the facts of a particular case supported the conclusion that a conversion had taken place,[1] that conclusion may have a bearing on the overall legal consequences in *Stour Valley Builders v Stuart*[2] the contrary view was taken. Lloyd L.J. said this:

3–46

3–47

---

[95] See, *e.g.* David Andrews, "Cheques sent in settlement" (1991) 13 C.J.Q. 7.
[96] See para.3–45, above.
[97] *Hudson v Yonkers Fruit Co* (1932) 179 North Eastern Reps. 373 at 375, *per* Cardozo C.J.
[98] *Pereira v Inspirations East Ltd* (1992) C.A.T. 1048, where, on the facts, the Court of Appeal suggested that "the highest that . . . it can be put against [C] . . . is that the paying in of the cheque by him may have been *attempted conversion*" (author's emphasis). Whilst the chose in action that is evidenced by the existence of a cheque cannot be converted, the cheque itself can and the true owner can recover the full extent of any loss thus occasioned: *Clerk and Lindsell on Torts* (18th ed., 2000), paras 22–35 *et seq.*
[99] See n.98, above.
[1] For example where the recipient of the cheque pays it in before communicating to the sender his intention merely to accept it on account, thus depriving the sender of the opportunity of stopping the cheque. In this situation Nolan L.J. said that "other considerations might well have arisen".
[2] See n.80, above.

> "[D] argues that by paying in the cheque . . . with knowledge of the conditions attached to the payment, the creditor acts unlawfully. But suppose he does; suppose the payment in is a conversion of the cheque or its proceeds. How does that help the debtor to establish that the creditor has accepted the condition which the debtor imposed?"

3-48   The only answer that can be given to the question posed by Lloyd L.J. in the passage referred to is that, by acting unlawfully, the creditor disentitles himself from contending that he accepted the cheque on a different basis from that on which it was offered.[3] However, there is a circularity about the argument which, it is submitted, is broken by concentrating, as the English courts do, on whether an accord (a meeting of minds) has been established. Whilst that factual issue remains at the forefront of the court's consideration, it is respectfully submitted that Lloyd L.J.'s approach in the *Stour Valley* case is correct and logical and that whether conversion has occurred in the circumstances plays no part in determining the outcome of that issue.[4]

A COMPLETE AND CERTAIN AGREEMENT

General principle

3-49   Although it may be possible to distill a form of agreement from the parties' negotiations, the agreement may not be sufficiently complete or certain to enable it to be upheld by the court. The position under the general law of contract has been stated thus:

> ". . . unless all the material terms of the contract are agreed there is no binding obligation. An agreement to agree in future is not a contract; nor is there a contract if a material term is neither settled nor implied by law and the document contains no machinery for ascertaining it".[5]

Failure to agree all material terms

3-50   Where it is plain that a material element in the negotiations remains unresolved, the court is likely to hold that no concluded agreement has been achieved because a material term has not been agreed.

---

[3] cf. *Homeguard Products (NZ) Ltd v Kiwi Packaging Ltd* [1981] 2 N.Z.L.R. 322, per Mahon J.
[4] A similar approach was adopted in *Stour Valley Builders v Stuart* to the argument that the payment-in of the cheque in the situation that forms the basis for the present discussion constitutes a breach of s.21(2)(b) of the Bills of Exchange Act 1908. Lloyd L.J. said that the section "does not help [D] establish substantively an agreement on the part of the creditor to accept a lesser sum in satisfaction of his claim".
[5] *Foley v Classique Coaches Ltd* [1934] 2 K.B. 1 at 3, per Maugham L.J.

In *Yorwerth v Sonnyplaster*,[6] D wrote to C's solicitors enclosing a cheque for £112 as an *ex gratia* payment saying that they did not consider that they were in any way liable for C's costs. C's solicitors replied acknowledging receipt of the cheque saying that they were "taking instructions regarding costs". They paid the cheque within a few days but did not communicate with D's solicitors again for four-and-a-half months, when they wrote saying that £112 was not an acceptable settlement figure. The Court of Appeal held that there was no concluded agreement because the question of costs was outstanding and, in the circumstances, the payment, in of the cheque and the silence for four-and-a-half months could not be construed as an acceptance.[7]

In the normal course of events, the court will not imply a term as to the payment of costs.[8]

Terms too vague

Where the parties' agreement is expressed in terms that are too vague to be enforced, the court will decline to hold that a sufficiently certain agreement has been reached.[9] 3–51

In *Wilson & Whitworth Ltd v Express & Independent Newspapers Ltd*,[10] C and D were newspaper publishers who became involved in a passing-off action in 1936. C's claim was dismissed at first instance, but its appeal was settled by a consent order in the "Tomlin" form in which one of the scheduled terms was to the effect that C would not do certain things in connection with the presentation of their newspapers and associated advertising "to any further extent than at the commencement of this action". When the matter had first been mentioned to the Court of Appeal it appeared to have been the parties' intention that this obligation should be recorded as an undertaking to the court. The Court of Appeal was unwilling to accept an undertaking in such vague terms and suggested that the parties agree more specific terms or, perhaps, deal with the settlement in a way that did not require an undertaking to the court. The parties were unable to agree more precise terms but asked the court to make a Tomlin order with the term indicated above as part of the schedule. The Court of Appeal made the order. In 1968 D alleged that C was acting in breach of the term and sought an injunction restraining C from breaking the agreement. Plowman J. held that, having regard to the observations of the Court of Appeal in 1936, an injunction could not be granted to enforce an obligation so vaguely expressed.

In *Tadmor v Tadmor*,[11] an order was made on W's application for an ouster order against H in the following terms: 3–52

---

[6] (1973) C.A.T. 255. See also *Gannon v Chubb Fire Limited* [1996] P.I.Q.R. P108, CA.
[7] *cf.* paras 3–28 *et seq.*, above.
[8] See paras 5–60–5–61, below.
[9] *Chitty on Contracts* (29th ed., 2004), Vol.1, paras 2–136 *et seq.* An argument to this effect was advanced and rejected in relation to the compromise considered in *Snelling v John Snelling Ltd* [1973] 1 Q.B. 87, the facts of which are recorded at para.3–69, below. See also *Hutchinson v Tamosius*, unreported, May 24, 1999, where His Honour Judge Hegarty Q.C., sitting as a High Court judge, rejected an argument to this effect in the context of the result of settlement discussions in relation to a partnership dispute.
[10] [1969] 1 W.L.R. 197. See Appendix 6.
[11] (1976) C.A.T. 432. The point that this was an interlocutory and an executory order does not appear to have been taken on W's behalf: see, *e.g.* para.32–29, below.

> Upon hearing counsel for the parties
>
>> And upon [cross undertakings by H and W not to assault molest or otherwise interfere with one another]
>> It is directed that [W] do occupy the first floor flat at the matrimonial home . . . (without [H] or the tenant) and that [H] do occupy such parts of the ground floor as he can arrange with the said tenant, subject to the tenant's approval.
>
> The order was never implemented in that W never returned to the matrimonial home, the tenant never moved out of his part of the first floor flat (possibly because he had some form of statutory protection) and no arrangement was made between H and the tenant concerning the occupation of the ground floor. W wanted the matter looked at on the merits, but H took the point that this was precluded because the order was a consent order. The Court of Appeal held that it was not a consent order because (a) it did not contain a recital to that effect[12] and (b) because a true consent order was equal to a contract between the parties and this order was too uncertain and subject to many conditions "such as the tenant moving from the first floor to the ground floor and arrangements being made with the tenant".

3-53   In *Assi v Leeds Metropolitan University*,[13] C became a full-time research student with D in 1991. Following various disputes C was told by D in 1992 that it was being recommended that the government funding for his work should cease and that he should not continue as a research student. C invoked D's grievance procedure and an apparent compromise was reached under which, on C's case, D would enrol him and grant him a three-year bursary subject to the selection of a suitable research topic and the appointment of a suitable supervisor. C complained that, in breach of that agreement, D had failed to provide him with a suitable supervisor and claimed damages for breach of contract. The Court of Appeal held that the judge had been correct in holding that the agreement reached was invalid for uncertainty in that it was not legally enforceable until a suitable research topic and supervisor had been identified.

3-54   However, where a provision in an agreement is merely incapable of any precise meaning, but can be severed from the rest of the agreement without doing violence to it, the court will do so.[14]

Agreement to agree and the "future document"

3-55 As indicated above,[15] an agreement to agree in the future is not a contract. For example, an agreement by the parties to stay[16] the proceedings between them "on terms that the issues arising therein be resolved by agreement"

---

[12] This is not necessarily fatal: see para.10–04, below.
[13] February 16, 2001.
[14] *Nicolene v Simmonds* [1953] 1 Q.B. 543. See *Chitty on Contracts* (29th ed., 2004), Vol.1, para.2–141.
[15] See para.3–49, above.
[16] See Ch.9, below.

would be unlikely to be upheld. This would constitute nothing more than an agreement to agree or negotiate.[17]

Problems occasionally arise when the parties have compromised their dispute but speak or write in terms which contemplate the drawing-up of some further document setting the seal, as it were, on their agreement. The question arises whether the compromise is immediately binding or not binding until such document is executed. The question has been formulated thus: 3–56

> ". . . it is a question of construction whether the execution of the further contract is a condition or term of the bargain or whether it is a mere expression of the desire of the parties as to the manner in which the transaction already agreed to will in fact go through. In the former case there is no enforceable contract either because the condition is unfulfilled or because the law does not recognise a contract to enter into a contract. In the latter case there is a binding contract and the reference to the more formal document may be ignored."[18]

Since the question is one of construction with a view to ascertaining the intention of the parties, it is impossible to describe any particular situation which arises in the context of compromise as being in one category or the other.[19] It is the significance attached by the parties to the future act which is the crucial factor. That is determined by construing the agreement as a whole.[20]

An agreement between husband and wife to enter into a separation agreement on specified terms has been held to be binding. 3–57

---

[17] *Walford v Miles* [1992] 2 A.C. 128, where the House of Lords upheld the well-established principle that a bare agreement to negotiate was unenforceable. See *Chitty on Contracts* (29th ed., 2004), Vol.1, paras 2–134–2–135. *Cf. Cable & Wireless Plc v IBM United Kingdom Ltd* [2002] EWHC 2059 (Comm Ct), where Colman J. upheld an agreement that the parties would "attempt in good faith to resolve the dispute or claim through an Alternative Dispute Resolution (ADR) procedure as recommended to the Parties by [CEDR]". See also *Beta Investments SA v Transmedia Europe Inc*, unreported, May 12, 2003, ChD, Justin Fenwick Q.C.
[18] *Von Hatzfeldt-Wildenburg v Alexander* [1912] 1 Ch. 284 at 288, *per* Parker J. See *Chitty on Contracts* (29th ed., 2004), Vol.1, paras 2–114 *et seq*.
[19] See, *e.g. Behar, Ellis & Parnell v Territorial Investments Ltd* (1973) C.A.T. 237, noted in para.37–18, below. In *Bishop v Berkshire Health Authority* [1999] P.I.Q.R. P92, Douglas Brown J. held that the then standard form of consent order entered into when a claimant is considering a structured settlement following agreement on the award of damages on a conventional basis is nothing more than an agreement to agree and thus does not constitute a binding obligation on the part of the claimant to accept that sum. *Cf. Gardiner v South Essex Health Authority*, unreported, December 10, 1998, (Longmore J., as he then was) and *Heselwood v Collett* [1999] P.I.Q.R. Q136 (Buckley J.), where the form of agreed order contained an undertaking on behalf of the claimant to limit the claim to the agreed conventional figure. See further Ch.35, below.
[20] *Chitty on Contracts* (29th ed., 2004), Vol.1, paras 12–041 *et seq*.

In *Morton v Morton*,[21] W had brought proceedings against H in a magistrates' court in 1930 for maintenance for herself and their son. The proceedings were compromised outside court and the terms were reflected in a document entitled "Heads of agreement" which was drawn up and signed by the respective solicitors. After reciting W's agreement to withdraw her summons, the document recorded that H and W "hereby mutually agree to enter a separation deed containing the following clauses", and the various terms were set out. Although the terms were carried out, no formal agreement was ever prepared or executed. In subsequent proceedings it was argued that the document was nothing more than a contract to contract. A Divisional Court of the Probate, Divorce and Admiralty Division held that there was a binding agreement (subject to the ultimate jurisdiction of the court). Lord Merriman P. said[22]:

> "[T]he commonest thing in the world, in these matrimonial causes, whether in the courts below or in this court, is to draw up heads of agreement, which are afterwards to be put into more solemn form, if the parties so require; but to say . . . that this is nothing more than a contract to make a contract seems to me to be impossible. . . . Every requisite of the agreement between the parties was here and I think it is the clearest possible case of a concluded agreement, which no doubt either party could have insisted on being put into more formal shape."[23]

Problem of the "conditional" compromise

3–58 Could it be argued on the foregoing basis that an agreement of compromise which, on its proper construction, contains a condition that a consent order or judgment reflecting it be made in due course, is not binding? The question is considered elsewhere,[24] but it is thought that the answer is "no". It is submitted that this is analogous to the position of a contract made subject to the fulfilment of some future condition which may or may not be satisfied. Such an agreement is not regarded as too vague or uncertain. It may have a number of different effects depending on how the agreement is interpreted.

3–59 **Not binding until future event.** If the parties expressly or impliedly stipulate that their compromise should not be binding upon them until the happening of some event, for example the approval of, or concurrence with its terms by, a third party, or until it has been reduced to writing,[25]

---

[21] [1942] 1 All E.R. 273. And see *Xydhias v Xydhias* [1999] 2 All E.R. 386, CA, discussed in Ch.32, below. Where parties negotiate on the basis that a binding agreement will only come into existence when the wording of a contemplated consent order is agreed, then in the absence of agreement to such wording no binding contract of compromise will have arisen: *Dalgety Foods Holland BV v Deb-Its Ltd* [1994] F.S.R. 125, Edward Nugee Q.C., sitting as a deputy High Court judge.
[22] [1942] 1 All E.R. 273 at 273.
[23] For settlements in matrimonial cases generally, see Ch.32, below.
[24] See Ch.5, paras 5–48 *et seq.*, below.
[25] Most mediation agreements contain a term to this effect: see paras 43–14 *et seq.*, below.

effect will be given to that stipulation and either party may withdraw from the agreement up to the moment of fulfilment of the condition.

3–60 In *Plumley v Horrell*,[26] T, by his will, left the bulk of his property to the six children of his two sisters. By a subsequent will, made about three months later, he left the bulk of his property to his half-sister, H. H's husband sought to prove the second will. This was opposed by two children of T's two sisters of the full blood, and proceedings were commenced. During the trial a compromise was effected, the terms of which were indorsed on the brief of counsel for one of the parties and signed and assented to by the others. The effect of the compromise was that H's husband would be entitled to prove the will upon his undertaking to charge the property passing under the will in favour of each of the six children of his full sisters for equal sums of £500, only two of those children being party to the proceedings. Although the other four children assented to the arrangement, none signed the agreement. After the agreement two of the children who were not parties to the previous proceedings entered *caveats* against the probate to which, under the compromise, H's husband would otherwise have been entitled. One of the children who had been a party to the compromise sought specific performance against H's husband of the obligation under the compromise to pay the sum of £500. Lord Romilly held:

(i) that the compromise was conditional upon the second will being admitted to probate;
(ii) that since not all the children of the full sisters were parties to the agreement, it could only become binding on all parties if they all accepted it; and
(iii) since certain of the children had repudiated the arrangement, it bound no one.

Binding obligation to await future event. Alternatively, the parties may **3–61** enter into a compromise, the operation of which is suspended until the fulfilment of the condition. There is a binding obligation on the parties to await the fulfilment of the condition.

In *Smallman v Smallman*,[27] the parties to a matrimonial dispute agreed all the essential terms of a compromise and expressed it to be dependent "on the approval of the court". The Court of Appeal rejected the argument that the agreement was not binding unless and until it was approved by the court. Lord Denning M.R.[28] expressed the position this way:

"There is an agreement but the operation of it is suspended until the Court approves it. It is the duty of one party or the other to bring the

---

[26] (1869) 20 L.T. 473. See also *Benstall v Swain* (1829) Tamlyn 288 at 295; *cf. Pym v Campbell* (1856) 6 E. & B. 370.
[27] [1972] Fam. 25; *cf. Amey v Amey* [1992] 2 F.L.R. 89.
[28] [1972] Fam. 25 at 31; *cf. Dietz v Lennig Chemicals* [1969] 1 A.C. 170 where the House of Lords held that an agreement of an infant's claim requiring the approval of the court under what was then RSC Ord.80 was not binding until the court gave its approval. Lord Pearson said (at 190) that "either party could lawfully have repudiated [the agreement] at any time before the court approved it". See further at Ch.35 below.

agreement before the Court for approval. If the Court approves it, it is binding on the parties. If the court does not approve it, it is not binding. But, pending the application to the court, it remains a binding agreement which neither party can disavow."

3–62 **Compromise unilaterally binding until future event.** The agreement may provide for the acceptance by one party of an obligation immediately binding upon him but the final compromise of the dispute being dependent on the fulfilment of a condition by the other. For example, A may agree with B that he will accept £1,000 in full settlement of his claim for unliquidated damages if B pays that sum into court within 28 days. A would not be permitted to resile from his agreement until B had the opportunity of fulfilling the condition.[29] If B paid the money into court within the prescribed period the compromise would be final.

3–63 **Immediately binding defeasible on condition subsequent.** Finally, the parties may enter into an immediately binding compromise which remains so until the fulfilment (more usually the failure) of some condition which causes it to cease to be binding. For example, one party to a dispute concerning the title to property (real or personal) may compromise the claim of the other by agreeing to pay him a specified sum within a specified period following the sale of the property, each party agreeing that neither shall be bound by the sum if the property realises less than a certain price. Parties to a claim for a liquidated sum may similarly agree that the creditor shall have in his favour a consent judgment for the full amount of the debt subject to a provision that the debtor may, within a specified period, pay a lesser sum in satisfaction of the claim, in default of which payment the creditor may enforce the judgment for the whole sum.[30]

In each of the situations referred to above, though the fulfilment (or failure) of the relevant condition may be uncertain, the terms of the compromise are sufficiently clear and complete for the appropriate effect to be given to it.[31]

3–64   In *Bartlett v Conley*,[31a] C and her late husband lent D1 and D2 £180,000 in November 1989 following their financial difficulties in the light of the problems at Lloyd's. C instituted proceedings for the recovery of £117,000,

---

[29] See the analysis of this type of situation under the general law of contract by Diplock L.J. (as he then was) in *United Dominions Trust (Commercial) Ltd v Eagle Aircraft Services Ltd* [1968] 1 W.L.R. 74 at 83–84. The use of the word "agree" in the text will be noted. If A merely offered B the opportunity of compromising on the terms suggested and B did not signify acceptance of the proposal, the question of revocability of the offer might arise prior to B actually paying the money into court: see, *e.g. Chitty on Contracts* (29th ed., 2004), Vol.1, paras 2–076 *et seq.*
[30] *Re South American and Mexican Co Ex p. Bank of England* [1895] 1 Ch. 37.
[31] For the rights and obligations of the parties in the event of the fulfilment or, as appropriate, non-fulfilment of the relevant condition, see Ch.8, below.
[31a] July 2, 1999, unreported.

being the balance of the foregoing sum outstanding, and the trial was due to commence on August 11, 1997. An agreement was reached on the morning of the trial which was recorded in a document entitled "Draft Heads of Agreement". The document was in these terms:

"The parties are agreed to compromise [C's] claims in these actions on the following terms, subject to

(1) [D1's and D2's] bank . . . (a) agreeing to the imposition of a second charge in favour of [C] as set out below; (b) agreeing to a ceiling upon the level of borrowings secured by way of its first charge being fixed at a maximum of £150,000 during the lifetime of the second charge referred to above;
(2) the parties agreeing upon the precise form of the charge to be entered into;
(3) [D1 and D2] retaining their Legal Aid status.

TERMS OF AGREEMENT

1. The Defendants and each of them do agree to pay to the Plaintiff the sum of £117,000 ('the principal sum') on a date no later than 11th day of August 2003.
2. In default of the payment as above of the principal sum on or before 11/8/03, the Defendants and each of them will become liable to pay on 12/8/03 the sum of £150,000 ('the default sum').
3. The Defendants and each of them agree to execute a legal charge upon the property known as Southlands Farm, Moretonhampstead, Devon to secure the payment of the principal and default sum.
4. No order for costs.
5. Legal Aid Taxation of the Defendants' costs.
6. Liberty to apply as to the interpretation and timing of this order."

No consent order giving effect to this draft was drawn up. Subsequent correspondence between the parties' solicitors showed that the intention underlying the provision concerning D1's and D2's "Legal Aid status" was that that status should remain until the making of the consent order whereupon their certificates would be discharged.

In June 1998 the Legal Aid Board decided that D1 and D2 were no longer entitled to Legal Aid and their certificates were discharged. C reinstated her proceedings against D1 and D2 on the basis that the condition for the compromise, namely the retention of their Legal Aid status, no longer obtained and, accordingly, there was no longer any effective agreement.

The Court of Appeal held that C was entitled to take that position since once D1's and D2's Legal Aid certificates ceased to operate for whatever reason prior to the making of the consent order, the condition in the agreement ceased to be satisfied. The court proceeded on the assumption, without deciding, that the original agreement was binding subject to the fulfillment of the various conditions.

Compromise of part of dispute

It is quite possible for the parties expressly to compromise a particular element or elements in their dispute without coming to an overall settlement.[32] This in no way results in the particular compromise being

3–65

---

[32] Positive encouragement to settle issues within a case is given in the CPR: see para.16–07, below.

regarded as incomplete. In accident cases involving personal injury, for example, the parties not infrequently agree an apportionment of liability, the assessment of damages being left to the court.[33] Where the question arises as to what was compromised the question is one of construction of the parties' agreement.[34]

3-66   The foregoing situation must, of course, be contrasted with that in which a material part of the dispute remains unresolved at a time when, as one of the parties subsequently seeks to argue, a complete agreement has been concluded.[35]

Agreement reached in "without prejudice" negotiations

3-67 A not unknown misapprehension is that a "without prejudice" agreement is neither complete nor binding until confirmed by an "open" agreement. This is not so. Once a "without prejudice" offer[36] is accepted, a complete contract is established which is binding on both parties.[37]

INTENTION TO CREATE LEGAL RELATIONS

3-68 Under the ordinary law of contract an agreement will not be enforced unless the parties intended to create a legally binding contract. The test for determining the existence of the intention is an objective one.[38] The problem of whether such an intention exists will rarely arise in the context of compromise. The dispute will usually be sufficiently constituted, either by way of correspondence involving solicitors or actual litigation, for it to be abundantly clear that any compromise is intended to affect the legal relations of the parties.[39] The issue has, however, arisen in a number of cases concerning husband and wife in relation to, as it were, amicable domestic arrangements.[40] Since the essence of compromise is the resolution

---

[33] *Tomlin v Standard Telephones* [1969] 1 W.L.R. 1378.
[34] See Ch.5, below.
[35] See para.3-50, above.
[36] See Ch.27, below.
[37] See, *e.g. Tomlin v Standard Telephones*, n.33, above.
[38] *Chitty on Contracts*, (29th ed., 2004), Vol.1, paras 2-156 *et seq.*
[39] See, *e.g. Bushwall Properties Ltd v Vortex Ltd* [1976] 1 W.L.R. 591. But see *Orion Insurance Co Plc v Sphere Drake Insurance Plc* [1992] 1 Lloyd's Rep. 239, where the Court of Appeal upheld a finding that an agreement made at a meeting of representatives of various insurance companies—the meeting having been designed to resolve differences over liabilities arising from the participation of the companies in two earlier insurance pool agreements—was a "goodwill agreement" only and was not intended to affect the legal relations of the parties.
[40] *Chitty on Contracts* (29th ed., 2004), Vol.1, paras 2-164 *et seq.*

of differences, it is not thought that this aspect of the law has much significance in this context. It is quite possible, of course, for members of a family to compromise a dispute, and intend thereby to be bound contractually, without the intervention of legal advisers.[41]

3–69 In *Snelling v John Snelling Ltd*,[42] C, D2 and D3, who were brothers, were directors of a family company, D1. Over a period of years, having regard to the policy of the brothers not to draw all of their earnings from the business, substantial loan accounts built up in favour of each. Serious differences arose between the brothers about the running of the company, culminating in C writing a letter to his father (who was chairman of the company) and to D2 and D3 in very uncomplimentary terms so far as the latter were concerned, but at the same time putting forward suggestions for reorganising the business. C threatened that if the principle of his proposals was not agreed to by a certain date, he would resign and withdraw his assets. This letter was written at a time when D1 was in the final stage of negotiations for the raising of additional finance for its operations by way of mortgage from a finance company. Efforts were made to overcome the differences between the brothers and on the same day as the mortgage was completed an agreement, prepared by D3 without legal assistance, was signed by all three. The agreement provided, *inter alia*, that in the event of any director resigning voluntarily he would immediately forfeit all monies due to him from D1 and its associated companies. It was further provided that the agreement would remain in force until the loan from the finance company had been repaid. About three months later C resigned his directorship and, in due course, sought to recover the balance outstanding on his loan account. It was contended on C's behalf that the agreement was not binding as it was not intended to give rise to legal relations. Ormrod J. (as he then was) held that the agreement was intended to have legal effect and drew attention to the following factors that led to this conclusion:

(i) the relationship between C and D2 and D3 had been destroyed by dissensions before the agreement was signed;
(ii) although drafted by a layman, the agreement contained words and phrases (including reference to "the court") which suggested that legal consequences were intended to flow from it.

3–70 Whilst there is as yet no reported English case in which the argument has been advanced, it is conceivable that a party to negotiations towards a compromise might seek to elevate a "comfort letter"[43] or a "letter of intent"[44] into a contractually binding commitment. The precise legal status of such a document is not settled[45] and it may well be that each such document would have to be construed appropriately in the light of all relevant and admissible material;[46] but generally it is thought that the use

---

[41] *Snelling v John Snelling Ltd* [1973] 1 Q.B. 87.
[42] [1973] 1 Q.B. 87.
[43] *Kleinwort Benson Ltd v Malaysia Mining Corporation Berhad* [1989] 1 W.L.R. 379, CA.
[44] *Wilson Smithett & Cape (Sugar) Ltd v Bangladesh Sugar and Food Industries Corporation* [1976] 1 Lloyd's Rep. 378.
[45] *Chitty on Contracts* (29th ed., 2004), Vol.1, para.2–176.
[46] See n.43, above.

of expressions such as "comfort" and, perhaps to a lesser extent, "intent" in relation to a letter or other similar communication would be regarded as negativing any intent to create legal relations in regard to its contents.[47]

FORMALITIES

3-71 Little or no formality is required for a contract to be upheld under English law.[48] Thus few situations arise where parties desirous of compromising their disputes need to have regard to the observance of any formalities. Three areas merit some attention:

Land

3-72 Any compromise involving a "sale or other disposition of an interest in land"[49] must be made in writing and "only by incorporating all the terms which the parties have expressly agreed in one document or, where contracts are exchanged, in each".[50] It is permissible for the terms to be incorporated into the relevant document by reference "to some other document",[51] but the document incorporating the terms "must be signed by or on behalf of each party to the contract".[52] Should any of these formalities not be observed there will be no contract.

3-73 In any case where a compromise involves a transfer of an acknowledged title or the creation of a lease,[53] these provisions must be observed. The most likely areas in which these matters will be of concern are the

---

[47] n.43, above.
[48] *Chitty on Contracts* (29th ed., 2004), Vol.1, Ch.4.
[49] The grant of an option to acquire an interest in land comes within the meaning of the section, but the notice by which such an option is exercised does not: *Spiro v Glencrown Properties Ltd* [1991] Ch. 537; *Trustees of Chippenham Golf Club v North Wiltshire District Council* (1991) 64 P. & C.R. 527.
[50] Law of Property (Miscellaneous Provisions) Act 1989, s.2(1). The Act affects all such transactions entered into after September 26, 1989. The Act replaced s.40 of the Law of Property Act 1925 (s.2(8)) with the result that the law of part performance cannot apply to contracts that fail to comply with its requirements. *Chitty on Contracts* (29th ed., 2004), Vol.1, Ch.4, paras 4–052—4–085 and paras 4–010—4–051. See previous decisions such as *Steadman v Steadman* [1976] A.C. 536 and *Sutton v Sutton* [1984] Ch. 184.
[51] Law of Property (Miscellaneous Provisions) Act 1989, s.2(2).
[52] *ibid.*, s.2(3).
[53] Other than an agreement to create a short lease (*i.e.* less than three years) within s.54(2) of the Law of Property Act 1925: s.2(5)(a). This includes a periodic tenancy. However, a "boundary agreement" is probably excluded from this requirement. In *Joyce v Rigolli* [2004] EWCA Civ 79, the Court of Appeal confirmed that the agreement concerned was "an agreement that merely demarcated the boundary. It did not purport to be a contract to convey any land from the appellant to the respondent. The parties' purpose was to fix the boundary at about the place where they thought it ought to have been". See Ch.38, below. See also *Nweze v Nwoko* [2004] EWCA Civ 379.

settlement of boundary disputes[54] and the compromise of landlord and tenant actions.[55]

Guarantee

A contract of guarantee must be in writing or evidenced by writing. Such a contract involves, on the part of the guarantor, a "promise to answer for the debt, default or miscarriage of another person".[56] Thus any compromise involving the introduction of a third party to act as guarantor of the obligations of one of the parties must comply with the statute to be enforceable as against him.

3–74

Deeds

Where parties decide for whatever reason to embody their agreement in a formal deed, the provisions of s.1 of the Law of Property (Miscellaneous Provisions) Act 1989[57] must be observed. In summary, these provisions require the deed to:

3–75

(a) make it clear on its face that it is intended to be a deed[58]; and
(b) be executed validly in accordance with the Act.[59]

The Act does not apply to deeds effected before s.1 became operative.[60]

---

[54] See Ch.38, below.
[55] See Ch.37, below.
[56] Statute of Frauds 1677, s.4. See *Chitty on Contracts* (29th ed., 2004), Vol.2, Ch.44.
[57] The Act applies to all deeds, not just those relating to land or property.
[58] s.1(2)(a).
[59] s.1(2)(b) and (3).
[60] s.1(11).

CHAPTER 4

Impeachment of a Compromise

4–01 At face value parties may appear to have reached a complete and valid compromise which satisfies all the essential requirements of the law, but circumstances may arise, as they do under the ordinary law of contract, which render that apparent agreement ineffectual. Those circumstances now fall to be examined.

INCAPACITY[1]

Children[2]

4–02 A child is not as a matter of law bound by a compromise.[3] Any such agreement is voidable at his option.[4] It would, however, be capable of ratification on attaining majority.[5] Nonetheless, a minor may become bound by a compromise of a dispute affecting him if the court approves the agreement.[6]

Mentally disordered persons and patients

4–03 At common law, it appears that a mentally disordered person will be held to a contract unless he did not know what he was doing and the other party was aware of the incapacity which resulted in him not knowing what

---

[1] For a general analysis, see *Chitty on Contracts* (29th ed., 2004) Vol.1, Ch.8.
[2] The word "child" is used in the text in place of either "minor" or "infant" to accord with the more modern approach of the CPR r.21.1(2)(a). A "child" is a person under the age of 18 years.
[3] *Overton v Bannister* (1844) 3 Ha. 504; *Mattei v Vautro* (1898) 78 L.T. 682.
[4] *Chitty on Contracts* (29th ed., 2004), Vol.1, para.8–005. See also *Rhodes v Swithenbank* (1889) 22 Q.B.D. 577.
[5] Minors' Contracts Act 1987, s.1(1)(a).
[6] See Ch.35, below. See CPR r.21.10.

he was doing. If the mentally disordered person can establish this, the contract would be regarded as voidable at his option.[7] An otherwise voidable contract for this reason may be ratified by the mentally disordered person after he has recovered or during a rational period.[8]

A "patient" for the purposes of Pt VII of the Mental Health Act 1983 is someone who, by reason of mental disorder, is incapable of managing and administering his property and affairs.[9] Any compromise entered into "personally" by a person to whom this description applies would be likely to be voidable at his option by reason of the principles referred to in the preceding paragraph. However, procedural provisions similar to those applicable in relation to children exist to enable binding compromises to be effected by or on behalf of "patients"[10] and, if the Court of Protection should become involved on the patient's behalf, the judge of that court has full powers to make orders or give directions so as to enable a valid compromise to be achieved on his behalf.[11] **4–04**

A judge cannot enter a consent to an order on behalf of a litigant before him because the litigant's counsel cannot obtain instructions and the judge feels that entering the consent is in that person's best interests.[12] **4–05**

Legal advisers[13]

Neither a solicitor nor a barrister has any implied or ostensible authority to compromise some matter "collateral to the action" in question.[14] **4–06**

Non-legal advisers and representatives

An accountant may have actual authority to compromise, pursuant to s.54 of the Taxes Management Act 1970, a dispute between his taxpayer client and the Revenue. Equally, in certain circumstances, the taxpayer may have held out an accountant apparently acting for him as having authority to **4–07**

---

[7] *Imperial Loan Co Ltd v Stone* [1892] 1 Q.B. 599; *Hart v O'Connor* [1985] A.C. 1000, PC.
[8] *Matthews v Baxter* (1873) L.R. 8 Ex. 132; *cf.* the analogous situation concerning children, above.
[9] s.94(2).
[10] CPR r.21.10.
[11] Mental Health Act 1983, ss.92–113. *The White Book*, Section 6B. See also Heywood and Massey, *Court of Protection Practice*.
[12] *Woodhead v Woodhead* (1978) C.A.T. 147.
[13] For the role of legal advisers and others in securing a "compromise agreement" in the employment setting, see Ch.36, below.
[14] See para.29–16, below.

enter into such an agreement, even though in fact the accountant had no express authority to do so.[15]

Expert witnesses

4–08 An expert witness engaged by a party, who takes part in a discussion with an expert witness instructed by another party to the litigation pursuant to a direction of the court, has no power to bind the party by whom he is instructed on any aspect of the case, unless the parties agree to be bound.[16] The practical effect of an agreement between experts may be effectively to bind a party, and indeed where a single expert is jointly instructed (whether by agreement or by direction of the court)[17] this practical consequence may be felt more acutely. However, the strict legal position in terms of an expert's authority is that he cannot bind the party or parties by whom he is instructed in relation either to the whole case or in respect of the issue or issues he is asked to address.

Companies

4–09 A trading company has an implied power to compromise claims brought by or against it,[18] but there may be circumstances in which the doctrine of *ultra vires* could vitiate a compromise entered into by a company.[19] The extent to which an individual director or employee has capacity to bind a company to a compromise will depend on the particular circumstances of the case.[20]

Local authorities

4–10 As with a company, a local authority's action may fall foul of the *ultra vires* doctrine. A local authority may act only within the powers conferred upon it by statute. Where it acts beyond those powers the doctrine of *ultra vires*,

---

[15] *Inland Revenue Commissioners v West* [1991] S.T.C. 357, CA; *cf. Sheppard v Inland Revenue Commissioners* [1992] 3 All E.R. 58, His Honour Judge Paul Baker Q.C., sitting as a judge at the High Court. For "ostensible authority" to operate to bind a principal it is necessary for the principal to hold the agent out as having authority. No representation by the agent as to the extent of his authority can amount to a holding-out by his principal: *Re Selectmove Limited* [1995] 1 W.L.R. 474 at 478.
[16] CPR r.35.12(5).
[17] CPR rr.35.7 and 35.8. Although see *D (A child) v Walker, The Times*, May 17, 2000, CA.
[18] *Dixon v Evans* (1872) L.R. 5 H.L. 606; *Bath's Case* (1878) 8 Ch.D. 334.
[19] *GNW Central Rail Co v Charlebois* [1899] A.C. 114; *Re Jon Beauforte (London) Ltd* [1953] Ch. 131.
[20] In *Hurst Stores and Interiors Ltd v M.L. Europe Ltd*, unreported, June 25, 2003, the issue arose as to whether the "project manager" of a company engaged to refit the toilet facilities in a large building had the authority to bind the company to a compromise.

the object of which is "the protection of the public",[21] will invalidate the act in question. Whilst it is perfectly permissible for a local authority to compromise disputes in which it becomes involved, entering into a compromise that lies beyond its powers is *ultra vires* and the agreement apparently reached will be struck down as void *ab initio*.[22]

Partners

The view traditionally expressed[23] that one partner may not compromise proceedings brought by or against the firm may be over-simplistic.[24] Since the settlement of a dispute with a partnership may be seen as part of the ordinary business of most types of firm,[25] a third party may ordinarily compromise a claim by or against a firm in the confidence that it would bind all partners even though he may not know whether all the partners either knew of or expressly approved it. However, an arrangement going beyond the usual nature of a compromise,[26] or one which was, to the knowledge of the other party to the settlement, in fraud of the other partners,[27] would be liable to be set aside.

4–11

Representative parties

Where a party represents others who have "the same interest in a claim",[28] a consent order or judgment reflecting a compromise of that claim will "unless the court otherwise directs"[29] be binding "on all persons represented in the claim . . . but may only be enforced by or against a person who is not a party to the claim with the permission of the court".[30] Although

4–12

---

[21] *Hazell v Hammersmith and Fulham London Borough Council* [1992] 2 A.C. 1 at 36, *per* Lord Templeman. See also paras 40–05 *et seq.*, below.

[22] *Eastbourne Borough Council v Foster*, unreported, December 20, 2000, Colin Mackay Q.C., as he then was, sitting as a deputy High Court judge. In this case the local authority entered into a "Compromise Agreement" with one of its senior employees under which he received a financial package on his ceasing employment which went beyond what the local authority could properly and legitimately have agreed with him. It was common ground at the trial that the agreement was void *ab initio*. For the decision on appeal to the Court of Appeal, see *Eastbourne Borough Council v Foster* [2001] EWCA Civ 1091.

[23] See para.4–08 of the 3rd edition and *35 Halsbury's Laws* (4th ed.), para.53.

[24] This view is based on *Crane v Lewis* (1887) 36 W.R. 480.

[25] *cf.* Partnership Act 1980, s.5. See *Lindley and Banks on Partnership* (17th ed., 1995), paras 12–08 *et seq.* Since a partner in general terms has an implied authority to commence or resist legal proceedings in the name of the firm (*Lindley, ibid.*, para.12–35), it would be illogical if a similar power to compromise those proceedings did not exist.

[26] See *Niemann v Niemann* (1890) 43 Ch.D. 198.

[27] *Lindley*, n.25, above, para.12–83. However, merely acting in excess of his powers will not make the actions of partner fraudulent in the sense required: *ibid.*, para.12–26.

[28] CPR r.19.6(1).

[29] CPR r.19.6(4).

[30] CPR r.19.6(4)(a) and (b).

the express approval of the court to a settlement of such a claim is not required, the court retains a degree of control over the effect of such a settlement both on parties represented in the claim and those who were not parties in the action. In proceedings to which CPR r.19.7 applies[31] the court's approval of a proposed settlement by a representative party is required.[32] Such approval will be given "where [the court] is satisfied that the settlement is for the benefit of all the represented persons".[33] Similar further protection to the represented parties is given under this rule as is afforded under CPR r.19.6 in relation to the binding nature of any judgment and its enforceability.[34]

Represented parties acting personally

4–13 Individual parties who have solicitors acting for them may, if they are *sui juris*, compromise an action without the intervention of their solicitors.[35] If their motives are dishonest with a view to depriving the solicitors of their costs or defeating their lien, the court will intervene for the solicitors' protection.[36]

MISTAKE

General

4–14 Mistakes occur in the contractual context in a number of ways. A clear and comprehensive classification of the various types of mistake that can operate to invalidate a contract is elusive.[37] In general terms the law recognises (i) mistakes where the parties have come to an agreement, but on the basis of some shared false assumption of fact, law[38] or state of affairs which renders performance of the agreement different from the performance the parties contemplated[39] and (ii) mistakes where there has been some misunderstanding about the terms of the agreement. So far as the latter are concerned, the mistake may either be mutual in the sense that

---

[31] Those relating to the estate of a deceased person, property subject to a trust or the meaning of a document (including a statute): CPR r.19.7(1).
[32] CPR r.19.7(5).
[33] CPR r.19.7(6).
[34] CPR r.19.7(7).
[35] *Brunsdon v Allard* (1859) 2 Ell. & Ell. 19; *Sullivan v Pearson* (1868) L.R. 4 Q.B. 153; *The Hope* (1883) 8 P.D. 144.
[36] *Re Margetson and Jones* [1897] 2 Ch. 314; *The White Book*, Vol.2, para.76-230.
[37] *Chitty on Contracts* (29th ed., 2004), Vol.1, paras 5–001—5–005.
[38] See para.4–20 below.
[39] *Great Peace Shipping Ltd v Tsavliris Salvage (International) Ltd* [2003] Q.B. 679 ("The Great Peace").

both parties have confused what the other intended, or unilateral in the sense that only one of them has confused what was intended. Where there has been a mutual mistake or mutual misunderstanding the contract will be regarded as void *ab initio*.[40] The position in the case of a unilateral mistake is less clear, but relief may be afforded in certain circumstances.[41]

Relief sought or given

Prior to *Great Peace Shipping Ltd v Tsavliris Salvage (International) Ltd*[42] ("*The Great Peace*") there had been a debate for many years about whether there was a separate equitable jurisdiction to set aside an agreement on the basis of a mutual (or common) mistake.[43] Since that case it is now clear that such a jurisdiction does not exist.[44] Where an operative *mutual* mistake (or misunderstanding) is found to have occurred, the contract will be void *ab initio*. Where there is disagreement about whether a mistake or misunderstanding of this nature occurred, the relief that the party asserting it will seek would seem to be a declaration to that effect, the setting aside of any such agreement (and any order or judgment made pursuant thereto) and an order directing repayment of any money paid thereunder.[45] Where a party asserts an operative unilateral mistake, his remedy is likely to be rectification of (as he would say) the erroneously expressed written agreement of compromise.[46] For a party resisting the attempts of the other to enforce the compromise, an operative unilateral mistake might afford a defence either to a claim for damages or to one for specific performance.[47]

4–15

Mistake in compromise

Mutual mistake about fundamental matter

Fact. A shared misapprehension of fact which goes to the root of the compromise renders the agreement void.

4–16

---

[40] *Chitty on Contracts* (29th ed., 2004), Vol.1, para.5–008.
[41] See para.4–22, below.
[42] [2003] Q.B. 679.
[43] *Chitty on Contracts* (28th ed., 1999), Vol.1, Ch.5.
[44] "If coherence is to be restored to this area of our law, it can only be by declaring that there is no jurisdiction to grant rescission of a contract on the ground of common mistake where that contract is valid and enforceable on ordinary principles of contract law": *The Great Peace*, n.39, above, at para.157, per Lord Phillips M.R. He went on to say that an "equitable jurisdiction to grant rescission on terms where a common fundamental mistake has induced a contract gives greater flexibility than a doctrine of common law which holds the contract void in such circumstances. . . . there is scope for legislation to give greater flexibility to our law of mistake than the common law allows".
[45] For a review of the remedies available when a compromise is treated as void *ab initio*, see *Eastbourne Borough Council v Foster* [2001] EWCA Civ 1091, CA.
[46] *Chitty on Contracts* (29th ed., 2004), Vol.1, para.5–100. See paras 4–31—4–35, below.
[47] *Chitty on Contracts* (29th ed., 2004), Vol.1, paras 5–066 and 5–100. Such a defendant could counterclaim for rectification: *cf. Re Roberts* [1905] 1 Ch. 704.

In *Allcard v Walker*,[48] a consent order was made in matrimonial proceedings following a divorce varying a post-nuptial settlement of certain property. The consent order was made on the mistaken assumption by all concerned that certain other property was bound by the settlement. In fact it was not so bound and Stirling J. held that the consent order made on this false premise should be set aside on terms. The contention that the mistake was one of law was rejected (private right of ownership being held to be a matter of fact), but Stirling J. said, in any event, that a mistake of law would not to be fatal to the application to set aside the order.

4–17   In *Huddersfield Banking Co Ltd v Henry Lister & Son Ltd*,[49] a consent order for the sale of a number of looms in a factory was made in the liquidation of the company to which the factory belonged. It was made upon the erroneous assumption that the looms were not fixtures. In fact, as subsequently appeared, they had been wrongfully loosened by a third party. The Court of Appeal held that the order had been made on the basis of a mutual mistake of fact and that the order should be set aside.

It was said by Kay L.J.[50]:

> "It seems to me that, both on principle and on authority, when once the Court finds that an agreement has been come to between parties who were under a common mistake of material fact, the Court may set it aside, and the Court has ample jurisdiction to set aside the order founded upon that agreement."

4–18   In *Grains & Fourrages SA v Huyton*,[51] C were buyers and D were sellers, pursuant to two separate contracts, of Chinese cotton expellers. The first contract was for 10,000 tonnes and the second for 1,983 tonnes respectively. The standard terms of the Grain and Feed Trade Association contract, upon which the parties traded, provided that the quality was to be '"final on representative samples drawn at discharge and analysed in London". Samples were taken at the port of discharge by jointly instructed superintendents and sent to London for analysis. On August 5, 1993 the analysts issued two certificates of analysis in respect of the expellers and extractions. On receiving the certificates and on re-checking, D advised C that there appeared to have been a typing error with the result that the results of the analyses had been interchanged, pointing out that the tonnages did not correspond with the commodity certified on each certificate. D asked that the analysts issue new and amended certificates. C took this up with the analysts who stated that the results corresponded with the samples provided and that the superintendents

---

[48] [1896] 2 Ch. 369.
[49] [1895] 2 Ch. 273. In previous editions of this work the case of *Magee v Pennine Insurance Co Ltd* [1969] 2 Q.B. 507 was given as an example of an operative false and fundamental assumption of fact that invalidated a compromise. Since the basis of the decision in this case can no longer be regarded as good law following *The Great Peace* (n.39 above), it is not now put forward as an example in this context. It would be interesting to see how similar facts would be decided on the basis of the law as it now is to be regarded. But the case of *Galloway v Galloway* (1914) 30 T.L.R. 531 (separation deed void because both parties assumed that they were validly married) is probably to be considered as correct whatever approach to the law applicable to mistake is adopted.
[50] [1895] 2 Ch. 273 at 284.
[51] [1997] 1 Lloyd's Rep. 628; *cf. The Ypatia Halcoussi* (see para.4–26, below) where no mutual mistake could be shown.

may have interchanged the labels on the samples. Proceeding on the assumption that this is what had happened, C and D agreed to treat each analysis as corresponding to the other contract. Payment was made on that basis. However, it emerged later that, contrary to the common assumption made by C and D, there was no transposition of results in relation to the cargoes named in the two certificates, but merely an incorrect transposition of the tonnages for each cargo. Mance J., as he then was, held that the agreement reached, which did not in the circumstances involve any element of compromise, should be set aside on the ground of a "common and fundamental mistake".

Opinion. Arguably, a mutual mistake of opinion will not vitiate a compromise, though what differentiates an opinion from fact or, in some circumstances, law may not always be that easy to determine: 4–19

> In *Cooper v Cooper (Preece)*,[52] H agreed to buy off any claim which W might have in the former matrimonial home for £400. The agreement was made in January 1972 and the agreed sum plus interest was to be paid by June 1972. Whilst the negotiations continued during 1971 both parties thought that the value of the house was about £4,000 (the sum outstanding on mortgage being about £3,800). In June 1972 H sold the property for £8,650. W sought to resile from the agreement on the basis that there had been a mutual mistake of fact, namely the value of the house. The Court of Appeal held that there had been no mistake of fact, merely one of opinion as to the value of the property. It was said that they both knew the house and all the material facts (for example, that it was very damp).[53]

Law. Characterising a mistake as one of law in contradistinction to one of fact or of opinion can be difficult.[54] For the purposes of the law of restitution the distinction between a mistake of law and a mistake of fact has been held by the House of Lords to be no longer maintainable.[55] Against that background the Court of Appeal held in *Brennan v Bolt Burden*[56] that a mutual mistake of law could in principle invalidate a 4–20

---

[52] (1973) C.A.T. 425B.
[53] cf. *Warren v Warren* (1983) 13 Fam. Law 49 (where the Court of Appeal granted W leave to appeal out of time against the making of a lump sum order based upon an agreed valuation of the former matrimonial home, when that valuation was exceeded on sale some eight months later by approaching 100 per cent. Griffiths L.J., as he then was, described the case as "atypical because of the extraordinary discrepancy"). Whatever the correctness of *Cooper v Cooper* may have been on the facts, and indeed on the principle of whether a mistake as to opinion can vitiate an agreement, it is thought that in the matrimonial finance context a significant discrepancy between a sale price of property and the value attributed to it by the parties in their negotiations leading to a consent order may afford a ground for setting aside the consent order, provided the order was substantially different from the order that would have been made if the true value had been known: see *Livesey v Jenkins* [1985] A.C. 424 and paras 32–98 et seq., below. cf. *L v L* (1981) 11 Fam. Law 57 (Balcombe J.). See also *Edmonds v Edmonds* (1990) Fam. Law 473, where *Warren v Warren* was distinguished and attention drawn to *Barder v Barder (Caluori intervening); sub nom. Barder v Caluori* [1988] A.C. 20. In many cases the precise boundary between a mistake of opinion and a mistake of fact will be difficult to identify: see, *e.g.* the discussion in *Chitty on Contracts* (29th ed., 2004), Vol.1, paras 6–004 et seq.
[54] *Chitty on Contracts* (29th ed., 2004), Vol.1, paras 6–011 and 29–040.
[55] *Kleinwort Benson Ltd v Lincoln City Council* [1999] 1 A.C. 153, HL.
[56] [2005] Q.B. 303.

compromise, although there was no operative mistake of law in that case.⁵⁷ The Court of Appeal was plainly uncomfortable with the prospect that the principle could, if applied too readily, undermine the finality normally associated with a compromise.⁵⁸ Indeed, there are indications in the judgments that had an exception to the general principle based upon "public policy" been proposed in argument, it would have afforded an answer to the issues raised in the case.⁵⁹ However, the case is authority for the principle, albeit one the application of which is likely to be scrutinised with particular care when raised. It is part of the everyday process of the compromise of actual or threatened litigation that views are taken on each side about the state of the law or its applicability to the facts of the particular case. Indeed, these views are frequently ventured in negotiation. It remains important to appreciate that the mere fact that parties compromise a dispute involving competing assertions of law which have debatable validity will not undermine the compromise. Provided the assertions are made in good faith⁶⁰ there would be no obvious grounds for calling the compromise into question. The need for a mutual mistake of law to render performance of the agreement different from the performance the parties contemplated, or indeed impossible,⁶¹ is difficult to apply in the case of a compromise.⁶²

4-21 **Mutual misunderstanding of terms** Assuming for present purposes that mistakes involving the identity of the other party are unlikely to arise in the context of compromise,⁶³ only one other situation falls to be considered under the general heading of "mutual mistake". It arises where each party interprets and accepts the offer of the other in a completely different sense from that which was intended. In such a situation, no contract comes into existence. An example would be afforded where A and B have two separate and distinct disputes running concurrently. A makes an offer of compromise intended to deal with both disputes; B believes that A is attempting to compromise one dispute only and accepts on that basis, and the actual

---

⁵⁷ It is easier to assert the principle than to identify the circumstances in which a mistake of law could invalidate a compromise. Suppose that A and B settle a dispute before proceedings are issued against the background of the shared erroneous belief that the limitation period applicable to the dispute in question had not expired. Would that be a mistake of law? If so, would it be right for the compromise to be set aside?
⁵⁸ [2005] Q.B. 303, *per* Maurice Kay L.J. at para.22, *per* Bodey J. at para.39 and *per* Sedley L.J. at paras 61–63.
⁵⁹ *ibid.*, *per* Maurice Kay L.J. at para.23 and *per* Bodey J. at para.52.
⁶⁰ See para.2–19, above.
⁶¹ See para.4–14 above.
⁶² [2005] Q.B. 303, *per* Maurice Kay L.J. at para.22, and *per* Sedley L.J. at paras 59–60.
⁶³ *Chitty on Contracts* (29th ed., 2004), paras 5–076 *et seq.*

agreement is inconclusive. Clearly there would be no contract, the parties being treated as not *ad idem*.[64]

Unilateral mistake. This sub-heading embraces the situation where the mistake about the terms of the agreement is unilateral in the sense that only one party has confused what was intended. Following *The Great Peace*[65] it is plain that, whatever other jurisdiction for giving relief to the mistaken party may exist, an equitable jurisdiction to set aside the agreement cannot now be invoked.[66] There is, however, some uncertainty about the way the courts will deal with this situation. Where one party to a compromise is labouring under some misapprehension about its terms that is known to, or has in some way been encouraged by, the other party, it is arguable that there is no genuine agreement between them even though, viewed objectively, it would appear that an agreement has been concluded.[67] That could render the whole agreement void *ab initio* or, alternatively, result in an agreement upon the basis of the understanding of the mistaken party for whom the remedy of rectification may be available in relation to any written agreement made pursuant to the negotiations.[68] 4–22

The cases to which reference is made below must now be viewed in the light of the restatement of the law of mistake in *The Great Peace* and the proposition that a mistake of law may now afford grounds for treating a compromise as void. 4–23

In *Wilding v Sanderson*,[69] a consent order was made directing the taking of accounts between the parties. One party thought that a particular form of account had been agreed not involving the payment of interest. The other party intended the converse. The terms of the consent order, on their true 4–24

---

[64] In previous editions the case of *Hickman v Berens* [1895] 2 Ch. 638 has been advanced as an example of the application of this principle. However, in *Chitty on Contracts* (29th ed., 2004) it is suggested that this case would not be followed today because of the objective nature of the test required by *The Great Peace* (see n.39, above) and since the compromise agreement did express "exactly what one of the parties meant". This approach might still afford a solution to the problems associated with a compromise of claims arising from a dispute which apparently settles both insured and uninsured losses, when one party intended that it should be so and the other did not so intend: *cf*. para.3–24, above. However, the actual terms of the agreement, properly construed, will probably determine the outcome of any such issue. See also *Chitty on Contracts* (29th ed., 2004), paras 2–030 and 5–056.
[65] See n.39, above.
[66] See n.44, above.
[67] This would seem to apply to a unilateral mistake of law affecting the appreciation by one party of the terms of a compromise, which is known to the other party: *Stone v Godfrey* (1854) 5 De G.M. & G. 76 at 90. A mistake as to the effect of the compromise will not of itself do so: *Taylor v Taylor* (1976) C.A.T. 228A; *Powell v Smith* (1872) L.R. 14 Eq. 85; *Hart v Hart* (1881) 18 Ch.D. 670.
[68] *Chitty on Contracts* (29th ed., 2004), para.5–067. It may also afford a defence to a claim for specific performance: *ibid.*, para.5–066.
[69] [1897] 2 Ch. 534.

construction, showed that interest was to be charged. The Court of Appeal held, however, that the mistake of one party as to the meaning of the words of the consent order had been contributed to by the other because of certain letters written on their behalf prior to the compromise, the minutes of judgment prepared by them and some remarks of their counsel. There was no real agreement between the parties.[70]

4–25 Where, however, the unilateral mistake is not known to, or contributed to by, the other party and can, therefore, be seen as a one-sided mistake simpliciter, the compromise will be upheld.

In *Taylor v Taylor*,[71] negotiations took place between the solicitors acting for H and W with a view to compromising financial issues. A concluded agreement was arrived at in correspondence whereby W would give up her right to periodical payments for herself (but not for the children) if H would transfer the matrimonial home into her sole name subject to a charge in his favour for a specified sum. H in fact entered into the agreement thinking that W had relinquished her rights to periodical payments for the children as well, his solicitors not having made this clear in the negotiations. The Court of Appeal held that H could not go behind the correspondence and say that he was mistaken about its effect. It was not a case of mutual or common mistake. It was a mistake of H himself "not known to the other party, nor contributed to by her".[72]

4–26 In *Olympia Sauna Shipping Co SA v Shinwa Kaiun Kaisha Ltd, The Ypatia Halcoussi*,[73] C chartered its vessel to D under a time charter on the New York Produce Exchange form for one round trip carrying a cargo of coal. The vessel arrived in Vancouver to load coal in March 1981, but there was a delay in berthing with the result that D claimed that the vessel had been off-hire for something over 13 days. On July 8, D submitted a hire statement to C which showed a deduction of $226,088 in respect of time lost at Vancouver and $28,636 in respect of bunkers. After an allowance for commission (which appears from the report to have been $5,652, representing 2.5 per cent of $226,088), the total deduction was shown as $249,072. The net result, if D was entitled to make these deductions, was a balance in D's favour of about $74,000. If the deductions were not permissible, the amount recoverable by C from D would be diminished by the $74,000 balance owed to D. This balance was not the subject of discussion or correspondence at that time. C and D were unable to agree on the deductions D was entitled to make for off-hire and bunkers and in July 1981 the dispute was referred to arbitration in London. C's points of claim claimed the amount deducted in respect of off-hire (less the commission), but at that stage made no reference to the deduction in respect of bunkers. In the points of defence and counterclaim D contended that the deductions were permissible and advanced a substantial (but unparticularised) counterclaim, but did not counterclaim for the $74,000 balance. The arbitration was due to take place on June 17 and 18, 1982. Negotiations with a view to resolving the dispute started in March 1982 and

---

[70] See *ibid.*, *per* Lindley L.J. at 550.
[71] (1976) C.A.T. 228A.
[72] *per* Lord Denning M.R.
[73] [1985] 2 Lloyd's Rep. 364.

at about that time C gave notice of its intention to increase its claim in order to pursue the deduction of $28,636 in respect of bunkers, thus making its total claim in the sum of $249,072. At no time during the negotiations between March and June 1982, when the compromise agreement hereafter referred to was concluded, did either party make reference to the $74,000 balance. On June 8, C indicated to D's solicitors by telex that C would be "prepared to accept [$]195,000 in total and final settlement of all outstanding claims and amounts whatsoever arising out of the ... time charter, both parties to forgo all claims and demands against the other". On June 9, D's solicitors replied by telex saying that D "accepts the terms of settlement" and indicating that the money would be paid on or before June 18. The cheque that D proffered to discharge the debt under the compromise was for $195,000 less the $74,000 balance which D said was not comprehended by the settlement, but which in fact D had overlooked and forgotten about at the time of the settlement. C refused to accept this and sued for the whole sum of $195,000. D counterclaimed for rectification of the agreement alleging common mistake or unilateral mistake. Bingham J. (as he then was) held:

(a) that there could have been no common mistake because D, having forgotten about it, had no intention with regard to the $74,000 balance at any relevant time before the compromise agreement, and C either had no intention with regard to it or did have intention, being that it should not be deducted from the sum to be paid;

(b) if there was a unilateral mistake (which there could not have been because D had forgotten about the $74,000 balance), P had no actual knowledge of such mistake.

In *O.T. Africa Line Ltd v Vickers plc*,[74] C and D had been negotiating the settlement of a dispute about the delayed shipment of four battle tanks from England to Nigeria. The claim was for about US $700,000 plus interest and costs, and the trial was fixed for January 15, 1996. In November 1995 D paid into court the sum of US $103,000 in settlement of the claim. This was not accepted and on December 8 C offered to settle for approximately US $185,000 for total detention costs plus a contribution to fixed costs of US $280,000, interest and costs. This offer was expressed to be open for 14 days. Various other discussions took place thereafter in which the figures mentioned by, or on behalf of, each side were expressed in US dollars. On December 22, D's solicitors faxed an offer to C's solicitors for "the total sum of £150,000 (including the sum in court)", the offer being expressed to be open until January 4 unless withdrawn sooner. An offer of £150,000 was not what D intended. It was intended that an offer of US $155,000, which had previously been made in oral discussions, be repeated. D's solicitors' fax was a mistake. D sought to argue, *inter alia*, that the agreement reached ought to be set aside on the grounds of unilateral mistake. Mance J., as he then was, held that since C "were ... not aware of, or in a position where they shut their eyes to, or responsible for or at fault in respect of any mistake made on [D's] side", there were no grounds for setting the agreement aside.

4–27

Traditionally, it has appeared that an interlocutory consent order made on the basis of a purely unilateral mistake not known to, or contributed to, by the other party may be set aside or varied.[75] Where, however, the

4–28

---

[74] [1996] 1 Lloyd's Rep. 700. See also *EasyFind (NSW) Pty Ltd v Paterson* (1987) 11 N.S.W.L.R. 98.
[75] See paras 6–21—6–24, below, and the implications of this in matrimonial finance cases at paras 32–29 *et seq.*, below.

consent order reflects a true compromise, it is unlikely that a purely unilateral mistake will afford grounds for the intervention of the court.[76]

4–29   Another instance of a unilateral mistake operating to defeat a compromise would arise where a successful plea of *non est factum* could be raised in relation, say, to proceedings to enforce the terms of a deed of compromise. In general terms,[77] a party who has signed a document essentially or fundamentally different from what was intended by him to be signed will not be bound by its terms. The plea does not, of course, avail a person who seeks merely to allege that he did not read the agreement or did not understand the scope or effect of its terms.[78]

4–30   **Mistaken record of compromise.**   Having reached agreement on all issues, the parties may proceed to incorporate the terms of the agreement in a formal written agreement. Where proceedings are extant they may wish to embody in a consent order or judgment such terms as are capable of embodiment in a court order or judgment. The situation may arise where the written agreement or court order does not properly and accurately reflect the agreement reached.

4–31   So far as a written agreement is concerned, if its inaccuracy has arisen as the result of a mutual mistake of the parties the court may well order its rectification.[79] Equally, if the document is inaccurate because of the mistake of one party which is known to the other who does not draw attention to the mistake, the court will order rectification because it would be inequitable not to do so.[80]

4–32   If a court order or judgment does not properly reflect the parties' agreement the court may have jurisdiction to amend it under the "slip rule"[81] or under its inherent jurisidiction.[82]

4–33   The principles and practice reflected in the foregoing two paragraphs have been applied in the context of an incorrectly drafted Tomlin order:

> In *Islam v Askar*,[83] C and D were partners in a restaurant business. In October 1991 C gave notice of dissolution of the partnership and in

---

[76] See para.4–22, above.
[77] *Chitty on Contracts* (29th ed., 2004), Vol.1, paras 5–086 *et seq*.
[78] *ibid.*, Vol.1, para.12–002. A misrepresentation as to the effect of a compromise may operate to invalidate it, however: See *Hirschfeld v The London, Brighton and South Coast Railway Company* (1876) 2 Q.B.D. 1, discussed at para.4–46, below.
[79] *Craddock Bros v Hunt* [1923] 2 Ch. 136; *USA v Motor Trucks Ltd* [1924] A.C. 196.
[80] *Thomas Bates Ltd v Wyndham's Ltd* [1981] 1 W.L.R. 505, CA. See also *Riverlate Properties v Paul* [1975] Ch. 133, CA; *Islam v Askar*, noted at para.4–37, below.
[81] CPR r.40.12.
[82] *The Bellcairn* (1885) 10 P.D. 161; *Ainsworth v Wilding* [1896] 1 Ch. 673; *Re South American and Mexican Bank Ex p. Bank of England* [1895] 1 Ch. 37 at 45; *Saunders v Saunders* (1978) 8 Fam. Law 206. See also *Islam v Askar*, noted at para.4–33, below.
[83] (1994) C.A.T. 1240; *The Times*, October 20, 1994. For Tomlin orders, see Chs 9 and 11, below.

November 1991 instituted proceedings for its winding-up. Various negotiations took place resulting in an exchange of faxes between solicitors by virtue of which D agreed to "buy out" C's interest in the partnership for £67,000. That sum was to be payable as to £20,000 immediately and the balance at the rate of £350 per week. It was also agreed that C would accept responsibility for a loan from his bank which had been used in connection with the partnership. D's solicitors suggested that a Tomlin order should be made and sent a draft to C's solicitors. That draft incorrectly provided for a starting figure for payment of the balance of £40,000 rather £47,000, monthly payments of the balance and an indemnity by C in relation to creditors other than the bank. The Tomlin order was made incorporating those mistakes in the schedule to the order, C's solicitors having failed to notice them. Shortly afterwards C's solicitors noticed the mistake as to the starting figure for the balance and drew the attention of D's solicitors to the mistake. A fresh Tomlin order was made rectifying this mistake, but the other two went unnoticed at that stage. When C's solicitors were eventually alerted to these other two mistakes, D's solicitors declined to agree to the rectification of the schedule to the Tomlin order, contending that the failure of C's solicitors to note and correct the mistakes earlier resulted in a binding agreement. It was further contended that, if this argument were wrong, but the agreement originally made had been incorrectly reflected in the Tomlin order, a fresh action was necessary to achieve rectification of the order. Finally, it was contended that there was no inherent jurisdiction to correct the schedule to the order as the schedule was not part of the order. The Court of Appeal rejected each of these arguments and held that:

(1) where the Tomlin order "mistakenly did not reflect the agreement correctly and the counter-party is aware of that fact, his conscience being affected in equity, and he seeks to take advantage of that mistake", there is an inherent jurisdiction to correct the Tomlin order;
(2) whilst the schedule to the order may not be part of the order, it is part of the record of the court and is consequently amenable to the inherent jurisdiction.

In the normal course of events, the court will play no part in the drafting of the terms reflected in a Tomlin order schedule. This will be a matter for the parties. Even if the parties include a provision which, for example, is too vaguely expressed to be capable of enforcement,[84] the court will not decline to make the order requested despite the difficulties which may subsequently arise.[85] However, it is not unusual for the court to propose alterations to draft consent orders prepared by the parties. The fact that such alterations are proposed and accepted does not render the order a nullity. The same principle applies when the court makes alterations to the schedule to a Tomlin order in order to give effect to the intention of the parties and to which no objection is subsequently taken.

4–34

In *Allied Irish Bank v Hughes and Fountain*,[86] D1's hotel was charged to C as mortgagees. After the terms of the mortgage had not been complied with C instituted proceedings for possession of the property. Discussions took place

4–35

---

[84] *Wilson and Whitworth Ltd v Express and Independent Newspapers Ltd* [1969] 1 W.L.R. 197, noted at para.3–51, above.
[85] *ibid.*
[86] (1994) C.A.T. 1055.

between C, D1 and D2's solicitors, D2 being D1's husband. In due course an agreement of compromise was reached which was to be incorporated into a Tomlin order. In order to give effect to the agreement D2 was to become a party to the proceedings brought by C. The agreement contained provisions for the payment of various sums by D1 and D2 upon or by certain dates. One of the provisions was in terms that "[the] Defendants will pay" to C a certain sum by a certain date and a subsequent term was that "[the] Defendants will further pay" to C interest upon that sum between the date of the agreement and the date for payment. When the proposed Tomlin order, in the schedule to which these two terms appeared, was placed before the district judge he added the words "jointly and severally" in relation to the obligations undertaken by D1 and D2 in respect of each of these two terms. He also added the provision into the order that there should be no order as to costs save that D1's costs should be taxed in accordance with the Legal Aid Regulations. The Tomlin order was thus made and entered into the court records. It was sent to the parties, including solicitors acting for D1 and D2. Those solicitors, who had not been in attendance before the district judge, raised no objection to the alterations and proceeded to tax their costs in accordance with the additional part of the order added by the district judge. The Court of Appeal held that what had occurred had not rendered the Tomlin order a nullity and, in any event, the order, having been referred back to D1 and D2's solicitors who acted upon it and took no point upon it, must in the circumstances be taken to have been accepted by the parties.

4–36   Where, of course, the provisions of a Tomlin order schedule are clear and unambiguous and truly reflect the parties' prior agreement, there are no grounds for altering the terms thus recorded.[87]

MISREPRESENTATION

General

4–37   A false representation of a material fact, made prior to a compromise and which induces it, may, at the instance of the party misled, operate to vitiate the compromise. The misrepresentation may be set up as a defence to a claim for specific performance of the agreement or as the basis of a claim to have it set aside. If any loss has been occasioned by the misrepresentation it may give rise to a claim for damages (for fraudulent or negligent misrepresentation) or an indemnity (in the case of innocent misrepresentation).[88] This latter aspect is unlikely to have much practical significance in the context of compromise. If the agreement has been embodied or reflected in a court order or judgment, the order or judgment may be set aside.[89]

---

[87] *Nolan Davis Ltd v Catton*, unreported, March 6, 2001, TCC, H.H. Judge Wilcox.
[88] *Chitty on Contracts* (29th ed., 2004), Vol.1, Ch.6, paras 6–041 *et seq.*
[89] See Ch.12, below.

Are compromises contracts *uberrimae fidei*?

Before looking at some instances of misrepresentation in this context, the question of whether contracts of compromise are *uberrimae fidei* must be considered. Ordinarily, the non-disclosure of a material fact will not constitute a misrepresentation[90] unless it makes that which is represented false.[91] But in certain classes of contract—called contracts *uberrimae fidei*—there must be full disclosure of all material facts. Without such disclosure a contract of this type is voidable. It has been suggested[92] that compromises belong to this class. However, modern textbooks[93] do not put ordinary compromises of disputes into this category and, it is submitted, that is the better view. All the cases relied upon as supporting the view that compromises are contracts *uberrimae fidei*[94] involved compromises of disputed rights under a will or settlement, often where infant beneficiaries were concerned. The Court of Equity insisted on full disclosure in such cases before being prepared to uphold any agreements reached.[95] It is inappropriate, it is submitted, to extend these authorities to suggest that all compromises belong to this class.

4–38

The better view, it is submitted, is supported by *Turner v Green*,[96] where a compromise of an action for an account was held to be specifically enforceable notwithstanding the suppression of a material fact prior to the

4–39

---

[90] See, *e.g.* per Lord Atkin in *Bell v Lever Bros Ltd* [1932] A.C. 161 at 227.
[91] *Dimmock v Hallett* (1866) L.R. 2 Ch. App. 21.
[92] Edwards, *The Law of Compromise and Family Settlements* (1925), pp.141–147; and Kerr, *Fraud and Mistake* (7th ed., 1952), p.96.
[93] *Chitty on Contracts* (29th ed., 2004), Vol.1, paras 6–139 *et seq.*; *Anson's Law of Contract* (28th ed.); *Cheshire, Fifoot and Furmston's Law of Contract* (14th ed.).
[94] For example *Gibbons v Caunt* (1799) 4 Ves. 849; *Brooke v Mostyn* (1864) 2 De G.J. & Sm. 373; *Gordon v Gordon* (1816–19) 3 Swans. 400; *Goymour v Pigge* (1844) 13 L.J. Ch. 322.
[95] In *Marshall v Marshall*, unreported, October 8, 1998, CA, Thorpe L.J. said this: "When the misfortune of a contested probate action falls on a family, the pressures and stresses are, in many respects, similar to those that afflict a family torn by contested proceedings following the dissolution of a marriage. In my judgment, the negotiation of compromise of such proceedings, whether in the Family Division or the Chancery Division, must be characterised by candour and not jeopardised by side deals, concealed from one or more of the negotiating parties. In other words, I would hold that there was a duty of full and frank disclosure of facts and circumstances relevant to the weighing of a proposal for the formation of the compromise".
[96] [1895] 2 Ch. 205. See N. Andrews, *Principles of Civil Procedure* (1994), para.13–047. The rationale for this principle was, it is respectfully submitted, put well by Rimer J. in *Clarion Ltd v National Provident Institution* [2000] 1 W.L.R. 1888, at 1905: "The compromise of litigation is a contractual exercise in which it is the commonest thing for each side to be aware of facts and matters of which it either knows or at least suspects the other side is ignorant. If each side knew all that the other side knew then either no or only a very different compromise would be reached. In the negotiation of such compromises the parties must be careful not to make any misrepresentations. But there is in my view no general duty imposed upon them in the nature of a duty of disclosure. The negotiations are in the nature of an arm's length commercial bargain. Each party has to look after his own interests and neither owes a duty of care to the other".

conclusion of the compromise by the party seeking specific performance. Chitty J., having cited the general proposition that mere silence in relation to a material fact is not a ground for rescission or a defence to specific performance unless there is "an obligation to disclose", said[97] that "[i]t cannot be contended that [there was] . . . any obligation to disclose" the material fact in that case. There is a further passage in the judgment[98] from which it is plain that the learned judge did not regard the contract of compromise in that case as requiring *uberrima fides*. Furthermore, in *Wales v Wadham*,[99] Tudor Evans J. had to consider the question of whether at common law a compromise of financial differences between estranged spouses was one requiring *uberrima fides*. He concluded that it was not. His decision was reinforced by the fact that, in the particular case, the parties had not insisted on full disclosure. Given that whether a contract was to be regarded as requiring *uberrima fides* "must depend upon its substantial character and how it came to be effected",[1] the learned judge concluded that this one was not.[2]

4-40   A suppression of a fact or document which, if its existence were revealed, would destroy totally (rather than, perhaps, merely undermine to some extent) a claim being advanced by a claimant would involve the claimant in pursuing a claim which he knew to be unfounded. A compromise of such a claim could be invalidated.[3]

4-41   It would appear, therefore, that each case would have to be looked at on its own facts to see whether a full disclosure was being insisted upon by the parties. In the general run of litigation this is unlikely to be so and indeed negotiations might be hindered by such insistence. Two areas where full disclosure would seem to be required as a matter of law are:

(a) the compromise of a partnership dispute;[4] and
(b) a compromise involving the actual or potential transfer of title to land.[5]

---

[97] [1895] 2 Ch. 205 at 208.
[98] *ibid.* at 209.
[99] [1977] 1 W.L.R. 199, not criticised on this point by the House of Lords in *Livesey v Jenkins* [1985] A.C. 424.
[1] *Seaton v Heath* [1899] 1 Q.B. 782 at 792, *per* Romer L.J.
[2] In *Livesey v Jenkins*, n.99, above, a statutory duty of disclosure was said to arise from the provisions of the Matrimonial Causes Act 1973, s.25. To the extent to which *Wales v Wadham* was contrary to this view it was disapproved by the House of Lords, but no doubt was cast upon the general proposition referred to in the text.
[3] See para.2–19, above. There is continuing obligation on parties during litigation to disclose documents that come to their notice: CPR r.31.11. A failure to disclose a material document discovered after the original list of documents is served, or which comes into existence thereafter, could afford grounds for alleging a misrepresentation: see Andrews, n.96, above, para.13–049.
[4] *Chitty on Contracts* (29th ed., 2004), Vol.1, para.6–157.
[5] *ibid.*, paras 6–152—6–153.

Some examples

It has been noted[6] that the assertion of a claim known by the claimant to be baseless, which induces the compromise, will be regarded in law as a fraudulent misrepresentation. Opinions may, of course, differ as to the validity of assertions made. Generally, a statement of unfounded opinion which induces a contract will not be an operative misrepresentation.[7] If, however, a person represents that he holds an opinion when in fact he does not, that will constitute a false representation.[8] The dividing line between statements of opinion and fact may be difficult to determine, particularly where the representor is in a better position than the representee to assess the accuracy and validity of the statement.[9] 4–42

Where, during the course of negotiations, a representation is made which at the time is true but which subsequently becomes false, a failure to disclose the changed position would be, in effect, a misrepresentation.[10] 4–43

> In *Gilbert v Endean*,[11] a claimant had, in effect, obtained a judgment against a debtor in a certain sum. Thereafter he agreed to accept a lesser sum on the basis of the debtor's represented poor financial position. It was known by all parties that the debtor's father was a wealthy man but that he had refused to help his son. Before the compromise agreement was signed the father died. The debtor's solicitor knew this at the time of the signing but failed to disclose it to the claimant's solicitor. The Court of Appeal held that the failure to disclose what was clearly a material fact given the earlier position was, in effect, a misrepresentation.

A statement of intention as to future conduct is not a representation of fact unless the intention of the person making the statement is, at the time of making it, the opposite of what is stated. Thus, a party to negotiations with a view to compromise who states his existing intention accurately and 4–44

---

[6] See para.2–19, above.
[7] *Anderson v Pacific Fire and Marine Insurance Co* (1872) L.R. 7 C.P. 65. "When an opinion is expressed the person who expresses it either does or does not know facts which justify that opinion. The existence of those facts, and his state of knowledge in relation to them, are themselves facts capable of being misrepresented by implication by the expression of opinion ... Sometimes an expression of opinion may carry with it no implication other than that the opinion is genuinely held. But on other occasions, as in this case, the circumstances may be such as to give rise to the implied representation that the person knew of facts which justified his opinion": *BG Plc v Nelson Group Services (Maintenance) Ltd* [2002] EWCA Civ 547, *per* Kennedy L.J.
[8] *Chitty on Contracts* (29th ed., 2004), Vol.1, para.6–006.
[9] cf. *Brown v Raphael* [1958] Ch. 636; *Esso Petroleum Co Ltd v Mardon* [1976] Q.B. 801; *Chitty on Contracts* (29th ed., 2004), Vol.1, paras 6–007 and 6–010.
[10] It might also be considered to give rise to a unilateral mistake of fact on the part of the party misled known to, or contributed to, by the other party: paras 4–24 *et seq.*, above.
[11] (1878) 9 Ch.D. 259. See also *With v O'Flanagan* [1936] Ch. 575, CA; *Davies v London and Provincial Marine Insurance Co* (1878) 9 Ch.D. 469; *Dietz v Lennig Chemicals Ltd* [1969]1 A.C. 170, considered at para.4–52, below.

honestly but who thereafter, but before the agreement is concluded, changes his mind is not under a duty to disclose it to the other party.[12] A representation by a party that he possesses a settled intention to pursue (or not to pursue) a particular course of conduct when no such settled intention exists can amount to a misrepresentation.[13]

4–45 The legal effect of a misrepresentation of law has hitherto been somewhat uncertain. As in the case of a mistake of law,[14] the dividing line between a misrepresentation of law and one of fact or opinion is often difficult to identify.[15] However, if a statement can fairly be characterised as one of law, such a statement, if incorrect or misleading, has usually been regarded as incapable of amounting to an actionable misrepresentation.[16] However, recent developments in the law of restitution[17] suggest that the distinction between a mistake of fact and one of law is not sustainable. It would seem to follow that such a distinction could not now also be made in the context of misrepresentation.[18] If that is a correct analysis of the recent authorities, a misrepresentation of law must now be regarded as capable of being relied upon to set aside an agreement concluded in reliance upon it. Since representations of law are frequently made in precontractual negotiations with a view to compromise, it is likely that it will be only in the most compelling of circumstances that a court would entertain the proposition that an incorrect assertion of law constitutes an actionable misrepresentation.[19]

4–46 Where, however, a misrepresentation is made as to the legal effect of a compromise, particularly where the representee is not independently legally advised, there are circumstances in which the court will intervene:

> In *Hirschfeld v The London, Brighton, and South Coast Railway Company*,[20] C was injured when travelling as a passenger in one of D's trains. Not long after the accident a representative of D called on C to see if C intended to make a claim. C said that he did and after discussion he agreed to accept a certain sum from D in full satisfaction of his claims. He signed a deed of release. Thereafter C sought to pursue a claim for a greater sum, alleging that D's representative had told him that if his injuries proved to be more serious than anticipated he could, notwithstanding the terms of the release, seek and obtain greater compensation. It was held[21] that C was entitled to rely upon the misrepresentation to avoid the terms of the release.

---

[12] *Wales v Wadham* [1977] 1 W.L.R. 199 at 211.
[13] *cf. Livesey v Jenkins* [1985] A.C. 424.
[14] See para.4–20, above.
[15] *Chitty on Contracts* (29th ed., 2004), Vol.1, para.6–011.
[16] *Beesly v Hallwood Estates Ltd* [1960] 1 W.L.R. 549.
[17] *Kleinwort Benson Ltd v Lincoln City Council* [1999] 1 A.C. 153, HL.
[18] *Chitty on Contracts* (29th ed., 2004), Vol.1, para.6–011.
[19] *cf.* para.4–23, above.
[20] (1876) 2 Q.B.D. 1. See also *West London Commercial Bank v Kitson* (1884) 13 Q.B.D. 360 at 362–363.
[21] Mellor and Lush JJ.

In *Saunders v Ford Motor Co Ltd*[22] C suffered an injury in the course of his 4–47
employment by D. D's insurers had an office at D's works. A representative of
those insurers had a conversation with C during which C agreed to accept
£200 in full settlement of all his claims. The insurers' representative told C
that the sum was "only for pain and suffering and for [his] absence from
work" and, in effect, that if C's condition got worse the position could be
reviewed. Paull J. held that C was not bound by the agreement because either
there was attached to the agreement an understanding that he could come
back if his condition deteriorated or because the parties were not *ad idem*.[23]

A misrepresentation may arise in a variety of ways:

In *Dietz v Lennig Chemicals Ltd*[24] a claim by a widow, on behalf of herself 4–48
and her child, under the Fatal Accidents Act, arising from the death of her
husband, was compromised and, in due course, put before the court for
approval. At the time the agreement was concluded she had not remarried, but
by the time it was put before the court she had. She had not told her solicitors,
who at all times up to and including the court hearing believed that she was
unmarried. Indeed, the title of the court papers remained in her old surname.
The House of Lords held that the failure to disclose the changed situation
(albeit completely innocent) and the use of the old surname in the court
proceedings constituted a misrepresentation.

In *Re Roberts*,[25] a solicitor misread or misunderstood counsel's opinion on a 4–49
particular matter and thereby misrepresented its effect to one of a number of
legatees he was advising. On the faith of what was represented a particular
legatee entered into a compromise of her claims against the estate with other
legatees. The Court of Appeal held that it should be set aside.

Needless to say, once a representation had been made it will be operative 4–50
only if:

(a) it has been addressed to the party misled; and
(b) it induced the compromise.

These will be matters of fact to be determined.[26]

Relief available

The principal equitable relief available in respect of any form of misrepre- 4–51
sentation (whether fraudulent, negligent or innocent) is that of rescission.
Provided the party misled has not affirmed the compromise or been guilty

---

[22] [1970] 1 Lloyd's Rep. 379.
[23] In *Arrale v Costain Civil Engineering Ltd* [1976] 1 Lloyd's Rep. 98 at 104–105, Stephenson L.J. said that he regarded the decision in *Saunders* "as based on a misrepresentation inducing the signing of the receipt ... and I would respectfully agree with it." It is submitted that this is indeed the better view of what fell for determination in the *Saunders* case.
[24] [1969] 1 A.C. 170.
[25] [1905] 1 Ch. 704.
[26] See, *e.g.* the analysis of the evidence covering these two matters in *Wales v Wadham* [1977] 1 W.L.R. 199 at 212–214.

of undue delay, or third-party rights have not intervened, or a substantial restoration of the status quo has not become impossible, the court will be prepared to set it aside together with any consent order or judgment based upon it.[27] Since for most practical purposes in the context of compromise that remedy (with appropriate consequential directions) is the one which will be sought, it is not proposed to examine the circumstances in which damages may fall to be awarded for a misrepresentation.[28]

DURESS AND UNDUE INFLUENCE

General

4–52 Certain forms of duress upon a contracting party have always operated to vitiate the agreement at common law.[29] Other forms of undue influence and pressure may operate to do so in equity. The precise extent of the circumstances in which undue influence and pressure operate are difficult to define.[30] Indeed, any attempt to do so has been firmly rejected by the House of Lords.[31] Each case depends upon its own particular facts. Whether the matter be approached on the basis of evidence of a particular factual situation or a presumption of undue influence in certain circumstances, the court will intervene only if an unfair advantage has been taken of one party by the other (in the sense of domination or victimisation) leading to a manifestly disadvantageous transaction. The concept of "inequality of bargaining power"[32] was also firmly rejected.

4–53 All earlier cases raising the issue of undue influence must be considered to be subject to this restatement of the law. As with the concept of "economic duress",[33] with which undue influence to some extent overlaps, it may have a significance in the context of compromise.[34]

Examples in the context of compromise

4–54 **Threat of proceedings.** Where a debt has arisen in circumstances which might render the debtor liable to criminal proceedings (for example, where a company employee or director has misappropriated company funds for

---

[27] *Chitty on Contracts* (29th ed., 2004), Vol.1, paras 6–100 *et seq.*; *Huddersfield Banking Co v Henry Lister* [1895] 2 Ch. 273, referred to at para.4–17, above.
[28] *Chitty on Contracts* (29th ed., 2004), Vol.1, paras 6–041 *et seq.*
[29] For example actual or threatened violence to the person or a near relative.
[30] *Chitty on Contracts* (29th ed., 2004), Vol.1, Ch.7.
[31] *National Westminster Bank plc v Morgan* [1985] 1 A.C. 686.
[32] *Lloyds Bank Ltd v Bundy* [1975] Q.B. 326 at 339, *per* Lord Denning M.R.
[33] See paras 4–62 *et seq.*, below.
[34] *cf. Backhouse v Backhouse* [1978] 1 W.L.R. 243 at 252 (Balcombe J.). See also *Horry v Tate & Lyle Refineries Ltd* [1982] 2 Lloyd's Rep. 416.

his own use), a threat of prosecution will not necessarily invalidate a compromise of the claim.[35] It will depend on the circumstances in which the threat is made.[36]

A threat of civil proceedings will not, of course, operate to invalidate a compromise of the claim.[37] A compromise of an unfounded claim known to be so by the claimant will be ineffective[38] and consequently a threat to pursue such a claim which results in a compromise will invalidate the agreement. 4–55

> In *Brent v Brent*,[39] C was the son of TB who died without making provision for his widow and family. On TB's death C became absolutely entitled to premises comprised in a settlement made by one of TB's forbears. He remained in possession of those premises for some 21 years until he entered into a contract to sell them. For some 14 years following his father's death C provided his mother, HB, with an annual allowance and, after this was discontinued, with certain other things and small sums of money. Some years after the allowance as such was discontinued, a conveyancer called Snell, acting on behalf of HB, caused a distress to be put upon the premises alleging arrears of the allowance. C, who was alarmed at this and at Snell's threats to sell his stock, signed an agreement prepared by Snell to pay the sum claimed together with the costs of the distress. Shortly thereafter Snell represented to C that HB and others had a claim to part of the property and that they were about to take proceedings. The claims advanced were unfounded and Snell knew this. As a result of Snell's representation C entered into a further agreement whereby the property was to be sold and the various "claimants", together with Snell, were to receive shares in the proceeds of sale. The Lord Chancellor held that the agreement could not be supported and should be set aside as a result of Snell's "threats and intimidation" on HB's behalf. 4–56

Threat of unlawful act. A compromise induced by a threat to do or abstain from doing something which it is unlawful to do or abstain from doing, when the party agreeing has no option but to agree, will be set aside: 4–57

> In *Ormes v Beadel*,[40] a building contractor in the course of erection of a building asked the architect for money, to which he was lawfully entitled, to pay his workmen. The money was urgently required. The architect threatened not to pay him unless he gave up the contract on distinctly disadvantageous terms. The agreement was set aside. 4–58

---

[35] *Flower v Sadler* (1882) 10 Q.B.D. 572, distinguishing *Williams v Bayley* (1866) L.R. 1 H.L. 200, and following *Ward v Lloyd* (1843) 7 Scott. N.R. 499. An agreement not to prosecute may be illegal: see para.4–77, below.
[36] *Chitty on Contracts* (29th ed., 2004), Vol.1, para.7–039.
[37] *cf. ibid.*, Vol.1, para.7–041.
[38] See para.2–19, above.
[39] (1841) 10 L.J. Ch. 84.
[40] (1860) 2 Giff. 166; reversed on appeal on the basis, in effect, that the contractor had affirmed the agreement: 2 De G.F. & J. 333.

4–59   In *D. & C. Builders Ltd v Rees*,[41] C was a small firm of builders which had done some work for D. It was lawfully entitled to £482 for the work it had done. After several months of delay, and at a time when C was in a parlous financial state, D told C that it could have £300 or it would get nothing. It accepted the sum in full settlement. The Court of Appeal held that C was not estopped from suing for the balance. D had unfairly taken advantage of C's position.

4–60   A threat that goods unlawfully detained will not be released unless some payment is made will invalidate the contract.[42] If, however, there is a genuine dispute between the parties as to whether the detention is unlawful, a valid compromise involving the release of the goods and payment may be made.[43]

4–61   **Threat of otherwise lawful act.** This is a difficult concept, but nonetheless one which cannot be ignored in this context. *Prima facie* it is difficult to see why a person may not threaten to do something which is lawful in order to induce another person to come to an agreement with him. A threat of civil proceedings is plainly lawful and a compromise of those threatened proceedings will not be set aside.[44] However, there may be rare situations in which the threat goes far beyond what is either normal or reasonable behaviour or, in the particular context in question, what is reasonable in relation to the dispute the parties are endeavouring to settle.[45] It appears[46]

---

[41] [1966] 2 Q.B. 617. This case could be seen as one involving "economic duress": see para.4-66, below. See also *Occidental Worldwide Investment Corp v Skibs A/S Avanti (The Siboen and The Sibotre)* [1976] 1 Lloyd's Rep. 293 at 335 (Kerr J.).
[42] *Somes v British Empire Shipping Co* (1860) 8 H.L.C. 338; *Green v Duckett* (1883) 11 Q.B.D. 275.
[43] *Atlee v Backhouse* (1838) 3 M. & W. 633.
[44] See para.4–55, above.
[45] In *CTN Cash and Carry Ltd v Gallagher Ltd* [1994] 4 All E.R. 713, Steyn L.J., as he then was, said that "[o]utside the field of protected relationships, and in a purely commercial context, it might be a relatively rare case in which 'lawful act duress' can be established. And it might be particularly difficult to establish duress if the defendant bona fide considered that this demand was valid. In this complex and changing branch of the law I deliberately refrain from saying 'never'". In *Huyton SA v Peter Cremer GmbH & Co* [1999] 1 Lloyd's Rep. 620, a case involving the suggestion that a compromise was voidable on the grounds of economic duress, Mance J., as he then was, said at 637, having quoted Steyn L.J.'s words, that the proposition that "good or bad faith may be particularly relevant when considering whether a case might represent a rare example of 'lawful act duress' is not difficult to accept. Even in cases where the pressure relied on is an actual or threatened breach of duty, it seems to me better not to exclude the possibility that the state of mind of the person applying such pressure may in some circumstances be significant, whether or not the other innocent party correctly appreciated such state of mind. 'Never' in this context also seems too strong a word". A little earlier in his judgment the learned judge had said this: "The law will of course be cautious about re-opening an apparent compromise made in good faith on both sides. But it seems, on the one hand, questionable whether a 'compromise' achieved by one party who does not believe that he had at least an arguable case is a compromise at all—though it may be upheld if there is other consideration . . and, on the other hand, difficult to accept that illegitimate pressure applied by a party who believes bona fide in his case could never give grounds for relief against an apparent compromise".
[46] See *Chitty on Contracts*, (29th ed., 2004), Vol.1, para.7–036.

that the US courts are more willing to employ this concept than their English counterparts. Chitty records a case in which a settlement of an injured employee's claim for damages at a manifestly low figure, procured by an otherwise lawful threat to dismiss him, was set aside on this ground.[47]

Economic duress. The pressure applied in the cases referred to in paras 4–58 and 4–59, above, was of an economic nature. It is now clearly established that "economic pressure may be sufficient to amount to duress for this purpose, provided at least that the economic pressure may be characterised as illegitimate and has constituted a significant cause inducing the [claimant] to enter into the relevant contract".[48] The suggestion that the coercion must have been such as to vitiate his consent[49] has been criticised and its utility in this context questioned.[50] However, whatever the precise parameters of the concept of economic duress may be, it could clearly have considerable significance in the context of compromise. 4–62

The dividing line between the type of economic pressure that is illegitimate and that which is legitimate may not always be easy to identify. Many pressures will be brought to bear in negotiations within a commercial context (including, of course, negotiations with a view to compromising a dispute, actual or potential) which will be regarded as both commonplace and acceptable.[51] Each case will depend upon its own facts, but the essential question will be whether the actual economic pressure exerted in the particular circumstances left the party upon whom it was imposed with no real choice (or no reasonable alternative) but to enter into the compromise.[52] Examples can be found on each side of the dividing line: 4–63

> In *Dorimix SRL v Visage Imports Ltd*,[53] C was an Italian company trading as a supplier of ladies' and men's clothing. D, a UK-based company, was an importer and wholesaler of such clothing. D placed orders with C for the delivery of goods over the period July to September 1989 so that the clothing could be in the retail market for the autumn/winter season. Delays in delivery occurred and the parties were in dispute about responsibility for these delays. On November 1 a compromise was reached and recorded in the following terms:
>
> "1. Re Ladies Shipments. 4–64

---

[47] *ibid.*; *Mitchell v CC Sanitation Co* (1968) 430 S.W. (2d) 933.
[48] *Dimskal Shipping Co SA v ITWF ("The Evia Luck")* [1992] A.C. 152 at 165, *per* Lord Goff of Chieveley.
[49] Beatson, *The Use and Abuse of Unjust Enrichment* (1991), pp.113–117; Birks [1990] 3 L.M.C.L.Q. 342.
[50] See n.48, above.
[51] *Chitty on Contracts* (29th ed., 2004), Vol.1, paras 7–006 and 7–022.
[52] *ibid.*, Vol.1, para.7–025.
[53] Unreported, May 18, 1999, CA. See also para.39–37, below.

"It was agreed today that all goods received into [D's] warehouse by Tuesday 7th November 1989 will be accepted at ordered price. Any goods received between Tuesday 7th November and Tuesday 21st November 1989 are subject to 25% discount. Any goods shipped after Friday 17th November 1989 are to be shipped free of charge.
2. Re Mens Shipments.
   a. [not relevant].
   b. Re all other mens outstanding purchase orders. If these goods are shipped before Friday 3rd November 1989 they are subject to 25% discount. If these goods are shipped after Friday 3rd November 1989 they are subject to 30% discount up until Friday 17th November 1989, after Friday 17th November any outstanding menswear orders will be shipped free of charge."

Because C had been concerned that D would not accept late delivery of the goods ordered earlier in the year, it had been looking for other outlets in the United Kingdom. C learned that garments such as those it was expecting to be delivered were on sale elsewhere at prices considerably lower than those at which C was proposing to sell them. D told C that it had been placed in an impossible situation as a result, but exaggerated the effect which this situation would have upon it to place pressure on C to agree, under threat of refusal by D to accept further deliveries or to pay the full price for those goods already shipped, to allow D a further discount. C agreed to a further significant discount on November 8. H.H. Judge Diamond Q.C. found that D's threat constituted "substantial and heavy economic pressure" on C which amounted to "illegitimate economic pressure". It constituted a threat not to perform the agreement of November 1 and amounted to a repudiation of that contract. It left C with only two practical alternatives: either to submit to D's demand or to accept the repudiation and sue for damages, the latter course being "financially unattractive and potentially disastrous". Although C lost the case on another issue and took that issue to the Court of Appeal, D did not appeal against the foregoing conclusion.

4-65   In *Hennessey v Craigmyle & Co Ltd*,[54] A was told by R that he would be summarily dismissed as from a week later, that his pay would stop, he would lose the use of his car and he would get no reference. The option was to be treated as having been made redundant with certain associated financial benefits. That option would only be available if he signed an agreement prepared by a conciliation officer of ACAS under s.134 of the Employment Protection (Consolidation) Act 1978, giving up his right to take proceedings before an industrial tribunal. He took legal advice, signed the agreement and was subsequently dismissed on the grounds of redundancy. Subsequently, A sought to argue, *inter alia*, that the agreement was voidable at common law on the grounds of "economic duress". The Court of Appeal held that the industrial tribunal had been entitled to reject this argument because A's will was not overborne: he had an alternative, albeit an unattractive one, of complaining to the industrial tribunal and drawing social security in the meantime.

---

[54] [1986] I.C.R. 461. It is questionable whether the decision in this case would be the same now following *Dimskal*, n.48, above. A case in which alleged "economic duress" in the context of a compromise was not upheld is *Hutchinson v Tamosious*, unreported, May 24, 1999 (H.H. Judge Hegarty Q.C.): see para.3-51, n.9, above.

A compromise entered into as a result of the undue influence of one 4–66
party over the other may, in certain circumstances, be set aside at the
instance of the party subjected to the undue influence.[55] The utility of
making the classification frequently made[56] between situations in which
actual undue influence operates and where (subject to disproof) it is
presumed to have operated because of the relationship of the parties, has
been questioned and labelled as "confusing" by the House of Lords.[57] The
issue is essentially one of fact depending on "the nature of the alleged
undue influence, the personality of the parties, their relationship, the
extent to which the transaction cannot readily be accounted for by the
ordinary motives or ordinary persons, and all the circumstances of the
case", presumptions in certain circumstances merely constituting tools in
resolving the issue.[58] Recourse to the question whether a transaction is to
the " manifest disadvantage" of the person influenced[59] has also been said
not to be helpful.[60] Where undue influence is established the transaction
may be set aside unless the person influenced loses the right to rescind.[61]

When the issue of undue influence arises the availability of independent 4–67
legal advice to the party subjected to the influence has always been
regarded as a material, though not always conclusive, factor in determining
whether the influence operated as a matter of fact.[62] Detailed guidance on
the duties of solicitors in the context of husband and wife cases has now
been given.[63] It will be a question of fact in every case whether, when
advice has been taken, it has had an "emancipating effect" in relation to
the undue influence exercised.[64]

Undue influence is perhaps, most likely to arise where members of a 4–68
family are in dispute; but it could as easily arise where a bank and its
customer compromise certain differences.[65] It has been held to operate in a

---

[55] *Chitty on Contracts* (29th ed., 2004), Vol.1, paras 7–047 *et seq.*
[56] *Barclays Bank plc v O'Brien* [1994] 1 A.C. 180 at 189–190, *per* Lord Browne-Wilkinson.
[57] *Royal Bank of Scotland v Etridge* [2001] UKHL 44; [2002] 2 A.C. 773.
[58] *ibid.*, *per* Lord Nicholls of Birkenhead at para.13, *per* Lord Clyde at para.92, *per* Lord Hobhouse of Woodborough at para.98 and *per* Lord Scott of Foscote at para.107.
[59] *National Westminster Bank plc v Morgan* [1985] 1 A.C. 686 at 704, *per* Lord Scarman.
[60] *Royal Bank of Scotland v Etridge*, n.57, above, *per* Lord Nicholls of Birkenhead at para.26.
[61] *CIBC Mortgages plc v Pitt* [1994] 1 A.C. 200. See para.4–70, below.
[62] *Powell v Powell* [1900] 1 Ch. 243, but now to read subject to *Royal Bank of Scotland v Etridge*, n.57, above.
[63] *Royal Bank of Scotland v Etridge*, n.57, above.
[64] *ibid.*, *per* Lord Nicholls of Birkenhead at para.20. See also *Boustany v Piggott* (1995) 69 P. & C.R. 298, PC. Merely having the opportunity to take advice may not suffice: *Claughton v Price* (1998) 30 H.L.R. 396. In that case Nourse L.J. said: "taking independent legal advice is neither always necessary nor always sufficient to rebut the presumption of undue influence. In many cases, I would say in most cases, it will be sufficient. But here it is clear that it was not, for the simple reason that [the influencer] could not reasonably have believed that a solicitor acting for [the influenced] would have advised him to go ahead without a crucial form of protection which had been offered originally and which there was every reason to believe would be given if requested". See also *Credit Lyonnais Bank Nederland NV v Burch* [1997] 1 All E.R. 144.
[65] *cf. National Westminster Bank plc v Morgan*, n.59, above.

case where an unrepresented employee compromised his personal injuries claim with his employers' insurance company.[66]

4–69 Husband and wife. Not infrequently allegations are made that arrangements apparently made between parties to a matrimonial dispute were made as the result of the undue influence or pressure exerted by one party over the other. It is well-established that, as a matter of law, there is no presumption of undue influence between husband and wife.[67] However, in many cases a wife may well be able to demonstrate that she reposed trust and confidence in her husband in relation to their financial affairs such that undue influence is to be presumed.[68] Nonetheless, married relationships may differ in respect of the responsibilities in these matters and each case will be looked at on its own facts.[69]

Effect

4–70 Where a compromise has been entered into as the result of duress or undue influence it becomes voidable at the option of the party so subjected. Early steps to disavow the apparent agreement must be taken otherwise it will be held to have been ratified or affirmed.[70]

ILLEGALITY

General

4–71 A court will not enforce a contract which, or the purpose of which, is illegal either under statute or under the general law.[71] Parties who are genuinely agreed on a compromise of their differences need to have an eye for any possible illegality if they wish it to be capable of enforcement.[72] The jurisdiction of the court to sever an illegal part of an agreement leaving the rest intact and capable of enforcement is somewhat limited.[73]

---

[66] *Horry v Tate & Lyle Refineries* [1982] 2 Lloyd's Rep. 416 (Peter Pain J.): a settlement was set aside where an employee accepted a low offer of compensation (a) without independent legal advice and (b) in ignorance of the contents of the insurers' medical report on him which was not shown to him.
[67] *Royal Bank of Scotland v Etridge*, n.57, above, *per* Lord Nicholls of Birkenhead at para.19.
[68] *Barclays Bank plc v O'Brien* [1994] 1 A.C. 180.
[69] *Royal Bank of Scotland v Etridge*, n.57, above, and see Ch.32, below.
[70] *Ormes v Beadel (on appeal)* (1860) 2 De G.F. & J. 333; *Occidental Worldwide Investment Corporation v Skibs A/S Avanti* [1976] 1 Lloyd's Rep 293; *North Ocean Shipping Co Ltd v Hyundai Construction Co Ltd* [1979] Q.B. 705. See *Chitty on Contracts* (29th ed., 2004), Vol.1, para.7–083.
[71] *Chitty on Contracts* (29th ed. 2004), Vol.1, Ch.16.
[72] *Tinsley v Milligan* [1994] 1 A.C. 340 at 362, HL.
[73] *Chitty on Contracts* (29th ed., 2004), Vol.1, paras 16–188 *et seq.* See *Carney v Herbert* [1985] A.C. 301, PC.

Compromise of disputes involving issues of illegality

The distinction between a compromise which is itself illegal and a compromise of a dispute which gives rise to questions of illegality should be noted. The former, of course, falls within the general principle stated above. The latter tends to be upheld.   4–72

> In *Binder v Alachouzos*,[74] the facts of which have previously been given,[75] the Court of Appeal rejected D's argument that the compromise itself was illegal, tainted, as it were, with the illegality that he alleged had affected the original financial transactions involving C.

Equally, at least for practical purposes, a distinction should be drawn between a compromise which is itself illegal and the compromise of a dispute on a contract which is indisputably illegal. The distinction may be more readily understood by reference to examples: 4–73

> (a) A and B have a dispute about the position of their boundary. A agrees not to commence proceedings for trespass against B in return for the latter's promise to destroy by fire a shed belonging to C, another neighbour. This is an illegal compromise of a legitimate dispute.
>
> (b) A and B have a bet by which A stands to gain £100 cash if he wins. He does win. B would have been obliged under the agreement to pay A within seven days. B asserts that he cannot do so and they agree that instead he will give A an antique chair within 14 days. The original agreement was indisputably illegal. The compromise would, if it were a compromise of an ordinary debt for £100, be indisputably legal.

Having made the distinction from the practical point of view, it should be noted that the legal effect is the same in each case: the compromise is illegal.[76] In the first, the purpose of the contract is illegal. In the second, the consideration for the compromise (the forbearance to pursue the wagering debt) is illegal.[77]   4–74

---

[74] [1972] 2 Q.B. 151.
[75] See para.2–17, above.
[76] *Chitty on Contracts* (29th ed., 2004), Vol.1, para.16–013.
[77] *Poteliakhoff v Teakle* [1938] 2 K.B. 816; *Hill v William Hill (Park Lane) Ltd* [1949] A.C. 530. See Ch.3, above.

Illegal compromises

4-75 **Ousting jurisdiction.** An agreement which purports to remove any recourse to the courts in the event of a dispute is void.[78] However, appropriately drafted arbitration clauses[79] or dispute-resolution clauses[80] may result in the determination of disputes by persons other than judicial *personae*. Not infrequently, terms of compromise provide for the settlement of disputes arising therefrom by an arbitrator, for example in cases where one party is obliged to carry out work under the terms of the agreement.

4-76 **Matrimonial financial provision.** Parties to a matrimonial dispute may not "contract out" of the right to apply to the court for financial relief.[81]

4-77 **Stifling a prosecution.** A dispute may give rise to both civil and criminal law consequences. A purported compromise of the civil aspects of a dispute will be void if it contains an express or implied term to the effect that no prosecution will be launched or that the appropriate authorities will not be

---

[78] *Lee v Showmen's Guild of Great Britain* [1952] 2 Q.B. 249; *Chitty on Contracts* (29th ed., 2004), Vol.1, para.16-045. Any attempt by a "public authority" to impose on an individual party to a compromise of a dispute an obligation not to pursue the authority to court for a remedy for breach would probably consitute a violation of Article 6(1) of the European Convention on Human Rights and Fundamental Freedoms. Following the introduction of the CPR, the jurisdictions of the High Court and county court have become a great deal closer in many areas. It is thought that it would not be contrary to public policy, and thus not a void provision, for parties to a dispute effectively to prevent the court from awarding the proper measure of damages, or the full extent of any relief, by agreeing to transfer the dispute from the High Court to the county court on the express condition that the claimant limits his claim for relief to that available in the county court: *cf. Basaran v Nevar Investments Ltd* (1979) C.A.T. 181. Indeed, parties not infrequently agree that a dispute should be dealt with on the small claims track (or indeed the fast track) even though the damages might otherwise exceed the relevant limit in order to avoid the costs consequences of the track appropriate to the true value of the claim.

[79] Now governed by the Arbitration Act 1996. See *Chitty on Contracts* (29th ed., 2004), Vol.1, Ch.16. And see Ch.41, below.

[80] *Channel Tunnel Group Ltd v Balfour Beatty Construction Ltd* [1993] A.C. 334, where it was held that the court has an inherent jurisdiction to inhibit proceedings brought in breach of an agreed method of resolving disputes. Parties to commercial agreements frequently provide for the determination by experts of issues that may arise during the currency of the contract: *e.g. Jones v Sherwood Computer Services Plc* [1992] 1 W.L.R. 277; *Nikko Hotels UK v M E P C* (1991) 28 E.G. 86; *Amoco (UK) Exploration Company v Amerada Hess Ltd* [1994] 1 Lloyd's Rep. 330. The terms of the agreement may result in an expert having to answer mixed questions of fact and law: *Norwich Union Life Insurance Society v P & O Property Holdings* (1993) 13 E.G. 108, CA; *Amoco (UK) Exploration Company v Amerada Hess Ltd*, above; *cf. Neste Production Ltd v Shell UK Ltd* [1994] 1 Lloyd's Rep. 447. A clause which seems to exclude completely the jurisdiction of the court from, *e.g.* reviewing the decision of the expert where there had been fraud or bias would be invalid: *Chitty on Contracts* (29th ed. 2004), Vol.1, para.16-047. See generally Kendall (1993) 109 L.Q.R. 385. See also *Cott UK Limited v F.E. Barber Limited* [1997] 3 All E.R. 540 (H.H. Judge Hegarty Q.C.); and *Halifax Financial Services Ltd v Intuitive Systems Ltd* unreported, December 21, 1998, McKinnon J.

[81] See Ch.32, below.

notified.[82] Indeed, it would appear that both parties to such an agreement could be guilty of conspiring to pervert the course of justice.[83] In a compromise of a dispute giving rise potentially to criminal proceedings in addition to the civil claims, great care should be taken to ensure that any agreement reached is clearly understood and expressed to be in respect solely of the civil claims.

Bankruptcy. A compromise tending to obstruct the course of bankruptcy proceedings is illegal and unenforceable: 4–78

> In *Kearley v Thomson*,[84] an agreement between a friend of the bankrupt and the petitioning creditor's solicitors that he should pay them their costs in return for their not opposing the bankrupt's discharge was held by the Court of Appeal to be unenforceable.

Assignment of right of action. A compromise involving the assignment by one party to the other of a right of action against another may be illegal. It may offend the rule which generally prohibits champertous agreements.[85] Broadly speaking, the principle applied is that an assignment of this nature will not be struck down if the assignee has a "genuine commercial interest in taking the assignment and in enforcing it for his own benefit".[86] 4–79

> In *Brownton Ltd v Edward Moore Inbucon Ltd*,[87] C, who were commodity brokers, sought and obtained advice from D1, who were computer systems consultants, concerning the installation of a computer system for their business. D1 recommended various manufacturers including D2. As a result, C entered into a contract with D2 for the supply, installation and maintenance of a computer system manufactured by them. The system never worked, was inadequate for C's needs and was scrapped. C sued D1 for damages for breach of contract, and negligence in connection with the advice given. D1 denied liability and alleged that any damages suffered by C were caused by D2's breach of their contract with C. C thereupon introduced D2 into the 4–80

---

[82] *Keir v Leemen* (1846) 9 Q.B. 371; *Windhill Local Board of Health v Vint* (1890) 45 Ch.D. 351, CA; *Rawlings v Coal Consumers Association* (1874) 30 L.T. 469; *Williams v Bayley* (1866) L.R. 1 H.L. 200; *Jones v Merionethshire Permanent Benefit BS* [1892] 1 Ch. 173. See *Chitty on Contracts* (29th ed., 2004), paras 16–035 *et seq.*

[83] *R. v Panayitou and Antoniades* [1973] 1 W.L.R. 1032. See criticism of this decision by Professor Glanville Williams Q.C. [1975] C.L.R. 609. For a critical analysis of the present law, see Hudson, "Contractual Compromises of Criminal Liability" (1980) 43 M.L.R. 532.

[84] (1890) 24 Q.B.D. 742. See *Chitty on Contracts* (29th ed. 2004), Vol.1 para.16–042.

[85] *ibid.*, Vol.1, paras 16–048 *et seq.* Given the introduction of conditional fee agreements in many areas of litigation, the approach of the courts to maintenance and champerty has already changed and will probably continue to change: see *Giles v Thompson* [1994] 1 A.C. 142, 164. However, *cf. Awwad v Geraghty & Co* [2001] Q.B. 570, CA, in relation to a "contingency fee". And see in relation to "conditional fees" *Kellar v Williams* [2004] UKPC 30 at [21], *per* Lord Carswell.

[86] *Trendtex Trading Corporation v Credit Suisse* [1982] A.C. 679 at 703, *per* Lord Roskill. See also *Chitty on Contracts* (29th ed., 2004), Vol.1, paras 16–057 *et seq.*

[87] [1985] 3 All E.R. 499. See also *South East Thames Regional Health Authority v Y.J. Lovell (London) Ltd* (1985) 32 B.L.R. 127 (H.H. Judge Newey Q.C., Official Referee).

proceedings alleging breach of contract. D2 denied liability, alleging that what had been supplied was in accordance with the contract, and denying that they had been made aware of C's requirements. They denied that they had been obliged contractually to provide a system fit for any particular purpose, but alleged that the goods supplied were of merchantable quality. D1 issued third-party proceedings against D2 and D2 issued a contribution notice against D1. Shortly before the trial (which was likely to be prolonged) D1 paid into court £302,002 in satisfaction of all the causes of action in respect of which C claimed against D1. C were prepared to accept this in settlement of their claims against both D1 and D2 provided they could secure a satisfactory arrangement with regard to their costs against D2 and D2's costs against them. D2 were unwilling to forgo their costs against C. Before C gave notice of acceptance of the payment into court an agreement was entered into between P and D1 whereby C would accept the sum in court on the usual terms as to costs, but would at the same time grant to D1 an assignment of their cause of action against D2. Notice of the assignment was given to D2, and D1 made it clear that all that they would be seeking was "an appropriate contribution in respect of the sum paid out in settlement" which they asserted would be to the extent of one half of the sum paid. At the trial, when D1 sought leave to amend the statement of claim to plead the agreement, the judge refused the application, accepting D2's contention that the agreement was champertous. The Court of Appeal, allowing D1's appeal, held that, looking at the totality of the transaction, D1 had a genuine commercial interest in taking the assignment. Although the contracts between C and D1 and C and D2 were separate, they arose out of the same commercial transaction and both D1 and D2 were sued in respect of the same damage. Consequently, any sum recovered by C from D2 would reduce the sum recoverable from D1 and, therefore, immediately before the assignment D1 had a genuine commercial interest in reducing the amount of their own loss. It was also said[88] that it was not fatal to such an agreement that the assignee might be better off or make a profit as a result.

4–81 Where a liquidator of a company or the trustee in bankruptcy of a bankrupt enters into such an arrangement, such an assignment will be valid.[89]

4–82 **Restrictive trade practices.** There is a substantial body of legislation, both European and within the United Kingdom, dealing with anti-competitive practices.[90] The common law continues to strike down agreements in unreasonable restraint of trade.[91] Plainly, any compromise, or any term within a compromise, which offends this framework of law will be susceptible to the argument that it is unenforceable.[92]

---

[88] [1985] 3 All E.R. 499 at 506, per Sir John Megaw, and at 508–509, per Lloyd L.J. Sir John Donaldson M.R. agreed with both judgments.
[89] *Norglen Ltd v Reeds Rains Prudential* [1999] 2 A.C. 1. In that case *Advanced Technology Structures Ltd v Cray Valley Products Ltd* [1993] B.C.L.C. 723 was overruled.
[90] *Chitty on Contracts* (29th ed., 2004), Vol.2, Ch.42; Whish, *Competition Law* (4th ed., 1999). See Competition Act 1998.
[91] *Chitty on Contracts* (29th ed., 2004), Vol.1, paras 16–075 et seq.
[92] cf. *Topliss Showers Ltd v Gessey & Son* [1982] I.C.R. 501, noted in para.3–44 of the 4th edition of this work, where a compromise involving restrictions on the ability of certain parties to sell goods other than at certain specified prices would have been unenforceable because of a failure to register the agreement pursuant to the Restrictive Trade Practices Act 1976 (now repealed by the Competition Act 1998).

Employment law. The common law approach to covenants in unreasonable restraint of trade apply to the employer-employee relationship and, in particular, to the position of the employee after the termination of the contract of employment.[93] Any compromise of a dispute between an employer and an employee that offends the principles encompassed within this approach will be unenforceable. Equally, certain agreements seeking to preclude the right of a dismissed employee to apply to an employment tribunal are unenforceable.[94]

4–83

---

[93] *Chitty on Contracts* (29th ed., 2004), Vol.1, paras 16–103 *et seq.*
[94] See Ch.36, below.

CHAPTER 5

Terms of a Compromise

PRELIMINARY

5–01 Much space will be devoted in a standard work on the law of contract to a discussion of terms[1]: whether a statement constitutes merely a representation or has become a term of the contract, the difference between a condition and a warranty, the body of law on exemption clauses, and so on. These are all matters of great significance in many situations but much less so in this context. Parties to a compromise, often guided by their legal advisers, will usually make clear what represents a fundamental term of the agreement and indeed the consequences which are to flow from a failure to comply with it.[2] An exemption clause in the usual sense is unknown. However, two matters in relation to the terms of a compromise do call for consideration: construction and implied terms.

CONSTRUCTION[3]

General problems and approach

5–02 Subsequent to the conclusion of a compromise, questions may arise as to its meaning and effect. This can occur even when those with the highest calibre of legal expertise have been responsible for the drafting of the agreement.[4] The task is to ascertain the common intention of the parties by construing the agreement.

---

[1] *Chitty on Contracts* (29th, ed., 2004), Vol.1 Pt.4.
[2] A full examination of the effects of a failure to observe the terms of a compromise appears in Ch.8, below.
[3] See also Ch.6, below.
[4] See, *e.g. Wilson and Whitworth Ltd v Express and Independent Newspapers Ltd* [1969] 1 W.L.R. 197; noted at para.3–51, above.

The means by which this objective is attained have been the subject of authoritative restatement in recent years. In *Investors Compensation Scheme Ltd v West Bromwich Building Society*,[5] Lord Hoffmann spelt out the principles in the following way[6]: 5–03

> "I do not think that the fundamental change which has overtaken this branch of the law, particularly as a result of the speeches of Lord Wilberforce in *Prenn v Simmonds* [1971] 1 W.L.R. 1381, 1384–1386 and *Reardon Smith Line Ltd v Yngvar Hansen-Tangen* [1976] 1 W.L.R. 989, is always sufficiently appreciated. The result has been, subject to one important exception, to assimilate the way in which such documents are interpreted by judges to the common sense principles by which any serious utterance would be interpreted in ordinary life. Almost all the old intellectual baggage of 'legal' interpretation has been discarded. The principles may be summarised as follows.
>
> > (1) Interpretation is the ascertainment of the meaning which the document would convey to a reasonable person having all the background knowledge which would reasonably have been available to the parties in the situation in which they were at the time of the contract. 5–04
> >
> > (2) The background was famously referred to by Lord Wilberforce as the 'matrix of fact', but this phrase is, if anything, an understated description of what the background may include. Subject to the requirement that it should have been reasonably available to the parties and to the exception to be mentioned next, it includes absolutely anything which would have affected the way in which the language of the document would have been understood by a reasonable man.[7] 5–05
> >
> > (3) The law excludes from the admissible background the previous negotiations of the parties and their declarations of subjective intent. They are admissible only in an action for rectification. The law makes this distinction for reasons of practical policy and, in this respect only, legal interpretation differs from the way we would interpret utterances in ordinary life. The boundaries of this exception are in some respects unclear. But this is not the occasion on which to explore them. 5–06

---

[5] [1998] 1 W.L.R. 896, HL.
[6] *ibid.* at 912–913. Lord Goff of Chievely, Lord Hope of Craighead and Lord Clyde expressly agreed with Lord Hoffmann's speech.
[7] In *Bank of Credit and Commercial International SA v Ali* [2002] 1 A.C. 251 at [39] Lord Hoffmann emphasised that he "meant anything which a reasonable man would have regarded as *relevant*" (Lord Hoffmann's emphasis).

5–07 (4) The meaning which a document (or any other utterance) would convey to a reasonable man is not the same thing as the meaning of its words. The meaning of words is a matter of dictionaries and grammars; the meaning of the document is what the parties using those words against the relevant background would reasonably have been understood to mean. The background may not merely enable the reasonable man to choose between the possible meanings of words which are ambiguous but even (as occasionally happens in ordinary life) to conclude that the parties must, for whatever reason, have used the wrong words or syntax: see *Mannai Investments Co Ltd v Eagle Star Life Assurance Co Ltd* [1997] A.C. 749.

5–08 (5) The 'rule' that words should be given their 'natural and ordinary meaning' reflects the common sense proposition that we do not easily accept that people have made linguistic mistakes, particularly in formal documents. On the other hand, if one would nevertheless conclude from the background that something must have gone wrong with the language, the law does not require judges to attribute to the parties an intention which they plainly could not have had. Lord Diplock made this point more vigorously when he said in *Antaios Compania Naviera S.A. v Salen Rederierna A.B.* [1985] A.C. 191, 201:

> 'if detailed semantic and syntactical analysis of words in a commercial contract is going to lead to a conclusion that flouts business commonsense, it must be made to yield to business commonsense.'"

5–09 This summary of the general principles of construction[8] has been treated as an authoritative framework within which issues concerning the interpretation of a compromise should be judged.[9] Whilst it is essentially a restatement of established principles in contemporary language, the "old intellectual baggage" associated with certain older canons of construction has been jettisoned in favour of a more down-to-earth, common-sense approach to determining what the parties meant by what they said. It does mean that some of the older authorities will now have to be viewed in a somewhat less rigid way than might have been the case hitherto.[10]

---

[8] *ibid., per* Lord Bingham of Cornhill at para.8.
[9] See, *e.g. National Bank of Sharjah v Dellborg*, unreported, July 9, 1997, CA (though Saville and Judge L.JJ expressed some misgivings about its assistance in that case); *Gibbs v Ebbetts*, unreported, October 20, 1997, CA; *Line Trust Corporation v Fielding*, unreported, July 26, 1999, CA; *Cape & Dalgleish v Fitzgerald*, unreported, November 15, 2000, CA.
[10] *Chitty on Contracts* (29th. ed., 2004), Vol.1, para.12–045.

Subjective intentions or understandings and extrinsic evidence

Until such time as the principle is revisited,[11] it is established law that in order to determine the common intention of the parties to an agreement reduced to writing, whether purely as a written contract or as an agreement embodied in a consent order or judgment, the intention of the parties must be construed by reference to the document or order itself: extrinsic evidence of what may or may not have been in the minds of the parties at the time of their agreement is not admissible for this purpose.[12] In the context of compromise this can be illustrated in a number of cases:

5–10

> In *Arrale v Costain Civil Engineering Ltd*,[13] the facts of which have been given previously,[14] the Court of Appeal held that in so far as the trial judge had taken into account evidence concerning the negotiations in order to construe the terms of the form of discharge, he was wrong to have done so. The evidence may have been relevant to the issues of misrepresentation and *non est factum* also raised, but should have been ignored for the purposes of construction.[15] It was also said[16] that it was doubtful whether the fact that the parties had permitted the giving of such evidence without objection rendered the same admissible for such purposes.

5–11

> In *Capon v Evans*,[17] the facts of which have also been given previously,[18] the Court of Appeal held that the judge should not have received evidence of C's "subjective understanding as to the effect of the words used" in the agreement. This evidence was neither relevant nor admissible "in the absence of any plea of mistake or rectification".

5–12

> In *Rees v West Glamorgan County Council*,[19] a personal injuries claim brought by C against D was settled in correspondence in April/May 1991 between C's solicitors and D's insurers on the basis that C would accept "£33,000 in full and final settlement of his claim together with [costs, details of which were supplied in the letter]". The letter from C's solicitor concluded

5–13

---

[11] *Investors Compensation Scheme Ltd v West Bromwich Building Society* [1998] 1 W.L.R. 896 at 913, *per* Lord Hoffmann; and *Bank of Credit and Commercial International SA v Ali*, n.7, above, *per* Lord Nicholls of Birkenhead at para 31.

[12] This passage was quoted with approval in *Dattani v Trio Supermarkets Ltd* [1998] I.R.L.R. 23, CA, referred to at para.5–15 below; *British Movietonews Ltd v London and District Cinemas Ltd* [1952] A.C. 166; *General Accident Fire and Life Assurance Corporation v IRC* [1963] 1 W.L.R. 1207, CA; *cf. Reardon Smith Line Ltd v Yngvar Hansen-Tangen* [1976] 1 W.L.R. 989 at 995–997. See also *Cadmus Shipping Co Ltd v Lakeview Trading Co SA* (1979) C.A.T. 317: not legitimate to look at contemporaneous note of party's representative to aid construction of undertaking as part of agreed order.

[13] [1976] 1 Lloyd's Rep. 98, CA.

[14] See para.3–15, above.

[15] *per* Lord Denning M.R. at 101, *per* Stephenson L.J. at 103–104 and *per* Geoffrey Lane L.J. at 105.

[16] *per* Stephenson L.J. at 104.

[17] (1986) C.A.T. 413; [1987] C.L.Y. 413.

[18] See para.3–24, above.

[19] [1994] P.I.Q.R. 37.

with the words "I await cheques to conclude this matter". On May 31, 1991 the Compensation Recovery Unit issued a certificate to D's insurers showing that, in respect of a compensation payment made in the week ending June 7, 1991, the sum to be deducted and paid to the Compensation Recovery Unit pursuant to s.22 of the Social Security Act 1989 (effective from September 3, 1990) was just over £10,000. C refused to accept any other sum than £33,000 and disputed D's right to deduct the amount provided for on the certificate. At first instance it was held that the contract of compromise, on its true construction, meant that C would receive £33,000 "in his hand" and that D would pay an additional sum to the Compensation Recovery Unit. In construing the agreement the recorder asked himself what P's solicitor had in mind when referring to the "cheques to conclude this matter" other than one for £33,000 and further said that the offer did not specify any deduction to be made. The Court of Appeal held the the recorder was wrong to conclude as he did:

(1) There was nothing in the correspondence to support the conclusion that C was to receive £33,000 "in his hand": the letters recorded an agreement to settle C's claim for £33,000 and s.22 of the 1989 Act simply directed what was to be done in performance of that agreement.
(2) The subjective state of mind of C's solicitor was not the correct test to apply and was irrelevant.

5–14 However, although evidence of the parties' negotiations is normally inadmissible for the purpose of construing their agreement, it may be admissible:

(a) to explain the meaning to be attached to an ambiguous word or expression; and
(b) along with other extrinsic evidence, to show the disputes which the parties, by their agreement, were endeavouring to resolve.[20]

5–15 In *Dattani v Trio Supermarkets Ltd*,[21] C had instituted proceedings for unfair dismissal against D. These came before an industrial tribunal on November 9, 1992. Before final adjudication a settlement was reached by which C was to be paid £5,000 by D. The formal record of the tribunal was in the following terms:

"This case has been settled on the basis that the Respondent pay the Applicant the sum of £5,000 at the rate of £1,000 per month, the first payment to be made on 16 November 1992. The Applicant remains free to return to the Tribunal should the sum agreed not be paid within the agreed time limits."

A further handwritten document addressed to C by a director of D and dated the same day as the settlement was reached recorded as follows:

---

[20] *Chitty on Contracts* (29th ed., 2004), Vol.1, paras 12–115 *et seq*. The passage in the text was cited with approval in *Dattani v Trio Supermarkets Ltd* [1998] I.R.L.R. 23, CA. In *National Bank of Sharjah v Dellborg*, unreported, July 9, 1997, CA, Saville L.J., as he then was, said: "where the words the parties have used are ambiguous or, read literally, are meaningless or nonsensical, the surrounding circumstances must be considered in order to select the appropriate meaning or to try to give the words meaning or sense".
[21] [1998] I.R.L.R. 23.

"In consideration of your accepting the sum of £5,000 from Trio Supermarkets Ltd in settlement of your claim for unfair dismissal by Trio Supermarket Limited in five installments [sic] of £1,000 per month I as director of Trio Supermarkets Limited hereby personally guarantee payment of each of the said sums of £1,000."

The terms of C's complaint to the industrial tribunal contained the allegation that certain wages were outstanding, but he did not pursue a claim for unpaid wages in the unfair dismissal proceedings although it would have been open to him to do so. About one year later C launched county court proceedings seeking unpaid wages of £11,800. D argued, *inter alia*, that this claim was embraced within the compromise made on November 9, 1992. D's counsel at the tribunal hearing had made two statements about the negotiations. In the first he indicated that negotiations during the luncheon adjournment broke down when C's solicitor made it clear that C would accept the sum of £3,500 offered, but only on the basis that it would be without prejudice to any other claim that C might bring in the county court. Counsel went on to say that the "less favourable settlement" in the sum of £5,000 was agreed when further evidence had been given and the tribunal had indicated informally that it was minded to find for C. His second statement was made after being reminded of the other document dated November 9, 1992 referred to above. Of that C said this: "Since writing my earlier statement I have now been shown [the document dated] 9th November 1992 which records the agreement made between [C's solicitor] and myself on behalf of Trio Supermarkets Limited. I can accordingly state that no basis for a settlement was discussed between us at the second adjournment other than that it was in respect of the Applicant's claim then being heard at the Industrial Tribunal". The Court of Appeal held that the statements of D's counsel were relevant and admissible on the issue of the identification of the claim compromised and, accordingly, that only the unfair dismissal claim was the subject of the agreement.[22]

Where the basis upon which an offer of settlement was made becomes an issue, it would seem that the course of the negotiations[23] and other extrinsic evidence[24] will be admissible to resolve that issue.

5–16

---

[22] *per* Mummery L.J. at para.52 of the judgment: "Taking account of its object, language, context and background this agreement should be construed as limited to a compromise of the unfair dismissal claim. Counsel's agreed statement is highly material on the issue of identification of the claim compromised. There was an initial offer to settle for £3,500. That was not accepted. An express reservation was made by [C's] solicitor of the right to bring proceedings in the county court. The sum, which was finally agreed at £5,000 was described by counsel for the company at that time as being 'less favourable' to the company. That was after [D's director] had given evidence and the tribunal had given an indication that they would find against the company".

[23] See paras 3–24 *et seq.*, above.

[24] See, *e.g. Neuchatel Asphalte Co Ltd v Barnett*, [1957] 1 W.L.R. 356; noted at para.2–06, above.

Post-compromise words and deeds

5-17 It is a well-established principle[25] that the words and deeds of parties after the conclusion of a contract cannot be used as an aid to the construction of the contract.[26]

"Rules" of construction

5-18 In the light of the restatement of the principles underlying the approach to the construction of contracts generally,[27] it may no longer be appropriate to describe as "rules" the propositions that have hitherto been treated as regulating the interpretation of contracts.[28] Nonetheless, many of the propositions traditionally called "rules of construction" will continue to inform the task of the court when seeking to put the correct interpretation on the parties' agreement. The propositions of particular relevance when considering a compromise have usually been the following:

(a) words are to be given their plain and literal meaning unless the result is absurd or the agreement is inconsistent within itself;
(b) words are to be interpreted in such a way as to effectuate the agreement rather than to invalidate it;
(c) the agreement should be considered as a whole, the meaning of words to be taken from their context with a view, if possible, to giving effect to the whole of it.[29]

5-19 In construing the meaning of the "release" in *Bank of Credit and Commercial International SA v Ali*,[30] Lord Bingham of Cornhill said this:

> "In construing this provision, as any other contractual provision, the object of the court is to give effect to what the contracting parties intended. To ascertain the intention of the parties the court reads the terms of the contract as a whole, giving the words used their natural and ordinary meaning in the context of the agreement, the parties' relationship and all the relevant facts surrounding the transaction so far as known to the parties. To ascertain the parties' intentions the court does not of course inquire into the parties' subjective states of

---

[25] Not controverted by anything said in *Investors Compensation Scheme Ltd v West Bromwich Building Society*, [1998] 1 W.L.R. 896.
[26] *Chitty on Contracts* (29th ed., 2004), Vol.1, at para.12–124; *Arrale v Costain Civil Engineering Ltd* [1976] 1 Lloyd's Rep. 98 at 103–104, *per* Stephenson L.J.
[27] See paras 5–03 *et seq.*, above.
[28] *Chitty on Contracts* (29th ed., 2004), Vol.1, para.12–045.
[29] This summary was quoted with approval in *Dattani v Trio Supermarkets Ltd* [1998] I.R.L.R. 23 at [40]–[41].
[30] *Bank of Credit and Commercial International SA v Ali*, n.7, above, at para.8.

mind but makes an objective judgment based on the materials already identified."

An example of the way in which this traditional approach led to an obviously common-sense result is afforded by the following case: 5–20

> In *Morss v Morss*,[31] parties to a matrimonial case had compromised on terms which provided, *inter alia*, that H would in due course make available for W's "use" a house then in the course of construction "rent free for her life or until . . . debarred by the court from access to the children of the family". As part of the agreement H undertook to furnish the house, to pay its outgoings and to maintain the insurance on the property and its contents. The Court of Appeal held, construing the agreement as a whole, that the word "use" meant "use as a residence and not otherwise". H was released from his undertaking to the court after W had ceased using the property herself as a residence, having gone to live with another man.

It needs to be emphasised that the process of construction and reference to the applicable principles only becomes necessary when there is uncertainty or ambiguity about the terms recorded by the parties. It has been said[32] that "where words used have an unambiguous and sensible meaning as a matter of ordinary language [there would be] serious objections in an approach which would permit the surrounding circumstances to alter that meaning". The strained interpretation of ordinary language should not be the product of the process of construction. 5–21

It is important to emphasise also that reference to cases in which the court has reached a particular conclusion in relation to a particular word or phrase will be of limited assistance in other cases. In this area, in particular, authorities "must be read in the context of their peculiar facts".[33] That having been said, certain phrases, hallowed by long and frequent usage, are likely to receive substantially the same response by way of construction in most compromises in which they appear. An obvious example would be the well-established formula "in full and final settlement of all claims that [C] has or may have arising from the accident".[34] Another example might be where parties agree a settlement "in respect of the subject-matter" of the action between them. Here a court is likely to interpret the words "in respect of" as connoting the widest possible connection between the settlement and the subject-matter of the action.[35] 5–22

---

[31] [1972] Fam. 264, in particular the judgment of Megaw L.J. at 277–279.
[32] *National Bank of Sharjah v Dellborg*, unreported, July 9, 1997, CA, *per* Saville L.J.
[33] *Bank of Credit and Commercial International SA v Ali*, n.7, above, *per* Lord Bingham of Cornhill at para.17.
[34] See paras 2–08 *et seq.*, above.
[35] *Line Trust Corporation v Fielding*, unreported, July 26, 1999, CA, *per* Chadwick L.J.

Releases

5–23 The release by one party of another from liability arising from whatever state of affairs brought them into dispute is, of course, the very essence of compromise.[36] Usually, parties will wish to see a resolution that wipes the slate clean and indeed that prevents further matters of disputation being added to the slate.[37] Many formulae have been devised to secure this objective, some fairly short, some more extensive.[38] Any such formula may be characterised as a "general release".[39] Releases of this nature have been utilised for very many years in a variety of contexts.[40] In some of the older authorities[41] there emerged the suggestion that there was a particular "rule of construction" applicable to deeds of release confining the ambit of the release to matters within the contemplation of the party making the release and in respect of which he had knowledge. Whatever the historical context in which these statements of principle found expression, the contemporary view is that no special rule of construction applies to a release. In *Bank of Credit and Commercial International SA v Ali*,[42] Lord Nicholls of Birkenhead said this[43]:

> ". . there is no room today for the application of any special 'rules' of interpretation in the case of general releases. There is no room for any

---

[36] See para.1–01, above and para.6–01, below.

[37] *cf. Bank of Credit and Commercial International SA v Ali*, n.7, above, *per* Lord Nicholls of Birkenhead at para.23: "General releases are often entered into when parties are settling a dispute which has arisen between them, or when a relationship between them, such as employment or partnership, has come to an end. They want to wipe the slate clean. Likewise, the problem which has arisen in this case is typical. The problem concerns a claim which subsequently came to light but whose existence was not known or suspected by either party at the time the release was given. The emergence of this unsuspected claim gives rise to a question which has confronted the courts on many occasions. The question is whether the context in which the general release was given is apt to cut down the apparently all-embracing scope of the words of the release".

[38] *ibid.*, *per* Lord Hoffmann at para.38. In *Heaton v AXA Equity & Law Life Assurance Society plc* [2002] 2 A.C. 329, the release in the settlement agreement was in these terms: "Each of the parties hereto hereby unconditionally and irrevocably releases and discharges each other, and their respective directors, officers and employees from all or any liabilities, actions, causes of action, suits, demands of whatever nature or kind and howsoever and whenever arising which any of them may be entitled to make, assert or pursue in any jurisdiction whatsoever in relation to or in any way connected with the matter specified in clause 2.1 above". Clause 2.1 provided that the "agreement is in full and final settlement of all claims and potential claims of whatsoever nature and kind (including interest and costs) which the parties have or may have against each other under or in respect of or arising out of or in connection with, whether directly or indirectly" in relation to certain identified and enumerated matters.

[39] See n.37, above.

[40] See, in particular, the historical review of the authorities in the speech of Lord Bingham of Cornhill in *Bank of Credit and Commercial International SA v Ali*, n.7, above, at paras 10–16.

[41] See the cases referred to in *Chitty on Contracts* (29th ed., 2004), Vol.1, at para.22–005.

[42] [2002] 1 A.C. 251.

[43] *ibid.* at para.26. See also Lord Bingham of Cornhill (with whom Lord Browne-Wilkinson agreed) at para.17, Lord Hoffmann (who dissented in the result) at paras 54–57 and Lord Clyde at para.79.

special rules because there is now no occasion for them. A general release is a term in a contract. The meaning to be given to the words used in a contract is the meaning which ought reasonably to be ascribed to those words having due regard to the purpose of the contract and the circumstances in which the contract was made. This general principle is as much applicable to a general release as to any other contractual term. Why ever should it not be?"

The case in which the foregoing words appeared is an important contemporary illustration of the circumstances in which a general form of release is agreed,[44] but which can then give rise to difficult problems of interpretation:

5–24

> C was an employee of the bank from June 1985 to June 1990. Following an extensive reorganisation of its worldwide business during the spring and early summer of 1990, and following consultation with ACAS and C's trade union, C was sent a redundancy notice terminating his employment with effect from June 30, 1990. The notice set out the terms of the redundancy package offered totalling £9,910. An additional option was offered, namely a further month's gross salary if he was willing to sign an ACAS form (COT-3)[44] acknowledging that the payment from the bank was in full and final settlement. Having discussed the matter briefly with an ACAS official, C agreed to accept this additional sum (£2,772) and signed the COT-3 form in the following terms:
>
>> "[C] agrees to accept the terms set out in the documents attached in full and final settlement of all or any claims whether under statute, common law or in equity of whatsoever nature that exist or may exist and, in particular, all or any claims rights or applications of whatsoever nature that the applicant has or may have or has made or could make in or to the industrial tribunal, except [his] rights under [the bank's] pension scheme."
>
> Unknown to C (and to the general body of D's employees) D's business had been carried on for a number of years in a dishonest and corrupt manner and had been seriously insolvent. In July 1991 the bank was put into compulsory liquidation. A number of former employees (including C) sought to claim in the liquidation for damages for handicap in the labour market caused by the stigma that association with D was likely to cause (known colloquially as "the stigma claims"). The liquidators of the bank rejected the claims, but in speeches delivered on June 12, 1997[45] the House of Lords held that such claims could proceed in principle. The liquidators then sought to argue, in relation to those former employees who had signed the form of release referred to above, that any such claim had thus been compromised. C's case was selected as a test case. The assumed facts included that D knew at the time of the agreement with C that its business was being carried out dishonestly and corruptly, that C did not know this and that he could not have been expected

---

[44] See Ch.36, below.
[45] *Mahmud v Bank of Credit and Commercial International SA* [1998] A.C. 20. In that case, according to Lord Nicholls of Birkenhead in *Bank of Credit and Commercial International SA v Ali*, n.7, above, at para.33, the House of Lords "developed or, put more bluntly, changed the law".

to appreciate that it might have been so carried out. The House of Lords held (Lord Hoffmann dissenting) that C's claim was not covered by the release.

5–25   Lord Bingham of Cornhill, having reviewed the old authorities (including *Turner v Turner* and *Arrale v Costain Civil Engineering Ltd*,[46] both of which are noted below[47]), and having expressed the reservations referred to above,[48] said that he shared the reluctance of the judges in those earlier cases "to infer that a party intended to give up something which neither he, nor the other party, knew or could know that he had".[49] He expressed himself thus[50]:

> "What, then, of the claim for stigma damages which lies at the heart of this appeal? The bank, through its senior employees, is fixed with knowledge of the bank's insolvency and nefarious practices, although it seems unlikely that those negotiating with the employees were alert to these facts, very carefully concealed from the world. [C] had no such knowledge. Neither the bank, even when fixed with such knowledge, nor [C] could realistically have supposed that such a claim lay within the realm of practical possibility. On a fair construction of this document I cannot conclude that the parties intended to provide for the release of rights and the surrender of claims which they could never have had in contemplation at all. If the parties had sought to achieve so extravagant a result they should in my opinion have used language which left no room for doubt and which might at least have alerted [C] to the true effect of what (on that hypothesis) he was agreeing."

5–26   Lord Nicholls of Birkenhead expressed himself as follows[51]:

> "I consider these parties are to be taken to have contracted on the basis of the law as it then stood. To my mind there is something inherently unattractive in treating these parties as having intended to include within the release a claim which, as a matter of law, did not then exist and whose existence could not then have been foreseen. This employee signed an informal release when he lost his job, in return for an additional month's pay. The ambit of the release should be kept within reasonable bounds. [C] cannot reasonably be regarded as having taken upon himself the risk of a subsequent retrospective change in the law. A claim arising out of such a change cannot be regarded as having been within the contemplation of the parties."

---

[46] (1880) 14 Ch.D. 829 and [1976] 1 Lloyd's Rep. 98, respectively.
[47] paras 5–30 and 5–32, below.
[48] para.5–22.
[49] [2002] A.C. 251 at para.17.
[50] *ibid*. at para.19.
[51] *ibid*. at para.35.

Lord Clyde was of the same view[52]:

5–27

> "The stigma claim is one which neither party could have contemplated even as a possibility as the law stood at the time when the agreement was made. At that time it would not be known whether or not the employee would have any difficulty at all in finding alternative employment. The bank's conduct had not yet achieved the notoriety which could create the stigma. But even if those facts had been even suspected as a possibility the prospect of any liability falling on the bank to a former employee is something which must have been far beyond the reasonable contemplation of the parties. Even without formulating any definition of the precise scope of the agreement, it seems to me that if the parties had intended to cut out a claim of whose existence they could have no knowledge they would have expressed that intention in words more precise than the generalities which they in fact used."

Whilst the facts of the case may be unusual—indeed unique in the sense that they are unlikely to be replicated precisely in another case—the expressions of principle concerning the way in which releases of this nature are to be interpreted are of considerable importance. A contemporary approach to the process of construction yielded what many may regard as a just result on a preliminary issue in a highly unusual situation. The principles thus enunciated will, of course, fall to be applied henceforth in other more mundane and less obviously meritorious cases.

5–28

All previous authorities must now be read in the light of the speeches in *Bank of Credit and Commercial International SA v Ali*. It is to be noted, however, that the majority was of the opinion articulated specifically by Lord Bingham of Cornhill (referred to in para.5–13, above) that the decisions in many of those previous authorities reflected a disinclination on the part of the court "to infer that a party intended to give up something which neither he, nor the other party, knew or could know that he had".

5–29

> In *Turner v Turner*,[53] disputes arose concerning the provisions made in T's will. In July 1868 a compromise of those disputes was achieved whereby the persons interested under the will, in consideration of certain payments by T's executrix, released by deed all claims on the estate "which they . . . then had, or could, should, or might at any time or times have". T had been one of the next of kin of J.M.W. Turner, R.A., and was entitled to one-fifth of the latter's estate. Part of that estate consisted of certain plates, pictures and engravings, which had been sold to J in 1858 for £2,500, of which T had received £500. In 1873, J put these items up for auction and received about £40,000. A suit

5–30

---

[52] *ibid.* at para.86.
[53] (1880) 14 Ch.D. 829.

was thereafter maintained against J by J.M.W. Turner's next of kin (including T's executrix) to have the sale to him set aside. In 1877, a decree to that effect was made with the result that T's executrix became entitled to a one-fifth share in the proceeds of the auction. It was common ground that when the deed of release was executed in July 1868 none of the parties was aware of the value of the items or of any right to set aside the original sale. Malins V.C. held that the one-fifth share of the proceeds of the auction was not subject to the general release because "it has always been the rule of this Court to construe releases and documents of that kind with regard to the intention of the parties, and to the state of the property which was known at the time".[54] All T's executrix had achieved under the deed of release was a "release of all claims and demands in respect of property which was then known to exist".[55]

5–31   In *Directors of the London and South Western Railway Co v Blackmore*,[56] in 1861, acting under compulsory purchase powers, D purchased some of C's land for railway purposes. In 1862, D sold to C some other areas of land. Various disputes arose between the parties culminating in an agreement in 1864. It contained various provisions concerning the erection and maintenance of boundary walls between C's land and D's land and also a release by C "of all claims and demands therein mentioned, or for or on any other account or ground whatsoever". In 1866 the land originally purchased by D from C became surplus to requirements and D proposed to sell it. C wanted to exercise a statutory right of pre-emption pursuant to the Act under which it had originally been purchased. D argued, *inter alia*, that any such right had been surrendered under the general release. In his opinion Lord Westbury said this[57]:

> "The general words in a release are limited always to that thing or those things which were specially in the contemplation of the parties at the time when the release was given. But a dispute that had not emerged, or a question which had not at all arisen, cannot be considered as bound and concluded by the anticipatory words of a general release."[58]

5–32   In *Arrale v Costain Civil Engineering Ltd*,[59] the facts of which have been given elsewhere,[60] Lord Denning M.R. was of the view that there could not have been an agreement to release the common law claim because no one gave any thought to it.[61]

5–33   Plainly, whatever may have been in the minds of the parties at the time the terms of a release are agreed, the release should not be interpreted so as to defeat the very object it set out to achieve:

---

[54] *ibid.* at 834.
[55] *ibid.* at 836; *cf.* paras 2–08 *et seq.*, above.
[56] (1870) L.R. 4 H.L. 610.
[57] *ibid.* at 623–624.
[58] In *Bank of Credit and Commercial International SA v Ali*, n.7, above, Lord Hoffmann (at para.42) said of the first sentence of this quotation from Lord Westbury's speech: "This is rather a sweeping statement. It is almost always dangerous to say 'always'. But, in cases of a release given in connection with the settlement of a dispute, it is a fair generalisation".
[59] [1976] 1 Lloyd's Rep. 98.
[60] See para.3–15, above.
[61] [1976] 1 Lloyd's Rep.98 at 102.

In *Re Perkins*,[62] L assigned the residue of a lease to A1 who, in due course, assigned the then residue of the term to A2. Each assignment contained a covenant by the assignee to pay the rent and to keep his assignor indemnified in respect of any breaches of the covenants in the lease. A2 died in December 1895 and A1 was adjudicated bankrupt in June 1897. After A1's bankruptcy, A2's executors assigned the then residue of the term to a man of straw who did not pay the rent or perform the covenants. L was required to pay, and did pay, the outstanding amounts for rent and insurance premiums under the lease. He pursued A1, through his trustee in bankruptcy, for these sums. A compromise was achieved whereby L took an assignment of A1's right to indemnity from A2 in return for which L released A1's estate in bankruptcy "from all claims and demands under or in respect of" A1's obligations to him under the (first) assignment. In L's action seeking a declaration that A2's estate was liable to him for payments made and to be made under the lease, it was argued by A2's executors that the release was to be construed as releasing all liability of A1 or his estate in bankruptcy to L under the covenants with L, with the effect that A2's executors were discharged from all liability under the covenant to indemnify A1. The Court of Appeal held that the release in the deed "although couched in very general terms, must, if possible, be so construed as not to defeat the object or purpose of the deed of which it forms part". Since the preservation of the right to sue A2's executors was essential to L's "recovery... of the asset assigned to him, and which asset he is to take in satisfaction of all demands", the "estate released must exclude that asset".[63]

The "*contra proferentem*" rule[64]

Despite the move away from the continued use of Latin expressions in everyday legal language, it is likely that the phrase "*contra proferentem*" will continue to trip off the tongue of lawyers engaged in commercial matters. The more important issue is whether the principle it enshrines still has a role to play in the construction of agreements. Expressed shortly and simply, the principle applied to the resolution of an ambiguity in an agreement which cannot be resolved by other principles of construction is that the ambiguity is resolved against the party responsible for putting it forward. 5–34

> In *Arrale v Costain Civil Engineering Ltd*,[65] the majority held that any ambiguity in the receipt put forward by D should be resolved against D.

It is submitted that the principle enshrines a pragmatic and workable means of resolving justly an ambiguity in a written document in a way that would appeal to the hypothetical reasonable man faced with having to choose between two alternative meanings.[66] If that proposition is justified, the principle (if not the expression itself) has a future. 5–35

---

[62] [1898] 2 Ch. 182.
[63] *ibid.*, *per* Sir Nathaniel Lindley M.R., giving the reserved judgment of the court, at 190.
[64] *Chitty on Contracts* (29th ed., 2004), Vol.1, paras 12–083 *et seq.*
[65] [1976] 1 Lloyd's Rep.98.
[66] *cf.* proposition 4 in Lord Hoffmann's summary in *Investors Compensation Scheme Ltd v West Bromwich Building Society*, set out in para.5–07, above.

Relevance of jurisdiction of court when construing consent order or judgment

5-36 The general approach to the construction of a consent order or judgment is identical to that of the construction of a contract of compromise. Since a consent order or judgment is itself evidence of the agreement it embodies or reflects, there would be no objection in principle to evidence of the terms of that agreement being received to assist in resolving any ambiguity in the terms of the order or judgment.[67] Where, however, there is a patent conflict between the terms of the order and the antecedent agreement, and the conflict is not susceptible of resolution by rectification of one or other,[68] the question arises as to which would prevail. It is difficult to give an answer which would necessarily apply in every situation of such an unusual nature, but overall, it is submitted, the order or judgment should prevail. As the final stage of the process by which the parties have sought to put to rest their previous disputation, they must be taken to have submitted themselves consensually to the jurisdiction of the court.[69] The consent order or judgment then falls to be interpreted in the way in which an order or judgment of a like nature, but not expressed to be by consent, would be interpreted. If there is any doubt about whether the order or judgment is within the powers of the court, it should be construed as being limited to the jurisdiction of the court and be enforced only to that extent.[70]

5-37 Consistent with the principle that, when parties agree that a consent order or a judgment should be made, they are to be taken as submitting themselves to the ordinary jurisdiction of the court, the court will approach the interpretation of the consent order or judgment by reference to the court's ordinary jurisdiction.

5-38 In *Allsuch v Kaye*,[71] an order by consent in the county court provided for payment of costs "to be taxed on scale 2". The Court of Appeal held that, properly construed, such an order did not preclude the exercise on taxation of the discretion on discretionary items provided for by the then Ord.38, r.9 of the County Court Rules.

5-39 In *Tucker v Woodroof*,[72] a building dispute between C, the builder, and D, the employer, was compromised by the acceptance by C of £1,600 and of D's undertaking to pay C's costs of the action "on an indemnity basis to be taxed

---

[67] For example *Cloutte v Storey* [1911] 1 Ch. 18 at 25–26.
[68] See paras 4–30 *et seq.*, above.
[69] See *Chanel Ltd v F. W. Woolworth* [1981] 1 W.L.R. 485 and 491, CA. In *Cornhill Insurance Plc v Barclay* (1992) C.A.T. 948 (noted more fully at para.6–05, below), Beldam L.J. said that "[when] the court is asked to make an order enforceable by the parties to give effect to their agreement, the parties should in the absence of express reservation be taken to have intended that the order has the same effect as it would have had if made after the court had resolved the underlying issues between them". See also *per* Staughton L.J. in *Balkanbank v Taher (No.2)* [1995] 1 W.L.R. 1056 at 1063. Though *cf. Morris v Wentworth-Stanley* [1999] Q.B. 1004, CA, considered in more detail at paras 6–29 *et seq.*, below.
[70] *Hinde v Hinde* [1953] 1 All E.R. 171 at 178, *per* Morris L.J.
[71] (1978) C.A.T. 840.
[72] *The Times*, March 18, 1993.

if not agreed". The Court of Appeal held that the effect of this agreement was not that taxation was to be at large, but it should be on the appropriate scale (scale 2), but on an indemnity basis. The discretion conferred by the then Ord.38, r.9, was not precluded.

5–40 In *Caudery v Finnerty*,[73] a consent judgment, reflecting the settlement of an action for breach of promise of marriage and an action for monies lent, was entered in the following terms: "By consent, it is ordered that judgment should be entered for [C] for £1,250, with costs of both actions to be taxed, to be paid by [D] by 8 equal payments half-yearly, the first of such payments to be made within a month of July 19, 1888". A further provision under the order related to the maintenance of premiums under a policy of security and the order continued as follows: "Execution not to issue provided that the payments of the instalments and of the premiums were regularly kept up; but that in case default were made in the payment of any instalment [C] be at liberty to issue execution for the whole amount remaining unpaid". D commenced paying the required instalments. After payment of the first instalment C intimated a claim for interest upon the whole sum under ss.17 and 18 of the Judgments Act 1838. D denied liability to make such further payment and the issue was agreed to be left until all payments had been made. It was held that the order could not be construed so as to include interest since the instalments were to be of equal amounts. *Per* Collins J: "The equality of the instalments *prima facie* excludes payment of interest, which would vary according to the amount remaining unpaid".

5–41 In *Balkanbank v Taher (No.2)*,[74] C, a bank, issued proceedings in Ireland against various defendants, D, claiming the return of certain monies that were alleged to belong to it and damages for fraud arising out of a joint venture agreement. C sought and obtained from the Irish court a Mareva injunction restraining D from dealing with their assets within the jurisdiction of the Irish court. Shortly after obtaining this injunction, C obtained a worldwide Mareva injunction from the English court in aid of its substantive proceedings in Ireland pursuant to s.25 of the Civil Jursidiction and Judgment Act 1982. The Mareva injunction was granted on the basis of various undertakings by C, including an undertaking in damages in the usual form, namely "to abide by any order which this court may make as to damages, in case this court may hereafter be of the opinion that the Defendants or any of them have suffered any by reason of this order which the [Claimant] ought to pay". Following the substantive trial, at which C's principal allegations of fraud failed, the Irish Mareva injunction was discharged and the Irish court directed an inquiry as to damages suffered by D arising from the injunction. Some three months later a consent order was made in the English court discharging the worldwide Mareva injunction and ordering that "there be an inquiry as to what damages [D] have . . . suffered as a result of the making of the [Mareva order] which [C] ought to pay". An issue arose thereafter as to whether the terms of this consent order precluded the court from considering, as a matter of discretion, whether the undertaking as to damages should be enforced. The Court of Appeal held that the order did not preclude such consideration. It was well

---

[73] (1892) L.J.Q.B. 496; (1892) 66 L.J. 684.
[74] [1995] 1 W.L.R. 1056. The first instance decision is reported at [1994] 4 All E.R. 239. See also *Cornhill Insurance Plc v Barclay* (1992) C.A.T. 948, noted at para.6–05, below.

established that when it came to enforcing an undertaking as to damages there were two separate points to consider: (i) as a matter of discretion, should the court order that the undertaking be enforced? (ii) if so, what loss had the defendants suffered in terms of money, was it caused by the order and was it too remote? *Per* Beldam L.J.: "the question is whether on the construction of the agreed order . . . the parties must be taken to have agreed that the court on the enquiry as to damages should only be concerned with the second question . . . namely, the amount of the damages, or whether the court can enquire into the first question, namely, whether the undertaking should be enforced". Beldam L.J. said that the following factors had to be taken into account: "firstly, that the parties had agreed that there would be an enquiry before a judge in the terms of the undertaking and the conventional order which was made. Secondly, the proceedings were unusual because the injunction was originally obtained pursuant to s.25 of the Civil Jurisdiction and Judgments Act 1982, when it was not expected by the parties that there would be proceedings in this jurisdiction . . . There was, therefore, no action or proceeding in this country in which a judge trying the case would be in a position to consider the matters bearing on the exercise of the discretion whether to enforce the undertaking. Thirdly . . . the words of the undertaking and the order 'which the [claimant] ought to pay' are capable of including the exercise by the court of its discretion." Beldam L.J. said further that, in the absence of any specific reference to the question of discretion in the correspondence leading up to the agreed order or on the occasion when the judge was asked to make that agreed order, "the terms of the order are wide enough to and do in fact include both questions".

IMPLIED TERMS

General

5-42   In addition to problems caused by imprecise drafting, parties may omit to include in their agreement a term which is necessary to render it effectual or complete. In these circumstances the court will be prepared to imply such term or terms as may be necessary to render the agreement effective[75] or complete[76] in the manner in which the parties are presumed to have intended. The court cannot, however, rewrite the parties' agreement, a principle sometimes overlooked by those contending for the existence of an implied term.

Implications as to time

5-43   Unless an agreement expressly provides that an obligation is to be fulfilled within a specified time or can be construed as such,[77] a term will be implied that the obligation must be fulfilled within a reasonable time.[78] What is a reasonable time depends on the circumstances.[79]

---

[75] *The Moorcock* (1889) 14 P.D. 64.
[76] *Liverpool City Council v Irwin* [1977] A.C. 239.
[77] As in *Board v Hoey* [1948] W.N. 448; (1949) 65 T.L.R. 43.
[78] *Chitty on Contracts* (29th ed., 2004), Vol.1, para.21-020. See, *e.g. Shears v Shears*, noted at para.3-23, above.
[79] *Chitty on Contracts* (29th ed., 2004), Vol.1, para.21-020.

Consistent with the approach referred to above,[80] where parties agree to 5–44
an order or judgment they will be taken to have submitted themselves to
the usual rules and jurisdiction associated with such an order or judgment
unless they have agreed otherwise. If they have agreed otherwise, that will
ordinarily be apparent from the terms of the order or judgment agreed.
Where there is no agreement to the contrary reflected in the judgment or
order itself (or no rule within the CPR makes provision to the contrary), a
consent order or judgment for the payment of a sum of money (including
costs) must be complied with within 14 days of its date.[81] A consent order
requiring an act (other than the payment of money) to be performed must
specify the time within which the act is to be performed.[82] Under the
previous rules[83] a judgment entered in default of compliance with an order
of this nature which did not specify a time for compliance would be set
aside, the original order being treated as a nullity since it was incapable of
enforcement.[84] Under the CPR a failure to comply with a rule or practice
direction "does not invalidate any step taken in the proceedings unless the
court so orders".[85] It is thought that the practice in relation to the
enforcement of mandatory orders will not have changed from that
obtaining under the former rules. If the antecedent agreement failed to
contain an express term as to the time for performance of the obligation to
be set out in the order, the court would imply an obligation to perform the
obligation within a reasonable time[86] and alter the order upon application.
If the antecedent agreement did contain an express provision concerning
the time for compliance, but the subsequent consent order failed to reflect
this, the order could be amended under CPR r.40.12.[87] However, until the
order was thus modified it would be incapable of enforcement.

"Permission to apply"[88] omitted

Parties may, when drawing up the order designed to embody and give 5–45
effect to their agreement, omit inadvertently the words "permission to
apply". The incorporation of these words into the order enables the court
to make further orders for the purpose of working out the order.[89] If the

---

[80] See paras 5–36 *et seq.*, above.
[81] CPR r.40.11.
[82] CPR PD40, para.8.1.
[83] RSC Ord.42, r.2; CCR Ord.22, r.3.
[84] *Hitachi Sales (UK) Ltd v Mitsui Osk Lines Ltd* [1986] 2 Lloyd's Rep. 574, CA.
[85] CPR r.3.10.
[86] See para.5–24, above.
[87] See *Bristol-Myers Squibb Company v Baker Norton Pharmaceuticals Inc* [2001] EWCA Civ 414; *Markos v Goodfellow* [2002] EWCA Civ 1542.
[88] In pre-CPR terminology the expression was "liberty to apply".
[89] *Cristel v Cristel* [1951] 2 K.B. 725; *Potts v Potts* (1976) 6 Fam. Law 217, CA. It does not enable the court to vary or alter the original order.

parties omit the expression, would the court imply it and entertain an application as if it had been expressly reserved? In cases of orders not made by consent which are not of a final character and which may require further orders for their working out, it is clear that the words will be implied[90] and permission given, if appropriate, to amend the order under the "slip rule".[91] There would seem no reason in principle why the same should not apply to consent orders of a similar character.

5–46   The implication of such a provision, in the circumstances indicated, should not be confused with the question of whether the expression might be implied where the parties agree to stay proceedings between them upon agreed terms, but omit to provide for it in relation to the enforcement of those terms.[92] It is clear that if the stay imposed consensually is absolute and unqualified (*i.e.* without the addition of words such as "save for the purposes of enforcing the agreed terms") and no "permission to apply" is reserved, the court will not imply such provision into the order.[93] If, however, the stay is qualified in the sense indicated, but the words "permission to apply for the purpose of enforcing the terms" are omitted, would the court imply them? On the basis of the approach discussed in the preceding paragraph, it is submitted that there is no reason in principle why not. It would merely involve the addition of a term to the agreement reflected in the consent order which is necessary to render it effectual or complete.[94]

No implication of consent order or judgment

5–47   The mere fact that a compromise has been reached whilst proceedings are pending will not, without more, result in a consent order or judgment being made. A term to the effect that an order should be made will not be implied[95]; express provision to this effect will be required.[96] It follows that

---

[90] *Penrice v Williams* (1883) 23 Ch.D. 353 at 356–357, *per* Chitty J., explaining *Fritz v Hobson* (1880) 14 Ch.D. 542.
[91] CPR r.40.12; *Websdell v Jenkins* (1902) 46 S.J. 484.
[92] See paras 9–18 *et seq.*, below.
[93] *Re Hearn* (1913) 108 L.T. 452 and 737, CA; *E.F. Phillips Ltd v Clarke* [1970] Ch. 322. But see *Atkinson v Castan*, The Times, April 17, 1991, considered at paras 11–29 *et seq.*
[94] See para.5–42, above.
[95] *McCallum v Country Residences Ltd* [1965] 1 W.L.R. 657, CA. The making of a consent order or judgment is not necessary to render an agreement of compromise effectual since means of enforcement (pursuant to a fresh action) exist to enable such an agreement to be effective. For the same reason it could not be said that such an agreement was incomplete. There may, however, be situations in which the express terms of the agreement so clearly contemplated the making of an order or judgment (even though not expressly saying so) that "it goes without saying" that this was intended: *cf. Chitty on Contracts* (29th ed., 2004), Vol.1, para.13–007. In this sense and in this kind of situation it is submitted that the court might "imply" a term to the relevant effect.
[96] *Graves v Graves* (1893) 69 L.T. 420. And see Ch.11, below.

merely because a judge is told that terms have been agreed, terms will not necessarily be incorporated in an order or judgment.[97]

Implied term pending agreed order

5–48 Assuming that a compromise contains an express term to the effect that an appropriate consent order or judgment will be made in due course, will the court use an implied term to bridge the gap, as it were, between the time when the compromise is concluded and the making of the order? The problem, which has already been highlighted to some extent,[98] may be illustrated by a simple example:

> A and B agree in correspondence that B will compromise A's claim for damages for personal injuries by payment to A of the sum of £1,500 inclusive of costs. It is stipulated by A and agreed by B (and thus a condition of the compromise) that a consent judgment in A's favour for £1,500, with no order as to costs, should be entered. What happens if A or B repents of this bargain before the judgment is entered?

5–49 If the agreement were construed merely as an agreement to agree, *i.e.* to agree to the judgment being entered in the proposed form on the day when the application for judgment is to be made, then it would not be binding and either party could change his mind before judgment is entered.[99] However, it is not thought that this construction and result in law would receive much favour: neither A nor B would be overburdened with merit if it were contended for.

5–50 It is submitted that the situation is readily met by regarding the agreement as immediately binding between A and B, one of the terms being that A will in due course accept in his favour a judgment for £1,500 and that B will consent to it being entered against him. By supporting this express term with an implied term to the effect that both parties will co-operate in securing the agreed judgment (or, conversely, that neither will prevent its realisation), each would be protected from the consequences of an attempted withdrawal from the agreement by the other. If A evinced an intention not to accept the judgment in due course, or refused to do so, and attempted to proceed with his claim, B could set up the agreement as a defence if he so chose or he could apply to stay the proceedings.[1]

5–51 If B failed to consent to the judgment or evinced an intention not to do so in due course, the question of A's remedy arises. There would be little doubt that he could sue upon the agreement in a fresh action and obtain

---

[97] *Green v Rozen* [1955] 1 W.L.R. 741.
[98] See paras 3–58 *et seq.*, above.
[99] *ibid.*
[1] See Ch.11, below.

judgment[2] or, in the circumstances, treat himself as discharged from his obligations under the agreement and pursue his original claim.[3] If he wished to hold B to the bargain struck, the commencement of a fresh action, with the associated additional costs and delay, would not be an attractive course. Would it be possible for him to invite the court to enter judgment in his favour, either by consent or otherwise, without having to take this unappealing course of action?

5–52   Although there is little direct authority on the issue of whether an implied term of the nature referred to above would be held to exist in the type of situation described, it is submitted that the view expressed above is consistent with the general law[4] and with the analogous situation disclosed by a case such as *Smallman v Smallman*.[5] Furthermore, in *Hargrave v Hargrave*,[6] Lord Langdale M.R., dealing with an argument to the effect that a compromise which provided that its terms should, if necessary, be made a rule of court,[7] was not binding if it were not made a rule of court, said, "It is unnecessary that such an agreement should ripen into an order of court before it can be made available".

5–53   If, therefore, such a term is to be implied, might it not be argued that its existence enables a court to regard itself as having jurisdiction to enter judgment in A's favour on the basis of the prior agreement even though B is no longer a consenting party to it? On one view of the decision of the Court of Appeal in *McCallum v Country Residences Ltd*[8] the answer would appear to be "no". However, closer analysis[9] and subsequent *dicta* in another case[10] suggest that this is not a correct reading of that decision.

5–54   In *McCallum v Country Residences Ltd*, C, a student architect, claimed damages and other relief against D, a property development company. D denied C's claim and counterclaimed for damages for defective work. Attempts were made to resolve the dispute in correspondence. The first offer made on D's behalf was for £400 plus C's costs to date. The offers were gradually increased over the ensuing months to £900, with no specific reference to costs save on one occasion when D's solicitors said that if the particular offer (£800) was not accepted, they had instructions to pay that sum into court forthwith. C's solicitors, when replying to the final offer of £900

---

[2] *ibid.*
[3] See Ch.8, below. Since the obtaining of a judgment was a condition imposed by A, the failure to satisfy this condition would give A this right if he accepted B's repudiation.
[4] *Chitty on Contracts* (29th ed., 2004), Vol.1, paras 13–011 and 13–012.
[5] [1972] Fam. 25, discussed at para.3–61, above.
[6] (1850) 12 Beavan 408 at 413.
[7] See para.9–06, below.
[8] [1965] 1 W.L.R. 657.
[9] See paras 5–57 *et seq.*, below.
[10] *Howard of Wyndham v Healthworks UK* (1989) C.A.T. 838, *per* O'Connor and Stocker L.JJ. See para.5–56, below.

made by D's solicitors, indicated that it was "of course, accepted on the understanding that [D] will pay the costs incurred to date". They also drew attention to the fact that, as C was legally aided, an order for legal aid taxation would be needed. They said that they would "issue a formal summons before the Official Referee that terms of settlement have been arrived at so that we can obtain the necessary order". They asked for D's cheque in settlement. The cheque was not forthcoming and D's solicitors made further complaints about C's work. C's solicitors took the line that the matter had been settled and, in due course, issued a summons seeking an order in Tomlin form staying the proceeding upon terms that D was to pay C £900 plus his taxed costs, with a legal aid taxation of C's costs. Apart from acknowledging service of the summons, D's solicitors said nothing further on the matter. When the matter came before the court, D's representative did not feel able to consent to the making of the Tomlin order (saying that he was not happy about the position on costs and that the compromise was not fully agreed or concluded). The Official Referee nevertheless made the order, considering that there had been an agreement to settle at £900 plus costs. The Court of Appeal (Danckwerts L.J. dissenting) held that the Official Referee had no jurisdiction to make the order. The majority (Lord Denning M.R. and Winn L.J.) took the view, on the correspondence, that whilst a concluded compromise had been achieved in the sum of £900 plus costs, there had been no agreement, express or implied, that a Tomlin order should be made.[11] There had been a simple compromise which gave rise to a new cause of action and which required a new action for the purposes of enforcement:

> "In the absence of a consent to the order, as distinct from a consent to the agreement, I do not think the Court has jurisdiction to make an order. . . . Of course, if there could have been found a consent to the order being made, it would have been a different matter."[12]

5–55 On the facts of *McCallum* no consent to the making of the Tomlin order was forthcoming on the day the court was invited to make such an order. Equally, the view of the majority was that there was no agreement at the time the compromise was concluded that such an order represented the means by which the compromise was to be implemented. To that extent the case does not address directly the issue presently under consideration. However, the case has been said to support the proposition that no order can be made in favour of an applicant in the category to which A in the example above[13] belongs where B reneges upon the agreement. This proposition has been rejected.

5–56 In *Howard of Wyndham v Healthworks UK*,[14] solicitors for C and D entered into written and oral negotiations with a view to resolving certain proceedings and did indeed reach agreement. The primary issue for the court was whether

---

[11] Danckwerts L.J. construed the correspondence as a final agreement to pay ££900 plus costs, together with an implied agreement that the action should be brought to an end in the cheapest and quickest way, namely by a summons in the Tomlin form.
[12] *per* Lord Denning M.R. at 660.
[13] See para.5–48, above.
[14] (1989) C.A.T. 838; [1990] 4 C.L. 376.

agreement had been reached on a certain date or on a subsequent date. If the conclusion had been that the agreement had been achieved on the subsequent date, then the agreement would have included a provision that a Tomlin order would be made in the form prepared by one of the solicitors. By the time the Tomlin order was sought from the court, D was unwilling to give his consent. It was argued on his behalf that, following *McCallum*, there was no jurisdiction to make the order. The Court of Appeal held that the agreement had in fact been concluded at the earlier of the two possible times and that, accordingly, the question did not arise. However, it was said that, had the agreement been reached at that later stage, with the provision for the Tomlin order included, there would have been "a term of that agreement that a Tomlin order should be made, and that the necessary consent was present". The court would have had jurisdiction to make such an order. It was said that where parties agree that terms of settlement are to be embodied in a Tomlin order, "it is not open, when one party seeks to get the order registered[15] by the Court for the purposes of enforcement, to a party who has previously consented to go back on his consent".

5–57   In the foregoing case, *McCallum* was explained on the basis that "the Court cannot have been satisfied that there was a true consent as to the cost part of the order and this lack of consent was manifested by the hesitancy of [D's representative] to consent to the costs order". It is, with respect, clear that in *McCallum* no consent was forthcoming on D's behalf to the order sought on C's behalf and, furthermore, that the costs aspect was what, so far as D was concerned, lay at the root of its unwillingness to agree to the order or even to accept that an agreement had been reached. However, all members of the court in *McCallum*[16] proceeded on the basis that a concluded agreement including the costs aspect had been reached. Some other explanation, therefore, would seem to be required for the conclusion that there was no jurisdiction to make the Tomlin order in that case. The explanation, it is submitted, is that the majority was unable to find that there was, as part of the compromise itself, any term that a Tomlin order should be made. Danckwerts L.J. had been prepared to find an implied agreement to this effect[17] and it seems clear that Winn L.J. would have been prepared to regard the court as having jurisdiction to make such an order if he had felt that the compromise could have been construed as Danckwerts L.J. had construed it.[18] Lord Denning M.R., of course, had said that the position would have been different "if there could have been found a consent to the order being made".[19]

---

[15] Although the word "registered" was used in O'Connor L.J.'s judgment, it is thought that this carries no further significance than the word "made".
[16] [1965] 1 W.L.R. 657, *per* Lord Denning M.R. at 660, *per* Danckwerts L.J. at 662, and *per* Winn L.J. at 662.
[17] See n.11, above.
[18] [1965] 1 W.L.R. 657 at 663.
[19] See n.12, above. In *Atkinson v Castan, The Times*, April 17, 1991, considered in detail at para.11–29, below, Staughton L.J. said that in *McCallum* case the court "by a majority held that the correspondence did not reveal an agreement to an order in Tomlin form".

5–58 On this basis, therefore, it would seem that a court would have jurisdiction to make an appropriate consent order giving effect to a previously concluded compromise notwithstanding the lack of formal consent to the making of the order by one of the parties, provided there was an express or implied term in that agreement that the order should be made. The court would find the consent to the order or judgment in the original agreement, a consent which, perhaps having regard to the implied term as to co-operation referred to previously,[20] is to be regarded as irrevocable. Any residual doubt there may be about the juridical basis for this approach can be dispelled by consideration of the following: using the example that gave rise to this discussion,[21] B was agreeing at the time of the compromise to consent to a judgment for £1,500 in the extant action. It would be a perversion of that agreement if he could resile from that position and argue that A should commence a fresh action to secure his (A's) rights under the agreement.[22]

5–59 Although each of the two cases considered above concerned the proposed making of a Tomlin order, there would not seem to be any practical or logical distinction to be drawn between agreements contemplating that form of consent order and any other form of order: the legal analysis of a compromise that includes provision for the making of any form of consent order or judgment must be the same.

If, of course, the agreement was construed as conditional in the sense that, until judgment is entered, there is no binding agreement, the position would be different.[23]

---

[20] See para.5–50, above. In *Cook v Cook* (1984) 14 Fam. Law 121, W had agreed in a deed of separation made prior to the institution of divorce proceedings that she would transfer her interest in the matrimonial home to H in return for ££5,000 whereupon all her claims for financial provision would be dismissed. She received the ££5,000 pursuant to the agreement and then instituted divorce proceedings as agreed. After dissolution of the marriage she gave notice of her claims for financial provision, submitting that the deed was void and that the court should not approve the agreement it reflected. At first instance her claims were rejected and an order dismissing them, including periodical payments, was made. (Note: this case was before s.25A of the Matrimonial Causes Act 1973 came into effect and was heard when the law was that a periodical payments claim could only be dismissed by consent.) On appeal W argued that the court should not have dismissed her periodical payments claim because she had resiled from the previous agreement. The Court of Appeal held that W's consent to the dismissal of the claim could be found in the deed and that there was, therefore, jurisdiction to make the order.
[21] See para.5–48, above.
[22] In *Atkinson v Castan*, n.19, above, the Court of Appeal held that where parties agree that their agreement should be (and is) set out in full in the recitals to a consent order, that of itself gives the court power to make orders in aid of the enforcement of the agreement in the existing action rather than requiring the institution of a fresh action. This case is considered fully at paras 11–29 *et seq.*, below.
[23] See para.3–58, above.

Costs

5-60 Whilst a court will always deal with the question of costs in contested proceedings, it is, of course, something for the parties to resolve by agreement if they settle those proceedings. If they do not mention it at all in their negotiations or their agreement, the only conclusion would seem to be that each side must bear its own costs. It is not necessary, in order to give efficacy to the agreement, for the court to imply a term relating to costs.

5-61 In *Somerset v Ley*,[24] disputed proceedings concerning a will were compromised and the court approved the settlement on behalf of an infant respondent. The proceedings were conducted in chambers, leading counsel having been briefed on behalf of several of the parties. The consent order embodying the compromise, although making provision for C's costs to be taxed and paid out of T's residuary estate, did not make express provision for the payment of leading counsel's fees, something required by the relevant Costs Rules in relation to proceedings in chambers. Cross J. (as he then was) held that he could not imply into the terms of settlement a provision that the fees of leading counsel were to be met.

5-62 If the matter of costs has been raised in negotiations and remains outstanding there may well be no concluded agreement.[25] An offer (which was accepted) to pay "reasonable costs" in a personal injuries claim was held to mean "costs to be taxed if not agreed".[26]

---

[24] [1964] 1 W.L.R. 640.
[25] *Yorweth v Sonnyplaster* (1973) C.A.T. 255; noted at para.3-50, above.
[26] *Zaniewski v Scales* (1969) 113 S.J. 525. See also *Gannon v Chubb Fire Limited* [1996] P.I.Q.R. P108, CA.

CHAPTER 6

Effects of a Compromise

EFFECTS AS BETWEEN THE PARTIES

End of dispute

An unimpeached compromise represents the end of the dispute or disputes 6–01 from which it arose.[1] Such issues of fact or law as may have formed the subject-matter of the original disputation are buried beneath the surface of the compromise. The court will not permit them to be raised afresh in the context of a new action.[2] If the parties have agreed that their original dispute may be resurrected in certain circumstances then, of course, the position may be different.[3] The principle has been neatly stated judicially on a number of occasions:

> In *Plumley v Horrell*,[4] Lord Romilly M.R. said this:
>
>> "Prima facie everybody would suppose that a compromise means that the question is not to be tried over again. That is the first meaning of compromise. When I compromise a law suit with my adversary, I mean that the question is not to be tried over again."
>
> In *Knowles v Roberts*,[5] Bowen L.J. expressed the position thus:
>
>> "As soon as you have ended a dispute by a compromise you have disposed of it".

This principle applies whether or not litigation was commenced in 6–02 relation to the dispute[6] and, if it was, whether or not the compromise has

---

[1] This sentence was cited with approval in *Prudential Assurance Co Ltd v McBains Cooper* [2000] 1 W.L.R. 2000 at 2005, CA.
[2] See paras 1–02 and 2–16, above.
[3] See paras 8–02 *et seq.*, below.
[4] (1869) 20 L.T. 473; noted at para.3–33, above.
[5] (1888) 38 Ch.D. 263 at 272.
[6] *Cook v Wright* (1861) 1 B. & S. 559; *Knowles v Roberts*, n.5, above.

been embodied in an order or judgment of the court.[7] The foundation of the principle lies in two aspects of public policy: the need for there to be an end to disputation[8] and the desirability of parties being held to their bargains. Where parties compromise without embodying their agreement in a court order or judgment, the latter aspect dominates the picture. Where the compromise is embodied in a judgment or order, both aspects are present, the former finding particular expression in the doctrine of *res judicata*.[9] This doctrine applies to a judgment or order notwithstanding that it is made pursuant to an agreement between the parties.[10] However, the nature and content of the agreement of compromise will be of particular relevance to the application of the doctrine in this context, both in its narrow and its wider sense.[11]

The consequences of an attempt by one party to ignore the existence of a compromise (whether or not embodied in an order or judgment) will be considered in due course.[12]

Identifying the disputes resolved[13]

6–03 An important aspect of the whole subject of compromise is the need, which may arise subsequent to the making of a compromise, for a court to identify precisely the disputes which have been settled.[14] The end result contemplated by this process of identification is the same whether the court is considering a compromise embodied in an order or judgment or one which is not. There may, of course, be differences in the materials which the court will have available and be prepared to examine for this purpose in each case. There may also be a possible distinction between the two situations in respect of the effect of the parties neglecting specifically to compromise a matter which could and should have been raised in their disputation.[15]

6–04 **Where no order or judgment.** Where a compromise is effected other than by a consent order or judgment, the court will have a variety of materials to examine: first and foremost, of course, will be the agreement itself,

---

[7] *Dixon v Evans* (1872) L.R. 5 H.L. 606; *Holsworthy UDC v Holsworthy RDC* [1907] 2 Ch. 62.
[8] *Interest reipublicae ut sit finis litium*.
[9] For the full expression, see Ch.1, n.5, above.
[10] *Re South American and Mexican Co Ex p. Bank of England* [1895] 1 Ch. 37; *Kinch v Walcott* [1929] A.C. 482, PC.
[11] See paras 6–07 *et seq.*, below.
[12] See Ch.8, below.
[13] Paras 6–03, 6–04 and 6–06, below; were cited with approval in *Dattani v Trio Supermarkets Ltd* [1998] I.R.L.R. 240 at 243–244, CA.
[14] See Ch.5 above.
[15] See paras 6–07 *et seq.*, below.

whether comprised in some formal document or merely the one or two communications which crystallised (or evidenced) the agreement.[16] Indeed, if the agreement was oral, the precise words used on the material occasion must be examined. However, the phraseology of the agreement may not always yield the answer to the question in hand. As observed previously,[17] in the normal course of events the parties' negotiations are inadmissible as an aid to construction of an agreement. However, they are relevant and admissible to assist in resolving any ambiguity of phraseology in the agreement or to identify the disputes the parties intended to resolve.[18] It is axiomatic that the analysis of these materials is an objective one, the subjective intentions of each party being irrelevant. An objective analysis of the "factual matrix" that formed the background to the compromise is required to enable the disputes settled to be identified.[19]

Where there is an agreed order or judgment. The same problem can arise 6–05 where a consent order or judgment sets the seal on the compromise of the disputes between the parties. In the normal course of events, it must be construed, as with the agreement it embodies, without direct evidence of the parties' intentions, although evidence of "surrounding circumstances" may be admissible.[20] The consent order itself may furnish evidence of the dispute or disputes it resolves.[21] Sometimes the parties will have drawn up a formal agreement which, it was proposed, should be effectuated by a court order. Reference to that agreement may be made to determine the extent of the disputes compromised.[22] If not, then the materials referred to in the preceding paragraph will be analysed.

---

[16] See Ch.3, above.
[17] See Ch.5, paras 5–06 *et seq.*, above.
[18] An example of this approach is afforded by the case of *Capon v Evans*, noted at paras 3–24 and 3–25, above, where the issue was whether both insured and uninsured losses arising from an accident had been compromised.
[19] See paras 5–03 *et seq.*, above. See also *Reardon Smith Line v Hansen-Tangen* [1976] 1 W.L.R. 989, HL; *Prenn v Simmonds* [1971] 1 W.L.R. 1381, HL. And see *Knowles v Roberts*, n.5, above. In *Cornhill Insurance Plc v Barclay*, noted at para.6–05, below, Beldam L.J. said that "[the] scope of an agreement of compromise by parties to proceedings before the Court is to be sought from its construction according to the principles used to determine the meaning of any other agreement. The intention of the parties is to be gathered from the terms of the agreement and such of the surrounding circumstances as may properly be called in aid". Stuart-Smith L.J. stated: "It is common ground that in construing the consent order which embodied the agreement reached between the parties the Court must have regard to the surrounding circumstances in which the agreement was reached which includes 'evidence as to the nature of the disputes compromised by the order': Plowman J. in *General Accident Fire and Life Assurance Corporation v I.R.C.* [1963] 1 W.L.R. 421, 431".
[20] *General Accident Fire and Life Assurance Corp v IRC* [1963] 1 W.L.R. 421 and 1207.
[21] *River Ribble Joint Committee v Croston UDC* [1897] 1 Q.B. 251; *Smith v Smith* (1974) 5 Fam. Law 125, CA.
[22] *Cloutte v Storey* [1911] 1 Ch. 18: the deed of agreement referred to questions "now in dispute" between the parties and the eventual court order confirming the compromise was construed as so referring.

In *Cornhill Insurance Plc v Barclay*,[23] C obtained an *ex parte* Mareva injunction against D1, D2 and D3 and gave the usual undertaking in damages. All defendants sought an order discharging the injunction on the basis that there was no evidence to support the suggestion that there was a risk that they would dissipate their assets. After the application had progressed for a while agreement was reached upon the basis that a sum of money (£1.3 million) be placed in an account in the joint names of the parties' solicitors, whereupon the Mareva injunction against D1 and D2 would be discharged. The injunction against D3 (a limited company) was agreed to continue with the proviso that it could continue to discharge its legitimate business expenses. A consent order was drawn up reflecting this, but making no express reference to the undertakings as to damages in the original Mareva order. Subsequently D1 sought to enforce the undertaking as to damages against C, contending that the consent order had not resulted in a discharge of that undertaking. The Court of Appeal held that the consent order, when construed in the light of the surrounding circumstances, was intended to compromise all matters arising from the grant of the injunction and the application to set it aside. Stuart-Smith L.J. stated:

> "The effect of the compromise was that in consideration of [C] abandoning such right as it had to an injunction until trial, the defendants agreed to abandon such rights as they had to apply for a discharge and to pay £1.3m into a joint account. The abandonment of such rights necessarily involved the abandonment of the contentions of fact upon which they were based."

6–06 Whilst it is extremely unlikely to arise in practice now, there have been occasions in the past when a consent order or judgment has appeared almost, as it were, out of the blue with the most insubstantial evidence of its background. Should this situation arise then, unless by inference from such evidence as there may be, the court can determine the disputes compromised, it would appear that all matters between the parties, except the terms of the actual judgment or order itself, are at large.[24]

---

[23] (1992) C.A.T. 948. *cf. Balkanbank v Taher (No.2)*, noted at para.5–41, above. In *Line Trust Corporation Ltd v Fielding*, unreported, July 26, 1999, CA, an issue arose as to whether a release in the schedule to a Tomlin order by which all parties released "all claims which they or any of them have or may have against each other in respect of the subject matter of this action or arising out of these proceedings" embraced claims against certain defendants for secret profit. The Tomlin order had been made on October 6, 1992 embodying a settlement reached in a substantial action in which those defendants had also been defendants. On October 5, 1992 a contribution notice was served upon one of those defendants in which a claim for secret profit had been intimated. The Court of Appeal treated the contribution notice as part of the factual background against which the Tomlin order was made and held that, objectively construed, the release was intended to embrace a compromise of the claim in respect of the secret profit given that it was a claim which arose "in respect of" the subject-matter of the earlier action.

[24] *cf. Goucher v Clayton* (1865) 13 W.R. 336.

Matters left out[25]

6-07 Not infrequently the analysis of the appropriate materials will disclose that the parties expressly or by necessary implication compromised certain matters of dispute but not others. In some cases it will be clear that certain matters were expressly or by implication not made part of the compromise.[26] However, there may be cases where, on any objective view, the parties could and should have dealt with a particular matter but neglected to do so. To what extent will they be permitted by the court to litigate that matter on some future occasion?

6-08 There is, at least in principle, a distinction between a compromise of a dispute achieved before the commencement of proceedings and one achieved thereafter. In the former situation (which will be governed solely by the law of contract), unless the court can imply a term that a particular matter was compromised, the agreement as construed must stand: the court will not rewrite the parties' bargain. It may be possible for the agreement to be effective without the matter in question having been embraced within it.[27]

6-09 Where, however, proceedings have been commenced and a settlement is achieved thereafter, what has traditionally been regarded as an extension of the doctrine of *res judicata* may operate to prevent the matter being litigated in a second action. The principle applied is often referred to as the rule in *Henderson v Henderson*. In that case Sir James Wigram V.C. said this:[28]

6-10 "... where a given matter becomes the subject of litigation in, and adjudication by, a court of competent jurisdiction, the court requires the parties to that litigation to bring forward their whole case, and will

---

[25] The analysis contained in this paragraph in the 4th edition (and which is substantially repeated here) was adopted with approval in *Dattani v Trio Supermarkets Ltd* [1998] I.R.L.R. 240 at 243, CA. However, that analysis must now be read in the light of *Johnson v Gore Wood & Co (a firm)* [2002] 2 A.C. 1, HL, referred to in paras 6–12 *et seq.*, below, in which, it should be noted, the House of Lords made it clear that the *Henderson v Henderson* principle could apply even though the first action resulted "in a compromise and not a judgment" (*per* Lord Bingham of Cornhill at 32). See also *per* Lord Millett at 59. In that case the proceedings in the first action were compromised by means of a written settlement agreement during the sixth week of the trial. It is not clear what order of the court, if any, was made. Usually, in this kind of situation, an order staying all further proceedings is made. However, it is not thought that the formal manner in which the proceedings are terminated is relevant. What is important is that there should have been proceedings which ultimately ended in a settlement. It follows that the alternative ground for the decision in *Dattani v Trio Supermarkets Ltd*, n.25, above, discussed at para.5–15 above, namely that the "decision" of the industrial tribunal was not a true decision, nor was it an order or judgment, to which the doctrine of *res judicata* applied, cannot now be regarded as the correct basis for rejecting the argument that C was precluded from pursuing his claim.

[26] For example *Worman v Worman* (1889) 43 Ch.D. 296. And see *Smith v Smith* (1974) 5 Fam. Law 125, CA, noted at para.2–03, above.

[27] See paras 5–42 *et seq.*, above.

[28] (1843) 3 Hare 100 at 115.

not (except under special circumstances) permit the same parties to open the same subject of litigation in respect of matter which might have been brought forward as part of the subject in contest, but which was not brought forward, only because they have, from negligence, inadvertence, or even accident, omitted part of their case. The plea of *res judicata* applies, except in special cases, not only to points upon which the court was actually required by the parties to form an opinion and pronounce a judgment, but to every point which properly belonged to the subject of litigation, and which the parties exercising reasonable diligence, might have brought forward at the time."

6–11 In *Greenhalgh v Mallard*,[29] it was said:

". . . *res judicata* for this purpose is not confined to the issues which the court is actually asked to decide, but . . . it covers issues or facts which are so clearly part of the subject matter of the litigation and so clearly could have been raised that it would be an abuse of the process of the court to allow a new proceeding to be started in respect of them."

6–12 These statements and subsequent expositions of the rule in *Henderson v Henderson* have been the subject of review by the House of Lords in *Johnson v Gore Wood & Co (a firm)*,[30] a case in which the previous proceedings had resulted in a compromise. Before considering the facts of the case[31] the contemporary approach to the rule should be noted. Lord Bingham of Cornhill[32] said this:

"It may very well be . . . that what is now taken to be the rule in *Henderson v Henderson* has diverged from the ruling which Wigram V-C made, which was addressed to *res judicata*. But *Henderson v Henderson* abuse of process, as now understood, although separate and distinct from cause of action estoppel and issue estoppel, has much in common with them. The underlying public interest is the same: that there should be finality in litigation and that a party should not be twice vexed in the same matter. This public interest is reinforced by the current emphasis on efficiency and economy in the conduct of litigation, in the interests of the parties and the public as a whole. The bringing of a claim or the raising of a defence in later proceedings may, without more, amount to abuse if the court is

---

[29] [1947] 2 All E.R. 255 at 257, *per* Somervell L.J. See also *Yat Tung Investment Co v Dao Heng Bank* [1975] A.C. 581, PC. *cf. Lawlor v Gray* [1984] 3 All E.R. 345. And see *Arnold v National Westminster Bank plc* [1991] 2 A.C. 93, HL.
[30] [2002] 2 A.C. 1, HL.
[31] See para.6–17, below.
[32] [2002] 2 A.C. 1 at 30–31.

satisfied (the onus being on the party alleging abuse) that the claim or defence should have been raised in the earlier proceedings if it was to be raised at all. I would not accept that it is necessary, before abuse may be found, to identify any additional element such as a collateral attack on a previous decision or some dishonesty, but where those elements are present the later proceedings will be much more obviously abusive, and there will rarely be a finding of abuse unless the later proceeding involves what the court regards as unjust harassment of a party. It is, however, wrong to hold that because a matter could have been raised in earlier proceedings it should have been, so as to render the raising of it in later proceedings necessarily abusive. That is to adopt too dogmatic an approach to what should in my opinion be a broad, merits-based judgment which takes account of the public and private interests involved and also takes account of all the facts of the case, focusing attention on the crucial question whether, in all the circumstances, a party is misusing or abusing the process of the court by seeking to raise before it the issue which could have been raised before. As one cannot comprehensively list all possible forms of abuse, so one cannot formulate any hard and fast rule to determine whether, on given facts, abuse is to be found or not. Thus while I would accept that lack of funds would not ordinarily excuse a failure to raise in earlier proceedings an issue which could and should have been raised then, I would not regard it as necessarily irrelevant, particularly if it appears that the lack of funds has been caused by the party against whom it is sought to claim. While the result may often be the same, it is in my view preferable to ask whether in all the circumstances a party's conduct is an abuse than to ask whether the conduct is an abuse and then, if it is, to ask whether the abuse is excused or justified by special circumstances. Properly applied, and whatever the legitimacy of its descent, the rule has in my view a valuable part to play in protecting the interests of justice."

Lord Millett put the matter thus[33]: 6–13

"It is one thing to refuse to allow a party to relitigate a question which has already been decided; it is quite another to deny him the opportunity of litigating for the first time a question which has not previously been adjudicated upon. This latter (though not the former) is prima facie a denial of the citizen's right of access to the court conferred by the common law and guaranteed by article 6 of the Convention for the Protection of Human Rights and Fundamental Freedoms (1953). While, therefore, the doctrine of *res judicata* in all its branches may properly be regarded as a rule of substantive law,

---

[33] *ibid.* at 59.

applicable in all save exceptional circumstances, the doctrine now under consideration can be no more than a procedural rule based on the need to protect the process of the court from abuse and the defendant from oppression."

6–14 As already indicated,[34] the House of Lords made it clear that the principle embodied in the rule in *Henderson v Henderson* could be applied where the first action concluded in a settlement. Lord Bingham of Cornhill put the considerations in this context as follows[35]:

"An important purpose of the rule is to protect a defendant against the harassment necessarily involved in repeated actions concerning the same subject matter. A second action is not the less harassing because the defendant has been driven or thought it prudent to settle the first; often, indeed, that outcome would make a second action the more harassing."

6–15 Lord Millett, having said that the principle was capable of applying where the first action was settled, said this[36]:

"Here it is necessary to protect the integrity of the settlement and to prevent the defendant from being misled into believing that he was achieving a complete settlement of the matter in dispute when an unsuspected part remained outstanding."

6–16 The rule in *Henderson v Henderson* has often been identified traditionally as having application where a matter "could and should" have been raised in the earlier litigation.[37] Where the settlement of such an action did not expressly deal with the matter that ought to have been raised, the argument in the second action was to the effect that the party now seeking to raise it was precluded from doing so.[38] Following *Johnson v Gore Wood & Co (a firm)* it is clear that that argument may, in some circumstances, still be maintained and may indeed succeed, although "too mechanical an approach" to the argument with little regard to the overall balance of justice is an approach which has been disavowed.[39] However, it is equally clear that where parties expressly agree to exclude from the settlement of the previous action the very matter about which complaint is

---

[34] See n.25, above.
[35] *Johnson v Gore Wood & Co (a firm)*, n.30, above, at 32–33.
[36] *ibid*. at 59.
[37] See, *e.g.* the approach of the Court of Appeal in *Johnson v Gore Wood & Co (a firm)* referred to at 81 in the opinions of the House of Lords.
[38] An argument to this effect was advanced in *Worman v Worman*, n.26, above, but on the facts was held not to apply. See also *Talbot v Berkshire CC* [1994] Q.B. 290.
[39] [2002] 2 AC 1 at 34.

made when it is raised in subsequent proceedings, the court will be very unlikely to treat those subsequent proceedings as an abuse of the process of the court.

In *Johnson v Gore Wood & Co (a firm)*,[40] C had conducted a property development business through a company, W Ltd. W Ltd was C's corporate embodiment. D was a firm of solicitors retained by C to act on W Ltd's behalf in connection with the proposed purchase of a piece of land for development purposes. D was also retained to act for and advise C in his personal capacity.[41] The property deal broke down and W Ltd commenced proceedings for professional negligence against D in January 1991. Those proceedings came to trial in 1992. In addition to the claim of W Ltd, C maintained that he had a personal claim against D arising from its alleged professional negligence. That claim was not brought at the same time or in the same proceedings as that brought by W Ltd, but it had been intimated on C's behalf at a very early stage in those proceedings when it was said that it would be pursued "in due course". In December 1991 C obtained a legal aid certificate to bring the personal claim. This was notified to D whose insurers, without admission, invited C's solicitors to give full details of the quantum of the claim. This was done. On the eve of the trial of W Ltd's claim, C's solicitors wrote to D's solicitors indicating that his personal claim would be pursued whether W Ltd's claim culminated in a judgment or settlement. The trial of W Ltd's claim began in October 1992 and was still proceeding in November 1992 when discussions took place about the possibility of an overall settlement embracing W Ltd's claim and C's claim. At a meeting on December 1, 1992, agreement was reached that C's claim would be capped at £250,000 exclusive of interest and costs, but that it was to be regarded as a separate claim. On December 2 W Ltd's claim was compromised by means of a settlement agreement which contained terms (a) which capped C's personal claim as previously agreed and (b) maintained confidentiality in relation to the agreement except "[in] connection with any action which [C] may bring against [D]". C issued a writ against D in April 1993 in respect of his personal claim. When those proceedings were well-advanced D indicated that it was proposing to apply to strike out the claim as an abuse of the process of the court. In relation to the argument that the rule in *Henderson v Henderson* should lead to C's claim being struck out, the House of Lords held unanimously that this should not be so. The parties to the settlement of W Ltd's action (in reality C and D) had proceeded on the basis of an underlying assumption that a further proceeding by C would not be an abuse of process. The settlement agreement itself contained terms which only made sense on the assumption that C was likely to make a personal claim. It would be unjust to permit D to resile from that assumption. 6–17

Other effects of compromise

The principal effect in law of an unimpeached compromise has been stated.[42] Not only does it represent, in general terms, finality so far as the original dispute is concerned, it represents a new situation giving rise to 6–18

---

[40] See n.30, above. See also *Perry v Day* [2004] EWHC 1398 (Ch), Rimer J.
[41] Since the proceedings which led to the arguments in the House of Lords were in the nature of a strike out application this fact was assumed for the purposes of the argument.
[42] See paras 6–01 and 6–02, above.

new causes of action.⁴³ The practical and procedural aspects of particular methods of compromise will be considered in due course.⁴⁴ A number of ancillary effects of compromise must not be overlooked and can conveniently be summarised here. Some arise directly because of the existence of a consent order or judgment; others arise in the context of the compromise remaining entirely contractual, no order or judgment having been made.

6–19 **Deriving from consent order or judgment.** Those matters which arise from the existence of a consent order or judgment can be summarised as follows:

6–20 *Fresh proceedings to set aside.*⁴⁵ A judgment or order by consent is binding until set aside.⁴⁶ Fresh proceedings must be commenced if it is sought to set aside a final judgment or order by consent.⁴⁷ If it appears, before the judgment or order has been drawn up or sealed, that a consent has been given by reason of any matter which would vitiate a contract of compromise, that consent may be withdrawn with the permission of the court and the order or judgment set aside.⁴⁸ Such an application will be entertained if instituted prior to, or contemporaneously with, the drawing-up or sealing of the order.⁴⁹

---

⁴³ *McCallum v Country Residences Ltd* [1965] 1 W.L.R. 657 at 660, *per* Lord Denning M.R.
⁴⁴ See Chs 9 and 10, below.
⁴⁵ For practice, see Ch.12, below.
⁴⁶ *Kinch v Walcott* [1929] A.C. 482, PC; *IRC v Hoogstraten* [1985] Q.B. 1077, CA.
⁴⁷ *Huddersfield Banking Co v Henry Lister* [1895] 2 Ch. 273; *Wilding v Sanderson* [1897] 2 Ch. 534; *Ainsworth v Wilding* [1896] 1 Ch. 673; *Page v Page* (1972) C.A.T. 383; *Kennedy v Claude Williams Motors Ltd* (1975) C.A.T. 135; *Kuwait Airways Corpn v Iraqi Airways Co (No.2)* [2001] 1 W.L.R. 429, HL. It cannot be set aside on appeal: *Re Elstein's Affairs* [1945] 1 All E.R. 272. *cf. De Lasala v De Lasala* [1980] A.C. 546. In *Skinner v The Thames Valley and Aldershot Co Ltd* (1995) C.A.T. 937, C's personal injuries claim against D1 was compromised on the basis that D1 would pay £525,000 and costs. A consent order was entered to that effect. During subsequent discussions as to the costs to be charged by C's solicitors, D1's solicitors considered that they had made a mistake in agreeing to pay costs because it seemed that C's solicitors may have agreed to act for the particular claimant for no charge. D1 sought leave to appeal against the consent order on that basis. In refusing the application for leave to appeal the Court of Appeal held that the only way in which D1 could challenge the agreed order as to costs was by bringing a fresh action.
⁴⁸ *Holt v Jesse* (1876) 3 Ch.D. 177; *Lewis v Lewis* (1890) 45 Ch.D. 281; *Hickman v Berens* [1895] 2 Ch. 638; *Stewart v Kennedy* (1890) 15 App. Cas. 75; *Neale v Gordon Lennox* [1902] A.C. 465; *Moore v Peachey* (1892) 66 L.T. 198; *Shepherd v Robinson* [1919] 1 K.B. 474; *Dietz v Lennig Chemicals Ltd* [1969] A.C. 170. See also paras 29–18, *et seq.*, below.
⁴⁹ *Shepherd v Robinson*, n.48, above; *Marsden v Marsden* [1972] Fam. 280. The cases confirming the jurisdiction of the court to intervene in these circumstances were decided when "perfection" of the order or judgment represented the time when this jurisdiction ceased to be available. The word "perfect" or "perfection" does not now appear in the CPR. Subject to the power of the court to dispense with the need to do so, every judgment or order must be "drawn up": CPR r.40.3(1). Every order that is drawn up, including a consent order made pursuant to r.40.6, must be "sealed": CPR rr.40.2, 40.3 and 40.6(2). It is submitted that the jurisdiction of the court to intervene in the circumstances mentioned will certainly exist until the order in question is "drawn up" and probably until it is "sealed": *cf. Stewart v Engel* [2000] 1 W.L.R. 2268. See also *Kirin Amgen Inc v Transkaryotic Therapies Inc, The Times,* June 1, 2001, Neuberger J.

An interim order[50] may be made by consent. Upon what basis and by 6–21
what means may it be set aside? The Civil Procedure Rules (CPR) have not
changed the substantive law. It follows that the pre-CPR authorities are
relevant to the question of the legal status of a consensual interim order.

An interim order made by consent may have a true contractual founda- 6–22
tion; but equally it may simply reflect an acceptance by the parties that the
order made is the correct order to make in the circumstances without the
trappings of an underlying contract.[51] It may be necessary for the court to
examine the basis of an interim order made by consent to see whether
there is a true contractual foundation. It is rare for the parties to utilise the
machinery of such an order to conclude a final compromise of their
dispute, but there is no reason in principle why they should not do so. If it
is plain that the parties did intend to conclude the whole case or, more
usually, some issue (for example, liability) by means of an interim order
made by consent, then full effect will be given to that contractual
foundation underlying the order.[52] When, however, there is no such
contractual foundation,[53] or the contractual foundation shows that the
parties are expressly submitting themselves to the jurisdiction of the court
to intervene further in the proceedings,[54] or that there is no contractual

---

[50] An interim order for this purpose is one that would have been called an "interlocutory order" before the CPR.
[51] *Siebe Gorman Ltd v Pneupac Ltd* [1982] 1 W.L.R. 185, CA. Lord Denning M.R., with whom Eveleigh and Templeman L.JJ. agreed, said this at 189: "We have had a discussion about 'consent orders.' It should be clearly understood by the profession that, when an order is expressed to be made 'by consent,' it is ambiguous. There are two meanings to the words 'by consent.' That was observed by Lord Greene M.R. in *Chandless-Chandless v Nicholson* [1942] 2 K.B. 321, 324. One meaning is this: the words 'by consent' may evidence a real contract between the parties. In such a case the court will only interfere with such an order on the same grounds as it would with any other contract. The other meaning is this: the words 'by consent' may mean 'the parties hereto not objecting.' In such a case there is no real contract between the parties. The order can be altered or varied by the court in the same circumstances as any other order that is made by the court without the consent of the parties. In every case it is necessary to discover which meaning is used. Does the order evidence a real contract between the parties? Or does it only evidence an order made without objection?".
[52] *Purcell v F.C. Trigell* [1971] 1 Q.B. 358. In that case, it was plain from the correspondence prior to the making of the consent order that the defendants were agreeing to their defence on liablity being struck out if they failed to answer some interrogatories within a certain period. It was an agreement going to a substantive issue in the case for which consideration was given on each side: see per Winn and Buckley L.JJ. in particular. And see *Tigner-Roche & Co v Spiro* (1982) 126 S.J. 526, CA; *cf. Greater London Council v Rush and Tompkins*, n.56, below.
[53] For example where the words "by consent" merely evidence an order made without objection: *Siebe Gorman Ltd v Pneupac Ltd*, n.51, above; *Chandless-Chandless v Nicholson* [1942] 2 K.B. 321 at 324.
[54] *cf. Chanel Ltd v F. W. Woolworth & Co* [1981] 1 W.L.R. 485, CA: an agreed order was made incorporating an undertaking by the second defendants not to do certain things "until judgment . . . or until further order in the meantime". On the assumption that the order had a contractual foundation, it was held that the order evidenced the underlying agreement which was itself to the effect that the undertaking should bind the second defendant until judgment or further order. See also paras 5–36 *et seq.*, above.

foundation depriving the court of the right to intervene further in the proceedings,[55] the dispute and any relevant issue remains at large.

6–23　Prior to the CPR the courts had always retained somewhat wider powers of interference with what were termed interlocutory consent orders than in the case of final consent orders. This reflected an exercise of the inherent jurisdiction by which the court retained a general control over interlocutory orders notwithstanding that they had been made by consent.[56] The approach manifested itself in various ways. For example, it was held that a mistake "on one side only" may afford grounds for setting aside the order.[57] Alternatively, rather than set aside the order, the court might decline to enforce it on the grounds that it would be inequitable to do so.[58]

6–24　Given the wide case management powers conferred by the CPR, it is unlikely that this jurisdiction (which, as indicated above, reflected an exercise of the court's inherent jurisdiction rather than one conferred by the Rules of the Supreme Court (RSC)) has been diminished. If anything, it is likely to have been reinforced and, arguably, widened. However, it is submitted that if it is clear that the parties agreeing to an interim order have reached a compromise intended to be binding, the court has no power to interfere with that agreement.[59]

6–25　*Appeals.* Virtually every appeal in either the High Court or the county court now requires permission to appeal.[60] It follows that any consent order or judgment made in either court would require permission to appeal.[61] The grounds of any appeal from a final consent order or judgment would doubtless be subjected to particularly close scrutiny.

---

[55] *Siebe Gorman Ltd v Pneupac Ltd*, n.51, above, *per* Eveleigh and Templeman L.JJ.
[56] *Purcell v F.C. Trigell Ltd*, n.52, above; *Burnholme and Forder Ltd v Warley* (1977) C.A.T. 236A; *Greater London Council v Rush and Tomkins* (1984) 128 S.J. 722, CA.
[57] *Purcell v F.C. Trigell Ltd*, n.52, above, *per* Lord Denning M.R.; *Mullins v Howell* (1879) 11 Ch.D. 763 at 766; *Brister v Brister* [1970] 1 W.L.R. 664.
[58] The view Buckley L.J. took in *Purcell v F.C. Trigell Ltd*, n.52, above, of what was done in *Mullins v Howell*, n.57, above. There must be evidence to show that it would be inequitable for the order to stand before the court will interfere: *Basaran v Nevar Investments Ltd* (1979) C.A.T. 181.
[59] In *Ropac Ltd v Inntrepreneur Pub Company (CPC) Ltd*, unreported, June 7, 2000, Neuberger J. appears to have concluded that an agreed "unless order", providing that T should be ordered to deliver up possession of premises to L unless a sum of money was paid to L by a specified date (time being expressly made of the essence), which he concluded was a "consent order of a binding nature", was, in principle, capable of being modified by the court in the sense of extending the time for compliance by T of the obligation to pay the sum of money. Having so decided (it appears), he decided not to extend the time for compliance. The transcript of the judgment is not entirely satisfactory and the case was complicated by the intervention of the jurisdiction to grant T relief from forfeiture notwithstanding the order for possession. Nonetheless, it is respectfully submitted that the decision of principle was wrong. The CPR were not intended to interfere with the parties' freedom to contract on whatever terms they choose: see, *e.g.* para.14–03, below. See also para.4–21 above.
[60] CPR r.52.3(1). See *Tanfern Ltd v Cameron-MacDonald* [2000] 1 W.L.R. 1311 at [20]–[22].
[61] This was a specific requirement under the RSC, Ord.59, r.1B(1)(b).

A consent order or judgment with implications for other parties. A consent 6–26
order or judgment may have legal and practical implications for parties
other than those to whom strictly it applies. Those parties may or may not
have been introduced into the proceedings by the time the consent order or
judgment is made.

Since, in general terms, the rules (statutory or otherwise) governing 6–27
orders or judgments made by the court following contested proceedings
apply to those made by consent, parties who agree to an order or judgment
are generally taken to have accepted that the normal rules applicable to
such an order or judgment will apply.[62] If those rules have implications for
other parties, generally those implications will apply in relation to a
consent order or judgment.

The approach outlined above may not, however, be of universal 6–28
application. For example, the Civil Liability (Contribution) Act 1978
provides that in relation to a claim for debt or damage a judgment against
one person liable in respect of the debt or damage "shall not be a bar to an
action, or to the continuance of an action, against any other person who is
(apart from any such bar) jointly liable with him in respect of the same debt
or damage".[63] It might be thought that if A and B settle a claim by A for
debt or damage in respect of which B and C are jointly liable expressly on
the basis that a judgment against B is entered, they are to be taken to be
recognising and agreeing that A's right to claim against C may proceed
(subject to any sanction in costs that might be imposed upon A if more
than one action is brought to establish C's liability if this could have been
achieved in one action[64]). However, it has been held that this is not
necessarily so.

> In *Morris v Wentworth-Stanley*,[65] C contracted to carry out work on land 6–29
> farmed in partnership by D1, his brother and his brother's wife, D2. D2 took
> no active part in the partnership. In 1991 the brother died and D1 continued
> the farming business. By September 1992 substantial sums were outstanding in
> respect of invoices submitted by C for his work. D1 gave notice terminating
> C's contract which he (C) treated as a repudiation. In July 1992 he, through
> his company, had commenced an action against the partnership for about
> £12,000 and interest in respect of work done up to that time. In February
> 1993 he commenced an action against D1, D1's brother and D2 "trading as
> the Stonards Farm Partnership" for about £48,000 plus interest. D1's solici-
> tors informed C's solicitors that the brother had died and that the partnership
> with D2 had been dissolved in December 1991. They suggested that to avoid
> the cost of seeking instructions from the brother's personal representatives and

---

[62] See para.5–36, above.
[63] Civil Liability (Contribution) Act 1978, s.3.
[64] *ibid.*, s.4.
[65] [1999] Q.B. 1004, CA.

from D2, C might wish to delete the brother's name and D2's name from the writ. C did so and the proceedings continued against D1 "trading as the Stonards Farm Partnership". D1 made a counterclaim on behalf of the partnership alleging breach of contract and negligent advice. During a period when the trial of the consolidated claims was adjourned part heard, a settlement was negotiated against the background of D1 being in financial difficulties. D1 agreed to pay £60,000 (about 75 per cent of the claim inclusive of interest), to abandon his counterclaim and to pay C's costs. The sum of £60,000 was to be paid in two instalments of £30,000 each. A judgment giving effect to this agreement was entered on November 13, 1995. On November 28, 1995 it was indicated on D1's behalf that he could not pay the agreed sums and was contemplating an individual voluntary arrangement under the Insolvency Act 1986. In January 1996 it was agreed that D1's son would pay £45,000 "in full and final settlement of the judgment". It was not suggested on C's behalf to D1 at the time of the original settlement, or to D1 or his son at this stage, that he intended to pursue D2 in respect of the balance of his claim. He did subsequently make such a claim giving credit for the sums received. The Court of Appeal held that, having failed to make any express reservation of the right to proceed against D2 at the time of the original settlement,[66] C's right to pursue a claim against her for the joint liability of the partnership was lost in the accord and satisfaction thus achieved and that s.3 of the Civil Liability (Contribution) Act 1978 did not permit the claim to be brought.[67]

6–30   As will be apparent from the discussion below,[68] the legal principles applicable in the general area of the settlement of cases arising from joint, concurrent and several obligations have been considered recently by the House of Lords. The principle in *Re EWA (A Debtor)*,[69] which underlay the primary basis for the decision in *Morris v Wentworth-Stanley*, did not fall

---

[66] See n.70, below.
[67] Although not necessary for the purposes of its decision, the Court of Appeal also held that C's second action amounted to an abuse of the process of the court within the rule in *Henderson v Henderson* (see paras 6–08 *et seq.*, above). It is at least questionable whether this view of the circumstances in *Morris v Wentworth-Stanley* could survive the restatement of the rule in *Henderson v Henderson* in *Johnson v Gore Wood & Co (a firm)*, n.30, above. Lord Millett said at 119: "The rule in *Henderson v Henderson* . . . cannot sensibly be extended to the case where the defendants are different. There is then no question of double vexation. It may be reasonable and sensible for a plaintiff to proceed against A first, if that is a relatively simple claim, in order to use the proceeds to finance a more complex claim against B. On the other hand, it would I think normally be regarded as oppressive or an abuse of process for a plaintiff to pursue his claims against a single defendant separately in order to use the proceeds of the first action to finance the second, at least where the issues largely overlap so as to form, in Sir James Wigram V-C's words . . . 'the same subject of litigation'".
[68] See paras 6–36 *et seq.*, below. Until then this area of the law was characterised as "developing": *Cape & Dalgleish v Fitzgerald* [2002] 2 Lloyd's Rep. PN 110, *per* Simon Brown L.J. In *Minton v Kenburgh Investments (Northern) Ltd*, unreported, June 28, 2000, Robert Walker L.J. said that it was a "difficult and developing area".
[69] [1901] 2 K.B. 642.

for review by the House of Lords and, accordingly, the principle remains good law despite being much criticised.[70] If the need in the settlement agreement for an express reservation of the right to pursue the other joint debtor had been disavowed, the whole basis for the decision concerning the effect of the settlement agreement reached would have been undermined. However, the question remains of how objectively to construe an agreement[71] containing a term which appears to sanction proceeding against D2 notwithstanding the settlement with D1 (namely, that a consent judgment should be made in due course to which s.3 of the Civil Liability (Contribution) Act 1978 applies), but which does not contain the express or implied term required by law to permit that course to be taken. The argument that an agreement containing a term that a consent judgment would be made must mean that the consequences provided for by s.3 have been accepted by the parties or, conversely, that unless they have expressly agreed to restrict the effect of the judgment it must have the same effect as one obtained adversely, was described as having "considerable force".[72] It was, however, rejected in the circumstances of the case.

Where a claimant is permitted to,[73] and does, maintain concurrent claims against a number of parties, he must give credit for sums received pursuant to any settlement or settlements reached with some, but not all, of those parties if he pursues to judgment another party (or parties) in respect of those concurrent claims.[74]

6–31

---

[70] The decision was described by Professor Glanville Williams Q.C. as "extraordinary" in *Joint Obligations* (1949). The Law Commission, in its report *The Law of Contract: Report on Contribution*, Law Com.79 (1977), described the rule as "somewhat technical" and said that "a plaintiff may find that settling with one tortfeasor prevents him from proceeding against the others although this was not what he really intended". The report recorded that the suggestion had been made that "it was time the common law rule on which this doctrine is founded should be abolished". In the event the Law Commission decided not to accede to this proposal (which, it said, "clearly has some force") because it had no immediate bearing on rights of contribution with which its report was primarily concerned. The view of the Commission (expressed in para.43 of the report) was that the problem was "not so serious as in the case of release by judgment because whereas release by accord and satisfaction involves the satisfaction of the claim, release by judgment operates even where the judgment is unsatisfied". That proposition is, of course, correct where there is satisfaction of the claim following the accord. In *Morris* there was no satisfaction.

[71] The decision was given before *Bank of Credit and Commercial International SA v Ali*, discussed at para.5–24, above. Applying also the test of what the reasonable man, armed with all the relevant facts and considerations, would have said of the settlement, it is at least arguable that he would have said that C was not intending to release any party other than D1 from liability to pay him what was due.

[72] The author declares an interest: he was leading counsel for the unsuccessful appellant.

[73] See paras 6–36 *et seq.*, below.

[74] *Townsend v Stone Toms & Partners* (1984) 27 B.L.R. 26, CA; *Banque Keyser Ullman SA v Skandia (UK) Insurance Co Ltd* [1988] 1 F.T.L.R. 360. See further on the manner in which credit is to be given in such cases, paras 6–55 *et seq.*, below.

6-32   As already indicated,[75] a judgment in a representative action is binding on all the parties represented, but it cannot be enforced without the court's permission against anyone not a party to the proceedings.

6-33   It should be noted that an agreed order for possession may be enforceable against all those found on the relevant premises irrespective of whether they were parties to the agreement giving rise to the order.[76]

6-34   *Deriving from compromise with no consequent court order.* Those ancillary matters that may derive from the existence of a compromise concluded other than by means of a court order or judgment can be summarised thus:

6-35   *Fresh action to set aside.* Where parties are unable to agree that, for whatever reason,[77] their agreement should be set aside and treated as rescinded, a fresh action instituted for the purpose will be required.[78]

6-36   *Effects in connection with other parties.* An agreement between a claimant and some, but not all, of the parties to a dispute may have an impact upon (i) the claimant's right to proceed against the other parties and (ii) the rights of those other parties to contributions in respect of the sum paid to the claimant in settlement. The general problem can be expressed as determining the extent to which a settlement between A and B in a dispute that also involves (or potentially involves) C precludes (or does not preclude, as the case may be):

(a) a claim by B against C for a contribution to his outlay in the settlement with A;
(b) a further claim directly by A against C in respect of loss or damage said by A to have been sustained as the result of some joint wrongdoing, or some concurrent wrongdoings, by B and C;
(c) if a claim by A against C is not precluded, a claim by C against B for contribution to his (C's) outlay towards A.

6-37   The paying party under a compromise will usually want to know that his liability for any further payment is at an end, though he may wish to preserve a right to claim a contribution to his liability from some other party. The party who has sustained loss or damage may be content to regard his settlement with one party as satisfying his claim fully, or he may

---

[75] See para.4–12, above.
[76] *R. v Wandsworth County Court Ex p. Wandsworth London Borough Council* [1975] 1 W.L.R. 1314. See also *Thompson v Elmbridge Borough Council* [1987] 1 W.L.R. 1425, CA and *Wiltshire County Council v Frazer (No.2)* [1986] 1 W.L.R. 109. See Ch.37, below.
[77] See Ch.4, above.
[78] See Ch.12, below.

wish to regard it as merely partial satisfaction with the opportunity to pursue the balance of his loss from another party. The law has been clarified significantly by the decision of the House of Lords in *Heaton v AXA Equity and Law Life*.[79] It still remains, however, more complex than it should be.[80]

The rules governing a settlement not embodied in a consent order or judgment are unaffected by the Civil Liability (Contribution) Act 1978. The relevant part of that Act (dealing with claims in respect of debt or damage against a number of parties) applies only to a judgment.[81] It is, nonetheless, the subsequent claim for a contribution (made pursuant to the Act[82]) brought against one or other of the parties to the original settlement by a party pursued for the first time subsequently that frequently brings into focus the scope and effect of the previous settlement.[83] 6–38

(i) Concurrent (or successive) contract-breakers and concurrent tortfeasors. When a court has to determine whether a further claim, including a contribution claim, has or has not been precluded by a settlement between A and B, its "primary focus of attention" will be upon the "terms of the settlement agreement between A and B ... construed in its appropriate factual context".[84] In *Heaton v Axa Equity and Law Life* Lord Bingham of Cornhill drew together a number of propositions that inform the process by which the postulated agreement between A and B may be interpreted. The case itself was one involving *successive contract-breakers* in the sense that each was in breach, or allegedly in breach, consecutively 6–39

---

[79] [2002] 2 A.C. 329.
[80] See, *e.g.* the comments of Steyn L.J., as he then was, in *Watts v Aldington*, n.93, below, quoted by Auld L.J. in *Jameson v Central Electricity Generating Board* [1998] Q.B. 323 at 336–337.
[81] s.3. See para.6–28, above.
[82] s.1.
[83] See, *e.g. Cape & Dagleish (a firm) v Fitzgerald*, unreported, November 15, 2000. D was, until his summary dismissal for gross misconduct (the perpetration of large scale systematic fraud), the managing director of a group of companies, I. I issued proceedings against D, but within days a settlement was agreed whereby D surrendered his 10 per cent holding in the group and each party mutually released each other from any claims. I, on behalf of the members of the group, released D from "any and all claims, rights and remedies which it has now or may have in the future, known or unknown . . . arising from his employment or office as director with, or as a shareholder of, any of them, or from the matters referred to in the [proceedings], or under the Shareholders' Agreement, or in any other way whatever, and any and all claims for expenses, legal costs or damages, arising from any of the same". Some while later I brought proceedings against its former auditors, C, alleging breach of duty in failing to detect D's frauds. C then issued contribution proceedings against D under the 1978 Act. The Court of Appeal held that I was not precluded by the agreement from pursuing the claim against C.
[84] *Heaton v Axa Equity and Law Life* [2002] 2 A.C. 329 at [9], *per* Lord Bingham of Cornhill. Presumably this means adopting the approach to the construction of a contract as set out in *Investors Compensation Scheme Ltd v West Bromwich Building Society* [1998] 1 W.L.R. 896 at 912–913, as modified in *BCCI v Ali* [2001] A.C. 251: see paras 5–03 *et seq.* above.

of separate contracts, but the statements of principle went beyond purely that situation and dealt also with the position of *concurrent tortfeasors*.[85] Lord Bingham said this[86]:

> "In considering whether a sum accepted under a compromise agreement should be taken to fix the full measure of A's loss, so as to preclude action against C in tort in respect of the same damage, and so as to restrict any action against C in contract in respect of the same damage to a claim for nominal damages, the terms of the settlement agreement between A and B must be the primary focus of attention, and the agreement must be construed in its appropriate factual context. In construing it various significant points must in my opinion be borne clearly in mind:
>
> (1) The release of one concurrent tortfeasor does not have the effect in law of releasing another concurrent tortfeasor and the release of one contract-breaker does not have the effect in law of releasing a successive contract-breaker.
> (2) An agreement made between A and B will not affect A's rights against C unless either (a) A agrees to forgo or waive rights which he would otherwise enjoy against C, in which case his agreement is enforceable by B, or (b) the agreement falls within that limited class of contracts which either at common law or by virtue of the Contracts (Rights of Third Parties) Act 1999 is enforceable by C as a third party.
> (3) The use of clear and comprehensive language to preclude the pursuit of claims and cross-claims as between A and B has little bearing on the question whether the agreement represents the full measure of A's loss. The more inadequate the compensation agreed to be paid by B, the greater the need for B to protect himself against any possibility of further action by A to obtain a full measure of redress.

---

[85] Concurrent (or several) tortfeasors (in contradistinction to joint tortfeasors) commit separate tortious acts which cause or contribute to the same damage: *Clerk & Lindsell on Torts*, (18th ed. 2000), paras 4–101 *et seq*. *Heaton* dealt with the issue of concurrent tortfeasors because the case of *Jameson v Central Electricity Generating Board* [2000] 1 A.C. 455, HL, which had been raised in argument, had been understood by some to indicate that the rule which applies to joint tortfeasors applied also to concurrent tortfeasors. See, *e.g.* the Fifth edition of this work at paras 6–42–6–57.
[86] [2002] 2 A.C. 329 at [9]. Where contract breakers can be regarded as successive in the sense that each is (or is allegedly) in breach *consecutively* of *separate contracts*, it is possible that the claims made are linked and the losses occasioned by the breaches overlap. Adjustments may have to be made to ensure against double recovery, but subject to that there is nothing to prevent a claimant who has settled with one such contract breaker from proceeding against the others. Indeed, where the damages obtainable against the succeeding contract breakers may only be nominal, there would be nothing wrong in principle for the claimant to proceed in order to obtain a declaration of the court that a breach of contract had been committed provided the pursuit of the action could not be characterised as an abuse of the process of the court.

(4) While an express reservation by A of his right to sue C will fortify the inference that A is not treating the sum recovered from B as representing the full measure of his loss, the absence of such a reservation is of lesser and perhaps of no significance, since there is no need for A to reserve a right to do that which A is in the ordinary way fully entitled to do without any such reservation.

(5) If B, on compromising A's claim, wishes to protect himself against any claim against him by C claiming contribution, he may achieve that end either (a) by obtaining an enforceable undertaking by A not to pursue any claim against C relating to the subject matter of the compromise, or (b) by obtaining an indemnity from A against any liability to which B may become subject relating to the subject matter of the compromise."

The case of *Jameson v Central Electricity Generating Board*[87] must now be seen in the light of the decision and analysis in *Heaton*. 6–40

> J worked for five years for E. During that time he was required by E to work at various locations including two power stations owned and occupied by D. During his employment, and during the period he worked at D's power stations, he was subject to exposure to asbestos. In 1987 J developed symptoms of malignant mesothelioma from which he died in April 1988. Before his death he had brought proceedings for damages for personal injuries against E alleging exposure to asbestos at various premises including those of D negligently and in breach of statutory duty. Shortly before his death he accepted £80,000 plus costs from E, the sum being expressed in a Tomlin order to be "in full and final settlement and satisfaction of all causes of action in respect of which [J] claims in the statement of claim". J's claim on the basis of full liability would have been worth approximately £130,000 and the sum of £80,000 was accepted to reflect the risks associated with the possibility of failing to establish liability against E. In April 1989, a year after J's death, the executors of his estate sought to bring proceedings against D seeking damages on behalf of J's widow under the Fatal Accidents Act, the claim being valued at about £142,000. The exposure to asbestos dust relied upon in this action was the same as part of the exposure relied upon in the previous action. The allegations of negligence and breach of statutory duty against D were similar, but not identical, to those previously made against E. D sought to argue that the settlement achieved in the action against E precluded pursuit of the claim against D.

D's argument prevailed in the House of Lords. In *Heaton* Lord Bingham said that, properly understood, the reasoning in *Jameson* was as follows[88]:

---

[87] [2000] 1 A.C. 455, HL. There can be no doubt that the tortfeasors in this case were rightly treated as concurrent, nor that the damage which ensued (the terminal illness and subsequent death of Mr Jameson) was the same whichever tort caused it; but it should be noted that the nature of the damages claim in each situation was different. Mr Jameson's personal claim was for damages for personal injuries. The claim brought by his estate on behalf of his wife was for the lost dependency.
[88] [2002] 2 A.C. 329 at [8].

> "(1) Proof of damage is an essential step in establishing a claim in tortious negligence . . .
> (2) Such a claim is a claim for unliquidated damages . . .
> (3) Such a claim is liquidated when either judgment is given for a specific sum or a specific sum is accepted in a compromise . . .
> (4) A judgment on such a claim will ordinarily be taken to fix the full measure of a claimant's loss . . .
> (5) A sum accepted in settlement of such a claim may also fix the full measure of a claimant's loss . . . whether it does so or not depends on the proper construction of the compromise agreement in its context . . .
> (6) On the facts of [J's] case, the sum accepted from [E] in settlement was to be taken as representing the full measure of [J's] loss: it followed that [J's] claim in tortious negligence was extinguished and he had no claim which could be pursued against [D] . . ."

6–41 *(ii) Joint tortfeasors.* On the law as it stands, it is clear that a release of one joint tortfeasor[89] by way of accord and satisfaction will operate to release all the others.[90] The rationale for the rule is that the cause of action against the joint tortfeasors is "one and indivisible"[91] and that it is extinguished by settlement with one of the tortfeasors. Where a claimant wishes to preserve the possibility of pursuing any of the other joint tortfeasors he must expressly (or impliedly[92]) reserve his right to do so at the time of the settlement. The rule has been subjected to trenchant criticism[93]:

6–42
> "These appeals illustrate the absurdity of the rule that the release of one of two joint and several tortfeasors operates as a release of the other. In Victorian times judges of great distinction reasoned that in a case involving joint and several liability of joint tortfeasors there is only a single cause of action, and accordingly a release of one of two joint tortfeasors extinguishes that single cause of action, or as it was usually put, releases the other joint tortfeasors. The rule has been relaxed by statute. The fact that joint tortfeasors can be sued

---

[89] The expression being used in the sense that the tortfeasors have committed the same wrongful act for which they are jointly and severally liable for the whole of the damage thus occasioned.
[90] *Clerk & Lindsell on Torts* (18th ed., 2000), para.4–104.
[91] *Duck v Mayeu* [1892] 2 Q.B. 511 at 513; *Apley Estates Co Ltd v De Bernales* [1947] Ch. 217 at 220–221; *Gardiner v Moore* [1969] 1 Q.B. 55. See also *per* Auld L.J. in *Jameson v Central Electricity Generating Board* [1998] Q.B. 323 at 335.
[92] *Gardiner v Moore*, n.91, above.
[93] *Watts v Aldington* (1993) C.A.T. 1578, *per* Steyn L.J., as he then was, quoted (and agreed with) by Auld L.J. in *Jameson v Central Electricity Generating Board*, n.91, above, at 336–337. Auld L.J. said that the rule as to joint tortfeasors is "in retreat".

successively heavily compromised the perceived rule of logic. But the old rule apparently still survives. In truth there is no inexorable march of logic. In a less formalistic age it is now clear that the question whether the release of a joint tortfeasor should operate to release the other tortfeasor is a policy issue. Either solution is logically defensible. But good sense, fairness and respect for the reasonable expectations of contracting parties suggests that the best solution is that the release of a joint tortfeasor should not release the other tortfeasor. On this basis the consequence that the unreleased tortfeasor may bring an action for contribution against the released tortfeasor must be faced. As far as the unreleased tortfeasor is concerned the settlement between the plaintiff and the released tortfeasor is *res inter alios acta*. If this solution is not perfect, it at least has the merit of promoting more sensible results than any other solution: see Glanville Williams, *Joint Obligations* (1949), pp. 137–138. The absurd consequences of applying the rule of logic invariably led judges, in the best common law tradition, to devise ways of escaping the rigours of its application. The first was the invention of the distinction between an agreement operating as a release of one joint tortfeasor from liability (which resulted in the discharge of the other joint tortfeasor from liability) and an agreement not to sue one joint tortfeasor (which did not involve a discharge of the other). The second technique was the creation of the rule that, even if the agreement operates as a release of one joint tortfeasor, nevertheless the other tortfeasor was not released if the agreement contained a reservation of the plaintiff's rights against the other tortfeasor. In combination these two subsidiary rules, generously interpreted, have ensured that in the majority of cases satisfactory solutions are achieved. But plainly the law is not in a satisfactory state. It is true that a claimant, who engages sophisticated lawyers, can by suitably drafted contractual stipulations avoid the application of the primary rule. But the rule is undoubtedly a trap for the unwary. And for those who are aware of the problem it is a potential disincentive to entering into bona fide and reasonable compromises. The rule requires re-examination, notably in the light of the suspect logic on which it was founded and, in any event, on the basis that the rationale of the rule disappeared once the 'one cause of action' theory was undermined by the statute which authorised successive actions against joint tortfeasors. The point is of considerable importance since it potentially affects a large number of transactions. But it seems to me that binding authority compels me to approach the problem in the traditional way."

In *Watts v Aldington*,[94] R had been plaintiff in defamation proceedings against A1 and A2. He had succeeded and in November 1989 was awarded £1.5 million against A1 and A2, together with his costs to be taxed if not

6–43

---

[94] See n.93, above.

agreed. R obtained an injunction against both A1 and A2 preventing repetition of the defamatory material. As at the entry of the judgment (i) R became entitled to enforce the judgment and (ii) A1 and A2 each became entitled to bring contribution proceedings against the other pursuant to the Civil Liability (Contribution) Act 1978, provided they did so within two years of the judgment. In September 1990 A2 was adjudicated bankrupt upon his own petition. In December 1990 A1 was adjudicated bankrupt on R's petition, relying upon the damages element of the judgment of November 1989. A1 instituted an appeal against this adjudication. Following a finding that A1 had breached the injunction against him, he was ordered to pay R indemnity costs. A1 intimated an intention to appeal against that order for costs and also indicated an intention to apply for leave to appeal out of time against the November 1989 judgment. A1 also, having failed to secure a variation of the terms of the injunction, intimated an intention to appeal against that refusal. Negotiations took place in early 1991 which led to a settlement of all outstanding issues between R and A1. The agreement recited all the orders referred to above, including the judgment of November 1989, and it provided, *inter alia*, that R would accept a certain sum of money from A1 which he undertook to accept "in full and final settlement of the judgment and orders referred to above and any liability howsoever arising before today's date which could involve any payment by [A1] directly or indirectly to [R]". One of the other terms was that the bankruptcy order against A1 would be annulled. This agreement was implemented. An issue arose subsequently as to whether the agreement had the effect of releasing A2 from his liability under the November 1989 judgment. The Court of Appeal held that it did not. The objective construction of the agreement, having regard to the surrounding circumstances and the express words of the agreement, was that the parties to the agreement were not intending that A2 should be forthwith discharged from all further liability. Neill L.J. stated that "The agreement was plainly subject to an implied term that [R's] rights against [A2] would be reserved". Steyn L.J. stated that "The implied term is established. It is the equivalent of an express reservation". The court eschewed any attempt to categorise the agreement as a release or discharge, on the one hand, or merely an agreement not to sue A1 or to enforce the judgment against him, on the other. It was said that the true inquiry was to determine the meaning and effect of the agreement.

6–44 This case involved the question of the effect upon the liability of a judgment debtor (who, with his fellow judgment debtor, was jointly and severally liable to the judgment creditor) of a release by the judgment creditor of the other judgment debtor.[95] Its relevance in the present context is to note the antipathy of the Court of Appeal towards the traditional rule relating to joint tortfeasors, the need for its re-examination and the undesirability of extending its ambit.

6–45 *(iii) Joint contractors.* A compromise by way of an accord and satisfaction between a claimant and one or more of a number of joint, or joint and several, contractors discharges his claim against all.

6–46 In *Deanplan Ltd v Mahmoud*,[96] L demised factory premises to T for 20 years. The lease contained the normal covenant for the payment of rent and the usual qualified covenant against assignment, with a proviso that every

---

[95] See also *Johnson v Davies* [1999] Ch. 117 at 127.
[96] [1993] Ch. 151. See also *Johnson v Davies* [1999] Ch. 117.

assignment should contain a covenant by the assignee directly with L to observe and perform the covenants and conditions of the lease. Some two years after the original lease was granted T (with L's consent) assigned the lease to D2, a company, which duly entered into the required covenant with L. Some 12 years later, and with L's agreement, D2 assigned the residue of the term to D1. D1 entered into direct covenants with L as was required. D1 fell into arrears with the rent and L obtained judgment in the county court for part of the rent owed. In due course the bailiffs took walking possession of the premises. Negotiations between L and D1 resulted in an agreement whereby L accepted certain goods (which in due course it sold) "in full and final settlement of all claims and demands against [D1] under the terms of the lease" and D1's surrender of the lease. L then sought to recover the balance of the rent from D2. H.H. Judge Paul Baker Q.C., sitting as a High Court judge, held that L was not entitled to recover the balance from D2. The agreement with D1 operated as a release, by way of accord and satisfaction, of all covenantors undertaking the same obligation. Since there were no words reserving rights against any other parties in the agreement between L and D1, and no surrounding circumstances rebutting the *prima facie* effect of the agreement, the agreement must take effect accordingly.

Judge Baker Q.C. summarised the law in this way[97]: 6–47

". . . a release of one joint contractor releases the others. There is only one obligation. A release may be under seal or by accord and satisfaction. A covenant not to sue is not a release. It is merely a contract between the creditor and the joint debtor which does not affect the liabilities of the other joint contractors or their rights of contribution or indemnity against their co-contractor. It is a question of the construction of the contract between the creditor and joint debtor in the light of the surrounding circumstances whether the contract amounts to a release or merely a contract not to sue."[98]

This statement must now be read subject to the judgments of the Court of Appeal in *Watts v Aldington* in which the categorisation of the agreement as a release or a contract not to sue was said no longer to be called for.[99] 6–48

(iv) Contribution claims between defendants and other parties.[1] As has been indicated,[2] it is frequently the case that the subsequent claim for a contribution against the original settling party by a party not a party to the original settlement brings into focus the terms of the original settlement. It is important to note that when one of two or more potential defendants to 6–49

---

[97] [1993] Ch. 151 at 170.
[98] *Watters v Smith* (1831) 2 B. & Ad. 889; *Nicholson v Revill* (1836) 4 Ad. & E. 675; *Re E. W. A. (A Debtor)* [1901] 2 K.B. 642.
[99] See n.93, above.
[1] See paras 6–28 *et seq.*, above.
[2] See para.6–38, above.

a claim for damage (whether the allegation is of joint or several liability) makes or agrees to make a payment in bona fide compromise of the claim, he may claim contribution from the others provided "that he would have been liable assuming that the factual basis of the claim against him could be established".[3] That proviso was apparently[4] added during the progress through its Parliamentary stages of the Bill which led to the Civil Liability (Contribution) Act 1978 as a means by which compromises based solely on the possibility of liability under foreign law were to be excluded from the potentiality of a contribution claim. Plainly, however, the phraseology is sufficiently wide to exclude compromises based on doubts as to the legal liability of the relevant defendant under English law.

6–50   It is also of significance to note that where the potential defendant to a claim for damage settles with the claimant and the claimant then (as he is entitled to do) commences proceedings against another defendant, that other defendant may seek contribution from the first defendant who has settled.

6–51   In *Logan v Uttlesford District Council and Hammond*,[5] C was employed by D Council and whilst working for it, was struck by a car driven by the third party. The third party settled C's claim for £2,000 before litigation commenced. C subsequently commenced proceedings against D alleging that the accident was caused by its negligence. D denied liability but brought in the third party claiming contribution. The third party applied to strike out the claim for contribution on the basis that, having settled C's claim as against him, D could not claim contribution. The Court of Appeal held that s.1(3) of the Civil Liability (Contribution) Act 1978 gave D a claim against the third party if C could show that D was liable. The section was not to be read as if the following words were added after "since the time when the damage occurred"—*otherwise than by a judgment on the merits or by reason of a bona fide settlement.*

6–52   The statutory requirement, pursuant to s.1(1) of the 1978 Act, is that any claim for a contribution must relate to "the same damage" as that in respect of which the claimant for the contribution was himself liable. The correct approach to this requirement was considered by the House of Lords in *Royal Brompton NHS Trust v Hammond*.[6] Lord Bingham of Cornhill referred[7] to the proposition "that one important object of the 1978 Act was to widen the classes of person between whom claims for contribution would lie and to enlarge the hitherto restricted category of causes of action capable of giving rise to such a claim". However, he emphasised that it is "a constant theme of the law of contribution from the

---

[3] Civil Liability (Contribution) Act 1978, s.1(4).
[4] See A. M. Dugdale, "The Civil Liability (Contribution) Act 1978" (1979) 42 M.L.R. 182.
[5] (1984) C.A.T. 263 (Sir John Donaldson M.R. and Griffiths L.J.).
[6] [2002] 1 W.L.R. 1397, HL. See also paras 39–28—39–31, below.
[7] *ibid.* at para.5.

beginning that B's claim to share with others his liability to A rests upon the fact that they (whether equally with B or not) are subject to a common liability to A". He said[8] that the three questions to ask are "(1) What damage has A suffered? (2) Is B liable to A in respect of that damage? (3) Is C also liable to A in respect of that damage or some of it?" He added the following observation:

> "I do not think it matters greatly whether, in phrasing these questions, one speaks (as the 1978 Act does) of 'damage' or of 'loss' or 'harm', provided it is borne in mind that 'damage' does not mean 'damages' (as pointed out by Roch LJ in *Birse Construction Ltd v Haiste Ltd* [1996] 1 WLR 675, 682) and that B's right to contribution by C depends on the damage, loss or harm for which B is liable to A corresponding (even if in part only) with the damage, loss or harm for which C is liable to A. This seems to me to accord with the underlying equity of the situation: it is obviously fair that C contributes to B a fair share of what both B and C owe in law to A, but obviously unfair that C should contribute to B any share of what B may owe in law to A but C does not."

(v) Joint contractor claimants. If a claimant is one of a number of joint contractors, a settlement with him by someone liable under the contract would not operate as a discharge of the obligations. However, any subsequent claim[9] for the whole amount of the debt would, in effect, require credit to be given for the amount paid under the settlement[10] assuming that the interests of the claimants are truly joint.

6–53

(vi) Torts (Interference with Goods) Act 1977. In a claim under the Torts (Interference With Goods) Act 1977 for a wrongful interference with goods, the claimant's title to the goods is extinguished by payment of a sum in compromise of the claim.[11] A settlement between the bailor of a chattel and a party who damaged the chattel in respect of damage thus caused, will bind the bailee of the chattel in respect of any claims arising from the bailment even though the settlement is expressed to be "without prejudice" to the bailee's claim.[12]

6–54

---

[8] *ibid.* at para.6.
[9] CPR r.19.3, provides that "[where] a claimant claims a remedy to which some other person is jointly entitled with him, all persons jointly entitled to the remedy must be parties unless the court orders otherwise".
[10] *cf. Steeds v Steeds* (1899) 22 Q.B.D. 537; *Powell v Broadhurst* [1901] 160. See further at paras 6–70 *et seq.*, below.
[11] s.5.
[12] *O'Sullivan v Williams* [1992] 3 All E.R. 385, CA.

Financial accounting involving other parties following a settlement

6–55 Where a claimant settles a claim against one or other of a number of parties against whom he is maintaining claims, he must generally bring into account the sums achieved from such a settlement if he is entitled to (and does) pursue to judgment any of the remaining parties to the action. In a case where a claimant has concurrent claims against more than one defendant, the whole amount recovered under a settlement with one must be brought into account in any claim against another.[13] However, the question of how sums such as these are to be treated is not always straightforward.

6–56 In *Townsend v Stone Toms & Partners*,[14] C appointed D1 as architects and D2 as building contractors in connection with certain building works, C and D2 in due course becoming parties to a JCT prime cost contract. C was dissatisfied with the quality of the works done and the ultimate cost and commenced proceedings against D1 and D2. The claim against D1 was for damages for defective design, defective supervision (both of D2 and a plumbing contractor) and for over-certification of monies paid to D2. The claims against D2 in contract were for defective work, its failure to rectify that work and a claim for sums allegedly overpaid. There was a substantial degree of overlapping between the claims against D1 and D2 where allegations of defective supervision and defective work were made respectively, on the one hand, and also in respect of overcertification and overpayment, on the other. D2 counterclaimed for a sum that it contended was the balance outstanding under the contract. In due course D2 paid the total sum of £30,000 into court in satisfaction of all the causes of action in respect of which C claimed and after taking into account its counterclaim. C accepted this sum and a consent order was made for the payment out of that sum, together with costs up to a specified date and the dismissal of the counterclaim. At the trial against D1 the judge found that had C pursued his claim against D2 to trial, he would have established a concurrent and co-extensive liability between D2 and D1 of about £25,000. (In C's pleaded case against D2 the amount claimed totalled about £229,000.) Given this finding, taken with the fact that C had already received £30,000 plus costs from D2, the judge decided that C had no further claim against D1 in respect of matters where its liability was concurrent and co-extensive with D2. Judgment was given against D1 for some £8,700 in relation to matters in respect of which there was no concurrent and co-extensive liability with D2. The Court of Appeal held that the judge's approach was correct and rejected suggestions:

(i) that if the £30,000 fell to be taken into account at all, it should only be taken into account at the time of executing the judgment against D1;
(ii) that it should be ignored altogether because it was impossible to say how much (if any) of the sum was attributable to claims for which D2 was responsible; and

---

[13] *Townsend v Stone Toms & Partners* (1984) 27 B.L.R. 26, CA; *Banque Keyser Ullman SA v Skandia (UK) Insurance Co Ltd* [1988] 1 F.T.L.R. 360, Steyn J.
[14] See n.13, above.

(iii) that if it was to be taken into account at all, it should be attributed to each claim against D1 in the proportion which £30,000 bore to the total amount of the claims brought against D2.

The judgments are, with respect, not entirely easy to distil into a series of succinct propositions.[15] It was emphasised that if it should be thought appropriate in any case to seek to apportion an amount received in settlement between the various claims advanced by a claimant, the onus is on the claimant to put forward material in support of the apportionment for which he contends.[16] Where the amount received in settlement resulted from the acceptance of a payment into court, attention was drawn to the opportunity for a claimant to obtain an order of the court under what was then RSC Ord.22, r.1(5), directing the party who made the payment into court to amend the notice to specify "the sum paid in respect of each cause of action".[17] Oliver L.J., as he then was, also made it plain that, even though the task of carrying out such an apportionment "may not be altogether straightforward", it was one which had to be attempted on the material available.[18] In carrying out that task, should it arise, Purchas L.J. said that the court "must restrict its attention to the effective benefits received by" the claimant.[19]

6–57

In *Banque Keyser Ullman SA v Skandia (UK) Insurance Co Ltd*,[20] C, syndicates of banks of which C was a member, succeeded in actions against two insurers of which D was one on the issues of liability and causation, quantum being left for subsequent adjudication save that damages would be in a sum equivalent to the amounts that would have been recoverable under certain insurance policies. At the conclusion of the trial it was ordered, *inter alia*, that D pay 40 per cent of C's costs. The purpose of the insurance policies had been to provide C with protection in the event of the failure of certain corporate borrowers to repay substantial loans. The insurances had been arranged by brokers, B, who were originally defendants in the proceedings. C's

6–58

---

[15] This may arise from the fact that the judge below approached the task in hand largely in the way he had apparently been invited to do on C's behalf, yet that approach was the subject of criticism on C's behalf in the Court of Appeal: see *per* Oliver L.J., as he then was, at 42. Purchas L.J., at 52, made it clear that the determination of this sort of issue "must depend very much upon the context and the conduct of each individual case" and it would be "unwise for this court to lay down general rules".
[16] See *per* Oliver L.J. at 41; *per* Purchas L.J. at 51 and 53; and *per* Waller L.J. at 56.
[17] By CPR r.36.6(2) a defendant who makes a Pt 36 payment must serve a notice stating "whether the payment relates to the whole claim or to part of it or to any issue that arises in it and if so to which part or issue". (A similar requirement relates to a Pt 36 offer: r.36.5(3)). The offeree may, within seven days of a Pt 36 offer or payment being made, request the offeror to clarify the offer or payment notice. If the offeror does not give the clarification requested under paragraph (1) within seven days of receiving the request, the offeree may, unless the trial has started, apply for an order that he does so: r.36.9.
[18] (1984) 27 B.L.R. 26 at 41.
[19] *ibid.* at 53.
[20] See n.13, above. See first instance decision on merits at [1990] 1 Q.B. 665. D eventually abandoned its appeal: *ibid*. The other defendant succeeded in the Court of Appeal and House of Lords: [1991] 2 A.C. 249.

claims against B were settled on the first day of the trial on the basis that B accepted liability in the sum of £10.5 million and this sum was paid on the express basis that it was in full and final settlement of C's claims "including the claims for costs". Under this settlement C received just over £3 million. C and D disagreed about the credit to be given by C for the sum received from B. Of that sum a little over £480,000 represented C's agreed costs of the action against B. C contended that that sum should be deducted from the credit that would otherwise have to be given to D since it had represented an additional separate claim against B. C also contended that the unrecovered costs of its action against D (*i.e.* the remaining 60 per cent)—some £416,000—should also represent a deduction from the necessary credit on the basis that, had it pursued B to trial, C would have recovered such unrecovered costs from B. Steyn J., as he then was, held that a deduction of the amount of C's agreed costs of the action against B should be made from the credit to be given since it represented a separate and additional claim against B; but that the unrecovered costs of the action against D were not to be deducted since C had not shown that a claim for such costs against B would have been sustainable. Referring to *Townsend*, Steyn J. said that the:

> "principle appeared to be that if a plaintiff who received payment from one of two tortfeasors established an additional separate claim against him, the payment was allocated first to that claim, and credit must be given in favour of the second tortfeasor only for the excess necessarily referable to the overlapping claim . . ."

Preservation of rights against other parties in partial settlements of multi-party litigation—some illustrations

6–59   Litigation, particularly commercial and construction litigation, has become increasingly complex. The complexity frequently arises from the number of parties that become involved. An all-embracing settlement is often not easy to achieve. Some of the problems that can arise have already been highlighted[21] and others remain to be discussed.[22] The path to the preservation of rights against parties other than those to whom the settlement applies can occasionally be somewhat perilous. Equally, the fact that rights are preserved in certain situations can lead to the appearance, at least, of injustice. Two cases in the field of construction litigation illustrate how problems such as these may arise.

6–60   In *Hydrocarbons Great Britain Ltd v Cammel Laird Shipbuilders Ltd and Automotive Products (t/a AP Precision Hydraulics) v (1) Redman Broughton Ltd (2) Black-Clawson International Ltd*,[23] C took delivery in March 1985 of an accommodation vessel for use in a sea-based gas field. The vessel was a platform with four legs which were lowered to stand on the sea bed, the

---

[21] See paras 4–79 *et seq.*, above (assignment); paras 6–26 *et seq.*, above (contribution proceedings); paras 6–55 *et seq.*, above (financial accounting).
[22] See Ch.39, below.
[23] (1991) 53 B.L.R. 84.

platform itself being capable of being jacked up above the sea surface by means of hydraulic jacking units. The vessel was manufactured by D who had subcontracted the design and supply of the jacking units to 3P1. 3P1 employed 4P1 to design, manufacture and supply 24 heavy-duty, double-action hydraulic cylinders for the jacking units and 4P1, in its turn, subcontracted the manufacture and supply of 48 cast steel clevises (which formed part of the hydraulic cylinders) to 4P2. By an agreement between 4P1 and 4P4, 4P4 witnessed the testing of the clevises and issued certificates in respect of them. In April 1986 cracks were discovered in a number of clevises and the accommodation vessel was taken out of service for repair. It did not return to service until March 1987. C sued D, who served a third-party notice on 3P1 claiming an indemnity. 3P1 served fourth-party proceedings on 4P1, who served contribution claims against 4P2 and 4P4.

In May 1989 C's claim against D was settled for £5.17 million. In November 1990, 3P1 and 4P1 entered into an agreement which provided, *inter alia*, as follows:

> "[4P1] admit their liability to [3P1] in the event that [3P1] are held liable to [D] . . . to indemnify [3P1] against [D's] claim against [3P1] . . . The amount of [4P1's] liability to [3P1] shall be limited to the amount of that sum of money to which [4P1] are or may become entitled under or by virtue of any order or judgment made or entered or any term of any settlement agreement made in the action in [4P1's] name against any other fourth party . . ."

In January 1991 D's claim against 3P1 was settled for £5 million.

At the trial between the remaining parties preliminary issues arose as to whether, by virtue of the above agreement, (a) 4P1 could recover anything but nominal damages from 4P2 and/or 4P4 in respect of its liability to 3P1 or (b) 4P1 could be entitled to recover any indemnity or contribution from 4P2 and/or 4P4 in respect of such liability.

The Court of Appeal held—

(1) On the true construction of the agreement 4P1 admitted its liability to indemnify 3P1 if the latter was held liable to D.
(2) 3P1 was held liable to D for £5 million.
(3) The amount of 4P1's loss was, therefore, £5 million, subject to any challenge to the reasonableness of the settlement between D and 3P1.
(4) 4P1's claim against 4P2 and/or 4P4 was for an indemnity in respect of the above loss of £5 million.
(5) By the above agreement 3P1 limited its claim against 4P1 to the sum for which 4P1 might obtain judgment against 4P2 and 4P4.
(6) The answer to each of the questions raised in the preliminary issues was "yes".

In *Wessex Regional Health Authority v HLM Design Ltd*,[24] C engaged D and 3P1 as architects and main contractor respectively in connection with the construction of a hospital. 3P1 engaged S as subcontractor. The contracts between C and 3P1 and 3P1 and S were JCT contracts containing arbitration clauses. The contract overran by 84 weeks at which stage practical completion was certified. D granted 3P1 an extension of time for 74 weeks and agreed to 3P1 giving S an equivalent extension. In July 1989 3P1 began arbitration

6–61

---

[24] (1995) 71 B.L.R. 84.

proceedings against C claiming a further 10 weeks' extension. C counterclaimed, contending that 3P1 was entitled only to a 30-week extension of time and that 44 weeks had been incorrectly granted by D. C also counterclaimed for just under £1 million in respect of defective work. In February 1992, shortly before the arbitration, C and 3P1 settled their disputes upon terms that C paid to 3P1 a further £1.65 million, each side bearing its own costs. The extension of time granted by D was left unchanged. The agreement was incorporated into a consent award.[25] In May 1992 C issued proceedings against D alleging that, as a result of D's breaches of contract and negligence, C had overpaid 3P1 and sought recovery of those sums from D. P contended that those sums included the sums C had agreed to pay 3P1 in the arbitration proceedings which had been settled. D raised the following defences:

(i) C's losses arose from the compromise in the arbitration proceedings and that if it was incorrectly made it was C's fault;
(ii) alternatively, C had failed to mitigate its loss;
(iii) C, as employer under a JCT contract, had no independent cause of action against his architect for over-certification save in limited circumstances (for example the contractor's insolvency);
(iv) the arbitration would establish the true contractual entitlement as between employer and contractor.

D brought third-party proceedings against 3P1 seeking, *inter alia*, a contribution under the Civil Liability (Contribution) Act 1978. In interlocutory proceedings a number of preliminary issues fell for determination, including the question of whether the consent award in the arbitration proceedings precluded D from proceeding. H.H. Judge Fox-Andrews Q.C., Official Referee, held that since C, as employer, had independent, concurrent and unlimited causes of action arising out of certification against both D (as architect) and 3P1 (as main contractor), C's claims were not precluded by the existence of the consent award. Had C and D wished to provide for this it should have been included within their contract. For the same reason, C's proceedings were not an abuse of the process of the court.

EFFECTS UPON AND IN CONNECTION WITH THIRD PARTIES

6–62 Some effects of a compromise upon persons not directly parties to it have already been considered.[26] Those instances concerned situations where the third party was to some extent a party to the dispute out of which the compromise arose. The discussion hereafter concerns third parties correctly so called: persons concerned neither with the original dispute nor with the process of compromise. The issues may conveniently be discussed in relation to four questions:

(1) How, if at all, may a compromise impose liabilities upon a third party?

---

[25] See Ch.41, below.
[26] See paras 6–26 *et seq.*, above.

(2) How, if at all, may a third party acquire rights under compromise?
(3) What rights, if any, does a third party have to impeach a compromise?
(4) What effects, if any, are felt by a third party who has become interested in the subject of a compromise following its impeachment by one of the parties to it?

Each will be considered separately.

Imposition of liability

The doctrine of privity of contract[27] generally precludes the imposition of contractual liabilities upon a third party by parties to the contract. This principle is unaffected by the Contracts (Rights of Third Parties) Act 1999 to which reference is made below. There may, of course, be a number of situations where the practical effect of an agreement of compromise between two parties may have an adverse effect upon a third party.[28]

6–63

Acquisition of rights

The same doctrine (privity of contract) has, in general terms, precluded a third party from suing to obtain the benefits which, by their contract, the parties have sought to confer upon him. Notwithstanding the efforts of Lord Denning M.R.[29] to displace it, the doctrine and its consequences has largely remained intact at common law.[30] However, the Contracts (Rights of Third Parties) Act 1999 will, in the circumstances in which it applies,[31] make a substantial inroad into the effects of the doctrine.

6–64

In the normal course of events, the only objects of benefit under a compromise will be the parties themselves. However, there may be circumstances in which a third party may be the person whom they agree to benefit.

6–65

> A not wholly unlikely example would be afforded where, say, two estranged brothers, A and B, become embroiled in proceedings over the ownership of a

---

[27] *Chitty on Contracts* (29th ed., 2004), Vol.1, paras 19–115 *et seq.*
[28] See, *e.g.*, para.6–33, above.
[29] *Drive Yourself Hire Co (London) Ltd v Strutt* [1954] 1 Q.B. 250; *Beswick v Beswick* [1966] Ch. 538, CA.
[30] *Dunlop Pneumatic Tyre Co Ltd v Selfridge and Co Ltd* [1915] A.C. 847; *Beswick v Beswick* [1968] A.C. 58, HL; *Scruttons Ltd v Midland Silicones Ltd* [1962] A.C. 446. See *Chitty on Contracts* (29th ed., 2004), Vol.1, paras 19–041 *et seq.* Though see *Linden Gardens Trust v Lenasta Sludge Disposals Ltd* [1994] A.C. 85.
[31] See paras 6–82 *et seq.*, below.

137

motor car. A alleges joint ownership by reason of a contribution to the purchase price; B, in whose name the car is registered, alleges sole ownership, saying that any contribution made by A was really a contribution by their mother, she being the source of the funds. They eventually come to an agreement whereby A agrees not to pursue his claim in return for a promise by B to pay the mother £1,000. Could this promise be enforced if B failed to keep it?

6–66   The common law doctrine of privity of contract would suggest that the mother, certainly, would have no right to enforce it. Unless the court was prepared to find that A was a trustee of the contractual right in favour of his mother, in which case proceedings could be taken with A and B as defendants,[32] there would appear to be nothing that the mother could do. The concept of the trust of a contractual right, as a device for circumventing the rigours of the doctrine of privity of contract, has met with less and less favour in the courts.[33]

6–67   The position now[34] would appear to be that if the contract between A and B expressly provided that the mother may enforce the agreement,[35] and that she is expressly identified by name within it,[36] then she may indeed do so "in her own right".[37]

6–68   Indeed, even if there is no express agreement to the above effect within a contract, but a term "purports to confer a benefit" on a third party, then that party may enforce the contract in his own right unless "on a proper construction of the contract it appears that the parties did not intend the term to be enforceable by the third party".[38]

6–69   The parties to the original contract cannot rescind or vary it without the consent of the third party subject to certain powers of the court to dispense with such consent.[39] Equally, the existence of a term that complies with s.1 of the Act does not affect the right of the promisee to enforce any term in the contract.[40]

6–70   Although a somewhat homely example was given in para.6–65, above, there is plainly considerable scope for the effect of the Act to be felt in compromises of all kinds, particularly in the commercial setting. For example, it is possible to envisage circumstances in which it may be utilised

---

[32] *Vandepitte v Preferred Accident Insurance Corporation of New York* [1933] A.C. 70 at 79.
[33] *ibid.*; *Re Schebsman* [1944] Ch. 83.
[34] Generally the Act applies to all contracts entered into from May 11, 2000 onwards: s.10(2).
[35] s.1(1)(a).
[36] s.1(3).
[37] s.1(1).
[38] s.1(1)(b) and (2).
[39] s.2.
[40] s.4.

to circumvent the problems associated with lifting the veil of incorporation. Parties will need to give careful consideration to the drafting of compromises that mention third parties to ensure either that the Act does apply, if that is what is desired, or that it does not, if it is not the intention.

It seems that if two parties compromise their differences, one of the terms being that a third party should not be sued in respect of some matter by one of the parties, the third party can effectively claim the benefit of that term provided the correct procedural steps are taken and all parties are before the court: 6–71

> In *Snelling v John Snelling Ltd*,[41] the facts of which have been given elsewhere,[42] C had sued the company, D1, for the monies outstanding on his loan account. D2 and D3, his brothers, applied to be joined as defendants to the action, adopted the defence that D1 had put in (pleading the agreement) and counterclaimed for a declaration that the sums which C claimed had been "forfeited" pursuant to the terms of that agreement. Ormrod J. (as he then was) held that, although D1 could not rely upon the agreement, not being a party to it, D2 and D3 could and, since all parties were before the court, there was jurisdiction to grant a stay of C's claim. Since, however, the reality was that C's claim failed, an order dismissing it was made. 6–72

Where a third party compromises a claim made by A against B and pays A the agreed sum, the court will intervene to prevent A pursuing B for the full amount. 6–73

> In *Hirachand Punamchand v Temple*,[43] C were money-lenders carrying on business in India. D borrowed money from them and gave them a promissory note in return. He also borrowed money from them on the security of a bond. When D failed to repay the loans with interest C approached D's father for payment at a time when the statement of account showed the total indebtedness to be Rs 3,600. After certain correspondence D's father sent a banker's draft in C's favour for a sum less than the amount claimed under the promissory note in full settlement of the claim. C took the draft and cashed it, keeping the money. C then pursued D for the balance under the loan. The Court of Appeal held that C could not pursue D for the balance on the basis that the debt was extinguished by the payment by D's father[44]; or that to permit the action would be a fraud on the father or an abuse of the process of the court;[45] or that from the moment of the cashing of the draft C would hold

---

[41] [1973] 1 Q.B. 87.
[42] See para.3–69, above.
[43] [1911] 2 K.B. 330. See also *Barclays Bank plc v Willowbrook International Ltd*, *Financial Times*, July 9, 1985 (Walton J.). In *Stour Valley Builders v Stuart*, noted at para.3–21, above, Lloyd L.J., as he then was, said that the *ratio decidendi* in the *Hirachand* case "is not easy to discern". Though see *Morris v Wentworth-Stanley* [1999] Q.B. 1004 at 1018.
[44] [1911] 2 K.B. 330 at 339–340 and 340–341, *per* Fletcher Moulton and Farwell L.JJ., respectively, relying upon *Cook v Lister* (1863) 13 C.B.(N.S.) 543. Vaughan Williams L.J. founded his decision upon other grounds, but expressly said that a defence to the claim on this basis "might be set up": at 337–338.
[45] *ibid*.

any monies received on the promissory note on trust for D's father and, since it was plain that he did not wish his son to pay anything further under the promissory note, C had no right to pursue the matter.[46]

Impeachment by or on behalf of third parties

6–74 Since, generally, parties cannot by virtue of a compromise impose liabilities upon a third party, a third party can rarely, if ever, have any legitimate interest in its impeachment (or, for that matter, its enforcement). However, since compromises almost invariably involve the payment of money or the disposition of property by one party to the other, the practical effect may be to diminish a fund upon which others may have legitimate claims. In some circumstances the court may intervene at the instance of a third party or on his behalf, usually in the context of bankruptcy or family disputes.

6–75 **Bankruptcy.** The most important area in which third parties may be interested in a diminishing fund is where a party to a compromise has become bankrupt since effecting the compromise. Such a person may, under the guise of compromising a dispute, deliberately seek to prefer one creditor over the others or simply put out of their reach a fund upon which they have claims. The trustee in bankruptcy is responsible for discovering, realising and distributing the bankrupt's property amongst his creditors in accordance with accepted principles. He may seek the court's aid in impeaching such a transaction[47] even though, it seems, it would not otherwise be open to attack.[48] The court's jurisdiction to "look behind" a compromise at the behest of the bankrupt himself or on his behalf will be used sparingly and only in "special circumstances" where the bankrupt was advised on it by his counsel.[49]

6–76 The intervention of the court will frequently be invited by the trustee in bankruptcy when a husband, who thereafter becomes bankrupt, has compromised certain disputes with his wife in such a way that all or a substantial part of the matrimonial assets become vested in her or the

---

[46] See *per* Vaughan Williams L.J. at 337.
[47] Insolvency Act 1986, ss.339–342.
[48] *Re Blythe Ex p. Banner* (1881) 17 Ch.D. 480; *Re Hawkins Ex p. Troup* [1895] 1 Q.B. 404; *Re Lennox Ex p. Lennox* (1885) 16 Q.B.D. 315 (see particularly, per Cotton L.J.). Whether as between parties the compromise would be binding was left open in *Banner*, though in *Hawkins* Lord Esher M.R., at 408, indicated that it would be: *cf.* para.2–19, above.
[49] *Re A Debtor* [1929] 1 Ch. 123 (some evidence of impropriety or lack of knowledge of facts on the part of counsel necessary); *Re Gregory Ex p. Norton v Trustee* [1935] Ch. 65. But where a consent order is made by virtue of which W's claim for periodical payments is dismissed and in return she obtains substantially more than that to which she otherwise would have been entitled by way of capital and property provision, she will have given valuable consideration and the transactions may be immune from attack: *Re Abbott* [1983] Ch. 45. See also *Re Windle* [1975] 1 W.L.R. 1628 and *cf. Re Kumar*, n.50, below.

children. A transfer or settlement of such property made pursuant to a consent order to that effect may still be open to impeachment under s.339 of the Insolvency Act 1986.[50] Such a consent order may be made only in proceedings for divorce or judicial separation. It is, of course, possible for a husband and wife living together amicably, but in the knowledge that the husband may become bankrupt before long, to "compromise" proceedings brought by the wife[51] to determine the extent of her interest in the matrimonial home which is in the husband's sole name. She may have made sufficient contributions to its acquisition, pursuant to an express or implied agreement that she should have a share in its beneficial ownership, to entitle her to an interest.[52] What would be the effect of a consent order declaring her interest to be 99 per cent when a court would not have assessed it at more than, say, 25 per cent? It is submitted, on the basis of the approach set out above,[53] that the court would look behind the agreement to the realities.[54]

The same approach would doubtless be adopted in respect of a "compromise" of claims by parties other than spouses to shared ownership of property made in similar circumstances.

6–77

Family disputes. The estrangement of a family offers a fertile environment for the growth of arrangements whereby assets "disappear", legitimate claims thereby being frustrated. Claims under the Matrimonial Causes Act 1973 ("the 1973 Act") and the Inheritance (Provision for Family and Dependants) Act 1975 ("the 1975 Act") depend on the existence of assets from which they can be met. Provisions exist under each Act to enable the impeachment or reversal of transactions intended to prevent or frustrate such claims.[55]

6–78

Voluntary transfers of assets are usually caught,[56] but transfers for valuable consideration to persons acting in good faith and without notice of the dishonest intention remain inviolate, certainly in proceedings under

6–79

---

[50] Matrimonial Causes Act 1973, s.39. In *Re Kumar (a bankrupt) Ex p. Lewis v Kumar* [1993] 1 W.L.R. 224, Ferris J. pursuant to s.339 of the Insolvency Act 1986, set aside a disposition by H by deed to W of his interest in the matrimonial home, the transfer being held to have been at an undervalue. A transfer of property order made by consent (or indeed other than by consent) between the date of the presentation of the bankruptcy petition against a husband and the date when the bankruptcy order is made constitutes a "disposition of property" within s.284 of the Insolvency Act 1986 and is, accordingly, void unless made with the consent, or subsequent ratification, of the Bankruptcy Court: *Re Flint (a bankrupt)* [1993] Ch. 319.
[51] Under the Married Women's Property Act 1882, s.17.
[52] The interest would be held on resulting or constructive trust by the husband for the wife and so would not form a part of his estate: Insolvency Act 1986, s.283(1) and (3).
[53] The authorities referred to in n.48, above.
[54] *cf. Re Densham* [1975] 1 W.L.R. 1519.
[55] 1973 Act, s.37; 1975 Act, s.10.
[56] 1973 Act, s.37(4); 1975 Act, s.10(2)(b).

the 1973 Act[57] and probably[58] under the 1975 Act. A genuine compromise of a dispute, whereby assets upon which such claims might be made are completely or substantially dissipated, would seem to be incapable of challenge by the claimant. But what of a compromise based on a concocted dispute? Or of a compromise of a genuine dispute whereunder the whole of the assets are transferred subject to an "undertaking" about the return of a proportion in due course? Or of a compromise of a genuine dispute in which the party against whom such claims are made is more than necessarily generous to the other party to the dispute?

6–80   In the first and second postulated situations there would be little difficulty in holding that there was no consideration for the compromise or that there was a lack of good faith. But the third situation could present difficulties. It is perhaps best illustrated by an example:

> H, who is old, uninsured and estranged from W, injures a young boy when he negligently drops something from his first-floor window to the street below. Knowing that he (H) has not long to live, he compromises the boy's claim for £25,000, his savings and only capital, when the claim was worth only £1,000. He does this intending to frustrate W's claim although the boy's advisers and representatives do not know this and accept in good faith.

It is thought that such a compromise could not be impeached under the 1973 Act[59] but that an order under s.10(2) of the 1975 Act might well be made.

6–81   **Other situations.**   Equity has always retained for itself the jurisdiction to grant relief against the consequences of fraud however it is sought to be covered.[60] A fraudulent dissipation of assets under cover of a compromise could, presumably, be set aside at the instance of a third party injuriously affected.[61]

Effects of impeachment by parties on third parties

6–82   By virtue of a compromise, A receives an item of property from B. A then sells it to C. If B then discovers the existence of a ground for impeaching the compromise and wishes to do so, what is the legal position?

---

[57] *ibid.*
[58] Under the 1975 Act a disposition made other than for "full valuable consideration" to a donee "may" result in an order that the donee, in effect, repays any money received or restores any property transferred: s.10(2). The court's discretion whether to exercise its powers will take into account "the circumstances in which the disposition was made, . . . the relationship . . . of the donee to the deceased, the conduct . . . of the donee and all the other circumstances of the case": s.10(6).
[59] Although, for what it is worth in the circumstances, his conduct in dissipating the assets in this way could be taken into account in W's application for financial relief: *Martin v Martin* [1976] Fam. 335.
[60] See Kerr, *Fraud and Mistake* (7th ed., 1952), p.6; quoted in *Cadogan v Cadogan* [1977] 1 W.L.R. 1051 at 1061, CA.
[61] *cf. Blenkinsopp v Blenkinsopp* (1852) 1 De G.M. & G. 495.

EFFECTS UPON AND IN CONNECTION WITH THIRD PARTIES

The answer depends on the effect in law of the ground for impeachment. **6–83**
If its effect is to render the compromise merely voidable (for example in the case of misrepresentation), the intervention of C's rights will operate to prevent its rescission,[62] provided C acted in good faith.[63] In this case C's position is secure. If, however, the compromise is void (for example for mistake) A will have acquired no title to pass on to C.[64]

It would appear that even if grounds exist for the setting aside of a **6–84**
consent order or judgment, it will not be so set aside, certainly at the joint instance of the parties, if a third party is likely to be prejudiced.[65] Where the original consent judgment sought to be set aside involved a third party, it is incumbent on the applicant to ensure that the third party is joined as a respondent to the application or that his interests are in some way protected.[66]

EFFECTS IN CONNECTION WITH ASSIGNMENT

As has already been observed,[67] the parties to a compromise will normally **6–85**
anticipate receiving the benefits from it and indeed performing the obligations under it. Occasionally, however, one party or the other may wish to place another in his shoes for the purpose of carrying it out or receiving the benefits. To what extent can this be done?

In general terms a party cannot shift the burdens of a contract onto the **6–86**
shoulders of another without the consent of the other contracting party.[68] If, however, an analysis of the terms of the contract, its subject-matter and other material circumstances suggests that the identity of the performer of the obligations is of no particular importance, performance by a substitute will suffice.[69] This is known as vicarious performance: it is not really an example of assignment.[70] Thus, for example, a building dispute might be compromised on terms which provide, *inter alia*, for the completion by the builder of certain items of work. Depending on the circumstances, vicarious performance by another builder may suffice.

At common law the benefit of a contract could not be assigned without **6–87**
the agreement of both contracting parties; in equity, subject to certain exceptions, it could. These exceptions still obtain notwithstanding the

---

[62] *Babcock v Lawson* (1880) 5 Q.B.D. 284; *Re L.G. Clarke* [1967] Ch. 1121. And see *Stone v Godfrey* (1854) 5 De G.M. & G. 76.
[63] *Scholefield v Templer* (1859) 4 De G.J.E. 429.
[64] For example *Cundy v Lindsay* (1878) 3 App. Cas. 459.
[65] *The Bellcairn* (1885) 10 P.D. 161; *Hammond v Schofield* [1891] 1 Q.B. 453.
[66] *Ranasingham v Cooray* (1978) C.A.T. 302.
[67] See para.6–80, above.
[68] *Robson v Drummond* (1831) 2 B. & Ad. 303; *Tolhurst v Associated Portland Cement Manufacturers Ltd* [1902] 2 K.B. 660, CA and [1903] A.C. 414, HL.
[69] *Davies v Collins* [1945] 1 All E.R. 247.
[70] *ibid.* at 249; *Chitty on Contracts* (29th ed., 2004), Vol.1, paras 19–080 *et seq.*

existence of the statutory form of assignment under the Law of Property Act 1925[71] and some may be of relevance in the context of compromise.

It would appear that parties to a contract may provide expressly that the benefits arising are not to be assignable.[72] This principle could, if the parties so wished, be extended to a compromise.

6–88 If the identity of a person entitled to the benefit of a contract is material to the person upon whom rests the burden, the benefit will not be assignable. The subjective wishes of the parties are, however, ignored. For example, if A compromises his dispute with B by virtue of which B owes him a sum of money, A will be entitled to assign the right to the money to C even though C intends to use the right to make B bankrupt.[73]

6–89 It is usually said that a "bare right to litigate" is not assignable since such an assignment would savour of maintenance or champerty.[74] That broad statement of principle still appears to be the law although the approach of the House of Lords in *Trendtex Trading Corporation v Credit Suisse*[75] has resulted in a less rigid approach to the question. In any event, the broad statement of principle had, prior to that decision, been subject to a number of significant exceptions. For example, a simple debt, which represents in effect merely a right to litigate, is assignable.[76] Thus a debt under a compromise can be assigned. A right to litigate ancillary to a transfer of property can be assigned.[77] Thus rights arising from the compromise of a boundary dispute between owners of adjacent properties would seem to be assignable provided some transfer of property is or may be involved.[78]

6–90 The right of a wife to maintenance is not assignable on the grounds of public policy.[79]

6–91 Superimposed upon the general principles of the law of contract must be the rules governing the assignability or otherwise of consent judgments. It is clear that a judgment debt is assignable,[80] as indeed is a judgment for

---

[71] s.136. The machinery of assignment is outside the scope of this work: see, *e.g. Chitty on Contracts* (29th ed., 2004), Vol.1, Ch.19.
[72] *cf. United Dominions Trust Ltd v Parkway Motors* [1955] 1 W.L.R. 719.
[73] *cf. Fitzroy v Cave* [1905] 2 K.B. 364. The leading authority on the subject is *Tolhurst v Associated Portland Cement Manufacturers Ltd*, n.68, above.
[74] *Chitty on Contracts* (29th ed., 2004), para.19–048.
[75] [1982] A.C. 679. See Ch.4, para.4–83, above, and the case of *Brownton Ltd v Edward Moore Inbucon Ltd*.
[76] For example *Fitzroy v Cave*, n.73, above.
[77] *Dawson v Great Northern and City Railway* [1905] 1 K.B. 260; *Glegg v Bromley* [1912] 3 K.B. 474; *Defries v Milne* [1913] 1 Ch. 98; *Ellis v Torrington* [1920] 1 K.B. 399.
[78] See Ch.37, below.
[79] *Watkins v Watkins* [1896] P. 222; *Clark v Clark* [1906] P. 331.
[80] *Goodman v Robinson* (1868) 18 Q.B.D. 332; *Harley v Samson* (1914) 30 T.L.R. 450. Whether an assignee of a judgment debt is in an identical position to the original judgment creditor is open to question: *Forster v Baker* [1910] 2 K.B. 636 at 642, *per* Fletcher Moulton L.J.

costs to be assessed if assessed.[81] A mere right to apply for costs is not assignable.[82] Where a part only of a judgment debt is assigned, the assignee will not be able to take enforcement proceedings without joining the assignor: the law permits only of execution in respect of the whole of a judgment debt.[83]

Assignment of rights and liabilities under a compromise may take place by operation of law on the death of one or other or both of the parties. Whilst not all rights and liabilities can be enforced by the estate,[84] a simple debt can be pursued and a judgment debt can be enforced. 6–92

Equally, by operation of law the trustee in bankruptcy of a bankrupt is the statutory assignee of his choses in action.[85] The trustee in bankruptcy may reassign the chose in action to the bankrupt.[86] 6–93

The resolution of a dispute by means of a consent judgment of a court outside the United Kingdom is a bar to proceedings on the cause of action thus compromised provided the judgment is enforceable and entitled to recognition in England and Wales (or, where appropriate, Northern Ireland).[87] 6–94

---

[81] *Hambleton v Brown* [1917] 2 K.B. 93.
[82] *Re Marley* [1952] 1 All E.R. 1057; cf. *Brownton Ltd v Edward Moore Inbucon Ltd*, discussed at para.4–84, above.
[83] *Forster v Baker*, n.80, above. *Chitty on Contracts* (29th ed., 2004), Vol.1, para.19–014.
[84] *Chitty on Contracts* (29th ed., 2004), Vol.1, paras 20–001 *et seq.*
[85] *Chitty on Contracts* (29th ed., 2004), Vol.1 paras 20–016 *et seq.*
[86] *Stein v Blake* [1996] 1 A.C. 243, HL.
[87] Civil Jurisdiction and Judgments Act 1982, s.34. For foreign arbitral awards, see Arbitration Act 1950, s.36.

CHAPTER 7

Satisfaction and Discharge of Obligations Under a Compromise

7–01 This chapter is concerned with situations in respect of which it can properly be said that:

(a) a party to a compromise has discharged or satisfied his obligations under it; or
(b) circumstances have arisen by virtue of which the law no longer demands performance of those obligations.[1]

PERFORMANCE

7–02 The problems which may arise in construing the terms of a compromise to determine the extent of the obligations imposed thereby have already been examined.[2] Once the extent of an obligation has been ascertained, the general principle, subject to the maxim *de minimis non curat lex*, is that complete and precise performance is essential. The other party will be bound to accept that performance as discharging the performer's obligations under the contract. In the absence of that performance, the other party will be entitled to say that there has been a breach of contract and the consequences of that will need to be addressed.[3] Normally, the nature and extent of the act or acts required to constitute performance of an obligation under a contract of compromise will be clear from the agreement. However, there will be situations in which the nature and extent of the obligations have not been spelt out with clarity and the court will have to decide what was intended.

---

[1] *Chitty on Contracts* (29th ed., 2004), Vol.1, Pt 6.
[2] See Ch.5, above.
[3] See Ch.8, below.

Payment by cheque

For example, the provision of a cheque in satisfaction of an obligation to pay money under a compromise may raise the question of whether the provision of the cheque itself is a sufficient discharge of the obligation or whether the receipt of cleared funds after presentation for payment of the cheque by the recipient is necessary.[4]

7–03

Payment by instalments

A compromise may provide for the satisfaction of an obligation to pay a sum of money by means of instalment payments.[5] In the normal course of events, the parties will have specified what is to happen in the event of less than complete payment of the sequence of instalments.[6] In this situation it will be plain, if it be what was agreed, that full and precise performance of the obligation is required. Where, however, the contract does not provide for what is to happen in the event of less than full payment, the question could arise as to whether virtually full performance is sufficient. The situation is best illustrated by an example:

7–04

> A and B resolve a boundary dispute over a strip of land in respect of which B asserts possessory title by an agreement whereby, upon payment to A by B of the sum of £10,000 by equal monthly instalments, A will execute a deed of conveyance of a specified part of the disputed strip of land to B. Apart from this, the agreement is silent about what should happen if B defaults in the payments. B makes nine of the 10 payments and then defaults.

Despite the apparent injustice to B in having discharged his obligation to the extent of 90 per cent, it is not thought that A would be under any obligation to execute the deed of conveyance. Unless the court was prepared to import into the situation the concept of "substantial performance" of an entire contract[7] or some approach analogous to that provided for in s.31(2) of the Sale of Goods Act 1979 (concerning contracts for the sale of goods by instalments),[8] nothing less than full and

---

[4] *Chitty on Contracts* (29th ed., 2004), Vol.1, paras 21–073 *et seq.*
[5] See, *e.g. Horizon Technologies International Ltd v Lucky Wealth Consultants Ltd* [1992] 1 W.L.R. 24, PC, noted at para.11–25, below. See also *Korea Foreign Insurance Company v Omne Re SA*, unreported, April 14, 1999, CA, noted at para.8–08, below.
[6] For example that the whole sum becomes due upon default in one payment (as in *Horizon Technologies International Ltd v Lucky Wealth Consultants Ltd*, n.5, above) or that the party to whom the payments are to be made shall be entitled to resort to his original claim (credits to be given for payments received).
[7] *Chitty on Contracts* (29th ed., 2004), Vol.1, paras 21–027 *et seq.* It is thought that this is unlikely in this situation, though *cf.* para.7–05, below.
[8] Benjamin, *Sale of Goods* (5th ed., 1997), paras 6–222 *et seq.* Again, it is thought that this is unlikely.

precise performance of B's obligation would suffice to trigger the performance of A's obligation.[9]

"Entire" compromise

7–05 If a contract of compromise is construed as "entire", *i.e.* that performance by one party is conditional upon full performance by the other, the failure by the latter fully to perform will entitle the former to treat himself as discharged from any performance on his part. For example, A and B compromise their differences over certain building work being done by B for A on the terms that A will pay B a sum of money if B completes a hot water system in his (A's) house which C had started but failed to complete.[10] Unless B performs substantially his obligation, *i.e.* does the work such that any defects and the costs of rectifying them are relatively small, A will not be obliged to pay him the agreed sum and will be regarded as discharged from so doing. If B does perform the work substantially he will be entitled to the agreed sum less the cost of rectifying the defects.

Agreement collateral to compromise

7–06 It should be noted that a party who complies with an obligation under a contract of compromise, but who fails to honour an agreement collateral to that contract, will still be regarded as having discharged the obligation under the compromise.

> In *Guy v Walker*,[11] C was a stock and share dealer who was in possession of a certificate of railway stock which D alleged belonged to her. She obtained an interlocutory injunction preventing C from parting with the certificate. C then advanced a claim against D for £1,955 which he alleged to be due in respect of certain dealings in stocks and shares. She disputed the claim, but a compromise was reached and she paid C £1,000 "in full discharge of all claims . . . and costs". C thereafter sought to pursue D for the balance of his claim, asserting that he had agreed to accept the reduced sum on the terms of D signing a written retraction of certain charges of fraud which she had made

---

[9] It is difficult to see how B could secure repayment of the £9,000 paid unless some restitutionary remedy could be relied upon. The question of the title to the disputed strip of land might, at first blush, seem difficult. However, it is submitted that the court would hold that the effect of the compromise was that in consideration of D's promise to convey part of the land to B upon completion of the payments, B gave up his right to assert ownership of the whole of the disputed strip by possessory title: *cf. Cornhill Insurance plc v Barclay*, noted at para.6–05, above.

[10] *cf. Bolton v Mahadeva* [1972] 1 W.L.R. 1009. See *Chitty on Contracts* (29th ed., 2004), paras 21–027.

[11] (1892) 8 T.L.R. 314.

publicly against him, and that she had not carried out that part of the agreement. The Court of Appeal held that C's action should be stayed. If there had been the agreement on the part of D as C alleged, it did not form part of the agreement embodied in the receipt. Any such agreement was a collateral agreement and C could bring an action for damages for breach of it.

Mutually dependent obligations

7–07 Just as a failure to fulfil an obligation under a collateral contract will not afford a basis for alleging a breach of the main contract of compromise, the failure to honour an obligation under a compromise which is independent of the performance by the other party of his obligations will not afford grounds for disregarding the agreement. This is a situation which is not likely to arise frequently since, in most cases, obligations under agreements are construed as mutually dependent.[12] However, in "all-embracing" matrimonial compromises it is likely that at least some of the obligations will be regarded as independent. For example, a compromise of differences in a separation deed whereby H agrees to indemnify W in respect of boarding school fees for their son is likely to be regarded as independent of W's agreement that they should share equally the boy's holidays by way of contact.[13]

DISCHARGE OTHER THAN BY PERFORMANCE

7–08 The circumstances in which complete or substantial performance of the obligations under a compromise are no longer expected by law and where the compromise is discharged can be summarised as follows:

(a) where the parties enter into a deed of release[14];
(b) where the parties enter into a fresh accord and satisfaction (in effect, a new compromise);
(c) where the parties agree to release each other from performance or further performance under the compromise (i.e. rescission) whether or not a new agreement is made thereafter;
(d) where the parties agree to vary the terms of the compromise;
(e) where waiver or estoppel operate to relieve a party from being obliged to perform an obligation;
(f) where there is an operative frustration of the compromise.

A detailed analysis of each of these situations is unnecessary for the purposes of this work.[15] The most likely areas for dispute in the context of

---

[12] *Chitty on Contracts* (29th ed., 2004), paras 24–034—24–036.
[13] cf. *Fearon v Earl of Aylesford* (1884) 14 Q.B.D. 792 at 800.
[14] For the interpretation of releases, see paras 5–23 *et seq.*, above.
[15] *Chitty on Contracts* (29th ed., 2004), Vol.1, Chs 22 and 23.

compromise would be where (e) and (f) arguably arise. The essential features of each should be noted although the following resumé is not intended to be exhaustive.

7–09 *Waiver* occurs where a party to an agreement "voluntarily agrees to forbear from insisting on the mode of performance or the time of performance fixed by the contract, or forbears from so insisting".[16] It disentitles the party forbearing from going back on his promise and insisting on his strict rights under the agreement.

7–10 *Estoppel* is not dissimilar to waiver but usually arises without an express request for forbearance when one party, by his words or conduct, induces the other to believe that strict compliance with the terms of the compromise will not be required. Putting the matter very broadly, if in all the circumstances it would be inequitable to allow the forbearing party to resile from the position he has taken, he will be precluded from insisting on strict performance.[17]

7–11 *Frustration* occurs when circumstances arise after the making of an agreement which render performance impossible or so totally different from that which was contemplated as to make performance inappropriate. If the changed circumstances render performance merely more difficult, onerous or expensive, the agreement will not be frustrated. Equally, the impossibility of giving effect to a subsidiary term of a compromise does not frustrate the whole agreement.[18] Examples of circumstances giving rise to frustration are afforded by the destruction of the subject-matter of the agreement, the death of a party to an agreement requiring personal performance and supervening illegality. But frustration will not be found where it has been induced by one or other of the parties to the agreement.[19]

7–12 In the matrimonial context it should be noted that a subsequent decree of divorce or nullity will not frustrate a prior compromise in the form of a separation agreement under which provision is made for maintenance payments.[20]

---

[16] *Anson's Law of Contract* (28th ed).
[17] For a detailed appraisal, see *Chitty on Contracts* (29th ed., 2004), Vol.1, paras 3–128 *et seq.*
[18] *Willis v Willis* [1928] P. 10, CA.
[19] See, generally, *Chitty on Contracts* (29th ed., 2004), Vol.1, Ch.23.
[20] *May v May* [1929] 2 K.B. 386; *Adams v Adams* [1941] 1 K.B. 386. It may afford grounds for a variation of the agreement under Matrimonial Causes Act 1973, s.35. See Ch.32, below.

CHAPTER 8

Effects of a Breach of a Compromise

GENERAL

The purpose of a compromise is to put an end to the disputation in which 8–01
the parties had hitherto been engaged.[1] Such cause or causes of action as each had, or may have had, prior to the conclusion of the agreement are discharged and, if the compromise is embodied in a consent judgment, those causes of action become merged in the judgment.[2] New causes of action arise from the existence of the compromise.[3] Do these principles mean that the original claims of a party can never be reasserted in the event of the compromise being disregarded by the other?

Given the normal meaning, purpose and effect of a compromise, the 8–02
natural inference is that the common intention of the parties is that the compromise will henceforth govern their legal relationship in connection with the disputes in which they had been engaged and that, accordingly, those disputes would still be regarded as "dead" even in the event of breach of the compromise.[4] In these circumstances, it is submitted that recourse to the original claims will not be permitted unless, upon a true construction of the compromise, it is clear that this is what the parties intended. In this context, whilst the matter is primarily one of construction, the nature of the consideration furnished by the party answering the claims being made by the claimant will operate as a pointer.

---

[1] See paras 6–01 and 6–02, above.
[2] *Thoday v Thoday* [1964] P. 181 at 197–198, *per* Diplock L.J.; *Chitty on Contracts* (29th ed., 2004), Vol.1, para.25–007.
[3] *McCallum v Country Residences Ltd* [1965] 1 W.L.R. 657 at 660. See paras 5–54 *et seq.*, above
[4] See, *e.g. Supamarl Ltd v Federated Homes Ltd* (1981) 9 Con. L.R. 25.

Promised or actual acts

8–03 In the discussion on consideration,[5] attention was drawn to the fact that the usual consideration furnished in the context of a compromise is the promised or actual forbearance of one party to pursue a claim against another in return for some promised or actual act by the other.[6] If the promised or actual forbearance to pursue the claim is construed as being in return for the promised performance of some act by the other party, such agreement will be regarded as one involving the immediate discharge of the claim.[7] Where, however, the promised or actual forbearance is construed as being in return for the actual performance of some act by the other party, the claim forborne will not be discharged until such performance takes place.[8] The propositions may be illustrated by reference to two simple examples:

(a) A agrees not to pursue his claim[9] against B in return for B's promise to pay A the sum of £1,000 within 28 days;
(b) A agrees not to pursue his claim against B if B pays to A the sum of £1,000 within 28 days.

If B fails to make the payment within the period specified, A's remedy under (a) would merely be to sue B for damages upon the compromise. Under (b) he would have the option of accepting B's repudiation of the agreement, treating himself as discharged from further performance of his obligations and reasserting his original claim, or of affirming the compromise and suing upon it.[10]

8–04 Although the illustrations given above involve merely the actual or promised payment of a sum of money, the analysis of the agreement to determine the consequences upon breach will be to the same effect where more complex terms are involved. Where there is a clear and unconditional discharge, abandonment or release of a claim by one party in return for the promised performance by the other of a series of acts, that original claim can never be revived. Where the agreement involves merely the suspension

---

[5] See paras 3–02 *et seq.*, above.
[6] See para.3–03, above.
[7] *Sibtree v Tripp* (1846) 15 M. & W. 23; *Crowther v Farrer* (1850) 15 Q.B. 677; *Henderson v Stobart* (1850) 5 Ex. 99. And see *Morris v Baron and Co* [1918] A.C. 1 at 35, *per* Lord Atkinson; *British Russian Gazette Ltd v Associated Newspapers Ltd* [1933] 2 K.B. 616. See *Chitty on Contracts* (29th ed., 2004), Vol.1, para.22–015.
[8] *Morris v Baron and Co*, n.7, above; *British Russian Gazette Ltd v Associated Newspapers*, n.7, above.
[9] A claim which, if liquidated, is disputed or alternatively is unliquidated: see paras 3–12 *et seq.*, above.
[10] He is not bound to accept the repudiation and revert to the original claim: *Smith v Shirley and Baylis* (1875) 32 L.T. 234, noted at para.8–10, below.

of the claim pending the carrying-out of the acts by the other party then the claim may not be lost forever.

In *Fraser v Elgen Tavern Property Ltd*,[11] C's claim for unliquidated damages against several defendants was settled upon terms of settlement which provided for a certain sum to be paid to C's solicitors within 21 days, time to be of the essence. The terms of settlement stated "The defendants to pay and the plaintiffs to accept the sum of $315,000 in full settlement of the plaintiff's claim" and "subject to an order for the taxation and payment of the plaintiffs costs, action to be struck out". The sum was not paid on the due date. C's solicitors gave notice that this non-payment constituted a repudiation of the terms of settlement and that C contended that he was no longer bound by the settlement. Late tender of the sum was refused. The defendants contended that there was accord and satisfaction in that C had agreed to accept their promise to pay the sum in satisfaction of the claim. Murphy J. held that: 8–05

(1) since time had expressly been made of the essence, it was a condition of the settlement that payment should be within 21 days;

(2) on a true construction of the agreement C was not agreeing to accept the promise of the defendants to pay the sum: he was agreeing to accept payment within 21 days, time being of the essence.

In *Hopmeyer v Silverman*,[12] a claim for possession under the Landlord and Tenant Act 1954 (to which, it appears, there was no defence) was the subject of a "compromise": the claim was adjourned upon certain terms with liberty to restore. The terms were that T undertook: 8–06

(1) to enter into a new tenancy agreement upon the terms of the draft tenancy agreement attached to the order within one month (the reference in the draft agreement to the inventory being understood to relate to an inventory drawn up by T and agreed between the parties within that period of one month); and

(2) to pay L's costs.

T simply failed, despite encouragement from L's solicitors, to produce the inventory. L restored his claim for possession and an order was granted. The Court of Appeal held that there had been an accord but no satisfaction since T had failed to produce the inventory.

Generally speaking, therefore, an agreement of compromise will discharge all original claims and counterclaims unless it expressly provides for their revival in the event of breach.[13] Where a party wishes to be able to revive his original claim in the event of the other party's failure to comply with his obligations under the compromise, he would be well-advised to insist that a term to that effect should be incorporated.[14] Any judgment or 8–07

---

[11] [1982] V.R. 398 (Supreme Court of Victoria).
[12] (1980) C.A.T. 147.
[13] This sentence was cited with approval in *Korea Foreign Insurance Company v Omne Re SA*, unreported, April 14, 1999, CA, *per* Evans L.J.
[14] In *Korea Foreign Insurance Company v Omne Re SA*, n.13, above, no express provision to this effect was incorporated in the agreement. However, the agreement was construed in such a way as to have this effect.

order made reflecting an agreement of this nature would need to be drafted so as to give effect to this intention.

8–08   In *Korea Foreign Insurance Company v Omne Re SA*,[15] D were reinsurers and C was the reinsured. They compromised certain disputes that arose between them under a number of reinsurance contracts in an agreement entitled "Commutation and Release Agreement". Under this agreement D agreed to pay C the sum of $1.35 million in full and final settlement of the outstanding claims. That sum was to be paid as to $100,000 on the execution of the agreement and the balance of $1,250,000 was to be paid in 12 instalments, 11 of $100,000 each and a final one of $150,000. The initial sum of $100,000 was paid but none of the further instalments was paid. The following clauses appeared in the agreement:

(i) "It is a condition precedent to this [agreement] that in the event [that D] makes default in [the payment] of USD 100,000.00 ... upon execution of this Agreement and/or any of the instalments within 5 to 10 bank working days from the ... dates [specified in the agreement] from [any] reason whatsoever, this [agreement] shall be wholly null and void, and [C] shall be entitled to reserve its full rights without prejudice to its rights under the Reinsurance Agreements and the claims recoveries."

(ii) "[C] and [D] in consideration of the execution of this Agreement by both parties hereto and upon the payment [specified], shall release and discharge each other ... from all past, present and future adjustments, obligations, offsets, actions, causes of action ... which either party ever had, now have, or hereafter may have ... it being the intention of the parties that this release operate as a full and final settlement of both parties' current and future liabilities and which arise out of the Reinsurance Agreements as defined ..."

Following D's failure to pay any of the instalments after the initial payment C instituted proceedings for the balance of $1.25 million. An issue arose as to whether C was entitled to sue D under the agreement (which provided that it became "null and void" in the event of a default by D) or whether C was obliged to revert to the original claims and pursue D in respect of those claims. D contended for the latter interpretation basing their argument on the proposition that, once they had been in default, the agreement was "null and void". The Court of Appeal held that since the general law of contract gave C the right upon D's repudiatory breach to elect whether to affirm the compromise agreement and to sue upon it, or to treat it as wholly discharged and to revert to the original claims, the clause referred to under (i) above gave D no basis for arguing that C was obliged to rely upon the original claims. It made no commercial sense to interpret that clause in the manner contended for by D since D could, by their own default, discharge their own liabilities under it and C would never have had any right to bring proceedings under it.

8–09   Where an agreement, on its proper construction, does provide for recourse to the original claim in the event of a breach by the other party, the question arises as to whether the innocent party is thereby obliged to

---

[15] n.13 above.

revert to that claim or whether he can proceed to enforce the compromise. Whilst it would not be impossible to conceive of an agreement which expressly provided that the innocent party in such a situation must revert to the original claim, the most likely formulation of such an agreement is that he *may* do so. If this is not spelt out expressly, it is likely to be implied in the sense that it is the obvious inference to be drawn from the agreement.[16] In this situation it would appear that the innocent party may elect between reverting to the original claim and pursuing his rights under the compromise.

8–10 In *Smith v Shirley and Baylis*,[17] C had resisted the grant of probate of the will and codicils of which D were executors. At the trial of the matter a compromise was concluded in the following terms:

> "In consideration of [C] withdrawing from opposition to proof of the will and codicils, [D] undertake to pay [C], within fourteen days, the sum of [£5,850], and a further sum of [£750] for costs; and thereupon [C] and the other residuary legatees will, if so required, release by deed all claim to the residue. Probate not to issue until after payment of the above sums, and the case to be adjourned for that purpose. In default of payment of the above sums within the time specified [C] to be entitled to have the case called on for hearing, and to take a verdict by consent upon all the issues."

D made default in payment and C sued upon the agreement and obtained judgment for £6,600. D appealed, arguing that the compromise merely entitled C either to the agreed sums, if paid, or to a verdict by consent in default of payment, but not to a right to the sums if not so paid. C argued that the true construction of the agreement was to the effect that D were absolutely bound to pay the agreed sums for a particular consideration, but that, if they should make default, C was to have another remedy, beyond and in addition to the ordinary remedy, by way of action for breach of promise to pay. The Court of Exchequer[18] held that the true construction of the compromise was as C had contended and that, accordingly, C was entitled to judgment.

ANTICIPATORY BREACH OF COMPROMISE

8–11 When an agreement permits recourse to the original claim in the event of a breach then, provided the specified breach is committed, the innocent party may elect to pursue his original claim or proceed on the compromise.[19] Is it necessary in every case to await the non-fulfilment of the particular obligation before the election is made? In accordance with the ordinary principles of the law of contract in relation to anticipatory breach, it would seem that, in certain circumstances, the end of the agreed period for

---

[16] *Chitty on Contracts* (29th ed., 2004), para.13–007.
[17] (1875) 32 L.T. 234. See also *Korea Foreign Insurance Company v Omne Re SA*, n.13, above.
[18] Cleasby, Pollock and Amphlett BB.
[19] *Smith v Shirley and Baylis*, n.10, above.

performance need not be awaited. Where a party upon whom the obligation rests:

(a) renounces the compromise, or
(b) does or omits to do something which renders performance of the obligation impossible,

the other party may treat the particular circumstances as a repudiation and act accordingly.

Renunciation

8–12 "A renunciation of a contract occurs when one party by words or conduct evinces an intention not to perform, or expressly declares that he is or will be unable to perform, his obligations under the contract in some essential respect."[20]

Thus, where A agrees to accept £10,000 from B in settlement of his claim and costs if B pays this sum within 28 days, B will be held to have renounced the compromise if, within the 28-day period, he shows that he does not in fact intend to make the payment.[21]

Self-created impossibility

8–13 Where a party to a contract, whether deliberately or otherwise, but, in any event, by his own act or default, creates circumstances which render performance by him impossible, he will be regarded as having repudiated the contract.[22] Such impossibility may arise at any time before performance is complete. An example of a non-deliberate impossibility is afforded by a compromise whereunder one party agrees to transfer to the other certain items of property, but before transfer a judgment creditor seizes the property in execution,[23] or the party upon whom the obligation to transfer rests is made bankrupt.[24] Either event will be regarded as a repudiation.

Implied term as to co-operation

8–14 A further aspect of this part of the law has already been highlighted.[25] The court will normally imply into any agreement a term to the effect that neither party will prevent performance or, looking at the matter the other

---

[20] *Chitty on Contracts* (29th ed., 2004), Vol.1, para.24–018.
[21] The problem of failure to make instalment payments is considered at para.7–04, above.
[22] *Universal Cargo Carriers Corporation v Citati* [1957] 2 Q.B. 401.
[23] *cf. Keys v Harwood* (1846) 2 C.B. 905.
[24] *Purcell v Marshall Parkes & Co* [1899] 1 Q.B. 710.
[25] See paras 5–48 *et seq.*, above.

way, that each party will do all that is reasonably necessary to see that it is carried out.[26] Thus, where a compromise provides that a court order shall be obtained or the agreement is "subject to the approval of the court", a term will be implied to the effect that both parties will co-operate in bringing the matter before the court and, where appropriate, in seeking its approval.[27] Any failure to do so will constitute a repudiation.[28]

INNOCENT PARTY'S CHOICE IF AVAILABLE

Where an innocent party finds himself in the position of being able to elect whether to pursue his original claim or to proceed under or by virtue of the compromise, careful consideration will have to be given to the practical and financial advantages of each course.[29] Indeed, those implications will probably have been considered before entering into the compromise in the first instance. Further, where the option to reassert the original claim is contemplated, care must be taken by the legal advisers of the innocent party in the drafting of letters to the guilty party or his advisers after becoming aware of his breach. Any statement or act which recognises unequivocally the continued existence of the compromise (such as continuing to request performance) after a repudiation in the sense referred to will result in an implied affirmation of the agreement precluding recourse to the original claim.[30]

8–15

---

[26] *Chitty on Contracts* (29th ed., 2004), Vol.1, paras 13–011—13–012.
[27] *Smallman v Smallman* [1972] Fam. 25. See also Ch.32 below.
[28] It will be a question of construction in cases of this nature whether the agreement consists of mutual promises to agree to the order sought, or whether it consists of an agreement by one party not to pursue fully his claims in return for the act of consent of the other party to the agreed order when the court is invited to make it. See paras 3–58 *et seq.*, above.
[29] The remedies available to an innocent party under or by virtue of the compromise are considered in Ch.11, below.
[30] *Chitty on Contracts* (29th ed., 2004), Vol.1, para.24–003. For an analysis of a situation in which the issue of affirmation arose in the context of the discussion of a possible compromise of a dispute arising from a breach of contract, see *Bell Electric Ltd v Aweco Appliance Systems* [2002] EWHC 872 (Elias J.).

PART 2

Machinery, Practice and Enforcement of a Compromise

This Part is concerned with the various means by which compromises are effectuated, the manner of achieving the course chosen and the steps which may be taken thereafter to enforce it.

CHAPTER 9

Means by which Compromises are Effectuated

GENERAL AND PRELIMINARY

9–01 This chapter is concerned with the means by which parties to a compromise give effect to their agreement. Before turning to the methods most commonly used, some preliminary matters should be noted.

The aim

9–02 Once a settlement has been achieved, the parties will wish to see:

(a) the terms properly and accurately recorded; and
(b) in so far as the mere recording of the terms is not sufficient for the purpose of achieving the agreed means of enforcement, the embodiment of those terms in some suitable document or court order to enable expeditious enforcement.

When a settlement of court proceedings is reached, the parties will usually agree to a machinery by virtue of which enforcement of the terms can be achieved within those proceedings rather than leaving the matter to be dealt with in fresh proceedings.[1]

Costs

9–03 In the normal course of events, specific provision will be made in the agreement in relation to the legal costs incurred. In the absence of any such provision, the court will not imply a term in relation to costs, the natural inference being that each party will bear its own costs.[2]

---

[1] See para.6–20, above.
[2] See para.5–60, above.

9–04 With the advent of the "issues-based" nature of the court's jurisdiction on costs following the introduction of CPR[3] there has been a tendency for parties to agree all substantive matters except costs and to invite the court to determine that issue. The practice is not really to be commended. The difficulties faced by a court in this situation were set out by Mummery L.J. in a case decided before the introduction of the CPR.[4] He said this:

> "All lawyers learn from experience that costs are often a stumbling block in negotiating a settlement of proceedings. A judge who is informed by the parties that they have agreed everything except costs may be placed in a difficult position. On the one hand, he may take the view that, if the parties have not agreed everything, including costs, then they have not settled their case: they must either reach an agreement on costs or, failing that, go on with the case. This is a matter for the discretion of the judge. He may be entitled in some circumstances to adopt that position in the hope that the case will not go on and that a settlement on costs will be achieved. On the other hand, a judge may not wish to risk jeopardising the settlement, and may agree to . . . decide the costs issue for the parties. There can be problems; as the case has not run its full course, the judge has not heard all the evidence and all the argument. He may face difficulty in knowing what materials he should take into account in the exercise of his judicial discretion."

The issue was revisited in a case after the introduction of the CPR.[5] Mummery L.J. again uttered words of caution:[6]

> "The arguments advanced on this appeal have demonstrated the real difficulties inherent in asking a judge to exercise his discretion in respect of the costs of an action, which he has not tried. There are, no doubt, straightforward cases in which it is reasonably clear from the terms of the settlement that there is a winner and a loser in the litigation. In most cases of that description the parties themselves will realistically recognise the result and the costs will be agreed. There will be no need to involve the judge in any decision on costs. If he becomes involved, because the parties cannot agree and ask him to resolve the costs dispute, the decision is not usually a difficult one for him to make.
>
> There are, however, more complex cases (and this is such a case) in which it will be difficult for the judge to decide who is the winner and

---

[3] CPR r.44.3(4) and (5).
[4] *Butcher v Wolfe*, unreported, October 30, 1998, CA.
[5] *BCT Software Solutions Ltd v C. Brewer and Sons Ltd* [2003] EWCA Civ 939.
[6] *ibid.*, paras 4–7.

who is the loser without embarking on a course, which comes close to conducting a trial of the action that the parties intended to avoid by their compromise. The truth often is that neither side has won or lost. It is also true that a considerable number of cases are settled by the parties in the belief that the terms of settlement represent a victory, or at least a vindication of their position, in the litigation, or in the belief that they have not lost; or, at the very least, in the belief that the other side has not won.

In my judgment, in all but straightforward compromises, which are, in general, unlikely to involve him, a judge is entitled to say to the parties 'If you have not reached an agreement on costs, you have not settled your dispute. The action must go on, unless your compromise covers costs as well.'

The disposition of a judge to help parties in negotiations for a settlement is understood and applauded. Good intentions are not, however, risk free. If acted upon too readily, commendable judicial intentions can make things far worse than they would have been if the judge had adopted the unpopular stance of requiring the parties to confront the realities of their litigation situation. The judge has a discretion to decline to do what the parties ask him to do. If, on the one hand, the action is for damages, it will be relatively easy for the judge to tell from the size of the settlement sum and from the litigation history (offers, payments in and so on) how the costs should be borne. As I have already said, it would be relatively unusual for the parties themselves not to agree on the costs of such cases. In more complex cases, however, involving a number of issues and claims for discretionary equitable relief, the costs position is much more difficult for the judge to resolve without actually trying the case."

Where parties have proceeded on this basis and the judge has acceded to the invitation, the question arises as to whether the parties should be able to appeal against that decision. There was a suggestion in a matrimonial finance case[7] that an appeal was prohibited in such circumstances because leaving the question of costs to the judge was part of the compromise. However, the Court of Appeal has said that "there is no such hard and fast limit to the jurisdiction of this court" and, accordingly, there is no formal prohibition to an appeal. However, it was also said that the Court of Appeal "is entitled to approach an appeal against a costs order, which has been made as part of a compromise, with an even greater degree of reluctance than is usually the case when it is asked to interfere with the discretion of the trial judge".[8]

9–05

---

[7] *Denne v Denne* (1977) C.A.T. 474B.
[8] *BCT Software Solutions Ltd v C. Brewer and Sons Ltd*, n.5, above, para.8.

9-06   An agreement to an order for costs entails a somewhat open-ended commitment.[9] Not infrequently the party agreeable to paying his opponent's costs in principle would prefer a more clearly defined obligation. This can be achieved either by agreeing an overall settlement sum inclusive of costs with no order as to costs, or by agreeing a specific sum as to costs.

Where either or both parties are in receipt of Legal Services Commission funding, an order for an appropriate public funding assessment will be required.[10]

THE METHODS OF COMPROMISE

Exchange of letters

9-07 Not infrequently, particularly when no proceedings are in existence, solicitors will engage in a formal exchange of letters confirming an agreement. Strictly speaking, this adds nothing to the agreement already reached and is unnecessary. However, it is often felt to be a convenient way of evidencing finality and is useful in that respect. An example would be afforded by a letter from a claimant's solicitor stating that his client agrees to accept £10,000 "in full and final settlement of all claims which he has or may have against [the defendant] arising from the accident on [date] and costs", such letter being in reply to one from the defendant's solicitor seeking confirmation of the agreement in those terms.[11]

A deed or memorandum of agreement

9-08 In some circumstances, particularly where the terms of compromise are not entirely straightforward, the parties may enter into a formal deed.[12]

This is often a convenient method of finalising the compromise of a partnership or boundary dispute which has not reached the stage of proceedings. It is not, of course, necessary in every case that the formalities of a deed should be observed. A memorandum of agreement drafted in terms normally associated with the content of a deed would, provided it is signed by or on behalf of both parties, be quite sufficient.

Making an agreement an order or rule of court

9-09 Where proceedings are in existence, the incorporation, so far as possible, of the terms of a compromise in the court record is often regarded as important, particularly from the point of view of enforcement. It has been

---

[9] The commitment includes one to pay interest at the judgment rate from the date the order for costs is made, even though the amount to be paid under that order will not be ascertained until the completion of detailed assessment: *Hunt v R.M. Douglas (Roofing) Ltd* [1990] A.C. 398. (In *Hunt* case the proceedings had been settled in Tomlin form, one of the terms being that D was to pay C the costs of the action to be taxed if not agreed.)
[10] See, *e.g.* Precedent No.12 at para.A1–12.
[11] See paras 2–08 *et seq.*, above.
[12] Certain formalities must be observed: see para.3–75, above.

suggested[13] that the parties may consent to an order directing themselves to perform the various obligations provided for under the settlement. It is submitted that in so far as the obligations sought to be imposed by the order are such as could have been imposed by the court under its normal jurisdiction, such a course is unobjectionable. However, it is clear that parties cannot by consent confer upon the court a jurisdiction which it does not otherwise possess.[14] Where terms go beyond the court's normal jurisdiction, yet the parties desire the agreement to be readily enforceable without the need for a fresh action, some other approach needs to be adopted. One such approach is for a consent order to be made directing that the agreement can be filed and made a rule of court.[15] Specific agreement to this effect is necessary.[16] The agreement is still a contract but is enforceable in the proceedings without the necessity of a fresh action.[17] The procedure is very similar to that of scheduling the terms of the agreement to a Tomlin order.[18] The disadvantage of this procedure is that there still remains a division of judicial opinion about the precise manner in which enforcement may be achieved.[19]

Simple consent judgment for the payment of money

This method will frequently be adopted where the basis of the agreement is the straightforward payment of a sum of money by one party to the other. It has the advantage from the judgment creditor's point of view of an immediate right to enforcement in default of payment.   9–10

Where there is any doubt about the other party's willingness to pay the agreed sum, it is prudent to insist upon a straightforward consent judgment with no provision as to time for payment.[20] The consequences of registration of the judgment[21] will be avoided by the judgment debtor if he pays immediately.   9–11

---

[13] *Green v Rozen* [1955] 1 W.L.R. 741 at 744, *per* Slade J. See also *Atkinson v Castan*, considered in detail at para.11–29, below.
[14] See paras 9–19 *et seq.*, and paras 10–06 *et seq.*, below.
[15] See Precedent No.17 in the fourth edition of this work.
[16] *Graves v Graves* (1893) 69 L.T. 420.
[17] *Re Shaw* [1918] P. 47.
[18] See paras 9–17 *et seq.*, below.
[19] See paras 11–06 *et seq.*, below. Indeed, for this reason, it seems that this particular approach has now largely fallen into disuse.
[20] The standard form of judgment provides for payment to be made within 14 days: CPR r.40.11. If no such period is contemplated under the consent judgment, care will have to be taken to ensure that the terms of the judgment drawn up by the court accurately reflect the terms of the draft agreed judgment and provide for payment forthwith.
[21] For example appearance on lists in various trades journals.

9–12   This is a convenient point to note the difference between a consent order or judgment and one to which the party against whom it is entered merely submits. The latter is not a judgment or order by consent.[22] Where there is a true agreement between the parties reflected in a consent order or judgment, the order or judgment does not itself constitute a contract. It affords evidence of the contract upon which it is based and that contract is "not less a contract and subject to the incidents of a contract because there is superadded the command of a judge".[23] A submission to judgment may involve an acceptance by one party that the other party is entitled to the judgment, or a conscious decision by that party not to pursue a defence to the claim, but it does not necessarily have the contractual foundation which lies at the root of a consent judgment.

Consent judgment providing time for payment

9–13   A party may be prepared to allow the other party time to pay the agreed sum whilst still wishing to have the security of an enforceable judgment without further application to the court. This can be achieved in a number of ways:

(a) by entering a consent judgment specifying the time within which the judgment debtor shall pay the agreed sum;[24]
(b) by entering a consent judgment with no provision as to time subject to a direction in one or other of the following terms:

(i) that the judgment not be drawn up for the agreed period;
(ii) that the judgment lies in the court office for the agreed period;
(iii) that execution is stayed for the agreed period.

A more usual alternative to one or other of these directions would be afforded by the recording of an undertaking by the judgment creditor not to enforce the judgment for the agreed period.[25]

9–14   In each instance, a failure on the part of the judgment debtor to pay the sum within the agreed period would entitle the judgment creditor to take immediate enforcement proceedings.[26]

---

[22] *Chandless-Chandless v Nicholson* [1942] 2 K.B. 321 at 324, *per* Lord Greene M.R.; *Levi v Taylor* (1904) 116 L.T.Jo. 64. See para.6–22, n.51, above. See also *Siebe-Gorman Ltd v Pneupac Ltd* [1982] 1 W.L.R. 185, CA.

[23] *Wentworth v Bullen* (1829) 9 B. & C. 840 at 850; *Lievesley v Gilmore* (1866) L.R. 1 C.P. 570; *Conolan v Leyland* (1884) 27 Ch.D. 632; *Worthington & Co v Abbot* [1910] 1 Ch. 588; *Brister v Brister* [1970] 1 W.L.R. 664. See also *Horizon Technologies International Ltd v Lucky Wealth Consultants Ltd* [1992] 1 W.L.R. 24, PC; and *Islam v Askar* (1994) C.A.T. 1240.

[24] CPR r.40.11.

[25] See Precedent No.13, at para.A1–13, below, modified to include the undertaking.

[26] See Ch.11, below.

In some cases time will be afforded to a judgment debtor by an 9–15
agreement whereby payments are made by instalments.[27] The usual method
of securing the position of the judgment creditor is for there to be a
forthwith judgment for the whole of the agreed sum, execution of which is
directed to be stayed on condition that the judgment debtor pays an agreed
figure at periodic intervals with a provision that the stay on execution be
removed in the event of a default in one of the periodic payments.[28]

Payment of money without judgment

Not infrequently the party to whom money is agreed to be payable will 9–16
not insist that judgment is entered immediately against the other party. A
convenient method of securing the creditor's position in such a case is for a
consent order to be made staying the proceedings[29] as follows:

(a) upon terms that the agreed sum is paid within a specified period with permission to remove the stay and enter judgment in that sum if not so paid;

(b) upon terms that the agreed sum is paid within a specified period in default of which the stay is removed and the proceedings restored; or

(c) upon terms scheduled to the order of the court save for the purpose of enforcement, with permission to apply for such purpose, the terms scheduled (or indorsed) being that the one party agrees to pay the other the agreed sum within the specified period.

The third method is more usually adopted where the terms of the 9–17
agreement are somewhat complex and it is felt that full reference to them
in the order is unnecessary or impossible.[30] However, it is also appropriate
in cases involving the payment of a sum of money (possibly by instalments)
where the parties do not want public reference to be made to it either on
the face of the order or by their representatives.[31] It is not a judgment and
cannot, without more, be enforced as such.[32]

---

[27] *cf. Re South American & Mexican Co* [1895] 1 Ch. 37; and *Horizon Technologies International Ltd v Lucky Wealth Consultants Ltd*, n.23, above. See CPR r.40.11(a).
[28] It is not always advisable for a judgment creditor to insist that in default of any one payment the whole balance becomes due because the judgment debtor may be able to use this to secure his own bankruptcy.
[29] For the significance and meaning of a "stay", see paras 9–24 *et seq.*, below.
[30] The order is a Tomlin order: see paras 9–19 *et seq.*, below.
[31] But note paras 10–28 *et seq.*, below and, in particular, para.10–31, below.
[32] See paras 11–21 *et seq.*, below.

Consent judgment or order involving terms other than mere payment of money, including Tomlin order

9–18   Compromises often comprise a series of terms not all of which involve the direct payment of money. Equally, terms of compromise often provide for arrangements which could not have been made the subject of a direct court order or judgment. For example, an action brought by the hirer (on hire-purchase) of a car against the finance company and the garage which originally supplied it in respect of alleged defects might be compromised on terms which include acceptance by the hirer of another car in exchange for the one of which complaint was made, with certain financial adjustments between the parties. Clearly, such an agreement is possible and enforceable as an agreement; but a court order directing the exchange of cars could not have been made. This problem does not arise where the parties are agreed on the manner in which a specific jurisdiction of the court is to be exercised in order to give effect to their compromise. In such a case an appropriate provision to the relevant effect may appear in the consent order or judgment.[33]

9–19   In cases where some or all of the terms of the compromise go beyond that which could be provided for by means of a straightforward consent order or judgment, care must be taken in selecting the most appropriate machinery for giving effect to the agreement. Where an agreement is reached which contains provisions of this nature, it is not good practice (nor indeed lawful) merely to recite the terms of the agreement in a document purporting to be a consent order or judgment and placing the words "by consent it is ordered" or by "by consent it is adjudged" at the beginning of the document.[34] A consent order or judgment which has been drawn up in a way which has not focused clearly upon whether any or all of its constituent provisions come within the normal jurisdiction of the court can present great problems when the question of enforcement arises.[35]

9–20   A variety of means exist by which terms of an agreement going beyond the normal jurisdiction of the court can be made amenable to the jurisdiction of the court for the purposes of enforcement. For example, provided it is sufficiently clearly expressed for the purposes of subsequent enforcement,[36] a court will be prepared to accept an undertaking given by a

---

[33] Although this arises most frequently in compromises of financial proceedings in the family jurisdiction, it can also arise in connection with, for example, disputes to which the Torts (Interference with Goods) Act 1977 or the Consumer Credit Act 1974 apply.
[34] This is what was done by the district judge in relation to the draft consent order presented to the court in *Atkinson v Castan*, noted at para.11–29, below.
[35] See, *e.g.* para.10–11, below.
[36] *Wilson and Whitworth v Express Newspapers and Independent Newspapers* [1969] 1 W.L.R. 197; noted at para.3–51, above.

party to the court which assumes an obligation going beyond what the court might have imposed upon that party by order.[37] Reference has already been made[38] to the procedure by which an agreement may be filed and made a rule of court, although it should be noted that this approach is now rarely, if ever, adopted.[39]

The method most commonly adopted to effectuate a compromise involving terms going beyond the court's normal jurisdiction is to incorporate the agreement into a "Tomlin order". This provides for a consensual stay of the proceedings on the agreed terms save for the purpose of carrying the agreed terms into effect, permission to apply to the court for this purpose being reserved.[40] The terms are usually incorporated into a schedule to the order or are recorded in a separate document[41] which is identified clearly on the face of the order. The great advantage of this procedure is that it enables the enforcement of the terms of the settlement within the existing action by a summary procedure. The terms may, of course, be complex and, as already indicated above, can be of a nature which go beyond the normal jurisdiction of the court. Indeed, the terms of settlement can go outside the ambit of the original dispute between the parties.[42]

9–21

Regular use has been made of the Tomlin form of order for many years.[43] The structure of the Tomlin order itself represents something of a compromise between competing legal and practical considerations. It is well established that once a compromise has been concluded a new legal relationship between the parties comes into existence replacing the previous relationship of disputation.[44] In the event of a failure by one of the parties to honour the agreement, the position in law is that the innocent party will have a cause of action represented by an action for damages, for specific performance, an injunction or other relief, depending upon the circumstances.[45] A cause of action is pursued procedurally by means of a

9–22

---

[37] *cf.* para.32–60, below.
[38] See para.9–07, above.
[39] *ibid.*
[40] Precedent No.14, at para.A1–14, below. In *Marchant v Marchant* (1967) C.A.T. 26, Danckwerts L.J. expressed the view that the words "liberty to apply" without more are ineffective to keep alive the proceedings for the purposes of enforcement. The full expression "liberty to apply for the purpose of enforcing the said terms" must be used. *cf.* para.11–29, below. The expression "permission to apply" will be used henceforth in the text reflecting the post-CPR terminology.
[41] See Precedent No.14, at para.A1–14, below.
[42] *Phillips (E. F.) & Co v Clarke* [1970] Ch. 322.
[43] At least since 1927 (Practice Note [1927] W.N. 290) and probably very much longer. The text of the author's lecture entitled "The Tomlin Order: Three Score Years and Ten", given to the London Common Law and Commercial Bar Association on November 19, 1997, to mark the seventieth anniversary of the Tomlin order, is reproduced in Appendix 6, below.
[44] See paras 6–01 and 6–02, above.
[45] See Ch.11, below.

new action. However, the full procedural panoply arising from the institution of new proceedings[46] is rarely necessary in this situation, is cumbersome and would, in most cases, result in unjustified delay in the implementation of the agreement.[47] But for the machinery afforded by a Tomlin order, parties to an agreement containing provisions which could not be made the subject of direct provision within a consent order would be forced to institute fresh proceedings for the purposes of enforcement.

9–23   The nature and effect of a Tomlin order was considered by the Court of Appeal in *Hollingsworth v Humphrey*[48]:

> Proceedings between C and D concerning the ownership of a property they had once shared, and which was subject to a joint mortgage, were compromised in Tomlin form on October 27, 1978. The material terms appearing in the schedule to the order were as follows:
>
> (a) The property should be sold within 3 months from the date of the order, D to have conduct of the sale.
> (b) Out of the proceeds of sale (as defined) C should receive £5,500, the balance to go to D, whereupon C was to be indemnified by D against liability under the joint mortgage.
>
> The order was not entered until June 15, 1979. D did nothing about the sale except to indicate in June 1979 that he was getting vacant possession from certain tenants to enable a sale to take place. Correspondence ensued between solicitors until about January 1982 during the course of which C's solicitors threatened proceedings for contempt. Nothing further happened until June 1983 when C's solicitors wrote a further letter. Finally, in June 1985, C served a notice of motion seeking:
>
> (a) an order lifting the stay so that she could proceed to trial; alternatively
> (b) an order that the terms be carried into effect with consequential directions;
> (c) an inquiry as to damages occasioned to C by D's delay in effecting the sale.
>
> Mervyn Davies J. refused (a) but ordered specific performance of the provisions in the schedule, substituting a new date for compliance. He also awarded C damages in an amount equal to 13.5 per cent per annum on the £5,500 from January 27, 1979. The Court of Appeal held that the judge was correct save to the extent of having awarded damages: that aspect had to be pursued by way of separate action.

9–24   On the issue of whether the stay should have been removed Fox L.J. expressed himself in this way, having recorded that there was no question in the instant case of the vitiation of the compromise by "for example, fraud or mistake":

---

[46] The payment of court fees on the institution of proceedings, exchange of pleadings, disclosure and so on.
[47] Arguably, any such action would be subject to the relevant Pre-Action Protocol.
[48] (1987) C.A.T. 1244; *Independent*, December 21, 1987, CA. See also *Wagstaff v Colls* [2003] EWCA Civ 469.

"The first question ... is the meaning of the agreement reached between the parties. That agreement ... consists not only in the scheduled terms of the compromise, but includes the provision for the stay itself which is an integral part of the compromise."

Having referred to the wording of the consent order, the learned Lord Justice continued as follows:

"As between the parties, ... while the action is not discontinued or dismissed, the bargain was that the action would not be resorted to thereafter save for the purpose of enforcing the terms. That is the plain meaning of the language used... The liberty to apply for the purpose of enforcing the terms gave [C] a summary method of securing compliance."

The argument that the compromise was merely a contract for the sale of C's beneficial interest in the property was rejected. That had been a matter in dispute and, as Fox L.J. observed, C had "asserted a cause of action and gave that up in consideration of the provisions of the Tomlin order". The reason why it was necessary for there to be a fresh action to claim damages for breach of the agreement reflected in the schedule to the Tomlin order was that a claim for damages did not represent enforcement of the agreement: the original action was only kept alive for that purpose and for no other. As he put it:

"... under the terms of the Tomlin order the only jurisdiction which [the judge] had in this action was to make an order for the purpose of carrying into effect the terms of compromise. An award of damages is not carrying the terms into effect. It is granting a remedy for breach of contract. In my view any claim by [the plaintiff] for breach of contract must be pursued in a separate action."

9–25

The decision of the Court of Appeal concerning the need for a fresh action to pursue a claim for damages for breach of a provision in a Tomlin order schedule has been perceived to reflect a somewhat restrictive interpretation of the words of a Tomlin order.[49] Indeed, when the CPR were drafted, the restrictive effect of this ruling was recognised and an effort made to circumvent it in the situation where a Pt 36 offer is accepted.[50] There is now authority to the effect that the overriding

9–26

---

[49] See, e.g. the author's view, at para.A6–17 below.
[50] See paras 21–15—21–16 below. The precedent for a Tomlin order put forward in the Fifth edition (and which continues to appear in this edition: see Precedent No.14, at para.A1–14, below), contains a provision in these terms: "AND IT IS RECORDED that the parties have agreed that any claim for breach of contract arising from an alleged breach of the terms set out in [the Schedule to this order] [the above-mentioned document] may, unless the court orders otherwise, be dealt with by way of an application to the court without the need to start a new claim". This is designed to circumvent the effect of *Hollingsworth v Humphrey*, n.48, above.

objective[51] enables the court to take a different view from that expressed in *Hollingsworth v Humphrey*.[52]

9–27   In *The Bargain Pages Ltd v Midland Independent Newspapers Ltd*[53] a passing off action between C and D was settled by means of a Tomlin order in 1996. The terms of settlement scheduled to the order imposed restrictions on D as to the name and get-up under which it might publish and distribute its papers. In addition it was required to procure that its parent, subsidiary and associated companies controlled by it should be bound by the terms of the agreement as if they themselves were party to it. The order provided in conventional terms that all further proceedings in the action were stayed "except for the purpose of carrying the said terms into effect" and for that purpose the parties were to be at liberty to apply. During the next six years corporate reorganisations took place on both sides. Issues arose between successors to C and D as to whether there were breaches by D's successors of the terms of the Tomlin order and, if so, how they might be pursued. On the issue of how C might pursue claims for damages against D, Sir Andrew Morritt V.C. held that a fresh action would not be necessary. He put matters thus:[54]

> "The first passing off action gave rise to a settlement to which effect was given by the Tomlin order. The Tomlin order is as much a part of the case as the original issues as to passing off. In my view it follows that the overriding objective applies as much to issues arising from the Tomlin order as it did to the original dispute about passing off. It appears to me to be contrary to the overriding objective to require that the remedy of damages for the breach of a term of the compromise be pursued in a second action if a remedy by way of mandatory injunction to enforce the terms of the compromise can be pursued in the first. Each arises from the terms of settlement scheduled to the Tomlin order. It is not suggested that those terms are liable to be set aside. Accordingly I do not consider that the decision of the Court of Appeal in *Hollingsworth v Humphrey* . . . would preclude an order for an enquiry as to damages sustained by [C] in consequence of a breach of the terms of the Agreement."

9–28   Irrespective of the issues raised concerning a potential claim for damages arising from breach of a Tomlin order, parties wishing to utilise the convenient machinery for enforcement afforded by such an order would be well-advised to use the standard form of words associated with it.[55] Since the effect of those words is so clearly established, it would be less than sensible to utilise some variant lest the court should be inclined to interpret the agreement underlying the consent order in a different manner from that which was intended. The importance of the words used in the usual form of Tomlin order is that a conditional stay of the proceedings is provided for, the action remaining alive for the purposes of enforcement.[56]

---

[51] CPR r.1.1.
[52] *The Bargain Pages Ltd v Midland Independent Newspapers Ltd* [2003] EWHC 1887 (Ch).
[53] *ibid.*
[54] *ibid.* at para.44.
[55] See Precedent No.14, at para.A1–14, below.
[56] See para.9–17, above.

The effect of a "stay" of proceedings in a context other than that of a Tomlin order has been much debated,[57] but the position now appears to be settled: an absolute or an unconditional stay is not to be equated with a dismissal or discontinuance of proceedings.[58] An operative stay prevents the action from moving forward any further,[59] or resuming "its active life",[60] without an order of the court, such an order not being granted lightly[61] and only in a "proper case".[62] The Court of Appeal has drawn attention to the "great difficulties" that would be faced by a party seeking the removal of a stay to an action "stayed by consent following a compromise".[63] Consistent with the analysis of the effect of a Tomlin order in *Hollingsworth v Humphrey*,[64] it is submitted that the "great difficulties" would lie in suggesting that the compromise itself was in some way conditional and not conclusive of the action and/or that the stay could be removed for the purpose of proceeding with the original claim. Any form of words that gives rise to an absolute or unconditional stay of the proceedings will result in the need for a fresh action to enforce the terms of any agreement scheduled to the order.[65]

In *Re Hearn*,[66] W had instituted proceedings by way of originating summons dated October 21, 1908 to determine, *inter alia*, whether H, from whom she was separated, had forfeited his life interest in an annuity of £500 provided for under his father's will, that annuity having been secured by the appropriation of certain properties. H was also entitled to a one-sixth share in the residue of the estate, his entitlement to that share being secured upon other properties. Those proceedings were compromised and a consent order was made on June 15, 1909 under which all further proceedings were stayed upon the terms mentioned in a schedule to the order. The terms provided, *inter alia*, that W should receive £315 per annum during the joint lives of H and W, such sum to be paid out of the income from the properties upon which H's annuity and his share of the residue were secured. It was also agreed that the trustees of the will of H's father (P) should take over the collection of the rents from, 9–29

---

[57] See, e.g. *Lambert v Mainland Market Deliveries Ltd* [1977] 1 W.L.R. 825, CA. See also *Wagstaff v Colls* [2003] EWCA Civ 469.
[58] *Rofa Sport Management AG v DHL International (UK) Ltd* [1989] 1 W.L.R. 902, CA.
[59] *Lambert v Mainland Market Deliveries Ltd*, n.57, above, *per* Lawton L.J at 834.
[60] *Rofa Sport Management AG v DHL International (UK) Ltd*, n.58, above, *per* Neill L.J at 911.
[61] See n.57, above, *per* Megaw and Lawton L.JJ.
[62] *Derrick v Williams* [1939] 2 All E.R. 559; *Cooper v Williams* [1963] 2 Q.B. 567; *Lambert v Mainland Market Deliveries Ltd*, n.57, above. A former bankrupt, who takes an assignment of a right of action against certain persons from his trustee in bankruptcy, is in no better position to apply to lift the stay imposed by a Tomlin order and to proceed against those persons than is his trustee in bankruptcy: *Re Ross (a bankrupt)*, unreported, April 17, 1997, CA, relying upon *Selig v Lion* [1891] 1 Q.B. 513.
[63] *Rofa Sport Management AG v DHL International (UK) Ltd*, n.58, above, *per* Neill L.J. at 911.
[64] See para.9–24, above.
[65] *Morton v Quick* (1878) 26 W.R. 441; *Green v Rozen* [1955] 1 W.L.R. 741 at 745–746. But see para.11–29, below.
[66] (1913) 108 L.T. 452 and 737.

and the general management of, the properties securing H's annuity. H was left in possession of the properties securing his share of the residue. By early 1910 the income from the properties securing the annuity was insufficient to pay the annuity in full after provision for prior charges had been made. The full amount of W's entitlement to £315 per annum under the agreement was not paid and, through her solicitors, she asked H to make good the deficiency out of the rents and profits of the property upon which his share of the residue was secured. This request was in accordance with the terms of the agreement reflected in the schedule to the order. H did not comply with this request and W issued a summons within the action stayed by the consent order seeking an order that H should give up possession of the properties securing or representing his one-sixth share of the residue, or that a receiver should be appointed in respect of those properties, so that the sums outstanding could be made good and the future payments rendered secure. There was no defence to W's application on the merits, but H took the point that the original action had been brought to an end by the consent order of June 15, 1909 and that an action for specific performance would be required to secure enforcement of those terms. Sargant J. held that W was not entitled to obtain the relief she sought by motion or summons in the original proceedings and that independent proceedings were required. The Court of Appeal[67] held that Sargant J. was "perfectly right" in this decision.[68]

9–30 It should be noted that the consent order made in *Re Hearn* did not provide for the qualified stay of proceedings required for a Tomlin order.[69] Equally, although the parties incorporated their agreement in the court record (namely the schedule to the order),[70] no suggestion was made that this gave the court a jurisdiction to grant relief by way of enforcement of the agreement without the need for a fresh action.[71]

9–31 A compromise embodied in a Tomlin order is just as susceptible to being set aside on any of the usual invalidating grounds[72] as any other compromise. The question arises of whether, as in most other cases,[73] a fresh action is required to set aside the order in such circumstances, or whether an application to remove the stay is the correct procedural course to adopt. It may be thought logical that, just as a judgment or other order by consent demands the institution of a fresh action for this purpose, so too would a settlement incorporated in a Tomlin order. Nonetheless, it appears to be possible for the matter to be dealt with purely by way of application. A stay imposed by virtue of the acceptance by one party of a Pt 36 payment may be set aside by application in the action.[74] Although not referring specifically to the procedural steps necessary for the purpose, in *Hollingsworth v*

---

[67] Cozens-Hardy M.R., Buckley and Kennedy L.JJ.
[68] (1913) 108 L.T. 737 at 738.
[69] See paras 9–19 *et seq.*, above.
[70] *Islam v Askar*, n.23, above.
[71] *cf. Atkinson v Castan*, discussed at paras 11–29 *et seq.*, below.
[72] See Ch.4, above.
[73] See Ch.12, below.
[74] *cf. Derrick v Williams*, n.62, above; *Lambert v Mainland Market Deliveries Ltd*, n.57, above.

Humphrey,[75] Fox L.J. said that it was "clear that a stay imposed as part of a compromise of an action may be lifted if the compromise is vitiated by, for example, mistake or fraud".

Whilst there is much to be said for this convenient approach from the practical point of view, it must be borne in mind that any process by which it is sought to set aside an agreement, or an order embodying that agreement, involves the assertion of a new cause of action based on whatever invalidating ground is relied upon. This would, in the normal course of events, require the institution of fresh proceedings. One answer to those proceedings might be the expiration of the appropriate limitation period. Presumably, such a point could also be taken in the context of an application to remove a stay in the circumstances under discussion.[76] 9–32

As emphasised below,[77] the schedule to a Tomlin order forms part of the court record and is amenable to the inherent jurisdiction of the court for the purposes of amendment in appropriate circumstances.[78] 9–33

Other cases

Other orders to which parties may consent in complete or partial resolution of the compromise involve adjournment, withdrawal, discontinuance or dismissal of the proceedings. 9–34

Adjournment. A party may be prepared for the trial of his claim (or the hearing of any interim application) to be adjourned generally (with liberty to restore) or for a specified period to enable the other party to carry out the terms of the agreement. A provision would normally be made whereby the claimant would undertake to apply for the discontinuance or dismissal of the claim on fulfilment of the terms by the other party. Should the terms not be carried out, the original claim could proceed.[79] 9–35

Many applications for an interim injunction are compromised on the basis of an adjournment of the application upon certain undertakings.[80]

---

[75] See para.9–21, above.
[76] Since a limitation point must, in the ordinary course of events, be pleaded, there must, it is submitted, be a clear written intimation of the facts alleged to support the defence to the application.
[77] See para.10–31, below.
[78] See paras 4–37, *et seq.*, above.
[79] For example *Hopmeyer v Silverman*, noted at para.8–06, above.
[80] See paras 11–33 *et seq.*, below.

9-36 **Withdrawal or discontinuance.** Subject to the appropriate rule,[81] an action may be withdrawn or discontinued by consent either unconditionally or upon terms. Both have the effect of putting an end to the proceedings even for the purposes of enforcement of any agreed terms unless they are "kept alive" specifically for such purpose.[82] Neither course precludes the commencement of fresh proceedings based on the same cause of action unless, on a true construction of the terms of the agreement underlying the consent, it is clear that a discharge of all claims was intended.[83]

9-37   In *Apple Computer Inc v Popiolek*,[84] C issued a writ against D seeking orders restraining him from selling computers, computer equipment and computer programmes not of C's manufacture under the name "Apple" and from passing off as manufactured by C similar items. C also claimed damages. At the hearing of C's summons for interlocutory relief in the terms of the indorsement on the writ, D consented to a perpetual injunction in the terms of the relief sought in the writ in consideration of which C agreed to, and did, file a notice of discontinuance of the action. In subsequent proceedings against D for alleged breaches of the injunction occurring after the notice of discontinuance, D sought to argue that the injunction did not survive the discontinuance and that, accordingly, no enforcement proceedings could be taken. In the Supreme Court of Victoria, Nicholson J. held that the injunction, which was a final order intended to dispose of part of C's claim, was not affected by the discontinuance: at the time of the agreement only the claim for damages remained alive and it was only that part of the subject-matter of the action which was affected by the notice of discontinuance.

9-38   In *"The Ardandhu"*,[85] a collision occurred between two vessels, K and A. The owners of K brought an action for damages against the owners of A. An agreement was drawn up between the respective solicitors in which the solicitors for A's owners said that they consented "to this action being discontinued without costs on the ground of inevitable accident". An order was subsequently made in the following terms: "Upon consent of both solicitors, it is ordered that this action be discontinued, without costs, on the ground of inevitable accident". The question arose subsequently of whether the agreement and the order giving effect to it represented a mutual release of all claims or whether, as the owners of K argued, there was merely a discontinuance with all matters remaining potentially open. The House of

---

[81] CPR Pt 38. In *Ernst & Young v Butte Mining Plc, The Times*, March 22, 1996, Robert Walker J. set aside as an abuse of the process of the court a notice of discontinuance of C's claim against D designed to frustrate the service by D of a substantial counterclaim which, but for the existence of C's claim, would have been statute-barred. The counterclaim could have been pursued provided C's claim was continued by virtue of s.35 of the Limitation Act 1980. The notice of discontinuance was served after a consent order had been agreed between C and D setting aside a judgment on C's claim obtained in default of defence.
[82] A "stay" is preferable in the circumstances and more certain in its effect: see paras 9-24 et seq., above.
[83] *The Ardandhu* (1887) 12 App. Cas. 256.
[84] [1984] V.R. 156, Supreme Court of Victoria.
[85] *The Owners of the Cargo of the "Kronprinz" v The Owners of the "Kronprinz": The "Ardandhu"* (1887) 12 App. Cas. 256.

Lords held that parties must be taken to have intended the words of the agreement and the order to have their natural and ordinary meaning, namely that of a discontinuance, leaving the possibility for each party to reassert its rights. Had the parties' solicitors used the words "this action should be dismissed", then no further proceedings would have been possible.

9–39 In *Macedonia Maritime Co v Austin & Pickersgill Ltd: The "FayrouzI-IV"*,[86] C were foreign shipowners for whom D constructed four vessels under separate contracts. C contended that at the time each of the vessels was delivered each was defective in a number of respects, including the welding. They claimed damages against D for about £3 million. D sought security for costs in the sum of £480,000 up to summons for directions stage (excluding discovery), but not beyond, approximately £350,000 of which was attributable to weld investigations on each of the vessels. C, who were in financial difficulties, indicated to D their willingness to withdraw some of their claims and provided D with a list set out under two headings entitled "claims to be withdrawn" and "claims which will be pursued". The welding claims were to be dropped on all vessels bar one and the one to be pursued involved a less costly weld investigation than the others. C offered D its reasonable costs to date in relation to the claims to be withdrawn and invited D to confirm its agreement in principle. C threatened to issue a summons returnable at the same time as D's summons for security, the costs of which would be sought if D failed to agree. D responded by accepting the offer and, following further discussions, C confirmed that their total claim after the withdrawals was $528,000 plus interest and costs. As a result D reduced its claim for security for costs to £75,000, including discovery, and agreement was reached that £45,000 of security should be provided. An order by consent in relation to the security was made subsequently and C were given leave to withdraw certain of the claims. C then sought to revive some of the withdrawn claims, including all those relating to welding. Hirst J., as he then was, held that they were not entitled to do so. They had carefully chosen which of the claims they were going to pursue, bearing in mind all the financial implications and those relating to the prospects of success, as a result of which they reduced substantially their potential liability to provide security for costs. The commercial background indicated "a permanent abandonment [of the claims withdrawn] and not a mere pause pending possible revival of the plaintiffs' fortunes".

9–40 **Dismissal.** The effect of a dismissal of proceedings by consent operates in the same way as a dismissal by adjudication, namely that the cause of action dies with the dismissal. The doctrine of *res judicata* applies and precludes the commencement of fresh proceedings upon the same or substantially the same grounds.[87] A straightforward consent order dismissing a claim for want of prosecution will not preclude fresh proceedings unless a true compromise underlies the consent.[88]

9–41 **"No order".** The expression "no order" is frequently used in the context of interim applications, and parties sometimes agree that "no order" should be made "by consent". Where this occurs in relation to an ordinary

---

[86] [1989] 2 Lloyd's Rep. 73.
[87] *The Ardandhu*, n.83, above; *The Bellcairn* (1885) 10 P.D. 161. See also *Kinch v Walcott* [1929] A.C. 482, PC; *Cohen v Jonesco* [1926] 1 K.B. 119 at 125.
[88] *Magnus v National Bank of Scotland* (1888) 57 L.J.Ch. 902.

interim application, the expression will usually be taken to imply that the parties have agreed that there is no (or no longer) reason for making an order at that time on the particular application hitherto being pursued. When it is used in the context of the final resolution of the differences between parties, it can give rise to problems because of its somewhat ambiguous meaning.[89] It is best avoided in that latter context.

Acceptance of Pt 36 payment

9–42 This procedure not only affords a means of accepting an offer of compromise but also a means by which the position of both parties is secured. It is sometimes used as a method of effecting a compromise already agreed. A claimant might, for example, say that he will accept a certain sum of money provided that it is paid into court within so many days.[90]

---

[89] See para.32–62, below, and also *Atkinson v Castan*, noted at para.11–29, below.
[90] See Ch.16, below.

CHAPTER 10

Practice of Compromise

GENERAL

Once parties have agreed the essential terms of their compromise and have 10–01
chosen the machinery by which it is to be given effect, the question arises of how, in practice, the machinery is set in place. Different practical steps will have to be taken depending on the stage at which the compromise is finalised and the court, if any, in which proceedings are extant. If no proceedings are involved and some written agreement is contemplated, this will, in the normal course of events, be arranged between the parties' solicitors. It is proposed merely to deal with the position when court proceedings are involved. A number of preliminary, but significant, matters should be considered first.

Attitude of the courts to compromise

No authority is needed to support the proposition that the courts welcome 10–02
and encourage compromise.[1] The reasons are manifest. In some instances[2] the approval of the court is necessary for a compromise to be effective. Generally speaking, however, this is not necessary and the court is not concerned with the terms of the compromise. This is a matter for the parties. Since they created the dispute, they can dispose of it as they please.[3] Indeed, it appears that the court cannot decline to enter a consent

---

[1] This has always been so. However, the reforms reflected in the CPR have given added emphasis to the proposition. A feature of the "active case management" demanded of the court is "helping the parties to settle the whole or part of the case": CPR r.1.4(2)(f).
[2] See, *e.g.* Chs 32 and 35, below.
[3] However, the fact that parties compromise litigation between the conclusion of the trial and before a reserved judgment is given may not necessarily result in the court not handing down the judgment: *Prudential Assurance Co Ltd v McBains Cooper* [2000] 1 W.L.R. 2000, CA.

order or judgment merely because it is suspicious of the terms or disapproves of them.[4] If the court is asked to make an order outside its jurisdiction,[5] or which is illegal, then it can properly decline to do so.

Equally, as a matter of practice, the court will not ordinarily make a binding declaration of right by consent,[6] and it is likely that it would wish to be informed of the facts and law applicable to any proposed consent order or judgment affecting the status of the parties.[7] Thus, although a court may make suggestions about the proposed terms of a compromise,[8] it cannot refuse to give effect to them by means of an order or judgment desired by the parties.[9]

> In *Arthur J.S. Hall v Simons* in the Court of Appeal,[10] Lord Bingham of Cornhill C.J., having referred to the above passage in the Fourth edition of this work, said this[11]:
>
> > "Adult parties of sound mind may ordinarily settle proceedings by an agreement made wholly out of court . . . They may for a variety of reasons choose to embody their agreement in a consent judgment of the court; this will not in the ordinary way call for any exercise of judgment by the court . . ."

Reality of the consent

10–03 Before the court will enter a consent order or judgment it must be satisfied that the appropriate consents have been given.[12] Without such consents no order can be made and the court cannot consent on behalf of a party.[13] Where parties are physically before the court, either in person or by

---

[4] *Noel v Becker* [1971] 1 W.L.R. 355, CA. See also *Re South American & Mexican Co* [1895] 1 Ch. 37, where it was acknowledged that agreed terms do not have to be mentioned by counsel to the court; *Bruce v Worthing Borough Council* 26 H.L.R. 223 at 228, per Staughton L.J.
[5] *Noel v Becker*, n.4, above, per Davies L.J. at 357; *Hinde v Hinde* [1953] 1 All E.R. 175. See further at paras 10–06 *et seq.*, below.
[6] *Wallersteiner v Moir* [1974] 1 W.L.R. 991. cf. *Patten v Burke Publishing* [1991] 1 W.L.R. 541. See also para.31–33, below.
[7] *R. v Bloomsbury and Marylebone County Court Ex p. Blackburne* (1985) 275 E.G. 1273 at 1274.
[8] cf. *Practice Direction (Ch.D.) (Minutes of Order)* [1960] 1 W.L.R. 1168.
[9] A refusal by a court to make such an order could, presumably, be enforced by a mandatory order, and an order in terms different in substance from those desired by the parties could be the subject of an appeal: cf. *Noel v Becker*, n.4, above. Indeed, a refusal to make an order at all could itself be regarded as an order dismissing a joint application of the parties for a consent order or judgment such that an appeal would lie.
[10] [1999] 3 W.L.R. 873.
[11] *ibid.* at 888. The implications of the judgments in the House of Lords ([2002] 1 A.C. 615) in this case in the context of compromise are dealt with in Ch.29, below.
[12] cf. para.3.2 of *Practice Direction—Judgments and Orders*, supplementary to CPR Pt 40.
[13] *Woodhead v Woodhead* (1978) C.A.T. 147.

representation, it is usual for the court to ask directly for confirmation of the consents. The consent of an unrepresented party is no less real than that of a represented party, but the court may enquire a little further to ensure that such consent is given voluntarily.[14]

If the parties are not physically before the court, but have invited the making of an order by consent, the draft order submitted to the court must be signed by the solicitors or counsel acting for each of the parties to the order.[15] If the consenting party is a litigant in person, he or she must sign the proposed order.[16] Unless the court has any reason to doubt the authenticity of the signature or that the consent was given voluntarily, the order will be made.[17]

Recording of the consent

Where a judgment or order truly represents the result of mutual consents, the fact of its consensual nature should be recorded on the face of the order or judgment.[18] The failure to do so will not affect the fact that it is of such a nature[19] and the court will be prepared to investigate the background if necessary to determine the true position.[20]

10–04

The distinction between a consent order or judgment and one to which a party "submits" has already been noted.[21] The mere fact that a party submits to an order or judgment does not accord it the status of one "by consent". This is so even if the submission is made pursuant to an agreement. The fact that an order or judgment is made "by consent" may have a number of practical and procedural implications.[22]

Indorsement of counsels' briefs

In those distant days when laptop computers were not taken to court habitually by junior counsel, the practice of indorsing counsels' briefs with the terms of an agreed order was often employed. It is thought that this

10–05

---

[14] The consent of a litigant in person to the making by a district judge of the county court of an injunction must be "real, genuine and informed"; non-dissent is not sufficient: *Simons and Simons v Winder and Winder* (1982) C.A.T. 369.
[15] See para.3.4(3)(a) of *Practice Direction—Judgments and Orders*, supplementary to CPR Pt 40. See further at paras 10–17 *et seq.*, below, for the practice.
[16] See para.3.4(3)(b) of *Practice Direction—Judgments and Orders*, Supplementary to CPR Pt 40.
[17] It has long ceased to be the practice that the personal attendance of a litigant in person before a judge is required, or that his signature is attested by a solicitor, before a consent order will be made.
[18] See para.3.4(2) of *Practice Direction—Judgments and Orders*, supplementary to CPR Pt 40; *Michel v Mutch* (1886) 54 L.T. 45; *Darley (Trustee of Baines) v Tulley* (1923) 155 L.T.Jo. 128; *Chandless-Chandless v Nicholson* [1942] 2 K.B. 321. See further at paras 10–17 *et seq.*, below.
[19] *Darley v Tulley*, n.18, above.
[20] *Magnus v National Bank of Scotland* (1888) 57 L.J.Ch. 902 at 904.
[21] See para.9–10, above.
[22] See Ch.6, above, and Ch.12, below.

will rarely, if ever, be a technique adopted in contemporary times. However, where it is utilised the usual practice is for each counsel to sign each other's indorsement. This precaution obviates the difficulties that might otherwise arise where the indorsement on one brief differed substantially from that on the other. In such an event, the court will not hear evidence of what was really intended and any order made in purported pursuance of the indorsements is regarded as a nullity.[23]

Jurisdiction

10–06 It has already been observed[24] that a court must enter a judgment or make an order by consent in the terms desired by the parties unless problems of jurisdiction (or illegality) arise. It is important, therefore, in practice for parties to ensure that no such problems remain before placing a draft agreed order or judgment before a court. Indeed, where problems of this nature have not been resolved, the court will often invite parties to reconsider the position and put matters in order.[25]

Problems of this nature can arise in a number of ways.

10–07 **The forum itself.** Parties may find themselves inviting a court to make an order or judgment outside the normal jurisdiction of that particular court or about which there is some doubt as to its jurisdiction. This will usually arise, if at all, in the county court. The problem is readily resolved by the filing of a memorandum pursuant to the appropriate section of the County Courts Act 1984.[26] Properly speaking, the agreement should be made before the judgment or order is made,[27] although it would appear that a failure to do so, and no point being taken by any party, would not render the order a nullity.[28]

10–08 **Tribunal within the appropriate forum.** A judge of the High Court or the county court possesses all the powers within the relevant jurisdiction. A master and district judge each possess a limited jurisdiction and, in some cases, an extended jurisdiction by the consent of the parties.[29] Parties should ensure that the correct tribunal is invited to make the order. In cases of doubt the directions of the court may be sought.

---

[23] *Practice Note* [1884] W.N. 91.
[24] At para.10–02, above.
[25] However, it is not unknown for the parties and the court to overlook a jurisdictional problem: see, *e.g. IRC v Hoogstraten*, noted at para.10–10, below. This can give rise to further difficulties at a later stage, particularly with regard to enforcement: *e.g. Hinde v Hinde* [1953] 1 All E.R. 175, noted at para.10–11, below.
[26] s.18 or 24.
[27] *cf. R. v Willes (Judge) Ex p. Abbey National Building Society* [1954] 1 W.L.R. 136.
[28] *cf. Williams v Settle* [1960] 1 W.L.R. 1072; [1960] 2 All E.R. 806.
[29] CPR r.2.4 and *The White Book*, Vol.1, paras 2.4.1–2.4.4.

Terms of the order or judgment are outside the ordinary jurisdiction.[30] It has already been noted[31] that the parties cannot by consent confer on the court a jurisdiction which it does not otherwise possess. If the point is noted, the court could properly decline to make an order outside its jurisdiction.[32] The rationale for this position is presumably that the court would not wish to, nor would wish to be seen to, act in a way that was arguably unlawful.

10–09

> In *IRC v Hoogstraten*,[33] C sued D for over £2.5 million, being the sum allegedly due in respect of unpaid taxes and interest, and obtained a Mareva order restraining any disposition of D's assets up to the amount claimed. Subsequently, D made certain dispositions of property in breach of this order. C sought his committal to prison for contempt, alternatively for the sequestration of his property. At a resumed hearing of this notice of motion negotiations took place and an agreement was reached. D accepted that he had been in breach of the order, but he contended (and this was common ground) that he had purged his contempt by, in effect, arranging for the recovery of the property the subject of the previous dispositions. In the circumstances C agreed not to seek D's committal to prison whilst he agreed to the sequestration of all his property. An agreed order to this effect was made by the judge. The Court of Appeal held that whilst the agreement was made in good faith and represented a sensible and constructive outcome of a contested committal application, the order "ought never to have been made" because an order for sequestration, under the then RSC, Ord.45, rr.1 and 5 could only be made against a person who was in contempt of court. At the time the agreed order was made, D was no longer in contempt of court. The order was, however, a valid order of the court until set aside.[34]

10–10

From the point of view of a client whose legal advisers have led him into the making of such an order, there may be unwanted consequences, particularly in connection with difficulties concerning enforcement.

10–11

> In *Hinde v Hinde*,[35] a consent order was made in 1936, upon W's application for maintenance from H, in a specified sum and was expressed to be payable to her "until remarriage". After H's death in 1952 no further payments were made and W, not having remarried, sought to enforce the order against H's estate. The Court of Appeal held that in so far as the consent order purported to confer upon W the right to receive payments from H beyond their "joint lives"—the period for which the court ordinarily had

---

[30] "Jurisdiction" in this context is used in the narrow sense of the term: *per* Diplock L.J. in *Garthwaite v Garthwaite* [1964] P. 356 at 387.
[31] See paras 9–18 *et seq.*, above.
[32] *Noel v Becker* [1971] 1 W.L.R. 355 at 357.
[33] [1985] Q.B. 1077.
[34] See also *Isaacs v Robertson* [1985] A.C. 97, PC; *cf. Nicholls v Kinsey* [1994] Q.B. 600, CA.
[35] [1953] 1 All E.R. 175. See also *Sugden v Sugden* [1957] P. 129 at 137, *per* Hodson L.J., and more generally in the family law context in Ch.32, below.

jurisdiction to provide[36]—the order was of no effect notwithstanding that it was made by consent.[37] Enforcement could not, therefore take place.

10–12 Terms of the order or judgment are outside the jurisdiction in the particular case. The parties may invite a court to make an order which it would ordinarily have jurisdiction to make but not in the context of the proceedings brought. The law affords certain relief in the event of a party establishing to judgment a cause of action or claim for relief. Unless the cause of action or claim for relief is actually asserted, the court would not, it is submitted, have jurisdiction to grant, even by consent, a relief which it would not otherwise be able to grant. The position is analogous to that described in para.10–09, above.

10–13 An example would be afforded by a claim by a landlord against a tenant for damages for breach of a repairing covenant which they agree to compromise on the basis that the tenant vacates the property. If the landlord wishes to obtain an order for possession (to which the tenant is prepared to consent or submit) to secure his position under the agreement, an appropriate amendment to the proceedings, or the institution of fresh proceedings (doubtless waiving all formalities), would, it is submitted, be necessary before the court could enter an order for possession.

10–14 It is likely that, with a view to saving expense and furthering the overriding objective, the court would be prepared to accept as conferring the appropriate jurisdiction a sentence in the preamble to a consent order to the effect that the parties have agreed to treat the existing proceedings as proceedings for the additional relief claimed, "abridging all time and waiving all formalities". However, depending on the circumstances, it may be more prudent, and the court may require, that a formal pleading be filed or an appropriate amendment be made to the existing proceedings, a suitable undertaking that this will be done being given.

In certain situations the permission of the court may be required before a new or amended pleading is filed. Where such permission is necessary to enable a compromise to be effectuated, and where the consent of both parties is readily forthcoming, it is inconceivable that the court would refuse it.

10–15 If attention is paid by the legal advisers of parties to a compromise to the jurisdictional aspects of any proposed consent order or judgment, no difficulty is likely to be found in the making and subsequent enforcement of the order. Much expense and frustration (particularly on the part of the lay client) will be saved by having everything in order.

---

[36] Supreme Court of Judicature (Consolidation) Act 1925, s.190(2); see now Matrimonial Causes Act 1973, s.28(1)(a).
[37] Such a provision could have been made in an agreement (*Kirk v Eustace* [1937] A.C. 491) and still could be (*cf.* Matrimonial Causes Act 1973, s.36), but not as part of an order.

10–16 The foregoing discussion has been directed at matters which, logically, are preliminary and incidental to the making of a consent order or judgment. Attention is now turned briefly to the practical aspects of securing the order or judgment once its terms have been agreed and all jurisdictional problems resolved.

PRACTICE OF OBTAINING A CONSENT ORDER

10–17 The introduction of the CPR has not resulted in any significant changes to the practice of obtaining a consent order or judgment once the parties are agreed. Where the proposed consent order or judgment is one of a number of fairly straightforward forms provided for in the rules,[38] and provided none of the parties is a litigant in person, nor is the approval of the court as such to the order required, a court officer may enter and seal the order.[39] If this procedure is followed, the order or judgment will not bear the name and judicial title of the person who made it,[40] because, of course, it will not have received any judicial scrutiny and will not have received any judicial authority as such. The order will, however, have the full authority of the court.

10–18 Where the foregoing procedure is adopted, the court officer will be concerned to ensure that the proposed order falls fairly and squarely within the terms of CPR r.40.6(3). If there is any doubt, he will refer the order to the master, district judge or judge. It will also be of concern to the court officer to ensure that none of the parties is a litigant in person. The purported making of an order pursuant to this procedure when one of the parties is a litigant in person would undoubtedly invalidate the order.[41] Where a represented party agrees a proposed consent order with a litigant in person, it would be prudent for the solicitor drawing up the order for submission to the court to write a covering letter to the court stating expressly that r.40.6(3) does not apply. This should ensure that judicial scrutiny is given to the order. The fact that it has been presented to a master, district judge or judge should be checked when the order is returned by the court.[42]

---

[38] CPR r.40.6(3). It will be noted that (b)(ii) refers to an order for "the stay of proceedings on agreed terms, disposing of the proceedings, whether those terms are recorded in a schedule to the order or elsewhere". This is intended to refer to a Tomlin order. The words "or elsewhere" were inserted to cater for the situation in which the parties (as they do with increasing frequency) wish to record the substance of their agreement other than in the schedule to the order (which is part of the court record and open for inspection) and thus keep it confidential: see paras 10–28 *et seq.*, below.
[39] CPR r.40.6(2).
[40] CPR r.40.2(1)(c).
[41] *National Westminster Bank Plc v Smillie*, unreported, February 4, 1999.
[42] *ibid.*

10-19 When the provisions of r.40.6(2) and (3) do not apply, an application to the court should be made.[43] The application, which will usually be dealt with by a master or district judge, can be dealt with without a hearing.[44] All applications are governed by CPR Pt 23. Since all parties are agreed that the particular consent order should be made, it is likely that the application will be made without serving an application notice.[45] The agreed order must be drawn up in the agreed terms, be expressed to be "by consent" and be signed by the legal representative acting for each party to whom the order relates or by the party if he is a litigant in person.[46] Where all parties affected by the order have written to the court consenting to the making of the order, a draft of which has been filed with the court, the draft will be treated as having been signed by all parties.[47] As indicated above, so far as litigants in person are concerned, the practice prior to the CPR had been for the court to accept a consent order signed by a litigant in person when satisfied that the signature was genuine and that the consent was also genuine and voluntarily given.[48] That practice continues. The master or district judge would be entitled to ask the litigant in person to attend before him, or to ask for some second written confirmation of agreement, if he had any reservations about the matter.

Information required by court

10-20 The Pt 23 Practice Direction places upon the parties who wish to follow the procedures available in r.40.6 the onus of ensuring that the court is provided "with any material it needs to be satisfied that it is appropriate to make the order".[49] This might include, for example, reference to some particular authority or statutory provision so as to demonstrate that the court does have jurisdiction to make a particular order which, at first sight, might seem unusual.

Settlements reached just before or during trial

10-21 Where a settlement is not achieved until just before or during the trial, the practice will vary slightly depending upon whether the court's approval to the settlement is required. If approval is not required, the judge will have been told by the advocates that a settlement has been reached and they will

---

[43] CPR r.40.6(5).
[44] CPR r.40.6(6); r.23.8(a).
[45] Pt 23 Practice Direction, para.3(3).
[46] CPR r.40.7.
[47] Pt 23 Practice Direction, para.10.2.
[48] See para.10-03, above.
[49] Pt 23 Practice Direction, para.10.4. A letter is usually acceptable for this purpose.

usually prepare a draft agreed order or judgment. That will be presented to the judge in open court who, provided he is satisfied that it displays all the proper features of a valid consent order or judgment,[50] will proceed to make the order. It is not strictly necessary for any terms of the settlement to be mentioned in open court, whether or not they appear on the face of the draft order.[51] Once an order is made it is a public document and is available for scrutiny, a factor which sometimes impels the parties to adopt a procedure designed to ensure confidentiality.[52] Where approval is required, the trial judge will be invited to give that approval.[53]

Settlements requiring approval of the court

A settlement involving a child or patient may be concluded prior to the commencement of proceedings. If so, the approval of the court will still be required for the agreement to be binding. The Pt 21 Practice Direction sets out the procedure to be adopted[54] and the information required. The Practice Direction deals with the information required when the settlement is of a claim arising from an accident. The information may need to be amplified where the claim arose out of alleged clinical negligence. For example, an issue which frequently arises in this context is causation. The defence may accept the alleged negligence (either in whole or in part), but deny that it caused or materially contributed to the condition of which complaint is made. Where the claimant is prepared to make a discount to reflect the risks of an adverse finding, the court will need to be informed about this and about how the claimant's advisers see the issue.[55]

10–22

Where counsel has advised on the settlement, it is normal for counsel's opinion to be placed before the court. It is not usually shown to the opposing side.

10–23

Where the settlement is concluded after the institution of proceedings, an application for approval will have to be made. If the settlement is concluded well before the trial, the application can be dealt with by the master or district judge under CPR r.40.6. In cases of difficulty, the application might be referred to a judge. If the settlement is achieved at or shortly before trial, the approval will be sought from the trial judge.

10–24

---

[50] See paras 10–06 et seq., above.
[51] See para.10–02, above.
[52] See paras 10–27 et seq., below.
[53] See para.10–22, below, and Ch.35, below.
[54] At paras 6.1–6.3: See Appendix 4, below.
[55] See Ch.35, below.

Notification of settlement to court

10–25   Where a settlement is reached which disposes of the whole claim for which a date or "window" has been fixed for trial, the parties must notify the listing officer for the trial court immediately.[56] Where a sealed order giving effect to the settlement has been obtained, a copy of the sealed order should be filed with the listing officer.[57]

10–26   A settlement of an appeal to the Court of Appeal should also be notified to the court as soon as possible.[58]

Settlement of appeals

10–27   The practice applicable when an appeal is made from a Master or district judge to a judge, or of any appeal to the Court of Appeal, is dealt with in Ch.42, below.

CONFIDENTIALITY

10–28   Parties may wish to keep the terms of their compromise confidential. There are two aspects that require to be considered: first, the agreement as to confidentiality itself; secondly, the means by which that agreement is given effect in any consent order reflecting it.

10–29   As between the parties, an express term as to confidentiality will usually be agreed if required. This will take the form appropriate to the nature of the case, but will normally provide that the terms of the compromise remain confidential to the parties save as may be necessary for the purposes of its implementation and as may be required by a court or other competent authority.[59] In *Horizon Technologies International Ltd v Lucky Wealth Consultants Ltd*,[60] the following provision appeared in the deed of settlement underlying the Tomlin order made in that case:

> "All parties hereto acknowledge that the provisions in this Deed of Settlement are confidential to all the parties hereto to include all

---

[56] Pt 39 Practice Direction, para.4.1.
[57] *ibid.*, para.4.2.
[58] This consideration applies where the parties settle the appeal whilst the court has reserved its judgment following the arguments: *HFC Bank Plc v HSBC Bank Plc, The Times*, April 26, 2000, CA.
[59] For example the taxation authorities.
[60] [1992] 1 W.L.R. 24. Another variant on this theme is as follows: "The parties are agreed that the terms of this settlement are to remain confidential between them and their legal advisers and are not to be disclosed in any circumstances to any other person without the prior written consent of all parties hereto or the permission of the court, such permission to be sought upon notice to all other parties".

officers, directors and servants thereof and each party undertakes in favour of all the others not to disclose any of these provisions to any person not a party to this deed, save as may be necessary for the purpose of implementing this Deed of Settlement. It is hereby agreed that neither party shall be in breach of this clause by disclosing any matters contained herein if compelled to do so by any Court or authority of competent jurisdiction."

10–30 If the compromise remains entirely contractual, the means of enforcing any threatened breach of the confidentiality clause would be by means of an application for an interim injunction in the context of a fresh action to enforce the agreement. If the agreement is embodied in some form of agreed order, the means of enforcement will depend upon the form of that order. If the confidentiality clause appears as a provision within the schedule to a Tomlin order, then an injunction may be sought since the terms of the schedule are contractual in status. Technically it would be possible to convert such a provision into an enforceable order by means of obtaining a mandatory order,[61] but this would offer little practical advantage over the obtaining of an injunction. Once an injunction has been obtained following a breach or threatened breach, notice of the existence of the injunction can be given to others (for example, the Press or television companies) who might otherwise be a conduit for the publication of the terms. Where, despite the apparent agreement between the parties as to confidentiality, there is doubt about the good faith of one or other of the parties, the existence of undertakings to the court would probably offer the most effective medium for the prevention of disclosure of the terms of the agreement.

10–31 There are a number of types of case where both parties do wish to ensure that no publicity is given to the terms of their settlement. Anything said in open court about a settlement can, of course, be reported. As already indicated,[62] in most cases it is not necessary for the terms of settlement to be mentioned in open court. However, any consent order or judgment will form part of the court record which is available for subsequent scrutiny. For example, the schedule to a Tomlin order, whilst not strictly part of the immediately enforceable court order, is part of the court record.[63] If the normal form of Tomlin order is utilised, a direction from the court could be obtained to the effect that the schedule to the order "be not released" to any party other than the parties or their advisers.[64] If concern is felt about the efficacy of this direction, the best

---

[61] See paras 11–21 *et seq.*, below.
[62] See para.10–02, above.
[63] *Islam v Askar* (1994) C.A.T. 1240.
[64] The author was involved in a case in which Sir Michael Davies suggested that such a direction be made where the parties wished the terms of the schedule to the Tomlin order to be kept confidential.

approach would be to ensure that the terms which would otherwise be scheduled to the order are incorporated on a separate document, suitably identified on the face of the Tomlin order.[65]

---

[65] See Precedent No.14 at para.A1–14, below.

CHAPTER 11

Enforcement of a Compromise

GENERAL

Where the terms of a compromise permit recourse to the original claim in the event of non-compliance with the agreement,[1] the innocent party will have the option of deciding whether to follow that course or to pursue such remedies as may be available under the compromise.[2] The discussion that follows presupposes a decision by the innocent party to rely upon his rights under the compromise.

11–01

The manner in which those rights may be enforced will depend upon the machinery chosen for giving effect to the compromise.[3] The essential primary consideration is whether or not what is to be enforced is a contract or an order or judgment.

WHERE THERE IS NO ORDER OR JUDGMENT

In the event that the compromise is entirely contractual, the usual remedies for breach of contract will be available depending on the circumstances.[4] Damages will often be the appropriate remedy, although there may be situations in which specific performance or an injunction will be granted.

11–02

Where a party to a compromise attempts to ignore its existence, either by continuing or commencing proceedings, the other party may either set up the agreement as a defence to the claim or apply to the court to stay the

11–03

---

[1] See Ch.8, above.
[2] See para.8–09, above.
[3] See Ch.9, above.
[4] *Chitty on Contracts* (29 ed., 2004), Vol.1, Pt 8.

proceedings.[5] In the latter event the party seeking to establish the existence of the compromise may apply for an order staying the proceedings. Usually, the question of whether a binding agreement exists is directed to be tried as a preliminary issue. Indeed, where no such application is made, but the pleadings disclose the issue, a direction to the same effect may be made.[6] When the question arises of whether an appeal to the Court of Appeal has been compromised, it can be dealt with by way of preliminary application to stay all further proceedings.[7]

WHERE THERE IS AN ORDER OR JUDGMENT

11-04 The courses open in respect of the enforcement of a consent order or judgment depend upon the form the order or judgment takes. Doubtless these courses will have been taken into account when the form of order was considered. As previously indicated,[8] unless the parties expressly agree and provide otherwise they are taken ordinarily to have agreed that any consent order or judgment drawn up to embody their compromise will take effect as if the court itself had made it following a contested hearing. In other words, the normal jurisdiction of the court applies to any such order or judgment.

11-05 The enforcement processes available to a party wishing to take proceedings arising from a failure by the other party to comply with an order or judgment will be governed by the relevant provisions of the CPR.[9]

Where an agreement is filed and made a rule of court

Where agreement is filed and made a rule of court

11-06 Where the agreement as a whole has been filed and made a rule of court the enforcement process will depend on the provision sought to be enforced. Where a particular provision has been made an order, then the

---

[5] *Eden v Naish* (1878) L.R. 7 Ch.D. 781; *Baker v Baker* (1886) 55 L.T. 723; *Re Mathews* [1905] 2 Ch. 460; *Guy v Walker* (1892) 8 T.L.R. 314. See also *Snelling v John Snelling Ltd* [1973] 1 Q.B. 87, considered at para.6–87, above. Where proceedings are extant and the claimant wishes to allege that an agreement has been reached compromising those proceedings, he may seek a determination of the point as a preliminary issue in those proceedings without the need for a fresh action. If the point is determined in his favour, an order staying the proceedings will be made and a declaration given as to the terms of the compromise. This was the course followed in the unreported case of *Metrostore Ltd v British Railways Board,* January 20, 1989, Warner J. See also *Eden v Naish*, above. Enforcement of the compromise as such would require a fresh action. *cf.* para.11–29, below.
[6] *Tomlin v Standard Telephones and Cables Ltd* [1969] 1 W.L.R. 1378.
[7] *cf. Harte v Harte* (1976) C.A.T. 423A.
[8] See paras 5–36 *et seq.*, above.
[9] CPR Pt 70 *et seq.*

enforcement process applicable to that order will be appropriate. Where a particular provision has not been made an order, but nonetheless remains part of the agreement, it is submitted that the approach will be similar to that which is appropriate to the enforcement of provisions in the schedule to a Tomlin order[10]: subject to one possible exception,[11] a further order of the court, converting the contractual obligation into an enforceable order, will be needed before enforcement steps can be taken.

Status of an agreement made a rule of court. The foregoing view is, it is submitted, the better one. There does, however, appear to be some doubt on the authorities as to the precise status of an agreement made a rule of court: is it equivalent to an order and enforceable as such or is it still merely an agreement which requires further steps to be taken in relation to it before it becomes an order or equivalent to an order?[12] The view expressed that it is the latter rather than the former is derived from, it is submitted, strong authority: 11–07

> In *Re Shaw*,[13] the precise question of the status of the provisions of such an agreement fell to be considered. The question, essentially, was whether or not payments made under provisions of an agreement made a rule of court were, for the purposes of taxation provisions, made under an order of the court. The Court of Appeal held that the payments were not made under an order and that the agreement was still a contract and nothing more. It was said[14] that the effect of making an agreement a rule of court was to enable enforcement of its provisions in a summary way without the need for a fresh action. 11–08

Thus, provisions of an agreement made a rule of court are accorded an identical status to the provisions in a Tomlin order schedule,[15] the whole purpose of such an order being to enable enforcement of those provisions within the existing action and without the need for instituting a new action. 11–09

Some support for the view that the making of an agreement a rule of court does not accord it the status of an order of the court may, it is submitted, be found, albeit *obiter*, in *Jessel v Jessel*.[16] 11–10

> In *Jessel v Jessel*, minutes of an order recording a matrimonial settlement were ordered to be made a rule of court. One provision, which H sought to uphold,[17] was an undertaking by W not to apply to increase a consent order 11–11

---

[10] See paras 11–21 *et seq.*, below.
[11] See paras 11–07 *et seq.*, below.
[12] The practice derives from the old Probate practice about which there is little evidence in contemporary books.
[13] [1918] P. 47, CA. See also *Croft v Croft* (1922) 38 T.L.R. 648; and *Aspden (Inspector of Taxes) v Hildesley* [1982] 1 W.L.R. 264.
[14] [1918] P. 47 *per* Warrington L.J. at 53–54, and at 53 *per* Swinfen-Eady L.J.
[15] See paras 9–19 *et seq.*, above.
[16] [1979] 1 W.L.R. 1148, CA.
[17] On the basis of *Minton v Minton* [1979] A.C. 593, HL; as to which see Ch.32, below.

for periodical payments made previously and an acknowledgment that the provision made in that order was to be in settlement of all her claims for periodical payments. One of H's arguments was that the making of the agreement a rule of court validated what was otherwise a void provision. The Court of Appeal held that the original order was a continuing order and dismissed H's contentions on that basis. However, all members of the court[18] doubted whether making a provision such as this a rule of court would validate it.[19]

11–12   The contrary view seems to have been taken in *Royal Society of Literature v Lowenthal*[20] and *Herbert v Herbert*.[21]

In *Royal Society of Literature v Lowenthal*, a summons to enforce a provision of an agreement made a rule of court was taken out under the former RSC Ord.45, r.8.[22] It was argued at first instance that the making of a compromise a rule of court did have the effect of making it an order and thus enforceable under the above-mentioned rule. At first instance[23] it was held that the terms of the compromise had to be treated as though they were themselves orders of the court and the point was conceded by counsel in the Court of Appeal. Since the decision of Jupp J. is not reported, and the matter was not argued in the Court of Appeal, it is respectfully submitted that little weight can be attached to it. It is not clear whether *Re Shaw* was cited at first instance: if it was not, the decision was clearly *per incuriam*.

11–13   In *Herbert v Herbert*, it was held that an agreement which had been made a rule of court had the same effect as an order or judgment and was enforceable as such. A summons to commit for an alleged breach of one of its terms was allowed to proceed. Although the argument to the contrary effect was advanced, it is clear that neither *Re Shaw* nor *Dashwood v Dashwood*[24] was cited in support. Had they been cited, the decision might well have been different.[25]

11–14   **Order or rule of court.**   It is possible that some confusion has arisen in this context by the use of the expressions "order of court" and "rule of court" as more or less synonymous.[26] Indeed, they are occasionally run together. In *Smythe v Smythe*,[27] an action for judicial separation was compromised

---

[18] See n.16, above: Lord Denning M.R., Browne and Geoffrey Lane L.JJ. at 1154, 1155 and 1156 respectively.
[19] *i.e.* the provision would not have assumed the status of an order.
[20] (1978) C.A.T. 182.
[21] (1978) 122 S.J. 826 (Mr Aubrey Myerson Q.C., sitting as a deputy High Court judge).
[22] This rule related to the enforcement, *inter alia*, of a "mandatory order" or a "judgment or order".
[23] Jupp J.
[24] [1927] W.N. 276.
[25] The term of the agreement alleged to have been breached was one by which H agreed not to remove certain items from the matrimonial home. It might have been an undertaking to W, not to the court: *cf. Marchant v Marchant* (1967) C.A.T. 26, at para.11–35, below.
[26] For example *Green v Rozen* [1955] 1 W.L.R. 741 at 743, *per* Slade J. (which, incidentally, was cited in *Herbert v Herbert*, n.21, above). See also n.37, below.
[27] (1887) 18 Q.B.D. 544, CA.

before trial upon certain terms, one of which was that the respondent was to pay the petitioner's taxed costs. It was provided that the agreement "may be made a rule of the High Court". The report shows[28] that an order was made subsequently "making the agreement of compromise an order of the Queen's Bench Division" and that thereafter it was "duly made an order". Counsel for the respondent argued there was no power to make the terms of compromise "a rule of court". Sir James Hannen, giving the leading judgment, referred to the long-established practice of making such agreements "a rule of court" and went on to say that he did not doubt that he "could have made this agreement an order of court".

Despite the apparent interchangeability of the two expressions, the case of *Smythe v Smythe*, it is submitted, supports the view that a further order is required before a provision in an agreement made a rule of court becomes an order. The case concerned a provision which without doubt was within the jurisdiction of the court to make, and this may afford an explanation for the use of expressions suggesting that the agreement itself could be made an order of court. It is noteworthy that Sir James Hannen, when referring to the practice, said[29] that agreements of compromise "frequently contain clauses providing that the agreement may be made a rule of court or that a judge's order may be obtained, if necessary",[30] reflecting, it is submitted, the very real distinction between the two. 11–15

If the converse view were taken it would mean that, by something of a "back-door" method, parties could make an obligation under an agreement immediately enforceable as a court order when such an obligation could not have been made the subject of an order under the normal jurisdiction of the court. As has been observed,[31] this cannot be done. Furthermore, an agreement which is a contract for one purpose[32] is surely a contract for all purposes.[33] 11–16

Enforcement. If the foregoing analysis is correct then, it is thought, the enforcement of a provision (other, perhaps, than one for the payment of money)[34] in an agreement made a rule of court has two stages: 11–17

(1) the obtaining of an appropriate court order directing compliance with the provision; and

---

[28] *ibid.* at 545.
[29] *ibid.* at 546.
[30] Words echoed by Barnes J. in *Graves v Graves* (1893) 69 L.T. 420.
[31] See paras 9–17 *et seq.*, above.
[32] *Re Shaw*, n.13, above.
[33] Once the terms of an agreement have been embodied in a consent order their legal effect is derived from the order not the agreement: *De Lasala v De Lasala* [1980] A.C. 546. This expression of principle has led to the view being formed in two Family Division cases that the agreement made a rule of court thereby becomes an order: see Ch.32, below.
[34] See para.11–20, below.

(2) in the event of non-compliance, the institution of the appropriate enforcement process.

The first order will doubtless be in the form of a mandatory order, an injunction or an order for specific performance if the provision is one requiring an act to be performed, the order fixing a time for performance. The party seeking such order may, of course, invite the court to provide for what is to happen in the case of default.[35] Subject to the matter referred to below, if the provision of the agreement was that a sum of money be paid over within a particular period and it was not so paid, the court could simply grant judgment for the sum. If the provision was that the other party perform a particular act within a specified period and that act is not carried out, the court could grant an appropriate sum by way of compensation for the breach.

11–18   The precise approach will depend on the provision sought to be enforced. The important point is that some further court order is necessary to secure redress, but that order may be obtained in the existing action (by application) rather than the institution of a completely fresh action.

11–19   It has to be acknowledged that if the view expressed above is correct, a somewhat cumbrous process to enforce is necessary involving, possibly, two applications to the court. However, matters of convenience cannot override the juridical basis of the process. At all events, of course, it is no more inconvenient than seeking to enforce the provisions of a Tomlin order schedule.[36] There is, as observed above, no reason why a default provision should not be incorporated in the order made by the court when an application to enforce the agreement is made.

11–20   Although the burden of the foregoing discussion has been to the effect that provisions in agreements made rules of court are still contractual in effect, it is possible that provisions by virtue of which "any sum of money, or any costs, charges or expenses" are payable to "any person" are directly enforceable as judgments. The provisions of the Judgments Act 1838, s.18 apply to "all rules of courts of common law" whereby sums such as those specified above are payable. The persons to whom such sums are payable

---

[35] Once an order has been made it is important to bear in mind the words of Megaw L.J. in *Royal Society of Literature v Lowenthal* n.20, above: "The Court has jurisdiction . . . to take whatever measures are appropriate, having regard to the circumstances of the case and bearing in mind the necessity of looking fairly to the interests of both parties, to see that a party in whose favour an order of the Court has been made shall not be left to suffer by reason of a breach of that order by another party. The Court is not to be hampered by technicalities of procedure". See also para.11–29, below.

[36] See paras 11–21 *et seq.*, below.

are "deemed judgment creditors within the meaning of" the Act.[37] The precise significance of these provisions is a little doubtful and in practice, it is thought, recourse should be had to an order for payment before enforcement steps are contemplated.

Where the terms are incorporated in a Tomlin order

The terms of the agreement are, in the normal course of events, scheduled to the order staying the proceedings.[38] They do not thereby become orders of the court and cannot, for example, be enforced directly by proceedings for contempt. In the event of default, the party wishing to enforce any of the scheduled terms as an order must apply to the court under the "permission to apply" provision in the order for such order or direction as may be appropriate to convert the contractual obligation into one enforceable by judicial process.[39]

11–21

Where the term sought to be enforced is one requiring the payment of money, the court will make an order that the sum be paid.[40] Unless the court specifies a different date for compliance, such an order will be enforceable after 14 days have elapsed from the date of the order.[41] Where the term relates to the performance of some other act, an order directing performance[42] must be obtained before proceedings for committal or for relief under any other provision[43] are instituted. Equally, where the term provides that a certain act shall not be performed, an injunction restraining commission must be obtained before the issue of any further enforcement process. Where the term relates to the execution of any conveyance, contract or other document, the court may direct its execution by the relevant party in the first instance, and, thereafter, in default of compliance, nominate another person to do so.[44]

11–22

---

[37] Quoted in full in *Hunt v Douglas (Roofing) Ltd* [1990] A.C. 398. In *Legal Aid Board v Russell* [1990] 2 Q.B. 607, Lord Donaldson of Lymington M.R. said that at the time the 1838 Act was enacted "rules" was a term "denoting decisions or rulings by the judiciary on a case by case basis, as is clear from contemporary law reports which constantly conclude with such expressions as 'rule nisi', 'rule absolute' or 'rule discharged' and it is clearly in this sense that section 18 refers to 'rules of courts of common law'". This view was indorsed by the House of Lords: [1991] 2 A.C. 317 at 326.
[38] See para.9–19, above.
[39] *Dashwood v Dashwood* [1927] W.N. 276. See also *Pubmaster Ltd v Gibb* [2002] EWHC 2236 (Ch.), Rimer J.
[40] The order made in *E.F. Phillips & Sons Ltd v Clarke* [1970] Ch. 322.
[41] CPR r.40.11.
[42] Practice Direction 40B, para.8.1.
[43] *ibid.*, para.9.1.
[44] Supreme Court Act 1981, s.39.

11-23 The court will decline to enforce terms that are too vague.[45] It is possible that the court would entertain a claim for damages arising from an alleged breach of a Tomlin order without requiring the institution of a fresh action.[46]

11-24 Circumstances may arise in which a party prima facie obliged to comply with a provision in a Tomlin order schedule will seek to resist the making by the court of an order to enforce that provision. Non-compliance by the party seeking the order with some other provision in the schedule may, in some circumstances, constitute a basis for the court refusing to make the order. This will depend upon an analysis of the contract reflected in the schedule. The question has arisen of whether terms forming part of the agreement between the parties, but not incorporated in the schedule to the Tomlin order, may be relied upon to resist the making of such an order.

11-25 In *Horizon Technologies International Ltd v Lucky Wealth Consultants Ltd*,[47] C and D settled certain proceedings between them by means of a deed of settlement which itself included a provision that upon execution of the deed both parties would apply jointly to the court for an order in the Tomlin form. The terms of the Tomlin order and its schedule were set out in one of the eight substantive clauses of the deed of settlement. The terms to be incorporated in the schedule provided, *inter alia*, for a series of payments to be made by D on or before specified dates, the first two such payments being direct to C and the remaining seven payments to a Chinese company. It was provided that default in payment of any of the sums would result in all the specified sums becoming due and payable forthwith. The other substantive clauses of the deed of settlement were to come into operation upon the making of the Tomlin order. One of those clauses provided that the terms set out in the deed were "interdependent on each other" and that "breach or failure to observe any of the provisions . . . shall forthwith discharge the parties of the other part from further performance". The Tomlin order was duly made and D made the first of the payments provided for in the schedule. Before the second payment fell due, a director of D (who was a party to the deed) alleged that C had failed to comply with one of the provisions of the deed (which was not incorporated in the schedule to the Tomlin order) and D, relying upon the clause referred to above, claimed to be released from any further performance of its obligations. On the issue of whether D was prima facie entitled to rely upon the clause referred to in order to resist C's claim for an order to enforce the provisions of the Tomlin order, the Judicial Committee of the Privy Council held that D was so entitled. It was said that the schedule to the Tomlin order was "clearly an integral part of the deed, but put, as it were, in parenthesis to take advantage of the Tomlin order procedure for summary judgment, so that the payments could be quickly and cheaply enforced". As part of the deed the provisions in the schedule remained "subject to all its provisions", including that referred to above.

---

[45] See para.3-51, above.
[46] See paras 9-25—9-27, above.
[47] [1992] 1 W.L.R. 24, PC; *cf. Hammond v Travers*, unreported, May 7, 1999 (Latham J.), where C sought unsuccessfully to argue that there were terms outside the Tomlin order made that constituted collateral warranties.

11-26 Parties who agree to a Tomlin order will usually seek to secure enforcement of its provisions in the manner described above.[48] However, it should be recalled that the agreement which led to the making of the Tomlin order still retains its own independent existence.[49] It follows that, in appropriate circumstances, a party may choose to seek a remedy under that agreement rather than pursuant to the Tomlin order.

11-27 In *Islam v Askar*, the facts of which have been given previously,[50] C sought to overcome the procedural difficulties he was experiencing by commencing a fresh action based upon the agreement reached in the exchange of faxes. The Court of Appeal held that, whilst the normal remedy would be to enforce the Tomlin order, there was no reason in principle why C should not be granted a remedy in this separate action.

Where the terms are part of an order that does not reflect finality

11-28 Whilst it might normally be anticipated that a party who had agreed to an adjournment of his claim to enable agreed terms to be carried out would restore his claim in default of those terms being fulfilled, there is no reason in principle why he should not take steps to enforce the agreed terms.[51] The same would apply to a withdrawal or discontinuance upon agreed terms. Enforcement could not take place in the context of the adjourned, withdrawn or discontinued proceedings: a fresh action would be necessary.

Agreed order that recites the terms of agreement

11-29 In certain circumstances it appears that the mere recitation of the terms of an agreement in an order will be sufficient to enable enforcement of these in the existing action.

In *Atkinson v Castan*,[52] C and D had been in dispute about a sycamore tree that grew on D's property close to its boundary with C's property. The tree grew close to a garage on C's land and at some stage the roots penetrated the garage, causing damage. On the advice of a tree surgeon, C, through their solicitors, requested D to have the tree removed. C commenced proceedings

---

[48] See para.11-21, above.
[49] See para.9-10, above. "Thus, as is common ground, the contract of settlement is capable of being distinct from the Tomlin order or any agreement to procure it. An example of such distinct contracts is afforded by *Horizon Technologies Ltd v Lucky Wealth Consultants Ltd* [1982]": *per* Sir Andrew Morritt V.C. in *Thakrar v Ciro Citterio Menswear* [2002] EWHC 1975 (Ch.).
[50] See para.4-37, above.
[51] *Smith v Shirley and Baylis* (1875) 32 L.T. 234; considered in para.8-10, above.
[52] (1991) C.A.T. 332; *The Times*, April 17, 1991.

for nuisance in the county court after D had not taken steps to have the tree removed. In due course D received advice from a chartered surveyor, which, amongst other things, accepted that in the long term, removal of the tree was the only action to be adopted. In April 1988, D's solicitors wrote to C's solicitors confirming that D would remove the tree and meet the cost of the remedial work. Shortly after that letter was written, D filed an admission in the county court in the form of a defence, which admitted the allegations in the particulars of claim save as to the question of damages. C's solicitors prepared a draft consent order which was headed "Draft Consent Order" and was in the following terms:

> "UPON the defendants having within the defence filed herein admitted paragraphs 1 to 6 (inclusive) of the plantiffs' particulars of claim in this action
> AND UPON the defendants having agreed to have removed at their expense the sycamore tree referred to in the aforesaid particulars of claim and each and every part thereof (including the roots)
> AND UPON the defendants having agreed to pay for the remedial work required to the garage of the plaintiffs as a result of the damage caused by the said tree and the removal of that tree and further to make good at their own expense any damage caused to the property of the plaintiffs as a result of and during the removal of the said tree and the aforesaid remedial work
> IT IS ORDERED that there be no order save that the defendants to pay the plaintiffs' costs of and incidental to the claim and to the action herein such costs to be taxed on Scale 3 if not agreed.
> WE, the undersigned hereby CONSENT to an order in the aforementioned terms."

This draft order was in due course signed by the parties' respective solicitors and submitted to the court. The order drawn up by the court and signed by the registrar in June 1988 differed from the draft consent order in that (a) the words "By Consent It Is Ordered That" were inserted before the preamble or recitals and (b) the word "further" was inserted in the expression "It Is Ordered" where the question of costs was provided for. Neither party at that stage complained about the form of the order drawn up by the court. Subsequently D obtained further expert advice indicating that no remedial work was necessary and neither was the removal of the tree. Consequently D took no steps to implement the agreement previously made. In July 1989, C took out an application in the existing action seeking orders that D should forthwith remove the sycamore tree and that there should be judgment for C for damages to be assessed. In March 1990, the county court judge made orders in the terms sought by C. D, who wished to take any point open to them in law to avoid the removal of the tree, had argued that, in the circumstances, C should have brought a fresh action to enforce the agreement and that they could not do so in the existing action. This argument was repeated on appeal, attention being drawn on behalf of D to the facts that:

- (i) C had not adopted one of the well-established methods of settling an action which obviated the need for a fresh action for the purposes of enforcement[53];
- (ii) the draft consent order provided for "no order" save in respect of costs; and

---

[53] See para.9–02 and para.6–11, above.

(iii) no "liberty to apply" was provided for.

Whilst doubting whether it was open to D to argue that the matter should be dealt with on the basis of the draft consent order rather than the order actually made by the county court, the Court of Appeal dealt with the appeal on the basis of the terms of the draft order. The Court of Appeal held that a fresh action was not necessary in the circumstances. Since the parties agreed that the order made by the court should recite the agreed terms, that was sufficient to enable those terms to be enforced by obtaining an appropriate order in the existing action.

The result in this case represented a robust despatch by the court of an unmeritorious point taken by parties trying to delay compliance with freely undertaken obligations. However, it is, with respect, questionable whether the reasons given for the decision are entirely consistent with established authority and practice.[54] The recitals to the order were effectively treated by the Court of Appeal as the equivalent of terms scheduled to a Tomlin order[55] or contained in an agreement filed and made a rule of court,[56] even though it is plain that the agreed order was not (and, apparently, not intended to be) a Tomlin order nor one directing that the agreement "be filed and made a rule of court". In his judgment, Woolf L.J. (with whom Staughton L.J. agreed), having referred to the practice of filing and making an agreement a rule of court, said that it was clear beyond doubt that "there is a long-established practice of compromising actions by making the agreement part of the decision of the court or, as it is often said, making it a rule of court". This is, of course, entirely correct; but hitherto the mere recitation of the terms of the agreement in the preamble to a consent order would, unless those terms had been framed as undertakings to the court,[57] normally have been looked upon simply as a means of recording what the parties' agreement had been, rather than as affording the means by which summary orders for enforcement of those terms could be achieved. The means by which parties had hitherto ensured that summary orders could be secured in aid of enforcement of the contractual obligations of a compromise was to agree that a Tomlin order should be made or that the agreement should be filed and made a rule of court. In either situation the court has normally looked for an express term to this effect within the compromise.[58] In *Atkinson* it seems that the Court of Appeal construed the agreement reflected in the draft consent order as involving either an express or an implied term to the effect that the terms set out in the recitals would be enforceable within the action. The matter was put thus by Woolf L.J.:

11–30

---

[54] For example *Re Hearn* (1913) 108 L.T. 452 and 737; noted at para.9–25, above, does not appear to have been cited in *Atkinson*. And see the comments made in para.9–26, above.
[55] See paras 9–19 *et seq.*, above.
[56] See para.9–07, above.
[57] See paras 11–33 *et seq.*, below.
[58] See paras 5–47 and 9–07, above.

11-31 "It is clear from [the draft order] first of all that the compromise was set out in full in the recitals; secondly, that it was intended that the compromise so set out should be included as part of the record of the decision of the court; thirdly, that the purpose of this being done was to ensure that the compromise would have the added status which results from a compromise being part of or incorporated into a decision of the court; fourthly, that the obvious purpose of this added status was to put the plaintiffs in a position where they would have the advantage, which would not otherwise be available, of going back to the court in the existing action to have the compromise enforced if the court was prepared to make the necessary orders to achieve this result; and fifthly and finally, that there should be liberty to apply for the purposes of enforcing the action."

11-32 That was, of course, the construction placed upon the agreement reached in this particular case. Since it appears that there was no defence to the claim brought by C in the first place (save, perhaps, as to the precise relief sought), it would seem to be, with respect, an entirely sensible and suitably purposive construction. Indeed, although the point does not appear to have been taken, the use of the expression "no order" might well have been held to connote the possibility of recourse to the court for an order in the event of the terms reflected in the recital not being complied with.[59] However, it is thought that the decision ought to be confined largely to its own facts: parties ought to be capable of choosing and securing a mechanism for the enforcement of their compromise about the nature of which there should be no need for prolonged debate.

Injunction by consent or undertaking

11-33 An injunction by consent may be enforced in the same manner as one obtained adversely, namely by sequestration or committal. Because of the serious nature of these remedies the rules governing them must be strictly observed.[60]

11-34 An undertaking to the court is enforceable in the same manner,[61] the only difference being that the undertaking does not have to be served on the person giving it before steps to commit for breach can be taken.[62]

---

[59] See para.9-37, above.
[60] *McIlraith v Grady* [1968] 1 Q.B. 468; *Wellington v Wellington, The Times*, March 22, 1978, CA; *Cinderby v Cinderby, Pekesin v Pekesin* (1978) 122 S.J. 436, CA; *cf. Palmer v Townsend* (1979) 123 S.J. 570, CA; and *Kavanagh v Kavanagh* (1978) C.A.T. 571.
[61] *Neath Canal Co v Ynisarwed Resolven Colliery Co* (1875) 10 Ch.App. 450; *Milburn v Newton Colliery Ltd* (1908) 52 S.J. 317.
[62] *D. v A. & Co* [1900] 1 Ch. 484; *Re Launder* (1908) 98 L.T. 554. See also *Hussain v Hussain* [1986] Fam. 134.

Furthermore, since an undertaking to the court is to be treated as an order of the court, enforcement processes other than committal may be taken where appropriate.[63]

It should clearly be understood that an order for committal can be made **11–35** only where there has been an undertaking to the court:

> In *Marchant v Marchant*,[64] H and W compromised proceedings brought by W against H on the basis of alleged wilful neglect to provide her with reasonable maintenance. The compromise consisted of a withdrawal of the summons on terms which included an undertaking by H "not to resort to the matrimonial home as from July 31, 1964 or to molest W", the words "liberty to apply" also being incorporated. The Court of Appeal held that W could not apply to commit H to prison for an alleged breach of the undertaking because it was not an undertaking to the court.

---

[63] *Gandolfo v Gandolfo* [1981] Q.B. 359.
[64] (1967) C.A.T. 26.

PART 3

Practice on Impeachment of a Compromise

CHAPTER 12

Practice on Setting Aside a Compromise

Assuming that grounds exist for setting aside a compromise,[1] the question of the practice to be followed to achieve this arises.   12–01

The practice varies according to whether or not the compromise has been embodied in a consent order or judgment.

COMPROMISE AGREEMENT

The procedure for seeking a judicial rescission of a compromise agreement is identical to that required in relation to any other contract. A fresh action is needed seeking an order setting aside the agreement with consequential directions.[2] Where appropriate, a counterclaim for the same purpose may be raised.[3]   12–02

COMPROMISE EMBODIED IN AN ORDER OR JUDGMENT

Prior to the drawing-up or sealing of a consent order or judgment there is a limited jurisdiction to set aside such an order or judgment.[4] An application seeking such relief must be issued prior to, or contemporaneously with, the drawing-up or sealing of the order.[5]   12–03

---

[1] See Ch.4, above.
[2] The principal remedy sought would be either a declaration of invalidity or an order setting aside the agreement (*i.e.* rescission) with consequential directions. The remedy granted may, of course, be different: *e.g.* damages in lieu of rescission in circumstances to which the Misrepresentation Act 1967, s.2(2) applies. See Ch.4, above.
[3] *Re Roberts* [1905] 1 Ch. 704.
[4] See paras 29–17 *et seq.*, below.
[5] *ibid.*

12–04 After the drawing-up or sealing of the order a final order or judgment by consent may be set aside only in a fresh action commenced for that purpose.[6] The relief sought will depend on the circumstances but will, in all probability, be the appropriate relief[7] in relation to the agreement underlying the order or judgment and an order setting aside that order or judgment.[8]

12–05 Interim order. An interim order may be set aside by an application in the action in appropriate circumstances.[9] However, if the order has been made without mistake on either side, the court will not set it aside (thus giving it its full contractual effect) but may decline to enforce it if it would be inequitable to do so.[10] The application would seek the appropriate relief and should be supported by evidence.

12–06 Tomlin order. Since a Tomlin order is determinative of the rights of the parties to an action following its resolution by agreement, such an order is, it is submitted, a final order. However, it is possible that an application to remove the stay on any of the usual invalidating grounds may be made by application in the action.[11]

12–07 Costs when agreement or order set aside. Where proceedings to set aside a compromise are successful, the court will examine carefully the question of the incidence of costs. The victor may not always be easy to identify.[12]

---

[6] See para.6–20, above.
[7] See n.2, above.
[8] The interests of third parties must be protected: See para.6–99, above.
[9] See paras 6–21 *et seq.*, above.
[10] *ibid.*
[11] See para.9–27, above.
[12] *cf. Hickman v Berens* [1895] 2 Ch. 638.

PART 4

The Settlement Process in Civil Justice

CHAPTER 13

Present Landscape in Civil Litigation

For as long as litigation has taken place there has always been an impetus 13–01
on the part of the parties to reach an accommodation if possible. Leaving aside all other factors, the high level of costs involved in pursuing a case to a full trial operated as an incentive to settle, particularly where the outcome of the case was difficult to predict. The making of an offer of settlement, particularly on the part of a defendant to an action, effective in relation to the costs of the action if not accepted, has long been an important feature of the litigation landscape. The system of payments into court[1] and the development of *Calderbank* offers[2] represented the most prominent features in that landscape before the reforms embodied in the CPR were implemented in April 1999.

Much had worked well in the practice that had developed over the years 13–02
in relation to offers of settlement, whether by means of a payment into court or other form of offer. Many of the good features of the previous system became transposed into the new regime, in some cases with modifications appropriate to a case-managed system of civil justice. Some additional features, designed to encourage early settlement, were also set in place.

Since 1999 the landscape of civil litigation has changed significantly. Less 13–03
cases are being dealt with in court[3] which means that more cases are being settled or, at least, are being settled earlier. To that extent one of the main objectives of the civil justice reforms has largely been achieved.[4] Whilst

---

[1] See the Fourth edition of this work, Ch.10.
[2] See *ibid.*, Ch.9.
[3] The Annual Judicial Statistics for 2003 demonstrated, *inter alia*, a 24 per cent reduction in proceedings begun in the Queen's Bench Division in 2003 compared with 2002.
[4] In his Interim Report, Lord Woolf had said that settlement "too often occurs at too late a stage in the proceedings", the twin consequences being the expenditure of unnecessary

changed funding arrangements for certain types of litigation will have made a substantial impact on the number of claims instituted, the structures and approach put in place by the reforms have had an impact on the process of settlement itself. The principal structure put in place to aid settlement was Part 36 and the general costs regime of the CPR[5]. Another increasing influence on the settlement process has been the encouragement by the courts of the use of alternative dispute-revolution (ADR), principally mediation.[6]

Before considering these features in the present landscape, a number of preliminary matters need to be noted.

NEGOTIATION

13-04 Every settlement emerges from a negotiating process. It is a hallmark of the English and Welsh legal system that the parties may conduct their negotiations ordinarily without revealing those negotiations, or any offers made as part of them, to the court in the event that a full trial is necessary. This traditional approach continues to find expression in the new system. Every Pt 36 offer[7] is treated automatically as "without prejudice"[8] (although not every offer of settlement is made pursuant to Pt 36[9]) and a Pt 36 payment cannot be revealed to the court until the trial is concluded.[10] It follows that a thorough understanding of the "without prejudice" rule is necessary.[11]

EXCHANGE OF INFORMATION

13-05 Generally speaking, a settlement that is satisfactory to both parties will only occur when each party to a dispute has had a fair opportunity to appraise the strengths and weaknesses of his own case and that of his opponent. Whilst opposing sides will still frequently arrive at differing perceptions of those strengths and weaknesses, the process often reveals an

---

costs and the difficulties associated with listing cases that do require a trial. Of the several working objectives put forward for the new system he envisaged, one was that whenever it is reasonable for the parties to do so, they should settle their dispute before resorting to the courts, but that where this was not achieved prior to the commencement of proceedings, they should do so at as early a stage thereafter as possible.

[5] See para.14–25, below.
[6] See Ch.43, below.
[7] See Ch.16, below.
[8] See paras 14–06 *et seq.*, below.
[9] See paras 14–02—14–04 and Ch.26, below.
[10] See para.14–07, below.
[11] See Ch.27, below.

acceptable middle ground resulting in a compromise. A "fair opportunity" to appraise a case depends at least partly upon the availability of relevant information and documentation to each party. A system designed to encourage the early settlement of disputes will, as a basic minimum, require the earliest possible exchange of relevant information and documentation. Inadequate disclosure of information and documentation before negotiations take place will often result in dissatisfaction on the part of one or other of the parties with the settlement achieved and can foment "post-settlement remorse".[12]

In a number of areas of litigation, some of which[13] accounted historically for the largest number of civil cases instituted, pre-action protocols[14] have been produced. Lord Woolf identified one of the purposes of such a code of practice as being "to enable [parties] to obtain the information they reasonably need in order to enter into an appropriate settlement".[15] The existence of a well-constructed pre-action protocol, supported by effective judicial sanctions in the event of non-compliance,[16] has been a significant influence on the earlier settlement of the particular type of litigation to which it relates. In his Foreword to the Civil Procedure Rules, the then Lord Chancellor emphasised that one of the tasks for the next phase of reform "is to increase the number of protocols so that the greatest number of cases fall within their scope". That process has continued.[17] 13–06

Merely because a pre-action protocol does not exist to cover a particular piece of litigation will not, of course, preclude the court from penalising in costs a party whose conduct in not providing relevant information prior to commencement of proceedings has disabled the making of an informed pre-action offer[18] or an informed evaluation of a claimant's offer. 13–07

---

[12] An expression coined by Sir Thomas Bingham M.R., as he then was, in *Arthur J. S. Hall & Co v Simons* [2002] 1 A.C. 615 at 643.
[13] For example personal injury litigation and litigation arising from alleged clinical negligence.
[14] Defined in the Glossary to the Rules as "[s]tatements of understanding between legal practitioners and others about pre-action practice and which are approved by a relevant practice direction".
[15] Final Report, Ch.10, para.1.
[16] The extent to which a pre-action protocol has been complied with is a factor the court must take into account in deciding what, if any, order for costs to make (CPR r.44.3(5)(a)) and which it will consider when deciding an application for relief from a sanction imposed for a failure to comply with any rule, practice direction or court order: r.3.9(1)(e). Rule 3.1(3)–(7) contains provisions enabling the court, in appropriate circumstances, to order a party to pay a sum of money into court if that party has, without good reason, failed to comply, *inter alia*, with "a relevant pre-action protocol".
[17] Protocols now exist in relation to personal injury claims, clinical negligence cases, professional negligence claims, technology and construction litigation, defamation cases, judicial review proceedings, disease and illness claims and housing disrepair cases.
[18] CPR r.44.3(5) is wide enough to cover this.

PRE-ACTION COSTS

13-08 Since the present discussion is focused primarily on the pre-action stage, it is important to note that the costs ordered to be paid by one party to another may include "costs incurred *before* proceedings have begun".[19] Since considerably more pre-action activity than occurred formerly is encouraged under the post-CPR system, it is only right that the costs arising in connection with a dispute should embrace appropriately incurred costs in that early stage. They will, of course, be subject to summary or detailed assessment by the court if they are not agreed. However, the significant point is that no party to a dispute can consider himself immune from paying his opponent's costs merely because they are being incurred during a period when no proceedings are on foot. Interest on those costs can be awarded.[20]

INDEMNITY COSTS

13-09 The opportunity to obtain, or the potential to be condemned in, indemnity costs[21] is a factor that may assist a party towards a realistic appraisal of the strength of his case. Built into the rules concerning claimant's offers[22] is a structure requiring the court to award indemnity costs (plus enhanced interest on any damages and upon those costs) if the claimant achieves more than his offer[23]. Does a similar opportunity exist for a defendant to obtain indemnity costs?

---

[19] CPR r.44.3(6)(d) (emphasis added).
[20] CPR r.44.3(6)(g).
[21] CPR r.44.4(2) and 44.4(3) "draw a distinction between the difference in substance between a standard order for costs and an indemnity order for costs. The differences are twofold. First, the differences are as to the onus which is on a party to establish that the costs were reasonable. In the case of a standard order, the onus is on the party in whose favour the order has been made. In the case of an indemnity order, the onus of showing that the costs are not reasonable is on the party against whom the order has been made. The other important distinction between a standard order and an indemnity order is the fact that, whereas in the case of a standard order the court will only allow costs which are proportionate to the matters in issue, this requirement of proportionality does not exist in relation to an order which is made on the indemnity basis. This is a matter of real significance. On the one hand, it means that an indemnity order is one which does not have the important requirement of proportionality which is intended to reduce the amount of costs which are payable in consequence of litigation. On the other hand, an indemnity order means that a party who has such an order made in its favour is more likely to recover a sum which reflects the actual costs in the proceedings. The question of whether an order for costs on a standard or indemnity basis is made in litigation of the sort with which we are here concerned may be a matter of substantial financial significance": *Excelsior Commercial and Industrial Holdings v Salisbury Hammer Aspden & Johnson* [2002] EWCA Civ 879 at [13], *per* Lord Woolf C.J.
[22] CPR r.36.21
[23] See, generally, Ch.23, below.

The mere rejection by a claimant of what in the event proves to have 13–10
been a reasonable offer is not, without more, sufficient to entitle the court
to award indemnity costs in the defendant's favour. In *Excelsior Commercial and Industrial Holdings v Salisbury Hammer Aspden & Johnson*[24]
Waller L.J. said this:

> "The question will always be: is there something in the conduct of the
> action or the circumstances of the case which takes the case out of the
> norm in a way which justifies an order for indemnity costs?"

In that case an award of indemnity costs was held to have been
appropriate because the claimant had proceeded with what was a very
speculative claim but had recovered merely nominal damages of £2 against
the fifth defendant, and failed entirely against the other defendant who was
then involved in the proceedings, against the background of various
attempts by the defendants to settle it, culminating in a joint payment into
court of £100,000.[25]

---

[24] [2002] EWCA Civ 879 at [39].
[25] *cf. Reid Minty v Taylor* [2002] 1 W.L.R. 2800 and *Kiam v MGN* (No.2) [2002] 1 W.L.R. 2810.

CHAPTER 14

Structure of Pt 36

INTRODUCTION

14-01 Part 36 of the CPR contains the detailed rules concerning offers to settle and payments into court. It replaced Ord.22 of the Rules of the Supreme Court, and Ord.11 of the County Court Rules, in relation to payments into court in respect of money claims and introduced provisions concerning offers to settle in respect of non-money claims. It also provides a machinery for making a combined offer to settle and a payment into court when the claim is for both monetary and non-monetary relief and the offeror wants to make a substantive offer in relation to each.

NOT A COMPLETE CODE

14-02 Part 36 does not represent a complete code for determining the effect that an offer to settle or a payment into court may have upon the costs of the litigation to which it relates. First, whilst any party who wishes his offer to settle to be judged by reference to the provisions of Pt 36 would be well advised to ensure that it is made precisely in accordance with those provisions, the court will not be precluded from giving effect to the normal consequences of Pt 36 if it is not strictly in accordance with those provisions.[1] However, the court will give effect to it in that way only "if [it] so orders", whereas strict adherence to the terms of Pt 36 will give rise automatically to the various consequences provided for in the provisions of Pt 36.[2] Secondly, Pt 36 says nothing about the costs consequences where a

---

[1] CPR r.36.1(2).
[2] CPR r.36.1(1)(b). The Practice Direction says, at para.1.3, that "[an] offer to settle which is not made in accordance with Pt 36 will only have the consequences specified in that Part if the court so orders and will be given such weight on any issue as to costs as the court thinks appropriate."

claimant (who has not himself made a claimant's Pt 36 offer[3]) does better than the amount paid in, or the terms offered by, the defendant. Whilst the claimant in this situation is regarded as the successful party and the defendant the "unsuccessful party", with the result that the latter will be ordered to pay the former's costs,[4] the costs rules require the court to consider the various matters set out in those rules before it exercises its discretion as to costs. There may be circumstances[5] which would dictate a departure from the general rule.

FREEDOM OF CONTRACT

Just as Pt 36 does not provide a complete code for determining the effect of a payment into court or an offer to settle, neither does it prevent a party from making an offer in a way which avoids some or all of its provisions. Rule 36.1(2) makes it plain that the existence of Pt 36 does not prevent a party making an offer to settle in whatever way he chooses. A pure "without prejudice" offer[6] would be outside Pt 36 and would not, of course, be capable of being referred to on the question of the costs between the parties.[7] An open offer would, strictly speaking, be outside Pt 36, although the offeror would probably wish to spell out that the intention is that it should have all the other consequences of Pt 36.[8] Any offer made orally would not be within Pt 36.[9] Ordinarily a mere offer of a sum of money in respect of a money claim (in contradistinction to a payment of money into court) would not be within Pt 36.[10] A claimant's offer which expressly disavowed reliance on the provisions permitting the court to award higher interest if the court's award was better than the offer[11] would not, strictly speaking, be within Pt 36.

14–03

It follows, therefore, that a party needs to "opt into" Pt 36 in order to guarantee that the court will treat the offer as one to which Pt 36 applies. Where the claim is a money claim and a payment into court is made, there

14–04

---

[3] For claimants' offers, see, in particular, paras 14–03, 14–05, 15–03, 16–12, 22–11 and 23–09 *et seq.*, below.
[4] r.44.3(2)(a).
[5] For example, a minimal improvement on a payment into court or offer to settle achieved at disproportionate expense: see Ch.24. Further, the court may make adverse orders for costs against a successful claimant in relation to certain issues: r.44.3(4) and (5).
[6] The intention of the Rules is to preserve the "without prejudice" privilege. For the "without prejudice" rule, see Ch.27, below.
[7] *Cutts v Head* [1984] Ch. 290, CA. It may still be possible to refer to a pure "without prejudice" offer on the issues that arise under s.17(1) of the Legal Aid Act 1988: see *McCallum v Westridge Construction Company* [1971] C.L.Y. 9360.
[8] See Precedent No.6 at para.A1–06, below.
[9] CPR r.36.5(1).
[10] CPR r.36.3. However, the decision in *Crouch v King's Healthcare NHS Trust* [2004] EWCA Civ 1332, discussed more fully at paras 18–05—18–07, below, suggests that there may be exceptions to this rule. A true exception is where the offer is a pre-action offer by a defendant to a money claim which then becomes supported by a payment into court within 14 days of the service of the claim form on the claimant: r.36.10(3). See further in Ch.15.
[11] CPR r.36.21. See Ch.23.

will be no doubt that the offeror intends Pt 36 to apply. Where, however, an offer is made in respect of a non-money claim (*e.g.* a claim for a declaration in relation to a disputed boundary), the offeror would be well advised to state expressly that it is intended to be made in accordance with Pt 36 if that is what he wishes.[12] However, even if this express statement is not made, but the manner in which the offer is phrased plainly brings it within Pt 36, it is likely to be treated by the court as having been "made in accordance with this Part".[13] Furthermore, as already indicated,[14] the court can give effect to the consequences provided for in Pt 36 even if the offer is not made "in accordance with" Pt 36.

14–05 Little problem is likely to be presented in this regard in relation to an offer made by a defendant in a non-money claim provided, of course, the right to refer to the offer on the question of costs has been reserved. In that situation, if a claimant does not secure a decision from the court which is more advantageous than the offer, the almost inevitable consequence would be that he would have to pay the defendant's costs from the date when the offer expired. This is precisely the consequence provided for in relation to a Pt 36 offer.[15] Where, however, a claimant makes a Pt 36 offer (whether in relation to a money claim or a non-money claim), it might arguably be unjust for him to seek higher interest on any damages awarded (if greater than his offer), indemnity costs from the date when the offer could have been accepted and higher interest on those costs[16] unless he made it absolutely clear at the time of the offer that he would be relying upon Pt 36.[17]

PRIVILEGED NATURE OF OFFERS WITHIN PT 36

14–06 A Pt 36 offer will be treated as being "without prejudice except as to costs".[18] This means that whilst it can be referred to the court on the issue of costs,[19] it cannot be referred to on any other issue except in the very restricted circumstances that the law permits.[20] The purpose of retaining the "without prejudice" privilege is to enable negotiations to take place on a "cards on the table" basis without fear that anything said or done will be

---

[12] See Precedent No.1 at para.A1–01, below. The Practice Direction (see Appendix 2) states that a Pt 36 offer "must . . . state that it is a Pt 36 offer . . .": para.5.1.
[13] CPR r.36.1(2).
[14] See para.2.2, above.
[15] CPR r.36.20.
[16] CPR r.36.21. See Ch.11, above.
[17] See Precedent No.4 at para.A1–04, below.
[18] CPR r.36.19(1).
[19] *cf. Calderbank v Calderbank* [1976] Fam. 93; *Cutts v Head*, above.
[20] See Ch.27, below.

translated into some kind of admission.[21] The advantage to the offeror of being able to refer to the offer on the question of costs is that the offeree's conduct in rejecting it can be fully reflected in any order as to costs at the trial if the offer is not bettered.[22] Under the former practice, which doubtless continues, offers of this nature may be referred to in appropriate circumstances during the pre-trial period.[23]

With the exception of certain specific situations,[24] the general rule is that the fact that a Pt 36 payment has been made must not be communicated to the trial judge "until all questions of liability and the amount of money to be awarded have been decided".[25] The purpose of the rule is, of course, to try to ensure that the trial judge is not influenced by knowledge of the offer made. Since the rule refers specifically to the "trial Judge", the ability exists, in appropriate circumstances, to draw the attention of the judge exercising the pre-trial case management functions to the existence (and indeed amount) of a Pt 36 payment. Under the former practice, this could occur in an application for an interim payment (once liability has been admitted or established) and in response to an application to strike out for want of prosecution.[26] Evidence of a Pt 36 offer may be given during the pre-trial period in similar circumstances.[27] This practice undoubtedly continues.

14–07

The rule as to non-disclosure is expressed in mandatory terms[28] as was its predecessor in the Rules of the Supreme Court.[29] Where, by inadvertence or otherwise, that rule had been breached, the practice had been for the trial judge to exercise a discretion as to whether to hear the case further. Where satisfied that no injustice would be done, particularly if the knowledge could be put to one side for the purpose of making his decision, the trial judge could proceed.[30] This practice continues. In *Garratt v Saxby*,[31] the Court of Appeal emphasised that a judge who learns inadvertently of a Pt 36 offer needs to have regard to the overriding objective "in deciding how to exercise [his] discretion to continue with the hearing or to recuse himself". The following additional guidance was given[32]:

14–08

---

[21] *ibid.*
[22] See Ch.23, below.
[23] See n.27, below.
[24] See para.14–09, below.
[25] CPR r.36.19(2).
[26] See paras 27–52 *et seq.*, below.
[27] *ibid.*
[28] "The fact that a Part 36 payment has been made shall not be communicated to the trial Judge": r.36.19(2). But see n.31, below.
[29] RSC Ord.22, r.7(1).
[30] *Millensted v Grosvenor Place (Park Lane) Ltd* [1937] 1 K.B. 717, CA; *Re An Action for Negligence* (1992 C. No.3063), *The Times*, March 5, 1993, Knox J.
[31] [2004] EWCA Civ 341.
[32] *ibid.* at para.20.

"It is for the judge to decide in each case whether the disclosure of a Pt 36 offer or payment makes a fair trial impossible and whether justice demands that he recuse himself. But judges should not be too ready to reach such a conclusion; the delay and extra cost occasioned by a recusal may be very considerable. Moreover, when exercising their discretion, judges should remind themselves that they ought to have little difficulty in analysing and deciding the issues in the case on their merits without being influenced by their knowledge of the amount of the Pt 36 offer or payment."

14-09 The existence of a Pt 36 payment would be a relevant factor for the trial judge if the defence of tender before claim[33] was raised. Accordingly, in this situation the rule against disclosure of a Pt 36 payment is expressly stated to be inapplicable.[34] Equally, there may be situations in which, once liability has been determined separately from the money claimed, the existence of the Pt 36 payment may be relevant to the costs of the trial on liability. An express exemption from the general rule is provided for in this regard[35] so that the trial judge at the liability hearing can be told of the existence of the payment. Having been so told, the principal option available to the judge is to reserve the question of the costs of the liability issue to the trial of the assessment of the money claim.[36] On the other hand, the absence of an offer at all on the question of liability, or the absence of an offer of a specified proportion (where, *e.g.* the issue of contributory negligence arises),[37] may result in the court granting the claimant the costs relating to that part of the proceedings.[38]

14-10 The third situation for which the rules provide an exception to the general rule is where the proceedings have been stayed "under r.36.15 following acceptance of a Part 36 offer or Part 36 payment".[39] By the time

---

[33] This is described in the Glossary to the Rules as being "[a] defence that, before the claimant started proceedings, the defendant unconditionally offered to the claimant the amount due or, if no specified amount is claimed, an amount sufficient to satisfy the claim."
[34] CPR r.36.19(3)(a).
[35] CPR r.36.19(3)(c).
[36] In *HSS Hire Services Group Plc v BMB Builders Merchants Limited* [2005] EWCA Civ 626, the Court of Appeal confirmed the interpretation of r.36.19 as permitting the revelation only of the existence of a Pt 36 payment at the conclusion of a liability only hearing. Waller L.J. said this: "In my view Part 36.19 does not allow for the disclosure of the amount of a payment in. On its language it allows simply the disclosure of the fact that there has been one or the fact that there has not. The consequences of that being the correct interpretation of Pt 36.19 seem to me to be as follows. If the court is told that there has been no payment in, then the court is free to exercise its discretion to award costs in relation to the preliminary issue and there is no difficulty with Part 44.3(4)(c). If however it is told that there has been a payment in, then, in any but perhaps the most exceptional case, I find it very difficult to think that there could be circumstances where if the issue of damages remains to be decided, the judge can do otherwise than to reserve the question of costs until after the determination of that issue".
[37] CPR r.36.5(4).
[38] CPR r.40.3(6)(f).
[39] CPR r.36.19(3)(b).

proceedings have been stayed under r.36.15,[40] it would be extremely rare for a "trial judge" to become involved subsequently. Nonetheless, in such circumstances as may arise, reference to the payment into court may be made.

The existence of the rule against disclosure cannot, of course, prevent a party from applying to the trial judge for permission to accept a Pt 36 payment in the circumstances where such an application may be entertained.[41] The previous rules were interpreted by the Court of Appeal in a way that required a plaintiff who wanted to accept a payment into court during a trial to obtain the consent of the defendant before making the application.[42] The view of the majority of the Court of Appeal was clearly influenced by a desire not to permit a plaintiff to try to gain a tactical advantage when a case was going badly by applying to take the payment into court, thus bringing it to the attention of the trial judge, and then seeking a re-trial before a different judge. However, the dissenting view drew attention to the lack of anything in the Rules which required the defendant's consent to such an application and to the existence of the discretion of the court to continue with the trial notwithstanding the judicial knowledge thus gained.[43] So far as the CPR are concerned, it is submitted that there is nothing that requires the consent of the defendant before a claimant may make such an application during a trial. Attention has already been drawn to the likely response of the court if a claimant then sought a trial before a different judge.[44]

14–11

---

[40] See paras 21–13 *et seq.*, below.
[41] CPR r.36.11(2)(a) and (b)(ii).
[42] *Gaskins v British Aluminium* Co [1976] Q.B. 524, *per* Lord Denning M.R. and Orr L.J. Browne L.J. dissented on the point, taking the view that a claimant could apply during the trial to take out a payment into court "whether or not the defendant consents".
[43] See para.14–08, above.
[44] *ibid.* See the course taken by H.H. Judge Kershaw Q.C. in *Capital Bank Plc v Stickland* [2004] EWCA Civ 1677, at para.2.

CHAPTER 15

Pre-action Offers

BACKGROUND

15–01 Under the previous rules, an offer to settle a case, whether involving a money claim or a non-money claim, achieved a status recognised by the rules only when proceedings were in existence. A payment into court could be made only when "an action for a debt or damages"[1] was in existence. A written offer made "without prejudice save as to costs" was, if made pursuant to the rules, only capable of being made by "[a] party to the proceedings" in relation "to any issue in the proceedings".[2] An offer of settlement "up to a specified proportion" on the issue of liability achieved a status under the rules only after an order for a split trial had been made.[3] An offer of contribution by a third party achieved recognition only after the third party became "a party to an action".[4] The rules did oblige the court to take into account offers of settlement of the nature mentioned above "in exercising his discretion as to costs",[5] but did not oblige it to take account of any pre-litigation offer.[6]

15–02   Consistent with the policy of encouraging earlier settlement,[7] the CPR give added status to a pre-action offer. If any such offer is translated into a settlement, then that, of course, ends the dispute. If, notwithstanding the offer, proceedings are instituted, r.36.10(1) provides that "the court will

---

[1] RSC Ord.22, r.1(1).
[2] RSC Ord.22, r.14(1).
[3] RSC Ord.33, r.4A.
[4] RSC Ord.16, r.10.
[5] RSC Ord.62, r.9(1).
[6] Notwithstanding the phraseology of the old rules, the practice was for the court to take account of an offer of settlement, certainly in a non-money claim, made before proceedings were issued: cf. *Snuggs v Seyd and Kelly's Credit Index Co* [1894] W.N. 95; *Butcher v Wolfe, The Times*, November 9, 1998, CA.
[7] Ch.13, above.

take that offer into account when making any order as to costs",[8] provided that the offer "complies with the provisions of this rule". How does the offeror comply with the provisions of the rule?

THE OFFER ITSELF

For the pre-action offer to achieve a status within the rules it must: 15–03

    (a) be kept open "for at least 21 days after the date it was made";
    (b) if made by someone who would be a defendant to any proceedings commenced, "include an offer to pay the costs of the offeree incurred up to the date 21 days after the date it was made".[9]

It must also "otherwise comply with" Pt 36.[10] In other words, it must contain the details required by Pt 36.[11]

An offer under this rule is "made" when it is received by the offeree,[12] as indeed is a Pt 36 offer made after proceedings have begun.[13] Although the formal provision within the rules enabling an offeree to seek clarification of a Pt 36 offer or payment notice[14] does not strictly apply to a pre-action offer, any failure to give clarification where it would have been a reasonable course to take is likely to be "conduct" that the court could take into account in relation to costs.[15]   15–04

As with any contractual offer, a pre-action offer may be withdrawn (or revoked) at any time before its acceptance.[16] It may be withdrawn before the time given for acceptance has run its course.[17] Once the specified period for acceptance has expired, it cannot thereafter be accepted.[18]   15–05

---

[8] This provision can, perhaps, be seen merely as a statement reflecting the mandatory obligation on the court to have regard to "any admissible offer to settle made by a party which is drawn to the court's attention (whether or not made in accordance with Part 36)": r.44.3(4)(c).
[9] CPR r.36.10(2)(a) and (b). A claimant's pre-action offer may say nothing about costs. If that is so and it is accepted, the natural consequence would be that each party would bear his own costs: see para.5–60, above. Alternatively, a claimant may invite the party who would be a defendant to agree to pay the claimant's costs either to the date of the offer, to the date of acceptance or to a date 21 days after the offer: see Precedent No.4 at para.A1–04, below.
[10] CPR r.36.10(2)(c).
[11] See Ch.17, below.
[12] CPR r.36.10(5).
[13] CPR r.36.8(1).
[14] r.36.9. See Ch.20, below.
[15] See para.13–10, above; *cf. Butcher v Wolfe, The Times*, November 9, 1998, CA.
[16] *Chitty on Contracts* (29th ed., 2004), paras 2–080 *et seq*.
[17] *ibid.*
[18] *ibid.*, para.2–087. An offer can, of course, be renewed after the expiration of such a period, but it effectively becomes a new offer.

15–06 A pre-action offer that is withdrawn is unlikely to have any significant impact on the question of costs at the end of a trial.[19] One which is refused or not accepted is, of course, in a different category. If the offeree ultimately succeeds in merely matching the offer, or achieves less, then the costs expended after refusing or not accepting the offer will have been wasted.

15–07 Where a claimant betters his own pre-action offer at trial he is entitled to rely upon the provisions of r.36.21[20] and seek enhanced interest and indemnity costs. It was argued in *Huck v Robson*[21] that a pre-action offer was not an offer within Pt 36 and, accordingly, was not subject to the provisions of r.36.21. This argument was rejected. Jonathan Parker L.J.[22] said this:

> "In my judgment the purpose and effect of rule 36.10 is to enable a party to make an offer which complies with Part 36, and which has all the consequences of a Part 36 offer, before proceedings are commenced."

He continued thus:

> "Read in context, the words "the court will take that offer into account" in rule 36.10 mean, in my judgment, that where an offer has been made before the commencement of litigation which complies with the requirements of the rule (which in turn requires that the offer comply with the remainder of Part 36) the court will take that offer into account as a Part 36 offer, and accordingly that where the offer has been made prior to the commencement of proceedings by the prospective claimant rules 36.20 or 36.21 (as the case may be) will apply to it."

15–08 What happens if the offeree changes his mind subsequently and decides that he would like to accept the offer? As already indicated,[23] the offer will have lapsed and will not be available for acceptance. In this situation, the offeree needs to become an offeror in his own right. In terms which are

---

[19] It would be difficult to say that such an offer was an wholly irrelevant factor given the wide ambit of the court's discretion on costs, but it is difficult to see how it could have any appreciable influence on the court's decision. In his Final Report, Lord Woolf said that "obviously the court would not take account of a withdrawn offer when considering costs except when considering the reasonableness of the parties' conduct generally" (Ch.11, para.5).
[20] See paras 23–09 *et seq.* below.
[21] [2002] EWCA Civ 398.
[22] *ibid.* at paras 51 and 53. Tuckey and Schiemann L.JJ. agreed with Jonathan Parker L.J. on this issue.
[23] See para.15–05, above.

appropriate to the particular dispute, he will need to state that he offers to settle the case on the terms previously offered by the original offeror, perhaps offering to pay the original offeror's costs arising after the period for acceptance had expired. Provided the offer complies with the requirements of Pt 36,[24] it would become a pre-action offer in its own right capable of being considered on the question of costs.

The process described in the preceding paragraph shows that there could be a number of unaccepted pre-action offers for the court to consider at the end of a trial. With the emphasis being placed on pre-litigation negotiations, this should not be regarded as an unwelcome scenario. Plainly, though, the resolution of the issue of costs could be somewhat complex. 15–09

FURTHER REQUIREMENTS—MONEY CLAIMS

Where the offeror is potentially a defendant in proceedings in which money is to be claimed, he must make a Pt 36 payment[25] "within 14 days of service of the claim form" in a sum which "must not be less than the sum offered before proceedings began".[26] 15–10

The proviso concerning the amount paid into court is important. Plainly, a Pt 36 payment in a sum less than the amount previously offered could not be referable to, or relate back to, the pre-action offer. Equally, a Pt 36 payment in a sum greater than the amount of the pre-action offer could be seen as not relating to that offer: the recipient of the Pt 36 payment notice in respect of a sum greater than the pre-action offer could quite reasonably interpret the payment into court as being a new offer of settlement. He might elect to accept it within 21 days on the usual terms as to costs.[27] As indicated below,[28] a Pt 36 payment made under this rule may not be accepted without the permission of the court. It would seem, therefore, that an offeror of a sum of money who wishes in subsequent proceedings to stand on his pre-action offer should pay into court a sum equal to that offer. It would not be necessary to add further interest to that sum in respect of the period between the offer and the date of the Pt 36 payment because the offer is to be judged by reference to the time it was made, not by reference to the time of the subsequent payment into court. 15–11

---

[24] See n.11, above.
[25] See Ch.18, below. The form of the Pt 36 payment notice will have to be modified to show that the payment is made in support of a pre-action offer: see Precedent No.11 at para.A1–11, below.
[26] CPR r.36.10(3).
[27] See paras 21–04 *et seq.*, below.
[28] See para.15–12, below.

FURTHER REQUIREMENTS—NON-MONEY CLAIMS

15–12   Unlike a money claim,[29] where a pre-action offer has been made in a non-money claim, the rules do not require any step to be taken by the offeror in relation to that offer at or about the time that the proceedings begin. The need for a payment into court in furtherance of a pre-action offer in a money claim reflects the policy of requiring the offeror to demonstrate his financial standing and of ensuring the existence of an inducement to the offeree to accept in the sense of knowing that "the money is there".[30] The payment in is made at the first opportunity there is to make one after the commencement of proceedings. No equivalent policy can operate in relation to a non-money claim and, accordingly, there is nothing further to be done once proceedings are on foot.

CAN A PRE-ACTION OFFER BE ACCEPTED AFTER PROCEEDINGS HAVE STARTED?

15–13   Given the legal effect of an unaccepted pre-action offer,[31] the answer to the question posed may seem obvious: it cannot be accepted. However, the reason for posing the question is that r.36.10(4) at first sight appears to contemplate the possibility of acceptance "after proceedings have begun", albeit not "without the permission of the court." How can the court give permission to the offeree to accept an offer (possibly made many months, or even years, previously) which is no longer open for acceptance? Can the rules have the effect of breathing new life into an offer that has expired? If so, is it right that the person who rejected the offer previously should be able to secure this by the unilateral step of commencing proceedings?

15–14   Phrased in the way that they were, the foregoing questions would each attract an essentially negative answer. On the other hand, in the case-managed system of civil justice there is at least an argument that a previously unwithdrawn offer is something of which the court, if it is asked to do so after the expiry of the offer, should be able to permit acceptance, albeit only upon terms which ensure justice for the offeror. The court would presumably not entertain sympathetically any such application if the offeree's prospects in the dispute had altered adversely compared with his prospects at the time of the offer. Equally, the court would need to ensure that the offeror was not out of pocket in relation to his costs. These are essentially the conditions that applied under the previous rules relating to

---

[29] See paras 15–09 and 15–10, above.
[30] But see paras 18–03—18–07, below.
[31] See para.15–05, above.

the acceptance of a payment into court after the normal time for acceptance had expired.[32] Indeed, under those rules the court did control the terms upon which the money in court might be accepted by the offeree after the normal period for acceptance[33] or be withdrawn by the offeror either before or after that period for acceptance had expired.[34]

15–15 It would appear that, in relation to money claims, the CPR will permit the court to entertain an application for acceptance of the money paid into court in furtherance of a pre-action offer even though the offer had not been accepted when made originally.[35] In a practical sense, the ability to do so is facilitated by the requirement that money should be paid into court by the offeror if he wishes his pre-action offer to be considered within the rules. Before making that payment into court the offeror will, of course, have made a conscious decision about the matter. The rule which enables the court to entertain such an application is expressed in precisely the same way in relation to pre-action offers in non-money claim cases.[36] Although at first sight this might suggest that a similar jurisdiction exists in relation to such cases, the intention underlying the rules was not to interfere with the freedom of a party to withdraw his offer at any time.[37] It is suggested, therefore, that a previously unaccepted pre-action offer cannot be the subject of an application to the court by the offeree for permission to accept once proceedings are on foot.

15–16 In some cases an offeror in a non-money claim (*e.g.* in claims for a declaration about a boundary) may wish to put his pre-action offer on effectively the same footing as a pre-action offer in a money claim which crystallises formally on the making of the requisite payment into court shortly after the commencement of the proceedings.[38] It is suggested that there are two ways of achieving this:

(i) by writing a suitable letter[39] within 14 days of the commencement of proceedings confirming the continued availability for acceptance of the offer "with the court's permission"; or

---

[32] *Gaskins v British Aluminium Co* [1976] Q.B. 524, CA; *Garner v Cleggs* [1983] 1 W.L.R. 862, CA; *Black v Doncaster Metropolitan Borough Council* [1999] 1 W.L.R. 53, CA. See also *Capital Bank Plc v Stickland* [2004] EWCA Civ 1677, discussed at para.22–12 below.
[33] *ibid.*; *Proetta v Times Newspapers Ltd* [1991] 1 W.L.R. 337, CA.
[34] *Metroinvest Ansalt v Commercial Union Assurance Co* [1985] 1 W.L.R. 513, CA; *Manku v Seghra* (1987) 7 Con.L.R. 90. See the Fourth edition of this work, para.10–07.
[35] CPR r.36.10(4).
[36] *ibid.*
[37] See para.15–05, above. See also para.14–03, above, and paras 17–03—17–04, below. The express reference in r.36.5(8) to the fact that a "withdrawn" Pt 36 offer is not to have the consequences set out in Pt 36 evidences the intention that an offeror should be able to withdraw an offer if he wishes to do so. And see *Scammell v Dicker* [2001] 1 W.L.R. 631, CA, noted at paras 17–04–17–05, below.
[38] See paras 15–09 and 15–10, above.
[39] See Precedent No.9 at para.A1–09, below.

(ii) by so phrasing the pre-action offer when it is made to make it clear that it will continue to be open for acceptance after it expires (including after the commencement of proceedings) albeit upon altered terms as to costs.[40] This approach is not infrequently adopted when making sealed offers in arbitration proceedings.[41]

---

[40] Precedent No.8. at para.A1–08, below.
[41] See paras 41–18—41–29, below.

CHAPTER 16

Essential General Requirements of a Pt 36 Offer and a Pt 36 Payment Notice

INTRODUCTION

This chapter deals with those requirements of the rules which are common (or effectively common) both to Pt 36 offers as such and Pt 36 payment notices. Chapter 17 deals with the additional specific requirements relating to a Pt 36 offer, Ch.18 deals with those relating to a Pt 36 payment notice and Ch.19 with those relating to offers of settlement in mixed claims.   16–01

FORM

A Pt 36 offer must be in writing.[1] A Pt 36 payment notice[2] is, of course, a document.   16–02

MATTERS TO WHICH EITHER CAN RELATE

A Pt 36 offer and a Pt 36 payment notice "may relate to the whole claim or to part of it or to any issue that arises in it"[3] and each must state whether "it relates to the whole of the claim or to part of it or to an issue that arises in it and if so to which part or issue".[4]   16–03

---

[1] CPR r.36.5(1).
[2] CPR r.36.6(2).
[3] CPR rr.36.5(2) and 36.6(1). A Pt 36 offer should relate to the substantive claim: *Mitchell v James* [2002] EWCA Civ 997 and *Bellamy v Sheffield Teaching Hospitals NHS Trust* [2003] EWCA Civ 1124, referred to at Ch.23, n.30, below.
[4] CPR rr.36.5(3)(a) and 36.6(2)(b). For "waiving irregularities" in a Pt 36 offer see Ch.18, n.18, below.

"THE WHOLE OF THE CLAIM"

16–04 The natural meaning of this expression connotes all issues that arise directly in the proceedings. It should be recalled that even issues which could have been raised, but were not raised specifically in the proceedings, could be treated as "settled" once a Pt 36 offer or payment has been accepted.[5]

16–05 In most cases, the "whole of the claim" will embrace primary liability, contributory negligence (where applicable), causation of loss and all issues relating to the remoteness and quantification of damages. Where relief in the form of an injunction or other equitable remedy is sought, it will include that relief as well.

INTEREST

16–06 Under the old rules, interest was deemed to be included in the plaintiff's cause of action in respect of a debt or for damages for the purposes of a payment into court.[6] The effect of the CPR is also to make any offer to settle a money claim to be inclusive of interest unless the contrary is expressed.[7] Any Pt 36 offer and any Pt 36 payment is required to give certain details in relation to interest "if it is expressed not to be inclusive of interest".[8] The details required in that event (and the details required in any non-inclusive claimant's Pt 36 offer to accept a sum of money[9]) are:

(a) whether interest is offered; and
(b) if it is, the amount offered, the rate or rates offered and the period or periods for which it is offered.[10]

PARTS AND ISSUES

16–07 The resolution of discrete issues represents one of the objectives of the "active case management" required by the CPR.[11] Encouraging parties to focus on the real issues in dispute ensures a more efficient and economical

---

[5] *i.e.* the kind of issues that might be treated as *res judicata* in the wider sense of the *Henderson v Henderson* (1843) 3 Hare 100 principle. See paras 6–08 *et seq.*, above.
[6] RSC, Ord.22, r.1(8).
[7] CPR r.36.22(1).
[8] CPR rr.36.5(3)(c) and 36.6(2)(e).
[9] CPR r.36.22.
[10] CPR r.36.22(2). See Precedent Nos 7, 10 and 11 at paras A1–07, A1–10 and A1–11, respectively, below.
[11] CPR r.1.4(2)(b), (d) and (f).

disposal of the case. Although, in practice, many issues were resolved in proceedings governed by the old rules, the rules themselves, particularly those relating to payments into court, were largely framed to facilitate the settlement of either the whole case or to particular "causes of action" within it.[12] After 1986, the rules permitted the making of a written offer to any other party to the proceedings (expressed to be "without prejudice save as to costs") in relation to "any issue in the proceedings"[13] and the court was obliged to take any such offer into account on the questions of costs unless, at the time it was made, the party making it "could have protected his position as to costs by means of payment into court".[14] Framing the offer correctly was often of great importance.[15]

The CPR enable, for example, the making of a Pt 36 payment by a defendant in a substantial personal injuries claim against a particular part of the claim. A significant feature of many such claims is the cost of future care for a severely disabled claimant. This can clearly be interpreted as "part" of the overall money claim or as an "issue" within it such that a Pt 36 payment in relation to it can be made.[16] 16–08

The plainly desirable objective of encouraging parties to resolve as many issues as they can must be balanced against the possibly undesirable fragmentation of an overall claim to the point where its true nature is no longer discernible. The prospect of a claimant facing, say, six different Pt 36 payments against six specific heads of claim, with another six having no offers made in respect of them, is not something, it is thought, the courts would generally wish to encourage. Furthermore, in cases where the court's approval to the acceptance of a Pt 36 payment is required,[17] the giving of such approval is not always easy unless the overall picture is available for consideration. However, there appear to have been no significant problems in practice in this regard and it is to be assumed that the operation of the new system has bedded down satisfactorily. 16–09

LIABILITY UP TO A SPECIFIED PROPORTION

A defendant can make a Pt 36 offer limited to accepting liability up to a specified proportion.[18] Such an offer made in the context of a money claim is not "an offer . . . to settle a money claim" within r.36.3(1) such that a Pt 16–10

---

[12] RSC Ord.22, rr.1–3. See, *e.g. Toprak Enerii Sanavi AS v Sale Tilney Plc* [1994] 1 W.L.R. 840.
[13] RSC Ord.22, r.14(1).
[14] RSC Ord.62, r.9(1)(d).
[15] *Hobin v Douglas*, *The Times*, December 29, 1998, CA.
[16] This has indeed become established practice since the introduction of the CPR. For the consequences of acceptance, see Ch.21, below.
[17] See Ch.22, below.
[18] CPR r.36.5(4).

36 payment is required for it to be effective.[19] It is merely an offer to settle the issue of liability, not an offer to settle all aspects of the claim including damages. Where a defendant wishes to make an offer to settle the whole claim (even where an order for a split trial has been made), it is open to him to do so by making a Pt 36 payment. Where he merely wishes to settle the issue of liability, he is not obliged by the CPR to make such a payment.

COUNTERCLAIMS

16–11 Where the party responding to a claim (either in the pre- or post-litigation stage) intimates a counterclaim, he must, if making a Pt 36 offer or a Pt 36 payment, "state whether it takes into account [the] counterclaim".[20] Since a Pt 36 offer may be made by a claimant, the same rule as applies to a defendant's Pt 36 offer will also apply to such an offer. Since Pt 36 applies to all parties who are or might become involved in an action,[21] the need to specify whether an offer takes account of "any"[22] counterclaim may be important if any such claim has been intimated or commenced by or against any such party. Any failure to do so could almost certainly entitle the offeree to seek and obtain clarification of the offer or Pt 36 payment notice.[23]

INTERIM PAYMENTS

16–12 A Pt 36 offer can be made by reference to an interim payment.[24] Furthermore, where a Pt 36 payment is made in respect of a money claim, the notice must state whether any interim payment already made has been taken into account.[25] Although this is the only provision in Pt 36 that requires an offer to settle to make specific reference to a prior interim payment, it would be advisable for a reference to the same effect to be made in any pre-action offer, whether by a claimant or a likely defendant, and in any claimant's Pt 36 offer made after proceedings have begun. A possible consequence of not doing so is that the offer will be treated as excluding the interim payment and any consequent settlement may be in a higher sum than the offeror truly intended. An "interim payment" is, by definition, a payment "on account of any damages, debt or other sum

---

[19] See para.18–01, below.
[20] CPR rr.36.5(3)(b) and 36.6(2)(c).
[21] *i.e.* those making a "Part 20 claim": r.20.2.
[22] See n.20, above.
[23] CPR r.36.9. See also Ch.20, below.
[24] CPR r.36.5(5).
[25] CPR r.36.6(2)(d).

(except costs) which the court may hold the defendant liable to pay".[26] These words suggest that any interim payment is to be regarded as part of the final sum awarded. However, without expressly so stating when an offer of settlement is made, it would be possible to interpret the offer as "£X plus the interim payment" rather than "£X inclusive of the interim payment".

---

[26] CPR r.25.1(1)(k).

CHAPTER 17

Particular Requirements of a Pt 36 Offer

DEFINITION

17–01 A "Part 36 offer" for this purpose is one which is made after proceedings have started[1] and relates solely to a non-money claim.[2] A pre-action offer in a non-money claim achieves a status within Pt 36 only when proceedings have begun.[3] The rules provide that such an offer is available for consideration by the court on the question of costs at the conclusion of the trial,[4] but the consideration given to it is "as a Part 36 offer" so that the provisions of CRP rr.36.20 and 36.21 may apply.[5]

TIME GIVEN FOR ACCEPTANCE

17–02 An offer made more than 21 days before the start of the trial will not fall within the provisions of Pt 36 if it fails to state expressly that it remains "open for acceptance for 21 days from the date it is made".[6] (A Pt 36 offer is "made" when it is "received by the offeree".[7]) It must also provide that after 21 days the offeree may accept it only if either "the parties agree the liability for costs" or "the court gives permission".[8] Those latter require-

---

[1] CPR r.36.2(4)(a).
[2] An offer to settle a money claim must be made by way of a payment into court called a "Pt 36 payment", though see paras 18–03—18–07, below.
[3] See Ch.15, below.
[4] CPR r.36.10(1).
[5] See para.15–07, above.
[6] CPR r.36.5(6)(a). See Precedent Nos 1, 3, 4 and 5 at paras A1–01, A1–03, A1–04 and A1–05, respectively, below.
[7] CPR r.36.8(1).
[8] CPR r.36.5(6)(b). See para.17–08, below.

ments are also mandatory in relation to an offer made "less than 21 days before the start of the trial".[9]

The rules recognise that any offer of this nature is a contractual offer and subject to the normal legal principles applicable to such an offer.[10] One option available to an offeror is the withdrawal of the offer before the time given for acceptance has expired. The rules provide that if a Pt 36 offer is withdrawn "it will not have the consequences set out in this part".[11] 17–03

Consistent with the normal principles of the law of contract, a Pt 36 offer may be withdrawn not merely within any period of 21 days or more granted for acceptance, but also at any time before the court gives permission for it to be accepted after that period of 21 days or more has expired.[12] Unlike a Pt 36 payment, which can be withdrawn only with the court's permission,[13] a Pt 36 offer can be withdrawn at any time.[14] 17–04

> In *Scammell v Dicker*,[15] in the context of a boundary dispute, D made a Pt 36 offer by a letter dated March 9, 2000 in relation to a trial listed for March 20, 2000. The letter drew attention to the fact that, because the offer was made less than 21 days before the trial, it could only be accepted if the parties could agree the liability as to costs or if the court gave permission.[16] By a letter dated March 13, 2000 D withdrew the offer. C argued that it could not be withdrawn unilaterally until a reasonable period had elapsed. The Court of Appeal held that D was entitled to withdraw the offer at any time prior to acceptance.

---

[9] CPR r.36.5(7). For the kind of considerations arising in relation to costs at this stage, see paras 22–06 *et seq*, below.
[10] See para.15–05, above.
[11] CPR r.36.5(8).
[12] CPR r.36.5(6)(b)(ii) requires the offeror to stipulate that the offer may be accepted after that period if the court gives permission. It remains to be seen whether a court would feel obliged to recognise the right of the offeror to withdraw the offer right up to the time it is about to give its ruling on an application by the offeree to accept it. That would seem to be the strict contractual position. However, it would be very unattractive to sanction a course which entitled the offeror to contest on its merits an application by the offeree for permission to accept the offer late, but then to withdraw it if it appeared to him that the decision of the court was going to be adverse.
[13] See para.18.17, below.
[14] A proposal that the rules should provide that a Pt 36 offer could not be withdrawn without the permission of the court was twice considered and twice rejected by the Civil Procedure Rule Committee. Two views were expressed: one was that to provide in this way would offend the normal contractual principles referred to in the text; the other was that the choice of "opting into" Pt 36 (with the consequent inability to withdraw the offer without the permission of the court) would be entirely the offeror's and that, having made that choice, the normal contractual principles would be offended no more than they are by the rules relating to payments into court. The former view prevailed. One aspect of the review of Pt 36 being undertaken by the Department for Constitutional Affairs is whether this rule should continue in this form or whether a Pt 36 offer should be capable of being withdrawn only with the permission of the court.
[15] [2001] 1 W.L.R. 631, CA.
[16] See para.17–02, above.

17-05 In the above case, Aldous L.J. (with whom Mance L.J. agreed) said this[17]:

> "The Civil Procedure Rules do not prevent a Part 36 offer being withdrawn at any time prior to acceptance. That I believe to be clear for six reasons. First, there is nothing in Part 36 which states that a Pt 36 offer cannot be withdrawn. If withdrawal was precluded, I would have expected the rule to have said so in clear terms. That is to be contrasted with rule 36.6(5), which prevents withdrawal of a payment without permission. Second, rule 36.5(6)(a) only requires the offer to 'be expressed to remain open for acceptance for 21 days . . .' If the intention had been that the offer had to remain open for 21 days then the word 'expressed' would not have been used. Third, there is no mention of a particular period for offers made close to trial: see rule 36.5(7). To read into the rules that such offers cannot be withdrawn for a reasonable period from the date of the offer would provide uncertainty which could not have been contemplated. Fourth, rule 36.5(8) expressly provides that a Part 36 offer can be withdrawn. There is no limitation on when the withdrawal can take place. The effect is set out, namely that the offeror cannot rely upon the consequences of having made a Part 36 offer. Fifth, a requirement that a Part 36 offer could not be withdrawn could impose hardship in certain circumstances. That being so, I would have expected a provision providing for withdrawal in certain circumstances, at least with permission of the court. Sixth, a Part 36 offer is an offer to enter into a contract with the offeree. To impose a term that the offer could not be withdrawn would result in an addition to the contractual terms offered by the offeror. That would be possible, but should not be done by implication. The purpose of making a Part 36 offer, as opposed to another type of offer, is to attain the advantages that the rules provide. It is only those offers which comply with the rules that are certain to attain those advantages . . . I do not believe that Part 36 seeks to exclude the general law of contract that an unaccepted offer can be withdrawn. All that it does is to lay down the requirements that are needed to attain the consequences of making a Part 36 offer."

His Lordship referred to para.17–04 as it appeared in the Fifth edition, and noted that the court's decision was consistent with it.

17-06 Since a withdrawn Pt 36 offer is unlikely to have any, or any significant, impact on the question of costs, it will probably be only in the rarest of circumstances that an offeror will elect to withdraw the offer. In a boundary dispute, the discovery of a previously unknown map, plan or statutory declaration which significantly altered the balance of the argu-

---

[17] [2001] 1 W.L.R. 631 at 637.

ment about the location of the disputed boundary affords an obvious example of the situation in which an offeror might wish to withdraw the offer. It would, if the matter ever got that far, give the court grounds for declining the grant of permission to the offeree to accept the offer after its period for acceptance had expired.[18]

ALTERATION OF PT 36 OFFER

17–07 Where a Pt 36 offer is altered, it constitutes a new offer. The rules provide that an "improvement to a Pt 36 offer will be effective when its details are received by the offeree".[19] Consistent with the need for a Pt 36 offer to be in writing,[20] it is likely that the "details" of any improved offer will need to have been reduced to writing.

COURT'S PERMISSION TO ACCEPT A PT 36 OFFER

17–08 The factors which the court will regard as relevant to the grant or refusal of permission to accept a Pt 36 offer after the time for acceptance has expired are likely to be the same as, or similar to, those applicable in relation to an application to accept a Pt 36 payment "out of time". Those factors will be reviewed later.[21]

---

[18] See Ch.15, n.28, below.
[19] CPR r.36.8(3).
[20] See para.16–02, above.
[21] See Ch.22, below.

CHAPTER 18

Particular Requirements of a Pt 36 Payment and a Pt 36 Payment Notice

DEFINITION OF PT 36 PAYMENT

18–01 A "Part 36 payment" is the payment of a sum of money into court after proceedings have commenced in pursuance of an offer to settle a money claim.[1] The policy underlying Pt 36 of the CPR was that an offeror would not be able to rely upon the provisions of Pt 36 in respect of a money claim unless he made a Pt 36 payment.[2] Two exceptions to this rule were expressly provided for by r.36.3(1).[3] Subject to those exceptions, an offer by a defendant to a money claim to settle that claim "will not have the

---

[1] CPR r.36.2(1) and (4); r.36.3.

[2] This policy is, it is submitted, clear from the words of r.36.3(1) (see n.4, below), from the heading to r.36.3, the words below r.36.2(1) and the provisions of r.36.10. In *Crouch v King's Healthcare NHS Trust*, n.11, below, Waller L.J. said: "Part 36 is quite clear that in relation to money claims to have the consequences that flow from Part 36, a payment into court is required. This flows from the words in brackets under Part 36.2(1), the heading above Part 36.3 and the wording of Part 36.3. It is also supported by the provisions of Part 36.10 relating to offers made prior to the commencement of the proceedings, where after commencement in a money claim the offer must be paid into court". The policy was endorsed by the formulation of r.36.2A, part of the thirty-seventh update of the CPR promulgated in August 2004 and added to the CPR by the Civil Procedure (Amendment No.3) Rules 2004, laid before Parliament on November 30, 2004. The original policy is demonstrated by the Minutes of the meeting of the Civil Procedure Rule Committee of March 27, 1998 which read as follows: "The Committee reconsidered the decision made at their previous discussion on this Part, that if a defendant was a public body or insured, no payment into court was required . . . On balance, the Committee agreed that there should be no exceptions to the requirement to make a payment into court".

[3] The first is where an offer to settle is made "by reference to an interim payment" within r.36.2(3). The second is where the offeror has applied for, but has not yet received, a certificate of recoverable benefit from the Compensation Recovery Unit at the time he makes his offer, provided that he does make a Pt 36 payment within seven days of receiving the certificate: r.36.23(2).

consequences set out in [Pt 36] unless it is made by way of a Pt 36 payment.[4] The expression "will not" and the absence of the words "unless the court orders otherwise" are to be noted. Since the original promulgation of Pt 36, r.36.2A has been added "to ensure that the scheme for offers to settle and payments into court can work in cases in which periodical payments may be awarded.[5] That provision indicates that an offer to settle a claim for future pecuniary loss "where such an offer is or includes an offer to pay the whole or part of any damages in the form of a lump sum, ... will not have the consequences set out in this Part unless a Part 36 payment of the amount of the lump sum offer is also made".[6]

Support for this policy was to be found in the following case, decided after the CPR were introduced: **18–02**

> In *Amber v Stacey*,[7] C did some work for D in August 1997. No price had been agreed. He rendered an invoice on September 2, 1997 for approximately £7,500 inclusive of VAT. He issued a summons in the county court on September 24. On October 1, 1997 D's solicitors wrote offering £4,000 plus VAT and costs to date. They said that if the offer was not accepted they would advise D to pay the sum into court. On October 10 C's solicitors wrote rejecting the offer saying that it would not be accepted "whether paid into Court or otherwise." No sum was paid into court until August 7, 1998 when £2,000 was paid in. A further £1,000 was paid in on January 20, 1999 (the 21-day period for acceptance ending on February 11, 1999). Following a three-day hearing which concluded on April 30, 1999 (four days after the CPR came into force) C was awarded approximately £2,300 inclusive of VAT. The recorder ordered C to pay D's costs not merely from February 11, 1999 (which was not disputed), but also from the date of D's letter of October 1, 1997. The Court of Appeal held that it was wrong for C to be ordered to pay D's costs for that period because it equated the situation with that which would have obtained had a payment into court been made at that time, whereas no such payment was made. Given C's unreasonably precipitate conduct in commencing proceedings when he did he was ordered to pay one half of D's costs from October 1, 1997 until January 20, 1999. *per* Simon Brown L.J.:
>
>> "There are to my mind compelling reasons of principle and policy why those prepared to make genuine offers of monetary settlement should do so by way of Pt 36 payments. That way lies clarity and certainty, or at any rate greater clarity and certainty than in the case of written offers ... Payments into court have advantages. They at least answer all questions as to (a) genuineness, (b) the offeror's ability to pay, (c) whether the offer is open or without prejudice, and (d) the terms on which the dispute can be

---

[4] CPR r.36.3(1). "An offer to settle which is not made in accordance with Part 36 will only have the consequences specified in that Part if the court so orders and will be given such weight on any issue as to costs as the court thinks appropriate": Pt 36 Practice Direction, para.1.3.
[5] See Notes to Accompany August 2004 thirty-seventh update of the CPR.
[6] This provision came into force on April 1, 2005.
[7] [2001] 2 All E.R. 88, CA.

settled. They are clearly to be encouraged, and written offers, although obviously relevant, should not be treated as precise equivalents."

18-03 However, some inroads into this policy have been made subsequently:

In *The MV "Maersk Colombo"*[8] C recovered £774,990 plus interest at trial in its claim for damages following a collision between D's container vessel and C's container terminal at Southampton. C's claim was a subrogated claim brought by its underwriters. On 27 May D's solicitors, acting on behalf of D's insurers, wrote to C's solicitors offering £956,867 plus interest, together with C's costs. This offer was stated to be open for 21 days and was in *Calderbank* form.[9] On 22 June C's solicitors wrote saying that in order for the offer to have "the costs consequences usually associated with such proposals" D should have made a payment into court. On 2 July D paid the sum of £956,867 into court, such sum being expressed to be exclusive of interest. However, interest of £361,701 was offered in addition. C did not accept the offer or the payment into court. The trial judge ordered D to pay C's costs to a date 21 days after the offer of 27 May and C to pay D's costs thereafter. The Court of Appeal upheld this exercise of the judge's discretion even though the offer of 27 May was not in the form of a Pt 36 payment. *per* Clarke L.J.[10]:

"I respectfully agree with [what Simon Brown L.J. said in *Amber v Stacey*] that offers should not be treated as precise equivalents of payments into court and that they have many advantages. In particular the money is then readily available and no question can arise as to whether the offeror can or will pay if the offer is accepted. It should thus be appreciated that offerors who do not make a payment-in do so at their peril in the sense that the court may not be willing to reflect the offer in its order for costs. However, the court retains a wide discretion under CPR 36.1(2) to make the same order as it would have made under CPR 36.20 even in the absence of a payment-in. All depends upon the circumstances of the particular case."

18-04 In *The MV "Maersk Colombo"* the dispute was effectively between the insurers of C and D. There could have been no doubt about the ability of D's insurers to pay the sum offered in the original letter of offer. The same consideration applies to an offer made by the National Health Service Litigation Authority on behalf of a defendant NHS Trust in respect of a clinical negligence claim. This factor led to the practice in such cases of no Pt 36 payment being made when an offer of settlement was put forward. The efficacy of this approach was tested in *Crouch v King's Healthcare NHS Trust*.[11] The issue was whether a letter making an offer of settlement against a claim for damages for clinical negligence (*i.e.* a money claim) which stated (i) that "the Defendant is an NHS public authority ... [and that therefore there should be] no doubt that its offer is a genuine one that

---

[8] *Southampton Container Terminals Ltd. v Schiffahrisgesellsch "Hansa Australia" Mgh & Co, The MV "Maersk Colombo"* [2001] 2 Lloyd's Rep. 275, CA.
[9] See paras 26-05 *et seq.* below.
[10] [2001] 2 Lloyd's Rep. 275 at [97] and [98].
[11] [2005] 1 W.L.R. 2015, CA.

it will pay promptly if the Claimant accepts it in accordance with the terms on which ... the offer [is made]", (ii) that "rather than paying NHS funds into Court, it is preferable for the amount of its offer (which would be paid out of NHS funds) to continue to be available for provision of patient services pending resolution of this case either by agreed terms of settlement or Court Order" and (iii) that "as an NHS body, there is no doubt that the Defendant will be able to pay the amount of its offer", was to be treated as of the same status as a Pt 36 payment. Such an offer is held open for 21 days from its receipt by the claimant. The offer was in the traditional *Calderbank* form.

In considering the efficacy of such an offer on the issue of costs the Court of Appeal drew on the approach in The *MV "Maersk Colombo"*[12] and in particular upon the use to which r.36.1(2)[13] can be put in this context. In the context of answering the question whether a *Calderbank* offer of the sort made was "admissible" on the issue of costs, Waller L.J. said this[14]: 18–05

> "It is in this context where it seems to me that Pt 36.1(2) has its most important impact. It seems to me that this provision was almost certainly aimed at the views expressed in *Cutts v Head*[15] and allows a Calderbank offer to be made even in money claims. It then provides the court with the power to make orders that such offers should have the consequences specified in Part 36. As regards Part 44.3, in my view the *dicta* of Oliver LJ and Fox LJ recognised that an offer "without prejudice save as to costs" would be strictly admissible in the context of costs even though they were of the view that in money claims such offers should usually be ignored where no payment in had been made. *Calderbank* offers even in money claims are therefore 'admissible' and by virtue of Part 44.3 can be taken into account amongst all other circumstances in considering the proper order for costs."

He also said this[16]:

---

[12] See para.18–03, above.
[13] This provides as follows: "Nothing in this Part prevents a party making an offer to settle in whatever way he chooses, but if that offer is not made in accordance with this Part, it will only have the consequences specified in this Part if the court so orders".
[14] [2005] 1 W.L.R. 2015.
[15] [1984] 1 Ch. 291 at 312, where Oliver L.J. (with whom Fox L.J. agreed) said: "I would add only one word of caution. The qualification imposed on the without prejudice nature of the *Calderbank* letter is, as I have held, sufficient to enable it to be taken into account on the question of costs; but it should not be thought that this involves the consequence that such a letter can now be used as a substitute for a payment into court, where a payment into court is appropriate. In the case of the simple money claim, a defendant who wishes to avail himself of the protection afforded by an offer must, in the ordinary way, back his offer with cash by making a payment in and, speaking for myself, I should not, as at present advised, be disposed in such a case to treat a *Calderbank* offer as carrying the same consequences as payment in". See also at paras 26–05 *et seq.*, below.
[16] [2005] 1 W.L.R. 2015 at [41].

> "If however the offer is admissible, and it is something to which the court should have regard, it is much less easy to see why, unless it could be shown the offer was sham or non-serious in some way, it should not in normal circumstances have the same result as if the sum had been paid in."

The letter was held to be both admissible and effective on the issue of costs as if a Pt 36 payment had been made.

18–05A   The foregoing approach was endorsed and clarified by the Court of Appeal in *The Trustees of Stokes Pension Fund v Western Power Distribution (South West) plc*.[16a] Guidance on the way in which the court's discretion is to be exercised was given by Dyson L.J. in the following terms:

> "In my judgment, and offer should usually be treated as having the same effect as a payment into court if the following conditions are satisfied . . . First, the offer must be expressed in clear terms so that there is no doubt as to what is being offered. It should state whether it relates to the whole of the claim or to part of it or to an issue that arises in it, and if so to which part or issue; whether it takes into account any counterclaim; and if it is expressed not to be inclusive of interest, giving details relating to interest equivalent to those set out in CPR 36.22(2). This condition does no more than reflect the requirements specified in CPR 36.5(2) in relation to payments into court. Secondly, the offer should be open for acceptance for at least 21 days and otherwise accord with the substance of a *Calderbank* offer. Thirdly, the offer should be genuine and not, to use the words of Waller LJ 'sham or non-serious in some way'. Fourthly, the defendant should clearly have been good for the money at the time when the offer was made . . . To the extent that any of these conditions is not satisfied, the offer should be given less weight than a payment into court for the purposes of a decision as to the incidence of costs. Where none of the conditions is satisfied, it is likely that the court will hold that offer affords the defendant no costs protection at all. But if all of the conditions to which I have referred are met, than I can see no reason in principle why the effect of an offer should differ from that of a payment into court."

18–06   These decisions do, of course, result in the consequence that, in appropriate circumstances, an offer of settlement in respect of a money claim may be made other than by way of a payment of money into court

---

[16a] [2005] EWCA Civ 845.

and yet have the consequences on the issue of costs that a true Pt 36 payment would have. It would be difficult to quarrel with the result of this approach in either of the two cases to which reference has been made: the defendant in each case was plainly good for the money and insistence on the money being paid into court would seem unnecessary. However, it does have to be observed that it was the intention behind the drafting of the CPR that there should be *no* exceptions to the requirement that an offer of settlement in a money claim case should be by way of a Pt 36 payment. Whether reference to the *travaux préparatoires* would have been permissible in the arguments before the Court of Appeal in either *The MV "Maersk Colombo"*, *Crouch* or *Western Power* is debatable, but recourse to them would have demonstrated the clear intention behind the drafting.[17] Furthermore, for the same reasons, a rather wider interpretation of r.36.1(2) has been given in those two cases than was intended even though the wording is indeed apt to permit the approach adopted. Generally, the intention behind r.36.1(2) was to reinforce the proposition that a party was not obliged to use Pt 36 as the means of making an offer and to permit the court to give effect to the provisions of Pt 36 where a party had endeavoured to comply with it, but had failed.[18]

Whilst there is much to be said for the approach suggested in *Western Power* in the case of govement departments and insurance companies, one of the advantages of requiring all offers of settlement in money claim cases to be by way of a Pt 36 payment was that there was consistancy of approach. A clear structure with clearly defined consequences can assist those engaged in the process of settlement. A disadvantage of a more liberal approach is the uncertainty it engenders. As matters stand, it would seem that offers on behalf of the NHS need not be made the subject of a Pt

18–07

---

[17] See the extract from the minutes of the meeting of the Civil Procedure Rule Committee referred to in n.2 above. At that meeting the Committee considered a draft rule (then numbered 36.2(4)) as part of a Second Revision of the proposed Pt 36 (the document bearing the reference CPR(98)69) which was in these terms: "Where the claim is a money claim, a defendant may only make a Part 36 offer by making a payment into court unless— (a) the defendant is insured to the full extent of the amount of the offer; or (b) is a public body". The Minutes of the meeting record in relation to that draft the following: "As had been agreed, there should be no exceptions to those required to make a payment into court and this rule should end at 'payment into court'". The final version of Part 36 was to this effect, the only exceptions to the rule being matters that do not go to its substance.

[18] See *Mitchell v James* [2002] EWCA Civ 997, where the offer, which was headed "Claimant's Part 36 offer to settle", failed to draw attention to the possibility of the offeree accepting the offer outside the normal 21-day period as required by r.36.5(6)(b). In that case, with the defendants having legal advisers and there having been no question that they had been misled by the terms of the offer, the defect was waived. See also *Neave v Neave* [2003] EWCA Civ 325; and *Charles v NTL Group* [2002] EWCA Civ 2004.

36 payment.[19] Does that mean that all government departments (and, possibly, all local authorities) are now also absolved from the requirement for money to be paid into court? What is the position of all insurers? And there is the unresolved question of whether an offer along the lines of the offer referred to in para.18–04, above is capable of being withdrawn without the permission of the court, as is the case with all Pt 36 offers.[20] It is submitted that a defendant, unless one plainly embraced by the principles established in the two cases discussed above, would be well-advised to make an offer of settlement in a money claim case by making a Pt 36 payment.[21]

PART 36 PAYMENT NOTICE

18–08 The requirements of a Pt 36 offer and a Pt 36 payment that are common to each other have already been reviewed.[22] These relate essentially to the matters in respect of which the offer to settle is made. Does it, for example, relate to the whole or part of a claim, or simply to an issue or issues, and if so what part or what issue or issues? When a Pt 36 offer is made, these matters will be identified in the offer itself; when a Pt 36 payment is made, they must be identified on the Pt 36 payment notice.[23]

18–09 Neither the rules nor the Practice Direction stipulate that a Pt 36 payment notice must be in a prescribed practice form. However, an offeror would be well advised to adopt the standard form or to model his own

---

[19] *Crouch v King's Healthcare NHS Trust* [2005] 1 W.L.R. 2015 at [45], *per* Waller L.J.: "the court is entitled to take into account the factors that the NHS Trust will stress in their latest standard letter which are the points ... emphasised on their behalf ... Essentially the Trust is bound to be good for the money. This form of offer from an NHS Trust is as sound as a payment in, and, unless there is some factor special about the circumstances of the case, a court should treat such an offer in the same way as a payment in".

[20] See paras 17–04 *et seq.*, above. In the appeal of *Murry*, considered at the same time as *Crouch*, n.11, above, it was said by the Court of Appeal that the offer "was one which ... the NHS Trust was entitled to withdraw". Since the letter in *Crouch* was, on this issue, in identical terms to that in *Murry*, it would seem that this also applied in that case. It does follow that, unless there is a binding commitment in the letter of offer not to withdraw the offer without the permission of the court, offers can be made without making a payment of money into court which can be withdrawn at any stage after they have been made: see para.17–04 above. Whether this is satisfactory will be one of the matters considered by the Civil Procedure Rule Committee in its review of this aspect of Pt 36.

[21] It was suggested in *Crouch*, n.11, above, that a party uncertain about whether a written offer would suffice might seek a direction from the court at an interim stage about its status. *Per* Waller L.J. at para.28: "I can see no reason why under Pt 36.1(2) a defendant may not during the currency of proceedings take an offer letter to the court and seek a direction that it should be treated as a Pt 36 payment with the consequences which flow from that being so". However, it respectfully questioned whether, as with the RSC, there is jurisdiction to give such a direction: *cf. Corby District Council v Holst & Co Ltd* [1985] 1 W.L.R. 427, CA.

[22] See Ch.16, above.

[23] CPR r.36.6(2).

upon it to ensure that the relevant information appears on the face of the notice.[24]

MECHANICS OF PAYMENT

The payment is made usually by way of a cheque in favour of the Accountant General of the Supreme Court and sent to the Court Funds Office.[25] 18–10

MECHANICS OF SERVICE OF THE NOTICE

When a Pt 36 payment is made, the Pt 36 payment notice must be filed with the court.[26] Unless the offeree informs the court at the time he makes the payment into court that he will serve the notice himself, the court will serve the Pt 36 payment notice.[27] Where the offeror is concerned to ensure the earliest possible service of the notice, he may well choose to serve it himself.[28] This had been the required practice in the High Court prior to the CPR and a practice frequently followed by solicitors in county court proceedings. Under the CPR, when the court effects service of a document, it may decide which of the various available methods of service[29] is to be used.[30] Where the offeror regards time as of the essence, he may, for example, wish to give notice by means of fax or other means of electronic communication.[31] Electing to serve a Pt 36 notice himself may give him greater control over the process. Where he does elect to serve the Pt 36 payment notice he must, after doing so, file a certificate of service.[32] The rules refer to the service of "*the* Part 36 payment notice". It would seem to follow that, so far as practicable, the original should be used for the purposes of service, the court doubtless retaining some form of copy for its records. The important objective, however, is to ensure that the offeree receives, at a time capable of identification, "written notice"[33] of the payment into court, including, of course, the terms upon which the payment is made. From the moment that information is conveyed in the required form to him, the period for acceptance[34] starts running. 18–11

---

[24] See Precedent No.11 at para.A1–11, below.
[25] Pt 36 Practice Direction, para.4.1(3).
[26] CPR r.36.6(2).
[27] CPR r.36.6(3).
[28] Unfortunately, there are instances where the court fails to serve the document: see, *e.g.*, *Chainrai v Boston* [2002] EWHC 1895 (QB), Henriques J.
[29] CPR r.6.3(2).
[30] CPR r.6.2(1).
[31] CPR r.6.2(1)(e) and the relevant Practice Direction.
[32] CPR rr.36.6(4) and 6.10.
[33] CPR r.36.8(2).
[34] See Ch.21, below.

PARTICULAR REQUIREMENTS OF A PT 36 PAYMENT AND A PT 36 PAYMENT NOTICE

INCREASED PAYMENT INTO COURT

18–12 Where the offeror decides to increase the amount of his Pt 36 payment, that further sum must be paid into court in accordance with the practice identified above and a new Pt 36 payment notice must be served. The increase in the Pt 36 payment will take effect "when notice of the increase is served on the offeree".[35]

THE 21-DAY RULE

18–13 As already noted, a Pt 36 offer made more than 21 days before the start of the trial must give the offeree 21 days from the date it is received by him to accept it. A Pt 36 offer made less than 21 days before the start of the trial may only be accepted without the permission of the court if the parties agree the liability for costs.[36] The same effect is given by the rules to a Pt 36 payment.

18–14 Unless sufficient circumstances exist to warrant the court giving permission for the withdrawal of a Pt 36 payment,[37] any such payment made not less than 21 days before the trial is capable of acceptance by the offeree within 21 days of it being made without the need for the court's permission.[38] A Pt 36 payment made less than 21 days before the trial may not be accepted without the permission of the court unless the parties agree the liability for costs.[39]

18–15 Unlike the position under the old rules, the only circumstance in which a Pt 36 payment can be accepted with the automatic costs consequences[40] is acceptance within 21 days of a payment into court made not less than 21 days before the trial.[41] In every other situation, as indicated above, the permission of the court is required unless the parties agree the liability for costs.[42]

---

[35] CPR r.36.8(4).
[36] See para.17–02, above.
[37] See para.18–17, below.
[38] CPR r.36.11(1).
[39] CPR r.36.11(2).
[40] See Ch.21, below.
[41] Under the old rules, the plaintiff had the right to accept a payment into court made before the trial whenever it was made provided it was accepted (a) within 21 days of the notice of payment into court having been received and (b) provided the trial or hearing had not begun: Ord.22, r.3(1). This interpretation was the interpretation assumed by the Court of Appeal in *King v Weston-Howell* [1989] 1 W.L.R. 579 at 584. Equally, any payment into court made for the first time after the trial had begun, or any increase during the trial of a payment into court made before the trial had begun, could be accepted within two days without the leave of the court.
[42] The rationale is that in a case-managed system of civil justice, with the early exchange of relevant information and documentation, there should be no reason why an appropriate Pt 36 payment (or, in non-money cases, an appropriate Pt 36 offer) should not be made at least 21 days before the trial. This rule may need reconsideration.

EFFECTIVENESS OF A PT 36 PAYMENT OUTSIDE THE 21-DAY RULE

The fact that a Pt 36 payment is made within 21 days of the trial will not necessarily disqualify it from consideration on the question of costs.[43] There is a positive obligation on the court to have regard to any "payment into court" when considering its order as to costs[44] and it should be recalled that a Pt 36 payment (and indeed a Pt 36 offer) "may be made *at any time* after proceedings have started".[45]

18–16

WITHDRAWAL OF A PT 36 PAYMENT

A Pt 36 payment may be withdrawn only with the permission of the court.[46] The circumstances in which, under the former rules, leave to withdraw a payment into court might be given have been stated previously.[47] The guiding factor was the change, if any, in the plaintiff's prospects in the action between the date of the payment in and the date of the application for withdrawal. In *Flynn v Scougall*,[48] the Court of Appeal considered the circumstances in which it is appropriate to give permission for a Pt 36 payment to be withdrawn. It held that "the same considerations apply to giving permission to withdraw money in court as to refusing permission to take it out" and that "Goddard LJ's phrase [in *Cumper v Pothecary*[49]] 'a sufficient change of circumstance since the money was paid to make it just that the defendant should have an opportunity of withdrawing or reducing his payment' was to be adopted as consistent with the overriding objective." New disclosure of information or documentation would be an obvious change of circumstances.

18–17

---

[43] This was also the position under the old rules: see *King v Weston-Howell*, n.41, above.
[44] CPR r.44.3(4)(c).
[45] CPR r.36.2(4)(a) (emphasis added).
[46] CPR r.36.6(5).
[47] See para.15–13, above, and the cases referred to in Ch.15, n.29, above.
[48] [2004] EWCA Civ 873. See also *Capital Bank Plc v Stickland* [2004] EWCA Civ 1677; referred to at para.22–12, below.
[49] [1941] 2 K.B. 58. He said, at 70, that "the defendant must show that there are good reasons for his application, such as the discovery of further evidence which puts a wholly different complexion on the case or a change in legal outlook brought about by a new judicial decision". He said that, "apart from matters such as fraud or mistake affecting the original payment, the court should consider whether there is a sufficient change of circumstance since the money was paid to make it just that the defendant should have an opportunity of withdrawing or reducing his payment".

CHAPTER 19

Mixed Money and Non-money Claims

THE OLD RULES

19-01 Under the former rules, a payment into court could be made only in an "action for a debt or damages" in satisfaction of "the cause of action in respect of which the plaintiff claims".24[1] Acceptance of the payment into court would result in the automatic stay of "all further proceedings . . . in respect of the specified cause of action".[2] This was seen as preventing a plaintiff from keeping open, for example, a claim for an injunction arising out of a cause of action in respect of which he was prepared to accept the sum in court in satisfaction of the damages claim.[3] This made the decision as to acceptance of a payment into court in this kind of situation difficult. Equally, a defendant could be placed in difficulty in making an offer of settlement effective on the question of costs.[4]

THE CPR

19-02 The phraseology of the CPR allows for greater flexibility in relation to making a Pt 36 payment in these circumstances. Where a defendant to what is solely a money claim wants to offer money in settlement, he must

---

[1] RSC Ord.22, r.1. A claim for an account of profits was not a claim for debt or damages: *Brahen v Emav Images Ltd* [1997] 1 W.L.R. 1507. See also *Malhotra v Dhawan* [1997] 8 Med. L.R. 319, CA.
[2] RSC Ord.22, r.3(4).
[3] *Hargreaves Construction (Limeside) Ltd v Williams, The Times,* July 3, 1982, Foster J. The counter-argument to this view is that the payment into court could only be made against the claim for damages and thus could not prevent the claim for the other relief from proceeding: *cf. Young v Black Sluice Commissioners* (1903) 73 J.P. 265.
[4] See Fourth edition of this work, para.9–15.

normally pay that sum of money into court.[5] However, if he is faced solely with a claim for an injunction (so that there is no claim for money), there is nothing to prevent him from making a Pt 36 payment in respect of that claim if he wishes. If the court eventually awards damages in lieu of an injunction there would be no reason in principle why the Pt 36 payment should not be fully effective on the question of costs. Equally, if a defendant is faced with a money claim and a non-money claim, and is prepared to settle one and argue against the other on the merits, he can either make a Pt 36 payment in respect of part of the case (or an issue within it),[6] or make no Pt 36 payment but make a Pt 36 offer in relation to the non-money claim. Provided the Pt 36 payment notice or the Pt 36 offer is sufficiently clear,[7] the offeror should be able to protect himself on costs and the offeree should not be troubled with the difficult choices that had to be made under the old rules.

AN OFFER TO SETTLE THE WHOLE OF A MIXED CLAIM

The foregoing discussion has been directed to attempts made to settle part of a mixed claim. A defendant to a mixed claim may wish to make an offer which is designed to dispose of the whole claim and afford him protection on costs if it is not accepted.   19–03

If he wishes to make solely a money offer in respect of the whole claim, he can do so by making a Pt 36 payment in the normal way. If he wishes, for example, to offer an undertaking or to consent to an injunction as his response to the whole claim, he can make a Pt 36 offer to that effect.[8] If, however, he wants to make a substantive offer in respect of each part of the whole claim in a way that disposes of the whole claim, the CPR make specific provision for this situation.   19–04

Essentially, what is required is the making of a Pt 36 payment in relation to the money claim and a Pt 36 offer in relation to the non-money claim,[9] the two elements being linked by the terms of the Pt 36 payment notice. That notice must: 19–05

(a) identify the document setting out the terms of the Pt 36 offer; and
(b) state that acceptance of the Pt 36 payment will be treated as acceptance also of the Pt 36 offer.[10]

---

[5] See Ch.18, above.
[6] See Ch.16, above.
[7] For the possibility of seeking clarification of either, see Ch.20, below.
[8] See para.19–02, above.
[9] CPR r.36.4(2).
[10] CPR r.36.4(3).

19–06 Notice of acceptance of the Pt 36 payment in respect of which such a Pt 36 payment notice has been served will result in the Pt 36 offer also being accepted.[11] The practical consequences of acceptance will be dealt with later[12] as will the costs consequences where one part of the offer is "beaten by" the claimant and the other is not.[13]

---

[11] CPR r.36.4(4).
[12] See Ch.21, below.
[13] See Ch.23, below.

CHAPTER 20

Clarification of Pt 36 Offers and Payment Notices

INTRODUCTION

The CPR require that the essential information about an offer that an offeree requires in order to give it proper consideration will be given in the Pt 36 offer or the Pt 36 payment notice.[1] The more clearly the terms are spelled out, the less likelihood there will be for post-settlement argument.[2] However, there may be circumstances where some clarification of the offer or payment notice is required. The rules provide for that situation.

20–01

THE RULE

Rule 36.9(1) entitles an offeree, within seven days of a Pt 36 offer or payment being made, to "request the offeror to clarify the offer or payment notice". If the clarification is not given within seven days of a request, the court can be asked to make an order to that effect provided the trial has not started.[3] The application for a "clarification order" must be made in accordance with Pt 23, and the application notice "should state the respects in which the terms of a Pt 36 offer or Pt 36 notice, as the case may be, are said to need clarification".[4] If the court makes the order it must specify the date when the Pt 36 offer or payment "is to be treated as having been made".[5] This will presumably normally be from the date when the clarification is received by the offeree.

20–02

---

[1] See Ch.16, above.
[2] Often the outward manifestation of "post-settlement remorse", a syndrome identified by Sir Thomas Bingham M.R., as he then was, in *Arthur J. S. Hall & Co v Simons* [2002] 1 A.C. 615 at 643.
[3] CPR r.36.9(2).
[4] Pt 36 Practice Direction, paras 7.2 and 7.3.
[5] CPR r.36.9(3).

20-03 The rule is framed to permit clarification of "the offer or payment notice" and the Practice Direction refers to clarification of the "terms" of the offer or payment notice. It is unlikely that the court will wish to encourage detailed and wide-ranging questions about an offer made under the guise of seeking "clarification". Whilst it is impossible to be definitive, it is likely that the court will, in the first instance, ask itself the broad question of whether making the order will help the parties to settle the whole or part of the case.[6] This may narrow down to the issue of whether the terms of the offer or notice are in any material respect unclear or ambiguous such that the offeree would be at a disadvantage in considering it.[7] If that is indeed the conclusion the court forms, a clarification order would be likely. The jurisdiction is, however, probably more flexible than the provision under the former rules which permitted merely the making of an order directing a defendant to amend his notice of payment to show how much of a single sum paid in respect of two or more causes of action was attributable to each cause of action. The court could do this only if the claimant was "embarrassed" by the unapportioned payment.[8]

OFFEREE'S OPTIONS AND THEIR IMPACT ON COSTS

20-04 The question will arise of what an offeree should do when the offeror neglects to specify in his offer or notice something that the rules require him to specify. Examples would be a failure to state that a counterclaim or an interim payment had been taken into account. Given that the rules do state expressly that these matters be specified,[9] the chances are that the omission was an oversight which a request for clarification would reveal immediately. From a purely contractual point of view, the offeror will be entitled to accept the offer as it stands and, subject to any issues as to mistake or misrepresentation, the contract thus formed will be binding. However, if the offeror elects not to accept the offer, it is unlikely that the court would be receptive to the argument, when the issue of costs is determined at the end of the trial, that the offer was not accepted because it was unclear or ambiguous. The remedy for that problem is the seeking of clarification, and the failure to do so, where it was plainly appropriate, would undoubtedly be one of the "circumstances"[10] that could be taken into account on costs. The culture embodied in the new rules demands a sensible and meaningful dialogue.

---

[6] CPR r.1.4(2)(f).
[7] See, e.g. *Kinetics Technology v Cross Seas Shipping*, unreported, 16 February 2001, David Steel J.
[8] RSC Ord.22, r.1(5). See Fourth edition of this work, paras 10–03—10–05.
[9] See Ch.16, above.
[10] CPR r.44.3(4).

CHAPTER 21

Acceptance other than with the Court's Permission

INTRODUCTION

The CPR provide for certain automatic consequences to follow when a Pt 36 offer or a Pt 36 payment is accepted within the time allowed for acceptance.[1] The circumstances in which an offer may be accepted with the permission of the court after the period has expired will be addressed later.[2]   21–01

THE MECHANICS OF ACCEPTANCE

A Pt 36 offer (whether by a defendant or a claimant) or a Pt 36 payment must be accepted by a "written notice of acceptance".[3] The rules require that this notice is "given" to the offeror,[4] which simply means that it must be sent (by whatever means of communication is appropriate) to the offeror. Any such notice must also be filed[5] with the court.[6] The contract formed by the acceptance of the offer will be concluded when notice of acceptance is received by the offeror.[7] The need for filing the notice with the court is for case management purposes only.   21–02

---

[1] The time will usually be 21 days from the date of the receipt of the offer or Pt 36 payment notice (see paras 18–07 *et seq.*, above), though it would be open to an offeror to specify a longer period in relation to a Pt 36 offer and the parties could agree to extend the time for acceptance of a Pt 36 payment under CPR r.2.11. The court may also order an extension or shortening of time for compliance with any rule: r.3.1(2)(a).
[2] See Ch.22, below.
[3] CPR rr.36.11(1) and 36.12(1).
[4] *ibid.*
[5] *i.e.* delivering it, by post or otherwise, to the Court Office: r.2.3(1).
[6] Pt 36 Practice Direction, para.8.6.
[7] CPR r.36.8(5).

21-03   The form of the notice of acceptance in respect of a Pt 36 payment is provided for in a form which also contains a request for payment.[8] The Practice Direction indicates[9] that the notice of acceptance in respect of a Pt 36 offer must also contain the same details as appear on that form: the claim number, the title of the proceedings, the identity of the Pt 36 offer to which it relates and the signature of the offeree or his legal representative.

COSTS CONSEQUENCES OF ACCEPTANCE OF A DEFENDANT'S OFFER

21-04   Where a claimant accepts a Pt 36 offer or a Pt 36 payment relating to the whole claim within the prescribed time for acceptance, he "will be entitled to his costs of the proceedings up to the date of serving notice of acceptance".[10] Those costs include any costs attributable to the defendant's counterclaim provided the Pt 36 offer or Pt 36 payment notice states that it takes account of the counterclaim.[11] The costs will be assessed on the standard basis if not agreed.[12]

21-05   Where the Pt 36 offer or Pt 36 payment relates to part only of the claim and the claimant, at the time of serving notice of acceptance, abandons the balance of the claim, the claimant will again be entitled to his costs on the basis referred to in the preceding paragraph "unless the court orders otherwise".[13] The purpose of the inclusion of the proviso is to permit a defendant to apply to the court for a different order from the normal order if he considers it appropriate to do so having regard to the costs associated with the abandoned parts of the claim. Under the old rules,[14] a plaintiff

---

[8] See Appendix 5, below.
[9] Pt 36 Practice Direction, para.8.7.
[10] CPR r.36.13(1).
[11] CPR r.36.13(3).
[12] CPR r.36.13(4). A costs order will be deemed to have been made on the standard basis: r.44.12(1)(b). There is no provision in this situation for obtaining indemnity costs: see *Dyson Ltd v Hoover Ltd* [2002] EWHC 2229 (Ch), Jacob J., as he then was. This has been seen by some as potentially causing an injustice where a claimant has made his own Pt 36 offer which is not accepted by the defendant, but then the defendant makes a Pt 36 payment or offer which exceeds that which the claimant in his offer said he would accept. If the claimant accepts the defendant's payment or offer he can only achieve standard costs, whereas by accepting it is he is achieving more than his own offer—something which, in the ordinary course of events, would result in an entitlement to indemnity costs and enhanced interest, if appropriate. In *Dyson*, Jacob J. suggested that the route out of the difficulty would be for the claimant not to take the money paid in as such, but to write to the defendant indicating the basis upon which the money is going to be taken out. If the defendant does not agree to that basis then an application could be made to the court for directions.
[13] CPR r.36.13(2).
[14] RSC Ord.62, r.5(4).

who accepted the sum paid into court in respect of one cause of action and abandoned the others was entitled to "his costs of the action incurred up to the time of giving notice of acceptance". The "costs of the action" embraced all the costs associated with the proceedings including those referable to the abandoned causes of action. Since the court had no discretion in the matter, this could cause an injustice.[15] The proviso enables the court to make an order more appropriate to the circumstances if invited to do so.

21–06 Where the Pt 36 offer or Pt 36 payment relates to part only of the claim, but the claimant does not abandon the other parts, the court will decide who is liable for the costs unless the parties have agreed.[16]

COSTS CONSEQUENCES OF ACCEPTANCE OF AN OFFER OR PAYMENT BY ONE OR MORE OF SEVERAL DEFENDANTS[17]

21–07 Where a Pt 36 offer or a Pt 36 payment relates to a claim brought against a number of defendants jointly or in the alternative[18] and is made by one or more, but not all, of those defendants, the claimant will be entitled to his costs on the basis previously described[19] provided that:

(a) he discontinues the claim against the other defendants; and
(b) those other defendants consent in writing to the acceptance of the the offer for payment.[20]

21–08 In this situation all the defendants are content with the acceptance by the claimant of the sum offered and that he should have his costs. Equally, the claimant is content not to continue his claims against those who were not directly party to the offer or payment. As between the defendants there may, of course, be outstanding disputes—for example, as to contribution

---

[15] *Hudson v Elmbridge Borough Council* [1991] 1 W.L.R. 880, CA.
[16] CPR r.36.15(3).
[17] For an analysis of the old rules, upon which the new rules are largely modelled, see Fourth edition of this work, paras 10–26 *et seq*. See also *Carrs Bury St Edmunds Ltd v Whitworth Partnership*, (1997) 13 Const. I.J. 199, where *Hodgson v Guardall* [1991] 3 All E.R. 823, was not followed.
[18] "Joint liability" is described in the Glossary to the CPR as being a situation in which "parties . . . share a single liability" for which each can be held wholly liable. The expression "sued jointly" was interpreted under the former rules as being sued "in respect of a joint liability", not merely being joined together in the same proceedings: *Townsend v Stone Toms & Partners* [1981] 1 W.L.R. 1153, CA.
[19] Pt 36 Practice Direction, para.9.4.
[20] CPR r.36.17(2).

or indemnity. Where the claimant is not prepared to discontinue his claim against the other defendants, or where one or more of them is or are not prepared to agree to the acceptance of the offer or payment, the claimant will require an order of the court permitting him to take the money out of court. At that time the court will make such order as to costs as it considers appropriate.[21]

21-09   Where a claimant has pursued a number of defendants jointly or alternatively (or indeed jointly and alternatively), it would be unusual for there to remain anything in issue between him and those defendants once a settlement has been achieved with one or more of the defendants.[22] Where, however, several liability[23] is alleged against some or all of those defendants, the position is different. Several liability connotes a separate claim and where a claimant accepts a Pt 36 offer or payment in respect of such a claim, but in the specified time for acceptance, he may do so without the court's permission and he will be entitled to his costs as well as being able to continue with a separate claim against the others provided the law permits this in the particular context.[24] The costs to which the claimant will be entitled are, as already indicated,[25] the "costs of the proceedings up to the date of serving notice of acceptance". This is likely to be interpreted as the costs attributable to the claim against the particular defendant whose several liability is discharged by acceptance of his offer or payment. In other words, the expression "costs of the proceedings" would be limited to the costs of proceedings against that defendant in respect of that liability.[26]

COSTS CONSEQUENCES OF ACCEPTANCE OF A CLAIMANT'S OFFER

21-10   Where a claimant's Pt 36 offer is accepted within the period set for acceptance, the claimant will be entitled to his costs of the proceedings to the date upon which the defendant serves notice of acceptance.[27] His right

---

[21] CPR r.36.17(4).
[22] But see para.22-05, below.
[23] "A person who is severally liable with others may remain liable for the whole claim even where judgment has been obtained against the others": Glossary to CPR.
[24] CPR r.36.17(3). See, generally, Ch.6 and paras 6-38 *et seq.*, above, in particular.
[25] See para.21-04, above.
[26] The previous rule, which governed the situation hitherto, used the expression "costs of the action" (RSC Ord.62, r.5(4)). That was interpreted as referring to the costs of the action "against that defendant": *QBE Ltd v Mediterranean Insurance*, [1992] 1 W.L.R. 573; *Carrs Bury St Edmunds Ltd v Whitworth Partnership*, n.17, above. This was to prevent possible injustice to a paying in defendant. It is submitted that the expression "costs of the proceedings" is even more susceptible to this interpretation than was the expression "costs of the action". A defendant who wishes to make the position absolutely clear might wish to phrase his Pt 36 payment notice in a way which demonstrates that the payment is made in respect of that "part of the claim" which relates to him.
[27] CPR r.36.14.

to costs in this situation results in a deemed order that he is entitled to those costs on the standard basis.[28]

THE MECHANICS OF PAYMENT OUT

In those cases where a Pt 36 payment is accepted and the costs consequences are automatic, the claimant obtains payment out to him of the sum in court by making a request for payment by means of the relevant form.[29] The form should be filed with the court and there may be other formalities to consider depending on whether the request for payment is made to the Royal Courts of Justice or elsewhere and whether the claimant wants a cheque or a direct transfer to his bank account.[30] The payment will be made to the claimant's legal representative if he is represented, or direct to him, unless he has been in receipt of legal aid at any time in respect of the proceedings, when the payment will be made to the Legal Services Commission by direction of the court.[31]

21–11

INTEREST

If the first Pt 36 payment made by a defendant is accepted within the 21-day period, no interest will have accrued whilst it is in court because it will not have been transmitted to an investment account.[32] If, however, an increased Pt 36 payment is accepted within the period for acceptance, interest will have accrued on any sum or sums previously paid into court. Unless the parties have agreed otherwise, accrued interest to the date of acceptance will be paid to the defendant and any interest accruing from the date of acceptance until payment out will be paid to the claimant.[33]

21–12

CONSEQUENCES OF ACCEPTANCE FOR THE PROCEEDINGS

Where a Pt 36 payment which relates to the whole claim is accepted, the claim will be stayed.[34] Where the payment expressly took into account any counterclaim,[35] the effect of acceptance will be to stay all proceedings

21–13

---

[28] CPR r.44.12(1)(c).
[29] CPR r.36.16. The form appears in Appendix 5, below.
[30] Pt 36 Practice Direction, paras 9.1–9.4
[31] *ibid.*, para.9.5.
[32] *ibid.*, paras 12.3 and 12.4.
[33] *ibid.*, para.8.10.
[34] CPR r.36.15(1). "A stay imposes a halt on proceedings, apart from taking steps allowed by the Rules or the terms of the stay. Proceedings can be continued if the stay is lifted": Glossary to CPR. See also paras 9–28 *et seq.*, above.
[35] See para.16–11, above.

including the counterclaim. There is no reason to suppose that the effect and operation of a stay thus imposed will be any different from that which obtained under the former rules.[36] The rules state expressly that any stay imposed in the situation described above will not affect the powers of the court to deal with any question of costs (including interest on costs[37]), or to order a payment out of court of any sum paid in.

21–14 Where a Pt 36 payment relating to part only of the claim is accepted, the claim will be stayed as to that part. If the parties have not agreed the liability for the costs of that part of the claim, the court will decide the issue.[38] The same result will follow if a Pt 36 offer relating to part only of a claim is accepted.[39] Although the rules do not state precisely what is to happen if a Pt 36 offer relating to an issue,[40] is accepted, it is likely that the purposive construction to be given to the rules[41] will result in the expression "issue" being treated as coterminous with "part" for this purpose. Liability is usually seen as an "issue" in a claim. An agreement as to apportionment of liability resulting from the acceptance of a Pt 36 offer will probably result, initially at least, in a stay of the proceedings in relation to that issue.[42]

21–15 When a Pt 36 offer relating to the whole of the claim is accepted, the stay imposed by the rules will be "upon the terms of the offer" and either party can apply to the court "to enforce those terms without the need for a new claim".[43] The effect is to translate the agreement into a rule-imposed Tomlin order,[44] although the stay is imposed by the rules and not by an order of the court as such. The equivalent of the former "liberty to apply" is, for this purpose, a right given by the rules to apply to the court for the purposes of enforcement. There may be circumstances in which the parties do require there to be some kind of order to give effect to their agreement:

---

[36] See para.9–18, above.
[37] See *Electricity Supply Nominees Ltd v Farrell* [1997] 1 W.L.R. 1149, CA.
[38] CPR r.36.15(3). The court will doubtless have regard to its power to limit the costs to, for example, a proportion of the costs or to a "distinct part of the proceedings": r.44.3(6).
[39] *ibid.*
[40] See para.16–07, above.
[41] CPR r.1.2(b).
[42] The agreement will probably be translated into a judgment on the issue as to liability (either 100 per cent or in some lesser proportion) at a later stage.
[43] CPR r.36.15(2).
[44] See further at para.21–16, below. See also paras 9–19 *et seq.*, above. The author claims (immodestly) some credit for the inclusion in Pt 36 of this provision which seemed to be the sensible practical response to the particular situation. He regrets, though, failure to keep the name "Tomlin" alive in the body of the rules at r.40.6(3)(b)(ii). In several early drafts of Pt 40 the words "a Tomlin order" appeared in parenthesis at the end of this sub-paragraph and remained there without objection from the Civil Procedure Rule Committee. It was, however, eventually spotted, and the last occasion Pt 40 was considered by the Committee these words were excised on the basis that if "Anton Piller" and "Mareva" had to go, so did "Tomlin"!

they might want a Tomlin order as such or, perhaps, an order incorporating an undertaking to the court or a declaration. The latter may be required particularly in the context of the acceptance by a claimant of an offer in relation to both aspects of a mixed claim under CPR r.36.4.[45] An order in relation to costs or legal aid taxation may also be required. If this is what is specified in the Pt 36 offer which is then accepted, the stay imposed by the rules will simply be upon the "term" that the parties cooperate in seeking an order by consent in the agreed terms. That term will be "implied" into the agreement if it is not expressed.[46]

Where a Pt 36 offer has been accepted an agreement will have been concluded. Enforcement of that agreement will normally take place by means of an application (made in accordance with Pt 23) for a suitable order pursuant to such rule as permits the order to be made.[47] A claim for damages arising from a breach of the agreement might be interpreted as something other than an application for "enforcement" of the agreement. Indeed, this was the view of the Court of Appeal in *Hollingsworth v Humphrey*[48] in relation to a claim for damages arising from the breach of the agreement contained in the schedule to a Tomlin order. The result of that view was that a fresh action was needed in order to pursue that claim for damages. In order to prevent the somewhat cumbersome process of starting wholly new proceedings in the event of a breach of a term of an accepted Pt 36 offer, provision is made in the rules that such a remedy may be claimed "by applying to the court without the need to start a new claim unless the court orders otherwise".[49]

21–16

---

[45] See para.19–05, above.
[46] See paras 5–47 *et seq.*, above. The parties may be able to utilise r.40.6 in appropriate circumstances: see paras 10–17 *et seq.*, above.
[47] CPR r.36.15(2).
[48] (1987) C.A.T. 1244; *Independent*, December 21, 1987. But see paras 9–23–9–27 above. Where parties agree a Tomlin order (rather than having the effect of one imposed on them pursuant to the rules), they may wish to overcome the consequences of *Hollingsworth v Humphrey* by agreeing that a new claim is not required if a claim for breach of the agreement has to be pursued; see Appendix 6, below.
[49] CPR r.36.15(6). The proviso "unless the court orders otherwise" entitles the court to direct a new claim, or some other form of proceeding than merely an application, if it considers it necessary and appropriate to do so.

CHAPTER 22

Acceptance with the Court's Permission

INTRODUCTION

22–01 In Ch.21 consideration was given to the costs and other consequences arising from acceptance of a Pt 36 offer or payment when the permission of the court prior to acceptance was not required. Consideration will now be given to the circumstances in which the permission of the court is required to enable acceptance and the consequences that do, or may, flow from the grant (or refusal) of that permission.

CHILDREN AND PATIENTS

22–02 Consistent with previous practice,[1] any settlement or compromise of a claim brought by or against a child or patient requires the approval of the court for it to be valid.[2] This means, in effect, that any Pt 36 offer or Pt 36 payment (and indeed any pre-action offer) could not be accepted without the permission of the court.[3] The CPR prescribe the practice to be adopted in order to obtain the court's approval[4] and they give the court power to direct how any money recovered by or on behalf or for the benefit of a child or patient is to be invested or otherwise dealt with.[5] Where permission to accept a Pt 36 payment is given, whether before or after the trial has started, no money can be paid out of court without an order of the court.[6] Where permission is given before the trial begins, the court will

---

[1] RSC, Ord.18; CCR Ord.10.
[2] CPR r.21.10(1). See Ch.35, below.
[3] CPR r.36.18(1).
[4] CPR r.21.10(2).
[5] CPR r.21.11.
[6] CPR r.36.18(1)(b) and (2)(a).

doubtless make an order as to costs which will almost certainly have been agreed. Where permission is given after the trial has begun, the court must "deal with the whole costs of the proceedings" in any order it makes.[7]

The effect upon the proceedings of permission being given to accept a Pt 36 offer or Pt 36 payment in relation to a child or patient will be the same as in any other case,[8] except that any stay that would otherwise arise on its acceptance will take effect only when the approval of the court has been given.[9] 22–03

So far as the costs consequences of acceptance are concerned, it is unlikely that they will differ to any material extent from the consequences that apply in litigation not involving a child or patient, certainly if the decision to accept the offer or payment into court subject to the approval of the court is intimated or made to the offeror within the normal time for acceptance. The position with regard to costs if permission is sought beyond that time is dealt with below,[10] as is the position if a child or patient claimant fails to improve on the Pt 36 offer or payment.[11] 22–04

SEVERAL DEFENDANTS

The circumstances in which a claimant may accept a Pt 36 offer or Pt 36 payment made by one or more, but not all, of several defendants without needing the permission of the court have been described.[12] In any case other than those described the claimant must apply to the court for an order permitting payment out to him of the sum in court.[13] The purpose of this requirement, which largely mirrors the requirements of the old rules,[14] is to enable the court to resolve any outstanding issue as to costs. An example of a situation in which the court might be required to adjudicate is where the claimant wants to accept a Pt 36 payment made by one of two defendants sued in the alternative, but there is an issue between the paying in defendant and the claimant as to who should be responsible for the costs of the other defendant. Under the former practice, the question as to primary liability for those costs was resolved on the basis of whether it was reasonable for the claimant to have joined the defendant whose costs are in issue. Once that had been resolved in the claimant's favour the remaining 22–05

---

[7] CPR r.36.18(2)(b).
[8] See paras 21–13 *et seq.*, above.
[9] CPR r.36.15(4).
[10] See paras 22–06 *et seq.*, below.
[11] See para.23–08, below.
[12] See paras 21–07—21–09, above.
[13] CPR r.36.17(4).
[14] RSC Ord.22, r.4.

matter for consideration was whether the non-paying in defendant recovered his costs directly against the paying in defendant or against the claimant, who then recovered them against the paying in defendant.[15] Issues of that kind continue to arise, although under the case-managed system the presence of a particular party within the proceedings will have been addressed at an early stage. That results in a less mechanistic, more flexible and better informed approach to this kind of dispute as to costs. The making of an order as to costs on the giving of permission for acceptance of a Pt 36 payment will reflect that approach.

LATE PT 36 OFFER OR PAYMENT AND/OR LATE ACCEPTANCE

22–06 As already indicated,[16] the only circumstance in which a Pt 36 offer or Pt 36 payment can be accepted without obtaining the court's permission is when it is made at least 21 days before the trial and is then accepted within the time prescribed (usually 21 days from the date it was made). In every other case, the court's permission is required for acceptance unless the parties agree the liability as to costs.

22–07 So that an appreciation of the difference between the former practice and the new practice can be obtained, it is worth restating the approach to a late payment into court made by a defendant, or the late acceptance by a claimant of a timeously made payment into court, under the former rules. A late payment into court could be accepted by a claimant with the usual consequences as to costs at any time prior to the commencement of the trial.[17] A payment into court made in good time could be accepted by a claimant after the usual 21-day period, albeit only with the leave of the court, that leave almost invariably being granted provided his prospects of success had not materially worsened since the date of the payment into court and also upon the terms that the claimant paid the defendant's costs after the time for acceptance had expired.[18] Furthermore, the former rules permitted the making by a defendant of a payment into court (or an increased payment into court) after the trial had begun which the claimant could accept within two days and obtain his costs in consequence.[19]

22–08 In each of the foregoing situations the costs consequences of the acceptance of the payment into court were clear to both sides. That made evaluation of the offer constituted by the payment into court tolerably easy

---

[15] See, e.g. *Goldsworthy v Brickell* [1987] Ch. 378 at 418.
[16] See paras 18–14—18–16, above.
[17] See para.18–14, n.40, above. If the late payment into court was caused by the failure of the claimant to give proper particulars of and information to support his case, there might have been arguments on the taxation of costs about what was or was not recoverable. However, the principle was clear: the claimant could obtain his costs to be taxed if not agreed.
[18] See para.15–14, above.
[19] See para.18–14, n.41, above.

and the overall settlement the more easily achieved. The removal of the certainty offered by the former rules was potentially controversial: the creation of a degree of uncertainty, by requiring the court's permission for acceptance (a permission which, theoretically, could be withheld) and leaving open the court's discretion as to costs, could militate against the desired objective of encouraging the settlement of cases.

It should, of course, be recalled that the prime objective is the early settlement of cases.[20] The observance of pre-action protocols and the court's active intervention in the management of a case once proceedings have started are designed to ensure that the wherewithal to achieve early settlement of a case is available. If a defendant, for example, is not able to make an informed and worthwhile offer well before the trial, the court's case management functions will arguably have failed in their intended purpose. If a claimant is unable to evaluate an offer made well before the trial, the same comment might be made. To that extent it is, therefore, logical that the rules which provide the framework for a case-managed system of civil justice should not contain provisions the existence of which might constitute an encouragement to parties not to co-operate with that system.[21] In a nutshell, therefore, that is the rationale for the omission from the new rules of provisions similar to those in the old. 22–09

Notwithstanding the need for the rules to reflect the philosophy of early settlement, there will remain those cases which, even in the best case-managed system, will not be capable of settlement until shortly before or during the trial. Case management techniques are unlikely to reveal how well a witness is likely to perform before he or she takes to the witness box. A defendant who feels that the credibility of a main witness for the claimant is likely to be damaged significantly in cross-examination, but whose expectations in this regard are unfulfilled, may feel that the time has arrived when a significant advance on a previous offer is necessary. Equally, a claimant the credibility of whose case has been undermined substantially may look with longing at an unwithdrawn Pt 36 offer or Pt 36 payment. The court will undoubtedly from time to time be confronted with applications for permission to accept an offer or payment in this kind of situation. Equally, there will be cases where, for some reason, a defendant has not been willing or able to make an offer or Pt 36 payment until shortly before the trial which, as it happens, the claimant would like to accept. Where the liability for costs is agreed, then no problem exists in any of these situations.[22] How, though, will a court respond where there is no agreement as to costs? 22–10

---

[20] See Ch.13, above.
[21] See para.4.33 of the Minutes of the Civil Procedure Rule Committee meeting of September 17, 1998.
[22] See para.22–06, above.

22-11   It is, of course, impossible to give an answer that will cover every situation. In exercising any power given to it by the CPR, the court must seek to give effect to the overriding objective.[23] Save to the extent that the court will want to ensure that the issue left between the parties is dealt with justly, there is no real guidance to be obtained by reference to the overriding objective. It is, perhaps, possible to envisage a situation in which both parties have been at fault in causing the delay in addressing settlement and, accordingly, "the need to allot [the court's] resources to other cases" may have a bearing on the permission sought. However, the starting point in every case will be to proceed on the assumption that both parties are content with the sum of money or the terms offered, one of the terms in either case being that the court will decide on the order as to costs.[24] It is very difficult to envisage any situation in which the court would decline to grant a claimant permission to accept a Pt 36 offer or Pt 36 payment unless (i) the time for acceptance had expired and (ii) his prospects of success in the proceedings have materially worsened.[25]

22-12   In *Capital Bank Plc v Stickland*,[26] C, as mortgagee, brought proceedings against D for interfering with the bank's immediate right to possession of a British registered vessel over which it held a charge. The claim form was issued in early 2003 for delivery-up of the vessel or payment of its value, limited to £88,818.12, plus interest. In June 2003 C's solicitors made a Pt 36 offer offering to accept £85,000 including interest. D did not respond, but put in a defence in which the only point of substance taken was that the vessel in respect of which the proceedings were brought was not the same vessel as had been mortgaged to the bank. D did not respond when the offer was repeated in December 2003. He did not co-operate with C in relation to its desire to inspect the vessel or with orders of the court designed to facilitate this. However, in January 2004 C managed to inspect the vessel when it emerged that the vessel was clearly the mortgaged vessel. Two days before the trial fixed in February 2004 D purported to accept the offers made in June and December 2003 even though each had expired. D made an application at the trial, which was opposed by C, for permission to accept those offers. The judge refused the application on the grounds that the strength of the claim had altered for the better from the bank's point of view, the defendant's persistent flouting of the court's orders, the absence of any security for payment of the £85,000 if he were to decide that it could be accepted and the lateness of the application made on the day of the trial. The Court of Appeal upheld the exercise of the judge's discretion.

Longmore L.J. said,[27] rejecting the submission that permission to accept out of time should only be refused if a claimant withdraws or reduces his Pt 36

---

[23] CPR r.1.2.
[24] This kind of arrangement is not unknown: see paras 9–04–9–05, above. However, its disadvantage is the uncertainty of the outcome from the parties' point of view and the difficulty of knowing how to reach the correct conclusion from the court's point of view: *ibid*.
[25] The same approach would probably apply in respect of a claimant's Pt 36 offer also: r.36.12(2) and (3).
[26] [2004] EWCA Civ 1677.
[27] *ibid*. at [14].

offer (or a defendant applies to withdraw or reduces his payment-in and is allowed to do so), that "the court's discretion should not be narrowed by saying that it can only be exercised if a claimant is to be treated as withdrawing his offer (or if a defendant is to be regarded as entitled to withdraw or reduce his payment-in) but the discretion should rather be as wide as possible so as to advance the overriding objective of dealing with cases justly".[28] He added that the "fact that there has been a change of circumstance is certainly relevant and may well be the most important factor to be taken into account" and here new evidence (which D had been endeavouring to delay) emerged confirming the identity of the vessel.

So far as the question of costs is concerned, it is likely that the starting point would be the proposition that the claimant has had to bring the proceedings in order to obtain the offer made and that, accordingly, he is to be treated as the successful party and thus entitled to his costs.[29] If, however, the claimant was himself largely responsible for impeding the defendant's ability to make a reasonable offer until very late in the day, that would doubtless be a factor for the court to reflect in the costs order. The court's full discretion as to costs would exist in this situation and it would, presumably, be open to the offeror to raise any point as to the costs of the proceedings that he wishes when the offeree seeks permission from the court to accept the offer. 22–13

Because of the open-ended nature of the court's discretion on costs, it is likely that the parties will endeavour to agree who should bear the costs and to what extent. However, when the defendant is not minded to agree that the claimant should have all his costs (which would, of course, be subject to assessment in the absence of agreement as to the amount), it may be good practice for the defendant to spell out at the time he makes his late Pt 36 offer or Pt 36 payment how he would invite the court to exercise its discretion in the absence of agreement.[30] The court's discretion will not necessarily be exercised in that way, but this approach will enable the claimant to know (i) what would be acceptable to the defendant and (ii) the probable outer limit of any adverse costs consequences from his point of view. 22–14

---

[28] Referring with approval to para.18–11 in the Fifth edition of this work which contained the following proposition: "The guiding factor was the change, if any, in the plaintiff's prospects in the action between the date of the payment in and the date of the application for withdrawal. It is likely, it is thought, that this will still remain a central factor in the court's approach to any such application under the new rules. However, given the nature of case management and the obligation on the parties to help further the overriding objective it is possible that the court would entertain such an application on wider grounds. If, for example, a claimant failed to give proper disclosure of documents in support of his claim, that may afford grounds for concluding that it would be unfair to hold a defendant to a particular Part 36 payment".
[29] CPR r.44.3(2).
[30] See Precedent No.12 at para.A1–12, below.

CHAPTER 23

Failing to Beat a Pt 36 Offer or Pt 36 Payment

INTRODUCTION

23–01 A trial which achieves nothing more than had previously been offered can be an expensive affair. An appreciation of this fact constitutes an incentive to settle, except for the few with unlimited resources.[1] Although the former rules merely required the existence of a payment into court to be taken into account in the exercise of the court's discretion as to costs, it became the established practice that a payment into court was the dominant consideration in a damages claim.[2] The general rule was that a claimant who beat the payment into court obtained his costs,[3] but a claimant who did not, obtained his costs only to the date of the payment into court and had to pay the defendant's costs thereafter. Subject to minor modifications this general principle found expression in the CPR.

DEFENDANT'S OFFER—MONEY CLAIM

23–02 A defendant to a money claim must normally make a Pt 36 payment to secure the protection afforded by Pt 36.[4] If the claimant fails to "better"[5] a Pt 36 payment, the normal result will be that he will be ordered to pay the

---

[1] *Cutts v Head* [1984] Ch. 290; *Roache v News Group Newspapers Ltd*, *The Times*, November 23, 1992.
[2] See Fourth edition of this work, para.10–19.
[3] But see *Charm Maritime Inc v Elborne Mitchell*, referred to at para.24–02, below.
[4] However, see paras 18–02–18–07 above.
[5] CPR r.36.20(1)(a). "Matching" it may not suffice because he will have achieved no more by proceeding with his claim than he was previously offered: see n.14, below. In *Blackham v Entrepose UK* [2004] EWCA Civ 1109, the Court of Appeal affirmed the approach that had obtained prior to the CPR, namely that when comparing the value of a judgment obtained

defendant's costs "after the latest date on which the payment . . . could have been accepted without needing the permission of the court."[6] As the successful party[7] to that date, he will be entitled to his costs. Since the effect of the rules is to permit a claimant 21 days in which to give notice of acceptance,[8] it is more equitable that any costs reasonably incurred by him during that time (which will, of course, be subject to assessment) should be paid by the defendant. This may have an important bearing on the amount of costs actually payable if a Pt 36 payment is left until a date only just outside the 21-day period before trial.

The normal order referred to above will be made unless the court 23-03 "considers it unjust to do so".[9] The considerations to be taken into account in determining whether it would be "unjust" so to order are referred to below.[10]

DEFENDANT'S OFFER—NON-MONEY CLAIM

The equivalent of the need to "better" a Pt 36 payment in the context of a 23-04 Pt 36 offer is "to obtain a judgment which is more advantageous" than the offer.[11] During consideration of the CPR the word "materially" appeared before the word "advantageous" for a while. However, it was eventually rejected on the basis that it could lead to unnecessary argument.[12] The question, therefore, that a court needs to ask is simply whether the claimant has secured something "more advantageous" than was previously offered. Given the possible approach of the court to the bettering of a Pt 36 payment by only a minimal amount,[13] it is possible to envisage the need to ask the question in some cases whether the marginal advantage

---

following a trial with the value of a Pt 36 payment plus interest made previously, it is important to "compare like with like" (*per* Brooke L.J.) and not to allow the interest that has accumulated since the date of the Pt 36 payment to count in deciding whether the Pt 36 payment has been bettered. As it was put at para.10: "If the defendants paid in, say, £39,000 plus £1,000 interest calculated up to the last day when the claimant could have accepted the payment without having to obtain permission, then if the claimant only received at trial £38,800 plus £950 interest up to that date, he will not have bettered the Pt 36 payment. It would be a misuse of language to say that he bettered it because he received at trial £38,800 plus £950 plus a further £500 of interest between the date he should have accepted the payment in and the date of trial". At para.13, Brooke L.J. continued thus: "when a judge applies this rule he should first ask himself what the payment into court represented . . . and then consider whether the amount for which he has directed judgment to be entered, as compared with that payment, is less than that amount".

[6] CPR r.36.20(2).
[7] CPR r.44.3(2).
[8] See paras 18–13 *et seq.*, above.
[9] CPR r.36.20(2).
[10] See paras 23–08 *et seq.*, below.
[11] CPR r.36.20(1)(b).
[12] Minutes of Civil Procedure Rule Committee meeting of September 17, 1998, para.4.50.
[13] See paras 24–02—24–03, below.

conferred by the decision of the court over that which was previously offered is such as to warrant an order for costs in a claimant's favour.[14]

23–05 If the claimant fulfils the requirement of obtaining a judgment which is "more advantageous" than the offer, he will be awarded his costs. If he fails, the normal result in the case of an unbettered Pt 36 payment will arise[15] subject to the court ordering the contrary because it "considers it unjust" that the usual order is made.[16]

DEFENDANT'S OFFER—MIXED CLAIM[17]

23–06 Where a defendant offers, for example, an undertaking in response to a mixed claim (and makes no Pt 36 payment in relation to the money claim), or makes a Pt 36 payment in response to the money claim but offers no undertaking in response to the non-money claim,[18] the offer will fall to be judged initially by reference to whether the court awards some substantive relief on that part of the claim in relation to which no offer or Pt 36 payment was made. If the court does so, the claimant will have bettered the offer or obtained a "more advantageous" judgment than the defendant's offer. If, however, no substantive relief is awarded on that element of the claim then, subject to the Pt 36 offer or Pt 36 payment (whichever is relevant) being more advantageous or better than the court's award, the claimant will have failed in beating the defendant's offer of settlement. The normal order will presumably be made in that situation subject to the "unjust" proviso.[19]

23–07 Where the defendant makes an offer pursuant to CPR r.36.4,[20] each aspect of the offer will have to be judged by reference to the test applicable to the relevant part of the offer. Is the Pt 36 offer in respect of the non-money "more advantageous" than the court's award? Is the Pt 36 payment "better" than the court's award? If the claimant fails to beat both features of the offer of settlement, the normal order (subject to the "unjust"

---

[14] The test is not substantially different from that applied to *Calderbank* offers prior to the implementation of the CPR. The question posed by Sir Thomas Bingham M.R., as he then was, in *Roache v News Group Newspapers Ltd*, n.1, above, was as follows: "Who, as a matter of substance and reality, had won? Has the plaintiff won anything of value which he could not have won without fighting the action through to the finish?" This approach was subsequently adopted in *Butcher v Wolfe* and *Hobin v Douglas*, The Times, December 9 and 29, 1998, respectively. cf. *Everglade Maritime Inc. v The Schiffahrtsgesellschaft*, ("The Maria") [1993] Q.B. 780.
[15] See para.23–02, above.
[16] See para.23–03, above.
[17] See, generally Ch.19, above.
[18] see para.19–02, above.
[19] See para.23–08, below.
[20] See para.19–05, above.

proviso) will be made. Where the claimant beats one, but not the other, the court will doubtless have to take a much broader view of its discretion in relation to costs than the more mechanistic view that would derive from a failure to beat both parts of the overall offer.

DEPARTURE FROM GENERAL RULE ON GROUNDS OF INJUSTICE

As indicated above,[21] the normal order made upon the failure of a claimant to achieve more than a previous Pt 36 offer or Pt 36 payment can be displaced if the court "considers it unjust" for that order to be made. Pt 36 gives no direct guidance as such on what might make it unjust for the normal order to be made.[22] Since there is an argument for saying that a marginal improvement on a Pt 36 offer or Pt 36 payment should not necessarily entitle the claimant to all his costs,[23] there may be a countervailing argument that a very narrow "miss" should not result in the very significant penalty as to costs which the normal order might cause in a particular case.[24]   23–08

FAILING TO "BEAT" A CLAIMANT'S OFFER

It is debatable whether the failure of a defendant to secure an award to a claimant of less than the claimant's offer can truly be described as a failure to "beat" that offer. However, this is a convenient point to note the consequences that may arise in this situation.   23–09

A claimant can make a pre-action offer[25] or one that is made after the proceedings have begun. In essence he will be offering to settle at a lesser figure, or upon less onerous terms to the defendant, than appears in his claim. If the defendant accepts the offer the dispute is ended. If the defendant makes a counter-offer which the claimant accepts, the dispute also comes to an end. If, however, the claim proceeds unresolved, various   23–10

---

[21] See paras 23–03 and 23–05, above.
[22] *cf.* the position in relation to an award of enhanced interest and indemnity costs against a defendant when a claimant does better than his offer: see paras 23–14 *et seq.*, below. The factors specified in r.36.21(5) may well be applicable more generally than simply in relation to claimants' offers.
[23] See Ch.24, below.
[24] However, there are significant arguments against taking that kind of approach: see para.24–04, below. It is unlikely that the fact that the claimant is a child or a patient and that his compensation would be reduced substantially by the normal order would be a reason for holding the normal order to be "unjust": *Abada v Gray, The Times*, July 9, 1997, CA.
[25] See Ch.15, above.

possible outcomes may be envisaged. First, the claimant achieves less than his offer, but more than any offer or Pt 36 payment made by the defendant. In this situation, the claimant is still *prima facie* to be regarded as the successful party and entitled to his costs, subject to the court exercising its discretion in some way adverse to him if, for example, he "exaggerated his claim".[26] Secondly, the claimant may achieve less than his offer and less than the defendant's offer or Pt 36 payment. In this situation, it is likely that he will obtain his costs to the expiration of the period for acceptance of the defendant's offer or Pt 36 payment and that he will be ordered to pay the defendant's costs thereafter.[27] Finally, of course, the claimant may achieve more than his offer or simply match it. What consequences flow from this?

23-11 If the result of a trial was that despite any offer made by the claimant he merely obtained his costs in the normal way, there would be no incentive to him to make any concession by way of an offer, and little incentive to the defendant to accept it. Prior to the CPR, the court was, in some circumstances, prepared to award a claimant indemnity costs after the date of expiry of the offer if the offer was ultimately bettered at trial.[28] The rationale was, presumably, that an unreasonable refusal of a reasonable offer designed to obviate the need for the continuation of the proceedings should not leave the claimant out of pocket. The opportunity to make such an order has been provided for expressly in the CPR[29] in the event of the defendant being held liable for more, or upon terms more advantageous to the claimant, than the proposals contained in the claimant's offer.[30]

---

[26] CPR r.44.3(5)(b). In *Quorum AS v Schramm (No.2)* [2002] 2 Lloyd's Rep. 72, C offered to accept $3.6 million, excluding matters of interest, by way of a Pt 36 offer. D made a Pt 36 payment of $600,000. Judgment was given in C's favour for $1.4 million. Thomas J., as he then was, declined to make a comparison between the award and the various offers. He concluded that C had to come to court to obtain the award which bettered D's offer by a substantial amount and awarded C its costs.

[27] See paras 23-02—23-05, above. Occasionally, the argument is attempted that C should be penalised in some way in this situation. However, this would result in a claimant being better off by not making an attempt to settle through an offer of his own. That cannot be consistent with the objective of the CPR to encourage settlement.

[28] *McDonnell v Woodhouse and Jones*, The Times, May 25, 1995, Waterhouse J.

[29] CPR r.36.21(3)(a). In *P & O Nedlloyd BV v Utaniko Limited* [2003] EWCA Civ 174 (the appeal in the *East West Corpn case* (see n.55, below), the Court of Appeal emphasised that an appellant must make a new offer in the context of the appeal in order to be able to rely upon r.36.21 and could not seek to rely on a pre-trial Pt 36 offer.

[30] CPR r.36.21(1). The word "more" is used in sub-paras (a) and (b) of this rule. It follows that, strictly speaking, r.36.21 would not become engaged if the claimant merely matched his offer at trial. However, such an offer would clearly be seen to have been a reasonable one in the light of the result of the trial and one that the defendant ought to have accepted. Given that the court has power to award indemnity costs where a party has behaved unreasonably, and has the power to award interest at such rate as it considers just (see *Petrotrade Inc v Texaco Ltd*, n.41, below), there would be no reason why orders similar to those contemplated in paras (2) and (3) should not be made in this situation. Indeed, this is precisely the conclusion reached in *Read v Edmed* [2004] EWHC 3274 (QB), Bell J. C had offered to accept an

Somewhat more controversially, the CPR give the court the power in this situation to award a higher than normal rate of interest on any sum of money awarded and upon any indemnity costs awarded.[31] Indeed, they suggest that the court has an automatic obligation[32] to award a higher rate of interest on some part of the money award[33] and on the relevant part of the costs[34] unless it considers it unjust to do so. Subject to that latter proviso, there are two areas where the court has a discretion in operating

23–12

---

apportionment of liability between herself and D on the basis of 50/50. That was rejected, but was the conclusion of the court at trial. *Per* Bell J.: "In my judgment, as a matter of general principle, where in a relatively uncomplicated claim for damages for personal injury and consequential losses such as this, the claimant makes a valid Part 36 offer or other admissible offer to settle an issue of liability at a given proportion of his or her claim, and the defendant refuses that offer and the court gives judgment for precisely that proportion of the claim, the claimant should be entitled to the benefit of an award of indemnity costs from the time of expiry of the offer and some interest on those costs just as he or she would if Part 36.21 had applied to the matter, in order to ensure, so far as possible, that she is not out of pocket, unless there is some particular circumstance, for instance a significant change in the complexion of the case or some unreasonable conduct by or on behalf of the claimant, which would make that conclusion unfair". *cf. Roache v News Group Newspapers Ltd* (1992) C.A.T. 1120, where C obtained precisely what D had paid into court. See also Ch.24, below in relation to a "near miss" offer by a claimant. In *Mitchell v James* [2002] EWCA Civ 997 it is made clear that a claimant who chooses to make an offer as to costs as part of his offer to settle cannot rely on the costs element of the offer to try to bring himself within r.36.21. The rule relates to the substantive claim, not to the quantum of costs. See also *Bellamy v Sheffield Teaching Hospitals NHS Trust* [2003] EWCA Civ 1124: "An offer to settle should not include any terms as to costs which are inconsistent with Part 36 itself. If it does so, then the offer has to be treated as an offer outside Part 36, to which the provisions of CPR Pt 36.1(2) apply: see the observations of this court in *Mitchell v James*": *ibid.*, *per* Chadwick L.J. at para.7.

[31] The controversy arose from a perception that a claimant who is awarded higher interest on his damages if he "beats" his own offer is the recipient of a windfall or uncovenanted bonus arising, in effect, from a previously placed wager. The loser is a defendant who is merely exercising his right to contest the claim. Whilst these concerns continue to be entertained in some quarters, it should be borne in mind that the maximum level of additional interest potentially payable (10 per cent above base rate) is considerably less than was once proposed in relation to certain levels of award. In *Access to Justice, Interim Report* (July 1995) Lord Woolf had suggested that the uplift should be 10 per cent above the rate that would otherwise be awarded on awards up to £50,000, 5 per cent from £50,000 to £100,000 and then 2.5 per cent thereafter. In *Access to Justice, Final Report* (July 1996) he recommended 25 per cent above the rate otherwise payable on awards up to £10,000, 15 per cent from £10,000 to £50,000 and 5 per cent thereafter. The rate would thus taper on an award exceeding £10,000, a 5 per cent uplift on the normal rate being the maximum uplift once £50,000 was exceeded. The other area of controversy arises from the suggestion that the rule embodies a breach of Article 6 of the European Convention for the Protection of Human Rights and Fundamental Freedoms on the basis that there is an inequality of treatment as between a claimant and a defendant. That the argument has not been advanced significantly in the six years since the introduction of the CPR suggests that it may not be considered maintainable, although there are those who believe that Pt 36 is more favourable to claimants than to defendants.

[32] CPR r.36.21(4) provides that where r.36.21(1) applies "the court *will* make the orders referred to in paragraphs (2) and (3) unless it considers it unjust to do so" (emphasis added). This would seem to override the apparently discretionary nature of the power deriving from the use of the word "may" in r.36.21(2) and (3). Consistency of approach is achieved in this way. In *Petrotrade Inc v Texaco Ltd*, n.41, below, Lord Woolf M.R. said: "The provisions of Part 36.21(2) and (3) are important because without them Part 36 offers would be of no value to a claimant. Part 36.21(2) and (3) create the incentive for a claimant to make a Part 36 offer. It is for this reason that paragraph (4) of the rule is worded in

this provision: the first relating to the amount of the sum of money to which, and the period over which, the higher rate of interest is applicable; the second being in relation to the actual rate of interest itself.

A. The amount on which, and the period for which, increased interest is payable

23-13 The enhanced rate of interest may be ordered to be paid "on the whole or part of any sum of money (excluding interest)[35] awarded to the claimant ... or some or all of the period starting with the latest date on which the defendant could have accepted the offer without needing the permission of the court".[36] This gives the court a wide discretion in relation to the sum of money on which the increased interest can be paid. At the top end of the scale, the court could award increased interest on the whole amount of the award, not merely on the difference between the amount referred to in the offer and the amount of the award. Equally, it can relate to any part of the sum awarded. The period over which it can be ordered is, however, confined to the period after the offer could have been accepted without needing the court's permission. The court can choose the whole or part of that period.

B. The rate of interest

23-14 The rule provides that the interest capable of being awarded may be "at a rate not exceeding 10 per cent above base rate".[37] This means that the court may add up to 10 per cent to the applicable base rate. It does not mean that the court is restricted to adding merely 10 per cent of the applicable base rate.[38] The rule does not specify the date on which the base rate is to be determined. If it has varied during the period between the date when the claimant's offer could have been accepted without the court's permission and the date of the award, doubtless an average could be taken.

---

terms which requires the court to make the orders referred to in paragraphs (2) and (3) 'unless it considers it unjust to do so'". He added that it "should be appreciated, even in cases to which paragraph (4) applies, that the court retains a considerable discretion as to the period during which the rate at which interest should be payable".

[33] See para.23-13, below.
[34] Costs may be awarded on the indemnity basis in the circumstances provided for in this rule only "from the latest date when the defendant could have accepted the offer without needing the permission of the court": r.36.21(3)(a).
[35] Any interest included within the claimant's offer must be excluded from the operation of the rule otherwise interest on interest might be awarded. It should be noted that the power to award higher interest under this rule "is in addition to any other power it may have to award interest": r.36.21(6).
[36] CPR r.36.21(2).
[37] CPR r.36.21(2) and (3)(b).
[38] If the applicable base rate is, say, 6 per cent, the court could award interest up to the rate of 16 per cent. It would not be restricted to 6.6 per cent.

C. How are these choices made?

23–15 As with all powers conferred by the CPR, the court must seek to give effect to the overriding objective when it makes its choice.[39] That requirement, with the emphasis in the overriding objective of the need to save expense, connotes in the context of this rule a concern that the parties should have focused on the resolution of their dispute.[40]

23–16 The approach to the way in which r.36.21 is to be applied has been set out by the Court of Appeal in *Petrotrade Inc v Texaco Ltd*,[41] in which the leading judgment was given by Lord Woolf M.R., as he then was. It was a commercial case in which C had made a Pt 36 offer (to accept just short of $143,000 inclusive of interest) that was not accepted by D but which C bettered (by about $7,000) on a summary judgment application. Since r.36.21 applies only to a judgment obtained "at trial", the rule did not strictly apply to the situation that obtained at the conclusion of the summary judgment application. The Court of Appeal concluded that the judge had been wrong not to award indemnity costs and a higher rate of interest. The following general observations of Lord Woolf M.R. are of relevance in this context[42]:

23–17 "... it would be wrong to regard the rule as producing penal consequences. An order for indemnity costs does not enable a claimant to receive more costs than he has incurred. Its practical effect is to avoid his costs being assessed at a lesser figure. When assessing costs on the standard basis the court will only allow costs 'which are proportionate to the matters in issue' and 'resolve any doubt which it may have as to whether costs were reasonably incurred or reasonably

---

[39] CPR r.1.2.
[40] In *Richard Little v George Little Sebire & Co*, The Times, November 17, 1999, the following view was expressed: "Many of the features of the overriding objective are more directly applicable to the pre-trial and trial periods of a case than to a decision made after a case has effectively been concluded. On the other hand, since one of the factors mentioned in the overriding objective is the saving of expense, the powers conferred by the rules are likely to be interpreted by the Courts in a way that encourages settlement. Settlement is achieved only if parties focus properly on the strengths and weaknesses of their respective cases. The powers conferred by r.36.21 are plainly designed to sharpen that focus. Unless the discretions conferred by the rule are exercised in a way that makes a material, albeit proportionate, difference to the eventual award in the case, the rule itself would become redundant". This view must be read in the light of the subsequent authoritative decision of the Court of Appeal in *Petrotrade Inc v Texaco Ltd*, n.41, below, but, with diffidence, it is not thought that the essence of the view has been affected by that decision. See, in particular, the quotation from Lord Woolf M.R.'s judgment in n.32, above.
[41] [2000] C.L.C. 1341. *cf.* Moore-Bick J., as he then was, in *Earl v Cantor Fitzgerald International*, unreported, May 2000, where he said that "whereas an award of standard interest is intended to be purely compensatory, an award of enhanced interest is more in the nature of a penalty for failing to compromise the proceedings". See *Hussain v Heywood* [2001] 7 C.L. 73.
[42] [2000] C.L.C. 134 at [62]–[65].

proportionate in amount in favour of the paying party'. On the other hand, where the costs are assessed on an indemnity basis, the issue of proportionality does not have to be considered. The court only considers whether the costs were unreasonably incurred or for an unreasonable amount. The court will then resolve any doubt in favour of the receiving party. Even on an indemnity basis, however, the receiving party is restricted to recovering only the amount of costs which have been incurred (see Part 44.4 and Part 44.5).

23-18 The ability of the court to award costs on an indemnity basis and interest at an enhanced rate should not be regarded as penal because orders for costs, even when made on an indemnity basis, never actually compensate a claimant for having to come to court to bring proceedings. The very process of being involved in court proceedings inevitably has an impact on a claimant, whether he is a private individual or a multi-national corporation. A claimant would be better off had he not become involved in court proceedings. Part of the culture of the CPR is to encourage parties to avoid proceedings unless it is unreasonable for them to do otherwise. In the case of an individual proceedings necessarily involve inconvenience and frequently involve anxiety and distress. These are not taken into account when assessing costs on the normal basis. In the case of a corporation, corporation senior officials and other staff inevitably will be diverted from their normal duties as a consequence of the proceedings. The disruption this causes to a corporation is not recoverable under an order for costs.

23-19 The power to order indemnity costs or higher rate interest is a means of achieving a fairer result for a claimant. If a defendant involves a claimant in proceedings after an offer has been made, and in the event, the result is no more favourable to the defendant than that which would have been achieved if the claimant's offer had been accepted without the need for those proceedings, the message of Part 36.21 is that, *prima facie*, it is just to make an indemnity order for costs and for interest at an enhanced rate to be awarded. However, the indemnity order need not be for the entire proceedings nor, as I have already indicated, need the award of interest be for a particular period or at a particular rate. It must not however exceed the figure of 10 per cent referred to in Part 36.

23-20 There are circumstances where a just result is no order for costs or no interest even where the award exceeds an offer made by a claimant. Part 36.21 does no more than indicate the order which is to be made by the court unless it considers it is unjust to make that order. The general message of Part 36.21, when it applies, is that the court will usually order a higher rate of interest than the going rate. As to what the additional rate of interest should be, it is not possible to give specific guidance. Reference for general guidance has to be made to the terms of Part 36.21 and, in particular, to the provisions of paragraph (5)."

Later in his judgment Lord Woolf gave some further indications of the factors that might be relevant to determining the rate of additional interest if r.36.21 applies. He said this[43]: 23–21

> "If it is accepted that a court has power to depart from the going rate because of a claimant's offer, the question then arises as to what additional interest it would be appropriate to offer? Quite clearly it should not exceed the 10 per cent referred to in Part 36.21. The court would have to take into account all the circumstances in considering whether it would be just to make an order of enhanced interest. Those include the matters which are set out in Part 36.21(5) . . .
>
> The amount of the claim is . . . a relevant factor. If a claim is small, enhanced interest has to be at a higher rate than if the claim is large, otherwise the additional advantage for the claimant will not be achieved."[44]

The underlying rationale for r.36.21 was also the subject of consideration by the Court of Appeal in *McPhilemy v Times Newspapers Ltd*[45] where Chadwick L.J. said this: 23–22

> "It is plain . . . that paragraphs (2) and (3) of CPR 36.21—in conjunction with paragraph (4)—are intended to provide an incentive to a claimant to make a Part 36 offer. The incentive is that a claimant who has made a Part 36 offer (which is not accepted) and who succeeds at trial in beating his own offer stands to receive more than he would have received if he had not made the offer. Conversely, a defendant who refuses a Part 36 offer made by a claimant and who fails to beat that offer at trial is at risk of being ordered to pay more than he would have been ordered to pay if the offer had not been made. But those incentives have to be set in the context that . . . CPR 36.21 is not to be regarded as producing penal consequences. The powers conferred by the rule . . . are intended to provide 'a means of achieving a fairer result for a claimant' [quoting Lord Woolf's judgment above]. Exercise of the powers cannot achieve 'a fairer result' if it leads to the claimant receiving more than can properly be regarded as a full and complete recompense for having to resort to, to pursue and to endure the strain and anxiety of, legal proceedings. An exercise of the powers which led to the claimant receiving more than could properly be regarded as compensation, in that enlarged sense,

---

[43] *ibid.* at paras 75 and 77.
[44] See also n.31, above, and the quotation from Lord Woolf's Interim and Final Reports.
[45] [2001] EWCA Civ 933 at [19] and [21].

would, necessarily in my view, be penal in nature. It could only be supported on the basis that there was a need to punish the defendant by requiring him to pay an amount which went beyond any amount needed to compensate the claimant. But, subject to the limitation that the powers are intended to be used in order to achieve a fairer result for the claimant and not to punish the defendant, it is plain that they are to be used in order to redress elements, otherwise inherent in the legal process, which can properly be regarded as unfair."

His conclusion was that:

"the power to award interest under paragraph (2) of CPR 36.21 at an enhanced rate . . . is conferred in order to enable the court, in a case to which CPR 36.21 applies, to redress the element of perceived unfairness, otherwise inherent in the legal process, which arises from the fact that damages, costs (even costs on an indemnity basis) and statutory interest will not compensate the successful claimant for the inconvenience, anxiety and distress of having to resort to and pursue proceedings which he had sought to avoid by an offer to settle on terms which (as events turned out) were less advantageous to him than the judgment which he achieved."

23–23 In the same case Simon Brown L.J.[46] said that regarding the rule as "penal" and that exercising it implied "condemnation of the defendant's conduct" reflected a misunderstanding of the rationale of the rule. He said:

"It is not designed to punish unreasonable conduct but rather as an incentive to encourage claimants to make, and defendants to accept, appropriate offers of settlement. That incentive plainly cannot work unless the non-acceptance of what ultimately proves to have been a sufficient offer ordinarily advantages the claimant in the respects set out in the rule."

23–24 Notwithstanding those views, it would appear also that the nature of the defence put forward may be relevant,[47] as is the manner in which the claimant has advanced his case.[48]

---

[46] *ibid.* at para.28.
[47] *Petrotrade Inc v Texaco Ltd*, n.41, above, para.76. See also the comments of Moore-Bick J. in *Earl v Cantor Fitzgerald International*, n.41, above, where he said that "it is appropriate when exercising the discretion under paragraph (2) to take into account, among other things, the conduct of the defendant in pursuing the matter to trial". In the context of that case he said that he "did not think that [the defendant's] conduct in continuing the litigation" warranted "a maximum award of enhanced interest" against the background of a submission that the case "raised serious issues of fact and law". In that case, where the award exclusive of interest was taken to be £500,000, an award of the maximum enhanced interest (16 per cent) for the relevant period would have yielded an award of over £53,000. The enhanced interest was awarded at the rate of 5 per cent above base rate (11 per cent in total), yielding a rounded-down figure of £35,000.
[48] *Petrotrade Inc v Texaco Ltd*, n.41, above, at para.78.

23-25 Although in *Petrotrade* the Court of Appeal was unwilling to give specific guidance on what the additional rate of interest should be in any case,[49] it indicated that it would be wrong to take 10 per cent above base rate as the starting point.[50]

23-26 In relation to enhanced interest on any indemnity costs awarded, it is no answer to the claim for enhanced interest that, at all material times, the claimant had been in receipt of legal aid (and thus not personally out of pocket) and that an award of enhanced interest could only provide a windfall to the Legal Services Commission.[51]

UNJUST TO MAKE THE ORDER?

23-27 The logical sequence of questions for the court to ask and answer would seem to be as follows:

(i) Has the claimant exceeded[52] his offer?
(ii) If so, is it unjust for an order for enhanced interest to be made?
(iii) If not, what should the amount of that interest be, on what sum and for what period?

23-28 It is likely that (ii) and (iii) will merge to some degree. The court is obliged to "take into account all the circumstances of the case", including certain specific matters, in deciding whether it would be unjust to make the orders for enhanced interest and indemnity costs.[53]

---

[49] The award made was 4 per cent above base rate for a period of 12 months, that period running from the time that a judgment had been given in the Court of Appeal on a previous occasion in relation to the particular litigation. Awards at 4–5 per cent above base rate are fairly frequent.
[50] In *Richard Little and others v George Little Sebire & Co*, n.40, above, the following view was advanced in relation to the approach to be adopted to choosing the appropriate rate of enhanced interest: "Whilst there are a number of ways in which the issue might be approached, one that strikes me as appropriate is to start with the proposition that enhanced interest of 10 per cent above base rate will be awarded on the whole of the judgment sum (excluding interest) from the earliest date when it can be awarded and then to evaluate whether the effect of doing so will itself work an injustice or result in a disproportionate advantage to the claimant or a disproportionate disadvantage to the defendant". In that case the offer had been to accept £30,000 inclusive of interest and the award was for £50,000 inclusive of interest. In *Earl v Cantor Fitzgerald International*, n.41, above, Moore-Bick J. said that he was not "persuaded that the court should award the maximum amount by way of enhanced interest unless there is some reason not to do so", but agreed that "it is . . . necessary to stand back and consider whether, viewed in the round, any given award would provide a disproportionate benefit to the claimant or impose a disproportionate burden on the defendant". In *Petrotrade Inc v Texaco Ltd*, n.41, above Lord Woolf referred to *Richard Little v George Little Sebire & Co* and to the suggestion that "the court should take as the starting point 10 per cent above base rate" and said that it was not an approach he would endorse.
[51] *Earl v Cantor Fitzgerald International*, n.41, above *per* Moore-Bick J.
[52] Or, perhaps, "matched": see n.30, above.
[53] CPR r.36.21(5).

23-29   The specific matters to which the court will have regard are the terms of the offer and the stage in the proceedings in which it was made, the information available to the parties at the time of the offer and the conduct of the parties with regard to the giving or refusing of information for the purpose of enabling the offer to be evaluated.[54] The rule is doubtless designed to benefit the claimant who makes a bona fide attempt to settle his claim at a reasonable figure. A failure to supply proper information so that the offer can be evaluated can hardly be said to be acting bona fide. Equally, the court is likely to be slow to assist a claimant who formulates an enormous claim, but who offers to accept something very small by comparison and then achieves slightly more than that figure. Again, this would hardly seem to be bona fide negotiation. A claimant who puts forward a whole series of offers (perhaps all on the same date), hoping that one will be exceeded so as to attract the benefits of the rule, is unlikely to receive an enthusiastic response from the court either.

THE "TACTICAL OFFER"

23-30   The opportunity to secure enhanced interest on any damages awarded, indemnity costs and enhanced interest on the costs is one that a claimant and his advisers may strive to seize. Efforts to secure those advantages may go beyond merely seeking in good faith to put forward an offer based upon a genuine evaluation of the risks involved in the dispute. It is in this context that the "tactical offer" has emerged. It has to be recalled that an offer is an "offer to settle"—in other words, an offer to accept something less than the full value of the claim or the full award sought.[55]

---

[54] When judging whether to award indemnity costs and/or enhanced interest when a claimant betters his own Part 36 offer the court is enjoined to consider the "information available to the parties at the time when the Part 36 offer ... was made": r.36.21(5)(c). The importance of disclosure of information and documentation to enable an offeree to assess an offer has been emphasised: see, *e.g. Ford v GKR Construction* [2000] 1 W.L.R. 1397; *Amber v Stacey* [2001] 1 W.L.R. 1225. It can potentially have an impact on costs: see *Factortame Ltd v Secretary of State for the Environment* [2002] 1 W.L.R. 2438. However, if the court concludes that the absence of the information or documentation at the time of the offer made no difference to the offeree's decision not to accept it, then the costs implications are unlikely to be significant. It could have an impact on the question of whether to award indemnity costs other than in the circumstances of an offer to which r.36.21 applies: see paras 13–09–13–10, above. In *The Maersk Company Ltd v Wilson* [2004] EWCA Civ 313, the discretion was exercised against the claimant because the claimant succeeded in beating his own offer only by a late change of approach to the case.

[55] An offer by a claimant to accept 100 per cent of his claim would not constitute an "offer to settle" since settlement implies making some concession: see *East West Corpn v Dampskibselskabet (No.2)* [2002] 2 Lloyd's Rep. 222, where Thomas J., as he then was, said that to engage these provisions there must be some "offer to settle in the ordinary sense of the word". See also para.1–01, above. Even if such an offer is seen as an offer to settle, it will not have been "beaten" when 100 per cent liability is established at trial: see *Gaynor v Blackpool Football Club Ltd*, April 10, 2002, Oldham County Court, H.H. Judge Armitage Q.C. (report via Lawtel); *East West Corpn case*. An offer to accept 99.9 per cent of a claim would probably founder upon a similar basis: see *Huck v Robson*, n.57, below, at para.71. *Cf.* n.59, below.

The issue arises as to when an offer is to be regarded as merely 23–31
"tactical", in the sense of being made simply to try to secure the
advantages conferred by r.36.21, or when it is an offer that ought to be
recognised as a genuine offer.[56] In *Huck v Robson*[57] the claimant in a road
traffic accident case offered to accept a judgment for 95 per cent of the full
value of the claim, the only issue on liability being that of contributory
negligence. Although a finding of 5 per cent contributory negligence is
unknown, the majority of the Court of Appeal concluded that this should
be viewed as a genuine offer. Tuckey L.J. said:

> "[in] this type of litigation a Claimant with a strong case will often be
> prepared to accept a discount from the full value of the claim to reflect
> the uncertainties of litigation. Such offers are not usually based on the
> likely apportionment of liability but merely reflect the reality that most
> claimants prefer certainty to the ordeal of a trial and uncertainty about
> its outcome. If such a discount is offered and rejected there is nothing
> unjust in allowing the claimant to receive the incentives to which he or
> she is entitled under the Rules."

The dividing line between a genuine and a "tactical" offer is not easy to 23–32
determine. It needs to be acknowledged that even a one per cent discount
on a very large sum is itself a large sum.[58] A very small concession on the
line of a boundary in a boundary dispute could be regarded as a significant
matter. Each case will depend on its own facts, but it is submitted that the
court should not be too astute to characterise an offer as "tactical".[59]

---

[56] It is, perhaps, legitimate to ask the question whether it matters. In *Huck v Robson*, n.57, below, Jonathan Parker L.J. said that "in order to qualify for the incentives provided by paragraphs (2) and (3) of [r.36.21] a claimant's Part 36 offer must represent at the very least a genuine and realistic attempt by the claimant to resolve the dispute by agreement. Such an offer is to be contrasted with one which creates no real opportunity for settlement but is merely a tactical step designed to secure the benefit of the incentives".

[57] [2002] EWCA Civ 398.

[58] *cf. per* Bell J. in *Read v Edmed*, n.30, above, at para.27: "A one per cent or even a 0.1 per cent concession from a realistic apportionment can mean a four or five figure sum in the seven figure claims which are not uncommon today".

[59] *ibid.* at para.23, where there was anecdotal evidence that "it was the settled practice for litigators acting for claimants to make offers such as 49 per cent, 65 per cent, 74 per cent and so on, to guard against findings of one half, one third and one quarter and so on of contributory negligence because of the clear wording of Part 36.21". As Bell J. observed, at para.26, "it does seem to me to be absurd if the wording of 36.21(1) has led to a practice of claimants offering to take marginally less than 75, 50, 33.3 or 25 per cent, or some other familiar fraction, simply to gain the benefit of Part 36.21".

CHAPTER 24

Narrow Beating of, or Failure to Beat, a Pt 36 Offer or Pt 36 Payment

24–01 The normal consequences of bettering a Pt 36 offer or payment have been described previously.[1] The claimant will obtain his costs. Merely matching the offer will not, of course, result in it having been "bettered" and, accordingly, the claimant will face potentially the same consequences as if he had failed to achieve the same as had previously been offered.

24–02 The question arises as to whether the bettering of a Pt 36 offer or Pt 36 payment by a very narrow margin, particularly if the marginal success has been achieved at disproportionate expense, should entitle the claimant to all his costs. The issue was brought into relief by a case decided under the former rules.

> In *Charm Maritime Inc v Elborne Mitchell*,[2] C sued D, its former solicitors, for damages of approximately $20 million representing its alleged losses arising from D's negligence in permitting C's claim in another action to be dismissed for want of prosecution. The trial lasted 30 days. One of the main issues was whether an allegation of fraud in the earlier action would have been sustained. Detailed expert accountancy reports were prepared, and lengthy expert evidence was given, in relation to this issue. The net result was that C achieved a judgment for $841,070. D had made payments into court totalling $822,368, the final increase being made in August 1995 before the trial commenced in the Autumn: C, therefore, "beat" the payment into court by about $19,000. The trial judge said that, on the assumption (which had to be made for the purposes of her decision) that C had beaten the payment into court by a narrow margin, she would have ordered D to pay C's costs to the date of the payment in and thereafter that C should pay D's costs. The Court of Appeal held that this was a wrong approach as it involved a double penalty

---

[1] See paras 14–02, 23–01 and 23–05, above.
[2] (1997) C.A.T. 1363; [1997] C.L.Y. 555.

on C which was the successful party: on this approach C would have failed to obtain its own costs and additionally would have to pay those of the losing party. The just result was that C should have its costs to the date of the payment in and that thereafter there should be no order as to costs. Of this result, it was said—*per* Evans L.J.:

> "Where the plaintiff recovers more than the amount of the payment in, the defendant cannot say that the plaintiff has failed to beat it, and claim an order in his favour on that ground. But the Court can say to both parties, where the defendant has made a payment in but without admitting that that sum was due, 'You have each tried for a higher or a lower figure, and in practical terms neither of you has succeeded. You should each pay your own costs of the Court time you have used'".

Per Swinton Thomas L.J.:

> "the basic rule [is] that costs follow the event and ... a Plaintiff who recovers more than the payment in will recover his costs unless there are special circumstances or it appears to the court that some different order should be made. There remains a discretion which must be exercised judicially but the courts are not tied in a mathematical straight jacket. In this case the Plaintiff has ... beaten the payment in by a few thousand dollars. On the facts of this case ... any reasonable bystander or onlooker, if told that the Plaintiff had recovered a few thousand dollars more than [it] had been offered well before the trial began, would ... take the view that the Plaintiff should pay the costs incurred since the date the offer was made".

> However, in the circumstances of this case, bearing in mind that "the [Plaintiff was] clearly at fault in that [it] should have accepted the sum ... offered" and that "the Defendants were at fault in not paying into court the amount that was eventually recovered by the [Plaintiff], broad justice can be achieved between the parties ... by ordering that the Defendants pay the Plaintiff's costs to the date of the payment into court, and that each party should bear its own costs thereafter."

The final result in relation to costs in the foregoing case is hardly surprising: to spend 30 days of very expensive time to obtain two per cent more than had previously been offered in the context of what, on the trial judge's findings, was a vastly exaggerated claim was clearly disproportionate. The facts of the case were stark and are unlikely to be replicated, even closely, with any great frequency. However, the greater flexibility adopted by the courts in relation to costs under the CPR may mean that close attention will be paid to the cost of achieving only a fairly small advance on what had previously been offered. Disproportionate costs in achieving only a marginal improvement on a Pt 36 offer or Pt 36 payment may make it appropriate for the general rule to be modified.[3] Whilst the

24–03

---

[3] See para.14–02, above. In the type of situation considered in the text, it would be open to the offeror, whose offer or Pt 36 payment had been beaten, but only just, to invite the court to exercise its discretion to make "a different order" from the normal order: r.44.3(2)(b). The provisions of r.44.3(4) and (5) would need to be applied in considering the offeror's

circumstances of every such case would vary, an order in the nature of that made in the *Charm Maritime* case would often do broad justice to the situation.

24-04   If the court is prepared to entertain the kind of argument foreshadowed above in relation to a narrow victory for a claimant, is there scope for a similar argument on the part of a claimant who narrowly fails to achieve what had previously been offered? There is no doubt that the discretion to modify the normal rule exists.[4] There may well be cases where the court would be tempted to try to ameliorate the consequences of the normal result of failure to better an offer or Pt 36 payment. A situation where the court is likely to be concerned would be where a severely disabled claimant "misses" a Pt 36 payment by only a very modest amount and the result of the normal costs order would be to reduce or even obliterate desperately needed compensation. It remains to be seen whether the greater flexibility of the new rules will permit this kind of argument to be advanced successfully.[5] The difficulty lying in the way of permitting it to succeed is that the defendant who has successfully judged the likely award of the court and who has made its arrangements around that judgment will suffer a financial penalty. Indeed, defendants may question whether there is much purpose in making a Pt 36 payment at all. Furthermore, any latitude given to a claimant in this kind of situation may encourage others not to address a reasonable offer with suitable care. The objective of early settlement on reasonable terms will be frustrated if too much benevolence is shown.

24-05   The jurisdiction to depart from the normal rule in either of the two situations referred to above plainly exists. It is, however, suggested that it would only be in exceptional circumstances that any significant departure from the normal or general rule would be entertained.

---

argument. The court will doubtless have in mind its powers under r.44.3(6) in this context. See also *Firle Investments Ltd v Datapoint International Ltd* [2001] EWCA Civ 1106; and *Kinetics Technology v Cross Seas Shipping*, unreported, 16 February 2001, David Steel J.

[4] See para.23-08, above.
[5] But see *Abada v Gray*, referred to in Ch.23, n.24.

CHAPTER 25

Miscellaneous Matters Relating to Pt 36

INTRODUCTION

This chapter deals with a number of miscellaneous matters arising from Pt 36. 25–01

PART 20 CLAIMS

Any claim other than one made by a claimant against a defendant is known as a "Part 20 claim". It includes a counterclaim by a defendant against the claimant or some other party, a claim by a defendant against any person (whether or not already a party) for contribution, indemnity or some other relief, and a claim made by someone against whom a Pt 20 claim has been made.[1] A Pt 20 claim is treated by the rules as if it were a claim[2] and, accordingly, Pt 36 applies to any such claim. 25–02

The effect of these provisions is to make it normally necessary for a defendant to a Pt 20 claim in which there is a money claim to make a Pt 36 payment if he wishes to protect his position in relation to costs.[3] A claim by an original defendant against another party for an indemnity or contribution in relation to a money claim brought against him would seem to be a money claim in its own right. On that basis, in general terms, a Pt 36 payment would normally need to be made to ensure protection on costs. However, the defendant to the Pt 20 claim may be in some difficulty in 25–03

---

[1] CPR r.20.2(1).
[2] CPR r.20.3(1).
[3] CPR r.36.3(1). However, see paras 18–03 *et seq.* above.

doing this. He may, for example, be prepared to contribute to, say, 50 per cent of the claimant's claim, but may have a different view as to the quantum of that claim than the view formed by the original defendant to that claim. That would make the assessment of what sum to pay into court very difficult. The sum paid in could be accepted by the original defendant who then either negotiates a settlement with the claimant, or secures a judgment from the court, in a sum less than the assessment of quantum made by the defendant to the Pt 20 claim. If the Pt 20 defendant is prepared to take that risk, then there is no problem in making a Pt 36 payment. If, on the other hand, he wishes merely to offer a proportion of the claimant's claim without making a Pt 36 payment,[4] it is likely that the purposive construction to be given to the rules[5] and the overall flexibility within Pt 36,[6] ought to allow such an offer to be made and to be effective on the question of costs.

25–04 A defendant to a Pt 20 claim who is thereafter joined as a defendant to the principal claim can, of course, make a Pt 36 payment against the original claimant's claim. If accepted by that claimant, that will end the dispute between them, although the original defendant may still be able to pursue a claim for a further contribution from the defendant who has settled with the claimant, but who remains a defendant to the Pt 20 claim.[7]

SMALL CLAIMS

25–05 Because of the limited costs provisions in relation to cases on the small claims track,[8] Pt 36 does not apply to small claims cases.[9] Rule 36.2(5) provides that a Pt 36 offer or a Pt 36 payment "shall not have the consequences set out in this Pt while the claim is being dealt with on the small claims track unless the court orders otherwise".

25–06 The foregoing provision is not designed to discourage offers of settlement, or payments into court, in relation to small claims cases. It merely provides that the automatic consequences of a Pt 36 offer or Pt 36 payment will not apply whilst a claim is on the small claims track. The proviso that the court may order otherwise is designed to enable the court to make a suitable order where, for example, a defendant has spent a considerable amount of money in costs in relation to an inflated claim which is subsequently reduced and transferred to the small claims track.[10]

---

[4] Which is permitted in non-money claims: r.36.5(4).
[5] CPR r.1.2(b).
[6] CPR r.36.1(2). See paras 18–05—18–07, above.
[7] *cf. Harper v Gray and Walker* [1985] 1 W.L.R. 1196. See paras 6–26 *et seq.*, above.
[8] CPR r.27.14(2), (3) and (4).
[9] CPR r.27.2(1)(g).
[10] Minutes of the Civil Procedure Rules Committee meeting, September 17, 1998, para.4.8.

PROVISIONAL DAMAGES

Where a defendant faces a claim which includes a claim for provisional damages, he has two options: he can either make a Pt 36 payment without offering to agree to an award of provisional damages or he can make a Pt 36 payment and at the same time specify whether he will agree to an award of provisional damages.[11] When he chooses the latter course, his Pt 36 payment notice[12] must so specify.[13] He must also give the appropriate details required by the rules so that the claimant will know the basis of the offer.[14]

25-07

Where the defendant makes a Pt 36 payment and offers to agree to a provisional damages award, and the claimant gives notice of acceptance within the usual 21-day period, the normal costs consequences[15] will result unless the court orders otherwise.[16]

25-08

If the claimant accepts the Pt 36 payment on the basis offered, he must apply to the court within seven days of doing so for an order for an award of provisional damages.[17] If the court makes the award,[18] the money in court will be paid out.[19]

25-09

PERIODICAL PAYMENTS AWARD IN A PERSONAL INJURY CASE

In a personal injuries case where there is a claim for future pecuniary loss, the court now has jurisdiction to award the damages wholly or in part by way of periodical payments.[20] An addition to Pt 36 (r.36.2A) has been made to enable offers effective on costs to be made in such cases.[21] An offer can be in the form of either a lump sum or periodical payments or a

25-10

---

[11] CPR r.36.7(1) and (2).
[12] See Chs 16 and 18, above.
[13] CPR r.36.7(2).
[14] CPR r.36.7(3).
[15] See para.21-04, above.
[16] CPR r.36.7(4).
[17] Pt 41 provides the machinery whereby this application is made.
[18] Since an award of provisional damages is, strictly speaking, a discretionary matter (*Willson v Ministry of Defence* [1991] 1 All E.R. 638), the court could theoretically decline to make an award notwithstanding the agreement of the parties. However, this would be a very unusual course to adopt.
[19] CPR r.36.7(6).
[20] The provisions of ss.100 and 101 of the Courts Act 2003 came into force on April 1, 2005 giving the power for the courts to order periodical payments in all cases where orders or settlements had not been made before April 1. The power to order variable periodical payments applies only to proceedings issued on or after April 1, 2005.
[21] See Appendix 2 at para.A2-03, below.

combination of both, but for the offer to be effective it must be made "by way of a Pt 36 offer under this rule".[22] Where the offer includes a lump sum then "it will not have the consequences set out in [Part 36] unless a Part 36 payment of the amount of the lump sum is also made.[23] A Part 36 offer to which r.36.2A applies must contain certain details about the terms of the offer.[24] Where a defendant makes a Pt 36 offer in accordance with r.36.2A by which there is an offer of both a lump sum and periodical payments, the claimant can only accept the offer as a whole.[25]

CONVERTING AN ORDERED PAYMENT INTO COURT TO A PT 36 PAYMENT

25–11 A party may be ordered to pay money into court under the CPR for various reasons.[26] Where that happens, the party may convert that enforced payment into court into a Pt 36 payment if he wishes to do so. All that he needs to do is to file a Pt 36 payment notice in accordance with r.36.6.[27] The court will serve it unless he notifies the court at the time of filing the Pt 36 payment notice that he intends to do so.[28]

APPORTIONMENT OF MONEY ACCEPTED IN SETTLE-MENT OF A FATAL ACCIDENTS ACT CLAIM

25–12 The CPR require the apportionment of a single sum of money paid into court in satisfaction of claims under the Fatal Accidents Act and the Law Reform (Miscellaneous Provisions) Act 1934 between the two claims.[29] The same requirement applies in relation to the claims of dependants under the Fatal Accidents Act 1976.[30]

---

[22] CPR r.36.2A(4) and r.36.2A(2).
[23] CPR r 36.2A(2). This phraseology follows closely that set out in r.36.3: see para.18–01, above. It is a moot point as to whether the need for a Part 36 payment in such a situation is to be regarded as mandatory: see paras 18–03—18–07, above.
[24] CPR r.36.2A(5)
[25] CPR r.36.2A(7).
[26] Under Pt 24 the court can make a conditional order on a summary judgment application requiring the defendant to pay a sum of money into court: Pt 24 Practice Direction, para.5. Further, under the general powers of case management, the court can order the payment of a sum of money into court: r.3.1(3) and (5). Although r.37.2(1) says that where a defendant makes a payment into court "following an order made under r.3.1(3) or 3.1(5) he may choose to treat the whole or any part of the money paid into court as a Part 36 payment", it is not thought that the intention was to restrict the ability to convert a payment into court solely to payments into court made under the rules thus specified.
[27] CPR r.37.2(2) and Pt 37 Practice Direction, para.3.2.
[28] CPR r.36.6(3).
[29] CPR r.37.4(1).
[30] CPR r.37.4(3).

CHAPTER 26

Offers outside Pt 36

Attention has already been drawn to the possibility that a party may, for whatever reason, deliberately choose not to make his offer of settlement within Pt 36.[1] For example, a party may wish to commence negotiations without the threat that, if his offer is not accepted, it may be referred to the court on the issue of costs or, if a claimant's offer, carry with it the prospect of enhanced interest and indemnity costs.[2] A straightforward "without prejudice" offer[3] may be advanced in the early stages of trying to resolve a dispute and it is, of course, possible that a party might choose to make a traditional *Calderbank* offer[4] in an ordinary piece of civil litigation.[5] Settlement meetings, whether with or without the intervention of a mediator, have become common events in all forms of litigation and they are invariably conducted on a "without prejudice" basis. For these reasons, and for the reason that Pt 36 offers[6] are treated automatically as "without prejudice except as to costs",[7] it is necessary to have an appreciation of the limits and effect of the "without prejudice" privilege. This will be dealt with in Ch.27, below. 26–01

For present purposes, it is proposed to put forward a brief review of the law and practice applicable to the relevance and, where appropriate, assessment of three types of offer which, strictly speaking, fall outside Pt 36: 26–02

(i) a "without prejudice" offer;

---

[1] See para.14–03, above.
[2] See paras 23–09 *et seq.*, above.
[3] See para.26–04, below.
[4] See para.26–05, below.
[5] The *Calderbank* offer is still the effective form of offer utilised in family finance proceedings: see Ch.34, below.
[6] See Ch.17, above.
[7] See para.14–06, above.

(ii) a *Calderbank* offer; and
(iii) an open offer.

26–03 It is important to note at the outset that the CPR provide that the court "must have regard to . . . any . . . admissible offer to settle made by a party which is drawn to the court's attention (whether or not made in accordance with Part 36)" in deciding what order, if any, to make about costs.[8] A party is, therefore, entitled to draw to the court's attention any admissible offer to settle which falls outside Pt 36 when inviting it to consider how to exercise its discretion as to costs, and the court must take it into account.

A "WITHOUT PREJUDICE" OFFER

26–04 It has long been an established principle that an offer made "without prejudice" cannot be referred to on the question of costs without the consent of both parties.[9] It follows that a pure "without prejudice" offer is not admissible on any issue as to costs[10] without the consent of both parties. The privilege afforded to "without prejudice" negotiations may be set aside in certain situations,[11] but the underlying philosophy of the rule is to enable "cards on the table" negotiations to take place without the fear that concessions made for the purposes of trying to reach an accommodation can then be used at trial to the disadvantage of the party making them.[12]

A *CALDERBANK* OFFER

26–05 This is an offer expressed to be "without prejudice except [or save] as to costs". In other words, it is intended to have all the features of a pure "without prejudice" offer,[13] but enables reference to it to be made on the issue of costs if it is not accepted. An offer of settlement of this nature first gained more widespread recognition following a Family Division case,[14]

---

[8] CPR r.44.3(4)(c).
[9] *Cory v Bretton* (1830) 4 C. & P. 462; *Paddock v Forrester* (1842) 3 Man. & G. 903; *Hoghton v Hoghton* (1852) 15 Beav. 278 at 321; *Jones v Foxall* (1852) 15 Beav. 388 at 396; *Walker v Wilsher* (1889) 23 Q.B.D. 335; *Statesbury v Turner* [1943] K.B. 370; *Computer Machinery Company Ltd v Drescher* [1983] 1 W.L.R. 1379 at 1382–1383; *Cutts v Head* [1984] Ch. 290; *Muller and Muller v Linsley and Mortimer* (1996) 1 P.N.L.R. 74.
[10] But see n.7 to para.14–03, above.
[11] See paras 27–15 *et seq.*, below.
[12] See para.27–02, below.
[13] See para.26–04, above and Ch.27, below.
[14] *Calderbank v Calderbank* [1976] Fam. Law 93. It is extraordinary that Mrs Calderbank should have lent her former husband's family name (probably in perpetuity if the Chancery Division permits it) to something which she never in fact did! Her effective offer for the purposes of costs was an open one. See also *McDonnell v McDonnell* [1977] 1 W.L.R. 34. The approach of courts exercising this jurisdiction to offers of this nature is discussed more fully in Ch.34, below.

although it had been used fairly widely in other Divisions, and its use had been commended and encouraged.[15] A challenge to the validity of such an offer in relation to costs failed in *Cutts v Head*[16] and, following that case, both the Rules of the Supreme Court and the County Court Rules were extended to make express provision for an offer of this nature.[17] The *Calderbank* offer is the blueprint for the Pt 36 offer.[18] A *Calderbank* offer is, of course, admissible on the question of costs and must, accordingly, be taken into account by the court if it is justified to do so.[19]

26–06 Shortly before the CPR came into force[20] the Court of Appeal had the opportunity to review the practice applicable to the assessment of a *Calderbank* offer in relation to the question of costs.[21] For an offer to have been effective in relation to the costs of the litigation the essential test is that propounded by Sir Thomas Bingham M.R., as he then was, in *Roache v News Group Newspapers Ltd*,[22] where he said this:

> "The judge must look closely at the facts of the particular case before him and ask: Who, as a matter of substance and reality, has won? Has the Plaintiff won anything of value which he could not have won without fighting the action through to a finish? Has the Defendant substantially denied the Plaintiff the prize which the Plaintiff fought the action to win?"[23]

26–07 The review of *Calderbank* offers in ordinary civil litigation shortly prior to the introduction of the CPR led to the rejection of the approach that had been adopted hitherto, namely that the recipient of such an offer was under no duty to seek clarification of the offer if it was unclear or ambiguous or to engage in any further negotiation.[24] This approach was rejected as being "altogether too narrow and inflexible".[25] Some meaningful engagement would thus be required.

---

[15] *Computer Machinery Company Ltd v Drescher* [1983] 1 W.L.R. 1379 at 1382–1383, *per* Sir Robert Megarry V.C. Under the RSC the court would not, however, declare at an interlocutory stage that such an offer will be considered on the question of costs in due course: *Corby District Council v Holst & Co Ltd* [1985] 1 W.L.R. 427, CA. *Cf.* Ch.18, n.20A, above.
[16] [1984] Ch. 290.
[17] RSC Ord.22, r.14; CCR Ord.11, r.10.
[18] See para.14–06, above.
[19] See para.26–03, above.
[20] April 26, 1999.
[21] *Butcher v Wolfe*, unreported, October 30, 1998; *Hobin v Douglas*, unreported, December 3, 1998.
[22] (1992) C.A.T. 1120.
[23] This test was accepted as the correct test in the two cases noted in n.21, above.
[24] *C & H Engineering v F. Klucznik & Son Ltd* [1992] F.S.R. 667 (Aldous J.).
[25] In *Butcher v Wolfe*, n.21, above, *per* Simon Brown L.J.

AN OPEN OFFER

26–08 This means exactly what its title conveys: it is not the subject of the privilege associated with the expression "without prejudice" and is available for all to see at all times. It is usually made or confirmed in a letter. It could be made in a witness statement prepared for the purposes of an interim application. It is not unknown for it to be made or confirmed by an advocate during the course of proceedings.

26–09 The particular value of the open offer (other, of course, than on the question of costs) is that it serves to demonstrate to the tribunal dealing with the substantive case (or any interim application) that a party who might otherwise be thought to be adopting a wholly unreasonable stance in the litigation is not doing so.[26] It also obviates the embarrassment caused by a witness who, forgetful of previous advice, refers to a "without prejudice" proposal. Its disadvantage is that the terms of the offer are known to the tribunal which might be influenced (or, more likely, be thought to be influenced) accordingly. The tendency, therefore, amongst practitioners is to reserve the making of such an offer to a case where it is felt that the offeree is being unduly optimistic of the outcome of the case and that there is virtually no prospect of the offer being bettered by the ultimate decision of the tribunal.

26–10 One important matter arising from the existence of an open offer is the extent, if any, to which the tribunal is entitled to draw inferences from it about the merits of the case or to which the claimant is entitled to point to it (or cross-examine upon it) for such purpose. There seems to be no direct authoritative guidance on the point. Clearly, if the open offer contains an express admission of fact, that fact could without more be relied upon. Equally, an express concession of an issue is clearly available for consideration. But can it go further than that? Does the opening of the offer enable investigation of the basis upon which the offer was made?

26–11 One reason for upholding the traditional meaning given to a "without prejudice" offer is to prevent the use by the party to whom it is made of the existence of the offer as some form of admission.[27] Arguably, discarding the "without prejudice" tag (which is, of course, the choice of the offeror) could legitimately lead to an investigation of the sort contemplated above. On the other hand, most questions asked in pursuance of such an investigation would trespass on the privilege given to legal advice and other

---

[26] In *Sampson v John Boddy Timber Ltd*, noted at para.27–11, below, Evans L.J. said that an open offer might be used by the party making it "to claim credit for being reasonable if no settlement is achieved and the dispute comes to trial".

[27] See para.26–04, above.

communications relating to litigation.[28] Each case would doubtless depend upon its own circumstances and, in particular, the phraseology of the communication making the offer.[29] But it is thought that, generally speaking, little, if any, investigation of the offer would be permitted and few, if any, inferences drawn from its existence.

---

[28] *Phipson on Evidence*, (16th ed., 2005), Ch.24.
[29] See the views of Sir Thomas Bingham M.R. on the without prejudice letter in *Sampson v John Boddy Timber Ltd*, n.26, above. An open letter from a defendant in a defamation action offering to make an apology on terms may be highly relevant to the issue of damages and can, therefore, be referred to and form the subject of questions to the plaintiff: *Dixons Stores Group Ltd v Thames Television Plc* [1993] 1 All E.R. 349 (Drake J.). Presumably, such a letter could be the subject of questions to the defendant.

CHAPTER 27

The "Without Prejudice" Rule

INTRODUCTION

27–01 The true foundation of the "without prejudice" rule has traditionally been seen as lying partly in public policy and partly in the express or implied agreement of the parties to the relevant negotiations.[1] In *Muller and Muller v Linsley and Mortimer*,[2] Hoffmann L.J., as he then was, having referred to *Cutts v Head*,[3] said this:

> "*Cutts v Head* shows that the rule has two justifications. First, the public policy of encouraging parties to negotiate and settle their disputes out of court and, secondly, an implied agreement arising out of what is commonly understood to be the consequences of offering or agreeing to negotiate without prejudice. In some cases both of these justifications are present; in others, only one or the other."

27–02 The net effect of negotiations being without prejudice is that, subject to certain exceptions,[4] a privilege[5] attaches to the content of those negotiations rendering their content inadmissible at the trial of the action to the settlement of which they were directed.

27–03 A number of issues need to be addressed in the context of the "without prejudice" rule. They can be enumerated as follows:

(i) When are negotiations without prejudice?

---

[1] *Cutts v Head* [1984] Ch. 290 at 306; *Rush & Tomkins Ltd v Great London Council* [1989] 1 A.C. 1280 at 1300; *Unilever Plc v The Procter & Gamble Company* [2000] 1 W.L.R. 2436 at 2442.
[2] (1996) 1 P.N.L.R. 74 at 77.
[3] [1984] Ch. 290.
[4] See paras 27–15 *et seq.*, below.
[5] *Sampson v John Boddy Timber Ltd*, noted at para.27–11, below, *per* Sir Thomas Bingham M.R., the relevant quotation from whose judgment appears in para.27–05, below.

(ii) When will the without prejudice veil be lifted or disregarded?
(iii) When will the disclosure of documents be protected by operation of the rule?
(iv) When can without prejudice negotiations be referred to at interim applications?
(v) At what stage in proceedings may objection be taken to a proposal to adduce evidence of the content of without prejudice negotiations?

WHEN ARE NEGOTIATIONS WITHOUT PREJUDICE?[6]

Negotiations may be conducted in many ways: by correspondence (whether by letters exchanged in the post, DX, by hand, facsimile or e-mail), orally (by telephone, in a specially arranged meeting or outside court) or in any combination. Parties may, of course, have agreed to alternative dispute resolution (ADR) or mediation.[7] However the negotiations are conducted, the House of Lords has made it clear in *Rush & Tompkins Ltd v Greater London Council* that genuine negotiations with a view to settlement are protected from disclosure whether or not the without prejudice stamp has been applied expressly to the negotiations. Lord Griffiths put the matter thus[8]:

27–04

> "The ['without prejudice'] rule applies to exclude all negotiations genuinely aimed at settlement whether oral or in writing from being given in evidence. A competent solicitor will always head any negotiating correspondence 'without prejudice' to make clear beyond doubt that in the event of the negotiations being unsuccessful they are not to be referred to at the subsequent trial. However, the application of the rule is not dependent upon the use of the phrase 'without prejudice' and if it is clear from the surrounding circumstances that the parties were seeking to compromise the action, evidence of the content of

---

[6] A thorough and helpful analysis of without prejudice communications and the earlier UK and Commonwealth authorities was made by Professor David Vaver, (1974) *University of Columbia Law Review*, 85. Although some of the learning in this article has now been overtaken by later authorities, it remains a "learned" and "exhaustive" analysis of the earlier cases (*per* Robert Walker L.J. in *Unilever Plc v The Procter & Gamble Company*, n.1, above, at 2445) and merits attention by all interested in this field. See also McEwan, "Without Prejudice—Negotiating the Minefield" (1994) 13 C.J.Q. 133.
[7] See paras 13–10 *et seq.*, above and see Ch.43, below.
[8] [1989] 1 A.C. 1280 at 1299. See also *Sampson v John Boddy Timber Ltd*, noted at para.27–11, below. The expression "genuinely aimed at settlement" means that the negotiations are aimed at the avoidance of litigation: *Forster v Friedland* (1992) C.A.T. 1052, noted at para.27–30, below, *per* Hoffmann L.J; *cf. The Prudential Insurance Company of America v The Prudential Assurance Company Limited* [2002] EWCA Civ 1154.

27–05   The impression of the without prejudice stamp upon the negotiations may, therefore, either be expressly achieved or impliedly so from the fact that the parties are genuinely seeking to compromise their dispute. This statement of principle lays to rest the possibility of an argument that the failure to use the well-known phrase "without prejudice" means that the party making the offer (or otherwise being engaged in negotiations) intends the offer (or negotiations) to be open. It follows that any party who wishes an offer of settlement to be regarded as an open one[9] must say so expressly. In *Sampson v John Boddy Timber Ltd*,[10] Sir Thomas Bingham M.R. said that "the rule is clear that unless a party makes plain its intention that such an offer should be treated as an open offer it is covered . . . by the cloak of privilege".

EXPRESS STIPULATION

27–06   The most common means by which negotiations are rendered without prejudice is by express stipulation to this effect. A letter, fax or email will be headed "without prejudice" or the position made clear at some suitable point within it. A telephone conversation in which negotiations are conducted will be prefaced with words such as "these discussions are 'without prejudice' and so would any offer made". Provided the material in the negotiations is such that the law permits the cloak of privilege to cover it,[11] an express stipulation of this nature will, of course, be upheld by the court.[12] It has also been held that a later letter may *ex post facto*, declare an earlier one to have been without prejudice.[13]

---

[9] See para.26–08, above.
[10] (1995) C.A.T. 552. In *Cheddar Valley Engineering Ltd v Chaddlewood Homes Ltd* [1992] 1 W.L.R. 820, Jules Sher Q.C., sitting as a deputy High Court judge, held that where one party to without prejudice negotiations wishes to change the basis of the negotiations and to make an open offer, it is incumbent on that party to spell out that changed basis to the other party with clarity. It was, however, said that if this changed basis "is made in circumstances in which the change would be brought home to the mind of a reasonable man in the position of the recipient of that information that would be enough". It was further suggested that the mere use of the word "open" may not be enough. It should, perhaps, be observed that these views were expressed in the context of a case where the representative of the party wishing to make the "open" offer did indeed use that expression when the relevant telephone call was made, but it was accepted that the legal executive receiving the offer did not hear it or realise its significance. The facts were somewhat unusual and, it is submitted, the use of the word "open" would in most circumstances operate to displace the without prejudice basis of the negotiations simply because it is a word the significance of which would be understood by the vast majority of practitioners.
[11] See paras 27–15 *et seq.*, below.
[12] *Rush & Tompkins Ltd v GLC*, n.8, above; *Walker v Wilsher* (1889) 23 Q.B.D. 335.
[13] *Peacock v Harper* (1887) 26 W.N. 109. In the light of *Rush & Tompkins Ltd v GLC*, n.8, above, it is thought that the inadvertent omission of the words without prejudice would not require some subsequent rectification if the parties were engaged in genuine negotiations with a view to settlement.

IMPLIED STIPULATION

Where the first of a series of letters is marked "without prejudice" it is likely that the rest of the series will be regarded impliedly as of the same character[14] unless it appears that there is a clear break in the chain of the subsequent correspondence showing that the privilege is not claimed.[15] Where without prejudice negotiations take place and it is agreed that further information should be obtained from a third party, the court may hold that the resulting documents are impliedly without prejudice and cannot be referred to.[16]

27–07

The statement of principle in *Rush & Tompkins Ltd v GLC*[17] applies to negotiations conducted by parties to a dispute, whether or not assisted by legal advisers. The character of the discussions, not the character of the participants, leads to the application of the "without prejudice" rule.[18]

27–08

"OPENING SHOTS"

As is plain from the foregoing discussion, communications (including specific offers) in negotiations genuinely aimed at settlement are generally protected from revelation at any subsequent trial of the action in the event that the negotiations do not produce a resolution. The question has arisen from time to time as to whether an "opening shot" or an intimation of a willingness to negotiate is similarly privileged. It is, perhaps, axiomatic that discussions cannot be treated as being "aimed at settlement" if at the time they take place there is no dispute (or no extant dispute) to settle.[19] The dividing line between that situation and one when the first tentative steps

27–09

---

[14] *Paddock v Forrester* (1842) 3 Man. & G. 903; *Re Harris* (1875) 32 L.T. 417.
[15] *India Rubber, Guttapercha, and Telegraph Works Company Ltd v Chapman* (1926) 20 B.W.C.C. 184, CA. See, however, the comment made in n.13, above. The case of *Dixons Stores Group Ltd v Thames Television Plc* [1993] 1 All E.R. 349 can be seen as a practical manifestation of this principle.
[16] *Rabin v Mendoza & Co* [1954] 1 W.L.R. 271 at 293, *per* Denning L.J., who referred to a "tacit agreement" that the documents should not be used to the prejudice of either party.
[17] [1989] 1 A.C. 1280.
[18] This also lays to rest consideration of the question of whether negotiations between members of the Bar and/or the solicitors' profession are impliedly without prejudice merely because of the professional status of the participants in the negotiations. See, *e.g. Chocoladefabriken Lindt & Sprungli AG v Nestle Co* [1978] R.P.C. 287 at 289, where Megarry V.C. recalled his experience of practice at the Bar which was to the effect that discussions "outside the doors of the Court" were never expressed to be without prejudice because it was "so plain . . . that the discussions were upon that footing".
[19] *Re Daintrey Ex p. Holt* [1893] 2 Q.B. 116 at 119. And see *Standrin v Yenton Minster Homes Ltd* (1991) C.A.T. 634 and *Buckingham County Council v Moran*, noted at para.27-12, below.

towards negotiations are taken may not always be that easy to determine. Cases on each side of the line are to be found reported.

27-10 In *South Shropshire District Council v Amos*,[20] C, as claimant, made a claim for compensation against the district council pursuant to s.120 of the Town and Country Act 1971 following a discontinuance order in respect of the business use of premises occupied by C. C's agents submitted a substantial document to the district council's district valuer containing full particulars of the claim with submissions in support of the claim. It was headed "without prejudice". The submission of this document had been preceded by a direct communication from C to the district council which stated that he wished the amount of compensation "to be negotiated with his agent". The Court of Appeal held that, given C's expressed intention to negotiate, the common practice for such claims to be the subject of negotiation before referral to the Lands Tribunal and a concession that there had been an ongoing dispute prior to the submission of the document, the document was protected by the without prejudice privilege even though it was an "opening shot".

27-11 In *Sampson v John Boddy Timber Ltd*,[21] an issue arose in a wasted costs application as to the status of a letter written by D's insurers. C had been injured at work and, through solicitors, intimated a claim against D. D's insurers, in a standard form letter, sought details of the claim which C's solicitors provided promptly. After a delay of some weeks C's solicitors wrote to D's insurers asking if they "were prepared to deal with the matter", failing which an application for legal aid would be made. D's insurers wrote back in the following terms:

> "We have now completed our investigations into the circumstances of your client's accident and confirm that we are prepared to negotiate a settlement on a compromise basis, arguing that your client ought not to have used the platform as a means of access. If you will provide us with a copy of any medical evidence you have in this case . . . our representative will arrange to discuss [the case]".

C's solicitors responded saying that they looked forward to meeting the insurers "and engaging in further negotiations". Eventually, some negotiations took place, but no agreement was reached. At the trial, at which liability was contested by D, C's counsel sought to rely upon the initial letter as an admission of liability subject to an argument about contributory negligence. The Court of Appeal held that the letter was to be regarded as without prejudice even though not marked as such. Sir Thomas Bingham M.R. stated: "the letter was a bona fide offer by the insurers to explore the possibilities of settlement on a compromise basis". Evans L.J. stated: "the letter was intended as an acknowledgement and as an offer to negotiate". Aldous L.J. stated: "the use of the words 'negotiate a settlement on a compromise basis' indicate that the writer was attempting to negotiate a settlement".

---

[20] [1986] 1 W.L.R. 1271. The Court of Appeal disapproved *Norwich Union Life Insurance Society v Tony Waller Ltd* (1984) 270 E.G. 42 (Harman J.). In *Schering Corporation v Cipla Ltd* [2004] EWHC 2587 (Ch), Laddie J. ruled as inadmissible an "opening shot" in seeking to initiate negotiations about a possible infringement of patent. C had sought to rely upon a without prejudice letter to obtain an injunction preventing an alleged infringement of patent.
[21] (1995) C.A.T. 552.

In *Buckinghamshire County Council v Moran*,[22] a plot of land acquired in **27-12**
1955 by C for possible use for a proposed road diversion adjoined D's
property. In 1967 D's predecessors in title began using the plot of land for
their own purposes. In 1971 D acquired the property together with such rights
as the vendors may have had over the plot of land. D continued to use the plot
as his own. In late 1975 C questioned D's use of the plot of land and he
replied in January 1976 saying that it had always been his "firm understanding
that the [plot] should be kept by the owner of the [property] if and until the
[proposed road diversion] was built". The letter was marked "without
prejudice". C challenged this view in subsequent correspondence, but took no
action to evict D from the the plot of land. In proceedings for possession
commenced by C in October 1985 D argued that he had acquired title to the
plot by adverse possession. The question of the admissibility of D's letter of
January 1976 arose. The Court of Appeal held that the letter was not an
"opening shot" in negotiations: it was an assertion of D's rights and contained
no or no clear indication of a willingness to negotiate.

"PARTING SHOTS" AND RESPONSES TO WITHOUT PREJUDICE LETTERS

Whilst examples from decided cases are thin on the ground, it would not **27-13**
be impossible to conceive of a situation where an issue as to the
admissibility of a closing salvo in an exhange of correspondence might
arise. The test must be similar to that relating to "opening shots",[23] namely
whether the letter is part of a sequence of correspondence aimed at the
avoidance of litigation or whether it merely represents an assertion of the
rights of the sender of the letter. However, an obstacle in the path to
admissibility is the fact that most letters of the nature described will be in
response to without prejudice letters and thus will be privileged from
exposure as a result.[24]

The question of the evidential significance or otherwise of letters written **27-14**
in response to without prejudice letters arises from time to time. The
answer to the question is normally quite straightforward: any letter in
response to a without prejudice letter will itself form part of the negotiations and thus will be privileged. The privilege, albeit to a degree imposed

---

[22] [1990] 1 Ch. 623. In *Standrin v Yenton Minster Homes Ltd*, (1991) C.A.T. 634, Lloyd L.J., after referring to *Norwich Union Life Insurance Society v Tony Waller Ltd, South Shropshire District Council v Amos* and *Buckinghamshire County Council v Moran*, said as follows: "The principle to be derived from those authorities, if it can be called a principle, is that the opening shot in negotiations may well be subject to privilege where, for example, a person puts forward a claim and in the same breath offers to take something less in settlement, or ... where a person offers to accept a sum in settlement of a yet unquantified claim. But where the opening shot is an assertion of the person's claim and nothing more than that, then prima facie it is not protected".
[23] See para.27–09, above.
[24] See para.27–14, below.

by the sender of the first letter, is in fact that of the writer of the response. Unless the writer of the response waives the privilege, the other party is not entitled to refer to it.[25] The same principles applies in respect of *Calderbank* offers.[26] The recipient of a *Calderbank* offer has no right to refer to that letter on any issue, including the issue of costs. The privilege remains that of the maker of the *Calderbank* offer.

WHEN WILL THE WITHOUT PREJUDICE VEIL BE LIFTED OR DISREGARDED?

27-15 The circumstances in which communications are properly to be regarded as without prejudice have been considered. In the course of that review it has emerged that unless at the time of the relevant communications there was an extant dispute between the parties, the communications are not covered by the privilege.[27] This does not in reality form any kind of exception to the "without prejudice" rule: it represents a manifestation of circumstances in which the rule never truly comes into play. When attention is focused upon apparent departures[28] from the rule, a somewhat similar analysis is revealed.[29]

27-16 When seeking to identify the circumstances in which the revelation of the contents of what are apparently without prejudice communications may be permitted, it is necessary to have regard to the underlying rationale for the "without prejudice" rule.[30] In *Rush and Tomkins v GLC*[31] Lord Griffiths said,[32] "the rule is not absolute and resort may be had to 'without prejudice' material for a variety of reasons when the justice of the case requires it".

27-17 The House of Lords endorsed the following appraisal of the rule by Oliver L.J., as he then was, in *Cutts v Head*[33]:

> "That the rule rests, at least in part, upon public policy is clear from many authorities, and the convenient starting point of the inquiry is

---

[25] See, *e.g. C & H Engineering v F. Klucznik & Son Ltd* [1992] F.S.R. 667 at 669–670.
[26] See paras 26–05 *et seq.*, above.
[27] See paras 27–19 *et seq.*, below.
[28] See paras 27–20 *et seq.*, below.
[29] See para.27–19, below.
[30] In *Muller and Muller v Linsley and Mortimer*, noted at para.27–49, below, Hoffmann L.J., as he then was, said that "[Some] of the decisions on the without prejudice rule show a fairly mechanistic approach, but the recent cases, most notably . . . *Cutts v Head* . . . and *Rush & Tomkins v G.L.C.* . . . . are firmly based on the analysis of the rule's underlying rationale". For Hoffmann L.J.'s extremely clear appraisal of the apparent exceptions to this rule and their relationship with its underlying rationale, see para.27–19, below.
[31] [1989] 1 A.C. 1280.
[32] *ibid.* at 1300.
[33] *ibid.*, quoting from [1984] Ch. 290 at 306.

the nature of the underlying policy. It is that parties should be encouraged so far as possible to settle their disputes without resort to litigation and should not be discouraged by the knowledge that anything that is said in the course of such negotiations (and that includes, of course, as much the failure to reply to an offer as an actual reply) may be used to their prejudice in the course of their proceedings. They should, as was expressed by Clauson J. in *Scott Paper Co. v Drayton Paper Works Ltd* [1927] 44 R.P.C. 151 at 156, be encouraged fully and frankly to put their cards on the table ... The public policy justification, in truth, essentially rests on the desirability of preventing statements or offers made in the course of negotiations for settlement being brought before the court of trial as admissions on the question of liability."

Lord Griffiths said that the "underlying purpose of the rule ... is to protect a litigant from being embarrassed by any admission made purely in an attempt to achieve a settlement".[34] He also emphasised[35] that the rule applies to "a genuine attempt to reach a settlement" and to "genuine negotiations". 27–18

The foregoing statement of the rationale for the rule was analysed further by Hoffmann L.J., as he then was, in *Muller and Muller v Linsley and Mortimer*,[36] when considering the basis for exceptions to the rule. That analysis forms an authoritative backdrop to the discussion of certain of the exceptions to the general rule. Hoffmann L.J. said this[37]: 27–19

"If one analyses the relationship between the without prejudice rule and the other rules of evidence, it seems to me that the privilege operates as an exception to the general rule on admissions (which can itself be regarded as an exception to the rule against hearsay) that the statement or conduct of a party is always admissible against him to prove any fact which is thereby expressly or impliedly asserted or admitted. The public policy aspect of the rule is not ... concerned with the admissibility of statements which are relevant otherwise than as admissions, *i.e.* independently of the truth of the facts alleged to have been admitted.

Many of the alleged exceptions to the rule will be found on analysis to be cases in which the relevance of the communication lies not in the

---

[34] [1989] 1 A.C. 1280 at 1300. In *Muller and Muller v Linsley and Mortimer*, noted at para.27–49, below, Hoffmann L.J. said that "the public policy rationale is ... directed solely to admissions".
[35] [1989] 1 A.C. 1280 at 1301 and 1305.
[36] (1996) 1 P.N.L.R. 74.
[37] *ibid.* at 79–80. This analysis did not purport to deal with the exception based upon the revelation of "unambiguous impropriety" perpetrated during without prejudice negotiations to which Hoffmann L.J. referred to in *Forster v Friedland*: see para.27–36 below.

truth of any fact which it asserts or admits, but simply in the fact that it was made. Thus, when the issue is whether without prejudice letters have resulted in an agreed settlement, the correspondence is admissible because the relevance of the letters has nothing to do with the truth of any facts which the writers may have expressly or impliedly admitted. They are relevant because they contain the offer and acceptance forming a contract which has replaced the cause of action previously in dispute. Likewise, a without prejudice letter containing a threat is admissible to prove that the threat was made. A without prejudice letter containing a statement which amounted to an act of bankruptcy is admissible to prove that the statement was made: *Re Daintrey*. Without prejudice correspondence is always admissible to explain delay in commencing or prosecuting litigation. Here again, the relevance lies in the fact that the communications took place and not the truth of their contents. Indeed, I think that the only case in which the rule has been held to preclude the use of without prejudice communications, otherwise than as admissions, is in the rule that an offer may not be used on the question of costs; a rule which, as I have said, has been held to rest purely upon convention and not upon public policy.

This is not the case in which to attempt a definitive statement of the scope of the purely convention-based rule, not least because . . . it depends upon customary usage which is not immutable. But the public policy rationale is, in my judgment, directed solely to admissions."

A. The fact of agreement

27–20 On Hoffmann L.J.'s analysis, the evidence showing that an agreement had been concluded is simply relevant to a fact that needs to be proved and there is no countervailing public policy requirement that the evidence to support the fact should be excluded. On any analysis it has always been the position that the contents of without prejudice negotiations can be revealed and considered by the court if an issue arises as to whether an agreement has been concluded.[38] The whole purpose of the privilege would be negated if it were not possible to lift the veil on the negotiations to determine whether an agreement had crystallised. If the result of that determination is that no agreement was concluded, the veil can be drawn again over the contents of the negotiations.[39]

---

[38] *Rush & Tomkins Ltd v GLC* [1989] 1 A.C. 1280; *Tomlin v Standard Telephones* [1969] WLR 1378.
[39] The misconception does still exist amongst some practitioners (and, perhaps, more widely amongst lay persons) that an agreement reached in without prejudice negotiations is not binding until confirmed by an "open" agreement. This is not so: see para.3–67, above.

B. Delay and adverse inferences from apparent lack of communication

Reference to the existence (though not normally the contents) of without prejudice communications may be made to rebut any suggestion of delay or laches[40] or, it seems, any adverse inference upon which a party seeks to rely derived from the apparent lack of correspondence or discussion of an issue.[41]

27–21

C. Where a without prejudice document would prejudice the recipient

It is often said that a without prejudice communication cannot be used to the disadvantage of the recipient. This proposition is derived from the case of *Re Daintrey Ex p. Holt*.[42] It is not wholly clear whether the principle underlying the case should be regarded as being in a different category of exception to the general rule from that referred to below (threats, abuse of rule and lack of good faith), or whether it should be seen as one example of the court not permitting the "without prejudice" rule to be abused.

27–22

> In *Re Daintrey Ex p. Holt*,[43] C commenced proceedings against D for recovery of a sum of money. In a letter headed "without prejudice", sent a short while after, D offered to compound the debt due from him to C. He also stated that he was unable to pay his debts and would suspend payment unless the composition was accepted. C presented a bankruptcy petition relying upon the letter as an act of bankruptcy. It was held[44] that the letter was admissible to prove the act of bankruptcy. It was said[45] that it was not possible to give a notice of bankruptcy without prejudice because "the document in question was one which, from its character, might prejudicially affect the recipient whether or not he accepted the terms offered thereby".

27–23

Hoffmann L.J. regarded this as an illustration of the principle that the evidence necessary to prove the fact of an act of bankruptcy was admissible. Whilst that may indeed be so, it is respectfully submitted that

27–24

---

[40] *Walker v Wilsher*, n.12, above.
[41] *McFadden v Snow* (1952) 69 W.N. N.S.W. 8; *Pitts v Adney* [1961] N.S.W.R. 535.
[42] [1893] 2 Q.B. 116.
[43] *ibid.*
[44] Vaughan Williams and Bruce JJ.
[45] [1893] 2 Q.B. 116 at 120. In *Cutts v Head*, n.3, above, both Oliver L.J. and Fox L.J. treated *Re Daintrey* as establishing that a without prejudice letter cannot be used to the disadvantage of the recipient. Oliver L.J. also said (at 304–305) that the Divisional Court in bankruptcy had, in holding that the letter was admissible, "relied upon the fact that there was no dispute and no offer of compromise". In fact, although stating that the existence of a dispute was necessary before a letter headed without prejudice could be regarded as such, the Divisional Court regarded the existence of the proceedings, commenced shortly prior to the letter, as constituting a "dispute" for this purpose: see [1893] 2 Q.B. 116 at 120.

Re Daintrey may, on one view, simply be seen as an exception to the general rule which is not easily categorised. Another view is that "the real point of the decision is that the veil was never there in the first place".[46] It is, however, a decision that has stood unchallenged for over 100 years and, it is thought, will probably be followed on similar or analogous facts.

D. Matters independent of or collateral to the subject-matter of the dispute

27–25 Although not referred to expressly in Hoffmann L.J.'s appraisal, an admission of a fact independent of, or collateral to, the subject-matter of the instant dispute between the parties has traditionally been treated as admissible in evidence subsequently to prove that fact. The foundation of this exception to the general rule is the ancient case of *Waldridge v Kennison*.[47] In that case an admission by one of the parties to a without prejudice discussion that his handwriting appeared on the bill of exchange upon which the action was based was held to be admissible evidence on that issue. Lord Kenyon C.J. justified the exception to the general rule on the grounds that "it was a matter no way connected with the merits of the cause, and which was capable of being easily proved by other means".

27–26   In *Rush & Tompkins Ltd v GLC*[48] Lord Griffiths made the following observation on *Waldridge v Kennison*:

> "I regard this as an exceptional case and it should not be allowed to whittle down the protection given to the parties to speak freely about all issues in the litigation both factual and legal when seeking compromise and, for the purpose of establishing a basis of compromise, admitting certain facts. If the compromise fails the admission of the facts made for the purpose of the compromise should not be held against the maker of the admission and should not therefore be received in evidence."

27–27   Vaver[49] draws attention to a case which would seem to illustrate a clear example of an admission which was rightly received in evidence:

> In *Barden v Barden*,[50] C and D were brothers who had been co-defendants in an action against them to recover judgment for goods supplied. During a

---

[46] *Unilever Plc v The Procter & Gamble Company* [2000] 1 W.L.R. 2436 at 2448, *per* Robert Walker L.J. But see n.45, above.
[47] (1794) 1 Esp. 142.
[48] [1989] 1 A.C. 1280 at 1300.
[49] See n.6, above.
[50] (1921) 21 S.R.N.S.W. 588, S.C.; *cf. Field v Commissioner for Railways for New South Wales* (1957) 32 A.L.J.R. 110. See also *McDowall v Hirschfield Lipson & Rumney* [1992] 2 F.L.R. 126.

without prejudice discussion between C and D, on the one hand, and the solicitor representing the plaintiff in the action, on the other, designed to discover whether D was also liable for the debt, D admitted that C was entitled to a half-share in a wheat-crop growing on certain land. This was irrelevant to the subject-matter of the discussion. Subsequently, C sued D for a declaration that the two had been partners in connection with the crop of wheat and sought to rely upon the admission. It was held that he was entitled to rely on the admission because it had nothing to do with the issues in the then pending action, but was only incidental thereto.

E. "Unambiguous impropriety"

The expression "unambiguous impropriety" is a convenient generic description applied to a variety of things said or done during without prejudice negotiations which may, in certain circumstances, be admitted in evidence. It was first used by Hoffmann L.J. in *Forster v Friedland*[51] and has since become part of the legal lexicon in this context. It may be helpful to put this exception to the general rule in its historical context.   27–28

In a brief review of circumstances in which the "without prejudice" tag may be disregarded by the court, Lord Griffiths in *Rush & Tompkins Ltd v GLC*[52] referred to the case of *Kitcat v Sharp*[53] as authority for the proposition that a threat will not be subject to the privilege. In fact that case involved letters written by a defendant to a clergyman plaintiff, marked "private and confidential", in which he threatened to publish the statement of claim with his abusive marginal comments appended to it to, amongst others, the plaintiff's bishop. The court treated this as a threatened contempt of court and granted the plaintiff an injunction. Whilst analogous to a threat made in a without prejudice letter, it is not, perhaps, the most direct example. Vaver[54] draws attention to two Commonwealth cases where threats, lack of good faith and abuse of the rule led the court to disregard the without prejudice tag: 27–29

> In *Underwood v Cox*,[55] a brother secured the agreement of his sister to, in effect, a rearrangement of the terms of their late father's will under a threat to expose the alleged illegitimacy of one of her children. The threat was made in a letter marked "without prejudice" which was sent in an envelope marked "Personal". When the brother sought to enforce the agreement the sister   27–30

---

[51] See para.27–36, below. In *Unilever Plc v The Procter & Gamble Company* [2000] 1 W.L.R. 2436 at 2444, Robert Walker L.J. identified an exception to the general rule as being one where "one party may be allowed to give evidence of what the other said or wrote in without prejudice negotiations if the exclusion of the evidence would act as a cloak for perjury, blackmail or other 'unambiguous impropriety'".
[52] See n.8, above.
[53] (1882) 48 L.T. 64 (Fry J.).
[54] See n.6, above.
[55] (1912) 4 D.L.R. 66 (Ontario Div. Ct.).

alleged misrepresentation, fraud, intimidation, undue influence and *non est factum*. When the brother denied the threats in cross-examination the trial judge disallowed reference to the letter because it had been written without prejudice. The Divisional Court held, without hesitation, that the letter should have been exposed since it contained no bona fide inducement to settle but a "dishonourable threat".

27-31 In *Greenwood v Fitts*,[56] D, during without prejudice negotiations, told C that if the matter went to trial he would perjure himself if necessary and bribe witnesses to perjure themselves to defeat the claim. He further threatened to leave the jurisdiction if C obtained judgment so as to defeat their entitlement. The trial judge disallowed C's attempt to rely on these matters to impeach D's credibility. The Court of Appeal held that the material should have been admitted since the without prejudice rule was never intended to protect threats of this nature. The evidence would tend to show that D did not believe that he had a good case or that on the issue in the case (i.e. whether D had made a fraudulent representation) he was not telling the truth.

27-32 In his commentary on these two cases, Vaver says this:

> "Compromises are regularly induced by such considerations as the desire to preserve good relations between the parties (especially if they are commercial men), the supposed weaknesses of a party's case, the supposed strength of the opponent's case, the costs and risks of litigation, etc. These are part and parcel of settlements in everyday life. On the other hand, misrepresentations, libels, threats of insolvency or bankrupcy in the event of non-acceptance, blackmail, threats of perjury, suborning or flight from the jurisdiction must all amount to the sort of improper pressure which ought to be admitted in evidence if relevant to some matter in issue—this notwithstanding they occur during 'without prejudice' negotiations."[57]

---

[56] (1961) 29 D.L.R. 260 (British Columbia Court of Appeal). See also *Kurtz and Co. v Spence & Sons* (1877) L.J.Ch. 238 (a patent case). In the latter case, D contended that C's manufacture of sulphate of alumina infringed D's patent and, during without prejudice negotiations to resolve the dispute, threatened legal proceedings if the manufacture was not abandoned. The Patents, Designs and Trade Marks Act 1883, s.32 enabled a party who was not in fact infringing the legal rights of a person claiming to be a patentee of an invention, to bring an action against that person if that person had himself threatened proceedings for infringement of patent. Kekewich J. held that C was entitled to rely upon D's threat for the purposes of injunction proceedings against D. This case was, it is submitted, one which turned very much on the application of the relevant statutory provisions and could not have been seen as having any wider application. Indeed, in *Unilever Plc v The Procter & Gamble Company* [2000] 1 E.L.R. 2436 at 2450, it was held that the decision "should no longer be regarded as good law".

[57] (1974) *University of British Columbia Law Review* 85 at 152-153.

The issue to which matters of this nature would go in most instances 27–33
would be the belief or otherwise in the merits of his case by the party
engaging in such conduct.[58] In the second edition of this work[59] it was
suggested that the two Commonwealth cases should influence an English
court in similar or analogous situations. Examples can be given:

> In *Finch v Wilson*,[60] C had sold D one of two adjacent plots of land and, by
> a separate contract, had undertaken to construct upon it a bungalow for the
> occupation of D. Various disputes arose and C brought an action for the
> unpaid balance of the price under the building contract. D contested C's right
> to this sum and counterclaimed for damages, including damages in respect of
> the cost of employing another builder to finish the works. C alleged that they
> were entitled to extensions under the building contract. A further element of
> D's counterclaim was for an injunction restraining C from carrying out threats
> made of assaults and trespass. One of the allegations made was that at a
> without prejudice meeting between C and D and their respective solicitors, C1
> had threatened that he would "ruin the lives of [D] and their family if the
> issues between him and them were not resolved". An order for exchange of
> proofs was made pursuant to the then RSC Ord.38, r.2A. D's solicitor had
> made a proof dealing with the circumstances of the without prejudice meeting
> and, *inter alia*, referred to C1's threats of the ruination of D's lives by
> harrassment derived from C's intention to occupy the adjoining plot of land.
> As a preliminary point, C objected to the admissibility of this aspect of the
> proof. H.H. Judge Stannard, Official Referee, held:
>
> (a) that the evidence was relevant both to the allegation of alleged threats
>   of trespass and assault and to the question of C's belief or otherwise in
>   the strength of their case; and
> (b) that "since the purpose of the [without prejudice] privilege is only to
>   protect negotiations bona fide entered into for the settlement of
>   disputes", threats of the nature involved in the instant case were not
>   privileged and the passage in the proof was admissible in evidence.

> In *Hawick Jersey International Limited v Caplan*,[61] C claimed repayment of 27–34
> a loan to D of £10,000 made by means of a cheque. D denied that the
> transaction was a loan because he had supplied £10,000 cash. D secretly tape-
> recorded a without prejudice meeting at which:
>
> (a) C did not dispute (and indeed accepted) D's repeated assertions that
>   the transaction was not a loan but one involving an exchange for
>   £10,000 in cash; and

---

[58] In *Moriarty v London, Chatham and Dover Railway Company* (1870) 5 Q.B.D. 314 at 319, Cockburn C.J. said that the: "conduct of a party to a cause may be of the highest importance in determining whether the cause of action . . . or the ground of defence . . . is honest and just . . . [I]t is always evidence which ought to be submitted to the consideration of the tribunal which has to be judged of the facts".
[59] See Ch.9, p.112.
[60] Unreported, May 8, 1987.
[61] *The Times*, March 11, 1988. In *Forster v Friedland*, noted at para.27–36, below, Hoffmann L.J. said that a party cannot use the without prejudice rule "as a cloak for blackmail" and, having referred to *Greenwood v Fitts* and *Hawick Jersey International Ltd v Caplan*, described them as "clear cases of improper threats".

(b) C expressly or impliedly said that the proceedings were brought to persuade D to reach a fairer settlement and to settle other differences.

Anthony May Q.C., as he then was, sitting as a deputy judge of the Queen's Bench Division, held that C was threatening to persist with dishonest proceedings and, accordingly, the without prejudice privilege did not apply to the discussion.

27–35 Each of the foregoing cases has illustrated how impropriety perpetrated under the cover of without prejudice discussions may properly be revealed at a subsequent trial. More recent decisions of the Court of Appeal have demonstrated the need for, and the desirability of, restricting the occasions when this is permissible to clear cases of "unambiguous impropriety".

27–36 In *Forster v Friedland*,[62] C (who were eight individuals) owned 4.5 million shares in S Plc. C alleged that on July 31, 1989 D1 agreed with C1 that he (D1) and others for whom he acted would purchase the shares at 73p. each. £100,000 was paid at once and completion, it was alleged, was to take place by October 31, 1989. D1 and D2 denied the existence of any legally binding agreement, saying that it was merely an agreement in principle. No completion took place on October 31, 1989 and a letter before action was written a few days later threatening proceedings if completion did not take place shortly. Various meetings and telephone conversations between the parties took place thereafter, all of which were covertly tape-recorded by C. D1 made his position clear that, if the matter came to litigation, he would deny that there was any legally binding agreement. However, he sought to reassure C that he regarded himself as honour bound to go through with the deal but that he wanted time to so arrange matters as to avoid the need to offer 73p. to all the other shareholders in accordance with the City Takeover Code. At first instance the judge held that the discussions were intended to be without prejudice but that they did not fall within the policy of the rule because there was no dispute which the parties sought to resolve and their purpose was merely for D1 to gain time. The Court of Appeal held that the discussions were protected by the "without prejudice" rule in that they were "genuinely aimed at settlement" in the sense of being aimed at the avoidance of litigation. There was an underlying dispute about whether the agreement was legally binding. Hoffmann L.J. stated: "Provided that this criterion is met, the nature of the proposals put forward or the character of the arguments used to support them are irrelevant". An argument that D1 was threatening to advance what he knew to be a sham defence, namely that there had been no agreement, whether legally binding or not, was rejected. Hoffmann L.J. stated: "The value of the without prejudice rule would be seriously impaired if its protection could be removed from [sic] anything less than unambiguous impropriety".

27–37 In *Fazil-Alizadeh v Nikbin*,[63] C and D1 became involved in a dispute, and proceedings ensued, about the circumstances of the acquisition and subsequent refurbishment of a house. In a second action issues concerning a cheque for

---

[62] (1992) C.A.T. 1052.
[63] (1993) C.A.T. 205.

£150,000 drawn in C's favour by D1 on D2's account arose. In July 1990 a settlement agreement was reached and was reduced to writing. Very considerable disputes arose thereafter about what had been agreed in that agreement. D1 alleged that the agreement had been altered in certain highly material respects by C. C contended that the alterations were made on the very day that the agreement had been drawn up. D2 covertly tape-recorded various conversations between the parties aimed at resolving their differences in the sense of resolving the underlying disputes reflected in the two actions. During one of the conversations, C made observations which, on one interpretation, could be seen as an acceptance that the alterations to the agrement were made at a date later than the date upon which the original agreement had been concluded. D1 and D2 wished to rely upon the contents of that conversation and that issue had been dealt with as a preliminary issue at an interlocutory stage by the county court judge. The Court of Appeal held that the observations in the conversation were ambiguous and did not represent "an unambiguous impropriety". Simon Brown L.J. stated: "There are powerful policy reasons for admitting in evidence as exceptions to the without prejudice rule only the very clearest of cases. Unless this highly beneficial rule is most scrupulously and jealously protected, it will all too readily become eroded".

This theme was taken up subsequently by the Court of Appeal in *Unilever plc v The Procter & Gamble Company*.[64]

C sought to bring proceedings against D under s.70 of the Patents Act 1977 for threatening C with proceedings for infringement of patent in relation to a particular product or process, the threat relied upon being asserted to have been made during a without prejudice meeting set up to discuss a number of issues between the parties. D applied to strike out C's claim on the grounds that it was an abuse of the process of the court for C to rely upon anything said during the without prejudice meeting. The Court of Appeal upheld the judge's decision to strike out the claim since what occurred at the meeting did not fall within the recognised exceptions to the normal "without prejudice" rule. There was nothing "oppressive, or dishonest, or dishonourable" in what was said on D's behalf.

Apart from its importance in the particular field of litigation to which it related, the *Unilever* case is important for the emphasis it places on the utility of the without prejudice privilege in encouraging full and frank exchanges between the parties. Robert Walker L.J. drew attention to the way in which practitioners treated the "without prejudice" rule, particularly in the context of meetings set up to discuss settlement. He said this:[65]

". . . I have no doubt that busy practitioners are acting prudently in making the general working assumption that the rule, if not 'sacred' . . . has a wide and compelling effect. That is particularly true where the 'without prejudice' communications in question consist not of

---

[64] [2000] 1 W.L.R. 2436.
[65] *ibid.* at 2443–2444.

letters or other written documents but of wide-ranging unscripted discussions during a meeting which may have lasted several hours.

At a meeting of that sort the discussions between the parties' representatives may contain a mixture of admissions and half-admissions against a party's interest, more or less confident assertions of a party's case, offers, counter-offers, and statements (which might be characterised as threats or as thinking aloud) about future plans and possibilities."

27–40   Robert Walker L.J.'s general conclusions are also of importance in what might be termed the post-Woolf culture. Having reviewed the earlier authorities he said this[66]:

"They show that the protection of admissions against interest is the most important practical effect of the rule. But to dissect out identifiable admissions and withhold protection from the rest of without prejudice communications (except for a special reason) would not only create huge practical difficulties but would be contrary to the underlying objective of giving protection to the parties, in the words of Lord Griffiths in the *Rush & Tompkins* case . . . 'to speak freely about all issues in the litigation both factual and legal when seeking compromise and, for the purpose of establishing a basis of compromise, admitting certain facts.' Parties cannot speak freely at a without prejudice meeting if they must constantly monitor every sentence, with lawyers . . . sitting at their shoulders as minders."

He continued by saying that "[the] expansion of exceptions should not be encouraged when an important ingredient of Lord Woolf's reforms of civil justice is to encourage those who are in dispute to engage in frank discussions before they resort to litigation".[67]

---

[66] *ibid.* at 2448–2449.
[67] *ibid.* at 2449–2450. This theme was reinforced in *W.H. Smith Ltd v Colman*, unreported, March 20, 2000, CA; *Dora v Simper* unreported, March 15, 1999, CA, noted at para.27–59, below; *Berry Trade Ltd v Moussavi* [2003] EWCA Civ 715; and *Savings & Investment Bank v Fincken* [2003] EWCA Civ 1630. In the latter case the issue in effect arose of whether C could give evidence at the trial of an alleged admission by D at a without prejudice meeting held a few days after D had sworn an affidavit inconsistent with the alleged admission. The circumstances were complicated, but the Court of Appeal held that the evidence could not be given. The policy approach referred to in the text was re-emphasised. In *Belt v Basildon & Thurrock NHS Trust* [2004] EWHC 783 (QB), Cox J. referred, *inter alia*, to paras 27–39 and 27–40, above, and concluded that she did not "accept [the] broad submission that the CPR and the Pre-Action Protocol require that an admission or partial admission made in the course of genuine 'without prejudice' negotiations aimed at settling a personal injury claim should automatically lose the cloak of privilege. In any event the approach being suggested by the claimant in this case, it seems to me, would have the effect of deterring parties from genuine attempts to settle claims, which would run completely contrary to the aims of the CPR and the Protocol".

27–41 Some of the cases considered above⁶⁸ involve the covert recording of without prejudice discussions. This seems to be occurring with greater frequency. In *Fazil-Alizadeh v Nikbin*, Simon Brown L.J. issued a timely warning about how readily the court should entertain the reception of evidence obtained in this way. Having expressed himself as noted above,[69] he said as follows:

> "Not least requiring of rigorous scrutiny will be claims for admissibility of evidence by those ... who have procured their evidence by clandestine methods and who are likely to have participated in discussions with half a mind at least to their litigious rather than their settlement advantages. That distorted approach to negotiation ... is itself to be discouraged, militating, as it inevitably must, against the prospects of successful settlement."

27–42 The criterion of "unambiguous impropriety" before the reception of evidence of what was said during without prejudice communications, and the need to protect admissions made during those communications, would seem to rule out from subsequent admissibility a number of things which, said in different circumstances, would either go to an issue in the case or to the credibility of a witness. For example, a changed version of the circumstances of an accident or a changed emphasis on material facts between the time of the without prejudice discussions and the trial would almost certainly not be admissible although plainly relevant. A previous inconsistent statement of a witness can, from the purely evidential point of view, be relied upon as an admission[70] and, of course, admissions made in without prejudice discussions are generally protected from subsequent disclosure.[71] Equally, the maintenance of a position during without prejudice negotiations designed to prevent subsequent litigation which is inconsistent with a position necessary to the success of that subsequent litigation if the negotiations fail, is not something that can be revealed in that litigation:

27–43
> In *Independent Research Services v Catterall*.[72] A brought proceedings for unfair dismissal before an industrial tribunal based upon the assertion that R, his employers, had acted in such a way as to cause a breakdown in the relationship of mutual trust and confidence that ought to subsist between employer and employee. R wished to put before the industrial tribunal at the substantive hearing evidence of a without prejudice letter written by A in which he put forward an offer of settlement which, *inter alia*, involved him

---

[68] For example, *Hawick Jersey International Ltd v Caplan*, *The Times*, March 11, 1988; *Forster v Friedland* (1999) C.A.T. 1052: and *Fazil-Alizadeh v Nikbin* (1993) C.A.T. 205.
[69] *i.e.* the quotation at the conclusion of the note of the case set out in para.27–37, above.
[70] Civil Evidence Act 1968, s.3(1)(a); *Phipson on Evidence* (16th ed., 2005). See n.67, above.
[71] See para.27–19, above.
[72] [1993] I.C.R. 1.

remaining as a full-time employee of the company. This, it was suggested, was inconsistent with the basis of the claim he wished to advance before the industrial tribunal. The Employment Appeal tribunal held that the negotiations were privileged and that none of the exceptions to the "without prejudice" rule permitted the reception of this evidence.

27-44　The authorities referred to in the foregoing analysis have set some parameters within which the issue of the reception of without prejudice material falls to be determined. It would be surprising if every potential scenario in which the issue will arise for consideration has been foreseen. New factual situations will almost inevitably arise which will require adaptation of the present parameters.[73] The court will doubtless have to adopt a pragmatic approach, balancing the primary consideration of ensuring protection for parties involved in true settlement negotiations against the need to ensure that the privilege afforded by the rule is not abused.[74]

F. Estoppel

27-45　It appears that evidence may be given of a clear statement made by one party during without prejudice negotiations upon which the other is intended to act (and did act) so as to give rise to an estoppel.[75]

G. Waiver and mutuality

27-46　Where a party entitled to claim the privilege associated with the "without prejudice" rule waives the privilege by relying on parts of the material at trial, it is established law that the whole of the without prejudice material

---

[73] Difficult situations can often arise in the matrimonial finance context.
[74] A proposition to like effect in the Third edition of this work was referred to without disapproval in *Independent Research Services v Catterall* [1993] I.C.R. 1 at 4. In *BNP Paribas v Mezzotero*, unreported, March 30, 2004, the EAT (Cox J.) upheld the decision of the chairman of the Employment Tribunal who ruled as admissible in her claim for sex discrimination what she alleged was said to her by her employers following her return from maternity leave at what they described as a "without prejudice" meeting at which she was told that her job was no longer viable and that it would be best for both parties if her contract was terminated. Cox J. held that there was no extant dispute at the time of the meeting and that the discussion was not genuinely aimed at settlement. She also held that it was "very much in the public interest that allegations of unlawful discrimination in the workplace are heard and properly determined by the Employment Tribunal to whom complaint is made, as the appropriate forum under the legislation". An application for permission to appeal was rejected: [2004] EWCA Civ 477. Pill L.J. said at para.21: "At the meeting the complainant was] plainly vulnerable and at a disadvantage. In the course of the meeting, the proposal is made to her, purportedly under without prejudice protection. Sensibly and reasonably she asked that it be put in writing. That request was refused. I simply do not understand how, if this was a genuine attempt at a without prejudice discussion with a view to settling the case, the applicants could refuse, as they did, to put the suggestion in writing. Indeed, their case would have been stronger had a properly worded letter been sent to her under a without prejudice heading".
[75] *Hodgkinson & Corby Ltd v Wards Mobility Services Ltd* [1997] F.S.R. 178 at 191, per Neuberger J.; referred to in *Unilever Plc v The Procter & Gamble Company* [2000] 1 W.L.R. 2436 at 2444.

may be admitted.[76] Where a party has relied on without prejudice material at an interim application (*e.g.* in seeking a freezing order) for the purposes of undermining the merits of the other party's case, the other party is entitled to deploy the contents of the without prejudice discussions or communications to advance its case at trial.[77]

WHEN WILL THE DISCLOSURE OF DOCUMENTS BE PROTECTED BY OPERATION OF THE RULE?

In *Rush & Tompkins Ltd v GLC*[78] the issue was whether without prejudice communications between parties to litigation are protected from disclosure to other parties in the litigation. The House of Lords upheld the claim for privilege contended for by one of the parties to a compromise achieved after without prejudice negotiations. Although the distinction between discoverability of a document and its admissibility was recognised, it was felt that the "without prejudice" rule (which essentially goes to the latter) should protect such communications from disclosure to third parties.[79]

27–47

> The facts were that D1 engaged C as main contractor in respect of a large housing development and C engaged D2 as subcontractors for the ground works. The completion of the contract was much delayed and D2 claimed for loss and expense against C who, in turn, sought to pass these claims on to D1. D1 would not agree D2's claim and, accordingly, C would not pay it. In August 1979 C commenced proceedings against D1 and D2 in which an inquiry as to the loss and expenses to which D2 were entitled under the subcontract was sought and a declaration that C was entitled to be reimbursed that sum by D1. Before the proceedings came to trial C and D1 reached an agreement whereby C accepted £1.2 million in settlement of all outstanding claims under the main contract. It was a term of the agreement that C would accept direct responsibility for all the sub-contractor's claims. The terms of

27–48

---

[76] *Great Atlantic Insurance Co v Home Insurance Co* [1981] 1 W.L.R. 529; as applied by concession in *Somatra Ltd v Sinclair Roche & Temperley* [2000] 1 W.L.R. 2453 at 2462–2463.
[77] See *Somatra*, n.76, at 2465 where Clarke L.J. said: "where, in support of its case on the merits of an action, a party deploys material which would not be admissible because it forms part of without prejudice communications the other party is entitled to refer to the contents of those same communications in order to advance its own case on the merits. It does not seem to me to be just to allow the first party to obtain an advantage by relying on the without prejudice material in one part of the litigation, as here on an application for Mareva relief, where the merits are relevant, and to rely upon the without prejudice nature of the communications when the other party wished to rely upon, say, an admission made in the same without prejudice discussions at the trial, where the merits are of course also relevant". He had previously said: "It seems to me that no party which has taken part in without prejudice discussions should be entitled to use them to his advantage on the merits of the case in one context, but then assert a right to prevent its opponent from doing so on the merits at the trial".
[78] [1989] 1 A.C. 1280.
[79] *ibid.* at 1305.

settlement were disclosed to D2, but the settlement did not disclose what valuation had been put on D2's claim in carrying out the global settlement. D2 sought specific discovery of the without prejudice correspondence leading to the settlement agreement. The House of Lords held that D2 could not have discovery of the documents. Lord Griffiths stated:

> "I would therefore hold as a general rule that the 'without prejudice' rule renders inadmissible in any subsequent litigation connected with the same subject-matter proof of any admissions made in a genuine attempt to reach a settlement. It of course goes without saying that admissions made to reach settlement with a different party within the same litigation are also inadmissible whether or not settlement was reached with that party."[80]

27–49   Where, however, the reasonablness of a compromise arrived at as a result of without prejudice negotiations is put in issue in subsequent proceedings, the without prejudice correspondence is admissible in those subsequent proceedings.

In *Muller and Muller v Linsley and Mortimer*[81] C1 was a director and shareholder in a computer software company, S company. He consulted D, solicitors, about a dispute with other directors and shareholders. D gave him advice about a certain course of action he should take in connection with his fear that the majority of the Board might dismiss him from his employment and thereby activate a provision that he be obliged to sell all his shares to the other shareholders at a fair value. Notwithstanding having attempted to take the advised course of action, C1's fears were realised. C1 and C2 brought proceeding against S company which, in due course, were settled in return for a cash payment and shares which became worth over £2 million when the company was floated. C1 and C2 then brought proceedings against D in connection with the advice alleging that, as a result of that advice, they became dispossessed of their original shares which would have been worth more than £4 million. C1 and C2 asserted that the earlier proceedings, and the settlement of those proceedings, had represented reasonable steps to mitigate their loss. As part of their defence, D denied the reasonableness of the settlement. D sought discovery of the without prejudice correspondence leading to the settlement. The Court of Appeal held that the correspondence was not privileged in the second action. The purpose of the revelation of the correspondence was not to establish the truth or otherwise of any express or implied admissions it might contain, but to determine the reasonableness of C's actions in reaching a settlement. Furthermore, by putting the reasonableness of the settlement in issue, C had impliedly waived any privilege that might exist.

27–50   In *Murrell v Healy*,[82] C was involved in two separate accidents six months apart. His claim in respect of the first accident, which included a claim for loss of earnings, was settled before the trial of the assessment of damages in relation to the second accident, his damages claim in that action also

---

[80] *ibid.* at 1301.
[81] (1994) C.A.T. 1461; *The Times*, December 8, 1994.
[82] Unreported, April 5, 2001, CA. See also *Gnitrow Ltd v Cape Plc* [2000] 1 W.L.R. 2327, CA; *cf. V.S.E.L. v Cape Contracts* [1998] P.I.Q.R. P207.

containing a claim for loss of earnings. The Court of Appeal held that the trial judge had been correct to admit documents showing how the compensation in respect of the first accident had been agreed. The settlement was relevant to the inquiry as to what injury C had suffered in the first accident.

A document created for the purpose of without prejudice discussions is privileged and an order for production in favour of one of the parties to the litigation will not be made.[83]   27-51

When can without prejudice negotiations be referred to at interim applications?

WANT OF PROSECUTION

Most substantive trials are preceded by various interim applications. The question arises as to the extent to which it is permissible for a without prejudice communication to be used as an aid to the determination of the outcome of a contested interim application.   27-52

Consistent with the principle that the existence of without prejudice negotiations may be referred to in order to rebut any inference of delay or laches that may otherwise arise,[84] without prejudice communications have frequently been referred to for that purpose on applications to dismiss for want of prosecution.[85] The practice was approved expressly by the Court of Appeal in *Family Housing Association v Michael Hyde & Partners*[86] in which the public policy considerations underlying the "without prejudice" rule generally[87] were held to have "little or no application"[88] in the particular context of applications to strike out for want of prosecution. Indeed, the content of the negotiations, as opposed merely to their existence, was recognised as having potential relevance in some cases.[89] Without prejudice communications may have a particular relevance in this   27-53

---

[83] *Rabin v Mendoza & Co* [1954] 1 W.L.R. 271, CA. In *Prudential Assurance Co. Ltd v Fountain Page Ltd* [1991] 1 W.L.R. 756, Hobhouse J., as he then was, held that witness statements served on D4 by P, pursuant to a direction under RSC Ord.38, r.2A, in an action which was subsequently settled, were not to be used by D4 in other proceedings because they remained privileged documents. The same limitation did not arise in relation to an expert's report served by P on D4 pursuant to a direction under RSC Ord.38, r.37.
[84] See para.27–21, above.
[85] Foe example, *Phipson on Evidence* (14th ed., 1990), pp.554–555; quoted in *Family Housing Association v Michael Hyde & Partners* [1993] 1 W.L.R. 354 at 361. See also *per* H.H. Judge John Newey, Q.C., Official Referee, in *Simaan General Contracting Company v Pilkington Glass Ltd* [1987] 1 W.L.R. 516 at 519.
[86] [1990] 1 W.L.R. 354.
[87] See para.27–19, above.
[88] [1993] 1 W.L.R. 354 at 363, *per* Hirst L.J.
[89] *ibid.*

context if a plaintiff seeks to argue[90] that a defendant is precluded from relying upon delay induced by the defendant's willingness for the case to proceed as manifested in those communications.[91]

Security for costs

27-54 It would seem that the normal "without prejudice" rule continues to apply in respect of things said and done by a defendant who applies for security for costs against the claimant. In *Kristjansson v R. Verney & Co Ltd*,[92] the Court of Appeal expressly said that it did "not wish to give any encouragement whatsoever to the notion there there is some general relaxation of the 'without prejudice' rule on an [interim] application for security for costs". The following reasoning of H.H. Judge Newey Q.C. Official Referee, was approved[93]:

> "To allow one party to give evidence of 'without prejudice' communications without the consent of another would be in direct conflict with the general rule excluding such evidence and with the public policy which supports it. Defendants sued by plaintiffs resident abroad or by companies likely to get into financial difficulties would be deterred from exploring possibilities of settlement and making sensible offers for fear of prejudicing their prospects of being able to obtain security for costs. In particular a defendant who has obtained an order for security intended to relate to preparations for trial only would be most unwilling to take any action which might prevent him from obtaining a second order for security in respect of trial costs."

27-55 The court is, however, entitled to take into account a Pt 36 payment or an open offer.[94] It is possible that it is entitled to take into account a Pt 36 offer.[95]

---

[90] See *Roebuck v Mungovin* [1994] 2 A.C. 224.
[91] [1993] 1 W.L.R. 354 at 363.
[92] Unreported, June 18, 1998, CA.
[93] *Simaan General Contracting Company v Pilkington Glass Ltd* [1987] 1 W.L.R. 516 at 520. It would seem that the case of *Rogers and Parry Ltd (in liquidation) v Thornham Construction Co Ltd*, referred to in para.9-49 of the Fourth edition of this work, must be treated as wrongly decided.
[94] *Sir Lindsay Parkinson & Co. Ltd v Triplan Ltd* [1973] Q.B. 609. See also *Keary Developments Limited v Tarmac Construction* [1995] 3 All E.R. 534 at 540, *per* Peter Gibson L.J. The open offer in the *Sir Lindsay Parkinson* case had been made in terms which were designed to give it the same effect as a payment into court.
[95] In *Simaan General Contracting Company v Pilkington Glass Ltd*, n.85, above, Judge Newey Q.C. said (at 520) that Lord Denning M.R. (in *Sir Lindsay Parkinson & Co Ltd v Triplan Ltd*, n.94, above) would "[no] doubt . . . today add *Calderbank* letters, which are the equivalent of payments in".

Interim payment applications

27–56 Where an application for an interim payment on account of damages is made in circumstances in which the defendant has not admitted liability or had judgment for damages to be assessed entered against him,[96] it will be necessary for the plaintiff to show that, if the action proceeded to trial, he "would obtain judgment for a substantial amount of money".[97] Whilst it might arguably be permissible to have regard to a without prejudice offer in order to see the extent to which a defendant has been prepared to entertain the claim,[98] some considerable caution would need to be applied to attaching too great a significance to it. To do so might be tantamount to treating the offer as some form of partial admission which, bearing in mind the express reference to an admission of liability as justifying the making of an order for an interim payment in the rules,[99] and to the rationale for the "without prejudice" rule generally,[1] would result in too liberal an approach. Issues of this nature are probably better determined on an overall analysis of the nature of the cases to be advanced on either side rather than on the consideration of without prejudice material. Where liability has been admitted, or a judgment has been obtained, it has been held possible to have regard to a payment into court when determining the amount of an interim payment.[2] It would follow, it is submitted, that a without prejudice offer should also be relevant in this context.

AT WHAT STAGE IN PROCEEDINGS MAY OBJECTION BE TAKEN TO A PROPOSAL TO ADDUCE EVIDENCE OF THE CONTENT OF WITHOUT PREJUDICE NEGOTIATIONS?

27–57 In the normal course of events, questions concerning the admissibility of evidence at trial are taken before the trial judge at a convenient point during the proceedings, normally when the evidence is about to be tendered. Not infrequently, it is necessary for the judge to hear (or hear about) the evidence *de bene esse* in order to decide the question. If ruled inadmissible, a judge will exclude it from his consideration of the case. This is a familiar judicial exercise[3] even though on occasions it may require what has been described as "mental gymnastics" in order to ensure exclusion of

---

[96] CPR r.25.7(1)(a) and (b).
[97] CPR r.25.7(1)(c).
[98] *cf.* para.27–53, above.
[99] See n.96, above.
[1] See para.27–17, above.
[2] *Fryer v London Transport Executive*, unreported, November 30, 1982.
[3] Characterised as "controlled forgetfulness" by Knox J. in *Re an action for negligence* (1992) (C No. 3063), *The Times*, March 5, 1993.

the material from the evaluation of the case.[4] Notwithstanding this generally adopted practice, there are cases where it has been regarded as desirable to determine issues of admissibility prior to the trial.[5] It can save a considerable amount of time and expense both in preparation for, and at, trial if inadmissible evidence is identified and excised early. It may also serve to pre-empt those rare cases where a party is, by having the issue determined by the trial judge, endeavouring to influence the judicial mind.

27–58   Overall, therefore, there is much to be said for having an issue such as this determined before the trial. Once determined, it will enable the parties to concentrate on deployment of the admissible evidence at the trial. However, it has been said that a decision to exclude evidence at an interim stage on the basis that to admit it would offend the "without prejudice" rule would only be made if the evidence was "plainly and obviously inadmissible". If it is "reasonably arguable" that the evidence is admissible, it may be more just and convenient that the final decision is left to the trial judge who, in the normal way, is better placed to appreciate the significance of the issues in the action and the relevance of the proposed evidence to those issues.[6] If, on the other hand, the preparations for trial would be seriously affected by the question being left to be resolved finally in this way, or substantial unnecessary costs would be incurred by this course, the balance might be tipped back in favour of making a clear decision at an interim stage.[7]

27–59   In *Dora v Simper*,[8] C sought relief from D1 and others arising from an alleged transfer of assets from a company of which they were directors, the transfer being alleged to have been at an undervalue. C also sought damages for conspiracy. The company had gone into liquidation. C obtained a freezing order against the defendants based upon an affidavit in which the contents of a without prejudice meeting were given during which, it was alleged, D1 had made an improper threat. The defendants sought to set aside the freezing order and, in a preliminary application, sought to exclude the evidence of the alleged improper threat. The Court of Appeal held that it should decide whether the evidence as it stood was capable of disclosing unambiguous impropriety. If it was, it would be for the judge hearing the application to discharge the freezing order to decide whether the threat was made and whether it was an improper threat. The court held that the alleged statement (namely that assets would be transferred so as to render any judgment nugatory) was capable of amounting to unambiguous impropriety.

---

[4] *Savings and Investment Bank Ltd v Gasco Investments (Netherlands) BV* [1984] 1 W.L.R. 271 at 278.
[5] *ibid.*; *Chocaladefabriken Lindt and Sprungli v Nestlé Co* [1978] R.P.C. 287; *Finch v Wilson*, noted at para.27–33, above.
[6] *Redifusion Simulation Ltd v Link Miles Ltd* [1992] F.S.R. 195, *per* Mummery J.
[7] *ibid.* at 200.
[8] Unreported, March 15, 1999.

PART 5

Role of Legal Advisers in Compromise

This Part is devoted to the role that a party's legal adviser, whether barrister, solicitor or other appropriate representative, plays in the process of compromise. Undoubtedly, many skills are required by those engaged in that process: not only the skills of negotiation which result in a compromise on satisfactory terms for the client, but also the skills of persuading a reluctant client to come to a compromise which is undoubtedly in his or her best interests. The role of a legal adviser can be looked at in terms of duties, obligations and responsibilities: to the client, to other members of the profession, to the court and, in some cases, to the public purse. It is from this standpoint that this Part is constructed.

CHAPTER 28

Professional Ethics and Responsibilities

General

The tradition of the Bar and of the solicitors' profession is one of honesty 28–01
and fair dealing.[1] This extends over many areas, not the least important of
which is the course of negotiation with a view to compromise. Dishonest
conduct will, of course, carry liability to disciplinary action. But, and in
some respects more significantly, a reputation for untrustworthiness,
unreliability and sharp practice is easily gained and by no means readily
displaced. It will result in an opponent aware of the reputation being far
less disposed to engage in compromise negotiations than might otherwise
be the case. Cases in which the interests of the litigants are not served by
arrival in court thus do arrive there. The administration of justice is
affected.

The putting forward of a false proposition on behalf of a client is often 28–02
inevitable if it forms part of the instructions received in good faith. But any
deliberate deception of an opponent in negotiations must never occur.
From the purely legal point of view, of course, it would, once discovered,
afford grounds for setting aside the agreement.[2]

"CONFIDENTIAL" MATTERS DISCLOSED BY CLIENT OR OPPONENT

There are occasions when the traditions and standards of the profession, 28–03
and indeed the requirements of the law of misrepresentation,[3] seem to

---

[1] Sir Malcolm Hilbery, *Duty and Art in Advocacy* (1959), pp.21–22; The Law Society, *The Guide to the Professional Conduct of Solicitors*.
[2] See Ch.4, above.
[3] *ibid*.

conflict with the duty to keep confidential matters disclosed by a client. Equally, the service of a client's interests may sometimes conflict with the convention of confidence between members of the profession when a conversation is said to be "off the record". Often decisions about the appropriateness or otherwise of a course of action have to be taken instantaneously without the opportunity for consultation with more experienced colleagues.[4] Sometimes the opportunity of testing a judgment against that of others is available. Occasionally, recourse may be had to the organs of the professional bodies regulating the professions responsible for assisting on such matters.[5]

28–04   It might be of assistance to record briefly two past rulings of these professional bodies which impinge on the process of compromise:

(a) Although negotiations between counsel with a view to compromise are impliedly "without prejudice",[6] certain admissions of fact made during the course of such negotiations are not so priviliged and may be used by an opponent if it be in his client's interests. For example, where a wife's counsel discloses to a husband's counsel that the wife is to remarry and this is of significance to the compromise of financial proceedings between them, it is legitimate for the husband's counsel to use this information in his client's interest.[7]

(b) Where a solicitor acts for a claimant in a personal injuries case and the defendants pay into court a sum arrived at on the basis of the plaintiff's medical condition shown in reports disclosed to them, he is entitled to act on the claimant's instructions to accept the sum paid in even if a further report becomes available showing that the client has only a short while to live, provided the defendants had originally been offered the opportunity of examining the claimant and had declined to do so.[8]

CONFLICTS OF INTEREST

28–05   A solicitor or barrister must not act for or advise a client when an actual or potential conflict of interest arises, whether the conflict of interest arises from some personal interest of the solicitor or barrister himself or by reason of having advised or represented some other party whose interests

---

[4] *cf.* the comments of Lord Diplock in *Saif Ali v Sidney Mitchell & Co* [1980] A.C. 198.
[5] For example. The Standard and Guidance Committee of the Law Society.
[6] *cf.* para.27–08, n.18, above.
[7] *Conduct and Etiquette at the Bar* (6th ed.), p.80.
[8] The Law Society *The Guide to the Professional Conduct of Solicitors* (1974), p.52.

conflict with the client in question.⁹ The most likely cause of such a problem in the context of compromise is where the legal adviser to a party is possessed of confidential information received from the other party to the dispute when previously acting for that other party.¹⁰

Clearly, it would be wrong for a legal adviser to act for a client in compromise negotiations when possessed of information about the other party's position in relation to the litigation, relevant to the negotiations, obtained when acting for that other party. Equally, a legal adviser is entitled to use, for the purpose of advancing his client's cause, only material which forms part of his instructions.¹¹ It would follow, it is thought, that it would be improper to seek to assist negotiations on behalf of a client by utilising information about the other party obtained other than by instructions received.¹² 28–06

UNFOUNDED CLAIMS

Reference was made at the beginning of this work[13] to the principle that a person who makes a claim knowing it to be unfounded shall not be entitled to retain any advantage derived from its compromise. A legal adviser instructed to pursue a claim acknowledged by a client to be baseless is entitled to refuse to act and indeed should not act. To do otherwise would conflict with his duty to the court where proceedings are involved and, whether or not proceedings are involved, would amount to complicity in his client's fraudulent attempt to obtain some wholly unjustified advantage.[14] It follows that a legal adviser should not act for a client who has 28–07

---

[9] Presumably, it is open to all relevant parties expressly to consent to the solicitor or barrister acting, although it would be rare for such consent to be forthcoming and, in any event, most practitioners would prefer not to be placed in a potentially embarrassing position.
[10] In *Bolkiah v KPMG* [1999] 2 A.C. 222 at 235–236 Lord Millett said this of a solicitor's duty of confidentiality to a former client: "Whether founded on contract or equity, the duty to preserve confidentiality is unqualified. It is a duty to keep the information confidential, not merely to take all reasonable steps to do so. Moreover, it is not merely a duty not to communicate the information to a third party. It is a duty not to misuse it, that is to say, without the consent of the former client to make any use of it or to cause any use to be made of it by others otherwise than for his benefit. The former client cannot be protected completely from accidental or inadvertent disclosure. But he is entitled to prevent his former solicitor from exposing him to any avoidable risk; and this includes the increased risk of the use of the information to his prejudice arising from the acceptance of instructions to act for another client with an adverse interest in a matter to which the information is or may be relevant".
[11] *cf.* Sir Malcolm Hilberry n.1, above, p.11.
[12] *cf. Re A Firm of Solicitors, The Times,* June 20, 1991, CA. See also The Law Society, *The Guide to the Professional Conduct of Solicitors* (1990), pp.86–87.
[13] See para.2–19, above.
[14] *ibid.*

intimated the hope that the assertion of a baseless claim will result in some offer of compromise by the other party.[15] Needless to say, there is nothing improper in acting for a party who has some arguable case, though not one thought to have much prospect of success, in the hope that some compromise will result.[16]

28-08   Equally, it appears that there is nothing professionally improper in acting for a party who pursues a claim or a defence which is plainly doomed to fail,[17] although the distinction between acting in that fashion and continuing unreasonably with an action with "no or no substantial chance of success"[18] is not always easy to define. The dividing line between that which is proper and that which is improper in this context is determined by distinguishing between the pursuit of a hopeless case, on the one hand, and the pursuit of one which amounts to an abuse of the process of the court, on the other.[19] Where either situation confronts a practitioner representing a legally aided client, there is a clear obligation to inform the Legal Services Commission so that the interests of the Legal Aid Fund may be protected.[20]

INFORMING CLIENT OF OFFER OF SETTLEMENT

28-09   A legal adviser must inform his client of an offer of compromise.[21] The obligation does not appear to go as far as reasoning the whole matter with the client and quoting authority,[22] although assistance in weighing balancing considerations would, and should, be undertaken.[23]

---

[15] See also the discussion on the question of an intention to proceed with a claim in Ch.3, paras. 3–10 *et seq.*, above
[16] *cf. Abraham v Jutsun* [1963] 1 W.L.R. 658. See para.2–19, n.34.
[17] *Ridehalgh v Horsefield* [1994] Ch. 205 at 253.
[18] *Davy-Chiesman v Davy-Chiesman* [1984] Fam. 48 at 67, *per* Dillon L.J.
[19] *Ridehalgh v Horsefield*, n.17, above, at 234. As Sir Thomas Bingham M.R. said, distinguishing "by definition" between the two is "not entirely easy", although recognition in practice is more straightforward. In the "wasted costs" jurisdiction, the legal representative is entitled to the benefit of any doubt. The same principle would presumably apply in other contexts. An area in the context of compromise in which the question arises of whether proceedings represent an abuse of the process of the court is that of the statutory demand procedure and the subsequent issue of a winding-up petition: See Ch.31, below. The tension between what is proper and improper in this context is reflected upon in *Philex Plc v Golban* [1994] Ch. 205 at 250–253, one of the individual cases decided along with *Ridehalgh v Horsefield*.
[20] Civil Legal Aid (General) Regulations 1989 (SI 1989/339), regs 67–69.
[21] *Sill v Thomas* (1839) 8 C. & P. 762 (solicitor).
[22] *Blair v Assets Co* [1896] A.C. 409 at 431. For a detailed analysis of the role of a barrister in giving advice on a settlement at court, see *Moy v Pettmann Smith (a firm)* [2005] 1 W.L.R. 581.
[23] See paras 28–10—28–11, below. See also para.5.1 of *Civil Litigation—A Guide to Good Practice*, prepared by the Civil Litigation Committee of the Law Society.

OVERALL DUTIES TO CLIENT IN COMPROMISE

How is the advisory role to be played in the context of compromise? The fact that the great proportion of disputes are resolved by agreement before being contested in court, not to mention those which are resolved before proceedings are even instituted, testifies to the existence of pressures on litigants or potential litigants to compromise. Such pressures may come from the litigant himself, from his family and friends, from his legal advisers, or from a combination of each. Despite the existence of some who are prepared to see the whole process of litigation through to its ultimate conclusion, many would prefer simply not to be involved in it at all. They are prepared to concede to the other side simply to avoid the personal anxiety involved. Others are more concerned about the dual problems of the uncertainties of litigation and the incidence of costs. Even the best prepared case on paper crumbles when the principal witness gives evidence. Tribunals are composed of human beings who are fallible. In many cases, particularly where a large element of discretion is conferred upon the tribunal, the uncertainties are even greater.[24] One advantage of a compromise, provided it is put into effect correctly, is that each party knows his position. Neither party may be completely satisfied with the result but, it is submitted, that is far better in many cases than one party facing a bill for legal costs far in excess of that which he ever really conceived as being his liability. 28–10

The vast majority of legal advisers will take an early opportunity of warning clients who have embarked, or are about to embark, on litigation of the uncertainties associated even with what may appear to be a good case and the costs which may be involved. In some cases, of course, such advice is unnecessary or goes unheeded. But, it is submitted, it is the height of professional irresponsibility not to give such warnings, particularly when clients of limited means are involved in a dispute the outcome of which, by its very nature, is even more uncertain than what might be termed the mainstream of litigation.[25] 28–11

---

[24] "I appreciate that . . . it is difficult for practitioners to advise clients in these cases because the rules are not very firm. That is inevitable when the courts are working out the exercise of the wide powers given by a statute like the Matrimonial Causes Act 1973. It is the essence of such a discretionary situation that the court should preserve, so far as it can, the utmost elasticity to deal with each case on its own facts. Therefore, it is a matter of trial and error and imagination on the part of those advising clients": per Ormrod L.J. in *Martin v Martin* [1978] Fam. Law 12 at 20.

[25] Following the implementation of Lord Woolf's proposals in the CPR and the introduction of pre-action protocols (see paras 13–07 *et seq.*, above) the need for legal advisers to give advice about the merits of settlement at an early stage has assumed greater prominence as a professional obligation. It remains important, of course, that sufficient information about the dispute is available to enable an informed view to be taken of any settlement proposal. A legal adviser who counsels settlement without such information runs the risk of an allegation of professional negligence: see Ch.29, below.

KEEP COURT INFORMED

28-12 Finally, in the context of professional responsibilities, members of both branches of the profession are required to keep the appropriate court officials informed of possible and actual settlements in cases in which they are involved.[26]

---

[26] See para.10-25, above.

CHAPTER 29

Authority to Compromise and Liabilities of Legal Advisers Arising from Compromise

AUTHORITY TO COMPROMISE—GENERAL

An extremely important topic for discussion in the context of compromise is the extent to which a legal adviser may bind a client to such an agreement.[1] It will be apparent from the discussion which follows that there may be circumstances in which a client is bound by a compromise entered into on his behalf which is not in accordance with his wishes or instructions. The question of the possible liability of the legal adviser to his client is dealt with later.[2] 29–01

A review of the law in this area prior to the decision of the House of Lords in *Arthur J.S. Hall v Simons*[3] revealed in some instances subtle differences between the extent to which a solicitor might bind a client to a compromise and that to which a barrister might bind a client.[4] Although not clearly articulated in the cases, it was thought that these distinctions arose at least to a degree because of the immunity from suit of barristers in relation to certain work undertaken by them compared with the lack of such immunity in relation to solicitors. There may have been a greater inclination to release a client from a compromise entered into on his behalf by a barrister because of the lack of remedy against the barrister. 29–02

---

[1] Persons other than legal advisers (*e.g.* partners and directors) may have authority to compromise. Generally speaking, the normal principles of agency apply, though see Ch.4, above. For the position of insurers in relation to compromise, see Ch.30, below.
[2] See paras 29–20 *et seq.*, below.
[3] [2002] 1 A.C. 615.
[4] See Fourth edition of this work, paras 12–04 *et seq.*

29-03   If that were the true explanation for the subtle differences that existed, the justification for those differences has now been removed by the repudiation by the House of Lords of the continued immunity from suit for barristers in relation to civil litigation.[5] Whether or not it was the true justification, the need for continued subtle distinctions in this area hardly seems appropriate with the developments in legal practice in recent years.

THE LAW

Actual authority and ostensible (or apparent) authority to compromise

29-04   A barrister or solicitor may be given *express* authority by a client in connection with a compromise. Vested with such authority he will be able to bind the client to a compromise. Although what follows is a discussion of situations in which a legal adviser may act in connection with a compromise without express authority, it is very unusual nowadays for a solicitor or barrister to take any step towards concluding an agreement of compromise without obtaining express authority from the client. Given the possibility of a claim in negligence this is plainly the only sensible course to adopt.[6]

In circumstances in which it may become relevant to inquire into the question of whether a client has given express authority in connection with a compromise,[7] the obtaining of information and relevant documentation will be permitted for the purpose, the area of inquiry not being covered by legal professional privilege.[8]

29-05   Where *express* authority to compromise is given, no question can arise as to the binding nature of the agreement entered into on a client's behalf. The authority of the legal adviser as the client's agent is conferred directly by the express instructions of the client. The law of agency does, however, in certain circumstances clothe an agent with an actual authority even though the principal has not conferred it directly and expressly upon the

---

[5] *Arthur J.S. Hall v Simons*, n.3, above.
[6] *Waugh v H.B. Clifford & Sons Ltd*, n.11, below, at 387 and 389.
[7] See paras 29-25 *et seq.*, below.
[8] *Conlon v Conlons Ltd* [1952] 2 All E.R. 462, CA: C's solicitors settled his personal injuries claim with D before proceedings were issued. When C subsequently commenced proceedings for damages generally, D raised the settlement by way of defence. C's reply alleged that the solicitors had acted without authority. D sought to interrogate on the scope of C's instructions in connection with the settlement. Although pre-CPR authorities in relation to matters of practice are generally to be treated as of no great assistance, the general approach of this case would, it is submitted, be followed in a similar situation. It would be impossible to arrive at a just result without the kind of information and documentation sought.

agent. The authority is *implied* from the nature of the agent's position or profession.[9] In this sense barristers and solicitors, according to the law as it stands, do possess certain implied powers to compromise on a client's behalf even though not given express powers to do so.[10]

The difference between an *implied* authority to compromise and an *ostensible* (or *apparent*) authority to compromise needs to be noted. It was brought into relief in *Waugh v H.B. Clifford and Sons Ltd*.[11] As Brightman L.J. (as he then was) said[12]: 29–06

". . . it is . . . necessary to bear in mind the distinction between on the one hand the *implied* authority of a solicitor to compromise an action without prior reference to his client for consent: and on the other hand the *ostensible* or *apparent* authority of a solicitor to compromise an action on behalf of his client without the opposing litigant being required for his own protection either (1) to scrutinise the authority of the solicitor of the other party, or (2) to demand that the other party (if an individual) himself signs the terms of compromise or (if a corporation) affixes its seal or signs by a director or other agent possessing the requisite power under the articles of association or other constitution of the corporation."

In *Waugh v H.B. Clifford and Sons Ltd*, by an error, a specific instruction from D to his solicitors not to agree to a matter which would conclude a compromise did not come to the attention of the person dealing with the matter until after he had sent a letter to C's solicitors confirming the agreement. The Court of Appeal held that D's solicitors had been able to agree the terms of the agreement within their ostensible authority, but not within their actual authority. The agreement was held to be binding on D. 29–07

In the course of his judgment, Brightman L.J. reviewed a number of the authorities on implied authority and said this[13]: 29–08

"The law has become well established that the solicitor or counsel retained in an action has an *implied* authority as between himself and his client to compromise the suit without reference to the client, provided that the compromise does not involve matters 'collateral to the action'; and *ostensible* authority, as between himself and the opposing litigant to compromise the suit without actual proof of authority, subject to the same limitation . . .."

---

[9] *Chitty on Contracts* (29th ed., 2004)), Vol.1, paras 31–042 *et seq.*
[10] But see the considerations referred to in paras 29–11 *et seq.*, below.
[11] [1982] Ch. 374. See also *Re Debtors No.78 of 1980, The Times*, May 11, 1985; *cf. Thompson v Howley* [1977] N.Z.L.R. 16. And see *Harford v Birmingham City Council* 66 P. & C.R. 468.
[12] [1982] Ch. 374 at 387.
[13] *ibid.* at 387.

29-09 Attention was drawn to the proposition that the implied authority may not be as extensive as the ostensible authority. It would be possible for a legal adviser to compromise a claim for a very substantial sum within his ostensible authority, whereas to do so may well be outside his implied authority. Agreeing a substantial figure without reference to the client might result in an allegation of negligence, but it would not affect the validity of the compromise as such.

29-10 It was emphasised that the only question an opposing litigant needs to ask himself is whether the compromise contains matters "collateral to the suit". The magnitude of the compromise, or the burden which its terms impose on the other party, is irrelevant.[14] Too restrictive an interpretation of "collateral" is not to be given.[15]

29-11 The judgments in *Waugh v H.B. Clifford & Sons Ltd* were given nearly 25 years ago.[16] All the principles reflected in those judgments in relation to implied authority were derived from decisions towards the end of the nineteenth century or the early part of the twentieth century.[17] The principles thus established arose from events that took place long before the modern world of communications technology inhabited by all lawyers and most, if not all, of their lay clients.[18] As already indicated,[19] no legal adviser would nowadays regard it as appropriate to reach a *final* settlement of a client's case relying upon an *implied* authority to do so: express instructions would be sought.

29-12 The same consideration would, it is thought, apply in relation to a significant agreement at the interim stages of a case. For example, an agreed resolution of a freezing order application or an application for a substantial interim payment would almost certainly not now be concluded without express authority from the client. However, some of the more everyday decisions that need to be made in the context of litigation (for example, extensions of time) will undoubtedly continue to be made as part of the incidental authority[20] of the particular level or status of the legal adviser concerned. It is submitted that, should the matter ever fall to be tested in contemporary times, the implied authority to settle matters within contemplated[21] or actual litigation will be confined to relatively mundane procedural issues.

---

[14] *ibid*. at 387.
[15] *ibid*. at 388.
[16] In December 1981.
[17] See para.29–13, below.
[18] The author recalls that the first fax machine was installed in his Chambers in 1988.
[19] See para.29–04, above.
[20] *Chitty on Contracts* (29th ed., 2004)), Vol.1, para.31-044.
[21] Given the emphasis placed in the post-CPR culture upon pre-action steps (including pre-action exchanges of information and possible alternative dispute-resolution (ADR)), it would be difficult to draw a distinction between the content of the implied authority to settle at that stage and the content of the implied authority to settle at the stage when proceedings have commenced.

29-13 If the foregoing analysis is correct, it remains to be seen whether the content of this residual implied authority is different as between solicitors and barristers. It was always the case that no implied authority to settle existed until proceedings were in existence[22] and, in relation to barristers, not until the barrister is present at court, either conducting or about to conduct the client's case.[23] The justification for that rule appears to have been that counsel is retained "to advise his client out of court, and to act for him in court".[24] Where counsel is indeed retained purely in that capacity, it is likely that a rule to the same effect would apply, although express confirmation of a proposed agreement is usually obtained either from the instructing solicitor if present, or by telephone if not. But it would almost certainly be a rule that would be moulded by the realities of present-day practice.

29-14 A barrister instructed in an interim application or in respect of a case management conference some days before it takes place may communicate with his opposite number in order to resolve matters. Whilst it would now be normal practice for the barrister to obtain authority from his instructing solicitor before agreeing anything, it is at least possible that in this kind of situation an implied authority equivalent to that of the solicitor would be accorded to the barrister.

Ostensible (or apparent) authority

29-15 As already indicated,[25] a legal adviser's ostensible (or apparent) authority may be more extensive than his actual authority, whether the actual authority is express or implied. It follows that ordinarily it is not necessary for the advisers for the other side in a dispute to question the extent of the actual authority when a settlement proposal is discussed. If the legal representative agreeing to a settlement is doing so on behalf of a party that needs to execute certain formal procedures before even it can be bound by the settlement,[26] then the ostensible authority of the legal representative will not be sufficient to make good that deficiency if it exists. Equally, if the other party knows that the actual authority of the representative acting for the opposing party is limited notwithstanding the position apparently being taken, the ostensible authority will not be operative.[27]

---

[22] *Macaulay v Polley* [1897] 2 Q.B. 122, CA.
[23] *Green v Crockett, Crockett v Green* (1865) 34 L.J. Ch. 606; *Harvey v Croydon Union Rural Sanitary Authority* (1884) 26 Ch.D. 249, CA.
[24] *Matthews v Munster* (1887) 20 Q.B.D. 141 at 143, *per* Lord Esher M.R. See also *Richardson v Peto* (1840) 1 Man. & G. 896. Counsel may, of course, be given express authority to negotiate a compromise at an earlier stage.
[25] See para.29-09, above.
[26] See, *e.g.* paras 4-09 *et seq.*, above.
[27] *Welsh v Roe* (1918) 87 L.J.K.B. 520 (McCardie J.); following *Brady v Curran* (1868) I.R. 2 C.L. 314, and reviewing fully all the authorities. *Scheyer v Wontner* (1890) 90 L.T. Jo. 116; *Marsden v Marsden* [1972] Fam. Law 280: The limitation must be "clear and unequivocal". *Strauss v Francis* (1866) L.R. 1 Q.B. 379.

29–16 The other limitation upon the operation of the principle of ostensible authority is that it does not extend to "collateral matters".[28] A matter obviously outside the ambit of the dispute being discussed would be regarded as "collateral" for this purpose, but presumably a legal representative may bind his client by the operation of the principle of ostensible authority to a general release of all claims, whether foreseen or unforeseen at the time of the settlement.[29]

Misunderstandings between client and legal adviser

29–17 Except in the circumstances indicated above,[30] the relationship between an opposing party and his legal adviser in relation to settlement discussions should be of no consequence to the other party. The remedy for a client whose legal adviser has agreed something in excess of his authority would ordinarily be a claim against the legal adviser. As the law now stands,[31] such a remedy is available against both solicitor and barrister.[32] Where, therefore, does the jurisdiction established in the following cases now fit into the picture?

29–18 In *Neale v Gordon Lennox*,[33] C authorised her counsel to compromise an action subject to a specified condition. He entered into a compromise which did not incorporate that condition. The order giving effect to the compromise was drawn up by C with a view to applying to set it aside. The House of Lords held that there was jurisdiction to set aside the order and, in the circumstances of the case, this should be done.

29–19 In *Shepherd v Robinson*,[34] counsel for D, with the agreement of D's solicitor, who was present, consented to judgment being entered against his client for part of the total sum claimed, the balance being abandoned. Unbeknown to that counsel, D had decided not to compromise and sent a message to her solicitor at court to that effect. The message had not arrived by the time of the agreement. Prior to the judgment being perfected D, in effect, applied to set it aside. The Court of Appeal held that there was jurisdiction to do so and exercised it in the circumstances of the case.

29–20 Both the foregoing cases concerned a situation where, on the facts, counsel misapprehended the extent of his authority. The jurisdiction is discretionary and exercised with caution.[35] As has been noted,[36] it has been

---

[28] See para.29–10, above.
[29] See paras 5–08 *et seq.*, above. Though *cf. Gardiner v Moore (No.2)* [1969] 1 Q.B. 55.
[30] See paras 29–15 and 29–16, above.
[31] Following *Arthur J.S. Hall v Simons*, n.3., above.
[32] *ibid.*
[33] [1902] A.C. 465.
[34] [1919] 1 K.B. 474.
[35] *Marsden v Marsden* [1972] Fam. 280.
[36] *ibid.*

extended to cover a situation where counsel has deliberately ignored instructions not to compromise.

As suggested above, the logical position is to say that the remedy of the wronged client in this situation is against his legal adviser. That having been said, it is not difficult to envisage situations in which "wires become crossed" without obvious fault on the part either of the client or the legal adviser. It would be unfortunate if there was no way of resolving a genuine misunderstanding. This jurisdiction, which until overruled by either the Court of Appeal or the House of Lords, is one which offers the potential for a pragmatic solution to such a situation. If it continues to exist, it will doubtless continue to be exercised with considerable caution and only where a clear injustice would arise if it were not exercised.[37] 29–21

LIABILITIES OF LEGAL ADVISERS ARISING FROM COMPROMISE

In *Saif Ali v Sydeny Nitchell & Co*[38] the House of Lords confirmed the immunity from suit of a barrister for: 29–22

(i) his conduct of a case in court; and
(ii) such pre-trial work as is "so intimately connected with the conduct of the cause in court that it can fairly be said to be a preliminary decision affecting the way the cause is to be conducted when it comes to a hearing".[39]

In the First edition of this work[40] it was suggested that the case of *Saif Ali* raised several more questions than it answered in relation to the extent to which a barrister (or solicitor) might be liable in negligence for work associated with a compromise.[41] On occasions subsequently the English courts have sought to grapple with some of the problems created by the test set out in (ii) in relation to work connected with compromise.[42] 29–23

---

[37] *ibid.*
[38] [1980] A.C. 198.
[39] The words of McCarthy P. in *Rees v Sinclair* [1974] 1 N.Z.L.R. 180 at 187, CA, which were adopted by the majority. The immunity, it was said, should not be given any wider application than was "absolutely necessary in the interests of the administration of justice".
[40] Published in 1980.
[41] A proposition repeated in all subsequent editions.
[42] See, *e.g. Kelley v Corston* [1998] Q.B. 686; and *Landall v Dennis Falconer & Alsop* [1994] 5 Med. L.R. 268. In *Arthur J.S. Hall v Simons*, n.3, above, Lord Hope of Craighead said (at 724) that "experience has shown that it is not an easy test to apply in regard to civil proceedings, especially in regard to allegations made about negligence in agreeing the terms of settlement" and that "[it] has not proved possible to devise a satisfactory alternative test for use in the field of civil justice, bearing in mind the overriding need to ensure that the protection given must not be any wider than is absolutely necessary".

29-24　Whatever the nature of the difficulties occasioned by the *Saif Ali* test, those difficulties have been removed by the abolition of any forensic immunity in relation to civil litigation. It is now not arguable that work associated with the compromise of litigation is covered by the immunity. A legal adviser, whether barrister or solicitor, can be sued for negligence in connection with advice given and work done in relation to the compromise of litigation.

WHAT CONSTITUTES NEGLIGENCE IN THIS CONTEXT?

29-25　Without intending to be exhaustive, it is submitted that the following actions of a legal adviser would be capable of amounting to negligence:

(a) giving positive advice to a client on a compromise having overlooked some matter (for example a limitation point) which would completely or significantly undermine the case advanced by the other party;
(b) compromising in defiance of express instructions on the matter;[43]
(c) (a solicitor) failing to communicate to counsel some express limitation of the client on compromise;
(d) giving positive advice to a client to settle, upon terms which no reasonably competent and well-informed member of the profession would have agreed or advised[44];
(e) failing to insist on a machinery of compromise under which the client's interests are adequately protected.[45]

29-26　These examples merely illustrate situations in which prima facie a breach of duty may arise. Proving one or another will not necessarily mean that a breach of duty is thereby established: that will depend on the circumstances of the case. In relation to heads (b) and (c) there will be no breach of duty if the client acts in a way which reasonably leads his legal adviser to believe that he has authorised the compromise.[46]

29-27　Furthermore, in any case it will be necessary for the dissatisfied client to establish that the breach of duty caused him some loss or damage. It may be necessary to show that, given proper advice, he would have acted

---

[43] *Re Newen* [1903] 1 Ch. 812, *per* Farwell J.
[44] See *Saif Ali v Sydney Mitchell & Co* [1980] A.C. 198; *Chown v Parrott* (1863) 14 C.B.(n.s.) 74; *Prestwich v Poley* (1865) 18 C.B.(n.s.) 806; *Re Newen*, n.43, above; *Waugh v Clifford*, n.11, above. See, in particular, in the context of advice on settlement, *Moy v Pettmann Smith (a firm)* [2005] 1 W.L.R. 581, HL.
[45] This might be regarded as an aspect of (d) above. See Ch.9, above.
[46] *Little v Spreadbury* [1910] 2 K.B. 658.

differently. In many cases the issue will be whether the client has, as a result of the negligence, lost the chance of a better result and, if so, what is the measure of that lost chance.[47] Where a breach of duty is established but no loss has been occasioned, nominal damages only will be awarded.[48]

> In *Butler v Knight*,[49] a solicitor, who thought that a judgment debtor had no funds, compromised the debt despite having instructions to enforce the judgment and not to accept any compromise. The solicitor was held liable for the difference between the whole amount of the judgment debt and the amount received under the compromise.

29–28

> In *McNamara v Martin Mears & Co*,[50] Peter Pain J. awarded W £8,000 against her solicitors who negligently advised her to accept £12,000 as a once-for-all settlement with H when she should have been looking for £24,000. The award was discounted for the costs and risks of litigation and for accelerated receipt.

29–29

> In *Dickinson v Jones Alexander & Co*,[51] C was negligently advised in connection with the financial aspects of her divorce from her husband. He was an extremely wealthy man, but the result of the advice she received in connection with the financial affairs was that she, together with the two children, found herself living in a small house in an unsatisfactory area with a mortgage she was unable to service as she was on supplementary benefit. At one stage she started selling her few assets and personal possessions to make ends meet. Douglas Brown J. held that the primary measure of damages was what a judge or registrar would have ordered C's husband to pay or transfer to her under the matrimonial legislation, taking into account subsequent variation orders. There was a negligible risk of C having obtained less than a proper award and the damages should be assessed on that basis. Since it was not clear that C's damages would not be taxable in her hands, she should receive the full sum, and not a sum which was assessed on the basis of tax having been deducted. Equally, since it was likely that supplementary benefits paid to her would be recoverable, it was not appropriate for credit to be given for those payments. In addition, she should be awarded damages for the distress and anxiety caused to her as a result of the inadequate settlement. In total she was awarded over £330,000.[52]

29–30

Where a compromise is concluded as a result of negligent legal advice or representation, but where no identifiable pecuniary loss can be identified, the court will be faced with seeking to place a monetary value on the consequences that flowed from the negligence, provided those consequences were reasonably foreseeable.[53]

29–31

---

[47] *Allied Maples Group Ltd v Simmons & Simmons* [1995] 1 W.L.R. 1602, CA.
[48] *Fray v Voules* (1859) 1 E. & E. 839.
[49] (1867) L.R. 2 Exch. 109.
[50] (1983) 127 S.J. 69.
[51] [1990] Fam. Law 137.
[52] An appeal by the defendants was settled on the basis of a reduction in the amount of damages awarded.
[53] See, *e.g. Heywood v Wellers* [1976] Q.B. 446, CA; *Al-Kandari v J.R. Brown & Co* [1988] 1 Q.B. 665, CA; *Dickinson v Jones Alexander & Co*, n.51, above.

LEGAL ADVISERS IN THE INVESTIGATION OF NEGLIGENCE

29-32 Where a legal adviser is a party to proceedings brought by a former client concerning a compromise, he will be entitled to give evidence in the usual way.[54] Where a legal adviser is called upon by a client to state the circumstances of a compromise in which he was involved, a solicitor may give evidence. It was once the view that the correct course for counsel was to make a statement from his place at the Bar without being sworn, but this does not now seem to reflect the current practice. Written statements by counsel have been received in such circumstances[55] and oral evidence is given in the usual way.[56]

---

[54] The duty of confidentiality would not operate in this context either by way of an express or implied waiver. A claim would be stayed if the former client refused to release the duty of confidence.
[55] *Gardiner v Moore (No.2)* [1969] 1 Q.B. 55.
[56] See, *e.g. Green v Collyer-Bristow and Pointer*, unreported, April 29, 1999, Douglas Brown J.

PART 6

Insurance Interests and Compromise

CHAPTER 30

Insurance Interests and Compromise

INTRODUCTION

A great deal of litigation is carried on by insurers exercising their rights of subrogation. The rights to which an insurer is subrogated are those of the insured with the result that any claim made by the insurer in pursuance of those rights must be brought in the name of the insured.[1] Equally, any resistance by an insurer to a claim brought by another party against its insured will be in the name of the insured. Given the volume of disputation that is conducted by or on behalf of insurers, it is clearly of importance to examine the effects that an insurance interest may have upon the settlement of a dispute.

30–01

In many cases, the existence of an insurer behind a party to a dispute will cause no complications in the context of the compromise of that dispute. However, problems may arise when both insured and uninsured losses constitute the subject-matter of the dispute.[2] Furthermore, the settlement of a dispute by either the insurer, on the one hand, or the insured, on the other, may have an impact upon the claims which the one may have on the other.[3] These two situations fall to be examined briefly.

30–02

---

[1] See, e.g. *Smith (M.H.) (Plant Hire) Ltd v Mainwaring (D.L.) (t/a Inshore)* [1986] 2 Lloyd's Rep. 244, CA.
[2] See paras 30–04 *et seq.*, below.
[3] See paras 30–09 *et seq.*, below.

SETTLEMENT WITH THIRD PARTY—THE EFFECTS FOR THE THIRD PARTY

The general principle

30–03 So far as a third party is concerned, the insurer and the insured represent a single entity or a composite unit.[4] Consequently, any compromise by the insured which constitutes a complete settlement of all issues between him and the third party will indeed be effective as such as between the third party and the composite unit, even though the insurer may not have authorised the settlement of the matters in respect of which it has interests.[5] Equally, it is likely that a similar form of settlement by the insurer will bind the insured.[6] However, the settlement may not be, or purport to be, a settlement of all issues including both insured and uninsured losses.[7]

Insured and uninsured losses

30–04 Usually the insurer will pay the insured his insured losses under the policy and then seek to recover its outlay against the party (often, of course, his insurers) responsible for causing those losses. The insured may have other claims against that party for which he was not covered by his insurance policy—in other words, the uninsured losses. Parallel (though, not infrequently, disjointed and disconnected) negotiations may be pursued by each in respect of each set of losses. It does happen, from time to time, that a settlement is concluded by either the insurer or the insured which seems to suggest that it represents a complete settlement of both sets of losses. However, where it is plain from the course of the negotiations that only one set of losses was intended to be embraced by the settlement, there will be no bar to the other claims being pursued.

---

[4] MacGillivray, *Insurance Law* (10th ed., 2003), para.22–52.
[5] ibid.; *West of England Fire Insurance Co v Isaacs* [1897] 1 Q.B. 226, CA. See also *Buckland v Palmer* [1984] 1 W.L.R. 1109, CA; and *Hayler v Chapman* [1989] 1 Lloyd's Rep. 490, CA.
[6] This, it is thought, will depend more upon the question of whether the insurer is to be treated, in the circumstances, as the insured's agent in the negotiations for matters not strictly the concern of the insurer. So far as the third party is concerned, the question that would arise would be whether it is correct to assume without more that the insurer had full authority to compromise all issues: *cf.* the position of a legal representative at paras 29–06 *et seq.*, above. If the insured had led the third party to believe that the insurer had such authority, even though actual authority may not have been conferred, then the ostensible authority thus created would be sufficient to bind the insured to the settlement. For a case in which the issue of whether the insured had the authority to bind the insured arose, see *Kitchen Design and Advice v Lea Valley Water Co* [1989] 2 Lloyd's Rep. 221, the facts of which have been given at para.2–09, above.
[7] See paras 30–04 *et seq.*, below.

30–05 In *Capon v Evans*,[8] the facts of which have been given previously,[9] the Court of Appeal held that the settlement concluded in correspondence embraced only the uninsured losses and that the insured losses remained capable of being pursued.

30–06 The position becomes a little more complicated if proceedings are commenced in respect of one or other set of losses and a Pt 36 payment is made and accepted, since the effect of acceptance of such a payment is to stay the further pursuit of the action.[10]

30–07 In *Lambert v Mainland Market Deliveries Ltd*,[11] C's stationary motor car was struck and severely damaged by a motor vehicle driven by D's employee. The accident occurred in January 1975. C's insurers paid C £982.97 in respect of the damage to his car and in March 1975 notified D's insurers of the amount they had paid to C and which they sought to recover from them (there being no "knock-for-knock" agreement between the two insurers). On July 2, 1975 C, acting personally, issued proceedings in the county court to recover his uninsured losses of £72.80, although the summons concerning this was not served on D until July 30, 1975. In the meantime, on July 3, C's insurers had written to D's insurers threatening to instruct C's own solicitors (whom C had previously consulted) to "include our claim" in proceedings to be brought on C's behalf unless payment was made within 14 days. On July 29, D's insurers, who were then unaware of the proceedings instituted by C, replied offering 50 per cent of the outlay. On August 7, by which time C's insurers had not responded to the letter of July 29, D's insurers became aware of C's personal claim. Immediately, they (a) paid £72.80 into court in respect of C's claim and (b) wrote to C's insurers withdrawing the offer previously made. C accepted the payment into court. When C's insurers, acting in C's name, sought to have the automatic stay of the proceedings lifted to enable them to pursue their outlay, D's insurers, acting in D's name, argued that there was no jurisdiction to lift the stay, but that if there was, it should not be lifted. The Court of Appeal held that there was jurisdiction to set aside the stay, albeit a jurisdiction that would be exercised "with very great care". It was appropriate to set aside the stay in this case as D's insurers were fully aware that C's insurers were pursuing the (much larger) balance of the claim and that D's insurers were simply trying to take advantage of a procedural provision to bar the pursuit of the rest of the claim. The stay was set aside on the undertaking of C's insurers to repay D's insurers the amount paid into court.

30–08 In *Buckland v Palmer*,[12] C's car was damaged in an accident caused by D's negligent driving in February 1982. When notified by C, C's insurers told her that they had a "knock-for-knock" agreement with D's insurers and that they (C's insurers) would meet the costs of the damage to her car less a £50 excess. In April 1982, C issued county court proceedings against D seeking to recover that £50. Within a few days D paid into court the full amount of the claim

---

[8] (1986) C.A.T. 413. See also *Taylor v Wray & Co. Ltd* [1971] 1 Lloyd's Rep. 497, CA.
[9] See para.3–24, above.
[10] CPR r.36.15(1).
[11] [1977] 1 W.L.R. 825.
[12] [1984] 1 W.L.R. 1109.

without admission of liability. At some stage after this, C's insurers discovered that D was not insured by the insurers he had mentioned to C at the time of the accident. In September 1982, C's insurers, acting in C's name, began county court proceedings against D personally for the amount of their outlay (some £1,142) less the sum of £50. D sought to strike out the action as an abuse of the process of the court. The Court of Appeal held that the second action should be struck out as an abuse of the process of the court since it constituted the bringing of two actions in respect of the same cause of action, but that the striking out should be without prejudice to an application by C's insurers to remove the stay on the first action imposed when the payment into court was accepted.

30–09   The position is less clear when one of the two types of claim proceeds to a consent judgment. In the normal course of events, a consent judgment would be seen as extinguishing the cause of action by merger.[13] This was recognised by Sir John Donaldson M.R. in *Buckland v Palmer*,[14] but who went on to say this:[15]

> "... I should be surprised and disappointed if this left the courts powerless to do justice if, for example, advantage had been taken of an ill-informed plaintiff by an experienced defendant who offered to submit to judgment in a small sum, well knowing that the plaintiff was under some misapprehension as to the effect upon his right thereafter to proceed with his substantial claim ... I would expect the courts to re-appraise the circumstances in which a judgment could be set aside, if justice so required."

30–10   Although the position is, perhaps, not entirely free from doubt,[16] it would seem that jurisdiction does exist for setting aside a consent judgment for one or other of the two types of loss (the matter usually arising with the settlement of uninsured losses) if the justice of the case requires it. It is thought likely, however, that the jurisdiction would be exercised sparingly[17] and with particular circumspection if third-party interests proper would be affected.[18]

---

[13] *Chitty on Contracts* (29th ed., 2004), Vol.1, para.25–007.
[14] Noted at para.30–08, above.
[15] [1984] 1 W.L.R. 1109 at 1115.
[16] In *Hayler v Chapman* [1989] 1 Lloyd's Rep. 490, a case where C, unknown to his insurers, recovered his uninsured losses against D following a contested county court arbitration hearing, the Court of Appeal assumed, without deciding, that the jurisdiction to set aside the award existed, but considered it right not to have done so in the circumstances.
[17] cf. *Lambert v Mainland Market Deliveries Ltd*, n.11, above, *per* Megaw L.J., at 833.
[18] See para.6–84, above.

SETTLEMENTS WITH THIRD PARTY—THE EFFECT AS BETWEEN INSURER AND INSURED

Under the general law of insurance, the insured is required not to do anything which would prejudice the insurer's rights. Indeed, most insurance policies contain express conditions concerning the insured's duties in this regard. Where, contrary to these duties, the insured compromises with a third party, he will be liable to the insurer for the full value of the rights he has compromised.[19]

30-11

Whilst there does not appear to be any direct authority on the point, it is thought that there would be an implied term in any contract of insurance to the effect that the insurer would not exercise its rights of subrogation so as to cause damage to the insured.[20] If an insurer mistakenly binds the insured to an overall compromise in a way that would leave the insured with no direct remedy against the third party, it is submitted that the insured should have a remedy against the insurer.

30-12

Where an insurer settles an insured's claim pursuant to the insured's policy and the insured then sues the person responsible for the loss and settles that claim, the insurer has, by virtue of the doctrine of subrogation, an equitable proprietary right in the form of a lien over the settlement moneys.[21]

30-13

SETTLEMENT WITH THIRD PARTY—THE EFFECT ON A CO-INSURER

An insured may be covered for the same risk in the same interest in the same subject-matter by more than one policy of insurance. In the normal course of events, where one insurer reasonably settles the claim of a third party brought against the insured, that insurer is entitled in equity to a contribution from the co-insurer.[22] Where, however, the insurer that settles the claim of the third party in full has in its policy with its insured a rateable proportion clause, it has been held[23] that it will be precluded from claiming the contribution from the co-insurer to which it would otherwise

30-14

---

[19] *West of England Fire Insurance Co v Isaacs* [1987] 1 Q.B. 226; *Horse, Carriage and General Insurance Co v Petch* (1916) 33 T.L.R. 131; *Boag v Standard Marine Insurance Co* [1937] 2 K.B. 113. See also *Faircharm Investments Ltd v Citibank International Plc* [1998] Lloyd's Rep. Bank. 127, CA.
[20] MacGillivray, *Insurance Law* (10th ed., 2003), para.22–59.
[21] *Napier and Ettrick (Lord) v Hunter* [1993] A.C. 713.
[22] *Chitty on Contracts* (29th ed., 2004), Vol.2, para.41–083.
[23] *Legal & General Assurance Society Ltd v Drake Insurance Co Ltd* [1992] Q.B. 887, CA; overruling *Monksfield v Vehicle & General Insurance Co Ltd* [1971] 1 Lloyds Rep. 139.

have been entitled because the amount paid to the third party in excess of the appropriate rateable proportion must be regarded as a voluntary payment and the right to claim a contribution in equity arises only where an insurer has been obliged under its policy to pay more than its rateable proportion. However, in *Eagle Star Insurance Co Ltd v Provincial Insurance Plc*[24] the Judicial Committee of the Privy Council held that where two insurers were under a statutory liability to indemnify a third party, the right of one insurer to a contribution from the other had to be determined in accordance "with the extent of their respective liabilities to the ... insured under the separate contracts of insurance".[25]

REINSURANCE AND "FOLLOW THE SETTLEMENTS" CLAUSES[26]

30–15 Reinsurance is the process by which an insurer of a risk takes out insurance of that risk with another insurer.[27] The original insurer is called the reinsured (or the reassured). A standard clause in the London reinsurance market between the reinsured and the reinsurer (called the "follow the settlements" clause) is in these terms:

> "All loss settlements by the reassured including compromise settlements and the establishment of funds for the settlement of losses shall be binding upon the reinsurers, providing such settlements are within the terms and conditions of the original policies and/or contracts and within the terms and conditions of this reinsurance."

---

[24] [1994] 1 A.C. 130.
[25] *ibid.* at 141. This approach was said to be more appropriate than that of determining the issue on the basis of their respective statutory liabilities because their respective contractual liabilities to the insured "will indicate the scale of the double insurance": *ibid.* The case of *Monksfield v Vehicle General Insurance Co Ltd*, n.23, above, was said to have been correctly decided.
[26] See MacGillivray, *Insurance Law* (10th ed., 2003), paras 33–71 *et seq.* "[The] effect of a clause binding reinsurers to follow settlements of the insurers, is that the insurers agree to indemnify insurers in the event that they settle a claim by their assured, *i.e.*, when they dispose, or bind themselves to dispose, of a claim, whether by reason of admission or compromise provided [1] that the claim so recognised by them falls within the risks covered by the policy of reinsurance as a matter of law, and provided [2] also that in settling the claim the insurers have acted honestly and have taken all proper and business like steps in making the settlement": *per* Robert Goff L.J. in *The Insurance Co of Africa v Scor (UK) Reinsurance Co Ltd* [1985] 1 Lloyd's Rep. 312 at 330.
[27] *Chitty on Contracts* (29th ed., 2004), Vol.2, para.41–091. Though see *per* Potter L.J. in *Skandia International Corporation v NRG Victory Reinsurance Ltd*, unreported, March 16, 1998, CA.

The effect of the provisos in the above clause was considered by the **30–16** House of Lords in *Hill v Mercantile and General Reinsurance Co Plc*.[28] A "compromise settlement" of the reassured will be excluded from the "follow the settlements" clause only if the provisos apply. Lord Mustill said this of the provisos[29]:

> "The intent of these seems clear in broad outline, although it may be difficult to apply on the margins. The crucial words are 'within the terms and conditions' of the original policies and of the reinsurance. To my mind these draw a distinction between the facts which generate claims under the two contracts, and the legal extent of the respective covers: the purpose of the distinction being to ensure that the reinsurer's original assessment and rating of the risks assumed are not falsified by a settlement which, even if soundly based on the facts, transfers into the inward or outward policies, or both, risks which properly lie outside them. This restriction is perhaps more clearly visualised in relation to the second proviso. Here, the reinsurers are entitled to say that they rated the policy by reference to its chronological and geographical extent, to the types of casualty insured, to the boundaries of the insured layer, the mode of calculating the loss, and so forth. These variables, defined by the terms of the policy, founded the bargain between reinsurers and reinsured on the basis of which the premium and other terms were set. The purpose of the second proviso is . . . to keep this foundation intact, and it would be undermined if an honest attempt by those further down the chain to ascertain the legal consequences of the facts could impose on the reinsurers responsibilities beyond those expressed in the policies. So also with the first proviso. The reinsurers undertake to protect the reinsured against risks which they have written, not risks which they have not written. To allow even an honest and conscientious appraisal of the legal implications of the facts embodied in an agreement between parties down the chain to impose on the reinsurers risks beyond those which they have undertaken and those which the reinsured have undertaken would effectively rewrite the outward contract: and it is this . . . which the provisos are designed to forestall."

The burden of establishing that an exception to the reinsurer's obligation **30–17** to follow the reinsured's settlements exists lies upon the reinsurer.[30]

---

[28] [1996] 1 W.L.R. 1239: "There are only two rules, and both obvious. First, that the reinsurer cannot be held liable unless the loss falls within the cover of the policy reinsured and within the cover created by the reinsurance. Second, that the parties are free to agree on ways of proving whether these requirements are satisfied": *per* Lord Mustill at 1251. See, generally, *Chitty on Contracts* (29th ed., 2004), Vol.2, paras 41–094—41–095. See also *Assicurazioni Generali SPA v CGU International Insurance Plc* [2004] EWCA Civ 429; and *Eagle Star Insurance Company Limited v J.N. Cresswell* [2004] EWCA Civ 602.
[29] [1996] 1 W.L.R. 1239 at 1252–1253.
[30] *Charman v Guardian Royal Exchange Assurance* [1992] 2 Lloyds Rep. 607, *per* Webster J.

NATURE OF THE "SETTLEMENT" OF AN INSURED'S CLAIM

30–18 Where an insured makes a claim upon his insurer pursuant to the contract of insurance between them and the insurer makes a payment in respect of that claim, it is traditional to refer to that payment as being "in settlement of" the claim. As previously indicated,[31] it has been suggested that this situation constitutes an "implied settlement" having a contractual status similar to that of a true compromise even though no articulated dispute between insurer and insured has emerged. However, as Clarke[32] has succinctly and pertinently stated, "[There] is a difference between settling a claim and settling a dispute". For reasons previously given,[33] it is submitted that "settlements" of claims made under insurance policies should be seen as forming a category of their own, some of which will have all the characteristics of the compromise of a dispute either as to liability or as to quantum or both, and some of which simply reflect the performance by the insurer of the obligations under the insurance contract.[34]

30–19 Unless there is evidence of bad faith or collusion between an insured and his insurer aimed at prejudicing a third party who has a claim against the insured, the court will not intervene to prevent the insured from accepting a sum in settlement of his claim against his insurer arising from the third party's claim against him even if that sum is substantially less than the amount of the third party's claim.[35]

---

[31] See paras 2–12 *et seq.*, above.
[32] Clarke, *The Law of Insurance Contracts* (3rd ed., 1997), para.30–6.
[33] See n.31, above.
[34] Clarke, n.32, above, para.30–06.
[35] *Normid Housing Association Ltd v Ralphs, Mansell* [1989] 1 Lloyd's Rep. 265, CA. This case involved a professional negligence claim by C against D (architects) who were insured in relation to claims of this nature.

PART 7

Chancery Litigation

This section is devoted to the settlement of disputes which are ordinarily dealt with within the Chancery jurisdiction of the court.

CHAPTER 31

The Settlement of Chancery Litigation

This chapter concerns the settlement of disputes which when pursued to litigation are likely to result in proceedings in the Chancery Division.[1] Certain business is assigned directly by statute to that division;[2] other business has been so assigned by virtue of rules and orders made pursuant to statutory authority.[3] A claimant may, of course, elect to commence proceedings in any division of the High Court, subject to the powers of the

31-01

---

[1] The *Chancery Guide* gives practical guidance on the conduct of cases in the Chancery Division. Its provisions are reproduced at *The White Book*, Vol.2, paras 1–1 *et seq*. At the time this edition went to press, a new edition of the *Chancery Guide* was due to be published in September 2005.

[2] By virtue of s.61(1) of, and Sch.1 to the Supreme Court Act 1981 the following matters are assigned specifically to the Chancery Division:
   (a) the sale, exchange or partition of land, or the raising of charges on land;
   (b) the redemption or foreclosure of mortgages;
   (c) the execution of trusts;
   (d) the administration of the estates of deceased persons;
   (e) bankruptcy;
   (f) the dissolution of partnership or the taking of partnership or other accounts;
   (g) the rectification, setting aside or cancellation of deeds or other instruments in writing;
   (h) probate business, other than non-contentious or common form business;
   (i) patents, trade marks, registered designs, copyright or design right;
   (j) the appointment of a guardian of a minor's estate.
and all causes and matters involving the exercise of the High Court's jurisdiction under the enactments relating to companies.

[3] For example, High court claims for the possession of land subject to a mortgage: *Practice Direction—Possession Claims*, para.1.6 (*The White Book*, Vol.1, para.55PD.1); landlord and tenant claims in the High Court: *Practice Direction—Landlord and Tenant Claims*, para.2.6 (*The White Book*, Vol.1, para.56PD.2); arbitration claims relating to a landlord or tenant or partnership dispute: Practice Direction—Arbitration, para.2.3(2)(*The White Book*, Vol.2, para.2E.41); probate claims in the High Court: CPR r.57.2(2); claims and applications for the substitution or removal of a personal representative: CPR r.57.13(2); and all proceedings in the High Court relating to the administration of the estates of deceased persons and trusts and all charity proceedings: CPR r.64.1(3).

court to transfer those proceedings elsewhere[4]; and certain types of litigation[5] are commonly to be found in both the Chancery Division and the Queen's Bench Division. Furthermore, some types of litigation, most notably in this context disputes under the Inheritance (Provision for Family and Dependants) Act 1975, are assigned to alternative divisions.[6] The discussion that follows, however, relates to those forms of dispute that are truly to be regarded as the exclusive province of the Chancery Division.[7]

31–02   As stated elsewhere,[8] the underlying legal basis for any compromise is the law of contract. That applies as much to the matters with which this Chapter is concerned as to any other. However, in some aspects of Chancery business the law demands attention to matters beyond the merely contractual; and, in some respects, the practice differs from that to be observed in relation to common law disputes. It is proposed to examine briefly certain aspects of Chancery business in which disputes may fall to be resolved by agreement and to deal with relevant matters of Chancery practice.

INSOLVENCY

Companies

31–03 The presentation and service of a creditor's petition seeking the compulsory winding-up of a corporate debtor may provoke the company to discharge the debt. If the company has repaid the debt out of its own moneys it will be in the interests of the petitioner as well as the company to seek to prevent the court from making any order to wind up the company,[9] because the winding-up will be deemed to have commenced at the time of the presentation of the petition for winding-up on which the order is based[10] and the payment will thereupon be invalidated unless the court otherwise orders.[11] If the petition has not been advertised, no notices (whether in support or in opposition) have been received by the petitioner

---

[4] Supreme Court Act 1981, ss.64 and 65.
[5] For example, professional negligence actions and claims by an employer for breach of a contract of employment by a former employee. The cases of *Platform Home Loans Ltd v Oyston Shipways Ltd* [2000] 2 A.C. 190, HL and *Faccenda Chicken Ltd v Fowler* [1987] Ch. 117, CA were commenced and pursued in the Chancery Division.
[6] CPR r.57.15(1). The settlement of these disputes is dealt with in Ch.33, below.
[7] And, in analogous cases, the preserve of the equity jurisdiction of the county court: County Courts Act 1984, ss.23 and 24.
[8] See Chs 1 and 3, above.
[9] Possibly after the substitution of another creditor for the petitioner under Insolvency Rules 1986, r.4.19.
[10] Insolvency Act 1986, s.129.
[11] *ibid.*, s.127.

with reference to the petition, and the company consents, the petitioner may, at least five days before the hearing, apply *ex parte* to the Court Manager of the Companies Court for leave to withdraw the petition on such terms as to costs as the parties may agree.[12] Otherwise the petitioner may appear at the hearing of the petition and ask for it to be dismissed. The usual practice, where a winding-up petition is dismissed on late payment of a debt by the company, is to make an order for costs in the petitioner's favour as against the company even if it does not appear. The petitioner is seen as having succeeded and the normal rule applies that costs follow the event. This general principle also applies to the costs of applications connected with the petition (such as applications to stay advertisement), unless there is good reason to the contrary.[13] The onus is on the company to lay before the court material as to why an order for costs should not be made against it; but this material does not have to be formal evidence properly so described. The court adopts a pragmatic approach to the acceptability of whatever material is put before it where an order for costs, other than in the petitioner's favour, is sought upon payment of the debt in full.[14] In earlier times, the threat by a petitioner who had been paid the petition debt that, if his costs were not paid in full, he would nonetheless press on with his petition and ask for a compulsory order, was very effective to avoid the airing of disputes as to costs, to avoid taxation of costs, and to avoid the risk of failure to honour an order for costs. However, the modern practice is now so entrenched that it has been said that such a threat has ceased to be a truly effective threat, at all events for the time being.[15]

31–04 If at the hearing of the petition the company seeks an adjournment with a view to paying the petitioning creditor, the court may stand the petition over to a future date. Whatever may be the rights of the parties to agree to the deferment of the hearing of other litigation, the special considerations which apply to creditors' winding-up petitions require, as a general rule, that they should be heard promptly. Thus, the court is reluctant to grant long or repeated adjournments, even with the consent of all concerned, unless there are cogent grounds for the application. In normal cases where the debt is not disputed, a period of four weeks from the date of the first hearing will normally be regarded as sufficient to enable the petitioning creditor, if still unpaid, to decide whether to press for a winding-up order or to rely on other arrangements. Usually this period will also be regarded

---

[12] Insolvency Rules 1986, r.4.15. See Sch.4, Form 4.8, reproduced as Precedent No.15, at para.A1–15, below, for an appropriate form of order.
[13] Re *Ryan Developments Ltd* [2002] EWHC 1121 (Ch); [2002] 2 B.C.L.C. 792 at [22], *per* Neuberger J.
[14] Re *Nowmost Co Ltd* [1996] 2 B.C.L.C. 492; following Re *Shusella Ltd* [1983] B.C.L.C. 505.
[15] Re *Nowmost Co Ltd*, n.14 above, *per* Lindsay J. at 496b–d.

31-05 Where the debt on which the petition is based is disputed by the company and the petition is dismissed pursuant to an agreement between the petitioner and the company, the court will imply a term into that agreement that no further winding-up petition will be presented in respect of the same debt. If thereafter the petitioning creditor successfully sues the company to judgment, the debt will merge in the judgment and may be relied upon to found a fresh petition.[17] An order in Tomlin form[18] is not appropriate to embody the terms of any compromise of a winding-up petition: it is inappropriate that the proceedings should be stayed while the terms of compromise are carried into effect since, if an order for the compulsory winding-up of the company were subsequently to be made, it would relate back to the service of the petition, thereby invalidating any intervening dispositions of the company's property in accordance with s.127 of the Insolvency Act 1986.[19]

Individuals

31-06 In suitable cases the Bankruptcy Court may make consent orders without attendance by the parties in personal insolvency matters.[20] The written consent of the parties will be required. Examples of such orders are as follows:

(1) On applications to set aside a statutory demand, orders:

(a) dismissing the application, with or without an order for costs as may be agreed (permission will be given to present a petition on or after the seventh day after the date of the order, unless a different date is agreed);

(b) setting aside the demand, with or without an order for costs as may be agreed; or

(c) giving permission to withdraw the application, with or without an order for costs as may be agreed.

---

[16] cf. *Practice Note (Companies: Winding Up)* [1977] 1 W.L.R. 1066. Although by para.1.2, *Practice Direction: Insolvency Proceedings* (*The White Book*, Vol.2, para.3E-1) replaces all previous Practice Notes and Practice Directions relating to insolvency proceedings, it is submitted that the former practice will still apply.

[17] *Re A Company (No.00928 of 1991) Ex p. City Electrical Factors Ltd* [1991] B.C.L.C. 514. For a suggested form of order dismissing a winding-up petition by consent, see Precedent No.16 at para.A1–16, below.

[18] See paras 9–19 *et seq.*, above.

[19] cf. *Re A Company (No.003324 of 1979)* [1981] 1 W.L.R. 1059 at 1060, *per* Vinelott J.; considered at para.31–11, below.

[20] *Practice Direction: Insolvency Proceedings*, para.16.3 (*The White Book*, Vol.2, para.3E-16).

(2) On petitions: where there is a list of supporting or opposing creditors in Form 6.21,[21] or a statement signed by or on behalf of the petitioning creditor that no notices have been received from supporting or opposing creditors, orders:

 (a) dismissing the petition, with or without an order for costs as may be agreed; or

 (b) if the petition has not been served, giving permission to withdraw the petition (with no order for costs).[22]

(3) On other applications, orders:

 (a) for sale of property, possession of property, disposal of proceeds of sale;

 (b) giving interim directions;

 (c) dismissing the application, with or without an order for costs as may be agreed; or

 (d) giving permission to withdraw the application, with or without an order for costs as may be agreed.

If (as may often be the case with orders under sub-paras (3)(a) or (b) above), an adjournment is required, whether generally with liberty to restore or to a fixed date, the order by consent may include an order for the adjournment. If adjournment to a date is requested, a time estimate should be given and the court will fix the first available date and time on or after the date requested.

The above list should not be regarded as exhaustive, nor should it be assumed that an order will be made without attendance as requested.[23] It is suggested that one situation in which the court may decline to make an order as requested is on an application for the bankruptcy petition to be dismissed (or for permission to withdraw it) where: (a) there is no evidence from the petitioner verifying the fact that since filing the petition no payment has been made to the petitioner out of the debtor's property by way of settlement (in whole or in part) of the debt in respect of which the petition was brought and no arrangement involving the debtor's property has been entered into for securing or compounding such debt; and (b) there are supporting creditors who may wish to apply for an order for the change of carriage of the petition.[24] The procedure outlined in para.31–06, above, is designed to save time and costs but is not intended to discourage attendance.[25] Applications for consent orders without attendance should be

31–07

---

[21] Insolvency Rules 1986, Sch.4.
[22] For an appropriate form of order, see Insolvency Rules 1986, Sch.4, Form 6.22, reproduced as Precedent No.17 at para.A1–17, below.
[23] *Practice Direction: Insolvency Proceedings*, para.16.4 (*The White Book*, Vol.2, para.3E-16).
[24] Under Insolvency Rules 1986, r.6.31. See also r.6.32.
[25] *Practice Direction: Insolvency Proceedings*, para.16.5 (*The White Book*, Vol.2, para.3E-16).

lodged at least two clear working days (and preferably longer) before any fixed hearing date.[26] Whenever a document is lodged or a letter sent, the correct case number, code (if any) and year (for example 123/SD/99 or 234/99) should be quoted. A note should also be given of the date and time of the next hearing (if any).[27] The attention of practitioners is specifically drawn[28] to para.4.4(4) of the Practice Direction relating to CPR Pt 44 under which the parties should agree a figure for any costs to be inserted in the court order or agree that there should be no order for costs. If the parties cannot agree the costs position, attendance on the appointment will be necessary; but unless good reason can be shown for the failure to deal with costs, no costs will be allowed for that attendance.

31–08 As in the case of winding-up petitions,[29] where, following the service of a bankruptcy petition, the debt is paid, the petitioning creditor will ordinarily be entitled to his costs on the dismissal of the petition, as he has in substance succeeded in his proceedings against the debtor. However, that inference can be displaced in a particular case, as where avoidable defects in the creditor's proceedings have led to costs being incurred unnecessarily for the debtor.[30]

Appeals

31–09 An appeal from a decision of a County Court (whether made by a district judge or a circuit judge) or of a registrar of the High Court in insolvency proceedings lies to a High Court judge of the Chancery Division without the permission of any court in accordance with s.375(2) of the Insolvency Act 1986 and rr.7.47(2) and 7.48(2) of the Insolvency Rules 1986 (as amended by s.55 of the Access to Justice Act 1999).[31] Such an appeal may be dismissed by consent; but the appeal court will not make an order allowing an appeal unless it is satisfied that the decision of the lower court was wrong. Any consent order signed by each party or letters of consent from each party must be lodged not later than 24 hours before the date fixed for the hearing of the appeal at the address of the appropriate venue and will be dealt with by the judge of the appeal court. Attention is drawn to para.4.4(4) of the Practice Direction relating to CPR Pt 44 regarding costs where an order is made by consent without attendance.[32]

---

[26] *Practice Direction: Insolvency Proceedings*, para.16.6.
[27] *ibid.*, para.16.7.
[28] *ibid.*, para.16.8.
[29] See para.31–03, above.
[30] *Re a Debtor (No.510 of 1997)*, The Times, June 18, 1998. On the facts, the proper order was that there should be no order as to costs.
[31] See *Practice Direction: Insolvency Proceedings*, paras 17.2(1) and 17.6 (*The White Book*, Vol.2, para.3E-18) and *Chancery Guide*, para.10.15 (*The White Book*, Vol.2, para.1–94).
[32] See *Practice Direction: Insolvency Proceedings*, para.17.22(8) (*The White Book*, Vol.2, para.3E-18); and compare n.28 at para.31–07, above.

LIQUIDATORS AND TRUSTEES IN BANKRUPTCY

A liquidator's power to compromise claims is exercisable only   **31–10**

(1) in the case of a members' voluntary winding-up, with the sanction of an extraordinary resolution of the company[33];
(2) in the case of a creditors' voluntary winding-up, with the sanction of the court or the liquidation committee (or, if there is no such committee, a meeting of the company's creditors)[34]; and
(3) when the company is being wound up by the court, with the sanction of the court or the liquidation committee.[35]

A trustee in bankruptcy's power to compromise claims is only exercisable with the permission of the creditor's committee or the court.[36]

The proper approach to the exercise of the court's power to sanction a compromise by a company liquidator was considered by the Court of Appeal in *Re Greenhaven Motors Ltd.*[37] The decision whether or not to sanction a proposed compromise was one for the court and not for the liquidator. It was therefore wrong in principle for the court to approach its task on the basis that the liquidator's wish to exercise the power should prevail unless it was satisfied that the liquidator was not acting bona fide or that he was acting in a way in which no reasonable liquidator should act. The correct approach was for the court to consider whether or not the interests of those creditors or contributories who had a real interest in the assets of the company in liquidation were likely to be best served by permitting the company to enter into the proposed compromise. In reaching its decision the court was entitled to give weight to the wishes of those creditors and contributories who would be affected by the decision and to the views of the liquidator; but ultimately it was for the court to decide whether or not to sanction the proposed compromise. If the exercise of the power was sanctioned, it was for the liquidator, in the absence of a direction from the court, to decide whether or not actually to exercise the power of compromise.[38]

---

[33] Insolvency Act 1986, s.165(2)(a), Sch.4, paras 2 and 3.
[34] *ibid.*, s.165(2)(b), Sch.4, paras 2 and 3.
[35] *ibid.*, s.167(1)(a), Sch.4, paras 2 and 3.
[36] *ibid.*, s.314(1)(a), Sch.5, paras 6 and 7.
[37] [1999] B.C.L.C. 635. It is submitted that the same principles would apply to a trustee in bankruptcy.
[38] See especially, *ibid.*, *per* Chadwick L.J. at 642h–643h. For a case in which the court sanctioned a compromise despite the opposition of preference shareholders on the grounds that they had no real or tangible interest in the assets available for distribution in the winding-up in any foreseeable circumstances, see *Re Barings Plc (No.7)* [2002] 1 B.C.L.C. 401.

UNFAIR PREJUDICE

31-11 Provided a petition under s.459 of the Companies Act 1985 does not seek an order for the compulsory winding-up of the company,[39] agreed terms of compromise may be embodied in an order in Tomlin form[40] and the petition allowed to remain on the file whilst the terms of compromise are implemented, subject to an undertaking by the petitioner to apply to dismiss the petition when the terms of the compromise have been fully implemented.[41]

DISQUALIFICATION ORDERS[42]

31-12 The Company Directors Disqualification Act 1986 empowers the court to make a disqualification order, that is to say an order that for a period specified in the order a person:

(a) shall not be a director of a company, act as a receiver of a company's property or in any way, whether directly or indirectly, be concerned or take part in the promotion, formation or management of a company unless (in each case) he has the leave of the court; and

(b) shall not act as an insolvency practitioner.[43]

31-13 In *Secretary of State for Trade and Industry v Rogers*[44] the Court of Appeal endorsed the summary form of procedure sanctioned by Ferris J. in *Re Carecraft Construction Co Ltd*[45] which enables disqualification proceedings to be dealt with summarily in cases where:

(1) facts regarding the director's conduct in managing the company or companies in question are either agreed or, at least, are not disputed;

---

[39] See *Practice Direction—Applications under the Companies Act 1985*, para.9(1) (*The White Book*, Vol.2, para.2G-10) as to the undesirability of asking as a matter of course for a winding-up order as an alternative to an order under s.459. The petition should not ask for a winding-up order unless that is the relief which the petitioner prefers or it is thought that it may be the only relief to which the petitioner is entitled.
[40] See paras 9–19 *et seq.*, above.
[41] *Re A Company (No.003324 of 1979)* [1981] 1 W.L.R. 1059. See Precedent No.18 at para.A1–18, below.
[42] For a more detailed discussion, see Walters and Davis-White, *Directors' Disqualification and Bankruptcy Restrictions* (2nd ed., 2005), Ch.9.
[43] The wording of the 1986 Act is reproduced with the amendments introduced by s.5 of the Insolvency Act 2000 as from April 2, 2001.
[44] [1996] 1 W.L.R. 1569.
[45] [1994] 1 W.L.R. 172.

(2) the Secretary of State is willing for the case to be dealt with by the judge on the agreed (or not disputed) facts and does not consider it necessary to endeavour to prove the additional facts that have been alleged in the evidence filed in support of the application;
(3) the director is willing for the case to be dealt with by the judge on the agreed (or not disputed) facts and does not dispute that those facts require the court to make a disqualification order; and
(4) the Secretary of State and the director have reached agreement either as to the length of the disqualification period that would be appropriate or, at least, as to the bracket of years into which the disqualification period should fall.

As explained by the Court of Appeal,[46] the *Carecraft* procedure can effectively, and without the judge's consent, limit the facts on which the judge can base his judgment as to the order that should be made[47] but the *Carecraft* procedure could not oblige the judge to make a disqualification order, and could not bind him as to the period of disqualification to be imposed. If the judge, on reading the papers in advance, had any doubts as to whether a disqualification order should be made or as to whether the period should fall within the agreed bracket, those doubts should be voiced at the earliest possible moment so that the parties could consider whether they, or either of them, would prefer a full trial. It was anticipated that it would be a very rare case in which any such doubts were entertained.

If the parties decide to invite the court to deal with the application under the *Carecraft* procedure they should inform the court immediately and obtain a date for the hearing of the application.[48] Whenever this procedure is adopted, the claimant must: 31–14

(1) except where the court otherwise directs, submit a written statement containing in respect of each defendant any material facts which (for the purposes of the application) are either agreed or not opposed (by either party); and
(2) specify in writing the period of disqualification which the parties accept that the agreed or unopposed facts justify or the band of years (*e.g.* four to six years) or bracket (*i.e.* two to five years; six to 10 years; 11 to 15 years) into which they will submit the case falls.[49]

---

[46] [1996] 1 W.L.R. 1569 at 1574H–1575B, *per* Sir Richard Scott V.C., as he then was.
[47] In this regard, the Court of Appeal differed from the approach of Ferris J in *Re Carecraft Construction Co Ltd* [1994] 1 W.L.R. 172 at 181B–C and 183G–H: see [1996] 1 W.L.R. 1569 at 1574A–C. Sir Richard Scott V.C. said this: "There is no impropriety in directors disqualification cases or in any other civil proceedings in placing before the court an agreed statement of facts and inviting the court to deal with the case on the basis of that statement".
[48] *Practice Direction: Directors Disqualification Proceedings*, para.13.1 (*The White Book*, Vol. 1, para.B1–013).
[49] *ibid.*, para.13.2.

355

Unless the court otherwise orders, a hearing under the *Carecraft* procedure will be held in private.[50] If the court is minded to make a disqualification order having heard the parties' representations, it will usually give judgment and make the disqualification order in public. Unless the court otherwise orders, the witness statement referred to above will be annexed to the disqualification order.[51] If the court refuses to make the disqualification order under the *Carecraft* procedure, it will give further directions for the hearing of the application.[52]

31–15 In *Secretary of State for Trade and Industry v Banarse*[53] it was said that a *Carecraft* statement of facts should not mince its words. Either the parties were in agreement as to the facts or they were not. If not, a trial would in the long run be the appropriate course. But if they were in agreement, the facts should be spelt out clearly and should leave no room or need for infilling or interpretation by way of inference of secondary fact. Where the court was faced with an admission that a respondent knew or ought to have known something, it could not proceed on the basis of actual knowledge. A defendant who wants to dispose of disqualification proceedings under the *Carecraft* procedure should consider insisting on the inclusion in the written statement of a provision limiting any admissions and concessions made by him to the purpose of facilitating a *Carecraft* disposal of the proceedings, and stating that they are wholly without prejudice to his position in relation to any other proceedings which may be brought against him, such as proceedings brought on behalf of the creditors of a company by its liquidator or other office holder.[54]

31–16 The then Vice-Chancellor (Sir Richard Scott V.C.) had recommended amending legislation enabling disqualification to be imposed by a formal undertaking entered into by the director, without the necessity of a court order.[55] Section 6 of the Insolvency Act 2000 accordingly amended the Company Directors Disqualification Act 1986 (as from April 2, 2001) by inserting a new s.1A relating to disqualification undertakings. Directors whom the Secretary of State considers unfit may consent to a period of disqualification without the need for court involvement by giving a disqualification undertaking. The Secretary of State has an unfettered discretion as to whether to accept an undertaking which has been offered, and is entitled to refuse to accept an otherwise satisfactory disqualification

---

[50] *ibid.*, para.13.4.
[51] *ibid.*, para.13.5.
[52] *ibid.*, para.13.6.
[53] [1997] 1 B.C.L.C. 653, especially at 658.
[54] The propriety of such a provision was accepted in *Official Receiver v Cooper* [1999] B.C.C. 115.
[55] See *Practice Note* [1996] 1 All E.R. 442; and *Secretary of State for Trade and Industry v Rogers* [1996] 1 W.L.R. 1569 at 1574G–H.

undertaking on the grounds that it does not refer to or incorporate a statement setting out the grounds of the director's unfitness.[56] The director should always seek expressly to limit the use of any admitted or undisputed facts recorded in a schedule of unfit conduct solely to the purposes of the Company Directors Disqualification Act 1986 or any purposes consequential thereto so as to prevent them from being used against him in other proceedings brought, for example, by an administrator, receiver or liquidator. The general rule is that the court will order the defendant to pay the costs of the Secretary of State (or official receiver) if a pending disqualification application is discontinued because the Secretary of State has accepted a disqualification undertaking; but the general rule will not apply where the court considers that the circumstances are such that it should make another order.[57] The editors of *The White Book* note[58] that since the introduction of disqualification undertakings, the use of the *Carecraft* procedure has largely dropped away, principally because undertakings have advantages in terms of reduced expense. However, it remains open for the parties to use it, in particular because the opportunity to include matters of mitigation is not (as a matter of the Secretary of State's policy) available in respect of disqualification undertakings, but (at least as matters currently stand) is available in the *Carecraft* procedure.

COURT-APPOINTED RECEIVERS

A receiver appointed by the court has a right to be indemnified in respect of his costs and remuneration out of all the assets subject to the receivership, not merely those in his possession. That right is not extinguished even though the receivership is discharged by consent and the receiver hands back control of the assets to their legal owners. Accordingly, the receiver can obtain an order charging all the assets over which he was appointed receiver with the amount of his costs and remuneration, whether or not he has ever reduced those assets into his possession.[59]

31–17

TRUSTEES AND PERSONAL REPRESENTATIVES

By s.15 of the Trustee Act 1925 a personal representative, or two or more trustees acting together, or (subject to the restrictions imposed in regard to receipts by a sole trustee not being a trust corporation) a sole acting trustee

31–18

---

[56] *Re Blackspur Group Plc (No.3)* [2001] EWCA Civ 1595; [2002] 2 B.C.L.C. 263.
[57] *Practice Direction: Directors Disqualification Proceedings*, paras 28.1 and 28.2 (*The White Book*, Vol.1, para.B1–028).
[58] *The White Book*, Vol.1, para.B1–013.1
[59] *Mellor v Mellor* [1992] 1 W.L.R. 517. The sum involved may be substantial: the receiver in *Mellor v Mellor* was seeking to recover a sum of a little under £40,000 (inclusive of VAT) in respect of his time, costs and disbursements during the three-and-a-half weeks' receivership.

where by the instrument (if any) creating the trust or by statute a sole trustee is authorised to execute the trusts and powers reposed in him may, if and as he or they think fit, compromise any debt, account, claim or thing whatever relating to the testator's or intestate's estate or to the trust, without being responsible for any loss occasioned by any act or thing so done by him or them if he has or they have discharged the duty of care set out in s.1(1) of the Trustee Act 2000.[60] The powers conferred by this section extend to a judicial trustee[61] and to the trustee of a deed of arrangement.[62] They also extend to the compromise by the trustees of an occupational pension scheme of a statutory debt from the employer arising under s.75 of the Pensions Act 1995.[63] These powers are to be given a wide construction.[64] Thus, trustees have power under s.15 to compromise a claim to property in the hands of the beneficiary by abandoning part of their claim in consideration of a beneficiary giving up a beneficial interest under the trust, provided the trustees consider in good faith that such a compromise would be beneficial to the trust estate, that is to say, to all the beneficiaries in accordance with their several interests in the trust estate holding the scale fairly between them.[65] However, neither the statutory power of compromise nor the court's inherent jurisdiction to sanction a compromise by an infant in a suit to which he is a party[66] can be extended to cover cases in which there is no real dispute as to rights but in which it is sought, by way of bargain between the beneficiaries, to rearrange the beneficial interests under the trust instrument and to bind infants and unborn persons.[67] Section 15 is concerned with what may be called external disputes in the sense of cases in which there is some issue between the trustees on behalf of the trust as a whole and a claimant whose claim is adverse to the trusts. It is not concerned with internal disputes where one beneficiary under the trusts is at issue with another beneficiary under the trusts.[68]

31–19 In exercising their powers under s.15 the trustees must listen to the beneficiaries and pay full attention to their views and wishes; but the decision rests with the trustees and even if all of the beneficiaries oppose

---

[60] The reference to the statutory duty of care is substituted for the words "in good faith" in the original section by Trustee Act 2000, s.40(1), Sch.2, Pt II, para.20, as from February 1, 2001. For a discussion of the statutory duty of care, see *Lewin on Trusts* (17th ed., 2000), paras 34–01E *et seq.*
[61] *Re Ridsdel* [1947] Ch. 597.
[62] *Re Shenton* [1935] Ch. 651.
[63] *Bradstock Group Pension Scheme Trustees Ltd v Bradstock Group Plc* [2002] EWHC 651 (Ch); [2002] I.C.R. 1427.
[64] *Re Earl of Strafford* [1980] Ch. 28, CA.
[65] *ibid.*
[66] See, *e.g.* Ch.35, below.
[67] *Chapman v Chapman* [1954] A.C. 429, HL. The Variation of Trusts Act 1958 gives the court an extensive jurisdiction to approve variations of trusts (including beneficial interests thereunder) on behalf of minors, unborn persons and others: see, generally, *Snell's Equity*, (31st ed., 2005), para.27–40; and *Lewin on Trusts* (17th ed., 2000), paras 45–31 *et seq.*
[68] *Re Earl of Strafford* [1980] Ch. 28 at 32–33 and 46, CA.

the proposed compromise the trustees have power to agree a proposed compromise.[69] However, the trustees must exercise some active discretion and must not adopt the mere passive attitude of leaving matters alone, as by failing to collect debts due to the trust.[70] In the case of a private (but not a public or charitable[71]) trust, no majority of trustees can bind a minority[72] unless the trust instrument expressly provides to the contrary.[73] Thus, where there are two or more trustees of a private trust they must all act together under s.15 unless the trust instrument expressly empowers the majority to bind the minority. But it is competent for an executor in a proper case to compromise a claim by his co-executor against the estate.[74]

The court has jurisdiction to exercise the discretion given to the trustees by s.15 and to direct them whether or not they should proceed with the compromise; and in exercising the jurisdiction the court will act in just the same way as any trustee, on the balance of possibilities and apparent advantages.[75] As stated elsewhere,[76] provided rights are in dispute, the court also has power to approve on behalf of beneficiaries under a disability compromises proposed by the beneficiaries who are *sui juris*.[77]

31–20

By CPR r.19.7(1) and (2) in a claim about the estate of a deceased person, property subject to a trust, or the meaning of a document (including a statute), the court may make an order appointing a person to represent any other person or persons in the claim where the person or persons to be represented:

31–21

(a) are unborn;
(b) cannot be found;
(c) cannot easily be ascertained; or
(d) are a class of persons who have the same interest in a claim and either:
   (i) one or more members of that class are within sub-paras (a), (b) or (c); or
   (ii) to appoint a representative would further the overriding objective of enabling the court to deal with cases justly.[78]

Where a party is acting as a representative under this rule, the court's approval of any settlement of the claim is required.[79] The court may

---

[69] *Re Ezekiel's Settlement Trusts* [1942] Ch. 230, CA.
[70] *Re Greenwood* (1911) 105 L.J. 509.
[71] *Re Whiteley* [1910] 1 Ch. 600.
[72] *Luke v South Kensington Hotel Co* (1879) 11 Ch.D. 121 at 125–126, CA, *per* Sir George Jessel M.R.; *Re Roth* (1896) 74 L.T. 50.
[73] *Re Butlin's S.T.* (1974) 118 S.J. 757.
[74] *Re Houghton* [1904] 1 Ch. 622.
[75] *Re Ezekiel's Settlement Trusts* [1942] Ch. 230, CA.
[76] See, *e.g.* Ch.35, below.
[77] *Chapman v Chapman* [1954] A.C. 429 at 457, HL.
[78] See CPR Pt 1.
[79] CPR r.19.7(5).

approve such a settlement where it is satisfied that the settlement is for the benefit of all the represented persons.[80] The former rules[81] expressly provided that in approving a compromise, the court could further order that the compromise should be binding on absent persons; but that such an order could be set aside where it was subsequently shown that the compromise order had been obtained by fraud or non-disclosure of material facts (thus making it unnecessary for absent persons to commence an action to set aside that order). CPR r.19.7(7) now provides that unless the court otherwise directs, any judgment or order given in a claim in which a party is acting as a representative under CPR r.19.7 is binding on all persons represented in the claim, but may only be enforced by or against a person who is not a party to the claim with the permission of the court. Where, under the former rules, proceedings between a single claimant and a single defendant, the latter of whom could not be found, raised issues of disputed fact, it was held that it was not appropriate to order that a third party, such as the Official Solicitor, should be appointed to represent the missing defendant with a view to the approval of a compromise binding on the latter.[82]

31–22 CPR r.19.8A[83] gives the court power to make judgments binding on non-parties. Its terms should always be borne in mind when considering the compromise of any claim to which its provisions apply. In any claim relating to (a) the estate of a deceased person or (b) property subject to a trust or (c) the sale of any property, the court may at any time direct that notice of any judgment or order given in the claim be served on any person who is not a party but who is or may be affected by it.[84] Any person served with notice of a judgment or order under this rule (a) shall be bound by the judgment or order as if he had been a party to the claim, but (b) may, provided he acknowledges service, (i) within 28 days after the notice is served on him, apply to the court to set aside or vary the judgment or order and (ii) take part in any proceedings relating to the judgment or order.[85]

CHARITIES

31–23 Charity trustees enjoy the wide powers conferred by s.15 of the Trustee Act 1925 to compromise claims relating to the assets of the charity.[86] Exceptionally, these powers may be exercised by a majority of the

---

[80] CPR r.19.7(6).
[81] RSC Ord.15, r.13(4); and CCR Ord.5, r.6(3).
[82] *Cotton v Official Solicitor* [1989] C.L.Y. 3045; cited in *The White Book*, Vol.1, para.19.7.5.
[83] The current rule came into effect on December 2, 2002. It replaces both the previous r.19.8A and the former CPR Sch.1, RSC Ord.44, r.2, thereby dispensing with the cumbersome procedure of reading the old and new rules together.
[84] CPR r.19.8A(1) and (2).
[85] CPR r.19.8A(8).
[86] See paras 31–18–31–20, above.

trustees.[87] In cases where the trustees disagree, or in complicated cases, they may consider it appropriate to apply to the Charity Commissioners for an order sanctioning the proposed compromise pursuant to s.26 of the Charities Act 1993. Anything done under the authority of such an order is deemed to be properly done in the exercise of the trustees' powers. The Charity Commissioners will normally require such an application to be supported by an opinion of properly instructed and suitably qualified counsel recommending the proposed compromise as expedient in the interests of the charity or (in a simpler case) by a letter from the charity's solicitors analysing the legal issues and commending the expediency of the proposed compromise.

31–24 Charity trustees' powers to compromise claims should be contrasted with the making of *ex gratia* payments. In *Re Snowden*[88] it was held that the court and the Attorney-General had power to authorise charity trustees to make *ex gratia* payments out of funds held on charitable trusts; but that it was a power which was not to be exercised lightly or on slender grounds and only in circumstances where it could fairly be said that if the charity were an individual it would be morally wrong of him to refuse to make the payment. Subject to the supervisory and directive powers of the Attorney-General, the Charity Commissioners are now empowered[89] to authorise charity trustees to make any application of the charity's property, or to waive to any extent on behalf of the charity its entitlement to receive any property, in any case where the charity trustees (apart from s.27) have no such power but in all the circumstances regard themselves as being under a moral obligation to do so. *Re Snowden* contains guidance as to the circumstances in which the power to make *ex gratia* payments may be exercised. In particular, Cross J. distinguished between cases where it appeared that the testator had never intended the charity to receive so large a gift as it did receive, and cases where the testator intended the charity to receive what it had received but the testator's relatives considered that he was not morally justified in leaving his money to charity rather than to them; and suggested that cases in which an *ex gratia* payment would be justified might be rarer in the second category than in the first.[90]

PROBATE CLAIMS

31–25 The procedure for contentious probate is now to be found in CPR Pt 57 and the Practice Direction supplementing Pt 57.[91] Because a probate claim is of the nature of a claim *in rem* a default judgment cannot be obtained in

---

[87] *Re Whiteley* [1910] 1 Ch. 600.
[88] [1970] Ch. 700.
[89] By the Charities Act 1993, s.27.
[90] [1970] Ch. 700 at 710–711.
[91] See also *Chancery Guide*, Ch.24 (*The White Book*, Vol.2, para.1–157). CPR Pt 57 and its Practice Direction do not apply to claims issued before October 15, 2001, which continue to be governed by the former *Practice Direction—Contentious Probate Proceedings*.

a probate claim[92]; and CPR Pt 38 (relating to discontinuance) does not apply to a probate claim.[93] A probate claim may be compromised in one of three possible ways.[94]

(1) By obtaining an order for the claim to be discontinued or dismissed under CPR r.57.11(2) (leading to a grant in common form)

31-26 At any stage of a probate claim the court, on the application of the claimant, or of any defendant who has acknowledged service, may order that the claim be discontinued or dismissed on such terms as to costs or otherwise as it thinks just; and may further order that a grant of probate of the will, or letters of administration of the estate, of the deceased person (as the case may be) which is the subject of the claim, be made to the person entitled thereto.[95] An application for such an order may be made by application notice in accordance with CPR Pt 23. An order for the discontinuance or dismissal of a probate claim under CPR r.57.11(2) will lead to a grant of probate or of letters of administration in common form. It should provide that on application for such a grant, any relevant *caveat* do, if still subsisting, cease to have effect. The advantage of this method of compromising a probate claim is that there is no need to ensure that all potential beneficiaries are either parties to the claim or have had notice thereof (pursuant to CPR r.19.8A[96]); and the order will be made without the expense of a trial of the claim on written evidence. The disadvantage of this method of compromising a probate claim is that since it leads only to a grant in common form, it will only bind the parties to the compromise. It is therefore sensible to ensure that the compromise will be acceptable to any non-parties who may be affected by it.

(2) By means of an order under s.49 of the Administration of Justice Act 1985

31-27 This section permits a probate claim to be compromised without a trial if every "relevant beneficiary"[97] has consented to the proposed order. It is only available in the High Court. Applications under s.49 may be heard by

---

[92] CPR r.57.10(1).
[93] CPR r.57.11(1).
[94] *Practice Direction 57—Probate*, para.6.1; and see *Chancery Guide*, para.24.1(7) (*The White Book*, Vol.2, para.1-157). For a suggested form of order, which should be adapted as appropriate, see Practice Form No.38CH (*The White Book*, Forms Volume), reproduced as Precedent No.19 at para.A1-19, below.
[95] CPR r.57.11 (2). The court retains a greater degree of control over probate claims than over ordinary litigation and permission to discontinue can be refused. In *Green v Briscoe*, May 9, 2005, unreported, David Richards J. held that in the circumstances a master had been entitled to take the view that it was not appropriate to give permission to an executrix to discontinue her counterclaim seeking an order for pronouncement of a will.
[96] See para.31-22, above.
[97] By s.49(2) "relevant beneficiary" in relation to a pronouncement relating to a will, or wills, of a deceased person means: (a) a person who under any such will is beneficially interested

a master or district judge and must be supported by written evidence identifying the "relevant beneficiaries" and exhibiting the written consent of each of them. The written evidence of testamentary documents will still be necessary.[98] The advantage of this method of compromising a probate claim is that it leads to a grant in solemn form yet it avoids the expense of a trial of the claim on written evidence. The disadvantage is that the consent of every "relevant beneficiary" must be obtained.

(3) Following a trial of the claim on written evidence

Where the parties to the claim agree to a compromise, the court may order the trial of the probate claim on written evidence.[99] The written evidence of testamentary documents required by CPR r.57.5 will still be necessary. It will also normally be necessary for an attesting witness to sign a witness statement or swear an affidavit of due execution of any will or codicil sought to be admitted to probate.[1] Since a trial of the claim on written evidence will lead to an order for a grant in solemn form, the court will generally ensure that all persons with any potential interest in the proceedings are either joined as parties or served with notice under CPR r.19.8A.[2] If the claim comes within CPR r.19.7,[3] the court can make a representation order with a view to approving the settlement if satisfied that it is for the benefit of all the represented persons. When satisfied that the matter is ready for trial, the master will order the case to be tried in the General List. Where any party to the proposed compromise is under a disability or is represented under CPR r.19.7, it will be necessary for the court to approve the compromise on their behalf. The application to have the compromise approved will be heard by the judge in private; and the evidence to prove the will can be heard immediately thereafter in open court.

31–28

In *Di Placito v Slater*[4] a claim by executors to distribute the deceased's estate in accordance with a particular will was compromised on the basis of an undertaking by the claimant not to bring proceedings to challenge the validity of that will after a specified date. The claimant breached the undertaking by commencing proceedings shortly after that date and then applied to the court

31–29

---

in the deceased's estate; and (b) where the effect of the pronouncement would be to cause the estate to devolve as on an intestacy (or partial intestacy), or to prevent it from so devolving, a person who under the law relating to intestacy is beneficially interested in the estate.

[98] *Practice Direction 57—Probate*, para.6.2.
[99] *ibid.*, para.6.1.
[1] *Chancery Guide*, para.24.2 (*The White Book*, Vol.2, para.1–157). At this stage, the will or codicil will be in the court's possession and cannot be handed out for use as an exhibit. The solution to the practical difficulties to which this gives rise is to be found at paras 24.2 and 24.3 of the *Chancery Guide*.
[2] See para.31–22, above.
[3] See para.31–21, above.
[4] [2003] EWCA Civ 1863; [2004] 1 W.L.R. 1605.

to vary the undertaking by retrospectively extending the specified time so as to validate the proceedings. In dismissing an appeal from an order refusing the extension of time, the Court of Appeal emphasised the need for the claimant to demonstrate "special circumstances" in the sense of circumstances so different from those which might properly be regarded as contemplated or intended to be governed by the order at the time that it was given that it was appropriate to release the undertaker from the burden of his undertaking.

PRACTICE AND PROCEDURE

Agreed orders

31–30 CPR r.40.6 and para.3 of *Practice Direction—Judgments and Orders*[5] apply where all the parties agree the terms in which a judgment should be given or an order should be made. Unlike the former RSC Ord.42, r.5A, they apply to claims proceeding in the Chancery Division. All consent orders lodged in Chancery Chambers are referred to the master for approval before the order is sealed.[6] Paragraph 10.4 of the *Practice Direction— Applications*[7] which supplements CPR r.23.8 (providing for applications to be dealt with without a hearing) emphasises that the parties to an application for a consent order must ensure that they provide the court with any material it needs to be satisfied that it is appropriate to make the order. Subject to any rule or practice direction a letter will generally be acceptable for this purpose. By para.10.5 of the same *Practice Direction*, the parties must inform the court immediately when a judgment or order has been agreed in respect of an application or claim where a hearing date has been fixed. Indeed, para.26 of the standard case management directions appended to the *Chancery Guide*[8] expressly provides that if the claim or part of the claim is settled, the parties must immediately inform the court, whether or not it is then possible to file a draft consent order to give effect to the settlement.

Appeals

31–31 The practice for compromising all appeals to the Chancery Division except first appeals in insolvency matters[9] is as set out in para.12 of *Practice Direction—Appeals*[10] supplementing CPR Pt 52. Where an appellant does

---

[5] *The White Book*, Vol.1, para.40 BPD.3. See paras 10–17 *et seq.*, above.
[6] *Chancery Guide*, para.9.13 (*The White Book*, Vol.2, para.1–86).
[7] *The White Book*, Vol.1, para.23PD.10.
[8] As Appendix 6 (*The White Book*, Vol.2, para.1–204).
[9] For which reference should be made to para.17.22(8) of *Practice Direction: Insolvency Proceedings* (*The White Book*, Vol.2, para.3E–18): see para.31–09, above.
[10] *The White Book*, Vol.1, para.52 PD.47

not wish to pursue an application or an appeal, he may request the appeal court for an order that his application or appeal be dismissed.[11] Such a request must contain a statement that the appellant is not a child or patient. If such a request is granted, it will usually be on the basis that the appellant pays the costs of the application or appeal. If the appellant wishes to have the application or appeal dismissed without costs, his request must be accompanied by a consent signed by the respondent or his legal representatives stating that the respondent is not a child or patient and consents to the dismissal of the application or appeal without costs. Where a settlement has been reached disposing of the application or appeal, the parties may make a joint request to the court stating that none of them is a child or patient, and asking that the application or appeal be dismissed by consent. If the request is granted the application or appeal will be dismissed. A document signed by solicitors for all parties must be lodged with the Chancery Listing Office requesting dismissal of the appeal. The appeal can be dismissed without any hearing by an order made in the name of the Vice-Chancellor. Any orders with directions as to costs will be drawn by the Chancery Associates.[12] The appeal court will not normally make an order allowing an appeal unless satisfied that the decision of the lower court was wrong, but the appeal court may set aside or vary the order of the lower court with consent and without determining the merits of the appeal if it is satisfied that there are good and sufficient reasons for doing so.[13] Where the appeal court is requested by all parties to allow an application or an appeal the court may consider the request on the papers. The request should state that none of the parties is a child or patient and set out the relevant history of the proceedings and the matters relied on as justifying the proposed order and be accompanied by a copy of the proposed order.[14]

If a claim is compromised at a time when an appeal is pending or contemplated, and the terms of compromise expressly identify different, specified results if the appeal is either dismissed or allowed, care should be taken to ensure that the terms of compromise clearly and adequately cater for all possible outcomes of the hearing of the appeal. In *Bayoumi v Women's Total Abstinence Educational Union Ltd (No.2)*[15] the court held that, since neither of the two prescribed results of the appeal had in fact

31–32

---

[11] This reflects the former practice under which the court was reluctant to allow an appeal to be withdrawn, as opposed to the appeal being dismissed by consent, because once an appeal was dismissed that was an end of the matter, whereas if the appeal was merely withdrawn, the appellant could, subject to obtaining any necessary extension of time, subsequently change his mind and launch the appeal again: *Buckbod Investments Ltd v Nana-Otchere* [1985] 1 W.L.R. 342.
[12] *Chancery Guide*, para.10.24 (*The White Book*, Vol.2, para.1–99).
[13] *Practice Direction—Appeals*, para.13–1 (*The White Book*, Vol.1, para.52 PD.48).
[14] ibid.
[15] Unreported, January 13, 2005, Chancery Division (Simon Berry Q.C.).

occurred, the judgment embodied in a consent order was not applicable in the events that had happened.

Declarations[16]

31-33 By CPR r.40.20 the court may make binding declarations, whether or not any other remedy is claimed. It is not the normal practice of the Chancery Division to make a declaration when giving judgment by consent.[17] But the rule is one of practice only and not of law and will give way to the paramount duty of the court to do the fullest justice to the claimant to which he is entitled, particularly where the declaration sought cannot affect the rights of anyone other than the parties and persons claiming through them.[18] Thus, where a contract has been brought to an end by reason of the defendant's repudiation of it, by consent the court may declare that the contract is at an end and that the claimant is no longer bound thereby.[19]

Interim applications

31-34 If all parties to an interim application agree, it can be adjourned for not more than 14 days by counsel or solicitors attending the Chancery Listing Office at any time before 4pm on the day before the hearing of the application and producing consents signed by solicitors or counsel for all parties agreeing to the adjournment. A litigant in person must attend before the listing officer as well as signing a consent. This procedure may not be used for more than three successive adjournments; and no adjournment may be made by this procedure to the last two days of any sitting.[20]

31-35 This procedure should also be used where the parties agree that the hearing of the application will take two hours or more and that, in consequence, the application should be adjourned to be heard as an interim application by order. In this event, the consents set out above should also contain an agreed timetable for the filing of evidence or confirmation that no further evidence is to be filed. Any application arising from the failure of a party to abide by the timetable and any application to extend the timetable must be made to the judge. Interim applications by order will, initially at least, enter the interim hearings warned list on the first Monday after close of evidence.[21]

---

[16] See also para.10–02, above.
[17] *Wallersteiner v Moir* [1974] 1 W.L.R. 991, *per* Buckley L.J. at 1029 and *per* Scarman L.J. at 1030.
[18] *Patten v Burke Publishing Ltd* [1991] 1 W.L.R. 541.
[19] *ibid., per* Millett J. at 544C.
[20] *Chancery Guide*, para.5.13 (*The White Book*, Vol.2, para.1–31).
[21] *ibid.*, para.5.14; (*ibid.*, para.1–32).

Undertakings given to the court may be continued unchanged over any adjournment. If, however, on an adjournment, an undertaking is to be varied or a new undertaking given, then that must be dealt with by the court.[22] 31–36

Where the respondent to an interim application does not appear, the applicant may invite the court to make a consent order based upon a letter of consent from the respondent or his or her solicitors, or a draft statement of agreed terms signed by the respondent's solicitors. This causes no difficulty where the agreed relief falls wholly within the relief claimed in the application notice. If, however, the agreed relief goes outside that which is claimed in the application notice, or even in the claim form, or when undertakings are offered, then difficulties can arise. A procedure has been established for this purpose to be applied to all applications in the Chancery Division.[23] Subject always to the discretion of the court, no order will be made in such cases unless a consent signed by or on behalf of the respondent to an application is put before the court in accordance with the following provisions: 31–37

(1) Where there are solicitors on the record for the respondent the court will normally accept as sufficient a written consent signed by those solicitors on their headed notepaper.
(2) Where there are solicitors for the respondent who are not on the record, the court will normally accept as sufficient a written consent signed by those solicitors on their headed notepaper only if in the consent (or some other document) the solicitors certify that they have fully explained to the respondent the effect of the order and that the respondent appeared to have understood the explanation.
(3) Where there is a written consent signed by a respondent acting in person the court will not normally accept it as sufficient unless the court is satisfied that the respondent understands the effect of the order either by reason of the circumstances (for example the respondent is himself a solicitor or barrister) or by means of other material (for example the respondent's consent is given in reply to a letter explaining in simple terms the effect of the order).
(4) Where the respondent offers any undertaking to the court:

    (a) the document containing the undertaking must be signed by the respondent personally;
    (b) solicitors must certify on their headed notepaper that the signature is that of the respondent; and

---

[22] *ibid.*, para.5.15; (*ibid.*, para.1–32).
[23] *ibid.*, paras 5.24–5.26; (*ibid.*, para.1–39).

(c) if the case falls within (2) or (3) above, solicitors must certify that they have explained to the respondent the consequences of giving the undertaking and that the respondent appeared to understand the explanation.

31–38   Where, upon an application for an interim injunction, the respondent chooses not to seek an adjournment of the application, but instead accepts that it should be dealt with and disposed of then and there by offering undertakings until trial or further order, there must be good grounds before the respondent is able to apply to discharge or modify the undertakings. Good grounds can consist of a significant change in circumstances or becoming aware of new facts which could not reasonably have been known or found out before the undertakings were given.[24] Where, however, an application for an interim injunction is not stood over to the trial of the action but is adjourned generally, it has not been dealt with and disposed of as an interim matter; and the respondent does not have to show any such grounds before he can apply to the court to modify the terms of the undertaking or to discharge it.[25] Where an undertaking is given to the court instead of an interim injunction, it is the practice in the Chancery Division to insert a cross-undertaking as to damages by the applicant unless the contrary is agreed and expressed at the time.[26] The position is less clear where the party applying for the injunction also gives an undertaking to the court. The parties should consider, and, if necessary, raise with the judge, whether the party in whose favour the undertaking is given must give a cross-undertaking in damages in those circumstances.[27] If the action is later compromised, the parties should expressly provide for their release from any cross-undertakings as to damages.[28]

31–39   There was a practice of long-standing in the Chancery Division whereby an ordinary interlocutory motion might, by agreement, be treated as a motion for judgment or as the trial of the action. Where an interim application is not contested and an agreed order is sought, the application may be treated as an application for final judgment. The order should recite the agreement of the parties that the application is to be treated as an application for judgment.[29] Where the application is contested, the consent of the parties is required for it to be treated as the trial of the action; and the order should contain a recital to this effect. If the judge is satisfied with the written evidence, he is at liberty to give final judgment thereon. The appropriate fee must be paid before the order will be passed and entered.

---

[24] *Chanel Ltd v F.W. Woolworth & Co Ltd* [1981] 1 W.L.R. 485, CA; *Butt v Butt* [1987] 1 W.L.R. 1351 at 1353, CA, *per* Nourse L.J.
[25] *Butt v Butt* [1987] 1 W.L.R. 1351, CA.
[26] *Chancery Guide*, para.5.22 (*The White Book*, Vol.2, para.1–37).
[27] *ibid.*
[28] And see paras 5–41 and 6–05, above.
[29] See Precedent No.20 at para.A1–20, below.

Masters

In proceedings in the Chancery Division, without the consent of the Vice-Chancellor a master or district judge may not approve compromises (other than applications under the Inheritance (Provision for Family and Dependants Act) 1975[30]: 31–40

(1) on behalf of a person under disability where that person's interest in a fund, or if there is no fund, the maximum amount of the claim, exceeds £100,000; or
(2) on behalf of absent, unborn and unascertained persons.[31]

A master or district judge has the power to make an injunction in terms agreed by the parties.[32] He may also make an order varying or discharging an injunction or undertaking given to the court if all parties to the proceedings have consented to the variation or discharge.[33]

When matters before the master settle, Chancery Chambers should be informed in writing as soon as possible and no later than 4pm on the day preceding the appointment. Failure to do so, and consequent waste of court time, may result in an adverse costs order being made.[34] 31–41

Release from undertaking

For the correct approach to be applied by the court when considering an application to be released from an undertaking, incorporated in a consent order settling an action, not to bring proceedings after a specified date, see *Di Placito v Slater*,[35] discussed at para.31–29, above. 31–42

---

[30] See Ch.33, below.
[31] *Practice Direction—Allocation of Cases to Levels of Judiciary*, para.5.1(a) (*The White Book*, Vol.1, para.2BPD.5).
[32] *ibid.*, para.2.3(a); (*ibid.*, para.2BPD.2).
[33] *ibid.*, para.2.4; (*ibid.*, para.2BPD.2).
[34] *Chancery Guide*, para.7.46 (*The White Book*, Vol.2, para.1–71).
[35] [2003] EWCA Civ 1863; [2004] 1 W.L.R. 1605.

PART 8

Matrimonial, Family and Inheritance Disputes

CHAPTER 32

Compromise of Disputes between Husband and Wife

Not every marriage breakdown ends in divorce, although in the vast majority of cases this occurs eventually. It is necessary, therefore, to consider a number of areas in which disputes may fall to be resolved by agreement. They can be enumerated as follows: **32–01**

(1) Agreements when no divorce or judicial separation proceedings are proposed or contemplated or, if proposed or contemplated, where they are likely to be delayed for a time.
(2) Agreements concerning the disposal of the divorce or judicial separation suit itself.
(3) Agreements involving the interim stages of divorce or judicial separation proceedings, particularly those involving interim financial provision.
(4) Agreements relating to the final disposal of financial and property applications.
(5) Agreements relating to children.

By far the most difficult of these areas is that relating to final financial and property applications. In relation to each area enumerated, it is proposed to examine briefly the law applicable, and the manner in which such agreements are reached, effectuated, enforced and, where necessary, set aside.

AGREEMENTS NOT NECESSARILY INVOLVING DIVORCE OR JUDICIAL SEPARATION

Two matters fall to be considered in this context: the compromise of proceedings brought under s.17 of the Married Womens Property Act 1882 (as amended) and maintenance agreements. **32–02**

Compromise of proceedings under Married Womens' Property Act 1882, s.17

32–03 **Preliminary.** Though much less important now than it was prior to the implementation of the Divorce Reform Act 1969 and its associated legislation, s.17 still has a role to play in the resolution of disputes between husband and wife (or engaged parties) concerning "the title to or possession of property". "Property" for this purpose is defined as including "real or personal property and any estate or interest therein, any money, negotiable instrument, debt or other chose in action and any other interest whether in possession or not".[1] Most commonly the matter in issue is the matrimonial home. What proportion does each party own? Has the share of one party increased by virtue of improvements carried out by that party?[2] What money did each contribute and what was the intention of the parties as to ownership? Should the property be sold either immediately or at some stage in the future?[3] However, issues concerning the ownership of property or rights in a family company or partnership can also be dealt with, as can issues relating to chattels.[4] S.17 may assume particular importance in circumstances where a claim for ancillary relief cannot be made—for example when the claimant has remarried before issuing an application for ancillary relief. Equally, s.17 may be utilised where it is important to establish the beneficial and legal interests of the parties—say, when bankruptcy has occurred or is threatened.

32–04 **Jurisdiction of the court and the parties' agreement.** The jurisdiction of the court under s.17 primarily concerns the declaration of existing rights, although the court has the power to prevent one party from enforcing those rights if to do so would be unjust to the other.[5] The court has power to order a sale of the property in question,[6] to assess the value of one party's share in that property and to order the other party to pay that assessed value.[7] It can also direct, in appropriate circumstances, that one party gives to the other credit in respect of the whole or part of mortgage instalments paid by the party who remains in occupation of a property the subject of a mortgage and require the party in occupation to pay an occupation rent to the other.[8]

---

[1] The definition was added by the Matrimonial Causes (Property and Maintenance) Act 1958, s.7.
[2] Matrimonial Property and Proceedings Act 1970, s.37.
[3] Matrimonial Causes (Property and Maintenance) Act 1958, s.7(7). See, *e.g. Jackson v Jackson* [1971] 1 W.L.R. 1539; and *Burke v Burke* [1974] 1 W.L.R. 1063.
[4] Forever etched in Mr Foskett's memory is an occasion when two parties to s.17 proceedings were contesting bitterly the "custody" of a stuffed woodpecker! (*The Times*, "Correspondence", January 19, 1995).
[5] *Pettitt v Pettitt* [1970] A.C. 777; *Gissing v Gissing* [1971] A.C. 886.
[6] See n.3, above.
[7] *Bothe v Amos* [1976] Fam. 46, CA.
[8] For example *Leake v Bruzzi* [1974] 1 W.L.R. 1528; *Suttill v Graham* [1977] 1 W.L.R. 819. In relation to the payment of an occupation rent, see *Dennis v McDonald* [1982] Fam. 63.

This statement of the powers of the court is important because any provisions of an agreement compromising s.17 proceedings which come to be reflected in a consent order must be within the jurisdiction of the court.[9] Any terms outside the normal jurisdiction would have to be dealt with by means of undertakings or in some other way (*e.g.* making the agreement a rule of court or the subject of a Tomlin order).[10]

Ousting the jurisdiction? As will be observed in due course,[11] the parties to an agreement over financial matters in the context of actual or contemplated divorce or judicial separation proceedings cannot oust the jurisdiction and ultimate discretion of the court. However, any concluded agreement[12] compromising s.17 proceedings does not require the sanction of the court[13] and it binds the parties and the court.[14] It would seem to follow that any consent order made would not be susceptible to future variation on account of changed circumstances, the agreement underlying the order being the governing factor.[15]

32–05

Setting aside—practice. If any grounds exist for setting aside the agreement underlying a consent order,[16] it seems that a fresh action should be commenced with a view to setting aside the agreement and the order.[17] If, of course, the view is taken (contrary to that suggested above) that even a consent order of this nature was susceptible to "a continuing power to vary its terms",[18] it would be regarded as an interlocutory order[19] and thus amenable to an appropriate application in the s.17 proceedings;[20] not only would there be jurisdiction to vary the order on account of changed circumstances,[21] but also to set it aside on appeal on any of the usual grounds[22] and the availability of fresh evidence.[23] If any part of the order

32–06

---

[9] *Livesey v Jenkins* [1985] A.C. 424; *Hinde v Hinde* [1953] 1 W.L.R. 175. See also Ch.10, above.
[10] See Ch.9, above.
[11] See para.32–35, below.
[12] See, *e.g. Shears v Shears* (1973) C.A.T. 288, considered fully at para.3–23, above.
[13] *ibid.*
[14] *Steadman v Steadman* [1976] A.C. 536. These authorities are, of course, very clear and binding. It should be observed, however, that s.17 itself provides that the judge "may make such order . . . *as he thinks fit*" (emphasis added) which suggests a discretion of sorts concerning a proposed agreed order notwithstanding what the parties may have agreed.
[15] In *Gee v Gee* (1972) 116 S.J. 219, the Court of Appeal held that there was jurisdiction to vary an order made, apparently, after a contested hearing.
[16] See Ch.4, above.
[17] *Page v Page* (1972) C.A.T. 383: "no order" was made on W's s.17 application upon certain agreed terms. H sought to appeal on the basis of W's non-disclosure of what he suggested was a material matter. The Court of Appeal held that even if H was right on the substantive matter there was no order from which to appeal—he should have brought an action to set aside the agreement.
[18] *De Lasala v De Lasala* [1980] A.C. 546 at 561, *per* Lord Diplock.
[19] *ibid.*
[20] See para.32–29, below.
[21] See n.15, above.
[22] See Ch.4, above.
[23] *cf. Thwaite v Thwaite* [1982] Fam. 1.

was executory, the court might be persuaded to intervene if circumstances arose suggesting that the agreement should not be enforced.[24] Regrettably, although the occasions when the problem might arise nowadays will be relatively few, there is here an area of uncertainty. It is still felt, however, that the better view is that any order made in pursuance of an agreement is to be regarded as final and, consequently, only open to attack in a fresh action commenced for the purpose.

32–07 **Intervention of third parties.** Unless any grounds existed for impeaching a compromise of s.17 proceedings, it would be binding on both parties to it. An agreement purporting to be a "compromise" of a dispute between H and W may, it is thought, at the instance of H's trustee in bankruptcy, be declared void as against him[25] if it is clear that H has granted W a far larger share in the property in question than was justified by the realities.[26] It is possible that any such "compromise" would be regarded as fraudulent if it was intended thereby to injure a third party and may, in such circumstances, be open to attack.[27]

Maintenance (and separation) agreements

32–08 **Preliminary.** A full definition of the expressions "maintenance agreement" and "separation agreement" for the purposes of the present statutory provisions appears in s.34(2) of the Matrimonial Causes Act 1973.[28] With one difference that definition first appeared in s.1(1) of the Maintenance Agreements Act 1957. The original requirement was that, to enable the intervention of the court for the benefit of one or other of the parties pursuant to the Act, the agreement had to be made "for the purposes of their living separately".[29] That requirement, though repeated in the Matrimonial Causes Act 1965,[30] was deleted by the Matrimonial Proceedings and Property Act 1970 and the definition thus produced was carried forward into the 1973 Act. Since the purpose of these statutory provisions from the outset was to enable the court to review maintenance and separation agreements previously governed only by the common law, and thus reviewable only by agreement of the parties,[31] it is thought that the statutory definition clearly evidences that which was (and still is where

---

[24] *ibid.*
[25] Insolvency Act 1986, ss.339 and 340.
[26] See paras 6–75 *et seq.*, above.
[27] See para.6–98, above.
[28] See para.32–10, below.
[29] This had the effect of excluding from review by the court an agreement made for the purpose of the parties effecting a reconciliation even if it did not last: *Ewart v Ewart* [1959] P. 23.
[30] s.23(2).
[31] See para.32–10, below.

appropriate) a "maintenance agreement" or "separation agreement" for the purposes of the common law. It is clear that such an agreement could include provisions making financial arrangements which went beyond what the Divorce Court could have ordered if called upon to do so.[32] Whether that fact has any bearing on the interpretation of the expression "financial arrangements" is considered below.[33]

Most, though not all, maintenance and separation agreements are reduced to writing and thereby become governed by ss.34–36 of the Matrimonial Causes Act 1973.[34] Those which are (or have been) made orally, or partly orally and partly in writing, would be governed by the common law save those relating to periodical payments provisions for children, which are now regulated by s.9 of the Child Support Act 1991.

The common law. A provision in an agreement governed solely by the common law which purports to exclude the jurisdiction of the court to award maintenance to a wife[35] or child[36] is contrary to public policy and void. If the provision to that effect represents "the whole, or substantially the whole"[37] consideration for the agreement, the whole agreement is void. If the provision "goes only to part of the consideration" the rest of the agreement may stand.[38] Nothing in the post-1969 legislation casts doubt on any of those principles where applicable.[39] It should be borne in mind that the common law principles were evolved when the range of reliefs available to the matrimonial courts was very much more limited than at present.[40] Although the authorities in which these principles were enunciated were concerned primarily with provisions for maintenance, there would seem to be no reason why, for example, an agreement not within s.34, but which purported to exclude the right of a party to apply for a lump sum or property adjustment order, should not be void at common law. Indeed, all contemporary authority supports this view.[41] 32–09

A valid maintenance or separation agreement governed solely by the common law is, of course, merely a contract and variable only with the agreement of the parties.[42] Equally, as with a written agreement of the same nature, it is enforceable as a contract by an action.[43]

---

[32] An example, though relating merely to maintenance for a wife, is afforded by *Kirk v Eustace* [1937] A.C. 491.
[33] See paras 32–10 and 32–16, below.
[34] See paras 32–10 *et seq.*, below.
[35] *Hyman v Hyman* [1929] A.C. 601.
[36] *Gaisberg v Storr* [1950] 1 K.B. 107; *cf. Hanlon v Hanlon* [1978] 1 W.L.R. 592, CA. But see now the effect of the Child Support Act 1991, paras 32–17 *et seq.*, below.
[37] *Bennett v Bennett* [1952] 1 K.B. 249 at 261, *per* Denning L.J.
[38] *ibid. Goodinson v Goodinson* [1954] 2 Q.B. 118.
[39] *Wright v Wright* [1970] 1 W.L.R. 1219; *Brockwell v Brockwell* (1975) 6 Fam. Law 46; *Dean v Dean* [1978] Fam. 161; *Minton v Minton* [1979] A.C. 593; *Edgar v Edgar* [1980] 1 W.L.R. 1410; *Camm v Camm* (1983) 4 F.L.R. 577, CA.
[40] See further at para.32–16, below.
[41] See cases cited in n.39, above. *cf. Ewart v Ewart*, n.29, above.
[42] For the position of separation deeds, see para.32–11, below.
[43] *De Lasala v De Lasala*, n.18, above. See also *Temple v Temple* [1976] 1 W.L.R. 701, CA.

Matrimonial Causes Act 1973, ss.34 and 35

32–10 **1. Definition of "maintenance agreement."**

The definition of a "maintenance agreement" which appears in s.34(2) is, subject to the one matter referred to above,[44] in identical terms to that originally set out in the Maintenance Agreements Act 1957, as is the definition of "financial arrangements". The definitions are as follows:

> "... 'maintenance agreement' means any agreement in writing made, whether before or after the commencement of this Act, between the parties to a marriage, being:
>
> (a) an agreement containing financial arrangements, whether made during the continuance or after the dissolution or annulment of the marriage; or
> (b) a separation agreement which contains no financial arrangements in a case where no other agreement in writing between the same parties contains such arrangements; ..."

> "... 'financial arrangements' means provisions governing the rights and liabilities towards one another when living separately of the parties to a marriage (including a marriage which has been dissolved or annulled) in respect of the making or securing of payments or the disposition or use of any property, including such rights and liabilities with respect to the maintenance or education of any child, whether or not a child of the family."[45]

It is worth recording that, at the time the definition of "financial arrangements" was first given statutory force in 1957, the financial provision which the Divorce Court could make by order was restricted to periodical payments orders (secured or otherwise) and their variation, the variation of ante-nuptial or post-nuptial settlements and the settlement of the property of a "guilty" wife. It was not until 1963[46] that lump sum orders could be made and, of course, not until the implementation of the Matrimonial Proceedings and Property Act 1970 that property adjustment orders could be made. For the reasons developed in due course,[47] this may be of importance in considering the powers of the court on an application

---

[44] See para.32–08, above.
[45] A "maintenance agreement" for the purposes of the Child Support Act 1991 is defined as "any agreement for the making or securing of periodical payments by way of maintenance to or for the benefit of any child": s.9(1). It should be noted that, unlike s.34(2), a maintenance agreement for this purpose does not have to be "in writing".
[46] Matrimonial Causes Act 1973, s.5(1).
[47] At para.32–16, below (in regard to the powers of the court on alteration) and para.32–41, below (in regard to the relationship of maintenance agreements to agreements compromising claims for financial relief).

to alter a maintenance agreement and, additionally, in the context of the relationship of "maintenance agreements" generally with agreements compromising proposed or actual applications to the Divorce Court for financial relief.

2. Form and content of a written maintenance agreement

Provided that good and lawful consideration[48] is given by each party to the agreement, no particular form is required by law.

32–11

A maintenance agreement which contains "a provision purporting to restrict any right to apply to a court for an order containing financial arrangements" is still valid even though that provision is void. All other terms are enforceable unless, of course, they are void or unenforceable for some other reason.[49] A maintenance agreement containing a provision whereby a party agrees to invite the court in due course to make a certain order (even one of dismissal of a claim) does not thereby seek to restrict a "right to apply" to the court.[50] Clearly, in the exercise of its ultimate discretion,[51] the court may decline the invitation. But that does not render the provision void under s.34(1) (or under the common law for that matter).

A maintenance agreement (which, for this purpose, tends to be called a "separation agreement" or a "deed of separation") is often made where the parties separate and decide to obtain a decree of divorce at a later stage.[52] Such an agreement may, of course, be made where a relatively immediate divorce is proposed, but where it is desired to have recorded an agreement relating to all matters before the divorce petition is filed. Whether the provisions in such an agreement relating to lump sum or property adjustment applications are, strictly speaking, matters which can be made the subject of a maintenance agreement under s.34 is mentioned in due course.[53] Whatever the effect of such provisions as part of a maintenance agreement as such, their existence in a document entitled "Deed of Separation" (or whatever other title may be chosen) will evidence the manner in which the parties, at the time of the agreement,

---

[48] See generally Ch.3, above.
[49] s.34(1).
[50] See, *e.g. Cook v Cook* (1984) 14 Fam. Law 121, where the Court of Appeal upheld a provision in a separation deed in which W agreed to the dismissal by the court in due course of her claims for periodical payments. All the provisions of the deed were approved and the dismissal of her periodical payments claim was ordered, her consent being found in the deed. *cf. Dipper v Dipper* [1981] Fam. 31. A maintenance agreement to which s.9 of the Child Support Act 1991 applies (n.45, above) and which "purports to restrict the right of any person to apply for a maintenance assessment" is void: s.9(4). For the effect which a maintenance assessment has upon a subsisting maintenance agreement making provision for a child or children, see para.32–19, below.
[51] See para.32–35, below.
[52] *cf. Cook v Cook*, n.50 above.
[53] See para.32–42, below.

3. Impeachment of a written maintenance agreement

32–12 As appears below,[55] there are circumstances in which a court may intervene and alter the terms of the maintenance agreement because of a change of circumstances since the agreement was concluded. Are there circumstances in which the original agreement could be set aside or rescinded at the instance of one of the parties? It is submitted that this must be so: a maintenance agreement is merely a contract and so should be impeachable upon any of the usual grounds.[56] A separation deed has been held void for mistake because it had been concluded on the false assumption (which was clearly fundamental) that the parties were validly married.[57]

4. Enforcement of a written maintenance agreement

32–13 The means adopted for enforcing an agreement of this nature are those appropriate to the term or terms of the agreement sought to be enforced. A fresh action will be required[58] and, in appropriate circumstances, proceedings under CPR Pt 24 may be used.[59] There is no power to remit arrears of periodical payments under an agreement.[60]

It appears that an accepted repudiation of a maintenance or separation agreement will result in the discharge of the agreement. If any repudiation is not accepted then the agreement remains operative.[61] A party who, despite the repudiation of the other, wishes the agreement to remain operative must show by word or deed that he (or she) does not accept the repudiation. The situation would usually arise where a wife decides that she is not satisfied with either the terms or existence of such an agreement and, so far as the former is concerned, she is not content merely with seeking a variation of the agreement.[62] An application to the court under, say, s.27 of the Matrimonial Causes Act 1973, the Guardianship of Minors Act 1971 or the Guardianship Act 1973 is then made or, if prima facie grounds for divorce or judicial separation exist, a petition is filed and ancillary relief claimed.

Clearly, nothing in any agreement can prevent this happening[63] but, equally clearly, if the agreement itself was reasonable it is something which

---

[54] See para.32–48, below. See in particular in this context *H v H* [1994] 2 F.L.R. 94 and *Smith v McInerney* [1994] 2 F.L.R. 1077 (Thorpe J.).
[55] See paras 32–14 *et seq.*, below.
[56] See Ch.4. And see *Hulton v Hulton* [1917] 1 K.B. 813; *Adamson v Adamson* (1907) 23 T.L.R. 434.
[57] *Galloway v Galloway* (1914) 30 T.L.R. 531.
[58] *De Lasala v De Lasala*, n.18, above.
[59] *Temple v Temple*, n.43, above.
[60] *MacDonald v MacDonald* [1964] P. 1.
[61] *Clark v Clark* [1939] P. 257; *Pardy v Pardy* [1939] P. 288.
[62] See paras 32–14 *et seq.*, below.
[63] See paras 32–09 and 32–11, above.

the court would wish to discourage. The relevance of a maintenance agreement in divorce or judicial separation ancillary relief proceedings is considered below.[64] It is prima facie regarded as of considerable significance. It is thought that a similar approach would (or should) be adopted in the context of proceedings such as those foreshadowed above. An agreement of this nature must be one of "all the circumstances of the case" which the court is enjoined by statute to consider.[65]

5. Alteration of a written maintenance agreement

Prior to the Maintenance Agreements Act 1957, a maintenance agreement could be altered in only two circumstances: first, by agreement of the parties and, secondly, where the maintenance agreement constituted a post-nuptial settlement, such a settlement could be varied under the powers given by statute since 1859.[66] After 1957 it was possible for the courts to intervene and review agreements of this nature on wider grounds. The present grounds were first made available by the Matrimonial Proceedings and Property Act 1970 and have subsequently[67] been redefined in relation to certain maintenance agreements for the benefit of a child or children of the parties to the agreement.

32–14

(i) Maintenance agreements governed only by ss.34–36 of the Matrimonial Causes Act 1973

Grounds for alteration. A subsisting[68] maintenance agreement may be varied if the court to which an application for variation is made is satisfied:

32–15

> "(a) that by reason of a change in the circumstances in the light of which any financial arrangements contained in the agreement were made or, as the case may be, financial arrangements were omitted from it (including a change foreseen by the parties when making the agreement), the agreement should be altered, so as to make different, or, as the case may be, so as to contain, financial arrangements, or (b) that the agreement does not contain proper financial arrangements with respect to any child of the family . . ."[69]

The question of whether there has been any change "in the circumstances in the light of which any financial arrangements contained in the

---

[64] See paras 32–33 *et seq.*, below.
[65] Matrimonial Causes Act 1973, s.27(3) and (3A); Guardianship of Minors Act 1971, s.12A.
[66] Matrimonial Causes Act 1859.
[67] Since October 14, 1991. See further at paras 32–17 *et seq.*, below.
[68] A maintenance agreement no longer subsists if it is transposed into an order of the court during divorce or judicial separation proceedings: *De Lasala v De Lasala*, n.18, above *per* Lord Diplock at 560.
[69] s.35(2).

agreement were made" is to be answered primarily by an objective analysis, although the factors which in fact influenced the particular parties are not to be ignored in a proper case.[70]

32–16 Powers on alteration. The Act provides that if the court[71] is satisfied of either of the matters referred to above, it has power to order "such alterations in the agreement . . . as may appear to the court to be just having regard to all the circumstances . . ." in either of the following ways:

> "(i) by varying or revoking any financial arrangements contained in it, or
> (ii) by inserting in it financial arrangements for the benefit of one of the parties to the agreement or of a child of the family . . ."[72]

The court has power to backdate the variation "to the point at which in justice it should be made"[73] and to entertain more than one application for a variation.[74]

The jurisdiction of the magistrates' court is limited to the insertion of periodical payments provision or the variation or termination of existing provisions for periodical payments.[75]

The High Court and county court may insert "financial arrangements" as defined previously.[76] Does this include a lump sum or property adjustment provision? The balance of authority suggests not, although the words of the statute are unlimited.[77] It is respectfully submitted that this is the correct view. Reference has already been made[78] to the powers of the Divorce Courts to make financial provision orders in 1957 when the precursor of the present statutory provision was enacted. The legislation

---

[70] *Gorman v Gorman* [1964] 1 W.L.R. 1440, CA. In *Simister v Simister* [1987] 1 F.L.R. 194, a maintenance agreement was entered into whereby W's maintenance was to be increased periodically to represent one-third of H's annual gross income. Within about five years of the agreement, H's income had increased from £16,000 per annum to £40,000 per annum and H was finding the obligation increasingly burdensome. Waite J. held that the payments under the agreement were in excess of W's "maximum reasonable needs" and that this was a relevant change of circumstances. The income provision was revoked and a periodical payments order of £10,000 per annum substituted.
[71] High Court, county court or, in certain cases, magistrates' court.
[72] s.35(2).
[73] *Warden v Warden* [1982] Fam. 10.
[74] *Orton v Orton* (1959) 109 L.J. 50.
[75] s.35(3).
[76] See para.32–10, above.
[77] In *Furneaux v Furneaux* (1974) 118 S.J. 204, Payne J. held that it was not possible to insert a provision for property adjustment. In *Pace v Doe* [1977] Fam. 18, Sir George Baker P. left open the question in a case where he held that certainly no such provision could be made in favour of a wife who had remarried after the agreement. *cf. D v D* (1974) 5 Fam. Law 61. It is submitted that the power of the court under s.31(7)A of the Matrimonial Causes Act 1973 to order a lump sum in lieu of periodical payments does not affect the situation since the power is limited to cases where a maintenance order is varied.
[78] See para.32–10, above.

subsequently has, to all intents and purposes, been of a consolidating nature and the definition of "financial arrangements" has not changed. If looked at in isolation from the historical context in which that expression first appeared in statutory form, it might be thought sufficiently wide to embrace all orders under ss.23 and 24. However, s.34(1) (which, again, finds its origin in the 1957 Act) declares void any provision in an agreement which purports to restrict "any right to apply to a court for an order containing financial arrangements". In 1957 there was no right to apply to a court for a lump sum order or a property adjustment order. Hence it was impossible for the 1957 Act to be referring to this type of provision as being within the expression "financial arrangements". If the definition is to be regarded as "always speaking"[79] then there would be an argument to the effect that, certainly by 1970, there would have been jurisdiction for either court to insert into a maintenance agreement provision by way of lump sum or property adjustment. However, the draftsman of the 1970 Act could so easily have clarified the definition as to put the matter beyond doubt that, it is submitted, the historical context cannot be ignored. If, as has been said,[80] an Act "must be construed as if one were interpreting it the day after it was passed", then the present-day definition must be taken to be the same as in 1957, with the consequence that no lump sum or property adjustment provision could be inserted by a court.

Any provision as to maintenance or increased maintenance ordered on an alteration must not extend beyond the joint lives of the parties or the remarriage of the party to whom the payments are made. Secured periodical payments are not to continue beyond the death or remarriage of the party to whom the payments are made.[81]

Special provisions exist in relation to the alteration of agreements after the death of one of the parties.[82]

---

[79] Bennion, *Statutory Interpretation*, s.146; Cross, *Statutory Interpretation* (2nd ed., 1987), pp.48–58.
[80] *The Longford* (1889) 14 P.D. 34 at 36–37, *per* Lord Esher. See also *A.-G. v Prince Ernest Augustus of Hanover* [1957] A.C. 436 at 465, *per* Lord Normand; and the approach of the House of Lords to the interpretation of the Judgments Act 1838 in *Legal Aid Board v Russell* [1991] 2 A.C. 317. It is probable, it is thought, that the words "the disposition or use of any property" in the definition of "financial arrangements" referred, *inter alia*, to matters concerning the continued occupation by one spouse, or the sale, of the matrimonial home—*i.e.* the types of orders which could be made under the Married Women's Property Act 1882, s.17. See paras 32-03—32-05, above. *cf. D v D*, n.77, above.
[81] s.35(4).
[82] s.36.

(ii) Maintenance agreements governed solely or partially by the Children Act 1989

32–17 Grounds for alteration. As indicated above,[83] the Children Act 1989 redefined the grounds upon which a subsisting maintenance agreement making provision for a child or children of the parties may be altered by the court. The provisions of this Act relate to maintenance agreements made both before and after the relevant commencement date.[84] The grounds upon which either the High Court or county court may intervene with a view to alteration of any such agreement are:

> "(a) that, by reason of a change in the circumstances in the light of which the financial arrangements were made (including a change foreseen by the parties when making the agreement) the agreement should be altered so as to make different financial arrangements; or
> (b) that the agreement does not contain proper financial arrangements with respect to the child."[85]

32–18 Powers on alteration. When the court is satisfied of either of the matters referred to above, it has the power to "make such alterations in the agreement by varying or revoking any financial arrangements contained in it as may appear to it to be just having regard to all the circumstances."[86]

Where the court decides to alter an agreement by inserting a provision for the making or securing of periodical payments for the maintenance of the child, or by increasing the rate of periodical payments required for the maintenance of the child, then, in deciding the term for which under the agreement as altered by the order the payments or (as the case may be) the additional payments attributable to the increase are to be made or secured for the benefit of the child, the court is obliged to apply sub-paras (1) and (2) of para.3 of Sch.1 to the Children Act 1989 as if the order were one made under the Acts referred to in s.15(1) of that Act.[87]

---

[83] See para.32–14, above. It is interesting to note that the draftsman decided, doubtless for the sake of clarity, to define a maintenance agreement for the purpose of these new statutory provisions. It is a more extensive definition than that employed for the purpose of the Child Support Act 1991 (see n.45, above), but bears a close similarity to the original definition now reflected in s.34 of the Matrimonial Causes Act 1973 (see para.32–10, above). It defines such an agreement as one in writing "made with respect to a child. . . . which contains provision with respect to the making or securing of payments, or the disposition or use of any property, for the maintenance or education of a child". Provisions such as those contemplated by this definition are "financial arrangements" within the terms of the Act. The definition does not carry any implication that this expression embraces lump sum or property adjustment provision: *cf.* para.32–16, above.

[84] Children Act 1989, Sch.1, para.10(1); and Children Act 1989 (Commencement and Transitional Provisions) Order 1991 (SI 1991/828).

[85] Children Act 1989, Sch.1, para.10(2).

[86] *ibid.*, Sch.1, para.10(3).

[87] *ibid.*, Sch.1, para.10(5). There is no reference in these provisions to any power in the court to insert a provision that a lump sum be paid or some property adjustment be made in favour of a child: *cf.* para.32–16, above.

(iii) Effect of the Child Support Act 1991 on maintenance agreements

Nothing in the Child Support Act 1991 is designed to preclude any person from entering into a maintenance agreement.[88] However, the existence of a maintenance agreement as defined in that Act[89] does not preclude the making of a maintenance assessment,[90] and the making of such an assessment generally results in the relevant provisions in the agreement becoming unenforceable.[91] The court is thus deprived of the power to alter any such provision. The statutory and regulatory provisions do not, of course, affect any capital or property dispositions made in respect of a child in a maintenance agreement, and there are certain limited exceptions to the general effect of a maintenance assessment as referred to above.[92]

32–19

AGREEMENTS CONCERNING DISPOSAL OF DIVORCE OR JUDICIAL SEPARATION SUIT ITSELF

Generally speaking, little dispute will arise between the parties on the "act" required to be proved before a decree can be granted.[93] This enables the obtaining of a decree in an uncontested suit, the whole procedure, except for the pronouncement of the decree, being masked from public gaze[94] except for those rare petitions ordered to be heard in open court by the judge. Even allegations of unreasonable behaviour are rarely disputed since "conduct" rarely has any great significance in disputes on ancillary matters. The full rigours of the doctrine of *res judicata* probably do not apply to undefended allegations of this nature and thus no detriment is suffered by a respondent who does not defend such allegations.[95]

32–20

However, there may be cases where a respondent feels sufficiently strongly to be disposed to defend: he or she may simply dispute the allegations or, in addition, make allegations of his or her own and cross-pray for divorce. Sometimes the strong feeling about the allegations can be

---

[88] s.9(2).
[89] s.9(1).
[90] s.9(3).
[91] s.10(2).
[92] ss.8(7) and 8(8).
[93] s.1(2).
[94] Family Proceedings Rules 1991 (SI 1991/1247), rr.2.24(3) and 2.36.
[95] See *Rowe v Rowe* [1980] Fam. 47. The point is not entirely free from doubt and it would be wise for a respondent's legal adviser to obtain the agreement of the petitioner's advisers to the effect that, in due course, they will not object to the raising of answers to the allegations if the matter should become relevant. In the absence of such agreement, a respondent will have to decide whether to contest the allegations or merely get his advisers to write a further letter giving his answers to the allegations but stating that, for the purposes of the divorce suit, he does not intend to contest them or, alternatively, simply saying that he denies the allegations and that if they are raised in the ancillary relief proceedings he reserves the right to defend them fully and make cross-allegations.

assuaged by a "toning down" or deletion of some of them. More often than not, the nature of the allegations against a respondent will be forgotten if the cross-allegations are not contested and each party obtains a decree.

32–21   Occasionally, divorce suits will not have been compromised prior to being listed for trial. Perhaps the "pre-trial review" will have failed in its objective.[96] As with other disputes, there are some which are incapable of compromise. However, further judicial encouragement towards agreement can be anticipated, and even where the parties have not themselves reached agreement the court may, in certain circumstances, impose its own will on the situation.[97] A court will be slow to declare an agreement seeking to avoid a contested suit as contrary to public policy:

> In *N v N*,[98] W presented a petition for divorce based upon H's alleged unreasonable behaviour. Some three or four weeks later, H and W agreed that there should be a five-month moratorium in which the possibility of a reconciliation should be explored. W agreed not to pursue her divorce suit for the agreed period so that the possibility of a reconciliation could be examined. H agreed that if at the end of the agreed period W did not withdraw her petition and proceeded with the suit, he would not defend the petition. At the end of the five-month period W decided to proceed with her petition. Ewbank J. held that she was entitled to proceed and H was bound by his agreement not to defend. There was nothing contrary to public policy in H agreeing not to defend the petition. The agreement was "entirely proper and indeed encouraged the possibility of a reconciliation".

32–22   Where agreement on the disposal of the suit is reached before trial or "at the doors of the court" and the agreement involves the filing of a new petition (for example on the basis of the fact of two years' separation and the consent of the other party), the leave of the court to file a new petition will be required.[99]

Where the parties acknowledge that the marriage has broken down irretrievably, circumstances would be rare indeed in which a contested suit would be justified.[1] Sensible and, in some cases, robust advice from legal advisers may be required: it will always receive judicial backing. In some cases, of course, a third party or parties will have been introduced into the suit and thus a compromise will have to provide for those wider interests. However, not even that should render agreement impossible provided satisfactory arrangements as to costs can be made.

---

[96] *Practice Direction (Divorce: Directions for Trial)* [1979] 1 W.L.R. 2.
[97] *Grenfell v Grenfell* [1978] Fam. 128, CA (where an undisputed allegation of adultery appeared in the proceedings).
[98] [1991] F.C.R. 690.
[99] Family Proceedings Rules 1991, rr.2.64.
[1] *cf. Welfare v Welfare* (1977) 121 S.J. 743; (1978) Fam. Law 55. There will be some rare cases where a grave hardship defence is being maintained in response to a five-year separation petition: see Matrimonial Causes Act 1973, s.5.

AGREEMENTS INVOLVING INTERIM STAGES OF DIVORCE OR JUDICIAL SEPARATION PROCEEDINGS, INCLUDING INTERIM FINANCIAL PROVISION

Interim applications proper

Preliminary. There are two principal areas in which interim[2] applications 32–23 proper are made to the court during the pendency of divorce or judicial separation proceedings—one relating to the occupation of the matrimonial home and the non-molestation of one party by the other and the other to the preservation and discovery of the assets of one of the parties.

Occupation of matrimonial home and non-molestation. Applications 32–24 relating to the occupation of the matrimonial home are made frequently.[3] When resolved by agreement they are usually so resolved by the giving of appropriate undertakings. For example, undertakings may be given unilaterally or by both parties as to the times when use will be made of certain rooms in the house or to the effect that certain rooms will not be entered. Equally, however, one party may be prepared to leave after a period of time and an undertaking to this effect may be given. Of course, it is open to a party to consent or submit to an appropriate order being made against him, although the provision of undertakings are more normal.[4]

The same applies to applications for non-molestation orders. Undertakings will normally be offered. Frequently the party against whom such an application is made does not accept the allegations relied upon by the applicant. Strictly speaking, a party against whom allegations are made who gives an undertaking is not taken as admitting the allegations. When an undertaking is offered and accepted it is not necessary for the court to have read or heard the evidence in support. However, a party often wishes to emphasise his or her non-acceptance of allegations by introducing the words "without admission" into the undertaking. This occurs frequently without objection and is a useful way of arriving at an "intermediate compromise" of what can be difficult and sensitive cases.

Preservation of assets and discovery of resources. The second area 32–25 concerns the preservation of financial resources and assets. Section 37 of the Matrimonial Causes Act 1973 affords one jurisdiction for obtaining orders preserving family assets; s.17 of the Married Womens' Property Act 1882 provides another. In addition (and, in some respects, more useful and

---

[2] *cf.* interim financial provision, below.
[3] For example under the Family Law Act 1996.
[4] An undertaking to the court is the equivalent of an order and does not, unlike an order, have to be served on the person who gave it before enforcement steps can be taken: *D v A & Co* [1900] 1 Ch. 484; *Re Launder* (1908) 98 L.T. 554.

flexible) is the court's inherent jurisdiction.[5] That jurisdiction also affords the basis for the grant in the Family Division of a search order.[6] Again, any agreement concerning these matters will usually be dealt with by way of undertakings to the court.

32–26 **Effect of undertakings "until further order".** One matter should be observed in relation to undertakings (or consent orders) of this nature: they are (if orders) interim or (if undertakings) equivalent to interim orders. They do not represent compromises of the substantive applications: they merely dispose of matters which arise in the course of proceedings. To that extent the court is likely to intervene and regulate such an order even if made pursuant to an agreement. In any event, parties usually consent to or undertake certain things "until the hearing of the substantive applications (or trial) or further order". Those last three words show that the parties are agreeable to placing themselves at the mercy of the court in the sense of recognising that some discharge, release or other variation of their agreement might be ordered at some later stage but prior to the hearing of the substantive issues.[7]

Interim financial provision

32–27 **Preliminary and nature of agreement.** Pending the resolution of the final financial issues between the parties, interim arrangements may be contemplated and made. Many of the issues which fall for consideration in relation to final orders arise in this context and it is not proposed to duplicate the discussion.[8]

Broadly speaking, the orders with which the court is likely to be concerned on an interim basis are those for maintenance pending suit and, to the extent permitted by the Child Support Act 1991,[9] interim periodical payments for any children of the family.[10] Where agreement concerning interim financial provision is reached, that agreement will usually be reflected or embodied in a consent order of this nature, suitable undertakings being given where appropriate in connection with, for example, the continued payment of mortgage instalments and other outgoings on the matrimonial home pending the final applications. The essential approach in

---

[5] *Roche v Roche* (1981) 11 Fam. Law 243, CA. See also *Shipman v Shipman* [1991] 1 F.L.R. 250.
[6] *Emanuel v Emanuel* [1982] 1 W.L.R. 669 (Wood J.).
[7] cf. *Chanel Ltd v F. W. Woolworth & Co Ltd* [1981] 1 W.L.R. 485, CA; *Thompson v Thompson* [1986] Fam. 38.
[8] See paras 32–31 *et seq.*, below.
[9] Child Support Act 1991, s.10.
[10] Matrimonial Causes Act 1973, ss.22 and 23(2)(d). There is also jurisdiction, pre-decree, to make secured periodical payments and lump sum provision for a child. The jurisdiction is rarely invoked, whether by consent or otherwise.

contested matters of this nature is to preserve the status quo so far as possible pending the final disposal of the financial issues and to ensure that the recipient has sufficient provision to meet immediate needs, including the payment of legal fees.[11] Agreements relating to these matters will, presumably, be directed towards this end and since, even in these matters, the ultimate discretion as to whether to make the proposed interim consent order remains with the court notwithstanding the parties' agreement,[12] it is important that this should be so. Doubtless, however, the fact that the parties have arrived at an agreement will be regarded by the court as important and will not lightly be disturbed.[13]

The court's practice. Since the ultimate discretion is that of the court, it is important that the court has the "correct, complete and up-to-date" information concerning the relevant matters in order that it can "lawfully and properly" exercise that discretion.[14] Since 1984[15] it has been necessary to lodge a statement of information with the court when applying for a consent order for interim financial provision so that the relevant information is available to the court before making the order sought. 32–28

Setting aside and variation. An order of this nature is clearly interim[16] and parties agreeing to one must be taken as submitting themselves to the jurisdiction of the court to interfere with such an order and to vary, discharge or suspend it or any part of it having regard to "all the circumstances of the case . . . [which] shall include any change in any of the matters to which the court was required to have regard when making the order to which the application relates . . .".[17] It appears that this statutory jurisdiction, and the inherent jurisdiction of the court to control interim orders (even those made by consent), enables the court, on an application in the suit,[18] to alter or discharge a consent order *ab initio* (or from some other date) where it is clear that the original order was inappropriate and it would be unjust to insist on its continuance.[19] 32–29

---

[11] See *A v A* [2001] 1 F.L.R. 377 and *G v G* [2003] 2 FLR 71.
[12] *Livesey v Jenkins* [1985] A.C. 424.
[13] See paras 32–48 *et seq.*, below.
[14] in *Livesey v Jenkins*, n.12, above, *per* Lord Brandon of Oakbrook at 437.
[15] When Matrimonial Causes Rules 1977, r.76A became operative. See now Family Proceedings Rules 1991, r.2.61.
[16] The court has a "continuing power to vary its terms" which, in *De Lasala v De Lasala*, [1980] A.C. 546 at 56 was held to be the appropriate test for an "interlocutory" order.
[17] Matrimonial Causes Act 1973, as amended by the Matrimonial and Family Proceedings Act 1984, s.31(7).
[18] Unlike certain final orders it may not be necessary or appropriate to appeal in these cases: if, *e.g.* the original consent order was a district judge's order, it would be appropriate to issue the application to vary or discharge before him. If, of course, the application raised particularly difficult issues it could be transferred to be heard by a judge.
[19] *Brister v Brister* [1970] 1 W.L.R. 664 (Ormrod J.); *Beighton v Beighton* (1974) 4 Fam. Law 119, CA; *Stephenson v Stephenson* (1974) 4 Fam. Law 124, CA.

Although it is clear that once a consent order of this nature has been made, the legal effect of the agreement which led to it is to be derived from the order, not the agreement,[20] it is likely that the grounds upon which such an agreement would have been set aside had it remained in the realm of contract[21] would be entertained as grounds for discharging or varying the order under the foregoing jurisdiction. Indeed, a mistake on one side only has afforded grounds for intervention[22] and, presumably, any non-disclosure of a material fact to the other side (and, in due course, indirectly to the court) would constitute a reason for intervention.[23]

In any case where intervention of this nature is sought, it is clear that the party seeking the intervention must show that the matter raised (for example, mistake or non-disclosure) led to the making of an order substantially different from that which otherwise would have been made.[24]

32–30 **Consent orders "without prejudice" to final orders.** The approach of the court to the making of interim financial provision orders following contested applications has been referred to above.[25] As a result of this approach it is not infrequently the case that an interim periodical payments order is different in quantum from the final order (normally lower because of a concentration on satisfying immediate needs). Furthermore, in the case of a consent order (whether or not incidental undertakings are given as well), a full appreciation of the evidence and the issues is not undertaken by the court save to the extent of consideration being given to the contents of the statement of information.[26] To that extent it would be wrong to suppose that the level of payments agreed should be regarded as influencing in any way those to be agreed or ordered in the final disposal.[27] However, in these cases the lay clients may prefer that fact to be acknowledged on the face of the order lest it be thought that positions are being "given away". At some suitable place in the agreed order can appear words such as "without prejudice to the final orders herein" to make the position clear.[28]

---

[20] *Livesey v Jenkins* [1985] A.C. 424; *De Lasala v De Lasala*, n.15, above.
[21] See Ch.4, above.
[22] *Brister v Brister*, n.19, above.
[23] *Livesey v Jenkins*, n.20, above.
[24] *Brister v Brister*, n.19, above; *Livesey v Jenkins*, n.20, above.
[25] See para.32–27, above. See also *Poon v Poon* [1994] 2 F.L.R. 857 (Johnson J.).
[26] See para.32–28, above.
[27] See also *F v F* [1995] 2 F.L.R. 45 where Thorpe L.J. suggested that on an interim provision application the Court should not indulge in an in-depth investigation and that any shortfall or over-provision could be compensated for at the final hearing.
[28] Usually in the preamble.

AGREEMENTS RELATING TO FINAL DISPOSAL OF FINANCIAL AND PROPERTY APPLICATIONS

Preliminary

As previously observed,[29] this is by far the most difficult area concerning compromises in the matrimonial sphere. In December 1980, the Court of Appeal was reminded by leading counsel[30] of the "confusion prevailing in the profession about consent orders in the matrimonial jurisdiction".[31] That there should have been confusion at any time is unfortunate. Practically speaking, the resolution by agreement of the financial and property affairs of the parties to a marriage breakdown assumes far greater significance than the resolution by agreement of the divorce or judicial separation itself. The process itself is one which commands full judicial support:

32–31

> "The law now encourages spouses to avoid bitterness after family breakdown and to settle their money and property problems."[32]

However, the context in which agreements of this nature operate is one in which a number of particular problems can arise in addition to those associated with compromises in other spheres. At all stages both parties may be exposed to emotional and financial pressures which result in unwise decisions being made in respect not only of themselves, but also of such children as there may be.[33] Equally, the bitterness sometimes associated with these situations can result in one or other or both of the parties seeking to conceal from the other the existence of assets and resources which otherwise would be relevant to rearranging their affairs. There is also the temptation to conceal proposed plans for remarriage which, again, may have an influence on the future resources of one or other or both of the parties. Sometimes, of course, circumstances may change after parties conclude an agreement (and a consent order) which makes continued reliance upon it (or the order) seem inappropriate.

The foregoing shows the need for the court to retain a fair degree of control over agreements and consent orders in this context. On the other hand, consistent with the approach which encourages settlement,[34] it is

32–32

---

[29] See para.32–01, above.
[30] The late Joseph Jackson, Q.C., then principal editor of *Rayden on Divorce* and co-author of *Jackson's Matrimonial Finance and Taxation*.
[31] *Thwaite v Thwaite* [1982] Fam. 1, *per* Ormrod L.J.
[32] *Minton v Minton* [1979] A.C. 593 at 608, *per* Lord Scarman. See also *Harris (formerly Manahan) v Manahan* [1997] 1 F.L.R. 205, *per* Ward L.J.
[33] See, *e.g. Backhouse v Backhouse* [1978] 1 W.L.R. 243 (Balcombe J.); *Edgar v Edgar* [1980] 1 W.L.R. 1410 at 1418, *per* Ormrod L.J.; *Camm v Camm* (1983) 4 F.L.R. 577.
[34] See para.32–31, above.

important that the court's control should not be used as a vehicle by which parties break their bargains and seek to reopen matters which were once fairly and properly concluded. It is inevitable that the legal principles applicable in this area endeavour to strike a balance between these competing considerations. The certainty, therefore, which legal advisers prefer to see in the statements of applicable principle is unlikely to be found to the extent seen in other contexts. That factor may have led to some of the confusion referred to above. Unfortunately, however, some of the earlier decisions in this area (all undoubtedly correct on their merits) often failed to reveal consistent statements of principle, whether relating to the law or practice applicable, leading to yet further confusion.[35]

Happily, a greater degree of clarity has emerged from a number of subsequent decisions, and certain propositions, particularly concerning the principles of law applicable, can now be advanced with a degree of confidence. There has also been the additional statutory intervention in the form of s.33A of the Matrimonial Causes Act 1973.[36] Regrettably, however, a number of "grey" areas have continued to exist. One of the greyest features of the landscape (the practice to be followed when seeking to set aside a consent order) has been the subject of judicial scrutiny in recent years. Some propositions can now be put forward with a sufficient degree of confidence so that practitioners can have a tolerably clear picture of what is expected in a given situation. However, some uncertainties do remain which, given the sensitive nature of the jurisdiction concerned, is neither helpful nor satisfactory. It remains[37] an area worthy of the attention of the appropriate Rules Committee. A simple unified[38] procedure should exist to enable a challenge to a consent order in this jurisdiction to be brought before a judge,[39] a suitable "filtration process" existing to prevent the obviously unmeritorious and unsustainable challenge proceeding beyond a "permission" stage.

Nature and relevance of an agreement in this context

32–33 **Nature.** It should be recalled at the outset that the topic under discussion is the compromise of proposed or actual applications for financial and property provision ancillary to a suit for divorce or judicial separation. Whilst a

---

[35] See also the comments of Lord Diplock in *De Lasala v De Lasala* [1980] A.C. 546.
[36] Introduced by the Matrimonial and Family Proceedings Act 1984, s.7.
[37] This view was put forward in the Second edition of this work and has been echoed in the commentary of Profesor Cretney Q.C. on the case of *Re C*, referred to at para.32–118, below, in (1993) 23 Fam. Law 675. In *Harris (formerly Manahan) v Manahan*, n.32, above, the Court of Appeal drew attention to the "far from clear" procedural position. Ward L.J. indicated that the Family Proceedings Rules Committee could usefully look again at r.8.1 of the Family Proceedings Rules: see further at paras 32–114 *et seq.*, below.
[38] In other words, not a choice of various alternatives: see paras 32–118 *et seq.*, below.
[39] See para.32–116, below.

"maintenance agreement" as previously defined[40] may well contain provisions which seek to compromise applications of this nature, it will not necessarily do so.[41] An agreement which does seek to resolve this kind of application, therefore, may or may not constitute a "maintenance agreement". The distinction between these two (potentially overlapping) forms of agreement is well recognised in practice. It is not wholly clear that the Judicial Committee of the Privy Council recognised fully the distinction in *De Lasala v De Lasala*.[42] Lord Diplock observed[43]:

> " ... the ... English legislation [recognises] two separate ways in which financial provision may lawfully be made for parties to a marriage which has been dissolved. One is by a maintenance agreement entered into between the parties without the intervention of the court; the other is by one party obtaining a court order against the other for periodical payments or for once-for-all[44] financial provision."[45]

In *De Lasala v De Lasala*, at a time when the relevant jurisdiction of the court[46] provided for the making merely of periodical payment orders (secured and unsecured) and lump sum orders, W consented to the dismissal of those claims when H had (a) paid to her a substantial lump sum referred to in a deed of arrangement which was approved by the court, and (b) settled upon trustees certain other substantial sums for the benefit of W and one child of the family, the relevant trust deeds being annexed to the deed of arrangement. These terms represented part of a global settlement which dealt with the manner in which W should obtain a decree of divorce, matters relating to the care and control of, and access to, the child and the basis upon which the outgoings of any residence purchased for W pursuant to the trusts were to be met.

It is clear, therefore, that the parties contemplated the intervention of a court in relation to these arrangements. The agreement did represent a compromise of proposed (and actual) applications to the court. It is not clear whether the Judicial Committee of the Privy Council decided that the agreement was a "maintenance agreement", but it is clear that, if it was, it

---

[40] See para.32–10, above.
[41] See para.32–11, above.
[42] [1980] A.C. 546.
[43] *ibid.* at 560.
[44] "Once-for-all provision" for this purpose is provision made by way of a lump sum order, a transfer of property order or a settlement of property order. For the sake of completeness it should, of course, be recalled that a settlement of property order made on or after a decree of judicial separation may be varied in a subsequent divorce suit: Matrimonial Causes Act 1973, s.31(1)(e) and (4). See also *Dinch v Dinch* [1987] 1 W.L.R. 252, HL, considered at paras 32–61 *et seq.*, below.
[45] A maintenance agreement can, of course, also be concluded by parties whose marriage has not been dissolved: see paras 32–10 *et seq.*, above.
[46] The consent order was made in May 1970 when the relevant Hong Kong Ordinance reflected the terms of the English Matrimonial Causes Act 1965.

was no longer "subsisting" to the extent that it was susceptible of variation in its own right.[47] The reason given was this[48]:

> "Financial arrangements that are agreed upon between the parties for the purpose of receiving the approval and being made the subject of a consent order by the court, once they have been made the subject of the court order no longer depend upon the agreement of the parties as the source from which their legal effect is derived. Their legal effect is derived from the court order . . ."

32–34   In the context of a case[49] concerning the basis upon which such a consent order could be set aside subsequently, the Court of Appeal interpreted the above statement of principle as representing "a significant departure" from the general principle applicable to consent orders in non-matrimonial cases and said that it had the effect of "eliminating the contractual basis" of matrimonial consent orders.[50] Whether or not that interpretation, for the purposes for which it was advanced, has survived the reaffirmation of the approach of the Privy Council by the House of Lords in *Livesey v Jenkins*[51] is a matter to which it will be necessary to return in due course.[52] However, one thing is clear from the quotation from the judgment of the Privy Council, namely that prior to the making of the consent order embodying the agreement of the parties the agreement of the parties must have some legal effect.

This, again, follows from the restatement of the principle in *Livesey v Jenkins*. A full analysis of the implications of that case appears below.[53] For present purposes, all that needs to be recorded is that it concerned the circumstances in which a consent order, reflecting a previously negotiated compromise of financial provision and property adjustment applications, could be set aside and the duty of disclosure of the parties. In the speech with which all their Lordships agreed, Lord Brandon of Oakbrook, referring to *De Lasala v De Lasala*,[54] said this[55]:

> ". . . when parties agree the provisions of a consent order, and the court subsequently gives effect to such agreement by approving the provisions concerned and embodying them in an order of the court, the legal effect

---

[47] See para.32–15, above.
[48] [1980] A.C. 546 at 560.
[49] *Thwaite v Thwaite* [1982] Fam. 1.
[50] *ibid.* at 8. In *Tommey v Tommey* [1983] Fam. 15, Balcombe J. said that the effect of *Thwaite v Thwaite* was that the "contractual basis of matrimonial consent orders is to be disregarded".
[51] [1985] A.C. 424.
[52] See para.32–88, below.
[53] See paras 32–82 *et seq.*, below.
[54] See n.35, above.
[55] *ibid.* at 55.

of those provisions is derived from the court order itself, and does not depend *any longer* on the agreement between the parties." (emphasis added)

Since the court's ultimate discretion cannot be ousted by an agreement between the parties, but an agreement arrived at is a very significant factor in exercising that discretion,[56] what is the legal effect of the agreement prior to the making of the consent order? Is it binding on the parties? If so, how is it enforced? What happens if the party entitled to apply for the relevant financial or property provision fails to bring the agreement before the court to enable the agreed orders to be made? 32–35

The agreement. Logically, the first step must be to decide if agreement has been reached at all. The whole subject of the nature of an agreement in this context was considered by the Court of Appeal in *Xydhias v Xydhias*.[57] 32–36

> There were lengthy pre-trial negotiations for settlement of W's ancillary relief claim. A series of draft consent orders were settled by counsel as working documents as the parties moved towards settlement. They had agreed the principal terms but were still at odds as to the terms of security and the duration of certain continuing obligations. The Court was told that the imminent hearing of the ancillary relief claims would not be needed but that a short appointment should be preserved for approval of a consent order or to allow time for negotiation of outstanding points. At that short appointment H withdrew from all negotiations. W sought to enforce an agreement which she asserted had been reached "between 22–29 August 1996". The district judge found that "by some time probably on 29 August 1996 (it is difficult to isolate clearly a defining moment) the essential building blocks of an agreement were in place". He excised from the final draft order those matters which H had not agreed. H's appeal to the judge was dismissed, as was his appeal to the Court of Appeal.

In dismissing the appeal Thorpe L.J. expressed himself thus[58]: 32–37

> "My cardinal conclusion is that ordinary contractual principles do not determine the issues in this appeal. This is because of the fundamental distinction that an agreement for the compromise of an ancillary relief application does not give rise to a contract enforceable in law. The parties seeking to uphold a concluded agreement for the compromise of such an application cannot sue for specific performance. The only way of rendering the bargain enforceable, whether to ensure that the applicant obtains the agreed transfers and payments or whether to protect the respondent from future claims, is to convert the concluded agreement into an order of the court. The decision of the Privy Council

---

[56] See paras 32–47, *et seq.*, below.
[57] [1999] 1 F.C.R. 289. H was granted permission to appeal to the House of Lords, but did not pursue the appeal.
[58] *ibid.* at 298–300.

in *De Lasala v De Lasala* . . . demonstrated that thereafter the rights and obligations of the parties are determined by the order and not by any agreement which preceded it. The order is absolute unless there is a statutory power to vary or unless vitiated by a fact that would vitiate an order in any other division. Additionally, as was demonstrated in *Robinson v Robinson* . . . an order in ancillary relief proceedings may be set aside if the product of a material breach of the duty of full and frank disclosure. An even more singular feature of the transition from compromise to order in ancillary relief proceedings is that the court does not either automatically or invariably grant the application to give the bargain the force of an order. The court conducts an independent assessment to enable it to discharge its statutory function to make such orders as reflect the criteria listed in s.25 of the Matrimonial Causes Act 1973, as amended . . .

In consequence, it is clear that the award to an applicant for ancillary relief is always fixed by the court. The payer's liability cannot be ultimately fixed by compromise as can be done in the settlement of claims in other divisions. Therefore the purpose of negotiation is not to finally determine the liability (that can only be done by the court) but to reduce the length and expense of the process by which the court carries out its function. If there is a dispute as to whether the negotiations led to an accord that the process should be abbreviated, the court has a discretion in determining whether an accord was reached. In exercising that discretion the court should be astute to discern the antics of a litigant who, having consistently pressed for abbreviation, is seeking to resile and to justify his shift by reliance on some point of detail that was open for determination by the court at its abbreviated hearing. If the court concludes that the parties agreed to settle on terms then it may have to consider whether the terms were vitiated by a factor such as material non-disclosure or tainted by a factor within the parameters set in *Edgar v Edgar*. Finally in every case the court must exercise its independent discretionary review applying the s.25 criteria to the circumstances of the case and to the terms of the accord. This approach particularly applies to accords intended to obviate delivery of briefs for trial. Different considerations may apply to agreements not negotiated in the shadow of an impending fixture . . .

Litigants in ancillary relief proceedings are subjected to great emotional and psychological stresses, particularly as the date of trial approaches. In my opinion there are sound policy reasons supporting the conclusion that the judge is entitled to exercise a broad discretion to determine whether the parties have agreed to settle. The pilot scheme depends on judicial control of the process from start to finish. The court has a clear interest in curbing excessive adversariality and in excluding from trial lists unnecessary litigation. A more legalistic approach, as this case illustrates, only allows the inconsistent or manipulative litigant to repudiate an agreement on the ground that some point of drafting, detail, or implementation had not been clearly resolved. Ordinarily heads of agreement signed by the parties or a clear exchange of solicitors' letters will establish the consensus. Hopefully a case such as this requiring the exercise of the judge's discretion will be a rarity . . .

In ancillary relief litigation a clear distinction has always been drawn between the determination of the liability and the determination of the security for the performance of the obligation. In the years when secured provision orders were commonplace counsel regularly settled cases on the footing that if the quantum of the annual payment could be agreed the mechanism that would be triggered to secure the recipient in the event of the payer's default would be separately and subsequently put into place either by further agreement or by determination of the Court. I have no doubt that that long-established practice informs and explains the communications between counsel as well as their readiness to regard the detail of the properties to be included within the schedule as ancillary and not precedent to a concluded agreement. Of course if the issue had to be decided on the stricter basis of pure contractual principle then the saga of the developing drafts and the complementary exchanges between the solicitors would have to be examined in much greater detail. The ambiguities and the inconsistencies that such an analysis would reveal would all tell against a finding of concluded contract on *Pagnan*[59] principles. However on the evidence before me I am in no doubt that the district judge rightly held that the parties had concluded a compromise during the week before the hearing. Throughout that week it was the husband who was pressing for a settlement and plainly there came a point at which the wife agreed his terms. All that remained unresolved was either mechanics or trivial."

This statement of the approach to agreements of this nature is, of course, important. Indeed, the merits of the case were such as undoubtedly justified the outcome. However, it is respectfully submitted that there are troubling uncertainties arising from the case. These can be summarised in the following comments and propositions:

32–38

(1) The court felt unable to define the moment when agreement was reached.
(2) More importantly, it is clear that no complete agreement was reached in the case. What to one person may be mechanics or trivial may be to another very important. The nature of the security might be critical to the husband who had to give it, but purely a matter of mechanics to the wife.
(3) Defining where the line is to be drawn between quantification and principle, on the one hand, and mechanics and mode of performance, on the other, may be very difficult.

---

[59] *Pagnan SpA v Tradax Ocean Transport SA* [1987] 3 All E.R. 565, CA.

32–39 The spectre of one party seeking to claim a concluded agreement relying upon *Xydhias*, whilst the other denies having reached that stage, is not illusory. It may be avoided if the parties agree to the two-stage process advocated by Thorpe L.J. whereby the agreement is concluded upon the heads of agreement being signed. However, negotiations are often not that formal and take place through a chain of correspondence and conversations, with new matters being introduced as negotiations develop. Whilst it is normally not too difficult to determine whether a complete agreement is reached at any point, it may be far more difficult to discern if the principles of agreement are agreed at some earlier stage.

32–40 From a practical point of view, it is suggested that it is now particularly important for negotiators to ensure that all material issues are raised at an early stage and that it is made clear that no agreement is to be regarded as concluded until final agreement is reached on all those material issues. Negotiations should remain expressly "subject to final agreement" until agreement is reached on all the material terms.

32–41 What other conclusions can be drawn from *Xydhias* and other authorities in this area? In the first place, there must be a sufficient agreement reached on the principal terms for it to have any impact at all on the court's discretion. If the parties are still negotiating, or they conclude an agreement and then agree to ignore it, there is no agreement to put forward for the court's consideration.

32–42 Secondly, it is beyond doubt that any provision in an agreement thus identified which seeks to restrict the right of a party to apply to the court for financial or property provision is unenforceable. If the agreement is a "maintenance agreement" within s.34 of the Matrimonial Causes Act 1973 then statutory force is given to the principle.[60] Notwithstanding the apparently wide ambit of the expression "financial arrangements" for the purpose of s.34, a fairly formidable argument exists for saying that only agreements including provision for periodical payments, the variation of ante-nuptial or post-nuptial settlements and/or the sale or retention of real or personal property qualify for recognition as a maintenance agreement within the terms of this section.[61] Furthermore, and in any event, it is by no means certain that a compromise of proposed or actual applications for financial relief actually contains "provisions governing the rights and liabilities . . . of the parties . . . in respect of the making or securing of payments or the disposition or use of any property".[62] It is not the provisions of the compromise which do this, but the provisions of the consent order to be

---

[60] See para.32–11, above.
[61] See paras 32–10 and 32–16, above.
[62] s.34(2).

obtained in due course.[63] Even if this be wrong, not all compromises of this nature will be in written form which is, of course, essential for an agreement to be within s.34.[64] Those which are not are undoubtedly covered by the principle established in *Hyman v Hyman*.[65]

Thirdly, if some legal effect is to be attributed to such a compromise it must, it is submitted, be along the following lines: a concluded compromise of proposed or actual applications for financial relief carries with it the express or, at the very least, implied agreement of the parties to invite the court in due course to exercise its discretion in accordance with the agreement unless some new circumstances, material in substance to the exercise of that discretion, arise between the conclusion of the agreement and the time when the court is invited to exercise it.[66] It follows, given the court's ultimate discretion, that the agreement is subject to the approval of the court. By analogy, therefore, with an agreement which is made expressly "subject to the approval of the court" the agreement: 32–43

(a) is not operative until approved by the court and made the subject of an order[67]; but
(b) is binding on the parties in the sense that it may be disavowed by neither pending the application to the court.[68]

---

[63] *cf. Sutton v Sutton* [1984] Ch. 184.
[64] Many will be oral by virtue of the fact that they are concluded "at the doors of the court". Subsequently reducing the agreement to writing does not mean that the agreement itself had not been concluded orally.
[65] [1929] A.C. 601. See para.32–09, above.
[66] *cf. Livesey v Jenkins*, n.51, above.
[67] Whence, thereafter, will be derived its legal effect: see paras 32–33 and 32–34, above.
[68] *Smallman v Smallman* [1972] Fam. 25. In *Amey v Amey* [1992] 1 F.C.R. 289 H and W were married in 1971. W had two children by a former marriage who, by the time of the relevant proceedings, were adults. In 1972, H purchased an inn for £12,000 which he and W improved and ran together in partnership. H and W were divorced in 1986 and an agreement as to their financial affairs was reached. In effect the agreement was to a 50/50 split of their assets. In pursuance of the agreement H paid £120,000 to W on October 1, 1986. On October 9, 1986, W's counsel drafted minutes of order with a view, as had been agreed, to an order being made by the court in due course. On December 8, 1986, W acquired the lease of another public house using, as H knew, part of the £120,000 for the purpose. On December 9, 1986, suddenly and unexpectedly, W died. The intended consent order had not by that time been made. H sought rescission of the agreement. Scott Baker J. held:

(a) that there was a binding agreement notwithstanding the fact that the proposed consent order had not been made,
(2) the agreement stood or fell by reference to common law,
(3) there was no basis in mistake or frustration to justify setting aside the agreement and, in any event
(4) it had already been performed.

See also the comments of Hoffmann L.J. in *Pounds v Pounds* [1994] 2 F.L.R. 1055 at 1072–1073. As to the choices available to the "innocent party" in the event of the other

32–44 FDR hearings. All ancillary relief applications are required to be listed for a hearing intended to resolve such disputes unless the court otherwise orders.[69] Often, such hearings result in consent orders which are drafted, approved and lodged on the day. Sometimes, however, agreement is reached, the court is told the essential terms and approves them, but the order is not drafted there and then, either because of the lateness of the hour or the need to obtain further advice, *e.g.* to minimise tax liabilities. What is the status of such an agreement? This was considered in *Rose v Rose*.[70] Having reconsidered the matter the husband was seeking to withdraw his consent to what had been agreed. The Court of Appeal concluded that the product of such a hearing is an unperfected order of the court, not merely a contractual agreement between the parties. Only in exceptional circumstances and for strong reasons will a party be allowed to escape the agreement. The whole purpose of an FDR is undermined if parties are free to re-evaluate their decisions and suggest that they have made the wrong choice. As a result it is now good practice to draw up and sign heads of agreement on the day of the FDR, which should be signed by both the parties and their advisers.

32–45 Even if the compromise of this nature in a particular case is a "maintenance agreement", the agreement to invite the court to exercise its discretion in a particular way does not give rise to a cause of action in the normal sense of that term in the event of one party seeking to ignore the agreement. The agreement is of a different nature from one where, for example, H agrees to pay W voluntary periodical payments at a certain rate. His failure to do so would give W a cause of action in relation to the arrears; she could bring an action, in effect, for damages.[71] The effect of an agreement such as the one under consideration is to give the innocent party the right to say to the district judge or judge:

> "We agreed not to have a contested hearing and leave the court's discretion completely at large; we agreed to invite you to exercise your discretion in this way; I want you still to do so; unless my wife/husband can adduce evidence of compelling reasons for taking a different course in the interests of justice, please give effect to our previously negotiated agreement."[72]

---

seeking to resile from any such agreement, see paras 32–65 *et seq.*, below.
[69] Family Proceedings Rules 1991, r.2.61D and E, as amended.
[70] [2002] 1 F.L.R. 978.
[71] See para.32–13, above.
[72] *cf. Edgar v Edgar* [1980] 1 W.L.R. 1410 at 1424 *per* Oliver L.J. In *Peacock v Peacock* [1991] 1 F.L.R. 324, a consent order in *Mesher* form was made between the parties in 1982 providing for the sale of the former matrimonial home not later than 1992 with an equal division of the net proceeds of sale. Agreed periodical payments provision in respect of W and the children was also incorporated in the order. In 1984 H and W negotiated direct on the basis that the small mortgage on the property would be discharged and that

That, it is thought, represents the right of the "innocent party" in the 32–46
event of the abandonment of the agreement by the other. Does it mean that
the innocent party is obliged to rely upon the agreement rather than taking
some different course on the substantive applications? If the compromise was
one of litigation of a different nature then, unless the terms of the agreement
had provided otherwise, the innocent party would be left merely with his
remedies under the compromise.[73] But this litigation is different. The essence
of the parties' agreement is this:

> "I agree to invite the court to exercise its discretion in this particular
> way on the basis that you also agree. And if you fail to abide by this at
> the hearing of the application, or you evince an intention before the
> hearing that you will not do so, I reserve the right either to invite the
> court's attention to our agreement and ask it to act upon it or to accept
> your new approach and leave all matters at large."

This approach is, it is submitted, in no way inconsistent with *Smallman v* 32–47
Smallman referred to above.[74] In that case W, the "innocent party", was
seeking to uphold the agreement upon which she (and another party) had
already acted. The question of what her position would have been had she
been content to accept H's "repudiation" of the agreement did not fall for
consideration.

If the foregoing represents an accurate statement of the nature and legal
effect of a compromise of these matters, the practice to be invoked to ensure
compliance with the agreement falls into place. There are one or two
situations where the position is not entirely straightforward, and these and
the general practice will be considered in due course.[75]

Relevance. In a large measure the relevance of an agreement in this context 32–48
has already been stated in the discussion of its nature and legal effect. For
completeness, however, the position should be stated clearly. Ever since
Hyman v Hyman[76] it has been clear:

---

the property would be transferred to W absolutely in return for H's release from the
periodical payments obligations under the order. They reached an understanding on this
basis and acted upon it to the extent that the mortgage was discharged and H ceased
making the periodical payments. Before steps were taken to transfer the house to W
disputes arose and, in due course, in response to H's application to vary the periodical
payments order, W issued a writ in the Chancery Division seeking specific performance of
the agreement made in August 1984. Thorpe J. held that the proceedings in the Chancery
Division were misconceived since the divorce court retained jurisdiction over the order of
1982 which, in effect, the parties by their agreement would need to vary. "How could the
court order specific performance of one side of the bargain, when the plantiff was not able
to perform her side of the bargain without the concurrence of another court having
completed a wide-ranging discretionary review?"

[73] See Ch.8, above.
[74] See n.68, above. It was a case arising before the new divorce legislation was fully in
operation. However, that does not make it any less relevant to the issues discussed in the
text although, of course, its binding nature relates only to the issues which were raised for
consideration.
[75] See paras 32–65 *et seq.*, below.
[76] [1929] A.C. 601. See para.32–09, above.

(a) that no provision in an agreement could preclude a party from applying to the court for financial relief; but that
(b) the fact of such agreement will be a very relevant factor when the court reaches a decision.[77]

32–49 This approach has found expression in cases since the legislation of 1970. If the court is satisfied that an agreement was freely negotiated with full knowledge of all the circumstances, particularly with the assistance of competent[78] legal advice, it is something "to which considerable attention"[79] is paid and constitutes "a very important factor in considering what is the just outcome of the proceedings".[80] The onus of showing sufficient grounds for disregarding it is on the party seeking to say that the agreement should not be reflected in the ultimate order of the court.[81]

32–50 As emphasised above,[82] once an agreement has been embodied in a consent order the legal effect of the agreement is derived from the terms of the order. The questions of the effect of an agreement of this nature (a) being filed and made a rule of court and/or (b) upon subsequent applications for a variation of the consent order are discussed below.[83]

32–51 **Statutory intervention—s.33A.** Section 33A of the Matrimonial Causes Act 1973[84] applies to a "consent order for financial relief" as defined, namely "an order in the terms applied for to which the respondent agrees". It provides as follows:

"Notwithstanding anything in the preceding provisions of this Part of this Act, on an application for a consent order for financial relief the

---

[77] *ibid., per* Lord Hailsham L.C. at 614 and 609 respectively; and quoted in *Edgar v Edgar*, [1980] 1 W.L.R. 1410, at 1415. See also, *Peacock v Peacock* [1991] F.L.R. 121, *per* Butler-Sloss L.J.
[78] *Camm v Camm* (1983) 4 F.L.R. 577. It is, with respect, questionable as to how far a court should go in investigating the quality of the legal advice which a person has received. The nature of the bargain struck should be manifest from its terms and the circumstances of the parties as revealed in the negotiations leading to it. If unfairness is to be a ground for rejecting an agreement, it would be unfair whether it was entered into against good advice or on the basis of bad legal advice. However, in *B v B* [1995] 1 F.L.R. 9, the quality of the advice received by W was examined in some detail and taken into account upon her application to vary and extend a consent order for periodical payments made some years earlier. See also *H v H* [1994] 2 F.L.R. 94 and *Smith v McInerney* [1994] 2 F.L.R. 1077. Since 1984 "first consideration" of all the circumstances to be considered by the court is the welfare of any minor children, a matter to be given appropriate weight in the balancing exercise when considering whether to give effect to the agreement of the parties: *N v N* [1994] 2 F.C.R. 275, CA. See further at paras 32–72 *et seq.*, below.
[79] in *Brockwell v Brockwell* (1975) 6 Fam. Law 46, *per* Stamp L.J.; quoted by Bush J. in *Dean v Dean* [1978] Fam. 161 at 166.
[80] *per* Ormrod L.J. in *Brockwell v Brockwell*, n.79, above; quoted in *Edgar v Edgar*, n.72, above, at 1417.
[81] *Edgar v Edgar*, n.72, above; *Dean v Dean*, n.79, above.
[82] See paras 32–33 to 32–34, above.
[83] See paras 32–128 *et seq.*, below.
[84] Introduced by Matrimonial and Family Proceedings Act 1984, s.7. Due to be repealed on a date to be appointed, with some saving provisions, by Family Law Act 1996, s.66.

court may, unless it has reason to think that there are other circumstances into which it ought to enquire, make an order in the terms agreed on the basis only of the prescribed information furnished with the application."

The prescribed information is now ordained by the terms of the Family Proceedings Rules 1991, r.2.61.[85]

Prior to the implementation of these provisions a court would rarely inquire into the appropriateness or otherwise of an order for which the parties applied by consent. The justification for taking this course, notwithstanding the mandatory obligation of the court to consider the circumstances prescribed by s.25 before making any order, was that an agreement reached with the assistance of the parties' legal advisers constituted sufficient evidence that it was reasonable and reflected the matters required to be taken into account by the section.[86]   32–52

It is not thought that the significance of the fact that the parties have reached agreement is in any way altered by these statutory provisions. They merely prescribe the procedure to be followed and the minimum amount of information which the court must have before it may make a consent order. In other words, the full appraisal of whether the agreement measures up to the requirements of section 25 is not required provided the prescribed information is made available to the court unless, of course, there is "reason to think that there are other circumstances" into which inquiry should be made. The essence of the prescribed information, however, is to draw the court's attention to "the kind of information which the court needs to have before making an order in accordance with the revised criteria contained in the new section 25 . . . of the Act of 1973".[87]   32–53

Securing an order reflecting a prior agreement

Where both parties are still in agreement

Practice on seeking. An application to the court should be made by the party having the carriage of the applications for financial relief to which the other party gives consent. The consent may be personal or by a legal adviser. In reality the application is often regarded as a joint application.[88]   32–54

---

[85] See *Livesey v Jenkins* [1985] A.C. 424.
[86] *Dean v Dean*, n.79, above.
[87] *Livesey v Jenkins*, n.85, above, at 444. See, *Pounds v Pounds* [1994] 2 F.C.R. 1055 at 1061–1062, *per* Waite L.J. and Harris (formerly Manahan) v Manahan, n.32, above, *per* Ward L.J.
[88] *Liversey v Jenkins* [1985] A.C. 424 at 437.

32–55　The manner in which the application is made depends upon when agreement is reached. Where, for example, agreement is reached during negotiations between solicitors (with or without the assistance of counsel) before any substantive hearing takes place, an application for a consent order will be made to the relevant district judge or judge. Where both parties have solicitors acting for them, no personal attendance before the court would seem to be necessary. This has been the case in the Divorce Registry for many years[89] and the practice became prevalent in many divorce county courts even though no Practice Direction expressly dealing with the matter was issued.[90] Nonetheless, the general practice in this regard seems to be implicit in the terms of r.2.61 of the Family Proceedings Rules 1991.[91] Agreement may, of course, be reached before any notice of application for financial relief is issued by or on behalf of either party. In this event, a notice of application in Form A[92] should be issued seeking an order in the terms agreed, those terms appearing in minutes of order annexed to the application. If (as will normally be the case) an order is proposed which impacts on both parties, it is preferable that each party issues a Form A even if only for the purposes of the dismissal of claims. The application will need to be indorsed with the consent of the solicitors on the record. Furthermore, a "statement of information"[93] must be lodged with the application. This may be signed by the solicitors on the record for the respondent to the application and, whilst it is not necessary for either party to sign the statement personally, the practice of obtaining both signatures has been commended.[94] The statement should indicate the capital and net incomes of the parties at the date of the statement and give the net equity of any property concerned, together with the effect of its proposed distribution and details of service on pension trustees and mortgagees if an order affecting a pension or property is sought.[95]

---

[89] *Practice Direction (Divorce Registry: Consent Summons)* [1974] 1 W.L.R. 937, as varied by *Practice Direction (Divorce Registry: Consent Summons) (No.2)* [1976] 1 W.L.R. 74. This practice was described as "experimental", but its long-term survival suggests that it is permanent. The original Practice Direction was said not to be intended to disturb the practice in Divorce County Courts.
[90] *ibid.*
[91] Sub-para.(3) of r.2.61 begins with the words "Where the parties attend the hearing of an application for financial relief", suggesting that there are situations where conversely they do not do so.
[92] Family Proceedings Rules 1991, r.2.53(2)(b).
[93] See para.32–51, above. But see para.32–59, below.
[94] *Practice Direction (Financial Provision; Consent Order)* [1986] 1 W.L.R. 381.
[95] *Practice Direction (Financial Provision: Consent Order) (No.2)* [1990] 1 W.L.R. 150. Although the prescribed form of the statement of information does not refer specifically to the likely size of each party's estate and the identity of those who might be regarded as having a prior claim on such estate in the event of each party's decease, it would seem that this sort of information should, either directly or indirectly, be conveyed to the court if, as is usual, an order by consent under s.15(1) of the Inheritance (Provision for Family and Dependants) Act 1975 is sought by the parties: *Whiting v Whiting* [1988] 1 W.L.R. 565 at 577.

Merely because these provisions have been complied with correctly does not mean, of course, that the district judge or judge is obliged to make the order sought or to deal with the application without attendance. The court retains its ultimate discretion in these matters[96] and it has a discretion as to whether to deal with the application on the basis only of the information provided in the statement.[97] Where there is "reason to think that there are other circumstances into which it ought to inquire", the court will undoubtedly decline to deal with the application in this way and will almost certainly require the personal attendance of the parties and/or their representatives. 32–56

Where either or both of the parties do not have solicitors acting for them, it is unlikely that a court would make a consent order without the personal attendance of the parties or, at the very least, compelling evidence of their genuine and informed consent.[98] This would be particularly so if the dismissal (or a restriction of the right to apply for a variation) of a wife's periodical payments claims is contemplated.[99] In any event, of course, all the other aspects of the practice described above[1] would need to be complied with before the court would act on an application for a consent order in such a situation. 32–57

Often, of course, an agreement is not concluded until arrival "at the doors of the court". Usually, the parties will be represented either by counsel or solicitors. When agreement is concluded in the discussions which take place, it is normal for the legal representative of the party who is effectively making the substantive application to the court to draw up, with the assistance and agreement of his opposite number, a draft agreed order for presentation to the court. Before the introduction of the procedure now set out in r.2.61 of the Family Proceedings Rules 1991 it was customary for the court to be told briefly of the reasons for, and the basis of, the agreement reflected in the draft order, although, more often than not, the court would accept the fact of the agreement as sufficient evidence that s.25 had been complied with. 32–58

Following the introduction of the new ancillary relief procedure nationally the court will have Form Es from both parties which should contain all the information as to the parties' means required by the rule. In those circumstances the court is unlikely to require a statement of information. Indeed, r.2.61(3) of the Family Proceedings Rules 1991 gives the court a 32–59

---

[96] See para.32–49, above.
[97] The use of the word "may" in s.33A yields the basis for this further discretion: see para.32–51, above.
[98] *cf.* para.10–03, above.
[99] *cf. Practice Direction (Family Division: Financial Statement)* [1984] 1 W.L.R. 674. This Practice Direction has largely been superseded by s.33A and r.2.61. However, it has not been withdrawn formally and probably represents the practice still adopted in the (unusual) situation being considered in the text.
[1] See paras 32–54 *et seq.*, above.

wide power to act "in such manner as it sees fit" as regards documentation when the parties attend court on a financial relief application.

32–60 Contents and phraseology of agreed order. It is essential that all the terms of the proposed consent order should come clearly within the court's powers conferred by ss.23 and 24. Any terms which cannot be brought within that jurisdiction should be formulated as undertakings or reflected in the recitals to the order to the court.[2] The parties cannot, by consent, confer on the court a power or jurisdiction which it does not otherwise possess.[3] Strictly speaking, the court can (and should) decline to make an order outside its jurisdiction.[4] If an order containing such provision is made, the provision will almost certainly be unenforceable unless it can be enforced in contract.[5]

32–61 It is important also that the proposed consent order truly reflects the agreement of the parties so that its essential purpose—the final resolution of unhappy differences—is not frustrated by future (costly) disputes about what the order was intended to achieve. The matter was put strongly by the House of Lords in *Dinch v Dinch*.[6] Lord Oliver of Aylmerton said this[7]:

> "I feel impelled once again to stress in most emphatic terms that it is in all cases the imperative professional duty of those invested with the task of advising the parties to these unfortunate disputes to consider with due care the impact which any terms that they agree on behalf of their clients have and are intended to have upon any outstanding application for ancillary relief and to ensure that such appropriate provision is inserted in any consent order made as will leave no room for any future doubt or misunderstanding or saddle the parties with the wasteful burden of wholly unnecessary costs."

32–62 The problem has arisen not infrequently when the consent order does not make plain whether an outstanding claim for ancillary relief has, or has not, been dismissed. It has often been said[8] that where it is intended to dismiss a claim for any particular relief that should be stated clearly in the order and that the expression "no order" should be avoided since it is ambiguous. A

---

[2] *Livesey v Jenkins*, [1985] A.C. 424 at 444. The procedure for making the terms a rule of court is considered below at paras 32–128 *et seq.*, below.
[3] *Hinde v Hinde* [1953] 1 W.L.R. 175, CA, and *Masefield v Alexander* [1995] 1 F.L.R. 100 at 102, CA. See also Ch.9, above. There is jurisdiction to dismiss one party's claims whilst keeping alive those of the other: *Thompson v Thompson* [1988] 1 W.L.R. 562 (Ewbank J.).
[4] *Noel v Becker* [1971] 1 W.L.R. 355. It is important that an order for financial relief is not made until after the *decree nisi*: *Pounds v Pounds* [1994] 2 F.C.R. 1055, CA.
[5] *Hinde v Hinde*, n.3, above. If the underlying agreement ceases to have effect once reflected in an order (see para.32–34, above), the provision cannot be enforced as an agreement.
[6] [1987] 1 W.L.R. 252.
[7] *ibid.* at 255.
[8] In *Gee v Gee* (1976) C.A.T. 278; *Rushforth v Rushforth* (1976) C.A.T. 91; *Carter v Carter* [1980] 1 W.L.R. 390; and *Dipper v Dipper* [1981] Fam. 31.

claim can, of course, be "kept alive" specifically by adjourning the application for it with liberty to restore.[9]

When a court is subsequently called upon to determine what was the true effect of a previous order for financial relief, the question is one of construction. The court will look at all the surrounding circumstances to give effect to its spirit and purpose. The view has been expressed[10] that the court will not readily imply or infer a dismissal of a wife's claim for ancillary relief when no express order was made in relation to that claim in the original order and that the burden of establishing the dismissal of that claim should be on the husband. The House of Lords has emphasised that the matter is one of construction to determine what the parties intended[11]:

> "There cannot . . . be any irrebutable presumption that an order which 32–63 is silent as to a claim which, on the record, appears to have been put in issue necessarily and always has to be construed as containing a dismissal of that claim. It must, in each case, be a question of construction of the particular order under consideration, and whilst I do not dissent from the proposition that a proper caution should be exercised before reaching a conclusion that will effectively preclude a wife from making a further claim for relief, I do not . . . derive much help from consideration of where the burden lies. One has . . . simply to look at the order and any admissible material available for its construction, and determine. . . . in the case of a consent order, what the parties intended . . . to effect by the order. If the conclusion is that what was intended was a final and conclusive once-for-all settlement, either overall or in relation to a particular property, then it must follow that that precludes any further claim in relation to that property."

Undertakings. The status of undertakings in ancillary relief orders has been 32–64 the subject of debate. They are routinely given by parties to cover matters which the court has no power to order: for example, the taking out of an insurance policy or provision of a tax indemnity. Although some regard the enforceability of such undertakings as uncertain in principle, it is submitted that they should be regarded as binding. To minimise difficulties in enforcement it is suggested that the party giving the undertaking should give it to the court as well as agreeing to like effect with the other party.

Where one party is resiling from the agreement. The circumstances in 32–65 which a court would feel entitled, either before or after a consent order is made, to disregard the prior agreement of the parties will be considered in

---

[9] cf. *Davies v Davies* [1986] 1 F.L.R. 497.
[10] *Brown v Kirrage* (1981) 11 Fam. Law 141, CA, a case involving the question of whether an application for a lump sum had in fact been dismissed or left open. See also *Atkinson v Atkinson* (1984) 14 Fam. Law 305, CA, a case involving a consent order.
[11] *Dinch v Dinch* [1987] 1 W.L.R. 252 at 263, HL. See also *Banyard v Banyard* (1985) 15 Fam. Law 120, CA; *Sandford v Sandford* [1986] 1 F.L.R. 412; *Potter v Potter* [1990] 2 F.L.R. 27; and *Richardson v Richardson* [1994] 1 F.L.R. 286.

due course.[12] The following discussion concerns the situation where parties agree on the orders (or the basis of the orders) which they would invite the court to make, but one of the parties has a change of heart. The change of heart may simply be of a wilful nature or may derive from a genuinely-held belief that, on reflection, the agreement was not fair. How should the party who wishes to abide by the agreement react? What procedural steps can be taken?

32–66 In the first place it is clear that, even though the agreement may not have what might be termed "full contractual force",[13] such a party should go on acting, so far as possible, as if the agreement stood. Without seeking to introduce into this area all the usual contractual concepts,[14] it is undeniably correct for the party not repudiating the agreement to show clearly that the other party's repudiation is not accepted; otherwise there would be a mutual abandonment of a previously agreed position to which it is not possible for either party to return with conviction.

32–67 Since the court's approach is to require the party trying to abandon the agreement to show good reason for the court to disregard it, the normal form of application made by the party seeking to uphold the agreement is one requiring the resiling party[15] "to show cause why an order" reflecting, or in the terms of, the previous agreement should not be made.[16] Once prima facie evidence of an agreement is adduced, the onus is placed squarely on the shoulders of the party resiling from it to adduce evidence of sufficient reasons to compel the court to ignore it. If, for example, an applicant for financial relief is satisfied with the provisions of the agreement, there is no reason why an order such as this should not be sought and obtained. Equally, however, the substantive applications could be pursued, an appropriate affidavit making it clear that all that is pursued, if the court thinks it right, is an order reflecting the previous agreement. If it is the respondent to an application who wishes to uphold the agreement, an application for a "show cause" order could be made even if the applicant by then is not actively pursuing the substantive applications. If, of course, the substantive applications are being pursued, in effect, in breach of the agreement, an order of this nature can be sought, coupled, perhaps, with an application for an order staying those applications save for the purpose of making orders reflecting, or in the terms of, the agreement.[17] It would, nevertheless, be

---

[12] See paras 32–71 *et seq.*, below.
[13] In the sense that no "cause of action" arises on the "breach" (or, more accurately, the "anticipatory breach") of the agreement: see paras 32–43 *et seq.*, above.
[14] *cf. Edgar v Edgar* [1980] 1 W.L.R. 1410 at 1417, *per* Ormrod L.J.
[15] See paras 32–48 *et seq.*, above.
[16] This was done in *Dean v Dean* [1978] Fam. 161.
[17] In *Harte v Harte* (1976) C.A.T. 423 the argument that the appeal had been compromised was raised by way of preliminary motion to stay the appeal.

possible merely to reserve the argument and the evidence about the agreement to the hearing of the substantive applications, but by then most of the objectives of the agreement in the first place (*i.e.* the saving of costs and the anxieties and uncertainty of litigation of this nature) will have been frustrated. One positive application is, it is thought, desirable from all points of view. That said, on many occasions the application for ancillary relief made by the resiling party will strike at the heart of the agreement (*e.g.* by alleging non-disclosure, or *material* change of circumstances) and the most economic course will often be to hear the "show cause" application together with the application(s) for ancillary relief.

On the assumption that the court considers that the agreement was, and remains, fair, what can it do? On one view an order "by consent" could not be made because the consent of one of the parties would not be forthcoming on the day the court was invited to make the order. On the other hand, the necessary consent could arguably be found in the agreement itself and an order "by consent" made.[18] This approach reflects the robust attitude which, it is submitted, a court can and should adopt when satisfied that an unmeritorious position is being adopted by the party seeking to resile from the agreement.

32–68

Nonetheless, whether or not the order made by the court is prefaced by the words "by consent", it will not allow itself to be frustrated by technical problems in connection with the order. Problems will arise only where terms going beyond the jurisdiction conferred by the Matrimonial Causes Act 1973[19] were included in the agreement. Matters such as these are usually dealt with by way of undertakings to the court.[20] It is extremely unlikely that a court would feel able, notwithstanding its desire to give effect to the agreement, to incorporate undertakings as such in the order made because:

32–69

(a) no undertaking is being volunteered to the court; and
(b) it would be inappropriate to bind a party to an obligation the breach of which could result in immediate steps for committal being taken.

A degree of ingenuity may have to be shown in utilising the jurisdiction of the court to secure the desired result. Although of no direct coercive

32–70

---

[18] *Cook v Cook* (1984) 14 Fam. Law 121, CA. See also Ch.5, paras 5–52 *et seq.*, above.
[19] Or Married Women's Property Act 1882 if invoked, s.17. See para.32–56, above.
[20] See para.32–60, above.

effect, the preamble to the order can make it clear, for example, why a particular level of periodical payments or lump sum order is being made, reflecting, perhaps, some additional element (*e.g.* payments under a life policy) which had been agreed but which cannot be made the subject of an order.[21] Alternatively, the value of the matter intended to have been covered by the undertaking no longer proffered can be adjusted and provided for accordingly.

Disregarding agreements and setting aside consent orders

Disregarding agreements *before* an order is made

32–71 **Preliminary.** The nature and effect of a compromise of proposed or actual ancillary relief applications has been stated.[22] So too has the influence which such an agreement will have on the court's ultimate discretion.[23] A number of factors have emerged which can be regarded as preliminary to a consideration of the circumstances in which the court is entitled to disregard a previously negotiated position:

(1) Clearly, if the negotiations never crystallised into a sufficient agreement there would be no agreement to put before the court.[24]
(2) If an agreement had been concluded, but both parties subsequently abandon reliance upon it, there will be no extant (and thus relevant) agreement to put before the court.[25]
(3) If there is no agreement to put before the court, it cannot be taken into account in exercising its discretion. The matter must be dealt with at large.

32–72 **Grounds for disregarding.** Even though full contractual force is not to be given to a compromise of this nature, the fact of an agreement is significant. As a matter of principle, the argument should be available to a party that, notwithstanding an agreement apparently concluded and not subsequently abandoned, such agreement should be regarded as of no significance because it was entered into on the basis of some ground which would invalidate an ordinary compromise such as an operative mistake, an effective misrepresentation (fraudulent or otherwise), duress or undue

---

[21] *Milne v Milne* [1981] 2 F.L.R. 286, CA.
[22] See paras 32–33 *et seq.*, above.
[23] See paras 32–49, *et seq.*, above.
[24] See para.32–35, above.
[25] It is not clear to what extent, if any, reference to the previously concluded agreement, which is thereafter abandoned by both parties, may be made at the hearing of a substantive application. It would not be inadmissible as such if relevant to any issues arising. It might, it is thought, be relevant to explain questions of delay or even, perhaps, the manner in which one party organised his or her finances or plans for a time.

influence.[26] Whilst it may be right not to try to adhere too strictly to precise common law contractual principles, regard must be had to the circumstances leading to the agreement and the parties' subsequent conduct. The matter was put thus in *Edgar v Edgar*[27]:

> "To decide what weight should be given, in order to reach a just result, to a prior agreement . . . regard must be had to the conduct of both parties, leading up to the prior agreement, and to their subsequent conduct, in consequence of it. It is not necessary in this connection to think in formal legal terms, such as misrepresentation or estoppel; *all*[28] the circumstances as they affect each of two human beings must be considered in the complex relationship of marriage. So, the circumstances surrounding the making of the agreement are relevant. Undue pressure by one side, exploitation of a dominant position to secure an unreasonable advantage, inadequate knowledge, possibly bad legal advice, an important change of circumstances, unforeseen or overlooked at the time of making the agreement, are all relevant to the question of justice between the parties."

32–73

Although the common law phraseology was thus eschewed, it is submitted that *Edgar v Edgar* is authority for the proposition that, when considering one party's contention that an agreement has been made which should influence the court's discretion, it is open to the other party to raise, *inter alia*, suggestions akin to misrepresentation or undue influence.[29] In *De Lasala v De Lasala*[30] the Judicial Committee of the Privy Council did not demur from the proposition that, as a matter of principle, an agreement to a consent order obtained by fraud or mistake was susceptible to being set aside. So far as fraud, mistake or misrepresentation are concerned in this context, they will often be embraced by the wider concept of the need for full and frank disclosure of all material facts between the parties when engaged in seeking to compromise proposed or actual applications for financial relief.[31]

32–74

Although it is submitted that it is clear that circumstances akin to the usual grounds for setting aside a compromise may be raised at some appropriate stage, it is equally clear, as a matter of practice, that the party relying on any of these grounds need not apply to the court to set aside an

32–75

---

[26] See Ch.4. *cf. Pounds v Pounds* [1994] 2 F.C.R. 1055 at 1073 *per* Hoffmann L.J.
[27] [1980] 1 W.L.R. 1410 at 1417, *per* Ormrod L.J. (with whom Oliver L.J. agreed); *cf. Allsop v Allsop* (1981) 11 Fam. Law 18, where the expression "misrepresentation" was used. See also *H v H* [1994] 2 F.L.R. 94.
[28] Ormrod L.J.'s emphasis.
[29] *cf.* the position after the making of an order. See also paras 4–66 *et seq.*, above.
[30] [1980] A.C. 546.
[31] *Livesey v Jenkins* [1985] A.C. 424.

agreement of this nature.[32] He or she may simply make it clear to the other party that the agreement is, for the relevant reason, no longer regarded as having effect. This may be emphasised, if it is the applicant for relief who takes this course, by taking active steps to pursue the substantive applications. Should the other party take any of the procedural steps suggested previously as being appropriate,[33] the matter of the invalidating ground can be raised then as the reason advanced for the court disregarding the agreement.

32–76   However, it is plain that wider grounds than merely those referred to above may be available in order that an agreement may be disregarded. The lack of full and frank disclosure of all material facts may, if significant to the agreement, cause the court to disregard it at the invitation of the party to whom the full disclosure was not made.[34] A material and unforeseen or overlooked change in circumstances since the agreement is another ground, although that, of course, represents an *ex post facto* basis for saying that the agreement is to be ignored. A "material change of circumstances" for this purpose may be one of many things. The most obvious example would be a significant change in the financial position of one or other or both of the parties, particularly if this had an adverse impact upon any children of the family.[35] Equally, of course, anything which occurs that invalidates the basis, or fundamental assumption, upon which the agreement was concluded would constitute a material change in circumstances.[36]

32–77   **Bad legal advice and "internal" undue pressure.** A further ground referred to in *Edgar v Edgar* was where a party entered into a disadvantageous agreement of this nature on the basis of "bad legal advice".[37] One of the factors held against Mrs Edgar by the Court of Appeal was that she entered into an agreement which was arguably less than generous to her against strong advice from her solicitor. Clearly, she did not receive bad legal advice.[38] One of the factors which led the Court of Appeal in *Camm v Camm*[39] to disregard an agreement made some seven-and-a-half years previously was that Mrs Camm had not received sufficiently strong and carefully thought-out legal advice.

---

[32] The relevance of the grounds for setting aside a consent order based upon the prior agreement is considered at paras 32–83 *et seq.*, below.
[33] See paras 32–65 *et seq.*, above.
[34] *cf. Livesey v Jenkins*, n.31, above.
[35] *N v N* [1994] 2 F.C.R. 275, CA.
[36] By analogy with such a change of circumstances after a consent order is made: *Barder v Barder* [1988] A.C. 20. See paras 32–97 *et seq.*, below.
[37] See para.32–72, above.
[38] A client who, against advice, insists on a speedy settlement without a prolonged investigation into the other party's resources cannot sustain a negligence claim against his or her solicitor alleging that the settlement was unsatisfactory: *Dutfield v Stephens (Gilbert H.) and Sons* (1988) 18 Fam. Law 473. See generally Ch.29, above.
[39] (1983) 4 F.L.R. 577.

32-78 The extent to which a court ought to investigate the quality of legal advice received has already been questioned.[40] Once embarked upon, the task is a difficult and sensitive one in an area of the law which is itself particularly difficult and sensitive.[41] Examination of the issue may be a prolonged affair.[42] Judges at first instance are, of course, bound to investigate these matters if raised[43] and the Court of Appeal is bound to apply the approach established authoritatively in *Edgar v Edgar* and *Camm v Camm*.[44] However, it is clear that there is not universal enthusiasm for the kind of investigation required, nor for the result which may emerge from that investigation. In *Pounds v Pounds*,[45] where the issue did not in the event fall for determination,[46] Hoffmann L.J., as he then was, when reflecting on the grounds upon which a court might refuse to give effect to a concluded agreement between the parties, said this[47]:

> "The result of the decision of this Court in *Edgar v Edgar* . . . and the cases which have followed it is that we have, as it seems to me, the worst of both worlds. The agreement may be held to be binding, but whether it will be can be demonstrated only after litigation and may involve, as in this case, examining the quality of the advice which was given to the party who wishes to resile. It is then understandably a matter for surprise and resentment on the part of the other party that one should be able to repudiate an agreement on account of the inadequacy of one's own legal advisers, over whom the other party had no control and of whose advice he had no knowledge."

32-79 It cannot be pretended that the resolution of the problems thrown up by cases in this jurisdiction where poor legal advice has been given is easy. The provision of a satisfactory legal framework within which these problems can appropriately be addressed is also not easily achieved. A simplistic

---

[40] See para.32–49, n.78, above.
[41] *cf.* the comments made in para.32–32, above.
[42] This appears to have been so in *Pounds v Pounds* [1994] 2 F.C.R. 1055: see *per* Waite L.J. at 1068 and 1072. It may involve the kind of detailed examination that the Court of Appeal has expressly said should be avoided in the "wasted costs" jurisdiction: *Ridehalgh v Horsfield* [1994] Ch. 205, CA.
[43] See, *e.g. B v B* [1995] 1 F.L.R. 9.
[44] (1983) 4 F.L.R. 577.
[45] [1994] 2 F.L.R. 1055.
[46] Because the Court of Appeal decided, contrary to the decision at first instance, that the order for financial relief was made with jurisdiction: *ibid.* at 1070–1071.
[47] *ibid.* at 1073. In *Harris (formerly Manahan) v Manahan*, discussed at para.32–93, below, Ward L.J. having reviewed *Edgar v Edgar, Camm v Camm, Pounds v Pounds* and *B v B* [1995] 1 F.L.R. 9, said this: "The effect of these authorities seem to me to amount to this: Because the Court is under a duty imposed by s.25 of the Matrimonial Causes Act 1973 to have regard to all the circumstances, and then under the duty itself to decide whether it will exercise any of its powers and if so how they are to be exercised, "bad legal advice" must be taken into account whether as a good justification or as a weak excuse for a party not being held to his or her bargain. The quality of advice clearly has a part to play".

(though not, it is submitted, an unrealistic) solution in a case where a plainly unfair and disadvantageous agreement has been reached following bad advice is for the court which comes to that conclusion simply to say so.[48] The route by which it came to be unfair is, perhaps, of very much less relevance. The same comment might be made of the "undue pressure" which was also relied upon by the Court of Appeal in *Camm v Camm*, certainly in so far as reliance was placed upon the "undue pressure" which came from "within" Mrs Camm. If an agreement is so plainly at variance with what would be fair having regard to the considerations set out in s.25, there is little need to conclude other than that a wholly unwise decision was made, for whatever reason, from which the court will relieve the party having made it. If it was wrong, it was wrong. Needless to say, the court will take a broad, rather than a particular, approach to whether the agreement was fair.[49]

32-80 **Other factors even if an "invalidating ground" exists.** Merely because one of the "invalidating grounds" has been raised and indeed proved does not necessarily mean that the agreement will be disregarded wholly or partially. First of all, it will be necessary to conclude that the ground was sufficiently important materially to affect the agreement.[50] Secondly, consideration will presumably have to be given to how long it has taken the party raising the issue to do so after discovering its existence and the extent to which the agreement has already been acted upon by both parties.[51] This should not be looked at in the strict common law way of affirmation or laches, but more as part of the general appraisal of the conduct of the parties or the general circumstances of the case.[52]

Setting aside consent orders—law and practice

1. Preliminary

32-81 The foregoing discussion has been directed at the circumstances in which a prior agreement could come to be disregarded by the court when invited to make an order by consent or where it is alleged that the parties have agreed terms concerning their financial affairs. It is now necessary to consider the position after a consent order has been made. Because the order is made by consent, it is made expressly at the joint invitation of the parties.[53] In what circumstances, if any, may the court, at the invitation of one of the parties, set aside the whole or part of that order and substitute another one?

---

[48] Indeed, the Court of Appeal did, in effect, say this in *Camm v Camm*, n.44, above.
[49] *Dean v Dean* [1978] Fam. 161; *cf. Wachtel v Wachtel* [1973] Fam. 72, CA.
[50] *cf.* para.32-84, below.
[51] *cf. Smallman v Smallman* [1972] Fam. 25; *Camm v Camm*, n.44, above.
[52] See paras 32-72—32-73, above.
[53] Or, using the phraseology of Matrimonial Causes Act 1973, s.33A, "an order in the terms applied for to which the respondent agrees".

32–82   Before embarking on that discussion two things should be emphasised: first, the discussion relates to, for want of a better expression, "getting rid" of the original order. It is not concerned as such with the subsequent variation of an order which is recognised as having been validly obtained in the first instance. The jurisdiction to vary orders appears in s.31 of the Matrimonial Causes Act 1973. As observed previously,[54] that jurisdiction has been invoked to vary a prior consent order for periodical payments on the ground of a mistake as to the practical effect of the order.[55] The mistake was one of "all the circumstances" which the court was entitled to take into account. Presumably, the same considerations could apply in relation to the other orders which s.31 ordains as being variable for this purpose.[56]

32–83   Secondly, the discussion does not relate to the situation where consent is given to an order containing arrangements for the use of a property until its subsequent disposition in certain events, one of those events being the "further order of the court", liberty to apply for such order being provided for.[57] Sometimes this is seen, incorrectly it is submitted, as a basis upon which the original agreement reflected in the order can be altered. Parties agreeing to such an order are expressly (or, at the very least, impliedly) submitting themselves to the jurisdiction of the court to make provision for the earlier disposition of the property in circumstances other than those otherwise provided for specifically in the parties' agreement.[58] The provision of "liberty to apply" generally, whether in a consent order or otherwise, does not give the court power to set aside, alter or vary the original order. It merely relates to applications for the implementation and enforcement of the original order.[59]

2. Grounds for setting aside a consent order

32–84   **General.** Subject to one area of uncertainty,[60] the grounds upon which a consent order in this jurisdiction may be set aside are now reasonably clear. The series of cases comprising *De Lasala v De Lasala*,[61] *Livesey v Jenkins*[62] and *Barder v Barder*[63] represents the source of all contemporary authoritative guidance on these matters. There is no need to set out for this purpose

---

[54] See para.32–29, above.
[55] *Brister v Brister* [1970] 1 W.L.R. 664; cited in *De Lasala v De Lasala* [1980] A.C. 546, but not referred to in the judgment.
[56] *De Lasala v De Lasala* [1980] A.C. 546.
[57] *Alonso v Alonso* (1974) 4 Fam. Law 164, CA; *Carson v Carson* [1983] 1 W.L.R. 285, CA; *Thompson v Thompson* [1986] Fam. 38, CA.
[58] *cf. Chanel v F. W. Woolworth & Co. Ltd* [1981] 1 W.L.R. 485, CA.
[59] *Cristel v Cristel* [1951] 2 K.B. 725; *Potts v Potts* (1976) 6 Fam. Law 217, CA.
[60] See paras 32–90—32–91, below.
[61] [1980] A.C. 546, PC.
[62] [1985] A.C. 424.
[63] [1988] A.C. 20.

the facts of any of these cases. Two broad propositions may be advanced on the basis of these authorities from which certain subsidiary propositions can be derived:

(a) once the provisions of the parties' agreement have become embodied in an order of the court, the legal effect of those provisions is thenceforth derived from the order and not from the agreement[64];

(a) any factor which undermines to a significant degree, or otherwise invalidates, the basis upon which one or other or both of the parties agreed to the making of that order may constitute a ground for setting aside the order.[65]

It is the second of these propositions from which the subsidiary propositions are to be derived.

32–85 **Failure to disclose all material facts before the order is made.** The failure of either or both of the parties to make full and frank disclosure of all material facts before the consent order is finally made will yield the basis for an application to set aside the order, provided, of course, the order made was substantially different from that which would have been made had the proper disclosure occurred.[66] Many of the older cases arise from a failure to disclose an intention to remarry; many of the more modern cases from a failure to disclose financial details.

> In *Livesey v Jenkins*,[67] W obtained a *decree nisi* of divorce in an undefended suit in March 1982, the decree being made absolute the following month. Negotiations concerning financial matters, which had commenced before then, continued until about August 12 when the form and terms of the consent order were agreed. The essential terms were to the effect that H would transfer to W all of his half share in the matrimonial home in return for the dismissal of all W's claims for herself. The purpose of the transfer of H's half share was to enable W to have a house of her own in which she could reside with the two children. On August 18, she became engaged to a man whom she had met on July 12. On August 19, the parties' solicitors issued a joint application to the court for the agreed order. On September 2, the registrar made the consent order as applied for and made no inquiries about its nature or basis. The order provided for the transfer to be made within 28 days and,

---

[64] *De Lasala v De Lasala*, n.61, above at 560; *Livesey v Jenkins*, n.62, above at 435; *Barder v Barder*, n.63, above at 40.
[65] *Livesey v Jenkins*, n.62 above at 443; *Barder v Barder*, n.63, above at 40–43.
[66] *Livesey v Jenkins*, n.62, above at 445–446 and 430. For cases in which it was held that the non-disclosure would not have made any substantial difference, see *Cook v Cook* (1988) 18 Fam. Law 163; *Chaudhuri v Chaudhuri* (1992) 22 Fam. Law 385, CA; *B v B* [1994] 1 F.C.R. 885 (Ward J.); *cf. Hope-Smith v Hope-Smith* [1989] 2 F.L.R. 56, CA.
[67] [1985] A.C. 424.

on September 22, H executed the appropriate conveyance. On September 24, W remarried. Neither the fact of, nor the possibility of, W's remarriage had ever been mentioned in the negotiations. After H learned of W's remarriage (on October 10), in due course, an application was made on his behalf for leave to appeal out of time against the original consent order, coupled with an application to set aside that order. The application was, in the first instance, dealt with by a circuit judge who gave leave, but dismissed his appeal. The Court of Appeal dismissed H's appeal. The House of Lords allowed H's appeal.

On the matters of principle directly of concern in the case, the decision of the House of Lords can be summarised thus: 32–86

(a) Whenever the court is invited to exercise the jurisdiction conferred by ss.23 and 24 of the Matrimonial Causes Act 1973 it is bound by s.25 to take into account all the circumstances of the case including the particular matters therein specified.[68]
(b) Unless the parties inviting the court to exercise its jurisdiction under these provisions provide the court, directly or indirectly, with correct, complete and up-to-date information about all the circumstances of the case, including the particular matters specified, "the court is not equipped to exercise and cannot therefore lawfully and properly exercise, its discretion in the manner ordained by section 25(1)".[69]
(c) The parties owe to each other and the court a duty "to make full and frank disclosure of all material facts".[70]
(d) If there is a failure in any case to comply with the duty referred to in (c) above which has led the court into making, whether by consent or otherwise, an order substantially different from the order which it otherwise would have made, the order actually made is liable to be set aside.[71]

On the facts of the case it was held: 32–87

(a) that, although not guilty of a misrepresentation, W was in breach of the duty referred to above by not disclosing the fact of her engagement as soon as it took place[72];
(b) that her failure to do so undermined the whole basis on which the consent order was agreed since H would undoubtedly have withdrawn his consent to the making of the order had he known[73];

---

[68] *ibid.* at 436–437.
[69] *ibid.*
[70] *ibid.* at 437–438.
[71] *ibid.* at 445–446.
[72] *ibid.* at 438.
[73] *ibid.* at 434 and 438.

(c) that in consequence the consent order was "invalid" and H was "entitled, in order to prevent injustice, to have it set aside".[74]

32–88 Fraud and misrepresentation. Each of these grounds would afford the basis for setting aside an ordinary contract of compromise[75] and fraud was recognised in *De Lasala v De Lasala*[76] as a ground for impeaching a matrimonial consent order. Even though there is some authority[77] for saying that it is not necessary to talk in terms of "misrepresentation" as such in this context, the House of Lords did not expressly eschew the expression in *Livesey v Jenkins*.[78] At all events, this semantic discussion is of little relevance: any misrepresentation (whether fraudulent, negligent or innocent) of a material factor is almost bound to result in the failure of the duty to disclose in full all material facts.

32–89 Mistake. Again, a sufficiently significant mistake may operate to undermine an ordinary compromise[79] and it has been acknowledged to be an invalidating ground so far as orders of the sort under consideration are concerned.[80] In most cases the mistake will lead to a situation in which the parties, and thus the court, are misinformed as to a material fact which itself will affect the validity of the consent of the parties and the order made pursuant to it. The problem is most likely to arise where mistaken valuations of property are relied upon in negotiations.[81]

32–90 Undue influence? On the basis of the second of the general propositions referred to previously,[82] anything that undermines significantly the consensual basis of the order must constitute a prima facie ground for setting aside the order. Where one party's agreement has been obtained as the result of the duress or undue influence of the other there would seem no reason in principle why any consent order made in pursuance of that agreement should not be vulnerable to attack by the party subjected to whatever pressure may have been applied. It has certainly been recognised

---

[74] *ibid.* at 438.
[75] See Ch.4, above.
[76] [1980] A.C. 546.
[77] *Edgar v Edgar*, referred to at para.32–72, n.27, above.
[78] [1985] A.C. 424.
[79] See Ch.4, above.
[80] *De Lasala v De Lasala*, n.61, above; *Robinson v Robinson* (1983) 4 F.L.R. 102, CA. In *Harris (formerly Manahan) v Manahan*, [1997] 1 F.L.R. 205, noted at para.32–93, below. Ward L.J. said that he could "imagine circumstances where the bad advice gives rise to a mistaken belief which, if shared by the other side, may enable the underlying agreement to be attacked on the ground of mistake".
[81] See para.4–19, above, and the cases referred to in n.53 under that paragraph. See also *Hope-Smith v Hope-Smith* [1989] 2 F.L.R. 56, CA; *Thompson v Thompson* [1991] 2 F.L.R. 530, CA; and *Rundle v Rundle* [1992] 2 F.L.R. 80, CA. See also paras 32–101 *et seq.*, below.
[82] See para.32–83, above. See also paras 4–66 *et seq.*, above.

as a ground for ignoring an apparently concluded agreement prior to an order being sought.[83]

In *Tommey v Tommey*[84] Balcombe J. (as he then was) concluded that 32–91
undue influence could not, as a matter of law, afford a basis for setting aside a consent order in this jurisdiction. That decision, however, was made before *Livesey v Jenkins* and, though carefully declining to express any concluded view on the matter, the House of Lords did venture the comment that it was "not persuaded that [the] decision on the question was necessarily correct".[85] Balcombe J. felt obliged, as he plainly was, to apply the decision of the Court of Appeal in *Thwaite v Thwaite*[86] to the problem in hand. As recorded previously,[87] the Court of Appeal interpreted the judgment of the Privy Council in *De Lasala v De Lasala*[88] as requiring the elimination of the "contractual basis" of consent orders in this jurisdiction and that "so far as possible" they should be dealt with, for the purpose of being set aside, in the same way as non-consensual orders.[89] That conclusion, it was said, followed from the proposition that the legal effect of agreed financial arrangements made the subject of a court order derived from the court order and not the prior agreement. With considerable diffidence, it is submitted that the conclusion does not necessarily follow from the premise. The legal effect of something is one thing; the basis upon which that something is deprived of legal effect is another. Merely because a party submits himself consensually to the exercise of this jurisdiction of the court in a particular way does not, it is submitted, mean that thereby he deprives himself of the right to say subsequently that his consent to that course was improperly obtained. There would be little justice in that. That principle is recognised clearly in *Livesey v Jenkins* and *De Lasala v De Lasala* in the sense that agreements to orders resulting from fraud, mistake or non-disclosure of material facts should be deprived of effect. It is but a small step to hold that an order obtained following an agreement induced by undue influence should similarly be deprived of effect. It may well be, as Balcombe J. said in *Tommey v Tommey*,[90] that it "will be a rare case where undue influence can be shown to exist right up to the making of the order", but if it can be shown that the prior agreement was induced by undue influence it is, with respect, difficult to see why the law should deprive the person subjected to it of remedy. It may well be that the particular part of *Thwaite v Thwaite* which Balcombe J.

---

[83] *Edgar v Edgar* [1982] 1 W.L.R. 1410; *Camm v Camm* (1983) 4 F.L.R. 577.
[84] [1983] Fam. 15.
[85] [1985] A.C. 424 at 440.
[86] [1982] Fam. 1.
[87] See para.19–34, above.
[88] [1980] A.C. 546.
[89] [1982] Fam. 1 at 8.
[90] [1983] Fam. 15 at 24–25.

was bound to follow cannot stand in the light of the approach of, and the principles enunciated by, the House of Lords. It must be noted, however, that, though cited both in *Livesey v Jenkins* and *Barder v Barder*,[91] no expression of disapproval of any part of the judgment in *Thwaite v Thwaite* is to be found in either of the speeches of Lord Brandon of Oakbrook.

32-92 **The bad deal?** Will a consensual "bad deal" afford grounds for the subsequent intervention by the court at the request of the victim of the "bad deal"? Whilst the logic behind cases like *Livesey v Jenkins* might suggest so, it is hard to see circumstances where a "bad deal" alone (*i.e.* without the presence of any other invalidating ground) might be grounds for setting aside a consent order. A "bad deal" is likely to arise from bad legal advice or from a refusal to accept reasonable legal advice, in which case the harm is self-inflicted. However there may be circumstances, particularly where children's interests have not been properly protected, where such a ground might be entertained.

32-93 **Bad legal advice?** Although bad legal advice is a factor to be taken into account by the court in determining whether to give effect to the parties' agreement before a consent order is made,[92] it is not something which *per se* affords a basis for setting aside a consent order.

> In *Harris (formerly Manahan) v Manahan*,[93] H and W attended a pre-trial review with their legal advisers, the purpose of which was to explore settlement. A clean-break agreement was reached on the basis that the former matrimonial home should be sold and H should receive a fixed sum of £25,000 if the property was sold for more than £185,000, and approximately 13 per cent of the gross sale price if sold for less than £185,000. A consent order reflecting this agreement was made. For some time prior to the making of the agreement the property had been the subject of an offer of £195,000, but W's solicitors advised against sale until the ancillary relief proceedings had been concluded. If a sale at that price had proceeded, W would have received about £29,000 net and H between £10–15,000 net. H, who was in his 50s, was still earning. W had no income of any significance and no prospect of such an income. Shortly before the making of the consent order, and because of the delay caused by the advice to W not to sell until the financial proceedings were concluded, the purchasers of the property withdrew. By the time of the consent order the parties had been separated for just over one year during which time H, despite being in employment, failed to pay the instalments due under the mortgage of about £87,000. With no further purchaser having been found, and given the increasing mortgage arrears, the building society secured a possession order in August 1994. Execution of this order was postponed for a while but, in due course, possession was obtained. At the price at which the property was likely to be sold, and given the parties' indebtedness, neither would receive anything once the property was sold. W had been advised badly

---

[91] [1988] A.C. 20.
[92] See paras 32–48 *et seq.*, above.
[93] [1997] 1 F.L.R. 205.

about agreeing to the consent order and, after a period of about 17 months, she sought to set aside the consent order on the grounds of the bad legal advice she had received. The court directed the determination as a preliminary point the question whether the ground relied upon by W for seeking to set aside a consent order was available to her. The Court of Appeal held that this ground was not available to her, principally on policy grounds that there must be finality in litigation. Ward L.J. stated:

> "To allow a bargain struck to be set aside is inevitably to fuel recrimination. Bitterness and anger are inevitable concomitants of the conflict which arises from contested claims. Parties suffer. So do their children. It is inevitable that the focus of recrimination will swing from the incompetent solicitor and will be heaped upon the other party even though his conduct in the negotiations may not fairly be capable of being impeached. If the policy of the law is to encourage the clean break, then the law should also ensure that break with the past is final and that there is no turning back."

This approach should be compared with the situation when a consent order is attacked by way of variation, as in *B v B*.[94] In that case a periodical payments order which was due to expire was extended. The order was entered into after bad legal advice.

32–94

Whether or not a lump sum order payable by instalments entered into as a result of bad legal advice could be attacked likewise by way of variation is a moot point. As with an order for periodical payments, such an order is variable under s.31 of the Matrimonial Causes Act 1973,[95] albeit the power to vary is only exceptionally utilised. It is anticipated that a court would strain to avoid such a result, but the issue has yet to be tested.

32–95

A failure to observe s.33A and the "prescribed rules". A consent order made following failure to lodge the statement of information with the application for it may result in the court being held subsequently not to have exercised its discretion on the basis of the required information and that the order is *ipso facto* invalid. The requirement for the statement of information appears to be mandatory.[96] However, if the information is available in any other manner—*e.g.* by counsel giving it orally—or if no injustice is done by the lack of information, the absence of it would be unlikely on its own to vitiate the order.

32–96

Supervening events. The foregoing discussion has been directed to events which precede the making of the consent order and which, if established subsequently, may lead to the setting aside of that order. The question arises of whether supervening events which falsify the basis upon which the

32–97

---

[94] [1995] 1 F.L.R. 9. See also *Richardson v Richardson* [1994] 1 F.L.R. 286; and *R v R (No.2)* [1996] 2 F.L.R. 617.
[95] *Tilly v Tilly* (1979) Fam. Law 79. And see *Westbury v Sampson* [2002] 1 F.L.R. 166.
[96] See para.32–28, above but subject to Family Proceedings Rules 1991, r.2.61.

consent order was made can be relied upon to have the order set aside and a fresh order made. The issue was raised starkly in the tragic circumstances of *Barder v Barder*[97]:

> In that case a consent order was made by the county court registrar whereby H was to transfer his interest in the jointly owned former matrimonial home to W in full and final settlement of all her claims. H also agreed to an order for substantial periodical payments in favour of the two children of whom W had previously been granted the custody, care and control. There were certain other ancillary undertakings concerning life policies held by the mortgagees. After the time limit for appealing against the order had expired, but before the order had been executed, W killed the two children and then committed suicide. H applied to the county court judge subsequently for, and was granted, leave to appeal out of time against the registrar's order. The judge allowed the appeal and set aside the order on the ground that it was made on the basis that for an appreciable time after the order was made W and the children would continue to live and benefit from the order. The House of Lords held that the judge had the jurisdiction to act as he did and that he was correct in setting aside the original order.

32–98   Lord Brandon of Oakbrook, with whom all the members of the House agreed, referred[98] to the conflicting principles of the need for finality in litigation and the need, in justice, for cases to be decided upon their true facts "and not on assumptions or estimates with regard to those facts which are conclusively shown by later events to have been erroneous". Having reviewed various authorities, Lord Brandon identified four conditions that would need to be satisfied to enable a court properly to exercise its discretion to grant leave to appeal out of time against an order for financial provision or property adjustment.[99] These can be summarised as follows:

> (a) the supervening events invalidate the basis, or fundamental assumption, upon which the order was made;
> (b) the events should have occurred within a relatively short time from the making of the order, usually "no more than a few months";
> (c) the application for permission to appeal out of time should be made reasonably promptly;
> (d) third-party rights in connection with property which is the subject-matter of the order should not be prejudiced.

32–99   Lord Brandon also emphasised[1] that the question of leave to appeal out of time should not be treated separately from the question of the merits of the appeal if leave is granted. This arose out of the first condition referred

---

[97] [1988] A.C. 20.
[98] *ibid.* at 41.
[99] *ibid.* at 43.
[1] *ibid.*

to above because, if established, it would mean that the appeal itself would be "certain, or very likely, to succeed".[2]

These principles have formed the basis for the court's consideration of applications in a number of cases since then, mostly[3] in less tragic circumstances than in *Barder v Barder* itself. These applications have arisen largely where a property valuation adopted at the time of the original consent order has been shown to have been erroneous, a subsequent unexpected death has occurred or where there has been an unanticipated remarriage or cohabitation by one of the parties.[4] The introduction of the Child Support Act 1991[5] led to an argument that the statutory provision for extra-judicial maintenance assessments it brought into effect represented a supervening event which undermined previously concluded "clean break" settlements.[6] It must be borne in mind, of course, that the principles enunciated in *Barder v Barder* are as applicable to cases where the original order followed a contested hearing as those where it followed an agreement between the parties. 32–100

(i) Erroneous valuations. There is an initial need to distinguish for this purpose between those situations in which the original order was based upon a valuation which was erroneous at the time because of a mistaken valuation[7] and those where some supervening event (which may be no more than a radical change in the property market) has caused a change in the valuation relied upon.[8] Strictly speaking, those cases which fall within the first category fall to be determined by reference to the principle set out in *Livesey v Jenkins*.[9] However, there is clearly some scope for overlap between the two[10] and cases which, on analysis, appear to fall into the first category have been determined on *Barder v Barder* principles: 32–101

> In *Thompson v Thompson*,[11] H and W were divorced in 1990 after 17 years of marriage, the decree being made absolute in January 1990. There were two children who continued to live with W. The ancillary relief proceedings were heard by the district judge on June 1, 1990. The matrimonial home was valued at £75,000 (provided that £3,000 repairs were carried out) subject to a 32–102

---

[2] *ibid.* The practice to be adopted when seeking to appeal out of time is dealt with below: see para.32–121, below.
[3] Though see *Smith v Smith* [1992] Fam. 69; noted at para.32–107, below.
[4] See *Salter* (1992) 22 Fam. Law 50. For a case in which two of these factors were alleged (unsuccessfully) by H to apply, see *B v B* [1994] 1 F.C.R. 585 (Ward J.).
[5] See para.32–27, above.
[6] See *Crozier v Crozier* [1994] Fam. 114, referred to at para.32–109, below.
[7] See para.32–89, n.81, above.
[8] The distinction was clearly articulated by the Court of Appeal in *Thompson v Thompson* [1991] 2 F.L.R. 530, noted at para.32–102, below.
[9] See paras 32–84 *et seq.*, above.
[10] *cf.* in *Cornick v Cornick* [1994] 2 F.L.R. 530 *per* Hale J, noted at para.32–103, below.
[11] [1991] 2 F.L.R. 530, CA.

mortgage of £5,600. H had life policies worth £8,500 and the equity of another house amounting to £9,800. H also had a travel agency business which was taken by the district judge to be worth £20,000. H had an indebtedness to the bank of £27,600 secured by way of second charge on the home, together with further debts of £6,000. Each party had liabilities for costs, quantified at £6,500 on W's side. The district judge transferred the matrimonial home to W subject to the first mortgage and ordered her to pay a lump sum of £7,500 to H, the basis of the order being a clean break. The time for appealing against the order expired on June 8, 1990. One week later H sold his business for £45,000. W applied for leave to appeal out of time against the district judge's order when she discovered what had happened. The judge rejected W's application on the basis that, although on the merits he would have granted it, he had no jurisdiction to entertain it because the valuation of £20,000 had been agreed by W. She had commissioned a valuation of the business prior to the hearing before the district judge which revealed a figure of £45,000, but her expert (who was present but not called at the hearing) did not feel able to sustain it. The Court of Appeal held that the sale at £45,000 represented a "new event" that changed the situation radically and which required a reconsideration of the district judge's order. Where an altered valuation is relied on, it may be relevant to inquire into whether the applicant was in some way responsible for the erroneous valuation because, if that be the case, it may (though it is not conclusive) be a reason for not granting the applicant the indulgence underlying an application for leave to appeal out of time (as in *Edmonds v Edmonds*[12]). Furthermore, if the cause of the altered valuation was foreseen and taken into account at the time of the original order, the altered valuation cannot be "new". Neither of these factors operated against W in this case since it was said that "all concerned acted reasonably on the assumption that the business was worth £20,000 at most". It was also said in this context that "percentages should be used with caution" and that it was "much better for the reviewing court, when considering the questions of degree to look in broad terms at the balance of the financial relationship created by the order under review, and then ask itself how this balance has been affected by the new state of affairs".

32–103   A general review of those cases reaching the Court of Appeal in which this kind of issue has arisen was conducted by Hale J., as she then was, in *Cornick v Cornick*.[13]

In that case the original order (not made by consent) in December 1992 was that the matrimonial home should be sold and H should pay W a lump sum of £320,000 and periodical payments for herself at the rate of £20,000 per annum. Periodical payments for the two children were ordered at the rate of £4,200 per annum, with further provision for the payment by H of their school fees. The value of each of H's shares in the company of which he was deputy chairman was taken by the court as £2.17. Excluding the value of certain share options of H falling due in 1996, the net assets of the parties in December 1992 totalled £649,000. The effect of the court order was to give W 51 per cent of those net assets or 36 per cent if the share options were taken into account. The value of H's shares increased substantially after the

---

[12] [1990] 2 F.L.R. 202, CA.
[13] [1994] 2 F.L.R. 530.

order was made. In the light of these increases the net effect of the order by November 1993 was to give W 26 per cent of 15 per cent of the assets, depending on whether the share options were taken into account. By May 1994 (when the application for leave to appeal was heard) the proportions were 20 per cent and 11 per cent respectively. W did not suggest that this dramatic rise in share value could reasonably have been foreseeen at the time of the hearing in December 1992. Hale J. held that W's application for leave to appeal out of time should be rejected because what occurred was nothing more than "a natural albeit dramatic change in the value of [H's] shareholding" reflecting a "natural process of price fluctuation".

Following her review of the authorities,[14] Hale J. drew the following conclusions:

32-104

> "(1) An asset which was taken into account and correctly valued at the date of the hearing changes value within a relatively short time owing to natural processes of price fluctuation. The court should not then manipulate the power to grant leave to appeal out of time to provide a disguised power of variation which Parliament has quite obviously and deliberately declined to enact.
>
> (2) A wrong value was put upon that asset at the hearing, which had it been known about at the time would have led to a different order. Provided that it is not the fault of the person alleging the mistake, it is open to the Court to give leave for the matter to be reopened. Although falling within the *Barder* principle it is more akin to the misrepresentation or non-disclosure cases than to *Barder* itself.
>
> (3) Something unforeseen and unforeseeable has happened since the date of the hearing which has altered the value of the assets so dramatically as to bring about a substantial change in the balance of assets brought about by the order. Then, provided that the other three conditions are fulfilled, the Barder principle may apply. However, the circumstances in which this can

---

[14] The following cases, *inter alia*, are referred to in the judgment: *Chaudhuri v Chaudhuri* [1992] 2 F.L.R. 73; *Cook v Cook* [1988] 1 F.L.R. 521; *Edmonds v Edmonds* [1990] 2 F.L.R. 202; *Hope-Smith v Hope-Smith* [1989] 2 F.L.R. 56; *Penrose v Penrose* [1994] 2 F.L.R. 621; *Rundle v Rundle* [1992] 2 F.L.R. 80; *Thompson v Thompson* [1991] 2 F.L.R. 530 and *Worlock v Worlock* [1994] 2 F.L.R. 689. *Heard v Heard* [1996] 1 F.C.R. 33, decided on June 20, 1994, was not referred to. It appears, however, to be consistent with Hale J.'s analysis. The original order (not a consent order) was made with the intention that H should have enough money from the sale of the former matrimonial home to re-house himself. It became apparent that the value upon which this expectation had been based was wrong. Sir Thomas Bingham M.R. (with whom Kennedy and Millett L.JJ. agreed) said that "the discovery that the valuation was unsound, or alternatively the discovery that the house could not be sold at the price which had been assumed as its market price, did amount to new events sufficient to satisfy Lord Brandon's first condition".

happen are very few and far between. The case law, taken as a whole, does not suggest that the natural processes of price fluctuation, whether in houses, shares or any other property, and however dramatic, fall within this principle."

32–105   Despite this helpful analysis, there has been no great consistency of approach to the reception of revaluation evidence, nor to the significance attached to it.

32–106   In certain circumstances the delaying tactics of one of the parties in connection with the implementation of a consent order (*e.g.* in the sale of a property) can operate to invalidate or falsify the basis upon which that order was made.[15] However, the other party will, in the normal course of events, be expected to take steps to enforce the order and a failure to do so will negative the suggestion that the delay constitutes a material supervening event.[16]

32–107   *(ii) Unexpected death of party.* This kind of event was starkly illustrated by the case of *Barder v Barder* itself.[17]

> In *Smith v Smith*,[18] H and W, who had been married in 1955, divorced in 1988, the decree having been made absolute on October 6, 1988. W's application for ancillary relief was heard by the registrar on December 7, 1988. At that time H was 62 and W was 52. The total family assets were approximately £107,000, comprising the equity in the house (which was in H's name and in which both parties were still living) of £63,000 and the balance of £46,000 representing accumulated savings and H's pension lump sum. H was earning £12,400 per annum and would receive a further pension of £5,300 per annum on his eventual retirement. H was not in good health. W was treated as having a potential income of £5,000 per annum The registrar ordered H to pay W a lump sum of £54,000 in full and final settlement of her claims for ancillary relief and directed that upon payment W should vacate the matrimonial home. The order was complied with by both parties. On May 17, 1989 W committed suicide. The Court of Appeal held, applying *Barder v Barder*, that it was correct in the circumstances for the judge to have granted leave to appeal out of time against the registrar's order and to allow H's appeal, but wrong to restrict himself to what was the predominant consideration before the registrar, namely the needs of the parties. It was necessary to consider the position in the light of the changed circumstances prevailing at the time when the reassessment was carried out. Having regard to all the criteria set out in s.25, the proper lump sum award in W's favour would be £25,000.

32–108   *(iii) Remarriage.* An undisclosed intention to remarry or cohabit at the time the original order was made will operate as a failure to make full disclosure.[19] If the possibility of an event of this nature was not or could

---

[15] *Hope-Smith v Hope-Smith* [1989] 2 F.L.R. 56, CA.
[16] *Rooker v Rooker* (1988) 18 Fam. Law 55, CA.
[17] See para.32–97, above.
[18] [1992] Fam. 69.
[19] See para.32–84, above.

not have been foreseen at the time of the original order, it is, of course, important that, had it been known or foreseen, it would have made a material difference to the order made and would have thus invalidated it.[20] If, of course, the possibility of remarriage by one of the parties had been foreseen at the time of the order and had been taken into account, then the fact that it took place subsequently could not be a supervening event within the *Barder v Barder* principle:

> In *Chaudhuri v Chaudhuri*,[21] H and W had separated in 1984 and the initial ancillary relief proceedings took place in February 1988. The principal issue was the matrimonial home. H wanted it sold so that both parties could rehouse themselves. W wished to remain there with the children. The registrar ordered that H should have one-third of the net equity, which was to be realised by an immediate lump sum payment of £27,000, out of which he was to discharge the mortgage on the house, and that he should have a charge on the house (which was then to be transferred to W) for one-sixth of the net proceeds of sale, the charge not to be realised without W's consent, or until the older child ceased full-time education, or until W's death or remarriage or permanent cohabitation with another man, whichever event should first occur. On H's appeal to the President in May 1988 the registrar's order was confirmed save that H's share in the proceeds of sale of the house was to be increased to one-quarter. W's case before the registrar and the President was that she needed to stay in the matrimonial home in order to provide a secure home for the children in a neighbourhood where she would have the support of friends. The house was transferred to her in July 1988. In June 1989 W's solicitors informed H that she intended to remarry and move to Chester. She did so in September 1989 and the elder son went to live with H. On H's application for leave to appeal against the order out of time the Court of Appeal held:
>
> (1) that the order contemplated the possibility of W remarrying and nothing was said as to what might happen in that event save that H's charge became realisable and, accordingly, it could not have been a fundamental assumption of the order that in the event of W remarrying she necessarily always had to stay in the same home with the children;
> (2) that the time which had elapsed, although near the borderline, was too great for it proper to grant leave to appeal out of time;
> (3) a suggestion that W had failed to disclose that she had opened a joint bank account with another man before the hearing before the President should be rejected as being something of no great significance.

32–109

(iv) Child Support Act 1991. In *Crozier v Crozier*[22] Booth J. rejected the suggestion that the introduction of the administrative machinery, outside the jurisdiction of the courts, for the assessment of a father's liability to maintain his children constituted a new event undermining the basis of a

32–110

---

[20] *B v B* [1994] 1 F.C.R. 885 at 888.
[21] (1992) 22 Fam. Law 385. See also *Cook v Cook* [1988] 1 F.L.R. 521, CA. See the comments of Hale J. in *Cornick v Cornick* [1994] 2 F.L.R. 530 at 534 noted at para.32–103.
[22] [1994] Fam. 114.

consensual attempt at a clean-break order made before the introduction of this machinery. Booth J. expressed herself in this way:

> "The fact that Parliament has chosen a new administrative method by which the State may intervene to compel a parent to contribute towards the maintenance of a child, by-passing the jurisdiction of the Courts, does not fundamentally alter the position as it was in law in February 1989. The parties were then unable to achieve a clean financial break in respect of their son. The legal liability to maintain him remained on them both as his parents. While the wife was prepared to assume that responsibility as between herself and the husband, she could not in fact fulfil that obligation without the assistance of State moneys. The State was never bound by the agreement or the order. At any time it could have intervened, through the Secretary of State, to seek an order through the Courts and the parties were not entitled to assume for the purposes of their agreement that it would not do so. I consider that it is immaterial for this purpose that the same parental liability will now be enforced through an agency outside the Courts. That is a difference only in the means by which the State may proceed to relieve itself of the obligation which it is the duty of the parents to discharge. The fact that the sum required of a parent may be greater under the new procedure than under the old is a consequence of the procedural change and not of any new and unforeseen power vested in the State. In my judgment, neither the existing order made in March 1993 under the statutory machinery which existed in February 1989 nor any anticipated liability which may be levied under the new machinery introduced by the Act of 1991, constitutes a new event, in fact or in law, sufficient to invalidate the basis of the consent order."

32–111 *(v) Change in the law.* In *S v S*[23] a wife sought to argue that the effect of the House of Lords' decision in *White v White*[24] was so fundamental that she should be entitled to reopen an order into which she entered by consent shortly before the decision. It was held that the decision could be deemed so fundamental as to entitle a party to reopen matters but that (i) the decision was so widely speculated upon that it was foreseeable and thus failed to meet the *Barder v Barder* criteria and (ii) a mistake of law as a vitiating factor *ab initio* had no place in consent orders for ancillary relief; public policy was against adopting an argument that would lead to the floodgates being opened.[25]

32–112 *(vi) Delay.* It is incumbent upon an applicant to proceed expeditiously with an application to set aside, or appeal out of time, a consent order. An applicant who, having ascertained the material facts, delays is likely to be

---

[23] [2002] 1 F.L.R. 992.
[24] [2001] 1 A.C. 596.
[25] *cf.* para 4–20 above.

unsuccessful. The court is inclined to be far more rigorous in applying Lord Brandon's test in *Barder v Barder* of a probable deadline of one year to cases of supervening events than it will be in cases of non-disclosure, the existence of which may not emerge for many years. In *Benson v Benson*,[26] a case in which a husband delayed for 15 months after his wife's death before applying to vary an order, Bracewell J. held the delay to be fatal to the application. Indeed, the husband had, through his former solicitors, compromised a variation of the order subsequent to the wife's death, before receiving fresh legal advice to challenge the original order.

This approach can be contrasted with cases such as *T v T*[27] and *C v C*[28] where bad cases of fraudulent non-disclosure were discovered nine and 14 years respectively after the consent orders. The court permitted the orders to be reopened. It remains clear, however, that once non-disclosure is discovered, the applicant must act with reasonable alacrity, although the court will not have much sympathy with a deliberate concealer of assets.

32–113

3. Practice

In *Benson v Benson*[29] no less than four actions were started in an attempt to reopen the case: (a) leave to appeal out of time; (b) a fresh action in the Queen's Bench Division for setting aside and substitution (an application to transfer to the Family Division was listed with the hearing); (c) an application to set aside and rehear under the County Court Rules (subsequently transferred to the High Court); and (d) for review of an executory order under the inherent jurisdiction. Bracewell J. expressed reservations about the second route, but observed that a litigant "must chose whatever route he considers the most appropriate and until the various procedures are unified the choice is that of the litigant".

32–114

That this multitude of choices presented itself for consideration is ample evidence of the confusion that permeates this area and it is hoped that the relevant Rules Committee will address this area to provide for a simple, fair and unified procedure. The existing practice was thoroughly scrutinised by Ward J., as he then was, in *B-T v B-T*,[30] but since then the rules governing procedure in the County Court have been changed more than once, and some doubts have been expressed upon some of his conclusions.

32–115

---

[26] [1996] 1 F.L.R. 692.
[27] [1996] 2 F.L.R. 640.
[28] [1994] 2 F.L.R. 272.
[29] [1996] 2 F.L.R. 690.
[30] [1990] 2 F.L.R. 1. See para.32–122, below.

32–116   Before reviewing *B-T. v B-T.* and the developments since, it is worth recalling the case of *Robinson v Robinson*.[31] In that case the Court of Appeal, in a passage of the judgment of Ormrod L.J. which was approved, albeit for a different purpose, in *Livesey v Jenkins*,[32] said this:[33]

> "From the point of view of convenience, there is a lot to be said for proceedings of this kind taking place before a Judge at first instance, because there will usually be serious and often difficult issues of fact to be determined before the power to set aside can be exercised. These can be determined more easily as a rule by a Judge at first instance. Moreover, he can go on to make the appropriate order which we cannot do in this court. I think that these proceedings should normally be started before a Judge at first instance, although there may be special circumstances which make it better to proceed by way of appeal."

In order to achieve this preferred destination for applications of this nature, somewhat circuitous routes have always[34] appeared to be necessary.

32–117   In *B-T v B-T*,[35] the procedural question arose in the context of a consent order made by a registrar of the Family Division in a cause treated as pending in the county court. The order contained lump sum provision in a manner designed to provide a roof over the heads of W and the one child of the family of whom she had the care and control. A periodical payments order in favour of the child was also incorporated. The ground upon which H relied was that of material non-disclosure by W arising from her failure to disclose in the negotiations leading to the order the fact that she had formed a permanent relationship with another man some three years previously and had had a child by him one month before the consent order had been made. H issued a notice of application returnable before the registrar seeking the setting aside of the order which W sought to strike out on the grounds that the court had no jurisdiction to make the order sought. Ward J. held that W's contention was well-founded and that the incorrect procedural approach had been adopted.

32–118   Towards the end of his judgment[36] Ward J., as he then was, set out in tabular form a summary of the available procedures and made comments relevant to the choice of those procedures. For historical purposes that summary is reproduced in Appendix 7, below. It should be noted that the judge was dealing with the procedure to be adopted when a final order was

---

[31] (1983) 4 F.L.R. 102.
[32] [1985] A.C. 424 at 442.
[33] (1983) 4 F.L.R. 102 at 113–114.
[34] At least until the judgment of Thorpe J., as he then was, in *Re C* [1995] 2 F.L.R. 799, referred to at para.32–121, below. But see the comments of the Court of Appeal in *Harris (formerly Manahan) v Manahan* [1997] 1 F.L.R. 205 referred to in n.54, below.
[35] [1990] 2 F.L.R. 1.
[36] *ibid.* at 24–25.

the subject of challenge. In essence he concluded as follows so far as consent orders are concerned:

(a) that a consent order made by a county court district judge could be set aside on appeal to the judge without leave,[37] or could be set aside in a fresh action constituted for the purpose, or could be the subject of an application to the district judge for a rehearing;
(b) that the same approaches could be adopted in relation to a consent order made by a district judge of the High Court save that the remedy of rehearing was not available[38];
(c) that a consent order made by a county court judge could be set aside on appeal to the Court of Appeal if leave is given, or could be set aside in a fresh action commenced for the purpose, or could be made the subject of an application to the judge for a rehearing;
(d) that the same approaches as those referred to in (c) could be adopted in relation to a consent order made by a High Court judge save that the remedy of rehearing was not available.

In relation to the various procedural avenues Ward J. commented as follows: 32–119

(1) An appeal to a judge is an appropriate procedure to enable a full rehearing, but is less satisfactory if made to the Court of Appeal because of the difficulty of that court receiving and resolving disputed fresh evidence and because it is likely to require a permission hearing, a full appeal if permission is granted and then a remitted new trial.
(2) A fresh action suffers from the disadvantage that the court can only set aside the order and cannot make a new order without a further hearing (albeit that the two hearings might be conducted

---

[37] In *Harris (formerly Manahan) v Manahan*, [1997] 1 F.L.R. 205, Ward L.J. acknowledged that whether or not permission is required "may be a matter of debate". The effect of the decision of the Court of Appeal in *Purcell v F. C. Trigell Ltd* [1971] 1 Q.B. 358, based upon its interpretation of s.31(1)(h) of the Supreme Court of Judicature (Consolidation) Act 1925, was that permission was required in relation to an appeal from a consent order made by a master or district registrar. Since the practice of the High Court is normally applied in the County Court (County Courts Act 1984, s.76), it seemed that permission would be required in the equivalent situation. However, it had been suggested in the notes to the Supreme Court Practice that the effect of *Purcell v Trigell* was overruled by the Supreme Court Act 1981. Given that the Supreme Court Act was essentially a consolidating Act it is, perhaps, questionable whether any change to the practice based upon the previous Act was intended. The need for permission represents a helpful filter in relation to unmeritorious and unsustainable appeals. Nevertheless, there had been an unresolved debate on the issue, although one which, in the particular context under discussion, was probably unimportant from the practical point of view.
[38] Because s.17 of the Supreme Court Act 1981, which could provide for a rehearing by a High Court judge, has never been implemented as no rules have been made under s.17(2). See also conclusion (d), below.

at the same time). However, it does provide a suitable vehicle for trying serious issues such as fraud.

(3) A rehearing is likely to be the best way forward. Serious allegations of fraud will be dealt with by a judge. The notice of application must fully set out the grounds relied upon.

32-120 The practice in relation to final orders, therefore, seemed to be as follows:

(a) Where the ground relied upon as invalidating the consent order was something which existed at the time the order was made (*i.e.* fraud, mistake, material non-disclosure, misrepresentation, undue influence or some other factor that, if appreciated at the time, would have made a material difference to the order that was agreed and made), the correct approach, if available, was to seek a rehearing, or to appeal or to bring a fresh action to set the order aside.

(b) Where some supervening event[39] was relied upon as falsifying the basis upon which the agreed order was made, the most appropriate course was to appeal.

32-121 With the introduction of the Family Proceeding Rules 1991 the avenue of appeal from a consent order made by a district judge of the county court to a judge of the county court appeared, perhaps unwittingly, to have been blocked.[40] If the change in the rules was intended to have this effect, the rationale was not entirely clear,[41] but it meant that Ward J.'s table needed amendment by deleting the possibility of appeal to the judge from a consent order of the district judge of a county court.[42] Given the

---

[39] See paras 32–97 *et seq.*, above.

[40] The effect of these rules was to render any order for ancillary relief a "final order" for the purposes of CCR Ord.37, r.6. That order precluded an appeal to the judge from a consent order of a final nature. The natural and ordinary meaning of the words used in the rules seemed to have been to this effect.

[41] It is not clear why the procedure should be different as between (a) consent orders for ancillary relief made in the High Court and the county court and (b) orders for ancillary relief made following a contested hearing and those made by consent given the nature of the grounds upon which such an order may be challenged. The only basis for the withdrawal of this particular procedural approach to the challenge of a consent order would seem to be that, given the availability of the process of rehearing, the appeal process became superfluous. However, in *Harris (formerly Manahan) v Manahan* [1997] 1 F.L.R. 205, the Court of Appeal did not see this to be a sufficient justification for not having both avenues available side by side save that the remedy of rehearing should be exhausted before pursuing the appeal process (*O'Connor v Mohammed Din* (1993) C.A.T. 150).

[42] See the helpful analysis of the situation following the introduction of the Family Proceedings Rules 1991 by Bennett (1993) 23 Fam. Law 84. This analysis undoubtedly influenced the profession to believe that an appeal was not an available procedural approach to the challenge of a consent order made by a district judge of the county court.

availability of an application for a re-hearing in the county court,[43] that procedure clearly represents the most advantageous approach when dealing with an order made in that jurisdiction.[44] A fresh action is always a cumbersome procedure to adopt and can have no advantages in this particular context. The practical implications of an application for a re-hearing are referred to below.[45] It must be remembered that a combination of approaches may be required or advisable.

The result of Ward J.'s conclusions (founded, it is submitted, on the basis of established authorities) was that an application to set aside a consent order on the grounds of material non-disclosure would, if the avenue of appeal was chosen, almost inevitably require the permission of the court because the likelihood was that the time for appealing would have expired well before the appeal was launched.[46] In order to obtain the permission of the court, a prima facie case of material non-disclosure must be made out.[47] The view has been expressed[48] that a case of material non-disclosure amounting to fraud "should not be subjected to any sort of prior filter by way of application for leave" and that "a litigant whose relief has been denied or depressed by fraud has an absolute right to bring the injustice to the Judge at trial". The issue of whether or not such a filter does exist in this kind of situation is referred to below.[49] However, this expression of view led Thorpe J., as he then was, to suggest that the practice fore-shadowed by the Court of Appeal in *Robinson v Robinson*[50] in relation to

32–122

However, this view must now be conditioned by the opinion of the Court of Appeal that "it is at least arguable that an appeal against a consent order will still lie": *Harris (formerly Manahan) v Manahan* [1997] 1 F.L.R. 205, *per* Ward L.J. Ward L.J. said that he did not find "the construction of these rules easy" and gave some convincing reasons for suggesting that the Family Proceedings Rules Committee should look again at the formulation of the rules; *cf.* n.37, above.

[43] See para.32–118, above. See also *Benson v Benson*, n.27, above.

[44] In *Crozier v Crozier* [1994] Fam. 114, referred to at para.32–110, above, H sought permission to appeal out of time against the original consent order. That order was made before the Family Proceedings Rules were implemented, but his appeal was launched thereafter. It was suggested on behalf of W that he should have sought to set aside the original order by way of application under CCR Ord.37, r.1. This submission was rejected by Booth J. who held that the correct procedure had been adopted. Booth J. referred to an application under Ord.37, r.1, as representing the issue of "fresh proceedings". There is very little practical difference between an application for a re-hearing of the application for the original consent order under Ord.37, r.1, and the issue of particulars of claim in order to bring a new action to set aside a previously concluded consent order. The result of each, if successful, would be that the original order would be set aside and, in due course, for a fresh look at the appropriate substantive order to make. However, it is, with respect, not correct to equate the two. See further at para.32–122, below.

[45] See para.32–124, below.

[46] *cf.* *S v S* [1994] 2 F.C.R. 1225. Indeed, the need for permission (in the sense of permission being given for an extension of time) would, for the same reasons, be required if an application for re-hearing under CCR Ord.37, r.1 was made: see para.32–124, below.

[47] *Worlock v Worlock* [1994] 2 F.L.R. 689, CA; *Re C* [1995] 2 F.L.R. 799 (Thorpe J.).

[48] *Re C* [1995] 2 F.L.R. 799 at 801, *per* Thorpe J.

[49] See para.32–127, below.

[50] (1983) 4 F.L.R. 102. See para.32–43, above.

matters of this nature was the issue of a "simple summons in existing proceedings".[51] This suggestion was, strictly speaking, *obiter*[52] and does require the reading into *Robinson* of something which is not expressly stated there[53] nor which has apparently been read into it by others.[54]

32–123   Notwithstanding the objections to the course proposed by Thorpe J., as he then was, on the basis of the present rules and previous authority, the attractions are obvious and there is much to commend it. It is a curious anomaly that whilst a district judge and a circuit judge may rehear a case, a High Court judge cannot do so; but that, it is submitted, appears to be the current position.

Practical considerations

32–124   **Application for rehearing.**   CCR Ord.37, r.1, provides that an application for a rehearing is to be made on notice and that the notice "shall be served on the opposite party not more than 14 days after the day of the trial".[55] It will be rare for the ground upon which reliance is to be placed to become known within such a short time after the order was made. Accordingly, in most cases an extension of time for making the application will be required. In such an event the grounds upon which the extension of time is sought should be set out in the notice of application, as should the grounds upon which the rehearing is sought on the assumption that the extension of time is granted.[56]

32–125   **Appeal.**   For reasons similar to those given above, it is likely that an extension of time for appealing or, if permission is necessary, for seeking permission to appeal will be required. Permission is required if the appeal is from a judge, whether county court or High Court. The notice of appeal

---

[51] *Re C* [1995] 2 F.L.R. 799 at at 800–801.
[52] As observed by Professor Cretney Q.C. in his commentary on the case at (1993) Fam. Law 675.
[53] As acknowledged by Thorpe J. in *Re C* [1995] 2 F.L.R. 799 at 800 (see n.52, above).
[54] It was patently not what Ward J. had considered to be the effect of *Robinson* in *B-T v B-T* [1990] 2 F.L.R. 1 nor what Booth J. had considered the position to be in *Crozier v Crozier* [1994] Fam. 114, above. In *Re C*, Thorpe J. expressed "no doubt at all" that the issue of the summons was what Ormrod L.J. had in mind. The learned judge had the advantage, not shared by his brother and sister judges, of having been leading counsel for the wife in *Robinson* and thus being a party to the way her case was prepared and argued. It is, with respect, difficult to know precisely how this kind of insight, not obviously apparent from the report of the case, should affect the appreciation of the case by others. In *Harris (formerly Manahan) v Manahan* [1997] 1 F.L.R. 205 Ward L.J. expressed himself in this way in relation to *Re C*: "Whilst I am ordinarily totally sympathetic to practicality overcoming technicality, nevertheless, where the rules sufficiently provide the remedy, as they do, I see no justification for importing ad hoc procedures. Thorpe J., as he then was, has far greater experience of these matters than I do and his judgment commands respect, but I venture to think that the extension he proposed goes further than is necessary".
[55] CCR Ord.37, r.1(5).
[56] CCR Ord.37, r.1(5).

must set out the basis upon which the application and, if granted, the subsequent appeal is to be advanced.

Fresh action. If this course is considered appropriate in any case (which, unless procedural obstacles exist in relation other courses, will be unusual), the question of the venue in which the proceedings are to be commenced will arise. If the jurisdictional limits of the county court cannot be overcome whether by agreement or otherwise, the proceedings will have to be begun in the High Court. Pursuant to s.64 of the Supreme Court Act 1981 proceeding's may be begun in any division of the High Court and it will probably be appropriate to commence in the Family Division. The proceedings are capable of being transferred, if desired, to the county court which made the order or the county court may transfer to the High Court pursuant to r.2.65 of the Family Proceedings Rules 1991. Often it will be advisable to start a fresh action and either an application for a rehearing or an appeal and have the two heard together. This has the added advantage that a fresh action will not be subject to the time limits applicable to either of the other two types of application. 32–126

Rejection of application to set aside *in limine*? The question of whether the court retains a residual discretion to reject an application (however it may have been advanced procedurally) to set aside a consent order in this jurisdiction has previously been addressed.[57] Since the House of Lords has given a firm warning of the need to permit such applications to succeed only where the invalidating ground, if established, is of sufficient significance to have caused the making of an order substantially different from what was ordered,[58] it is likely that a court would, in an appropriate case, decline to permit the application to proceed. Where, for example, it is clear beyond doubt that even if the non-disclosure was established it would have made no difference to the order made, the court might wish to act at an early stage to prevent the wastage of costs and the resurrection of bitterness.[59] This could be achieved by exercising adversely to the applicant any discretion concerning the granting of leave to appeal or, where a rehearing is sought, the granting of a rehearing. Where a fresh action is launched an application to strike out the proceeding summarily[60] might succeed in these circumstances. However, in many cases the court will feel obliged to investigate the evidence fully before coming to a decision.[61] 32–127

---

[57] See paras 19–65 and 19–66, above.
[58] See para.32–84, above.
[59] This raises the difficult question of whether deliberate but inconsequential fraud is something which should enable the "victim" to bring the matter before the court. It is not thought that Thorpe J. in *Re C* [1995] 2 F.L.R. 799 (see para.32–118, above) was necessarily suggesting that this should be so because his comments were directed at a victim whose relief had been "denied or depressed" by fraud. However, any litigant who chooses to bring a fresh action, which, though not to be recommended, is certainly an available avenue, would not need any leave to bring the proceedings.
[60] CPR r.3.4.
[61] *Redmond v Redmond* [1986] 2 F.L.R. 173 H.H. Judge Stannard.

Agreements made "a rule of court" and variations

32–128 Preliminary. None of the main authorities on agreements and consent orders in this jurisdiction have dealt specifically with:

(a) an agreement "filed and made a rule of court"; or
(b) an agreement in respect of which a "side letter" has been written; and
(c) he effect, if any, of such an agreement or "side letter" on subsequent applications for a variation of those parts of a consent order susceptible to variation.[62]

These matters are of some significance in this context.

32–129 Agreements "filed and made a rule of court". A practice once encouraged[63] in this jurisdiction is for the total agreement of the parties to be "filed and made a rule of court".[64] This had a number of advantages: it ensured that the totality of the parties' agreement was available to see as part of the court record and it enabled the recording and summary enforcement of terms which went beyond the court's normal jurisdiction. As to the latter, the use of undertakings has always been available and has been encouraged.[65] If the view of the authorities expressed elsewhere in this work[66] is correct, namely that the provisions of an agreement made a rule of court are contractual and do not, by being so made, *ipso facto* become orders of the court, then, in some cases, the parties may still prefer this choice. Indeed, their choice in certain circumstances may be dictated by the taxation consequences.[67]

32–130 The view referred to above is founded primarily on *Re Shaw*[68] together with a number of other considerations. In two Family Division cases the view has been expressed that the provisions of an agreement made a rule of court are, having been so made, orders and enforceable as such. In *M v M*,[69] Wood J. so held in relation to a separation deed made a rule of court on the grant of a *decree nisi* in 1974. The judge founded his judgment on *De Lasala v De Lasala*[70] and *Thwaite v Thwaite*,[71] although it seems that *Re*

---

[62] *i.e.* pursuant to Matrimonial Causes Act 1973, s.31.
[63] *Hall v Hall, The Times,* June 30, 1972, Ormrod J.; *cf.* [1972] 1 W.L.R. 1215.
[64] *Practice Direction (Decrees and Orders: Agreed Terms)* [1972] 1 W.L.R. 1313.
[65] *Livesey v Jenkins* [1985] A.C. 424 at 444.
[66] See Ch.11, paras 11–06 *et seq.*, above.
[67] *Aspden v Hildesley* [1982] 1 W.L.R. 264.
[68] [1918] P. 47, CA.
[69] *The Times,* January 9, 1982.
[70] [1980] A.C. 546.
[71] [1982] Fam. 1. In neither case did the court purport to deal with the situation of an agreement filed and made a rule of court.

Shaw and *Aspden v Hildesley*[72] were not cited. In *Tommey v Tommey*,[73] Balcombe J. appears to have taken the same view though the matter was, strictly speaking, *obiter*. The judge was referred to *Aspden v Hildesley*, but distinguished the case from the case before him on the basis that in *Tommey* the agreement was not "filed and made a rule of court".

Although Balcombe J. felt that the distinction drawn was a fine one (and, it is respectfully submitted, for many practical purposes it almost certainly is) it still remains an important distinction. It is correct to say that when the terms of an agreement are embodied in an order of the court the legal effect of the agreement is to be derived from the order. However, if the order of the court is that the terms of agreement be filed and made a rule of court, it does not necessarily follow that these terms thereby become orders of the court. If they did, then this could result in one of the matters occurring which the House of Lords in *Livesey v Jenkins*[74] forbade, namely the making of orders which do not fall within the jurisdiction conferred by ss.23 and 24.[75] There would be nothing wrong in incorporating in an agreement filed and made a rule of court a provision, for example, requiring H to effect a life assurance policy on his own life to secure the payment of future school fees in the event of his death. That cannot be made an order of the court.[76] If the making of the agreement a rule of court rendered all its provisions orders, the forbidden would be achieved.

32–131

Two matters arise immediately from this:

32–132

(1) There is, of course, no reason why those provisions of an agreement filed and made a rule of court which can be embodied as orders of the court should not be so embodied. There would be many advantages in so doing.
(2) Since there is this division of judicial view on the legal effect of provisions filed and made a rule of court, any party seeking to enforce a term of such an agreement would be well advised to issue an application seeking relief in the alternative—*i.e.* seeking enforcement of the term as an order or, if not an order, as a term of an agreement with default provisions incorporated to enable enforcement of the order thus created in the event of non-compliance.[77]

---

[72] [1982] 1 W.L.R. 264.
[73] [1983] Fam. 15.
[74] [1985] A.C. 424.
[75] See para.32–60, above.
[76] *cf. Milne v Milne* [1981] 2 F.L.R. 286.
[77] See Precedent No.43 in the Fourth edition of this work.

32-133   Having referred to the practice and stated the effect of filing and making an agreement a rule of court, it does seem that the practice once encouraged[78] has largely fallen into disuse. The practice of "side letters" seems to have emerged in more recent times.[79]

32-134 **Agreements, side-letters and variations of consent orders.** One of the reasons parties sometimes wished to make their agreement a rule of court was so that reference could be made to it in the event of some future application for a variation of a provision made the subject of an order.[80] An example is afforded when W agrees to accept lesser provision by way of periodical payments for herself in return for a greater eventual share of the capital assets. In order that the basis of the periodical payments order should not be forgotten in the event of an application for variation, H would clearly prefer to see the basis of the agreement recorded somewhere so that, if necessary, reference to it could be made. Although, certainly in the past, the making of the agreement a rule of court has enabled a provision such as this to be referred to later, it is not a necessity that it be so made for this purpose. If agreements on matters such as these are relevant and admissible on the subsequent application, it will not matter where and how they are recorded.

32-135   In *N v N*,[81] contrary to legal advice received at the time, W agreed in 1987 that her maintenance would cease after five years except in the "quite unforeseen circumstances of serious illness or disability". She did this in anticipation of having established a career by then. No direction under s.28(1A) was made, but W's agreement to the above effect was contained in a side letter written shortly before a consent order dealing with ancillary relief matters was made. It was unlikely that this letter was shown to the district judge who made the order. The Court of Appeal held, *inter alia*, that the side letter was "highly relevant and [could not] be disregarded in the overall consideration of all the circumstances".

AGREEMENTS RELATING TO CHILDREN

32-136 It is difficult to conceive of an agreement between parents concerning their child as being a compromise in the usually accepted sense of that term. Hopefully, parents agree on a particular course of action because they both

---

[78] See para.32–119, above.
[79] *N v N* [1994] 2 F.C.R. 275 at 288, *per* Roch L.J., noted at para.32–135, below: side letters reflect a "well-established practice".
[80] See Precedent Nos 95 and 96 in the fourth edition of this work.
[81] See n.80, above. In *Garner v Garner* [1992] 1 F.L.R. 573, the Court of Appeal made it clear that a court dealing with a subsequent variation application in respect of a prior consent periodical payments order "would expect to pay full regard to any special terms agreed between the parties at the time the original order was made—as, *e.g.* when indorsements on briefs or contemporaneous correspondence show that an agreed order had, for some particular reason, been set at an artificially low figure" (*per* Cazalet J. at 582, with whom Neill L.J. agreed).

regard it as in the child's best interests without regard to their own selfish concerns. Unhappily, experience in practice suggests that this is not always the case. However, agreements concerning children are frequently made, whatever might be said of the motives of the parties.

It was clear that the discretionary jurisdiction conferred by s.42 of the 1973 Act[82] could be exercised irrespective of the wishes or agreement of the parties. A similar approach is almost certainly applied in relation to agreed "section 8" orders under the Children Act 1989.[83] Since, however, co-operation between parties over a child is clearly desirable in the child's interests, it would be unusual for a court to decline to reflect an agreement in an order if an order was required. Furthermore, the enforcement of an order which did not reflect the wishes of the parties would be virtually impossible. Nevertheless, it is not unknown for a judge (or district judge) to ask parents to think again over, say, excessive visiting arrangements for a very young child or an agreement whereby children are to be split, if the view is taken that the plans have not been adequately considered. It is likely that the order sought will be made if it has been fully considered even if the judge might not regard it as entirely sensible.

32–137

A court faced with a dispute between parents over a child or children will, understandably perhaps, find itself even more frustrated than in other cases that the dispute cannot be resolved by agreement. A judge with great experience of this kind of jurisdiction has said this [84]:

32–138

"... Whilst in other jurisdictions it is open and often desirable for the Court to exercise its influence to induce parties to compromise, it can only be in the rarest of cases an appropriate course to take where sensitive and delicate decisions must be taken to achieve the welfare of children."

Consent orders entered into in this sphere are not, or do not always remain, satisfactory to one or other of the parties. Unless permission is granted,[85] an appeal can rarely be entertained.[86] In most cases, certainly where interim orders are concerned, an application to vary the order would be the most appropriate course to follow. The court will always be guided by what is in the best interests of the child irrespective of what may have been agreed at some earlier stage in his or her life.

32–139

---

[82] "The court may make such order as it thinks fit for the custody and education of any child of the family.": s.42(1). "Custody" includes access: s.52(1); *cf. Wood v Wood* (1979) C.A.T. 49.
[83] By s.10(1) of the Act it is said that the court "may make a section 8 order" at the instance of the parties specified and s.1(1) and 1(5) appear to be applicable in relation to consideration of a proposed agreed order.
[84] *Re R.* [1995] 1 F.L.R. 123 at 135, *per* Sir Francis Purchas.
[85] *ibid.*
[86] *Re F* [1992] 1 F.L.R. 561, CA.

CHAPTER 33

Settlement of Inheritance Act Disputes

PRELIMINARY

33–01 The Inheritance (Provision for Family and Dependants) Act 1975 provides the court with jurisdiction, in appropriate circumstances, [1] to make orders that alter the provisions of a will or the effect of the laws of intestacy where no will was made. Such orders may be made at the instance of a limited class of persons[2] and a time limit is applicable to claims brought under the Act.[3] A range of orders may be made which is very similar to the range available under the ancillary relief jurisdiction provided for by the Matrimonial Causes Act 1973.[4] A number of questions arise in connection with the law and practice applicable to the settlement of potential or actual disputes under this jurisdiction. The settlement of disputed claims arising under the Act should be seen against the background of the general proposition that such claims are claims against the individual rights of the beneficiaries of the estate and not against the estate as a whole. The consequence is that the personal representatives have no power to compromise claims under the Act pursuant to s.15 of the Trustee Act 1925 without reference to the beneficiaries.

CONTRACTING OUT

33–02 It is not clear whether a potential applicant other than a spouse or former spouse may, during the deceased's lifetime, "contract out" of the right to

---

[1] s.2.
[2] s.1(1), as amended by the Law Reform (Succession) Act 1995.
[3] s.4.
[4] s.2; *cf.* Matrimonial Causes Act 1973, ss.23 and 24.

apply to the court for an order under the Act.[5] Under the general law, spouses or former spouses cannot do so.[6] Provision is, however, made under the Act to enable the making (by consent or otherwise) of an order disentitling recourse to this jurisdiction on or after a decree of divorce, judicial separation or nullity[7] or on the making of a financial provision or property adjustment order following an overseas decree to like effect.[8] Section 15(1) of the Act[9] provides that the court:

"... if it considers it just to do so, may on the application of either party to the marriage, order that the other party to the marriage shall not on the death of the applicant be entitled to apply for an order under s.2 of this Act."

The "court" in question is the court dealing with the parties' ancillary relief applications. Plainly, it has a discretion whether or not to make an order in the terms indicated notwithstanding that the parties agree. However, since the previous phraseology of s.15(1) permitted such an order only if the parties were in agreement and the court thought it right, it is unlikely, except in the most exceptional circumstances, that the court would stand in the way of making such an order. Where parties contemplate that their property and capital settlement is "once for all", it is a provision which will doubtless find its way into most consent orders. Where the disentitlement provision is incorporated by agreement, the usual order will provide for it to come into operation only upon the final dismissal of the periodical payments claim, whether immediately or at some future date. 33–03

It has been said[10] that it is not possible for the court to be satisfied that it is "just" to make such an order unless it is given "some indication of what the estate is likely to consist of and some details of the persons whom the applicant considers to have a prior claim on his estate in the event of his decease". This comment was made in the context of a somewhat unusual 33–04

---

[5] The position was not clear under the Inheritance (Family Provision) Act 1938: see *Zamet v Hyman* [1961] 1 W.L.R. 1442, where the Court of Appeal expressed no view on the matter in relation to a dependant.
[6] *Re M* [1968] P. 174. See also *Re S* [1965] P. 165.
[7] s.15.
[8] s.15A.
[9] As introduced by the Matrimonial and Family Proceedings Act 1984, s.9, with effect from October 12, 1984. Section 15A was introduced by s.25 of that Act. The order may be made "on making an order under section 17" of the 1984 Act. Subject to that, s.15A(1) is in identical terms to s.15(1).
[10] *Whiting v Whiting* [1988] 1 W.L.R. 565 at 577, *per* Balcombe L.J. at 577, with whom, on this issue, Stocker and Slade L.JJ. agreed.

situation[11] and, whilst strictly speaking applicable also to a consensual application for such an order, it is very unlikely that any very detailed (and specific) information on these matters would be required by the court. No specific provision has been made in the statement of information required to be lodged in support of an application for a consent order in ancillary relief proceedings[12] relating to these matters, but it is thought that the information required in such a statement would give the court sufficient material in all but the most exceptional cases upon which to approve the making of the order requested.

33–05   It should, perhaps, be said that even in cases where parties may not "contract out" of the Act, the fact that they made an agreement to that effect may be one of the "relevant" matters which the court may consider in exercising its jurisdiction.[13]

EFFECT OF PREVIOUS COMPROMISE OR CONSENT ORDER

33–06   If two spouses have not "contracted out" of the Act pursuant to s.15(1) at the time of their divorce, will the fact that they have compromised everything else at that time be of any significance on an application under the Act by the surviving former spouse? The question would arise in the context of considering whether the deceased former spouse had failed "to make reasonable financial provision" for the surviving former spouse.[14]

33–07   Whilst every case would, in the final analysis, depend upon its own facts, the answer to the question posed must clearly be "Yes". The prior agreement is obviously one of the circumstances the court must take into account. In *Re Fullard*[15] Ormrod L.J. said this[16]:

> "Where the application is made by an ex-wife (or ex-husband) of the deceased, the fact that the parties have been divorced and the result of

---

[11] H had applied to the court for an order discharging a consent order for nominal periodical payments in favour of W, made several years previously following their divorce, and at the same time applied for an order under s.15(1). All the evidence adduced by H before the judge was directed to his application to discharge the periodical payments order. The judge rejected his application *in toto*. On his appeal against this rejection, the Court of Appeal by a majority dismissed his appeal "on the simple ground that [H had] not made out a case to support his application under section 15". The appeal was dismissed "without prejudice to [H's] right to renew his application under section 15".

[12] See paras 32–49 *et seq.*, above.

[13] s.3(1)(g): *cf. Re Fullard* [1982] Fam. 42, CA; but see *Re Farrow* [1987] 1 F.L.R. 205 (Hollings J.).

[14] s.1(2)(b).

[15] [1982] Fam. 42, CA.

[16] *ibid.* at 46–47.

that divorce in financial terms is plainly [a] matter which is relevant—and which is highly relevant."

In that case, in answering the question whether it was reasonable for the deceased to make no provision for his former wife upon his death, the court took into account the size of the estate (which was modest) and the consideration that the deceased had "made arrangements with his former wife which settled their financial affairs". It was held emphatically that the deceased had acted perfectly reasonably. A similar conclusion was reached in *Brill v Proud*.[17]

EFFECT AND VARIATION OF PREVIOUS "MAINTENANCE AGREEMENT"

It is presumed that, consistent with the approach referred to above, the existence of a "maintenance agreement" and its terms would be taken into account by the court considering the exercise of its jurisdiction. There is specific provision, in relation to a maintenance agreement which subsisted at the deceased's death and which provided for the continuation of payments after his death, for the court to vary or revoke the agreement. In exercising its power in such matters the court must have regard "to all the circumstances of the case, including any order which the court proposes to make under section 2 or section 5 of this Act and any change (whether resulting from death of the deceased or otherwise) in any of the circumstances in the light of which the agreement was made".[18] Likewise the court has the jurisdiction, in the context of applications under the Act to vary a pre-existing order for secured periodical payments or a maintenance agreement, to exercise its powers under s.2.[19]

COMPROMISE PROPER OF CLAIMS UNDER THE ACT

Any compromise by virtue of which the parties seek the making of a consent order under the Act must ensure that the order made is within the jurisdiction conferred on the court by the Act.[20]

The jurisdiction conferred by the Act, in the sense of the reliefs available, is very similar to that conferred by the Matrimonial Causes Act 1973. The differences for present purposes are immaterial, but there is one difference

---

[17] (1984) 14 Fam. Law 59, CA.
[18] s.17(2).
[19] s.18.
[20] cf. *Livesey v Jenkins* [1985] A.C. 424; *Hinde v Hinde* [1953] 1 W.L.R. 175. See paras 32–58 *et seq.*, above.

between the jurisdictions in the wider sense which is of some relevance: once the divorce court comes to adjudicate on applications for financial relief, the *sine qua non* of those applications (the decree) will have been pronounced. In virtually all such cases the parties will have co-operated in relation to the obtaining of the decree. By implication they will have exposed themselves to the jurisdiction of the court in relation to ancillary matters.

33–12   Under the 1975 Act the equivalent two-tier process is carried out at one and the same time. The right to make application and the making by order of provision, if appropriate, is dealt with by the same tribunal at the same time. Furthermore, the factors to be taken into account by the court in deciding whether an applicant is within the jurisdiction conferred by the Act are the same as those to be taken into account by the court in determining what, if any, provision should be made.[21]

33–13   For the court to exercise its jurisdiction to make orders there is a condition precedent[22] which states that the court must be satisfied that the financial provision made for the applicant (whether by testamentary disposition or the rules of intestacy) is not reasonable.[23] That is, almost by definition, an area ripe for argument. It may, therefore, be that the parties to an application of this nature, recognising the uncertainty of this matter (putting aside for the moment the uncertainties associated with the exercise of the discretionary jurisdiction conferred by the Act so far as orders are concerned), will wish to reach an overall settlement without putting to the test whether the applicant can surmount the first hurdle associated with an application.[24] This is unlikely to be discouraged by the court, particularly having regard to the question of costs, but equally, strictly speaking, the court could not make orders within its jurisdiction unless satisfied of this first matter. Whilst bona fide admissions of fact[25] would doubtless be accepted to bring an applicant within the Act, there are always those cases where such an admission will not be forthcoming and yet a compromise be desired. This, it is thought, is a situation where the compromise might be best effectuated by means of a Tomlin order[26] or by making the agreement a rule of court.[27]

---

[21] s.3.
[22] *Re Fullard*, n.13, above, *per* Ormrod L.J. at 46.
[23] s.2(1).
[24] Indeed, some intending applicants may be concerned as to whether they can show that they were being "maintained" for the purposes of the Act: s.1(1)(e).
[25] *cf*. paras 37–12 *et seq.*, below, *Re Carecraft Construction Co Ltd* [1994] 1 W.L.R. 172 at 182, *per* Ferris J. See paras 31–12 *et seq.*, above.
[26] See Ch.9, paras 9–19 *et seq.*, above.
[27] Since the practice of "filing and making an agreement a rule of court" found its origin in the old Probate practice, this might be thought the appropriate course. There is, however, some doubt about how such an agreement is enforced: see paras 32–129 *et seq.*, above. See also *Practice Direction (Probate: Compromised Action)* [1972] 1 W.L.R. 1215.

When the court is invited to exercise its powers by consent it will be under a dual duty:

(a) to consider whether the financial provision actually made for the applicant is reasonable; and, if not;
(b) to consider how, if at all, its powers are to be exercised.

The duty is carried out by means of a yet further duty, namely that of having regard to the specific matters enumerated in s.3(1), the last of which being "any other matters . . . which in the circumstances of the case the court may consider relevant".

33–14

Although no rules have been made[28] ordaining the information which the parties should put before the court when applying for a consent order, it is thought that the court must require them to give it sufficient up-to-date and accurate information to enable it to exercise its discretion.[29] The scheme of the Act is so similar to that of the Matrimonial Causes Act 1973 that it must be presumed that Parliament intended commensurate concern to be shown for the disposition of the assets of the dead as for those of the living.

33–15

SETTING ASIDE AND ENFORCEMENT

For the reasons adumbrated above,[30] it is thought that grounds similar to those available for setting aside a compromise of matrimonial ancillary relief applications will be available to set aside the compromise of these proceedings.[31] It should, however, be noted that an order for provision under the Act is to be treated as a legacy or something which devolves on intestacy.[32] Any such provision is not, therefore, to be treated for the purposes of enforcement as an order. The correct way to enforce such a provision is to take proceedings for the administration of the estate.[33]

33–16

PRACTICE

Rules exist to facilitate the identification of all relevant parties and their incorporation as parties into the proceedings. Where all the parties who are or may be interested in the estate are not parties to the proceedings, it

33–17

---

[28] *cf.* Family Proceedings Rules 1991, r.2.61.
[29] *cf. Livesey v Jenkins*, n.20, above.
[30] See paras 33–10 *et seq.*, above.
[31] See Ch.32, above.
[32] s.19(1).
[33] *Re Jennery* [1967] Ch. 280, CA.

seems that the correct course to adopt is to ask the court for administration of the estate which will enable it to authorise the executors to enter a compromise on agreed terms.[34]

33–18 Where an applicant or a beneficiary is a minor or a patient, he or she will be represented by a next friend or guardian ad litem. As with all compromises affecting the rights of such persons, the court will have to approve any proposed settlement and will be guided by the views of the legal advisers.[35]

33–19 A copy of any consent order made under the Act, whether in the Family Division or the Chancery Division (or, of course, any county court), must be sent to the Principal Registry of the Family Division for entry and filing, and a memorandum of the order is to be endorsed on, or permanently annexed to, the grant of probate or letters of administration under which the estate is being administered. Applications under the Act may be made in either the Family or the Chancery Division of the High Court, or in a county court.

---

[34] *Re Knowles* [1966] Ch. 386; *Re Lofts* [1968] 1 W.L.R. 1949.
[35] s.19(3); *Practice Direction (Family Provision: Endorsement of Order)* [1979] 1 W.L.R. 1.

CHAPTER 34

Offers of Settlement in Matrimonial Finance Cases

Preliminary

The costs involved in contested ancillary relief proceedings have always been a matter of concern. Whether one or other or both of the parties has assistance from public funds for the purposes of the proceedings, or whether the legal costs are being met directly from one or both pockets, in most cases (bearing in mind the Legal Services Commission's charge in such cases), the costs are met from the family's resources. Except where those resources are very substantial, their division, in whatever proportions, involves sufficient hardship in its own right without the need for aggravating the position by running up legal bills beyond that which is necessary. **34–01**

Even where the resources of the parties are substantial, legal costs can assume disproportionately high levels.[1] The direction of the lay client's mind towards the question of costs in this context has received repeated judicial encouragement.[2] **34–02**

In *E v E*,[3] the family assets consisted of two homes belonging to each party and H's shareholding in a small company that provided his livelihood. W was legally aided. The costs incurred by H and W respectively were £35,000 and £25,000. Booth J. found herself unable to make the appropriate provision for the parties and the children because of the very substantial costs of each party. With the concurrence of Sir Stephen Brown P., her Ladyship issued a series of guidelines for the preparation of substantial ancillary relief cases. Of those guidelines two related specifically to the duties of the parties' legal advisers in connection with the possibility of settlement. Booth J. said in this regard[4]:

---

[1] *Re T (Divorce: Interim Maintenance)* [1990] 1 F.L.R. 1; *Newton v Newton* [1990] 1 F.L.R. 33; *E v E.* [1990] Fam. Law 297; *Piglowska v Piglowski* [1992] 2 F.L.R. 763, HL.
[2] See, *e.g. Singer (formerly Sharegin) v Sharegin* [1984] F.L.R. 114, CA.
[3] [1990] 1 F.L.R. 318.
[4] *ibid.*

"(10) Solicitors and counsel should keep their clients informed of the costs at all stages of the proceedings and, where appropriate, should ensure that they understand the implications of the legal aid charge . . .

(11) The desirability of reaching a settlement should be borne in mind throughout the proceedings. While it is necessary for the legal advisers to have sufficient knowledge of the financial position of both parties before advising their clients on a proposed settlement, the necessity to make further inquiries must always be balanced by a consideration of what they were realistically likely to achieve and the increased costs which were likely to be incurred by making them."[5]

34–03 This approach *crystallised* under the new ancillary relief procedures introduced in June 2000. This required costs estimates to be produced at every hearing or appointment so that the court and the parties could be aware of the extent of the costs incurred.[6] However, notwithstanding initiatives of this nature the level of costs has continued to be a major problem confronting judges dealing with all but those ancillary relief cases involving the wealthiest parties, and anxiety has frequently been expressed over the level of costs incurred in relation to the value of the assets in issue.[7]

GENERAL APPROACH TO COSTS

34–04 In matrimonial disputes, there is often no obvious successful or unsuccessful party.[8] This is particularly so in relation to disputes about children, but may also extend to financial matters. A party may lose on some issues and win on others. A degree of flexibility in costs is, therefore, exercised:

"The practice as to costs in the Family Division especially at first instance is, and rightly, much less rigid than it has become in ordinary litigation."[9]

34–05 However, broadly speaking and particularly in financial disputes, where a party has to go to court (other than for a consent order previously agreed) in order to obtain an order for relief sought, and the other party has either made no offer of settlement at all or one which is bettered at the hearing, then *prima facie* the respondent to the application will be

---

[5] See further at paras 34–04 *et seq.*, below.
[6] Family Proceedings Rules 1991, r.2.61F(1), as introduced by the Family Proceedings (Amendment No.2) Rules 1999 (SI 1999/3491).
[7] See, *e.g. S v B* [2005] 1 F.L.R. 474 and *P v P* [2005] 1 F.L.R. 548.
[8] *cf.* para.14–02, above. *Gooday v Gooday* [1969] P. 1; *Povey v Povey* [1972] Fam. 40; *Martin v Martin* [1976] Fam. 335.
[9] *McDonnell v McDonnell* [1977] 1 W.L.R. 34 at 37, *per* Ormrod L.J. And see *Grenfell v Grenfell* [1978] Fam. 128 at 143.

considered responsible for the costs thus occasioned. This is the order usually made where the respondent is not funded by the Legal Services Commission.[10]

34–06 The provisions of CPR r.44(3)(2)(a), which provides that generally the unsuccessful party is to pay the successful party's costs,[11] are specifically disapplied in relation to family proceedings,[12] but the factors referred to in r.44.3(4) and (5), to which the court must have regard when considering what order to make about costs, are not disapplied.[13] Furthermore, in relation to ancillary relief proceedings, the Family Procedings Rules 1991 (FPR) provide that when an opponent's *Calderbank* offer[14] is beaten, the losing party must be ordered to pay the costs incurred after the date beginning 28 days after the offer was made unless the court considers it unjust so to order.[15] However, the Court of Appeal has taken the opportunity subsequently[16] to review carefully the law and practice in this area and has pointed out that the discretion is much wider than sometimes thought[17]:

> "It [FPR r.2.69D(e)]may enable a judge or district judge to mitigate, to some extent the uncomfortable consequences of a *Calderbank* situation in a case where there is some but not a substantial amount of property and/or money to divide and costs will have to be paid from the available capital. The judge, in such a case, may make an order, often just enough to buy a suitable property for the wife, and then find that effect of the *Calderbank* offers may totally destabilise his order . . . In my judgment , therefore r.2.69B and 2.69D can be managed and, where the court considers it unjust to apply r.2.69B, it can make a different costs order to reflect the justice of the case."

Moreover, the Court has at times been drawn to making issue-based orders, penalising a party who has pursued and lost a particular issue.[18]

34–07 Where the respondent is funded by the Legal Services Commission, the court's ability to make an order against him is limited. Often, no order for costs is made in this situation or an order to the extent of the respondent's

---

[10] *Singer (formerly Sharegin) v Sharegin*, n.2, above, *per* Cumming-Bruce L.J. at 119. See also *Moorish v Moorish* (1984) 14 Fam. Law 26, CA; and *Gojkovic v Gojkovic (No.2)* [1992] Fam. 40.
[11] See para.14–02, above.
[12] Family Proceedings (Miscellaneous Amendments) Rules 1999, r.4(1)(6).
[13] See, generally, Ch.13, above.
[14] See paras 34–08 *et seq.*, below.
[15] FPR r.2.69B.
[16] In *Norris v Norris; Haskins v Haskins* [2003] 2 F.L.R. 1124.
[17] *ibid.* at paras 24–25, *per* Butler-Sloss P.
[18] See *P v P* [2002] 2 F.L.R. 1075; and *C v C* [2004] 1 F.L.R. 291.

contribution, if any.[19] Equally, where an applicant's application fails then, subject to similar public funding considerations, that "consequence" will be followed by an order in the respondent's favour.

All this may change. The Court of Appeal has expressed its approval of the proposal of the Costs Sub-Committee of the President's Ancillary Relief Advisory Group that the governing principle should be that no orders for costs will be made unless a particular party has behaved in such an unreasonable manner that the court feels that a sanction should be imposed.[20] Draft amendments to the FPR have apparently been prepared, but an anticipated date for their introduction is not clear.

MAKING AN OFFER THAT MAY AFFECT THE COSTS ORDER[21]

34–08 It is as plain in this jurisdiction as in any other that a "without prejudice" offer cannot be referred to on costs.[22] The offers made are usually open[23] or in the *Calderbank* form.[24] In ancillary relief cases which proceed to a final hearing there will often be both open and *Calderbank* proposals since the FPR require the parties to file and serve open proposals.[25] Bearing in mind the way the question of costs is dealt with in family matters, particularly having regard to the way the incidence of costs is sometimes taken into account in achieving the final orders of the court in contested matters,[26] there is a *strong* argument that the court should be made aware of how the parties have conducted themselves in the negotiations. *Calderbank* offers, it has been suggested, inhibit the court in exercising its jurisdiction since it cannot know "all the circumstances of the case" if offers in negotiations are concealed from the court until after its discretion has been exercised.[27]

In *S v B*[28] Wilson J said this of the proposed new rule of no order for costs absent unreasonable conduct:

---

[19] Legal Aid Act 1988, s.17(1), ordains that the liability must not exceed "the amount (if any) which is a reasonable one for him to pay having regard to all the circumstances, including the financial resources of all parties and their conduct in connection with the dispute".
[20] See *Norris v Norris*; *Haskins v Haskins*, n.16, above, at paras 28–31 and 64.
[21] See Ch.27, above. See Bennett, "The Mechanism of the Offer" [1990] Fam. Law 249.
[22] See para.26–04, above.
[23] The form of offer actually made in *Calderbank v Calderbank* [1976] Fam. 93. See also *E v E* [1990] Fam. Law 297.
[24] See paras 26–05, *et seq.*, above.
[25] FPR r.2.69E.
[26] *Practice Direction (Family Division) (Ancillary Relief: Costs Estimates)* [1988] 1 W.L.R. 561. See *Thompson v Thompson* [1994] 1 F.C.R. 7, CA; and *Wells v Wells* [2002] 2 F.L.R. 97, where the purist approach of leaving costs entirely out of account until after judgment was disapproved in a case of limited assets.
[27] See Berkin, "*Calderbank* offers—An Unwelcome Intrusion in the Family Division?" (1984) 14 Fam. Law 61.
[28] [2005] 1 F.L.R. 474 at [49].

"Of at least equal significance, if duly introduced, will be the suggested provision that no without prejudice offer can be taken into account in any determination as to costs. The consignment to history of *Calderbank* correspondence in proceedings for ancillary relief and thus the emergence of an ability to treat a party's outstanding costs as one of his liabilities definitively within the substantive judgment, ie without the need or indeed opportunity for such subsequent consideration as may demand that their earlier treatment be undermined, is hugely attractive."

However, until new rules emerge, the use of *Calderbank* offers is likely to remain in the process of these matters, since they have been encouraged judicially, directly[29] and indirectly.[30] 34–09

In financial proceedings it is specifically provided[31] that either party may make a *Calderbank* offer. Furthermore, present practice is that a *Calderbank* offer has to be replied to unless there is a very good reason not to do so. Such reason is only likely to exist in cases where material non-disclosure is reasonably suspected or where there is an important uncertainty that first needs resolving—for example, where the life expectancy of a relevant person is in doubt. 34–10

In *Gojkovic v Gojkovic (No.2)*,[32] Butler-Sloss L.J., having stated that there are certain preconditions to the effectiveness of an offer for the purpose of influencing the court's discretion on costs, said this[33]: 34–11

"Both parties must make full and frank disclosure of all relevant assets and put their cards on the table. Thereafter the respondent to an application must make a serious offer worthy of consideration. If he does so then it is incumbent on the applicant to accept or reject the offer and, if the latter, to make her/his position clear and indicate in figures what she/he is asking for—a counter offer. It is incumbent on both parties to negotiate if possible and at least to make the attempt to settle the case . . ."

On the facts of *Gojkovic* the Court of Appeal did not regard the absence of a counter-offer on W's part reprehensible. However, Butler-Sloss L.J. emphasised subsequently in her judgment[34] that "the failure to make a counter-offer may be a matter for considerable criticism by the court and 34–12

---

[29] *Moorish v Moorish* (1984) 14 Fam. Law 26, CA; *Gojkovic v Gojkovic*, n.10, above.
[30] By allowing them to influence the costs order: see paras 34–15 *et seq.*, below.
[31] FPR r.2.69(1).
[32] [1992] Fam. 40.
[33] *ibid.* at 59.
[34] *ibid.* at 60.

may properly be penalised in costs at the hearing". This must now be read also in the light of her comments in the Court of Appeal as President in *Norris v Haskins*.[35]

34–13 Furthermore, under the ancillary relief rules, shortly before the FDR,[36] all offers, whether open, *Calderbank* or "without prejudice", must be notified to the court. If the case is not settled the offers are not kept on the court file but returned to the parties.[37]

THE EFFECT, IF ANY, OF THE OFFER ON COSTS

34–14 In ancillary relief proceedings the situation is now governed by FPR r.2.69B–D. The general principle has already been stated in para.34–05, above. The factors that the court will take into account when the it considers exercising its costs jurisdiction include the terms of the offers, the stages of the litigation when they were made, the information then available, the conduct of the parties and their respective means.[38]

34–15 Where an applicant is in receipt of Legal Services Commission funding and is awarded a lump sum which equals or is less than a sum previously offered on a *Calderbank* basis, an order for costs could be made in similar terms to that in *Pick v Pick*,[39] the court being entitled to take into account the lump sum as part of the applicant's means.[40] When an application for a lump sum is pursued and the application is rejected, the court would be entitled to take account of the applicant's contribution to his public funding in determining what, if any, adverse order for costs ought to be made.[41]

34–16 Where an applicant is in receipt of Legal Services Commission funding with either a nil or relatively small contribution (*i.e.* small in relation to the bill of costs of the respondent), the existence of an unbettered *Calderbank* offer may well influence the court in ordering the respondent's costs after the offer to be paid by the Legal Services Commission[42] provided, of course, that the other factors governing the making of such an order can be established.[43]

---

[35] See para.34–06, above. Thorpe and Mantell L.JJ. agreed with her judgment.
[36] FPR r.2.61E(3).
[37] FPR r.2.61E(5).
[38] FPR r.2.69D.
[39] (1981) 11 Fam. Law 187 (Wood J.).
[40] See also *Lockley v National Blood Transfusion* [1992] 1 W.L.R. 492.
[41] It would doubtless be one of the circumstances permitted to be considered under s.17(1) of the Legal Aid Act 1988.
[42] *McDonnell v McDonnell*, n.9, above.
[43] Legal Aid Act 1988, s.18.

CHILDREN'S CASES

In children's cases the usual order is that there is no order as to costs. However, that general approach may be displaced if one party has been behaving particularly unreasonably or there is a large disparity between the respective means of the parties.[44] The court will take into account the risk of an order in such a case exacerbating hostility between the parents, to the child's detriment.[45]

34–17

---

[44] For example *M v H* [2000] 1 F.L.R. 394.
[45] See *R v R* [1997] 2 F.L.R. 95; *Q v Q* [2002] 2 F.L.R . 668; and *C v FC* [2004] 1 F.L.R. 362.

PART 9

Settlement of Serious Personal Injury Claims Involving Children or Patients

PART IV

CHAPTER 35

Settlement of Serious Personal Injury Claims Involving Children or Patients[1]

INTRODUCTION

Cases involving serious personal injury to the claimant present special problems for practitioners. They will invariably involve consideration of how best to provide for the claimant's future needs out of the compensation received. The problems are accentuated where the claimant cannot conduct the litigation on his own behalf, either because he is a child (*i.e.* he is under 18[2]) or because he is incapable by reason of a mental disorder (as defined in the Mental Health Act 1983) of managing and administering his own affairs.[3]

35–01

The determination of capacity is of the first importance and will invariably require some medical evidence in support. For a case in which problems arose as to capacity long after the case was thought concluded, see *Masterman-Lister v Brutton & Co.*[4] A claimant who is a patient at the time of the issue of proceedings must litigate via a litigation friend. However, where the claimant was a patient at the date of the tortious injury but has recovered capacity since and before issue, he need not be so represented. Capacity is time-specific and function-specific.[5] Furthermore, a patient may have capacity for some purposes, *e.g.* administering a small income-stream, and not for

35–02

---

[1] See, generally, *Kemp & Kemp*, Vol.1. As this chapter does not set out to deal in detail with the underlying law, the reader is referred for more detailed discussion to *Kemp & Kemp*, which should be the *vade mecum* of all practitioners in this field.
[2] CPR r.21.1(2)(a).
[3] Mental Health Act 1983, ss.1(2) and 94(2); CPR r.21.1.(2)(b).
[4] [2002] EWCA Civ 1889; [2003] P.I.Q.R. Q1, CA.
[5] See *Masterman Lister*, n.4 above.

others, *e.g.* managing a very large lump sum. Equally, a claimant who is a patient at the date of trial may not be considered likely to remain one throughout the period covered by the court's award.[6] Consideration of the capacity of a patient, or of what measures are required to manage that patient's affairs on his behalf, may be influenced by the Mental Capacity Act 2005, which favours the "least restrictive alternative", *i.e.* the least intervention consistent with protection.

35–03 As has already been noted,[7] the foundation of the law of compromise is the law of contract. It is, therefore, no surprise to find that the law makes special provision for those who may be incapable of entering into valid contracts or whose ability to make contracts may be restricted by age.[8]

35–04 The procedure governing actions brought by or against patients or children is set out in Pt 21 of the CPR. A patient must proceed through a litigation friend.[9] A child will normally proceed through a litigation friend, although the court may dispense with this in appropriate circumstances.[10]

35–05 No settlement, compromise or payment and no acceptance of any money paid into court is valid, so far as it relates to a claim by, on behalf of or against a child or patient without the approval of the court.[11]

35–06 The effect of this rule is that a defendant who "settles" a claim against a patient or child which does not have the approval of the court does not secure his discharge from liability.

35–07 A claimant who, through a litigation friend, reaches an agreement to settle a claim before proceedings are begun, must nevertheless seek the approval of the court. An application for this purpose must be issued. The procedure is governed by Pt 8 of the CPR, but see the discussion of *Drinkall v Whitwood* below at para.35–12 for the procedure governing approval of a partial settlement arrived at before proceedings.[12]

35–08 Where a settlement of a personal injury claim is reached during proceedings, approval of the proposed settlement may be sought from a district judge, master or judge, depending on the circumstances of the case.[13] The court will require information (amongst other things) as to:

---

[6] See *Mitchell v Alasia* [2005] EWHC 11 (QB), *per* Cox J.
[7] See, *e.g.* Ch.1, above.
[8] For a general discussion of contractual capacity see *Chitty on Contracts* (29th ed., 2004), Vol.1, Ch.8; and see paras 4–02 *et seq.*, above. The normal principle is that contracts made by minors are, with some exceptions, voidable at their instance.
[9] CPR r.21.2(1).
[10] CPR r.21.1(2) and (3).
[11] CPR r.21.10(1).
[12] CPR r.21.10(2)(a) and (b); and PD21, para.6.1.
[13] See paras 10–22 *et seq.*, above.

(i) whether and to what extent the defendant admits liability;
(ii) the age and occupation of the child or patient;
(iii) the litigation friend's approval of the terms of settlement;
(iv) the circumstances of the incident or state of affairs giving rise to the claim;
(v) relevant medical reports;
(vi) a schedule of loss and damage;
(vii) details of the evidence on liability, if it is not admitted, and an appreciation of the perceived litigation risks, with an assessment of the discount against a full liability award considered appropriate having regard to those risks;
(viii) an opinion from counsel or the solicitor acting for the child or patient endorsing the settlement figure[14];
(ix) in a complex case, a draft order[15];
(x) suggestions as to investment, where appropriate.

Circumstances may dictate that further information needs to be put before the court. For example, where the claim has been discounted to reflect the risk of defeat on a difficult and undecided point of law, it may be necessary to provide the court with authorities.

CONSEQUENCES OF FAILING TO OBTAIN APPROVAL

Until such time as approval has been given it is open to either side to withdraw from the agreement.[16] Once the court has given its approval it seems that even if the order has not been drawn the agreement will still be binding.[17] Neither party would, on this analysis, be permitted to withdraw its consent. It is arguable, however, that even after this point, and even once the consent order has been drawn, the court may still allow the terms to be set aside and the action to proceed.

The court's approval must be sought to the making of interim payments to or on behalf of a patient.[18]

It should be appreciated that the restriction on enforceability applies not only to an overall settlement but also to a compromise of individual issues within a case. The very great importance of securing the court's approval to a settlement of even a single issue to ensure that it is binding is shown by the case of *Drinkall v Whitwood*.[19]

---

[14] CPR PD21, para.6. This opinion should also deal, where appropriate, with the amount to be paid out to those who have provided gratuitous care.
[15] See Precedent Nos 21 and 22 at paras A1–21 and A1–22, below.
[16] *Dietz v Lennig Chemicals Limited* [1969] A.C. 170 at 190, *per* Lord Pearson.
[17] *Re Barrell Enterprises* [1973] 1 W.L.R. 19, CA.
[18] CPR PD21, para.1.7.
[19] [2003] EWCA Civ 1547; [2004] 1 W.L.R. 462.

C- was a minor who suffered serious injuries when the bicycle she was riding collided with a car. The issue of contributory negligence arose before proceedings were issued and the parties agreed an 80:20 split in C's favour. No agreement was reached on quantum issues and proceedings were issued. About 18 months later, and just before the claimant reached her majority and would have been capable of adopting the agreement and making it binding, D sought to resile from it and allege a higher degree of contributory negligence, the ground being that C had not been wearing a cycle helmet. C opposed the right of D to withdraw from what she said was a binding agreement.

The Court of Appeal, applying *Dietz v Lennig Chemicals*[20] held that the acceptance of a partial settlement offer in these circumstances did not constitute a binding agreement until and unless the settlement was approved by the court. The court went on to say that advisers of claimants in such circumstances would be well advised to issue proceedings with the specific purpose of securing approval of a partial settlement. Where this occurred pre-proceedings it seems, *per* Simon Brown L.J., that this should be done by proceedings under CPR Pt 7 rather than Pt 8. It should also be noted that the Court of Appeal left open the possibility, not raised in this case, of an argument based on estoppel and change of position.

35–13 In a case where proceedings have been issued, such a concession as was made in *Drinkall* could be secured by obtaining judgment with damages to be assessed.

EFFECT OF APPROVAL AND SETTING ASIDE CONSENT ORDERS ON THE BASIS OF A CHANGE OF CIRCUMSTANCES

35–14 A consent order is, for all that it is made by agreement, nevertheless an order of court. Where a child or patient is involved, the court, in making the order, is exercising a supervisory jurisdiction and is anxious to scrutinise the terms of the proposed settlement. It is not performing a mere rubber-stamping exercise. It requires information to be placed before it to enable it to fulfill its function. Thus, the order made reflects the view and decision of the court and is, therefore, something against which an appeal may lie. The right to appeal against a consent order has existed since 1873[21] and is now contained in s.18(1)(f) of the Supreme Court Act 1981. With few exceptions[22] there is no distinction between appealing against a final and an interim order. Permission is required to appeal against a consent order. If the validity and enforceability of the order stem from the order itself, and not from the agreement underpinning it, the order and, in effect, the agreement may, if the court thinks fit, be set aside on appeal.

---

[20] [1969] 1 A.C. 170.
[21] Supreme Court of Judicature Act 1873, s.49.
[22] For example as to appealing an order extending time for a step to be taken within proceedings.

Where there has been a contested trial, it has long been accepted that an appeal may lie if the factual basis for the decision is falsified by events, even if those events occurred after judgment and could not possibly have been predicted at the time of trial.[23] Granted that the vitiating events have, in all the reported cases, occurred during the currency of appeals on other grounds, this does not seem to be a reason in principle for restricting the operation of the doctrine to cases where there is coincidentally an extant appeal.

35–15

In the matrimonial jurisdiction, it is well established that a consent order providing for ancillary relief may be appealed, even out of time, on the grounds of a change of circumstances which falsifies the basis upon which the order was made.[24] As when it is dealing with patients and children, the court, in family matters, is exercising a supervisory jurisdiction. It was expressly recognised in *Barder v Caluori (Barder)*[25] that the principles expounded in *Mulholland v Mitchell*[26] and *Murphy v Stone-Wallwork (Charlton) Limited*[27] applied to cases involving financial relief on divorce.[28]

35–16

It is suggested that there is no good reason why the court should not, in appropriate circumstances, allow an appeal against a consent order or judgment where there has been a change of circumstances such that the basis upon which the order or judgment was made has been falsified. It is, however, likely that this jurisdiction will be used rarely and with caution and, in the personal injury context, it is probable that only something as extreme as the death of the claimant shortly after the order is made will suffice.[29] The courts will, of course, strive to ensure that parties keep to bargains freely struck except where it would be grossly unfair (and, perhaps, contrary to the public interest) to hold them to the consequences of those bargains.

35–17

It is submitted that appeal will ordinarily be allowed only where:

35–18

(i) a change of circumstances has occurred which renders the terms of the consent order manifestly and significantly unfair; provided that
(ii) the changed circumstances relate to matters which were the subject of an assumption common to both parties[30];

---

[23] See *Murphy v Stone-Wallwork (Charlton) Ltd* [1969] 1 W.L.R. 1023, HL; *Mulholland v Mitchell* [1971] A.C. 666, HL; *Curwen v James* [1963] 1 W.L.R. 748; *McCann v Shepherd* [1973] 1 W.L.R. 540; *Hughes v Singh*, unreported, April 13, 1989, CA.
[24] See *Barder v Caluori (Barder)* [1988] A.C. 20; *Burns v Burns* [2004] EWCA Civ 1258; *Lindsay v Lindsay (Evans)*; and the discussion at Ch.32, above.
[25] [1988] A.C. 20.
[26] [1971] A.C. 666.
[27] [1969] 1 W.L.R. 1023, HL.
[28] [1988] A.C. 20 at 41, *per* Lord Pearson.
[29] Assuming, of course, that the settlement figure contained a large element for future loss, particularly for the claimant's care.
[30] *i.e.* they were not part of the litigation risk posed by rival contentions.

(iii) the changed circumstances were not foreseeable at the time the consent order was made and falsify the common assumption upon which both parties had acted[31];
(iv) the changed circumstances occur within a short time of the order[32];
(v) the party seeking to set aside the order acts promptly on discovering the changed circumstances[33];
(vi) third party rights will not be affected significantly by the setting-aside of the order.

COURT OF PROTECTION[34]

35–19 The Court of Protection supervises the financial affairs of patients. It must be involved where a patient who is litigating has, or will soon have, assets. There is no means of avoiding its involvement. Its procedures are governed by the Court of Protection Rules 2001.[35] It approves approximately 400 new damages awards every year.

35–20 It is appropriate for the Court of Protection to be involved when, and only when, the patient has assets to administer. This may, of course, arise relatively early in proceeding if an interim payment is made. If more than £30,000 is paid in this way the Court of Protection should be asked to appoint a receiver, who alone is empowered to deal with these assets. If between £20,000 and £30,000 is paid in this way, the advice of the master of the Court of Protection should be sought.

35–21 The Court of Protection will charge for the administration and management of funds entrusted to it, and those charges should always be claimed by the claimant in personal injury proceedings, although precise quantification of the anticipated costs will often not be possible until the overall damages sum is known. Fee rates are published by the Court of Protection within the Court of Protection Rules 2001.

35–22 The Court of Protection has wide powers, including the right to grant enduring powers of attorney.[36] Procedures exist for hearings and appeals.[37]

The approval of the Court of Protection should be sought and, if obtained, brought to the attention of the court being asked to approve the settlement of the claim.

---

[31] For example, a change in the multiplier discount rate would normally be foreseeable and foreshadowed by debate, a first instance decision or consultation exercise.
[32] It is probable that this will be measured in months rather than years.
[33] For a matrimonial case in which it was held that the proposed appellant had waited too long, see *Burns v Burns* [2004] EWCA Civ 1258.
[34] See Heywood and Massey, *Court of Protection Practice*.
[35] SI 2001/824, in force from April 1, 2001, as amended.
[36] Under the Enduring Powers of Attorney Act 1985 and the Court of Protection (Enduring Powers of Attorney) Rules 2001 (SI 2001/825), as amended.
[37] See the 2001 Rules, n.35, above.

VARIOUS PRINCIPLES IN SETTLEMENT IN PERSONAL INJURY CASES

Whilst it is not appropriate in this work to consider in detail the quantification of claims for personal injury of the utmost severity, there are some areas which are of particular importance to the question of compromise. These are now dealt with. 35-23

A. Provisional damages

It is well known that in most personal injury cases where there is uncertainty about the future duration and extent of the claimant's losses the court will make the best estimate it can on the evidence, and award damages for future loss on a once-for-all basis. As has been acknowledged candidly by the House of Lords, the one inevitable feature of the product of such guesswork is that it will be shown in time to have been wrong.[38] The courts compensate for lost chances when considering quantum, if not in relation to matters of causation.[39] 35-24

Where, however, the claimant at the time of trial has only a small possibility of a significant deterioration in health which, if it occurred, would markedly increase his losses beyond what could legitimately then be claimed, Parliament has provided that he can protect himself by seeking an award of provisional damages.[40] 35-25

A detailed examination of the criteria for an award of provisional damages is beyond the scope of this work,[41] but the general principle is that the claimant must show "a chance[42] that at some definite or indefinite time in the future [he] will, as a result of the act or omission which gave rise to the cause of action, develop some serious disease or suffer some deterioration in his physical or mental condition". Even if the claimant can show a personal injury carrying with it the risk of the development of a serious disease or deterioration the court still retains a discretion as to whether to make an award of provisional damages. 35-26

---

[38] "There is only one certainty: the future will prove the award to be either too high or low": *Lim Poh Choo v Camden and Islington Health Authority*, [1980] A.C. 174 at 184, *per* Lord Scarman. See also *Thompson v Smiths Shiprepairers (North Shields) Limited* [1984] Q.B. 405 at 443E, *per* Mustill J.: "The whole exercise of assessing damages is shot through with imprecision".

[39] See *Davies v Taylor* [1974] A.C. 207, HL; *Doyle v Wallace* [1998] P.I.Q.R. Q147; *Langford v Hebran & Nynex Cablecom* [2001] EWCA Civ 361, CA.

[40] Supreme Court Act 1981, s.32A; inserted by Administration of Justice Act 1981, s.6 as from July 1, 1985 and County Courts Act 1984, s.52.

[41] See *Kemp & Kemp*, Vol.1, Ch.25.

[42] The chance must be "measurable rather than fanciful": *Wilson v Ministry of Defence* [1991] 1 All E.R. 638.

35-27 A claim for provisional damages must be pleaded.[43] If a claim which includes a claim for provisional damages is settled before proceedings then, whether or not approval would otherwise be necessary, proceedings under CPR Pt 8 should be issued. Whenever, and at whatever stage, a claim is settled on terms which include an award of provisional damages it is vital to comply with the requirements of CPR Pt 41, in particular the requirement for an agreed statement of facts.[44] By definition in such a case there will not have been a reasoned judgment on quantum and, equally plainly, the case may not be reactivated until many years after the settlement is reached. The judge dealing with the case then will have to reconstruct the way in which the immediate damages figure was reached and determine the nature of the condition(s) agreed to be capable of triggering a claim for further damages. Although the court is obliged to keep the case file safe, it would be good practice for the solicitors acting for the parties to make special archiving arrangements for the whole file, at least for the period specified in the order as being the time within which the claimant could return to court.

35-28 Under *Practice Direction: Provisional Damages*,[45] the consent order submitted to the court being invited to approve an award of provisional damages must:

   (i) specify the disease or type of deterioration, or diseases or types of deterioration, which for the purposes of the immediate award have been assumed will not occur and will entitle the claimant to further damages if they do occur;
   (ii) give an award of immediate damages;
   (iii) specify the period or periods within which an application may be made in respect of each disease or deterioration[46];
   (iv) contain a direction as to the documents to be preserved (which will normally be the consent judgment itself, the statements of case, an agreed statement of facts and the agreed medical reports).

B. Structured settlements/orders for periodical payments

35-29 The uncertainty which accompanies once-for-all awards of damages, and which gives the need for the jurisdiction to award provisional damages in suitable cases, can also affect the mechanics of settlement in some high-value cases. Where the severely injured claimant depends upon his compensation for amelioration of his condition (particularly in respect of his care regime),

---

[43] CPR r.41.2(1)(a).
[44] The application itself is made under CPR Pt 23: see PD41, para.4.1.
[45] CPR PD41, para.4.1. See also paras 25-07—25-09 above,
[46] Although it is far from clear that a fixed cut-off point could or should be inserted into all such orders: see *Middleton v Elliott Turbomachinery*, unreported, October 10, 1995, CA.

then as soon as that compensation runs out (which it is likely to do if he outlives the life-expectancy predictions of the medical experts or if his investments do not perform as expected) he will be left dependent upon publicly funded or charitable services.

Where, therefore, the claimant requires an annual income for life, a structured settlement[47] could provide a vehicle for guaranteeing that income. The fashion for structured settlements has ebbed and flowed over the years since their arrival on the scene, but they remain an important part of the machinery available for compensating the seriously injured claimant. Indeed, their availability has now been extended with the dispensation of the consent of the parties as a requirement. 35–30

Until April 2005 structured settlements could not be imposed by the court on either party[48] nor, even if the defendant was in principle prepared to agree a structure, could the defendant be forced to purchase an annuity rather than to fund the structure itself.[49] A decision by a defendant not to offer a structured settlement (or structured settlements generally) was not amenable to judicial review.[50] 35–31

This situation has now altered fundamentally but it may be helpful to give some short detail about how the present picture has emerged. 35–32

Historically, the mechanism by which a structured settlement was achieved in most cases[51] has been that an annuity was purchased (or, in suitable circumstances, the defendant proposed self-funding) on behalf of the claimant.[52] The annuity provided an annual income for life which could be index-linked or guaranteed to rise in some other predetermined manner. Over the years the ambit of structured settlements widened. Any party liable for damages for personal injuries could enter into a structured settlement: for example, the Motor Insurers' Bureau and the Criminal Injuries Compensation Authority could enter into such an arrangement. Mutual insurers could agree to a structured settlement. 35–33

---

[47] Neatly defined at the former CPR PD40, para.1 as "a means of paying a sum awarded or accepted by a claimant by way of instalments for the remainder of the claimant's life".
[48] See *Cowan v Kitson Insulation Ltd* [1992] P.I.Q.R. Q19; *Clegg v Burnley, Pendle and Rossendale HA* unreported, July 17, 2001, Penry-Davey J. The Law Commission rejected a suggestion that claimants be given the right to insist on a structure and the court the power to impose one: Law Com. No.224.
[49] *Clegg v Burnley*, ibid.
[50] See *R. v Liverpool Health Authority NHLSA and Department of Health Ex P. Hopley* [2002] Lloyd's Rep. Med. 494.
[51] Self-funded structures are possible for the National Health Service Litigation Authority. Security for the claimant against future insolvency of the defendant is provided by the National Health Service (Residual Liabilities) Act 1996. Other government bodies may enter into self-funded structures.
[52] It was no longer necessary for it to be purchased from the defendant public liability insurer's life arm.

35-34 The principal advantages of a structured settlement to a claimant were, and remain:

(i) The certainty that the fund cannot be exhausted save by the insolvency of the life company.[53] It cannot be dissipated and the patient will, literally and figuratively, be able to budget on the basis of continued payments for life.
(ii) The tax-free status of the payments. Whilst income tax levels are currently low, a long-term settlement should sensibly take account of fluctuations in their levels, making the absence of a liability to tax potentially very desirable;
(iii) ease of calculation of future income and reduced role for legal, financial and other advice[54];
(iv) Security. If the courts are to take a restrictive approach to incapacity it is perfectly foreseeable that a vulnerable claimant who falls short of strict incapacity could be much better served by a secure (and untouchable) stream of income for life.
(v) Non-interference with means-tested benefits. The effect of the decision in *Beattie v Secretary of State for Social Security*[55] was reversed by the Social Security Amendment (Personal Injury Payments) Regulations 2002[56] and the National Assistance (Assessment of Resources) (Amendment) (No.2) Regulations 2002.[57] Claims for income support—and of course for non-means-tested benefits—are not affected by receipts from a structured settlement.

35-35 The main disadvantage has been perceived to be the inflexibility of compensation based on an annuity which cannot be surrendered once taken out. Nevertheless, structured settlements have on balance, and subject to variations in economic conditions, been considered a welcome development in the law. Other disadvantages are the fluctuating investment market, which makes annuities from time to time unduly expensive, the time-limited nature of many RPI annuities[58] and the failure of annuities to keep pace—even when pegged to RPI—with the actual cost of providing services, particularly care.

35-36 Traditionally, structured settlements have been termed either "top down" or "bottom up". The former concentrates on the true value of the claim (expressed as a lump sum) and calculates from that value what annuity

---

[53] In which case s.4 of the Damages Act 1996 provides for 100 per cent indemnity under the Policyholders Protection Act 1975.
[54] This is particularly important given the reluctance of the courts to compensate for the cost of obtaining such advice: see *Eagle v Chambers* [2004] EWCA Civ 1033; and *Page v Plymouth Hospitals* [2004] EWHC 1154, Davis J].
[55] [2001] 1 W.L.R. 1404.
[56] SI 2002/2442.
[57] SI 2002/2531.
[58] They are not available in products which last beyond 2035.

payments can be secured. Where this type of structure is contemplated it is important to agree the lump sum (and obtain approval for it) with the option of pursuing a structured settlement. That way, if the investigations of a structure do not bear fruit, both sides are committed to the lump sum settlement. A "bottom up" structure concentrates on the needs of the claimant and the income required to meet those needs, rather than the litigation value of the claim taken as a whole.

35–37 The world of structured settlements has been materially altered by the amendment to s.2 of the Damages Act 1996 effected by s.100 of the Courts Act 2003.[59] Since the coming into force of this provision on April 1, 2005 the court is required in all cases involving claims for future pecuniary loss in respect of personal injury to consider making an order that the damages are paid wholly or partly by way of periodical payments. The need to consider this is required in all cases where settlement had not been reached at the time this provision came into force. An additional power (to order variable periodical payments) is likely to apply only to claims issued after April 1, 2005. The court may also order periodical payments in respect of other damages (*i.e.* those not in respect of future pecuniary loss) with the consent of the parties.

35–38 Crucial features of the new regime will be that the payments will be tax free, with the starting point of linkage to RPI (though this may be altered by the court) and the continuity of payment must be secure. This latter provision may cause some practical problems. Certain organisations which are regular litigants in this field may be neither entitled to self-fund structures, for want of established financial security, nor able to purchase suitable products on the market. This is likely to be a real problem in many cases.

35–39 The way in which the new regime will operate in practice will doubtless emerge over time; however, certain Practice Directions have been issued which give some guidance.

35–40 CPR Pt 41, the new Practice Direction and the relevant statutory instruments set out some of the requirements to which the court should have regard, for example the size of annual payments and the (reasoned) wishes of both claimant and defendant. Whilst the key criterion is the claimant's needs rather than his wishes, it must be open to doubt whether the court would impose an order for periodical payments upon an unwilling claimant, provided always that the reasons he advanced against it were acceptable and his fund is suitably protected, perhaps by its administration by the Court of

---

[59] The change has even extended to terminology. "Periodical payments" has now replaced "structured settlements", though the meaning is the same.

Protection. Procedurally, Pt 41 sets out the matters which must be dealt with in any order for periodical payments, whether made by consent or by the court.

35–41   The parties may, in their statements of case, set out whether they consider an order for periodical payments or lump sum to be more appropriate. Particulars may be ordered by the court of any such plea.[60] The court will give an indication "as soon as practicable" as to which way it is thinking. This is likely to be at a case management conference and at an early stage.

35–42   Part 36 has been amended to reflect the changes effected by the new system of periodical payments. The Civil Procedure (Amendment No.3) Rules 2004[61] make such amendments. Costs consequences follow if the claimant fails to secure an award which is "more advantageous" than a Pt 36 offer including an offer in relation to periodical payments (or, as the case may be, does secure an award which is "more advantageous"), but the phrase "more advantageous" is not defined in the rule.[61a]

35–43   However that may be, the new CPR r.36.2A(5) provides that an offer must state the amount of the lump sum element, what part of the offer (if any) relates to periodical payments, the amount and duration of any such periodical payments, the basis of variation (*i.e.* by reference to what indexation) and the security of the funding. A party may also state what part of the offer relates to future pecuniary loss in the form of a lump sum and what amount relates to other damages by way of lump sum.

35–44   Such offers may only be accepted as a whole and not in part, and the defendant must actually pay the lump sum element to have costs protection.

35–45   How far the courts will permit a departure from RPI as the indexation method (*e.g.* in response to submissions that actual costs of care have always risen more steeply than RPI in the past), is unclear. RPI will be the starting point and, it seems, is to be used in the majority of cases.[62]

35–46   Security of continuity of payment is a crucial feature of the new regime. There is, after all, little point in having an award for annual income payments if the paying party is unlikely in the future to be solvent and to be

---

[60] CPR r.41.5.
[61] See Appendix 2 at para.A2–03 and para.25–10, above.
[61a] *cf.* paras 23–04—23–07, above.
[62] *Cooke v United Bristol Healthcare* [2003] EWCA Civ 1370 appears to have laid to rest the argument that the courts may depart from the discount rate set by the Lord Chancellor using his powers under s.1(1) of the Damages Act 1996, but this decision is not determinative of the issue of when the court may depart from RPI as the indexation benchmark. Parliament plainly intended that there be circumstances where such a departure should take place, but there is as yet no useful judicial guidance as to when this will happen.

able to make such payments. In such circumstances, a traditional lump sum award would be much to be preferred. Section 2(4) of the Act sets out how payments are to be secured, but there is a power in that subsection, and expanded upon in CPR r.41.9, to vary this. It is likely that this power will only rarely be used.[63]

In high value cases, therefore, such as will in many cases be brought by patients and minors, the financial security of the paying party is of the first importance. This will probably be a matter for expert evidence, save where the paying party is a government body or protected by ministerial guarantee.

35–47

Periodical payments: procedure

Hitherto, consideration of the viability of a structured settlement has tended to await trial or lump sum offer, with the issue being adjourned for further consideration. The relevant Practice Direction (to CPR Pt 40) did require the parties to raise the issue of a structured settlement at case management hearings wherever the claim for future losses was likely to exceed £500,000, but now the ability to order periodical payments will be possible in all personal injury claims containing an element of future losses. It is likely that this will be raised at an early stage in all such cases, and practitioners should give early thought to this possibility and to obtaining the necessary evidence.

35–48

The terms of any order adjourning for consideration of a structured settlement were important. Crucial features were that:

35–49

(i) it could not be a final order, nor could the money pass to the claimant. If this happened the tax advantages of structuring were lost;
(ii) it had to contain the court's approval to the settlement figure in principle, with the lump sum or future periodical payments identified;
(iii) it should not have entered judgment for the claimant;
(iv) it should have provided for the funding of the financial intermediary who was to investigate the structure, possibly with a ceiling on the expenditure. By the PD40C (which came into force in October 2003) the costs of such advice were to be treated as costs of the litigation);
(v) it should have contained cross-undertakings: from the claimant to limit his claim to the sum agreed and from the defendant to keep the offer open pending investigation of the structure;
(vi) it should have provided for the consolidation in one place (preferably) of the full sum agreed, which could be made up of sums in court and sums to be paid.

---

[63] For a more detailed analysis, see *Kemp & Kemp*, Ch.23.

35-50 Where a consent order for a structured settlement was sought, the procedure was governed by PD40C and Pt 23. The evidence required was as set out in PD40C (4) and (5).

35-51 Under the new regime, if the possibility of an order for periodical payments has been identified and researched in sufficient time, such adjournments as were commonplace in the past may become less frequent, and the trial judge can make such orders as he thinks fit. Otherwise, some elements of the adjournment order set out above will be suitable.

35-52 Under the new regime, whether by agreement or order, periodical payments orders may be varied. The Damages (Variation of Periodical Payments) Order 2004[64] flows from s.2B of the Damages Act 1996 (introduced by s.100 of the Courts Act 2003) and contains guidance on the circumstances in which an order for periodical payments may be made. As with provisional damages, the order may be varied if there is a significant deterioration in condition. Importantly, and unlike in the case of provisional damages, periodical payments may be varied—if the order so provides—where the claimant enjoys a significant improvement in his condition. Defendants will wish to be alive to this possibility. The procedural code (art.5 of the 2004 Order) is very similar in its effect to the terms of traditional orders for provisional damages.

35-53 Practice Direction 41B provides some examples of circumstances in which the court may make a variable order under the new law. The examples given are:

    (i) where a claimant's condition may change leading to an increase/decrease in needs and, thus, recurring costs;
    (ii) where gratuitous carers (whose care costs will not be assessed on a full professional basis) may cease to provide such care;
    (iii) where the claimant's educational circumstances may change;
    (iv) where the claimant would have received a promotion and/or increase in pay;
    (v) where the claimant will cease to earn.

Clearly, this list is not intended to be exhaustive.

C. The recoupment of benefits[65]

35-54 The Social Security (Recovery of Benefits) Act 1997, and the regulations made under it,[66] form a detailed code dealing with the recoupment by the State from a tortfeasor of benefits paid to an injured person by reason of injuries caused by the tort.

---

[64] SI 2004/841.
[65] For further reading, see *The Means Tested Benefits Legislation* (Sweet & Maxwell) and Richard Lewis, *Deducting Benefits from Damages for Personal Injury* (OUP, 1999).
[66] Social Security (Recovery of Benefits) Regulations 1997 (SI 1997/2205).

So far as settlement is concerned, the following points should be noted: 35–55

(1) No case should be settled without sight of a current certificate of recoverable benefits.
(2) It has been argued that where the claimant is a patient or a child, the consent order giving effect to the settlement of the case should specify the sums awarded for each head of loss claimed in the same way that the court is obliged by s.15 of the 1997 Act to do when delivering judgment after a contested hearing.[67] The argument advanced is that since the claimant is by definition incapable of giving consent, the exemption given at s.15(1) of the Act[68] does not apply. It is submitted that this is an unduly technical argument and that actions settled by or on behalf of children and patients are settled by consent, albeit that this consent is given by a litigation friend and subject to the approval of the court.
(3) Where a Pt 36 payment is made by the defendant the claimant must beat the gross figure stated to escape the adverse consequences of Pt 36.[69]
(4) If a certificate is appealed after the settlement of an action, it seems that the benefit of such an appeal—absent agreement to the contrary—will inure to the claimant. Where, however, the agreement is for payment of a sum of money only—and the benefits position is not addressed—it seems that the claimant is entitled only to the net sum, after deduction of benefits.[70]

D. Costs

A litigation friend must give an undertaking to be responsible for any costs awarded against the child or patient, subject to a right to recoupment from the assets of the claimant under a disability. The litigation friend does, however, enjoy the protection afforded by the existence of a Legal Services Commission funding agreement. 35–56

Just as the court will be careful to ensure that the claim of a patient or child has not been undervalued, whether negligently or otherwise, by his legal advisers, so too will it look to see that he is not overcharged by those same advisers. 35–57

Wherever an order is made for money to be paid to or by a patient or child the court will generally assess the costs payable by the patient or child to his solicitor as well as those payable by any other party to the patient or 35–58

---

[67] See *Personal Injury Handbook* (2nd ed., Sweet & Maxwell), Chs 16–19.
[68] Which exempts consent orders from the requirements of s.15.
[69] CPR r.36.23(4) and the Practice Direction.
[70] *Rees v West Glamorgan County Council* [1994] P.I.Q.R. P37. See para.5–13 above.

child. This latter step is not necessary where there has been a default costs certificate. Only that which the court assesses as payable may be paid to the solicitor by or on behalf of the patient or child.[71]

35–59　A detailed assessment of the solicitor/client costs may be dispensed with (a) where one is not necessary to protect the patient or child, (b) where another party has agreed to pay those costs and the solicitor has waived any right to seek more from his client, (c) where there has been a summary assessment and a waiver by the solicitor of any right to claim more and (d) where there is a legal expenses or other insurer liable to pay those costs and the court is satisfied that it has the means to do so.[72]

35–60　A practice grew up over time of bodies which were undoubtedly "good for" the payment of lump sums making offers by way of letter rather than payments in. Those who made these payments relied upon decisions since *Calderbank* and the terms of the CPR. Their avowed reason was that since the length of time the defendant would be deprived of the use of funds would be unascertainable in the event the offer were refused, and since many such bodies (*e.g.* the Department of Health) had other calls on their funds, it was contrary to the public good to deprive them of those funds when no one could be in any doubt that they would be in a position to meet any award or agreed settlement sum whenever that was arrived at.

35–61　The Court of Appeal has now considered such letters specifically in the case of the National Health Service Litigation Authority, a body funded by the Department of Health. In *Crouch v King's Healthcare Trust*; *Murry v Blackburn Hyndburn & Ribble Valley Healthcare NHS Trust*[73] the court considered the complementary powers under CPR rr.36.1(2) and 44.3. It held on the facts of those cases that the letter of offer should for all litigious purposes be treated as a payment in and attract similar costs protection.

35–62　It should be noted that in *Crouch* and *Murry* the defendant conceded that its letter of offer should be treated for all purposes as a payment in, *i.e.* that restrictions on its being withdrawn should apply similarly to those which apply to payments in. Attention should also be given to the precise status of the Department of Health, protected as it is by the National Health Services (Residual Liabilities) Act 1996 making its liabilities secure beyond doubt. Without those two protections, it must be doubted whether a letter of offer would be treated as equal to a payment in in other cases.

35–63　There is a continuing interest in, and encouragement for, alternative dispute resolution (ADR). In serious personal injury cases, for example major clinical negligence actions, it is routine for the Queen's Bench masters to

---

[71] CPR r.48.5.
[72] CPR PD51.
[73] [2005] 1 W.L.R. 2015, discussed at paras 18–03—18–07, above.

make an order requiring the parties to address their minds to ADR well in advance of trial and, if they cannot agree upon it, to set out their reasons in a sealed document to be opened by the trial judge only when costs come to be considered. Costs consequences can, though not always will, follow a refusal to enter into ADR. In *Halsey v Milton Keynes*[74] the Court of Appeal took the opportunity of considering the circumstances in which a refusal to enter into mediation might be penalised in costs. Without attempting an exhaustive list of factors relevant to the exercise of the court's discretion it held that they may include (i) the nature of the dispute, (ii) the merits of the case, (iii) the extent to which other settlement methods had been attempted, (iv) whether the costs of ADR would be disproportionately high, (v) whether any delay in setting up and attending the ADR would have been prejudicial, and (vi) whether the ADR had a reasonable prospect of success. The court went on to say that where a successful party had refused to agree to ADR despite the court's encouragement, that was a factor which could be taken into account.

E. Money laundering

Practitioners concerned about the impact of the money-laundering provisions of the Proceeds of Crime Act 2002 upon the settlement of litigation should take some comfort from the decision of the Court of Appeal in the case of *Bowman v Fels*.[75] In this case the Court of Appeal, effectively overturning the earlier case of *P v P*,[76] held that s.328 of the Act, held that settling litigation does not amount to becoming concerned in an arrangement which facilitates the acquisition, retention, use or control of criminal property.

35–64

---

[74] n.73 above.
[75] [2005] EWCA Civ 226.
[76] [2003] EWHC 2260 (Fam).

PART 10

Employment Contracts and Compromise

CHAPTER 36

Employment Contracts and Compromise

INTRODUCTION

For many years the contractual relationship between employer and employee has been augmented by a number of statutory protections provided to employees. This process of statutory protection has increased such that it now includes protection in regard to dismissal (*i.e.* the right not to be unfairly dismissed); on the transfer of the business in which the employees have been employed under the Transfer of Undertakings (Protection of Employment) Regulations 1981[1]; against discrimination based on sex, race or disability; and in connection with the conditions of employment (for example, under the Working Time Regulations 1998[2] and National Minimum Wage Age 1998). 36–01

It follows that, when considering the settlement of disputes arising in the employment setting, it is frequently necessary to consider both contractual claims (for example, for wrongful dismissal or alleged breach of restrictive covenants) and statutory claims. This distinction is reflected in the different forums in which such disputes can be heard. Generally, contractual claims are heard in the ordinary civil courts (although Employment Tribunals now have a limited jurisdiction to determine some claims of breach of contract).[3] Statutory claims are determined by Employment Tribunals. 36–02

In regard to the compromise of claims arising from disputes in the employment setting, important differences exist between the compromise of contractual and common law claims, on the one hand, and the 36–03

---

[1] SI 1981/1794.
[2] SI 1998/1833.
[3] See the Industrial Tribunal Extension of Jurisdiction Orders 1994.

compromise of statutory claims, on the other. In essence, contractual claims (including those which can be heard by Employment Tribunals) are subject to the same general principles that apply to compromise agreements in other civil disputes. This is in sharp contrast to the compromise of statutory claims. With regard to the latter, stringent limitations on the ability to compromise such claims are designed to protect employees from entering into ill-advised settlement agreements.

CONTRACTUAL CLAIMS

36–04 Relatively little needs be said in this chapter about the compromise of these claims, because, as already stated, they are subject to the general principles that apply to the compromise of other civil law claims. Reference should, however, be made to three particular matters.

General release

36–05 The first of these matters arises from the decision of the House of Lords in *Bank of Credit and Commerce International SA v Ali*,[4] the facts of which have been given elsewhere.[5] As indicated previously,[6] the majority of the House of Lords (Lord Hoffmann dissenting) held that, on its true construction, the compromise agreement did not extend to claims for stigma damages. In particular, the majority held that, whilst a party was capable of agreeing to release claims of which he was not, and could not have been, aware, any such agreement had to use clear and unambiguous terms to that effect. That was not the case with the compromise agreement of 1990. Lord Hoffmann dissented. He was of the view that the compromise agreement of 1990 was sufficiently wide in its terms to include a claim for stigma damages. Lord Hoffmann did recognise that, in the context of a general release, a party should not be allowed to rely on that release when that party has failed to disclose the existence of a claim of which it had knowledge and of which it believes the other party is unaware. However that did not, in Lord Hoffmann's view, apply to the facts of the *Ali* case. The other members of the House of Lords did not express any view on this aspect of the case.

36–06 As is apparent from the above, a variety of views were expressed by the individual members of the House of Lords in this case. At present there is no doubt that those who wish to compromise all possible claims (whether or not known by the parties and/or recognised by the law at the time of the

---

[4] [2002] 1 A.C. 251.
[5] See para.5–24, above.
[6] See paras 5–23—54–28, above.

compromise) must be careful to use clear and comprehensive express terms to obtain this effect. Further, a party seeking to obtain a general release from another who is aware of the existence of some possible claim of which the other party is unaware, is at risk of being prevented from relying on that general release on the basis that any such reliance would be unconscionable.

Stress-related personal injury

The first of the two further matters to be discussed in the context of contractual or common law claims between employers and employees arises from the recognition of claims for stress-related injury caused by unreasonable working practices. 36–07

It has long been a common practice to exempt from the scope of a "full and final settlement" between an employer and employee any claim that the employee has or may have in regard to personal injury. This practice may need to be considered with greater care in the light of the development of the line of authority that employees may be able to claim damages for personal injury from their employer for breach of duty of care in relation to failing to protect the employee from work-related stress.[7] 36–08

References

Finally in this context, a further development in the law of employment is the blossoming of a duty of care in regard to the giving of references by an employer. The employer owes a duty of care both to the employee (or ex-employee) with regard to whom the reference is provided and to the recipient of the reference. The basis for this liability was set out by the House of Lords in *Spring v Guardian Assurance Plc*.[8] 36–09

It is not uncommon for a settlement agreement in the employment setting to include a term that the employer will provide a reference in regard to the employee to any interested parties and will do so in agreed terms. An agreement of this nature can give rise to difficult issues. Thus, for example, it is often the case that those seeking references will require the referee to complete a questionnaire relating to the employee. Indeed, in some activities (such as the provision of financial services) the completion of a questionnaires about the employee is mandatory—for example, as to their compliance or non-compliance with financial regulations. The issue 36–10

---

[7] See *Hartman v South Essex Mental Health and Community Care NHS Trust* [2005] EWCA Civ 6.
[8] [1995] A.C. 296.

may arise as to whether completion of any such questionnaire in addition to providing the agreed reference constitutes a breach of the settlement agreement.

36–11 Again, difficult questions can arise as to the relationship between the duty of an employer to provide an agreed reference and the duty of honesty owed to the recipient of that reference. The range of difficult questions that can arise in the context of an agreement to provide a particular reference was recognised by the Court of Appeal in *John Cox v Sun Alliance Life Ltd*.[9] However, those issues did not need to be determined on the facts of that case.

36–12 Those involved in settling employment disputes in which the settlement includes an agreement to provide an agreed reference would be well advised to bear in mind the words of Mummery L.J. in that case:

> "I would add a final word for the benefit of employers and employees who prefer to avoid time consuming, costly litigation about job references. In a case where the terms of an agreed resignation or of the compromise of an unfair dismissal claim make provision for the supply of a reference, the parties should ensure as far as possible that the exact wording of a fair and accurate reference is fully discussed, clearly agreed and carefully recorded in writing in COT3 at the same time as other severance terms."

36–13 Before leaving the compromise of contractual, common law claims, it should be noted that, as already mentioned, in respect of the limited jurisdiction enjoyed by Employment Tribunals to determine claims for breach of contract, the same rules apply in regard to compromise agreements as apply to the settlement of contractual and common law claims in the civil courts.[10]

STATUTORY CLAIMS

36–14 As indicated above,[11] the rules that apply to the compromise of statutory claims by employees are very different from those applicable to the compromise of common law claims. The basic scheme adopted in connection with the compromise of statutory claims is for these to be rendered

---

[9] [2001] I.R.L.R. 448.
[10] *Sutherland v Network Alliance Ltd* [2000] I.R.L.R. 12. In that case a compromise agreement that did not meet the statutory requirements to be an effective compromise of statutory claims was held to be effective in barring a claim for breach of contract brought in the Employment Tribunal.
[11] See para.36–03, above.

void and ineffective unless certain conditions are met as to the involvement of third parties in the making of those agreements, whose involvement is intended to ensure a degree of protection for the interests of the employee. Two broad categories of third parties are recognised for these purposes: conciliation officers of ACAS and "independent advisers".

36–15 Section 203(1) of the Employment Rights Act 1996 (ERA 1996) sets out the general prohibition against contracting out of rights contained within the Act. Section 203(1) declares "void" any contractual term that purports to exclude the operation of the ERA 1996 or which precludes a person from bringing proceedings thereunder before an Employment Tribunal. This provision, and its predecessors, have been given a liberal interpretation by the courts against the background of arguments designed to escape from its consequences.[12]

3–16 In *Igbo v Johnson Matthey Chemicals Ltd*,[13] A wished to visit her husband and children in Nigeria and R, her employers, agreed to an extended holiday entitlement (by some three days) to enable her to do this. She was required to agree to a term of this arrangement to the effect that if she did not return to work on the day following the termination of the extended holiday her contract of employment would "automatically terminate on that date". She was unwell on her return from the holiday and unable to return to work as required. She had a medical certificate confirming her illness, but R decided to treat her contract as terminated in accordance with the agreement. The Court of Appeal held, rejecting the suggestion that there had been a consensual termination of the contract, that she had been dismissed and that the effect of the agreement was to "limit the operation" of the provisions in the Act that gave A the right not to be unfairly dismissed. Hence the agreement was void.

3–17 In *Courage Take Home Limited v Keys*,[14] A was dismissed and an industrial tribunal adjudged that the dismissal was unfair. The question of the remedy was adjourned. Before the restored hearing, and without the intervention of a conciliation officer, A accepted the sum of £9,500 from R in full and final settlement of his claim. Subsequently, A sought to pursue his claim for compensation. The Employment Appeal Tribunal held that the agreement concerning the £9,500 was void within s.140(1)(b) of the Employment Protection (Consolidation) Act 1978 (the predecessor to s.203 ERA 1996) in that it precluded or sought to preclude A from bringing proceedings for compensation under the Act. A was, nonetheless, held not entitled to seek further compensation as it would not be "just and equitable" under s.74 of that Act.

36–18 However, the broad terms of s.203(1) of the ERA 1996 are subject to s.203(2), which sets out a number of exceptions to this general prohibition against contracting out of rights accorded to employees within the Act. By far the two most important of these exceptions are set out at s.203(2)(e) and (2)(f). These provide:

---

[12] *Council of Engineering Institutions v Maddison* [1977] I.C.R. 30; *Naqvi v Stephens Jewellers Ltd* [1978] I.C.R. 631, EAT.
[13] [1986] I.C.R. 505.
[14] [1986] I.C.R. 874.

"(2) Subsection (1)—

. . .

(e) does not apply to any agreement to refrain from instituting or continuing proceedings where a conciliation officer has taken action under section 18 of the Industrial Tribunals Act 1996; and

(f) does not apply to any agreement to refrain from instituting or continuing proceedings within section 18(1) of the Industrial Tribunals Act 1996 if the conditions regulating compromise agreements under this Act are satisfied in relation to the agreement."

36–19 The reference to a conciliation officer is, of course, a reference to an ACAS conciliation officer. The reference to "the conditions regulating compromise agreements" includes reference to the involvement of "independent advisers" in the making of those agreements.

36–20 Hence, there can be a valid and effective compromise of various statutory rights enjoyed under the ERA 1996 that are or can be enforced before an Employment Tribunal only if the compromise agreement has been made under the auspices of ACAS or with the involvement of an independent adviser acting on behalf of the employee. The particular rights enjoyed under the ERA 1996 that fall within these terms are:

(1) the right to an itemised pay statement *per* s.8 of the ERA 1996;
(2) the right not to suffer unauthorised deductions from wages *per* s.13 of the Act;
(3) the right not to have to make payments to an employer *per* s.15 of the Act;
(4) the right not to be obliged to be subject to more than the maximum permitted deductions from wages in retail employment *per* ss.18 and 21 of the Act;
(5) the right to guarantee payments *per* s.28 of the Act;
(6) the right to parental leave *per* s.80 of the ERA;
(7) the right to a written statement of reasons for dismissal *per* s.92 of the Act;
(8) the right to a redundancy payment *per* s.135 of the Act;
(9) protection from suffering detriment in employment under Pt V of the Act;
(10) the right to time off from work under Pt VI of the Act;
(11) rights in connection with suspension from work under Pt VII of the Act;
(12) the right not to be unfairly dismissed under Pt X of the Act.

36–21 Provisions similar to those found in the ERA 1996 apply in regard to the compromise of rights enjoyed under other legislation. These are in particular:

(1) the Equal Pay Act 1970 and the Sex Discrimination Act 1975 (SDA 1975) (s.77 of the SDA 1978);
(2) the Race Relations Act 1976 (RRA 1976) (s.72 of the RRA 1976);
(3) the Disability Discrimination Act 1995 (DDA 1995) (s.9 of the DDA 1995);
(4) the National Minimum Wage Act 1998 (s.49 of that Act);
(5) the Working Time Regulations 1998[15] (reg.35);
(6) the Transnational Information and Consultation of Employees Regulations 1999[16] (reg.41);
(7) the Part-Time Workers (Prevention of Less Favourable Treatment) Regulations 2000[17] (reg.9);
(8) ss.10–13 of the Employment Relations Act 1999 which are concerned with rights associated with the right to be accompanied at a disciplinary or grievance hearing. These sections are to be treated as provisions within Pt 5 of the ERA 1996 for the purposes of s.203;
(9) the Fixed-Term Employees (Prevention of Less Favourable Treatment) Regulations 2002[18];
(10) the Employment Equality (Sexual Orientation) Regulations 2003[19];
(11) the Employment Equality (Religion or Belief) Regulations 2003[20];
(12) the Merchant Shipping (Working Time: Inland Waterways) Regulations 2003[21];
(13) the European Public Limited Liability Company Regulations 2004.[22]

Likewise a number of rights accorded by the Trade Union and Labour Relations (Consolidation) Act 1992 ("TULRCA 1992") are subject to the same scheme whereby compromise agreements are rendered void unless made through the officers of ACAS or with the involvement of an independent adviser on behalf of the employee.[23] Those rights under TULRCA 1992 are:

(1) the right of trade union members not to be unjustifiably disciplined or suffer unauthorised or excessive deductions from subscriptions, *per* ss.64, 68 and 86;
(2) the rights in regard to union membership and activities set out at ss.137, 138, 146, 168–170 and 164, being rights not to suffer

---

[15] SI 1998/1833.
[16] SI 1999/3323.
[17] SI 2000/1551.
[18] SI 2002/2034.
[19] SI 2003/1661.
[20] SI 2003/1660.
[21] SI 2003/3049.
[22] SI 2004/2326.
[23] TULRCA 1992, s.288.

detriment in relation to union membership or expulsion or exclusion from a union and rights in connection with time off for trade union duties and activities;

(3) rights in connection with the recognition of unions within s.70(B) and para.156 of Sch.A1.

36–23 In addition, there can be an effective compromise of rights in connection with consultation with employers' representatives (see ss.188 and 190) through an ACAS-conciliated agreement, but not through a compromise agreement effected with the involvement of an independent adviser.[24]

36–24 So far in this chapter only the general scheme that applies to the settlement of statutory claims has been described. The details relating to agreements achieved both with the assistance of ACAS conciliation officers and through the involvement of independent advisers will now be addressed.

SETTLEMENT ACHIEVED THROUGH INTERVENTION OF CONCILIATION OFFICER

36–25 Under s.18(2) of the Employment Tribunals Act 1996[25] it is the duty of a conciliation officer, where he has been invited to act, or where he decides that he should act, "to endeavour to promote a settlement of the complaint without its being determined by an Industrial Tribunal".[26] When an agreement has been achieved through the intervention of a conciliation officer, the usual procedure is for the conciliation officer to record the terms on what is known as Form COT3, a document that each of the parties or his representative[27] is asked to sign before onward transmission to the Employment Tribunal. Consistent with ordinary principles,[28] the reduction of the agreement to writing is not essential to its enforceability unless, of course, it is a condition of the agreement that a form of document such as form COT3 is executed.[29]

---

[24] TULRCA 1992, s.288(2c).
[25] See also s.18(3) in relation to other matters in respect of which Employment Tribunal proceedings can be brought.
[26] The meaning of this expression and the scope of a conciliation officer's duties in this regard were considered by the House of Lords in *Moore v Duport Furniture Products Ltd* [1982] I.C.R. 84. See also *Hennessey v Craigmyle & Co Ltd* [1996] I.C.R. 461, CA.
[27] The signature of a representative will bind the party upon whose behalf it is purportedly written provided the representative has ostensible authority to act: *Freeman v Sovereign Chicken Ltd* [1991] I.C.R. 853, where the signature of a representative of the Citizens Advice Bureau was held by the Employment Appeal Tribunal to bind the party on whose behalf it was written. However, in *Gloystarne & Co Ltd v Martin* [2001] I.R.L.R. 15, the trade union representative was found to lack ostensible authority to conclude a settlement agreement on behalf of the employee through ACAS.
[28] See Ch.3, paras 3–30 *et seq.*, above.
[29] *Gilbert v Kembridge Fibres Ltd* [1984] I.C.R. 188; *Gloystarne & Co Ltd v Martin* [2001] I.R.L.R. 15.

36-26 A settlement achieved through the medium of a conciliation officer is extremely difficult to challenge subsequently. It would probably require evidence that the conciliation officer acted in bad faith or adopted unfair methods in seeking to achieve a settlement before consideration would be given to setting aside the agreement.[30] It should be noted that, unlike the situation which had obtained prior to the passing of s.39 of the Trade Union Reform and Employment Rights Act 1993,[31] a conciliation officer will not simply "nod through" an agreement already concluded between the parties. His active involvement[32] in promoting the agreement is required for an agreement to be regarded as one made through his intervention and thus binding by virtue of s.203(2)(e) of the ERA 1996. An agreement entered into other than with the active intervention of the conciliation officer will need to fulfil the statutory requirements of a "compromise agreement" or "compromise contract" for it to be binding. Indeed, it was because of ACAS's refusal to "nod through" agreements reached between the parties that the alternative method of settling disputes through the involvement of an independent adviser was introduced.

36-27 As has already been noted, conciliation officers may be called upon to assist in connection with disputes other than simply unfair dismissal claims, including those arising from alleged sex, race and disability discrimination under the SDA 1975, the RRA 1976 and the DDA 1995, respectively. Not infrequently a settlement of proceedings for unfair dismissal is achieved through the intervention of a conciliation officer and a payment is made by the employer said expressly to be "in full and final settlement of all claims which [the employee] has or may have against [the employer] arising from [his/her] employment or out of its termination". The Employment Appeal Tribunal has held[33] that the use of such a formula in an unfair dismissal case will not operate to prevent the pursuit of claims which otherwise might be settled through the intervention of a conciliation officer. The use of such words will be confined to "those matters which are within [the parties'] presumed intention at the time". On that basis it would seem, therefore, that express reference to the other possible claims for relief would need to be made in any such formulation to achieve also a final resolution of those matters.

36-28 The role of ACAS officers has been extended by regs 22–24 of Sch.1 to the Employment Tribunals (Constitution and Rules of Procedure) Regulations 2004.[34] In essence these provisions impose a compulsory period of

---

[30] *Slack v Greenbaum (Plant Hire) Ltd* [1983] I.C.R. 617.
[31] This section of the Act became operative on August 30, 1993.
[32] s.203(2)(e) refers to an agreement concluded after the conciliation officer has "taken action" under s.18 of the Employment Tribunals Act 1996.
[33] *Livingstone v Hepworth Refractories Ltd* [1992] I.C.R. 287. This case might have to be looked at afresh in the light of *Bank of Credit and Commerce International SA v Ali*, n.4, above.
[34] SI 2004/2351.

conciliation through ACAS before there can be a substantive hearing of a relevant claim presented to an Employment Tribunal. A relevant claim is any claim in which ACAS would otherwise have authority to seek to effect conciliation other than a claim for discrimination (including a claim in connection with the protected disclosure provisions) or a claim for national security proceedings. Relevant claims will either fall within the category of claims to which the "standard period" of imposed conciliation will apply (*i.e.* 13 weeks) or within those to which the shortened period applies (*i.e.* 7 weeks). Provisions exist which allow for the extension or abbreviation of those periods and, indeed, for the removal of the compulsory period of conciliation.

COMPROMISE AGREEMENTS

36–29 For an agreement between the parties, achieved other than through the intervention of a conciliation officer, to be binding, it must satisfy the conditions that regulate the form and content of a "compromise agreement" or "compromise contract" (which is the expression used in the SDA 1975 and RRA 1976). Section 203(3) of the ERA 1996 provides that:

    (a) the agreement must be in writing;
    (b) the agreement must relate to the particular complaint;
    (c) the employee must have received advice from a relevant independent adviser as to the terms and effect of the proposed agreement and in particular its effect on his ability to pursue his rights before an Employment Tribunal;
    (d) there must be in force, when the adviser gives the advice, a policy of insurance covering the risk of a claim by the employee in respect of loss arising in consequence of the advice;
    (e) the agreement must identify the adviser; and
    (f) the agreement must state that the conditions regulating compromise agreements under the Act are satisfied.

36–30 As already made clear, similar provisions apply to compromising claims through the involvement of an independent adviser under other legislation such as the SDA 1975, the RRA 1996 or the DDA 1995. In regard to each type of claim compromised through the involvement of an independent adviser, it is vital that the compromise agreement stipulates that the conditions relating to each relevant enactment have been satisfied. A number of further matters need to be discussed in regard to these statutory compromise agreements or contracts.

Independent advisers

36–31 Originally the requirement was that the employee be assisted by a legal adviser (a solicitor or barrister). However, the definition of relevant advisers has been extended (and can be further extended by order of the Secretary of State).

"Independent advisers" currently comprise:

(1) qualified lawyers (which includes certain legal executives);
(2) representatives of trade unions who have been certified to be competent to give advice;
(3) advisers who work for an advice centre so long as that advice is provided without charge and they have been certified as competent to give advice.

As to the expression "qualified lawyers", anyone acting for the employer or an associated employer involved in the matter in dispute does not constitute an "independent" adviser. Similarly, representatives of trade unions and advisers from advice centres are not "independent" if the trade union or advice centre is the employer or an associated employer of the employee. 36–32

The particular complaint or proceedings

The legislation confines the scope of effective "compromise agreements" or contracts to the compromise of the particular "complaint" or "proceedings". It appears that these words are used interchangeably and there can be no doubt that these agreements can be effective to compromise both potential, as well as actual, proceedings. The intention behind this restriction is to ensure that compromise agreements cannot be used effectively to constitute a blanket "full and final settlement" of all claims that an employee "has or might have" against an employer. The involvement of an independent adviser can only render effective compromise agreements which seek to settle the specific dispute or disputes raised between employee and employer. However, if a number of disputes exist between an employee and an employer, each can be compromised in the single compromise agreement provided the proper formulation is used in connection with each claim. There is no need for separate agreements in relation to each.[35] The confinement of a "compromise agreement" to the particular complaint or proceedings involved means that such an agreement is more limited in its scope than an agreement effected through an ACAS conciliation officer. 36–33

STATUTORY COMPROMISE AGREEMENTS, ACAS CONCILIATION AND CONTINUITY OF EMPLOYMENT

In a number of circumstances where an employee has been dismissed but has been reinstated or re-engaged by his or her employer, continuity of employment is preserved. These circumstances include those where an 36–34

---

[35] See *Lunt v Merseyside TEC Ltd* [1999] I.C.R. 17.

employee who has alleged unfair dismissal or sex or race discrimination is re-employed after the intervention of an ACAS conciliation officer or after the making of a compromise agreement through the involvement of an independent adviser. The full provisions are set out in the Employment Protection (Continuity of Employment) Regulations 1996.[36]

TRANSFER OF UNDERTAKINGS (PROTECTION OF EMPLOYMENT) REGULATIONS 1981 ("TUPE")

36-35 TUPE govern the rights and duties of employees where the undertaking in which they work is transferred as a going concern to another undertaking (the transferee). Thus, reg.5 of TUPE has the effect of transferring automatically those employees on their existing terms and conditions to the transferee. TUPE also makes provision in respect of such matters as dismissals in connection with transfers and the provision of information to workers' representatives. TUPE provides that the parties are not able to contract out of its protections.[37] There is authority,[38] based both on the EC Directive on which TUPE are based and under TUPE, that the prohibition against contracting out demands that agreements with employees entered into as a result of, or in connection with, a transfer which alters those employees' rights are void and ineffective. This has important implications. Thus, a transferee employer, and staff automatically transferred to it as a result of TUPE, cannot enter into a binding and effective agreement to vary the transferred employees' terms and conditions if a reason for that agreement is the existence of the transfer.

However, the EAT has held in *Solectron Scotland Ltd v Roper*[39]:

> "that this principle does not apply to a compromise agreement entered into after the employment has ended which settles a financial claim of transferred ex-employees that arose at the end of the employment. This is because the compromise agreement cannot be said to have arisen out of the transfer and the agreement did not purport to alter terms and conditions of employment because the employment had terminated. As a result, the compromise is in principle capable of being valid even though it compromised a claim which related to a transferred right to enhanced redundancy payments."

36-36 TUPE is anomalous in that, apart from regs 10-11, neither TUPE nor legislation such as the ERA 1996 or Employment Tribunals Act 1996, nor indeed the enactments dealing with discrimination, contain any provision

---

[36] SI 1996/3147.
[37] See reg.12.
[38] *Foreningen of Arbeijdslederei Danmark v Daddy's Dance Hall AS* [1988] I.L.R. 315; *Credit Suisse First Boston (Europe) Ltd v Lister* [1998] I.R.L.R. 700.
[39] [2004] I.R.L.R. 4.

extending the provisions relating to ACAS agreements or compromise agreements to TUPE. This may well reflect the fact that, in general, the claims of employees who come within TUPE will be made either against the transferor or the transferee based upon the substantive rights provided by other legislation—for example, the right not to be unfairly dismissed or the right not to be discriminated against on grounds of sex, race or disability.

The exception to the above concerns regs 10–11 of TUPE which create a 36–37 distinct cause of action justiciable in an Employment Tribunal. Regulations 10 and 11 deal with the right of representatives of affected staff to be kept informed (and, in some circumstances, consulted) about the effect of a transfer of an undertaking. Regulation 11(9) permits disputes relating to claims under regs 10–11 to be resolved by a conciliation officer from ACAS. No provision exists, however, which allows effective compromise agreements of claims under regs 10–11 through the involvement of "independent advisers". In this respect TUPE mirrors the provisions that relate to ss.188 and 190 of TULRCA 1992, discussed at para.36–23 above.

In regard to the remainder of TUPE, as already noted, there are no 36–38 express provisions dealing with the compromise of claims of employees who fall within TUPE. As already indicated, this may be because any statutory claims such employees make will be through other substantive legislation (such as the ERA 1996). Nevertheless, it is surprising that the (potentially complex) relationship between TUPE and compromise agreements (both at common law and under the statutory provisions) has given rise to such little litigation.[40] In the absence of case law, it is suggested that tribunals and courts may well adopt the following approach:

(1) Where employees who are embraced within the provisions of TUPE institute statutory claims (for example, for unfair dismissal) which fall within the existing structure of the resolution of such claims through ACAS or compromise agreements, then the statutory provisions which permit ACAS settlements or compromise agreements through independent advisers of those claims will apply.
(2) Where employees who are embraced within TUPE seek to compromise common law claims against their employers then, for so long as the reason for that compromise agreement is not connected with the transfer, the compromise will be an effective common law compromise.

---

[40] An exception to this lack of case law is the case of *Thompson v Walon Car Delivery* [1997] I.R.L.R. 343. The case concerned an ACAS agreement entered into between the transferor and the employees, but not with the transferee. The agreement was not concluded until after the transfer. It was held that the benefit did not transfer to the transferee of the undertaking.

(3) Where employees who are embraced within TUPE purport to compromise common law claims against their employers, and those claims and the compromise agreement arise as a result of, or for a reason connected with, the transfer, the purported compromise will be void.

MECHANICS OF SETTLEMENT IN EMPLOYMENT TRIBUNALS

36-39 A settlement achieved through the intervention of a conciliation officer is, as previously indicated, usually embodied in Form COT3, although this is not a requirement of a valid ACAS agreement: indeed, the same can be oral. "Compromise agreements" (or "compromise contracts" as they are referred to in the SDA 1975 and the RRA 1976) must be reduced to writing. Any agreement of this nature would have its own contractual status and could, without more, be enforced as such. Where there are extant proceedings before an industrial tribunal, or where the settlement is not achieved until the parties are "at the doors of the tribunal", some form of consent order may be considered appropriate.

36-40 The consent order may consist of a simple dismissal of the complaint, the applicant indicating an intention to withdraw upon terms agreed.[41] If that course is adopted, the terms of settlement will have a simple contractual status and will be susceptible to enforcement only by the bringing of a fresh action in the civil courts. Another possibility is the imposition of a "stay" on the proceedings.[42] This would also, without more, mean that the terms of settlement would fall to be enforced by a fresh action in the civil courts.

36-41 Where an applicant is prepared to allow his claim to be adjourned to enable the respondent to comply with the terms of an agreement, an appropriate order to that effect can be made.[43]

36-42 It is always open to the parties, of course, to agree a consent order to the effect that the former employer should pay an agreed sum by way of compensation. However, the disadvantage of this course from the applicant's point of view is that it will almost certainly activate the recoupment

---

[41] A decision by an Employment Tribunal to dismiss an originating application on withdrawal gives rise to the application of the principles of cause of action estoppel: see *Barber v Staffordshire County Council* [1996] I.C.R. 379.
[42] Whilst there is no specific reference to a power to order a stay in the Employment Tribunals (Constitution and Rules of Procedure) Regulations 1993 (SI 1993/2687), r.13(1) provides Employment Tribunals with the ability to administer wide powers including, it is submitted, the imposition of a "stay".
[43] *cf. The Milestone School of English Ltd v Leakey* [1982] I.R.L.R. 3, EAT.

provisions concerning certain benefits received,[44] provisions which will not come into play if a settlement not involving an order for payment (a "monetary award") is concluded.

SETTING ASIDE AN AGREED SETTLEMENT

As observed previously, it is difficult to set aside an agreement entered into pursuant to the intervention of a conciliation officer. This proposition is largely derived from the obstacles that exist in the path of suggesting that such an officer exceeded his duties or carried them out improperly. However, there would seem to be no reason in principle why an agreement thus concluded (or, of course, a compromise agreement involving an independent adviser) could not be set aside if any of the usual invalidating grounds for a contract[45] could be established as between the parties to the agreement. Indeed this is recognised implicitly in the decision of the Court of Appeal in *Hennessey v Craigmyle & Co Ltd*[46] where an allegation that the agreement was concluded following "economic duress" was entertained, albeit rejected.[47] Naturally, the same principle would apply to compromise agreements relating to contractual and common law claims which fall outside the statutory provisions.

36–43

SETTING ASIDE A CONSENT ORDER

It has been said[48] that in order to justify the setting aside of a consent order, whether made by an employment tribunal or by the Employment Appeal Tribunal, it is necessary to set aside the underlying agreement and that, accordingly, since the Employment Appeal Tribunal has no jurisdiction to do that, it has no jurisdiction to set aside a consent order made

36–44

---

[44] Employment Protection (Recoupment of Jobseekers' Allowance and Income Support) Regulations 1996 (SI 1996/2349).
[45] See Ch.4, above.
[46] [1986] I.C.R. 461. In the EAT judgment in *Hennessey*, it was specifically held that an agreement within s.140 of the Employment Protection (Consolidation) Act 1978 could be avoided on all the grounds available at common law: see [1995] I.C.R. 879.
[47] In so far as the decision of the Employment Appeal Tribunal in *Larkfield of Chepstow Ltd v Milne* [1988] I.C.R. 1 at 7 tentatively suggests the contrary, it is respectfully submitted that it is wrong. It does appear that the passage in the judgment was more directed to the question of whether the Employment Appeal Tribunal had the jurisdiction (in the narrow sense of the term) to entertain an appeal designed to secure the setting-aside of a concluded settlement rather than to the broader issue of whether, if established in the appropriate forum (see below), the usual invalidating grounds could afford a reason for setting aside such an agreement.
[48] *Times Newspapers Ltd v Fitt* [1981] I.C.R. 637 at 642. The decision rested partly upon *Eden v Humphries & Glasgow Ltd* [1981] I.C.R. 183 which is discussed at paras 36–45 and 36–46, below.

pursuant to that agreement. However, there can be little doubt that it would be open to a party to seek to challenge a consent order made either by an employment tribunal or by an Employment Appeal Tribunal by instituting a fresh action for the purpose.[49] This is the normal course to adopt in relation to a consent order designed to dispose finally of a case, and there would seem to be no reason why such a course should not be available.

36–45   An employment tribunal and the Employment Appeal Tribunal each possesses jurisdiction under the rules applicable to them to review and revoke any decision or order if "the interests of justice" require such a review.[50] In the absence of authority to the contrary, these words would seem to confer a wide discretionary jurisdiction to intervene and revoke or vary a consent order in appropriate circumstances. One such circumstance, it is submitted, would be where the consent to the making of the order is shown to have been invalidated. In *Larkfield of Chepstow Ltd v Milne*,[51] the Employment Appeal Tribunal appeared to confirm that an employment tribunal does have power under the relevant rule to review a consent order staying proceedings following a compromise, although in the particular case it held that the industrial tribunal was wrong to have set aside the order.[52] In *Eden v Humphries & Glasgow Ltd*,[53] however, whilst apparently entertaining an application under the equivalent rule dealing with its own proceedings to review a consent order giving leave for an appeal to be withdrawn, the Employment Appeal Tribunal declined to say that the

---

[49] This is effectively what the EAT invited the appellant in *Eden v Humphries & Glasgow Ltd*, n.48, above, to do if he wished to pursue the matter further.

[50] Employment Tribunals (Constitution and Rules of Procedure) Regulations 1993 (SI 1993/2687), r.11, and Employment Appeal Tribunal Rules 1993 (SI 1993/2854), r.33, respectively.

[51] [1988] I.C.R. 1.

[52] The circumstances of the case were very unusual. At the conclusion of the hearing on whether the dismissal had been unfair the employment tribunal reserved its decision, but encouraged the parties to consider the possibility of settlement. As a result they did agree, following the conciliation procedure, on effectively a 50/50 basis, and a consent order staying the proceedings was made. Some while later the employment tribunal contacted the parties and indicated that prior to reserving its decision it had already reached a unanimous decision in favour of the applicant. The applicants were, in effect, invited by the tribunal to apply for a review under what was then r.10(1)(e) of the 1985 Procedural Regulations. When they did so the tribunal removed the stay and directed that the issue of compensation be dealt with by a different tribunal. The Employment Appeal Tribunal drew a clear distinction between the agreement (which was reflected in Form COT3) and the order, but did acknowledge that if the agreement could be attacked (*e.g.* on the basis of a mistake or misrepresentation) then the consent order could also be attacked. The judgment, however, seemed to be based at least partly on the question of whether the Employment Appeal Tribunal itself could set aside the agreement. Plainly, it could not do that, but the essential question (which was not very clearly addressed) was whether the employment tribunal had the power to set aside the order if satisfied that the agreement was invalidated for some reason.

[53] [1981] I.C.R. 183.

interests of justice required a review of the order since its jurisdiction did not extend to setting aside the agreement underlying that order.[54]

36–46 Neither of these two decision is, with respect, very satisfactory, a situation possibly contributed to by the fact that there may not have been the fullest argument on what are, it is submitted, important issues. However, in so far as the jurisdiction of an employment tribunal to review a consent order is confirmed by *Larkfield*, it is submitted that the case is correct. In so far as the Employment Appeal Tribunal in *Eden* said that it did not have jurisdiction to review one of its own consent orders, it is submitted that it was fettering its own powers unnecessarily. Each of the rules relating to the powers to review would, it is submitted, afford a satisfactory alternative to the institution of a fresh action.

STATUTORY ARBITRATION SCHEME

36–47 On May 25, 2001 a new scheme for arbitration in claims of unfair dismissal was introduced, which scheme was subsequently applied to Scotland, as well as England and Wales. The scheme has also now been extended, originally within England and Wales and subsequently within Scotland, to apply to claims relating to flexible working arrangements.[55] Further, the Secretary of State may extend the scheme to claims other than for unfair dismissal and claims in connection with flexible working.

36–48 An agreement to engage in such an arbitration is, of course, an agreement to oust the jurisdiction of the Employment Tribunal. This is an effective ouster for so long as the arbitration agreement is in writing, and is made either through an ACAS-conciliated agreement or a compromise agreement involving an independent adviser. The parties must agree to a written waiver of rights, including the waiver of the right to return to the Employment Tribunal in regard to the dispute. ACAS appoints the arbitrator from its Panel of Arbitrators, although the arbitrator cannot be an ACAS employee.

36–49 Provision is made in the ACAS Arbitration Scheme (England and Wales) Order 2001[56] to deal with the situation where the parties to a valid arbitration agreement are able to settle their dispute. Paragraphs 31–34 of the Schedule to the Order provide that:

---

[54] *ibid*. at 186.
[55] See TULRCA 1992, s.212A, introduced under the power set out in s.7 of the Employment Rights (Dispute Resolution) Act 1998, and the ACAS Arbitration Scheme (Great Britain) Order 2004 (SI 2004/753) and the ACAS (Flexible Working) Arbitration Scheme (Great Britain) Order 2004 (SI 2004/2333).
[56] SI 2001/1185.

"31. Parties are free to reach an agreement settling their dispute at any stage.

32. If such an agreement is reached:

- (i) upon the joint written request of the parties to the arbitrator or the ACAS Arbitration Section, the arbitrator (if appointed) or the ACAS Arbitration Section (if no arbitrator has been appointed) shall terminate the arbitration proceedings;
- (ii) if so requested by the parties, the arbitrator (if appointed) may record the settlement in the form of an agreed award (on a covering pro forma).

33. An agreed award shall state that it is an award of the arbitrator by consent and shall have the same status and effect as any other award on the merits of the case.

34. In rendering an agreed award, the arbitrator:

- (i) may only record the parties' agreed wording;
- (ii) may not approve, vary, transcribe, interpret or ratify a settlement in any way;
- (iii) may not record any settlement beyond the scope of the Scheme, the Arbitration Agreement or the reference to the Scheme as initially accepted by ACAS."

36–50   It is too early to say how much use will be made of this alternative to a full hearing before an Employment Tribunal. The scheme can be seen as representing an attempt to return, in appropriate cases, to the philosophy that underpinned Employment Tribunals when first established (*i.e.* that they were to represent a quick, cheap and informal method of dispensing justice in the context of employment disputes).

CONCLUSION

36–51   It is clear from the review of the law and practice associated with the resolution by agreement of disputes in the employment setting that the rules surrounding the compromise of statutory rights enforced in Employment Tribunals are considerably more tightly defined than those that govern the compromise of contractual and other common law claims between employers and employees. That there should be this difference of emphasis is, of course, consistent with the philosophy of the protection of workers that underpins the ever-increasing (and increasingly EC-led) edifice of employees' rights.

PART 11

Landlord and Tenant and Disputes over Land

CHAPTER 37

Landlord and Tenant

Landlord and tenant relationships remain at the root of a wide range of litigation. The parties involved generally have significantly different interests in the property concerned and often have different perceptions of its future. The tenancies involved may be business tenancies or residential tenancies; the law involved may be common law or statute-based. 37–01

Many landlord and tenant disputes are resolved by compromise. In some instances the complex statutory intervention complicates the settlement process. In other instances it is necessary to focus upon the exact nature of the landlord and tenant relationship which may result from the compromise and its impact on the rights and obligations of the parties or the rights of third parties. 37–02

As indicated above, the two broad areas of landlord and tenant litigation that are subject to differing statutory control are, of course, those involving: 37–03

(a) business tenancies; and
(b) residential tenancies.

BUSINESS TENANCIES

Introduction

The Landlord and Tenant Act 1954 ("the 1954 Act"), Pt II, as amended by the Regulatory Reform (Business Tenancies) 2003 Order,[1] provides significant security of tenure for business tenants and, in some instances, 37–04

---

[1] SI 2003/3096.

compensation in the event that the tenant's security of tenure is lost. The 1954 Act enables a business tenant to apply to the court for a new tenancy following the service of notices by either the landlord or the tenant seeking to determine an existing tenancy and then restricts the circumstances in which a landlord can refuse to grant a new tenancy. Given the commercial background to the premises and their use and the valuable nature of protection under the 1954 Act, it is an area ripe for both dispute and compromise.

Contracting out

37–05 Except as provided by s.38(A) of the 1954 Act, it is not possible for the parties to a business tenancy to contract out of its provisions.[2] The relevant part of s.38(A) reads as follows:

> "(1) The persons who will be the landlord and the tenant in relation to a tenancy to be granted for a term of years certain which will be a tenancy to which this Part of this Act applies may agree that the provisions of ss.24 to 28 of the Act shall be excluded in relation to that tenancy.
>
> (2) The persons who are the landlord and the tenant in relation to a tenancy to which this Part of this Act applies may agree that the tenancy shall be surrendered on such date or in such circumstances as may be specified in the agreement and on such terms (if any) as may be so specified.
>
> (3) An agreement under subsection (1) above shall be void unless:
>
> > (a) the landlord has served on the tenant a notice in the form or substantially in the form, set out in Schedule 1 to the Regulatory Reform (Business Tenancies) (England and Wales) Order 2003; and
> > (b) the requirements specified in Schedule 2 to that Order are met.
>
> (4) An agreement under subsection (2) above shall be void unless:
>
> > (a) the landlord has served on the tenant a notice in the form or substantially in the form, set out in Schedule 3 to the Order 2003; and
> > (b) the requirements specified in Schedule 4 to that Order are met.
>
> (5) The requirements specified in Schedule 2 to that Order are met."

---

[2] s.38(1). Prior to June 1, 2004 the relevant exceptions were contained in s.38(4).

37–06 This provision, like its predecessor, is of considerable commercial importance and is widely invoked. Where previously it was common for agreements for leases were entered into conditional upon the court granting the requisite authority under the subsection but not otherwise, the exclusion of the security of tenure under the Act now lies within the parties' control.[3] Despite being of such importance and a purely paper exercise, no doubt the apparently straightforward requirements of the section will be subject to interpretation and errors will be made. This can give rise to a number of unwanted consequences including costly litigation. It is worth noting that the structure and content of the section and the procedure to be adopted will not fit well with a last-minute compromise of litigation that involves the grant of a new tenancy excluded from the protection of the 1954 Act.

37–07 Under the new scheme a business tenancy can be granted outside the provisions of the Act provided the following conditions are complied with:

(a) The intended landlord must serve on the intended tenant a notice in writing 14 days before the tenancy is to start, or before the tenant becomes contractually bound to enter into it, in prescribed form containing a "health warning" to the effect that the proposed tenancy does not enjoy the protection of the 1954 Act. There is a prescribed form of landlord's notice.[4] The notice contains a "health warning" informing the intended tenant clearly that the security of tenure given by the 1954 Act will not apply.

(b) The intended tenant must sign a declaration to the effect that the notice has been served on him, read by him and that he accepts the consequences of the notice. There is a prescribed form of the tenant's simple declaration.[5] This is referred to as a "simple" declaration because the intended tenant simply makes the declaration by signing it and need not formalise it by swearing to it.

(c) If the landlord's notice is served less than 14 days before the grant of the tenancy the tenant may still accept it by confirming receipt, reading and acceptance of the notice including the "health warning", but in this case the statement must be supported by statutory declaration. There is a prescribed form of the tenant's statutory declaration.[6] The tenant is thereby forced into the arms of a solicitor even if only for the purpose of having his declaration sworn. Nothing in the Order or the form of the declaration requires the tenant to seek, or the solicitor to give, advice.

---

[3] *Essexcrest Ltd v Evenlex Ltd* [1988] 1 E.G.L.R. 69 at 71, *per* Dillon L.J. For the effect of an agreement "subject to the approval of the court", see para.3–61, above.
[4] See the Regulatory Reform (Business Tenancies) (England and Wales) Order 2003 (SI 2003/3096).
[5] *ibid.*
[6] *ibid.*

(d) The notice, the declaration or statutory declaration, and the agreement to contract out (or at least a reference to it) have to be endorsed on the instrument creating the tenancy.

It follows that if a proposed settlement includes the grant of a new tenancy outside the Act the settlement must accommodate the giving of the necessary notices and declarations.

37–08 Secondly, the court has jurisdiction to make an order excluding the effect of the 1954 Act only if s.38(A) applies. As with the previous regime it appears that if the tenancy is one where the statute confers no jurisdiction (*e.g.* where the proposed tenancy is not for a term of years certain) the effect of the 1954 Act will not be excluded in relation to any tenancy granted on the basis of an agreement made in the mistaken belief that there was jurisdiction to make the order.[7] Even where the parties have proceeded in the belief that the effects of the 1954 Act have been excluded, and so have entered the tenancy on that basis, any tenancy granted will nevertheless attract the protection of the 1954 Act.

37–09 In addition, s.38(A) relates to proposed landlords and tenants and therefore proposed tenancies, not to tenancies already granted. Thus it should be noted that compliance with the notice regime can be effective to exclude a tenancy from the protection of the 1954 Act only if it pre-dates the grant of the tenancy (namely the execution of the lease) itself.[8]

37–10 Finally, it is essential that the notice and declaration or statutory declaration and the agreement to contract out or reference to the same be endorsed on the instrument creating the tenancy.[9] It has been said, in relation to the equivalent requirement under the old regime,[10] that this requirement exists "in order that third parties, prospective assignees, or prospective mortgagees of the tenant's interest under a lease" of this nature should know that the provisions of Pt II of the Act have been excluded. Whatever the rationale for the requirement, compliance with it would seem to be a condition precedent to the efficacy of the exclusion of the protection under the 1954 Act in relation to any lease granted pursuant to the parties' agreement and notice procedure. In the normal course of events, a provision will be included in the lease when executed to the effect that the parties have agreed that the provisions of ss.24–28 of the Act are excluded from the tenancy and that the necessary notice and declaration were given on specified dates pursuant to s.38(A).[11]

---

[7] *Nicholls v Kinsey* [1994] Q.B. 600; *Coop v Hastings Borough Council* (1993) 91 L.G.R. 608.
[8] s.38A; and, by analogy, *Essexcrest Ltd v Evenlex Ltd*, n.3, above.
[9] See para.37–05, above and Precedent No.27 at para.A1–27.
[10] *Tottenham Hotspur Football & Athletic Co Ltd v Princegrove Publishers Ltd* [1974] 1 W.L.R. 113 at 119, *per* Lawson J.
[11] See suggested form in Precedent No.27 at para.A1–27.

The case of *Tottenham Hotspur Football & Athletic Co Ltd v Princegrove* 37-11
Publishers Ltd,[12] demonstrates the additional dangers under the new regime
for those compromising on the basis the grant of a new tenancy.

> In that case C and D compromised proceedings for a new business tenancy brought by D on the basis that a new lease for one year should be granted upon certain agreed terms. One of those terms was that C and D should apply jointly for an order under s.38(4) authorising an agreement excluding the provisions of ss.24–28. The county court judge made a consent order granting D the new tenancy upon the agreed terms and authorising the agreement to be included in the new lease. No formal lease was executed in pursuance of the order but D, pursuant to the agreement and the order, remained in occupation of the premises and paid rent accordingly. In proceedings for possession brought by C after the expiration of the term provided for in the agreement and order, D sought to argue that the agreement authorised by the order was not valid since it was not contained in or endorsed on the instrument specified in the order, namely the new lease. Lawson J. held that since D continued to occupy the premises following the agreement and consent order on the basis of the agreement embodied in that order, they were to be taken as occupying pursuant to an agreement for a lease in accordance with the principle of *Walsh v Lonsdale*.[13] Accordingly, the consent order itself was to be regarded as the "instrument creating the tenancy" and, since the order contained the agreement excluding ss.24–28, the requirements of s.38(4) had been met.

It follows since the event necessary for exclusion of the 1954 Act protection was a court order and the consent order both created the tenancy and amounted to compliance with the steps for exclusion those steps were treated as meeting the requirement to pre-date the grant of the tenancy. Under the new regime the steps required are to be taken by the parties and not the court. If a consent order has the effect of creating a tenancy, and the necessary notice and declaration have not been given, it appears that the tenancy created will not be excluded from the 1954 Act regardless of any express indication in the consent order that it was to be.

Parties agree upon the grant of a new tenancy

Previously, where a tenant's claim for a new tenancy was properly before 37-12
the court and the parties were agreed on the period and terms of a new
tenancy and desired the new tenancy to be provided for pursuant to an
order of the court, then, subject only to the court's discretion, if invited to
authorise an agreement under s.38(4), it had to order a new tenancy on the
terms agreed.[14] In light of the new regime for contracting out of the
protection of the 1954 Act, the parties have to take the necessary steps and

---

[12] [1974] 1 W.L.R. 113.
[13] (1882) 21 Ch.D. 9.
[14] s.29.

cannot achieve the desired result simply by court order.[15] The parties will normally seek a consent order embodying the agreed terms, although there is no reason why an appropriately drafted Tomlin order[16] might not be utilised. Where the parties are agreed and the necessary notice and declaration have been dealt with, the master or district judge[17] can make the appropriate order depending on whether the proceedings are in the High Court or county court, and the grant of the tenancy will be complete subject to any requirement to register the lease. In the alternative the parties may elect to embody their agreement in a Tomlin order that does not amount to the grant of a tenancy but provides a timetabled process for the grant of the tenancy it is agreed will be granted.

37–13   It follows even more than ever that parties who reach an agreement in principle for the grant of a new tenancy need to appreciate whether they have in fact concluded a legally binding agreement and, if so, whether all formalities have been undertaken and, if they have not, how to protect their position pending the finalisation of all necessary formalities. An appreciation of the nature of contractual relationship they may or may not be entering is the key to these matters. In the past many landlords and tenants have taken a very relaxed attitude both to the proceedings for the grant of a new tenancy and to their negotiations, often allowing the status quo to drift on for years. That approach has caused problems if one or other changes his mind, third parties acquire rights in the property or the court steps in before anything is formalised.

37–14   Given the movement to greater court control of litigation and the drive to bring proceedings to a conclusion within a reasonable period, such an approach may be counter-productive. Prior to the making of an order for the grant of a new tenancy or the creation of an enforceable contract for the grant of a new lease, a tenant who relaxes simply because there is broad agreement between him and his landlord, and who allows his proceedings to be struck out for failing to take such steps as the court requires, is at risk of losing his right to a new tenancy altogether. Once agreement has been reached in principle the tenant and his legal advisers need to ensure that the position is secured either by court order or the creation of an enforceable contract as soon as possible. Pending either of those events, it is essential that the tenant takes care to ensure that his proceedings are not struck out.

37–15   In this context it may be important to distinguish between the two types of agreement that the parties may actually have made, namely:

---

[15] see para.37–11, above.
[16] See paras 9–17 *et seq.*, above.
[17] CPR PD28, para.4.1 and r.56.3(2).

(i) an agreement for the grant of a new lease; or
(ii) a contract of compromise which compromises proceedings under the Act or any dispute about the tenant's rights under the Act.

37–16 The distinction between the two types of agreement is brought into relief by two cases:

37–17 In *R. J. Stratton Ltd v Wallis Tomlin & Co Ltd*,[18] L1 served on T a notice to terminate the business tenancy between them in accordance with s.25, to which T responded by serving a counter-notice indicating an unwillingness to give up possession at the end of the tenancy. Thereafter solicitors and surveyors instructed by both parties sought to achieve an agreed position. In correspondence in January 1982 the surveyors for both parties agreed the terms "of the new lease which . . . will commence on March 26, 1982". In February 1982 a receiver of L1 was appointed and shortly thereafter the premises were conveyed, subject to the residue of the existing lease, to L2. The land upon which the premises were sited was unregistered land and the agreement reached previously had not been registered before the transfer of the reversion to L2. The question arose of whether the agreement constituted an agreement for a new lease and, if so, whether its existence precluded T's application to the court for a new tenancy under the Act. The Court of Appeal held:

(1) that there was nothing in the correspondence to suggest that the agreement was "subject to the execution of a formal lease" and hence not binding until such a lease had been executed;
(2) that the agreement was a binding agreement for a new lease within s.28; and, accordingly,
(3) T was precluded from invoking the Act.

Furthermore, since the agreement had not been registered, it was not binding on L2.

37–18 In *Behar, Ellis and Parnell v Territorial Investments Ltd*,[19] T made an application for a new tenancy and proceedings were adjourned pending negotiations. The correspondence showed that the parties were agreed on all the terms, the expression "subject to contract" or "subject to lease" never being used. L sought to resile from the agreement and contended that, even though it was clear that the parties' solicitors intended to short-circuit the problems of going to court and obtaining an order for a new tenancy, he was not bound to execute the lease because it was contemplated during negotiations that the parties would not be bound until formal execution of it had taken place. The Court of Appeal held that L was bound by the agreement: it

---

[18] [1986] 1 E.G.L.R. 104. In *Derby & Co Ltd v I.T.C. Pension Trust Ltd* [1977] 2 All E.R. 890, T applied to the court for the grant of a new tenancy under the 1954 Act. Negotiations ensued during which terms were agreed, but those terms were expressly stated by T to be without prejudice to their rights under the Act and subject to contract. Oliver J., as he then was, held that L could not in those circumstances insist on the grant of a new tenancy on those terms.
[19] (1973) C.A.T. 237. See also *Boots the Chemists Ltd v Pinkland Ltd* (1992) 28 E.G. 118, for the position where T's counsel refers to a particular period of tenure in the opening of proceedings for a new tenancy.

was a case of trying to compromise pending litigation and not one of a proposed lessor and lessee negotiating for a lease.

37–19 Where the parties' agreement in principle operates purely as an agreement to grant a new lease and does not extend to compromising the proceedings for the tenant's claim for a new tenancy, it is necessary to consider whether the agreement is legally enforceable. It is particularly important for a tenant who does not commence proceedings on the basis that the matter has been resolved to ensure that the agreement reached is enforceable, enabling him to obtain his new lease even after his ability to apply to the court for one has been lost. As highlighted by *R.J. Stratton Ltd v Wallis Tomlin & Co Ltd* it is also necessary to protect against the intervention of third party rights when a third party may have acquired an interest in the property in the period between the agreement in principle and the actual grant of the new lease.

37–20 As with all other transactions relating to dispositions of land since September 27, 1989, an agreement for the grant of a lease of more than three years will only be enforceable as such if it is in writing, the document contains all the terms expressly agreed, both parties have signed a copy and the written agreement has been exchanged.[20]

37–21 Even a written agreement, copies of which have been signed by both parties, may not create a binding and enforceable contract for the grant of the lease if the agreement was "subject to contract" and has not been "exchanged" in the technical conveyancing sense.

37–22 In *Salomon v Akiens*,[21] L served a s.25 notice objecting to a new tenancy on the basis of persistent delay in the payment of rent, to which T served a counternotice. The parties then proceeded to negotiate the terms of a new tenancy. In correspondence marked "Subject to contract" and "Subject to lease" the parties agreed the form of the lease. L's solicitors sent a counterpart lease for signature which was, after some delay, signed and returned. L refused to proceed. No claim for a new tenancy had ever been issued on behalf of T. It was held that there was nothing in the circumstances to justify a departure from the well-established principle that the expressions "subject to contract" and "subject to lease" mean that either party may withdraw at any point prior to exchange of the lease and the counterpart. Further, since L made no promise to grant a lease there was no consideration for T not commencing proceedings and no estoppel was created. Such representation would be very unlikely to have been made in the face of the indication that the negotiations and agreement were "subject to contract" or "subject to lease".

37–23 Provided the compromise between the parties is enforceable as an agreement for a lease, it will be open to either party, in the event of any subsequent difficulty, to rely on that contract and seek specific perfor-

---

[20] Law of Property (Miscellaneous Provisions) Act 1989, s.2. See paras 3–72 and 3–73, above.
[21] [1993] 1 E.G.L.R. 101.

mance. The tenant who has protected his position by registering the agreement for a lease, will also be able to enforce that agreement against any third party purchaser from the landlord.

Where the agreement reached is a compromise of the proceedings and one party seeks to resile from the agreement, it will be possible for the other to be able to rely on the compromise so as to prevent the resiling party seeking anything other than that which has been agreed. That would usually be achieved by raising the compromise as a preliminary issue and seeking an appropriate declaration or other relief so as to give effect to the compromise.[22] 37–24

Whether a party can use an agreement compromising 1954 Act proceedings to insist on the grant of a new lease when that agreement does not itself amount to an enforceable agreement for a lease remains to be tested in the courts. However, the safest course is clearly to ensure that the agreement settling the proceedings contains all the terms agreed, all the terms of the new tenancy or mechanisms for determining them and that it is signed by all parties or their representatives authorised for that purpose. Clearly, practitioners acting for tenants involved in negotiations with a view to settling 1954 Act proceedings should think very carefully before allowing the tenant's statutory rights to cease, whether by bringing no claim or by allowing the claim to be struck out, until the new tenancy is actually granted. 37–25

Parties agree that a business tenant will vacate

The resolution of a dispute under or in connection with an existing business tenancy may involve the surrender of the tenancy. In the normal course of events, any such surrender is void.[23] However, s.38(A) permits the parties to make an effective agreement with such effect is certain conditions are complied with.[24] Similar procedural provisions and requirements apply in this situation as exist in relation to an agreement to exclude the provisions of ss.24–28 of the 1954 Act in relation to a proposed business tenancy.[25] 37–26

Some tenants quitting business premises on the termination of their tenancy are entitled to compensation. The right to compensation arises where the tenant's potential right to a new tenancy fails in the face of the 37–27

---

[22] See para.11–03, above.
[23] s.38(1).
[24] s.38(A).
[25] See paras 37–06 *et seq.*, above.

landlord's reliance on only grounds (e), (f) and/or (g) under s.30 of the 1954 Act.[26] The entitlement to compensation arises only at the end of the business tenancy.[27] It is not unusual in such cases for a landlord who does not actually require the premises immediately to be willing to allow the tenant a short-term lease provided it is excluded from the Act.[28] In such circumstances the tenant actually quits upon the termination of the new short lease, not on the termination of his business tenancy. There is a good argument that as the quitting of the premises is not connected to the termination of the business tenancy, the tenant's right to compensation was lost when the short intervening lease was taken and that, accordingly, no compensation is payable.[29]

37–28   If it is the intention in these circumstances that the tenant should receive both the value of his compensation and a short lease, care should be taken to ensure that a binding agreement is reached which places the landlord under a contractual obligation to pay a sum of money such as would have been paid in connection with the right to compensation.

RESIDENTIAL TENANCIES

Introduction

37–29   For many years the relationship of landlord and tenant in the field of residential lettings has been almost exclusively governed by statute.[30] The statutory structure by virtue of which tenants have received qualified security of tenure has remained essentially the same since the early days, although the emphasis of the grounds upon which (a) rents have been controlled and (b) possession of premises may be regained has changed from time to time according to the economic and political climate. As things stand, the relationship of landlord and tenant in this area is likely to be regulated by one of a number of Acts depending on when the relationship commenced.

37–30   In the context of private residential landlord and tenant relationships most tenancies entered into after February 28, 1997 will be assured shorthold tenancies, and those entered into after January 15, 1989, but before February 28, 1997, will be assured tenancies (unless the parties had

---

[26] s.37.
[27] *International Military Services v Capital and Counties* [1982] 1 W.L.R. 575; *Cardshops v John Lewis Properties* [1983] Q.B. 161.
[28] See paras 37–05 *et seq.*, above.
[29] See Woodfall, Vol.2, Ch.22, para.22.170.2.
[30] The first rent controls were introduced in 1915 and the first major statutory intervention was the Increase of Rent and Mortgage Interest (Restrictions) Act 1920.

complied with the necessary formalities to make the tenancy an assured shorthold tenancy). Any such relationship formed prior to January 15, 1989 would be dependent upon the Rent Act 1977 and/or the Rent (Agriculture) Act 1976. In the context of a residential landlord and tenant relationship where the landlord is a local authority or other social landlord the relationship is likely to be governed by the Housing Act 1985.[31]

No contracting out

It has long been an established principle that parties cannot contract out of the protection afforded by the Rent Acts.[32] This principle does not prevent parties engaged in a genuine dispute about whether or not the tenancy with which they are concerned is fully protected by the Acts from compromising the dispute in a manner inconsistent with the tenant having or having had that protection.[33] 37–31

> In *Bruce v Worthing Borough Council*,[34] T was a disabled man who, at all material times, owned a specially adapted property in Kent. In March 1983 he obtained the tenancy of a flat from L, a local authority in Sussex, for a period of 11 months. At the expiration of that term the tenancy was extended and T remained in occupation. In 1985 T sought to exercise a right to buy the freehold of the flat from L pursuant to the provisions of the Housing Act 1985 which conferred such a right upon someone having a "secure tenancy". For a person to have a "secure tenancy" it was for the premises to be occupied "as his only or principal home" (s.81 of the Housing Act 1985). L entertained T's application for a while until the view was taken that T had not occupied the flat as his sole or principal residence. L served a notice to quit on T, and sought possession of the premises and arrears of rent. T issued proceedings seeking, *inter alia*, a declaration that he was and had always been a "secure tenant". After T and three other witnesses had given evidence in the county court proceedings over a period of two days, an agreement was concluded which was reflected in the consent order which provided, *inter alia*, that "[T's] claim be dismissed with no order as to costs". Subsequently, T sought to contend that this order should not have been made since he had not made an express admission to the effect that he was not a secure tenant and that the judge should have made inquiries as to T's status before making the order. The Court of Appeal held that the judge was not required to make any further inquiry in the circumstances. The consent order amounted to an express admission that T did not enjoy the protection of the Housing Act 1985 or, if it did not, it amounted to an implied admission to the same effect, which was sufficient. 37–32

---

[31] The 1985 Act consolidated a large number of enactments including, in this context, the Housing Act 1980.
[32] See, *e.g. AG Securities v Vaughan* [1990] 1 A.C. 417. See also *Appleton v Aspin* [1988] 1 W.L.R. 410, CA.
[33] *cf. Binder v Alachouzos* [1972] 2 Q.B. 151, considered at para.2–17, above. See also *Syed Hussain bin Abdul Rahman bin Shaik Alkaff v A.M. Abdullah Sahib & Co* [1985] 1 W.L.R. 1392, PC.
[34] (1993) 26 H.L.R. 223.

37-33   It is also established by authority[35] that a landlord and tenant may agree that the tenant will vacate premises of which he is a statutorily protected tenant in return for the payment by the landlord to him of a sum of money. In the event of the tenant complying with the obligation to vacate, he will be able to recover the promised sum of money even though the landlord would not have been able to enforce the agreement to vacate. The inability of the parties to contract out of the protection afforded by the Acts that confer protection is derived from the way in which those Acts have been structured.

Statutory framework and the court's jurisdiction

37-34   Each of the Acts[36] capable of conferring a degree of protection on a residential tenant contains a mandatory obligation on the court not to make an order for possession except where the circumstances prescribed in the relevant Act are established.[37] In this context, as in others,[38] the courts have held that the parties cannot, by agreement or default, confer upon the court a jurisdiction which it does not otherwise have.[39] It is, therefore, incumbent on the court to satisfy itself and be seen to satisfy itself that the statutory provisions are met irrespective of any agreement between the parties.[40]

37-35   In *Plaschkes v Jones and Jones*,[41] the judge gave possession of a flat subject to a protected tenancy effectively "by consent", although this did not appear in the order, without having considered the validity of the notice to quit (which had been put in issue in a defence and a letter from the defendants' solicitor to the court) or whether it was reasonable to make an order. Contrary to expectations, the housing authority "looked behind" the order, considered that it should not have been made and declined to re-house the defendants. On the defendants' appeal, the Court of Appeal held that the judge should have considered these matters. A re-trial was ordered.

37-36   In *R. v Newcastle upon Tyne County Court Ex p. Thompson*,[42] L issued proceedings against T seeking possession of a flat. L accepted that the premises were premises to which the Rent Act 1977 applied and sought possession on

---

[35] *Rajbenback v Mamon* [1955] 1 Q.B. 283, CA; *cf.* comments of the Privy Council in *Syed Hussain v A.M. Abdullah Sahib & Co*, n.33, above, at 1397. See Stocker, "Compromise of possession claims" 83 L.S.Gaz. 1701.
[36] See para.37-28, above.
[37] Rent Act 1977, s.98(1); Rent (Agriculture) Act 1976, s.6(1); Housing Act 1985, s.84; Housing Act 1988, s.7.
[38] See paras 10-09 *et seq.*, above.
[39] *Barton v Fincham* [1921] 2 K.B. 291, CA; *R. v Bloomsbury and Marylebone County Court Ex p. Blackburne* [1985] 2 E.G.L.R. 1571, CA; *R. v Newcastle upon Tyne County Court Ex p. Thompson* [1988] 2 E.G.L.R. 119; *Wandsworth v Fadayomi* [1987] 1 W.L.R. 1473, CA.
[40] *Barton v Fincham*, n.39, above; *Salter v Lask* [1924] 1 K.B. 754; *Smith v Poulter* [1947] K.B. 3393. *cf. Bruce v Worthing Borough Council*, n.33, above.
[41] (1982) C.A.T. 438.
[42] [1988] 2 E.G.L.R. 119; (1988) 20 H.L.R. 430.

the ground that the flat was reasonably required by them for occupation as a residence for themselves and their two sons. This assertion was put in issue in T's defence and the issue of greater hardship raised. At the hearing before the district registrar an order was made by consent (although not so expressed) to the effect that T should give up possession of the flat by a specified date approximately six months later. No order for costs was made. None of the matters that it would have been necessary for L to establish in order to obtain an order for possession were admitted or conceded on T's behalf, and no evidence was called. McNeill J. held that in the absence of any admissions or concessions of the grounds entitling L to possession, the order was made without jurisdiction and should be quashed.

In *Chinwe Gil v Baywater*[43] the Court of Appeal made it clear that whilst it was desirable but not essential that the grounds for an order for possession be recorded on the order, where the order was made pursuant to the tenants' consent the recording of admissions may be necessary. The court would only have jurisdiction if there were express or implied admissions going to sufficient grounds. Accordingly, the court would only have jurisdiction if the material before it contained such admissions. It follows that where were a consent order is simply presented to the court without any other material on which the court could exercise its discretion, the consent order itself would have to contain the admissions in order for it to be effective. 37-37

Essentially, the court must be satisfied that grounds for possession are made out, including the requirement that the making of an order is reasonable. The tenant's agreement to an order for possession may indicate an admission that there are grounds and that the making of an order is reasonable, but it may simply constitute a submission to the giving-up of possession. Consequently, the court cannot rely simply on the fact that the order for possession is effectively by consent to satisfy itself that the order should be made.[44] The court must have material upon which to form a view as to its jurisdiction to grant the order. That material might be evidence in the form of statements, admissions made expressly, or which can be implied from the documentation or other matters put before the court. The ability to point to the material from which the court's jurisdiction derived is important. For the landlord who wishes to avoid any prospect of the tenant subsequently challenging the jurisdiction of the court to have made the order for possession recording admissions by the tenant that establish grounds for and the reasonableness of the order is the safest way of dealing with the matter.[45] 37-38

Obtaining an "agreed" order in practice

The jurisdictional matters referred to above[46] can present difficulties in obtaining an effective order for possession. Not infrequently, a protected tenant will desire to have an order for possession against him with a view 37-39

---

[43] [2002] EWCA Civ 1340.
[44] *London Borough of Hounslow v McBride*, unreported, March 19, 1998, CA.
[45] See suggested form in Precedent No.23 at para.A1-23, below
[46] See para.37-34, above.

to assisting his position over re-housing by the local authority. Such tenants will be concerned to ensure that the terms of the order, including admissions, will not enable a local authority to conclude that they are intentionally homeless.[47] Whatever the merits or otherwise of that matter may be (and, from the strictly legal point of view, it is of no concern to the court), the jurisdictional problems to which reference has been made can arise. This has been recognised on the highest authority[48] as being overcome by admissions of fact by the tenant of the basis of the landlord's claim:[49]

37–40 "If the parties before the court admit that one of the events has happened which give the court jurisdiction and there is no reason to doubt the bona fides of the admission, the court is under no obligation to make further enquiry as to the question of fact; but apart from such an admission the court cannot give effect to an agreement, whether by way of compromise or otherwise, inconsistent with the provisions of the Act."

37–41 The matter has been put in similar terms more recently:[50]

"If it is desired to reach terms of agreement to be embodied in an order whereby possession of premises covered by section 98 of the Rent Act 1977 is to be given up, for the court to have jurisdiction to make an order there must be plain admissions of the qualifying conditions which must be fulfilled before such an order can be made. That is to say, a concession that it is reasonable for the order to be made, that, whichever the case may be, suitable alternative accommodation is or will be available to the tenant, or that the relevant circumstances specified in the appropriate case exist, and, where relevant, that it is accepted by the tenant that greater hardship would not be caused by granting the order than by refusing to grant it."

37–42 Where such admissions of fact are made in good faith, it is open to the court to regard the tenant as submitting (rather than consenting) to an order for possession and drawing the order as such. Such difficulties as the tenant might face with the local authority by having "consented" to an order for possession are at least reduced.[51] The tenant's legal representa-

---

[47] See Housing (Homeless Persons) Act 1977.
[48] *Barton v Fincham*, n.40, above *per* Atkin L.J, at 299.
[49] See Precedent No.23 at para.A1–23, below.
[50] *R. v Newcastle upon Tyne County Court Ex p. Thomson*, n.39, above, at 122.
[51] It is apparent from cases such as *Plaschkes v Jones and Jones*, n.40, above, that even in cases where the words "by consent" are omitted from an order, some housing authorities will look closely at whether any admissions or concessions made were correctly and appropriately made.

tives will need to consider carefully with the tenant how such admissions will be viewed.

Residential occupants without statutory protection or with "restricted contracts"

Where a residential occupant has no statutory protection[52] no jurisdictional obstacles exist in the path of securing an agreed order for possession. Similarly, where the occupant occupies under a "restricted contract,"[53] *i.e.* where a degree of protection is afforded by virtue of the right to apply to a rent assessment committee (when sitting as a rent tribunal) for limited security of tenure, it is in order for the tenant to contract out of that right if he chooses to do so.

It follows that where the parties agree that the tenant's status does not attract statutory protection the court has no duty to investigate the facts before it makes the order for possession which the parties seek.[54]

37–43

> In *Alcove Properties v Fraser and Fraser*,[55] the defendants were tenants under a furnished tenancy to which the Furnished Houses (Rent Control) Act 1946 applied. At a time when they had a clear defence to the possession proceedings brought against them,[56] and a further application to the rent tribunal for time was pending, they consented to an order for possession, suspended until a specified date, a claim for damages being abandoned. Subsequently, they applied to set aside the consent order on the basis that it was made without jurisdiction and that they could not contract out of their rights under the Act. The Court of Appeal held that there was nothing in the Act to deprive the consent order of having "its full efficacy". Russell L.J. emphasised that under the Act in question it was "entirely for the individual to decide whether to put the Rent Tribunal procedure into operation and whether and when to withdraw from that procedure". Such an individual is in no way debarred from bargaining away his right to invoke that procedure if he wishes to do so.[57]

37–44

Subsequent variation and enforcement of orders

It should be recalled that a possession order may, it appears, be enforced against any person on the premises when it is executed.[58]

37–45

---

[52] Foe example where there is a genuine licence or a genuine holiday letting.
[53] Rent Act 1977, s.19. By virtue of the Housing Act 1988, s.36 no new "restricted contracts" may be made after the commencement of the Act save where the contract is granted pursuant to a contract made before the commencement of the Act.
[54] *Syed Hussain Bin Abdul Rahman Bin Shaikh Alkaff v A.M. Abdullah Sahib & Co* [1985] 1 W.L.R. 1392.
[55] (1966) C.A.T. 124A.
[56] The proceedings were premature.
[57] In *R. v Bloomsbury and Marylebone County Court Ex p. Blackburne*, n.39, above, Sir John Donaldson M.R., at 158, explained the case on the basis that "the Rent Acts operated in relation to premises, whereas the rent tribunal scheme operated *in personam* and it was open to the tenant to agree to waive his personal contractual rights".
[58] See para.6–33, above.

37–46　It should be borne in mind that where a tenant is a protected tenant, the court retains a statutory jurisdiction to vary an order for possession even if it is made by consent.[59] In addition, the fact that the court retains jurisdiction to vary an undertaking or release a party from his undertaking even where the undertaking is given in conjunction with a consent order[60] should not be forgotten.

37–47　It is possible that the compromise of a claim for possession may provide for the making of a possession order suspended on terms. If it be alleged that the order ought to be enforced because of some failure to observe those terms, leave to issue execution will be required and in the High Court the defendant will be given an opportunity to be heard.[61] In the county court the landlord can secure a warrant of possession by filing the appropriate request,[62] the practical effect is often the same as the tenant may apply to suspend or set aside the warrant.

37–48　An order for possession secured with the agreement of a party may be set aside on the same grounds, as may other orders obtained by consent.[63] Where a landlord obtains a possession order by misrepresentation a tenant may have a statutory right to compensation.[64] The fact that the tenant effectively consented to the order does not prevent the court making an order for compensation.[65]

Tenancy springing from the compromise

37–49　Where possession proceedings have run their course, whether in connection with a tenancy protected under the Rent Act 1977 or the Housing Act 1985 or an unprotected tenancy, it is not unknown for the parties to make an arrangement whereby the tenant remains in occupation of the premises on the basis of a commitment to pay the current rent and a regular sum in reduction of the arrears or any damages. In order for a new tenancy to arise where a tenant holds over following the determination of his tenancy, the parties must intend to create a new tenancy, to create a new legal relationship.[66] The courts are generally slow to impute the necessary

---

[59] See Rent Act 1977, s.100; Housing Act 1988, s.9; Housing Act 1985, s.85. See also *Rossiter v Langley* [1925] 1 K.B. 741; *Mouat-Balthasar v Murphy* [1967] 1 Q.B. 344.
[60] *Kensington Housing Trust v Oliver*, unreported, July 24, 1997, CA.
[61] *Fleet Mortgage and Investment Co Ltd v Lower Maisonette, 46 Eaton Place Ltd* [1972] 1 W.L.R. 765.
[62] *The White Book* (2005), cc.26.17.
[63] See Ch.4, above.
[64] Rent Act 1977, s.2; Housing Act 1988, s.12.
[65] *Thorne v Smith* [1947] K.B. 307.
[66] *Vaughan-Armatrading v Sarsah* (1995) 27 H.L.R. 631; *London Borough of Greenwich v Regan* (1996) 28 H.L.R. 469.

intention to create a new tenancy. The simple facts of continued occupation and payment of compensation to the landlord for that use will not on their own be sufficient. In the context of a secure tenancy the continuing occupation and payment of rent will generally not give rise to a new tenancy and the tenant will effectively be a tolerated trespasser whose tenancy is in limbo though potentially capable of revival if the order for possession was varied.[67]

FORFEITURE AND RELIEF FROM FORFEITURE

Proceedings seeking forfeiture of a lease and proceedings seeking relief from forfeiture are frequently compromised. It is important for the parties compromising such claims to be clear in their understanding and intent so far as the impact of the compromise on the existence of the lease and of third parties interests are concerned. 37–50

The issue of forfeiture proceedings by a landlord is an act of forfeiture like peaceable re-entry. However, as against the tenant the lease and its covenants are not immediately determined. Pending judgment of the claim for forfeiture or relief from forfeiture there is a "twilight period"[68] or "period of limbo"[69] when the lease has a shadowy existence during which the landlord cannot rely upon the covenants, but the lease and covenants have not actually been brought to an end.[70] If the forfeiture proceedings are compromised then, as long as the compromise does not provide for a forfeiture, the landlord may then rely on obligations under the lease which arose during that twilight period. 37–51

> In *Ivory Gate Ltd v Spetale*,[71] L served a s.146 notice and commenced forfeiture proceedings which were compromised on the basis that L discontinued the forfeiture proceedings without releasing any of its rights against the sureties, and the lease itself would be transferred to L. The lease was transferred to L. L commenced proceedings against the sureties claiming rent arrears up to the date of the transfer. It was held that the issue of forfeiture proceedings itself did not determine the lease. The lease was determined only by merger upon the transfer, and until that point the sureties' obligations subsisted. 37–52

> In *Weaver v Mogford*,[72] L commenced forfeiture proceedings against the current tenant on the basis of rent arrears. L obtained a default judgement which was challenged subsequently. The proceedings were ultimately compro- 37–53

---

[67] *Burrows v Brent London Borough Council* [1996] 1 W.L.R. 1448.
[68] *Associated Deliveries v Harrison* (1984) 50 P. & C.R. 91.
[69] *Liverpool Properties v Oldbridge Investments* [1985] 2 E.G.L.R. 65.
[70] See *Woodfall*, Vol.1, Ch.17, para.17.091.1
[71] [1998] 2 E.G.L.R. 44.
[72] [1988] 2 E.G.L.R. 48.

513

mised on the basis that L obtained an order for possession which would not be executed for three months on conditions, it being acknowledged that the current tenant and its mortgagee had no further interest in the property. L had taken proceedings against the original lessee for damages for disrepair, who claimed that the effect of the order was a waiver of the forfeiture followed by a surrender, thereby relieving him of his obligations. It was held that the order for possession in the forfeiture proceeding confirmed that the lease was forfeit. The fact that in correspondence there had been discussion of reinstating the lease did not alter the effect of the order made. The original lessee remained liable until the date of the forfeiture.

Similarly, dismissal of a claim for forfeiture, even by consent, has the effect of restoring the lease fully, the legitimacy of the act of forfeiture not having been established with the effect that it is to be treated as a nullity.[73] It follows that both parties are then treated as having the same rights and obligations they would have had if the forfeiture proceedings had never taken place.

37-54 Where the effect of the compromise of such proceedings is a forfeiture and the granting of relief subject to conditions, the position is not so clear. It is clearly established that if the court itself decides to grant relief from forfeiture subject to conditions, the court retains jurisdiction to modify those conditions by extending time, if not varying the conditions, in so far as it considers that it would be just and equitable even if the order itself did not record a "liberty to apply".[74] The power of the court to intervene and extend time or otherwise modify the conditions of relief expressly agreed between the parties and incorporated in a consent order has been doubted judicially, but not conclusively ruled out.[75] Similarly, the ability of the tenant to seek to avoid his failure to comply with the conditions for relief in a consent order by making a second application for relief has been doubted. However, if it appears to the court that the tenant submitted to an order for relief upon terms, rather than genuinely consenting to such an order, it would seem that the court does retain the power to intervene.[76]

37-55 In this regard it appears that a distinction may need to be drawn between a final order by consent and an interim order by consent. Where the parties agree an adjournment of forfeiture proceedings upon compliance with conditions and provide in default of compliance that there will be an order for possession against the tenant, it is possible that the court's case management powers will enable it, if it concludes that it is necessary to satisfy the overriding objective, to intervene.[77]

---

[73] *Hynes v Twinsectra* [1995] 2 E.G.L.R. 69.
[74] *Chandless-Chandless v Nicholson* [1942] 2 K.B. 321.
[75] *ibid.*; *Crawford v Clark*, unreported, March 2, 2000, CA.
[76] *Chandless-Chandless v Nicholson*, n.74, above.
[77] *Ropac Ltd v Inntrepreneur Pub Co (CPC) Ltd, The Times,* June 21, 2000. But see para.6-24, above.

CHAPTER 38

Disputes over Land

GENERAL

A dispute between co-owners of land or neighbours is a practitioner's **38–01** nightmare. Ownership, boundaries, fences, adverse possession, rights of way and so on, are a fertile source of acrimonious litigation into which, strive as he might, the practitioner finds it well nigh impossible to inject a modicum of common sense and rationality. With the possible exception of co-ownership disputes, costs escalate out of all proportion to the nature and significance of the dispute and the value of the land or rights at stake.[1] That fact will occasionally lead parties to see sense and come to an amicable compromise, although all too often at the door of the court.

Where such a settlement provides for or will actually be a disposition of **38–02** land the practitioner drafting and advising on such a settlement must be conscious of the necessary formalities, the potential implied terms and the fact that the transaction may have taxation implications. Compliance with s.2 of the Law of Property (Miscellaneous Provisions) Act 1989 and registration requirements[2] should be considered. Further the switch from the "voluntary" system of stamp duty to stamp duty land tax which gives rise to a liability for tax for the "purchaser" upon the occurrence of a "land transaction" necessarily involves the practitioner in consideration of the tax implications of a settlement. Any acquisition of a chargeable interest in land, including a transfer of the legal and/or beneficial interest in land or the grant, release or surrender of a lease, will be an event that gives rise to potential liability.

---

[1] *cf. Jones v Price* [1965] 2 Q.B. 618, CA.
[2] Land Registration Act 2002.

38–03   It should be noted that whilst both the High Court and county court have power to grant declarations concerning land, it is not the practice of the court to grant such declarations by consent.[3] Since a declaration relating to interests in land affects the position of third parties it is very unlikely that the court would be prepared to abandon that rule of practice whatever the circumstances.[4] It follows that the best the parties compromising such disputes can do at court is to ensure that the consent order records all matters agreed between them.

38–04   Whilst a "bare right to litigate" is not normally assignable,[5] a right to litigate ancillary to a transfer of property can be assigned.[6] This probably means that rights arising from the compromise of a dispute over interests in land or boundaries are capable of assignment provided that some transfer of property is involved in it.

38–05   It would seem consistent with the position under the general law[7] that, where a compromise involving a possible change of title is contemplated, all defects in the transferor's title must be disclosed to render the agreement fully effective.

38–06   Given the significant implications that flow from the fact that a contract of compromise contains a contract for the disposal of any interest in land, it is important to accurately characterise compromises in property disputes. A compromise providing for the sale of a property to a third party, as opposed to between the parties to the compromise, does not amount to a contract for the disposition of land. The parties to a contract for the disposal of the interest in land will include a vendor and a purchaser, someone obliged to dispose of the interest and someone obliged to take it.[8]

BOUNDARIES

38–07   If, as is normal, the compromise agreement in a boundary dispute involves a redefinition of the boundaries, it is prudent to finalise the agreement by deed in case, in reality, some small part of the land changes ownership. In any event, a properly prepared plan, having certain fixed points of reference, should be drawn up and incorporated in the agreement, and the agreement should comply with the relevant formalities.[9]

---

[3] *Wallersteiner v Moir* [1974] 1 W.L.R. 991 at 1029 and 1030, CA.
[4] *Patten v Burke Publishing Ltd* [1991] 1 W.L.R. 541.
[5] See para.6–104, above.
[6] ibid.
[7] *Chitty on Contracts* (29th ed., 2004), Vol.1, paras 6–152–6–143.
[8] *Nweze v Nwoke* [2004] EWCA Civ 379.
[9] Law of Property (Miscellaneous Provisions) Act 1989, s.2(1); see Ch.3, para.3–72, above.

When the implementation of a consent order defining a boundary results in practical difficulties, the court is always available to assist in interpreting orders and will make every effort to ensure certainty.[10] **38–08**

If the agreement involves a reorganisation of the boundary, for instance as a result of a trade of different areas of land, consideration should be given to the need to register the transaction to achieve completion and whether any liability for stamp duty land tax arises. **38–09**

DURING COURT PROCEEDINGS

Where court proceedings are extant and there is any question of land changing hands, the best and safest course is, usually, for an order in the Tomlin form[11] to be prepared, one of the agreed terms being that the parties will execute a deed giving effect to their agreement so far as the boundary is concerned. It is sensible expressly to provide which party will have carriage of any documentation and at whose expense it will be undertaken. In any event this is one situation in which, for several reasons, it would be sensible for the parties themselves to be required by their legal advisers to sign the schedule to the order. This approach to the settlement will provide for the problem referred to in para.38–07 above and will enable eventual recourse to s.9 of the Supreme Court Act 1981 in the event of one party failing or refusing to execute the deed. Equally, in so far as the provisions of the agreement concern positive steps to be taken by one party or the other, or the prevention of interference or trespass, they can be enforced in the action provided the necessary steps are taken.[12] **38–10**

---

[10] *Dicker v Scammell* [2003] EWHC 1601.
[11] See Ch.9, paras 9–19, *et seq.*, above.
[12] See Ch.11, above.

PART 12

Construction Litigation

CHAPTER 39

Construction Disputes

INTRODUCTION

Construction disputes are usually dealt with in three *fora*: in the Technology and Construction Court[1]; by arbitration[2]; and by adjudication under the Housing Grants Construction and Regeneration Act 1996.[3] 39–01

Particular issues. Although the general law of compromise applies to construction disputes in the same way as it does to any other form of dispute, certain problems occur frequently by reason of the complexity of the subject-matter and the interaction of dispute-resolution machinery which often highlight particular issues. These issues include problems associated with: 39–02

(i) the long-term nature of construction contracts;
(ii) certificates and retentions;
(iii) multiple issues;

---

[1] See CPR Pt 60.
[2] See Ch.41, below.
[3] In numerical terms, after negotiation, adjudication appears to be the principal method of dispute-resolution in the construction industry. On the latest figures available, the Technology and Construction Court in London dealt with about 380 new cases in 2003. It is unlikely that the number of cases dealt with in other centres would exceed that number. The only available figures in relation to construction arbitrations are those published by the Royal Institution of Chartered Surveyors, which appointed around 200 construction arbitrators in the same period. Research (P. Fenn, *Survey of Domestic Arbitration in United Kingdom*; and Michael Black Q.C., *Arbitration*, Vol.65, No.3, August 1999) indicates that the arbitral appointments made by the Royal Institution of Chartered Surveyors account for about 25 per cent of the annual total number of construction arbitrations. By contrast, in the year to August 2003 the Glasgow Caledonian University's Adjudication Reporting Centre recorded over 2,000 appointments by Adjudicator Nominating Bodies ("*Research Analysis of The Trends of Adjudication Based on Returned Questionnaires from Adjudicator Nominating Bodies (ANBs)*" (Report No.6.) March 2004; available at http://www.adjudication.gcal.ac.uk/report6.doc).

(iv) multiple parties;
(v) claims for contribution to settlements reached with other parties;
(vi) the amendment of pleadings between the date of offer and judgment or award;
(vii) value added tax; and
(viii) adjudication.

LONG-TERM ISSUES

39-03 Problems often arise during the course of a construction project as to the contractor's progress and/or responsibility for defects. While these issues are now subject to adjudication, they are often settled by agreements intended either to be a temporary resolution pending final negotiation or more formal procedures, or to be final and binding.

39-04 **Disputes concerning progress.** Disputes concerning progress are often compromised by an "acceleration agreement" by which the contractor or subcontractor undertakes to adopt accelerative measures in order to maintain completion dates. Such an agreement is predicated on the basis that the accelerative measures require work additional to the original contractual obligations.[4] The precise draftsmanship of an acceleration agreement will depend upon the terms of the underlying contract and, in particular, whether or not the contractor or subcontractor already has the benefit of an extension of time.[5] If an extension of time has been granted or claimed, it may be agreed that the extension of time or the claim be withdrawn; if no extension of time has been granted, the original contract may be varied to provide an earlier completion date. It is usually the case that the contractor or subcontractor will be paid additional sums for the deployment of the additional resources to accelerate progress. Often the payment is made conditional upon the achievement of the new completion date.

39-05 In the negotiation of acceleration agreements it is essential that the parties consider what is to happen if progress is delayed further and to specify whether the original allocation of risk in the underlying contract is to remain or whether, having regard to the additional rewards available to the contractor or subcontractor, a reallocation of risk is required.

39-06 **Disputes concerning existing defects.** So far as disputes concerning defects are concerned, these may also arise during the course of the works and the parties, recognising that liability may require extensive investiga-

---

[4] This itself is fertile ground for dispute: see the comments of H.H. Judge Hicks Q.C. in *Ascon Contractors Limited v Alfred McAlpine Construction Isle of Man Limited* (2000) 16 Const. L.J. 316 at [50] and [51]. See also Andrew Tweeddle, "What are Acceleration Costs?" (2004) 20 C.L.J. 115.
[5] Precedents can be found in Robert Fenwick Elliott, *Building Contract Disputes: The Practice and Precedents* (1998 looseleaf, Release 14, 2004), para.14-175; Marshall Levine, *Construction and Engineering Precedents*, (1999), Vol.1, A38.

tion, may nevertheless agree that rectification of the defects is necessary so as to ensure satisfactory and timely completion of the project. In such circumstances, they may wish to enter into an interim agreement by which the contractor will undertake the necessary remedial works, the employer will continue making payments to the contractor and the question of responsibility for the defects will be resolved subsequently.[6]

It has been pointed out[7] that the following issues should be borne in mind when negotiating such an agreement: 39–07

(i) whether the agreement is intended to be without prejudice to the parties' rights or without prejudice in the sense that it will be privileged from production[8];
(ii) whether existing rights of set-off should be excluded. An unscrupulous employer might take the benefit of the remedial works, but thereafter refuse to make payment on the ground that the remedial works were going to have to be undertaken by the contractor in any event. The employer could not, of course, refuse to make payment for the works in accordance with the contract in those circumstances, but might seek to raise by way of set-off losses consequent on the delay in remedying work not in conformity with the contract;
(iii) when and in what manner the dispute as to the quality of the works should be determined.

Additionally, the parties should be careful to ensure that the agreement is either expressed as a deed or supported by consideration.[9] It is an almost inevitable feature of this and other forms of agreement that one of the parties is obliged to do no more than it had agreed to do under the construction contract.[10] 39–08

CERTIFICATES AND RETENTIONS

Structure of construction contracts. The traditional construction contract, whereby there is "an entire contract for the sale of goods and work and labour for a lump sum price payable by instalments as the goods are delivered and the work is done",[11] is often (although not invariably) 39–09

---

[6] For example by expert determination, adjudication, arbitration, litigation, or some form of ADR. For a thorough review of the range of available methods of dispute-resolution, see Brown and Marriott, *ADR Principles and Practice* (2nd ed., 1999).
[7] Fenwick Elliott, n.5, above, Ch.14, which also includes a precedent for a form of agreement (para.14–170).
[8] See Ch.27, above.
[9] See Ch.3, above.
[10] See *Westminster Building Company v Beckingham* [2004] B.L.R. 163 in which an adjudicator held that a variation agreement was unenforceable because it was not supported by consideration. It was held that the adjudicator had jurisdiction to decide as he did.
[11] Lord Diplock in *Modern Engineering v Gilbert-Ash* [1974] A.C. 689 at 717.

predicated on the basis that the price and its instalments will be certified, either by a third party acting impartially as between the parties,[12] or by one of the parties itself acting under a duty of good faith.[13] Often an agreed percentage is held back from certified amounts by way of "retention" to be released in stages on satisfactory completion of the works.

39-10 In many forms of contract certificates issued during the course of the works are not conclusive as to compliance with the contract. However, there may be a provision requiring the issue of a final certificate which gives rise to evidential or procedural bars to claims by any party.[14] Some standard forms attempt to accommodate settlement agreements reached between the parties. An example is cl.30.2.2 of the JCT Standard Form of Building Contract (1998 edition):

> "If any adjudication, arbitration or other proceedings have been commenced by either Party before the Final Certificate has been issued the Final Certificate shall have effect as conclusive evidence as provided in clause 30.9.1 after either:
>
> 2.1 such proceedings have been concluded, whereupon the Final Certificate shall be subject to the terms of any decision, award or judgment in or settlement of such proceedings; or
> 2.2 a period of 12 months after the issue of the Final Certificate during which neither Party has taken any further step in such proceedings, whereupon the Final Certificate shall be subject to any terms agreed in partial settlement, whichever shall be the earlier."

39-11 The terms of settlement of any proceedings (including adjudication) commenced before the issue of the final certificate may override the conclusive effect of the certificate. Although the expression "agreed in partial settlement" is somewhat obscure, it is suggested that if proceedings have been commenced before the issue of a final certificate, but have lain dormant for 12 months, the final certificate will be conclusive,[15] subject to any issue that may have been compromised during the course of those proceedings.

39-12 **Certificates.** If the parties have agreed to settle a dispute arising under a contract containing certification provisions, they must consider whether their agreement is intended to operate within the context of those

---

[12] See the analysis by Lord Hoffmann in *Beaufort Developments (NI) Ltd v Gilbert-Ash (NI) Ltd* [1999] 1 A.C. 266 at 275–282.
[13] *Balfour Beatty Civil Engineering Ltd v Docklands Light Railway Ltd* (1996) 78 B.L.R. 42 at 57, *per* Sir Thomas Bingham M.R.
[14] *Crown Estates Commissioners v John Mowlem & Co Ltd* (1994) 70 B.L.R. 1; *Matthew Hall Ortech v Tarmac Roadstone* (1997) 87 B.L.R. 96.
[15] *Blackpool Borough Council v F Parkinson Ltd* (1991) 58 B.L.R. 85 at 108.

provisions or to replace them. Generally, construction contracts provide, either through the evolution of standard forms or through individual negotiation, a complex interaction of the allocation of risk. Parties should be cautious of interfering with the structure of a contract, particularly during the course of the works to which it relates.

Agreements as to the content of certificates. An agreement operating within the context of the provisions of the contract will allow specific issues to be compromised while preserving the contractual machinery for dealing with outstanding matters, both contentious and non-contentious, in the manner agreed between the parties. This may be achieved by an agreement that operates only to settle the content or quantum of a certificate to be issued by the certifier. 39–13

Parties must exercise care when dealing with certificates from which deductions have been made, otherwise they run the risk, if not actually of creating a compromise of the disputes inherent in such a certificate, at least of prejudicing their ability subsequently to claim the sums deducted.

> In *CPL Contracting Ltd v Cadenza Residential Ltd*,[16] C (the contractor) made application for payment. The employer's agent issued a certificate for a lesser sum. C issued an invoice said to be for the valuation "as agreed". Two days later D (the employer) issued an ineffective notice of withholding deducting further sums and paid the net amount. Several months later C served a notice to adjudicate. H.H. Judge Kirkham held that at no stage prior to the notice to adjudicate did C indicate that it pursued the balance under its application, consequently there was no dispute to refer to adjudication and the adjudicator had no jurisdiction. Judge Kirkham did, however, reject the submission that there was a binding agreement whereby C had agreed that it would not seek payment as regards any under-valuation in relation to the application.

Since the decision was limited to the jurisdiction of an adjudicator appointed at a particular point in time, it is unclear whether C might subsequently have been able to raise a dispute that could have been referred to adjudication or arbitration.

"Clean break" agreements. On the other hand, parties are often attracted by "clean break" agreements (usually in terms of the agreement of the final account after allowance for cross-claims), particularly after the works are physically, although not contractually, complete. Such an agreement usually discharges the contract and also the jurisdiction of the certifier. Parties should ensure that the agreement addresses all outstanding financial matters (such as retentions) and should also consider liability for latent defects and whether the provisions of the original contract giving a discharge by way of final certificate are to apply[17] or whether liability is to 39–14

---

[16] [2005] T.C.L.R. 1.
[17] For an example of the difficulties that can arise where this is not done, see: *Tameside Metropolitan Borough Council v Barlow Securities Group Services Ltd* [2001] B.L.R. 113.

be preserved. Additionally, if the jurisdiction of the certifier is to be discharged before the opportunity finally to review the sums comprised in interim certificates, consideration should be given to declaring in any agreement that the certifier is also discharged from any liability to any party arising out of the interim certificates.[18]

39-15 Retentions. As indicated above, a specific point that should not be overlooked in a "clean break" settlement is the treatment of retentions. If the payment of a single further sum is agreed, it is advisable to state whether it is inclusive or exclusive of retentions. While the employer might be negotiating on the basis of the actual payments made to date, the contractor might regard the retentions as a fund of money that has already been earned, but has not yet been paid. Under certain forms of contract the contractor would be correct, but other forms allow the employer to have recourse to the retention fund and to deduct, for example, liquidated damages for delay.[19]

MULTIPLE ISSUES

39-16 Historically, construction disputes have involved multiple issues. This has given rise to the development of techniques such as the Scott Schedule and, more recently, the practice of the Technology and Construction Court to order trials of preliminary issues and sub-trials. The compromise of discrete issues in construction cases raises a number of matters to be addressed:

 (i) multiple causes of action causative of the same or similar damage;
 (ii) causes of action in respect of which damage has not yet accrued or been discovered;
 (iii) latent defects; and
 (iv) the effect of offers to settle in litigation and arbitration.

39-17 Multiple causes of action causative of the same or similar damage. It is not uncommon for a party to a construction dispute to frame its claim not only in terms of breach of the substantive contract, but also in tort (for misrepresentation, negligence or breach of statutory duty), in quasi-contract (for restitutionary remedies) or for breach of a collateral contract. The reasons for such strategies are to take advantage of the limitation periods applicable in tort or equity or of different measures of damage. If particular

---

[18] A certifier will usually be liable to the employer by whom the certifier is retained (see *Sutcliffe v Thackrah* [1974] A.C. 727), but it is more doubtful that there will be liability to the contractor following the decision in *Pacific Associates v Baxter* [1990] Q.B. 993 (for a discussion of the circumstances in which a certifier might be liable to a contractor, see *Jackson & Powell on Professional Negligence* (5th ed., 2002), paras 2–64—2–68.
[19] See *Henry Boot Building Ltd v The Croydon Hotel & Leisure Co Ltd* (1985) 36 B.L.R. 41.

issues are to be compromised, the parties should ensure that they are clearly identified in any agreement or order embodying the compromise. The problems associated with failing to do so have been addressed elsewhere.[20]

Causes of action in respect of which damage has not yet accrued or been discovered. The ordinary limitation period for actions founded on a simple contract is six years (or 12 if the contract is a "speciality", *i.e.* deed) from the date on which the cause of action accrued.[21] The cause of action will accrue on the date of breach of the contract. In conventional construction contracts the cause of action in respect of defects will run from the date on which possession of the relevant part of the works was handed over, not when the defective works were carried out.[22] The exception to this is claims under the Defective Premises Act 1972: the proviso to s.1(5)of the Act provides that if, after completion of the dwelling, any further work is done to rectify defective work, any cause of action in respect of the further work is deemed to have accrued when the further work was finished. Accordingly, a fresh cause of action accrues when further work is carried out that does not rectify the original defect[23]

39–18

Section 32 of the Limitation Act 1980 provides that:

39–19

"(1) Subject to subsection (3) below, where in the case of any action for which a period of limitation is prescribed by this Act:

(a) . . .

(b) any fact relevant to the claimant's right of action has been deliberately concealed from him by the defendant; or

(c) . . .

the period of limitation shall not begin to run until the claimant has discovered the . . . concealment . . . or could with reasonable diligence have discovered it . . .

(2) For the purposes of subsection (1) above, deliberate commission of a breach of duty in circumstances in which it is unlikely to be discovered for some time amounts to deliberate concealment of the facts involved in that breach of duty."

In the previous edition of this book it was suggested that the importance of this section had been greatly increased by the decision of the Court of Appeal in *Brocklesby v Armitage & Guest*,[24] in which it was held that it is not

39–20

---

[20] See paras 6–07 *et seq.*, above.
[21] Limitation Act 1980, ss.5, 8.
[22] *Tameside Metropolitan Borough Council v Barlow Securities Group Services Ltd* [2001] B.L.R. 113 at 124.
[23] *Alderson v Beetham Organisation Ltd* [2003] B.L.R. 217.
[24] [2001] 1 All E.R. 172.

necessary for the purpose of extending the limitation period pursuant to s.32(1)(b) of the 1980 Act to demonstrate that the fact relevant to the claimant's right of action has been deliberately concealed in any sense greater than that the commission of the act was deliberate (in the sense of being intentional) and that that act or omission, as the case may be, did involve a breach of duty whether or not the actor appreciated that legal consequence.[25] The case was followed in *Liverpool Roman Catholic Archdiocese Trustees Incorporated v Goldberg*.[26] It was also suggested that this decision arguably rendered it difficult for any professional to raise a limitation defence. In *Cave v Robinson Jarvis and Rolf*,[27] the House of Lords overruled both cases, and held that the section did not include a failure to disclose a negligent breach of duty that the actor was not aware of committing.

39–21 Latent defects. Problems can arise in connection with the compromise of claims for defects where there is the potential for further defects to manifest themselves at some point in the future. In *Brunsden v Humphrey*[28] it was said that it is a "well settled rule of law that damages resulting from one and the same cause of action must be assessed and recovered once for [*sic*] all". That case was followed in *Conquer v Boot*[29]:

> In that case D contracted to build a bungalow for C in a good and workmanlike manner. C brought an action in the county court "for breach of contract to complete in a good and workmanlike manner", setting forth particulars of what he alleged required to be done to fulfill the contract, and he obtained damages. He afterwards brought another action, claiming in identical terms for breach of the same contract except as to amount claimed, and the addition that the contract was to build "with proper materials". This was followed by particulars different from, but of the same character as, those in the first action. D pleaded *res judicata*.

Sankey L.J. held thus[30]:

> "The cause of action here is: (1) the contract to complete in a good and workmanlike manner a bungalow, and (2) the breach of it. I do not think that every breach of it—every particular brick or particular room that is faulty—gives rise to a separate cause of action. I am of opinion that the cause of action here was the contract and the breach of it, both of which had been assigned in the original action. I do not think it is possible to say that every one of these breaches is a separate cause of action."

---

[25] *ibid.*, *per* Morritt L.J. at 181
[26] [2001] 1 All E.R. 182 at 190.
[27] [2003] 1 A.C. 384.
[28] [1884] 14 Q.B.D. 141 at 147, *per* Bowen L.J.
[29] [1928] 2 K.B. 336.
[30] *ibid.* at 342.

Thus, settlement of a claim for defective workmanship may preclude a **39–22** further action in respect of defects emerging subsequently.[31] It has been said that if an employer is sued for the balance of the contract price and is apprehensive lest all the defects have not yet manifested themselves, his correct course is to pay the claim and bring a separate action for the defects at a later stage[32] based on the decision in *Davis v Hedges*.[33]

> In *Mostcash Plc (formerly UK Paper Plc) v Fluor Ltd (No.1)*,[34] the parties had compromised earlier proceedings "in full and final settlement of all claims and in satisfaction of all causes of action . . . arising out of or in connection with [the project] . . . excluding only any cause of action that may in future accrue to [the claimant] (a) for any latent defect arising from [the defendant's] design . . .". Subsequent proceedings were commenced claiming damages for breach of contract or negligence in respect of design. The Court of Appeal held that the case of *Bank of Credit and Commerce International SA v Ali*[35] did not require the court to approach the compromise on the basis that the parties did not intend their compromise to extend to future causes of action of which they would not have had knowledge at the date of the compromise. But for the exclusion, the claims in the subsequent proceedings would have fallen within the compromise. The parties clearly contemplated that there might be existing causes of action for latent defects in design, and those causes of action fell within the settlement agreement.

Care must also be exercised in settling claims for professional negligence: **39–23**

> In *Hamlin v Edwin Evans*,[36] C appealed against a decision that their claim in negligence against D in relation to a survey of their house was out of time under the Limitation Act 1980, s.14A. C had settled a claim for negligent omission in the survey in respect of dry rot, but subsequently the consequences of more serious structural defects were discovered and a fresh writ was issued eight years after the report was made and six years from the discovery of the dry rot. On a preliminary issue, the judge found that time ran from the date of knowledge of the dry rot and therefore the writ for the structural defects was out of time. On appeal it was held that possessed only one single and indivisible cause of action arising out of one negligent act, the making of a single report.

---

[31] An exception to this is where the terms of the contract indicate that latent defects give rise to separate causes of action. Further, in *Steamship Mutual Underwriting Association Ltd v Trollope & Colls (City) Ltd* (1986) 33 B.L.R. 81 at 101, Lloyd L.J. held that in each case it will depend on the facts whether or not the damage gives rise to a separate cause of action.

[32] *Keating on Building Contracts* (7th ed., 2001), para.17–12.

[33] (1871) L.R. 6 Q.B. 687 where, in an action for damages for the non-performance and improper performance of certain work which the claimant had employed the defendant to do, the defence set up was that the defendant had sued the claimant for the price of the work alleged to have been improperly done, and the claimant had settled by paying the whole amount then sued for. As the claimant might have given the non-performance and the defective performance complained of in evidence in reduction of damages, the claimant was precluded from bringing a cross action for them, and it was held that though the claimant might have used the causes of action for which he sued in reduction of the claim in the former action, he was not bound to do so, but might maintain a separate action for them.

[34] [2002] B.L.R. 411.

[35] [2002] 1 A.C. 251.

[36] (1996) 80 B.L.R. 85.

39–24 Effect of offers to settle. Parties are encouraged by the Civil Procedure Rules to make offers in respect of parts of an action or issues that arise within it.[37] The question may arise whether a party may accept such an offer and continue to dispute the other parts of, or issues in, the action.

39–25 In *Stock v London Underground Ltd*,[38] C brought a negligence action against D on the basis that commercial premises owned by C had been damaged as a result of D's tunnelling. The damage suffered was both structural and economic. C presented particulars of claim setting out several varied and distinct heads of damage and D made a payment into court to cover the entire cost of repairs. There was, in addition, a claim for consequential loss arising from damage to a recording studio located in the same building in the sum of £25 million. The payment into court was declared ineffective at first instance as it was held to satisfy only part of the cause of action. D appealed, contending that the types of damage represented separate causes of action as they differed in nature, extent and the proof required. The Court of Appeal held, dismissing the appeal, that the principle applicable in personal injury cases that various heads of claim did not create several causes of action applied also to building disputes. The central issue was the definition of a "cause of action". The fact that all the damage complained of was caused by the same breach of duty was a crucial factor. It was not correct to distinguish between the differing mechanisms by which each of the aspects of damage were caused because there was a single breach of duty by a single tortfeasor, and *Steamship Mutual Underwriting Association Ltd v Trollope and Colls (City) Ltd*[39] was distinguished. The fact that the extent and nature of the heads of damage were substantially different was not a factor which would create different causes of action, as in the instant case the claims formed a single composite claim.

39–26 On the other hand, claims and counterclaims will usually be separate causes of action and settlement agreements should ensure that where an employer is offering to pay a sum to a contractor it is expressly declared whether the sum is intended to take account of any counterclaims of the employer or whether the employer will seek to pursue its counterclaims notwithstanding. An example of the difficulties that arise where an offer is unclear is found in *John Mowlem Construction v Secretary of State for Defence*.[40]

MULTIPLE PARTIES

39–27 Construction disputes frequently involve multiple parties, employers, occupiers, contractors, subcontractors, materials suppliers, professional advisors, guarantors and insurers. The presence of numerous parties with different relationships, liabilities and interests complicates settlement.[41]

---

[37] See para. 16–07, above.
[38] *The Times*, August 13, 1999.
[39] (1986) 33 B.L.R. 77. Pt 36 does not refer to an offer in respect of a "cause of action".
[40] (2001) 82 Con. L.R. 140.
[41] See paras 6–26 *et seq.*, above.

"The same damage" and Civil Liability (Contribution) Act 1978.[42] An illustration of these difficulties is provided by the case of *Birse Construction Ltd v Haiste Ltd*.[43]   39–28

> A water authority contracted with C for the design and construction of a reinforced concrete storage reservoir. C retained D as consulting engineers. 3P was employed by the water authority, who appointed him as engineer for the purpose of the contract with C and as the construction engineer for the purpose of s.7 of the Reservoirs Act 1975 to issue all necessary certificates. After completion the reservoir was found to be defective. The water authority's claim against C in respect of the defective reservoir and consequential losses was settled by an agreement under which C was to construct a new reservoir at its own expense. C sued D, who in turn claimed contribution from 3P pursuant to s.1 of the Civil Liability (Contribution) Act 1978. The judge held that 3P's liability to D was in respect of the "same damage" within the meaning of s.1(1) of the Act of 1978 as the liability of D to C, and that D was entitled to claim contribution from him. On appeal by 3P the Court of Appeal held, allowing the appeal, that on the true construction of s.1(1) of the Civil Liability (Contribution) Act 1978 "the same damage" referred to the damage suffered by the person to whom the party seeking contribution was liable; that the damage suffered by the water authority, namely the physical defects in the reservoir, and the damage suffered by C, namely the financial loss of having to construct a second reservoir for the water authority, were not, therefore, "the same damage" within the meaning of the section and that, accordingly, D had no right to contribution from 3P under the Act.   39–29

The ruling of the Court of Appeal avoided the possibility of liability passing back to the water authority by circuity of action[44]: C settled with water authority, D liable to C, water authority (by its employee) liable to D. Parties to the settlement of a complex construction dispute should always be alive to this possibility.   39–30

Birse was followed in the Court of Appeal in *Royal Brompton Hospital NHS Trust v Watkin Gray International*[45]:   39–31

> In that case the employer had settled an arbitration against the contractor and pursued the professional team. The arbitration settlement contained an indemnity from the employer to the contractor in respect of any claims against it made by the professional team. The professional team sought to join the contractor to the employer's action against them. The joinder was disallowed on the grounds that the employer claimed from the contractor in the arbitration sums allegedly

---

[42] See para.6–52, above.
[43] [1996] 1 W.L.R. 675.
[44] In *Co-operative Retail Services Ltd v Taylor Young Partnership* [2000] B.L.R. 461 (a case concerning the relationship between the liability of parties to a construction contract to make contribution to losses caused by a fire and the insuring obligations under the contract), the Court of Appeal held that the formal defence of circuity of action ought to be "jettisoned" (*per* Brooke L.J. at 475). This decision was affirmed in the House of Lords ([2002] B.L.R. 272). Lord Hope observed (at 286) that there was much force in the point and that the true basis of the rule is to be found in the contract between the parties.
[45] [2001] 3 T.C.L.R. 2.

overpaid in consequence of the professional team's extensions of time and liquidated damages for delay which would have been claimed but for their certificates, but the damage claimed in the employer's action against the professional team was the detriment to, or impairment of, employer's bargaining position *vis-à-vis* the contractor in relation to the costs and expenses overpaid pursuant to the certificates and the liquidated damages which were not recovered. This was held not to be the same damage as the employer's claims against the contractor in the arbitration and, accordingly, there was no right to contribution under the Civil Liability (Contribution) Act 1978.[46]

The decision was affirmed by the House of Lords.[47]

39–32 In the Court of Appeal Stuart-Smith L.J. observed that this was not a case of a defective building in which both the contractor and the architect could be liable in respect of the same damage. Clearly, in such a case settlement with a contractor could lead to the contractor seeking contribution from the architect and the architect seeking contribution from the employer, either (if the architect were an independent professional), for example, on the basis of instructions given by the employer, or (if the architect were an employee of the employer)[48] on the basis of an implied right of indemnity.[49] In the House of Lords, Lord Steyn contemplated the same possibility[50]:

> "The characterisation of the Employer's claim against the Contractor is straightforward. It is for the late delivery of the building. This is not a claim which the Employer has made against the Architect. Moreover, notionally it is not damage for which the Architect could be liable merely by reason of a negligent grant of an extension of time. It is conceivable that an Architect could negligently cause or contribute to the delay in completion of works, *e.g.* by condoning inadequate progress of the work or by failing to chivvy the Contractor. In such a case the Contractor and the Architect could be liable for the same damage."

39–33 **Indemnities, subrogation rights and assignments.** Each of these may present problems similar to those outlined above. As in the *Royal Brompton* case,[51] parties may only be willing to settle if they are indemnified against future claims by other parties. As in the *Co-operative Retail Services*

---

[46] *Birse* was also followed by a differently constituted Court of Appeal in *BICC Limited and Cumbrian Industrials Limited v Parkman Consulting Engineers* [2002] B.L.R. 64. The *Brompton Hospital* case was not referred to in the judgment. It was observed, the case being concerned with the respective contributions to an employer's losses from design and workmanship, that it was artificial to categorise the damage suffered by the employer as the physical damage rather than the cost in dealing with the physical damage.
[47] [2002] B.L.R. 255.
[48] Possibly a more frequent situation after the decision of the Court of Appeal in *Merrett v Babb* [2001] EWCA Civ. 214.
[49] See *Chitty on Contracts* (29th ed., 2004), para.39–110.
[50] [2002] B.L.R. 255 at [22].
[51] See n.45, above.

case,[52] if parties claim the benefit of an insurance policy as co-insured, insurers may be unable to exercise subrogated rights[53] against them.

Parties may sometimes agree that, as a term of the settlement, one party is to take an assignment of the rights of another and pursue those rights for its own benefit. The circumstances in which the law permits such assignments have been considered above.[54] In the context of construction litigation this has been held permissible where the assignee had a genuine commercial interest in the subject-matter and there was only a very slight possibility of making a profit out of the litigation.[55] On the other hand, it has not been allowed where the assigned share of the proceeds of the litigation was disproportionate to the assignee's interest.[56] 39–34

Claims against joint contractors. 39–35

In *Connex South Eastern Limited v MJ Building Services Group Plc*,[57] D entered into a contract with C and an associated company. There was an agreement between D and the associated company which released the associated company. C claimed that the agreement also had the effect of releasing C because it was a joint contractor with its associated company. The Court of Appeal held that on the facts the settlement agreement did not release C.

The case does, however, serve to remind parties that where joint contractors are involved, discharge of one joint contractor will discharge all unless express words are used.

Claims against successive contract breakers. Where A, having sued B for damages for breach of contract, enters into a settlement with B expressed to be in full and final settlement of all its claims against B, is A thereafter precluded from pursuing against C a claim for damages for breach of another contract to the extent that this claim is for damages which formed part of A's claim against B? 39–36

In *Heaton v AXA Equity and Law Life Insurance Security Plc*[58] it was argued that the receipt of a sum in full and final settlement of a claim in tort or for breach of contract operated in the same way as a judgment so as to preclude any further claim against a third party for the same damage. The House of Lords held[59] that in considering whether a settlement agreement has this

---

[52] See n.44, above.
[53] See Ch.30, above.
[54] See para.4–83, above.
[55] *South East Thames Regional Health Authority v Y J Lovell (London) Ltd* (1985) 32 B.L.R. 127 at 138.
[56] *Advanced Technology Structures Ltd v Cray Valley Products* (1992) 63 B.L.R. 59 at 73ff. But see *Norglen Ltd v Reeds Rains Prudential* [1999] 2 A.C. 1, where this case was overruled.
[57] [2005] EWCA Civ 193.
[58] [2002] 2 A.C. 329. See paras 6–39 *et seq.*, above.
[59] *ibid.* at [81], *per* Lord Rodger.

effect, the proper question is whether, when construed against the appropriate matrix of fact, the terms of the settlement show that the parties intended that the agreed sum should be in full satisfaction of the wrong done to the claimant. In that connection, an indication in the agreement whether express or implied that the claimant envisages the possibility of further proceedings against another wrongdoer may, of course, be of significance but only as a pointer to the conclusion that the parties did not intend that the agreed sum should be in full satisfaction of the harm suffered by the claimant. Equally, an indication in the agreement to the opposite effect will be a pointer that the parties intended that the agreed sum should constitute full satisfaction. In either event, the court will draw the appropriate conclusion as to the effect of the agreement on any claims against another wrongdoer.

39–37 Impugning settlements for duress.

In *Carillion Construction Limited v Felix (UK) Limited*[60] C was the main contractor and engaged D as a subcontractor. D breached its delivery obligations and told C that future deliveries were dependent on agreement by C of its final account in the sum of £3.3 million. C did not agree to that amount. C considered its position but was advised that adjudication would take too long and that an application for injunctive relief was unlikely to succeed. Accordingly, C reached an agreement with D to settle the final account in the sum of £3.2 million. C made a written complaint to D, mentioning duress. The settlement agreement was put into effect and D completed its deliveries. C sought an order rescinding the agreement on the grounds of duress. It was held by Dyson J., allowing the application, that duress required illegitimate pressure to be applied which compelled the victim's agreement to enter into a contract, following *DSND Subsea Limited (formerly DSND Oceantech Ltd) v Petroleum Geo Services ASA*.[61] D's threat to withhold deliveries until settlement of its final account was a threat to breach the contract when it was already guilty of culpable delay. The pressure exerted by D in threatening to withhold deliveries was illegitimate and gave C no real choice but to enter into the settlement agreement.

39–38 Global settlements.

The difficulties attendant upon seeking contribution by way of damages where a party has entered into a global settlement with another (typically the main contractor settling with the employer and seeking contribution from the subcontractors) will be explored in the next section, but a situation can also arise where one party has settled with another and a third party seeks a part of that payment (for example, where the employer settles with the main contractors and the subcontractors seek payment from the main contractor).

In *Durabella Limited v Jarvis & Sons Limited*[62] C was a subcontractor to D on "pay when paid" terms. D had been involved in previous proceedings with the employer which had been compromised on terms which, at the behest of D, included the following "no value is included within the settlement figure

---

[60] [2001] B.L.R. 1.
[61] [2000] B.L.R. 530.
[62] (2001) 83 Con.L.R. 145.

for works undertaken in connection with the Development by [C] the subject of [the action by C] and [the employer] has taken account of its counterclaim . . . in calculating the sum to be paid to [D]". H.H. Judge Humphrey Lloyd Q.C. held that the settlement had no evidential value whatsoever as showing whether or not D received payment for C's work. The relevant clause inserted by D had the deliberate intention of misleading readers as to the employer's supposed position.

This case clearly demonstrates that the court will look behind the form or words used in a global settlement to ascertain the underlying position and to ensure that third parties rights are not unjustly affected.

CLAIMS FOR CONTRIBUTION TO SETTLEMENTS REACHED WITH OTHER PARTIES

Given the prevalence of arbitration clauses in construction contracts and the difficulties in English law attendant on joining further parties to an arbitration,[63] it is not uncommon for parties, bound to resolve their disputes by arbitration, to reach terms of settlement within the context of the arbitration and then to pursue other parties for contribution to the settlement. This has led to a considerable jurisprudence on the topic arising from construction disputes. 39–39

THE PRINCIPLE IN *BIGGIN V PERMANITE*[64]

In this case manufacturers of specialised products from bitumen prepared an adhesive called "Permasec" for use with roofing felt which was to be capable of being applied cold owing to the scarcity of fuel at that time in Holland where it was to be used. They sold it to roofing contractors who resold it to specialists in roofing materials for supply to the Dutch Government, which disposed of it to numerous Dutch roofing contractors. The Permasec was used in the repair of house roofs mainly during the winter of 1945, and in the spring of 1946 it began to "creep" (drip and run). The roofs had to be repaired or renewed and claims were made against the Dutch Government. In May 1946, the Dutch Government asked its suppliers, the specialists in roofing materials, to take back 1,400 tons of Permasec unused, but they refused. The Dutch Government withheld £55,000 which it owed to its suppliers for roofing felt. It refused to submit to the jurisdiction of the English courts but consented to arbitration in England. The suppliers, on the advice of counsel on the day of the commencement of the arbitration, settled the claim for £43,000. They brought an action for damages for breach of warranty for this sum against the roofing contractors from whom they had bought it, who 39–40

---

[63] See the commentary on s.35 of the Arbitration Act 1996, in Mustill and Boyd, *Commercial Arbitration* (2nd ed., 2001 Companion), at p.309.
[64] [1951] 2 K.B. 314. See T.O. Trotman, "Relying on settlements: the rationale of Biggin v Permanite", L.M.C.L.Q., May 2, 2000, 222–229.

brought in the manufacturers of products from bitumen as third parties. Liability was admitted but on the question of damages. At first instance,[65] Devlin J. held that since a defendant required to indemnify a claimant against his liability to another party was entitled to have the existence and precise extent of that liability proved against him in proceedings to which he was a party, and since the compromise between the claimants and the Dutch Government was not a foreseeable consequence of the making of a claim but flowed from the voluntary act of the claimants, such compromise was irrelevant to the issue of damages between the claimants and the defendants. Evidence of that settlement was irrelevant and inadmissible, and the claim for the £43,000 as a lump sum failed. On appeal[66] the Court of Appeal reversed Devlin J. and held that the amount paid under the settlement being admittedly an upper limit *prima facie* led to the conclusion that, if reasonable, it should be taken as the measure of damages, and whether or not it was reasonable, was a question to be determined by evidence; and in the circumstances the evidence in the case established that it was reasonable.

39–41 Somervell L.J. said this[67]:

"I think that the judge here was wrong in regarding the settlement as wholly irrelevant. I think, though it is not conclusive, that the fact that it is admittedly an upper limit would lead to the conclusion that, if reasonable, it should be taken as the measure. The result of the judge's conclusion is that [the claimants] must prove their damages strictly to an extent to show that they equal or exceed £43,000; and that if that involves, as it would here, a very complicated and expensive inquiry, still that has to be done. The law, in my opinion, encourages reasonable settlements, particularly where, as here, strict proof would be a very expensive matter. The question, in my opinion, is: what evidence is necessary to establish reasonableness? I think it relevant to prove that the settlement was made under advice legally taken. The client himself could do that, but I do not think that the advisers would normally be relevant or admissible witnesses. I say 'normally'. It may be that in special cases they might be. [The claimant] must, I think, lead evidence, which can be cross-examined to, as to facts which the witnesses themselves prove and as to what would probably be proved if, as here, the arbitration had proceeded, so that the court can come to a conclusion whether or not the sum paid was reasonable. The defendant may, by cross-examination, as was done here, seek to show—and perhaps successfully show—that it was not reasonable. He may do so, or call evidence which leads to the same conclusion. He might in some cases show that some vital matter had been overlooked. In the present case, of course, Sir Walter Monckton relies, rightly, on the judge's finding with regard to the first head of damage, on the fact that the

---

[65] [1951] 1 K.B. 422.
[66] [1951] 2 K.B. 314.
[67] *ibid.* at 321.

evidence showed that too much was bought, and so on; but if there is evidence at the end of the matter of the kind which I have indicated, on which the court can come to the conclusion that this was a reasonable settlement in the circumstances, then I think that it should be the measure. Parties, Bowen L.J. said, have been held to contemplate litigation in the sort of circumstances which have arisen here. It would, I think, be unfortunate if they were not also held to contemplate reasonable settlements in the type of circumstances which have arisen here."

Singleton L.J. said[68]:

39–42

"Therefore, in a case such as this, the claimants must call evidence to establish their case. If the evidence which they call satisfies the judge or jury that the settlement was a reasonable one, the damages awarded will be the amount of the settlement and the costs reasonably incurred. I do not think that any good purpose is served by calling counsel who advised the settlement to say that he did so advise, even if the evidence is admissible. It could only be followed by questions why he so advised, and that would be asking him to do the work of the judge. Moreover, the duty of the judge at the trial is to determine the damages; and the facts proved before him might be quite different from those known to counsel at the time of his advice to settle for so much. The trial judge must make up his own mind on the facts he finds proved before him. At the same time, I am far from saying that the settlement ought to be disregarded. No one can think that a person or a company will agree to pay £43,000 damages lightly. It is a matter for consideration that the settlement was arrived at under advice, the more so as the party settling may be quite uncertain as to whether he can recover anything against someone else. If, upon the evidence, the judge is satisfied that the damages would be somewhere around the figure at which the claimants had settled, he would be justified in awarding the settlement figure. I do not consider that it is part of his duty to examine every item in those circumstances. The claimants put forward their claim and call evidence to establish it. The defendants have an opportunity of cross-examining the claimants' witnesses and of calling evidence themselves. The claimants must establish a prima facie case that the settlement was a reasonable one. If the defendants fail to shake that case, the amount of the settlement can properly be awarded as damages. The position is much the same, though perhaps not quite so strong, as in a case in which damages have been assessed in a suit between other parties involving the same facts. The judgment is not binding, but the court will not lightly disregard it in the absence of fresh evidence or new factors . . .

---

[68] *ibid.* at 325–326.

The question is not whether the claimants acted reasonably in settling the claim, but whether the settlement was a reasonable one; and, in considering it, the court is entitled to bear in mind the fact that costs would grow every day the litigation was continued. That is one reason for saying that it is sufficient for the purpose of the claimants if they satisfy the judge that somewhere around the figure of settlement would have been awarded as damages."

39–43   These judgments have been considered subsequently in several cases, both at first instance and on appeal. The decisions are sometimes not easy to reconcile. The differences appear to have centred on:

(i) what must be proved to demonstrate a reasonable settlement;
(ii) (as a sub-issue) the relevance and admissibility of advice received; and
(iii) the position in multi-party cases.

Additionally, consideration must be given to situations where there are express indemnities.

39–44   **What must be proved to demonstrate a reasonable settlement.** In *Fletcher & Stuart v Jay & Partners*[69] the Court of Appeal approved the statement of the *Biggin* principle by the Official Referee, namely that it was concerned only with the question whether a reasonable sum paid in settlement can be regarded as the proper measure of damages in a subsequent action where liability is not in issue. A defendant cannot impose liability on a third party by settling the claimant's claim against him, where the obligations of the defendant to the claimant are the same as those of the third party to the defendant. Geoffrey Lane L.J. pointed out that *Biggin* has nothing to do with proving the liability of a third party to a defendant.[70]

39–45   In *Holland Hannen v WHTSO*,[71] the Court of Appeal emphasised that the court has to consider not the reasonableness of the conduct of the parties, but the reasonableness of the compromise itself.

39–46   In *Fairfield-Mabey Limited v Shell UK*[72] the settlement was reasonable, but the claim failed because it could not be established that the third party was liable.

39–47   *Seven Seas Properties Ltd v Al-Essa (No.2)*[73] is an example of a case where the settlement was not held to be reasonable. Gavin Lightman Q.C., sitting as a deputy High Court judge, held that it is not sufficient for the

---

[69] (1976) 17 B.L.R. 38.
[70] *ibid.* at 44 and 46.
[71] (1985) 35 B.L.R. 1 at 15.
[72] (1989) C.I.L.L. 514.
[73] [1993] 1 W.L.R. 1083 at 1089.

claimant merely to plead the compromise without any explanation as to how the settlement figure was made up or arrived at, or any evidence as to how or why or on what advice it was entered into. He rejected the claim because he considered that it over-valued certain matters.

39–48 In *P&O Developments v Guy's and St Thomas' National Health Service Trust*[74] H.H. Judge Bowsher Q.C. held that an agreement made with a person not a party to the action is relevant and admissible on two bases: (a) as a rule of evidence—the settlement may be some evidence of the true value of the claim settled, it sets a maximum to the claim and may reduce the degree and detail of evidence required to prove the claim; and (b) the reasonable settlement of claims may be a matter which parties may be held to have in their reasonable contemplation under the second rule in *Hadley v Baxendale*.[75] By "reasonable settlement" the judge meant that it was based on an assessment of what was legally due to the third party.

39–49 In *Royal Brompton National Health Service Trust v Hammond*[76] H.H. Judge Hicks Q.C. held, after a detailed analysis of what was in fact in dispute in *Biggin*, that the principle extends not only to cases where liability is not in dispute, but also where the settlement involves a compromise of issues of liability on a claim and counterclaim as well as issues of quantum.

39–50 It follows from the above that in each case the claimant must first show that the party from whom contribution is sought is liable to him for the loss, before going on to demonstrate that the sum paid by way of compromise was reasonable. It is not enough for the claimant to prove that a claim had been made and that it was reasonable to settle it. The apparent difference between the approaches in the *Fletcher & Stuart* and *Royal Brompton* cases may be explained on the basis that in the former case the liability referred to was that of the parties to the instant action, not that of the claimant to the party with whom the settlement was negotiated. It would rob the principle of any practical utility if it were not to apply to claims for contribution to settlements of disputed claims.

RELEVANCE AND ADMISSIBILITY OF ADVICE RECEIVED

39–51 In *Oxford University Press v John Stedman Design Group*[77] H.H. Judge Esyr Lewis Q.C. held that it was neither necessary nor indeed permissible to call evidence from any legal adviser to explain why the settlement was

---

[74] [1999] B.L.R. 3 at 13.
[75] (1854) 9 Ex. 341.
[76] [1999] B.L.R. 162, 170.
[77] (1990) 34 Con. L.R. 1, 101.

made and its basis. The court has to decide whether the settlement was reasonable in the light of the circumstances that are shown to have obtained when the settlement was made. The opinion of the lawyers who advised the party who settled is irrelevant.

39–52   In *The Society of Lloyds v Kitson's Environmental Services*[78] H.H. Judge Havery Q.C., however, held that where a party contends or accepts that the existence, nature and terms of any advice received are material facts to the issue of the reasonableness of the settlement, privilege in respect of the advice is waived.

39–53   In *DSL Group v Unisys International*[79] H.H. Judge Hicks Q.C. took a different view. He held that the defendant to the original claim must prove that the settlement was reasonable, not that he acted reasonably. The advice he received will go to the latter not the former. Accordingly, the nature of the advice is legally irrelevant and, therefore, privilege in respect of it is not waived automatically by any reference to it. This analysis was said to be "lucid and helpful" by H.H. Judge Humphrey Lloyd Q.C. in *J Sainsbury plc v Broadway Malyan*.[80] He held that the test is an objective one and so the fact that settlement was reached following legal advice is irrelevant.[81] In the *P&O*[82] case, H.H. Judge Bowsher Q.C. took another view. He held that advice received by a party might go either to the question whether the claimants acted reasonably or to the question whether the settlement was reasonable, or both. Moreover, whether the claimants acted reasonably may have an evidential bearing on whether the settlement was reasonable.

39–54   The editors of *Keating on Building Contracts*[83] suggest that the view in *DSL* is to be preferred to that in *P&O*. The judgments in *Biggin* recognise that the fact that the settlement was reached with advice is relevant, but Singleton L.J. expressed the view that there is no good purpose to be served by calling counsel who advised the settlement to say that he did so advise because it could only be followed by questions as to why he so advised. That would be asking him to do the work of the judge. On the other hand, the mere fact that advice was received must be of limited probative value: the advice may have been rendered on incomplete or inaccurate facts, or might simply have been wrong.

---

[78] (1994) 67 B.L.R. 102 at 116.
[79] (1994) 67 B.L.R. 117 at 137.
[80] (1998) 61 Con. L.R. 29 at 64.
[81] This statement appears to go somewhat further than H.H. Judge Hicks Q.C. went in the *DSL* case and is difficult to reconcile with Somervell L.J.'s statement in *Biggin* that "I think it relevant to prove that the settlement was made under advice legally taken" and Singleton LJ's that, "It is a matter for consideration that the settlement was arrived at under advice".
[82] (1999) B.L.R. 3 at 14.
[83] 7th ed., 2001, para.8–42, n.44.

Multi-party cases. In the *P&O*[84] case, H.H. Judge Bowsher Q.C. rejected 39–55
the submission that if a global settlement is reasonable, it is unnecessary to
prove the sums allocated to individual parties against whom contribution is
sought. He held that it was necessary to prove that the sums allocated were
each reasonable. H.H. Judge Hicks Q.C. came to a similar, but differently
expressed, conclusion in the *Royal Brompton* case[85]: the *Biggin* principle
applies to the issue where there are multiple defendants, but the liability of
each must be proved independently. It would be open to any defendant to
argue that its liability should not exceed a due proportion of the settlement
figure.

> In *Bovis Lend Lease Ltd (formerly Bovis Construction Ltd) v RD Fire* 39–56
> *Protection Ltd*,[86] following the settlement of claims and counterclaims brought
> by C against the employer, certain preliminary issues fell to be determined
> between C and its subcontractors, D1 and D2. C appointed D1 to carry out
> fire protection and dry lining works, but disputes arose and C progressively
> removed work from D1 and employed D2 to complete the outstanding work.
> C contended that defaults by both D1 and D2 had caused it to be in breach of
> the main contract, which had led the employer to bring substantial claims
> against C. It fell to be determined whether the global settlement between C
> and the employer precluded C from claiming for the alleged defaults against
> D1 and D2 where the settlement did not provide a means of determining the
> fault attributable to each of them and, further, whether C could rely on
> hypothetical remedial schemes instead of on the settlement to support its loss
> claims.

H.H. Judge Anthony Thornton Q.C. in a lengthy judgment which repays
study, considered the law concerning reliance on settlement agreements.
He derived eight conclusions from the *Biggin* line of authorities. His eighth
principle addressed multi-party cases:

> "8. The *Biggin* principles are not confined to cases where there is only
> one party causing the loss being settled or where the claims being
> settled are confined to those based on the defendant's breaches of
> contract. It is necessary, however, for the court to determine what part
> of an overall settlement of a multi-party or multi-issue dispute is
> attributable to the relevant breaches of contract of the defendant, or
> to each separate defendant where a *Biggin* claim is being made against
> more than one defendant. Any allocation of part of a reasonable
> overall settlement must itself be reasonable."

He then went on to identify six disputed issues as to the application of
the *Biggin* principles that arose on the facts of the case, but will arise in
many other cases:

---

[84] (1999) B.L.R. 3 at 11ff.
[85] (1999) B.L.R. 162 at 168–16.
[86] (2003) 89 Con. L.R. 169. See also Lewis Cohen, "Reasonableness of Settlements Revisited" (2005) 21 Const. L.J. 216.

39–57
(1) Where a potentially relevant settlement had been entered into, is it for the claimant or the defendant to establish what sum has been paid for, or a loss caused by, potentially relevant claims or causes of action? He held that it was for the claimant.

(2) What is the consequence when the wording of a settlement, particularly a multi-issue or multi-party settlement, does not identify what sum is included for the settlement of relevant claims or causes of action and there is no allocation of the overall sum to the relevant claims or causes of action? He held that it ought to be possible for a court to undertake the two necessary tasks of placing an appropriate value on the settlement and of apportioning from that an appropriate and reasonable overall value for the works in respect of which contribution is being sought. The court should not accept the assertion that these tasks are impossible unless there is clear and satisfactory factual and expert evidence to support it.

(3) Can a main contractor elect to bypass the settlement and seek to recover from its subcontractor its potential liability to the employer in full? He held that even if a claimant elects to prove its claim in some other way than by relying on a settlement, it is prevented from recovering more than the sum included in the settlement, even if a greater sum is proved by that alternative means.

(4) If a claimant cannot establish what part of the settlement related to or was allocatable to the defendant's breaches of contract, does it follow that that claimant recovers nothing? He held that in such circumstances, either the claimant fails to establish that any sum is included in the settlement, or the evidence might establish that certainly something was included in the settlement and the court should assess a reasonable sum. However, it might not be possible or reasonable to make such an assessment; if the unreasonableness had been the result of inequitable or self-induced conduct of the claimant, the claim would fail because the claimant could not establish what sum it lost. On the other hand, if the unreasonableness arose from factors outwith the claimant's control, it might be concluded that there was no significant reduction in the loss incurred by the claimant as a result of the settlement and the claimant may proceed to seek damages unconstrained by the settlement.

(5) Can the settlement be considered as reasonable and as one which has incurred the claimant in relevant loss given that it appears to be based on a larger claim for works than was being made by the employer and given further the limited size of the works claims relative to all other claims and counterclaims covered by the settlement? He held as to the former, following *Comyn Ching &*

Co (London) Limited v Oriental Tube Company Limited[87] that the inclusion of unpleaded claims does not automatically render a settlement unreasonable but must depend on the possibility that the claimant's ultimate liability might include those claims. As to the latter, he held that that was a matter of evidence.

(6) If the settlement is unreasonable so that its terms cannot be relied on by a claimant, what is the consequence and, in particular, do the claimant's claims fail completely? He held that if a settlement (or a part of a settlement) is found unreasonable it can provide no evidential foundation to establish the claimant's loss, but it would still provide a ceiling on recovery if the claim were sought to be established by conventional means. On the other hand, if it could be shown that the settlement constituted a break in the chain of causation or was a wholly unreasonable failure to mitigate the claimant's loss, nothing would be recoverable.

Payment in kind. Where a contractor has agreed with an employer to carry out remedial works that will nevertheless amount to "payment" within the meaning of s.1(4) of the Civil Liability (Contribution) Act 1978, at least where the payment in kind was capable of valuation in monetary terms. Accordingly, the contractor would not be precluded from seeking contribution under the 1978 Act from another party alleged to be liable in respect of the same damage.[87a]

39–57A

Indemnities. The existence of indemnities in the contract between the claimant and those from whom contribution is sought will affect the extent of recovery. An indemnity may be expressed to be against claims made, as opposed to liabilities[88] or be limited to specific liabilities.[89] It remains an undecided question whether the existence of a limited contractual right of indemnity will also limit the right of recovery under the *Biggin* principle. Some indication of the answer may be given by analogy to contracts of insurance. In *Lumbermen Mutual Casualty Company v Bovis Lend Lease Limited*[90] D was insured by C under a construction engineering and design

39–58

---

[87] (1979) 17 B.L.R. 47.
[87a] *Baker & Davies Plc v Leslie Wilks Associates (A Firm)* [2005] 3 All E.R. 603.
[88] See *Comyn Ching & Co Ltd v Oriental Tube Co Ltd* (1979) 17 B.L.R. 47 at 92, *per* Brandon L.J., *i.e.* it is not necessary to establish primary liability on the part of the person against whom secondary liability under the indemnity is sought.
[89] The editors of *Keating* (7th ed., 2001), point out that a special difficulty sometimes arises with management contracts, which often provide in substance that the management contractor's liability to the employer for defects or delay shall be limited to any amount that he actually recovers from the subcontractor responsible. Can the subcontractor successfully avoid liability by arguing that the management contractor has suffered no loss? They suggest that that while each case depends on the construction of the particular management contract and the subcontract and no general principle can be stated, the subcontractor's argument is likely to be thought unmeritorious.
[90] [2005] B.L.R. 47.

professional liability policy and a commercial excess liability policy. D commenced proceedings against its employer relating to the design and construction of a leisure and retail complex. The employer served a defence and counterclaim alleging, amongst other things, mismanagement of the project. The litigation was settled, but the settlement agreement did not identify how the sum paid to D was calculated or what elements of the counterclaim were recognised as valid. D then made claim under the policies. C sought a negative declaration. In the course of the argument C relied on the *Biggin* and *P&O* cases. The Commercial Court[91] held that the function of ascertainment of loss in the context of liability insurance is not identical to the process of proving the amount of loss caused by breach of contract where the consequence of such breach is liability of the claimant to a third party with whom a settlement has been entered into. In the context of liability insurance the process of ascertainment is not merely the process of evidencing loss, but represents that stage in the assured's relationship with the third party by which he sustains those compensatory liabilities to the third party specifically identified by the judgment, award or settlement agreement which, by the terms of the policy, is an essential element in the cause of action against insurers. There is no similar mechanism which operates as a precondition to the cause of action for an ordinary breach of contract. The claimant has his cause of action regardless of whether there was a judgment, award or settlement of a third party's claim against him. His only concern is to establish the measure of damages, and for this purpose the judgment, award or settlement is likely to provide the necessary evidence, although, as appears from the *P&O* case, this may not be of great weight in the case of the settlement agreement, especially if it is a global settlement.

AMENDMENT OF PLEADINGS BETWEEN DATE OF OFFER AND JUDGMENT OR AWARD

39–59 In construction disputes (in common with other types of complex litigation) parties' cases often develop as issues are investigated, necessitating extensive amendment to the pleadings. It may be that a claim succeeds or fails by reason, wholly or in part, of a late amendment.

39–60 **Claimant succeeds on late amendment.** In *Beoco Ltd v Alfa Laval Co Ltd*,[92] the Official Referee allowed the claimant to amend its case on the first day of trial and gave judgment for the claimant on the basis of the amendment. Stuart-Smith L.J. held that, as a general rule, where a claimant makes a late amendment which substantially alters the case the defendant has to meet, but without which the action will fail, the defendant is entitled to the costs of the action down to the date of the amendment.

---

[91] *ibid.* at [54], *per* Colman J.
[92] [1995] Q.B. 137.

Defendant succeeds on late amendment. In *Blexen Ltd v G Percy Trentham*,[93] in a construction arbitration an amendment by the respondent just before the hearing meant that the claimant failed to better a sealed offer. The arbitrator awarded the claimant its costs down to the date of the sealed offer and the respondent its costs thereafter. On appeal, the Official Referee held that the costs award should be remitted because the arbitrator misconducted himself in treating the amendments as irrelevant, whereas he should have asked whether the claimant acted reasonably in continuing the arbitration after the date of the offer. The Court of Appeal reversed the Official Referee on the ground that he did not have jurisdiction to make such an order under the Arbitration Act 1950, but it did consider what was the correct question for the arbitrator to have asked himself. Lloyd L.J. said[94]: 39–61

> "... the general rule should apply where the defendant amends to plead a new defence on which the burden rests on him, for example, a plea of limitation for liability or of some relevant contractual exception. In such a case, if the effect of the amendment is to reduce what would otherwise have been awarded below the sum paid in, it would usually be just to give the claimant his costs. In addition, it is normally preferable for the judge or an arbitrator to consider what would have been the result but for the amendment, rather than the simple question whether the claimant acted reasonably in continuing with the arbitration or action on the pleadings as they stood, or the more elusive question, whether the claimant would or would not have accepted the offer, had he known of the future amendments."

The point was revisited in *Cadmus Investment Company Ltd v Amec Building Ltd*,[95] a decision of the Commercial Court on appeal from a construction arbitrator. 39–62

> In 1992 C claimed an extension of time and loss and expense of £4.3 million. D made two sealed offers. The first, made in 1993, was rejected almost immediately. Just before the commencement of the hearing in 1995, D amended its defence alleging that C's claim had been compromised in 1990. During the hearing D made a second (increased) sealed offer. In August 1995 the arbitrator awarded C £437,356 which was approximately £25,000 less than the first sealed offer when adjusted for interest. The arbitrator decided that D should not have the benefit of the first sealed offer because of the late amendment. Costs should follow the event until the second sealed offer, after which D would have its costs. His reasoning was that had the compromise not been pleaded it was likely that C would have beaten the first offer, albeit by a narrow margin and, accordingly, C should have the benefit of the doubt because the late amendment was D's fault. Further, while the evidence

---

[93] (1990) 54 B.L.R. 37.
[94] *ibid.* at 47.
[95] [1998] A.D.R.L.J. 72.

suggested that C might well have rejected the first offer even if it had known of the defence, it would not be right to speculate about such a hypothetical situation. Tuckey J. upheld the arbitrator's decision on the basis that he properly directed himself in accordance with *Blexen*.

VALUE ADDED TAX

39–63 Construction claims often include some elements that attract VAT and others that do not. It is outwith the scope of this work to consider when VAT is applicable,[96] but parties engaged in the negotiation of a compromise of a construction dispute should consider whether any particular item attracts VAT and whether the receiving party is able to recoup the VAT element of the claim. It is generally good practice for any settlement to state the extent to which it includes or excludes VAT.

ADJUDICATION

39–64 **Interim nature of adjudication.** As stated at the opening of this chapter, adjudication is probably currently the principal formal method for resolving construction disputes. The law of compromise generally applies equally to disputes the subject of adjudication as it does to any other form of dispute resolution.

However, there is a specific point that should be borne in mind: the Housing Grants, Construction and Regeneration Act 1996, s.108, provides that a party to a construction contract[97] has the right to refer a dispute arising under the contract for adjudication under a procedure complying with the section. By s.108(3) of the 1996 Act one of the criteria with which the procedure must comply is that the contract must provide that the decision of the adjudicator is binding until the dispute is finally determined by legal proceedings, by arbitration (if the contract provides for arbitration or the parties otherwise agree to arbitration) or by agreement. If a dispute referred to adjudication is to be compromised, therefore, it must be decided whether the compromise is intended to be final or whether the dispute can be reopened in subsequent litigation or arbitration proceedings.

---

[96] Elliott, n.5, above, paras 6–135 *et seq.*, and paras 14–107 *et seq.*
[97] "(1) By s.104 of the Act a "construction contract" means an agreement with a person for any of the following—
  (a) the carrying out of construction operations;
  (b) arranging for the carrying out of construction operations by others, whether under sub-contract to him or otherwise; or
  (c) providing his own labour, or the labour of others, for the carrying out of construction operations.
(2) References in this Part to a construction contract include an agreement—
  (a) to do architectural, design, or surveying work; or
  (b) to provide advice on building, engineering, interior or exterior decoration or on the laying-out of landscape in relation to construction operations."

In *Bracken v Billinghurst*[98] C (the employer) had the benefit of two adjudicator's decisions, but nevertheless offered to compromise "the whole case" for a lesser sum. Solicitors acting for the contractor (D) and his company (which was found not to be the contracting party) made a counter-offer of a yet lower sum and enclosed a cheque drawn by the company. After a considerable lapse of time C presented the cheque, which was duly honoured. Very shortly thereafter C wrote to D stating that he intended to pursue the full amount of the adjudicators' awards. Simultaneously, C's solicitors wrote to D's solicitors stating that the cheque was accepted as a payment of account. H.H. Judge Wilcox held that since the counter-offer was made by a third party (the company), presentation and encashment of the cheque constituted acceptance of the offer of compromise. While this decision is an example of the rules governing acceptance of offers of compromise by banking cheques,[99] Judge Wilcox did refer to the fact that a valid adjudication award is only final pending the ultimate resolution of the disputes by agreement, arbitration or litigation,[1] and stated that had the offer of compromise been made by D he would have had no difficulty in concluding that there was an accord as C had acted in such a way as to induce D to think that the money was taken in satisfaction of the claims in dispute and had caused him to act on that view.

Adjudication and compromised disputes. Disputes that have been, or have been claimed to have been, compromised have been referred to adjudicators. 39–65

In *Lathom Construction Ltd v Cross*,[2] following the appointment of the adjudicator a compromise was reached and reduced to writing. There was a subsequent dispute as to whether the settlement was valid. The matter was referred back to the adjudicator. C argued that the claim was under the original contract and that the alleged compromise was a defence to that claim. The adjudicator found that there was a valid compromise but that on its true construction there was still an amount due to the C. D refused to pay on the grounds that the adjudicator had no jurisdiction to construe the settlement agreement. C commenced proceedings for summary judgment under CPR Pt 24. The judge found that the application before the adjudicator was properly made, but that D need only show a triable issue on an application for summary judgment and that the argument that, having found that there was a valid compromise, the adjudicator did not have any jurisdiction to consider the terms of the settlement, had a reasonable prospect of success.

The brief report of *Lathom* seems to indicate that the finding that the application before the adjudicator was properly made proceeded on the basis that the original dispute and the compromise could subsist simultaneously, with the result that in the event that the compromise was not observed, an award under the original dispute could be made. This appears to be contrary to the principle that a valid compromise ends the dispute from which it arose.[3] That principle was referred to by H.H. Judge Humphrey Lloyd Q.C. in *Shepherd Construction v Mecright Ltd*[4]: 39–66

---

[98] [2004] T.C.L.R. 41.
[99] See paras 3–30 *et seq.*, below.
[1] [2004] T.C.L.R. 41 at [21].
[2] (1999) C.I.L.L. 1568.
[3] See paras 6–01 *et seq.*, above.
[4] [2000] B.L.R. 489.

D were subcontractors employed by C in October 1998 under a subcontract for the supply and erection of steelwork. D carried out the work during 1999, but the subcontract was subject to variations. On March 15, 2000, D entered into a compromise agreement with C to settle the amount due under the subcontract. In July 2000, D requested an adjudication in respect of further sums they claimed were due. C relied on the settlement agreement in its reply to the adjudication request to contend that no further sums were due. D responded by arguing that the agreement had been obtained under duress, because of their financial difficulties. C sought a declaration that the settlement agreement meant that there was no dispute arising under the subcontract capable of being referred to adjudication; further, that the duress claim was not a dispute capable of adjudication. It was held that once parties had reached an agreement settling a dispute no further dispute existed that could be referred to adjudication. The Housing Grants, Construction and Regeneration Act 1996 provided for the referral of disputes arising "under" a construction contract and a dispute as to the terms of a settlement agreement was not a dispute under the original subcontract. The question of duress had not occurred prior to D's adjudication request, so that at that date there was no dispute between D and C upon which there could be an adjudication.

39–67   In an earlier edition of this work it was suggested that, if there was any inconsistency between *Lathom* and *Mecright*, the decision in the latter was to be preferred. In *Westminster Building Company v Beckingham*,[5] H.H. Judge Anthony Thornton Q.C. distinguished the decision in *Mecright*. He drew the distinction between, on the one hand, a settlement agreement settling all disputes or a stand alone agreement and, on the other, a variation agreement varying the terms of the underlying contract. Where the underlying contract contains a provision for adjudication allowing reference for any dispute arising "under the contract", a dispute as to the enforceability of the former will not fall within the jurisdiction of an adjudicator appointed under the underlying contract, whereas a dispute as to the enforceability of the latter will. Judge Thornton said[6]: "a dispute as to whether it is enforceable is one arising under the contract since its terms form part of, and are to be read with, the underlying contract".

39–68   **Forbearance from adjudication.**   Forbearance to sue has long been recognised as furnishing consideration for a compromise.[7] In *Joseph Finney Plc v Gordon Vickers and Gary Vickers t/a Mill Hotel*,[8] H.H. Judge David Wilcox gave summary judgment in a claim based on a compromise whereby the defendant agreed to pay an interim certificate in consideration of the claimant's promise not to proceed with an adjudication to enforce the claimant's rights under the contract.

---

[5] [2004] B.L.R. 163, cited at n.10 above.
[6] *ibid.* at [25].
[7] See paras 3–03 *et seq.*, above.
[8] Unreported, March 7, 2001.

PART 13

Administrative Court Proceedings

CHAPTER 40

The Resolution by Agreement of Administrative Court Proceedings

INTRODUCTION

A wide variety of proceedings in which the decisions or actions of public bodies are challenged are allocated to the Administrative Court, formerly known as the Crown Office List.[1] Most significant of these is the application for judicial review.[2] It is beyond the scope of this work to consider the practice applicable to Administrative Court cases generally, or to consider in detail the circumstances in which relief may be granted by the court.[3]

40–01

A very significant number of Administrative Court matters "settle". The Crown Office List Review chaired by Sir Jeffery Bowman, which reported in March 2000, obtained statistics for the year ending June 30, 1999.[4] Appendix E to the review team's report showed that in that year 1,622 cases had proceeded to the substantive hearing stage, of which 785 had been disposed of by consent or withdrawn. The rate of such disposals varied considerably between different categories of case.

40–02

---

[1] *Practice Direction (QBD) (Trials in London)* [1981] 1 W.L.R. 1296; *Practice Direction (Administrative Court: Establishment)* [2000] 1 W.L.R. 1654.
[2] Judicial review procedure is the procedure under Pt 8 of the Civil Procedure Rules as modified by CPR Pt 54: see CPR r.54.1(2)(e). Other Administrative Court business includes case stated appeals, certain statutory appeals and statutory applications to quash, habeas corpus proceedings and a miscellany of other matters.
[3] See, *e.g.* De Smith, Woolf and Jowell, *Judicial Review of Administrative Action* (5th ed., 1995); Lewis, *Judicial Remedies in Public Law* (3rd ed., 2004).
[4] Although Ch.2 of the report expressed doubts as to the accuracy of the statistics. See also Eynon, "Uncontested Proceedings in the Crown Office" [1999] J.R. 153.

40-03 It is relatively unusual for the resolution of Administrative Court proceedings to represent an instance of compromise in its true sense.[5] Generally speaking, one party or the other ceases to contest the claim, rather than there being a settlement involving an element of "give and take". This may be because the claimant or defendant comes to accept that its position is untenable, but often it is because it does not make sense in practical terms to take the matter further, irrespective of the merits. A particular reason for this is that many applications for judicial review and statutory appeals allocated to the Administrative Court seek to do no more than to compel a reconsideration of the original decision—inevitably so, because the court cannot normally substitute its own view of the proper outcome even if the decision-maker has erred in law. Where the claimant has a plausible case but the outcome of the litigation is uncertain, it will often be more sensible for the defendant to agree to take a fresh decision than to incur cost and delay by contesting the proceedings. For example, it is a very frequent practice[6] for the defendant in immigration and asylum cases to resist the application for permission to apply for judicial review, but to consent to a quashing order[7] if permission is granted.

40-04 Nonetheless, there may be cases where the outcome accords more closely with a conventional compromise. For example, a claimant may be prepared to withdraw an application for judicial review of a housing authority's decision to take possession proceedings against him, in return for a commitment by the authority to permit him to remain in his present accommodation for longer than would have been the case if the decision under challenge had been upheld by the court. Another example is a case in which the parties agree upon an order granting some but not all of the relief originally claimed (*e.g.* a quashing order but no mandatory order). Another form of compromise, in a case where a decision has been challenged on a number of grounds (say, lack of jurisdiction and a failure to take account of relevant considerations), might involve the defendant consenting to a quashing order and to reconsideration of its decision in return for the claimant agreeing not to challenge the new decision for want of jurisdiction.

ALTERNATIVE DISPUTE RESOLUTION

40-05 It is a long established principle that judicial review is a remedy of last resort, in the sense that permission to apply for judicial review will not normally be granted where there is some alternative remedy open to the

---

[5] See para.1–03, above.
[6] *e.g. Gnanavarathan v A Special Adjudicator* [1995] Imm. A.R. 64 at 72; *R. v Immigration Appeal Tribunal Ex p. Probakaran* [1996] Imm. A.R. 603 at 606. The practice was noted in Appendix E of the Bowman Report as explaining the particularly high incidence of consent orders in such cases.
[7] Note that the former orders of *mandamus*, *prohibition* and *certiorari* are now known as mandatory orders, prohibiting orders and quashing orders respectively.

claimant. Such alternative remedies may include not only other statutory rights of appeal or review, but also the ability to pursue the defendant's internal complaints procedures or to complain to some external regulator. The detail of these matters is outside the scope of this work. However, in *R. (Cowl) v Plymouth CC*[8] the Court of Appeal built upon the discretionary nature of the power to grant or withhold permission for judicial review proceedings, in order to encourage the use of alternative dispute resolution. The court held that even where no alternative remedy in the technical sense was available, there was no absolute right to proceed with an application for judicial review. It was held that except for good reason, the application should be stayed and not permitted to proceed "if a significant part of the issues between the parties could be resolved outside the litigation process". In *Cowl* itself the defendant had offered to establish a modified form of complaints procedure to deal with the matter. The rationale is obviously also capable of being applied to a proposal to mediate. The court's power to make adverse costs orders against a party which unreasonably refuses to mediate is also capable of being applied in judicial review proceedings as elsewhere.[9]

Despite the considerable attention received by *Cowl* when first decided, it is not thought that a large number of cases have been stayed or refused permission on the basis there set out, nor that great use has been made of mediation in judicial review proceedings, by comparison with other forms of civil litigation. The potential for mediation in public law disputes is probably greater than is often recognised, not least because it allows for a more substantive outcome than the mere reconsideration of a decision. Nonetheless, there are valid reasons why mediation may sometimes be inappropriate in judicial review. If the defendant believes that a particular course of action would be improper in public law, through lack of vires or otherwise, it will probably regard itself as barred from taking that step without a ruling of the court. Where a judicial or quasi-judicial decision is under challenge, then again the decision-maker may feel that this cannot appropriately be made the subject of negotiation or compromise. Finally, given the relatively short nature of most judicial review hearings, the incentive to spend money on mediation in the hope of avoiding hearing costs may be comparatively limited. **40–06**

---

[8] [2002] 1 W.L.R. 803. See also *Anufrijeva v Southwark LBC* [2004] Q.B. 1124 at [81], holding that damages claims under the Human Rights Act 1998 should normally be referred to ADR or pursued through internal procedures or to an ombudsman as complaints of maladministration.

[9] See Ch.43, below. For an example of a successful defendant being refused its costs on this basis (in part), see *R. (Nurse Prescribers Ltd) v Secretary of State for Health* [2004] EWHC 403 (Admin). For an example the other way, see *R. (A, B, X and Y) v East Sussex CC* (2005) 8 C.C.L.R. 228 at [42] to [45]. In *Halsey v Milton Keynes General NHS Trust* [2004] 1 W.L.R. 3002 at [34]–[35] the court rejected any suggestion that it should be more willing to impose costs sanctions against public bodies than against other litigants on this ground.

THE POWER TO COMPROMISE

40–07 In most Administrative Court cases, the defendant will be a public body, and often a statutory corporation whose powers are therefore limited to those expressly or impliedly conferred upon it by statute.[10] It follows that such a body, before entering into a compromise, must be satisfied not only that the proposed compromise would represent a proper exercise of its powers having regard to the merits of the claim, the likely cost of the litigation and so forth (these are matters which it may be called upon to justify to its external auditor),[11] but also that any positive step which the agreement requires it to take would be *intra vires*.[12] For example, if a local authority is forbidden by statute from allocating its housing stock to certain persons, it could not validly agree to make such an allocation as part of a compromise of litigation.

40–08 However, in the absence of some such express prohibition, it is thought that it will not generally be too difficult to identify a power to conclude a compromise. In the case of a local authority, such power may be found either in reading together s.222 of the Local Government Act 1972 (power to prosecute, defend or appear in legal proceedings) and s.111 of that Act (power to take steps incidental to discharge of functions), or in the very general "well-being" power now conferred by s.2 of the Local Government Act 2000. Also significant in local authority cases is the power under s.92 of the Local Government Act 2000 to make payments to, or provide other benefits for, persons whom an authority considers may have been adversely affected by action that may amount to maladministration.

40–09 In *R. (Hooper) v Secretary of State for Work and Pensions*[13] the court had to consider an argument that, having settled the claims of some individuals, the defendant was under a public law obligation to treat others in a like position in the same way. In relation to persons refused a certain type of benefit on allegedly discriminatory grounds, the state's policy had been to settle any such claim once it was brought to the European Court of Human Rights and declared admissible, but not otherwise. The court upheld this approach, saying that a settlement without admission of liability, whether

---

[10] Ministers of the Crown, by contrast, are corporations sole having all the capacity of a natural person. For the implications of this status, and the extent to which any power to make payments might be cut down by the existence of statutory powers of more limited scope, see the discussion in *R. (Hooper) v Secretary of State for Work and Pensions* [2003] 1 W.L.R. 2623 at [120] to [137] (CA) and [2005] 1 W.L.R. 1681 at [6], [45]–[47] and [123] (HL).

[11] See Sch.2 to the Audit Commission Act 1998 for the bodies whose accounts are subject to audit.

[12] See *Hazell v Hammersmith and Fulham LBC* [1992] 2 A.C. 1 at 38. See also para.4–10, above.

[13] [2003] 1 W.L.R. 2623 at [103] to [108]. This issue was not debated in the House of Lords.

at Strasbourg or in any other proceedings, did not require equivalent payments to be made to others in a like position—"A well recognised motive for settling a case is to avoid the risk of an adverse decision and a settlement cannot be considered as carrying the same consequences as such a decision."

40–10 In some cases where the claimant seeks the quashing of an existing decision and/or the taking of a fresh decision, or the variation of some prior decision, the defendant may have no power to embark upon that course unless the existing decision is quashed by an order of the court.[14] In other words the decision-maker, having once reached a decision, is *functus officio* for so long as that decision continues to subsist. This is most obviously true of judicial and quasi-judicial determinations involving the resolution of competing claims, but the doctrine may apply in other situations as well. This is notwithstanding the general rule that, unless the contrary intention appears, a statutory power may be exercised and a statutory duty must be performed "from time to time as occasion requires".[15] In the context of a proposed compromise, the issue may be of practical importance if a change of heart by the decision-maker will affect a third party who may seek to persuade the court not to make a quashing order.[16]

NATURE, ENFORCEMENT AND EFFECT OF COMPROMISE

40–11 The nature of the compromise may be of importance where a term of the compromise is that the defendant should take certain positive steps, particularly where those steps entail something more complex than the mere retaking of a decision.

40–12 If the court is invited to, and does, make a mandatory order requiring certain steps to be taken, then the position is straightforward. The order of the court must be obeyed, and failure to comply with a mandatory order is

---

[14] See *e.g. R. v Parliamentary Commissioner for Administration Ex p. Balchin* [1998] 1 P.L.R. 1, where Sedley J., having found the Ombudsman's decision on an investigation to be unlawful, indicated that he would quash it formally if this was necessary in order for the matter to be reconsidered.
[15] Interpretation Act 1978, s.12. See the discussion in Wade & Forsyth, *Administrative Law* (9th ed., 2004), pp.229–232.
[16] See para.40–18 below, and the *Towry Law case* cited at para.40–23. In *R. v Aylesbury Vale DC Ex p. Chaplin*, The Times, July 23, 1996, Keene J. and the Court of Appeal ([1997] 3 P.L.R. 55) rejected a submission that it was improper for a local planning authority to grant a fresh application for planning permission where its original refusal was under appeal, and the objector to permission would have been able to make representations in opposition to the appeal at the inquiry. However, Keene J. did acknowledge that the grant of permission would have been unlawful if it had been motivated by the authority's desire to avoid the costs of the appeal rather than by its assessment of the likely outcome.

a contempt of court. That is one reason why it is undesirable to agree terms of compromise which involve the court making an order against the defendant the effect of which is unclear.[17] Where the material terms of the agreement between the parties do not form part of an order of the court,[18] they may well amount to a contract of compromise, enforceable in the same way as any other contract to compromise civil proceedings. In other cases, the true construction of the "agreement" may be that it amounts to no more than a giving of the assurance by the defendant as to how it proposes to exercise its powers in future. Such an assurance would undoubtedly give rise to a legitimate expectation that it would be fulfilled, of a substantive and not merely a procedural kind,[19] so that a failure to do what had been promised without some compelling reason would constitute grounds for a fresh application for judicial review.

40–13 It should be noted that, in R. v Commissioner for Local Administration Ex p. PH,[20] it was held by Turner J. that the Local Government Ombudsman was not entitled to investigate a complaint of maladministration, with a view to the award of compensation, where the complainant had already ventilated the matters in question by way of judicial review.[21] That was a case in which the judicial review proceedings had led to a judgment, but the result would presumably have been the same if they had ended in settlement. Accordingly, a judicial review claimant who wishes to preserve the possibility of complaint to the Ombudsman or some similar avenue of redress should ensure that this is reflected in the terms of any compromise of the judicial review proceedings (even then it would be a matter for the Ombudsman's discretion whether to accept the complaint).

---

[17] See, e.g. R. (Lloyd) v Barking and Dagenham LBC (2001) 4 C.C.L.R. 196, where the defendant gave undertakings to the court as part of an agreement pursuant to which judicial review proceedings were adjourned, but disputes later arose as to whether there had been compliance with those undertakings. At 206A–C, the Court of Appeal criticised the undertakings on various grounds: in part they stated merely that the Council would comply with its duties under statute, which it was obliged to do in any event (see also R. v ILEA Ex p. Ali (1990) 2 Ad. L.R. 822 at 837B); they imposed positive obligations which it was outside the defendant's power to achieve; and they required the implication of terms as to reasonableness. The possibility of sanctions for contempt "merely complicates an already difficult situation".

[18] The Tomlin form of order (see paras 9–19 et seq., above) does not appear to be common in Administrative Court proceedings, but there is no reason in principle why it should not be used.

[19] See the discussion in R. v North & East Devon Health Authority Ex p. Coughlan [2001] Q.B. 213.

[20] The Times, January 8, 1999 (permission to appeal refused by Simon Brown L.J., March 8, 1999). See also R. (Scholarstica Umo) v Commissioner for Local Administration [2004] E.L.R. 265.

[21] Conversely, in R. v Secretary of State for the Environment, Transport and the Regions Ex p. Garland (Turner J., November 10, 2000) the claimant was held to be barred from applying for judicial review of a determination of the Secretary of State concerning his pension entitlement, where that would undermine the effect of a settlement entered into between the claimant and the district auditor in a way which would be inequitable.

WITHDRAWAL OF PROCEEDINGS

Under the Civil Procedure Rules, it appears that an application for judicial review is a claim within the meaning of CPR Pt 38,[22] and so may be discontinued by the claimant filing and serving a notice of discontinuance, save in the specific cases where the consent of the court is needed pursuant to CPR r.38.2(2).[23] Eynon[24] indicates that it is the practice of the Administrative Court Office to permit applications to be withdrawn without consent,[25] but to seek written confirmation from other parties who have been given notice of the proceedings that they do not object to the withdrawal, and in particular that they do not seek any costs order, before closing the court file. If necessary, the case may be listed on the issue of costs alone.

40-14

In the case of statutory appeals assigned to the Administrative Court, para.12.2 of the Practice Direction to CPR Pt 52 will apply. The appellant may seek an order that the appeal be dismissed,[26] which will if it is granted usually be on the basis that the appellant pays the costs of the appeal.

40-15

OBTAINING AGREED ORDER

In judicial review proceedings, the practice to be adopted when a consent order (as opposed to mere withdrawal of the proceedings) is required, and the parties are agreed on the terms of the order they seek, is set out in

40-16

---

[22] The phrase "claim for judicial review" is specifically used in CPR Pt 54. This interpretation, if correct, means that the position is now significantly different from what it was held to be by Laws L.J. in *Estate of Kingsley (deceased) v Secretary of State for Transport* [1994] C.O.D. 358. The then RSC Ord. 21, r.2(4) permitted the withdrawal of an action without the leave of the court if all the parties consented, but it was held that in the context an "action" did not include proceedings in the Crown Office List, because the role of the court in public law proceedings was to guard the public interest as it might be affected by the decision under challenge, and that on that account it was important for the withdrawal of proceedings to be subject to the court's approval.

[23] *cf.* para.9–36, above.

[24] n.4, above at paras 10–14 of the article.

[25] para.14 of Eynon's article (above, n.4) indicates that the leave of the court is required to withdraw proceedings involving the liberty of the subject, *i.e.* applications for writs of habeas corpus or for committal for contempt. It is respectfully suggested that under the CPR there is no very clear basis for such a requirement in habeas corpus cases, and that the true reason for it in contempt cases may be the court's own interest in securing that its orders are upheld. No suggestion of a need for leave in proceedings of this nature appears in s.16 of the current Administrative Court Notes for Guidance (January 2005). *R. v Secretary of State for the Home Department Ex p. Gashi* (CO/3559/1999, June 15, 2000) is an example of a case in which the court appears to have accepted a defendant's argument that the withdrawal of certain claims should not be permitted, because they raised points on which a judgment was required in order to dispose of a large number of other outstanding applications for judicial review.

[26] Again, therefore, the position has changed under the CPR. Previously, in the absence of any express provision requiring it, the appellant was entitled to withdraw an appeal by way of case stated (and presumably a statutory appeal) without the permission of the court: see *Collet v Bromsgrove DC* [1997] Crim. L.R. 206.

para.17 of the Practice Direction to CPR P.54, the terms of which are as follows:

> "17.1 If the parties agree about the final order to be made in a claim for judicial review, the claimant must file at the court a document (with two copies) signed by all the parties setting out the terms of the proposed agreed order together with a short statement of the matters relied on as justifying the proposed agreed order and copies of any authorities or statutory provisions relied on.
> 17.2 The court will consider the documents referred to in paragraph 17.1 and will make the order if satisfied that the order should be made.
> 17.3 If the court is not satisfied that the order should be made, a hearing date will be set.
> 17.4 Where the agreement relates to an order for costs only, the parties need only file a document signed by all the parties setting out the terms of the proposed order."

40–17   This is similar to the former procedure in the Crown Office List.[27] In practice, it is highly unusual for the court not to make the order sought, and the statement of matters relied upon can in most cases properly be made extremely concise. Cases in which the court may require rather more by way of justification are likely to be those in which some unusual form of order is sought, or in which it is apparent that the order that the court is asked to make may have an impact upon third parties. That would include cases where the proposed form of relief includes a declaration which is not strictly limited to the relationship between the claimant and the defendant.

40–18   Real difficulties are only likely to arise in cases where the defendant is amenable to the grant of certain relief sought by the claimant, but a third party is opposed to that relief being granted. There are numerous instances in which a third party will be more closely interested in the outcome of an application for judicial review than the nominal defendant. A challenge to a planning authority's grant of planning permission to a developer is an obvious example, as are most instances in which judicial review is sought of a decision made by magistrates. In *R. v Independent Appeals Tribunal of Hillingdon BC Ex p. Governing Body of Mellow Lane School*,[28] the statutory appeal panel decided to allow a pupil's appeal against his permanent exclusion from school. When faced with an application for

---

[27] See *Practice Direction (Crown Office List: Consent Orders)* [1997] 1 W.L.R. 825, and previously *Practice Direction (Crown Office List: Uncontested Proceedings)* [1982] 1 W.L.R. 979.
[28] [2001] E.L.R. 200.

judicial review by the school governing body for which permission was granted, the panel decided not to contest the matter, and signed a consent order providing for the original decision to be quashed. The consent order was made by the court notwithstanding the opposition of the pupil, and without an examination of the merits. It is respectfully submitted that to take this course was contrary both to principle and to authority.[29] In *Kingsley's case*[30] Laws L.J. said that where the defendant conceded that relief should be granted, there was "no question" but that the court had to approve any order carrying that into effect. In *R. (Wirral Health Authority) v Finnegan*[31] the Mental Health Review Tribunal was willing to agree to the quashing of its decision to discharge a patient, but the patient was not. The court held[32] that, in the circumstances, it was plainly not appropriate to make a consent order and the matter had to be "properly considered" by the court to see whether judicial review was appropriate.[33] Additionally, it is submitted that "the parties" within the meaning of para.17 of the Practice Direction include not only the claimant and the defendant, but also any interested party[34] who has been served pursuant to CPR r.54.7(b) and has filed an acknowledgment of service.

Where the proceedings are by way of a statutory appeal, para.12.4 of the Practice Direction to CPR Pt 52 permits the parties to make a joint request to the court for the appeal to be dismissed by consent. However, para.13.1 of the Practice Direction provides that the appeal court will not make an order allowing an appeal unless satisfied that the decision of the lower court was wrong. Where the appeal court is requested by all parties to allow an appeal, that request may be considered on the papers. The request should state that none of the parties is a child or patient and set out the relevant history of the proceedings and the matters relied on as justifying the proposed order and be accompanied by a copy of the proposed order. **40–19**

---

[29] Newman J. appears to have taken the view that the pupil suffered no deprivation of rights, because he would be entitled to a fresh appeal panel hearing, and that the panel could have agreed to reconsider its decision regardless of any application for judicial review. It is respectfully suggested that neither of these propositions is sustainable.

[30] n.19, above.

[31] Scott Baker J., March 6, 2001 (CO/202/01).

[32] Judgment para.28. This was approved as a correct approach by the Court of Appeal in the same case (*R. (Wirral Health Authority) v Mental Health Review Tribunal* [2001] EWCA Civ 1901 at [7]).

[33] Compare *R. v Bassetlaw DC Ex p. Oxby*, *The Times*, December 18, 1997, where the court was prepared to entertain an application for judicial review made by the leader of the defendant authority as a means of enabling that authority to attack one of its own earlier decisions, but held that the fact that the defendant was in substance seeking judicial review of its own decision was to be taken into account in deciding how the court should exercise its discretion. See also *R. (Meredith) v Merthyr Tydfil CBC* [2002] EWHC 634 (Admin).

[34] Defined as any person (other than the claimant and defendant) who is directly affected by the claim: see *R. v Liverpool CC Ex p. Muldoon* [1996] 1 W.L.R. 1103.

COSTS UPON WITHDRAWAL OR SETTLEMENT OF JUDICIAL REVIEW PROCEEDINGS

40–20 As noted above, judicial review proceedings are inherently likely to be overtaken by events. Sometimes they will cease to be of practical utility to the claimant: for example, an application for judicial review is made in respect of a pupil's permanent exclusion from school, but before it can be heard the pupil obtains a place in another school and no longer wishes to return to the school from which he was excluded. Perhaps more frequently, the defendant will agree to take a fresh decision. In such circumstances, which party should bear the costs? There is a significant body of authority as to the approach which the court will take if an application for costs comes before it. If the parties allow this case-law to inform their negotiations, it will usually be possible to agree what costs order should be made.

40–21 The current approach of the court is derived from *R. v Liverpool CC Ex p. Newman*.[35] A challenge to a decision to propose a programme of redundancies became academic when the relevant redundancy notices were rescinded. The claimants sought to discontinue without being obliged to pay the defendant's costs and succeeded in obtaining an order that each party should bear its own costs. Simon Brown J. held that in the event of discontinuance a defendant would generally recover its costs, provided that the discontinuance was shown to be consequent upon the claimant's recognition of the likely failure of the challenge.[36] But if the defendant had pre-empted a high likelihood of the challenge succeeding by doing that which the challenge was designed to achieve, it might well be just that it should pay the claimant's costs as well as bearing its own. If the defendant had merely decided to short-circuit the proceedings to avoid expense, inconvenience or uncertainty, and without accepting the likelihood of their success, or if the challenge had been rendered academic by some development independent of the parties, it would normally be appropriate for the costs to lie where they fell. An in-depth investigation of the merits to determine which party should pay costs would seldom be an appropriate use of the court's time.

40–22 Many of the relevant authorities were reviewed by Scott Baker J. in *R. v Waltham Forest LBC Ex p. Boxall*, which is now the leading case.[37] The judge indicated that, in cases which settled before permission was granted,

---

[35] (1992) 5 Ad. L.R. 669.
[36] The position might be different if the claimant had given the defendant no adequate warning of the intention to bring proceedings, and so no sufficient opportunity to reconsider its decision without the need for litigation. See, *e.g. R. v Inland Revenue Commissioners Ex p. Opman International UK* [1986] 1 W.L.R. 568.
[37] (2001) 4 C.C.L.R. 258.

it was only in plain and obvious cases that a costs order should be made against the defendant.[38] In other cases, the extent to which the court would be prepared to look into the previously unresolved substantive issues would depend upon the circumstances of the particular case, including the amount of costs at stake and the conduct of the parties.[39] In *Boxall* itself, the judge considered the allegations and response "broadly", concluded that there was little doubt that the defendant would have been found to have acted unlawfully in at least some respect, and awarded the claimants their costs up to a particular point.[40]

There are some types of case, most typically a challenge by case stated or judicial review to a decision of the magistrates' court, in which the nominal respondent or defendant (the justices) is not normally expected to appear to defend its decision, and will not generally be liable for costs if it does not appear, even if the decision is overturned. However, such a party is under a duty to consider whether it is appropriate to sign a consent order quashing the decision, and if its refusal to do so is unreasonable in all the circumstances, it may be liable for the costs unnecessarily incurred.[41] Conversely, it was held in *R. (Towry Law Financial Services plc) v The Financial Ombudsman Service Ltd*[42] that the defendant Ombudsman, although recognising a flaw in its determination, was not entitled to re-open the matter without the consent of both parties to the underlying complaint (see para.40–10 above). Since the ombudsman could not have

40–23

---

[38] See *R. v Kensington & Chelsea RLBC Ex p. Ghrebegiosis* (1994) 27 H.L.R. 602 (costs order granted); *R. v Hackney LBC Ex p. Rowe* [1996] C.O.D. 155 (order refused); *R. v Bassetlaw DC Ex p. Aldergate Estates Ltd* (CO/4387/99, Jackson J., April 17, 2000, order granted).

[39] Cases where it was regarded as appropriate to deal fully with the substantive issue, because of the amount of costs involved and/or because the point was a reasonably short one, include *R. v Holderness BC Ex p. James Robert Developments Ltd* (1992) 66 P. & C.R. 46, and *Freud Lemos Properties Ltd v Secretary of State for the Environment* (CO/2839/91, David Widdicombe Q.C., March 23, 1994); see also *R. v Central Criminal Court Ex p. Propend Financial Property Ltd* [1996] 2 Cr.App.R. 26. Contrast *R. v Independent Television Commission Ex p. Church of Scientology* [1996] C.O.D. 443. Defendants who make concessions late in the day may be at risk of adverse costs orders for that reason alone (see e.g. *R. (Veja) v Secretary of State for the Home Department* [2004] EWHC 1788 (Admin)).

[40] See also *R. (Bowhay) v North and East Durham Health Authority* [2001] A.C.D. 159, where the court performed a similarly brisk review of the merits and awarded a proportion of the costs against the defendant.

[41] *R. v Newcastle-under-Lyme Justices Ex p. Massey* [1994] 1 W.L.R. 1684. Relevant considerations include the attitude of the body which instituted the original proceedings before the magistrates, and the nature and obviousness of the flaw in the justices' decision. A similar approach was applied to the Special Educational Needs Tribunal whose decision was the subject of a statutory appeal in *S v Metropolitan Borough of Dudley* [2000] Ed. C.R. 410. The subject of the award of costs against inferior courts, tribunals and coroners in judicial review and statutory appeal proceedings was comprehensively reviewed in *R. (Davies) v HM Deputy Coroner for Birmingham (No.2)* [2004] 1 W.L.R. 2739. The present acknowledgment of service form in judicial review proceedings caters specifically for such defendants.

[42] [2002] EWHC 1603 (Admin).

done more to avoid or resolve the proceedings, no costs award against it would have been appropriate in any event.

CONTINUATION OF PROCEEDINGS AFTER FRESH DECISION

40–24 How far should the court permit a defendant to bring the proceedings to an enforced end by means of its own willingness to take a fresh decision? Apart from the issue of costs, the claimant may be reluctant to withdraw the claim because it suspects that it may wish to challenge the fresh decision, and would prefer to do so by way of amendment to the existing proceedings rather than by having to commence entirely fresh proceedings. Alternatively, the claimant may have an interest in obtaining the court's adjudication upon some question of principle.

40–25 In *R. v Secretary of State for the Home Department Ex p. Alabi*[43] the Court of Appeal gave guidance as to the former situation. Where the defendant offers to reconsider its original decision, but the facts are or may be such that a challenge might lie against any future decision adverse to the claimant, the judicial review proceedings should be put on hold, the Administrative Court Office being alerted accordingly. The fresh decision should then be reached as soon as possible. If it goes against the claimant, the parties should consider whether the outstanding review proceedings are an appropriate vehicle for the ventilation of any fresh challenge. If the defendant contends that they are not, or that an existing permission is being used in an attempt to pursue an impossible case, it should apply to strike the proceedings out. Sometimes the defendant may purport to reconsider its decision or to perform its statutory duty at a very late stage before the substantive hearing of the judicial review, or otherwise in circumstances such that it is unclear whether the defendant's duty has now been properly performed. In *Parr v Wyre Forest BC*[44] Donaldson L.J. indicated that the court should not refuse relief "merely because at the eleventh hour the authority had done something which might be, but was not necessarily, a compliance with their duty".

40–26 The leading case on the question of whether a case in which the claimant no longer requires substantive relief should go forward as a "test case" is the decision of the House of Lords in *R. v Home Secretary Ex p. Salem*[45]:

---

[43] [1997] I.N.L.R. 124, applied in *R. v Entry Clearance Officer Ex p. Makkari*, Moses J., February 18, 1999.
[44] (1982) 2 H.L.R. 71 at 83. See also *R. v Lambeth LBC Ex p. A1 and A2* (1997) 30 H.L.R. 933 at 947.
[45] [1999] 1 A.C. 450.

there is a discretion to hear disputes in public law cases even when they are academic as between the parties, but it should be exercised with caution and only where there is a good reason in the public interest for doing so. Whether a case should proceed as a test case is a matter to be determined by the court, if the parties cannot agree, and not unilaterally by the claimant or its advisers.[46]

AGREEMENT AT THE PERMISSION STAGE

There is no provision in the CPR for permission to apply for judicial review to be granted by consent, and CPR r.4.5(2) specifically provides that the time limit for filing the claim form may not be extended by agreement between the parties.[47] This no doubt reflects the wider interest in the speedy resolution of disputes concerning the validity of determinations by public bodies. But in cases where third party rights are not materially affected, it is highly likely in practice that permission to apply for judicial review will be granted, along with any necessary extension of time, where the defendant raises no objection.

40–27

There will often be scope for agreement between the parties at the permission stage concerning the directions which the court will be invited to give, particularly in relation to expedition and the abridgement of time for the defendant's evidence. Typically, in a case in which the claimant would otherwise seek interim relief, the defendant may be willing to give undertakings over to the substantive hearing if the court is prepared to expedite that hearing.

40–28

Finally, it should be noted that CPR r.54.18 enables the court to decide a claim for judicial review without a hearing (*i.e.* on the papers) where all the parties agree. To date, it is not thought that much use has been made of this facility.

40–29

---

[46] *R. (Tshikangu) v Newham LBC*, The Times, April 27, 2001.
[47] The position on statutory appeals is the same: CPR r.52.6(2).

PART 14

Arbitrations

CHAPTER 41

Settlement of Arbitrations

GENERAL

A great many disputes which otherwise would be resolved by the ordinary litigious process are dealt with by arbitration. An arbitration of this nature usually arises out of an agreement between the parties to the effect that their disputes shall be so resolved.[1] Most, though not all, arbitration agreements arise in the commercial context. An arbitration agreement is almost invariably written, with the result that the Arbitration Act 1996 ("the 1996 Act") governs the situation. The process of arbitration under consideration is one of a judicial nature.[2]

41–01

ESSENTIAL PRINCIPLES CONCERNING COMPROMISE

Since the process of arbitration is merely a means parallel to the ordinary court process by which disputes are resolved, the essential principles and practice of compromise are the same. By s.51 of the 1996 Act if during arbitral proceedings the parties settle the dispute, unless otherwise agreed by the parties the tribunal will terminate the substantive proceedings and, if so requested by the parties and not objected to by the tribunal,[3] shall record the settlement in the form of an agreed award. The agreed award shall state that it is an award of the tribunal and shall have the same status and effect as any other award on the merits of the case. The provisions of

41–02

---

[1] Arbitration agreements "imposed" by the small print in consumer contracts are subject to ss.89–91 of the Arbitration Act 1996. Subject to that, in addition to arbitrations pursuant to an agreement, statute provides for compulsory or optional arbitration in certain cases: for a full treatment of statutory arbitrations see *Russell on Arbitration* (22nd ed., 2003), Appendix 4, p.594.
[2] *ibid.*, paras 1–000–1–009, pp.1–7.
[3] For example, on the grounds of illegality.

the Act relating to awards generally[4] apply to agreed awards and, unless the parties have also settled the matter of the payment of the costs of the arbitration, the provisions of the Act relating to costs[5] will also apply.

41–03 While any settlement of a dispute referred to arbitration will be contractual in nature and enforceable as such, an agreed award has the benefit of certainty, and so enforcement is likely to be easier. In addition, if it is intended to enforce the award overseas, an agreed award may be recognised and enforced under the New York Convention.[6]

41–04 It has been suggested that s.51 does not apply where the parties do not settle the whole of the dispute.[7] Notwithstanding that suggestion, a tribunal may embody a settlement of part only of a reference in an award relating to that part under s.47 of the 1996 Act.

41–05 As has been observed in relation to the non-arbitral process,[8] if the parties come to an agreement without providing for the making by the court of some suitable consent order, the court will have no jurisdiction to make any such order. The court's jurisdiction to determine the dispute will have been taken away in the sense that there is no extant dispute to resolve. Unless the parties agree specifically to the making of an order to embody their compromise, the court will have no further interest in the matter. An analogous position arises in the arbitral process. Since an arbitral tribunal is appointed by agreement of the parties to resolve their dispute, their compromise of that dispute removes the very foundation of the appointment. The tribunal becomes *functus officio* in relation to the dispute and has no further authority in the matter[9] unless requested by the parties to make an agreed award and the tribunal does not object to making of the agreed award. Once the award reflecting the compromise is made the tribunal is yet again *functus officio*.[10]

---

[4] ss.52–58.
[5] ss.59–65.
[6] Russell n.1, above, paras 8–011 *et seq.*, p.368.
[7] *ibid.*, para.6–023, p.236.
[8] See para.5–47, above.
[9] *Chimimport Plc v G. D'Alesio SAS* [1994] 2 Lloyd's Rep. 366, the parties to an arbitration agreement settled their dispute and provided expressly that, by signing the settlement agreement, "the parties settle their differences, cease the arbitrary case in London and will have no claims whatsoever towards one another". Rix J. held, on the agreed assumption for the purposes of the hearing that the settlement agreement was valid, that the arbitrator had no further jurisdiction in the arbitration. The decision must now however be read in the light of the power conferred on an arbitral tribunal to rule on its own substantive jurisdiction by s.30 of the 1996 Act.
[10] *Sutherland & Co v Hannevig Bros Ltd* [1921] K.B. 336.

ENFORCEMENT OF COMPROMISE

The normal procedure to enforce an award whether made in England or abroad is by the summary procedure under s.66 of the 1996 Act. Section 66 provides that an award made by the tribunal pursuant to an arbitration agreement may, by leave of the court, be enforced in the same manner as a judgment or order of the court to the same effect. Where leave is given, judgment may be entered in terms of the award. The procedure extends to an agreed award.[11] **41–06**

Every arbitration award is enforceable by a fresh action brought for the purpose.[12]

An action on the award is normally appropriate where leave to enforce an award is not given because the person against whom it is sought to be enforced shows that the tribunal lacked substantive jurisdiction to make the award[13] or where the procedure under s.66 of the 1996 Act is not available.[14] **41–07**

Machinery analogous to that of a Tomlin order is not available as a means of compromising an arbitration. Since enforcement is not a matter for the arbitral tribunal, which will be *functus officio* once it has delivered its award, there is no summary process available to be invoked in such a manner. Leave to enforce an award as a judgment or order[15] is the nearest equivalent. **41–08**

WHO DECIDES WHETHER COMPROMISE CONCLUDED?

An issue may arise between two parties to extant arbitration proceedings as to whether they have concluded a compromise.[16] Does the arbitral tribunal decide the issue or is it a matter for the court? How is the issue brought before the appropriate forum? **41–09**

As Rix J. put it in *Chiminport Plc v G. D'Alesio*,[17] the validity of a settlement agreement "is critical to [the arbitrators] jurisdiction". Section 30 of the 1996 Act provides that unless otherwise agreed by the parties, **41–10**

---

[11] CPR r.62.18(5) provides that where an application is made to enforce an agreed award both the arbitration claim form and the order itself must state that that the award which it is sought to enforce is an agreed award.
[12] *Bremer Deltransport GmbH v Drewry* [1933] 1 K.B. 753, CA. See also *The Saint Anna* [1983] 1 W.L.R. 895; *Agromet Motoimport v Maulden Engineering Co (Beds)* [1985] 1 W.L.R. 762.
[13] Under s.66(3) of the 1996 Act.
[14] For example, where the arbitration agreement does not fall within the broad statutory definition in ss.5 and 6 of the 1996 Act.
[15] See para.41–06, above.
[16] See Ch.3, above.
[17] [1994] 2 Lloyd's Rep. 366 at 370.

the arbitral tribunal may rule on its own substantive jurisdiction, namely whether there is a valid arbitration agreement, whether the tribunal is properly constituted, and what matters have been submitted to arbitration in accordance with the arbitration agreement. It is therefore suggested that in the first instance the arbitral tribunal is the appropriate forum before which to bring the issue of the validity of any compromise.[18] Indeed, if a party were to seek to bring the matter before the courts, it could well be met with an application to stay the proceedings under s.9 of the 1996 Act.[19] On such an application the court might, however, determine the validity of the compromise under s.9(4) in answer to the question whether the arbitration agreement is "inoperative".

41-11 It could be argued that the court is the more appropriate jurisdiction: an arbitrator who has been invited to consider an issue of this nature will of necessity have seen evidence of the parties' negotiations. This might be considered an impediment to the future determination of the substantive dispute in a wholly detached fashion if the arbitrator should decide that the dispute had not been settled. While undoubtedly this could be a problem, it is one that is inherent in other powers conferred on the tribunal by the 1996 Act, especially s.38(3), which empowers a tribunal to order a claimant to provide security for the costs of the arbitration. Various expedients have been adopted to address the problem of a tribunal being shown "without prejudice" correspondence admissible on applications for security for costs, including the appointment of a new arbitrator whose sole function is to determine the application.

41-12 If the court is considered the appropriate forum, how is the issue brought before it? The appropriate procedure would appear to be to make application under s.32 of the 1996 Act, which provides that the court may, on the application of a party to arbitral proceedings, determine any question as to the substantive jurisdiction of the tribunal with the agreement in writing of all the other parties to the proceedings with the permission of the tribunal. If the opposing parties refuse, for whatever reason, to agree to the application, the applicant party may seek the

---

[18] Section 67 of the 1996 Act provides that a party to arbitral proceedings may (upon notice to the other parties and to the tribunal) apply to the court challenging any award of the arbitral tribunal as to its substantive jurisdiction; or for an order declaring an award made by the tribunal on the merits to be of no effect, in whole or in part, because the tribunal did not have substantive jurisdiction.

[19] Section 9 states:
  (1) A party to an arbitration agreement against whom legal proceedings are brought (whether by way of claim or counterclaim) in respect of a matter which under the agreement is to be referred to arbitration may (upon notice to the other parties to the proceedings) apply to the court in which the proceedings have been brought to stay the proceedings so far as they concern that matter. . . .
  (4) On an application under this section the court shall grant a stay unless satisfied that the arbitration agreement is null and void, inoperative, or incapable of being performed."

permission of the tribunal. It is suggested that any tribunal, mindful of the problems expressed above, would be likely to give its permission.

Alternatively if the respondent to an arbitration seeks to ignore a concluded compromise, the claimant could commence an action (utilising proceedings for summary judgment) to enforce the agreement[20] or perhaps seek a declaration that a compromise has been concluded. The making of a declaration is, of course, discretionary and does not operate as a judgment susceptible of enforcement in the usual way.

41–13

SETTING ASIDE CONSENT AWARD

It is thought that any grounds which would justify the setting-aside of a contract would be sufficient to justify the setting-aside of an arbitral award made by consent.[21] Section 68(1) of the 1996 Act provides that a party to arbitral proceedings may apply to the court challenging an award in the proceedings on the ground of serious irregularity affecting the award. "Serious irregularity" includes the award being obtained by fraud or the award or the way in which it was procured being contrary to public policy.[22] By s.70(3) any application or appeal must be brought within 28 days of the date of the award, although that period may be extended by the court under CPR Pt 62. These rules must, it is submitted, have been drafted with awards made after contested arbitrations in mind. Such time limits are plainly inappropriate in relation to an action to set aside the agreement underlying a consensual arbitral award. The circumstances in which the court may act under s.68 are limited and the time limits are strictly enforced. An alternative course of action is to pursue proceedings to set aside the award in the same manner as if it were a final order or judgment.

41–14

OFFERS AND COSTS

General. Unless an arbitration agreement provides to the contrary, the costs of the reference to arbitration and of the award are at the tribunal's discretion.[23] An arbitral tribunal possessed of this discretion has the same discretion as a High Court judge.[24] The discretion must be exercised judicially and the taking into account of a "without prejudice" offer does not amount to a judicial exercise of the discretion.[25] Furthermore, in

41–15

---

[20] cf. para.11–02, above.
[21] See Ch.4, above.
[22] s.68(2)(g).
[23] Arbitration Act, 1996, s.61.
[24] *Stotesbury v Turner* [1943] K.B. 370.
[25] ibid. See, generally, *L. Figueiredo Navegacas SA v Reederei Richard Schroeder KG* [1974] 1 Lloyd's Rep. 192. The rule preventing consideration of without prejudice offers is not confined to offers of settlement but extends to efforts to resolve disputes by other means: *Reed Executive Plc v Reed Business Information Ltd* [2004] 1 W.L.R. 3026.

considering the question whether the claimant has achieved more by rejecting the offer and continuing the arbitration than accepting it,[26] an arbitral tribunal should not have regard to the incidence of costs in the reference, but only to the claim for principal and interest.[27] Since the Civil Procedure Rules do not apply to arbitrations, the process of a Pt 36 payment[28] is not available as a protection on costs. How, then, can an offer be made which, if not bettered on the award, will influence the award as to costs?

41–16 **The form and substance of an effective offer.** As Donaldson J. (as he then was) made clear in *Tramountana Armadora SA v Atlantic Shipping Co SA*,[29] there are two methods of making an offer potentially effective on costs in arbitration proceedings:

(1) an "open offer"; and
(2) a "sealed offer".

The former will have a status identical to that in ordinary litigation.[30] The latter has been described as[31]:

"... the arbitral equivalent of making a payment into court on settlement of the litigation or of particular causes of action in that litigation."

41–17 The procedures are not, of course, identical. A "sealed offer" does not involve an actual payment of a sum of money as part of the offer of settlement. An offeree disposed to accept the sum of money proffered might be well-advised to accept the offer on condition that the sum of money (or a banker's draft in the appropriate sum) is paid (or the banker's draft received) within a specified period. Any failure to observe this condition would leave the original claim open or, arguably, if he elected to waive the condition in his favour, enable recourse to a cause of action on the compromise.

41–18 As with a Pt 36 payment, the fact that a sealed offer has been made is usually concealed from the tribunal. This is usually achieved by an invitation to the tribunal at the conclusion of the arbitration to make an interim award on the substance of the dispute and to receive further representations on the question of costs subsequently.[32] Another (rather

---

[26] See paras 41–19 *et seq.*, below.
[27] *Everglade Maritime Inc v Schiffahrtgesellschaft* [1993] Q.B. 780, CA.
[28] See Chs 13 *et seq.*, above.
[29] [1978] 1 Lloyd's Rep. 391 at 396.
[30] See para.26–08, above.
[31] [1978] 1 Lloyd's Rep. 391, *per* Donaldson J.
[32] *King v Thomas McKenna Ltd* [1991] 2 Q.B. 480 at 492.

archaic) means by which this is achieved is if the tribunal invites the parties to give it a sealed envelope, the contents of which would reveal whether an offer had been made and, if so, in what terms.[33]

When the arbitral tribunal comes to consider the relevance of a "sealed offer" the approach has been described thus:[34] **41–19**

> "... he should ask himself the question: 'Has the claimant achieved more by rejecting the offer and going on with the arbitration than he would have achieved if he had accepted the offer?' This is a simple question to answer, whether the offer does or does not include interest. The arbitrator knows what the claimant would have achieved if he had accepted the offer. He would have received that sum and could not have asked the arbitrator to award any interest.[35] The arbitrator knows what he has in fact awarded to the claimant both by way of principal and interest. In order that like should be compared with like, the interest element must be recalculated as if the award had been made on the same date as the offer. Alternatively, interest for the period between offer and award must notionally be added to the amount of the sealed offer. But, subject to that, the question is easily answered.
>
> If the claimant in the end has achieved no more than he would have achieved by accepting the offer, the continuance of the arbitration after that date has been a waste of time and money. Prima facie, the claimant should recover his costs up to the date of the offer and should be ordered to pay the respondent's costs after that date. If he has achieved more by going on, the respondent should pay the costs throughout."

An important feature of a Pt 36 payment is that the offer constituted thereby includes an offer to pay the claimant's costs to the date when the payment would be accepted without the permission of the court.[36] For a "sealed offer" to have the equivalent effect in terms of protection on costs, the terms offered must make this plain. **41–20**

> In the *Tramountana* case,[37] the offer had been for a lump sum effectively to include interest and costs. The question of whether the offer was sufficient in

---

[33] *ibid.* at 492–493.
[34] *Tramountana Armadora SA v Atlantic Shipping Co SA* [1978] 1 Lloyd's Rep. 391 at 397.
[35] Since this comment in the *Tramountana* case, arbitrators have been given the power to award interest: Arbitration Act of 1996, s.49.
[36] See paras 21–04 *et seq.*, above. *In Mitchell v James* [2004] 1 W.L.R. 158 it was held that as CPR r.36.1(2) states, nothing in Pt 36 prevents a party making an offer to settle in whatever way he chooses. However, nothing in r.36.1(1)(2) permits a party to include a term as to costs as part of a Pt 36 offer for the purpose of obtaining an order for costs on an indemnity basis.
[37] See n.29, above.

relation to the capital sum and interest was a relatively easy exercise. But the costs to the date of the offer were an unknown factor and it was not possible for the arbitrator to make the comparison between the offer and the eventual award.[38]

The difficulty which arose in the *Tramountana* case led Donaldson J. to say[39]:

"If a party wishes to make a 'sealed offer' and to have it considered in the context of an order for costs, he must offer to settle the action for £x plus costs."

41–21   In *Archital Luxfer Ltd v Henry Boot Construction Ltd*[40] Peter Gibson J., as he then was, concluded that Donaldson J. was merely "dealing with the essential substance and purpose of sealed offers and was not intending to lay down any universal requirements as to form". The judge continued thus[41]:

"In order for the essential task of the arbitrator to be performed, namely, of deciding the question whether the party to whom the offer is made has achieved more by rejecting the offer and going on with the arbitration, than he would have achieved if he had accepted the offer, the offer must be in such terms as will enable the question to be answered. When the structure of the litigation is such that settlement on the terms offered will entitle the party to whom the offer is made, to payment of his costs to that date, then unless the offer includes an offer to pay the costs the arbitrator cannot in most circumstances know whether the claimant has or has not achieved more.

If an offer should be made in terms which specifically included a named sum to cover costs, and the arbitrator is satisfied that the amount so offered must without question have covered any costs therein incurred, there is no reason why the arbitrator should not give effect to the offer if the sum offered to settle the claim was insufficient. It will always be prudent to offer to pay taxed costs, because of the risk of error, but the sufficiency of an offer is concerned with its demonstrable substance and not with its form.

A party to whom an offer is made cannot be expected or required to enter upon any detailed investigations as to his position on costs in order to decide whether or not an offer made fairly reflects his prospect of success; nor, in my judgment, should an arbitrator enter

---

[38] See the quotation from the judgment of Donaldson J., at para.29–10, above.
[39] [1978] 1 Lloyd's Rep. 391 at 398.
[40] [1981] 1 Lloyd's Rep. 642.
[41] *ibid.* at 654.

upon any such investigation in order to discover whether an offer made was such that a claimant has or has not achieved more by rejecting it. Such offers are required to be plain and self-evident in their terms."

In *Archital Luxfer Ltd v Henry Boot Construction Ltd*, there was a claim and a counterclaim. The sealed offer of the respondents was that they would allow the claimants £12,000 on their claim and accept £17,000 on their counterclaim. They proposed that the £5,000 thus owing to them be paid out of a sum of £12,000 held in a joint deposit account in the names of the parties pending the outcome of the proceedings with the accumulated interest in that account being duly apportioned on that sum. They proposed that there should be no order as to costs. At the end of the arbitration the claimants were awarded substantially less on their claim than the £12,000 offered and the respondents recovered a little more than the £17,000 they said they would accept. It was conceded that as at the date of the offer there was no reason to suppose that the costs of either side were significantly different. Peter Gibson J. held that the offer was a valid and effective sealed offer and should have been acted upon by the arbitrator when considering his order as to costs. 41–22

In that case the position on costs as at the time of the offer was clear. In other cases where the respondent is the net creditor of the claimant it may not be, and the judge suggested[42] a means by which this problem could be dealt with: 41–23

"There is no reason . . . why the substance of such an offer should not conclude with the proposal that there should be no order as to costs but that, if the party to whom the offer is made does not accept that part of the offer, the question of costs be referred to and decided by the arbitrator upon the basis that the other terms of settlement of the action are accepted. The offer could further provide that if the arbitrator then directed that the costs be paid in terms no more favourable to the offeree than as first proposed, the arbitrator would be asked to direct the offeree to pay the costs thus wasted. If the offer were in those terms and was rejected; and the claimant received no more than the sum offered in settlement the arbitrator could determine what costs ought to be allowed to the claimant on the basis that he had accepted the offer when made."

Whilst, plainly, this is a course which could be adopted it is, it is respectfully submitted, open to the objection that the offer is not sufficiently certain to be readily capable of acceptance.[43] The offer by a respondent to pay £X plus costs on the claim and to accept £Y plus costs on the counterclaim with mutual set-offs represents exactly what the 41–24

---

[42] [1981] 1 Lloyd's Rep. 642 at 655–656.
[43] See also para.9–03, above, and n.2 referred to in that paragraph.

arbitral tribunal could award eventually. It may, therefore, be safer to do this and then make a further offer in the assessment of costs if unreasonableness from the other side is anticipated or shown.

An offer that excludes the payment of costs may be given relatively little weight, although it may not be disregarded if its value can be ascertained relatively easily. In *Lindner Ceilings Floors Partitions Plc v How Engineering Services Limited*[44] the respondent made an offer of a defined sum in respect of the claimant's claim exclusive of interest and costs, both of which were to be assessed by the arbitrator. The arbitrator took account of the offer notwithstanding that it was not in the form "£X plus costs". On appeal the judge held[45] that the form of the offer allowed the tribunal to answer the question posed in the *Tramountana* case[46] and it was not difficult to see that the claimant should have accepted the offer.

41–25 Conversely, in determining whether the sum awarded exceeds the offer the costs awarded are to be disregarded. In *Everglade Maritime Inc v Schiffahrtgesellschaft*[47] the arbitrators awarded US$16,215.99, plus interest. The respondent had made a sealed offer of US$15,000, plus interest and the claimant's costs to the date of the offer. The arbitrators found that, in the absence of an offer, they would have directed that each party bear its own costs and pay half of the costs of the reference. They concluded that the claimant would have received more by accepting the offer and therefore the claimant should pay the respondent's costs from the date of the offer. The Court of Appeal held that they were wrong, that they should have disregarded costs and simply considered whether the claimant had recovered more in the award than it would have recovered had it accepted the offer.

41–26 So far as interest is concerned, in the *Tramountana* case, Donaldson J. suggested[48] that in order to compare the offer and the award on a "like for like" basis either the interest may be recalculated as if the award had been made on the same date as the offer, or the interest between the offer and the award may be added to the offer. An added complication is that by s.49(3) of the 1996 Act arbitrators now have the power to award compound interest. A prudent offeror may wish to take account of the possibility of an award of compound interest in the offer. In the *Lindner* case, H.H. Judge Seymour Q.C. suggested the simpler approach of leaving interest out of account altogether.[49]

---

[44] [2001] B.L.R. 90.
[45] *ibid.* at 96.
[46] See para.41–19, above.
[47] [1993] Q.B. 780, CA.
[48] See para.41–19, above.
[49] [2001] B.L.R. 90 at [6].

The foregoing discussion, though reflecting on the form of a "sealed **41–27**
offer", has centred largely on its substance. The form is likely to vary from
case to case. In the *Archital Luxfer* case the concluding paragraph of the
respondent's offer was in these terms:[50]

> "This offer is made on terms that its existence and contents are not to
> be disclosed to the Arbitrator until he has determined all issues of
> liability and debt or damages, and it will be brought to his attention on
> the issue of costs. The offer made in this letter is intended to have the
> effect of a payment into court pursuant to RSC, Ord.22. This offer
> will remain open for acceptance at any time, with the proviso that if it
> is not accepted within one month from the date upon which it is
> received, [our clients] will propose that [your clients] should pay any
> further costs incurred by [our clients] after the expiry of that period."

It is thought that this would provide a useful model upon which offers of **41–28**
this nature could be based. Presumably, a 21-day period for acceptance of
the offer would be regarded as sufficient for this purpose: it is the period
provided for in connection with the acceptance of a Pt 36 payment.
Arbitral tribunals may however, have an even wider discretion than the
courts under CPR r.36.[51] Indeed, it is suggested that there is no reason why
the practice of claimants' offers introduced by Pt 36 should not be adopted
in arbitrations.

The foregoing discussion has centred upon offers of settlement involving **41–29**
payment of money. If the terms of the arbitration agreement and the
content of the dispute provide for other or additional remedies, considerations concerning the sufficiency of the offer would arise much as they arise
in the context of *Calderbank* offers in the ordinary sphere of civil
litigation.[52]

---

[50] [1981] 1 Lloyd's Rep. 642 at 646.
[51] *Argolis Shipping Co SA v Midwest Steel & Alloy Corp, The "Angeliki"* [1982] 2 Lloyd's Rep. 594 at 597, *per* Lloyd J.
[52] See paras 26–05 *et seq.*, above.

PART 15

Appeals and ADR

CHAPTER 42

Settlement of Appeals

Parties may decide, even after a full-scale battle below and the lodging of appropriate appeals, to cut short the appellate process and compromise their differences. Such an agreement is as binding as if made at any other stage of the proceedings.[1] No additional approval of the court, other than that required by the nature of the particular proceedings, is required to validate such an agreement. The procedure may vary according to whether the appeal is in the Court of Appeal or before a judge by way of appeal from a district judge or master. **42–01**

COURT OF APPEAL

Parties may decide to settle a pending appeal by modifying the effects of the order or judgment obtained below. In some cases this can be achieved without the need for any formal variation of the order or judgment the subject of the appeal. For example, an appeal by the defendant against the quantum of an award of damages may be compromised by the agreement of the plaintiff to accept a lower figure than the amount of the award below. While the judgment might stand as the judgment between the parties, a contractual commitment to the acceptance of a lower sum is sufficient to dispose of the matter. In this situation the appeal may safely be dismissed by consent, the defendant relying upon that contractual commitment. **42–02**

Indeed, the procedure whereby an appeal is dismissed by consent (the "DBC" procedure)[2] is the preferred procedural course since it does not involve the Court of Appeal in permitting an appeal to be allowed by consent.[3] This procedure can, of course, be employed in cases where the **42–03**

---

[1] *National Benzole Co Ltd v Gooch* [1961] 1 W.L.R. 1489.
[2] Known, certainly under the former practice, as the "DBC" procedure.
[3] See further at para.42–06, below.

terms of settlement are more complex than as foreshadowed in the example given. The only drawback is that a fresh action will be necessary for the purposes of enforcement unless, of course, an order in Tomlin form is agreed.[4]

42–04   Where parties are agreed that an appeal should be dismissed by consent, a joint request to the court to that effect should be made.[5] The procedure does not apply where any party to the proceedings is a child or a patient[6] and the joint request must so state.[7] Unless there appear to be any difficulties, it is likely that the Head of the Civil Appeals Office will initial the request, the effect being that the appeal will thereby be dismissed. An order to this effect will be drawn up and sent to the parties. Once this has been done the Court of Appeal will have no jurisdiction to reinstate the appeal or to permit the appellant to begin a fresh appeal.[8]

42–05   Where a Tomlin order is required by the parties it is likely that the practice prior to the introduction of the Civil Procedure Rules will be followed. The Court of Appeal is prepared to make such an order if satisfied that the dismissal by consent procedure is not appropriate or sufficient. The parties would submit a draft order to the Head of the Civil Appeals Office. If the office entertained any concerns about the matter that could not be dealt with relatively informally through the Head of the Civil Appeals Office or the Clerk to the Lord Justice assigned to consider the proposed order, the application for the order could be listed for mention. Where a Tomlin order is made, it is usual for the permission to apply for the purpose of enforcing the agreed terms[9] to be directed to the court below.

42–06   Where the parties are agreed that the order of the court below was wrong and are agreed on the order that ought to be substituted they can invite the Court of Appeal to allow the appeal. This must be dealt with by means of a joint request to the court, setting out the relevant history of the proceedings and the matters relied on as justifying the proposed order, a copy of which must accompany the application.[10] If the Court of Appeal is satisfied that it is appropriate to make the order it will do so on the papers. It will list the appeal for mention only if it considers that there are problems about the proposed order which cannot be resolved in any other way.[11]

---

[4] See paras 9–17 *et seq.*, above; and see para.42–05, below.
[5] Pt 52 Practice Direction, para.12.4.
[6] *ibid.*, para.12.1. For the provisions concerning cases involving a child or a patient, see para.42–07, below.
[7] Pt 52 Practice Direction, para.12.4.
[8] *Ogur Borough Council v Knight* [1994] T.L.R. 22, CA.
[9] See para.9–14, above.
[10] Pt 52 Practice Direction, para.13.1.
[11] *cf. Hadfield v Knowles, The Times*, May 27, 1996.

42–07 Where an appeal which relates to a child or patient is settled, the approval of the Court of Appeal to the settlement is required. In either case the parties' solicitors should send a copy of the proposed order to the Court of Appeal together with an opinion from the advocate representing the child or patient and, in the case of a patient, any relevant reports prepared for the Court of Protection and a document evidencing the formal approval of that court where required.[12]

42–08 An ADR scheme exists within the Court of Appeal for suitable cases.[13]

JUDGE

42–09 In addition to providing for appeals to the Court of Appeal, Pt 52 of the CPR applies to appeals to a High Court judge "from the decision of a county court or a district judge of the High Court" or from a master to a High Court judge.[14] It applies also to appeals from a county court district judge to a circuit judge.[15]

42–10 Any such appeal will, if pursued, be a "rehearing (as opposed to a review of the decision of the lower court)".[16] Parties may, of course, compromise any such appeal, subject only to the court's case management powers which may be exercised independently of the parties' agreement.[17] Since many appeals of this nature will be in relation to interim matters, those case management functions may result in the court looking carefully at what has been agreed when invited to make a consent order disposing of an appeal.

42–11 Nonetheless, where an appeal is compromised, it would seem that the same procedure as that described in relation to appeals to the Court of Appeal[18] obtains. The Pt 52 Practice Direction applies to "all appeals to which Pt 52 applies"[19] and, given that paras 12 and 13 of that Practice Direction (relating to consent disposals of an appeal) refer to the documents specified as being sent to "the appeal court",[20] it would appear that the procedure set out in those paragraphs should be followed when an appeal to a judge is resolved.

---

[12] Pt 52 Practice Direction, para.13.3 and 13.4.
[13] See *Practice Direction (Court of Appeal (Civil Division))* [1999] 1 W.L.R. 1027, para.11.
[14] Pt 52 Practice Direction, para.8.1.
[15] *ibid.*, para.8.10.
[16] *ibid.*, para.9.1.
[17] CPR Pt 3.
[18] See paras 42–04 *et seq.*, above.
[19] Pt 52 Practice Direction, para.2.1.
[20] The "appeal court" is defined as "the court to which an appeal is made": CPR r.52.1(3)(b).

CHAPTER 43

Settlement through ADR

INTRODUCTION

43–01 The increased use of alternative dispute resolution (ADR) to achieve settlement has already been noted.[1] The true definition of ADR is much debated.[2] For the purposes of this work it is taken to be any process that involves the active intervention of a third party in helping to achieve a settlement of a dispute between others.[3] The principal and best known process of this nature is mediation, although conciliation needs also to be identified as a process within the working definition adopted.

43–02 Much has been written about the technique of mediation as a process.[4] This is outwith the scope of this work. The areas of legal and practical relevance that need to be considered can be summarised thus:

(i) the court's role in encouraging mediation and the costs consequences to the parties of failing to embrace it;
(ii) the legal parameters of a mediation and a mediated settlement.

COURT'S ROLE IN ENCOURAGING MEDIATION AND COSTS CONSEQUENCES TO PARTIES OF FAILING TO EMBRACE IT

---

[1] See Ch.13, para.13–03, above.
[2] See, *e.g.*, Boulle and Nesic, *Mediation, Principles Process Practice*, Ch.1.
[3] This means that arbitration, adjudication, expert determination and other decision-making options are excluded, as indeed is neutral evaluation. In *Halsey v Milton Keynes General NHS Trust* [2004] 1 W.L.R. 3002 at [5] it was said, that the "term 'alternative dispute resolution' is defined in the Glossary to the CPR as a 'collective description of methods of resolving disputes otherwise than through the normal trial process'. In practice, however, references to ADR are usually understood as being references to some form of mediation by a third party".
[4] See n.2, above.

Under the CPR there is an obligation on the court to "further the overriding objective by actively managing cases".[5] "Active case management" includes: 43–03

> "(e) encouraging the parties to use an alternative dispute resolution procedure if the court considers that appropriate and facilitating the use of such procedure;
> (f) helping the parties to settle the whole or part of the case; . . ".[6]

These words do not confer upon the court explicit power to order ADR.[7] They merely confer upon the court an obligation to "encourage" the parties to use ADR if it considers it appropriate. In two cases decided very shortly after the CPR came into force, the court assumed jurisdiction to make an order that the parties engage in ADR even though one of the parties are objected to it.[8] In *Shirayama Shokusen Co Ltd v Danovo Ltd*,[9] Blackburne J. said that he took the view "that the court does have jurisdiction to direct ADR even though one party may not be willing to have the dispute submitted to ADR". In *Halsey v Milton Keynes General NHS Trust*,[10] the Court of Appeal said, however, that "if (contrary to our view) the court does have jurisdiction to order unwilling parties to refer their disputes to mediation, we find it difficult to conceive of circumstances in which it would be appropriate to exercise it". It was said that it "is one thing to encourage the parties to agree to mediation, even to encourage them in the strongest terms. It is another to order them to do so. It seems to us that to oblige truly unwilling parties to refer their disputes to mediation would be to impose an unacceptable obstruction on their right of access to the court".[11]   43–04

It is submitted, therefore, that the better view is that the court does not have jurisdiction to order a reluctant party to submit his dispute to ADR. The traditional wisdom of those engaged in the mediation process is that it is a voluntary process. The distinction between ordering a reluctant party to engage in ADR and encouraging it "in the strongest terms" may be a fine one in some circumstances, but the courts do make such a distinction at the present time.   43–05

---

[5] CPR r.1.4(1).
[6] CPR r.1.4(2).
[7] Neither does r.26.4, which provides that the court may "stay" proceedings, initially "for one month" and thereafter for longer specified period "as it considers appropriate" if "a party [makes] when filing the completed allocation questionnaire . . . a written request for the proceedings to be stayed while the parties try to settle the case by alternative dispute resolution or other means".
[8] See *Guinle v Kirreh*, unreported, August 3, 1999, *per* Arden J. (as she then was) and *Muman v Nagasena* [2000] 1 W.L.R. 299, CA.
[9] [2004] 1 W.L.R. 2985.
[10] [2004] 1 W.L.R. 3002, CA.
[11] *ibid.* at para.9.

43–06 Prior to the case of *Halsey v Milton Keynes General NHS Trust*, a number of cases had given strong encouragement for the use of mediation.[12] *Halsey* offered the Court of Appeal the opportunity to review the general considerations applicable to the issue and to give guidance on the correct approach. Although the case itself was a clinical negligence case (and the other appeal heard at the same time was a personal injury case) the Court of Appeal said that whilst "mediation and other ADR processes do not offer a panacea, and can have disadvantages as well as advantages", nonetheless "most cases are not by their very nature unsuitable for ADR". It was said that "[all] members of the legal profession who conduct litigation should now routinely consider with their clients whether their disputes are suitable for ADR". Consideration must, therefore, be given in almost[13] every case at some stage[14] to the issue of whether it might be suitable for some form of ADR, particularly mediation.

43–07 In order to encourage such consideration the court will frequently give a direction to that effect at an appropriate case management stage. In the Admiralty and Commercial Court the parties are directed "to exchange lists of neutral individuals who are available to conduct ADR procedures", to endeavour in good faith to agree a neutral individual or panel and to take "such serious steps as they may be advised to resolve their disputes by ADR procedures before the neutral individual or panel so chosen". The order also provides that if the case is not settled, "the parties shall inform the court what steps towards ADR have been taken and (without prejudice to matters of privilege) why such steps have failed".[15] A direction devised by Master Ungley in the field of clinical negligence litigation, which the Court of Appeal in *Halsey* said was a "less strong form of encouragement" but which should "also routinely be made at least in general personal injury litigation, and perhaps in other litigation too", is in these terms:

---

[12] See, in particular, *R. (Cowl) v Plymouth City Council* [2002] 1 W.L.R. 803; *Dunnett v Railtrack Plc* [2002] 1 W.L.R. 2434; *Hurst v Leeming* [2003] 1 Lloyd's Rep 379. *Dunnett v Railtrack* was decided in February 2002: D, which had successfully defended a county court claim concerning C's horses brought in person by C, refused to consider mediation in the context of her appeal against the loss of her claim despite being encouraged to do so by the Court of Appeal prior to the appeal. D successfully resisted the appeal, but was not awarded its costs of the appeal, as would normally have been the case, because of its attitude to mediation.

[13] In *Halsey* it was said that "most cases are not by their very nature unsuitable for ADR." However, it was recognised that some disputes "do not lend themselves to ADR procedures". Examples given were where the parties want the court to determine issues of law or construction which may be essential to the future trading relations of the parties, or where the issues are generally important for those participating in a particular trade or market. Some issues involving allegations of fraud or other commercially disreputable conduct might not be mediated successfully. Other examples are cases where a party wants the court to resolve a point of law which arises from time to time, or cases where injunctive or other relief essential to protect the position of a party is sought. See, generally, *Halsey*, n.10, above, at para.17.

[14] Generally, it is submitted, there should have been a good degree of disclosure and exchange of information: see Ch.13, para.13–05, above.

[15] Quoted in *Halsey*, n.10 above, at para.30.

"The parties shall by [specified date] consider whether the case is capable of resolution by ADR. If any party considers that the case is unsuitable for resolution by ADR, that party shall be prepared to justify that decision at the conclusion of the trial, should the judge consider that such means of resolution were appropriate, when he is considering the appropriate costs order to make. The party considering the case unsuitable for ADR shall, not less than 28 days before the commencement of the trial, file with the court a witness statement without prejudice save as to costs, giving reasons upon which they rely for saying that the case was unsuitable".[16]

It was said that where such a direction is given it will "bring home to [the parties] that, if they refuse even to consider [the question of whether the case is suitable for ADR], they may be at risk on costs even if they are ultimately held by the court to be the successful party".[17] As that passage indicates, the sanction available to the court if a party, despite encouragement from the court in the form of such a direction, fails to agree to mediation, is to make some adverse order for costs at the end of the trial. The order may deprive that party of its costs or require that party to pay the other party's costs despite the eventual result of the trial in favour of the party having refused mediation.[18] The Court of Appeal in *Halsey* emphasised, however, that taking such a course required appropriate justification:

43–08

"In deciding whether to deprive a successful party of some or all of his costs on the grounds that he has refused to agree to ADR, it must be borne in mind that such an order is an exception to the general rule that costs should follow the event. In our view, the burden is on the unsuccessful party to show why there should be a departure from the general rule. The fundamental principle is that such departure is not justified unless it is shown (the burden being on the unsuccessful party) that the successful party acted unreasonably in refusing to agree to ADR. We shall endeavour in this judgment to provide some guidance as to the factors that should be considered by the court in deciding whether a refusal to agree to ADR is unreasonable".

---

[16] See *ibid.* at paras 32–33. A variant on this theme is to require the reasons given for the unsuitability of ADR to be recorded in a sealed envelope to be filed with the court which is not to be opened until the conclusion of the trial.
[17] *ibid.*, at para.33.
[18] CPR r.44.3(2) provides that "if the court decides to make an order about costs (a) the general rule is that the unsuccessful party will be ordered to pay the cost of the successful party; but (b) the court may make a different order". Rule 44.3(4) provides that "in deciding what order (if any) to make about costs, the court must have regard to all the circumstances, including—(a) the conduct of the parties . . .". Rule 44.3(5) provides that the conduct of the parties includes "(a) conduct before, as well as during, the proceedings and in particular the extent to which the parties followed any relevant pre-action protocol".

43–09   The factors identified by the Court of Appeal as being potentially relevant to the question of whether a party has unreasonably refused ADR "will include (but are not limited to) the following: (a) the nature of the dispute; (b) the merits of the case; (c) the extent to which other settlement methods have been attempted; (d) whether the costs of the ADR would be disproportionately high; (e) whether any delay in setting up and attending the ADR would have been prejudicial; and (f) whether the ADR had a reasonable prospect of success".[19] Of these, (b), (c) and (f) are likely to be the most contentious, although (d) could certainly arise if the costs involved in a proposed mediation were disproportionately high compared with the sums at stake in the dispute.[20]

MERITS OF THE CASE

43–10   "The fact that a party reasonably believes that he has a strong case is relevant to the question whether he has acted reasonably in refusing ADR". So stated the Court of Appeal when indicating that courts needed to be aware of the danger of a "claimant [using] the threat of costs sanctions to extract a settlement from the defendant even where the claim is without merit".[21] It was said that "the fact that a party *reasonably* believes that he has a watertight case may well be sufficient justification for a refusal to mediate". In *Halsey* the Court of Appeal agreed with the view of the trial judge, who had rejected the claimant's claim, that the defendant trust had been entitled to reject the repeated suggestions for mediation on the claimant's side because of the speculative nature of the claim to which it reasonably believed it had a strong defence. It was said that the claimant had "come nowhere near showing that the trust acted unreasonably in refusing to agree to a mediation", nor had it been established that "mediation had a reasonable prospect of success".[22]

OTHER ATTEMPTS AT SETTLEMENT

43–11   "The fact that settlement offers have already been made, but rejected, is a relevant factor. It may show that one party is making efforts to settle, and that the other party has unrealistic views of the merits of the case". This is the way that the matter was put by the Court of Appeal in *Halsey*.[23] However, only negotiations conducted under the rubric or principle of

---

[19] *Halsey*, n.10, above, at para.16.
[20] *ibid.*, at para.21.
[21] *ibid.*, at para.26.
[22] *ibid.*, at paras 36–54.
[23] *ibid.*, at para.20.

"without prejudice except as to costs" could be referred to on this issue.[24] In *Halsey* it was recognised that the issue of previous attempts at settlement was "in truth no more than an aspect of" the issue of whether "ADR had a reasonable prospect of success".

WHETHER MEDIATION HAD REASONABLE PROSPECTS OF SUCCESS

In *Halsey* the Court of Appeal identified "the fundamental question" as being "whether the successful party acted unreasonably in refusing to agree to mediation".[25] As already indicated,[26] the burden of showing a reason for departing from the normal rule as to costs lies on the unsuccessful party in the litigation. It follows from that that the burden should be on the "unsuccessful party to show that there was a reasonable prospect that mediation would have been successful".[27] This was said to be "not an unduly onerous burden to discharge" because "he does not have to prove that a mediation would *in fact* have succeeded". 43–12

It is, of course, important to identify where the true responsibility for declining mediation rests. As was said in *Halsey*, a "successful party cannot rely on his own unreasonableness in such circumstances".[28] If, however, the successful party reasonably took the view that a mediation would have had no reasonable prospect of success because the party that ultimately lost the case was "most unlikely to accept a reasonable compromise" then that would constitute a basis for concluding that the refusal to mediate was reasonable.[29] 43–13

LEGAL PARAMETERS OF A MEDIATION AND MEDIATED SETTLEMENT

In *Halsey* the Court of Appeal recognised the importance of respecting the integrity and confidentiality of the mediation process itself. It was put in this way[30]: 43–14

---

[24] In *Reed Executive Plc v Reed Business Information Ltd* [2004] 1 W.L.R. 3026, the Court of Appeal reaffirmed the well-established principle that without prejudice negotiations cannot be referred to on questions going to the issue of costs. To that extent, the without prejudice correspondence was inadmissible on the issue of the reasonableness or otherwise of a party's stance to mediation.
[25] *Halsey*, n.10, above, at para.25.
[26] See para. 43–08, above.
[27] *Halsey*, n.10, above, at para.28 on.
[28] *ibid.*, at para.26.
[29] *ibid.*, at para.25. A case which preceded *Halsey* in the Court of Appeal which indicates the approach of the court where parties have "postured" and "jockeyed for position" in respect of the issue of mediation is *Macmillan Williams v Grange* [2004] EWCA Civ 294.
[30] *Halsey*, n.10, above, at para.14.

"We make it clear at the outset that it was common ground before us (and we accept) that parties are entitled in an ADR to adopt whatever position they wish, and if as a result the dispute is not settled, that is not a matter for the court. . . . if the integrity and confidentiality of the process is to be respected, the court should not know, and therefore should not investigate, why the process did not result in agreement."

43–15 This is an important policy statement. Leaving aside all other actual or potential advantages of embarking on a mediation in a particular case, the twin advantages of the confidential and the "without prejudice" nature of the process, allied to its informality, are fundamental. If the courts are to encourage parties to engage in mediation to maximum effect, the principles underlying the process will need to be respected fully.

43–16 Since any mediation taking place against the background of actual or threatened litigation will almost invariably be designed to achieve a settlement, either in whole or in part, of the underlying disputes, the discussions forming part of the mediation will be impliedly without prejudice.[31] However, most mediators, whether acting on behalf of one of the main service providers[32] or as an individual, will ask the parties to sign a mediation agreement incorporating an express provision confirming the without prejudice nature of the process. The confidentiality of the process is secured in a similar fashion.[33]

43–17 As set out elsewhere in this work,[34] there are exceptions to the "without prejudice" rule. If called upon to permit an exception to apply in respect of some aspect of a mediation, the courts will have to tread a fine line

---

[31] See paras 27–04 *et seq.*, above.

[32] For example, CEDR, ADR Group or the Chartered Institute of Arbitrators.

[33] An obligation of confidentiality will be implied as a matter of law into an arbitration agreement: *Ali Shipping Corporation v Shipyard Trogir* [1999] 1 W.L.R. 314, CA. Perhaps *a fortiori* in relation to a mediation agreement. The standard CEDR confidentiality clause was considered in *Instance v Denny Bros Printing*, unreported, December 21, 1999, Lloyd J. It was in these terms: "Every person involved in the mediation will keep confidential and not use for any collateral or ulterior purpose all information, (whether giver orally, in writing or otherwise), produced for, or arising in relation to, the mediation including the settlement agreement (if any) arising out of it, except insofar as it is necessary to implement and enforce any such settlement agreement". It was held that "communications preceding the mediation agreement that . . . led to it [were] within the scope of the confidentiality clause". Lloyd J. said that "given that embarking on mediation is a consensual process which may well, as it did in this case, involve quite lengthy discussion before an agreement is reached for mediation, let alone any ultimate settlement agreement, it seems to me that it would be natural to read the phrase: 'arising in relation to the mediation' as not being limited to things done after the signature of the mediation agreement. Mediation is defined as the attempt to settle the dispute by mediation. The process of getting to entry into the mediation agreement is itself, albeit at a preliminary stage, an attempt to settle the dispute by mediation. No doubt in practice all or most discussions at such a stage will be on a without prejudice basis".

[34] See Ch.23, above.

between seeing that justice is done in the individual case and ensuring that precedents are not set which undermine the whole foundation, and thus the consequent strength, of the mediation process. Too ready a willingness to permit an exception to apply, particularly the "unambiguous impropriety" exception,[35] could have that effect. It is likely that the general approach of the Court of Appeal in *Unilever Plc v The Procter & Gamble Company*,[36] followed in subsequent cases,[37] will be the approach adopted when this kind of issue arises. Robert Walker L.J.'s description of a without prejudice meeting as consisting of "wide-ranging unscripted discussions . . . which may have lasted several hours"[38] is a description which could be applied readily to a mediation.

One exception to the "without prejudice" rule is that which permits evidence of without prejudice discussions to be given in order to prove that an agreement has been reached.[39] Technically, this exception could be called into play in the context of a mediation, but it is the almost invariable practice for a mediation to be conducted on the basis that an agreement will only be treated as having been concluded when it is reduced to writing and signed by or on behalf of the parties.

43–18

It is not, of course, an exception to the "without prejudice" rule to permit the reception in evidence of something said during without prejudice negotiations which is alleged to have constituted a material misrepresentation inducing the settlement achieved. This is a natural consequence of the law that entitles a party to seek to set aside a compromise on the basis of a misrepresentation.[40] The extent to which a mediator may be drawn into this process, directly or indirectly, is considered below.[41]

43–19

So far as confidentiality is concerned, whether it springs from an express or implied contractual provision, the remedy for breaching such a provision will usually be, in the first instance, a claim for an injunction and then damages or restitutionary relief.

43–20

As things stand in the United Kingdom, no particular privilege or immunity attaches to a mediator under the general law.[42] On that basis a mediator could be called as a witness to speak about what occurred at a

43–21

---

[35] See paras 27–28 *et seq.*, above.
[36] [2000] 1 W.L.R. 2436.
[37] See Ch.27, n.67, above.
[38] See Ch.27, para.27–39, above.
[39] See para. 27–20, above.
[40] See Ch.4, above.
[41] See para.43–21, below.
[42] The position varies worldwide.

mediation subject, of course, to matters of objection available to the parties themselves. Many mediators would see the prospect of being called as a witness for or against a party to a mediation as anathema to his or her role as the trusted intermediary between the parties. To that extent most mediation agreements provide expressly that the parties will not call the mediator as a witness in any proceedings concerning the matters in dispute or what occurred at the mediation. The efficacy of such an agreement has yet to be tested, but the policy statement enunciated in *Halsey*[43] would suggest that the courts will be most reluctant to see a mediator being required to testify about such matters.

---

[43] See para.43–14, above.

APPENDIX 1

Precedents

This Appendix is divided into six parts:

Section 1: Precedents for Part 36
Section 2: Draft Consent Orders and Judgments—General
Section 3: Chancery Precedents
Section 4: Precedents for Serious Personal Injury Claims by Children or Patients
Section 5: Landlord and Tenant Cases and Boundary Disputes
Section 6: Administrative Court Proceedings

Section 1

Precedents for Part 36

CONTENTS

1. General form of Part 36 offer relating to the whole claim made more than 21 days before the trial.
2. General form of Part 36 offer relating to the whole claim made less than 21 days before the trial.
3. General form of Part 36 offer relating to part of the claim made more than 21 days before the trial.
4. General form of a claimant's Part 36 offer relating to the whole of a money claim made more than 21 days before the trial.
5. General form of a claimant's Part 36 offer relating to part of a money claim made more than 21 days before the trial.
6. General form of Part 36 offer as an open offer.
7. General form of pre-action offer by a defendant in a money claim.
8. General form of pre-action offer by a defendant in a non-money claim.
9. Letter written by defendant in non-money claim who had made pre-action offer to be sent to the claimant on the institution of proceedings.
10. General form of claimant's pre-action offer in a money claim.
11. Defendant's letter to claimant when making or increasing a Part 36 payment during the trial.

APPENDIX 1

1

General form of Part 36 offer relating to the whole claim made more than 21 days before the trial[1]

A1–01 Dear Sirs,   PART 36 OFFER

<u>C v D</u>

We refer to the above matter in which we act for D.

Our client has instructed us to make the following offer to settle, the offer being made in accordance with Part 36, Civil Procedure Rules.

He offers to settle the whole claim on the terms that [*set out precise terms offered*]. [This offer takes into account/does not take into account his counterclaim for . . .]

This offer will remain open for acceptance for 21 days from the date you receive it. If your client gives notice of acceptance within that period, he will be entitled to his costs of the proceedings (assessed on the standard basis if not agreed) to the date of the service of that notice. If your client does not accept the offer within that period, then it can be accepted thereafter if we can agree the liability for the costs of the proceedings or the court gives permission.

[If our client's offer is accepted, or is permitted to be accepted by the court, we propose that it is embodied in a consent order/judgment in the terms set out in the enclosed draft or terms to like effect.][2]

Yours, etc.

2

General form of Part 36 offer relating to the whole claim made less than 21 days before the trial[3]

A1–02 Dear Sirs,   PART 36 OFFER

<u>C v D</u>

We refer to the above matter in which we act for D.

Our client has instructed us to make the following offer to settle, the offer being made in accordance with Part 36, Civil Procedure Rules.

He offers to settle the whole claim on the terms that [*set out precise terms offered*]. [This offer takes into account/does not take into account his counterclaim for . . .]

---

[1] See Ch.17, above.

[2] If an order beyond the rule-imposed Tomlin order is required, a paragraph to this effect may be sensible: see para.21–15, above.

[3] See Ch.17, above.

Your client may accept it at any time before the trial begins if we can agree the liability for the costs of the proceedings or the court gives permission.

Our proposal in relation to the costs of the proceedings is [*set out details*]. If your client rejects that proposal, he can seek the permission of the court to accept the offer. Our client will contend that, if the court gives its permission, the order for costs should be [*set out details*]. However, our client makes it clear that he will abide by the decision of the court in this regard.

[If our client's offer is accepted, or is permitted to be accepted by the court, we propose that it is embodied in a consent order/judgment in the terms set out in the enclosed draft or terms to like effect.][4]

Yours, etc.

3

General form of Part 36 offer relating to part[5] of the claim made more than 21 days before the trial[6]

Dear Sirs, PART 36 OFFER **A1–03**

<u>C v D</u>

We refer to the above matter in which we act for D.

Our client has instructed us to make the following offer to settle, the offer being made in accordance with Part 36, Civil Procedure Rules.

Our client offers to settle [the part of the claim relating to . . .] on the following terms, namely [*set out details*]. [The offer takes account/does not take account of our client's counterclaim.]

This offer will remain open for acceptance for 21 days from the date you receive it. If your client gives notice of acceptance within that period and at the time of serving it he abandons the balance of the claim, [our client accepts that your client will be entitled to his costs of the proceedings (assessed on the standard basis if not agreed) to the date of the service of that notice][7] [our client will apply to the court to seek a different order as to costs from that provided for in r.36.13(2). The order as to costs we propose is . . .][8]

---

[4] If an order beyond the rule-imposed Tomlin order is required, a paragraph to this effect may be sensible: see para.21–15, above.
[5] This precedent could be adapted to make an offer to settle an "issue": see paras 16–07 *et seq.*, above.
[6] See Ch.17, above.
[7] The usual order if C abandons the balance of his claim: r.36.13(2).
[8] This would be appropriate where, for example, the defendant considers that it would be unfair that C should have all the costs associated with the abandoned parts of his claim: see para.21–05, above. This approach does not, it is submitted, offend the principle that for a Pt 36 offer to be effective it must relate only to the substantive dispute: see Ch.23, n.30, above.

APPENDIX 1

If your client serves notice of acceptance within 21 days, but does not abandon the balance of his claim, we propose that the order for costs following the stay of the proceedings[9] is that [*set out proposal*]. If that proposal is not acceptable to your client, the court will have to decide the liability for costs.[10]

If your client does not accept the offer on either basis within that period, then it can be accepted thereafter if we can agree the liability for the costs of the proceedings or the court gives permission.

[If our client's offer is accepted, or is permitted to be accepted by the court, we propose that it is embodied in a consent order/judgment in the terms set out in the enclosed draft or terms to like effect.][11]

Yours, etc.

4

General form of claimant's Part 36 offer relating to the whole of a money claim made more than 21 days before the trial[12]

A1–04 Dear Sirs,   PART 36 OFFER

<u>C v D</u>

We refer to the above matter in which we act for C.

Our client has instructed us to make the following offer to settle, the offer being made in accordance with Part 36, Civil Procedure Rules.

As you know, our client's claim is for [damages arising from . . .] [the sum of £X arising from . . .] plus interest. He offers to settle the whole of his claim for the sum of £Y [which, for the avoidance of doubt, is inclusive of interest to 21 days from now.][13]

This offer will remain open for acceptance for 21 days from the date you receive it. If your client gives notice of acceptance within that period, our client will be entitled to his costs of the proceedings (assessed on the standard basis if not agreed) to the date of the service of that notice.[14]

If your client does not accept the offer within that period, then it can be accepted thereafter if we can agree the liability for the costs of the proceedings or the court gives permission.

---

[9] CPR r.36.15(3)(a).
[10] CPR r.36.15(3)(b).
[11] If an order beyond the rule-imposed Tomlin order is required, a paragraph to this effect may be sensible: see para.21–15, above.
[12] See Ch.17, above.
[13] These words are not strictly necessary since interest to the expiration of the 21-day period is deemed to be included: r.36.22(1). If interest is not included, but interest is demanded within the offer, details must be given: r.36.22(2).
[14] CPR r.36.14.

[If your client does not accept this offer and is held liable at the trial for more, it would be our client's intention to rely on the provisions of r.36.21.][15]

Yours, etc.

5

General form of claimant's Part 36 offer relating to part[16] of a money claim made more than 21 days before the trial[17]

Dear Sirs,   PART 36 OFFER **A1–05**

<u>C v D</u>

We refer to the above matter in which we act for C.

Our client has instructed us to make the following offer to settle, the offer being made in accordance with Part 36, Civil Procedure Rules.

As you know, our client's claim is for [damages arising from . . .] [the sum of £X arising from . . .] plus interest. One part of his overall claim relates to [*give details*]. He offers to settle that part of his claim for the sum of £Z [which, for the avoidance of doubt, is inclusive of interest to 21 days from now.][18]

This offer will remain open for acceptance for 21 days from the date you receive it. If your client gives notice of acceptance within that period, we propose that the order for costs following the stay of the proceedings[19] is that [*set out proposal*]. If that proposal is not acceptable to your client, the court will have to decide the liability for costs.[20]

If your client does not accept the offer within that period, then it can be accepted thereafter if we can agree the liability for the costs of the proceedings or the court gives permission.

---

[15] Again, these words are not strictly necessary because r.36.21 arises automatically once a claimant does better than his offer. However, there would be no harm in emphasising that reliance will be replaced upon it.
[16] See paras 16–07 *et seq.*, above.
[17] See Ch.17, above.
[18] These words are not strictly necessary since interest to the expiration of the 21-day period is deemed to be included: r.36.22(1). If interest is not included, but interest is demanded within the offer, details must be given: r.36.22(2).
[19] CPR r.36.15(3)(a).
[20] CPR r.36.15(3)(b).

[If your client does not accept this offer and is held liable at the trial for more, it would be our client's intention to rely on the provisions of r.36.21.][21]

Yours, etc.

6

General form of Part 36 offer as an open offer

A1–06   Dear Sirs,   PART 36 OFFER

C v D

We refer to the above matter in which we act for D.

Our client has instructed us to make the following offer to settle, the offer being made in accordance with Part 36, Civil Procedure Rules. We would draw attention to the fact that it is our client's wish that this offer should be treated as an open offer. For the avoidance of doubt, therefore, we make it plain that our client waives any privilege attaching to the offer by reason of r.36.19(1).[22]

[continue with substance of offer]

Yours, etc.

7

General form of pre-action offer by a defendant in a money claim[23]

A1–07   Dear Sirs,   PRE-ACTION OFFER

C v D

We refer to the above matter in which we act for D.

Your client has intimated a claim for [damages arising from . . .] [£X arising from . . .].

Our client offers to settle the whole claim in the sum of £Y [inclusive of interest until 21 days hence] [exclusive of interest which is offered at the rate of . . . % p.a.

---

[21] Again, these words are not strictly necessary because r.36.21 arises automatically once a claimant does better than his offer. However, there would be no harm in emphasising that reliance will be placed upon it. It should, however, be noted that, whilst r.36.21 is not precluded from operation when part only of a claim forms the subject of the claimant's offer, its practical implementation may generally be difficult in cases other than where the offer is for settlement of the whole claim.
[22] See paras 26–08 *et seq.*, above.
[23] See Ch.15, above.

from . . . to . . .].[24] He also offers to pay your client's reasonable costs up to 21 days from the date you receive this offer.

This offer remains open for 21 days after you receive it. [It takes account/does not take account of the counterclaim our client has intimated.]

If your client does not accept the offer, but in due course begins proceedings in relation to this matter, it will be our client's intention to pay the above-mentioned sum into court within 14 days of the service of the claim form so that the provisions of r.36.10 will apply.

Yours, etc.

8

General form of pre-action offer by a defendant in a non-money claim[25]

Dear Sirs,   PRE-ACTION OFFER **A1–08**

C v D

We refer to the above matter in which we act for D.

Your client has intimated a claim for [*set out details*].

Our client offers to settle the whole claim on the terms/basis that [*set out details of offer*]. [If this offer is accepted, we would suggest that a formal deed is executed so that the boundary is henceforth clearly defined.][26]

He also offers to pay your client's reasonable costs up to 21 days from the date you receive this offer [together with the reasonable costs of preparing and executing the above-mentioned deed].

This offer remains open for 21 days after you receive it. [It takes account/does not take account of the counterclaim our client has intimated.]

[OR—This offer remains open on the terms we have mentioned for 21 days from the date you receive it. Should your client elect not to accept it within that period, it will remain open until proceedings are begun except that our client would require payment of his reasonable costs incurred after 21 days have elapsed from the date you receive it.] [If the offer is not accepted before proceedings are begun, it will remain open for acceptance thereafter, but only with the permission of the court. We would invite the court to give permission only on the basis that our client's

---

[24] These details are required to ensure that the offer complies with Pt 36 (see paras 15–03 *et seq.*, above): r.36.5(3)(c).
[25] See Ch.15, above. There will not be many claims which are purely "non-money". However, a claim for a declaration about a disputed boundary where there is no additional claim for damages is one example.
[26] This would probably be sensible in a boundary dispute: see Ch.38, above.

costs from 21 days after you receive this offer should be met by your client on an indemnity basis.][27]

Yours, etc.

9

Letter written by defendant in non-money claim who had made pre-action offer to be sent to the claimant on the institution of proceedings[28]

A1–09 Dear Sirs,

C v D

We refer to our pre-action offer dated . . . which your client did not accept within the time given for acceptance.

Now that he has instituted proceedings, may we state that the offer can be treated as open for acceptance with the permission of the court within r.36.10(4)(a). We would invite the court to give permission only on the basis that our client's costs from 21 days after you received the pre-action offer should be met by your client on an indemnity basis.[29]

Yours, etc.

10

General form of claimant's pre-action offer in a money claim

A1–10 Dear Sirs,   PRE-ACTION OFFER

C v D

We refer to the above matter in which we act for C.

Our client has intimated a claim for [damages arising from . . .] [£X arising from . . .].

Our client is prepared to, and offers to, settle the whole claim in the sum of £Y [inclusive of interest until 21 days hence] [exclusive of interest which he offers to accept at the rate of . . . % p.a. from . . . to . . .].[30]

---

[27] If the offeror wants to put his pre-action offer on virtually the same footing as a pre-action offer in a money claim, a paragraph along these lines would be sensible: see para.15–03, above. Another alternative is to make a pre-action offer as shown in the above Precedent down to the part in square brackets starting "*OR*" and then to write a letter as shown in Precedent 9, below.

[28] See Precedent 8, above.

[29] Any other suggestion as to costs could, of course, be made, but this is thought to be the most likely suggestion in the situation. Ultimately, it will be for the court to decide.

[30] These details are required to ensure that the offer complies with Pt 36 (see paras 15–03 *et seq.*, above): r.36.5(3)(c).

He would, of course, expect that his reasonable costs up to 21 days from the date you receive this offer would be met.

This offer remains open for 21 days after you receive it. [It takes account/does not take account of the counterclaim your client has intimated.]

Should our client's offer not be accepted and it becomes necessary for him to commence proceedings, it will be his intention to rely on r.36.21 if the award of the court exceeds his present offer.

Yours, etc.

11

Defendant's letter to claimant when making or increasing a Part 36 payment during the trial[31]

Dear Sirs, A1–11

<u>C v D</u>

We refer to the trial taking place between the above parties.

We enclose with this letter a Part 36 payment notice in which we give notice that our client has paid a further £ . . . into court.

Our client's appraisal of this case has changed with the recent disclosure of the documents relating to . . . Had he seen those documents earlier he would have taken a different view on the merits of your client's claim.

Because it is this late disclosure that has prompted the further payment into court, we do not consider it right for your client to have his full costs to date. Our offer is, therefore, that your client should have his costs to . . . and that there should be no order as to costs thereafter. If your client agrees to this, the full Part 36 payment can be accepted without seeking the court's permission. [We would propose an order in accordance with the enclosed draft.]

If your client does not agree that order as to costs, he can, of course, still seek the court's permission to accept the sum offered. If he does this, we will be contending that the permission should only be granted on the basis of the order for costs proposed above.

Since the trial is in progress and your client has access to his legal advisers, our proposal in relation to costs will be available until the conclusion of tomorrow's proceedings. If the payment is not accepted on the above basis by then, we will be seeking an order for our client's costs thereafter on the indemnity basis.

Yours, etc.

---

[31] See paras 22–10 *et seq.*, above.

APPENDIX 1

Section 2

Draft Consent Orders and Judgments—General

CONTENTS

    12. General form of draft consent order.
    13. General form of draft consent order for a sum of money.
    14. Tomlin order—general.

12

General form of draft consent order

A1–12

[*Title of action*]

[BEFORE, etc.]

UPON the parties having agreed terms of settlement

BY CONSENT

IT IS ORDERDERED/DIRECTED

[SET OUT PRECISE TERMS OF ORDER]

AND IT IS FURTHER ORDERED that the costs of this matter/application are [agreed in the sum of £....] [to be the subject of a detailed assessment] and to be paid by the claimant/defendant [*or such other agreed order as to costs even if it is that* "there shall be no order as to costs"].

[AND IT IS FURTHER ORDERED that the claimant's/defendant's costs shall be the subject of [a]/[an immediate] detailed assessment on the standard basis in accordance with Regulation 107 of the Civil Legal Aid (General) Regulations 1989, as amended, Article 5 of the Access to Justice Act 1999 (Commencement No.3) Order 2000, Article 4 of the Community Legal Services (Funding) Order 2000 and the Civil Legal Aid (General) (Amendment) Regulations 2000].[1]

[AND IT IS FURTHER ORDERED that either party shall have permission to apply][2]

DATED, etc.

Counsel/Solicitor
for Claimant

Counsel/Solicitor
for Defendant

---

[1] If one or other of the parties is in receipt of assistance from the Legal Services Commission.
[2] If this is appropriate.

13

General form of draft consent judgment for a sum of money

A1–13

[*Title of action*]

[BEFORE, etc.]

UPON the parties having agreed terms of settlement

BY CONSENT
IT IS ORDERED that the defendant pay the claimant the sum of £...., inclusive of interest[1] [to be paid within .... days] [to be paid by equal weekly/monthly instalments of £...., commencing on ...., the whole sum to be immediately payable if the defendant should fail to make any one payment].

[*continue as in Precedent 12*]

14

Tomlin order—general

A1–14

[*Title of case*]

UPON [hearing Counsel for the parties] [hearing the solicitors for the parties] [reading the letter from the claimant's solicitor and the defendant's solicitor/defendant in person]

AND UPON the parties having agreed terms of settlement

BY CONSENT

IT IS ORDERED that all further proceedings in this [matter/case] be stayed upon the terms set out in the [Schedule to this order] [document entitled "Settlement of Claim No. between [C] and [D]" dated and signed by (Counsel

for each party) (the solicitors for each party) (the solicitor for C and the defendant in person), the original of which has been retained by (C's solicitors) and a copy of which has been retained by (D's solicitors)(D)][1] except for the purpose of enforcing those terms.

AND IT IS FURTHER ORDERED that either party may be permitted to apply to the court to enforce the terms upon which this [matter/case] has been stayed without the need to bring a new claim.

---

[1] If the terms of the judgment continue no further than this point, the judgment will be enforceable after 14 days: CPR r.40.11.
[1] If the parties wish to keep the terms of their agreement confidential by recording it elsewhere than in a Schedule to the order, which is part of a record that can be made public, then a formula such as that suggested will need to be adopted.

AND IT IS RECORDED that the parties have agreed that any claim for breach of contract arising from an alleged breach of the terms set out in the [Schedule to this order] [the above-mentioned document] may, unless the Court orders otherwise, be dealt with by way of an application to the Court without the need to start a new claim.[2]

AND IT IS FURTHER RECORDED [*set out agreed order as to costs and include any legal aid taxation*]

SCHEDULE

[*set out terms of agreement here unless they are to be recorded on a separate document*]

---

[2] This agreement may be necessary if the parties wish to avoid the consequences of the case of *Hollingsworth v Humphrey* (1987) C.A.T. 1244 referred to in para.21–16, above. But see paras 9–23—9–27, above.

Section 3

Chancery Precedents

CONTENTS

15. Order for permission to withdraw winding-up petition.
16. General form of order dismissing a winding-up petition by consent.
17. General form of order dismissing or giving permission to withdraw a bankruptcy petition.
18. General form of Tomlin Order compromising a petition under s.459 of the Companies Act 1985
19. Order in Probate Claim involving Compromise.
20. Agreed order in passing-off action where hearing of interim application treated as application for judgment.

15

Order for permission to withdraw winding-up petition

[*Title of petition*]   A1–15

Winding-up petition presented on

UPON THE EX PARTE APPLICATION OF

AND UPON READING

AND UPON HEARING

and the Court being satisfied that the petition has not been advertised, that no notices in support of or in opposition to the petition have been received by the Petitioner and that the Company consents to this Order

IT IS ORDERED that the Petitioner have permission to withdraw the said petition

and that [*insert any further terms of the order*].

16

General form of order dismissing a winding-up petition by consent

[*Title of petition*]   A1–16

UPON THE PETITION OF _____ a creditor of the above-named Company

AND UPON HEARING Counsel for the Petitioner and for the Company

APPENDIX 1

AND UPON READING the evidence

IT IS by consent ORDERED

1. That the said Petition do stand dismissed out of this Court.
2. That the Petitioner be restrained, whether by himself or by his servants or agents or otherwise howsoever, from presenting any further petition for the winding-up of the above-named Company based on the sum of £—— claimed in the said Petition.
3. That the costs of and occasioned by the said Petition be treated as costs in the cause in any subsequent court proceedings for the recovery of the said sum.

17

General form of order dismissing or giving permission to withdraw a bankruptcy petition

A1–17

[*Title of petition*]

Mr Registrar _____ in Chambers.

IN THE MATTER of a bankruptcy petition filed on

UPON THE APPLICATION of

AND UPON HEARING

AND UPON READING the evidence

BY CONSENT

IT IS ORDERED THAT [this petition be dismissed] [the petitioner has permission to withdraw this petition]

and that [*insert any further terms of the order, e.g. as to costs*]

AND IT IS ORDERED that the registration of the petition as a pending action at the Land Charges Department of HM Land Registry on _____ under Reference No _____ be vacated upon the application of the debtor under the Land Charges Rules.

DATED

NOTICE TO DEBTOR

It is your responsibility, and it is in your interest, to ensure that the registration of the petition as an entry, both in the Land Charges Register and your registered titles, is cancelled.

18

General form of Tomlin order compromising a petition under s.459 of the Companies Act 1985

[*Title of petition*]   A1–18

UPON THE PETITION of

AND UPON HEARING Counsel for the Petitioner and for the Respondents

AND UPON READING the evidence

AND the Parties having agreed to the terms set out in the attached Schedule.

AND the Petitioner by his Counsel undertaking to apply to dismiss the Petition when the said terms have been fully implemented.

IT IS BY CONSENT ordered that all further proceedings herein be stayed except for the purpose of carrying such terms into effect

AND for that purpose the parties have permission to apply.

SCHEDULE

[*set out the agreed terms*]

19

Order in probate claim involving compromise

[*Title of claim*]   A1–19

AN APPLICATION by notice dated_____was made on_____by [Counsel/Solicitor] for_____and was attended by

THE COURT heard_____for_____

[THE COURT read_____]

[Probate of the alleged last will and testament dated_____/Letters of administration of the estate] of_____deceased [was/were] granted on_____to_____

THE COURT is satisfied that:

(1) consents by or on behalf of every relevant beneficiary (as defined by s.49 of the Administration of Justice Act 1985) have been given to the making of this order; and
(2) this order is for the benefit of the relevant beneficiaries who are children.

THE COURT pronounces for/against the force and validity of the last will and testament of the deceased a completed copy of which is the testamentary document dated_____and marked exhibit_____referred to in the [witness

APPENDIX 1

statement/affidavit] of testamentary documents of_____[made/sworn] on_____and against the force and validity of the last will and testament of the deceased a completed copy of which is the testamentary document dated_____and marked exhibit_____referred to in the [witness statement/affidavit] of testamentary documents_____[made/sworn] on_____

IT IS ORDERED that

(1) this claim [and counterclaim] be discontinued.
(2) the probate/letters of administration be revoked
(3) the terms set out in the Schedule be carried into effect
(4) [probate of the will] [and codicil(s)] [letters of administration of the estate] of deceased late of [*address*] be granted to [the claimant/the defendant] named as executor if entitled thereto
(5) on application for such a grant the caveat numbered and entered on [*date*], do if still subsisting cease to have effect
(6) there be assessed if not agreed

   (a) the costs of this claim [and counterclaim] of the claimant/defendant the executor named in the will
   (b) the costs of this claim [and counterclaim] of the claimant /defendant and
   (c) the costs of the claimant/defendant in accordance with the provisions of the Legal Aid Act 1988/the Access to Justice Act 1999.

(7) the costs specified in 6(a) and (b) above be paid out of the estate of the deceased in the due course of administration.

SCHEDULE

[*set out the agreed terms*]

20

Agreed order in passing-off action where hearing of interim application treated as application for judgment

A1–20

[*Title of claim*]

UPON APPLICATION for an injunction made by Counsel for the Claimant

AND UPON HEARING Counsel for the Defendant

AND UPON READING the documents recorded on the court file as having been read

AND the Parties by their respective Counsel

   (a) agreeing to the application being treated as an application for judgment and
   (b) consenting to this Order

IT IS BY CONSENT ORDERED

   1. That the Defendant be restrained (whether by itself, its directors, officers, servants or agents or otherwise howsoever) from using or carrying on

business under the name or style of_____ or under any name or style which includes the word or so nearly resembles the same as to be calculated to deceive members of the public into or to induce the belief that the business carried on by the Defendant is the same as the business presently carried on by the Claimant or is in any way connected therewith.
2. That the operation of this injunction be suspended until after so as to enable the Defendant to take all necessary steps to change the name of the Defendant company to one not containing the word_____.
3. That the Defendant do pay to the Claimant its costs of this action in the agreed sum of £.

APPENDIX 1

Section 4

Precedents for Serious Personal Injury Claims by Children or Patients

CONTENTS

21. Consent order for settlement of action brought by a minor patient which involves RPI-linked periodic payments within subsequent variations

21

Consent Order for Settlement of Action Brought by a Minor Patient Which Involves RPI-Linked Periodic Payments With Subsequent Variations

A1–21

[*Title of the action*]

BEFORE The Honourable sitting in the High Court of Justice, [*insert center*] on [*insert date*].

UPON HEARING [*name(s)*] of Counsel on behalf of the Claimant and [*names*] of Counsel on behalf of the Defendant.

WHEREAS the Claimant has made a claim ("the Claim") against the Defendant arising out of [*type of claim, e.g. a medical incident or series of incidents*] on or around [*date(s) of negligence*] from which the Claimant suffered personal injuries and in respect of which proceedings were commenced by the Claimant against the Defendant in the High Court of Justice on [*date*].

AND WHEREAS the Claimant is a Minor, [*currently also a Patient under the Court of Protection*], and brings this Claim by his [*description, e.g. mother/father/uncle, etc.*] and Litigation Friend, [*name*].

AND UPON the Claimant and the Defendant having agreed to the terms set forth herein.

AND UPON the Claimant having agreed to accept the sum of [*insert amount of gross settlement sum exclusive of periodic payments*] (inclusive of interim payments received and payments made to the CRU) plus the periodic payments referred to in the Schedule attached to this order in satisfaction of the Claim.

AND WHEREAS the said sum of [gross settlement sum as above] (inclusive of interim payments received and payments made to the CRU) includes the sum of [*insert*] in respect of the claim for future loss of earnings; and the periodic payments referred to in the Schedule attached to this Order are paid in respect of future care and medical costs and other recurring or annual costs.

AND UPON THE COURT:

1. Reading the advices [*NB theses advices may be both legal and financial. The names of the advisers and the dates of the advices may be put in the order if desired*] obtained on behalf of the Claimant as to the desirability and appropriateness of the terms in the Schedule to this Order.
2. Being satisfied that continuity of payment under the order is reasonably secure under s2(4)(c) of the Damages Act 1996 (as amended).
3. Being satisfied that the terms of CPR Parts 21 and 41 (in respect of periodic payments) have been complied with.
4. Being informed that the Master of the Public Guardianship Office has signified his approval [*delete if not applicable*].

AND UPON THE CLAIMANT BY HIS LITIGATION FRIEND:

1. Acknowledging receipt of the sum of [*amount of any interim payments*] paid to the Claimant's solicitors as an interim payment on account of past expenses and losses.
2. Acknowledging payment of [*amount if applicable*] to CRU in respect of recoverable benefits.
3. Undertaking to the Court that:

    (a) The Claimant, whether acting by his/her Litigation Friend or his/her Receiver, shall forthwith to take all necessary steps to stay the Claim and any proceedings which have begun or have been threatened against the Defendant in connection with the Claim;

    (b) The Claimant, his/her Litigation Friend and his Receiver shall not institute any proceedings against the Defendant or any other party or person whomsoever in connection with the Claim, save by way of enforcement of this order.

AND UPON THE COURT HAVING APPROVED the terms of this Order and the Schedule annexed to this Order.

BY CONSENT IT IS ORDERED THAT:

1. The Defendant shall make payment to or for the benefit of the Claimant in full and final settlement of the Claim as follows:

    (a) [*Net settlement sum to be paid over*] (being the sum of [*gross settlement sum*] less the interim payment of [*insert*] and CRU of [*insert*]) be paid into Court by 4.00 pm on [*date*]. Such sum shall thereafter be dealt with as follows:

    (i) The sum of [*insert any sum to be paid out to past carers*] to be paid out forthwith without further order to the Claimant's solicitors for distribution to the Litigation Friend on account of past care and interest and miscellaneous expenses and interest;

    (ii) The further sum of [*insert amount*]) to be paid out forthwith without further order to the Claimant's solicitors on behalf of the Claimant then to be transferred to the Legal Services Commission in respect of any Legal Aid statutory charge pending final resolution of the payment of costs;

    (iii) The balance to be paid into the Court Special Account for the benefit of the Claimant; and the Claimant's solicitors shall use their best endeavours to arrange with the Court of Protection as soon as practicable for the appointment of a Receiver for the

Claimant and that upon such appointment being made the said balance, together with all accrued interest, shall be transferred to the Claimant's account at the Public Guardianship Office, there to be dealt with as the Public Guardianship Office in its discretion shall think fit;

    (b) Further payment to the Claimant by way of periodic payments of damages as specified in the attached Schedule.

2. The Defendant do pay the Claimant's costs of the action, such costs to be subject to detailed assessment on the standard basis if not agreed.
3. There be detailed assessment of the Claimant's costs in accordance with Regulation 107 of the Civil Legal Aid (General) Regulations 1989 as amended, Article 5 of the Access to Justice Act 1999 (Commencement No.3) Order 2000, Article 4 of the Community Legal Services (Funding) Order 2000 and the Civil Legal Aid (General) (Amendment) Regulations 2000. [*delete if not legally aided*]
4. All further proceedings in this Claim be stayed except for the purpose of carrying such terms into effect.
5. Both parties have permission to apply to carry the terms of this Order into effect.

DATED the

SIGNED (1) (Litigation Friend on behalf of the Claimant)

        (2) (for the Defendant)

STRUCTURED SETTLEMENT AGREEMENT

PARTIES

1. [*Name of Claimant*] by his/her [*insert description of relationship*] and Litigation Friend, [*insert name*] (the "Claimant").
2. [*Insert name of Defendant*] (the "Defendant").

WHEREAS:

1. The Claimant has made a Claim against the Defendant arising out of [*short description, e.g. "medical negligence"/"a road traffic accident"*] in or about [*date*] ("the Claim").
2. The Claimant is a Minor and currently also a Patient under the Court of Protection and brings the Claim by his/her [*relationship*] and Litigation Friend, [*name*].
3. It is agreed, subject to the approval of the High Court of Justice, that the Claim shall be settled on terms and in the amounts set out in this Agreement.
4. The High Court of Justice has approved the Agreement and the Court of Protection has authorised the Litigation Friend to sign this agreement in the name and on behalf of the Claimant.

IT IS HEREBY AGREED AS FOLLOWS:

1. By way of settlement of the Claim the Defendant shall pay or procure to be paid for the benefit of the Claimant the sums as specified or referred to

in paragraph 2 below and the Claimant shall accept such sums together with the sum of [*insert*] already paid by the Defendants to the Compensation Recovery Unit and the sum of [*insert amount of any interim, delete if none*] already paid to the Claimant by way of an interim payment (receipt of which the Claimant acknowledges) in full and final settlement of the Claim, which shall thereby be discharged.

2. The Defendant shall make payments to or for the benefit of the Claimant as follows:

    2.1 the sum of [*insert immediate amount of net settlement lump sum*] (being the sum of [*insert the overall gross settlement figure*] less the interim payment of [*insert amount if applicable*] and CRU of [*insert amount*]) to be paid into court within [*insert*] days hereof;

    2.2 the further sums as specified in the attached Schedule.

DATED:

SIGNED: (1) (the Claimant acting by his/her Litigation Friend)

(2) (for the Defendant)

SCHEDULE TO THE ORDER

1. The following sums shall be paid:

    1.1 The sum of [*insert amount*] to be paid within [*insert*] days to represent all and any periodic payments due under this order in respect of the period from [*insert for period covering date of the order to first annual periodical payment and calculate sum accordingly*].

    1.2 The sum of [*insert annual periodical payment sum*] per annum (recalculated by reference to the additional conditions in 2.5(a) below) payable annually on [*insert*] in each year, the first such payment to be made on [*insert first payment date*] (each such annual payment being a "Periodic Payment"), up to and including [*insert last date of payment of the initial sum*].

    1.3 The sum of [*insert varied sum*] per annum (recalculated by reference to the additional conditions in 2.5(b) below) payable annually on [*insert date*] in each year, the first such payment to be made on [*insert first payment date of first varied payment*] (each such annual payment being a "Periodic Payment"), up to and including [*insert last payment date of first varied payment*].[1]

    1.4 The sum of [*insert amount of second varied payment*] per annum (recalculated by reference to the additional conditions in 2.5(c) below) payable annually on [*date of first payment of second varied payment*] (each such annual payment being a "Periodic Payment").[2]

2. Each Periodic Payment shall be subject to the following additional conditions:

---

[1] The purpose of this paragraph is to provide that any variation sums be subject to RPI in the years before payment even though not in fact paid over; thus, what the claimant receives is the value of the agreed variation sum at the date of first payment.

[2] The same principle applies to subsequent variations.

2.1 The Periodic Payments will continue during the lifetime of the Claimant;
2.2 No minimum number of Periodic Payments shall be made;
2.3 Liability to make payment of any further Periodic Payment will cease on the death of the Claimant with a pro rata return to cover the period remaining should the death of the Claimant occur part way through a year;
2.4 The Defendant shall be entitled to require the Claimant to produce evidence in a form reasonably satisfactory to the Defendant that the Claimant remains alive before making any Periodic Payment;
2.5 The said Periodic Payments shall be recalculated on the [*annual recalculation date, e.g. 1 January*] in each year from the [*date of first anniversary of first periodic payment*[3]] in accordance with the following formulae:

(a) in NF = relation to the Periodical Payment on [*insert date of first variation*] OF x NIF

$$\text{OIF}$$

Where

NF = the new Periodic Payment figure being calculated;

OF = on [*date of first variation*], the sum of [*insert amount of first periodic payment*] or, as the case may be, the relevant Periodic Payment figure calculated on [*date of annual recalculation*] in the year preceding the year in which the calculation is being carried out;

NIF = the Index applicable to April in the year in which the calculation is being carried out, the first NIF being in respect of April [*year of first recalculation*];

OIF = the Index applicable to April in the year prior to the year in which the calculation is being carried out, the first OIF being in respect of April [*year of first periodic payment*];

Index = the United Kingdom General Index of Retail Prices for all items published by the Central Statistical Office (January 1987 = 100) or any equivalent or comparable index which in the Defendant's reasonable opinion replaces such index from time to time;

(b) in relation to the Periodical Payments on or after [*date of first variation*] up to and including [*date of last payment of first variation*] the payments shall be calculated as if the preceding periodical payments commencing on [*date of first periodic payment*] had been paid and calculated in accordance with paragraph 2.5 (a) above by reference to an initial annual periodic payment of [*amount of variation*] by applying the formula:

NF = OF x NIF

OIF

---

[3] Assuming, as will surely become normal, that calculating the uplift is done annually.

Where

NF = the new Periodic Payment figure being calculated;

OF = on [*date of first payment*], the sum of [*amount of first variation*], as the case may be, the relevant Periodic Payment figure calculated on [*annual date of recalculation*] in the year preceding the year in which the calculation is being carried out;

NIF = the Index applicable to April in the year in which the calculation is being carried out, the first NIF being in respect of April [*year of first variation*];

OIF = either:

(a) in relation to the first Periodic Payment payable on [*date of first variation payable*] the [*publication of RPI for the year preceding that year*]; or
(b) in relation to each Periodic Payment payable from [*date of first varied payment*], the Index applicable to April in the year prior to the year in which the calculation is being carried out, the first OIF being in respect of [*publication of RPI for the year preceding that year*];

Index = the United Kingdom General Index of Retail Prices for all items published by the Central Statistical Office (January 1987 = 100) or any equivalent or comparable index which in the Defendant's reasonable opinion replaces such index from time to time.

REPEAT IN RELATION TO ANY SUBSEQUENT VARIATIONS.

APPENDIX 1

Section 5

Landlord and Tenant Cases and Boundary Disputes

CONTENTS

22. Agreed order for possession in non-Housing Act case.
23. Agreed order for possession in Housing Act case.
24. Agreed order for new tenancy under Landlord and Tenant Act 1954.
25. Claim Form seeking authorisation for excluding ss.24–28 of the Landlord and Tenant Act 1954.
26. Witness Statement supporting 67.
27. Provision in (or indorsement on) lease in respect of which ss.24–28 have been excluded.
28. An offer in a boundary dispute.

22

Agreed order for possession in non-Housing Act case

A1–22   [*Title of action*]

UPON hearing counsel/solicitors for the parties

AND UPON the parties having agreed 1. the defendant does not have the protection for the Rent Act 1977 etc., and 2. terms of settlement.

BY CONSENT

IT IS ADJUDGED that the plaintiff do recover against the defendant possession of the land and premises mentioned in the particulars of claim attached to the claim form in this action, namely [*set out details*].

23

Agreed order for possession in Housing Act case[1]

A1–23

[*Title of action*]

UPON hearing counsel/the solicitors for the parties

---

[1] See para.37–40, above.

AND UPON counsel [*or the solicitor*] for the defendant expressly admitting the several matters set out in the schedule to this order

IT IS ADJUDGED that the claimant do recover against the defendant possession of the land and premises mentioned in the particulars of claim attached to the claim form in this action, namely: [*here describe the land and premises as set out in the particulars of claim*]

AND that the claimant do recover against the defendant the sum of £—for rent and mesne profits and £——for costs [or his costs of this action to be subject to detailed assessments]

IT IS ORDERED that the defendant do give the claimant possession of the said land and premises on or before the [*set out the agreed date*].

SCHEDULE

1. That suitable alternative accommodation will be available to him when the order for possession takes effect, namely [*here set out the relevant details of the accommodation available*] or [*set out in this paragraph the ground or grounds relied upon by the plaintiff which is or are admitted by the defendant*]
2. That it is reasonable for the court to make an order for possession.[2]

24

Agreed order for new tenancy under Landlord and Tenant Act 1954

[*Title of application*]   A1–24

BEFORE District Judge

UPON hearing [*as appropriate*]

BY CONSENT

IT IS ORDERED that a new tenancy of the premises described in the schedule to this order be granted to the applicant for the period, at the rent and on the terms set forth in the said schedule.

AND IT IS FURTHER ORDERED that authorisation be given to the term of the said schedule excluding in relation to the tenancy therein referred to the provisions of sections 24 to 28 of the Landlord and Tenant Act 1954[1]

and it is further ordered that [*insert agreed provision as to costs*]

DATED,

---

[2] *ibid*. This admission is necessary when any of the grounds in Part II of Sch.2 to the Act are relied upon and admitted: s.7(4).
[1] To be added where appropriate, see Landlord and Tenant Act 1954, s.38(4).

APPENDIX 1

25

Claim Form seeking authorisation for excluding ss.24–28 of the Landlord and Tenant Act 1954

A1–25

IN THE COUNTY COURT

NO. OF MATTER

IN THE MATTER OF the Landlord and Tenant Act 1954

AND IN THE MATTER OF a proposed lease by AL to AT

AL	Claimant
and	
AT	Defendant

The Claimant and the Defendant jointly apply to the court for an orders:

Pursuant to section 38(4) of the Landlord and Tenant Act 1954 that they be permitted to enter into an agreement excluding sections 24 to 28 of the said Act in relation to the proposed lease between AL, as lessor, and AT, as lessee, of the premises known as [address].

The grounds on which the parties claim to be entitled to the order are set out in the witness statement of XY sworn on [date].[1]

It is not intended to serve any person with notice of this.

Part 8 of the Civil Procedure Rules 1998 applies to this claim.

DATED,

STATEMENT OF TRUTH

I believe etc . . .

26

Witness Statement supporting Precedent No.25

A1–26

[Heading as in 25]

I, XY, of [address] will state as follows:

1. I am a partner in the above-named firm of solicitors which has been retained to advise the proposed landlord, AL, in relation to the lease

---

[1] See Precedent No.26, below.

intended to be granted to AT. And I am authorised to make this claim on his behalf. As appears from the letter from AT's solicitors, a true copy of which is now produced and shown to me marked "XY 1," my firm has also been instructed to act on behalf of AT in connection with this claim under section 38(4) of the 1954 Act. Save where the contrary is indicated the matters set out in this witness statement are within my own knowledge or contained in my firm's files relating to this matter.

2. AL and AT wish to enter into a lease concerning the premises at and known as [address] in relation to which lease the provisions of sections 24–28 of the Act are to be excluded.
3. AL is the freehold owner of the premises and I am informed by AL that he hopes to be in a position to demolish the same and redevelop the site in about 18 months' time. Accordingly, he is unwilling to let the premises for more than that period.
4. AT is in the car-repairing business and must leave his present premises shortly. I am informed by AT's solicitor that he is actively seeking more suitable premises but is prepared to rent the premises referred to above for 18 months as an interim arrangement.
5. There is now produced and shown to me marked "XY 2" a draft of the proposed lease incorporating a clause excluding the provisions of sections 24–28.
6. I have discussed the matter with CD who has been retained by AT and it is clear that following discussions with our respective clients they and we have agreed that it is in their joint interests to make this claim.
7. On behalf of AL and AT I respectfully ask the court to make an order under section 38(4) authorising them to enter into an agreement in relation to their proposed lease excluding the provisions of sections 24–28.

STATEMENT OF TRUTH.

27

Provision in (or indorsement on) lease in respect of which ss.24–28 have been excluded

It is expressly agreed between the lessor, AL, and lessee, AT, that the provisions of ss.24–28 of the Landlord and Tenant Act 1954 shall not apply to this lease, authorisation for such agreement having been granted by order of District Judge of the county court on [date]. **A1–27**

We would emphasise that this offer is, and is intended to be, an open offer.[1]

Yours faithfully,

etc.

---

[1] It is essential to say this if an open offer is intended: para.26–08, above.

28

An offer in a boundary dispute

A1-28

1. Our client will abandon his counterclaim for damages if your client will abandon his claim for damages.
2. The true boundary between our respective clients' pieces of land to be taken henceforth to be along the red line on the scale plan enclosed herewith.
3. Our client will remove or have removed the post and wire fence erected along with the line depicted on the plan within 14 days of the making of the order we suggest below.
4. Our client will have erected at his own expense within 28 days of the making of the order suggested below a sound stockproof fence between points X and Y shown on the boundary as defined above and will maintain the same in good condition thereafter. We should, of course, emphasise that he cannot impose an obligation on his successors in title to maintain the fence in good condition or at all.
5. Bearing in mind the expense to which our client will be exposed in relation to 4 above, we would propose that each party should bear his own costs.

If the terms set out above are accepted, we would suggest a consent order in Tomlin form, terms 2 to 4 being incorporated as specific terms of the schedule, a further term of the schedule being that both parties will execute a deed giving effect to the agreement in paragraph 2.

The provision as to there being no order as to costs would appear on the face of the court order. We would suggest that our respective clients personally sign the schedule to the order. If the terms set out above are acceptable, but our suggested consent order is not, please advise us of any alternative proposal so that we can consider the matter.

Section 6

Adminstrative Court Proceedings

CONTENTS

29. Document in support of agreed order.

29

Document in support of agreed order[1]

A1–71

IN THE HIGH COURT OF JUSTICE NO.

QUEEN'S BENCH DIVISION

ADMINISTRATIVE COURT

IN THE MATTER OF AN APPLICATION FOR JUDICIAL REVIEW

BETWEEN

R

on the application of

AB	Claimant
v	
CD	Defendant

1. Subject to the approval of the court, the Claimant and the Defendant jointly seek an order that [set out terms of order sought].

    Either

2. For the reasons set out in paragraph 3 below, each party accepts that the decision of CD cannot stand/the order made by CD cannot stand [or as appropriate] and that the relief sought under paragraph 1 above is the appropriate relief in the circumstances.
3. The reasons why the decision/order of CD cannot stand are agreed by AB and CD to be as follows: [*set out reasons, referring to any authorities or statutes as may be necessary*].

    or

    AB and CD differ on why the decision/order of CD cannot stand, but do not consider that the time of the Court could properly be utilised in

---

[1] See Ch.27, paras 27–05 *et seq.*, above.

APPENDIX 1

determining which of the competing views is correct. In summary the competing views are as follows: [*set out the situation*].

or

2. AB contends that the decision of CD is unlawful. CD disputes that, but accepts that in the interests of avoiding delay and costs, it is appropriate to reconsider its decision. No third party interests will be materially affected by such reconsideration.

---------------   ---------------

Solicitors for AB   Solicitors for CD

DATED, etc.

APPENDIX 2

CPR Part 36 and Part 36 Practice Direction

PART 36—OFFERS TO SETTLE AND PAYMENTS INTO COURT

Contents of this part

Scope of this Part	Rule 36.1
Part 36 offers and Part 36 payments—general provisions	Rule 36.2
Personal injury claims for future pecuniary loss	Rule 36.2A
A defendant's offer to settle a money claim requires a Part 36 payment	Rule 36.3
Defendant's offer to settle the whole of a claim which includes both a money claim and a non-money claim	Rule 36.4
Form and content of a Part 36 offer	Rule 36.5
Notice of a Part 36 payment	Rule 36.6
Offer to settle a claim for provisional damages	Rule 36.7
Time when a Part 36 offer or a Part 36 payment is made and accepted	Rule 36.8
Clarification of a Part 36 offer or a Part 36 payment notice	Rule 36.9
Court to take into account offer to settle made before commencement of proceedings	Rule 36.10
Time for acceptance of a defendant's Part 36 offer or Part 36 payment	Rule 36.11
Time for acceptance of a claimant's Part 36 offer	Rule 36.12
Costs consequences of acceptance of a defendant's Part 36 offer or Part 36 payment	Rule 36.13
Costs consequences of acceptance of a claimant's Part 36 offer	Rule 36.14
The effect of acceptance of a Part 36 offer or a Part 36 payment	Rule 36.15
Payment out of a sum in court on the acceptance of a Part 36 payment	Rule 36.16
Acceptance of a Part 36 offer or a Part 36 payment made by one or more, but not all, defendants	Rule 36.17
Other cases where a court order is required to enable acceptance of a Part 36 offer or a Part 36 payment	Rule 36.18
Restriction on disclosure of a Part 36 offer or a Part 36 payment	Rule 36.19
Costs consequences where claimant fails to do better than a Part 36 offer or a Part 36 payment	Rule 36.20
Costs and other consequences where claimant does better than he proposed in his Part 36 offer	Rule 36.21
Interest	Rule 36.22
Deduction of benefits	Rule 36.23

Scope of this Part

36.1

(1) This Part contains rules about—

(a) offers to settle and payments into court; and
(b) the consequences where an offer to settle or payment into court is made in accordance with this Part.

(2) Nothing in this Part prevents a party making an offer to settle in whatever way he chooses, but if that offer is not made in accordance with this Part, it will only have the consequences specified in this Part if the court so orders.

(Part 36 applies to Part 20 claims by virtue of rule 20.3)

Part 36 offers and Part 36 payments—general provisions

36.2

(1) An offer made in accordance with the requirements of this Part is called—

(a) if made by way of a payment into court, "a Part 36 payment";
(b) otherwise "a Part 36 offer".

(Rule 36.3 sets out when an offer has to be made by way of a payment into court)

(2) The party who makes an offer is the "offeror".
(3) The party to whom an offer is made is the "offeree".
(4) A Part 36 offer or a Part 36 payment—

(a) may be made at any time after proceedings have started; and
(b) may be made in appeal proceedings.

(5) A Part 36 offer or a Part 36 payment shall not have the consequences set out in this Part while the claim is being dealt with on the small claims track unless the court orders otherwise.

(Part 26 deals with allocation to the small claims track)
(Rule 27.2 provides that Part 36 does not apply to small claims)

Personal injury claims for future pecuniary loss

36.2A

(1) This rule applies to a claim for damages for personal injury which is or includes a claim for future pecuniary loss.

(2) An offer to settle such a claim will not have the consequences set out in this Part unless it is made by way of a Part 36 offer under this rule, and where such an offer is or includes an offer to pay the whole or part of any damages in the form of a lump sum, it will not have the consequences set out in this Part unless a Part 36 payment of the amount of the lump sum offer is also made.

(3) Where both a Part 36 offer and a Part 36 payment are made under this rule—

(a) the offer must include details of the payment, and

(b) rules 36.11(1) and (2) and 36.13(1) and (2) apply as if there were only a Part 36 offer.

(4) A Part 36 offer to which this rule applies may contain an offer to pay, or an offer to accept—

(a) the whole or part of the damages for future pecuniary loss in the form of—
  (i) either a lump sum or periodical payments, or
  (ii) both a lump sum and periodical payments,
(b) the whole or part of any other damages in the form of a lump sum.

(5) A Part 36 offer to which this rule applies—

(a) must state the amount of any offer to pay the whole or part of any damages in the form of a lump sum;
(b) may state what part of the offer relates to damages for future pecuniary loss to be accepted in the form of a lump sum;
(c) may state, where part of the offer relates to other damages to be accepted in the form of a lump sum, what amounts are attributable to those other damages;
(d) must state what part of the offer relates to damages for future pecuniary loss to be paid or accepted in the form of periodical payments and must specify—
  (i) the amount and duration of the periodical payments,
  (ii) the amount of any payments for substantial capital purchases and when they are to be made, and
  (iii) that each amount is to vary by reference to the retail prices index (or to some other named index, or that it is not to vary by reference to any index); and
(e) must state either that any damages which take the form of periodical payments will be funded in a way which ensures that the continuity of payment is reasonably secure in accordance with section 2(4) of the Damages Act 1996 or how such damages are to be paid and how the continuity of their payment is to be secured.

(6) Where a Part 36 payment includes a lump sum for damages for future pecuniary loss, the Part 36 payment notice may state the amount of that lump sum.

(7) Where the defendant makes a Part 36 offer to which this rule applies and which offers to pay damages in the form of both a lump sum and periodical payments, the claimant may only give notice of acceptance of the offer as a whole.

A defendant's offer to settle a money claim requires a Part 36 payment

36.3

A2–04

(1) Subject to rules 36.2A(2), 36.5(5) and 36.23, an offer by a defendant to settle a money claim will not have the consequences set out in this Part unless it is made by way of a Part 36 payment.

(2) A Part 36 payment may only be made after proceedings have started.
(Rule 36.5(5) permits a Part 36 offer to be made by reference to an interim payment)
(Rule 36.10 makes provision for an offer to settle a money claim before the commencement of proceedings)

(Rule 36.23 makes provision for where benefit is recoverable under the Social Security (Recovery of Benefit) Act 1997).[1]

Defendant's offer to settle the whole of a claim which includes both a money claim and a non-money claim

36.4

(1) This rule applies where a defendant to a claim which includes both a money claim and a non-money claim wishes— A2–05

  (a) to make an offer to settle the whole claim which will have the consequences set out in this Part; and
  (b) to make a money offer in respect of the money claim and a non-money offer in respect of the non-money claim.

(2) The defendant must—

  (a) make a Part 36 payment or Part 36 offer made under rule 36.2A in relation to the money claim; and
  (b) make a Part 36 offer in relation to the non-money claim.

(3) The Part 36 payment notice or Part 36 offer made under rule 36.2A must—

  (a) identify the document which sets out the terms of the Part 36 offer made under this rule; and
  (b) state that if the claimant gives notice of acceptance of the Part 36 payment or Part 36 offer made under rule 36.2A he will be treated as also accepting the Part 36 offer made under this rule.

(Rule 36.6 makes provision for a Part 36 payment notice)

(4) If the claimant gives notice of acceptance of the Part 36 payment or Part 36 offer made under rule 36.2A, he shall also be taken as giving notice of acceptance of the Part 36 offer in relation to the non-money claim.

Form and content of a Part 36 offer

36.5

(1) A Part 36 offer must be in writing. A2–06
(2) A Part 36 offer may relate to the whole claim or to part of it or to any issue that arises in it.
(3) A Part 36 offer must—

  (a) state whether it relates to the whole of the claim or to part of it or to an issue that arises in it and if so to which part or issue;
  (b) state whether it takes into account any counterclaim; and
  (c) if it is expressed not to be inclusive of interest, give the details relating to interest set out in rule 36.22(2).

(4) A defendant may make a Part 36 offer limited to accepting liability up to a specified proportion.

---

[1] 1997 c.27.

(5) A Part 36 offer may be made by reference to an interim payment.
(Part 25 contains provisions relating to interim payments)
(6) A Part 36 offer made not less than 21 days before the start of the trial must—

    (a) be expressed to remain open for acceptance for 21 days from the date it is made; and

    (b) provide that after 21 days the offeree may only accept it if—
        (i) the parties agree the liability for costs; or
        (ii) the court gives permission.

(7) A Part 36 offer made less than 21 days before the start of the trial must state that the offeree may only accept it if—

    (a) the parties agree the liability for costs; or
    (b) the court gives permission.

(Rule 36.8 makes provision for when a Part 36 offer is treated as being made)

(8) If a Part 36 offer is withdrawn it will not have the consequences set out in this Part.

Notice of a Part 36 payment

36.6

A2–07

(1) A Part 36 payment may relate to the whole claim or part of it or to an issue that arises in it.

(2) A defendant who makes a Part 36 payment must file with the court a notice ("Part 36 payment notice") which—

    (a) states the amount of the payment;
    (b) states whether the payment relates to the whole claim or to part of it or to any issue that arises in it and if so to which part or issue;
    (c) states whether it takes into account any counterclaim;
    (d) if an interim payment has been made, states that the defendant has taken into account the interim payment; and
    (e) if it is expressed not to be inclusive of interest, gives the details relating to interest set out in rule 36.22(2).

(Rule 25.6 makes provision for an interim payment)
(Rule 36.4 provides for further information to be included where a defendant wishes to settle the whole of a claim which includes a money claim and a non-money claim)
(Rule 36.23 makes provision for extra information to be included in the payment notice in a case where benefit is recoverable under the Social Security (Recovery of Benefit) Act 1997)

(3) The offeror must—

    (a) serve the Part 36 payment notice on the offeree; and
    (b) file a certificate of service of the notice.

(4) Omitted

(5) A Part 36 payment may be withdrawn or reduced only with the permission of the court.

Offer to settle a claim for provisional damages

36.7

(1) A defendant may make a Part 36 payment in respect of a claim which includes a claim for provisional damages.
(2) Where he does so, the Part 36 payment notice must specify whether or not the defendant is offering to agree to the making of an award of provisional damages.
(3) Where the defendant is offering to agree to the making of an award of provisional damages the payment notice must also state—

  (a) that the sum paid into court is in satisfaction of the claim for damages on the assumption that the injured person will not develop the disease or suffer the type of deterioration specified in the notice;
  (b) that the offer is subject to the condition that the claimant must make any claim for further damages within a limited period; and
  (c) what that period is.

(4) Where a Part 36 payment is—

  (a) made in accordance with paragraph (3); and
  (b) accepted within the relevant period in rule 36.11,
  the Part 36 payment will have the consequences set out in rule 36.13, unless the court orders otherwise.

(5) If the claimant accepts the Part 36 payment he must, within 7 days of doing so, apply to the court for an order for an award of provisional damages under rule 41.2.
(Rule 41.2 provides for an order for an award of provisional damages)
(6) The money in court may not be paid out until the court has disposed of the application made in accordance with paragraph (5).

Time when a Part 36 offer or a Part 36 payment is made and accepted

36.8

(1) A Part 36 offer is made when received by the offeree.
(2) A Part 36 payment is made when written notice of the payment into court is served on the offeree.
(3) An improvement to a Part 36 offer will be effective when its details are received by the offeree.
(4) An increase in a Part 36 payment will be effective when notice of the increase is served on the offeree.
(5) A Part 36 offer or Part 36 payment is accepted when notice of its acceptance is received by the offeror.

Clarification of a Part 36 offer or a Part 36 payment notice

36.9

(1) The offeree may, within 7 days of a Part 36 offer or payment being made, request the offeror to clarify the offer or payment notice.
(2) If the offeror does not give the clarification requested under paragraph (1) within 7 days of receiving the request, the offeree may, unless the trial has started, apply for an order that he does so.

(3) If the court makes an order under paragraph (2), it must specify the date when the Part 36 offer or Part 36 payment is to be treated as having been made.

Court to take into account offer to settle made before commencement of proceedings

36.10

A2–11 (1) If a person makes an offer to settle before proceedings are begun which complies with the provisions of this rule, the court will take that offer into account when making any order as to costs.

(2) The offer must -

(a) be expressed to be open for at least 21 days after the date it was made;
(b) if made by a person who would be a defendant were proceedings commenced, include an offer to pay the costs of the offeree incurred up to the date 21 days after the date it was made; and
(c) otherwise comply with this Part.

(3) Subject to paragraph (3A), if the offeror is a defendant to a money claim—

(a) he must make a Part 36 payment within 14 days of service of the claim form; and
(b) the amount of the payment must be not less than the sum offered before proceedings began.

(3A) In a claim to which rule 36.2A applies, if the offeror is a defendant who wishes to offer to pay the whole or part of any damages in the form of a lump sum—

(a) he must make a Part 36 payment within 14 days of service of the claim form; and
(b) the amount of the payment must be not less than the lump sum offered before proceedings began.

(4) An offeree may not, after proceedings have begun, accept—

(a) an offer made under paragraph (2); or
(b) a Part 36 payment made under paragraph (3) or (3A), without the permission of the court.

(5) An offer under this rule is made when it is received by the offeree.

Time for acceptance of a defendant's Part 36 offer or Part 36 payment

36.11

A2–12 (1) A claimant may accept a Part 36 offer or a Part 36 payment made not less than 21 days before the start of the trial without needing the court's permission if he gives the defendant written notice of acceptance not later than 21 days after the offer or payment was made.
(Rule 36.13 sets out the costs consequences of accepting a defendant's offer or payment without needing the permission of the court)
(2) If—

(a) a defendant's Part 36 offer or Part 36 payment is made less than 21 days before the start of the trial; or
(b) the claimant does not accept it within the period specified in paragraph (1)—
  (i) if the parties agree the liability for costs, the claimant may accept the offer or payment without needing the permission of the court;
  (ii) if the parties do not agree the liability for costs the claimant may only accept the offer or payment with the permission of the court.
(3) Where the permission of the court is needed under paragraph (2) the court will, if it gives permission, make an order as to costs.

Time for acceptance of a claimant's Part 36 offer

36.12

(1) A defendant may accept a Part 36 offer made not less than 21 days before the start of the trial without needing the court's permission if he gives the claimant written notice of acceptance not later than 21 days after the offer was made.

(Rule 36.14 sets out the costs consequences of accepting a claimant's offer without needing the permission of the court)

(2) If—
(a) a claimant's Part 36 offer is made less than 21 days before the start of the trial; or
(b) the defendant does not accept it within the period specified in paragraph (1)—
  (i) if the parties agree the liability for costs, the defendant may accept the offer without needing the permission of the court;
  (ii) if the parties do not agree the liability for costs the defendant may only accept the offer with the permission of the court.
(3) Where the permission of the court is needed under paragraph (2) the court will, if it gives permission, make an order as to costs.

A2–13

Costs consequences of acceptance of a defendant's Part 36 offer or Part 36 payment

36.13

(1) Where a Part 36 offer or a Part 36 payment is accepted without needing the permission of the court the claimant will be entitled to his costs of the proceedings up to the date of serving notice of acceptance.
(2) Where—
(a) a Part 36 offer or a Part 36 payment relates to part only of the claim; and
(b) at the time of serving notice of acceptance the claimant abandons the balance of the claim,

the claimant will be entitled to his costs of the proceedings up to the date of serving notice of acceptance, unless the court orders otherwise.

A2–14

(3) The claimant's costs include any costs attributable to the defendant's counterclaim if the Part 36 offer or the Part 36 payment notice states that it takes into account the counterclaim.

(4) Costs under this rule will be payable on the standard basis if not agreed.

Costs consequences of acceptance of a claimant's Part 36 offer

36.14

A2–15   Where a claimant's Part 36 offer is accepted without needing the permission of the court the claimant will be entitled to his costs of the proceedings up to the date upon which the defendant serves notice of acceptance.

The effect of acceptance of a Part 36 offer or a Part 36 payment

36.15

A2–16   (1) If a Part 36 offer or Part 36 payment relates to the whole claim and is accepted, the claim will be stayed.

(2) In the case of acceptance of a Part 36 offer which relates to the whole claim—

   (a) the stay will be upon the terms of the offer; and
   (b) either party may apply to enforce those terms without the need for a new claim.

(3) If a Part 36 offer or a Part 36 payment which relates to part only of the claim is accepted—

   (a) the claim will be stayed as to that part; and
   (b) unless the parties have agreed costs, the liability for costs shall be decided by the court.

(4) If the approval of the court is required before a settlement can be binding, any stay which would otherwise arise on the acceptance of a Part 36 offer or a Part 36 payment will take effect only when that approval has been given.

(5) Any stay arising under this rule will not affect the power of the court—

   (a) to enforce the terms of a Part 36 offer;
   (b) to deal with any question of costs (including interest on costs) relating to the proceedings;
   (c) to order payment out of court of any sum paid into court.

(6) Where—

   (a) a Part 36 offer has been accepted; and
   (b) a party alleges that—
      (i) the other party has not honoured the terms of the offer; and
      (ii) he is therefore entitled to a remedy for breach of contract,

the party may claim the remedy by applying to the court without the need to start a new claim unless the court orders otherwise.

Payment out of a sum in court on the acceptance of a Part 36 payment

36.16

Where a Part 36 payment is accepted the claimant obtains payment out of the sum in court by making a request for payment in the practice form.

Acceptance of a Part 36 offer or a Part 36 payment made by one or more, but not all, defendants

36.17

(1) This rule applies where the claimant wishes to accept a Part 36 offer or a Part 36 payment made by one or more, but not all, of a number of defendants.
(2) If the defendants are sued jointly or in the alternative, the claimant may accept the offer or payment without needing the permission of the court in accordance with rule 36.11(1) if—

   (a) he discontinues his claim against those defendants who have not made the offer or payment; and
   (b) those defendants give written consent to the acceptance of the offer or payment.

(3) If the claimant alleges that the defendants have a several liability to him the claimant may—

   (a) accept the offer or payment in accordance with rule 36.11(1); and
   (b) continue with his claims against the other defendants if he is entitled to do so.

(4) In all other cases the claimant must apply to the court for—

   (a) an order permitting a payment out to him of any sum in court; and
   (b) such order as to costs as the court considers appropriate.

Other cases where a court order is required to enable acceptance of a Part 36 offer or a Part 36 payment

36.18

(1) Where a Part 36 offer or a Part 36 payment is made in proceedings to which rule 21.10 applies—

   (a) the offer or payment may be accepted only with the permission of the court; and
   (b) no payment out of any sum in court shall be made without a court order.

(Rule 21.10 deals with compromise etc. by or on behalf of a child or patient)

(2) Where the court gives a claimant permission to accept a Part 36 offer or payment after the trial has started—

   (a) any money in court may be paid out only with a court order; and

(b) the court must, in the order, deal with the whole costs of the proceedings.

(3) Where a claimant accepts a Part 36 payment after a defence of tender before claim has been put forward by the defendant, the money in court may be paid out only after an order of the court.
(Rule 37.3 requires a defendant who wishes to rely on a defence of tender before claim to make a payment into court)

Restriction on disclosure of a Part 36 offer or a Part 36 payment

36.19

A2–20 (1) A Part 36 offer will be treated as "without prejudice except as to costs".
(2) The fact that a Part 36 payment has been made shall not be communicated to the trial judge until all questions of liability and the amount of money to be awarded have been decided.
(3) Paragraph (2) does not apply—

(a) where the defence of tender before claim has been raised;
(b) where the proceedings have been stayed under rule 36.15 following acceptance of a Part 36 offer or Part 36 payment; or
(c) where—
  (i) the issue of liability has been determined before any assessment of the money claimed; and
  (ii) the fact that there has or has not been a Part 36 payment may be relevant to the question of the costs of the issue of liability.

Costs consequences where claimant fails to do better than a Part 36 offer or a Part 36 payment

36.20

A2–21 (1) This rule applies where at trial a claimant—

(a) fails to better a Part 36 payment;
(b) fails to obtain a judgment which is more advantageous than a defendant's Part 36 offer; or
(c) in a claim to which rule 36.2A applies, fails to obtain a judgment which is more advantageous than the Part 36 offer made under that rule.

(2) Unless it considers it unjust to do so, the court will order the claimant to pay any costs incurred by the defendant after the latest date on which the payment or offer could have been accepted without needing the permission of the court.
(Rule 36.11 sets out the time for acceptance of a defendant's Part 36 offer or Part 36 payment)

Costs and other consequences where claimant does better than he proposed in his Part 36 offer

36.21

(1) This rule applies where at trial—
   (a) a defendant is held liable for more; or
   (b) the judgment against a defendant is more advantageous to the claimant,
   than the proposals contained in a claimant's Part 36 offer (including a Part 36 offer made under rule 36.2A).

(2) The court may order interest on the whole or part of any sum of money (excluding interest) awarded to the claimant at a rate not exceeding 10% above base rate for some or all of the period starting with the latest date on which the defendant could have accepted the offer without needing the permission of the court.

(3) The court may also order that the claimant is entitled to—
   (a) his costs on the indemnity basis from the latest date when the defendant could have accepted the offer without needing the permission of the court; and
   (b) interest on those costs at a rate not exceeding 10% above base rate.

(4) Where this rule applies, the court will make the orders referred to in paragraphs (2) and (3) unless it considers it unjust to do so.
(Rule 36.12 sets out the latest date when the defendant could have accepted the offer)

(5) In considering whether it would be unjust to make the orders referred to in paragraphs (2) and (3) above, the court will take into account all the circumstances of the case including—
   (a) the terms of any Part 36 offer;
   (b) the stage in the proceedings when any Part 36 offer or Part 36 payment was made;
   (c) the information available to the parties at the time when the Part 36 offer or Part 36 payment was made; and
   (d) the conduct of the parties with regard to the giving or refusing to give information for the purposes of enabling the offer or payment into court to be made or evaluated.

(6) Where the court awards interest under this rule and also awards interest on the same sum and for the same period under any other power, the total rate of interest may not exceed 10% above base rate .

Interest

36.22

(1) Unless—
   (a) a claimant's Part 36 offer which offers to accept a sum of money; or
   (b) a Part 36 payment notice,

   indicates to the contrary, any such offer or payment will be treated as inclusive of all interest until the last date on which it could be accepted without needing the permission of the court.

(2) Where a claimant's Part 36 offer or Part 36 payment notice is expressed not to be inclusive of interest, the offer or notice must state—

(a) whether interest is offered; and
(b) if so, the amount offered, the rate or rates offered and the period or periods for which it is offered.

Deduction of benefits

36.23

A2–24 (1) This rule applies where a payment to a claimant following acceptance of a Part 36 offer or Part 36 payment into court would be a compensation payment as defined in section 1 of the Social Security (Recovery of Benefits) Act 1997[2].

(2) A defendant to a money claim may make an offer to settle the claim which will have the consequences set out in this Part, without making a Part 36 payment if—

(a) at the time he makes the offer he has applied for, but not received, a certificate of recoverable benefit; and
(b) he makes a Part 36 payment not more than 7 days after he receives the certificate.

(Section 1 of the 1997 Act defines "recoverable benefit")

(3) A Part 36 payment notice must state—

(a) the amount of gross compensation;
(b) the name and amount of any benefit by which that gross amount is reduced in accordance with section 8 and Schedule 2 to the 1997 Act; and
(c) that the sum paid in is the net amount after deduction of the amount of benefit.

(4) For the purposes of rule 36.20(1)(a), a claimant fails to better a Part 36 payment if he fails to obtain judgment for more than the gross sum specified in the Part 36 payment notice.

(4A) For the purposes of rule 36.20(1)(c), where the court is determining whether the claimant has failed to obtain a judgment which is more advantageous than the Part 36 offer made under rule 36.2A, the amount of any lump sum paid into court which it takes into account is to be the amount of the gross sum specified in the Part 36 payment notice.

(5) Where—

(a) a Part 36 payment has been made; and
(b) application is made for the money remaining in court to be paid out,

the court may treat the money in court as being reduced by a sum equivalent to any further recoverable benefits paid to the claimant since the date of payment into court and may direct payment out accordingly.

---

[2] 1997 c.27.

PRACTICE DIRECTION—OFFERS TO SETTLE AND PAYMENTS INTO COURT

This Practice Direction supplements CPR Part 36

Part 36 offers and Part 36 payments

1.1 A written offer to settle a claim[1] or part of a claim or any issue that arises in it made in accordance with the provisions of Part 36 is called:

(1) if made by way of a payment into court, a Part 36 payment[2], or
(2) if made otherwise, a Part 36 offer[3] (including an offer under rule 36.2A).

1.2 A Part 36 offer or Part 36 payment has the costs and other consequences set out in rules 36.13, 36.14, 36.20 and 36.21.

1.3 An offer to settle which is not made in accordance with Part 36 will only have the consequences specified in that Part if the court so orders and will be given such weight on any issue as to costs as the court thinks appropriate.[4]

Parties and Part 36 offers

2.1 A Part 36 offer, subject to paragraph 3 below, may be made by any party.
2.2 The party making an offer is the "offeror" and the party to whom it is made is the "offeree".
2.3 A Part 36 offer may consist of a proposal to settle for a specified sum or for some other remedy.
2.4 A Part 36 offer is made when received by the offeree.[5]
2.5 An improvement to a Part 36 offer is effective when its details are received by the offeree.[6]

Parties and Part 36 payments

3.1 An offer to settle for a specified sum made by a defendant[7] must, in order to comply with Part 36, be made by way of a Part 36 payment into court.[8]
3.2 A Part 36 payment is made when the Part 36 payment notice is served on the claimant.[9]
3.3 An increase to a Part 36 payment will be effective when notice of the increase is served on the claimant.[10]

(For service of the Part 36 payment notice see rule 36.6(3) and (4).)

---

[1] Includes Part 20 claims.
[2] See rule 36.2(1)(a).
[3] See rule 36.2(1)(b).
[4] See rule 36.1(2).
[5] See rule 36.8(1).
[6] See rule 36.8(3).
[7] Includes a respondent to a claim or issue.
[8] See rule 36.3(1).
[9] See rule 36.8(2).
[10] See rule 36.8(4).

3.4 A defendant who wishes to withdraw or reduce a Part 36 payment must obtain the court's permission to do so.

3.5 Permission may be obtained by making an application in accordance with Part 23 stating the reasons giving rise to the wish to withdraw or reduce the Part 36 payment.

Making a Part 36 payment

A2–28

4.1 Except where paragraph 4.2 applies, to make a Part 36 payment in any court the defendant must—

(1) serve the Part 36 payment notice on the offeree;
(2) file at the court—
   (a) a copy of the payment notice; and
   (b) a certificate of service confirming service on the offeree; and
(3) send to the Court Funds Office—
   (a) the payment, usually a cheque made payable to the Accountant General of the Supreme Court;
   (b) a sealed copy of the claim form; and
   (c) Court Funds Office form 100.

4.2 A litigant in person without a current account may, in a claim proceeding in a county court or District Registry, make a Part 36 payment by—

(1) lodging the payment in cash with the court;
(2) filing at the court—
   (a) the Part 36 payment notice; and
   (b) Court Funds Office form 100.

Part 36 offers and Part 36 payments—general provisions

A2–29

5.1 A Part 36 offer or a Part 36 payment notice must:

(1) state that it is a Part 36 offer or that the payment into court is a Part 36 payment, and
(2) be signed by the offeror or his legal representative.[13]

5.2 The contents of a Part 36 offer must also comply with the requirements of rule 36.5(3), (5) and (6).

5.3 The contents of a Part 36 payment notice must comply with rule 36.6(2) and, if rule 36.23 applies, with rule 36.23(3).

5.3A The contents of a Part 36 offer to which rule 36.2A applies must comply with the requirements of rule 36.2A(5).

5.4 A Part 36 offer or Part 36 payment will be taken to include interest unless it is expressly stated in the offer or the payment notice that interest is not included, in which case the details set out in rule 36.22(2) must be given.

5.5 Where a Part 36 offer is made by a company or other corporation, a person holding a senior position in the company or corporation may sign the offer on the offeror's behalf, but must state the position he holds.

5.6 Each of the following persons is a person holding a senior position:

(1) in respect of a registered company or corporation, a director, the treasurer, secretary, chief executive, manager or other officer of the company or corporation, and

---

[13] For the definition of legal representative, see rule 2.3.

(2) in respect of a corporation which is not a registered company, in addition to those persons set out in (1), the mayor, chairman, president, town clerk or similar officer of the corporation.

Clarification of Part 36 offer or payment

6.1 An offeree may apply to the court for an order requiring the offeror to clarify the terms of a Part 36 offer or Part 36 payment notice (a clarification order) where the offeror has failed to comply within 7 days with a request for clarification.[14] **A2–30**

6.2 An application for a clarification order should be made in accordance with Part 23.

6.3 The application notice should state the respects in which the terms of the Part 36 offer or Part 36 payment notice, as the case may be, are said to need clarification.

Acceptance pf a Part 36 offer or payment

7.1 The times for accepting a Part 36 offer or a Part 36 payment are set out in rules 36.11 and 36.12. **A2–31**

7.2 The general rule is that a Part 36 offer or Part 36 payment made more than 21 days before the start of the trial may be accepted within 21 days after it was made without the permission of the court. The costs consequences set out in rules 36.13 and 36.14 will then come into effect.

7.2A Where a Part 36 payment is made as part of a Part 36 offer made under rule 36.2A, the payment is ignored for the purposes of determining the times set out in rules 36.11 and 36.13.

7.3 A Part 36 offer or Part 36 payment made less than 21 days before the start of the trial cannot be accepted without the permission of the court unless the parties agree what the costs consequences of acceptance will be.

7.4 The permission of the court may be sought:

(1) before the start of the trial, by making an application in accordance with Part 23, and

(2) after the start of the trial, by making an application to the trial judge.

7.5 If the court gives permission it will make an order dealing with costs and may order that, in the circumstances, the costs consequences set out in rules 36.13 and 36.14 will apply.

7.6 Where a Part 36 offer or Part 36 payment is accepted in accordance with rule 36.11(1) or rule 36.12(1) the notice of acceptance must be sent to the offeror and filed with the court.

7.7 The notice of acceptance:

(1) must set out—
  (a) the claim number, and
  (b) the title of the proceedings,
(2) must identify the Part 36 offer or Part 36 payment notice to which it relates, and
(3) must be signed by the offeree or his legal representative (see paragraphs 5.5 and 5.6 above).

7.8 Where:

---

[14] See rule 36.9(1) and (2).

(1) the court's approval, or
(2) an order for payment of money out of court, or
(3) an order apportioning money in court—
  (a) between the Fatal Accidents Act 1976 and the Law Reform (Miscellaneous Provisions) Act 1934, or
  (b) between the persons entitled to it under the Fatal Accidents Act 1976, is required for acceptance of a Part 36 offer or Part 36 payment, application for the approval or the order should be made in accordance with Part 23.

7.9 The court will include in any order made under paragraph 7.8 above a direction for;

(1) the payment out of the money in court, and
(2) the payment of interest.

7.10 Unless the parties have agreed otherwise:

(1) interest accruing up to the date of acceptance will be paid to the offeror, and
(2) interest accruing as from the date of acceptance until payment out will be paid to the offeree.

7.11 A claimant may not accept a Part 36 payment or Part 36 offer made under rule 36.2A which is part of a defendant's offer to settle the whole of a claim consisting of both a money and a non-money claim unless at the same time he accepts the offer to settle the whole of the claim. Therefore:

(1) if a claimant accepts a Part 36 payment or Part 36 offer made under rule 36.2A which is part of a defendant's offer to settle the whole of the claim, or
(2) if a claimant accepts a Part 36 offer which is part of a defendant's offer to settle the whole of the claim,

the claimant will be deemed to have accepted the offer to settle the whole of the claim.[15]

(See paragraph 8 below for the method of obtaining money out of court.)

Payment out of court

A2–32

8.1 To obtain money out of court following acceptance of a Part 36 payment, the claimant should—

(1) file a request for payment in Court Funds Office form 201 with the Court Funds Office; and
(2) file a copy of form 201 at the court.

8.2 The request for payment should contain the following details:

(1) where the party receiving the payment—
  (a) is legally represented—
    (i) the name, business address and reference of the legal representative, and
    (ii) the name of the bank and the sort code number, the title of the account and the account number where the payment is to be transmitted, and

---

[15] See rule 36.4.

(2) where the party is acting in person—
   (a) his name and address, and
   (b) his bank account details as in (ii) above.

8.3 Where a trial is to take place at a different court to that where the case is proceeding, the claimant must also file notice of request for payment with the court where the trial is to take place.

8.4 Subject to paragraph 8.5(1) and (2), if a party does not wish the payment to be transmitted into his bank account or if he does not have a bank account, he may send a written request to the Accountant-General for the payment to be made to him by cheque.

8.5 Where a party seeking payment out of court has provided the necessary information, the payment:

(1) where a party is legally represented, must be made to the legal representative,
(2) if the party is not legally represented but is, or has been, in receipt of legal aid in respect of the proceedings and a notice to that effect has been filed, should be made to the Legal Aid Board by direction of the court,
(3) where a person entitled to money in court dies without having made a will and the court is satisfied—
   (a) that no grant of administration of his estate has been made, and
   (b) that the assets of his estate, including the money in court, do not exceed in value the amount specified in any order in force under section 6 of the Administration of Estates (Small Payments) Act 1965,

may be ordered to be made to the person appearing to have the prior right to a grant of administration of the estate of the deceased, e.g. a widower, widow, child, father, mother, brother or sister of the deceased.

Foreign currency

9.1 Money may be paid into court in a foreign currency:

(1) where it is a Part 36 payment and the claim is in a foreign currency, or
(2) under a court order.

9.2 The court may direct that the money be placed in an interest bearing account in the currency of the claim or any other currency.

9.3 Where a Part 36 payment is made in a foreign currency and has not been accepted within 21 days, the defendant may apply for an order that the money be placed in an interest bearing account.

9.4 The application should be made in accordance with Part 23 and should state:

(1) that the payment has not been accepted in accordance with rule 36.11, and
(2) the type of currency on which interest is to accrue.

Compensation recovery

10.1 Where a defendant makes a Part 36 payment in respect of a claim for a sum or part of a sum:

(1) which falls under the heads of damage set out in column 1 of Schedule 2 of the Social Security (Recovery of Benefits) Act 1997 in respect of

recoverable benefits received by the claimant as set out in column 2 of that Schedule, and

(2) where the defendant is liable to pay recoverable benefits to the Secretary of State, the defendant should obtain from the Secretary of State a certificate of recoverable benefits and file the certificate with the Part 36 payment notice.

10.2 If a defendant wishes to offer to settle a claim where he has applied for but not yet received a certificate of recoverable benefits, he may, provided that he makes a Part 36 payment not more than 7 days after he has received the certificate, make a Part 36 offer which will have the costs and other consequences set out in rules 36.13 and 36.20.

10.3 The Part 36 payment notice should state in addition to the requirements set out in rule 36.6(2):

(1) the total amount represented by the Part 36 payment (the gross compensation),
(2) that the defendant has reduced this sum by £   , in accordance with section 8 of and Schedule 2 to the Social Security (Recovery of Benefits) Act 1997, which was calculated as follows:
Name of benefit   Amount
and
(3) that the amount paid in, being the sum of £   is the net amount after the deduction of the amount of benefit.

10.4 On acceptance of a Part 36 payment to which this paragraph relates, a claimant will receive the sum in court which will be net of the recoverable benefits.

10.5 In establishing at trial whether a claimant has bettered or obtained a judgment more advantageous than a Part 36 payment to which this paragraph relates, the court will base its decision on the gross sum specified in the Part 36 payment notice.

General

11.1 Where a party on whom a Part 36 offer, a Part 36 payment notice or a notice of acceptance is to be served is legally represented, the Part 36 offer, Part 36 payment notice and notice of acceptance must be served on the legal representative.

11.2 In a claim arising out of an accident involving a motor vehicle on a road or in a public place:

(1) where the damages claimed include a sum for hospital expenses, and
(2) the defendant or his insurer pays that sum to the hospital under section 157 of the Road Traffic Act 1988, the defendant must give notice of that payment to the court and all the other parties to the proceedings.

11.3 Money paid into court:

(1) as a Part 36 payment which is not accepted by the claimant, or
(2) under a court order,

will be placed after 21 days in a basic account[17] (subject to paragraph 11.4 below) for interest to accrue.

---

[17] See rule 26 of the Court Funds Office Rules 1987.

11.4 Where money referred to in paragraph 11.3 above is paid in in respect of a child or patient it will be placed in a special investment account[18] for interest to accrue.

(A practice direction supplementing Part 21 contains information about the investment of money in court in respect of a child or patient.)

(Practice directions supplementing Part 40 contain information about adjustment of the judgment sum in respect of recoverable benefits, and about structured settlements.)

(A practice direction supplementing Part 41 contains information about provisional damages awards.)

Personal injury claims for future pecuniary loss

12.1 A Part 36 offer to settle a claim for damages (whether in the form of a lump sum, periodical payments or both) for personal injury which includes a claim for future pecuniary loss must contain the details of the offer which are set out in rule 36.2A.

12.2 Section 2(4) of the Damages Act 1996 sets out the circumstances in which the continuity of periodical payments will be taken to be secure. Section 2(8) and (9) of the Act deal with the index-linking of periodical payments.

12.3 Except where otherwise stated in this Practice Direction, the rules in Part 36 will apply to offers to settle made under rule 36.2A as they apply to other Part 36 payments and to Part 36 offers.

A2–36

---

[18] See rule 26 as above.

APPENDIX 3

Extract from CPR Part 21 and Part 21 Practice Direction

PART 21

Compromise etc. by or on behalf of child or patient
21.10

    (1) Where a claim is made—   **A3–01**

        (a) by or on behalf of a child or patient; or
        (b) against a child or patient,
    no settlement, compromise or payment and no acceptance of money paid into court shall be valid, so far as it relates to the claim by, on behalf of or against the child or patient, without the approval of the court.

    (2) Where—

        (a) before proceedings in which a claim is made by or on behalf of, or against a child or patient (whether alone or with any other person) are begun, an agreement is reached for the settlement of the claim; and
        (b) the sole purpose of proceedings on that claim is to obtain the approval of the court to a settlement or compromise of the claim, the claim must—
            (i) be made using the procedure set out in Part 8 (alternative procedure for claims); and
            (ii) include a request to the court for approval of the settlement or compromise.

    (3) In proceedings to which Section II of Part 45 applies, the court shall not make an order for detailed assessment of the costs payable to the child or patient but shall assess the costs in the manner set out in that Section.

(Rule 48.5 contains provisions about costs where money is payable to a child or patient)

PART 21 PRACTICE DIRECTION

Settlement or compromise by or on behalf of a child or patient prior to the start of proceedings

    6.1 Where a claim by or on behalf of a child or patient has been dealt with by agreement prior to the start of proceedings and only the approval of the court to the agreement is sought, the claim: **A3–02**

        (1) must be made using the Part 8 procedure,
        (2) must include a request for approval of the settlement or compromise, and
        (3) subject to paragraph 6.4 in addition to the details of the claim, must set out the terms of the settlement or compromise or have attached to it a draft consent order in practice form N292.

    6.2 In order to approve the settlement or compromise, the information concerning the claim that the court will require will include:

        (1) whether and to what extent the defendant admits liability,

(2) the age and occupation (if any) of the child or patient,
(3) the litigation friend's approval of the proposed settlement or compromise, and
(4) in a personal injury case arising from an accident—
   (a) the circumstances of the accident,
   (b) any medical reports,
   (c) where appropriate, a schedule of any past and future expenses and losses claimed and any other relevant information relating to personal injury as set out in the practice direction which supplements Part 16 (statements of case), and
   (d) where considerations of liability are raised—
      (i) any evidence or police reports in any criminal proceedings or in an inquest, and
      (ii) details of any prosecution brought.

6.3 (1) An opinion on the merits of the settlement or compromise given by counsel or solicitor acting for the child or patient should, except in very clear cases, be obtained.

(2) A copy of the opinion and, unless the instructions on which it was given are sufficiently set out in it, a copy of the instructions, must also be supplied to the court.

(3) A copy or record of any financial advice must also be supplied to the court.

6.4 Where in any personal injury case a claim for damages for future pecuniary loss is settled, the provisions in paragraphs 6.4A and 6.4B must in addition be complied with.

6.4A The court must be satisfied that the parties have considered whether the damages should wholly or partly take the form of periodical payments.

6.4B Where the settlement includes provision for periodical payments, the claim must—

(1) set out the terms of the settlement or compromise; or
(2) have attached to it a draft consent order,
which must satisfy the requirements of rules 41.8 and 41.9 as appropriate.

6.5 Applications for the approval of a settlement or compromise will normally be heard by a Master or district judge.
(For information about provisional damages claims see Part 41 and the practice direction which supplements it)

Settlement or compromise by or on behalf of a child or patient after proceedings have been commenced

A3–03

6.6 Where in any personal injury case a claim for damages for future pecuniary loss, by or on behalf of a child or patient, is dealt with by agreement after proceedings have been commenced, an application should be made for the court's approval of the agreement.

6.7 The court must be satisfied that the parties have considered whether the damages should wholly or partly take the form of periodical payments.

6.8 Where the settlement includes provision for periodical payments, an application under paragraph 6.6 must—

(1) set out the terms of the settlement or compromise; or
(2) have attached to it a draft consent order,
which must include the requirements of rules 41.8 and 41.9 as appropriate.

6.9 The court must be supplied with—

(1) an opinion on the merits of the settlement or compromise given by counsel or solicitor acting for the child or patient, except in very clear cases; and
(2) a copy or record of any financial advice.

Apportionment under the Fatal Accidents Act 1976

7.1 A judgment on or settlement in respect of a claim under the Fatal Accidents Act 1976 must be apportioned between the persons by or on whose behalf the claim has been brought.

7.2 Where a claim is brought on behalf of a dependent child or children, the money apportioned to any child must be invested on his behalf in accordance with rules 21.10 and 21.11 and paragraphs 8 and 9 below.

7.3 In order to approve an apportionment of money to a dependent child, the court will require the following information:

(1) the matters set out in paragraph 6.2(1),(2) above, and
(2) in respect of the deceased
   (a) where death was caused by an accident, the matters set out in paragraph 6.2(3)(a),(b) and (c) above, and
   (b) his future loss of earnings, and
(3) the extent and nature of the dependency.

APPENDIX 4

Extract from CPR Part 40 and Part 23 Practice Direction

PART 40 EXTRACT FROM CPR

Consent judgments and orders

40.6

A4–01

(1) This rule applies where all the parties agree the terms in which a judgment should be given or an order should be made.
(2) A court officer may enter and seal an agreed judgment or order if—
  (a) the judgment or order is listed in paragraph (3);
  (b) none of the parties is a litigant in person; and
  (c) the approval of the court is not required by these Rules, a practice direction or any enactment before an agreed order can be made.
(3) The judgments and orders referred to in paragraph (2) are—
  (a) a judgment or order for—
    (i) the payment of an amount of money (including a judgment or order for damages or the value of goods to be decided by the court); or
    (ii) the delivery up of goods with or without the option of paying the value of the goods or the agreed value.
  (b) an order for—
    (i) the dismissal of any proceedings, wholly or in part;
    (ii) the stay of proceedings on agreed terms, disposing of the proceedings, whether those terms are recorded in a schedule to the order or elsewhere;
    (iii) the stay of enforcement of a judgment, either unconditionally or on condition that the money due under the judgment is paid by instalments specified in the order;
    (iv) the setting aside under Part 13 of a default judgment which has not been satisfied;
    (v) the payment out of money which has been paid into court;
    (vi) the discharge from liability of any party;
    (vii) the payment, assessment or waiver of costs, or such other provision for costs as may be agreed.
(4) Rule 40.3 (drawing up and filing of judgments and orders) applies to judgments and orders entered and sealed by a court officer under paragraph (2) as it applies to other judgments and orders.
(5) Where paragraph (2) does not apply, any party may apply for a judgment or order in the terms agreed.
(6) The court may deal with an application under paragraph (5) without a hearing.
(7) Where this rule applies—
  (a) the order which is agreed by the parties must be drawn up in the terms agreed;
  (b) it must be expressed as being "By Consent";
  (c) it must be signed by the legal representative acting for each of the parties to whom the order relates or, where paragraph (5) applies, by the party if he is a litigant in person.

PART 23 PRACTICE DIRECTION

Consent orders

A4–02
10.1 Rule 40.6 sets out the circumstances where an agreed judgment or order may be entered and sealed.

10.2 Where all parties affected by an order have written to the court consenting to the making of the order a draft of which has been filed with the court, the court will treat the draft as having been signed in accordance with rule 40.6(7).

10.3 Where a consent order must be made by a judge (i.e. rule 40.6(2) does not apply) the order must be drawn so that the judge's name and judicial title can be inserted.

10.4 The parties to an application for a consent order must ensure that they provide the court with any material it needs to be satisfied that it is appropriate to make the order. Subject to any rule or practice direction a letter will generally be acceptable for this purpose.

10.5 Where a judgment or order has been agreed in respect of an application or claim where a hearing date has been fixed, the parties must inform the court immediately. (Note that parties are reminded that under rules 28.4 and 29.5 the case management timetable cannot be varied by written agreement of the parties.)

APPENDIX 5

Part 36 Forms

APPENDIX 5

A5–01

Notice of payment into court
(in settlement - Part 36)

In the	
Claim No.	
Claimant (including ref)	
Defendant (including ref)	

To the Claimant ('s Solicitor)

Take notice the defendant _____ has paid £ _____ (a further amount of £ _____)
into court in settlement of
(tick as appropriate)

☐ the whole of your claim
☐ part of your claim *(give details below)*
☐ a certain issue or issues in your claim *(give details below)*

The (part) (issue or issues) to which it relates is(are):*(give details)*

☐ It is in addition to the amount of £_____ already paid into court on _____ and the total amount in court now offered in settlement is £_____ *(give total of all payments in court to date)*
☐ It is not inclusive of interest and an additional amount of £_____ is offered for interest *(give details of the rate(s) and period(s) for which the amount of interest is offered.)*

☐ It takes into account all(part) of the following counterclaim:*(give details of the party and the part of the counterclaim to which the payment relates)*

☐ It takes into account the interim payment(s) made in the following amount(s) on the following date(s): *(give details)*

Note: This notice will need to be modified where an offer of provisional damages is made (CPR Part 36.7) and/or where it is made in relation to a mixed (money and non-money) claim in settlement of the whole claim (CPR Part 36.4).

N242A Notice of payment into court (in settlement) (04.03) The Court Service PublicationsBranch

A5–02

For cases where the Social Security (Recovery of Benefits) Act 1997 applies
The gross amount of the compensation payment is £_____

The defendant has reduced this sum by £_____ in accordance with section 8 of and Schedule 2 to the Social Security (Recovery of Benefits) Act 1997, which was calculated as follows:

Type of benefit   Amount

The amount paid into court is the net amount after deduction of the amount of benefit.

Signed [   ]   Position held [   ]
       Defendant('s solicitor)   (If signing on
                                   behalf of a firm
                                   or company)

Date [   ]

Name of bank [   ]

Account number [   ]

Sort code [   ]

Note: To the Claimant

If you wish to accept the payment made into court without needing the court's permission you should:
- complete N243A/Form201 and send to the Court Funds Office, 22 Kingsway, London, WC2B 6LE.
  (Copies are available from any court office or from the Court Funds Office or the Court Service website at www.courtservice.gov.uk)
- you must also send copies to the defendant and to the court

APPENDIX 5

A5–03 Notice of acceptance and request for payment (Part 36)

In the _____

Claim No. _____

Claimant (including ref.)

Defendant (including ref.)

On _____ I accepted the payment(s) into court totalling £ _____ net of CRU benefits in settlement of (the whole of) (part of) (certain issue(s) in) my claim as set out in the notice of payment into court received on _____

I declare that:-

☐ the claim has been accepted [within 21 days] [after 21 days but costs have been agreed] [less than 21 days before trial but costs have been agreed]

☐ the payment into court was not made in defence of tender

☐ the offeree is not a child or patient

☐ payment into court was not made under the Fatal Accidents Act 1976 and/or the Law Reform (Miscellaneous Provisions) Act 1934

(If any of the above declaration have not been made, the money in court can only be paid out by order of the court)

☐ the claimant [is] [is not] a person in receipt of legal aid under section 9 of the Access to Justice Act 1999

☐ a copy of this notice has been served on the defendant('s)(solicitor) named below and the court and I request payment of this money held in court to be made to:

For CFO use

A/c No.
Schedule number
Date received
Withdrawn
Inits / Date
Inits / Date
Write on/off
Date
Inits / Claimant's Cheque
Cheque issued stamps
Inits / Defendant's Cheque

Claimant or Solicitor's full name
Address
Ref. No.
Postcode

Name of bank
Account number
Sort code

Defendant('s)(Solicitor) full name
Address
Ref. No.
Postcode

Name of bank
Account number
Sort code

Signature

Note: Before signing this form please read the notes for guidance overleaf. Incorrectly signed forms may be returned unactioned.

Signed _____ Date _____

SOLICITOR'S DETAILS
Partner's name (PLEASE PRINT)
Name of firm
Solicitor for the

WITNESS DETAILS
Witnessed by
Occupation of witness
Date
Solicitor or Witness address

N243A/Form 201 Notice of acceptance and request for payment (Part 36) (10.04)

APPENDIX 6

Lecture given by David Foskett Q.C. to the London Common Law and Commercial Bar Association on November 19, 1997 entitled "The Tomlin Order: three score years and ten"

APPENDIX 6

A6–01 The opportunity to celebrate an official birthday as well as a real one presents itself to very few. The club to which one must belong in order to have this particular distinction has somewhat restricted entry requirements.

It may be an overstatement to suggest that the Tomlin Order is a monarch among the multifarious forms of order that a Court can make; but it has become a sufficiently important figure in the legal landscape for it now to be acknowledged that it has both an official and an actual birthday. Today, 19th November is its official birthday. Today 70 years ago the existence of what has become known as "the Tomlin Order" was first made public through the medium of the reports called The Weekly Notes, the series that preceded the Weekly Law Reports. That which appeared was a report of the Practice Note issued by Mr Justice Tomlin, as he then was, on Wednesday, 2nd November. That day must surely represent the actual birthday of the Tomlin Order. It might have been the day on which this lecture, designed to celebrate this important anniversary, ought to have been held. However, that day this year was a Sunday. The London Common Law and Commercial Bar Association would have been risking rather more of its reputation for being able to pull in three more than two men and a dog to one of its lectures than it was prepared to sacrifice by holding this lecture on a Sunday.

I suggested a moment or two ago that this anniversary, whether it be of an official or an actual nature, was important. It must be for others to judge whether that assertion is justified. However, since today I am freed from the constraints imposed upon me in my more accustomed role as an advocate, I can express a personal opinion. I do think that the celebration is both important and, as it happens, timely in a different sense.

In the course of this lecture I will endeavour to explain why this should be so. I shall say something about the long gestation period leading to the birth of the Tomlin Order, about the birth process itself and about what has happened in the span of three score years and ten that we salute today. I shall also address the question of whether the Tomlin Order has now outlived its purpose or whether it will survive into the new millennium, either in its existing or some modified form. Not unnaturally, I shall have to address these matters in the wider context of the settlement of litigation generally.

A6–02 Unable as I am wholly to shrug off the role of advocate, I must say something which engages the attention of those who are present listening in an endeavour to hold it for as long as necessary. I undertake, therefore, to put forward what I have to say as briefly as I can. Any Judge will know that that kind of promise from an advocate is completely worthless.

Judges are, however, known to respond enthusiastically to words from an advocate of the following nature: "I am happy to be able to tell your Lordship that you will not be troubled by this case; the parties have settled their differences." As Lord Lane, an enthusiastic golfer, once said of those words, they herald an unexpected round of golf for the Judge.[1] He did, however, continue by saying that they meant something of rather greater substance, namely, that but for the high proportion of cases that were settled, the administration of justice would soon grind to a halt because the Courts would be overwhelmed by the volume of work.

It was, I suppose, just possible that when Lord Lane was first appointed a Judge in 1966, a settlement at the doors of the Court would have enabled the Judge to have a round of golf. Nowadays, the gap in the list would be filled with alacrity by those responsible for ensuring the continuing throughput of cases. Students of Lord Woolf's proposals will know that he would like a settlement at the doors of the Court to be an even greater exception to the general rule that it is at present. One

---

[1] Foreword to the First Edition, *Law and Practice Compromise*, 1980.

consequence of achieving that objective would be the yet more efficient despatch of unsettlable disputes. If those who promote Alternative Dispute Resolution are justified in their belief that it offers the prospect of the resolution of disputes without litigation, some Judges of my acquaintance will be able to contemplate the professional golf careers that have eluded them thus far.

Settlement of litigation is important. Not merely because without it the administration of justice would, as Lord Lane said, "grind to a halt"; but also because in a civilised society, it must surely be desirable that those who do find themselves in dispute should, if at all possible, resolve their differences without resort to the costly, time- and emotion-consuming process of litigation. For many, life is too short to be involved in prolonged disputation. However, as any litigation lawyer will know, the impetus that drives a would-be litigant into a solicitor's office often reflects a sufficiently strong underlying feeling of grievance that settlement at less than total vindication is impossible to contemplate, certainly at that stage. Equally, there are those whom the law will regard as having benefited unjustly at the expense of another who will not lightly give up the fruits thus achieved. This also makes settlement an elusive objective. When settlement is achieved, perhaps somewhat against the odds, the one thing that it is (unfortunately) necessary to contemplate is the possibility that one or other party will not stick by and honour the agreement reached. It is that possibility that the Tomlin Order addresses by providing a convenient machinery for the enforcement of a compromise achieved during the pendency of litigation.

So what is it, why is it important and how did it come about?

Let us start with some fundamental propositions. Firstly, where parties agree a settlement of their dispute, they conclude a contract. Each gives up the right to pursue further the stance adopted in relation to the dispute. Secondly, any such contract, unless it preserves expressly (or by necessary implication) the right to revert to the original disputation in the event of a breach by one or other of the parties, will mean that the original disputation cannot be resurrected. As Bowen LJ put it in a case decided over 100 years ago[2]—

A6–03

> "As soon as you have ended a dispute by a compromise you have disposed of it."

The effect of this is that the contract of compromise henceforth governs the legal relationship of the parties in relation to the matters which gave rise to the dispute and it is to that contract that either must go for assistance from the Court for the purposes of enforcement. As Lord Denning MR said in a case some 30 years ago[3] in which the settlement involved the payment of a sum of money in satisfaction of the claim—

> "When an action is compromised by an agreement to pay a sum in satisfaction, it gives rise to a new cause of action. This arises since the Writ in the first action, and must be the subject of a new action. The Plaintiff, in order to get judgment, has to sue on the compromise. That is the only course which the Plaintiff can take in order to enforce the settlement . . ."

As that quotation reveals, since the enforcement of a compromise involves the assertion of a new cause of action, the rules of procedure (which, for this purpose,

---

[2] *Knowles v Roberts* (1888) 38 Ch.D. 263 at 272.
[3] *McCallum v Country Residences Ltd* [1965] 1 W.L.R. 657 at 660. See also *Green v Rozen* [1955] 1 W.L.R. 741 at 746.

have not varied greatly over the years) would require the commencement of a fresh action.

A6–04   In the High Court that would mean the issue and service of a new Writ, perhaps endorsed with a Statement of Claim, followed by all the panoply of further pleadings, discovery and so on. Even if the matter could have been dealt with under Order 14, Rules of the Supreme Court, or in some other reasonably summary fashion, there would be delay and expense. For the litigant seeking the enforcement of the obviously enforceable, there would be much frustration.

Long before the expression "fast track" was coined, the Courts of the day provided the means by which the need for a fresh action could be obviated and relatively summary justice dispensed. I say "*could* be obviated" because, in order to avail themselves of this useful procedure, the parties had to settle their litigation in a particular form. As I will demonstrate in a moment, deviation from that form could prove costly.

Before dealing with that, I should, perhaps, emphasise that what we are concerned with here is the kind of compromise that generally involves more than just, for example, the mere payment of a sum of money or the giving up of possession of premises. In cases like that, a straightforward consent judgment or order is often entered, although not necessarily so in every case. We are concerned with cases where relatively complicated terms of settlement are agreed, perhaps involving a number of inter-related obligations. Some of the obligations may be such that they could not, even had the parties wished otherwise, have been made orders of the Court. There is, it should be noted, no jurisdiction to make an order or judgment by consent which the Court would not otherwise have jurisdiction to make.[4] What the parties need in this situation (or in any other situation where they do not seek an immediately enforceable consent judgment or order), is a process for active enforcement of the agreement without the need to bring an entirely new action. So how has that need been met?

A6–05   My researches have not revealed precisely when it was that the beginnings of what later became known as "the Tomlin Order" first emerged clearly into legal practice. I did discover a case that took place in August 1848[5] in which an injunction was agreed to and the proceedings were stayed "unless the Defendants committed any breach of the injunction already awarded; and any of the parties were to be at liberty to apply to the Court, as there should be occasion". As we will discover, that has some similarities to the eventual form of Tomlin order. However, it is plain that there was, as might be expected, a considerable rigidity of approach in the first half of the last century. When litigants settled, they either had a contract or they had an enforceable consent judgment or order. There was indeed an enforceable order, in the form of an injunction, in the case to which I have just referred. The Judges found it difficult to recognise a kind of halfway house. My belief, however, is that the Judicature Act 1873 and the new rules introduced in the ten years thereafter provided the springboard for the development of a more flexible approach.

Those of us who, incidentally, happen to be members of the new Civil Procedure Rule Committee would, I think, give anything to be able to have a playback of the deliberations of our illustrious predecessors in what for them must have been radical and reforming days. I am inclined to think that they too might be interested in, and perhaps even horrified by, what they would hear if they could listen to our discussions. But I digress.

---

[4] See, *e.g. Re Aylmer,* (1887) 20 Q.B.D. 258 at 262; *Livesey v Jenkins* [1985] A.C. 424; *IRC v Hoogstraten* [1985] Q.B. 1077.
[5] *MacRae v Holdsworth,* 2 De G. & Sm. 496.

What had emerged, certainly by the early part of this century, was a practice whereby parties agreed to the stay of the proceedings upon the terms of the agreement between them. Those terms were recorded in a Schedule to the Order and the intention was that the Court should be able to make orders in aid of the enforcement of those terms as the result of an application made by summons *within the stayed action*. In other words, no fresh action was required, although, of course, a further step in the proceedings was necessary in order to obtain a suitable form of Order.

A "stay" needs to be contrasted with a "dismissal" or "discontinuance" of the action. Those two expressions connote a degree of finality about the action, whereas a "stay" suggests that there may yet be a spark of life in the proceedings for some purposes. What the parties were looking for, having agreed a stay of the action upon the terms of their agreement, was the odd spark to ignite the process of enforcement if the agreement was not honoured.

Since it is only just a fortnight since 5th November, perhaps I can continue the pyrotechnic theme a little further. Along the path that led ultimately to the Tomlin Order, the odd damp squib failed to ignite. In October 1908 a Mrs Florence Hearn took some proceedings against her estranged husband, Colonel George Hearn.[6] As you might imagine, the focus of the proceedings was money. Those proceedings related to the question of whether Colonel Hearn was still entitled to an annuity of £500 under his late father's will, that annuity being secured on certain properties. Those proceedings were settled on fairly complicated terms. In essence, however, Mrs Hearn was to receive £315 per annum (which must have been a sizeable sum then) during the joint lives of herself and Colonel Hearn, that sum to be paid out of the income from the properties on which his annuity and his share of the residue of the estate was secured. The trustees of Colonel Hearn's father's will were put in charge of the management of the properties securing the annuity, although Colonel Hearn himself was left in possession of the properties securing his share of the residue. The settlement was concluded by means of a consent order made in June 1909 under which all further proceedings were stayed upon the terms of the agreement as set forth in the schedule to the order.

Within six months of the agreement, the net income from the properties securing the annuity was insufficient to pay the full sum of £315 per annum. As she was entitled to do under the agreement, Mrs Hearn asked Colonel Hearn to make up the deficiency from the income of the properties upon which his share in the residue was secured. He failed to deliver. Mrs Hearn issued a summons *in the old proceedings* seeking enforcement of the obligation. She wanted the properties securing his share in the residuary estate either transferred to the trustees of the will to manage, or the appointment of a receiver and manager, so that she could receive the monies rightfully due to her.

She had all the merits. Unfortunately, her Counsel, Mr Arnold Herbert, did not have a good day when he appeared before Mr Justice Sargant. The Judge accepted the argument put forward on Colonel Hearn's behalf that in order to achieve the result she wished, it was necessary that she commence a fresh action. Mr Justice Sargant said that the effect of the stay was that the original proceedings were "spent and exhausted" and he refused Mrs Hearn's application.

Undeterred, Mr Herbert took Mrs Hearn's case to the Court of Appeal. It took only four weeks to get there, but he had an even worse day before the then Master of the Rolls, Sir Herbert Cozens-Hardy, and Lords Justice Buckley and Kennedy. Without even calling on his opponent, they said that Mr Justice Sargant was absolutely right and dismissed the appeal with costs.

---

[6] *Re Hearn* (1913) 108 L.T. 452 and 738.

A6–07   This was one case where the technicalities got in the way of the merits. Had the consent order provided a qualified form of stay, the result would almost certainly have been different. By "qualified" I mean that the stay of the proceedings could have been expressed to be "except as may be necessary to enforce the terms of the agreement set out in the schedule." The basis upon which the existing proceedings could be said still to have been alive, rather than "spent and exhausted", would then have been clear.

In fairness to Mr Herbert, that was not the sole, nor even the principal, ground upon which he lost. But the views of Mr Justice Sargant and the Court of Appeal were expressed in such a way as to suggest that had it been the sole ground, it would have resulted in the failure of his client's application.

Looking back, as perhaps only a lecturer can do, it does seem surprising that the case did not prompt some clearer guidance to the profession from the Court of Appeal on how a settlement might best be concluded to overcome such an obviously unjust result and one which must have been obtained at considerable wasted costs. We might, perhaps, be celebrating the 84th anniversary of the Cozens-Hardy Order had that opportunity been taken. But such was not the practice then.

Sir Herbert Cozens-Hardy did have an ingenious trait within his character. In a later case, in order to accommodate the unfortunate death of Lord Justice Kennedy (with whom he had sat on the *Hearn* case) between the composition of the judgment of the court and the giving of the judgment, he back-dated the date of the judgment. He is also the person who, as a mere Lord Justice and before he became Master of the Rolls, is reported in a case in 1903[7] as having said "I agree" immediately after one of his brethren had just concurred with the judgment of the then Master of the Rolls and had said "and I do not think I can usefully add anything." This apparent lack of fraternal tact did not constitute an impediment to Sir Herbert's future judicial career.

A6–08   I had at one stage thought that I would be able to tell you of a happy ending so far as Mr Herbert was concerned, because I noticed that in 1913 a Mr A. Herbert was made King's Counsel. Some kind of consolation prize, perhaps. More detailed research did, however, reveal that that was Mr *Arthur* Herbert—not Mr *Arnold* Herbert. Arthur Herbert had the extraordinary distinction, according to his entry in Who's Who, of possessing a paternal grandmother who was a sister of the two ladies who composed "Twinkle Twinkle Little Star". His lesser distinctions were a double first in the Classical and Law Tripos at St John's College, Cambridge, the Yorke Prize at Cambridge and the Equity Scholarship at the Inner Temple.

In the same list of King's Counsel in 1913 appeared the name of a fellow Chancery practitioner, Thomas James Cheshyrre Tomlin. I do have this mental picture of these two distinguished gentlemen, in full bottomed wigs and all the traditional regalia, discussing what could be done to ensure that the kind of misfortune that befell the namesake of one of them (and, more importantly, his client, Mrs Hearn) should not arise again.

Given what I shall say in a moment, it is plain that the profession, perhaps in the light of the *Hearn* case, was beginning to get its act together. But before I leave the biographical dimension, I should tell you that, as these things happen, there was only one vacancy on the High Court Bench in the Chancery Division in October 1923. The Lord Chancellor must have been blessed with an embarrassment of riches, given the credentials of those who had been in silk for 10 years. For reasons upon which, by tradition, the profession would have speculated, Thomas Tomlin emerged as the man most fitted to the task. Perhaps "Twinkle Twinkle Little Star"

---

[7] *Jaeger v Mansions Consolidated Ltd* (1903) 87 L.T. 690 at 697.

did not count amongst the Lord Chancellor's favourite tunes. But from that moment on, the Tomlin Order was destined to be just that. There is, perhaps, just the faintest of ironies in the fact that the person who, by his elevation to the Court of Appeal, created the vacancy in the Chancery Division was none other than Mr. Justice Sargant.

Lawyers are accustomed to applying the "but for" test in relation to causation. We all know that but for the decomposed remains of a snail in a bottle of ginger beer in Paisley in August 1928, the modern law of negligence might not have assumed the shape that it has. Well, but for a squabble in a firm of undertakers in Portsmouth in 1926, the Tomlin Order might never have come into existence in the shape that we know it.

The Dashwood family were undertakers. They fell out and a partnership action ensued brought by Mr William Dashwood. It was settled. A consent order was made staying the proceedings. According to the report of the case[8], the stay was expressed to be "except so far as may be necessary for the purpose of carrying this Order and the terms agreed between the parties and set out in the schedule hereto into effect." One of the terms was that Mr William Dashwood was not to canvass or solicit for funeral business in any part of the City of Portsmouth for a period of 3 years. His former partners said that he had breached this obligation and applied to have him committed. Mr Dashwood's solicitors briefed the appropriately named Mr Swords to defend him. He took the point that there was no power to commit because the terms set out in the schedule were not orders of the Court. He argued that it was necessary for the applicants first to have taken proceedings, either independently or in the action, to enforce the terms by means of an Order for specific performance or an injunction. It would only then be possible to apply for committal if, following the making of such an Order, his client failed to obey.

A6–09

Mr Justice Tomlin, having expressed surprise that there was no authority directly on the point, acceded to those submissions. He expressed himself in this way:

"In the present case the Court was staying the action on terms which the parties had agreed, and only keeping it alive to the extent necessary to enable any party thereafter to enforce the terms. It seemed to follow that the terms in the schedule were not an order of the Court which ought directly to be enforced by proceedings for contempt. The proper course was to apply for specific performance or an injunction, and then to base proceedings for contempt on any subsequent breach."

This decision was taken on 1st November 1927, according to the edition of The Weekly Notes dated 12th November 1927. According to the edition published a week later, and exactly 70 years ago today, it is clear that Mr Justice Tomlin had applied his mind overnight (perhaps having consulted some of his brethren) to the way in which a consent order of the type used in the Dashwood case should be phrased. On 2nd November a Practice Note bearing his name was issued. He said that in future, where an action was proposed to be stayed on agreed terms to be scheduled to the Order, the minutes of order should be drawn up to read as follows:

"And the Plaintiff and Defendant having agreed to the terms set out in the Schedule hereto, it is ordered that all further proceedings in this action be stayed, except for the purpose of carrying such terms into effect.
Liberty to apply as to carrying such terms into effect."

---

[8] [1927] W.N. 276.

A6–10   And with modest stylistic changes from time to time, that is how a Tomlin Order has been drawn ever since.

Again, I regret to say that I cannot tell you precisely when this form of Order was christened "a Tomlin Order". Mr Justice Tomlin was appointed, direct from the High Court Bench, to the House of Lords in February 1929 and died (as Lord Tomlin of Ash) in August 1935. All I can tell you is that there is unequivocal evidence available that a certain Mr Denning was, as Counsel, party to the drawing up of a Tomlin Order in the following year. I will mention that case in a few moments.

Looking back, as we are, to the first days of life of the Tomlin Order, it is surprising that something that has become such an established part of everyday practice did not have its birth announced in The Times. Try as I might, I have found no reference to the Practice Note in any of The Times law reports of that period. The reporters from The Times were, I think, elsewhere than Mr Justice Tomlin's Court on 2nd November 1927.

Some might have been watching proceedings before Mr Justice Wright, as he then was, who had before him, representing the Plaintiff in a case called *Dalton v Jones*, a 28 year old A.T. Denning. They might not have lingered long there. Lord Devlin has described Mr. Justice Wright as "a great lawyer, but no orator." He said that he was "a master of the monotone sinking sometimes to the mumble." I suspect most were in the Lord Chief Justice's Court.

A6–11   The Lord Chief Justice then was Lord Hewart, about whom much has been said. Lord Devlin has described him as "a horror". Lord Hewart was trying an action in negligence with the assistance of a special jury. The Plaintiff was a Miss Marjorie Beckh; the Defendant, a Mr Neil Sinclair, Fellow of the Royal College of Surgeons. Miss Beckh had the advantage of being represented by Mr Malcolm Hilberry, as he then was—another figure whose reputation lives on.

Miss Beckh was claiming damages for personal injuries arising from a burn to her knee caused by a hot water bottle. The hot water bottle was a necessary adjunct to the operation that Mr Sinclair was performing, namely, that of sigmoidoscopy. For the medically uninitiated, this involves passing a sigmoidoscope (a kind of telescope) into that part of the anatomy in the vicinity of which can be found the sigmoid colon. For those who still remain ignorant, it is about the last place on earth that most of us would wish to spend our days looking!

You may be interested to know how The Times reported some of the exchanges in Court.

In the first place, Mr Hilberry asked the Lord Chief Justice if his client could show her injury to the jury. The report indicates that the response was—

"It is quite usual to exhibit knees nowadays isn't it?" (Laughter)

Later an expert witness gave evidence that the burn was "of the third degree". The following interchange is reported:

"Mr Hilberry: What is a burn of the third degree?
Lord Chief Justice: I always thought it was a form of cross-examination." (Laughter)

At the end of this day, whilst Mr Sinclair was being cross-examined, the Lord Chief Justice is reported as saying this:

"I think that Mr Serjeant Buzfuz in a well known . . . case described a warming-pan as a useful, comforting article of domestic furniture." (Laughter)

At lightning speed, Mr Hilberry retorted as follows:

"That is if it were withdrawn from the scene of the operation before it did any harm." (Laughter)

When I was called to the Bar by Gray's Inn I, along with all those then called, was presented with a copy of a book entitled "Duty and Art in Advocacy"—by Sir Malcolm Hilberry. I suppose the duty of an advocate must be to permit the Judge, particularly if he is the Lord Chief Justice, to have three jokes at your expense—and the art is to ensure that you get the last laugh. Whilst that might be said of what happened on 2nd November, I am afraid I must tell you that, perhaps predictably, the Lord Chief Justice did have the very last laugh on the following day: he withdrew the case from a jury, saying that there was no evidence of negligence. Poor Miss Beckh: all that unconscious indignity, a scalded knee and no compensation.

By the time his Practice Note had been reported in The Weekly Notes 17 days later, Mr Justice Tomlin had probably forgotten all about it. For him, though, November had been a month of compromise. On the day before the report in The Weekly Notes, he had presided over a hearing in which the Daily Express had given undertakings not to breach the copyright of those perennial favourite songs—

"Sister Suzie's Sewing Shirts for Soldiers"
"Pack up your troubles in your old kit bag", and
"Goodbyee".

Mention of a newspaper bearing the title "Express" brings me neatly to that case in which Mr Denning was involved in 1936. The parties on each side were publishers of certain newspapers in various parts of Essex. For over 50 yeas they had respected each other's "patches". But in 1935 the publishers of the "Stratford Express" took proceedings against the publishers of newspapers entitled "The Express and Independent" alleging that they were passing off their business as that of the Plaintiffs by representing that there was an association between them. The Plaintiffs wanted an injunction preventing the Defendants from using the words "Express" or "Express and Independent" in connection with any of the newspapers.

Those proceedings failed at first instance. The Plaintiffs appealed and the appeal was compromised. The basis of the agreement was that neither party would, in an agreed area of common circulation, change the way in which their newspapers were entitled by reference to the way those newspapers were entitled at the beginning of the proceedings. The Plaintiffs, therefore, committed themselves not to use the word "Express" with any greater prominence, or dropping the word "Stratford" to any greater extent, "than at the commencement of this action". The Defendants made similar commitments.

As you might imagine, expressing the obligations of each party in this way begged some important questions about what practice had prevailed "at the commencement of [the] action".

When Mr Denning, who was Junior Counsel for the Plaintiffs, appeared before the Court of Appeal, presided over by Lord Wright, Master of the Rolls (as Mr Justice Wright had by then become), the suggestion was that cross-undertakings of the nature I have described would be given. Lord Wright said on several occasions that an undertaking in those terms would be too vague for the Court subsequently to enforce and also said that a contractual term to this effect would also fail for uncertainty. Despite the efforts of Mr Denning and Mr Vaisey, for the Defendants, to persuade the Court to a different view, Lord Wright sent them away to "think it over", with the comment that "We are not here to settle in open Court the appropriate form of terms on which the appeal is dismissed". (It is, is it not, reassuring to know that those who achieve the highest judicial office have, in their time at the Bar, been spoken to somewhat testily, even if in a monotone, by those who have already achieved high office?)

When the parties came back to Court a fortnight later, they had not changed the substance of their agreement, nor had they defined the obligations of either party with any greater precision. What they did was to make a Tomlin Order in which the obligations were expressed as terms in the Schedule to the Order. The Court of Appeal was prepared to make that Order because it did not bind the Court to anything.

And until 1968 that was the end of the story. By then, of course, Mr Denning had been a High Court Judge, Lord Justice of Appeal, a Lord of Appeal in ordinary and for some 6 years, Master of the Rolls.

A6–14 In 1968, the Defendants complained that, within the common area of circulation, the Plaintiffs had started giving greater prominence to the word "Express" than the word "Stratford" and that in the case of one of their newspapers, "The Ilford & Redbridge Express", they had dropped the name "Stratford" altogether. They issued a Notice of Motion (making use of the "liberty to apply" in the Tomlin Order) asking for an injunction restraining the Plaintiffs from breaching their agreement.

Perhaps not surprisingly, given the terms of the discussion between Lord Wright and Mr Denning in 1936, in a reserved Judgment given on St Valentine's Day 1969, Mr Justice Plowman declined to make the requested Order because the obligation in the agreement had been too vaguely expressed. It made no difference that what he was being asked to enforce was a contractual undertaking and not one given to the Court.[9]

Apart from its anecdotal interest, the case does highlight clearly the distinction between terms of a compromise which are embodied in an Order of the Court as such (as an undertaking to the Court would have been) and those which remained entirely contractual in status. The terms of a Tomlin Order schedule come within the latter category, even though they appear in the Court record.

A6–15 When reading the report of that case again for the purpose of preparing this lecture, I was surprised to see that one of the points that the Plaintiffs' Leading Counsel, Mr Mervyn Davies QC, took was that the Defendants were not entitled to proceed by way of application under the "liberty to apply", but should have proceeded by way of a fresh action. He was proposing to rely upon a passage in Daniell's Chancery Practice, 8th Edition (1914), which read as follows:

> "A consent order, embodying a new agreement between the parties beyond the scope of the action, can only be enforced in a fresh suit."

The authority relied on for that proposition was Mrs Hearn's case.

Because it was unnecessary for the purposes of his decision, Mr Justice Plowman did not express any view about this argument. However, given the phraseology of a Tomlin Order, with its provision for a qualified stay, it is surprising that it was thought that this kind of argument could be sustained, certainly some 40 years after Mr Justice Tomlin's Practice Note. In the case I mentioned towards the beginning of this lecture, in which Lord Denning MR spoke of new causes of action springing from a compromise, Danckwerts LJ had said that it was precisely to avoid the need for the issue of fresh proceedings "that the Tomlin form of Order was evolved."

A few months after Mr Justice Plowman's decision in what I will call the "the Essex Express" case, Mr Justice Goff (that is Mr Justice *Reginald* Goff) finally

---

[9] *Wilson and Whitworth Ltd v Express and Independent Newspapers Ltd* [1969] 1 W.L.R. 197.

exorcised the ghost that had stalked the corridors of the Chancery Division since the 8th Edition of Daniell's Chancery Practice. He said that the bald proposition stated in that work was not supported by the *Hearn* case and expressed himself thus:

> "In my judgment, provided an Order is in the normally appropriate form with a qualified stay and a liberty to apply, and provided the application is strictly to enforce the terms embodied in the Order and the schedule, and does not depart from the agreed terms, an Order giving effect to the terms may be obtained under the liberty to apply in the original action, notwithstanding the compromise itself goes beyond the ambit of the original dispute and the provision sought to be enforced is something which could not have been enforced in the original action and which, indeed, is an obligation which did not then exist but arose for the first time under the compromise."

With just a faint expression of caution, he concluded his judgment with these words:

> "That, I think, until the Court of Appeal says I am wrong, should resolve the doubt which has hitherto existed."[10]

Well, the Court of Appeal has never said that he was wrong. Indeed, he was plainly right. He went on to make an order that the Defendant should pay the Plaintiffs the sum of £100 by way of agreed damages and £275 by way of agreed costs, the first obligation being set out explicitly in the schedule and the second arising under a term which provided that if the Plaintiffs' costs were agreed, they should be paid forthwith to the Plaintiffs.

The Court of Appeal did have occasion to reflect on the nature and effect of a Tomlin Order in 1987.[11] Ironically, the opportunity arose on an appeal from Mr Justice Mervyn Davies, as Leading Counsel for the Plaintiffs in the "Essex Express" case had in the meantime become.

Property proceedings between the Plaintiff and the Defendant had been compromised in Tomlin form. The material terms set out in the schedule were, firstly, that the property should be sold within 3 months and, secondly, that out of the net proceeds of sale, the Plaintiff should receive a specific sum whereupon she would be indemnified by the Defendant in respect of liability under a joint mortgage. There was enormous delay during which nothing really happened. Eventually, some 6 or 7 years later, the Plaintiff took steps to enforce the agreement. She did this by Notice of Motion in the existing action. Mr Justice Mervyn Davies ordered specific performance of the provisions of the schedule, substituting a new date for compliance. He also awarded the Plaintiff damages for the Defendant's delay in effecting the sale of the property.

When reflecting on the effect of a Tomlin Order, Fox LJ said that the agreement between the parties consisted "not only in the scheduled terms of the compromise", but also the "provision for the stay itself, which is an integral part of the compromise." He went on in this way:

> "As between the parties . . . while the action is not discontinued or dismissed, the bargain was that the action would not be resorted to thereafter save for the purpose of enforcing the terms. That is the plain meaning of the language used

A6–16

---

[10] *E.F. Phillips Ltd v Clarke* [1970] Ch. 322.
[11] *Hollingsworth v Humphrey* (1987) C.A.T. 1244.

... The liberty to apply for the purpose of enforcing the terms gave [the Plaintiff] a summary method of securing compliance."

So there it is: confirmation at the level of the Court of Appeal that the Tomlin Order provides a "summary method of securing compliance" with the scheduled terms. I do not think Lord Tomlin would have been at all surprised by this decision, though he might have wondered why it had taken 60 years to emerge.

A6–17 The Court of Appeal upheld the Judge's decision as to the Order for specific performance, but (and here is the sting in the tail) they said that he was wrong to award damages. That, it was said, required a fresh action. It was, you might think, a case of their Lordships giving with one hand and taking away with the other.

The basis for the decision that a fresh action was required for this purpose was that a claim for damages for breach of the agreement did not constitute *enforcement* of the agreement and it was only the *enforcement* of the agreement for which the original action was kept alive.

For what my view is worth, that does seem to be a strictly correct interpretation of the words always used in the Tomlin Order, albeit a somewhat narrow one. I wonder how many Counsel or Solicitors, if asked at the time they were agreeing a Tomlin Order whether they anticipated a fresh action if damages for breach were claimed, would answer in the affirmative. One of my suggestions for the modification of the present standard form of Tomlin Order would be expressly to *include* a potential claim for damages as part of the summary process provided for unless the Court orders otherwise. It is difficult to see what advantage there is in requiring a fresh action in such a situation. Any directions that might be required in relation to setting out the basis of the claim, discovery and so on, could doubtless be given in the context of the pending application pursuant to the "liberty to apply".

If that decision of the Court of Appeal is to be seen as reflecting a somewhat restrictive approach to a Tomlin Order, a decision some 7 years later can be seen as almost directly the converse.

A6–18 Parties to a partnership dispute settled their differences on the basis that the Defendant would buy out the Plaintiff's share for a specified sum. That sum was to be paid by an initial down payment and the balance by *weekly* payments. It would have taken about a year to pay off the balance at this rate. It was agreed that the settlement should be embodied in the Tomlin Order. When the Defendant's solicitors prepared the draft Tomlin Order, the word "monthly" rather than "weekly" appeared in relation to the instalment payments. Some other differences from what had been agreed in the correspondence also appeared. Although some of the differences were noticed by the Plaintiff's then solicitors, the crucial one, namely, the rests between periodical payments, was not.

When it was eventually noticed, the Defendant was not prepared to agree to a rectification of the terms of the schedule. One of the arguments advanced on behalf of the Defendant, at the hearing of the appeal from the refusal of the Judge at first instance to amend the schedule to reflect what had been agreed, was that it required a fresh action for that to be possible.

It took 19 months for that appeal to be heard. Unlike Mr Arnold Herbert, Counsel for the Plaintiff, who was the Appellant, had rather a good day in the Court of Appeal. I cannot remember his name, but "sources close" to him have confirmed that his knees were hardly unbent as he stood up to open the appeal when it became apparent that the writing was on the wall for the other side. Indeed he was not called on. In relation to the "fresh action" argument, Steyn LJ, as he then was, said this[12]:

---

[12] *Islam v Askar* (1994) C.A.T. 1240.

"That is a curious submission because the purpose of a Tomlin Order is that these matters should all be dealt with in the same proceedings."

The Court of Appeal held that, whilst the schedule to a Tomlin Order is not part of the Order, it *is* part of the Court record and is thus amenable to the inherent jurisdiction of the Court. That jurisdiction was wide enough to correct a mistake of the sort made in this case.

Because of the procedural difficulties he was facing in relation to the rectification of the Tomlin Order, the Plaintiff had also instituted a fresh action seeking judgment for the money he was owed pursuant to the agreement he had entered into. That had been struck out by the Judge at first instance. The Court of Appeal held that he was entitled to proceed in that way and indeed granted judgment for the whole sum.

That is a useful reminder that, as with any consent order or judgment in the ordinary civil jurisdiction, there is in existence an underlying contract which retains its own independent legal force. In a case from Hong Kong that went to the Privy Council a few years ago,[13] the whole of the agreement between the parties settling the particular piece of litigation had not been transposed into the schedule to the Tomlin Order. When one of the corporate parties applied for an Order enforcing the terms of the schedule, it was met with the argument that it was itself in breach of a term of that larger agreement and, accordingly, was not entitled to the Order sought. The Privy Council decided, as a preliminary point, that that argument could indeed be taken by the party resisting enforcement.

Before drawing all this to some form of conclusion, let me draw attention to one feature of the standard Tomlin Order procedure which parties do from time to time adapt. Since the Schedule to the Order is part of the Court record, it is open to public inspection. Parties may wish, for an assortment of reasons, to keep their settlement confidential. This can, at least in part, be achieved by recording the terms of the settlement on a separate document rather than in the schedule. Provided that that document is clearly identified on the face of the Tomlin Order, there can be no objection to dealing with things in that way. I have myself been involved in a number of cases where this has been done.

In this brief review I have mentioned what seem to me to be the important cases concerning Tomlin Orders. There are others.

The Tomlin Order started its life as a means by which terms of settlement could be enforced without the need for a fresh action. The emphasis was on expedition and the saving of costs. Nothing has changed. In the Privy Council case to which I referred a short while ago, Lord Lowry spoke of advantage being taken "of the Tomlin Order procedure for summary judgment, so that the payment could be quickly and cheaply enforced."

Are there any features of the Tomlin Order procedure that do not meet the criteria of quick and cheap enforcement?

I have mentioned the need for a fresh action in order to claim damages. In order to get round that, all the parties need to do is to define "enforcement" as including a claim for damages "unless the Court otherwise directs". That would give the Court the power to overrule the parties' agreement if it thought that a fresh action was, in the particular circumstances, required or was desirable.

The other, more obvious, comment that one might make is that, whilst no fresh action is needed for enforcement, a further application to the Court is required. That, of course, itself involves delay and expense. Is there any way round that?

Well, in the first instance, it seems to me to be important, where a Court Order is being sought, that the Court itself should be the final arbiter of whether the Order

---

[13] *Horizon Technologies Ltd v Lucky Wealth Consultants Ltd* [1992] 1 W.L.R. 24.

sought should indeed be made. Although there is often a fair amount of "rubber stamping" in the Court's processes, for the most part the making of a Court Order is a judicial act and requires proper consideration. The "Essex Express" case perhaps demonstrates the need for the Court to have control over the making of Orders for enforcement. Having said that, however, I do not see why the parties could not, if they wished, agree an abridged procedure for obtaining any enforcement order, with provision for non-attendance unless there is a dispute about the making of the Order. This provision could appear on the face of the Tomlin Order itself.

I have seen attempts made to circumvent the need to apply for a further Court Order by providing, on the face of the purported Tomlin Order, that the terms of the Schedule be made Orders of the Court. This is, in my view, a very cockeyed approach. If it is possible for the terms of the Schedule to be made Orders of the Court, what is the point of using the Tomlin form of Order at all? But, and perhaps more significantly, the Tomlin Order is used most frequently where some or all of the provisions in the Schedule could *not* be made Orders of the Court because they go beyond the Court's normal jurisdiction. In such a case a consensual direction that the terms of the Schedule be made Orders of the Court would offend the principle, to which I referred earlier, that the Court cannot by consent make Orders outside its normal jurisdiction.

If anyone would like to see *a* (and I emphasise it is only *a*) suggestion as to how a slightly modernised Tomlin Order might be phrased under the present Rules, a precedent will be annexed to the written version of this lecture. For a modest sum, that written version can be purchased. Lest it be thought that I shall profit from this, let it be clearly understood that the proceeds will go to the Barristers Benevolent Association!

A6–21   Mention of the "present Rules" leads me finally to the new Rules which will be made in due course. The trailer for this lecture suggested that I might be in a position to offer predictions as to the future use of the Tomlin Order in the context of those Rules. It would, I think, be a little presumptuous (and, perhaps, somewhat foolhardy in any event) for me to make any predictions about the future. The Civil Procedure Rule Committee will formulate a set of Rules that will, in due course, be considered by the Lord Chancellor. He will decide in what form those Rules are placed before Parliament and, of course, Parliament will decide finally.

Since the deliberations of the Committee are not confidential, I shall not have to code what I am about to say with expressions like "sources close to" or "friends of the Committee"! I can, with some degree of confidence, predict that consideration will be given by the Committee to the question of whether what I will call a "Rule-imposed" Tomlin Order has a role to play in the future.

Lord Woolf's proposals place emphasis on "offers to settle", the role of a payment into Court being less central than it has been hitherto to the regime by which the Court gives support to offerors. If that balance is carried through into the Rules then, unless everything is left to the parties, the Rules will have to make some provision as to what will happen if an offer to settle is accepted. As things stand at present, if a payment into Court is accepted, the Rules impose an automatic stay on the proceedings[14] in respect of the cause or causes of action to which the payment relates. Apart from the administrative requirement of paying the money out to the intended recipient, and dealing with the taxation of costs, there is nothing else for the Court to do. Under any regime which places less emphasis on monies being in Court in support of an offer of settlement, or indeed where support is given by the Rules to the making of offers to settle in cases involving claims for more than just

---

[14] RSC Ord.22, rr.3(4) and (5); CCR Ord.11, rr.3(3) and (6).

damages or other monetary relief, then, as I have said, the Rules will have to indicate what is going to happen when an offer is accepted. Unless the Rules say something about the consequences of acceptance of such an offer, the parties will either have to have specified what is to happen or be left to enforce the settlement in a fresh action. I cannot believe that anyone would welcome that last possibility.

I suggest, but merely suggest, that the Tomlin Order has a role here. My colleagues on the Civil Procedure Rule Committee may have better ideas; but, as presently advised, I have been unable to think of a better approach than to impose upon an offer made and accepted in accordance with the new Rules a Tomlin form of Order. That would enable the Court to assist in the enforcement of the terms of the offer without the need for fresh proceedings. All I feel able to say, therefore, is that there must be a fighting chance that the Tomlin Order will become "institutionalised" under the new Rules. Since the philosophy that underpins the new rules will be the saving of costs and increased speed in securing justice, it surely would have found a natural home.

The phraseology of any such Order, whether under the new Rules as such or simply made by the parties after the Rules have become effective, will doubtless change from its traditional form. The Committee is enjoined by the enabling Act to draft the Rules in uncomplicated language. I am looking forward with keen anticipation to the debate about how we should express simply the concept of a "notice of motion"! **A6–22**

Whilst I think that the expression "stay" is likely to be retained, the days of the expression "liberty to apply" are probably numbered. I would, I think, be holding rather too many hostages to fortune if I appended to the written version of this lecture a precedent for the Tomlin Order after the new Rules are in place.

The Tomlin Order was born in a rather different age from the present. Its full legal and practical implications have taken some years to be appreciated and indeed refined. It does, however, have at least a partial international following. My limited enquiries have revealed that, in addition, of course, to Hong Kong, it has travelled as far afield as New Zealand. Apparently, it has not yet made the final leap to Australia. I have suggested to the President of the Australian Bar Association, with whom I have been in contact about the Tomlin order, that we might be prepared to trade the idea for a return of The Ashes!

I rather suspect that Mr Justice Tomlin, as he then was, never really thought that his Practice Note would gain the fame that it has. I am sure he never thought that his name would be applied to the form of Order set out in that Note. It is strange how these names do come to be applied in the legal world. I am sure that Mrs Calderbank would never have thought (and maybe does not even know to this day) that her former husband's family name has been applied by lawyers to a form of offer of settlement that was never in fact made in the *Calderbank* case itself! She might be even more surprised to find that the Family Law Bar Association and the Solicitors Family Law Association compete annually in a golf match for the Calderbank Cup. Perhaps there is scope for such a match between the London Common Law and Commercial Bar Association and the Chancery Bar Association, the prize being the Tomlin Trophy.

Whatever Lord Tomlin might have thought about his Practice Note if he ever applied his mind to it again, I have no doubt that he would have been delighted to know that we celebrate today the 70th birthday of the Order that bears his name. Whilst three score years and ten is the biblical limit of life, I believe that the Tomlin Order will survive for many years to come and will probably outlive all of us.

If I had a glass in my hand at this precise moment, I would propose a toast to the Tomlin Order and wish it "many happy returns".

APPENDIX 7

Extract from *B-T v B-T*

B-T v B-T [1990] 2 F.L.R. 1[1]

(This table is included for historical purpose[2])

Summary of the available procedures

The differences between the various remedies are most graphically represented by my setting them out in tabular form.

A7–01

Type of order	Appeal	Fresh Action	Rehearing
1. County Court registrar,* by consent	Yes, without leave. Fresh evidence admissible without leave. Hearing *de novo*[3]	Yes	Yes, apply to the registrar*
2. High Court registrar,* by consent	ditto	Yes	No
3. County court judge, by consent	Yes, but only with leave of the judge. Need leave of the Court of Appeal to admit fresh evidence	Yes	Yes, apply to the judge
4. High court judge, by consent	ditto	Yes	No
5. County court registrar,* after contested hearing	Yes, without leave. Fresh evidence admissible. Hearing *de novo*	Yes	Maybe not
6. High Court registrar,* after contested hearing	ditto	Yes	No
7. County court judge after contested hearing	Yes, but with leave of judge or Court of Appeal. Need leave to admit fresh evedence	Yes	Maybe not
8. High Court judge	ditto	Yes	No

---

* Now "district judge".
[1] See paras 31–114, *et seq*.
[2] See para.32–118, above
[3] In the light of the Family Proceedings Rules introduced since the decision in *B-T v B-T*, this should now read "no": Ch.32, above. For an up-dated version of this table, see Bennett (1993) Fam. Law 84.

INDEX

ACAS conciliation officer
active involvement of, 36–36
continuity of employment, 36–34
disability discrimination claims and, 36–27
COT3 form, 36–25, 36–39
Employment Tribunals Act 1996, provisions of, 36–25
race discrimination claims and, 36–27
role of, 36–14, 36–19—36–22, 36–28
sex discrimination claims and, 36–27
unfair dismissal claims and 36–27

Accountants
authority to compromise, 4–07

Administrative court proceedings, resolution by agreement
agreed order, obtaining, 40–16—40–19
alternative dispute resolution, 40–05—40–06
costs upon withdrawal or settlement, 40–20—40–23
effect of compromise, 40–11—40–13
enforcement of compromise, 40–11—40–13
fresh decision, continuation of proceedings after, 40–24—40–26
introduction, 40–01—40–04
judicial review applications, 40–01—40–04

Administrative court proceedings, resolution by agreement—*cont.*
mediation in judicial review proceedings, 40–06
nature of compromise, 40–11—40–13
permission stage, 40–27—40–29
precedents for, A1–34
power to compromise, 40–07—40–10
withdrawal of proceedings, 40–14—40–15

Agreement
see also **Compromise**
binding agreement reached, examples of, 3–23—3–26
complete and certain agreement,
agreement to agree and the "future document", 3–55—3–57
failure to agree all material terms, 3–50
general principle, 3–49
terms too vague, 3–51—3–55
conditional compromise, 3–58
binding obligation to await future event, 3–61
condition subsequent, 3–63
not binding until future event, 3–59—3–60
part of a dispute, 3–65
unilaterally binding until future event, 3–62
"without prejudice" negotiations, 3–67

675

INDEX

Agreement—*cont.*
  formalities,
    deeds, 3–75
    generally, 3–71
    guarantee, 3–74
    land, 3–72—3–73
  identifiable agreement,
    binding, examples of, 3–23—3–26
    general, 3–22
    no binding agreement reached, examples of, 3–27—3–29
    presentation of cheque sent in settlement, 3–30—3–48
  intention to create legal relations, 3–68—3–70
  no binding agreement reached, examples of, 3–27—3–29
  presentation of cheque sent in settlement,
    American rule, 3–45
    conversion of cheque, 3–47
    determination of issue, 3–33—3–44
    "full and final settlement", sent in, 3–31
    issue, 3–30
    must seek to settle a dispute, 3–32
  rule of court or order,
    enforcement of a compromise, 11–17—11–20
    making agreement a, 9–09, 11–06

Alternative dispute resolution
  administrative court proceedings and, 40–05—40–06
  clinical negligence litigation and, 43–07
  encouragement by courts, 13–03, 43–03—43–09
  mediation, 43–06
  mediation agreements, provisions of, 43–21

Alternative dispute resolution—*cont.*
  personal injury cases and, 35–63
  settlement through,
    civil procedure rules and, 43–03—43–05
    confidentiality of, 43–14—43–20
    costs, consequences to parties failing to mediate, 43–03—43–09
    introduction, 43–01—43–02
    mediation, court's role in encouraging, 13–03, 43–03—43–09
    mediator, lack of privilege or immunity, 43–21
    merits of the case, relevance of, 43–10
    other attempts at settlement, relevance of, 43–11
    unreasonableness in refusing to agree to, mediation, 43–12—43–13
    "without prejudice" nature of the process, 43–14—43–19

Appeals, settlement of
  Court of Appeal, to,
    alternative dispute resolution and, 42–08
    child, relating to, 42–07
    "DBC" procedure, 42–03
    patient relating to, 42–07
    Tomlin orders and, 42–05
  judge, to,
    civil procedure rules and, 42–09—42–11
    "rehearing" provision, 42–10

Arbitrations
  compromise of, 1–02, 41–01—41–13

INDEX

Arbitrations—*cont.*
  construction disputes,
    claims to contribution to settlements, 39–39—39–50
  open offers, 41–16
  sealed offers,
    comparison with Part 36 payment, 41–18—41–29
    generally, 15–16, 41–17—41–20
  settlement of,
    costs, 41–15—41–29
    decision as to whether compromise concluded, 41–09—41–13
    enforcement of compromise, 41–06—41–08
    essential principles concerning compromise, 41–02—41–05
    form of an effective offer, 41–16—41–29
    setting aside consent award, 41–14
    substance of an effective offer, 41–16—41–29
  statutory scheme, 36–47—36–50
  unfair dismissal claims, 36–47—36–50

Assertions
  good faith and, 2–16
  want of good faith, 2–19

Assignments
  bare right to litigate, 6–89
  right of action,
    possibility of illegality in compromise, 4–79

Bad deal
  setting aside a consent order and, 32–92

Bankruptcy
  assignment, effects in connection with, and, 6–93
  illegal compromise, 4–78
  third parties, and, 6–75—6–77
  trustees in bankruptcy, 31–10

Barristers
  authority to compromise,
    differences between, and solicitors, 29–02, 29–14
  immunity from suit, 29–02—29–03, 29–22—29–24
  implied or ostensible authority,
    cannot compromise matter "collateral to the action", 4–06
  independent advisers,
    employment contracts and compromise, 36–31

Benefits
  recoupment of,
    personal injury claims, in, 35–54—35–55

Biggin v Permanite
  principle in, 39–40—39–58

Boundary disputes
  compromise agreement and, 38–07—38–09
  consent order and, 38–08
  finalise agreement by deed, 38–07
  precedents for, A1–27—A1–33
  Tomlin order and, 38–10

Breach of compromise
  acts amounting to, 8–03—8–10
  anticipatory,
    generally, 8–11
    implied term as to co-operation, 8–14
    renunciation, 8–12
    self-created impossibility, 8–13
  effects generally, 8–01—8–02
  innocent party's choice on, 8–15
  promised acts, 8–03—8–10

INDEX

Business tenancies
  contracting out,
    generally, 37–05—37–11
    notice regime, 37–05—37–07
    order excluding effect of 1954 Act, 37–08
    statutory provisions, 37–05—37–06
  new tenancy,
    conclusion of legally binding agreement, 37–13
    Tomlin order and, 37–12
    risk of losing right to, 37–14
    specific performance remedy, 37–23
    "subject to contract", 37–21
    types of agreement, 37–15—37–25
  introduction, 37–04
  surrender of tenancy, 37–26—37–28
  vacation, agreement for,
    compensation, entitlement to, 37–27

***Calderbank* offers**
  admissibility as to costs, 27–05
  costs and matrimonial finance cases, 34–08—34–13
  outside Part 36, 26–02, 26–05—26–07
  responses to "without prejudice" letters, 27–14
  review of, 26–07
  settlement process in civil justice prior to 1999, 13–01

Case management
  active intervention to achieve early settlement, 22–09—22–12

Champertous agreements
  assignment of right of action, 4–79

Chancery litigation
  agreed orders, 31–30
  appeals, 31–31—31–32
  application to be released from undertaking, 31–42
  business assigned to Chancery Division, by statute, 31–01
  charities, 31–23—31–24
  declarations, 31–33
  court-appointed receivers, 31–17
  disqualification orders, 31–12—31–16
  insolvency,
    appeals, 31–09
    companies, 31–03—31–05
    individuals, 31–06—31–08
  interim applications,
    adjournments, 31–34—31–36
    consent order, 31–37
    final judgment, 31–39
    injunction, 31–37
    undertakings, 31–36
  liquidators, 31–10
  masters,
    informing Chancery Chambers of settlement, 31–41
    powers of, 31–40—31–41
  personal representatives, 31–18—31–22
  practice and procedure,
    agreed orders, 31–30
    appeals, 31–31—31–32
    declarations, 31–33
    interim applications, 31–34—31–39
    masters, 31–40—31–41
    release from undertaking, 31–42
  precedents for, A1–15—A1–20
  probate claims, 31–25—31–29
  trustees, 31–18
  trustees in bankruptcy, 31–10
  unfair prejudice, 31–11

678

INDEX

Charities
  application to Charity Commissioners, 31-23
  ex gratia payments, 31-24
  statutory powers of trustees, 31-23

Cheque
  payment by as performance, 7-03
  sent in settlement,
    American rule, 3-45
    conversion of cheque, 3-47
    determination of issue, 3-33—3-44
    "full and final settlement" offer, 3-31
    issue of, 3-30
    must seek to settle a dispute, 3-32

Children
  agreements relating to, 32-136—32-139
  incapacity, 4-02
  matrimonial finance cases and, 34-17
  Part 36 offer or payment, acceptance on behalf of, 22-02—22-04
  personal injury claims involving,
    approval of the court, obtaining, 35-05—35-09
    change of circumstances and setting aside consent orders, 35-14
    costs, 35-56—35-63
    failure to obtain approval, 35-10—35-13
    introduction, 35-01—35-09
    litigation friend, 35-07
    money laundering, 35-64
    periodical payments, order for, 35-29—35-47

Children—*cont.*
  personal injury claims involving
    periodical payments, procedure for obtaining, 35-48—35-53
    provisional damages, 35-24—35-28
    recoupment of benefits, 35-54—35-55
    setting aside consent orders, 35-14
    structured settlements, 35-29—35-47

Civil justice reforms, post 1999
  Part 36 and, 13-03

Civil procedure rules
  alternative dispute resolution and, 43-03—43-05
  appeals to judge, settlement of, 42-09—42-11
  consent order, practice of obtaining, 10-17—10-20
  mixed money and non-money claims and the,
  flexibility in making Part 36 payment, 19-02—19-05
  Part 20, *see* **Part 20**
  Part 36, *see* **Part 36**
  payment into court and the, 13-02
  pre-action offers and, 15-03—15-04
  pre-action protocols, 13-06

Companies
  capacity to compromise, 4-09

Compromise
  see also **Agreement**
  breach of, *see* **Breach of compromise**
  complete and certain agreement, agreement to agree and the "future document", 3-55—3-57

679

INDEX

Compromise—*cont.*
  complete and certain
    agreement—*cont.*
      failure to agree all material
        terms, 3–50
      general principle, 3–49
      terms too vague, 3–51—3–55
  condition subsequent, 3–63
  conditional compromise,
    binding obligation to await
      future event, 3–61
    condition subsequent, 3–63
    not binding until future event,
      3–59—3–60
    part of a dispute, 3–65
    unilaterally binding until
      future event, 3–62
    "without prejudice"
      negotiations, 3–67
  consideration, 3–02—3–21
  effect,
    see **effects of compromise**
  formalities,
    deeds, 3–75
    generally, 3–71
    guarantee, 3–74
    land, 3–72—3–73
  identifiable agreement,
    binding agreement, examples
      of, 3–23—3–26
    general, 3–22
    no binding agrement, examples
      of, 3–27—3–29
    presentation of cheque sent in
      settlement, 3–30—3–48
  illegal,
    assignment of a right of action,
      4–79—4–81
    bankruptcy, 4–78
    compromise of disputes
      involving illegality,
      4–72—4–74

Compromise—*cont.*
  illegal—*cont.*
    employment law, 4–83
    generally, 4–71
    matrimonial financial
      provision, 4–76
    ousting jurisdiction, 4–75
    restrictive trade practices,
      4–82—4–83
    stifling a prosecution, 4–77
  impeachment of a,
    see **impeachment of a**
    compromise
  intention to create legal
    relations, 3–68—3–70
  part of a dispute, 3–65—3–67
  unilaterally binding until future
    event, 3–62
  valid, essential requirements of,
    complete and certain
      agreement, 3–49—3–64
    consideration, 3–02—3–21
    formalities, 3–71—3–75
    identifible agreement,
      3–22—3–29
    intention to create legal
      relations, 3–68—3–70
    introduction, 3–01
    terms of agreement, 3–64
Confidentiality
  alternative dispute resolution
    and, 43–14—43–20
  legal advisers, role of in
    compromise, 28–03—28–04
  securing confidentiality of
    agreement, 10–28—10–31
Conflicts of interest
  professional ethics and
    responsibilities,
    28–05—28–06
Consent judgment
  see **Consent order**

Consent order
  boundary disputes, 38–08
  Chancery litigation,
    interim applications, 31–37
  effects of compromise,
    deriving from consent order or judgment, 6-19—6-24
  employment contracts and, 36-42—36-44
  implication for other parties of, 6-26—6-33
  Inheritance Act disputes,
    entry and filing of consent order, 33–19
    previous consent order, effect of, 33-06—33-08
  insolvency, 31-06—31-08
  jurisdiction,
    relevance of, in construing a consent order, 5-36—5-41
    terms of consent order outside ordinary, jurisdiction, 10-09—10-16
  practice of obtaining consent order,
    civil procedure rules and the, 10-17—10-20
    notification of settlement to court, 10–25
    recording of the consent, 10–04
    settlement of appeals, 10-26—10-27
    settlements reached just before or during trial, 10–21
    settlements requiring approval of the court, 10-22—10-24
  precedents for draft consent orders, A1-12—A1-14

Consent order—*cont.*
  setting aside,
    Employment Tribunal or Employment Appeal Tribunal order, 36–44
    matrimonial proceedings, in *see* **Matrimonial disputes**
    mentally disordered persons and patients, personal injury claims, 35–14
    personal injury claims, children, 35–14
    structured settlements and, 35–50
    terms of compromise, implied terms as to, 5–47
  variation of,
    matrimonial proceedings, 32-134—32-135

Consideration
  actual forbearance to sue, 3–03
  compromise proper, 3-07—3-09
  definition of, 3–02
  executed, 3–02
  executory, 3–02
  intention to pursue claim, 3-19—3-21
  lack of,
    baseless claim, 3–11
    courts finding, 3–10
    existing debts, 3–12
    frivolous claim, 3–11
    illegal claim, 3–11
    part payment of debt, 3-12—3-18
    past consideration, 3–12
    vexatious claim, 3–11
  promised forbearance to sue, 3–03

Construction disputes
  adjudication,
    compromised disputes and, 39-65—39-67

INDEX

Construction disputes—*cont.*
  adjudication—*cont.*
    forbearance from, 39–68
    Housing Grants, Construction and Regeneration Act, 1996, 39–64
    interim nature of, 39–64
  amendment of pleadings between date of offer and judgment,
    claimant succeeds on late amendment, 39–60
    defendant succeeds on late amendment, 39–61—39–62
  arbitration,
    claims for contribution to the settlement, 39–39—39–50
  claims for contribution to the settlement,
    admissibility of advice received, 39–51—39–54
    indemnities, 39–58
    multi-party cases, 39–55—39–57
    principle in *Biggin v Permanite*, 39–40—39–43
    proof of a reasonable settlement, 39–44—39–50
    relevance of advice, 39–51—39–54
  construction contracts,
    certificates, 39–12—39–13
    "clean break" agreements, 39–14
    retentions, 39–15
    structure of, 39–09—39–11
  contractor's progress,
    "acceleration agreements", 39–04—39–05
    reallocation of risk, 39–05
  defects, responsibility for existing, 39–06—39–08
  introduction, 39–01

Construction disputes—*cont.*
  issues to be addressed in compromise of dispute,
    causes of action in respect of which damage has, not yet accrued, 39–18—39–20
    effects of offers to settle, 39–24—39–26
    latent defects, 39–21—39–22
    multiple causes of action, 39–17
    settling claims for professional negligence, 39–23
  multiple parties,
    assignments, 39–33—39–34
    claims against joint contractors, 39–35
    claims against successive contract breakers, 6–39—6–40, 39–36
    global settlements, 39–38
    impugning settlements for duress, 39–37
    indemnities, 39–33—39–34
    "same damage", 6–52, 39–28—39–32
    subrogation rights, 39–33—39–34
  Scott schedule, 39–16
  trials of preliminary issues, 39–16
  value added tax, 39–63

Costs
  acceptance of Part 36 offer or payment,
    consequences of, 21–10
    number of claimants jointly or in the alternative, 21–07—21–08
    relating to part only of claim, 21–05—21–06

Costs—*cont.*
acceptance of Part 36 offer or payment—*cont.*
several liability and, 21–09
with court's permission, 22–13—22–14
within prescribed time, 21–04
arbitration and, 41–15—41–29
clarification of Part 36 offer and, 20–04
clarification of payment notice, 20–04
failure to beat a Part 36 offer or payment and, 23–19
indemnity,
settlement and, 13–09—13–10, 23–18—23–19
issue left to court, 9–03—9–05
no order as to, 23–20
on setting aside a compromise, 12–07
Part 36 and, 14–02—14–11
pre-action,
settlement and, 13–08
standard costs,
distinction between indemnity costs and, 13–09
unaccepted pre-action offers and, 15–09

Counter-assertions
good faith and, 2–16

Court of Protection
settlement of personal injury claims,
patients and, 35–19—35–21

Court proceedings
attitude of courts to compromise, 10–02—10–03
ensuring reality of consent, 10–03
indorsement of counsels" brief, 10–05

Court proceedings—*cont.*
jurisdiction problems,
forum, 10–07
generally, 10–06
terms of consent order outside ordinary, jurisdiction, 10–09—10–16
tribunal within the appropriate forum, 10–08
practice of obtaining consent order,
civil procedure rules and the, 10–17—10–20
notification of settlement to court, 10–25
settlement of appeals, 10–26—10–27
settlements reached just before or during trial, 10–21
settlements requiring approval of the court, 10–22—10–24
recording of the consent, 10–04

Damages
nominal,
legal advisers and breach of duty, 29–27
personal injury case,
periodical payment award and Part 36, 25–10
provisional, and Part 36, 25–07—25–09

Disputes
actual,
assertion of claim, 2–02—2–07
examples of, 2–03—2–07
existence of, 2–02, 2–14
adjudication on, 1–01
adversarial system, 1–02
bona fide nature of, 2–16
construction,
see **Construction disputes**

INDEX

Disputes—*cont.*
  law or fact, 2-15—2-18
  land,
    see **Land disputes**
  matrimonial,
    see **Matrimonial disputes**
  potential dispute,
    "buying off" of, 2-10
    existence of, 2-14
    meaning of, 2-08
    unarticulated, 2-12—2-14

Divorce
  see **Matrimonial disputes**

Duress
  see also **Undue influence**
  contracting party,
    generally, 4-52—4-53
  examples in the context of compromise,
    economic duress, 4-62—4-65
    threat of proceedings, 4-54—4-55
    threat of otherwise lawful act, 4-61
    threat of unlawful act, 4-57—4-60

Effect of compromise
  appeals, 6-25
  assignment, effects in connection with,
    bankruptcy, 6-93
    "bare right to litigate", 6-89
    common law provisions, 6-87
    death, 6-92
    express provision by parties, 6-87
    identity of a person material to, 6-88
    right of wife to maintenance, 6-90
    vicarious performance, 6-86

Effect of compromise—*cont.*
  as between the parties,
    agreed judgment, 6-05—6-06
    agreed order, 6-05—6-06
    end of dispute, 6-01—6-02
    identifying the disputes resolved, 6-03
    matters left out, 6-07—6-17
    no judgment, 6-04
    no order, 6-04
  commercial litigation,
    complexities, 6-59—6-61
  concurrent obligations, 6-30—6-31
  consequent order, without,
    concurrent contract-breakers, 6-39
    concurrent tortfeasors, 6-39
    effects in connection with other parties, 6-36
    fresh action to set aside, 6-35
    unaffected by Civil Liability (Contribution) Act, 1978, 6-38
  construction litigation,
    complexities, 6-59—6-61
  contribution claims between defendants and other parties, 6-49—6-52
  enforceability of agreed order for possession, 6-33
  financial accounting involving other parties, 6-55—6-59
  joint contractor claimants, 6-53
  joint contractors, 6-45—6-48
  joint obligations, 6-30
  joint tortfeasors, 6-41—6-44
  other effects,
    deriving from consent order or judgment, 6-19
    fresh proceedings to set aside, 6-20
    interim order by consent, 6-21—6-24

INDEX

Effect of compromise—*cont.*
  third parties,
    bankruptcy and, 6–75—6–77
    Civil Liability (Contribution) Act 1978 exception, 6–28—6–29
    effects upon, 6–62—6–84
    family disputes, 6–78
    fraud, 6–81
    impeachment by or on behalf of, 6–74—6–77
    implications on, 6–26—6–27
    voluntary transfers of assets, 6–79
  Torts (Interference with Goods) Act 1997, 6–54

Effectuation of a compromise
  generally, 9–01—9–02
  methods of,
    consent judgment for the payment of money, 9–10—9–11
    consent judgment providing time for payment, 9–13—9–15
    deed or memorandum of agreement, 9–08
    exchange of letters, 9–07
    making agreement an order or rule of court, 9–09
    memorandum of, 9–08
    payment of money without judgment, 9–16—9–17
    Tomlin order, 9–17, 9–21—9–33
  other methods,
    acceptance of Part 36 payment, 9–42
    adjournment of proceedings, 9–34—9–35
    discontinuance of proceedings, 9–36—9–39

Effectuation of a compromise—*cont.*
  other methods—*cont.*
    dismissal of proceedings, 9–40
    "no order" by consent, 9–41
    withdrawal of proceedings, 9–36—9–39

Employment contracts
  ACAS conciliation officer, settlement achieved through intervention of,
    active involvement of, 36–36
    continuity of employment, 36–34
    disability discrimination claims and, 36–27
    COT3 form, 36–25, 36–39
    Employment Tribunals Act 1996, provisions of, 36–25
    race discrimination claims and, 36–27
    role of, 36–14, 36–19—36–22, 36–28
    sex discrimination claims and, 36–27
    unfair dismissal claims and 36–27
  compromise agreements,
    independent advisers, 36–31—36–32
    scope of, 36–33
    statutory provisions to create a binding, 36–29
  continuity of employment, reinstated or re-engaged employee, 36–34
  employment tribunals,
    "interests of justice" review by, 36–45
    mechanics of settlement, 36–39—36–42

INDEX

Employment contracts—*cont.*
introduction, 36–01—36–03
mechanics of settlement,
employment tribunals,
36–39—36–42
compensation, 36–42
consent order, 36–40
COT3 form, 36–39
"interests of justice" review
by, 36–45
setting aside a consent order,
36–44
setting aside an agreed
settlement, 36–43
references, 36–09—36–13
restraint of trade, unreasonable,
covenants unenforceable, 4–83
statutory arbitration scheme,
36–47—36–50
statutory claims by employees,
ACAS conciliation officers,
role of, 36–14,
36–19—36–22
compromise agreements and
Employment Rights Act,
1996, 36–20
compromise of rights under
other legislation, 36–21
exceptions to prohibition
against contracting-out,
36–18
"independent advisers", role
of, 36–14
prohibition against contracting
out of statutory rights,
36–15—36–17
stress-related personal injury,
36–07—36–08
Transfer of Undertakings
(Protection of Employment)
Regulations 1981
absence of express provisions,
compromise of claims,
36–38

Employment contracts—*cont.*
Transfer of Undertakings
(Protection of Employment)
Regulations 1981—*cont.*
ACAS agreements, 36–36
compromise agreements,
36–36
rights and duties of employees,
36–35
Enforcement of compromise
generally, 11–01
no order or judgment,
11–02—11–03
order or judgment,
agreed order reciting terms of
agreement, 11–29—11–32
agreement filed and made a
rule of court, 11–06
enforcement, 11–17—11–20
enforcement of Tomlin order,
11–21—11–27
generally, 11–04—11–05
injunction by consent or
undertaking,
11–33—11–35
order not reflecting finality,
11–28
"order of court" or "rule of
court", 11–14—11–16
status of agreement made a
rule of court,
11–07—11–13
Estoppel
discharge of obligation under a
compromise, 7–10
"without prejudice" negotiations
and, 27–45
Exchange of information
disclosure prior to negotiations,
documentation, 13–05
information, 13–05
letters,
method of compromise, 9–07
pre-action protocols,
13–06—13–07

INDEX

Expert witnesses
capacity to compromise, 4–08

Formalities of a valid compromise
boundary disputes, 3–73
contract of guarantee, 3–74
creation of a lease, 3–73
deeds, 3–75
generally, 3–71
land, 3–72—3–73
transfer of an acknowledged title, 3–73

Fraud
matrimonial disputes,
  setting aside consent order, 32–88
relief against consequences of, equity and, 6–81

Frustration
discharge of obligations under a compromise, 7–08
examples of, 7–11

"Good faith"
counter-assertions and, 2–16
denials and, 2–16
want of "good faith", 2–19

Husband and wife
assignability of right of wife to maintenance, 6–90
divorce, see **Matrimonial disputes**
impeachment by third parties when husband becomes bankrupt, 6–76
undue influence,
  independent legal advise and, 4–69

Illegality
assignment of a right of action, 4–79—4–81

Illegality—*cont.*
bankruptcy, 4–78
compromise of disputes involving issues of, 4–72—4–74
employment law, 4–83
generally, 4–71
matrimonial financial provision, 4–76
ousting jurisdiction, 4–75
restrictive trade practices, 4–82—4–83
stifling a prosecution, 4–77

Impeachment of a compromise
duress,
  effect, 4–70
  examples of, 4–54
  generally, 4–52
incapacity,
  children, 4–02
  companies, 4–09
  expert witnesses, 4–08
  legal advisers, 4–06
  local authorities, 4–10
  mentally disordered persons, 4–03
  mentally disordered patients, 4–03—4–05
  non-legal advisers, 4–07
  partners, 4–11
  representatives, 4–07
  representative parties, 4–12
  represented parties acting personally, 4–13
illegality,
  assignment of a right of action, 4–79—4–81
  bankruptcy, 4–78
  compromise of disputes involving issues of, 4–72—4–74
  employment law, 4–83
  generally, 4–71

687

Impeachment of a compromise—*cont.*
illegality—*cont.*
matrimonial financial provision, 4–76
ousting jurisdiction, 4–75
restrictive trade practices, 4–82—4–83
stifling a prosecution, 4–77
misrepresentation,
contracts *uberrimae fidei*, 4–38—4–44
effect of a, 4–45—4–50
generally, 4–37
relief available, 4–51
mistake,
generally, 4–14
relief sought or given, 4–15
mistake in compromise,
law, of, 4–20
mistaken record of compromise, 4–30—4–36
mutual mistake about fundamental matter, 4–16—4–20
mutual mistake of opinion, 4–19
mutual misunderstanding of terms, 4–21
unilateral mistake, 4–22—4–29
undue influence,
effect, 4–70
generally, 4–66—4–68
husband and wife, 4–69

Incapacity
impeachment of a compromise,
accountants, 4–07
children, 4–02
companies, 4–09
expert witnesses, 4–08
legal advisers, 4–06

Incapacity—*cont.*
impeachment of a compromise—*cont.*
local authorities, 4–10
mentally disordered persons, 4–03
mentally disordered patients, 4–03—4–05
non-legal advisers, 4–07
partners, 4–11
representative parties, 4–12
represented parties acting personally, 4–13

Inheritance Act disputes
compromise of claims under the Act,
jurisdiction, 33–10—33–15
contracting out, 33–02—33–05
enforcement, 33–16
entry and filing of consent order, 33–19
practice, 33–17—33–19
preliminary, 33–01
previous compromise, effect of, 33–06—33–08
previous consent order, effect of, 33–06—33–08
setting aside, 33–16
variation of previous maintenance agreement, 33–09

Insolvency
appeals, 31–09
companies, 31–03—31–05
consent orders, 31–06—31–08
court-appointed receivers, 31–17
individuals,
consent orders, 31–06—31–08
liquidator,
power to compromise claims, 31–10
trustee in bankruptcy,
power to compromise claims, 31–10

INDEX

Insurance interests
co-insurer,
  contribution from, 30–14
  rateable proportion clause, 30–14
"follow the settlements" clause and reinsurance, 30–15—30–17
introduction, 30–01
insured's claim,
  nature of the "settlement", 30–18
re-insurance and "follow the settlements" clause, 30–15—30–17
third parties, settlement with and effects on,
  consent judgment, 30–09—30–10
  general principle, 30–03
  insured losses, 30–04—30–05
  Part 36 payment, 30–05—30–08
  uninsured losses, 30–04—30–05
third parties, settlement with and effects as between insurer and insured,
  general law of insurance, 30–11
  rights of subrogation, 30–12—30–13

Judicial review
administrative court proceedings, resolution by agreement, 40–01—40–04
costs upon withdrawal or settlement of, 40–20—40–23
mediation in, 40–06

Jurisdiction
ousting,
  illegal compromise, 4–75

Jurisdiction—*cont.*
relevance of, in construing a consent order, 5–36—5–41
terms of consent order outside ordinary jurisdiction, 10–09—10–16

Land disputes
compromise involving transfer of title to land, 4–41
compromise of,
  assignment of rights arising from a compromise, 38–04
  boundaries, 38–07—38–09
  declarations, 38–03
  disclosure of defects, 38–05
  introduction, 38–01—38–06
  third parties and, 38–06
formalities of a valid compromise, 3–72—3–73

Landlord and tenant
business tenancies,
  contracting out, 37–05—37–11
  new tenancy, 37–12—37–25
  introduction, 37–04
  surrender of tenancy, 37–26—37–28
forfeiture,
  compromise of proceedings, 37–50—37–55
precedents for, A1–27—A1–33
relief from forfeiture,
  compromise of proceedings, 37–50—37–55
residential tenancies,
  court's jurisdiction, 37–34
  enforcement of orders, 37–45
  introduction, 37–29—37–30
  no contracting out, 37–31—37–33

689

INDEX

Landlord and tenant—*cont.*
residential tenancies—*cont.*
obtaining an "agreed" order, 37–39—37–42
occupants without statutory protection, 37–43—37–44
setting aside order for possession, 37–48
statutory provision, 37–34—37–38
tenancy springing from a compromise, 37–49
variation of order for possession, 37–46—37–47

Legal advice
bad legal advice,
disregarding agreements in matrimonial disputes, 32–77—32–79
setting aside consent orders, 32–93—32–95
independent,
undue influence and, 4–67—4–69
relevance to reasonableness of settlement, 39–51—39–57

Legal advisers
see also individual headings
Barristers and Solicitors
authority to compromise,
actual, 29–04—29–05
express, 29–04—29–05, 29–12
differences between barristers and solicitors, 29–02, 29–14
immunity from suit, 29–02—29–03
implied, 29–05—29–14
incidental, 29–12
interim stages of case, 29–12, 29–14
liability to client, 29–01
ostensible, 29–06—29–09, 29–15—29–16

Legal advisers—*cont.*
bad advice of,
disregarding agreements in matrimonial disputes, 32–77—32–79
setting aside consent orders, 32–93—32–95
barristers,
immunity from suit, 29–02—29–03, 29–22—29–24
construction disputes and, 39–51
evidence of,
proceedings brought by former client, 29–32
impeachment of a compromise and, 4–06
landlord and tenant negotiations, 37–25
liabilities of,
abolition of immunity in civil litigation, 29–24
breach of duty, 29–26—29–30
court determination of monetary value of loss, 29–31
immunity from suit of barrister, 29–02—29–03, 29–22—29–24
negligence, 29–24—29–26, 29–31
nominal damages where no loss occasioned, 29–27
misunderstandings between client and,
discretionary jurisdiction to set aside compromise, 29–18—29–21
extent of authority, 29–18—29–20
generally, 29–17

INDEX

Legal advisers—*cont.*
 role of in compromise,
  "confidential" matters disclosed by client or opponent, 28–03—28–04
  conflicts of interest, 28–05—28–06
  generally, 28–01—28–02
  informing client of offer of settlement, 28–09
  keeping the court informed, 28–12
  overall duties to client in compromise, 28–10
  unfounded claims, 28–07—28–08

Legal aid
 consent orders, 3–64
 costs, 9–06

Liquidator
 power to compromise claims, 31–10
 right of action assigned to, 4–81

Local authorities
 capacity to compromise, 4–10

Maintenance agreements
 alteration of, 32–14—32–19
 Child Support Act 1991, effect of on, 32–19
 Children Act 1989 and, 32–17—32–18
 common law and, 32–09
 definition of, 32–10
 Matrimonial Causes Act 1973 and, 32–08—32–16
 preliminary, 32–08
 written agreements,
  enforcement of, 32–13
  impeachment of, 32–12

Mareva injunction
 effects of a compromise, 6–05

Matrimonial disputes
 agreements, types of,
  children, relating to, 32–01, 32–136—32–139
  disposal of divorce or judicial separation suit, 32–01, 32–20—32–22
  divorce or judicial separation proceedings not necessarily involved, 32–01—32–19
  final disposal of financial and property, applications, 32–01, 32–31—32–135
  interim financial provision, 32–01, 32–23—32–30
 Child Support Act 1991
  effect of, on maintenance agreements, 32–19
 Children Act 1989
  grounds for alteration of maintenance agreements, 32–17
  maintenance agreements governed solely or partially by, 32–17—32–18
  powers on alteration, 32–18
 children, agreements relating to, 32–136—32–139
 costs,
  Calderbank offers and, 34–08—34–13
  children's cases, 34–17
  effect of the offer on, 34–14—34–16
  general approach as to, 34–04—34–07
  preliminary, 34–01—34–03
  "without prejudice" offer and, 34–08—34–09

INDEX

Matrimonial disputes—*cont.*
  disregarding agreements before an order is made,
    bad legal advice, 32–77—32–79
    grounds for, 32–72—32–76
    "internal" undue pressure, 32–77—32–79
    other factors even if invalidating ground exists, 32–80
    preliminary, 32–71
  divorce or judicial separation, agreement where no, proceedings for,
    Child Support Act 1991, effect of, on maintenance, agreements, 32–19
    Children Act 1989, maintenance agreements governed, by, 32–17—32–18
    maintenance and separation agreements, 32–08—32–16
    Married Womens" Property Act 1882, 32–03—32–07
    Matrimonial Causes Act 1973, 32–08—32–16
  divorce or judicial separation, where proceedings for,
    generally, 32–20
    agreement involving new petition, 32–22
    no compromise prior to, 32–21
  final disposal of financial and property applications,
    costs, 34–01—34–17
    disregarding agreements before an order is made, 32–71—32–80
    FDR hearings, 32–44—32–50

Matrimonial disputes—*cont.*
  final disposal of financial and property applications—*cont.*
    nature of an agreement, 32–33—32–43
    preliminary, 32–31—32–33
    prior agreement, securing an order reflecting, 32–54—32–70
    relevance of an agreement, 32–33—32–43
    "rule of court", agreements filed and made, 32–128—32–133
    setting aside consent orders, 32–81—32–127
    statutory intervention, 32–51—32–53
    variation of consent orders, 32–134—32–135
  illegal compromises and, 4–76
  interim financial provision, consent orders "without prejudice" to final,
  orders, 32–20
    court's practice, 32–28
    nature of agreement, 32–27
    preliminary, 32–27
    setting aside, 32–29
    variation, 32–29
  interim stages of proceedings,
    discovery of resources, 32–25
    financial provision, 32–27—32–30
    non-molestation, 32–24
    occupation of matrimonial home, 32–24
    preliminary, 32–23
    preservation of assets, 32–25
    undertakings, effect of "until further order", 32–26
  maintenance agreements, alteration of, 32–14—32–19

Matrimonial disputes—*cont.*
  maintenance agreements—*cont.*
    Child Support Act 1991, effect of on, 32–19
    Children Act 1989 and, 32–17—32–18
    common law and, 32–09
    definition of, 32–10
    enforcement of written agreements, 32–13
    impeachment of written agreements, 32–12
    Matrimonial Causes Act 1973 and, 32–08—32–16
    preliminary, 32–08
    written agreements, 32–11
  Married Women's Property Act 1882, proceedings under,
    definition of property, 32–03
    intervention of third parties, 32–07
    introduction, 32–03
    jurisdiction of the court, 32–04
    ousting the jurisdiction of the court, 32–05
    parties' agreement, 32–04
    setting aside, 32–06
  Matrimonial Causes Act 1973
    alteration of maintenance agreements governed only by, 32–15
    definition of maintenance agreement, 32–10
    enforcement of a written agreement, 32–13
    final disposal of financial and property,
  applications, 32–51—32–53
    powers on alteration, 32–16
    written maintenance agreements, 32–11

Matrimonial disputes—*cont.*
  prior agreement, securing an order reflecting a,
    both parties still in agreement, 32–54—32–64
    contents of agreed order, 32–60—32–63
    phraseology of agreed order, 32–61—32–63
    resiling from agreement, by one party, 32–65—32–70
    undertakings, 32–64
  setting aside consent orders,
    appeals, 32–125
    application for rehearing, 32–124
    bad deal, 32–92
    change in the law, 32–111
    Child Support Act 1991, 32–110
    death of party, unexpected, 32–107
    delay, 32–112—32–113
    erroneous valuations, 32–101—32–106
    failure to disclose material facts before order is made, 32–85—32–87
    failure to observe statutory provision, 32–96
    fraud, 32–88
    fresh action, 32–126
    grounds for, 32–84—32–113
    legal advice, bad, 32–93—32–95
    misrepresentation, 32–88
    mistake, 32–89
    practice, 32–114—32–123
    preliminary, 32–81—32–83
    rejection of application *in limine*, 32–127
    remarriage, 32–108

Matrimonial disputes—*cont.*
setting aside consent orders—*cont.*
supervening events, 32–97—32–113
undue influence, 32–90—32–91

Mediation
see **Alternative dispute resolution**

Mentally disordered persons and patients
capacity to compromise, 4–03—4–05
definition of, 4–04
Inheritance Act settlements, approval by court, 33–18
guardian ad litem, representation by, 33–18
Part 36 offer, acceptance of, 22–02—22–04
personal injury claims involving,
approval of the court, obtaining, 35–05—35–09
change of circumstances and setting aside consent orders, 35–14
costs, 35–56—35–63
Court of Protection, 35–19—35–21
failure to obtain approval, 35–10—35–13
introduction, 35–01—35–09
litigation friend, 35–07
money laundering, 35–64
periodical payments, order for, 35–29—35–47
periodical payments, procedure for obtaining, 35–48—35–53
provisional damages, 35–24—35–28
recoupment of benefits, 35–54—35–55

Mentally disordered persons and patients—*cont.*
personal injury claims involving—*cont.*
setting aside consent orders, 35–14
structured settlements, 35–29—35–47

Methods of compromise
consent judgment for the payment of money, 9–10—9–11
consent judgment providing time for payment, 9–13—9–15
deed or memorandum of agreement, 9–08
exchange of letters, 9–07
making agreement an order or rule of court, 9–09
memorandum of, 9–08
payment of money without judgment, 9–16—9–17
Tomlin order, 9–17, 9–21—9–33

Misrepresentation
contracts *uberrimae fidei*, 4–38—4–50
effect of a, 4–45—4–50
generally, 4–37
obtaining order for possession by,
residential tenancies, 37–48
relief available,
rescission, 4–51
setting aside consent orders, 32–88

Mistake in compromise
generally, 4–14
law, of, 4–20
mistaken record of compromise, 4–30—4–36
mutual mistake about fundamental matter, 4–16—4–20

INDEX

Mistake in compromise—*cont.*
  mutual mistake of opinion, 4–19
  mutual misunderstanding of terms, 4–21
  setting aside consent orders, 32–89
  unilateral mistake, 4–22—4–29
  relief sought or given, 4–15

Multi-party litigation
  construction disputes,
    claims for contribution to the settlement, 39–55—39–57
  effect of compromise,
    third parties, impeachment by or on behalf of, 6–74—6–77

Negligence
  legal advisers,
    abolition of immunity in civil litigation, 29–24
    actions of, amounting to, 29–25—29–26

Negotiation
  Part 36 offers, 13–04
  "without prejudice" rule, 13–04

Non-legal advisers
  capacity to compromise, 4–07

Obligations, satisfaction and discharge under compromise
  other than by performance,
    estoppel, 7–10
    frustration, 7–11—7–12
    generally, 7–08
    waiver, 7–09
  performance,
    agreement collateral to compromise, 7–06
    "entire" compromise, 7–05
    generally, 7–02
    mutually dependent obligations, 7–07
    payment by cheque, 7–03
    payment by instalments, 7–04

Offers
  see also **Part 36**
  Calderbank offer, 26–02, 26–05—26–07
  open,
    arbitration and, 41–16
    outside scope of Part 36, 26–02, 26–08—26–10
    value of, 26–09
  outside scope of Part 36
    Calderbank offer, 26–02, 26–05—26–07
    costs, 26–03
    open offer, 26–02, 26–08—26–10
    "without prejudice", 26–02, 26–04, 26–11
  sealed,
    arbitration and, 41–16—41–29
  tactical, 23–30—23–32
  "without prejudice", 26–02, 26–04, 26–11

Part 20 claim
  definition of, 25–02
  effect of, 25–03—25–04

Part 36
  acceptance of offer other than with the court's permission,
    consequences of, 21–13—21–16
    costs, 21–04—21–10
    enforcement of, 21–16
    filing with court, 21–02
    interest, 21–12
    introduction, 21–01
    mechanics of payment out, 21–11
    written notice, 21–02
  acceptance with the court's permission,
    children, 22–02—22–04

695

INDEX

Part 36—cont.
    costs, 22–13—22–14
    late acceptance, 22–06—22–12
    late Part 36 offer or payment,
        22–06—22–12
    patients, 22–02—22–04
    several defendants, 22–05
apportionment of money
    accepted in Fatal Accidents
    Act claims, 25–12
arbitration and, 41–15—41–29
clarification of offer,
    costs and, 20–04
    introduction, 20–01
    rule, 20–02—20–03
clarification of payment notice,
    costs and, 20–04
    introduction, 20–01
    rule, 20–02—20–03
converting an ordered payment
    into court into a Part 36
    payment, 25–11
costs and, 14–02, 18–14
effectuation of a compromise,
    acceptance of Part 36 offer,
        9–42
failure to beat offer or payment,
    claimant's offer,
        23–09—23–11
    defendant's offer: mixed claim,
        23–06—23–07
    defendant's offer: money
        claim, 23–02—23–05
    defendant's offer: non-money
        claim, 23–04—23–05
    enhanced rate of interest,
        23–12—23–26
    exception to rule on grounds
        of injustice, 23–08
    introduction, 23–01
    matters court has regard to,
        23–27—23–32
    narrow beating,

Part 36—cont.
    forms, A5–01
    introduction to, 14–01
    means of enforcement of a
        compromise, 9–42
    mixed money and non-money
        claims,
    payment under the old rules,
        19–01
    payment under the civil
        procedure rules, 19–05
negotiation and, 13–04
offers outside,
    Calderbank offers,
        26–05—26–07
    open offer, 14–03,
        26–08—26–10
    oral, 14–03
    "without prejudice", 14–03,
        26–02, 26–04, 26–11
offers within,
    exceptions to rule of non
        communication,
        14–08—14–11
    rule of non communication to
        trial judge, 14–07—14–08
    "without prejudice except as
        to costs", 14–06
"opt into"
    money claim, 14–04
    non-money claim,
        14–04—14–05
payment,
    definition of, 18–01
    effectiveness of, outside 21 day
        rule, 18–16
    mixed money and non-money
        claims, 19–01—19–05
    withdrawal of, 18–14, 18–17
periodical payment award in
    personal injury case, 25–10
precedents for, A1–01—A1–11
provisional damages and,
    25–07—25–09

Part 36—*cont.*
  requirements of Part 36 offers,
    acceptance of liability up to specified proportion, 16–10
    alteration of offers, 17–07
    counterclaims, 16–11
    court's permission to accept, 17–08
    definition of "Part 36 offer", 17–01
    form, 16–02
    interest provision, 16–06
    interim payments, 16–12
    introduction, 16–01
    resolution of parts and issues in disputes, 16–07—16–09
    time given for acceptance, 17–02
    "whole of the claim" meaning, 16–04—16–05
    withdrawal of offer, 17–03—17–06
  requirements of Part 36 payment notices,
    21 day acceptance rule, 18–13—18–15
    acceptance of liability up to specified proportion, 16–10
    counterclaims, 16–11
    form, 16–02
    identification of parts and issues, 18–08
    increased payment into court, 18–12
    interest provision, 16–06
    interim payments, 16–12
    introduction, 16–01
    mechanics of payment, 18–10

Part 36—*cont.*
  requirements of Part 36 payment notices—*cont.*
    mechanics of service of the notice, 18–11
    resolution of parts and issues in disputes, 16–07—16–09
    standard form, 18–09
    "whole of the claim" meaning, 16–04—16–05
  settlement and, 13–03
  small claims and, 25–05—25–06
Partnership disputes
  capacity to compromise, partners, 4–11
  full disclosure required in a compromise of a, 4–41
Payment into court
  see also **Part 36**
  acceptance of, client having short time to live, 28–04
  settlement prior to 1999, 13–01
Performance
  agreement collateral to compromise, 7–06
  cheque, payment by, 7–03
  entire compromise of, 7–05
  impossibility, self-created, 8–13
  instalments, payment by, 7–04
  mutually dependent obligation, 7–07
  promised or actual acts, 8–03—8–10
  satisfaction and discharge of obligations, 7–02—7–07
Personal injury claims, settlement of
  children and patients, involving, approval of the court, obtaining, 35–05—35–09
  change of circumstances, 35–14

INDEX

Personal injury claims, settlement of—*cont.*
  costs, 35–56—35–63
  Court of Protection, 35–19—35–21
  failure to obtain approval, 35–10—35–13
  introduction, 35–01—35–09
  litigation friend, 35–07
  money laundering, 35–64
  periodical payments, order for, 35–29—35–47
  periodical payments, procedure for obtaining, 35–48—35–53
  provisional damages, 35–24—35–28
  recoupment of benefits, 35–54—35–55
  setting aside consent orders, 35–14
  structured settlements, 35–29—35–47
  precedents for, A1–21—A1–26
"Post settlement remorse"
  inadequate disclosure of information, 13–05
Pre-action offers
  acceptance after proceedings have started of,
    money claims, 15–13—15–15
    non-money claims, 15–15—15–16
  background, 15–01—15–02
  bettering of, at trial, 15–07
  civil procedure rules and,
    conditions for achieving status within the, 15–03—15–04
  claimant's, to settle, 23–10
  non-money claim,
    status within Part 36 when proceedings have begun, 17–01

Pre-action offers—*cont.*
  proviso as to amount paid into court,
    money claims, 15–10—15–11
    non-money claims, 15–12
  unaccepted, and costs, 15–09
  withdrawal of, 15–05—15–6
Pre-action protocols
  assistance in early settlement of cases, 22–09
  disclosure of information and, 13–06
Precedents
  administrative court proceedings, A1–34
  boundary disputes, A1–27—A1–33
  Chancery litigation, A1–15—A1–20
  draft consent orders and judgments, A1–12—A1–14
  Landlord and Tenant cases, A1–27—A1–33
  Part 36, A1–01—A1–11
  personal injury claims by children or patients, A1–21—A1–26
Private law
  compromise in context of, 1–02, 1–05
Probate claims
  compromise of,
    order under Administration of Justice Act 1985, 31–27
    order under the civil procedure rules, 31–26
    trial of claim on written evidence, 31–28
  nature of claim, 31–25
Professional ethics and responsibilities
  "confidential" matters disclosed by client or opponent, 28–03—28–04

INDEX

Professional ethics and responsibilities—*cont.*
conflicts of interest, 28–05—28–06
generally, 28–01—28–02
informing client of offer of settlement, 28–09
keeping the court informed, 28–12
overall duties to client in compromise, 28–10
unfounded claims, 28–07—28–08

Prosecution
application for want of, "without prejudice" negotiations and, 27–52—27–53
stifling,
illegal compromise, 4–77

Public law
compromise in the context of, 1–05

Receivers
court-appointed, 31–17

Representative parties
capacity to compromise, 4–07, 4–12

Represented parties
acting personally,
capacity to compromise, 4–13

Res judicata
agreements concerning disposal of divorce or judicial, suit, 32–20
application to settlement of first action, 6–09—6–17
meaning of, 1–02
rule of substantive law, 6–13

Rescission
relief for misrepresentation, 4–51

Residential tenancies
court's jurisdiction, 37–34

Residential tenancies—*cont.*
enforcement of orders, 37–45
introduction, 37–29—37–30
no contracting out, 37–31—37–33
obtaining an "agreed" order, 37–39—37–42
occupants without statutory protection, 37–43—37–44
setting aside order for possession, 37–48
statutory provision, 37–34—37–38
tenancy springing from a compromise, 37–49
variation of order for possession, 37–46—37–47

Restraint of trade
unreasonable and compromise, 4–83

Restrictive trade practices
illegality and, 4–82—4–83

Setting aside a compromise
discretionary jurisdiction, 29–18—29–21
misunderstanding between legal advisers and client, 29–18—29–21
practice on,
compromise embodied in order or judgment, 12–03—12–04
costs, 12–07
interim order, 12–05
judicial rescission, 12–02
Tomlin order, 12–06

Setting aside a consent judgment
third parties interests,
insured and uninsured losses, 30–10

Setting aside consent orders
appeals, 32–125

699

INDEX

Setting aside consent orders—*cont.*
application for rehearing, 32–124
arbitration, 41–14
bad deal, 32–92
change in the law, 32–111
Child Support Act 1991, 32–110
death of party, unexpected, 32–107
delay, 32–112—32–113
erroneous valuations, 32–101—32–106
failure to disclose material facts before order is made, 32–85—32–87
failure to observe statutory provision, 32–96
fraud, 32–88
fresh action, 32–126
grounds for,
  bad deal, 32–92
  failure to disclose all material before order is made, 32–85
  failure to observe statutory provision, 32–96
  fraud, 32–88
  generally, 32–84
  legal advice, bad, 32–93—32–95
  misrepresentation, 32–88
  mistake, 32–89
  supervening events, 32–97
  undue influence, 32–90—32–91
Inheritance Act disputes, 33–16
legal advice, bad, 32–93—32–95
misrepresentation, 32–88
mistake, 32–89
personal injury cases,
  children and patients, 35–14
practice,
  appeal, 32–125

Setting aside consent orders—*cont.*
practice—*cont.*
  application for rehearing, 32–124
  fresh action, 32–126
  provision of a unified procedure, 32–114—32–123
  rejection of application to set aside *in limine* 32–127
preliminary, 32–81—32–83
rejection of application *in limine*, 32–127
remarriage, 32–108
supervening events,
  change in the law, 32–111
  Child Support Act 1991, 32–110
  delay, 32–112—32–113
  erroneous valuations, 32–101—32–106
  remarriage, 32–108
  unexpected death of party, 32–107
undue influence, 32–90—32–91
Settlement
see also **Structured settlements**
civil justice and,
  case-managed system, 13–02
  exchange of information before negotiation, 13–05—13–07
  negotiation, 13–04
  Part 36, 13–03
  prior to 1999, 13–01
Small claims
Part 36 and, 25–05—25–06
Solicitors
authority to compromise,
  differences between, and barristers, 29–02, 29–13
immunity from suit, 29–02—29–03, 29–22—29–24

INDEX

Solicitors—*cont.*
  implied or ostensible authority,
    compromise matter "collateral to the action", 4–06
  independent advisers,
    employment contracts and compromise, 36–31

Stay of proceedings
  consequences of acceptance of Part 36 payment,
    part only of claim, 21–14
    whole claim, 21–13, 21–15
  reference of Part 36 payment made to judge, 14–10

Structured settlements
  advantages of, 35–34
  "bottom up" structure, 35–36
  children and patients,
    personal injury claims, 35–29—35–47
  consent order for, 35–50
  Courts Act 2003, effect of, 35–37
  disadvantages of, 35–35
  terms of order adjourning for consideration of, 35–49
  "top down" structure, 35–36

Terms of compromise
  construction,
    consent judgment, relevance of jurisdiction of court, 5–36—5–41
    consent order, relevance of jurisdiction of court, 5–36—5–41
    "contra proferentem" rule, 5–34
    extrinsic evidence, 5–10—5–16
    general problems, 5–02—5–09
    "natural and ordinary" meaning of words, 5–08

Terms of compromise—*cont.*
    post compromise words and deeds, 5–17
    releases, 5–23—5–53
    relevance of jurisdiction of court, 5–36—5–41
    rules of, 5–18—5–22
    subjective intentions or understandings, 5–10—5–16
  construing the agreement,
    ascertaining common intention of parties, 5–02—5–09
  construing a consent order or judgment,
    relevance of jurisdiction of court, 5–36—5–41
  implied terms,
    consent order or judgment, no implication of, 5–47
    costs, 5–60—5–62
    general, 5–42
    "pending agreed order", 5–48—5–59
    "permission to apply" omitted, 5–45
    time, as to, 5–43—5–44
  legal advisers and, 5–01

Third parties
  effects of compromise on,
    bankruptcy and, 6–75—6–77
    Civil Liability (Contribution) Act 1978 exception, 6–28—6–29
    effects upon, 6–62—6–84
    family disputes, 6–78
    fraud, 6–81
    impeachment by or on behalf of, 6–74—6–77
    implications on, 6–26—6–27
    voluntary transfers of assets, 6–79

INDEX

Third parties—*cont.*
insurance interests and,
settlement with and effects on, 30–03—30–10
settlement with and effects as between insurer and insured, 30–11—30–13
want of good faith and, 2–19

Tomlin order
appeals, settlement of and, 42–04—42–05
breach of provision in schedule to,
fresh action, need for, 9–26—9–27
confidentiality and, 10–30—10–31
disputes over land, 38–10
effect of, 9–23
enforcement under,
generally, 11–21—11–27
standard form of words, 9–28—9–30
incorporation of compromise agreement into, 9–21
mistaken record of compromise and, 4–33—4–36
nature of, 9–23
setting aside a compromise and, 12–06
structure of, 9–22
susceptibility to being set aside, 9–31
text of lecture, A7–01

Tortfeasors
concurrent, 6–39—6–40
joint, 6–41—6–44

Undue influence
see also **Duress**
effect, 4–70
husband and wife, 4–69
setting aside of compromise due to, 4–66—4–68

Unfair prejudice
Chancery litigation, 31–11

Value added tax
construction disputes, 39–63

Voidable compromise
effect of duress and undue influence, 4–70

Waiver
discharge of obligations under a compromise, 7–09
lifting veil of "without prejudice" rule, 27–46—27–50

"Without prejudice" rule
alternative dispute resolution and, 43–14—43–21
application of principle,
negotiations genuinely aimed at settlement, 27–09—29–10
whether or not assisted by legal advisers, 27–08
foundation of, 27–01
generally, 13–04
lifting veil of "without prejudice"
adverse inferences from apparent lack of communication, 27–21
circumstances for, 27–15—27–19
estoppel, 27–45
fact of agreement, 27–20
introduction, 27–03
matters independent of subject matter of dispute, 27–25—27–27
prejudice the recipient, 27–22—27–24
public policy rationale, 27–03, 27–20—27–28

INDEX

"Without prejudice" rule—*cont.*
  lifting veil of "without
    prejudice"—*cont.*
    "unambiguous impropriety",
      27–28—27–44
    waiver and mutuality,
      27–46—27–50
  manner of conducting,
    express stipulation, 27–07
    implied stipulation, 27–07
    introduction, 27–04
  matrimonial disputes,
    compromise of,
    interim financial provision,
      32–30
  mediation and, 43–14—43–21
  objections to adduce evidence of
    content of, 27–03
  "opening shots" and the,
    27–09—27–12

"Without prejudice" rule—*cont.*
  "parting shots" 27–13—27–14
  protection of, 27–04—27–05
  protection of disclosure of
    documents, 27–03
  referral at interim applications,
    interim payment applications,
      27–56—27–59
    introduction, 27–03
    security for costs,
      27–54—25–55
    want of prosecution,
      27–52—27–53
  responses to without prejudice
    letters, 27–13—27–14
  when are negotiations, 27–03
  offers outside Part 36, 26–02,
    26–04, 26–11